Lecture Notes in Computer Science 7636

Commenced Publication in 1973
Founding and Former Series Editors:
Gerhard Goos, Juris Hartmanis, and Jan van Leeuwen

Services Science

Subline of Lectures Notes in Computer Science

Chengfei Liu   Heiko Ludwig
Farouk Toumani   Qi Yu (Eds.)

Service-Oriented Computing

10th International Conference, ICSOC 2012
Shanghai, China, November 12-15, 2012
Proceedings

 Springer

Volume Editors

Chengfei Liu
Swinburne University of Technology, Faculty of ICT
John Street, Hawthorn, VIC 3122, Australia
E-mail: cliu@swin.edu.au

Heiko Ludwig
IBM, Almaden Research Center
650 Harry Road
San Jose, CA 95120, USA
E-mail: hludwig@us.ibm.com

Farouk Toumani
Blaise Pascal University, LIMOS - UMR 6158
Complexe scientifique des Cézeaux, 63177 Aubiere, France
E-mail: ftoumani@isima.fr

Qi Yu
Rochester Institute of Technology
College of Computing and Information Sciences
1 Lomb Memorial Drive, Rochester, NY 14623, USA
E-mail: qi.yu@rit.edu

ISSN 0302-9743   e-ISSN 1611-3349
ISBN 978-3-642-34320-9   e-ISBN 978-3-642-34321-6
DOI 10.1007/978-3-642-34321-6
Springer Heidelberg Dordrecht London New York

Library of Congress Control Number: 2012949454

CR Subject Classification (1998): D.2, C.2, H.4, H.3, H.5, J.1, F.3

LNCS Sublibrary: SL 2 – Programming and Software Engineering

Typesetting: Camera-ready by author, data conversion by Scientific Publishing Services, Chennai, India

Printed on acid-free paper

Springer is part of Springer Science+Business Media (www.springer.com)

Preface

This volume contains the conference proceedings of the 10th International Conference on Service-Oriented Computing (ICSOC 2012), which took place in Shanghai, China, November 12–15, 2012. The ICSOC conference series is the prime forum for academics and industry researchers and developers to report and share ground-breaking work in service-oriented computing. The series provides cross-community scientific excellence by the gathering of experts from various disciplines, such as business process management, distributed systems, computer networks, wireless and mobile computing, grid computing, networking, service science, management science, and software engineering. ICSOC 2012 placed an emphasis on results that solve open research problems and have significant impact on the field of service-oriented computing and also in particular cloud services.

ICSOC 2012 attracted 185 research paper submissions, out of which 32 full papers and 21 short papers were selected for this volume after a careful review by the Program Committee (PC) for originality, novelty, rigor, and relevance. Each paper was reviewed by at least three reviewers and the discussion on each paper was moderated by an experienced senior PC member. The research track was very competitive with an acceptance rate of 17% for full papers, and an additional 11% for short papers. Furthermore, this volume contains nine industrial papers (six full papers and three short papers selected out of 20 submissions to the industrial track).

The conference program was complemented by an invited talk, three outstanding keynotes, a panel discussion, demonstrations, a PhD symposium as well as a collection of workshops.

We would like to express our gratitude to everyone who helped make ICSOC 2012 a success: the conference Organizing Committee for providing an excellent environment for the conference, the Research and Industrial Program Committee members as well as the additional reviewers for their conscientious and diligent work to ensure the high quality of the conference scientific program. Finally, and most importantly, we want to thank all the authors for their high-quality contributions.

November 2012

Chengfei Liu
Heiko Ludwig
Farouk Toumani

Organization

Honorary Chair

Junliang Chen   Beijing Post and Communication University, China

General Chairs

Jian Yang   Macquarie University, Australia
Liang Zhang   Fudan University, China

Advisory Committee

Jifeng He   Eastern China Normal University, China
Jian Lv   Nanjing University, China
Baile Shi   Fudan University, China
Zhaohui Wu   Zhejiang University, China

Program Chairs

Chengfei Liu   Swinburne University, Australia
Heiko Ludwig   IBM Almaden Research Center, USA
Farouk Toumani   Université Blaise Pascal, France

Workshop Chairs

Aditya Ghose   University of Wollongong, Australia
Huibiao Zhu   Eastern China Normal University, China

Industry Chairs

Yanbo Han   Chinese Academy of Sciences
Nanjangud C. Narendra   IBM India Software Lab, Bangalore, India
Surya Nepal   ICT CSIRO, Australia

Demonstration Chairs

Alex Delis   University of Athens, Greece
Quang Z. Sheng   Adelaide University, Australia

Panel Chairs

Cesare Pautasso   University of Lugano, Switzerland
Thomas Sandholm   HP Labs, USA

PHD Symposium Chairs

Olivier Perrin   Nancy 2 University, France
Jianmin Wang   Tsinghua University, China
Yan Wang   Macquarie University, Australia

Publicity Chairs

Florian Daniel   University of Trento, Italy
Yunzhan Gong   Beijing Post and Communication University,
                                 China
Zaki Malik   Wayne State University, USA

Local Organization Chairs

Jian Cao   Shanghai Jiaotong University, China
Zhenying He   Fudan University, China
Guohua Liu   Donghua Univesity, China
Budan Wu   Beijing Post and Communication University,
                                 China

Corporate Sponsor Chairs

Genxing Yang   Shanghai Software Industry Association, China
Shiyong Zhang   Fudan University, China
Yingsheng Li   Fudan University, China

Financial Chair

Weiwei Sun   Fudan University, China

Publication Chair

Qi Yu   Rochester Institute of Technology, USA

Web Chair

Xiang Fu   Hofstra University, USA

Senior Program Committee Members

Benatallah Boualem	UNSW, Australia
Bouguettaya Athman	RMIT, Australia
Casati Fabio	University of Trento, Italy
Curbera Paco	IBM, USA
De Paoli Flavio	Università di Milano Bicocca, Italy
Dustdar Schahram	TU Wien, Austria
Hacid Mohand-Said	Université Claude Bernard Lyon 1, France
Maximilien Michael	IBM Research, USA
Motahari-Nezhad Hamid Reza	HP, USA
Pernici Barbara	Politecnico di Milano, Italy
Quang Z. Sheng	Adelaide University, Australia
Rinderle-Ma Stefanie	University of Vienna, Austria
Rossi Gustavo	UNLP, Argentina
Su Jianwen	U C Santa Barbara, USA
Tai Stefan	Karlsruhe Institute of Technology, Germany
Tari Zahir	RMIT University, Australia
Weske Mathias	HP / University of Potsdam, Germany
Wolf Karsten	University of Rostock, Germany

Research Program Committee Members

Accorsi Rafael	University of Freiburg, Germany
Aiello Marco	University of Groningen, The Netherlands
Akkiraju Rama	IBM/USA, USA
Arenas Alvaro	Instituto de Empresa Business School, Spain
Bagheri Ebrahim	Athabasca University, Canada
Bartolini Claudio	HP Labs, Palo Alto, USA
Basu Samik	Iowa State University, USA
Basu Sujoy	HP Labs, USA
Benbernou Salima	Université Paris Descartes, France
Bertolino Antonia	ISTI-CNR, Italy
Binder Walter	University of Lugano, Switzerland
Bussler Christoph	Analytica, Inc., USA
C. Narendra Nanjangud	IBM India Software Lab, Bangalore, India
Carro Manuel	UPM and IMDEA Software Institute, Spain
Chen Shiping	CSIRO ICT, Australia
Chung Lawrence	The University of Texas at Dallas, USA
Coquery Emmanuel	Université de Lyon, France
D'Andrea Vincenzo	University of Trento, Italy
Daniel Florian	University of Trento, Italy
Demirkan Haluk	Arizona State University, USA
Deng Shuiguang	Zhejiang University, China
Drira Khalil	LAAS Toulouse, France
Engels Gregor	University of Paderborn, Germany

Eshuis Rik   Eindhoven University of Technology,
                                The Netherlands
Friesen Andreas   SAP AG, Germany
Gasevic Dragan   Athabasca University, Canada
Ghezzi Carlo   Politecnico di Milano, Italy
Ghose Aditya   University of Wollongong, Australia
Giorgini Paolo   University of Trento, Italy
Graupner Sven   HP Labs, Palo Alto, USA
Grefen Paul   Eindhoven University of Technology,
                                The Netherlands
Hacid Hakim   Bell Labs France, France
Han Peng   Chongqing Academy of Science and
                                Technology, China
Han Yanbo   Chinese Academy of sciences, China
Khalaf Rania   IBM T.J. Watson Research Center, USA
Kirchberg Markus   Hewlett-Packard Labs, Singapore
Kongdenfha Woralak   Naresuan University, Thailand
Kotonya Gerald   Lancaster University, UK
Lago Patricia   VU University Amsterdam, The Netherlands
Lelli Francesco   European Research Institute on Service
                                Science, Tilburg, The Netherlands
Leymann Frank   Univerisity of Stuttgart, Germany
Li Jun   HP Labs, USA
Li Ying   Zhejiang University, China
Lin Fu-ren   National Tsing Hua University, Taiwan, R.O.C.
Liu Xumin   Rochester Institute of Technology, USA
Maamar Zakaria   Zayed University, United Arab Emirates
Maglio Paul   IBM Research Amaden, USA
Malik Zaki   Wayne State University, USA
Mecella Massimo   SAPIENZA Università di Roma, Italy
Mrissa Michael   University of Lyon, France
Nepal Surya   CSIRO, Australia
Paik Helen   UNSW, Australia
Pautasso Cesare   University of Lugano, Switzerland
Perez Christian   INRIA, France
Perrin Olivier   Lorraine University, France
Pisipati RadhaKrishna   Infosys Technologies Limited, India
Poizat Pascal   University of Evry and LRI, France
Psaier Harald   Vienna University of Technology, Austria
Puhlmann Frank   inubit AG, Germany
Qiao Mu   The Pennsylvania State University, USA
Reichert Manfred   University of Ulm, Germany
Reisig Wolfgang   Humboldt-Universität zu Berlin, Germany
Roland Colette   Université Paris 1 Panthéon Sorbonne, France
Rosenberg Florian   IBM Research, USA
Ruiz-Cortés Antonio   University of Seville, Spain

Saint-Paul Regis	Create-Net, Italy
Shwartz Larisa	IBM T.J. Watson Research Center, USA
Silva-Lepe Ignacio	IBM, USA
Singh Munindar P.	North Carolina State University, USA
Smirnov Sergey	SAP Research, Germany
Spanoudakis George	City University London, UK
Stroulia Eleni	University of Alberta, Canada
Tan Wei	IBM T.J. Watson Research Center, USA
Toledo Beatriz	UNICAMP, Brazil
van Hillegersberg Jos	University of Twente, The Netherlands
Venugopal Srikumar	UNSW, Australia
Wang Changzhou	Boeing, USA
Wang Yan	Macquarie University, Australia
Weber Ingo	NICTA, Australia
Wombacher Andreas	Univeresity of Twente, The Netherlands
Xu Lai	Bournemouth University, UK
Yahyapour Ramin	University of Goettingen, Germany
Yu Jian	Swinburne University of Technology, Australia
Zadeh Hossein	RMIT University, Australia
Zhao Weiliang	University of Wollongong, Australia
Zhao Xiaohui	Unitec Institute of Technology, New Zealand
Zheng Yan	Aalto University/Xidian University, Finland/China
Zisman Andrea	City University London, UK

Industry Program Committee Members

Roman Vaculin	IBM Research, T.J. Watson Research Center, USA
Ryan Ko	HP Laboratories, Singapore
Liam O'Brien	CSIRO, Australia
Jenny Yan Liu	Pacific Northwest National Laboratory, USA
G.R. Gangadharan	IDRBT, Hyderabad, India
Karthikeyan Ponnalagu	IBM Research, India
Vladimir Tosic	NICTA, Australia
Guiling Wang	North China University of Technology, China
Jun Wei	Chinese Academy of Sciences, China
Jianwu Wang	University of California, San Diego, USA
D. Janaki Ram	IIT Madras, India
Mathias Weske	Hasso Plattner Institute, Germany
Bernhard Holtkamp	Fraunhofer ISST, Germany
Zhongjie Wang	Harbin Institute of Technologies (HIT), China
Umesh Bellur	IIT Bombay, India
Abdelkarim Erradi	Qatar University, Qatar
Andreas Wombacher	University of Twente, The Netherlands
Sami Bhiri	DERI, Ireland

Gero Decker   Signavio GmbH, Germany
Sergey Smirnov   Hasso Plattner Institute, Germany
Daniel Gmach   HP Labs, USA
Zakaria Maamar   Zayed University, UAE

External Reviewers

David Allison   Maude Manouvrier
Mohsen Asadi   Riccardo De Masellis
Kelly R. Braghetto   Emna Mezgani
Pavel Bulanov   Bardia Mohabbati
Marco Comerio   Carlos Muller
Daniel de Angelis Cordeiro   Richard Müller
Paul de Vreize   Nicolas Mundbrod
Codé Diop   Daniel Oberle
Ando Emerencia   Marcio K. Oikawa
Marios Fokaefs   Giuliano Andrea Pagani
José María García   José Antonio Parejo
Marcela O. Garcia   Fabio Patrizi
Ilche Georgievski   Achille Peternier
Morteza Ghandehari   Robert Prüfer
Christian Gierds   Manuel Resinas
Genady Ya. Grabarnik   Szabolcs Rosznyal
Victor Guana   Jonathan Rouzaud-Cornabas
Joyce El Haddad   Alessandro Russo
Riadh Ben Halima   Johannes Schobel
Dan Han   Ankit Srivastava
Chung-Wei Hang   Steve Strauch
Mohamed Amine Hannachi   Yutian Sun
Florian Haupt   Jen Sürmeli
Konstantin Hoesch-Klohe   Osvaldo K. Takai
Zhengxiong Hou   Julian Tiedeken
Keman Huang   Hiroshi Wada
Aymen Kamoun   Sebastian Wagner
Nesrine Khabou   Haiqin Wang
David Knuplesch   Yonghong Wang
Jens Kolb   Ehsan Ullah Warriach
Andreas Lanz   Wei Xu
Jim Zhanwen Li   Jinghui Yao
Zhenwen Li   Jun Yuan
Qinghua Lu   Sema Zor

Table of Contents

Research Papers

Service Engineering 1

Service Management 1

Cloud

Service Engineering 2

Service Management 2

Service QoS

Service Engineering 3

Service Security, Privacy and Personalization

Service Applications in Business and Society

Service Composition and Choreography

Service Scaling and Cloud

Research Papers – Short

Service Composition and Choreography

Process Management

Service Description and Discovery

Service Management

Service Security, Privacy and Personalization

Industrial Papers

Service Applications

Cloud Computing

Industrial Papers – Short

Erratum

Specification and Detection of SOA Antipatterns

Naouel Moha[1], Francis Palma[1,2], Mathieu Nayrolles[1,3],
Benjamin Joyen Conseil[1,3], Yann-Gaël Guéhéneuc[2],
Benoit Baudry[4], and Jean-Marc Jézéquel[4]

[1] Département d'informatique, Université du Québec à Montréal, Canada
moha.naouel@uqam.ca
[2] Ptidej Team, DGIGL, École Polytechnique de Montréal, Canada
{francis.palma,yann-gael.gueheneuc}@polymtl.ca
[3] École Supérieur en Informatique Appliquée, France
{mathieu.nayrolles,benjamin.joyen-conseil}@viacesi.fr
[4] INRIA Rennes, Université Rennes 1, France
{bbaudry,jezequel}@irisa.fr

Abstract. Like any other complex software system, Service Based Systems (SBSs) must evolve to fit new user requirements and execution contexts. The changes resulting from the evolution of SBSs may degrade their design and quality of service (QoS) and may often cause the appearance of common poor solutions, called *Antipatterns*. Antipatterns resulting from these changes also hinder the future maintenance and evolution of SBSs. The automatic detection of antipatterns is thus important to assess the design and QoS of SBSs and ease their maintenance and evolution. However, methods and techniques for the detection of antipatterns in SBSs are still in their infancy despite their importance. In this paper, we introduce a novel and innovative approach supported by a framework for specifying and detecting antipatterns in SBSs. Using our approach, we specify 10 well-known and common antipatterns, including *Multi Service* and *Tiny Service*, and we automatically generate their detection algorithms. We apply and validate the detection algorithms in terms of precision and recall on *Home-Automation*, an SBS developed independently. This validation demonstrates that our approach enables the specification and detection of SOA antipatterns with the precision of more than 90% and the recall of 100%.

Keywords: Antipatterns, Service based systems, Specification, Detection, Quality of service, Design, Software evolution and maintenance.

1 Introduction

Service Oriented Architecture (SOA) [8] is an emerging architectural style that is becoming broadly adopted in industry because it allows the development of low-cost, flexible, and scalable distributed systems by composing ready-made services, *i.e.*, autonomous, reusable, and platform-independent software units that can be accessed through a network, such as the Internet. This architectural style can be implemented using a wide range of SOA technologies, such as OSGi,

C. Liu et al. (Eds.): ICSOC 2012, LNCS 7636, pp. 1–16, 2012.
© Springer-Verlag Berlin Heidelberg 2012

SCA, and Web Services. SOA allows building different types of Service Based Systems (SBSs) from business systems to cloud-based systems. Google Maps, Amazon, eBay, PayPal, and FedEx are examples of large scale SBSs.

However, the emergence of such systems raises several challenges. Indeed, like any other complex software system, SBSs must evolve to fit new user requirements in terms of functionalities and Quality of Service (QoS). SBSs must also evolve to accommodate new execution contexts, such as addition of new devices, technologies, or protocols. All of these changes may degrade the design and QoS of SBSs, and may often result in the appearance of common poor solutions to recurring problems, called *Antipatterns*—by opposition to *design patterns*, which are good solutions to such problems that software engineers face when designing and developing systems. In addition to the degradation of the design and QoS, antipatterns resulting from these changes make it hard for software engineers to maintain and evolve systems.

Multi Service and *Tiny Service* are two common antipatterns in SBSs and it has been shown, in particular, that *Tiny Service* is the root cause of many SOA failures [15]. *Multi Service* is an SOA antipattern that corresponds to a service that implements a multitude of methods related to different business and technical abstractions. Such a service is not easily reusable because of the low cohesion of its methods and is often unavailable to end-users because of its overload. Conversely, *Tiny Service* is a small service with just a few methods, which only implements part of an abstraction. Such service often requires several coupled services to be used together, resulting in higher development complexity and reduced flexibility.

The automatic detection of such antipatterns is an important activity to assess the design and QoS of SBSs and ease the maintenance and evolution tasks of software engineers. However, few works have been devoted to SOA antipatterns, and methods and techniques for the detection of antipatterns in SBSs are still in their infancy.

Our goal is to assess the design and QoS of SBSs. To achieve this goal, we propose a novel and innovative approach (named SODA for Service Oriented Detection for Antipatterns) supported by a framework (named SOFA for Service Oriented Framework for Antipatterns) to specify SOA antipatterns and detect them automatically in SBSs. This framework supports the static and dynamic analysis of SBSs, along with their combination. Static analysis involves measurement of structural properties related to the design of SBSs, while dynamic analysis requires the runtime execution of SBSs for the measurement of runtime properties, mainly related to the QoS of SBSs. The SODA approach relies on the first language to specify SOA antipatterns in terms of metrics. This language is defined from a thorough domain analysis of SOA antipatterns in the literature. It allows the specifications of SOA antipatterns using high-level domain-related abstractions. It also allows the adaptation of the specifications of antipatterns to the context of the analyzed SBSs. Using this language and the SOFA framework dedicated to the static and dynamic analysis of SBSs, we generate detection algorithms automatically from the specifications of SOA antipatterns and apply them on any SBSs under analysis. The originality of our approach stems from the ability for software engineers to specify SOA antipatterns at a high-level of abstraction using a consistent vocabulary and from the use of a domain-specific language for automatically generating the detection algorithms.

We apply SODA by specifying 10 well-known and common antipatterns and generating their detection algorithms. Then, we validate the detection results in terms of precision and recall on *Home-Automation*, an SBS developed independently by two Masters students. We consider two different versions of *Home-Automation*: (a) an original version, which includes 13 services, and (b) a version modified by adding and modifying services to inject intentionally some antipatterns. We show that SODA allows the specification and detection of a representative set of SOA antipatterns with a precision of 92.5% and a recall of 100%.

The remainder of this paper is organized as follows. Section 2 surveys related work on the detection of antipatterns in general, and in SBSs in particular. Section 3 presents our specification and detection approach, SODA, along with the specification language and the underlying detection framework, SOFA. Section 4 presents experiments performed on *Home-Automation* for validating our approach. Finally, Section 5 concludes and sketches future work.

2 Related Work

Architectural (or design) quality is essential for building well-designed, maintainable, and evolvable SBSs. Patterns and antipatterns have been recognized as one of the best ways to express architectural concerns and solutions. However, unlike Object Oriented (OO) antipatterns, methods and techniques for the detection and correction of SOA antipatterns are still in their infancy.

Unlike OO antipatterns, fewer books and papers deal with SOA antipatterns: most references are Web sites where SOA practitioners share their experiences in SOA design and development [4; 13; 17]. In 2003, Dudney *et al.* [7] published the first book on SOA antipatterns. This book provides a catalog of approximately 50 antipatterns related to the architecture, design and implementation of systems based on J2EE technologies, such as EJB, JSP, Servlet, and Web services. Most antipatterns described in this book cannot be detected automatically and are specific to a technology and correspond to variants of the Tiny and Multi Service. Another book by Rotem-Gal-Oz *et al.* [22] on SOA patterns and antipatterns will soon be published in Summer 2012. In a recent paper, Král *et al.* [15] described seven SOA antipatterns, which are caused by an improper use of SOA standards and improper practices borrowed from the OO design style. Other books exist on SOA patterns and principles [6; 9] that provide guidelines and principles characterizing "good" service oriented designs. Such books enable software engineers to manually assess the quality of their systems and provide a basis for improving design and implementation.

Several methods and tools exist for the detection [14; 16; 19; 24] and correction [1; 25; 26] of antipatterns in OO systems and various books have been published on that topic. For example, Brown *et al.* [2] introduced a collection of 40 antipatterns, Beck, in Fowler's highly-acclaimed book on refactoring [10], compiled 22 code smells that are low-level antipatterns in source code, suggesting where engineers should apply refactorings. One of the root causes of OO antipatterns is the adoption of a procedural design style in OO system whereas for SOA antipatterns, it stems from the adoption of an OO style design in SOA system [15]. However, these OO detection methods and tools cannot be directly applied to SOA. Indeed, SOA focuses on services as first-class entities whereas OO focuses on classes, which are at the lower level of granularity. Moreover, the highly dynamic nature of an SOA environment raises several challenges that are not faced in OO development and requires dynamic analysis.

Other related works have focused on the detection of specific antipatterns related to system's performance and resource usage and–or given technologies. For example, Wong *et al.* [27] used a genetic algorithm for detecting software faults and anomalous behavior related to the resource usage of a system (*e.g.,* memory usage, processor usage, thread count). Their approach is based on *utility functions*, which correspond to predicates that identify suspicious behavior based on resource usage metrics. For example, a utility function may report an anomalous behavior corresponding to spam sending if it detects a large number of threads. In another relevant work, Parsons *et al.* [21] introduced an approach for the detection of performance antipatterns specifically in component-based enterprise systems (in particular, JEE applications) using a rule-based approach relying on static and dynamic analysis.

Although different, all these previous works on OO systems and performance antipattern detection form a sound basis of expertise and technical knowledge for building methods for the detection of SOA antipatterns.

3   The SODA Approach

We propose a three-step approach, named SODA, for the specification and detection of SOA antipatterns:

Step 1. Specify SOA antipatterns: This step consists of identifying properties in SBSs relevant to SOA antipatterns. Using these properties, we define a Domain-Specific Language (DSL) for specifying antipatterns at a high level of abstraction.
Step 2. Generate detection algorithms: In this step, detection algorithms are generated automatically from the specifications defined in the previous step.
Step 3. Detect automatically SOA antipatterns: The third step consists of applying, on the SBSs analyzed, the detection algorithms generated in *Step 2* to detect SOA antipatterns.

The following sections describe the first two steps. The third step is described in Section 4, where we detail experiments performed for validating SODA.

3.1   Specification of SOA Antipatterns

We perform a domain analysis of SOA antipatterns by studying their definition and specification in the literature [7; 15; 22] and in online resources and articles [4; 13; 17]. This domain analysis allows us to identify properties relevant to

SOA antipatterns, including static properties related to their design (*e.g.,* cohesion and coupling) and also dynamic properties, such as QoS criteria (*e.g.,* response time and availability). Static properties are properties that apply to the static descriptions of SBSs, such as WSDL (Web Services Description Language) files, whereas dynamic properties are related to the dynamic behavior of SBSs as observed during their execution. We use these properties as the base vocabulary to define a DSL, in the form of a rule-based language for specifying SOA antipatterns. The DSL offers software engineers high-level domain-related abstractions and variability points to express different properties of antipatterns depending on their own judgment and context.

```
1  rule_card      ::= RULE_CARD: rule_cardName { (rule)+ };
2  rule           ::= RULE: ruleName { content_rule };

3  content_rule   ::= metric | relationship | operator ruleType (ruleType)+
4                     | RULE_CARD: rule_cardName

5  ruleType       ::= ruleName | rule_cardName

6  operator       ::= INTER | UNION | DIFF | INCL | NEG

7  metric         ::= id_metric ordi_value
8                     | id_metric comparator num_value
9  id_metric      ::= NMD | NIR | NOR | CPL | COH | ANP | ANPT | ANAM | ANIM
10                    | NMI | NTMI | RT | A
11 ordi_value     ::= VERY_HIGH | HIGH | MEDIUM | LOW | VERY_LOW
12 comparator     ::= EQUAL | LESS | LESS_EQUAL | GREATER | GREATER_EQUAL

13 relationship   ::= relationType FROM ruleName cardinality TO ruleName cardinality
14 relationType   ::= ASSOC | COMPOS
15 cardinality    ::= ONE | MANY | ONE_OR_MANY | num_value NUMBER_OR_MANY

16 rule_cardName, ruleName, ruleClass ∈ string
17 num_value ∈ double
```

Fig. 1. BNF Grammar of Rule Cards

We specify antipatterns using rule cards, *i.e.,* sets of rules. We formalize rule cards with a Backus-Naur Form (BNF) grammar, which determines the syntax of our DSL. Figure 1 shows the grammar used to express rule cards. A rule card is identified by the keyword **RULE_CARD**, followed by a name and a set of rules specifying this specific antipattern (Figure 1, line 1). A rule (line 3 and 4) describes a metric, an association or composition relationship among rules (lines 13-15) or a combination with other rules, based on set operators including intersection, union, difference, inclusion, and negation (line 6). A rule can refer also to another rule card previously specified (line 4). A metric associates to an identifier a numerical or an ordinal value (lines 7 and 8). Ordinal values are defined with a five-point Likert scale: very high, high, medium, low, and very low (line 11). Numerical values are used to define thresholds with comparators (line 12), whereas ordinal values are used to define values relative to all the services of a SBS under analysis (line 11). We define ordinal values with the box-plot statistical technique [3] to relate ordinal values with concrete metric values while avoiding setting artificial thresholds. The metric suite (lines 9-10) encompasses

```
1 RULE_CARD: MultiService {                     1 RULE_CARD: TinyService {
2  RULE: MultiService {INTER MultiMethod       2  RULE: TinyService {INTER FewMethod
3  HighResponse LowAvailability LowCohesion};   3                            HighCoupling};
4  RULE: MultiMethod {NMD VERY_HIGH};           4  RULE: FewMethod {NMD VERY_LOW};
5  RULE: HighResponse {RT VERY_HIGH};           5  RULE: HighCoupling {CPL HIGH};
6  RULE: LowAvailability {A LOW};               6 };
7  RULE: LowCohesion {COH LOW};
8 };
```

(a) Multi Service   (b) Tiny Service

Fig. 2. Rule Cards for Multi Service and Tiny Service

both static and dynamic metrics. The static metric suite includes (but is not limited to) the following metrics: number of methods declared (NMD), number of incoming references (NIR), number of outgoing references (NOR), coupling (CPL), cohesion (COH), average number of parameters in methods (ANP), average number of primitive type parameters (ANPT), average number of accessor methods (ANAM), and average number of identical methods (ANIM). The dynamic metric suite contains: number of method invocations (NMI), number of transitive methods invoked (NTMI), response time (RT), and availability (A). Other metrics can be included by adding them to the SOFA framework.

Figure 2 illustrates the grammar with the rule cards of the Multi Service and Tiny Service antipatterns. The Multi Service antipattern is characterized by very high response time and number of methods and low availability and cohesion. A Tiny Service corresponds to a service that declares a very low number of methods and has a high coupling with other services. For the sake of clarity, we illustrate the DSL with two intra-service antipatterns, *i.e.*, antipatterns within a service. However, the DSL allows also the specification of inter-service antipatterns, *i.e.*, services spreading over more than one service. We provide the rule cards of such other more complex antipatterns later in the experiments (see Section 4).

Using a DSL offers greater flexibility than implementing ad hoc detection algorithms, because it allows describing antipatterns using high-level domain-related abstractions and focusing on *what* to detect instead of *how* to detect it [5]. Indeed, the DSL is independent of any implementation concern, such as the computation of static and dynamic metrics and the multitude of SOA technologies underlying SBSs. Moreover, the DSL allows the adaptation of the antipattern specifications to the context and characteristics of the analyzed SBSs by adjusting the metrics and associated values.

3.2   Generation of Detection Algorithms

From the specifications of SOA antipatterns described with the DSL, we automatically generate detection algorithms.

We implement the generation of the detection algorithms as a set of visitors on models of antipattern rule cards. The generation is based on templates and targets the services of the underlying framework described in the following subsection. Templates are excerpts of JAVA source code with well-defined tags. We use templates because the detection algorithms have common structures.

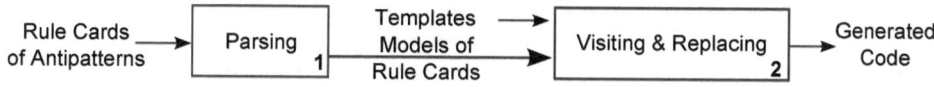

Fig. 3. Generation of Detection Algorithms

Figure 3 sketches the different steps and artifacts of this generation process. First, rule cards of antipatterns are parsed and reified as models. Then, during the visit of the rule card models, the tags of templates are replaced with the data and values appropriate to the rules. The final source code generated for a rule card is the detection algorithm of the corresponding antipattern and this code is directly compilable and executable without any manual intervention.

This generative process is fully automated to avoid any manual tasks, which are usually repetitive and error-prone. This process also ensures the traceability between the specifications of antipatterns with the DSL and their concrete detection in SBSs using our underlying framework. Consequently, software engineers can focus on the specification of antipatterns, without considering any technical aspects of the underlying framework.

3.3 SOFA: Underlying Framework

We developed a framework, called SOFA (Service Oriented Framework for Antipatterns), that supports the detection of SOA antipatterns in SBSs. This framework, designed itself as an SBS and illustrated in Figure 4, provides different services corresponding to the main steps for the detection of SOA antipatterns (1) the automated generation of detection algorithms; (2) the computation of static and dynamic metrics; and (3) the specification of rules including different sub-services for the rule language, the box-plot statistical technique, and the set operators. The rule specification and algorithm generation services provide all constituents to describe models of rule cards as well as the algorithms to visit

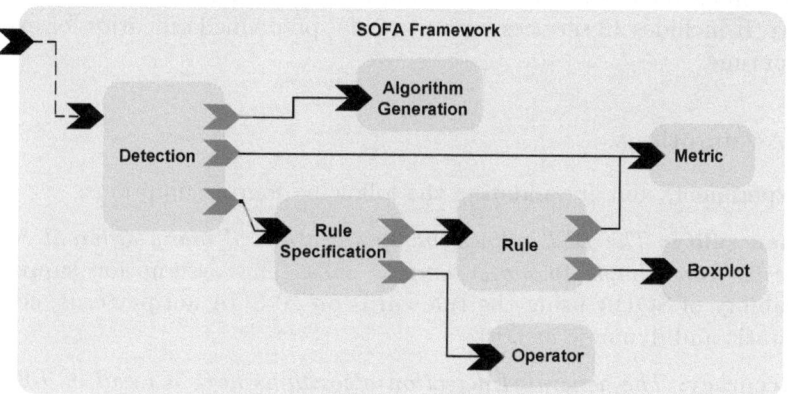

Fig. 4. The SOFA Framework

rule card models and to generate detection algorithms from these models. These different constituents rely on Model Driven Engineering techniques, which provide the means to define a DSL, parse it, and check its conformance with the grammar. We also use Kermeta [18], an executable metamodeling language, for generating the detection algorithms based on models of rule cards.

With respect to the computation of metrics, the generated detection algorithms call sensors and triggers implemented using the modules of the Galaxy framework [12]. These sensors and triggers, implemented as join points in an aspect-oriented programming style, allow, *at runtime*, the introspection of the interface of services and the triggering of events to add non-functional concerns, such as transactions, debugging, and, in our case, the computation of metrics such as response time.

We chose Kermeta and Galaxy for the sake of convenience because they are developed and maintained within our research team. Galaxy [12] is an open agile SOA framework supporting the SCA (Service Component Architecture) standard [20]. SCA is a relatively new standard, advocated by researchers and major software vendors, like IBM and Oracle, for developing technology agnostic and extensible SBSs. Galaxy encompasses different modules for building, deploying, running, and monitoring SBSs. Such a framework is essential for allowing the detection of SOA antipatterns at execution time through FraSCAti [23], which provides runtime support for the SCA standard. Furthermore, the SOFA framework is implemented itself as an SCA component to ease its use and evolution and to offer it as a service to end-users concerned by the design and QoS of their SBSs.

4   Experiments

To show the completeness and extensibility of our DSL, the accuracy of the generated algorithms, and the usefulness of the detection results with their related performance, we performed experiments with 10 antipatterns on a service-based SCA system, *Home-Automation*. This SBS has been developed independently for controlling remotely many basic household functions for elderly home care support. It includes 13 services with a set of 7 predefined scenarios for executing it at runtime.

4.1   Assumptions

The experiments aim at validating the following four assumptions:

A1. Generality: *The DSL allows the specification of many different SOA antipatterns, from simple to more complex ones.* This assumption supports the applicability of SODA using the rule cards on 10 SOA antipatterns, composed of 14 static and dynamic metrics.

A2. Accuracy: *The generated detection algorithms have a recall of 100%, i.e., all existing antipatterns are detected, and a precision greater than 75%, i.e., more*

Table 1. List of Antipatterns. (The first seven antipatterns are extracted from the literature and three others are newly defined.)

Multi Service also known as *God Object* corresponds to a service that implements a *multitude of methods* related to different business and technical abstractions. This aggregates too much into a single service, such a service is not easily reusable because of the *low cohesion* of its methods and is often **unavailable** to end-users because of its *overload*, which may induce a **high response time** [7].

Tiny Service is a small service with **few methods**, which only implements part of an abstraction. Such service often requires **several coupled** services to be used together, resulting in higher development complexity and **reduced usability**. In the extreme case, a *Tiny Service* will be limited to **one method**, resulting in many services that implement an overall set of requirements [7].

Sand Pile is also known as *'Fine-Grained Services'*. It appears when a service is **composed** by multiple smaller services sharing **common data**. It thus has a **high data cohesion**. The common data shared may be located in a **Data Service** antipattern (see below) [15].

Chatty Service corresponds to a set of services that exchange a lot of **small data of primitive types**, usually with a **Data Service** antipattern. The *Chatty Service* is also characterized by a **high number of method invocations**. *Chatty Service* chats a lot with each other [7].

The Knot is a set of **very low cohesive** services, which are **tightly coupled**. These services are thus less reusable. Due to this complex architecture, the **availability** of these services can be **low**, and their **response time high** [22].

Nobody Home corresponds to a service, defined but actually never used by clients. Thus, the **methods** from this service are **never invoked**, even though it may be **coupled** to other services. But still they require deployment and management, despite of their no usage [13].

Duplicated Service a.k.a. *The Silo Approach* introduced by IBM corresponds to a set of **highly similar** services. Since services are implemented multiple times as a result of the silo approach, there may have **common** or **identical methods** with the **same names and/or parameters** [4].

Bottleneck Service is a service that is highly used by other services or clients. It has a **high incoming and outgoing coupling**. Its **response time** can be **high** because it may be used by too many external clients, for which clients may need to wait to get access to the service. Moreover, its **availability** may also be low due to the traffic.

Service Chain a.k.a. *Message Chain* [10] in OO systems corresponds to a **chain of services**. The *Service Chain* appears when clients request consecutive service invocations to fulfill their goals. This kind of **dependency** chain reflects the action of **invocation** in a **transitive** manner.

Data Service a.k.a. *Data Class* [10] in OO systems corresponds to a service that contains **mainly accessor methods**, *i.e.*, getters and setters. In the distributed applications, there can be some services that may only perform some simple information retrieval or **data access** to such services. *Data Services* contain usually **accessor methods** with **small parameters** of **primitive types**. Such service has a **high** data **cohesion**.

---

than three-quarters of detected antipatterns are true positive. Given the trade-off between precision and recall, we assume that 75% precision is significant enough with respect to 100% recall. This assumption supports the precision of the rule cards and the accuracy of the algorithm generation and of the SOFA framework.

A3. Extensibility: *The DSL and the SOFA framework are extensible for adding new SOA antipatterns.* Through this assumption, we show how well the DSL, and in particular the metrics, with the supporting SOFA framework, can be combined to specify and detect new antipatterns.

A4. Performance: *The computation time required for the detection of antipatterns using the generated algorithms is reasonably very low, i.e., in the order of few seconds.* This assumption supports the performance of the services provided by the SOFA framework for the detection of antipatterns.

4.2   Subjects

We apply our SODA approach using the SOFA framework to specify 10 different SOA antipatterns. Table 1 summarizes these antipatterns, of which the first seven are from the literature and three others have been newly defined, namely, the *Bottleneck Service*, *Service Chain*, and *Data Service*. These new antipatterns are inspired from OO code smells [10]. In these summaries, we highlight in bold the key concepts relevant for the specification of their rule cards given in Figure 5.

```
1 RULE_CARD: DataService {
2   RULE: DataService {INTER HighDataAccessor
3   SmallParameter PrimitiveParameter HighCohesion};
4   RULE: SmallParameter {ANP LOW};
5   RULE: PrimitiveParameter {ANPT HIGH};
6   RULE: HighDataAccessor {ANAM VERY_HIGH};
7   RULE: HighCohesion {COH HIGH};
8 };
```
(a) Data Service

```
1 RULE_CARD: TheKnot {
2   RULE: TheKnot {INTER HighCoupling
3   LowCohesion LowAvailability HighResponse};
4   RULE: HighCoupling {CPL VERY_HIGH};
5   RULE: LowCohesion {COH VERY_LOW};
6   RULE: LowAvailability {A LOW};
7   RULE: HighResponse {RT HIGH};
8 };
```
(b) The Knot

```
1 RULE_CARD: ChattyService {
2   RULE: ChattyService {
3   INTER TotalInvocation DSRuleCard};
4   RULE: DSRuleCard {RULE_CARD: DataService};
5   RULE: TotalInvocation {NMI VERY_HIGH};
6 };
```
(c) Chatty Service

```
1 RULE_CARD: NobodyHome {
2   RULE: NobodyHome {
3   INTER IncomingReference MethodInvocation};
4   RULE: IncomingReference {NIR GREATER 0};
5   RULE: MethodInvocation {NMI EQUAL 0};
6 };
```
(d) Nobody Home

```
1 RULE_CARD: BottleneckService {
2   RULE: BottleneckService {
3   INTER LowPerformance HighCoupling};
4   RULE: LowPerformance {
5   INTER LowAvailability HighResponse};
6   RULE: HighResponse {RT HIGH};
7   RULE: LowAvailability {A LOW};
8   RULE: HighCoupling {CPL VERY_HIGH};
9 };
```
(e) Bottleneck Service

```
1 RULE_CARD: SandPile {
2   RULE: SandPile {COMPOS FROM
3   ParentService ONE TO ChildService MANY};
4   RULE: ChildService {ASSOC FROM
5   ContainedService MANY TO DataSource ONE};
6   RULE: ParentService {COH HIGH};
7   RULE: DataSource {RULE_CARD: DataService};
8   RULE: ContainedService {NRO > 1};
9 };
```
(f) Sand Pile

```
1 RULE_CARD: ServiceChain {
2   RULE: ServiceChain {INTER TransitiveInvocation
3   LowAvailability};
4   RULE: TransitiveInvocation {NTMI VERY_HIGH};
5   RULE: LowAvailability {A LOW};
6 };
```
(g) Service Chain

```
1 RULE_CARD: DuplicatedService {
2   RULE: DuplicatedService {ANIM HIGH};
3 };
```
(h) Duplicated Service

Fig. 5. Rule Cards for Different Antipatterns

4.3   Objects

We perform the experiments on two different versions of the *Home-Automation* system: the original version of the system, which includes 13 services, and a version modified by adding and modifying services to inject intentionally some antipatterns. The modifications have been performed by an independent engineer to avoid biasing the results. Details on the two versions of the system including all the scenarios and involved services are available online at http://sofa.uqam.ca.

4.4   Process

Using the SOFA framework, we generated the detection algorithms corresponding to the rule cards of the 10 antipatterns. Then, we applied these algorithms at runtime on the *Home-Automation* system using its set of 7 predefined scenarios. Finally, we validated the detection results by analyzing the suspicious services manually to (1) validate that these suspicious services are true positives and (2) identify false negatives (if any), *i.e.*, missing antipatterns. For this last validation step, we use the measures of precision and recall [11]. Precision estimates the ratio of true antipatterns identified among the detected antipatterns, while recall estimates the ratio of detected antipatterns among the existing antipatterns. This validation has been performed manually by two independent software engineers, whom we provided the descriptions of antipatterns and the two versions of the analyzed system *Home-Automation*.

4.5   Results

Table 2 presents the results for the detection of the 10 SOA antipatterns on the original and evolved version of *Home-Automation*. For each antipattern, the table reports the involved services in the second column, the version analyzed of *Home-Automation* in the third column, the analysis method: *static* (S) and–or *dynamic* (D) in the fourth, then the metrics values of rule cards in the fifth, and finally the computation times in the sixth. The two last columns report the precision and recall.

4.6   Details of the Results

We briefly present the detection results of the *Tiny Service* and *Multi Service*. The service `IMediator` has been identified as a *Multi Service* because of its very high number of methods (*i.e.*, NMD equal 13) and its low cohesion (*i.e.*, COH equal 0.027). These metric values have been evaluated by the *Box-Plot* service respectively as high and low in comparison with the metric values of other services of *Home-Automation*. For example, for the metric NMD, the *Box-Plot* estimates the median value of NMD in *Home-Automation* as equal to 2. In the same way, the detected *Tiny Service* has a very low number of methods (*i.e.*, NMD equal 1) and a high coupling (*i.e.*, CPL equal 0.44) with respect to other values. The values of the cohesion COH and coupling CPL metrics range from 0 to 1. In the original version of *Home-Automation*, we did not detect any *Tiny Service*. We then extracted one method from `IMediator` and moved it in a new service named `MediatorDelegate`, and then this service has been detected as a *Tiny Service*.

We also detected 7 other antipatterns within the original version of *Home-Automation*, namely, *Duplicated Service, Chatty Service, Sand Pile, The Knot, Bottleneck Service, Data Service*, and *Service Chain*. All these antipatterns involve more than one service, except *Data Service* and *Duplicated Service*. The service `PatientDAO` has been detected as a *Data Service* because it performs

Table 2. Results for the Detection of 10 SOA Antipatterns in the Original and Evolved Version of *Home-Automation* System *(S: Static, D: Dynamic)*

ANTIPATTERNNAME	SERVICESINVOLVED	VERSION	ANALYSIS	METRICS	DETECTTIME	PRECISION	RECALL
Tiny Service	[MediatorDelegate]	evolved	S	NOR: 4 CPL: 0.440 NMD: 1	0.194s	[1/1] 100%	[1/1] 100%
Multi Service	[IMediator]	original	S, D	COH: 0.027 NMD: 13 RT: 132ms	0.462s	[1/1] 100%	[1/1] 100%
Duplicated Service	[Communication-Service] [IMediator]	original	S	ANIM: 25%	0.215s	[2/2] 100%	[2/2] 100%
Chatty Service	[PatientDAO] [IMediator]	original	S, D	ANP: 1.0 ANPT: 1.0 NMI: 3 ANAM: 100% COH: 0.167	0.383s	[2/2] 100%	[2/2] 100%
Nobody Home	[UselessService]	evolved	S, D	NIR: >0 NMI: 0	1.154s	[1/1] 100%	[1/1] 100%
Sand Pile	[HomeAutomation]	original	S	NCS: 13 ANP: 1.0 ANPT: 1.0 ANAM: 100% COH: 0.167	0.310s	[1/1] 100%	[1/1] 100%
The Knot	[IMediator] [PatientDAO]	original	S, D	COH: 0.027 NIR: 7 NOR: 7 CPL: 1.0 RT: 57ms	0.412s	[1/2] 50%	[1/1] 100%
Bottleneck Service	[IMediator] [PatientDAO]	original	S, D	NIR: 7 NOR: 7 CPL: 1.0 RT: 40ms	0.246s	[2/2] 100%	[2/2] 100%
Data Service	[PatientDAO]	original	S	ANAM: 100% COH: 0.167 ANPT: 1.0 ANP: 1.0	0.268s	[1/1] 100%	[1/1] 100%
Service Chain	[IMediator] [SunSpotService] [PatientDAO] [PatientDAO2]	original	D	NTMI: 4.0	0.229s	[3/4] 75%	[3/3] 100%
AVERAGE					0.387s	[15/17] 92.5%	[15/15] 100%

simple data accesses. Moreover, in the evolved version, we detected the *Nobody Home* antipattern, after an independent developer introduced the service Use-lessService, which is defined but never used in any scenarios. We detected a consecutive chain of invocations of IMediator → SunSpotService → Patient-DAO → PatientDAO2, which forms a *Service Chain*, whereas engineers validated IMediator → PatientDAO → PatientDAO2. Therefore, we had the precision of 75% and recall of 100% for the *Service Chain* antipattern. Moreover, we detected the HomeAutomation itself as *Sand Pile*. Finally, an important point is that we use in some rule cards the dynamic property *Availability* (A). However, we did not report this value because it corresponds to 100% since the services of the system were deployed locally.

4.7 Discussion on the Assumptions

We now verify each of the four assumptions stated previously using the detection results.

A1. Generality: *The DSL allows the specification of many different SOA antipatterns, from simple to more complex ones.* Using our DSL, we specified 10 SOA antipatterns described in Table 1, as shown in rule cards given in Figure 2 and 5. These antipatterns range from simple ones, such as the *Tiny Service* and *Multi Service*, to more complex ones such as the *Bottleneck* and *Sand Pile*, which involve several services and complex relationships. In particular, *Sand Pile* has both the `ASSOC` and `COMPOS` relation type. Also, both *Sand Pile* and *Chatty Service* refer in their specifications to another antipattern, namely *DataService*. Thus, we show that we can specify from simple to complex antipatterns, which support the generality of our DSL.

A2. Accuracy: *The generated detection algorithms have a recall of 100%, i.e., all existing antipatterns are detected, and a precision greater than 75%, i.e., more than three-quarters of detected antipatterns are true positive.* As indicated in Table 2, we obtain a recall of 100%, which means all existing antipatterns are detected, whereas the precision is 92.5%. We have high precision and recall because the analyzed system, *Home-Automation* is a small SBS with 13 services. Also, the evolved version includes two new services. Therefore, considering the small *but* significant number of services and the well defined rule cards using DSL, we obtain such a high precision and recall. For the original *Home-Automation* version, out of 13 services, we detected 6 services that are responsible for 8 antipatterns. Besides, we detected 2 services (out of 15) that are responsible for 2 other antipatterns in the evolved system.

A3. Extensibility: *The DSL and the SOFA framework are extensible for adding new SOA antipatterns.* The DSL has been initially designed for specifying the seven antipatterns described in the literature (see Table 1). Then, through inspection of the SBS and inspiration from OO code smells, we added three new antipatterns, namely the *Bottleneck Service*, *Service Chain* and *Data Service*. When specifying these new antipatterns, we reused four already-defined metrics and we added in the DSL and SOFA four more metrics (`ANAM`, `NTMI`, `ANP` and `ANPT`). The language is flexible in the integration of new metrics. However, the underlying SOFA framework should also be extended to provide the operational implementations of the new metrics. Such an addition can only be realized by skilled developers with our framework, that may require from 1 hour to 2 days according to the complexity of the metrics. Thus, by extending the DSL with these three new antipatterns and integrating them within the SOFA framework, we support A3.

A4. Performance: *The computation time required for the detection of antipatterns using the generated algorithms is reasonably very low, i.e., in the order of few seconds.* We perform all experiments on an Intel Dual Core at 3.30GHz with 3GB of RAM. Computation times include computing metric values, introspection delay during static and dynamic analysis, and applying detection algorithms. The computation times for the detection of antipatterns is reasonably low, *i.e.*, ranging from 0.194s to 1.154s with an average of 0.387s. Such low computation times suggest that SODA could be applied on SBSs with larger number of services. Thus, we showed that we can support the fourth assumption positively.

4.8 Threats to Validity

The main threat to the validity of our results concerns their *external validity*, *i.e.*, the possibility to generalize our approach to other SBSs. As future work, we plan to run these experiments on other SBSs. However, we considered two versions of *Home-Automation*. For *internal validity*, the detection results depend on the services provided by the SOFA framework but also on the antipattern specifications using rule cards. We performed experiments on a representative set of antipatterns to lessen this threat to the internal validity. The subjective nature of specifying and validating antipatterns is a threat to *construct validity*. We try to lessen this threat by defining rule cards based on a literature review and domain analysis and by involving two independent engineers in the validation. We minimize *reliability validity* by automating the generation of the detection algorithm. Each subsequent detection produce consistent sets of results with high precision and recall.

5 Conclusion and Future Work

The specification and detection of SOA antipatterns are important to assess the design and QoS of SBSs and thus, ease the maintenance and evolution of SBSs. In this paper, we presented a novel approach, named SODA, for the specification and detection of SOA antipatterns, and SOFA, its underlying framework. We proposed a DSL for specifying SOA antipatterns and a process for automatically generating detection algorithms from the antipattern specifications. We applied and validated SODA with 10 different SOA antipatterns on an original and a evolved version of *Home-Automation*, a SBS developed independently. We demonstrated the usefulness of our approach and discussed its precision and recall.

As future work, we intend to enhance the detection approach with a correction approach to suggest refactorings and automatically, at runtime, correct detected SOA antipatterns, enabling software engineers to improve the design and QoS of their SBSs. Furthermore, we intend to perform other experiments on different SBSs from different SOA technologies, including SCA, Web Services, REST and EJB. The approach may require some adaptations from one technology to another because although SOA technologies share some common concepts and principles, they also have their own specific characteristics. Another targeted SBS is the SOFA framework itself since because this SBS will certainly evolve to handle various antipatterns and SBSs. We will thus ensure that the evolution of the SOFA framework does not introduce itself antipatterns.

Acknowledgments. The authors thank Yousri Kouki and Mahmoud Ben Hassine for their help with the implementation of *Home-Automation*. This work is partly supported by the NESSOS European Network of Excellence and a NSERC Discovery Grant. And, this work is in memory of Anne-Françoise Le Meur, our dearly departed colleague, who initiated the work.

References

1. Bart Du Bois, J.V., Demeyer, S.: Refactoring - Improving Coupling and Cohesion of Existing Code. In: Proceedings of the 11th IEEE Working Conference on Reverse Engineering, pp. 144–151 (2004)
2. Brown, W., Malveau, R., McCormick III, H., Mowbray, T.: Anti Patterns: Refactoring Software, Architectures, and Projects in Crisis. John Wiley and Sons (1998)
3. Chambers, J., Cleveland, W., Tukey, P., Kleiner, B.: Graphical methods for data analysis. Wadsworth International (1983)
4. Cherbakov, L., Ibrahim, M., Ang, J.: SOA Antipatterns: The Obstacles to the Adoption and Successful Realization of Service-Oriented Architecture, www.ibm.com/developerworks/webservices/library/ws-antipatterns/
5. Consel, C., Marlet, R.: Architecturing Software Using a Methodology for Language Development. In: Palamidessi, C., Meinke, K., Glaser, H. (eds.) ALP 1998 and PLILP 1998. LNCS, vol. 1490, pp. 170–194. Springer, Heidelberg (1998)
6. Daigneau, R.: Service Design Patterns: Fundamental Design Solutions for SOAP/WSDL and RESTful Web Services. Addison-Wesley (November 2011)
7. Dudney, B., Asbury, S., Krozak, J., Wittkopf, K.: J2EE AntiPatterns. John Wiley & Sons Inc. (2003)
8. Erl, T.: Service-Oriented Architecture: Concepts, Technology, and Design. Prentice Hall PTR (2005)
9. Erl, T.: SOA Design Patterns. Prentice Hall PTR (2009)
10. Fowler, M.J., Beck, K., Brant, J., Opdyke, W., Roberts, D.: Refactoring: Improving the Design of Existing Code. Addison-Wesley (1999)
11. Frakes, W.B., Baeza-Yates, R.A. (eds.): Information Retrieval: Data Structures & Algorithms. Prentice-Hall (1992)
12. Galaxy INRIA: The French National Institute for Research in Computer Science and Control, http://galaxy.gforge.inria.fr
13. Jones, S.: SOA Anti-patterns, http://www.infoq.com/articles/SOA-anti-patterns
14. Kessentini, M., Vaucher, S., Sahraoui, H.: Deviance From Perfection is a Better Criterion Than Closeness To Evil When Identifying Risky Code. In: Proceedings of the IEEE/ACM International Conference on Automated Software Engineering, ASE 2010, pp. 113–122. ACM, New York (2010)
15. Král, J., Žemlička, M.: Crucial Service-Oriented Antipatterns, vol. 2, pp. 160–171. International Academy, Research and Industry Association, IARIA (2008)
16. Lanza, M., Marinescu, R.: Object-Oriented Metrics in Practice. Springer (2006)
17. Modi, T.: SOA Management: SOA Antipatterns, http://www.ebizq.net/topics/soa_management/features/7238.html
18. Moha, N., Sen, S., Faucher, C., Barais, O., Jézéquel, J.M.: Evaluation of Kermeta for Solving Graph-based Problems. Journal on Software Tools for Technology Transfer 12(3-4), 273–285 (2010)

19. Munro, M.J.: Product Metrics for Automatic Identification of "Bad Smell" Design Problems in Java Source-Code. In: Proceedings of the 11th International Software Metrics Symposium. IEEE Computer Society Press (September 2005)
20. Open SOA: SCA Service Component Architecture - Assembly Model Specification, version 1.00 (March 2007), www.osoa.org
21. Parsons, T., Murphy, J.: Detecting Performance Antipatterns in Component Based Enterprise Systems. Journal of Object Technology 7(3), 55–90 (2008)
22. Rotem-Gal-Oz, A., Bruno, E., Dahan, U.: SOA Patterns. Manning Publications Co. (2012), to be published in Summer 2012
23. Seinturier, L., Merle, P., Fournier, D., Schiavoni, V., Demarey, C., Dolet, N., Petitprez, N.: FraSCAti - Open SCA Middleware Platform v1.4, http://frascati.ow2.org
24. Settas, D.L., Meditskos, G., Stamelos, I.G., Bassiliades, N.: SPARSE: A symptom-based antipattern retrieval knowledge-based system using Semantic Web technologies. Expert Systems with Applications 38(6), 7633–7646 (2011)
25. Simon, F., Steinbruckner, F., Lewerentz, C.: Metrics Based Refactoring. In: Proceedings of the 5th European Conference on Software Maintenance and Reengineering, pp. 14–16 (March 2001)
26. Trifu, A., Dragos, I.: Strategy-Based Elimination of Design Flaws in Object-Oriented Systems. In: Proceedings of the 4th International Workshop on Object-Oriented Reengineering. Universiteit Antwerpen (July 2003)
27. Wong, S., Aaron, M., Segall, J., Lynch, K., Mancoridis, S.: Reverse Engineering Utility Functions Using Genetic Programming to Detect Anomalous Behavior in Software. In: Proceedings of the 2010 17th Working Conference on Reverse Engineering, WCRE 2010, pp. 141–149. IEEE Computer Society, Washington, DC (2010)

Verification of GSM-Based Artifact-Centric Systems through Finite Abstraction

Francesco Belardinelli[1], Alessio Lomuscio[1], and Fabio Patrizi[2]

[1] Department of Computing, Imperial College London
{f.belardinelli,a.lomuscio}@imperial.ac.uk
[2] DIIAG, Sapienza Università di Roma
patrizi@dis.uniroma1.it

Abstract. The GSM framework provides a methodology for the development of artifact-centric systems, an increasingly popular paradigm in service-oriented computing. In this paper we tackle the problem of verifying GSM programs in a multi-agent system setting. We provide an embedding from GSM into a suitable multi-agent systems semantics for reasoning about knowledge and time at the first-order level. While we observe that GSM programs generate infinite models, we isolate a large class of "amenable" systems, which we show admit finite abstractions and are therefore verifiable through model checking. We illustrate the contribution with a procurement use-case taken from the relevant business process literature.

1 Introduction

The *artifact-centric paradigm* [8, 9] has recently gained considerable prominence in the business processes and services communities as a promising and novel methodology for quick and inexpensive deployment of data-intensive web-services. In the artifact-centric approach *data* feature prominently and drive the execution of the system, together with the associated process-based description of the services. The Guard-Stage-Milestone (GSM) language [15], together with its Barcelona production and execution suite, provides a declarative framework to deploy artifact-centric systems. In a nutshell, GSM offers the constructs for the definition of *artifacts* as typed records of data, their evolution (or *lifecycles*) through a dedicated rule-driven semantics, and the interface for the interaction of the artifacts with the users. This interface is composed of services that agents can invoke thereby affecting the artifacts in the system through chains of operations.

We see two deficiencies in the GSM approach as it currently stands. Firstly, similarly to database-inspired techniques, GSM programs only define the evolution of the artifacts and provide no precise mechanism for accounting for any users or automatic agents interacting with the system. Yet, if we wish to follow an approach of implementing services through agents, these need to be present in the model. Secondly, GSM currently lacks any support for automatic verification. Yet, validation through verification is increasingly being regarded as an important aspect of service deployment [17].

This paper aims to make a direct contribution towards these two key problems. To solve the first concern, we provide a semantics, based on multi-agent systems, to GSM

C. Liu et al. (Eds.): ICSOC 2012, LNCS 7636, pp. 17–31, 2012.
© Springer-Verlag Berlin Heidelberg 2012

programs, where we give first-class citizenship to human actors and automatic agents present in the service composition. To solve the second, we observe that GSM programs generate infinite-state systems thereby making traditional model checking impracticable. Our contribution here is to show that GSM programs admit, under some rather general conditions, finite models, thus opening the way for their effective verification. The rest of the paper is organised as follows. In Section 2 we introduce artifacts and GSM programs, which are illustrated by the *Requisition and Procurement Orders* scenario in Section 3. In Section 4 we adopt the semantics of artifact-centric multi-agent systems (AC-MAS) to deal with the verification of GSM programs. Finally, in Section 5 we show how to embed GSM programs into AC-MAS; thus obtaining finite abstractions for the former.

Related Work. The exploration of finite abstraction in the context of artifact-centric environments has attracted considerable attention recently [2–5, 10, 11, 14]. While these make a noteworthy contribution and are in some cases used here as a stepping stone for our results [2–4], the key point of departure from the literature of the present contribution is that we here operate directly on GSM programs and not on logical models derived manually from them. We see this as an essential step towards the construction of *automatic* verification techniques for GSM programs.

2   GSM Programs

Artifact-centric systems are based on the notion of *artifact*, i.e., a record of structured data, that are born, evolve, and die during a system run either as a consequence of chains of internal actions of other artifacts, or through external actions performed by actors. GSM [15] is a declarative language, interpreted by specialised toolkits, that enables the user to implement guard-stage-milestone models for artifact systems.

For simplicity, here we work on an untyped version of GSM programs in which we also neglect timestamps: while GSM programs are richer, the version we consider enables us to present decidability results concisely while at the same time supporting complex use-cases as we show in Section 3. The present section makes use of notions and definitions from [15].

Definition 1 (Artifact Type). *An* artifact type *is a tuple* $AT = \langle P, x, Att, Stg, Mst, Lcyc \rangle$ *such that*

- *P is the* name *of the artifact type;*
- *x is a variable that ranges over the IDs of instances of AT; this is the* context variable *of AT, which is used in the logical formulas in Lcyc;*
- *Att is the set of* attributes, *which is partitioned into the set* Att_{data} *of data attributes and* Att_{status} *of status attributes;*
- *Stg is the set of* stages;
- *Mst is the set of* milestone;
- *Lcyc is the* lifecycle model *of the artifact type AT, which is formally defined below.*

Intuitively, artifact types can be seen as records of structured data. The set Att_{data} includes the attribute $mostRecEventType$, which holds the type of the most recent event. Milestones and stages describe the evolution of the artifact type. We associate a Boolean *milestone status* attribute, denoted as m, to each milestone $m \in Mst$ in Att_{status}. Analogously, for each stage $S \in Stg$, in Att_{status} there is a Boolean *stage status* attribute $active_S$.

While the data content of an artifact type is specified by its datamodel, i.e., all its attributes excluding the lifecycle, its execution is described by its lifecycle.

Definition 2 (Lifecycle). *The lifecycle of an artifact type AT is a tuple $Lcyc = \langle Substg, Task, Owns, Guards, Ach, Inv \rangle$ such that*

- *$Substg$ is a function from Stg to finite subsets of Stg, where the relation $\{(S, S')|S' \in Substg(S)\}$ is a forest. The leaves of the forest are called* atomic *stages.*
- *$Task$ is a function from the atomic stages in Stg to tasks.*
- *$Owns$ is a function from Stg to finite, non-empty subsets of Mst. A stage S owns a milestone m if $m \in Owns(S)$.*
- *$Guards$ is a function from Stg to finite sets of* sentries*, as defined in Section 2.1. An element of $Guards(S)$ is called a* guard *for S.*
- *Ach is a function from Mst to finite sets of* achieving *sentries.*
- *Inv is a function from Mst to finite sets of* invalidating *sentries.*

More details are given in Section 2.1. Intuitively, every artifact goes through a number of stages, which are activated by the relevant guards. A stage is closed when the tasks associated with it and its substages are fulfilled. When this happens, the milestones associated with the stage become true and possibly trigger the guards associated with another stage. We now introduce GSM programs.

Definition 3 (GSM program). *A GSM program Γ is a set of artifact types AT_i for $i \leq n$.*

For convenience, we assume that all context variables are distinct. Artifact instances are then defined as mappings from artifact types to a possibly infinite interpretation domain U of data values.

Definition 4 (AT and GSM snapshot). *A snapshot for the artifact type AT is a mapping σ from x, Att to the interpretation domain U. A snapshot for the GSM program Γ is a mapping Σ from each type $AT \in \Gamma$ to a set $\Sigma(AT)$ of snapshots for type AT.*

Intuitively, a snapshot for the artifact type AT is an assignment of the values in U to the attributes of AT. A GSM snapshot is then a collection of AT snapshots. Notice that different instances of the same artifact type are distinguished by their IDs $\sigma(x)$, hereafter denoted as ρ.

2.1 Execution of GSM Programs

Events are responsible for the evolution of a GSM system from one snapshot to the next. Three types of incoming events are considered: 1-way messages M, 2-way service call returns F^{return}, and artifact instance creation requests $create_{AT}^{call}$. A ground event e has a *payload* $(A_1 : c_1, \dots, A_n : c_n)$ where A_i is a data attribute and c_i is a value in the domain U. Intuitively, incoming events are processed by the sentries associated with guards and milestones, and the payload determines the evolution of the stage as detailed below.

Definition 5 (Immediate effect). *The* immediate effect *of a ground event e on a snap-shot* Σ, *or ImmEffect(Σ, e), is the snapshot that results from incorporating e into Σ, including (i) changing the values of the* mostRecEventType *attribute of affected (or created) artifact instances; (ii) changing the values of data attributes of affected artifact instances, as indicated by the payload of e.*

The operational semantics for GSM programs is given through the notion of *business step*, or B-step, which represents the impact of a single ground incoming event e on a snapshot Σ. The semantics of B-steps is characterised by 3-tuples (Σ, e, Σ') where

1. Σ is the *previous* snapshot;
2. e is a ground incoming event;
3. Σ' is the *next* snapshot;
4. there is a sequence $\Sigma_0, \Sigma_1, \ldots, \Sigma_n$ of snapshots such that (i) $\Sigma_0 = \Sigma$; (ii) $\Sigma_1 = ImmEffect(\Sigma, e)$; (iii) $\Sigma_n = \Sigma'$; and (iv) for $1 \leq j < n$, Σ_{j+1} is obtained from Σ_j by a PAC rule (see below).

Business steps follow *Prerequisite-Antecedent-Consequent* (PAC) rules [15]. To intro-duce PAC rules we first define formally event expressions and sentries. In what follows τ_{AT} is a path expression $x. < path >$ where x is the ID variable for some artifact type $AT \in \Gamma$. An example of a path expression is $\rho.S.m$, which refers to the milestone m of stage S, for some AT instance ρ.

Definition 6 (Event expression). *An* event expression $\xi(x)$ *for an artifact type AT with ID variable x has one of the following forms:*

– *Incoming event expression $x.e$: (i) $x.M$ for 1-way message type M; (ii) $x.F^{return}$ for service call return from F; (iii) $x.create_{AT}^{call}$ for a call to create an artifact instance of type AT.*
– *Internal event expression: (i) $+\tau_{AT'}.m$ and $-\tau_{AT'}.m$, where m is a milestone for type AT'; (ii) $+\tau_{AT'}.active_S$ and $-\tau_{AT'}.active_S$, where S is a stage of type AT'.*

Intuitively, an event occurrence of type $+\tau_{AT'}.m$ (resp. $-\tau_{AT'}.m$) arises whenever the milestone m of the instance identified by $x. < path >$ changes value from false to true (resp. true to false). Similarly, an event occurrence of type $+\tau_{AT'}.active_S$ (resp. $-\tau_{AT'}.active_S$) arises whenever the stage S of the instance identified by $x. < path >$ changes value from closed to open (resp. open to closed).

We can now define sentries for guards and milestones. These represent the conditions to open and close stages.

Definition 7 (Sentry). *A* sentry *for an artifact type AT is an expression $\chi(x)$ having one of the following forms: **on** $\xi(x)$ **if** $\varphi(x) \wedge x.active_S$, **on** $\xi(x)$, or **if** $\varphi(x) \wedge x.active_S$ such that (i) $\xi(x)$ is an event expression; and (ii) $\varphi(x)$ is a first-order (FO) logical formula over the artifact types occurring in Γ that has exactly one free variable.*

We now discuss the interpretation of sentries, i.e., when a snapshot Σ satisfies a sentry χ, or $\Sigma \models \chi$. Satisfaction of an FO-formula φ at Σ is defined as standard. Further, the expression $\rho.e$ for an artifact instance ρ is true at Σ if $\rho.mostRecEventType = e$. Finally, the internal event expression $\odot \rho.\tau.s$ for polarity $\odot \in \{+, -\}$, path expression τ, and status attribute s, is true at Σ if the value of $\rho.\tau.s$ matches the polarity.

We can now introduce PAC rules.

Definition 8 (PAC rules). *A PAC rule is a tuple* $\langle \pi(x), \alpha(x), \gamma(x) \rangle$ *such that*

- $\pi(x)$ *is of the form* $\tau.m$, $\neg\tau.m$, $\tau.active_S$, *or* $\neg\tau.active_S$;
- $\alpha(x)$ *is of the form* $\chi(x) \wedge \psi(x)$, *where* $\chi(x)$ *is a sentry and* $\psi(x)$ *is of the form* $\tau.m$, $\neg\tau.m$, $\tau.active_S$, *or* $\neg\tau.active_S$;
- $\gamma(x)$ *is an internal event expression as in Def. 6.*

Given a B-step $\Sigma = \Sigma_0, \Sigma_1, \ldots, \Sigma_j$ for a ground event e, the PAC rule $\langle \pi, \alpha, \gamma \rangle$ is applicable if $\Sigma \models \pi$ and $\Sigma_j \models \alpha$. Applying such a rule yields a new snapshot Σ_{j+1}, which is constructed from Σ_j by applying the effect called for by γ.

Additional conditions can also be assumed for the application of PAC rules, which notably ensure the absence of cycles [15].

3 The RPO Scenario

The *Requisition and Procurement Orders* (RPO) scenario is a business process use-case. We analyse an implementation in which a GSM program is used to instantiate the procurement process [15]. We illustrate the notions presented in Section 2 in the context of a fragment of this scenario. In the RPO scenario a *Requisition Order* is sent by a Customer to a Manufacturer to request some goods or services. The Requisition Order has one or more *Line Items*, which are bundled into *Procurement Orders* and sent to different Suppliers. A Supplier can either accept or reject a Procurement Order. In the latter case, the rejected Line Items are bundled into new Procurement Orders. Otherwise, the order is fulfilled by the Supplier and sent to the Manufacturer, who in turn forwards it to the Customer.

In GSM programs it is natural to model the Requisition and Procurement Orders as artifact types RO and PO respectively. In particular, the *datamodel* of the Requisition Order, i.e., all its attributes excluding the lifecycle, can be encoded as in Fig. 1, which is adapted from [15]. The definition of the Procurement Order datamodel is similar. Notice that in the datamodel we have both data and status attributes; the latter contain milestone and stage data as detailed in Def. 1.

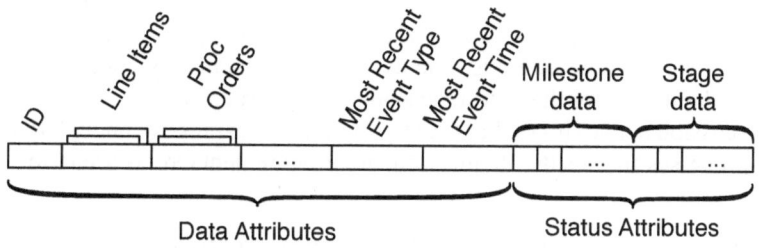

Data Attributes   Status Attributes

Fig. 1. The Requisition Order datamodel

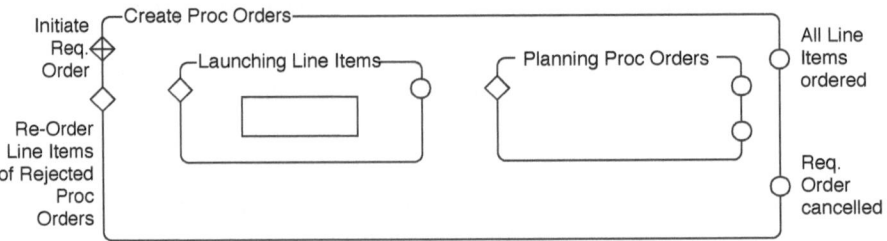

Fig. 2. A stage of the Requisition Order lifecycle

Fig. 2 illustrates part of the lifecycle for the Requisition Order [15]. Stages are represented as rounded boxes. The stage **Create Proc Orders** contains the child-stages **Launching Line Items** and **Planning Proc Orders**; the former is atomic. Milestones are shown as small circles associated with stages. For instance, the milestones **All Line Items ordered** and **Req. Order cancelled** are associated with the stage **Create Proc Orders**. The former is an achieving milestone, i.e., when **All Line Items ordered** becomes true the stage is closed; while the latter is invalidating, that is, when **Req. Order cancelled** holds, the stage is reopened. The diamond nodes are guards. The stage **Create Proc Orders** is triggered by guards **Initiate Req. Order** and **Re-order Line Items of Rejected Proc Orders**. A diamond with a cross represents a "bootstrapping" guard, which indicates the conditions to create new artifact instances. Similar representations can be given for all other stages in the Requisition and Procurement Orders.

As mentioned in Section 2 the execution of GSM programs is governed by PAC rules. To illustrate these we consider PAC2 as given in [15]:

	Prerequisite π	Antecedent α	Consequent γ
PAC2	$x.active_S$	**on** $e(x)$ **if** $\varphi(x)$	$+x.m$

where stage S has milestone m and **on** $e(x)$ **if** $\varphi(x)$ is an achieving sentry for m. Suppose that $\Sigma_0, \Sigma_1, \ldots, \Sigma_j$ is a sequence of snapshots in a B-step. Intuitively, if $\Sigma \models \pi$, then there is an artifact instance ρ s.t. $\rho.active_S$ is true, i.e., the stage S is active for ρ. Furthermore, if $\Sigma_j \models \alpha$ then $\rho.mostRecEventType = e$ and the achieving condition φ for milestone m holds. Finally, Σ_{j+1} is obtained by applying $+\rho.m$, i.e., by toggling the flag m for the milestone status of S to true.

The discussion above shows that GSM programs are expressive enough to formalise business processes such as the Requisition and Procurement Orders scenario.

4   Artifact-Centric MAS with Parametric Actions

In Section 5 we introduce a sufficient condition for obtaining finite abstractions for a notable class of the GSM programs. In order to define an embedding into an agent-based semantics, as well as to state precisely the model checking problem for these structures, we here generalise the framework of [4] to parametric actions. This is required to obtain effective model checking procedures. The material below extends [4] and follows its structure and some of the definitions. We start by introducing some terminology on databases [1].

Definition 9 (Database schema and instance). *A* database schema *is a set* $\mathcal{D} = \{P_1/q_1, \ldots, P_n/q_n\}$ *of predicate symbols* P_i *with arity* $q_i \in \mathbb{N}$.

A $\mathcal{D}$-instance *on a (possibly infinite) domain* U *is a mapping* D *associating each predicate symbol* P_i *with a finite* q_i-*ary relation over* U, *i.e.,* $D(P_i) \subseteq U^{q_i}$.

The set $\mathcal{D}(U)$ denotes all $\mathcal{D}$-instances on the domain U. The *active domain* $ad(D)$ of D is the *finite* set of all individuals occurring in some predicate interpretation $D(P_i)$. The *primed version* of a database schema $\mathcal{D}$ as above is the schema $\mathcal{D}' = \{P'_1/q_1, \ldots, P'_n/q_n\}$. Given two $\mathcal{D}$-instances D and D', $D \oplus D'$ is the $(\mathcal{D} \cup \mathcal{D}')$-instance such that (i) $D \oplus D'(P_i) = D(P_i)$; and (ii) $D \oplus D'(P'_i) = D'(P_i)$. The $\oplus$ operator will be used later in relation with temporal transitions in artifact systems.

We now extend the definition of AC-MAS in [4] to accommodate parametric actions, where U is the interpretation domain.

Definition 10 (Agent). *An agent is a tuple* $i = \langle \mathcal{D}_i, L_i, Act_i, Pr_i \rangle$ *such that*

– $\mathcal{D}_i$ *is the* local database schema;
– $L_i \subseteq \mathcal{D}_i(U)$ *is the set of* local states l_i;
– Act_i *is the set of* local actions $\alpha_i(\vec{x})$ *with parameters* $\vec{x}$;
– $Pr_i : L_i \mapsto 2^{Act_i(U)}$ *is the* local protocol function, *where* $Act_i(U)$ *is the set of* ground actions $\alpha_i(\vec{u})$ *for* $\vec{u} \in U^{|\vec{x}|}$.

Given a set $Ag = \{0, \ldots, n\}$ of agents, we define the *global* database schema of Ag as $\mathcal{D} = \mathcal{D}_0 \cup \cdots \cup \mathcal{D}_n$, i.e., the set of all predicate symbols appearing in some local database schema. Agent 0 is usually referred to as the *environment* E.

AC-MAS are models representing the evolution of a system of agents.

Definition 11 (AC-MAS). *Given a set* Ag *of agents, an* artifact-centric multi-agent system *is a tuple* $\mathcal{P} = \langle \mathcal{S}, U, s_0, \tau \rangle$ *such that*

– $\mathcal{S} \subseteq L_E \times L_1 \times \cdots \times L_n$ *is the set of* reachable global states;
– U *is the* interpretation domain;
– $s_0 \in \mathcal{S}$ *is the* initial global state;
– $\tau : \mathcal{S} \times Act(U) \mapsto 2^{\mathcal{S}}$ *is the* transition function, *where* $Act = Act_E \times Act_1 \times \cdots \times Act_n$ *is the set of* global actions, $Act(U)$ *is the set of* ground actions, *and* $\tau(\langle l_E, l_1, \ldots, l_n \rangle, \vec{\alpha}(\vec{u}))$ *is defined iff* $\alpha_i(\vec{u}) \in Pr_i(l_i)$ *for every* $i \in Ag$.

We can interpret a global state $s = \langle l_E, l_1, \ldots, l_n \rangle$ as the $\mathcal{D}$-instance D s.t. $D(P_i) = \bigcup_{j \in Ag} l_j(P_i)$, for $P_i \in \mathcal{D}$. Notice that for each $s \in \mathcal{S}$ there exists a unique $\mathcal{D}$-instance D as above, however the converse is not true in general. The way D has to be interpreted will be clear from the context. We define the *transition relation* $s \to s'$ if there exists $\vec{\alpha}(\vec{u}) \in Act(U)$ and $s' \in \tau(s, \vec{\alpha}(\vec{u}))$. The notion of *reachability* is defined as in [4]. In what follows we assume that the relation $\to$ is serial, and that $\mathcal{S}$ is the set of states reachable from s_0. Notice that by definition $\mathcal{S}$ is infinite in general. Hence, the AC-MAS $\mathcal{P}$ is an infinite-state system. Finally, s and s' are *epistemically indistinguishable* for agent i, or $s \sim_i s'$, if $l_i(s) = l_i(s')$. This is consistent with the standard definition of knowledge as identity of local states [12].

We are interested in temporal-epistemic specifications in a first-order setting.

Definition 12 (FO-CTLK). *Given a set Var of* individual variables *and a set $Con \subseteq U$ of* individual constants, *the first-order CTLK formulas φ on the database schema $\mathcal{D}$ are defined in BNF as follows:*

$$\varphi ::= t = t' \mid P_i(\vec{t}) \mid \neg\varphi \mid \varphi \to \varphi \mid \forall x \varphi \mid AX\varphi \mid A\varphi U\varphi \mid E\varphi U\varphi \mid K_i\varphi$$

where $P_i \in \mathcal{D}$, $\vec{t}$ is a q_i-tuple of terms, *and t, t' are terms, i.e., elements in $Var \cup Con$.*

The language FO-CTLK is the extension to first-order of the branching-time logic CTL enriched with an epistemic operator K_i for each agent $i \in Ag$ [2]. For a formula φ we denote the set of variables as $var(\varphi)$, the set of free variables as $fr(\varphi)$, and the set of constants as $con(\varphi)$. We consider also the non-modal first-order fragment of FO-CTLK, obtained by omitting the modal operators in Def. 12.

An *assignment* is a function $\sigma : Var \mapsto U$. We denote by $\sigma\binom{x}{u}$ the assignment s.t. (i) $\sigma\binom{x}{u}(x) = u$; and (ii) $\sigma\binom{x}{u}(x') = \sigma(x')$ for $x' \neq x$. We assume that no confusion will arise between assignments in AC-MAS and snapshots in GSM programs. Also, we assume a Herbrand interpretation of constants.

Definition 13 (Semantics of FO-CTLK). *We define whether an AC-MAS $\mathcal{P}$ satisfies a formula φ in a state s under assignment σ as usual (see, e.g., [4]). In particular,*

$$(\mathcal{P}, s, \sigma) \models P_i(t_1, \ldots, t_{q_i}) \quad \textit{iff } \langle\sigma(t_1), \ldots, \sigma(t_{q_i})\rangle \in s(P_i)$$
$$(\mathcal{P}, s, \sigma) \models t = t' \qquad\qquad \textit{iff } \sigma(t) = \sigma(t')$$
$$(\mathcal{P}, s, \sigma) \models \forall x \varphi \qquad\qquad \textit{iff for all } u \in ad(s), (\mathcal{P}, s, \sigma\binom{x}{u})) \models \varphi$$
$$(\mathcal{P}, s, \sigma) \models K_i\varphi \qquad\qquad \textit{iff for all } s', s \sim_i s' \textit{ implies } (\mathcal{P}, s', \sigma) \models \varphi$$

A formula φ is true *at s, written $(\mathcal{P}, s) \models \varphi$, if $(\mathcal{P}, s, \sigma) \models \varphi$ for all assignments σ; φ is* true *in $\mathcal{P}$, written $\mathcal{P} \models \varphi$, if $(\mathcal{P}, s_0) \models \varphi$.*

Note that we adopt an *active domain* semantics, that is, quantified variables range over the active domain of s.

Given an AC-MAS $\mathcal{P}$ and an FO-CTLK formula φ, the *model checking problem* amounts to finding an assignment σ such that $(\mathcal{P}, s_0, \sigma) \models \varphi$. Note that the model checking problem for this logic is undecidable in general [2].

4.1 Finite Abstractions

We now extend the techniques in [4] to define finite abstractions for AC-MAS with parametric actions. We fix a finite set $C \supseteq ad(s_0)$ of constants. Further, whenever we consider an FO-CTLK formula φ, we assume w.l.o.g. that $con(\varphi) \subseteq C$. Finally, the states s and s' are defined on the interpretation domains U and U' respectively, and $\mathcal{P} = \langle \mathcal{S}, U, s_0, \tau \rangle$ and $\mathcal{P}' = \langle \mathcal{S}', U', s_0', \tau' \rangle$ are AC-MAS. To introduce the notion of *bisimulation* as defined in [4], we first need to state when two states are *isomorphic*.

Definition 14 (Isomorphism). *The states s and s' are* isomorphic, *or $s \simeq s'$, iff there exists a bijection $\iota : ad(s) \cup C \mapsto ad(s') \cup C$ s.t. (i) ι is the identity on C; and (ii) for every $P_i \in \mathcal{D}$, $j \in Ag$, and $\vec{u} \in U^{q_i}$, $\vec{u} \in l_j(P_i)$ iff $\iota(\vec{u}) \in l'_j(P_i)$.*

Any function ι as above is a *witness* for $s \simeq s'$. Notice that isomorphic instances preserve first-order (non-modal) formulas:

Proposition 1. *Let φ be an FO-formula, assume that $s \simeq s'$, and let $\sigma : Var \mapsto U$ and $\sigma' : Var \mapsto U'$ be assignments s.t. (i) there is a bijection $\gamma : ad(s) \cup C \cup \sigma(fr(\varphi)) \mapsto ad(s') \cup C \cup \sigma'(fr(\varphi))$; (ii) γ is a witness for $s \simeq s'$; and (iii) $\sigma' = \gamma \circ \sigma$. Then $(\mathcal{P}, s, \sigma) \models \varphi$ iff $(\mathcal{P}', s', \sigma') \models \varphi$.*

Prop. 1 states that isomorphic instances cannot distinguish FO-formulas. We now generalise this result to the language FO-CTLK.

Definition 15 (Similarity). *An AC-MAS $\mathcal{P}'$ simulates $\mathcal{P}$, or $\mathcal{P} \preceq \mathcal{P}'$, iff there exists a simulation relation on $\mathcal{S} \times \mathcal{S}'$, i.e., a relation $\preceq$ s.t. (i) $s_0 \preceq s'_0$; and (ii) if $s \preceq s'$ then*

1. $s \simeq s'$;
2. for every t, if $s \rightarrow t$ then there is t' s.t. $s' \rightarrow t'$, $s \oplus t \simeq s' \oplus t'$ and $t \preceq t'$;
3. for every t, if $s \sim_i t$ then there is t' s.t. $s' \sim_i t'$, $s \oplus t \simeq s' \oplus t'$ and $t \preceq t'$.

Moreover, we say that $\mathcal{P}$ and $\mathcal{P}'$ are *bisimilar*, or $\mathcal{P} \approx \mathcal{P}'$, iff there exists a *bisimulation relation* on $\mathcal{S} \times \mathcal{S}'$, i.e., a relation $\approx$ s.t. both $\approx$ and $\approx^{-1} = \{\langle s', s \rangle \mid s \approx s'\}$ are simulation relations.

We can now introduce the class of AC-MAS of interest here.

Definition 16 (Uniformity). *An AC-MAS $\mathcal{P}$ is* uniform *iff for every $s, t, s' \in \mathcal{S}$, $t' \in \mathcal{D}(U)$, if $t \in \tau(s, \alpha(\vec{u}))$ and $s \oplus t \simeq s' \oplus t'$ for some witness ι, then for every bijection ι' extending ι, $t' \in \tau(s', \alpha(\iota'(\vec{u})))$.*

Intuitively, uniformity requires that the definition of transitions does not depend on the data content of each state, apart from constants in C. This definition of uniformity extends [4] as parametric actions are considered explicitly, thus allowing for effective abstraction.

We now show that uniformity, together with bisimilarity and boundedness, is sufficient to preserve FO-CTLK formulas, where an AC-MAS $\mathcal{P}$ is *b-bounded*, for $b \in \mathbb{N}$, if for all $s \in \mathcal{S}$, $|ad(s)| \leq b$ [3].

Observe that boundedness imposes no restriction on the domain U of $\mathcal{P}$. Thus, if U is infinite, so is the state space of $\mathcal{P}$ in general.

The next results show that, although infinite-state, a uniform and b-bounded AC-MAS $\mathcal{P}$ can be verified by model checking its *finite abstraction*. In what follows $N_{Ag} = \max_{\alpha(\vec{x}) \in Act} \{|\vec{x}|\}$.

Definition 17. *Let Ag be a set of agents and let U' be a set. For each agent $i = \langle \mathcal{D}, L, Act, Pr \rangle$ in Ag we define an agent $i' = \langle \mathcal{D}', L', Act', Pr' \rangle$ s.t. (i) $\mathcal{D}' = \mathcal{D}$; (ii) $L' = \mathcal{D}'(U')$; (iii) $Act = Act$; (iv) $\alpha(\vec{u}) \in Pr'(l')$ iff there is $l \in L$ s.t. $l' \simeq l$ for some witness ι, and $\alpha(\iota'(\vec{u})) \in Pr(l)$ for some bijection ι' extending ι. Let Ag' be the set of all i' thus defined.*

Notice that the definition of i' depends on the set U'. However, we omit U' when it is clear from the context.

Definition 18 (Abstraction). *Let $\mathcal{P}$ be an AC-MAS over Ag, the* abstraction $\mathcal{P}'$ *over Ag' is defined as follows:*

- $s_0' = s_0$;
- $t' \in \tau'(s', \alpha(\vec{u}))$ *iff there are s, t, and $\vec{u}'$ s.t. $t \in \tau(s, \alpha(\vec{u}'))$, $s \oplus t \simeq s' \oplus t'$ for some witness ι, and $\vec{u} = \iota'(\vec{u}')$ for some bijection ι' extending ι;*
- $\mathcal{S}'$ *is the set of reachable states.*

Notice that $\mathcal{P}'$ is an AC-MAS. In particular, $\mathcal{P}'$ satisfies the conditions on protocols and transitions, and it is finite whenever U' is.

We can now prove the main result of this section, which extends Theorem 4.7 in [4] to AC-MAS with parametric actions.

Theorem 1. *Given an infinite, b-bounded and uniform AC-MAS $\mathcal{P}$, an FO-CTLK formula φ, and a finite set $U' \supseteq C$ s.t. $|U'| \geq 2b + |C| + \max\{var(\varphi), N_{Ag}\}$, the abstraction $\mathcal{P}'$ is finite, uniform and bisimilar to $\mathcal{P}$. In particular,*

$$\mathcal{P} \models \varphi \text{ iff } \mathcal{P}' \models \varphi$$

This result states that by using a sufficient number of elements in $\mathcal{P}'$, we can reduce the verification of an infinite AC-MAS to verifying a finite one. Also notice that U' can be taken to be any finite subset of U satisfying the condition on cardinality. By doing so, the finite abstraction $\mathcal{P}'$ can be defined simply as the restriction of $\mathcal{P}$ to U'. Thus, every infinite, b-bounded and uniform AC-MAS is bisimilar to a proper finite subsystem, which can be effectively generated.

5   AC-MAS Associated to GSM Programs

In this section we associate GSM programs to AC-MAS. By doing so we achieve two results. Firstly, we provide a formal semantics to GSM programs via AC-MAS that can be used to interpret FO-CTLK specifications. Secondly, this enables us to apply the finite abstraction methodology in Section 4 to GSM programs.

To begin with, for each artifact type $AT = \langle P, x, Att, Stg, Mst, Lcyc \rangle$ we introduce a predicate symbol P with attributes x, Att. Hence, the arity of P is $q_P = 1 + |Att|$.

Definition 19. *Given a GSM program $\Gamma = \{AT_j\}_{j \leq n}$ we define a database schema $\mathcal{D}_\Gamma = \{P_j\}_{j \leq n}$ such that each P_j is the predicate symbol corresponding to the artifact type AT_j.*

We now introduce agents in GSM programs.

Definition 20. *Given a GSM program Γ and an interpretation domain U, an agent is a tuple $i = \langle \mathcal{D}_i, L_i, Act_i, Pr_i \rangle$ s.t.*

- $\mathcal{D}_i \subseteq \mathcal{D}_\Gamma$ *is the* local database schema, *and $\mathcal{D}_E = \mathcal{D}_\Gamma$;*
- $L_i = \mathcal{D}_i(U)$ *is the set of* local states, *and $L_E = \mathcal{D}_\Gamma(U)$;*

- Act_i is the set of actions $\alpha_e(\vec{y})$ for each event type e with payload $\vec{y}$. Further, we introduce a skip action $skip_i$ for each agent i. Act_E is defined similarly.
- For every ground action $\alpha_i(\vec{u})$, for every local state l_i, $\alpha_i(\vec{u}) \in Pr_i(l_i)$, i.e., a ground action $\alpha_i(\vec{u})$ is always enabled.

We observe that the original formulation of GSM programs in [15] does not account for agents. In fact, artifacts are bundled together in the *Artifact Service Center* (ASC), which interacts with the external environment through incoming and generated events. According to Def. 20 the Artifact Service Center of GSM programs is mapped into the environment of AC-MAS; while the environment of GSM programs is mapped to the agents in an AC-MAS. So, the notion of environment corresponds to different entities in GSM programs and AC-MAS. We keep the original terminology, as the distinction is clear. Furthermore, each agent, including the environment, perform actions corresponding to sending an event to the ASC. As illustrated in Section 2.1, these include 1-way messages M, 2-way service call returns F^{return}, and artifact instance creation requests $create_{AT}^{call}$. We assume that actions are always enabled as no protocol is explicitly given for GSM programs.

Given a set of agents defined as above, the AC-MAS $\mathcal{P}_\Gamma$ associated to the GSM program Γ is defined according to Def. 11.

Definition 21. *Given a set Ag of agents over the GSM program Γ and a snapshot Σ_0, the AC-MAS associated with Γ is a tuple $\mathcal{P}_\Gamma = \langle \mathcal{S}, U, s_{\Sigma_0}, \tau \rangle$ s.t.*

- $\mathcal{S} \subseteq L_e \times L_1 \times \cdots \times L_n$ *is the set of* reachable global states;
- U *is the interpretation domain;*
- $s_{\Sigma_0} \in \mathcal{S}$ *is the* initial global state *corresponding to Σ_0;*
- $\tau : \mathcal{S} \times Act(U) \mapsto 2^{\mathcal{S}}$ *is the global transition function s.t. $t \in \tau(s, \alpha(\vec{u}))$ iff (i) if $\alpha = \langle \alpha_e, \alpha_1, \ldots, \alpha_n \rangle$ then at most one α_i is different from $skip_i$; (ii) if $\alpha_i = \alpha_e$ then (Σ_s, e, Σ_t) holds in Γ, where $\vec{u}$ is the payload of event e.*

Notice that, given a set Ag of agents, there is a one-to-one correspondence between snapshots in Γ and states in the AC-MAS $\mathcal{P}_\Gamma$. Given a snapshot Σ we denote the corresponding state as s_Σ. Similarly, Σ_s is the snapshot corresponding to the global state s. Also, GSM programs do not specify initial states; therefore the definition of $\mathcal{P}_\Gamma$ is parametric in Σ_0, the snapshot chosen as the initial state of Γ. Most importantly, the transition function τ mirrors the B-step semantics of GSM programs. Since each B-step consumes a single event, we require that at most one agent performs an event action at each given time, while all other agents remain idle. This has correspondences with other approaches in multi-agent systems literature, such as interleaved interpreted systems [16].

5.1 Finite Abstractions of GSM Programs

In this section we show that GSM programs admit finite abstractions. Specifically, by suitably restricting the language of sentries we can prove that the AC-MAS $\mathcal{P}_\Gamma$ obtained from a GSM program Γ is uniform. So, by applying Theorem 1 we obtain that if $\mathcal{P}_\Gamma$ is also bounded, then it admits a finite abstraction, hence its model checking problem is decidable. Hereafter, $\mathcal{L}_{\mathcal{D}_\Gamma}$ is the first-order (non-modal) language of formulas built on the predicate symbols in the database schema $\mathcal{D}_\Gamma$ in Def. 19.

Definition 22 (Amenable GSM programs). *A sentry* $\chi(x)$ *is amenable iff the FO-formula* $\varphi(x)$ *in* $\chi(x)$ *belongs to the language* $\mathcal{L}_{\mathcal{D}_\Gamma}$. *A GSM program is amenable iff all sentries occurring in any guard or milestone are amenable.*

It is known that, given a database schema $\mathcal{D}$, the language $\mathcal{L}_{\mathcal{D}}$ built on it is sufficiently expressive to define a wide range of systems [4, 14]. As an example, the scenario in Section 3 adheres to this property. Therefore we see amenable GSM programs as a rather general class of GSM programs with potentially wide applicability.

The next results show that the AC-MAS $\mathcal{P}_\Gamma$ is uniform whenever Γ is amenable.

Lemma 1. *For every states* $s, t \in \mathcal{P}_\Gamma$, *if* $s \simeq t$ *for some witness* ι, *then* $\Sigma_t = \iota(\Sigma_s)$.

Proof. Notice that if ι is a witness for $s \simeq t$, then in particular the attributes x and Att in Σ_s are mapped to the corresponding attributes in Σ_t. Further, the attributes in Stg, Mst and $Lcyc$ remain the same. □

The next result is of essence in the proof of uniformity for $\mathcal{P}_\Gamma$.

Lemma 2. *For every* $s, t, s' \in \mathcal{S}$, $t' \in \mathcal{D}_\Gamma(U)$, *if* $s \oplus t \simeq s' \oplus t'$ *for some witness* ι, *then* (Σ_s, e, Σ_t) *implies* $(\Sigma_{s'}, \iota'(e), \Sigma_{t'})$ *where* ι' *is any bijection extending* ι

Proof. Assume that (Σ_s, e, Σ_t) and ι is a witness for $s \oplus t \simeq s' \oplus t'$. We show that $(\Sigma_{s'}, \iota'(e), \Sigma_{t'})$ where ι' is a bijection extending ι. If (Σ_s, e, Σ_t) then there is a sequence $\Sigma_0, \ldots, \Sigma_k$ of snapshots s.t. $\Sigma_0 = \Sigma_s$, $\Sigma_1 = ImmEffect(\Sigma_s, e)$, and $\Sigma_k = \Sigma_t$. Also, for $1 \le j < k$, Σ_{j+1} is obtained from Σ_j by the application of a PAC rule. We show that we can define a sequence $\Sigma'_0, \ldots, \Sigma'_k$ s.t. $\Sigma'_0 = \Sigma_{s'}$, $\Sigma'_1 = ImmEffect(\Sigma_{s'}, \iota'(e))$, $\Sigma'_k = \Sigma_{t'}$, and for $1 \le j < k$, Σ'_{j+1} is obtained from Σ'_j by the application of a PAC rule. This is sufficient to show that $(\Sigma_{s'}, \iota'(e), \Sigma_{t'})$. First, for $0 \le j \le k$ define $\Sigma'_j = \iota'(\Sigma_j)$. By Lemma 1 we have that $\Sigma'_0 = \iota'(\Sigma_s) = \Sigma_{s'}$ and $\Sigma'_k = \iota'(\Sigma_t) = \Sigma_{t'}$. Also, it is clear that if $\Sigma_1 = ImmEffect(\Sigma_s, e)$, then we have that $\Sigma'_1 = \iota'(\Sigma_1) = \iota'(ImmEffect(\Sigma_s, e))$ is equal to $ImmEffect(\iota'(\Sigma_s), \iota'(e)) = ImmEffect(\Sigma_{s'}, \iota'(e))$. Finally, we show that if Σ_{j+1} is obtained from Σ_j by an application of a PAC rule, then also Σ'_{j+1} is obtained from Σ'_j by the same PAC rule. Consider the PAC rule $\langle \pi(x), \alpha(x), \gamma(x) \rangle$. We have that if $\Sigma_s \models \pi(\rho)$ for some artifact ID ρ in Σ_s, then clearly $\Sigma_{s'} \models \pi(\iota'(\rho))$. Further, let $\Sigma_j \models \alpha(\rho) \equiv \chi(\rho) \wedge \psi(\rho)$, where $\chi(x)$ is an amenable sentry and $\psi(x)$ is of the form $\tau.m$, $\neg\tau.m$, $\tau.active_S$, or $\neg\tau.active_S$. Clearly, if $\Sigma_j \models \psi(\rho)$ then $\Sigma'_j \models \psi(\iota'(\rho))$. Further, since $\chi(x)$ is of the form **on** $\xi(x)$ **if** $\varphi(x)$ and $\varphi(x)$ is an FO-formula in $\mathcal{L}_{\mathcal{D}_\Gamma}$, then by Prop. 1 we have that $\Sigma'_j \models \chi(\iota'(\rho))$. Hence, $\Sigma'_j \models \alpha(\iota'(\rho))$. Finally, if Σ_{j+1} is constructed from Σ_j by applying the effect called for by $\gamma(\rho)$, then Σ'_{j+1} is constructed from Σ'_j by applying the effect called for by $\gamma(\iota'(\rho))$. Thus, we have the desired result. □

Lemma 2 enables us to state the first of our two key results.

Theorem 2. *If the GSM program* Γ *is amenable, then the AC-MAS* $\mathcal{P}_\Gamma$ *is uniform.*

Proof. Let us assume that $t \in \tau(s, \alpha(\vec{u}))$ for some ground action $\alpha(\vec{u}) \in Act(U)$, and $s \oplus t \simeq s' \oplus t'$ for some witness ι. We prove that $t' \in \tau(s', \alpha(\iota'(\vec{u}))$, where ι' is a bijection extending ι. By the definition of τ in $\mathcal{P}_\Gamma$, $t \in \tau(s, \alpha(\vec{u}))$ if (Σ_s, e, Σ_t), where e is a ground event with payload $\vec{u}$, and $\alpha_i = \alpha_e$ for exactly one of the components in α. By Lemma 2 we have that $(\Sigma_{s'}, \iota'(e), \Sigma_{t'})$, and again by definition of τ we obtain that $t' \in \tau(s', \alpha(\iota'(\vec{u})))$. As a result, $\mathcal{P}_\Gamma$ is uniform. $\square$

By combining Theorems 1 and 2 we obtain a decidable model checking procedure for amenable GSM programs. Specifically, a GSM program Γ is b-bounded if the cardinality of all snapshots is bounded, i.e., there is a $b \in \mathbb{N}$ s.t. $|\Sigma| \leq b$ for all snapshots $\Sigma \in \Gamma$. Hence, we have the following result.

Corollary 1. *Assume a b-bounded and amenable GSM program Γ on an infinite domain U, an FO-CTLK formula φ, and a finite set $U' \supseteq C$ such that $|U'| \geq 2b + |C| + \max\{var(\varphi), N_{Ag}\}$. Then, the abstraction $\mathcal{P}'$ of $\mathcal{P}_\Gamma$ is uniform and bisimilar to $\mathcal{P}_\Gamma$. In particular, $\mathcal{P}_\Gamma \models \varphi$ iff $\mathcal{P}' \models \varphi$.*

Thus, to verify a GSM program we can model check the finite abstraction of the corresponding AC-MAS. Notice that by the remarks at the end of Section 4.1 the latter procedure can be computed effectively.

To conclude, in [4] it was proved that the model checking problem for finite AC-MAS is PSPACE-complete in the size of the state space $\mathcal{S}$ and the specification φ. So, we obtain the following:

Proposition 2. *Model checking bounded and amenable GSM programs is in PSPACE in the number of states of its corresponding finite abstraction and the length of the specification.*

Notice that amenability is a sufficient condition for decidability, but may not be necessary. Indeed, a larger class of GSM programs may admit finite abstraction. This point demands further investigations.

5.2   The RPO Scenario as an AC-MAS

We briefly show how the GSM program RPO for the Requisition and Procurement Orders scenario of Section 3 translates into its corresponding AC-MAS $\mathcal{P}_{RPO}$. Firstly, we associate the RPO program with the database schema $\mathcal{D}_{RPO}$ containing a predicate symbol P_{RO} for the Requisition Order artifact type, as well as a predicate symbol P_{PO} for the Procurement Order artifact type. In particular, the predicate symbol P_{RO} has data and status attributes as specified in the datamodel in Fig. 1. The definition of P_{PO} is similar.

A number of agents appears in the RPO scenario: a Customer C, a Manufacturer M, and one or more Suppliers S. According to Def. 20 each agent has a partial view of the database schema $\mathcal{D}_{RPO} = \{P_{RO}, P_{PO}\}$. We can assume that the Customer can only access the Requisition Order (i.e., $\mathcal{D}_C = \{P_{RO}\}$), and the Supplier only the Procurement Order (i.e., $\mathcal{D}_S = \{P_{PO}\}$), while the Manufacturer can access both (i.e., $\mathcal{D}_M = \{P_{RO}, P_{PO}\} = \mathcal{D}_{RPO}$). Finally, the AC-MAS $\mathcal{P}_{RPO} = \langle \mathcal{S}, U, s_0, \tau \rangle$ defined according to Def. 21, is designed to mimic the behaviour of the RPO program. In particular, $\mathcal{S}$ is the set of reachable states; U is the interpretation domain containing relevant items and data; s_0 is an initial state (e.g., the one where all relations are empty); τ is the transition function as in Def. 21. We define a temporal transition $s \to s'$ in $\mathcal{P}_{RPO}$ iff there is some ground event e s.t. $\langle \Sigma_s, e, \Sigma_{s'} \rangle$ holds in RPO.

By means of the AC-MAS $\mathcal{P}_{RPO}$ we can model check the RPO program against first-order temporal epistemic specifications. For instance, the following FO-CTLK formula specifies that the manufacturer M knows that each Procurement Order has to match a corresponding Requisition Order:

$$\phi = AG \, \forall ro\_id, \vec{x} \, (PO(id, ro\_id, \vec{x}) \to K_{\mathsf{M}} \, \exists \vec{y} \, RO(ro\_id, \vec{y}))$$

We remark that the RPO program can be defined so that any clause $\varphi(x)$ in any sentry $\chi(x)$ belongs to the FO-language $\mathcal{L}_{\mathcal{D}_{RPO}}$. Hence, the RPO program is amenable and by Theorem 2 the AC-MAS $\mathcal{P}_{RPO}$ is uniform. Finally, if we also assume that the RPO program is bounded, then according to Def. 18 we can introduce a finite abstraction $\mathcal{P}'$ of $\mathcal{P}_{RPO}$. This can be effectively constructed as the subsystem $\mathcal{P}'$ of $\mathcal{P}_{RPO}$ defined on a finite subset of the interpretation domain satisfying the cardinality condition, that is, $\mathcal{P}'$ is defined as $\mathcal{P}_{RPO}$ but for the domain of interpretation U', which can be taken as the finite $U' \supseteq C$ s.t. $|U| = 2b + |C| + \max\{var(\phi), N_{Ag}\}$. By Corollary 1 we can check whether the RPO program satisfies ϕ by model checking the finite abstraction $\mathcal{P}'$.

This leaves open the problem of checking whether the RPO program is actually bounded. A partial answer to this is provided in [14], which isolates a sufficient condition that guarantees boundedness of processes operating on artifacts.

6   Conclusions

GSM environments currently lack support for full verification. While abstraction methodologies for various artifact-inspired systems and multi-agent systems have been put forward [4, 6, 7, 10, 14], they all lack support for program verification and operate on logical models, thereby making automatic model checking impracticable. Our objective in this paper was to overcome this limitation and provide GSM with an agent-based semantics, so that information-theoretic properties such as knowledge of the participants could be verified. We achieved this by extending minimally the semantics of AC-MAS [4] to account for parametric actions, while at the same time maintaining the key results concerning finite abstractions. We then proceeded to map GSM constructs into the corresponding notions in AC-MAS, and identified what we called "amenable GSM programs" that we showed to admit finite abstractions. We remarked that amenability is not a significant limitation in applications and demonstrated the approach on a fraction of a use-case from [15]. In further work we intend to use the results here presented to improve GSMC, an experimental model checker for artifact-centric systems [13].

Acknowledgements. This research was supported by the EC STREP Project "ACSI" (grant no. 257593) and by the UK EPSRC Leadership Fellowship "Trusted Autonomous Systems" (grant no. EP/I00520X/1).

References

1. Abiteboul, S., Hull, R., Vianu, V.: Foundations of Databases. Addison-Wesley (1995)
2. Belardinelli, F., Lomuscio, A., Patrizi, F.: A computationally-grounded semantics for artifact-centric systems and abstraction results. In: Proc. of IJCAI (2011)
3. Belardinelli, F., Lomuscio, A., Patrizi, F.: Verification of Deployed Artifact Systems via Data Abstraction. In: Kappel, G., Maamar, Z., Motahari-Nezhad, H.R. (eds.) ICSOC 2011. LNCS, vol. 7084, pp. 142–156. Springer, Heidelberg (2011)
4. Belardinelli, F., Lomuscio, A., Patrizi, F.: An abstraction technique for the verification of artifact-centric systems. In: Proc. of KR (2012)
5. Calvanese, D., De Giacomo, G., Lenzerini, M., Rosati, R.: View-based query answering in description logics: Semantics and complexity. J. Comput. Syst. Sci. 78(1), 26–46 (2012)
6. Cohen, M., Dam, M., Lomuscio, A., Russo, F.: Abstraction in model checking multi-agent systems. In: Proc. of AAMAS (2) (2009)
7. Cohen, M., Dam, M., Lomuscio, A., Qu, H.: A Data Symmetry Reduction Technique for Temporal-epistemic Logic. In: Liu, Z., Ravn, A.P. (eds.) ATVA 2009. LNCS, vol. 5799, pp. 69–83. Springer, Heidelberg (2009)
8. Cohn, D., Hull, R.: Business Artifacts: A Data-Centric Approach to Modeling Business Operations and Processes. IEEE Data Eng. Bull. 32(3), 3–9 (2009)
9. Damaggio, E., Hull, R., Vaculín, R.: On the Equivalence of Incremental and Fixpoint Semantics for Business Artifacts with Guard-Stage-Milestone Lifecycles. In: Rinderle-Ma, S., Toumani, F., Wolf, K. (eds.) BPM 2011. LNCS, vol. 6896, pp. 396–412. Springer, Heidelberg (2011)
10. Deutsch, A., Hull, R., Patrizi, F., Vianu, V.: Automatic verification of data-centric business processes. In: Proc. of ICDT (2009)
11. Deutsch, A., Sui, L., Vianu, V.: Specification and Verification of Data-Driven Web Applications. J. Comput. Syst. Sci. 73(3), 442–474 (2007)
12. Fagin, R., Halpern, J.Y., Moses, Y., Vardi, M.Y.: Reasoning About Knowledge. The MIT Press (1995)
13. Gonzalez, P., Griesmayer, A., Lomuscio, A.: Verifying GSM-based business artifacts. In: Proc. of ICWS (2012)
14. Bagheri Hariri, B., Calvanese, D., De Giacomo, G., De Masellis, R., Felli, P.: Foundations of Relational Artifacts Verification. In: Rinderle-Ma, S., Toumani, F., Wolf, K. (eds.) BPM 2011. LNCS, vol. 6896, pp. 379–395. Springer, Heidelberg (2011)
15. Hull, R., Damaggio, E., De Masellis, R., Fournier, F., Gupta, M., Heath, F.T., Hobson, S., Linehan, M.H., Maradugu, S., Nigam, A., Sukaviriya, P.N., Vaculín, R.: Business artifacts with guard-stage-milestone lifecycles: managing artifact interactions with conditions and events. In: Proc. of DEBS (2011)
16. Lomuscio, A., Penczek, W., Qu, H.: Partial Order Reductions for Model Checking Temporal-epistemic Logics over Interleaved Multi-agent Systems. Fundamenta Informaticae 101(1-2), 71–90 (2010)
17. Lomuscio, A., Qu, H., Solanki, M.: Towards verifying contract regulated service composition. Journal of Autonomous Agents and Multi-Agent Systems 24(3), 345–373 (2012)

Service Component Architecture Extensions for Dynamic Systems

João Claudio Américo and Didier Donsez

Grenoble University, LIG Erods Team, Grenoble, France
{Joao.Americo,Didier.Donsez}@imag.fr

Abstract. The Service Component Architecture (SCA) is a set of specifications which defines a model in which components may interact by means of services. SCA is supported by major software vendors due to its several advantages, such as technology independence and portability. However, SCA in its current form does not address components substitutability, one of the goals of the Service-Oriented Architectures style. This paper discusses this limitation and proposes a set of extensions to SCA in order to manage dynamic substitutability of services and their life cycle, which allows components to change service providers at run-time whenever they need to. These extensions are validated by NaSCAr, an iPOJO-based tool which enables the dynamic deployment and adaptation of SCA composites on the OSGi service platform.

Keywords: SCA, Software Engineering, Service-Oriented Architectures, Component-Based Design, Dynamic Adaptability.

1 Introduction

Structuring systems as interacting components is the result of years of research in software engineering [1][2]. It is also one of the solutions proposed in order to deal with software scalability, evolution, and complexity issues. Component-Based Design (CBD) [3] and Service-Oriented Architectures (SOA) [4] are two software engineering approaches widely used for structuring systems. The former primes for the separation of concerns, independence between software units, and explicit functional dependencies; while the latter defines a communication model between software units based on the provision and the consumption of entities called *services*, resulting in increased scalability and decreased integration issues.

Although these two approaches address different concerns [5], service oriented component models (SOCMs) are component models which conciliate both paradigms. Service-oriented components interact through the requirement and provision of services [6]. SOCMs merge modularity and separation of concerns of the CBD approach with loose coupling, late binding and substitutability of the SOA approach. It is also worth to mention that most of SOCM frameworks deal automatically with dynamism issues and SOA basic mechanisms (such as service publication, discovery and selection), allowing developers to focus on applications business logic. Some examples are Declarative Services [6], iPOJO [7], and the Service Component Architecture (SCA) model [8]. Among the existing SOCMs today, only SCA proposes a technology-independent model, since

C. Liu et al. (Eds.): ICSOC 2012, LNCS 7636, pp. 32–47, 2012.

all the others target OSGi and Java consequently. SCA targets business solutions and provides a programming model that allows exploiting many SOA benefits.

The service-oriented approach can be extended to incorporate dynamic (*i.e.* at runtime) modifications regarding software architecture. Dynamic evolutions are motivated by the need of updating software without interrupting its execution and adapting it to context changes (for instance, to substitute software components by others more appropriate in a given moment) [9][10]. Generally, dynamic service frameworks allow components to be deployed, updated, and stopped without interrupting both the platforms on which the application is executed and the services that are not related to the adaptation. In the context of network devices, some examples of dynamic service platforms are Apache River [1], Universal Plug and Play (UPnP) [12], Devices Profile for Web Services (DPWS) [13], and the OSGi Service platform [14]. Most SOCMs integrate dynamism on their models, allowing components to be installed and uninstalled at runtime. As components are dynamically deployed and undeployed, their services must be respectively published and unpublished. By this, components may consume the same service from different providers during its execution. However, this feature is not enabled in SCA, where links between components are indicated statically in a configuration file.

This paper provides a SCA extension which supports components binding dynamic reconfiguration. Just as SCA, the extension is technology-independent, which allows developers to implement it on the top of any dynamic service platform and even switch between different platforms depending on the context of the execution (*e.g.* using a particular technology to bind devices located on the same network and a different one which fits better for distributed applications).

The remainder of this paper is organized as follows: Section 2 gives an outline of the SCA model. Section 3 presents a set of extensions for dynamism issues, whose implementation and validation are discussed in Section 4. Section 5 relates the extensions presented in this paper with other solutions. Finally, Section 6 concludes the paper and presents our perspectives for future works.

2 Service Component Architecture

The Service Component Architecture (SCA) [8] was created in 2005 by a group of major software vendors, such as IBM and Oracle. This group was called the Open SOA Collaboration and it aimed to create a programming model to facilitate the development of service-oriented applications. SCA specification core has four major parts:

- the **Assembly** specification defines components packaging, composition and wires. Components assembly is defined outside implementation code, which increases software reuse.
- the **Client and Implementation Model** specification defines how services must be accessed and packaged for each programming language. This mechanism allows SCA components to be technology-independent.
- the **Binding** specification defines mechanisms for accessing components. It allows SCA to be independent from communication protocols.

---
[1] Available at http://river.apache.org, based on Sun's ancient Jini [11] platform.

– the **Policy Framework** specification defines policies for quality of service (QoS) aspects. These QoS attributes are defined outside the code.

The main entities of the SCA assembly model are software *components*. A component is a configured instance of an *implementation*, which may implement or not business functions. Components may interact with each other by means of a set of abstractions. The ones that implement business functions may expose them as *services*. Services are composed by operations which may be accessed by component's clients. Service description depends on the technology used to implement the component (Java interfaces for Java implementations, WSDL for BPEL implementations and so forth). Components may consume services from other components by means of *references*, which contain the operations that the component needs to invoke. A reference is linked to a service through an abstraction called *wire*. Components can be combined into larger logical constructs called *composites*. Component services and references can be *promoted* to composite services and references, allowing them to be visible to other composites. This assembly is described in a configuration file which uses a XML-like language called Service Component Definition Language. Non-functional aspects in SCA can be specified in two ways. The first one is the *policy sets*, which holds one or more policies. A policy is a constraint or capability which can be applied to a component or to an interaction between components, and which is expressed in a concrete form. An example of a policy is *Encryption*, which can be described by WS-Policy assertions and be applied to service interactions. The second way is by means of *intents*, which are high-level abstract forms of policies, independent of configuration. An example of an intent is confidentiality, which indirectly means that the developer must use a policy set containing an encryption policy.

An application contains one or more composites. Component implementations and the artifacts necessary for their deployment are packaged into *contributions* (typically, a zip archive containing a file that lists deployable composites). At runtime, composites and components are contained in a *domain*, which corresponds to a set of SCA runtimes from a specific SCA vendor managed by a single group. In the context of distributed applications, the domain is responsible for defining how components from different machines (but in the same domain) will communicate. Components and composites are limited to one domain, but they may communicate with applications outside their domain through the protocols defined on the bindings of their services and references.

3   Dynamic Binding Extensions for SCA

Several implementations and runtimes for SCA are available, including open source projects such as Apache Tuscany[2], Fabric3[3], the already extinct Newton project, and OW2 FraSCAti [16]. One of the most remarkable features of the SCA specification is that it allows for developers to extend its assembly model for supporting new implementations, bindings, and interfaces. In this section, a set of SCA extensions is presented. These extensions enable SCA components to deal with dynamism and its related issues, such as life cycle management.

---

[2] Available at http://tuscany.apache.org
[3] Available at http://fabric3.org

3.1 Motivations

Typically, an application which follows the service-oriented architecture model is a system with three main elements: service registries that store service descriptions and associate them with their respective providers; service providers, which implement business functions and publish the description of its services in a service register; and service consumers, which query the registry to find a required service. This three-part architecture enables loose coupling and late binding, as consumers only know the service descriptors and through this description they may invoke operations on any service implementation which provides this service [17].

In SCA, this model consists basically of service providers and service consumers. Developers must inform which provider is bound to a given reference inside a composite, through an abstraction called *wire*. The *auto-wire* feature in the SCA Assembly Model enables the automatic wiring of references to services, but it is limited to services and references inside the same composite. Thus, if a developer wants to bind a reference with services from other composites, this must be done manually at design time. Furthermore, since there is no registry to publish services, a composite has no knowledge of other composites which are not included on its description, and thus can not establish wires towards them. In addition, the auto-wire feature does not have a selection mechanism in order to filter service providers and to find the best fit service. A solution based on the dynamic update of the composite files could improve the flexibility of SCA applications; however, the developers would still need to modify the composite files and know all the composites present in the system.

3.2 Dynamic Binding Extension

Dynamic Publication and Discovery. The Dynamic Binding Extension proposed in this work is an extension to the SCA Assembly Model allowing providers to publish their services and for consumers to query for and select services implementations. This is done by adding three concepts to SCA: service registry, filters and service properties.

```
<sca:component name="DigitalSecurityCamera">
  <sca:implementation.java class="com.video.Camera"/>
  <sca:service name="MotionImageService">
    <interface.java interface="IFrameService.java" />
    <xdyn:binding.dynamic>
      <xdyn:property name="frameRate" value="30" />
      <xdyn:property name="resolution" value="640x480" />
    </xdyn:binding.dynamic>
  </sca:service>
  <sca:service name="PanTiltZoomService">
    <interface.java interface="IPTZService.java" />
    <xdyn:binding.dynamic>
      <xdyn:property name="panAngle" value="180" />
      <xdyn:property name="tiltAngle" value="90" />
      <xdyn:property name="zoomRatio" value="10" />
    </xdyn:binding.dynamic>
  </sca:service>
</component>
```

Listing 1: SCA Dynamic Binding Extension - Service Publication

Listing 1 shows the configuration of a component which publishes two services through the dynamic binding extension. The first one, named MotionImageService, has a Java interface called IFrameService as service description. Along with the description, two properties are published in the registry: its frame rate and its resolution. Similarly, the second service, called PanTiltZoomService and described by Java interface IPTZService, is published with information related to its covering angle and zoom ratio.

Listing 2 exemplifies a query for the IFrameService in the service registry. This query contains an LDAP filter expression[4]. For instance, although the service description is the same, this query would not return the service depicted in Listing 1, due to the fact that it searches for cameras whose resolution is 800x600, and not 640x480.

```
<sca:component name="MotionDetector">
  <sca:implementation.java class="com.module.MotionDetector"/>
  <sca:reference name="MotionImageReference">
    <interface.java interface="IFrameService.java" />
    <xdyn:binding.dynamic>
      <xdyn:filter ldap:query="(&(resolution='800x600')(frameRate>15))"/>
    <xdyn:binding.dynamic>
  </sca:reference>
</sca:component>
```

Listing 2: SCA Dynamic Binding Extension - Service Active Discovery

The binding.dynamic element can be used on services and references. Two types of service registries are used: a local service registry, whose scope is limited to unpromoted services inside the composite; and a global service registry, whose scope includes the whole SCA domain, allowing references to invoke services from other composites. Besides this scope rule, very few assumptions are made about the registries: first, registries are passive, that is, instead of pushing information to the components, it awaits components query; second, their query take as input an interface I_1 and a set of contraints C and must return a set of service references whose interfaces $I_2 \supseteq I_1$ and whose set of properties satisfies C; and third, the access to the registry is somehow synchronized, that is, at any given instant t, at most one component is accessing the registry, either for publishing, unpublishing or for querying. SCA's autowire feature could have been used to bind references to services intra-composite, but it does not contain mechanisms for filtering service providers. When used on services, the binding.dynamic element has the following sub-nodes and attributes, here presented in XPath notation:

- **(service/)binding.dynamic**: this binding type informs the SCA runtime that this service must be published in the service registry. This publication respects SCA's visibility rules: if the published service is not promoted, it can solely be found by references contained in the same composite; however, promoted services can be found by other composites inside the domain.
- **(service/)binding.dynamic/property** (Optional): This element is optional and identifies an exported property. Based on the exported properties, service consumers may select an implementation among the potential service providers. A service

---

[4] LDAP (Lightweight Directory Access Protocol) is a protocol for accessing information services over IP networks [18].

published without any property can only be selected by references which do not specify filters. Services may publish more than one property.

- **(service/)binding.dynamic/property/@name**: Name of the property.
- **(service/)binding.dynamic/property/@value**: Value of the property.

In turn, when used on a reference, the binding.dynamic element has the following attributes and nodes:

- **(reference/)binding.dynamic**: Through this binding type, components inform the SCA runtime that this reference will be dynamically wired to a service. This service may be provided by components from the same composite or from other composites inside the domain (promoted references only). In the first case, the framework looks for services published in the local service registry; the global service registry is used only in the second case.
- **(reference/)binding.dynamic/filter**: This element is optional and identifies a filter for performing service selection based on the properties exported by the services. If no filter is specified, any provider can be bound to the corresponding reference.
- **(reference/)binding.dynamic/filter/@expression**: The query to be executed over the service providers properties. In the example, filters are expressed in LDAP syntax, but other types of filter/query expressions can be used.

As we add the capabilities of dynamic component deployment[5], service selection and service substitutability, references may end up with no services to get linked to. Next subsections introduce others aspects which must be taken considered for dynamic service-oriented composites and their corresponding elements in the proposed SCA extension.

Components Life Cycle: Since references may not find matching services at runtime, the concept of *valid* and *invalid* components was introduced in SCA. A SCA valid component is a SCA component which has all its references satisfied; otherwise, it is considered as invalid. Although at deployment time it is not known whether a component is valid or not (it depends on the already deployed components), only valid components may publish services. Not all references might be necessary to activate a given component though. This type of reference is called *optional*. Thus, revisiting the definition of a valid SCA component, a *SCA valid component* is a component whose mandatory (*i.e.* non-optional) references are all satisfied (that is, have a service which matches its interface and its defined filters); otherwise, the component is considered invalid. These concepts are represented in Figure 1 as a SCA components life cycle state diagram.

The initial and final states correspond to the moments when a SCA component is respectively added to and removed from the SCA domain (*i.e.*, installed/uninstalled in the SCA runtime platform). Started components can be either valid or invalid (transitions 1 and 2, respectively), depending on the services which are present on the domain.

---

[5] For sake of simplicity, from this point on the term component is used for both components and composites, since composites may be seen as components of components.

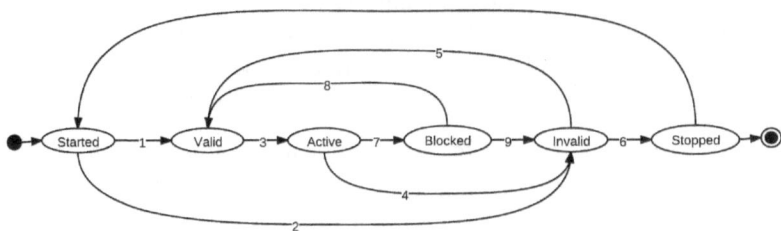

Fig. 1. SCA Components Life Cycle

Only valid components become active (transition 3), that is, it may publish and consume services. As components may be dynamically installed and uninstalled in the platform, active components may eventually become invalid (transition 4). The component then has two options: either it waits until a new provider of its unsatisfied mandatory references is deployed in the SCA domain (transition 5), or it is stopped (transition 6), erasing its published services from service registries and releasing its consumed services. Active services that are stopped by an administrator must also pass by the transition 4 before their full stop. Components may also be updated: in that case, components are first invalidated, stopped and then a new version is started.

Another concept added to the SCA Dynamic Binding Extension that affects components life cycle is that of a *blocking reference*. Its semantics are slightly different from optional references: as optional references, the absence of a blocking reference do not invalidate a component; however, when the service corresponding to a blocking reference is invoked inside the component, it is blocked (transition 7) either until a service that corresponds to its requirements is published or until a given timeout. In the first case, the service is revalidated (transition 8), whereas in the second case the service is invalidated afterwards (transition 9).

Since SCA allows informing whether a reference is optional by means of its multiplicity, an element was included in the SCA Dynamic Binding Extension to specify blocking references.

- **(reference/)binding.dynamic/@blocking**: A boolean field that informs whether a component reference is blocking or not. This field is optional and its default value is FALSE.
- **(reference/)binding.dynamic/@timeout**: A field that indicates how long the platform must wait before invalidating a blocking reference. This field is only present if there is also a blocking field in the reference. If this field is not informed, the platform will keep the component blocked until a new matching service is found.

Service-Level Dependencies: Missing references may also indirectly affect provided services. For instance, if a component has a reference towards an email service and provides a service which sends reports to company shareholders. The fact that no email service is present at the platform should consequently imply that the report dispatch service should not be published, as it will not work. This is called a *service-level dependency*.

Although the SCA specification does not address this issue, the SCA Dynamic Binding Extension does, by means of the following elements:

- **(service/)binding.dynamic/dependency**: In this sub-element, developers describe which references a given service depends on. More than one dependency element can be described for a given service.
- **(service/)binding.dynamic/dependency/@ref_name**: This field indicates the name of the reference that the service depends on. This name must match exactly with one existing component reference.

A service can only be published in the service registry if all its dependencies are satisfied. That means, for instance, that components may not have all of their services published in a given instant. They may also be active and do not publish any of their services due to dependency on optional or blocking references.

Life Cycle Management Callbacks: In several SOCMs, changes in components' life cycle generate events that are treated by callbacks. Although SCA itself has a callback mechanism, it is not related to components' and services' life cycle (SCA does not contain a life cycle model); it is used instead to provide bi-directional asynchronous services. Callbacks corresponding to changes in the life cycle of components and services can be indicated in the SCA Dynamic Binding Extension. Today, two event types are taken into account in the extension: Reference binding/unbinding and service registration/unregistration[6]. The following elements correspond to the definition of life cycle management callbacks:

- **(service/)binding.dynamic/lccallback**: In this sub-element, developers indicate callbacks corresponding to changes in the service life cycle (registered/ unregistered).
- **(service/)binding.dynamic/lccallback/@event**: Event type the callback refers to. Two types are possible here: REGISTER and UNREGISTER. At most one callback can be specified to each type of event.
- **(service/)binding.dynamic/lccallback/@handler**: The function (or method, or procedure, depending on the language that is being used to implement the component) that must be called in case of the given event.
- **(reference/)binding.dynamic/lccallback**: In this sub-element, developers indicate callbacks corresponding to changes in the state of component references. Components references state directly affects components' life cycle, because components validation depends on it.
- **(reference/)binding.dynamic/lccallback/@event**: In this field, developers must specify the event type the callback refers to. Two types are possible here: BIND and UNBIND. At most one callback can be specified to each type of event.
- **(reference/)binding.dynamic/lccallback/@handler**: Similar to services' callback handler field, the developer can specify the function that must be called in case of the given event.

---

[6] The component validation/invalidation could also be taken into account, but SCA current specifications do not allow us to introduce component-level data.

Service Level Agreements: Service Level Agreement (SLA) is an agreement established between the service consumer and provider, associated with a specific service specification, whose negotiated quality of service guarantees are enforced and monitored at runtime [19]. The Dynamic Binding Extension allows the expression of contracts from both service providers and consumers. When a service consumer reference specifies a contract, only service providers who have specified a contract can be linked to them. The framework will then analyze both contracts and establish an agreement for the service utilization. SLAs can be specified by means of the following elements:

- **(service/)binding.dynamic/sla**: Through this sub-element, developers indicate that the service provided has a contract.
- **(service/)binding.dynamic/sla/@contract**: In this field, developers specify the file containing the service contract.
- **(reference/)binding.dynamic/sla**: Through this sub-element, developers indicate that the reference has an associated contract and that it will only get bound to services which also have a contract.
- **(reference/)binding.dynamic/sla/@contract**: Similarly to its service counterpart, this field specifies the file which contains the reference contract.

Several languages exist for specifying SLA contracts, such as WSLA [20] and SLAng [21]. Different implementations of the extension may support different SLA languages.

4   Implementation and Validation

4.1   Dynamic Deployment and Substitution of SCA Components

A proof-of-concept implementation of the extension presented above was created on top of the OSGi Service Platform [14]. Instead of developing an extension to a static SCA runtime, it was preferred to create a tool to parse SCA composites and deploy them as dynamic components in the OSGi Platform. This way, the OSGi Service Registry could be used to bind services and references from different composites dynamically.

Composites promoted services containing a dynamic binding are published in the OSGi Service Registry with an special property that enables the differentiation between OSGi and SCA services. Consequently, SCA and non-SCA applications can be hosted on the same platform and virtual machine, which could decrease the cost of invocations to external applications through Java-based bindings. Since non-promoted references can only be bound to services inside the composite, and the composite is a static unit of deployment (new components cannot be dynamically added to a composite), the resolution of non-promoted references can be performed before its execution.

The tool that deploys SCA contributions onto the OSGi platform is called NaSCAr [7], and it uses the iPOJO's component model and composite API to create OSGi bundles that provide and require SCA services. Contributions may be conditioned into artifacts such as zip files (as preconized in SCA standard) or OSGi bundles, which allows to benefit from OSGi deployment tools like Apache ACE, OBR and Eclipse P2. NaSCAr parses the contribution file to identify deployable composites; then, for each composite file, it creates its containing components and includes them inside an iPOJO composite.

---

[7] NaSCAr stands for "Not another SCA runtime".

IPOJO composites have their own internal service registry and may publish and discover services published by other composites, which corresponds exactly to the behavior expected for the SCA Dynamic Binding Extension.

Mapping concepts from SCA and the SCA Dynamic Binding Extension to iPOJO is very straightforward. IPOJO already contains the basic SCA concepts, such as composites, components, services, references (known in iPOJO as dependencies), properties, and services and references promotions (which are presented in the iPOJO API as Exported and Imported services respectively). The 'optional reference' flag and life cycle callbacks from the SCA Dynamic Binding Extensions are already present in iPOJO dependencies. Same for service properties, which are native from the OSGi Service Platform service layer. Blocking services are implemented by using iPOJO's Temporal Dependency handler. SLA support is based on the works of Touseau *et al.* [15]. Service-level dependencies combine two iPOJO mechanisms: service callbacks and service controllers. In fact, NaSCAr instruments the component class byte-code in order to inject two methods: the first is invoked every time a service is bound to the component reference; the second is called when a consumed service is unregistered (respectively "bind" and "unbind" callback methods). In addiction, a boolean field is added to the class; this field, called service controller, indicates whether a service must be registered or not, *i.e.* setting this field to **true** causes a service to be registered, and it is automatically unregistered when the same field is set to **false**. Thus, NaSCAr injects a bind (and unbind) method associated to the reference indicated by a given service that sets the controller field linked to the latter to **true** (and **false**, respectively).

Currently, IPOJO has one strong limitation: components and composites may publish at most one service. Consequently, as NaSCAr is currently based on iPOJO, only SCA components and composites that contain at most one service may be deployed.

4.2 Evaluation

NaSCAr processes composites in three stages: first, it parses the contributions composite files and creates an object model representation of the applications' assembly; then it creates iPOJO composites from this representation; finally, it starts composites instances in the OSGi platform. Its real (uncompressed) bundle size is 79.7 kB (where 17.4 KB correspond to classes used to represent the SCA component model and 40.9 KB correspond to the implementation itself). NaSCAr publishes a service in the OSGi registry which contains four operations: *deploy, undeploy, list and info*. A second module, NaSCAr-Shell, retrieves this service and enables the deployment of SCA composites by means of Apache Karaf Shell commands.

NaSCAr was tested against a container microbenchmark available at https://github.com/rouvoy/container-benchmark. This benchmark is composed by a Fibonacci calculator application: a client invokes a method on the Fibonacci calculator object which returns the nth member of the Fibonacci series (n being a method parameter). The microbenchmark is based on Google Caliper microbenchmark framework, which is responsible for running the benchmark and publishing its results. Figure 2 shows the microbenchmark application architecture for the different tested containers.

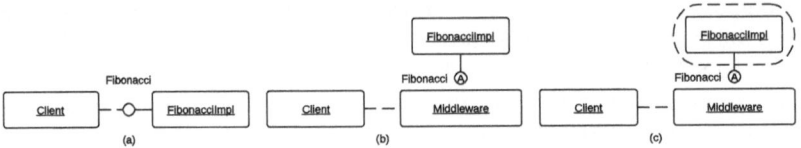

Fig. 2. Microbenchmark application architecture

A standard Java version of the benchmark follows the architecture style (a): a client is connected directly to the Fibonacci implementation. An OSGi application would fit the architecture style (b): the client must first retrieve the service implementation in order to access the object and directly invoke the service. NaSCAr, SCA containers and iPOJO follow the architecture style (c): the implementation has a membrane which is automatically created and managed by the container based on the component's metadata.

Figure 3 presents a chart in logarithmic scale containing results of the benchmark in terms of ns/service call and a comparison with results obtained by the standard Java, OSGi, iPOJO (simple components with direct injection), Apache Tuscany and OW2 Frascati SCA runtimes (with request scope) versions. A detailed version of the benchmark, containing the execution times and a complete description of the environment is available at `http://microbenchmarks.appspot.com/user/jcamerico @gmail.com`. NaSCAr presents a slightly higher overhead compared to iPOJO and OSGi components, due to the fact that components' services and references must be respectively exported and imported by the iPOJO composite that wraps them.

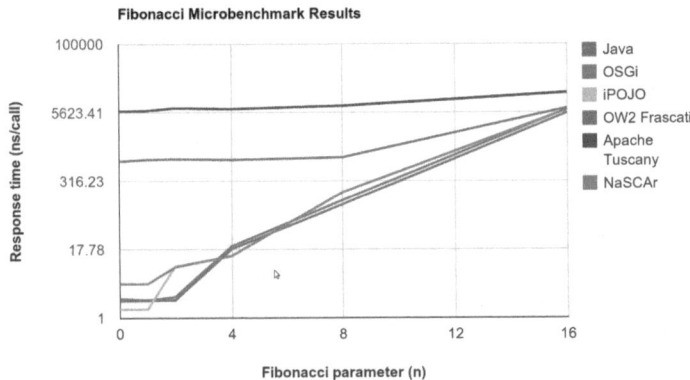

Fig. 3. Microbenchmark results

4.3 Case Study

The following use case illustrates the dynamic reconfiguration capabilities of the SCA Dynamic Binding Extension and its implementation on NaSCAr. The example represents a building automation application where devices (sensors and actuators) can be installed and uninstalled (*e.g.* faulty or powered-out devices) in rooms without interrupting the application's execution. This example focuses on the lighting control (which depends on the presence of persons in a given room), the light intensity (for optimal visual comfort) and room occupancy schedule.

In the lighting control application, each instance of the 'Room Lighting Manager' (RLM) component manages a room or a hall section. A singleton instance of the 'Building Lighting Manager' (BLM) component coordinates the RLM component instances through a reference towards the Room Lighting Service provided by them. A RLM instance is active if there is at least one active actuator for its corresponding room. RLM and actuators are bound by means of services too. These actuators can be, for example, UPnP and DPWS devices implementing the SwitchPower and DimmingLight services described in the UPnP Lighting Control standard profile. RLMs are also bound to sensors, in order to detect human presence and luminosity. These presence sensing devices could be either UPnP Digital Security Cameras or motion sensors. Luminosity sensors can be implemented with photo-resistors. Optionally, the system may connect to a Google Calendar component, in order to verify a room occupancy schedule and turn the lights on in case of an event scheduled for a given time.

Since sensors and actuators can be dynamically added, removed, turned on and off, RLMs can not establish a static wire towards their services. In addition, its Room Lighting Service depends on the presence of actuators, which characterizes a service-level dependency. The BLM also needs dynamic bindings towards RLMs, as their may register and unregister their services during the system execution.

In order to connect UPnP devices in SCA, a tool called UPnPServiceFactory was developed. It is implemented by a SCA composite whose components serve as proxy with UPnP. In total, 54 proxy classes were generated for different devices service interfaces. 49 of these proxy classes correspond to the services described by the UPnP Forum Standard Specifications. After the code generation, classes are conditioned in bundles.The code generation is based on XSTL stylesheets. Figure 4 illustrates the complete use-case architecture.

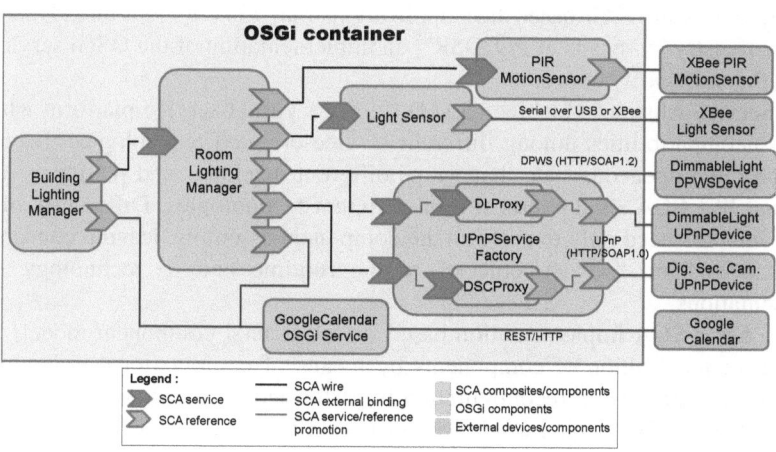

Fig. 4. Use Case Application Architecture

5   Related Work

In the CBD approach, software components are independent software units, which are composed in order to build a complete system, with contractually specified interfaces and explicit context dependencies. Dynamic adaptation can be performed using late binding mechanisms, which allows coupling components at runtime through well-defined interfaces [3]. Service-oriented component models, such as iPOJO[7] and Declarative Services[6] are good alternatives for creating dynamically adaptable software, but they are OSGi (and consequently Java)-based. Although SCA is considered as being a technology-agnostic service-oriented component model, no works about dynamic availability have been done until now. In fact, SCA may offer some forms of dynamism (mechanisms that change references in case of absence of a given reference, for instance). But those solutions are extremely limited due to the use of statically-defined wires between services and references. In addition, most dynamic features are considered as some of many possible behaviors in the SCA specification.

Pautasso *et al.* have classified in [22] the different bindings types between service providers and consumers. According to their definition, SCA wires would constitute a *binding by reference*, since developers must inform the component and the service to be invoked. The auto-wire feature in SCA would turn this binding model more flexible, just like a *binding by constraint*, where the binding specifies a set of services S. In this model, each service $s \in S$ satisfies the set of constraints C. In this specific case, C includes two constraints: 1) the services must have the same interface and 2) the services must be in the same composite. The dynamic binding extension removes the second constraint and enables developers to customize the set of constraints.

The use of service registries instead of static links increases software flexibility and component substitutability. The OSGi-based service-oriented component models use them in several different ways, either locally or remotely (as defined by the OSGi Remote Services specification and implemented by frameworks such as ROSE [23] and R-OSGi[24]). Non OSGi-based Java applications may benefit from the advantages of a service registry by means of POJOSR[8], an implementation of the OSGi service layer without the modularity concerns.

The Service Abstract Machine (SAM) [25] is a virtual service platform which addresses incompatibilities among different service-oriented technologies. It creates a global and homogeneous state that wraps different machines and platforms dynamically. Just like SCA, it supports several different technologies. Differently of SAM, SCA developers need only to perform the component assembly, leaving concepts such as "instances" and "service objects" to the runtime and its technology specific implementations.

FraSCAti, a SCA implementation based on the Fractal component model, enables dynamic reconfiguration of components by means of computational reflection [16]. However, this application reconfiguration is performed by means of an API and follows the standard SCA style, where we must specify the source and the target of each wire. So, the burden of substituting a component by another is entirely on the assembler. Our approach to dynamic reconfiguration applies the late binding paradigm: rewiring

---

[8] Available at http://pojosr.googlecode.com

is automatic and based on a selection among the available services. CEVICHE[26], a framework which enables the runtime adaptation of web services partner links and activities within a business process, is based on FraSCAti. Recently, FraSCAti has added OSGi support, which allows components to publish and discover services. The dynamic binding extension however is not bound to OSGi and can be implemented in other technologies. TuSCAny and Fabric3 do not present dynamic reconfiguration mechanisms.

When a query returns more than one service provider, NaSCAr just injects either an unsorted list of all implementations or the first implementation of the list. Bottaro and Hall [27] have extended the Declarative Services component model by adding a utility function-based mechanism for ranking services. This utility function is based on published service properties. Injected service providers may be dynamically substituted by newly deployed services whose rank are higher than the former ones.

6 Conclusions and Perspectives

SCA is a technology-agnostic service-oriented component model which combines benefits from the SOA and CBD approaches, such as late binding and loose coupling. SCA focuses on the hierarchical assembly of components independently of the technology they use, which increases reuse and decrease development cost. However, SCA does not address dynamic reconfiguration, which limits its use on several domains of applications. This paper proposed a set of extensions for the SCA model in order to address this issue. These extensions were implemented by a tool that generates iPOJO composites from SCA composites, called NaSCAr. NaSCAr presented a very small overhead compared to other SCA runtimes. Differently of the currently most used open source SCA runtimes, NaSCAr targets memory and space-limited devices, as pictured in the use case. Nonetheless, it still has some limitations: for instance, since it is based on iPOJO, components may provide at most one service. This issue could be overcome if NaSCAr was based directly on the OSGi API, but the latter does not present a hierarchical composition model onto which SCA composites may be mapped.

Future works include taking into account other policies related to composites lifecycle. For instance, since NaSCAr composites may be dynamically started and stopped, some components could keep its state before being stopped, or transfer its state to another instance of the same composite. It is also important to enable an extension mechanism for allowing NaSCAr to deploy custom implementation and binding types.

Acknowledgements. The authors would like to acknowledge the OW2 FraSCAti team for their comments and their support on the container benchmark.

References

1. Parnas, D.: On the criteria for decomposing systems into modules. Communications of the ACM 15(12), 1053–1058 (1972)
2. Garlan, D., Shaw, M.: An Introduction to Software Architecture. In: Advances in Software Engineering and Knowledge Engineering, vol. I. World Scientific (1993)
3. Szyperski, C.: Component Software - Beyond Object-Oriented Programming, 2nd edn. Addison-Wesley, ACM Press (2002)

4. Papazoglou, M., Georgakopoulos, D.: Service-oriented computing. Communications of the ACM 46, 25–28 (2003)
5. Papazoglou, M., Andrikopoulos, V., Benbernou, S.: Managing Evolving Systems. IEEE Software 28(3), 49–55 (2011)
6. Cervantes, H., Hall, R.: Autonomous Adaptation to Dynamic Availability Using a Service-Oriented Component Model. In: ICSE 2004, pp. 614–623 (2004)
7. Escoffier, C., Hall, R., Lalanda, P.: iPOJO: An Extensible Service-Oriented Component Framework. In: Proc. IEEE Int'l Conf. Services Computing (SCC 2007), pp. 474–481 (2007)
8. Open Service-Oriented Architecture Collaboration: Service Component Architecture Specifications (2007), http://www.osoa.org/display/Main/Service+Component+Architecture+Specifications
9. Oreizy, P., Medvidovic, N., Tayler, R.N.: Runtime Software Adaptation: Frameworks, Approaches and Styles. In: Proceedings of the 30th Int'l Conference on Software Engineering, pp. 899–910 (2008)
10. Kramer, J., Magee, J.: Analysing Dynamic Change in Software Architectures: A case study. In: 4th IEEE Int'l Conference on Configuration Distributed Systems, pp. 91–100 (1998)
11. Edwards, K.W.: Core Jini, 2nd edn. Prentice Hall (2001)
12. UPnP: Universal Plug and Play, http://www.upnp.org/
13. Zeeb, E., Bobek, A., Bohn, H., Golatowski, F.: Service-oriented architectures for embedded systems using devices profile for web services. In: Proceedings of the 2nd Int'l IEEE Workshop on SOCNE 2007, pp. 956–963 (2007)
14. The OSGi Alliance: OSGi service platform core specification, release 4.3 (2011), http://www.osgi.org/Specifications
15. Touseau, L., Donsez, D., Rudametkin, R.: Towards a SLAbased Approach to Handle Service Disruptions. In: Proceedings of the 2008 IEEE Int'l Conference on Services Computing, pp. 415–422 (2008)
16. Seinturier, L., et al.: Reconfigurable SCA Applications with the FraSCAti Platform. In: Proceedings of the 6th IEEE Int'l Conference on Service Computing, pp. 268–275 (2009)
17. Michlmayr, A., et al.: Towards recovering the broken SOA triangle: a software engineering perspective. In: 2nd Int'l Workshop on SoSE, pp. 22–28 (2007)
18. IETF: Lightweight Directory Access Protocol (LDAP) Syntaxes and Matching Rules. IETF RFC 4517
19. Verma, D.: Supporting Service Level Agreements on IP Networks. Macmillan Technical Publishing (1999)
20. Ludwig, H., Keller, A., Dan, A., King, R., Franck, R.: Web Service Level Agreement (WSLA) Language Specification. IBM (2003)
21. Lamanna, D.D., Skene, J., Emmerich, W.: SLAng: A Language for Service Level Agreements. In: Proceedings of the 9th IEEE Workshop on Future Trends in Distributed Computing Systems, pp. 100–106 (2003)
22. Pautasso, C., Alonso, G.: Flexible Binding for Reusable Composition of Web Services. In: Gschwind, T., Aßmann, U., Wang, J. (eds.) SC 2005. LNCS, vol. 3628, pp. 151–166. Springer, Heidelberg (2005)
23. Bardin, J., Lalanda, P., Escoffier, C.: Towards an automatic integration of heterogeneous services and devices. In: Proceedings of the 2010 Asia-Pacific Services Computing Conference, pp. 171–178 (2010)
24. Rellermeyer, J.S., Alonso, G., Roscoe, T.: R-OSGi: Distributed Applications Through Software Modularization. In: Cerqueira, R., Campbell, R.H. (eds.) Middleware 2007. LNCS, vol. 4834, pp. 1–20. Springer, Heidelberg (2007)

25. Estublier, J., Simon, E.: Universal and extensible service-oriented platform feasibility and experience: The service abstract machine. In: Proceedings of the 33rd IEEE Int'l Computer Software and Applications Conference, pp. 96–103 (2009)
26. Hermosillo, G., Seinturier, L., Duchien, L.: Creating Context-Adaptive Business Processes. In: Maglio, P.P., Weske, M., Yang, J., Fantinato, M. (eds.) ICSOC 2010. LNCS, vol. 6470, pp. 228–242. Springer, Heidelberg (2010)
27. Bottaro, A., Hall, R.S.: Dynamic Contextual Service Ranking. In: Lumpe, M., Vanderperren, W. (eds.) SC 2007. LNCS, vol. 4829, pp. 129–143. Springer, Heidelberg (2007)

Who Do You Call? Problem Resolution through Social Compute Units

Bikram Sengupta[1], Anshu Jain[1], Kamal Bhattacharya[1],
Hong-Linh Truong[2], and Schahram Dustdar[2]

[1] IBM Research - India
{bsengupt,anshu.jain,kambhatt}@in.ibm.com
[2] Distributed Systems Group, Vienna University of Technology, Austria
{truong,dustdar}@infosys.tuwien.ac.at

Abstract. Service process orchestration using workflow technologies have led to significant improvements in generating predicable outcomes by automating tedious manual tasks but suffer from challenges related to the flexibility required in work especially when humans are involved. Recently emerging trends in enterprises to explore social computing concepts have realized value in more agile work process orchestrations but tend to be less predictable with respect to outcomes. In this paper we use IT services management, specifically, incident management for large scale systems, to investigate the interplay of workflow systems and social computing. We apply a recently introduced concept of Social Compute Units, and flexible teams sourced based on various parameters such as skills, availability, incident urgency, etc. in the context of resolution of incidents in an IT service provider organization. Results from simulation-based experiments indicate that the combination of SCUs and workflow based processes can lead to significant improvement in key service delivery outcomes, with average resolution time per incident and number of SLO violations being at times as low as 52.7% and 27.3% respectively of the corresponding values for pure workflow based incident management.

1 Introduction

Business process management (BPM) and workflow systems have had tremendous success in the past two decades with respect to both mindshare and deployment. We can safely consider service-oriented architecture (SOA) to be a business-as-usual design practice. On the other hand, we are observing enterprises embracing social computing as an alternative for executing more unstructured yet team-based collaborative, outcome-based strategies. Gartner [1] predicts that by 2015, we will observe a deeper penetration of social computing for the business as enterprises struggle to deal with the rigidity of business process techniques. Current workflows are suitable for automation of menial tasks but inflexible when it comes to supporting business users who must deal with complex decision making. However, a significant conceptual gap clearly exists between workflows on the one hand, and social computing as it is known today.

C. Liu et al. (Eds.): ICSOC 2012, LNCS 7636, pp. 48–62, 2012.

The goal of this paper is to introduce a framework that establishes the interactions of business processes and workflows with a concept called Social Compute Units (SCU) [8], recently introduced by some of the authors. A SCU is an abstraction of a team consisting of human resources that bring together the appropriate expertise to solve a given problem. The SCU abstraction treats the SCU as a programmable entity. The resources that make up a SCU are socially connected. The term *socially* implies connectedness of an individual beyond his or her organizational scope. The reason for connectedness could be prior ad-hoc collaborations but also collaboration within a given scope of responsibility where the scope is distributed across organizational verticals.

The context in which we propose the use of SCUs in this paper is the IT Service Management (ITSM) domain. More specifically, we are interested in the Incident Management process within ITSM. IT service vendors maintain large, complex IT infrastructure on behalf of their clients, and set up skill-based teams with the responsibility of maintaining different infrastructure components, such as applications, servers, databases and so on. When an interruption or degradation in service in some part of the IT infrastructure is detected, service requests are raised in the form of *tickets* that describe the incident. However, due to inherent dependencies between different system components, identifying the root cause of the problem is a complex, and often time-consuming, activity. The traditional approach to incident management is to have a human dispatcher intercept the ticket and review the incident description. Using his/her knowledge of the system and dependencies, the dispatcher then determines the most likely component that may be faulty and forwards the ticket to the relevant team, where it is assigned to a practitioner for investigation. The practitioner may determine the presence of a fault in the component and the incident may be resolved by taking corrective action to remove the fault. However, often the practitioner may discover that the fault does not lie in the component s/he is managing, and sends the ticket back to the dispatcher, who then needs to decide on the next team the ticket should be sent to, and this process continues till the right team receives the ticket and resolves the incident.

Such a process-driven approach may be reasonable when the problem description is detailed and clear. In reality, we find the end user reporting the incident to state the symptom at best. It is the human dispatcher's responsibility to guess the root-cause and identify the right person for the resolution job. This may be appropriate for simple and low severity incidents, but is risky in more complex situations. In those cases the overall resolution time may exceed the contractually agreed upon response time as manifested in Service Level Objectives (SLO). The consequences can be degradation of client satisfaction and/or monetary penalties. Our proposal is to demonstrate the benefits of bringing together appropriate resolution units, conceptualized as a SCUs, that possess the right skills composition to deal with the eventualities of the given context, as defined by the system where the incident occurs. The members of a SCU may be drawn from components where there is a higher likelihood of a fault, and component dependency information may be used to on/off-board members as investigation proceeds. Such an agile way of managing incident resolution should help facilitate parallel investigations and thereby quicker resolution. However, SCUs may also incur a higher cost (since multiple practitioners are investigating a problem at once), hence its use has to be judiciously interleaved with the more standard workflow-driven sequential investigation of incidents, so that the right trade-off between quicker resolution and higher cost may be achieved.

The main contributions of the paper are as follows:

1. The development of a technical framework for SCU sourcing, invocation and evolution in the context of IT incident management spanning multiple teams and organizational verticals.
2. A simulation based approach to study the efficiencies that may be gained through SCUs over standard process management approaches, and the trade-offs involved.

The rest of the paper is organized as follows. In Section 2 we present a motivating example and introduce the concept of SCUs. In Section 3 we introduce the formal system model for the use of SCUs in incident management, and describe the life-cycle of a SCU from its invocation, evolution to dissolution. Section 4 presents a simulation based method to demonstrate the benefits that may be achieved through a combination of SCUs and workflow based approaches. After discussing related work in Section 5, we conclude with a discussion on future work and extensions of our framework in Section 6.

2   Motivating Example

Consider an IT service provider that manages applications on behalf of a client. Each application is a complex eco-system of its own, consisting of actual application code, the hosting middleware and operating system, servers, storage components, network and firewall configurations etc. An incident in any application may have its root-cause in any of its sub-systems. Resolving the incident for the application may henceforth require multiple skills, from programming skills to networking skills. IT service providers that manage hundreds or thousands of applications cannot scale by assigning individual teams to manage individual applications. Instead, it is more cost-efficient to form organizational units that are formed around skills and manage specific, similar system components.

Figure 1 shows an example of a component dependency graph for an application and its management context. The connectors between nodes indicate the nature of relationship or dependency between the components. For example, the straight line between *Application* and *Application Server* denotes a tight coupling as in a component being hosted on another (thus the dependency type is *isHostedOn*). Each dotted line, e.g. between *Web Server* and *Application Server* denotes a loose coupling between components as in one component being connected to the other through a web-service call or an HTTP request (*isConnectedTo* being the dependency type).

Each layer of an application is managed by an organizational entity as denoted on the left side. The *Application* component is managed by the Application Management team, which has the right set of coding skills and application knowledge to debug issues or extend functionality. The middleware layer (web server, application server and DBMS) is managed by the Application Hosting team that knows how to manage application servers and databases. In principle each management entity can be modeled as another node in the dependency graph but for simplicity we have depicted management entities as dotted line boxes around the components they are responsible for. For example, the dotted line box around the DBMS component could also be represented by a DBMS node connected to a Database Management node through a connector stereotyped as *isManagedBy*.

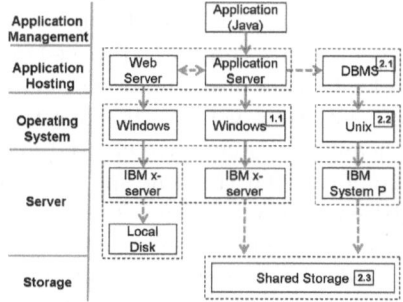

Fig. 1. Dependencies between application components and their management context

Let us now consider incident management - an important area in ITSM [3] - for the above example. An incident is an event which is not part of the standard operation of a service and causes, or may cause, an interruption to or a reduction in, the quality of that service. The goal of incident management is to restore the service functionality as quickly as required. The service restoration time is tied to the Service Level Objective (SLO) the client and provider have agreed upon and usually depends on the severity of the incident. An incident may be caused by a known problem for which there exists an action plan, or, may also require problem resolution as the root-cause is not known. Let us now examine incident resolution through two scenarios, with a focus on who is resolving an issue.

1. An incident states an issue with capacity exceeded on the server hosting the Application Server. The action plan (1.1 in Figure 1) is to delete all unnecessary temporary files using a pre-defined sequence of steps. The resource required is a member of the Operating System team and has Windows skills.
2. An incident indicates an issue with slow performance of the database management system (DBMS). The root cause needs to be identified. The IT Help Desk responsible for dispatching the ticket will route the ticket to the Application Hosting team and a resource will be assigned to look for standard causes, such as full log files (2.1 in Figure 1). The assigned resource determines that the cause is capacity exceeded on the server and hence passes

the incident on to the Server support to free up capacity (2.2 in Figure 1). The Server support team member executes some pre-defined steps to free up space, however notices that this is not solving the issue as the problem lies in the growth of the tables. This requires the ticket to be passed on to the storage team (2.3 in Figure 1). The storage team allocates space and takes necessary steps to resolve the issue and close the incident.

In the first scenario, the incident description has sufficient clarity for a dispatcher to quickly identify the relevant component and required skills. The ticket can be dispatched to the Windows Operating System team, where an available practitioner will execute a standard set of actions to resolve the issue. Thus such a ticket is amenable to a well-defined, repeatable incident management process. On the other hand, the second case involves a ticket where the symptom reported can be due to one of several possible causes. Using the standard sequential approach to incident management, we can try to proceed one component at a time, ruling out the presence of a fault in one component, before passing on the ticket to the next likely component. However, by the time the actual problem is discovered and fixed, significant time may have elapsed and a SLO may also have been breached. It may be noted that the time spent is not only due to the investigations that have to be carried out by each team, but also due to the delays that occur when a ticket has to be transferred across organizational boundaries, and the time that is wasted when a ticket is pending in a queue, waiting for a practitioner to become available and accept the ticket.

We posit that tickets such as in the second case above, need a different approach to incident management. Instead of being investigated by one practitioner from one component team at a time, they may need simultaneous attention from multiple practitioners and teams. In this paper we will apply the concept of a Social Compute Unit (SCU) [8] to address the second scenario above. A SCU is a "loosely coupled, virtual and nimble" team of socially-connected experts with skills in domains relevant to the problem at hand. Socially connected in common terms is widely understood outside of the work context. We define connectedness with respect to a *social fabric*. We believe that in general a human resource is a connected entity represented as a point (or node) in the social fabric. The social fabric consists of a continuum of network expressions such as an organizational network or a collaboration network. The former is typically well defined with specific roles and responsibilities assigned to nodes in the network. The latter is an expression of an individual's ability to transcend organizational boundaries to act as a source or sink of information.

A SCU team member may not be a dedicated resource, but someone who can invest a certain amount of time towards solving a problem, when the requirement comes up. A SCU is created on request (e.g. from the problem domain's business owner), has a certain amount of computing power derived from the skills and availability of its members and from their collaboration, uses its computing power towards addressing the problem which triggered its creation, and is dissolved upon problem resolution. These characteristics make the SCU an attractive approach for incident resolution management in an IT service organization. For more details on the SCU concept, the interested reader is referred to [8]. In the rest of the paper, we will describe in detail how SCUs may be used within an IT service management environment for facilitating collaborative incident resolution spanning multiple teams/organizations.

3   Incident Management Using SCUs: A Technical Framework

We first describe our system model, and then outline the basic principles that guide a SCU through its life-cycle. There may be different ways of realizing the abstract framework presented in this section and a concrete instantiation will be described and evaluated in the following section.

3.1   System Model

We assume a component dependency model represented as a graph $G = (V, E)$, where V is a set of nodes, each representing a component of the overall IT infrastructure being managed, and E is a set of directed edges representing dependency relationships between the nodes. Each edge may be represented by a triple $< C_i, C_j, DT_k >$, where $C_i, C_j \in V$ and represent system components, and $DT_k \in DT$ is the dependency relationship that exists between C_i (source) and C_j (target), drawn from a set DT of possible relationships relevant to the domain. A component $C_i \in V$ has a set of possible *features* C_i^F through which it provides services to the end-user. A *ticket* T_i is raised when an interruption or degradation in IT performance is detected, and may be initially represented as $< TS_i, D_i, P_i >$, where TS_i is the time-stamp when the ticket was raised, D_i is a textual description of the problem, P_i is a priority level indicating the criticality of the problem that may be drawn from an ordered sequence of numbers $\{1, 2, ...p\}$, with 1 representing the highest priority and p the lowest. Based on its priority P_i, a ticket will also have a Service Level Objective $SLO(P_i)$ which is the window of time W_i within which the incident needs to be resolved, thereby setting a deadline $TS_i + W_i$ that the ITSM team has to strive to meet. Each ticket is also implicitly associated with a fault profile $FP = \{(C_i, f_j) | C_i \in V, f \in C_i^F\}$, which is a set of features in a set of system components that have developed a fault, and need to be investigated and fixed. In the majority of cases, we may expect a ticket to be associated with a single malfunctioning feature in one component. Of course, the fault profile is not known when a ticket arrives, but needs to be discovered in course of the incident management process.

When a ticket is raised, it is the dispatcher's responsibility to review the problem description, and try to identify the likely component(s) that are not functioning correctly, so that the ticket may be dispatched to the relevant team(s). The dispatcher is aided in this task by the component dependency graph, and in general, s/he may be expected to devise a dispatch strategy that contains an ordered sequence of components $\{C_{i_1}, C_{i_2}, ..., C_{i_{|V|}}\}$, which we call the *Likelihood*

Sequence (LS(t)) for a ticket t, going from the most to the least likely component that may be the cause for this incident. $LS(t)$ represents the order in which the ticket should be dispatched to the different components for investigation, till the root cause is identified and fixed. Note that we assume a fully ordered sequence only for simplicity; the likelihood of some of the elements may be deemed to be equal, in which case any of them may be picked as the next component to be investigated. $LS(t)$ would depend on the ticket description, which may contain some indicators of the potential source of the problem, while the component dependency graph would make certain related components candidates for investigation as well, based on the nature of the relationship they have with the sources. The Likelihood Sequence is a key construct in our incident management framework. It not only drives the dispatch strategy for the business-as-usual (BAU) way of routing tickets one team at a time, but is also the sequence our SCU-based approach would refer to, to help decide on the composition and dynamic reconfiguration of the SCU during an incident resolution activity. The Likelihood Sequence may be expected to evolve as investigation proceeds and better understanding is achieved regarding the nature of the problem.

ITSM services will be provided by a set of practitioners (human resources) R. Each $R_i \in R$ has a skill profile $SP(R_i) = \{(C_p, f_q, l_r) | C_p \in V, f_q \in C_p^F, l_r \in L\}$, where L is an ordered sequence of skill levels $\{1, 2, ..., l\}$, with 1 being the lowest (most basic) and l being the highest skill level for any skill. A skill is the ability to investigate and correct a particular feature in a given component. Most practitioners will possess a set of skills, with varying skill levels, and the skills of a practitioner will usually be centered around different features in a single IT component, although there may be a few experienced practitioners with skills that span multiple components. Given this, each component is immediately associated with a *team* - a group of practitioners who have skills in one or more of the component features and may be called upon to investigate an incident that may have potentially been caused by the component. For a component C_i, this is given by $Team(C_i) = \{R_i | R_i \in R, \exists l \in L, \exists f \in C_i^F.(C_i, f, l) \in SP(R_i)\}$. For each combination (f, l) of a feature f and skill level l, we have an effort tuple $< E_{inv}(f, l), E_{res}(f, l) >$, which indicates representative (e.g. average) effort needed by a practitioner with skill level l in feature f to investigate if the feature is working correctly ($E_{inv}(f, l)$), and to restore the feature to working condition ($E_{res}(f, l)$) in case a fault is detected.

A Social Compute Unit $SCU(T_p, t)$ for a ticket T_p at a point in time t, may be represented by $< \mathcal{C}(t), \mathcal{R}(t), \mathcal{S}(t) >$, where $\mathcal{C}(t) \subseteq V$ is the set of components currently being investigated (i.e. at time t), $\mathcal{R}(t) \subseteq R$ is the set of practitioners that are part of the SCU at time t, and $\mathcal{S}(t)$ is an abstraction of the current *state* of the investigation, encompassing all components/features that have been verified to be functioning correctly till this point, all the faulty features that have been restored, and the all features that are currently under investigation or restoration. Thus a SCU is a dynamic entity whose composition (in terms of components and practitioners) as well as state (in terms of features investigated or restored), will continually evolve with time.

The management of an incident - from its creation to closure - will incur a cost, primarily due to effort spent by practitioners on various investigation tasks. We assume that when a practitioner joins an investigation effort, s/he will need to spend a certain amount of effort E_{init} to familiarize with the problem and the current investigation state. Subsequently, s/he will expend effort on feature investigation and restoration, commensurate with her skill levels. If s/he is part of a SCU, she will be expected to spend E_{collab} effort to collaborate with the larger team through the sharing of findings. This effort may be proportional to the duration of her stay in the SCU, as well as the size of the SCU during that period (in terms of the number of practitioners and components/features involved). If we wish to monetize the effort spent, we may assume a function $UnitSalary(R_i) : SP(R_i) - > \mathcal{R}$ (where $\mathcal{R}$ is the set of Real numbers), that returns the cost of unit effort spent by the practitioner, based on his/her skill profile. We also assume there is a certain amount of effort needed to set up and dissolve a SCU, given by SCU_{setup} and $SCU_{disolve}$ respectively. Also, in the process-driven sequential way of incident management, there will be a certain delay $D_{transfer}$ imposed each time a ticket is transferred from one team to the next. Finally, delays may be introduced due to unavailability of practitioners.

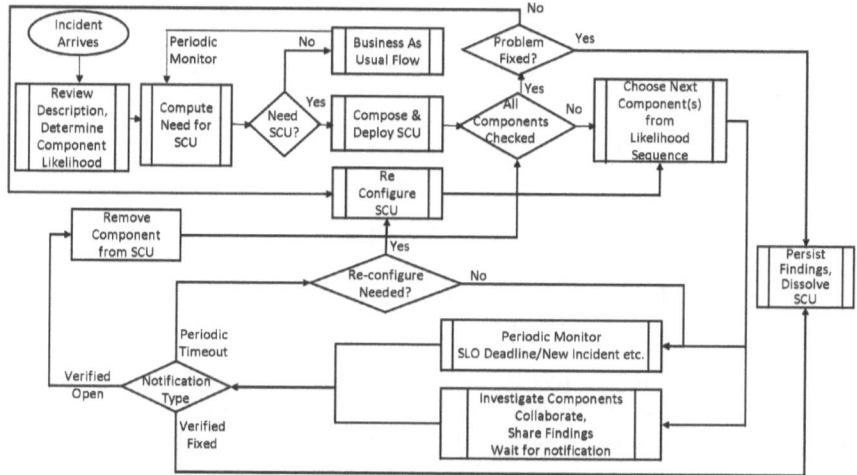

Fig. 2. Incident Management Using SCUs

3.2   SCU Based Incident Management

Figure 2 depicts the overall incident management process that we propose. It is important to note that our SCU approach complements, rather than replaces, sequential process-driven incident management, represented in Figure 2 as the Business As Usual (BAU) flow. We do not expect a SCU to be required for every ticket, rather we base this decision upon the specific context of a ticket at a given point in time. When an incident arrives, the problem description should be reviewed, and the relative likelihood of different components being the source of the problem, has to be evaluated. This may be done by a human agent (e.g. a dispatcher) who uses a combination of ticket description and knowledge of component dependencies to identify potential faulty components. Supervised learning techniques such as Support Vector Machine (SVM) [15] may also be used to suggest for new tickets the likelihood (represented by a probability distribution) of each component being the source of the problem [2]. A combination involving a human dispatcher being assisted by an automated agent is also possible. It may be noted that such a likelihood evaluation is anyway done (even if implicitly) as part of a standard incident management process, since the dispatcher has to decide each time s/he receives a ticket, which component team needs to be contacted next to investigate the problem. Also, it is not necessary for the entire likelihood sequence to be generated as soon as an incident arrives. Instead, this may also be done incrementally, by considering at any point in time which are the most likely components that may be the cause for the incident (taking into account components that have already been investigated), and involve only those teams in the next phase of investigation.

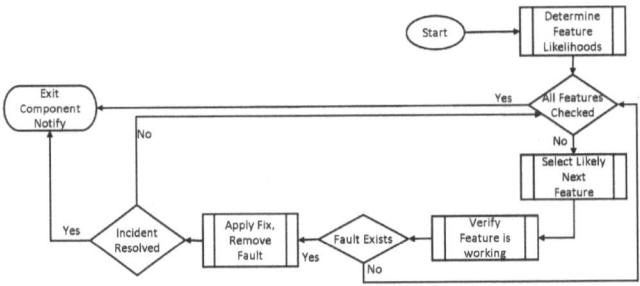

Fig. 3. Investigation Within A Component

Once this initial analysis has been done, we need to decide whether or not to invoke a SCU. In case the ticket deadline is sufficiently far away and/or there is a very strong likelihood of one particular component being the source of the problem, then the system may decide to follow the BAU mode, in which the ticket is dispatched to the most likely faulty component, where a practitioner will have to investigate it (this is explained in more detail later in the context of Figure 3). However, there will still be a need to monitor the situation so that in case the deadline is approaching without the root cause been detected, then a decision may be taken to set up a SCU to accelerate the investigation.

In case the BAU mode is not deemed appropriate in view of an impending deadline or lack of clarity in the problem description, a SCU may be invoked. Here, a few of the more likely faulty components are identified, and a set of practitioners who have the necessary skills in these components are on-boarded to the SCU. The decision on how many such components to consider, how many practitioners to on-board, what their skill levels should be etc. may be taken based on availability and the urgency of the situation. For example, if there is a crisis situation with the deadline of a high priority ticket being near at hand, then highly skilled practitioners from most/all of the component teams may have to be involved. In less urgent cases, one practitioner per component, for a small number of components at a time (say, 2-3) may be sufficient. Once on-boarded, the practitioners representing a component would try to determine if the incident has been caused by a fault in one of its features, using the process depicted in Figure 3. Here, a practitioner would proceed through the feature list of a component in the order of their relative likelihood of having a fault (as inferred by him/her based on the ticket description and understanding of features), and for each feature, investigate if it is correctly functioning, and if not, apply a fix to restore the feature. If the fix resolves the incident as well, then any ongoing investigation will be stopped across all components. Suitable findings from the investigation process will be harvested for later reference, and the SCU will be dissolved (Figure 2). Otherwise, the practitioner may move on to the next feature. If the current practitioner(s) representing a component do not have all the skills needed to cover the complete feature set, then on completion of their investigation, they may be replaced by other suitable practitioners. Note that this basic approach towards investigating a component remains the same whether a BAU or SCU mode is used. In case multiple practitioners are investigating the same component together in a SCU, they may partition the feature list amongst themselves to ensure there is no redundancy of effort. Also, within a SCU, a practitioner will be expected to collaborate with others e.g. through the sharing of findings, as shown in Figure 2.

As investigation proceeds, it is necessary to periodically monitor the situation and take appropriate action (Figure 2). For example, if the incident deadline is approaching, then there would be a need to re-configure the SCU by on-boarding more practitioners to cover other components. In case a high priority ticket arrives that needs the attention of a practitioner who is currently part of another (relatively less urgent) ticket's SCU, then the practitioner may have to leave the SCU and be replaced by another suitably skilled colleague who is available. Again, if all the features of a component have been verified to be functioning correctly, then the component may be removed from the SCU and the corresponding practitioners off-boarded. New SCU members may then be added from the next likely set of component(s). Finally, in the unusual case when all components have been investigated without the defect being identified, the SCU may be re-constituted and re-run, with higher skilled practitioners if needed.

4   Experiments

To experimentally evaluate our proposed SCU-based approach for incident management, we have designed an event driven simulator that mimics the flow of tickets through an IT service delivery environment. We first describe the experimental set-up, and then present the results.

4.1 Experimental Set-Up

The simulation framework is built on java and has 4 major components: Events Generator that generates standard events related to incidence creation and management; Ticket Lifecycle Simulator, which manages various timers and notifications related to a ticket; Delivery Model, which includes the basic models of all the system entities (tickets, components, features, resources etc.) and relationships, and whose generated runtime is directly used within the simulation framework; and SCU Runtime Manager, designed as a library for implementing a SCU model in a service delivery environment.

For our experiments, we have considered an IT system with 30 components, with each component having between 0 to 5 dependencies generated as a random graph. For generating ticket data, we used a power law probability distribution of tickets across components, which is suitable for generating Pareto-like long tailed distributions. Based on our experience from working with large ITSM organizations, we have set this closer to a 70:30 distribution, which means that only 30% of the components cause 70% of the tickets. Overall, we generated 1154 tickets to cover a 1 week period of study, and maintained a resource pool of 200 practitioners to ensure a reasonable service rate. The ticket arrival rate is modeled as a stochastic process using a Poisson distribution initialized by average hourly arrival rates of tickets as we have seen in several actual service delivery environments. We assumed 4 different priority levels for tickets, with SLOs of 4 hours (highest priority), 8 hours, 24 hours and 48 hours (lowest priority) respectively. The relative distribution of the priority levels, were 2% (highest priority), 8%, 20% and 70% (lowest probability). All these values were selected based on our review of multiple ticket sets and SLOs. We assumed each practitioner to have skills in all the features of one component (which is often the case since practitioners in such environments are usually specialists in a particular technical domain). The staffing levels of each component were determined based on their relative workload (in terms of number of tickets received, the number of features, and the effort needed to investigate and fix each feature). Each ticket was assigned a fault profile of a single feature in one component. The likelihood sequence of each ticket was generated carefully by assuming the faulty component to be amongst the most likely ones in a high percentage of cases, but we also generated tickets with unclear root causes, where the faulty component occurred later in the sequence (with a probability that decreased progressively as the likelihood decreased). Moreover, we adjusted each sequence to ensure that the position of a likely component correlated well with that of some of its neighbours in the dependency graph, so that these neighbours were likely candidates as well.

We studied two modes of incident management - a fully process driven BAU mode, and a heterogeneous mode of BAU and SCUs. In the former, a ticket is investigated by one practitioner from one component at a time, and whenever a ticket has to cross organization boundaries, we assumed a delay of 30 minutes to account for the process-related overheads. This is actually a conservative estimate, since in real life service environments we have found tickets to be stuck for hours or days together in transfer between the components, and this was a key motivation for the SCU. In the heterogeneous mode, SCUs were automatically assembled for every highest priority ticket. For the rest of the tickets (including those initially dispatched in BAU mode), the decision to compose a SCU was based on the urgency of the situation at a given point in time. We used 4 levels of urgency, based on distance from the SLO deadline, and gradually increased the span of a SCU to cover more components (while having a single practitioner per SCU component) as the ticket moved from one urgency level to the next higher one.

4.2   Results and Discussion

The table in Figure 4 presents the results obtained from our simulation-based experiments. The column BAU stands for the mode where only process-driven sequential investigation was carried out for each ticket, while the rest of the columns involve situations where the BAU mode was complemented by SCUs. We experimented with different variations of this latter mode. We started with a conservative policy of initializing each SCU with a single component (Start1), but still investing in the SCU set-up cost (e.g. for getting the collaboration platform ready) in anticipation of the need to onboard more practitioners. In the other variations, we initialized each SCU with 2, 3 and 5 components. Once set up, a SCU was, of course, allowed to expand in size by onboarding more components, as the ticket progressed towards its deadline.

		SCU Performance in different modes with % Variation over BAU							
All times are in hours	**BAU**	**Start 1**		**Min 2**		**Min 3**		**Min 5**	
Avg. No. of Resources Per Ticket	4.79	5.49	114.6%	5.81	121.3%	6.45	134.8%	7.20	150.2%
Avg. Person Hours Per Ticket	17	16	95.1%	18	106.8%	21	122.1%	23	135.0%
Avg. Time To Resolve	20.6	12.13	58.9%	11.2	54.3%	11.12	53.9%	10.87	52.7%
Avg. Time Investigating	15.3	10.23	66.7%	9.233	60.2%	9.283	60.5%	9.1	59.3%
Max Time to Resolve	133	70.52	53.1%	67.93	51.2%	73.3	55.2%	69.42	52.3%
No. of SLO Violations	165	67	40.6%	77	46.7%	75	45.5%	45	27.3%
Average SCU Strength	1.00	2.20	220.0%	2.49	249.0%	3.18	318.5%	4.03	403.5%
Social Interaction**	0	12	N/A	20	N/A	34	N/A	55	N/A
Ticket = 1154 | Components = 30 | Resources = 200 | Duration = 7 days									
**Avg no. of colleagues the resources encountered at least once during the simulation period									

Fig. 4. Experimental Results

We compare the performance of BAU and SCU modes along two main dimensions: effort and time to resolve. In terms of effort spent, the BAU mode is, in general, more efficient than the SCU mode. This is because in the former, only a single practitioner is being assigned at a time to conduct an investigation (on the most likely component at that point), while in the latter, multiple practitioners are assigned, and the aggregate effort invested is likely to be higher. Thus both the metrics Average Number of Resources Per Ticket and Average Person Hours Effort Per Ticket (aggregated across all resources who worked on a ticket) shows an increase as we go from BAU to SCU mode, and across the different variants of SCU modes. The only exception to this is when we start a SCU with a single component, in which case the Average Person Hours Effort Per Ticket decreases by about 5% relative to the BAU mode. This is an interesting case, and one probable reason for this may be that the Start1 mode, being at the boundary between full BAU and SCU modes, is able to effectively leverage the advantages of both, combining the power of quicker resolution with the low initial effort to bring down the total effort per ticket.

While the overall effort spent in SCU mode is, in general, higher, the collaborative investigation power of a SCU also significantly reduces the time to resolution, as seen from the values of the metrics Average Time To Resolve, Average Time Investigating and Max Time to Resolve. In all of these, the performance of the BAU mode lags far behind that of the SCU modes. From the business impact perspective, the most compelling case for the SCU comes from the dramatically improved SLO performance that results from its faster resolution of tickets, with Number of SLO Violations ranging between only 27.3% to 46.7% of the corresponding number for BAU. With the stringent penalties that IT vendors have to pay for poor SLA performance, the financial implications of this are far reaching. It may also be noted that while the SCU approach may consume more aggregate effort from practitioners, this does not necessarily translate to higher costs for the vendor. This is because, vendors typically maintain a dedicated team to provide production support to customer systems, and the effort available from these practitioners, if not utilized, may go waste and result in under-utilization, even though the vendor would still have to bear the same costs in terms of employee salary.

While a SCU has the flexibility to scale up as needed, we find that the average SCU size at any point in time (or its "strength") ranges from 2.2 to 4.03. While this may also partly be due to resource unavailability that prevents it from growing very large (since there will be many other tickets that keep practitioners engaged), the size is small enough for easy governance. Finally, we see that by virtue of being in a SCU, a practitioner is able to increase his/her sphere of interaction substantially, and the average number of colleagues they collaborate with during this brief period of study ranges from 12 to as high as 55. There are several long-term benefits an organization can derive from this that we intend to study in detail going forward, as mentioned in Section 6.

5   Related Work

We believe the novelty of our work is in the usage of SCU teams in problem resolution of otherwise sequential services processes. For example, the authors of [5] developed SYMIAN, a simulation framework for optimizing incident management via a queueing model based approach, which identifies bottlenecks in the sequential execution of ticket resolution. SYMIAN is based on the current implementation of incident management in the IT service provider organizations. Our approach is different from [5] as it takes into account optimization of resolution time through parallelization of work effort in the context of otherwise sequential execution of work.

A number of researchers have looked at the problem of mapping tickets to teams based on the problem description. For example, [14] develops a Markov model by mining ticket resolution sequences of historical tickets that were transferred from one team to another before being resolved. In [10] supervised learning techniques are used to determine the likelihood that a service request corresponds to a specific problem symptom; prior performances of teams are then analyzed to identify groups that have the necessary skills to resolve these problems. In [12] an auction-based pull model for ticket allocation is proposed, along with incentive mechanisms for practitioners to be truthful about expected resolution time when bidding for tickets. Unlike our approach, however, none of these works consider dynamic team formation to facilitate faster resolution of tickets through collaborative problem solving. The use of component dependency graphs in the incident management process has also been explored [11,9]. However, these have mainly been used to correlate problems and to search possible solutions rather than to automatically establish a suitable team for solving problems.

Human-based tasks, e.g., in BPEL4People [4], can be used to specify human capabilities or certain management tasks, e.g., by utilizing human-specific patterns [13]. However, this model relies on specific, pre-defined management processes which are not suitable for complex problem resolution, as we have discussed in this paper. Crowdsourcing [6,7] has been employed for solving complex problems, but while it also offers parallel computation power, our approach is distinct in its use of *social collaboration* to harness complementary skills within an organization and drive towards a common goal.

6   Conclusions and Future Work

This paper is a starting point into a broader mission to investigate the interplay of service-oriented and social computing concepts. So far we have introduced the fundamental concept of Social Compute Units and in this paper demonstrated the cost-benefit aspects of SCU's for a typical enterprise process. Whereas we believe the initial results from our simulations based on real-world experiences from the service delivery business of a large IT Service provider are very promising, future work will address the following:

1. Our current model assumes the SCU to be an organizationally implemented work model, i.e. skill and availability of resources will drive SCU formation. Social computing has a richer set of mechanisms, such as incentive and rewards, that are not yet part of our framework
2. The culture of collaboration that an SCU will nurture should have several long-term benefits in terms of knowledge management and enhancement in skill profiles. We will incorporate these in our framework going forward.
3. An important next step is to realize this approach in a real service delivery environment.

References

1. http://www.gartner.com/it/page.jsp?id=1470115
2. IBM SPSS, http://spss.co.in/
3. IT infrastructure library. ITIL service support, version 2.3. Office of Government Commerce (June 2000)
4. WS-BPEL Extension for People (BPEL4People) Specification Version 1.1 (November 2009), http://docs.oasis-open.org/bpel4people/bpel4people-1.1-spec-cd-06.pdf
5. Bartolini, C., Stefanelli, C., Tortonesi, M.: SYMIAN: A Simulation Tool for the Optimization of the IT Incident Management Process. In: De Turck, F., Kellerer, W., Kormentzas, G. (eds.) DSOM 2008. LNCS, vol. 5273, pp. 83–94. Springer, Heidelberg (2008)
6. Brew, A., Greene, D., Cunningham, P.: Using crowdsourcing and active learning to track sentiment in online media. In: Proceeding of the 2010 Conference on ECAI 2010: 19th European Conference on Artificial Intelligence, pp. 145–150. IOS Press, Amsterdam (2010)
7. Doan, A., Ramakrishnan, R., Halevy, A.Y.: Crowdsourcing systems on the worldwide web. Commun. ACM 54(4), 86–96 (2011)
8. Dustdar, S., Bhattacharya, K.: The social compute unit. IEEE Internet Computing 15(3), 64–69 (2011)
9. Gupta, R., Prasad, K.H., Mohania, M.: Automating ITSM incident management process. In: International Conference on Autonomic Computing (2008)
10. Khan, A., Jamjoom, H., Sun, J.: AIM-HI: a framework for request routing in large-scale IT global service delivery. IBM Journal of Research and Development 53(6) (2009)
11. Marcu, P., Grabarnik, G., Luan, L., Rosu, D., Shwartz, L., Ward, C.: Towards an optimized model of incident ticket correlation. In: Integrated Network Management (IM), pp. 569–576. IEEE Press, Piscataway (2009)
12. Deshpande, P.M., Garg, D., Suri, N.R.: Auction based model for ticket allocation in IT service delivery industry. In: IEEE SCC (2008)
13. Russell, N., van der Aalst, W.M.P.: Work Distribution and Resource Management in BPEL4People: Capabilities and Opportunities. In: Bellahsène, Z., Léonard, M. (eds.) CAiSE 2008. LNCS, vol. 5074, pp. 94–108. Springer, Heidelberg (2008)
14. Shao, Q., Chen, Y., Tao, S., et al.: Efficient ticket routing by resolution sequence mining. In: 14th ACM SIGKDD International Conference on Knowledge Discovery and Data Mining (2008)
15. van Gestel, T., Suykens, J.A.K., Baesens, B., et al.: Benchmarking least squares support vector machine classifiers. Machine Learning 54(1), 5–32 (2004)

Relationship-Preserving Change Propagation in Process Ecosystems

Tri A. Kurniawan*, Aditya K. Ghose, Hoa Khanh Dam, and Lam-Son Lê

Decision Systems Lab., School of Computer Science and Software Engineering,
University of Wollongong, NSW 2522, Australia
{tak976,aditya,hoa,lle}@uow.edu.au

Abstract. As process-orientation continues to be broadly adopted – evidenced by the increasing number of large business process repositories, managing changes in such complex repositories becomes a growing issue. A critical aspect in evolving business processes is change propagation: given a set of primary changes made to a process in a repository, what additional changes are needed to maintain consistency of relationships between various processes in the repository. In this paper, we view a collection of interrelated processes as an ecosystem in which inter-process relationships are formally defined through their annotated semantic effects. We also argue that change propagation is in fact the process of restoring consistency-equilibrium of a process ecosystem. In addition, the underlying change propagation mechanism of our framework is leveraged upon the well-known Constraint Satisfaction Problem (CSP) technology. Our initial experimental results indicate the efficiency of our approach in propagating changes within medium-sized process repositories.

Keywords: inter-process relationship, semantic effect, process ecosystem, change propagation, constraint network.

1 Introduction

Nowadays, modeling and managing business processes is an important approach for managing organizations from an operational perspective. In fact, a recent study [11] has shown that the business process management (BPM) software market reached nearly $1.7 billion in total software revenue in 2006 and this number continues to grow. In addition, today's medium to large organizations may have collections of hundreds or even thousands of business process models (e.g. 6,000+ process models in Suncorp's process model repository for insurance [16]). Therefore, it becomes increasingly critical for those organizations to effectively manage such large business process repositories.

In recent years, the ever-changing business environment demands an organization to continue improving and evolving its business processes to remain competitive. As a result, the most challenging aspect of managing a repository of business processes is dealing with changes. Since business processes within

---

* On leave from a lecturership at University of Brawijaya, East Java, Indonesia

C. Liu et al. (Eds.): ICSOC 2012, LNCS 7636, pp. 63–78, 2012.
© Springer-Verlag Berlin Heidelberg 2012

a repository can be inter-dependent (in terms of both design and execution), changes to one process can potentially have impact on a range of other processes. For example, changes initially made to a sub-process (e.g. removing an activity) may lead to secondary changes made to the processes that contain this sub-process. Such changes may lead to further changes in other dependent processes. The ripple effect that an initial change may cause in a process repository is termed *change propagation*. In a large business process repository, it becomes costly and labor intensive to correctly propagate changes to maintain the consistency among the inter-dependent process models. Therefore, there is an emerging need for techniques and tools that provide more effective (semi-)automated support for change propagation within a complex process repository.

There has been however very little work on supporting change propagation in process model collections [7]. Our proposed framework aims to fill that gap. We view a collection of interrelated process models as an ecosystem [9]. In such ecosystem, process models play a role analogous to that of biological entities in a biological ecosystem. They are created (or discovered, using automated toolkits [10]), constantly changed during their lifetimes, and eventually discarded. Changes made to a process may cause perturbations (i.e. inconsistencies) in the ecosystem in the form of critical inter-process relationships being violated. In this view, a process ecosystem is considered to be in an (consistency-)equilibrium if its all inter-process relationships are mutually consistent. Change propagation is therefore reduced to finding an equilibrium in a process ecosystem.

We further view the problem of finding an equilibrium in a process ecosystem as a constraint satisfaction problem (CSP) in which each process model is mapped to a node and each relationship (between two process models) is a constraint (between the corresponding nodes) in a CSP. This paper is also built on top of our previous work [15], which provides formal definitions for three common types of inter-process relationships (namely part-whole, generalization-specialization and inter-operation) based on concepts of semantic effect-annotated business processes [12]. Specifically, in this paper we propose a machinery to automatically establish relationships between process models in a process repository based on these formalizations. Based on these established relationships, we construct a constraint network [6] of a process ecosystem containing a violated relationship. Candidate values for each individual process node in a CSP can be obtained from the redesign of the process, which can be implemented using existing business process redesign approaches (see, e.g. [13, 19]) or manually produced by the analysts. The CSP encoding allows us to plug different individual process redesign modules without affecting the remaining parts of the architecture.

The rest of the paper is organized as follows. Sec. 2 briefly describes semantic effect-annotated process model and inter-process relationships. Sec. 3 explains how such relationships can be established. Sec. 4 proposes our approach to preserve such relationships in propagating changes within a process ecosystem. In Sec. 5, we present an empirical validation of our approach. We then discuss related work in Sec. 6, and conclude and layout some future work in Sec. 7.

2   Preliminaries

Semantic Effect-Annotated Process Model. An effect annotation relates to a particular result or outcome to an activity in a process model [14]. An activity represents the work performed within a process. Activities are either atomic (called a *task*, i.e. they are at the lowest level of detail presented in the diagram and can not be further broken down) or compound (called a *sub-process*, i.e. they can be broken down to see another level of process below) [21]. In an annotated BPMN process model, as our approach relies on, we annotate each activity with its (immediate) effects. We define these immediate effects as the immediate results or outcomes of executing an activity in a process model. We consider that multiple effects can be immediately resulted in such execution. We shall leverage the ProcessSEER [12] tool to annotate process model with the semantic effects. This annotation allows us to determine, at design time, the effects of the process if it were to be executed up to a certain point in the model. These effects are necessarily non-deterministic, since a process might have taken one of many possible alternative paths through a process design to get to that point. We define a procedure for *pair-wise effect accumulation*, which, given an ordered pair of activities with effect annotations, determines the cumulative effect after both activities have been executed in contiguous sequence.

Let t_i and t_j be an ordered pair of activities connected by a sequence flow such that t_i precedes t_j. Let $e_i = \{c_{i1}, \ldots, c_{im}\}$ and $e_j = \{c_{j1}, \ldots, c_{jn}\}$ be the corresponding pair of effect annotations, respectively. If $e_i \cup e_j$ is consistent, then the resulting cumulative effect is $e_i \cup e_j$. Otherwise, we define $e'_i = \{c_k\}$ where $c_k \in e_i$ and $\{c_k\} \cup e_j$ *is consistent*, and the resulting cumulative effect to be $e'_i \cup e_j$. In the following, we shall use $ACC(e_p, e_q)$ to denote the result of pair-wise effect accumulation of two contiguous activities t_p and t_q with the immediate effects e_p and e_q, respectively.

Effects are only accumulated within participant lanes (i.e. role represented as a pool) and are not including inter-participant within inter-operation business process. In addition to the effect annotation of each activity, we also denote E_t as the cumulative effect of activity t. E_t is defined as a set $\{es_{t1}, \ldots, es_{tm}\}$ of alternative *effect scenarios* based on the $1, \ldots, m$ alternative paths reaching the activity. Alternative effect scenarios are introduced by AND-joins or XOR-joins or OR-joins. We accumulate effects through a left-to-right pass of a participant lane, applying the pair-wise effect accumulation procedure on contiguous pairs of activities connected via control flow links. The process continues without modification over splits. Joins require special consideration. In the following, we describe the procedure to be followed in the case of 2-way joins only, for brevity. The procedure generalizes in a straightforward manner for n-way joins.

In the following, let t_p and t_q be two activities immediately preceding a join. Let their cumulative effect annotations be $E_p = \{es_{p1}, \ldots, es_{pm}\}$ and $E_q = \{es_{q1}, \ldots, es_{qn}\}$, respectively. Let e be immediate effect and E be cumulative effect of an activity t immediately following the join.

For **AND-joins**, we define $E = \{ACC(es_{pi}, e) \cup ACC(es_{qj}, e)\}$ where $es_{pi} \in E_p$ and $es_{qj} \in E_q$. Note that we do not consider the possibility of a pair of

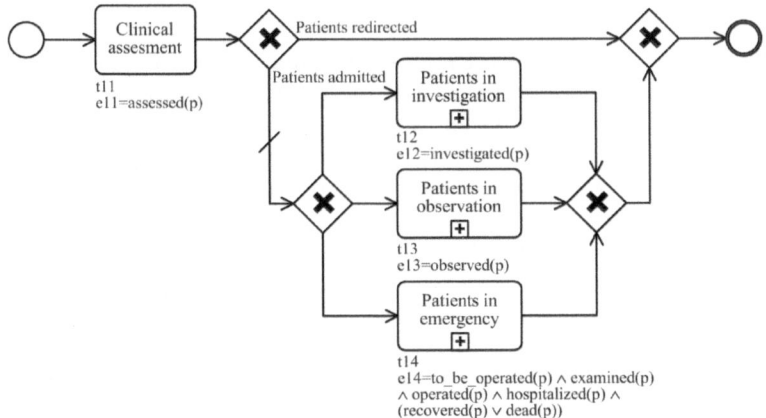

Fig. 1. *Management of patients on arrival* process

effect scenarios es_{pi} and es_{qj} being inconsistent, since this would only happen in the case of intrinsically and obviously erroneously constructed process models. The result of effect accumulation in the setting described here is denoted by $ANDacc(E_p, E_q, e)$. For **XOR-joins**, we define $E = \{ACC(es_r, e)\}$ where $es_r \in E_p$ or $es_r \in E_2$. The result of effect accumulation in the setting described here is denoted by $XORacc(E_p, E_q, e)$. For **OR-joins**, the result of effect accumulation in such setting is denoted by $ORacc(E_p, E_q, e) = ANDacc(E_p, E_q, e) \cup XORacc(E_p, E_q, e)$.

Figure 1 illustrates a semantic effect-annotated BPMN process model. The immediate effect e_i of each activity t_i is represented in a Conjunctive Normal Form (CNF) allowing us to describe such effect as a set of outcome clauses. Let p be patient to be observed and treated. For example, activity t_{13} has an immediate effect $e_{13} = observed(p)$ which depicts the outcomes of executing such activity. The cumulative effects of execution the process until t_{13} can be computed by accumulating the effects starting from t_{11} until t_{13}, i.e. $assessed(p) \wedge observed(p)$. We can also compute for the other activities in a similar way.

Inter-process Relationships. We recap relationships formalization described in our previous work [15]. We classify these relationships into two categories: *functional dependencies* and *consistency links*. A functional dependency exists between a pair of processes when one process needs support from the other for realizing some of its functionalities. In this category, we define two relationship types, i.e. *part-whole* and *inter-operation*. A consistency link exists between a pair of processes when both of them have intersecting parts which represent the same functionality, i.e. the outcomes of these parts are exactly the same. They are functionally independent. We identify one type in this category, i.e. *generalization-specialization*. Our framework focuses on these three types.

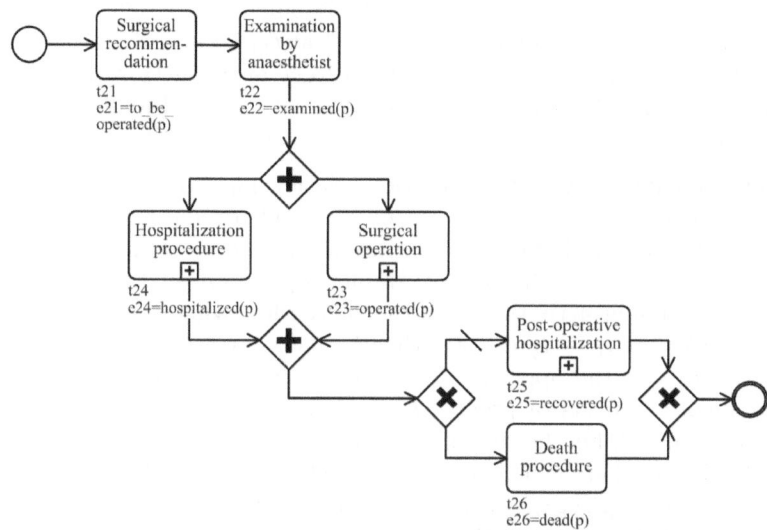

Fig. 2. Expansion of *Patients in emergency* sub-process in Figure 1

We use $acc\,(P)$ to denote the end cumulative effects of process P; $CE\,(P, t_i)$ to describe cumulative effect at the point of activity t_i within process P; and es_j to denote an effect scenario j-th. Noted, each of $acc\,(P)$ or $CE\,(P, t_i)$ is a set of effect scenarios. Each effect scenario is represented as a set of clauses and will be viewed, implicitly, as their conjunction.

(i) Part-Whole. A part-whole relationship exists between two processes when one process is required by the other to fulfill some of its functionalities. More specifically, there must be an activity in the 'whole' process representing the functionalities of the 'part' process. The 'part' process is also commonly referred to as a sub-process within the 'whole' process. Logically, there is an insertion of the functionalities of the 'part' into the 'whole'.

We define the insertion of process $P2$ in process $P1$ at activity t, $P1 \uparrow^t P2$, is a process design obtained by viewing $P2$ as the sub-process expansion of t in $P1$. We then define the part-whole as follows: $P2$ is a direct part of $P1$ iff there exists an activity t in $P1$ s.t. $CE\,(P1, t) = CE\,(P1 \uparrow^t P2, t)$. Let us consider an example[1] of the part-whole relationship which is illustrated in Figures 1 and 2 (called $P1$ and $P2$, respectively). Such relationship is reflected by the activity *Patients in emergency* (t_{14}) in $P1$ whose functionality represents $P2$. This means that the result of executing activity t_{14} in $P1$ is solely the result of executing $P2$, and vice-versa. The insertion point here is at t_{14} in $P1$. The cumulative effect of $P1$ at this point is $CE\,(P1, t_{14}) = \{es_{14}\}$; $es_{14} = assessed\,(p) \wedge to\_be\_operated\,(p) \wedge examined\,(p) \wedge operated\,(p) \wedge$

---

[1] We will only exemplify the part-whole relationship due to space limitation. In this paper, we only address direct relationships for the shake of efficiency in propagating the changes. The indirect ones can be referred in our previous work [15].

hospitalized $(p) \wedge (recovered\,(p) \vee dead\,(p))$. We only have one effect scenario, i.e. es_{14}. Furthermore, the cumulative effect of $P1$ at t_{14} by inserting $P2$ at this activity is $CE\,(P1 \uparrow^{t_{14}} P2, t_{14}) = assessed\,(p) \wedge to\_be\_operated\,(p) \wedge examined\,(p) \wedge operated\,(p) \wedge hospitalized\,(p) \wedge (recovered\,(p) \vee dead\,(p))$. Finally, we can infer that $P2$ is a part of $P1$ since $CE\,(P1, t_{14}) = CE\,(P1 \uparrow^{t_{14}} P2, t_{14})$.

(ii) Inter-operation. An inter-operation relationship exists between two processes when there is at least one message exchanged between them and there is no cumulative effect contradiction between tasks involved in exchanging messages. Formally, given processes $P1$ and $P2$, an inter-operation relationship exists between them including activities t_i and t_j iff the following holds: (i) $\exists t_i$ in $P1$ $\exists t_j$ in $P2$ such that $t_i \rightharpoonup t_j$ denotes that t_i sends a message to t_j, or $t_j \rightharpoonup t_i$, if the message is in the opposite direction; (ii) let $E_i = \{es_{i1}, es_{i2}, \ldots, es_{im}\}$ be the cumulative effects of process $P1$ at task t_i, i.e. $CE\,(P1, t_i)$, and $E_j = \{es_{j1}, es_{j2}, \ldots, es_{jn}\}$ be the cumulative effects of process $P2$ at task t_j, i.e. $CE\,(P2, t_j)$. Then, there is no contradiction between E_i and E_j for all $es_{ip} \in E_i$ and $es_{jq} \in E_j$ s.t. $es_{ip} \cup es_{jq} \vdash \perp$ does not hold, where $1 \le p \le m$ and $1 \le q \le n$.

Effect contradiction exists if the expected effects differ from the given effects. If this is the case, we do not consider such relationship as an inter-operation one even though there is a message between both processes.

(iii) Generalization-Specialization. A generalization-specialization relationship exists between two processes when one process becomes the functional extension of the other. More specifically, the *specialized* process has the same functionalities as in the *generalized* one and also extends it with some additional functionalities. One way to extend the functionalities is by adding some additional activities so that the intended end cumulative effects of the process are consequently extended. Another way involves enriching the immediate effects of the existing activities. In this case, the number of activities remains the same for both processes but the capabilities of the *specialized* process is extended. Noted, the *specialized* process inherits all functionalities of the *generalized* process, as formally defined as follows. Given process models $P1$ and $P2$, $P2$ is a specialization of $P1$ iff $\forall es_i \in acc\,(P1)$, $\exists es_j \in acc\,(P2)$ such that $es_j \models es_i$; and $\forall es_j \in acc\,(P2)$, $\exists es_i \in acc\,(P1)$ such that $es_i \models es_j$.

3   Establishing Inter-process Relationships

The formal definitions of inter-process relationships that we discussed in the previous section empower us to systematically specify (manually or automatically) which process models are related to others in a process repository. To do so, analysts who need to manage the large and complex process repositories must effectively explore the space of all possible pairings of process designs to determine what relationships (if any) should hold in each instance. Note that this generates a space of $\binom{n}{2}$ possibilities, where n is the number of distinct process designs in the repository. Clearly, this has the potential to be an error-prone exercise. An analyst may normatively specify a relationship that does not actually hold (with regard to our definition of the relationship) between a pair of process designs. In some cases, an analyst might need help in deciding what relationship ought to hold. We therefore develop a *user-interactive* machinery to assist analysts in deciding what type of *normative* relationship should hold between a pair of processes. We consider two approaches in such assistance, i.e. *checking* and *generating* modes. In the *checking* mode, we will assess whether a relationship specified by an analyst does indeed hold with regard to our formal definition. If this is the case, the relationship between the two processes can be established. Otherwise, the tool would alert the analyst and also suggest the actual relationship that may be found between the two processes[2]. In the *generating* mode, our machinery systematically goes through all process models in the repository, generates all possible relationships between them, and present these to the analyst for confirmation. Note that the space of alternative relationships can be large, specially in the case of part-whole relationships. For example, given 4 processes $P1, P2, P3$ and $P4$ where $P2$ is part of $P1$, $P3$ is part of $P2$ and $P4$ is part of $P3$. Not only direct relationships, the tool would also suggest all indirect relationships among them, e.g. $P4$ is (indirectly) part of $P1$, $P4$ is (indirectly) part of $P2$. However, these indirect relationships would not be useful to be maintained since change propagation can still be performed through the direct ones. Hence, the decision should be made by the analyst in both approaches.

Once a relationship is established, a *relationship descriptor* is created. Such a descriptor contains details that are relevant to its associated relationship including identities of each pair of processes and their established relationship type. However, a descriptor can also be enriched with any additional information relevant to the existing relationship types, e.g. the insertion point activity in a part-whole relationship. Relationship descriptors are maintained (i.e. created, updated, and removed) during the relationships establishment and maintenance.

The relationship-establishing algorithms for both approaches, require transformation of each process model into a graph, i.e. transforming each activity, gateway and start/end events into a node and each flow into an edge. These algorithms may involve two runs in evaluating a given pair of processes for each relationship type excluding the inter-operation. On the first run, we evaluate the first process with respect to a normative relationship constraint to the second one. If the constraint does hold, we establish the relationship between the two processes. Otherwise, in the second run we evaluate the second process with respect to the constraint to the first one. For example, the part-whole establishment algorithm can be described as follows[3]. The inputs are two process graphs, i.e. denoted pa and pb, and the outputs are either an instance of relationship descriptor or *null*. The algorithm will assess whether pa is part of pb by computing $CE(pb, n)$ and $CE(pb \uparrow^n pa, n)$ of each sub-process node $n \in pb$. If $CE(pb, n) = CE(pb \uparrow^n pa, n)$ then it returns an instance of relationship descriptor of such relationship. Otherwise, it returns *null*. On the first run, we evaluate the first process to the second one. If it is not satisfied, we then evaluate the

---

[2] If it is "unknown" relationship (refers to our formal definitions), it is not maintained.

[3] Algorithms for the two other relationships are not explained due to space limitation.

second process to the first one on the second run. If a given relationship type cannot be established, we continue the evaluation with the other relationships between the processes in consideration. Note that the part-whole relationship evaluation must be performed before the generalization-specialization relationship evaluation, since the former is a special case of the latter. Inappropriate evaluation ordering of these two relationships might have unexpected result, i.e. every part-whole will be suggested as generalization-specialization. There is no evaluation ordering constraint for inter-operation relationship type.

4   Relationship-Preserving Change Propagation

To preserve the established relationships, the changes need to be propagated across different processes. To do so, the process ecosystem containing the initial changes should firstly defined as the boundary of such propagation. We then deal with how to redesign a process for resolving the relationships violations. Further, we apply our CSP approach to find an equilibrium in a process ecosystem.

Process Ecosystem. We view a collection of interrelated process models within a process repository as an ecosystem [9]. However, we further restrict that any process model in a process ecosystem must be traceable to any other process models in the ecosystem. This traceability may involve many relationships with regard to the relationships we formally defined earlier. A process model may have more than one relationship with the others in the ecosystem. In addition, there may be more than one process ecosystem within a process repository. Furthermore, since a change made to a process would only affect other processes in the same ecosystem, we will only propagate changes within this process ecosystem. A process ecosystem is in *(consistency-)equilibrium* if and only if every inter-process relationship in the ecosystem is consistent with our earlier definitions. We shall refer to a process ecosystem that violates the consistency equilibrium condition a *perturbed-equilibrium* ecosystem. Consistency perturbation is often the outcome of change to one or more process models in an ecosystem. Restoring consistency-equilibrium involves making further changes to other process models in the ecosystem and so on, which is, in fact, change propagation. We shall refer to an ecosystem resulted from such restoration a *restored-equilibrium* ecosystem.

Resolving Relationship Violations. To resolve a relationship violation, the processes involving in this relationship need to be changed. There can be many options to do such changes, each of which results in a variant of the original process (called process variant). Generating a process variant for a given process can be done automatically by a machinery[4] or manually by the analyst. The procedure required to resolve a relationship violation between a pair of processes $P1$ and $P2$ due to changes to one of them, e.g. $P1$, can be described as follows.

---

[4] The techniques for automatically generating all process variants are out of scope of this paper. We leave them as our future investigations. We have used only analyst-mediated process redesign in our implementation and current evaluation.

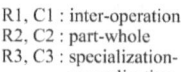 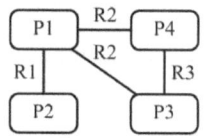 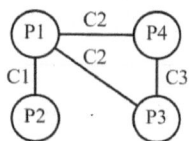

(a) Process ecosystem of processes P1..P4 with the corresponding inter-process relationships R1..R3

(b) Constraint graph of process ecosystem illustrated in (a) with the corresponding constraints C1..C3

Fig. 3. Transforming a process ecosystem into a constraint graph

We identify such changes in $P1$ that can trigger the violation with regard to our formal definitions. Based on the relationship type, the changes must be propagated to $P2$ to get its variant such that the relationship constraint can be re-satisfied. For example, let $P1$ and $P2$ be the whole and the part, respectively. Let t_i in $P1$, with immediate effects e_{t_i}, be a sub-process representing $P2$ s.t. the condition C is satisfied, i.e. $CE(P1, t_i) = CE(P1 \uparrow^{t_i} P2, t_i)$. The possible change introduced in $P1$ that can cause violations is a change to t_i, i.e. either by: (i) changing e_{t_i} to be e'_{t_i} s.t. $e_{t_i} \neq e'_{t_i}$ or (ii) dropping t_i. In the first case, we need to change $P2$ to be $P2'$ by either adding or deleting some activities or reducing or extending some immediate effects of some particular activities s.t. C is satisfied with e'_{t_i}. We no longer need to maintain the relationship for the second case. Note that changing $P1$ by excluding t_i will not cause any violation.

CSP in Process Ecosystems. A CSP consists of a set of variables X, for each variable there exists a finite set of possible values D, and a set of constraints C restricting the values that the variables can simultaneously take [2]. Each constraint defines a relation between a subset of variables and constraints the possible values for the involved variables. We consider a constraint involving only one variable as a unary constraint, two variables as a binary, and so on.

A solution to a CSP is an assignment of a value from its domain to every variable, in such a way that every constraint is satisfied. We may want to find only one solution, all solutions or an optimal solution [2]. Solutions to a CSP can be performed by searching systematically for the possible values which can be assigned to a variable. There are generally two search methods. The first method involves either traversing the space of partial solutions [2] (e.g. backtracking, backjumping and backmarking algorithms) or reducing the search space through constraint propagation (i.e. look-ahead). In variable selection, the look-ahead strategy seeks to control the size of the remaining search space. In value selection, it seeks a value that is most likely to lead to a consistent solution. Performing constraint propagation at each variable will result a smaller search space, but the overall cost can be higher since the cost for processing each variable will be more expensive. The second method involves repairing an inconsistent complete assignment/solution (e.g. min-conflicts and repair-based algorithms [17])

Algorithm 1: Generating a restored-equilibrium process ecosystem : *repair* approach

---

Input:
    p, a changed process model
    PE_p, graph of a perturbed-equilibrium process ecosystem
Result: a restored-equilibrium PE_x or *null*

1   **begin**
2   V_{done}, a set of evaluated process identifiers, initially empty
3   p_{var}, the selected variant of a redesigned process, initially *null*
4   p_m, the process to be changed, initially *null*
5      $PE_x \leftarrow PE_p$; $p_{var} \leftarrow p$;
6      $V_{done} \leftarrow V_{done} \cup$ {identifier of p};
7      $p_m \leftarrow$ **GetNextProcess**(PE_x, V_{done});
8   **while** $p_m \neq null$ *and* $p_{var} \neq null$ **do**
9          $p_{var} \leftarrow$ **ProcessChangeForMinConflicts**(p_m, PE_x, V_{done});
10   **if** $p_{var} \neq null$ **then**
11   replace p_m in PE_x by p_{var};
12             $V_{done} \leftarrow V_{done} \cup$ {identifier of p_m};
13             $p_m \leftarrow$ **GetNextProcess**(PE_x, V_{done});
14   **else**
15             $PE_x \leftarrow null$;
16   **end**
17   **end**
18   **return** PE_x;
19   **end**

Empirically, it is shown that ordering variables for value assignment can have substantial impacts on the performance of finding CSP solution [2]. The ordering variables could be either: (i) *static ordering*, the order of variables is defined before the search starts and not be changed until the search complete or (ii) *dynamic ordering*, the next variables to be assigned are dynamically defined at any point depends on the current state of the search. There are some heuristics in selecting variable ordering, i.e. variable with the smallest domain (in dynamic ordering) or variable which participates in the most constraints.

We argue that maintaining the equilibrium in a process ecosystem can be casted as a binary CSP. We can build a constraint network [6], represented in a constraint graph, of the process ecosystems to depict a binary CSP in which each node represents a process model, all possible variants of redesigning a process can be considered as domain value of each node and each edge represents a relationship constraint between processes, as in Figure 3. Process $P1$ in Figure 3a can be mapped into a node $P1$ in Figure 3b, as well as its relationship to process $P2$, i.e. $R1$, which is mapped into an edge between nodes $P1$ and $P2$, and so forth for the remaining processes and relationships. Indeed, the domain value of each node is finite since there exist constraints (at least, end cumulative effects and activity temporal constraints) that must be satisfied by process variants. We consider

---

Algorithm 2: Generating a restored-equilibrium process ecosystem : *constructive* approach

---

Input:

    p, a changed process model

    PE_p, graph of a perturbed-equilibrium process ecosystem

Result: a restored-equilibrium PE_x or *null*

```
 1  begin
 2  │   V_done, a set of evaluated process identifiers, initially empty
 3  │   p_var, the selected variant of a redesigned process, initially null
 4  │   p_m, the process to be changed, initially null
 5  │   PE_x ← PE_p; p_var ← p;
 6  │   V_done ← V_done ∪ {identifier of p};
 7  │   p_m ← GetNextProcess(PE_x, V_done);
 8  │   while p_m ≠ null and p_var ≠ null do
 9  │   │   p_var ← a process variant of p_m which maintains the existing
    │   │       relationships with other processes identified in V_done, if no possible
    │   │       variant then p_var = null;
10  │   │   if p_var ≠ null then
11  │   │   │   replace p_m in PE_x by p_var;
12  │   │   │   V_done ← V_done ∪ {identifier of p_m};
13  │   │   │   p_m ← GetNextProcess(PE_x, V_done);
14  │   │   else
15  │   │   │   I_pm ← a path running from p to p_m;
16  │   │   │   p_mdb ← the preceding of p_m in I_pm ;
17  │   │   │   if p_mdb = p then
18  │   │   │   │   PE_x ← null;
19  │   │   │   else
20  │   │   │   │   remove identifier of p_mdb from V_done;
21  │   │   │   │   p_m ← p_mdb;
22  │   │   │   │   p_var ← p_mdb;
23  │   │   │   end
24  │   │   end
25  │   end
26  │   return PE_x;
27  end
```

---

constraint graph of a process ecosystem as a tuple $G_e = (V, C)$ where V and C denote a set of process nodes and a set of relationship constraints between processes, respectively. In the resulting constraint graph G_e, each process node is of the form $(id, T, E, G, start, end)$ where $id, T, E, G, start, end$ represent ID, set of activities, set of edges, set of gateways, start and end events of a process, respectively. And, each relationship constraint is of the form $(id, source, target, type)$ where $id, source, target, type$ represent ID, source node, target node and type of an inter-process relationship, respectively. An equilibrium in process ecosystem then is considered as a solution in CSP once all constraints are satisfied by value assigned to each node, i.e. a variant of each process. We might not have a solution for a given perturbed-equilibrium process ecosystem since there does not exist a variant of a particular process node for resolving the violations[5].

Algorithms. We propose two algorithms, i.e. *repair* and *constructive*, for generating a restored-equilibrium process ecosystem, as shown in Algorithms 1 and 2, respectively. The analyst can perform either one or both of them to generate a restored-equilibrium process ecosystem. We implement dynamic ordering in searching process to be evaluated through one which participates in the most constraints, represented by **GetNextProcess** function. We search a process in the perturbed-equilibrium process ecosystem which is in the following conditions: (i) not yet evaluated, (ii) violates its relationship constraints with the previously evaluated processes and (iii) participates in the most constraints.

In the repair approach, inspired by Min-Conflicts algorithm [17], we search the new equilibrium of process ecosystems by minimizing conflicts between variants of process being changed with the other processes which are not yet evaluated, and satisfying relationship constraint with the previously evaluated processes. It is represented by **ProcessChangeForMinConflicts** function which searches a variant of changed process by satisfying the following criteria: (i) satisfies all relationship constraints with the previously evaluated processes and (ii) has the minimal violations with all the rest processes in the ecosystem. Finally, we would select a variant which has the minimum conflict and continue until all constraints satisfied, shown in Algorithm 1.

In the constructive approach, inspired by Graph-based backjumping algorithm [5], we search a new equilibrium of a process ecosystem by redesigning the process being evaluated to satisfy its constraint with the previous evaluated process until all constraints are satisfied. Once there is no variant of the process being evaluated to satisfy the constraint, we would jump back to the most recent related process (with respect to the process being evaluated) which is already evaluated, as shown in Algorithm 2. Then, this recent process should be redesigned to make the following process to be evaluated satisfy its constraint.

5   Evaluation

We have performed an empirical validation[6] to assess how the repair and constructive approaches perform on different sizes of the process ecosystem. Specifically, we established process ecosystems with sizes ranging from 10 to 80 processes. All these processes have 5-20 activities. We also annotated each activity with immediate effects and had the tool compute the cumulative effects in each process at every stage. The established process ecosystems are equipped with the inter-process relationships discussed earlier. Our framework generates all possible relationships between different processes and presents the constraint graph of every process ecosystem.

---

[5] Finding an optimal solution would be our next investigation.

[6] All experiments were run on a i3 Intel Core-2.27 GHz, RAM 2.85 Gb laptop.

The experiments are conducted as follows. A process, denoted as $P1$, was selected to have some initial changes, which are then propagated to other related processes to maintain the consistency of the process ecosystem. In general, the total time required to establish a restored-equilibrium process ecosystem is $(s + nt)$ where s is the time our CSP algorithms compute, n is the number of processes needing to be changed (as identified by our tool) and t is the average time for making changes to a process. In our experiments, we assume that when a process is flagged as needing changing, the actual changes would be done by the analyst. As such, we are only interested in the time elapsed for propagating changes in our CSP algorithms.

Table 1. Elapsed time for searching the process ordering and checking the constraints of various sizes of process ecosystems

No. of processes	No. of violated constraints	No. of redesigned processes n	Elapsed time	
			Repair mode (sec)	Constructive mode (sec)
10	3	3	64	63
20	8	8	331	329
30	11	11	875	844
40	12	12	1,316	1,272
50	12	12	1,642	1,512
60	13	13	2,199	1,988
70	14	14	2,699	2,443
80	18	18	3,395	3,163

Table 1 describes how the repair and constructive approaches perform in proportion to the size of the process ecosystem in terms of the elapsed time for establishing a new equilibrium of process ecosystem. Our experimental results suggest that the proposed approach is efficient (i.e. helps analysts propagate changes regardless of the complexity of the inter-process relationships in the process ecosystem) and scalable in propagating changes to maintain the equilibrium of a medium-sized process ecosystem (up to 80 processes). Additionally, performing the repair approach to get a restored-equilibrium process ecosystem takes longer time than performing the constructive approach. This could be explained as follows. In the repair approach, we need to verify the consistency between all processes that are related to the process being modified whereas in constructive approach, we only check the consistency between the process being modified and related processes that were already modified. However, we have not taken into account the complexity of redesigning an individual process in our experiments (i.e. how long it would take, for the analyst, to redesign a process that needs changing). Furthermore, we have not analyzed the complexity of our algorithms in order to correlate the elapsed time with parameters represented by the three leftmost columns of Table 1. The scalability of our framework for dealing with a large-sized ecosystem will be addressed in our future investigations.

6   Related Work

Change propagation approaches have been intensively investigated in software evolution/maintenance, engineering management and software modeling (see, e.g. [1,3,4]). Recently, this approach has also been applied to BPM and service computing (see, e.g. [18,20]). However, there exist little work on change propagation in process model collections [7], as can be seen in [8]. Weidlich *et al.* [20] attempt to determine a change region in another model by exploiting the behavioral profile of corresponding activities due to a model change. Their behavioral profile relies on three relations, which are based on the notion of weak order, between nodes in a process graph. Wang *et al.* [18] present analysis of dependencies between services and their supporting business processes. On the top of this analysis, they define change types and impact patterns which are used to analyze the necessary change propagation occurring in business processes and services. To the best of our understanding, these researches are only dealing with a pair of business artifacts. The closely related work to our proposed framework is done by Ekanayake *et al.* [8], which deals with processes in a collection. They propose change propagation based on the shared fragments between process models. To propagate changes, they develop a special data structure for storing these fragments and process models. Once changes are made to a fragment, all processes which this fragment belongs to are considered to be changed. This fragment-based approach would be closely related to one of our research interests, namely change propagation for the specialization-generalization relationship.

We leverage constraint networks [6] using CSP approach in propagating the changes between processes. To the best of our knowledge, CSP technology has not been used in the existing researches to deal with change propagation in a complex process repository. We are interested in how changes on one process can be properly propagated to the related processes to maintain the consistency-equilibrium of a process ecosystem. We focus on three kind of relationships between semantic effect-annotated BPMN models, i.e. part-whole, specialization-generalization and inter-operation.

7   Conclusion and Future Work

Being inspired by CSP approach, we have proposed a novel framework for managing relationship-preserving change propagation in process ecosystems. This framework can assist the process analysts in maintaining the equilibrium of their process ecosystems within a complex process repository. Future work includes development of techniques for generating process variants for a given process, finding the optimal solution with minimal change strategy of restored-equilibrium process ecosystem and performing experiments on our framework using case-studies taken from the industry.

References

1. Aryani, A., Peake, I.D., Hamilton, M.: Domain-based change propagation analysis: An enterprise system case study. In: 2010 IEEE International Conference on Software Maintenance (ICSM), pp. 1–9. IEEE (2010)
2. Bartak, R.: Constraint propagation and backtracking-based search. Charles Universität, Prag (2005)
3. Chua, D.K.H., Hossain, M.A.: Predicting change propagation and impact on design schedule due to external changes. IEEE Trans. on Eng. Management (99), 1–11
4. Dam, H.K., Winikoff, M.: Supporting change propagation in UML models. In: 2010 IEEE International Conf. on Software Maintenance (ICSM), pp. 1–10. IEEE (2010)
5. Dechter, R.: Enhancement schemes for constraint processing: Backjumping, learning, and cutset decomposition. Artificial Intelligence 41, 271–312 (1990)
6. Dechter, R.: Constraint Processing. Morgan Kaufmann Publishers (2003)
7. Dijkman, R., Rosa, M., Reijers, H.: Managing large collections of business process models-current techniques and challenges. Comp. in Industry 63(2), 91–97 (2012)
8. Ekanayake, C.C., La Rosa, M., ter Hofstede, A.H.M., Fauvet, M.-C.: Fragment-Based Version Management for Repositories of Business Process Models. In: Meersman, R., Dillon, T., Herrero, P., Kumar, A., Reichert, M., Qing, L., Ooi, B.-C., Damiani, E., Schmidt, D.C., White, J., Hauswirth, M., Hitzler, P., Mohania, M. (eds.) OTM 2011, Part I. LNCS, vol. 7044, pp. 20–37. Springer, Heidelberg (2011)
9. Ghose, A., Koliadis, G.: Model eco-systems: preliminary work. In: The Fifth Asia-Pacific Conf. on Conceptual Modelling, pp. 19–26. Australian Comp. Society (2008)
10. Ghose, A., Koliadis, G., Chueng, A.: Rapid Business Process Discovery (R-BPD). In: Parent, C., Schewe, K.-D., Storey, V.C., Thalheim, B. (eds.) ER 2007. LNCS, vol. 4801, pp. 391–406. Springer, Heidelberg (2007)
11. Hill, J.B., Cantara, M., Deitert, E., Kerremans, M.: Magic quadrant for business process management suites. Tech. rep., Gartner Research (2007)
12. Hinge, K., Ghose, A., Koliadis, G.: Process SEER: A tool for semantic effect annotation of business process models. In: IEEE International Enterprise Distributed Object Computing Conference, EDOC 2009, pp. 54–63. IEEE (2009)
13. Koliadis, G., Ghose, A.: A Conceptual Framework for Business Process Redesign. In: Halpin, T., Krogstie, J., Nurcan, S., Proper, E., Schmidt, R., Soffer, P., Ukor, R. (eds.) BPMDS 2009 and EMMSAD 2009. LNBIP, vol. 29, pp. 14–26. Springer, Heidelberg (2009)
14. Koliadis, G., Ghose, A.: Verifying semantic business process models in interoperation. In: Int. Conf. on Services Computing 2007, pp. 731–738. IEEE (2007)
15. Kurniawan, T.A., Ghose, A.K., Lê, L.-S., Dam, H.K.: On Formalizing Inter-process Relationships. In: Daniel, F., Barkaoui, K., Dustdar, S. (eds.) BPM Workshops 2011, Part II. LNBIP, vol. 100, pp. 75–86. Springer, Heidelberg (2012)
16. La Rosa, M., Dumas, M., Uba, R., Dijkman, R.: Business process model merging: an approach to business process consolidation. ACM Transactions on Software Engineering and Methodology (TOSEM) (in press, 2012)
17. Minton, S., Johnston, M.D., Philips, A.B., Laird, P.: Minimizing conflicts: A heuristic repair method for constraint satisfaction and scheduling problems. Artificial Intelligence 58, 161–205 (1992)

18. Wang, Y., Yang, J., Zhao, W.: Change impact analysis for service based business processes. In: IEEE International Conference on Service-Oriented Computing and Applications, SOCA 2010, pp. 1–8. IEEE (2010)
19. Weber, B., Rinderle, S., Reichert, M.: Change Patterns and Change Support Features in Process-Aware Information Systems. In: Krogstie, J., Opdahl, A.L., Sindre, G. (eds.) CAiSE 2007. LNCS, vol. 4495, pp. 574–588. Springer, Heidelberg (2007)
20. Weidlich, M., Weske, M., Mendling, J.: Change propagation in process models using behavioural profiles. In: Int. Conf. on Services Computing, SCC 2009, pp. 33–40. IEEE (2009)
21. White, S.A., Miers, D.: BPMN: Modeling and Reference Guide. Future Strategies Inc. (2008)

Scheduling Service Tickets in Shared Delivery

Hari S. Gupta and Bikram Sengupta

IBM Research, Bangalore, India
{hsgupta1,bsengupt}@in.ibm.com

Abstract. We study the problem of optimally scheduling tickets in
shared delivery of IT services. Such delivery models are characterized
by a common pool of skilled agents who collectively support the service
needs of several customers at a time. The ticket scheduling problem becomes interesting in this scenario due to the need to provide satisfactory
experience to multiple customers with different Service Level Agreements
(SLAs) in a cost-efficient and optimal way, by intelligently leveraging the
available skill set and balancing workload across agents. We present a detailed description of the problem domain and introduce a novel metric
for estimating the relative criticality of tickets from different customers
at any point in time, taking into account several factors such as the distance from SLA breach, the SLA penalty and the expected volume of
tickets during the rest of the service time window. This criticality measure is used within a Mixed Integer Programming (MIP) based solution
approach to the ticket scheduling problem, where we consider the objectives of SLA penalty minimization, balancing breaches across customers,
load balancing across agents, and maximizing skill match. Due to the
complexity of the problem, optimization engines may not always return
feasible or efficient solutions within reasonable time limits. Hence, we also
develop a custom heuristic algorithm that returns acceptable solutions
very fast. Detailed simulation experiments are used to compare these approaches and to demonstrate their efficiency in meeting the scheduling
objectives of shared delivery.

1 Introduction

IT service delivery organizations (henceforth called service vendors) employ
skilled practitioners to address service requests from customers. Many of these
requests are relatively small, atomic tasks that require a specific skill and may be
handled by a single practitioner within a short duration (e.g., a few minutes to
a few days). Such requirements, which the vendor receives in the form of service
tickets, may represent a specific IT problem experienced by the customer (e.g.,
"server down", "transaction failed" etc.) or may be a request for a new capability
(e.g., "create a new disk partition"). These requirements are generally of some
business priority, with the expectation that it will be completed in a time-bound
manner, as specified in Service Level Agreements (SLAs) between the customer
and the vendor. If there are delays, then the customer's business may be severely
impacted, leading to significant financial losses. The consequent degradation in

C. Liu et al. (Eds.): ICSOC 2012, LNCS 7636, pp. 79–95, 2012.
© Springer-Verlag Berlin Heidelberg 2012

customer satisfaction may have implications on the vendor's future business with the customer. Moreover, vendors would need to compensate the customer by paying a penalty for any additional breach beyond the SLA threshold. Thus business imperatives and economic reasons call for timely, careful and intelligent handling of service tickets.

In this paper, we will study the problem of efficiently scheduling tickets in a service delivery organization. In particular, we study ticket scheduling in the context of the shared delivery or factory model [5,1], which is increasingly being used by IT vendors. What distinguishes these models is that instead of dedicated, customer-specific teams, a common pool of agents belonging to a specialization area (e.g., say a packaged application system) supports the needs of several customers who need services in that area. These customers may have different SLAs with the vendor, depending on the criticality of their business, and the price they are willing to pay for the vendor's services. Such shared delivery makes the assignment of tickets to agents an involved balancing exercise: for example, the vendor has to strive to reduce the aggregate SLA penalty it has to pay, while trying to maintain some parity between the service experiences provided to the different customers; at the same time, the vendor has to ensure that, to the extent possible, the workload of different agents are balanced (to prevent agent fatigue or reduce idle time), and tickets are assigned to agents with high levels of skill in the relevant areas (so that customers are satisfied with the quality of service provided). Naturally, as the number of tickets and customers scale up, balancing the various ticket assignment criteria and analysing the trade-offs, are way beyond what a human dispatcher will be capable of. There is a need to explore automated decision-making systems that can intelligently schedule tickets through an expert knowledge of shared service delivery, and that is encoded through a robust optimization or heuristic formulation.

Towards that end, this paper makes the following important contributions. After discussing related work (Sec. 2), we present a detailed description of the problem domain of scheduling tickets in a shared delivery system (Sec. 3), including its differences with the traditional model of delivery via customer-specific teams. We then develop a set of scheduling objectives for shared delivery, that attempts to balance the vendor's needs for profitability and delivery efficiency, with the need to ensure parity in the service experience of individual customers. To the best of our knowledge, this is the first work that investigates the complexities of work scheduling in a shared environment to this depth. After introducing the problem, over the next few sections, we present a number of solution approaches: a mixed integer programming (MIP) based formulation (Sec. 4) that attempts to optimize the scheduling objectives in a priority order; a heuristic algorithm that attempts to balance the objectives over multiple phases guided by several policies (Sec. 6); and two greedy algorithms (Sec. 5) that each tries to optimize on a specific objective, and represent baselines with which we can compare our approaches. In Sec. 7, we report on detailed simulation-based experiments to study the performance of all the approaches and analyse their scheduling effectiveness. We find that both MIP and heuristic approaches do very well in balancing the various scheduling objectives for moderate-sized problems, but the heuristic algorithm scales much better. Finally, Sec. 8 presents our conclusions and directions for future research.

2   Related Work

There is a rich body of literature related to the general problem of scheduling jobs on machines (job shop scheduling or JSS) [8,6], and different variants (e.g., online or offline scheduling, related or unrelated machines) have been investigated in depth. The most common scheduling objectives of JSS are minimization of makespan, total completion time, total tardiness, and load balancing. While these are standard objectives with wide applicability, scheduling of tickets need specific focus on the management of SLAs. In particular, shared delivery calls for scheduling objectives that are sensitive to the SLA and expertise needs of individual customer, even as they seek to maximize a vendor's profitability and delivery efficiency.

The allocation of tickets to agents also has (superficial) similarities with the routing of calls in a call-center. Skill-based routing (SBR) [3,11] segments calls based on the skills needed to handle them and routes a call to an available agent with appropriate skill. Given the low limits of caller patience, the objective is to minimize waiting time and calls drop rate, and thus there is no scope for batch scheduling. In contrast, service tickets can be batched together at the start of a shift and then at specific intervals, and dispatched to agent queues. Moreover, unlike a call that will naturally drop off beyond a waiting time, each ticket that arrives has to be serviced, even if its service level objective (SLO) has been breached; these tickets thus impose an additional burden that can potentially delay other tickets.

In recent years, there has been considerable interest on automation, measurement and optimization of service delivery. For example, [4] proposes a solution for efficient seat utilization to reduce infrastructure costs. [12] models the cost overheads in distributed service delivery and proposes relevant metrics to assess the same. Our work combines automation and optimization is scheduling of service tickets in shared delivery, using the novel metric of relative ticket criticality. There has been limited research on the topic of optimal allocation of service tickets, and the few papers in the area mostly address issues that are complementary to our work. For example, [10] studies game theoretic aspects of the problem and designs incentive mechanisms for ticket complexity elicitation in a truthful way from agents. In [2], an auction-based pull model for ticket allocation is proposed, along with incentive mechanisms for agents to be truthful about expected resolution time when bidding for tickets. While theoretically appealing, it is unlikely that large-scale service delivery bound by SLAs can function effectively when it completely depends on agents to bid for tickets. [9] develops a Markov model by mining ticket resolution sequences of historical tickets that were transferred from one group to another before being resolved. This model is then used to guide future ticket transfers and reduce mis-routing. In [7], supervised learning techniques are used to determine the likelihood that a service request corresponds to a specific problem symptom; prior performances of support groups are then analyzed to identify groups that have the necessary skills to resolve these problems. While expertise is indeed an important consideration for ticket assignment, there are other practical objectives (e.g., manage SLAs, balance load etc.) that need to be taken into account in a real-life delivery organization.

3   Domain Description

The traditional mode of delivery of IT services has been through a dedicated team of agents for every customer. In practice, this simplifies the task of assigning and scheduling tickets within the team. All agents work towards a common goal (of serving the customer's interests in the best possible way) and this synergy of purpose helps in prioritization of tasks, often in consultation with the customer. However, while this model is responsive to the needs of individual customers, it has a number of drawbacks from the vendor's perspective. The most significant of these are that utilization of agents may be poor/uneven across teams due to variability in demand, and that dedicated teams tend to operate in silos making knowledge sharing and deployment of best practices difficult. For these reasons, many vendors [5,1] are now adopting a shared delivery model, wherein groups of agents who specialize in a particular domain are pooled together and made responsible for addressing the needs of multiple customers who require services in that domain. What makes this approach feasible is that for a significant body of IT services, the skills needed are more domain-specific than customer-centric. Such a model can translate to reduced service costs (due to increased sharing of resources and practices), whose benefits may then be shared with the customer. However, in a shared delivery model, the vendor needs to assume greater ownership of scheduling work. Tickets from different customers would compete for the attention of the same set of agents, and this would introduce a natural conflict into the system. How well the vendor manages this conflict will determine the service experience of individual customers from the shared delivery system, as well as the financial returns of the vendor. It is in this context that we study the ticket scheduling problem.

We begin with an informal description of the problem domain, introducing the main concepts and their relationships. An IT service vendor will be employing a pool of *agents* for each specialization area that it supports (for example, management of servers, packaged application systems etc.) Within the specialization area, different *categories of service requests* may arise. An agent will be *skilled* in handling one or more of these request categories. Each pool of agents from a given specialization area will be servicing tickets received from a set of *customers*. A *ticket* usually contains a description of the problem or request, based on which it may be assigned the appropriate service category at the time of its creation. A ticket will also contain a *priority level*, which reflects its business urgency from the perspective of the customer. The service vendor and customer would have entered into a *Service Level Agreement (SLA)* for resolving tickets within a specific time limit, based on their priority. For example, for priority 1 tickets (having the highest urgency) from customer X, the agreement may be that 90% of such tickets within a given service delivery time window (e.g., a month) will be resolved within 4 hours. If the SLA is breached, the vendor is generally required to pay a *penalty* to the customer, per additional ticket that exceeds the time limit. A *Service Level Objective (SLO)* represents the manifestation of a SLA at a per-ticket level and is the time-limit by which a vendor attempts to resolve each ticket of a given priority from a customer. Thus for the SLA example introduced above, the SLO for priority 1 tickets from customer X would be 4 hours. While an agent needs to have specific skill(s) to be eligible to resolve a ticket of a given category, the *resolution effort* i.e., the time spent by the agent on the ticket to resolve it, would depend on the agent's degree of expertise for the ticket (higher the expertise, lower the effort). There may be different ways to estimate expertise e.g., by number of relevant tickets successfully resolved, level of training received, number of years of experience in the area etc. In this paper, we will assume that expertise values are available, without going into specific computation methods. We will consider the following *states* of a ticket: *New Arrival* (a ticket has just arrived), *Queued,* (it has been placed in an agent's queue), *Work-in-Progress or WIP* (an agent is working on it), and *Closed* (it has been resolved).

Relative Criticality Measure

In order to help a vendor prioritize tickets coming in from different customers to the same pool of agents, we now introduce a notion of relative *criticality* of tickets. For a given customer c and priority p, let

- r_{cp} = % of tickets allowed to breach SLA
- q_{cp} = Penalty of a SLO breach beyond SLA
- u_{cp} = Number of tickets to be scheduled now
- v_{cp} = Number of tickets closed in the past
- w_{cp} = Number of tickets expected to come in future
- n_{cp} = Number of tickets breached SLO in the past (among the closed tickets)

Given the above information, we can compute the estimated number of tickets allowed to breach (at max) among present and future tickets (m_{cp}) by:

$$m_{cp} = \frac{(u_{cp} + v_{cp} + w_{cp}) * r_{cp}}{100} - n_{cp}$$

Now, we define a ticket's criticality belonging to the given customer-priority as:

$$C_{cp} = \begin{cases} \frac{(u_{cp}+w_{cp})*q_{cp}}{m_{cp}+1} & \text{if } m_{cp} < u_{cp} + w_{cp} \\ 0 & \text{otherwise} \end{cases}$$

Intuitively, the criticality of a ticket is less when the number of allowed SLO breaches (m_{cp}) is more; criticality is more when the volume of tickets $(u_{cp}+w_{cp})$ over which these breaches are allowed is more; criticality is more when the SLA penalty is more; and criticality is negligible (zero) when the number of allowed SLO breaches that remain is more than or equal to the current and future ticket volume. It may be noted that the criticality measure depends on knowledge of the future volume of tickets. Usually the volume of tickets from a specific customer over a given service window can be reasonably estimated based on historical data, and this estimate is also used by the vendor to draw up staffing plans. The more accurate this information, the more refined will the criticality measure be. Of course, the vendor can also update this estimate at any time during a service window (e.g. based on some unanticipated event) and the criticality measure would be adjusted accordingly for subsequent tickets.

Problem Objectives and Constraints

Given this background, we consider the following problem: assume we have a pool of agents, where each agent has a queue of tickets, and may have a *WIP* ticket she is working on; given a set of new tickets that have arrived, how do we optimally allocate the new and queued tickets to the agents? Below, we introduce our scheduling objectives in the order of their (decreasing) relative importance, from the vendor's perspective.

The first objective (*SLA Penalty Minimization*) that the vendor will try to meet is minimization of the penalty it has to pay due to SLO breaches beyond the SLA limit. Assume there is a ticket t from a customer c with priority p, where the permitted number of breaches for priority p tickets from c under the SLA has already been reached or exceeded. The vendor would then want to schedule t in a way that it does not breach its SLO, since otherwise the vendor will have to pay a penalty. Note that, to achieve this, the vendor may have to breach (in some cases) other ticket(s) that are either within their respective SLA limits, or carry a lower penalty.

The above objective helps a vendor minimize financial losses *after a SLA has already been violated*. However, the vendor would want to schedule tickets in a way that minimizes the chance of a SLA breach in the first place. This leads to our second objective set *SLO Breach Balancing and Minimization*, which (i) helps a vendor reduce SLO breaches for high criticality tickets (thereby reducing the risk of an SLA breach) by minimizing the maximum criticality value of a ticket with SLO breach, and (ii) minimizes the total number of SLO breaches.

Our third objective (*Load Balancing*) is to ensure that some agents are not overloaded with work, while others are relatively idle. An inequitable load distribution need not always lead to an SLO breach, but it would adversely impact agent's motivation, thereby justifying a separate objective to ensure fairness. In general, of course, a balanced workload distribution also helps in reducing delays, thus this objective complements the first two introduced above.

Our fourth objective (*Expertise Maximization*) helps in assigning tickets to agents who are highly skilled in resolving the associated problem categories while maintaining the fairness across customers (achieved by a sub-objective). In particular, for the shared delivery system, we want to ensure this not only at an aggregate level, but for each customer being supported, since it will help ensure that tickets are resolved faster and the solution quality is high, both of which will positively impact customer satisfaction.

As is usually the case with multi-objective optimization, the solutions motivated by individual objectives will differ, even conflict. For example, expertise
maximization without load balance may lead to some highly skilled people being
assigned excessive work, which can de-motivate them as well as lead to delays
and SLO breaches. Hence it is essential to arrange the objectives in the right
sequence (as introduced above), so as to address the vendor's scheduling goals
most optimally.

In addition to finding an efficient solution for the given objectives, we adhere to
a few constraints, a couple of which need some explanation. First, once a ticket has
been assigned to an agent, we do not re-assign it to another agent subsequently
(even if it improves the scheduling objectives), although, as new tickets arrive,
we may change its position in the queue. This is to prevent a ticket from hopping
from one agent to another multiple times, which would be an irritant for the agents
(since, they may have already reviewed tickets in queue) and will also confuse customers (who are notified of ticket assignments). There may indeed be a few cases
where re-assignment is a practical necessity, but for now we leave it to the agents
and supervisors to identify these instances and manually re-assign. Secondly, once
a ticket has breached its SLO, we limit the number of tickets in the queue that arrived later than this ticket but are placed ahead of it. This ensures that no ticket
starves, since otherwise such tickets can get indefinitely delayed as the scheduler
tries to avoid further SLO breaches in new tickets.

4   MIP Formulation

We will now develop a Mixed Integer Programming (MIP) based formulation for
optimal assignment of tickets in shared delivery. This will formalize the objectives
and constraints introduced in Sec. 3.

The set of inputs for the given problem are: **(a)** a set of customers S_C, a set of
priorities S_P, a set of ticket categories T_C and a set of (Min, Max) resolution time
tuples R_T for the different ticket categories; **(b)** a set of SLAs (SLA_{CP}) applicable over a specific service time window (e.g., a month) for different (customer,
priority) combinations, from which we can further derive the sets, (i) SLO_{CP}
representing the time-limits by which tickets of different (customer, priority)
combinations are expected to be solved, (ii) R_{CP}, representing the maximum
percentage of tickets that are allowed to breach the SLO time-limits for different
(customer, priority) combinations, and (iii) Q_{CP}, which denotes the penalty per
additional SLO breach beyond maximum allowed percentage limits, for different customers and priorities; **(c)** a set of agents S_A {1, 2, ..., M}, and for each
agent $a \in S_A$, (i) a set of skills $SK_a \subseteq T_C$, comprising the set of ticket categories the agent can resolve, and (ii) existing load on the agent L_a due to *WIP*
ticket's remaining resolution time in the agent's queue; **(d)** a set of (*New Arrival*
and *Queued*) tickets S_T {1, 2, ..., N} that need to be assigned to the agents,
where each ticket t_k contains, (i) information about the customer ($Cust(t_k)$),
priority ($Pri(t_k)$) and category ($Cat(t_k)$) to which it belongs, (ii) time stamp
representing the arrival time of the ticket into the system, denoted by TS_k, and

(iii) information about any existing agent assignment, which needs to be maintained in the next run; **(e)** expertise value f_{ij} for each ticket j and agent i; **(f)** resolution time t_{ij} for each ticket j and agent i (calculated from the min and max resolution times of the category to which the ticket belongs, and from f_{ij}).

Note: In the MIP model of the problem, for compactness we have used the logical expressions at several places, all of which are linearisable, and have been linearised for the implementation.

Before describing the MIP model, we first describe the set of decision variables used in the formulation, secondly the constraints on these variables, and finally the objectives.

A $N \times M$ decision variables matrix (A) is used to record assignment, in which each entry $a_{ij} \in \{0,1\}$ represents whether a ticket j is assigned to an agent i or not. The value of any entry a_{ij} should result 1 if the ticket j is assigned to agent i, or 0 otherwise. Similarly, we define two more decision variables matrices S and E, in which each entry $s_{ij} \geq 0$ ($e_{ij} \geq 0$) represents the start time (end time) of the ticket j if it is assigned to the agent i, or 0 otherwise.

We maintain another $N \times M$ Assignment History Matrix (H) to constrain the decision matrix (A), and each entry $h_{ij} \in \{0,1\}$ in H is 1 if ticket j was assigned to agent i (when j is a *Queued* ticket), or 0 otherwise. Therefore,

$$\forall j \in S_T, \sum_{i \in S_A} h_{ij} \leq 1$$

Let β_{ij} represents the number of tickets in *Closed* or *WIP* state, which arrived later than ticket j, but scheduled before ticket j on agent i. We define also, $\alpha_{ijk} \in \{0,1\}$ as an indicator variable identifying whether a ticket k arrived later than a ticket j, and is assigned to agent i ahead of j, i.e.,

$$\alpha_{ijk} = \begin{cases} 1 \text{ if } a_{ij} = a_{ik} = 1 \wedge TS_k > TS_j \wedge s_{ij} \geq e_{ik} \\ 0 \text{ otherwise} \end{cases}$$

The completion time for each ticket can be defined as the sum of its end times on all agents, as the end time of the ticket would be 0 for the agents to whom ticket is not assigned, i.e., $\forall j \in S_T, c_j = \sum_{i \in S_A} e_{ij}$

For a ticket j, we use $b_j \in \{0,1\}$ to record if j will breach its SLO or not. The variable $b_j = 1$ if the ticket's completion time (c_j) is greater than its remaining SLO time, and 0 otherwise Let t_c is the current time (i.e., time when scheduling starts), then

$$b_j = \begin{cases} 1 \text{ if } (Pr(j) = p) \wedge (Cust(j) = c) \\ \quad \wedge (c_j > SLO_{cp} - (t_c - TS_j)) \\ 0 \text{ otherwise} \end{cases}$$

Let for a customer c and priority p, n_{cp} denotes the set of tickets with already breached SLO's, r_{cp} denotes the max percentage of tickets allowed to breach according to SLA, u_{cp} denotes the *New Arrivals* and the existing tickets which are in *Queued* state, v_{cp} denotes the tickets *Closed* in the past and the tickets in *WIP* state, w_{cp} denotes the expected number of tickets in future, m_{cp} denotes the maximum number of tickets allowed to breach in the current and future schedules, q_{cp} denotes the penalty for an SLO breach beyond SLA, and z_{cp} denotes the number of tickets breaching SLO beyond SLA. Also, an indicator values matrix G is given, in which each entry $\gamma_{jcp} \in \{0,1\}$, is 1 if a ticket j belongs to customer c and is of priority p, or is 0 otherwise. Now, we can define m_{cp} and z_{cp} as follows:

$$m_{cp} = \lfloor (|u_{cp}| + |v_{cp}| + |w_{cp}|) * \frac{r_{cp}}{100} \rfloor - |n_{cp}|$$

$$z_{cp} = \max(\sum_{j \in S_T} (\gamma_{jcp} * b_j) - m_{cp}, 0)$$

Next we specify the set of constraints using the variables and other elements mentioned earlier.

C_1 : Each ticket is *assigned to one and only one agent.*

$$\forall j \in S_T, \sum_{i \in S_A} a_{ij} = 1$$

C_2 : A ticket can only be assigned to an agent who has the required skill to resolve it.

$$\forall i \in S_A, j \in S_T, (a_{ij} = 1 \Rightarrow Cat(j) \in SK_i)$$

C_3 : The difference between the end time and start time of a ticket i on agent i should be equal to the resolution time t_{ij} if the ticket is assigned to the agent, and 0 otherwise:

$$\forall i \in S_A, j \in S_T, (e_{ij} - s_{ij} = t_{ij} * a_{ij})$$

C_4 : If a ticket j is assigned to an agent i then the start time (s_{ij}) would be $\geq L_i$, as agent cannot start working on the ticket without closing the ticket in *WIP* state with the agent, i.e.,

$$\forall i \in S_A, j \in S_T, (s_{ij} \geq a_{ij} * L_i)$$

C_5 : Since a ticket assigned to an agent is never transferred to another agent in a subsequent run of the scheduler, and to put this constrain we use the History Assignment Matrix (H) defined earlier.

$$\forall i \in S_A, j \in S_T, (h_{ij} = 1 \Rightarrow a_{ij} = 1)$$

C_6 : To prevent *starvation* of any ticket j breaching SLO, we put a bound MDC on the number of tickets which can be scheduled before ticket j and have arrived later than j in the system (i.e., the number of tickets having time stamp greater than the time stamp of ticket j):

$$\forall i \in S_A, \forall j \in S_T, (b_j = 1 \Rightarrow (\sum_{k \in S_T} \alpha_{ijk} + \beta_{ij}) \leq MDC)$$

C_7 : The constraint that the tickets do not have overlapping schedule (i.e., an agent works on one ticket at a time), is defined as follows:

$$\forall i \in S_A, j, k \in S_T (j \neq k \Rightarrow (s_{ij} \geq e_{ik} \vee s_{ik} \geq e_{ij}))$$

Subject to the constraints given above, the *MIP* tries to optimize for the following objectives. The objectives are defined in the order of their priority, as we discussed in Sec. 3.

Objective 1: Minimizing the total penalty due to SLO breaches beyond SLA's of different customer-priority tickets:

$$minimize(\sum_{c \in S_C} \sum_{p \in S_P} z_{cp} * q_{cp})$$

Objective 2: While the above objective is concerned with SLO breaches beyond the SLA limit, we have to try and minimize SLO breaches at each step, well before the SLA limit has been reached. In addition, we need to ensure that the SLO breaches, when they must occur, are balanced to the extent possible across different (customer, priority) combinations, taking into account the relative *criticality* of each breach. Since a further $m_{cp} + 1$ breaches will lead to a penalty of q_{cp} for a customer c and priority p, we estimate the criticality of each individual breach as $\frac{q_{cp}*(u_{cp}+w_{cp})}{m_{cp}+1}$. We thus have the following two goals:

$$minimize(\max_{c \in S_C, p \in S_P, m_{cp} > 0} (\frac{q_{cp} * (u_{cp} + w_{cp})}{m_{cp} + 1} * \sum_j b_j * \gamma_{jcp}))$$

$$minimize \sum_{j \in S_T} b_j$$

Objective 3: Load balancing across agents:

$$minimize(\max_{i \in S_A}(L_i + \sum_{j \in S_T} t_{ij} * a_{ij}))$$

Objective 4: To ensure that tickets are assigned to agents with high expertise whenever possible, we try to maximize the aggregate agent expertise across all tickets. However, in shared delivery, we also need to ensure that every customer individually receives a fair share of available expertise, hence we try to maximize the minimum average expertise of assignments received by any customer. This is handled through the following objectives:

$$maximize(\min_{c \in S_C} \frac{F_c + \sum_{j \in u_c} \sum_{i \in S_A} (a_{ij} * f_{ij})}{u_c + v_c})$$

$$maximize(\sum_{j \in S_T} \sum_{i in S_A} (a_{ij} * f_{ij}))$$

In the above, $u_c = \sum_{p \in S_P} u_{cp}$ and $v_c = \sum_{p \in S_P} v_{cp}$. F_c represents the aggregate expertise received by customer c for all closed and WIP tickets. For a ticket $j \in v_c$, let $Ag(j)$ return the agent who was assigned j. Then, $F_c = \sum_{j \in v_c, Ag(j) = i} f_{ij}$.

As the overall problem is multi-objective and there are trade-offs involved while optimizing for these objectives, we solve for the objectives in the order of their relative importance, and use the results from one solution as a constraint when solving the next objective. Although one can go for a dynamic prioritization of objectives considering the knowledge of their relative importance, but to our knowledge the presented prioritization of objectives best referred to the current service delivery environment.

5   Greedy Algorithms

In this section, we present two greedy algorithms which we have used to compare the MIP approach and the heuristic algorithm that we will propose next. The first algorithm (*GTMin*), tries to greedily minimize the number of tardy tickets (i.e., tickets breaching SLO's), while the second algorithm (*GEMax*), maximizes the average expertise of ticket assignments. In a way, these algorithms represent baselines for standard scheduling/assignment objectives.

Algorithm: Greedy Tardy Tickets Minimization (GTMin): First sort the tickets in the increasing order of SLO time limits; Pick the tickets one by one in the sorted order: (a) assign a *Queued* ticket to an agent whom it was assigned previously, and (b) assign a *newly arrived* ticket to an agent a such that the ticket's completion time is least, if is assigned to a. Whenever a ticket is assigned to an agent, the ticket is added in the end of the agent's ticket queue.

Algorithm: Greedy Expertise Maximization (GEMax): First sort the tickets in the increasing order of SLO time limits; Pick the tickets one by one in the sorted order: (a) assign a *Queued* ticket to an agent whom it was assigned previously, and (b) assign a *newly arrived* ticket to an agent a such that a's expertise level is maximum for the category to which the ticket belongs. Whenever a ticket is assigned to an agent, the ticket is added in the end of the agent's ticket queue.

6   Heuristic Algorithm

The heuristic algorithm runs in two phases. The first phase is a variant of *GTMin*, in which the heuristic tries to minimize the number of SLO breaches along with load balancing (lines 1 to 6), and additionally tries to increase the expertise if possible (line 6). In the second phase, it tries to reposition a ticket in the same agent's queue to whom the ticket is assigned (line 13), or swap the tickets across agents with repositioning after swapping (line 15), so that the total penalty decreases. It is guided by 3 policies: *pick-ticket* defines the order of selecting tickets one at a time and either repositioning it in the same queue using *tuning-policy* or swapping it with some other ticket along with repositioning according to *swap-policy*. Overall, the heuristic considers all objectives during its run, while meeting constraints.

Algorithm: Heuristic

Phase 1:

1. Sort the tickets in the increasing order of SLO time limits (deadlines);
2. For each ticket t in sorted order, do
3. C_T = minimum completion time, if t is assigned to any agent at the last position in the agent's queue;
4. s_a = set of agents: $\forall a \in s_a$, t's completion time is within $x\%$ (we use $x = 20$) of C_T, if t is assigned to a at the last position in a's ticket-queue;
5.   If t is in *Queued* state and previously assigned to agent a', then
            assign t back to agent a' at last position in a''s ticket-queue;
6.   Otherwise, assign t to an agent $a \in s_a$ such that a's expertise is maximum among all the agents in s_a for the category to which t belongs;

Phase 2:

7. P_T = total penalty due to SLO breaches so far including past breaches, beyond SLA's for all customer-priority pairs;
8. For $N = 1$ to *#tickets*, do
9.   Pick a ticket t using algorithm **pick-ticket**;
10. P_{tuning} = total penalty on tuning the position of t using **tuning-policy**;
11. P_{swap} = total penalty on swapping t with other tickets using **swap-policy**;
12.   If $P_{tuning} < P_T$ AND $P_{tuning} \le P_{swap}$
13.   Readjust the positions of the tickets as suggested by **tuning-policy**;
14.   Else If $P_{swap} \le P_T$
15.   Readjust the positions and assignments of the tickets as suggested by **swap-policy**;

Pick-Ticket: Choose a ticket from the unpicked tickets abide by the following rules: (a) choose a ticket which is breaching SLO and for corresponding customer-priority pair the percentage of SLO breaches is more than the SLA, (b) in case of a tie from the rule-a, then choose a ticket, the penalty of which is maximum among all the penalized breaching unpicked tickets, (c) to break a tie further, choose a ticket having highest criticality value, (d) in case of further tie, choose a ticket having least deadline (SLO time limit) which can be negative also, (e) if more than one ticket follow all the three rules, then pick any of them and return.

Tuning-policy(t): Shift the ticket t backward and forward in the same agent's queue to whom the ticket is assigned, by shifting other tickets in the queue appropriately. Pick a shift among all the positions tried, such that the total penalty after the shift is minimum among the total penalties after other shifts, and is also less than the total penalty before the shift. If more than one shifts induce same amount of reduction in the total penalty, then choose the position such that the shift is minimum from the original position. While shifting the tickets maintain the starvation constraints (i.e., any *Queued* ticket is not delayed by more than MDC number of tickets arrived later than t). Suggest the new positions of the tickets.

Swap-policy(t): Swap the ticket t with each of the other tickets t', one by one. Let t is assigned to agent a and t' is assigned to agent a'. If t and t' are assigned to same agent (i.e., $a = a'$) then do nothing. Otherwise, swap the positions and assignments of the tickets (i.e., assign t to a' and t' to a). Tune the positions of t in a''s queue and t' in a's queue respectively, such that the reduction in total penalty after tuning the positions is maximum. Restore the assignments and positions of the tickets, and repeat the swapping of t with other tickets. Among all the swaps, pick a swap such that the total penalty is minimum among all the swaps with different tickets. Suggest the new assignments and positions of the tickets.

7   Experiments

7.1   Methodology

To test the efficacy of our scheduling approaches (MIP, heuristic) through experiments, we have designed *an event driven simulator*, which mimics the service delivery system by tracking events such as: ticket generation, dispatch event, start ticket event (which occurs when an agent picks a ticket from queue), and ticket departure event (when a ticket is closed). For our experiments, data sets were designed with utmost care, by studying historical data sets and through interactions with service delivery practitioners. We consider 10 different ticket categories, 5 different customers and 4 priority levels P_1 (highest priority) through P_4 (lowest priority). Approximate distribution of tickets across different priority levels is as follows: $P_1 : 5\%$, $P_2 : 10\%$, $P_3 : 35\%$, $P_4 : 50\%$. For each (customer, priority) combination, the SLOs are generated in the range of 3 to 40 time units, the maximum allowed breaches are varied from 5% to 20%, while SLA penalties are generated in the range of 1 to 20 monetary units. To ensure realistic SLAs, the data generation procedure was constrained so that for each customer, SLOs for higher priority tickets are smaller than for lower priority tickets, maximum allowed breach level %s are lower, while SLA penalties are higher, reflecting the higher criticality associated with higher priority. For each category c, we assume we have a minimum ($t_{c_{min}}$) and a maximum ($t_{c_{max}}$) observed resolution time (ORT), through historical analysis of tickets of that category. With each agent, we associate between 2 to 6 categories reflecting his/her skills, generated from a Gaussian distribution. For each (agent, category) pair, we set an expertise level $= 0$ if the agent does not have the corresponding skill, otherwise an expertise value is assigned in the range of 0.1 to 0.9, using a Gaussian distribution. We define the Estimated Resolution Time (ERT) t_{ij} for a ticket j (of category c) and agent i as follows, where α the expertise of the agent for the category c:

$$t_{ij} = t_{c_{max}} - \frac{t_{c_{max}} - t_{c_{min}}}{2} * \alpha^2$$

For an agent with very high expertise, this means that the resolution time is estimated to be around the middle of the (min, max) ORT range. This is a realistic approach, since the historical minimum time observed for a ticket of a given category cannot be directly and completely linked to the expertise of the agent who had resolved it. Also, we use α^2, so that ERT grows sub-linearly with decrease in expertise. To predict the future volume (used in computing the criticality value) corresponding to a customer and priority, we perturb the future volume from the dataset randomly within $\pm 20\%$ for a period of 1000 time units. We do all the experiments for a stream of 1000 tickets, and with number of agents varying from 10 to 50. The frequency of scheduling is set to 0.3 time units, i.e., after every 0.3 time units the scheduler (*MIP, heuristic, GTMin,* or *GEMax*) is invoked to schedule and reposition, the *new arrivals* within this period and *Queued* tickets respectively.

We consider a Poisson model for tickets arrival, where the inter-arrival times follow an exponential distribution, with bursts following Gaussian distribution (as bursts are periodic, occurring mostly at the start of a service shift). To generate the ticket arrivals, (i) first, we generate a large number of tickets (normal stream) with exponentially distributed inter-arrival times (mean arrival rate $\lambda = \frac{1}{avg.\ ERT}$), (ii) then, generate a sequence of bursts (burst-stream) following Gaussian distribution with independent exponentially distributed inter-arrivals within each burst, (iii) for each experiment, as the number of agents (m) is varied, the inter-arrival times in the normal stream is adjusted uniformly to match the arrival rate of the merged stream (normal-stream merged with burst-stream) with the service rate (y), where $m = y + y^{1/3}$. This makes the overall utilization more aggressive than the well-known square-root staffing approach [11]. Finally, we set maximum delay count (MDC) to 8, to avoid starvation for tickets that breach SLO. To solve the *MIP* formulation, we used Java APIs of ILOG-CPLEX, with a time bound of 3 min. for each of the objectives.

7.2 Results

To analyze the efficacy of our scheduling algorithms for shared delivery, we measure a set of metrics in course of our simulation experiments. These metrics follow directly from the scheduling objectives introduced earlier.

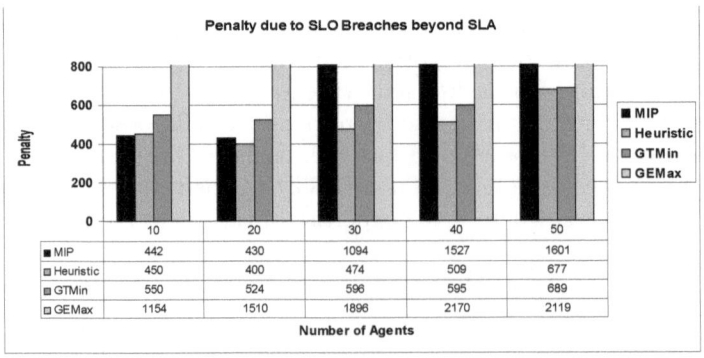

Fig. 1. Total penalty due to SLO breaches beyond SLAs of customer-priority pairs

The first metric (corresponding to SLA Penalty Minimization) is the *total penalty induced by the SLO breaches beyond SLAs*, the results of which are shown in Fig 1 along with the table of values in the bottom. As we see, for the first two experiments (with 10 and 20 agents), *MIP* and *Heuristic* induce the least penalty. *GTMin* causes a penalty increase of 24.4% and 21.8% over *MIP* penalties for the two experiments respectively. The *GEMax* algorithm does not perform well, as it is concerned mainly with the maximization of expertise in assignments. Starting from the third experiment (with 30 agents), we found that *MIP* fails to return any feasible assignment within the allotted time. On deeper investigation, we discovered that due to bursty arrival and queued tickets, the number of tickets to be scheduled in some runs was around 50. This led to a huge increase in the number of internal variables and constraints (>70,000), since these are of the order of $O(MN^2)$ where M and N refer to #agents and #tickets respectively. To circumvent this problem, for *MIP* experiments with (30, 40, 50) agents, we did not consider all the *Queued* tickets at every scheduling run, but fixed many of them at their existing queue positions. This made scheduling tractable, but led to a sharp increase in SLA penalty for *MIP*, as seen in Fig 1. This demonstrates that by usually allowing ticket positions to change in a queue, we are able to save on a lot of SLO breaches and SLA penalty.

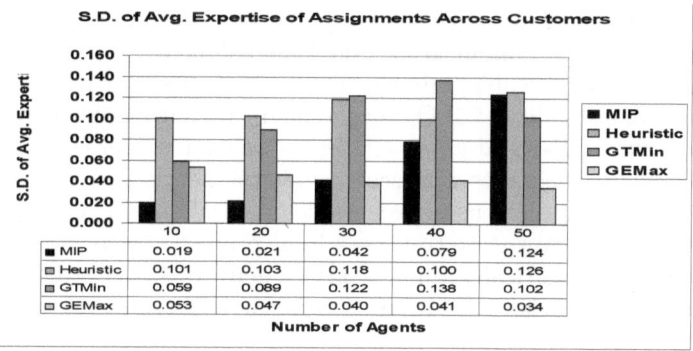

Fig. 2. Standard deviation of average expertise of assignments of tickets belonging to different customers

Next, we measure the S.D. of agent load at every run (corresponding to the load balancing objective). *MIP, heuristic* and *GTMin* all did well on this metric, showing that load is well-balanced by all of them. For example, for 20 agents, the S.D. value for *MIP* ranges from (1.78 to 36.7), and is only slightly higher for the *heuristic* and *GTMin*. Expectedly, *GEMax* returns poor results, with a S.D. range of (4.09 to 631.19) across all the runs for 20 agents. This is because there are a few multi-skilled people with high expertise in our experimental set-up, who attract many tickets due to expertise maximization, irrespective of their current load (which also leads to high SLA penalty, as seen above).

We then compute the S.D. of average expertise of assignments across all customers (Fig. 2). We find that while *GEMax* performs consistently well on the fourth objective, the other approaches show slightly higher S.D., which means that each customer is given a lesser balanced share of the available expertise. We also measured the average expertise of all assignments across all customers, and found that it ranges between [0.73, 0.86] for *GEMax* when aggregated over all runs, while the corresponding values for *GTMin* are [0.59, 0.63]. *MIP* and *heuristic* performed comparably with ranges from [0.60, 0.67] and [0.63, 0.71] respectively.

Finally, we measure the average time taken by various algorithms per run. *MIP* takes comparatively large time (235.8 - 416.9 sec.) per run for all the experiments across different numbers of agents, while all other approaches take negligible time (< 6 seconds at most). It should be noted that for the *MIP*, we accepted whatever feasible solution it provided in cases where optimal solution could not be reached in the bounded time.

8   Discussions

Our experimental results demonstrate the effectiveness of our scheduling approaches for shared service delivery. Compared to *GTMin* which greedily reduces *SLO breaches*, the *MIP* and *heuristic* approaches give comparable or better results for SLA penalty minimization and load balancing. Another highlight of the results is that we are able to balance individual customer interests very well, both in terms of criticality of SLO breaches and the sharing of expertise. We also observe that the MIP-based approach works well for moderate sized problems but its performance degrades with scale, while the heuristic scales very well and can rapidly generate solutions of acceptable quality. Thus a combination of the two approaches can allow us to traverse a large problem space very effectively. In future, we plan to empirically study a service delivery system to determine how well we can estimate ticket resolution effort, agent expertise, and the relationship between the same.

References

1. Application assembly optimization: a distinct approach to global delivery. White Paper, IBM GBS (2010)
2. Deshpande, P.M., Garg, D., Rama Suri, N.: Auction based models for ticket allocation problem in it service delivery industry. In: IEEE Intl. Conf. on Ser. Comp., SCC (2008)
3. Gans, N., et al.: Telephone call centers: Tutorial, review, and research prospects. Manf. & Ser. Op. Mgmt. 5 (2003)
4. Gupta, P., Parija, G.R.: Efficient seat utilization in global it delivery service systems. In: IEEE SCC, pp. 97–103 (2009)
5. Kakal, C.S.: Global shared support service: Leveraging expertise, sharing costs, and deriving value. White Paper, Infosys (May 2005)

6. Karger, D., Stein, C., Wein, J.: Scheduling algorithms. In: Algorithms and Theory of Computation Handbook (2010)
7. Khan, A., et al.: Aim-hi: a framework for request routing in large-scale it global service delivery. IBM J. Res. Dev. 53 (2009)
8. Lawler, E.L., et al.: Sequencing and scheduling: Algorithms and complexity. In: Logistics of Production and Inventory, vol. 4, pp. 445–522. Elsevier (1993)
9. Shao, Q., Chen, Y., Tao, S., Yan, X., Anerousis, N.: Efficient ticket routing by resolution sequence mining. In: KDD (2008)
10. Subbian, K., et al.: Incentive compatible mechanisms for group ticket allocation in software maintenance services. In: APSEC (2007)
11. Wallace, R.B., Whitt, W.: A staffing algorithm for call centers with skill-based routing. Manufacturing & Service Operations Management 7 (2005)
12. Zhou, N., Ma, Q., Ratakonda, K.: Quantitative modeling of communication cost for global service delivery. In: IEEE SCC, pp. 388–395 (2009)

Programming Hybrid Services in the Cloud

Hong-Linh Truong[1], Schahram Dustdar[1], and Kamal Bhattacharya[2]

[1] Distributed Systems Group, Vienna University of Technology
{truong,dustdar}@infosys.tuwien.ac.at
[2] IBM Research - India
kambhatt@in.ibm.com

Abstract. For solving complex problems, we advocate constructing "social computers" which combine software and human services. However, to date, human capabilities cannot be easily programmed into applications in a similar way like software capabilities. Existing approaches exploiting human capabilities via crowds do not support well on-demand, proactive, team-based human computation. In this paper, we explore a new way to virtualize, provision and program human capabilities using cloud computing concepts and service delivery models. We propose novel methods for modeling clouds of human-based services and combine human-based services with software-based services to establish clouds of hybrid services. In our model, we present common APIs, similar to APIs for software services, to access individual and team-based compute units in clouds of human-based services. Based on that, we propose frameworks and programming primitives for hybrid services. We illustrate our concepts via some examples of using our cloud APIs and existing cloud APIs for software.

1 Introduction

Recently the concept of building social computers has emerged, in which the main principle is to combine human capabilities and software capabilities into composite applications solving complex problems [1, 2]. Furthermore, concrete technologies have been employed to provide human capabilities via standard, easy-to-use interface, such as Web services and Web platforms [3–5] and some efforts have been devoted for modeling and coordinating flows of human works in the process level [6, 7]. In all these works, a fundamental issue is how to program human capabilities. We observed two main approaches in utilizing human capabilities: (i) passively proposing tasks and waiting for human input, such as in crowd platforms [5], and (ii) actively finding and binding human capabilities into applications. While the first one is quite popular and has many successful applications [8–10, 5, 11], it mainly exploits individual capabilities and is platform-specific. In the second approach, it is difficult to proactively invoke human capabilities in Internet-scale due to the lack of techniques and systems supporting proactive utilization of human capabilities [2].

In this paper, we conceptualize human capabilities under the service model and combine them with software establishing clouds of hybrid services. In our approach, we explore novel ways to actively program and utilize human capabilities in a similar way to software services. Our research question is how to provision and program human capabilities using cloud service and deployment models for high level frameworks and programming languages to build "social computers".

C. Liu et al. (Eds.): ICSOC 2012, LNCS 7636, pp. 96–110, 2012.

1.1 Motivation

Hybrid services, in our notion, include software-based services (SBS) and human-based services (HBS). We argue that we could provide a cloud of HBS working in a similar manner to contemporary clouds of SBS (such as Amazon services and Microsoft Azure services) so that HBS can be invoked and utilized in a proactive manner, rather than in a passive way like in crowdsourcing platforms. Furthermore, HBS can be programmed together with SBS in a composite application, instead of being used separately from SBS as in contemporary crowdsourcing platforms.

Our goal is to program HBS and SBS together in an easier way because several complex applications need to utilize SBS and HBS in a similar way. For example, several Information Technology (IT) problems, such as in incident management for IT systems, software component development, and collaborative data analytics, can be described as a dependency graph of tasks in which a task represents a unit of work that should be solved by a human or a software. Solving a task may need to concurrently consider other relevant tasks in the same graph as well as introduce new tasks (this in turns expands the task graph). Utilizing team and hybrid services is important here as tasks are interdependent, but unlike crowdsourcing scenarios in which different humans solving different tasks without the context of teamwork and without the connectedness to SBS. Teamwork is crucial as it allows team members to delegate tasks when they cannot deal with the task as well as newly tasks can be identified and created that need to be solved. SBS for teamwork is crucial for team working platforms in terms of communication, coordination, and analytics. Therefore, it is crucial to have solutions to provision individual- and team-based human capabilities under clouds of human capabilities, in parallel with the provisioning of SBS.

These clouds require novel service models and infrastructures to provide and support on-demand and elastic HBS provisioning. We need solutions allowing us to buy and provision human capabilities via simple interfaces in a similar way to buying and provisioning virtual machines in contemporary clouds of Infrastructure-as-a-Service (IaaS) and Software-as-a-Service (SaaS). However, so far, to our best knowledge, there is no proposed solution towards a cloud model for human capabilities that enables to acquire, program, and utilize HBS in a similar way to that of IaaS, Platform-as-a-Service (PaaS) and SaaS.

1.2 Contributions and Paper Structure

We concentrate on conceptualizing the cloud of HBS and how clouds of HBS and SBS can be programmed for solving complex problems. Our main contributions are:

 - a novel model for clouds of HBS and hybrid services provisioning
 - a framework for solving complex problems using clouds of hybrid services
 - programming primitives for hybrid services

The rest of this paper is organized as follows. Section 2 discusses our model of clouds of hybrid services. Section 3 describes a generic framework for using hybrid services. Section 4 describes programming primitives and examples utilizing clouds of hybrid services. We discuss related work in Section 5. Section 6 concludes the paper and outlines our future work.

2   Models for Clouds of Hybrid Services

In our work, we consider two types of computing elements: software-based computing elements and human-based computing elements. In software-based computing elements, different types of services can be provided to exploit machine capabilities and
we consider these types of services under Software-based Service (SBS) category. Similarly, human-based computing elements can also offer different types of services under
the HBS category. We consider a cloud of hybrid services as follows:

Definition 1 (Cloud of hybrid services). *A cloud of hybrid services includes SBS and*
HBS that can be provisioned, deployed and utilized on-demand based on different pric-
ing models.

In principle, a cloud of hybrid services can also be built atop clouds of SBS and clouds
of HBS. As SBS and clouds of SBS are well-researched, in the following we will discuss
models for clouds of HBS and of hybrid services.

2.1   Models for HBS

In principle, human capabilities can be provisioned under the service model, e.g., our
previous work introduced a technology to offer individual human capabilities under
Web services [3]. However, at the moment, there exists no cloud system that the consumer can program HBS in a similar way like IaaS (e.g., Amazon EC) or data (e.g.,
Microsoft Azure Data Marketplace). Before discussing how clouds of hybrid services
can be used, we propose a conceptual model for clouds of HBS.

HBS Communication Interface. Humans have different ways to interact with other
humans and ICT systems. Conceptually, we can assume that HBS (and corresponding
HBS clouds) abstracting human capabilities can provide different communication interfaces to handle tasks based on a request and response model. *Requests* can be used
to describe tasks/messages that an HBS should perform or receive. In SBS, specific
request representations (e.g., based on XML) are designed for specific software layers
(e.g., application layer, middleware layer, or hardware layer). In HBS we can assume
that a single representation can be used, as HBS does not have similar layer structures
seen in SBS. Requests in HBS can, therefore, be composed and decomposed into different (sub)requests. The use of the request/response model will facilitate the integration
between SBS and HBS as via similar service APIs.

   Unlike SBS in which communication can be synchronous or asynchronous, in HBS
all communication is asynchronous. In general, the upper bound of the communication
delay in and the internal request processing mechanism in HBS are unknown. However,
HBS intercommunication can be modeled using:

- message-passing in which two HBS can directly exchange requests: $hbs_i \xrightarrow{request}$
  hbs_j. One example is that hbs_i sends a request via SMS to hbs_j. Similarly, an SBS
  can also send a request directly to an HBS.
- shared-memory in which two HBS can exchange requests via a SBS. For example, hbs_i stores a request into a Dropbox[1] directory and hbs_j obtains the request

---

[1] www.dropbox.com

from the Dropbox directory. Similarly, an SBS and HBS can also exchange requests/responses via an SBS or an HBS (e.g., a software can be built atop Dropbox to trigger actions when a file is stored into a Dropbox directory (see http://www.wappwolf.com)).

Similarly to machine instances which offer facilities for remote job deployment and execution, an HBS communication interface can be used to run requests/jobs on HBS.

Human Power Unit (HPU). The first issue is to define a basic model for describing the notion of "computing power" of HBS. Usually, the computing capability of a human-based computing element is described via human skills and skill levels. Although there is no standard way to compare skills and skill levels described and/or verified by different people and organizations, we think that it is feasible to establish a common, comparative skills *for a particular cloud* of HBS.

- the cloud can enforce different evaluation techniques to ensure that any HBS in its system will declare skills and skill levels in a cloud-wide consistency. This is, for example, similar to some crowdsourcing systems which have rigorous tests to verify claimed skills.
- the cloud can use different benchmarks to test humans to validate skills and skill levels. Each benchmark can be used to test a skill and skill level. This is, for example, similar to Amazon which uses benchmarks to define its elastic compute unit.
- the cloud can map different skills from different sources into a common view which is consistent in the whole cloud.

We define HPU for an HBS as follows:

Definition 2 (Human Power Unit). *HPU is a value describing the computing power of an HBS measured in an abstract unit. A cloud of HBS has a pre-defined basic power unit, hpu_θ, corresponding to the baseline skill bs_θ of the cloud.*

Without the loss of generality, we assume $hpu_\theta = f(bs_\theta)$. A cloud C provisioning HBS can support a set of n skills $SK = \{sk_1, \cdots, sk_n\}$ and a set of m cloud skill levels $SL = \{1, \cdots, m\}$. C can define the human power unit wrt sk_i for sl_j as follows:

$$hpu(sk_i, sl_j) = hpu_\theta \times \frac{f(sk_i)}{f(bs_\theta)} \times sl_j \qquad (1)$$

For the cloud C, $\frac{f(sk_i)}{f(bs_\theta)}$ is known (based on the definition of SK). Given the capability of an $hbs - CS(hbs) = \{(sk_1, sl_1), \cdots, (sk_u, sl_u)\}$ – the corresponding hpu can be calculated as follows:

$$hpu(CS(hbs)) = \sum_{i=1}^{u} hpu(sk_i, sl_i) \qquad (2)$$

Note that two HBS can have the same hpu value, even their skills are different. To distinguish them, we propose to use a set of "architecture" types (e.g., similar to different types of instruction set architectures such as x86, SPARC, and ARM), and the cloud provider can map an HBS into an architecture type by using its skills and skill levels. Given a human offering her capabilities to C, she can be used exclusively or shared among different consumers. In case an hbs is provisioned exclusively for a particular consumer, the hbs can be associated with a theoretical utilization u – describing the utilization of a human – and $CS(hbs)$; its theoretical HPU would be $u \times hpu(CS(hbs))$. In case a hbs is provisioned for multiple consumers, the hbs can be described as a set of multiple instances, each has a theoretical power as $u_i \times hpu(CS_i(hbs))$ where $u = \sum(u_i) \leq 1$ and $CS(hbs) = CS_1(hbs) \cup CS_2(hbs) \cup \cdots \cup CS_q(hbs)$.

Using this model, we can determine theoretical power for individual HBS as well as for a set of individual HBS. Note that the power of a set of HBS may be more than the sum of power units of its individual HBS, due to teamwork. However, we can assume that, similar to individual and cluster of machines, theoretical power units are different from the real one and are mainly useful for selecting HBS and defining prices.

2.2 HBS Instances Provisioning

Types of HBS Instances For HBS we will consider two types of instances:

Definition 3 (Individual Compute Unit instances (iICU)). *iICU describe instances of HBS built atop capabilities of individuals. An individual can provide different iICU. Analogous to SBS, an iICU is similar to an instance of a virtual machine or a software.*

Definition 4 (Social Compute Unit instances (iSCU)). *iSCU describe instances of HBS built atop capabilities of multiple individuals and SBS. Analogous to SBS, an iSCU is similar to a virtual cluster of machines or a complex set of software services.*

In our approach, iICU is built based on the concept that an individual can offer her capabilities via services [3] and iSCU is built based on the concept of Social Compute Units [12]) which represents a team of individuals.

HBS Instance Description. Let C be a cloud of hybrid services. All services in C can be described as follows: $C = HBS \cup SBS$ where HBS is the set of HBS instances and SBS is the set of SBS instances. The model for SBS is well-known in contemporary clouds and can be characterized as $SBS(capability, price)$. The provisioning description models for HBS instances are proposed as follows:

- For an $iICU$ its provisioning description includes $(CS, HPU, price, utilization, location, APIs)$.
- For an $iSCU$ its provisioning description includes $(CS, HPU, price, utilization, connectedness, location, APIs)$.

From the consumer perspective, $iSCU$ can be offered by the cloud provider or the consumer can build its own $iSCU$. In principle, in order to build an SCU, the provider or the consumer can follow the following steps: first, selecting suitable $iICU$ for an $iSCU$ and, second, combining and configuring SBS to have a working platform for $iSCU$. The $connectedness$ reflects the intercommunication topology connecting members of $iSCU$, such as ring, star, and master-slave, typically configured via SBS. $APIs$ describe how to communicate to and execute requests on HBS. Moreover, similar to SBS, HBS can also be linked to user rating information, often managed by third-parties.

Pricing Factors. Similar to existing SBS clouds, we propose clouds of HBS to define different pricing models for different types of HBS instances. The baseline for the prices can be based on hpu_θ. We propose to consider the following specific pricing factors:

- utilization: unlike individual machines whose theoretical utilization when selling is 100%, ICU has much lower theoretical utilization, e.g., normal full time people have a utilization of 33.33% (8 hours per day). However, an SCU can theoretically have 100% utilization. The real utilization of an HBS is controlled by the HBS rather than by the consumer as in machine/software instances.
- offering communication APIs: it is important that different communication capabilities will foster the utilization of HBS. Therefore, the provider can also bill consumers based on communication APIs (e.g., charge more when SMS is enabled).
- connectedness: similar to capabilities of (virtual) networks between machines in a (virtual) cluster, the connectedness of an $iSCU$ will have a strong impact on the performance of $iSCU$. Similar to pricing models in existing collaboration services[2], the pricing factor for connectedness can be built based on which SBS and collaboration features are used for iSCU.

Furthermore, other conventional factors used in SBS such as usage duration and location are considered.

2.3 Cloud APIs for Provisioning Hybrid Services

Services in a cloud of hybrid services can be requested and provisioned on-demand. As APIs for provisioning SBS are well developed, we will focus on APIs for provisioning HBS. Table 1 describes some APIs that we develop for hybrid services in our VieCOM (Vienna Elastic Computing Model). These APIs are designed in a similar manner to common APIs for SBS.

Figure 1 shows main Java-based classes representing HPU, HBS and its subclasses (ICU and SCU), requests and messages for HBS (`HBSRequest` and `HBSMessage`), and skills (`CloudSkill`, `Skill`, and `SkillLevel`). Currently, we simulate our cloud of HBS. For SBS, we use existing APIs provided by cloud providers and common client APIs libraries, such as JClouds (`www.jclouds.org`) and boto (`http://docs.pythonboto.org/en/latest/index.html`).

3   Framework for Utilizing Hybrid Services

By utilizing hybrid services in clouds, we could potentially solve several complex problems that need both SBS and HBS. In our work, we consider complex problems that can be described under dependency graphs. Let DG be dependency graph of tasks to be solved; DG can be provided or extracted automatically. In order to solve a task $t \in DG$, we need to determine whether t will be solved by SBS, HBS or their combination. For example, let t be a virtual machine failure and the virtual machine is provisioned by

---

[2] Such as in Google Apps for Business (`http://www.google.com/enterprise/apps/business/pricing.html`)

Table 1. Main APIs for provisioning HBS

APIs	Description
APIs for service information and management	
listSkills ();listSkillLevels()	list all pre-defined skills and skill levels of clouds
listICU();listSCU()	list all iICU and iSCU instances that can be used. Different filters can be applied to the listing
negotiateHBS()	negotiate service contract with an *iICU* or an *iSCU*. In many cases, the cloud can just give the service contract and the consumer has to accept it (e.g., similar to SBS clouds)
startHBS()	start an *iICU* or an *iSCU*. By starting, the HBS is being used. Depending on the provisioning contract, the usage can be time-based (subscription model) or task-based (pay-per-use model)
suspendHBS ()	suspend the operation of an *iICU* or *iSCU*. Note that in suspending mode, the HBS is not released yet for other consumers yet.
resumeHBS ()	resume the work of an *iICU* or *iSCU*
stopHBS()	stop the operation of an *iICU* or *iSCU*. By stopping the HBS is no longer available for the consumer
reduceHBS()	reduce the capabilities of *iICU* or *iSCU*
expandHBS()	expand the capabilities of *iICU* or *iSCU*
APIs for service execution and communication	
runRequestOnHBS()	execute a request on an *iICU* or *iSCU*. By execution, the HBS will receive the request and perform it.
receiveResultFromHBS()	receive the result from an *iICU* or *iSCU*
sendMessageToHBS()	send (support) messages to HBS
receiveMessageFromHBS()	receive messages from HBS

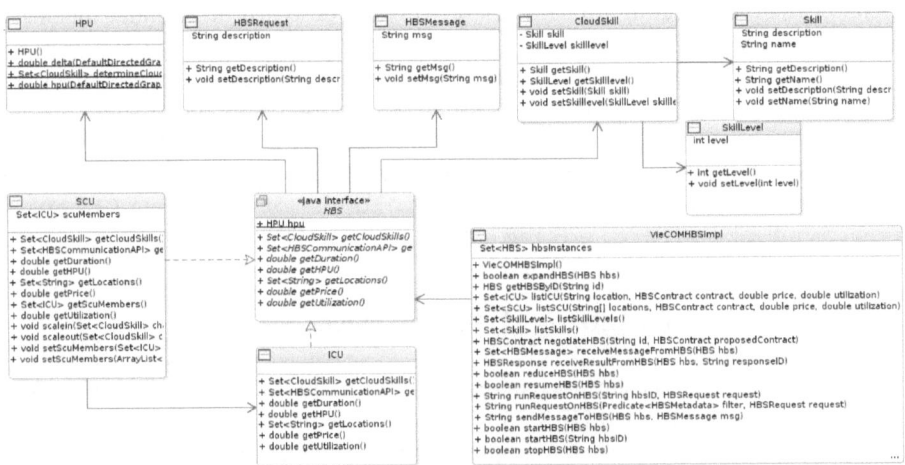

Fig. 1. Example of some Java-based APIs for clouds of HBS

Amazon EC2. Two possibilities can be performed: (i) request a new virtual machine from Amazon EC and configure the new virtual machine suitable for the work or (ii) request an HBS to fix the virtual machine. In case (i) SBS can be invoked, while for case (ii) we need to invoke an HBS which might need to be provisioned with extra SBS for supporting the failure analysis.

Our approach for utilizing hybrid services includes the following points:

- link tasks with their required human power units via skills and skill levels, before programming how to utilize HBS and SBS.
- form or select suitable $iSCU$ or $iICU$ for solving tasks. Different strategies will be developed for forming or selecting suitable $iSCU$ or $iICU$, such as utilizing different ways to traverse the dependency graph and to optimize the formation objective.
- program different strategies of utilizing $iSCU$ and $iICU$, such as considering the elasticity of HBS due to changes of tasks and HBS. This is achieved by using programming primitives and constructs atop APIs for hybrid services.

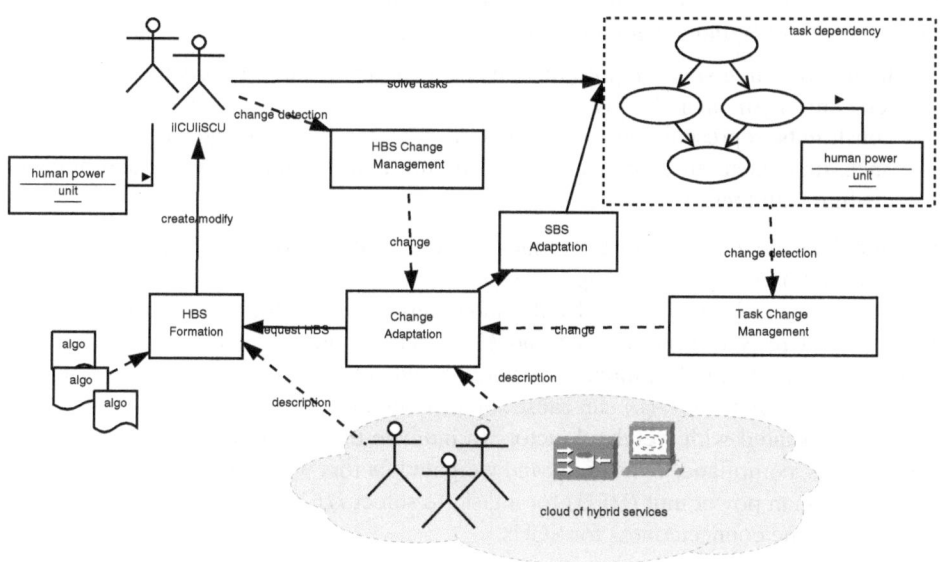

Fig. 2. Conceptual architecture

Figure 2 describes the conceptual architecture of our framework for solving complex problems. Given a task dependency graph, we can detect changes in required human computing power by using *Task Change Management*. Detected required power changes will be sent to *Change Adaptation*, which in turns triggers different operations on HBS usage, such as creating new HBS or adapting an existing HBS. The operations on HBS are provided via different algorithms, each suitable for specific situations.

When an HBS deals with a task graph, the HBS can change the task graph and its required human power units (this will trigger HBS operations again). During the solving process, HBS can change and this can be detected by *HBS Change Management*. The HBS change will be sent to *Change Adaptation*.

4   Programming Hybrid Services

In this section, we discuss some programming primitives for hybrid services that can be applied to complex application framework that we mentioned before. Such a primitives can be used in different components, such as *HBSFormation* and *ChangeAdaptation*, in our framework described in Figure 2. In illustrating programming examples, we consider a virtualized cloud of hybrid services that are built atop our cloud of HBS and real-world clouds of SBS. Consequently, we will combine our APIs, described in Section 2.3, with existing client cloud API libraries.

4.1   Modeling HPU-Aware Task Dependency Graphs

Our main idea in modeling HPU-aware task dependencies is to link tasks to required *management skills and compliance constraints*:

- human resource skills: represent skill sets that are required for dealing with problems/management activities.
- constraints: represent constraints, such as resource locations, governance compliance, time, cost, etc., that are associated with management activities and humans dealing with these activities.

Given a dependency graph of tasks, these types of information can be provided manually or automatically (e.g., using knowledge extraction). Generally, we model dependencies among tasks and required skills and compliance constraints as a directed graph $G(N, E)$ where N is a set of nodes and E is a set of edges. A node $n \in N$ represents a task or required skills/compliance constraints, whereas an edge $e(n_i, n_j) \in E$ means that n_j is dependent on n_i (n_i can cause some effect on n_j or n_i can manage n_j). Edges may be associated with weighted factors to indicate the importance of edges. The required skills, compliance constraints and weighted factors will be used to determine the required human power unit (HPU) for a task, to select $iICU$ and members for $iSCU$, and to build the connectedness for SCUs.

Examples and Implementation. Figure 3 presents an example of a dependency graph of an IT system linked to management skills. In our implementation of dependency graph, we use JGraphT (http://jgrapht.org/). We define two main types of Node – *ITProblem* and *Management*. All relationships are dependency. It is also possible to use TOSCA [13] to link people skills and map TOSCA-based description to JGraphT.

4.2   Combining HBS and SBS

Combining HBS and SBS is a common need in solving complex problems (e.g., in evaluating quality of data in simulation workflows). In our framework, this feature can

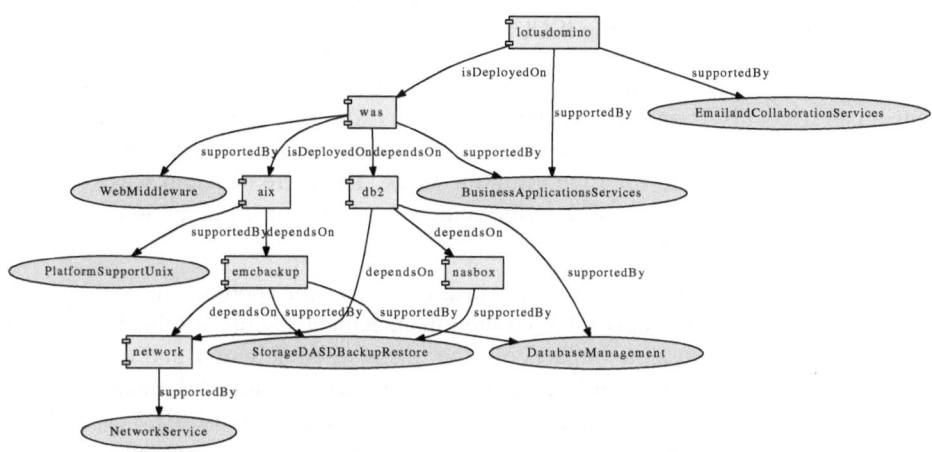

Fig. 3. An example of HPU-aware dependency graph. A component box describes a software and its problems (*ITProblem* node). An eclipse describes management skills (*Management* node).

be used for preparing inputs managed by SBS for an HBS work or managing outputs from HBS work. Furthermore, it can be used to provision SBS as utilities for HBS work (e.g., requiring HBS to utilize specific SBS in order to produce the result where SBS is provisioned by the consumer).

Examples. Listing 1.1 shows an example of programming a combination of HBS and SBS for a task using our cloud APIs and JClouds. In this example, we want to invoke Amazon S3 to store a log file of a Web application sever and invoke an HBS to find problems. Using this way, we can also combine HBS with HBS and of course SBS with SBS from different clouds.

```
//using JClouds APIs to store log file of web application server
BlobStoreContext context =
    new BlobStoreContextFactory().createContext("aws-s3","REMOVED
        ","REMOVED");
BlobStore blobStore = context.getBlobStore();
//.... and add file into Amazon S3
Blob blob = blobStore.blobBuilder("hbstest").build();
blob.setPayload(new File("was.log"));
blobStore.putBlob("hbstest", blob);
String uri = blob.getMetadata().getPublicUri().toString();
VieCOMHBS vieCOMHBS = new VieCOMHBSImpl();
//assume that WM6 is the HBS that can analyze the Web Middleware
        problem
vieCOMHBS.startHBS("WM6");
HBSRequest request = new HBSRequest();
request.setDescription("Find possible problems from " + uri);
vieCOMHBS.runRequestOnHBS("WM6", request);
```

Listing 1.1. Example of HBS combined with SBS

4.3   Forming and Configuring iSCUs

A cloud provider can form an $iSCU$ and provide it to the consumer as well as a consumer can select $iICU$ and SBS to form an $iSCU$. An $iSCU$ not only includes HBS ($iICU$ or other sub $iSCU$) but also consists of possible SBS for ensuring the connectedness within $iSCU$ and for supporting the work. There are different ways to form SCUs. In the following, we will describe some approaches for forming SCUs to solve a dependency graph of tasks.

Selecting Resources for iSCU. Given a task $t \in DG$, our approach in dealing with t is that we do not just simply take required management resources suitable for t but we need to consider possible impacts of other tasks when solving t and the chain of dependencies. To this end, we utilize DG to determine a set of suitable human resources to deal with t and t's possible impact. Such human resources establish HBS capabilities in an $iSCU$. Overall, the following steps are carried out to determine required SCU:

- Step 1: determine $DG_{BAU} \subseteq DG$ where DG_{BAU} includes all $t_j \; \exists$ a walk (t_j, t), t_j is the task that must be dealt together with t in typical Business-As-Usual cases.
- Step 2: determine $DG_{CA} \subseteq DG$ that includes tasks that should be taken into account under corrective action (CA) cases. $DG_{CA} = \{t_r\} \; \exists$ a walk(t_r, t_j) with $t_j \in DG_{BAU}$.
- Step 3: merge $DG_{SCU} = DG_{BAU} \cup DG_{CA}$ by (re)assigning weighted factors to links between $(t_k, t_l) \in DG_{SCU}$ based on whether (i) t_k and t_l belong to DG_{BAU} or DG_{CA}, (ii) reaction chain from t to t_k or to t_l, and (iii) the original weighted factor of links consisting of t_k or t_l.
- Step 4: traverse DG_{SCU}, $\forall t_i \in DG_{SCU}$, consider all (t_i, r_i) where r_i is management resource node linking to t_i in order to determine human resources.

Based on the above-mentioned description different SCU formation strategies can be developed. Note that our principles mentioned above aim at forming $iSCU$ enough

Table 2. Examples of SCU formation strategies

Algorithms	Description
SkillWithNPath	Select $iICU$ for $iSCU$ based on only skills with a pre-defined network path length starting from the task to be solved.
SkillMinCostWithNPath	Select $iICU$ for $iSCU$ based on only skills with minimum cost, considering a pre-defined network path length starting from the task to be solved.
SkillMinCostMaxLevelWithNPath	Select $iICU$ for $iSCU$ based on skills with minimum cost and maximum skill levels, considering a pre-defined network path length starting from the task to be solved.
SkillWithNPathUnDirected	Similar to $SkillWithNPath$ but considering undirected dependency
MinCostWithNPathUnDirected	Similar to $MinCostWithNPath$ but considering undirected dependency
MinCostWithAvailNPathUnDirected	Select Select $iICU$ for $iSCU$ based on skills with minimum cost, considering availability and a pre-defined network path length starting from the task to be solved. Undirected dependencies are considered.

```
DefaultDirectedGraph <Node, Relationship> dg; //graph of problems
//...
double hpu = HPU.hpu(dg); //determine
SCUFormation app = new SCUFormation( dg);
ManagementRequest request = new ManagementRequest();
//define request specifying only main problems to be solved
//....
//call algorithms to find suitable HBS. Path length =2 and
    availability from 4am to 19pm in GMT zone
ResourcePool scu = app.
    MinCostWithAvailabilityNPathUnDirectedFormation(request, 2,
    4, 19);
if (scu == null) { return ; }
ArrayList <HumanResource> scuMembers = scu.getResources();
SCU iSCU = new SCU();
iSCU.setScuMembers(scuMembers);
//setting up SBS for scuMember ...
```

Listing 1.2. Example of forming iSCU by minimizing cost and considering no direction

for solving main tasks and let $iSCU$ evolve during its runtime. There could be several possible ways to obtain DG_{BAU} and DG_{CA}, dependent on specific configurations and graphs for specific problems. Therefore, potentially the cloud of HBS can provide several algorithms for selecting HBS to form SCUs. As we aim at presenting a generic framework, we do not describe here specific algorithms, however, Table 2 describes some selection strategies that we implement in our framework. Listing 1.2 describes an example of forming an SCU.

Setting up iSCU connectedness. After selecting members of $iSCU$, we can also program SBS and HBS for the $iSCU$ to have a complete working environment. $iSCU$ can have different connectedness configurations, such as

- ring-based $iSCU$: the topology of $iSCU$ is based on a ring. In this case for each $(hbs_i, hbs_j) \in iSCU$ then we program $hbs_i \xrightarrow[request]{} hbs_j$ based on message-passing or shared memory models. For example a common Dropbox directory can be created for hbs_i and hbs_j to exchange requests/responses.
- star-based $iSCU$: a common SBS can be programmed as a shared memory for $iSCU$. Let sbs be SBS for $iSCU$ then $\forall hbs_i \in iSCU$ give hbs_i access to sbs. For example, a common Dropbox directory can be created and shared for all $hbs_i \in iSCU$.
- master-slave $iSCU$: an $hbs \in iSCU$ can play the role of a shared memory and scheduler for all other $hbs_i \in iSCU$.

Listing 1.3 presents an example of establishing the connectedness for an $iSCU$ using Dropbox. Note that finding suitable configurations by using HBS information and compliance constraints is a complex problem that is out of the scope of this paper.

```
SCU iSCU ;
// ... find members for SCU
DropboxAPI<WebAuthSession> scuDropbox; // using dropbox apis
// ...
AppKeyPair appKeys = new AppKeyPair(APP_KEY, APP_SECRET);
WebAuthSession session =
        new WebAuthSession(appKeys, WebAuthSession.AccessType.
        DROPBOX);
// ...
session.setAccessTokenPair(accessToken);
scuDropbox = new DropboxAPI<WebAuthSession>(session);
// sharing the dropbox directory to all scu members
// first create a share
DropboxAPI.DropboxLink link = scuDropbox.share("/hbscloud");
// then send the link to all members
VieCOMHBS vieCOMHBS = new VieCOMHBSImpl();
for (HBS hbs : iSCU.getScuMembers()) {
    vieCOMHBS.startHBS(icu);
    HBSMessage msg = new HBSMessage();
    msg.setMsg("pls. use shared Dropbox for communication " +
        link.url);
    vieCOMHBS.sendMessageToHBS(hbs, msg);
// ...
}
```

Listing 1.3. Example of star-based iSCU using Dropbox as a communication hub

```
SCU iSCU ;
// ...
iSCU.setScuMembers(scuMembers);
// setting up SBS for scuMember
// ...
double hpu = HPU.hpu(dg); // determine current hpu
// SCU solves/adds tasks in DG
// ....
// graph change − elasticity based on human power unit
double dHPU = HPU.delta(dg,hpu);
DefaultDirectedGraph<Node, Relationship> changegraph;
// obtain changes
Set<CloudSkill> changeCS = HPU.determineCloudSkill(changegraph);
if (dHPU > SCALEOUT_LIMIT) {
    iSCU.scaleout(changeCS); // expand iSCU
}
  else if (dHPU < SCALEIN_LIMIT) {
    iSCU.scalein(changeCS); // reduce iSCU
// ...
}
```

Listing 1.4. Example of elasticity for SCU based on task graph change

4.4   Change Model for Task Graph's Human Power Unit

When a member in an $iSCU$ receives a task, she might revise the task into a set of sub-tasks. Then she might specify human compute units required for sub tasks and revise the task graph by adding these sub-tasks. As the task graph will change, its required human power unit is changed. By capturing the change of the task graph, we can decide to scale in/out the $iSCU$. Listing 1.4 describes some primitives for scaling in/out $iSCU$ based on the change of HPU.

5   Related Work

Most clouds of SBS offering different possibilities to acquire SBS on-demand. However, similar efforts for HBS are missing today. Although both, humans and software, can perform similar work and several complex problems need both of them in the same system, currently there is a lack of programming models and languages for hybrid services of SBS and HBS. Most clouds of SBS offering different possibilities to acquire SBS on-demand, however, similar efforts for HBS are missing today.

Existing systems for utilizing crowds for solving complex problems [14, 5] do not consider how to integrate and virtualize software in a similar manner to that for humans. As we have analyzed, current support can be divided in three approaches [2]: (i) using plug-ins to interface to human, such as BPEL4People[4] or tasks integrated into SQL processing systems[11], (ii) using separate crowdsourcing platforms, such as MTurk[15], and (iii) using workflows, such as Turkomatic [8]. A drawback is that all of them consider humans individually and human capabilities have not been provisioned in a similar manner like software capabilities. As a result, an application must split tasks into sub-tasks that are suitable for individual humans, which do not collaborate to each other, before the application can invoke humans to solve these sub-tasks. Furthermore, the application must join the results from several sub-tasks and it is difficult to integrate work performed by software with work performed by humans. This is not trivial for the application when dealing with complex problems required human capabilities. In terms of communication models and coordination models, existing models such as in MTurk and HPS are based on push/pull/mediator but they are platforms/middleware built-in rather than reusable programming primitives of programming models.

In our work, we develop models for clouds of HBS. Our techniques for virtualizing HBS and programming HBS in a similar way to SBS are different from related work. Such techniques can be used by high-level programming primitives and languages for social computers.

6   Conclusions and Future Work

In this paper, we have proposed novel methods for modeling clouds of HBS and describe how we can combine them with clouds of SBS to create hybrid services. We believe that clouds of hybrid services are crucial for complex applications which need to proactively invoke SBS and HBS in similar ways. We describe general frameworks and programming APIs where and how hybrid services can be programmed.

In this paper, we focus on designing models, frameworks and APIs and illustrating programming examples. Further real-world experiments should be conducted in the future. Furthermore, we are also working on the integration with programming languages for social collaboration processes [7] using hybrid services. Other related aspects, such as pricing models and contract negotiation protocols, will be also investigated.

References

1. The Social Computer - Internet-Scale Human Problem Solving (socialcomputer.eu) (last access: May 3, 2012)
2. Dustdar, S., Truong, H.L.: Virtualizing software and humans for elastic processes in multiple clouds – a service management perspective. International Journal of Next-Generation Computing 3(2) (2012)
3. Schall, D., Truong, H.L., Dustdar, S.: Unifying human and software services in web-scale collaborations. IEEE Internet Computing 12(3), 62–68 (2008)
4. WS-BPEL Extension for People (BPEL4People) Specification Version 1.1 (2009),
   http://docs.oasis-open.org/bpel4people/
   bpel4people-1.1-spec-cd-06.pdf
5. Doan, A., Ramakrishnan, R., Halevy, A.Y.: Crowdsourcing systems on the world-wide web. Commun. ACM 54(4), 86–96 (2011)
6. Oppenheim, D.V., Varshney, L.R., Chee, Y.-M.: Work as a Service. In: Kappel, G., Maamar, Z., Motahari-Nezhad, H.R. (eds.) ICSOC 2011. LNCS, vol. 7084, pp. 669–678. Springer, Heidelberg (2011)
7. Liptchinsky, V., Khazankin, R., Truong, H.-L., Dustdar, S.: Statelets: Coordination of Social Collaboration Processes. In: Sirjani, M. (ed.) COORDINATION 2012. LNCS, vol. 7274, pp. 1–16. Springer, Heidelberg (2012)
8. Kulkarni, A.P., Can, M., Hartmann, B.: Turkomatic: automatic recursive task and workflow design for mechanical turk. In: Proceedings of the 2011 Annual Conference Extended Abstracts on Human Factors in Computing Systems, CHI EA 2011, pp. 2053–2058. ACM, New York (2011)
9. Barowy, D.W., Berger, E.D., McGregor, A.: Automan: A platform for integrating human-based and digital computation. Technical Report UMass CS TR 2011-44, University of Massachusetts, Amherst (2011), http://www.cs.umass.edu/~emery/pubs/
   AutoMan-UMass-CS-TR2011-44.pdf
10. Baird, H.S., Popat, K.: Human Interactive Proofs and Document Image Analysis. In: Lopresti, D.P., Hu, J., Kashi, R.S. (eds.) DAS 2002. LNCS, vol. 2423, pp. 507–518. Springer, Heidelberg (2002)
11. Marcus, A., Wu, E., Karger, D., Madden, S., Miller, R.: Human-powered sorts and joins. Proc. VLDB Endow. 5, 13–24 (2011)
12. Dustdar, S., Bhattacharya, K.: The social compute unit. IEEE Internet Computing 15(3), 64–69 (2011)
13. Binz, T., Breiter, G., Leymann, F., Spatzier, T.: Portable cloud services using tosca. IEEE Internet Computing 16(3), 80–85 (2012)
14. Brew, A., Greene, D., Cunningham, P.: Using crowdsourcing and active learning to track sentiment in online media. In: Proceeding of the 2010 Conference on ECAI 2010: 19th European Conference on Artificial Intelligence, pp. 145–150. IOS Press, Amsterdam (2010)
15. Amazon mechanical turk (2011) (last access: November 27, 2011)

QoS-Aware Cloud Service Composition Based on Economic Models

Zhen Ye[1,2], Athman Bouguettaya[3], and Xiaofang Zhou[1]

[1] The University of Queensland, Australia
[2] CSIRO ICT Centre, Australia
[3] Royal Melbourne Institute of Technology, Australia

Abstract. Cloud service composition is usually long term based and economically driven. We consider cloud service composition from a user-based perspective. Specifically, the contributions are shown in three aspects. We propose to use discrete Bayesian Network to represent the economic model of end users. The cloud service composition problem is modeled as an Influence Diagram problem. A novel influence-diagram-based cloud service composition approach is proposed. Analytical and simulational results are presented to show the performance of the proposed composition approach.

1 Introduction

Cloud computing is increasingly becoming the technology of choice as the next-generation platform for conducting business [1]. Big companies such as Amazon, Microsoft, Google and IBM are already offering cloud computing solutions in the market. A fast increasing number of organizations are already outsourcing their business tasks to the cloud, instead of deploying their own local infrastructures [2]. A significant advantage of cloud computing is its economic benefits for both users and service providers.

Cloud computing has been intertwined with SOC since its inception [3]. Service oriented computing (SOC) has been widely accepted as the main technology enabler for delivering cloud solutions [4]. Service composition is an active research area in service-oriented computing [5]. Compared to traditional service composition, cloud service composition is usually long-term based and economically driven. Traditional quality-based composition techniques usually consider the qualities at the time of the composition [6]. This is fundamentally different in cloud environments where the cloud service composition should last for a long period. Specifically, we identify the following problems in existing solutions: First, end users in cloud environment are usually large companies and organizations who aim to construct long-term business relationships with cloud service providers [4]. This aspect is largely lacking in existing service composition solutions, e.g., [5] [6]. Besides, end users and service providers participant in service composition according to their economic models [7]. However, existing models addressing economic aspects do not consider service composition but mostly focus on resource provision to specific applications [8] (e.g. cloud cache, scientific applications).

C. Liu et al. (Eds.): ICSOC 2012, LNCS 7636, pp. 111–126, 2012.
© Springer-Verlag Berlin Heidelberg 2012

This paper presents a novel quality-based cloud service composition approach. The research focuses on the selection of composition plans based solely on non-functional (Quality-of-Service, or QoS) attributes. Our main contributions include: (1) Economic models are constructed for end users to model their long-term behaviors. (2) The cloud service composition problem is considered from a decision analysis perspective. Specifically, this research proposes to use *Influence Diagrams* [9] to represent and solve cloud service composition problem. (3) An exemplary scenario is considered where the composition framework aids a department in a university compose cloud services to process tenure cases. Analytical and simulational results are presented to show the performance of the proposed approach.

The remainder of the paper is structured as follows: Section 2 presents a motivating scenario. Section 3 provides an overview of the cloud service composition problem. Section 4 gives a detail analysis of the research challenges and then elaborates the proposed composition approach. Section 5 evaluates the proposed approaches and shows the experiment results. Related work are presented in section 6. Section 7 concludes this paper and highlights some future work.

2   Motivating Scenario

We use the tenure process [10] in the US to motivate and illustrate the cloud service composition problem. American universities take great care in making tenure decisions. A junior professor is usually not promoted to a tenured position without demonstrating a strong record of research and teaching. Specifically, tenure decisions are made based mainly on the evaluation of a candidate's publication and citation records. A university typically includes dozens of colleges. Each college includes dozens of departments. Each department deals with multiple (most likely 5 to 10) tenure cases per year. The tenure process is highly labor intensive. The whole process is usually error prone and conducted manually. To overcome these problems, universities tend to outsource the tenure tasks (e.g., analysis, storage, computation) to clouds.

Let us consider a simple example, where University A contains only one college and the college contains only one department. Suppose the university outsources three main tasks to the clouds during 2012 and 2015. The proposed composition framework would generate a composite tenure application for University A. Specifically, the tenure application (Fig. 1) has three abstract SaaS. Tenure application will first search and find the publication and citation records of a candidate (task 1, T_1). It will then find the the publication and citation records of the comparable professors (task 2, T_2). Finally, the tenure application will generate the evaluation report (task 3, T_3). Besides these abstract SaaS, the composite tenure application also needs CPU, network and storage resources from IaaS providers. CPU services (denoted as CPU) are used to do computations on data. Storage services (denoted as Sto) are used to keep intermediate data. The whole tenure application should be as fair as and as transparent as possible. Therefore, all the input and output data, should be stored in case some

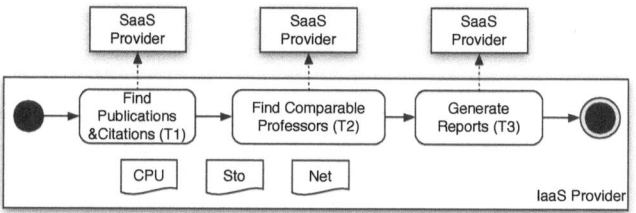

Fig. 1. Tenure application for University A

appeals arise. Network services (denoted as Net) are needed to transfer data between end users and the application, and between components in the composite application.

University A would have different QoS requirements (response time, cost etc.) on the composite tenure application during the long period, i.e., from 2012 to 2015. University A presents these preferences through a *Score Function* [6]. Composite services with higher score are more preferred. University A changes the preferences by change the weights in the score function for different periods. For example, in 2012, University A may prefer composite service that has less response time. While in 2013, University A may find response time is less important but want to save the cost as much as possible. To obtain an optimal composition, the composition framework needs a long-term economically driven model to model the preferences of the end users. Based on the user's economic model, the composition framework makes decisions to select concrete SaaS providers and IaaS providers for university A. The ultimate goal of the composition is to find an optimal plan during a long period, which has the maximal score.

3   Background

This section presents the background of the cloud service composition problem. First, the cloud environment is presented followed by the composition procedure. The adopted QoS model is then explained. Cloud service composition problem is defined at the end of this section.

3.1   Cloud Service Composition Framework

In this research, we identify four actors in the cloud environment (Fig. 2): *End Users, Composer, SaaS (Software as a Service) Providers* and *IaaS (Infrastructure as a Service) Providers*. Platform as a Service (PaaS) layer is omitted as we assume that it is included in the IaaS layer. *End Users* are usually large companies and organizations, e.g., universities, governments. The composer in this paper represents the proposed composition framework. SaaS providers supply SaaS [4] to end users. IaaS providers supply IaaS [4], i.e., CPU services, storage services, and network services, to SaaS providers and end users. The composer

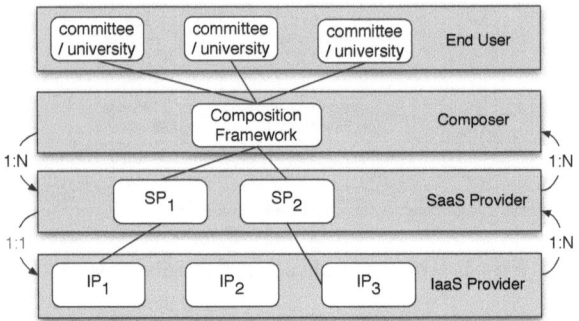

Fig. 2. Four actors in cloud computing

acts on the behave of the end users to form composite services that contains services from multiple SaaS providers and IaaS providers (Fig. 2). Here, we make the assumption that the composer interact directly with SaaS providers, SaaS providers interact directly with IaaS providers. The composer can interact with IaaS providers indirectly only through SaaSs. This assumption is reasonable since even if the composer aims to use some CPU/Network/storage resources, it must invoke these resources through some kind of software interfaces.

Similar to traditional service composition [11], cloud service composition is conducted in two steps. First, a composition schema is constructed for a composition request. Second, the optimal composition plan is selected. A composition plan is formed by choosing concrete cloud service providers for each abstract SaaS and abstract IaaS in the composition schema. Since the research focuses on the selection of composition plans based solely on QoS attributes, we assume that existing composition techniques for matching functional attributes will be used, e.g., [5] to generate composition schema.

A *Composition Schema* (or *Abstract Composite Service*) is constructed using *abstract SaaS* and *abstract IaaS*, and combined according to a set of *composition patterns*. There are four *Composition Patterns* according to the data-flow and control-flow: *S*equential Pattern (SP), *P*arallel Pattern (PP), *O*ptional Pattern (OP) and *L*oop Pattern (LP) [12]. To simplify the discussion, we initially assume that all the abstract composite services we deal with are acyclic. If an abstract composite service contains cycles (LP), a technique [6] for unfolding it into an acyclic composition schema will be applied. Composition schema is represented using Directed Acyclic Graph (DAG). Ovals denote abstract SaaS. Rectangles denote abstract IaaS. Arcs among nodes (i.e., ovals and rectangles) represent the control flow and data flow. To differentiate PP from CP, we use normal lines to represent PP and dotted lines to represent CP. A composition schema may have multiple *Execution Paths*[6] if the schema contains CP patterns. For example, in the motivating scenario, the composition schema for the tenure requests is presented in Fig. 3. T_1, T_2, T_3 are abstract SaaSs. CPU_i denotes the computation request for the output data from T_i. For example, the composite application

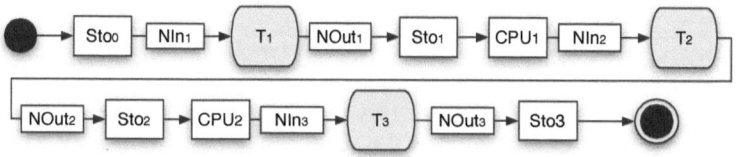

Fig. 3. Composition schema for University A

needs CPUs after receives output data from T_1. These CPUs adapt the output data to the input of T_2. Sto_i denotes the storage request for the intermediate data $NOut)i$. All the intermediate data are stored in case someone will appeal the decisions in the following years. NIn_i denotes the network resources for inputs, $NOut_i$ represents the network resources for outputs.

3.2   QoS Model

To differentiate composition plans during selection, their non-functional properties need to be considered. For this purpose, we adopt a discrete QoS model that is applicable to all the SaaS and IaaS. Without loss of generality, we only consider the QoS attributes listed as follows. Although the adopted QoS models have a limited number of attributes, they are extensible and new QoS attributes can be added. We assume IaaS are homogeneous. One unit of IaaS, i.e., *CPU, network* or *storage*, possess the same resources.

QoS Model for Elementary Services. Three QoS attributes are considered for component services: throughput, response time, and cost.

- Throughput. Given an SaaS provider SP, the throughput of its SaaS $q_{sr}(SP)$ is the number of requests the SaaS provider is able to process per second. Given an IaaS provider IP, the service rate of its IaaS $\overrightarrow{q_{sr}(IP)} = [q_{sr}^{CPU}(IP), q_{sr}^{Net}(IP), q_{sr}^{Sto}(IP)]$ is a three-attribute vector, where $q_{sr}^{CPU}(IP)$ ($q_{sr}^{Net}(IP)$, $q_{sr}^{Sto}(IP)$) represents the number of CPU (network, storage) requests the IaaS provider is able to process per second.
- Response time. Given an SaaS provider SP, the response time of its SaaS $q_{rt}(SP)$ measures the expected delay in seconds between the moment when a request is sent and the moment when the results are received. Given an IaaS provider IP, the capability of its IaaS $\overrightarrow{q_{cap}(IP)} = [q_{cap}^{CPU}(IP), q_{cap}^{Net}(IP), q_{cap}^{Sto}(IP)]$ is a three-attribute vector, where $q_{cap}^{CPU}(IP)$ ($q_{cap}^{Net}(IP)$, $q_{cap}^{Sto}(IP)$) is the number of CPU (network, storage) units used for processing a computation (data transfer, storage) request. For CPU request, the response time to adapt the output data from task t_i is calculated as: $q_{rt}^{CPU}(t_i) = \frac{CPU_i}{q_{cap}^{CPU}(IP)}$. For network request, the response time of transferring input data for task t_i is denoted as: $q_{rt}^{IN}(t_i) = \frac{NIn_i}{q_{cap}^{Net}(IP)}$. The response time of transferring output

QoS Attribute	Aggregation Functions
Throughput (q_{sr})	$q_{sr}(aCS) = min(q_{sr}(SP_1), q_{sr}(SP_2), \ldots, q_{sr}(SP_n), q_{sr}^{CPU}(IP), q_{sr}^{Net}(IP), q_{sr}^{Sto}(IP))$
Response time (q_{rt})	$q_{rt}(aCS) = CPA(aCS)$
Cost (q_{cost})	$q_{cost}(aCS) = \sum_{i=0}^{n}(q_{cost}(SP_i) + q_{cost}^{CPU}(t_i) + q_{cost}^{IN}(t_i) + q_{cost}^{OUT}(t_i) + q_{cost}^{Sto}(Sto_i)) \cdot q_{sr}(aCS)$

Fig. 4. Aggregation functions for computing the QoS of a composite service

data for task t_i is denoted as: $q_{rt}^{OUT}(t_i) = \frac{NOut_i}{q_{cap}^{Net}(IP)}$. For storage request, no response time is needed to compute, since we do not consider setup time or other time for storage resources in this research.

- Cost. Given an SaaS provider, the execution cost $q_{cost}(SP)$ is the fee that a customer needs to pay for a single request. If the SaaS provider agrees to supply SaaS at service rate $q_{sr}(SP)$. The total execution cost is computed using the expression: $cost = q_{sr}(SP) \cdot q_{cost}(SP)$. Given an IaaS provider IP, the cost for using unit IaaS for one second is denoted as a three-attribute vector $\overrightarrow{q_{cost}(IP)} = [q_{cost}^{CPU}(IP), q_{cost}^{Net}(IP), q_{cost}^{Sto}(IP)]$, where $q_{cost}^{CPU}(IP)$, $q_{cost}^{Net}(IP)$ and $q_{cost}^{Sto}(IP)$ are the price for using unit CPU IaaS, unit network IaaS and unit storage IaaS for one second correspondingly. For CPU request, the cost of computing output data from task t_i is represented as: $q_{cost}^{CPU}(t_i) = q_{cost}^{CPU}(IP) \cdot q_{cap}^{CPU}(IP) \cdot q_{rt}^{CPU}(t_i)$. The cost to transfer input data for task t_i is calculated using: $q_{cost}^{IN}(t_i) = q_{cost}^{Net}(IP) \cdot q_{cap}^{Net}(IP) \cdot q_{rt}^{IN}(t_i)$. The cost to transfer output data for task t_i can be calculated as: $q_{cost}^{OUT}(t_i) = q_{cost}^{Net}(IP) \cdot q_{cap}^{Net}(IP) \cdot q_{rt}^{OUT}(t_i)$. The cost to store intermediate data Sto_i is computed as: $q_{cost}^{STO}(Sto_i) = q_{cost}^{Sto}(IP) \cdot Sto_i \cdot time$, where $time$ denotes the seconds the intermediate data should be stored.

QoS Model for Composite Services. The quality criteria defined above are in the context of elementary cloud services. Aggregation functions are used to compute the QoS of the composite service. Fig. 4 presents these aggregation functions:

- Throughput. The throughput of a composite service denotes the number of requests it serves per second. For an abstract composite service aCS, the throughput $q_{sr}(aCS)$ is the minimal service rate of the selected SaaS providers $q_{sr}(SP)$ and the IaaS provider $q_{sr}(IP)$.
- Response time. The response time $q_{rt}(aCS)$ of an abstract composite service aCS is computed using the Critical Path Algorithm (CPA) [13]. Specifically, the CPA is applied to the execution path $Path(aCS)$ of the abstract composite service aCS. The critical path is a path from the initial node to the final node which has the longest total sum of weights labeling its nodes. In the case at hand, a node corresponds to an abstract SaaS or IaaS in an execution path, and its weight is the response time of the SaaS or IaaS.
- Cost. The cost of an abstract service is the sum of execution cost of all the selected SaaS and IaaS.

3.3   Problem Definition

Based on the analysis above, this section presents the general definition of the cloud service composition problem. Suppose an end user has a set of requests during a long period. Each request demands the same execution path (denoted as $Path = \{Sto_0, NIn_1, t_1, NOut_1, Sto_1, CPU_1, NIn_2, t_2, NOut_2, Sto_2, CPU_2,$ $\ldots, NIn_{n_j}, t_{n_j}, NOut_{n_j}, Sto_n\}$). The end user represents its QoS preferences by determining the weights in the score function during a long period. We denote the QoS requirements of the end user as: $W(Path) = \{W(1), W(2), W(3), \ldots, W(t)\}$. Each tuple $W(t)$ represents the weights for different QoS attributes for the composite service at period $period_t$. To illustrate the composition problem, we use the three QoS attributes for saaS discussed earlier, other QoS attributes can be used instead without any fundamental changes. The QoS dimensions are numbered from 1 to 3, with 1 = throughput, 2 = response time and 3 = cost. Hence, Each $W(t)$ is further denoted as a matrix: $W(t) = [w_1(t), w_2(t), w_3(t)]$, where $w_a(t)$ denotes the weight of QoS attribute a for the composite service at period $period_t$.

For task T_i, a set of k_i candidate SaaS providers can be used to implement the task: $SP_i = \{SP_i(1), SP_i(2), \ldots, SP_i(k_i)\}$. A set of p_p candidate IaaS providers supply IaaS to composite services: $SP_0 = SP_0(1), SP_0(2), \ldots, SP_0(p_p)\}$. A candidate composition plan (denoted as $Plan[SP_0(k_0), SP_1(k_1), SP_2(k_2), \ldots, SP_n(k_n)])$) is formed by selecting certain SaaS providers and IaaS providers for an end user. In the composition plan, the composite service is supported by the IaaS provider $SP_0(k_0)$. Task T_i is implemented by SaaS provider $SP_i(k_i)$. The QoS values for a composition plan $Plan$ is denoted as: $q(plan) = \{q(1), q(2), q(3), \ldots, q(t)\}$. Each tuple $(q(t))$ is further denoted as a matrix: $[q_1^0(t), q_1^1(t), \ldots, q_1^i(t), q_2^0(t), q_2^1(t), \ldots, q_2^i(t), q_3^0(t), q_3^1(t), \ldots, q_3^i(t)]$, where $q_a^i(t)$ denotes the advertising QoS value of attribute a for the abstract SaaS T_i at period $period_t$. Each composite plan has an aggregated QoS values computed using the aggregation functions stated above. These values are then scaled using the SAW method in [6] to a real number in $[0, 1]$. $q_a^t(Plan)$ denotes the scaled value of QoS attribute a for the composition plan at period $period_t$. Each composition plan is associated with a "score" from the end user's perspective. A commonly used score function is the weighted sum of QoS values of the composite service:

$$S^t(Plan) = w_1(t) \cdot q_1^t(Plan) + w_2(t) \cdot q_2^t(Plan) + w_3(t) \cdot q_3^t(Plan), \qquad (1)$$

The score function over the long period is then represented as: $S(Plan) = \int_1^t s^t(Plan)dt$. The composition problem is to find an optimal composition plan, which has the maximal score value.

4   ID-Based Composition Approach

This section first presents the economic model for end users. Influence diagram approach is then detailed. The proposed composition approach is presented at the end of this section.

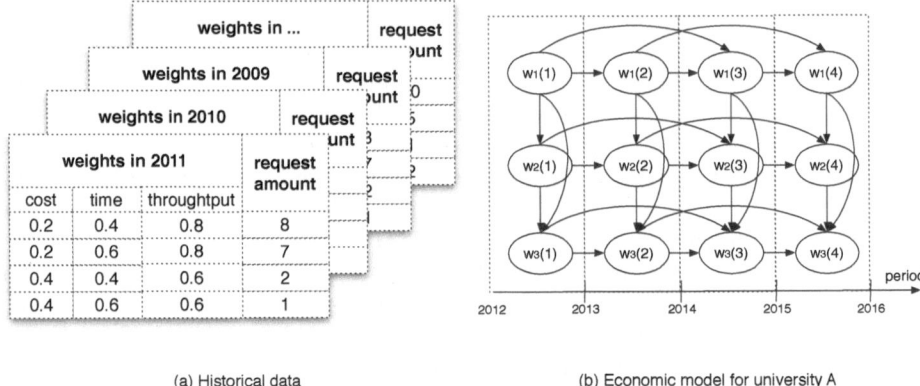

(a) Historical data   (b) Economic model for university A

Fig. 5. Economic model: an example

4.1   Cloud Economic Model

When the composition system makes decisions on which concrete SaaS providers and IaaS providers should be selected for the end user, it has no idea about how will the ultimate composite service behave during a long period. To enable long-term cloud service composition, economic models are needed to predict the long-term preferences of the end users. An economic model is defined as "a theoretical construct that represents economic processes by a set of variables and a set of logical and quantitative relationships between them. "[14].

We adopt Bayesian Networks (BN) [15] to represent the economic model for the end users. BN is a probabilistic graphical model that represents a set of random variables and their conditional dependency using a directed acyclic graph. A BN consists of a set of random variables as nodes which are connected through directed links (arcs). Each node has a conditional probability table that quantifies the effects the parents have on the nodes. If we represent the weights at different periods as nodes in a BN, we can then leverage the network as a means to represent the economic model for the end users.

For end users, we make the assumption that all the requests, initialised at the same period, have the score function with the same weights. However, requests initialised at different periods have different score functions. For example, Fig. 5 shows the economic model of university A in the tenure example. This economic model is constructed based on historical data (Fig. 5(a)) from university A. Fig. 5(a) shows the QoS preferences of university A for the last several years. The weight for each QoS attribute is a real number between 0 and 1. The larger the weight the more important is the corresponding QoS attribute to university A. The last column represents the number of tenure requests that have the preferences. Based on these historical data, we construct the economic model for university A as shown in Fig. 5(b). $w_a(t), a = 1, 2$ denotes the weight for QoS attribute a at period $period_t$. In the same period $period_t$, the weights have conditional probability relationship with each other, i.e., $w_2(t)$ depends on the value of $w_1(t)$. For different periods, a weight $w_a(t)$ at period $period_t$ would depend on the weights in the previous periods, i.e., $w_a(1)$, $w_a(2)$, ..., $w_a(t-1)$. However, this research only considers two previous weights, since it is reasonable to assume that the weights at the most recent periods will have more affection on the weights at present. Hence, as shown in Fig. 5(a), $w_a(t)$ depends on the values of $w_a(t-1)$ and $w_a(t-2)$.

4.2   Influence Diagram Problem

Based on the economic models for the end users, we adopt *Influence Diagram* to represent and solve the cloud service composition problem. Influence diagrams (IDs) [9] are graphical models for representing and solving complex decision-making problems based on uncertain information. IDs are directed acyclic graphs that is seen as BN augmented with decision and value nodes.

An ID is a directed acyclic graph (N, A): $N = D \cup C \cup U$. D correspond to a set of decision variables under the control of the decision maker. C is the set of chance nodes correspond to random variables. U is a set of utility nodes that represent the objective functions of the model. A is the set of directed arcs between the nodes. Arcs pointing to a decision node indicate what information will be known to the decision maker at the time the decision is made. Arcs to a chance node indicate which variables condition the probability distribution for the associated random variables. Arcs to a utility node indicate which variables condition the associated expected utility. Each node in an ID is associated with a frame of data. For a chance node x, this data includes the outcome space of x, Ω_x, and the conditional probability distribution of x, π_x. For each decision node d, this data includes the alternatives of the associated decision variable, Ω_d. Finally, the data frame for utility node r contains the conditional expected value of r conditioned on the predecessors of r. The conditional expectation of r is actually a deterministic function of the conditioning variables: $U[r|C(r)] = g(C(r))$. The outcome space of r is Ω_r. To solve an ID problem (or to evaluate an ID problem) is to find the maximal utility value and the decision values at the time when the utility values are maximised.

Regarding cloud service composition problem stated above, we model cloud service composition problem to an ID problem as follows. We represent the weights from end users and the advertising QoS values from cloud providers as chance nodes in an ID.The QoS values from cloud service providers have conditional probabilistic relationship. All the selection decisions on abstract SaaS and IaaS are represented as decision nodes in the ID. Utility nodes represent the score of a composition plan. For example, Fig. 6 shows the influence diagram representation for the tenure example. In Fig. 6, node $q_a^i(t)$ in denotes the advertising value of QoS attribute a for task T_i at period $period_t$. $wq_a(t)$ denotes the weighted score for QoS attribute a at period $period_t$. $S(t) = wq_1(t) + wq_2(t) + wq_3(t)$, denotes the score for the composition plan at period $period_t$, which can be computed using Equ. 1. $S_{total} = S(1) + S(2) + S(3)$, denotes the total score

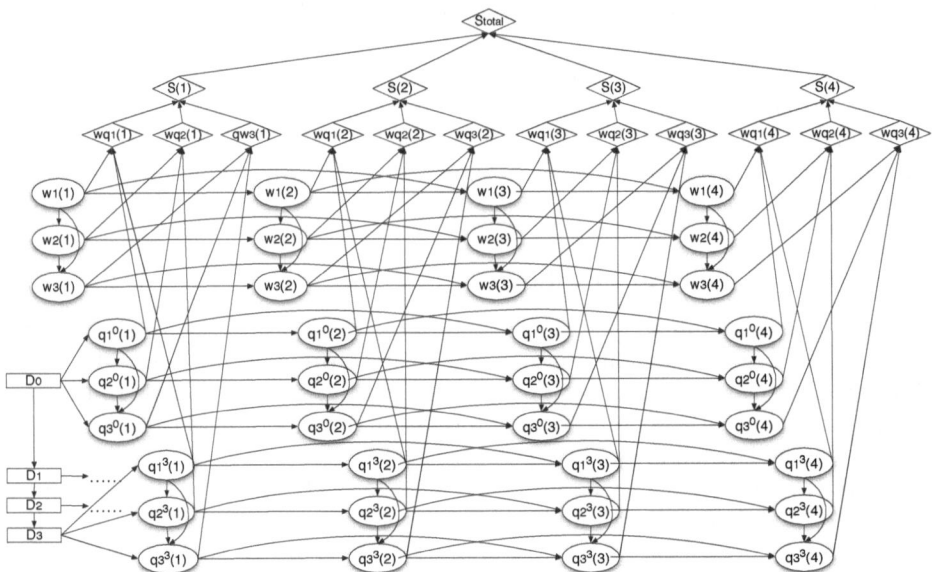

Fig. 6. Influence diagram for the tenure example when one QoS attribute is considered

for this ID. The separable nature of the utility function is represented in the structure of the graph using these multiple utility nodes. In the cloud service composition problem, there are two kinds of utility nodes. A *super utility node* is either a sum node or product node (e.g., $S(1)$, $S(2)$, S_{total}), and a *non-super utility node* is any other utility node (e.g., $wq_1(1)$, $wq_2(1)$). There is exactly one utility node, the *terminal utility node* (e.g., S_{total}), which has no successors in an ID. This represents the objective function for the model. Super utility nodes can only have utility nodes (either super or non-super) as conditional predecessors. Non-super utility nodes, on the other hand, can only have chance and decision nodes as conditional predecessors.

4.3   Dynamic Programming Algorithm

ID problems can be solved using two types of solutions [16]: A brute force solution is first transfer the ID to the corresponding decision tree, then compute all the possible scenarios with their probability and finally obtains the optimal decision variables that maximise the utility value. Another type of solution is to iteratively reduce the diagram using influence diagram reductions [17]. Considering the properties of cloud service composition, we propose a dynamic programming reduction algorithm to solve the ID problem.

Solving an ID problem using reductions involves applying a sequence of maximization and expectation operators to the utility function. In the influence diagram, these operators correspond to remove decision and chance nodes at the

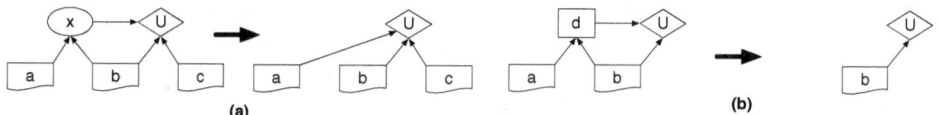

Fig. 7. Influence diagram reductions

utility node by performing maximizations or expectations. The special properties of the maximization and expectation operators when applied to separable functions are foundation of the proposed dynamic programming algorithm. They allow maximizations and expectations to be performed over an addend or factor in the utility function instead of over the entire utility function. In those cases, only a subspace of the utility function needs to be examined. This may significantly reduce the dimensionality of the operations necessary to solve a decision problem.

Two main reductions to solve an ID problem are: removing a chance node by expectation and removing a decision node by maximization. Removal of a chance node by expectation, as in Fig. 7(a), can be performed whenever the only successor of a chance node is the utility node. In the mathematics this corresponds to: $Utility[U|a, b, c] \leftarrow Utility_{\Omega_x}[Utility[U|x, b, c]|a, b]$. Note that in this case, the utility node U inherits the predecessors of chance node x. The removal of a decision node by maximization, as in Fig. 7(b), can be performed whenever the decision node has the utility node as its only successor and all conditional predecessors of that utility node, other than the decision node, are informational predecessors of the decision node. In the mathematics, decision node removal corresponds to: $Utility[U|b] \leftarrow max_d\{Utility\ [U|b, d]\}$ and $d^* = argmax_d\{Utility[U|b, d]\}$. Note that the utility node U does not inherit any predecessors of d as a result of this operation. Consider the motivating example in Fig. 6, the cloud service composition problem can always be solved by reducing the chance nodes and decision nodes in the following sequence: $q_a^i(t)$, $w_a(t)$, D_i. Nodes $q_a^i(t)$ can be removed using expectation operators as in Fig. 7(a). Nodes D_i can be removed using maximisation operators as in Fig. 7(b). Interested readers can refer to [17] for the details of other basic reductions of ID: e.g., arc reversal using Bayes theorem, summing a variable out of the joint.

Algorithm. 1 presents the dynamic programming algorithm to solve the composition problem as an ID problem. The algorithm will continue reducing nodes from the ID until there is only one terminal utility node left (line 2). If two utility nodes r_1 and r_2 have the same successor, a super value node r, and $C(r_1)$ is contained in $C(r_2)$, then removing r_1 and r_2 (if they are the only predecessors of r, or merging r_1 and r_2, into new value node r' if they are not) will not increase the size of any operation necessary to solve the influence diagram and so we should remove them (line 3:4). After each step of the algorithm (line 6:11), the net change in total number of nodes in the diagram will be at least one less. The algorithm always reduces an influence diagram to the terminal value node thus producing the optimal policy and maximum expected value for the problem.

Algorithm 1. Dynamic programming approach to evaluate ID
_____

1: $ID \leftarrow$ The influence diagram with the terminal utility node U
2: **while** $C(U) \neq \emptyset$ **do**
3:     **if** there is removable utility nodes **then**
4:         remove all the necessary utility nodes
5:     **else**
6:         **if** there is a removable decision node d **then**
7:             remove d and the necessary utility nodes
8:         **else**
9:             there must be a removable chance node x
10:            remove x and the necessary utility nodes
11:        **end if**
12:    **end if**
13: **end while**
_____

5   Experiments and Results

We conduct a set of experiments to assess the performance of the proposed approach. We use the tenure scenario as our testing environment to setup the experiment parameters. We run our experiments on a Macbook Pro with 2.2 GHz Intel Core i7 processor and 4G Ram under Mac OS X 10.7.3. Since there is not any sizable cloud service test case that is in the tenure application domain and that can be used for experimentation purposes, we focus on evaluating the proposed approach using synthetic cloud services.

We compare the proposed approach with the brute force ID approach. The brute force approach is to generate all the possible candidate composition plans, consider all the possible scenarios for each plan regarding the economic models and compute the score and the probability for each scenario (i.e., transfer ID to a corresponding decision tree). The optimal composition plan is the one that has the maximal weighted sum score. We implement the brute force approach in Java. The dynamic programming approach is implemented using Elvira [18] and Java. Computation times are measured in experiments to compare the two approaches. In this process, the number of alternatives for each chance node and decision node is varied from 2 to 10 with the step of 1 and the length of the considered periods is varied from 2 to 5 with steps of 1. All experiments are conducted 5 times and the average results are computed.

Fig. 8 presents the computation time when the number of alternatives of the decision nodes is varied from 2 to 10. For these experiments, we set the other parameters as follows: the number of the decision nodes is set to be 4. The number of alternatives of chance nodes ($\Omega_{w_a(t)}$ and $\Omega_{q_a^i(t)}$) is set to be 2. This means there are two options for all the chance nodes in the ID. The considered period is set to be $t = 2$, i.e., we consider the tenure example for the period during 2012 and 2013. And the number of QoS attributes is set to be 3. From Fig. 8, we can see that both approaches will have polynomial time complexity. But the dynamic programming has better performance than the brute force approach.

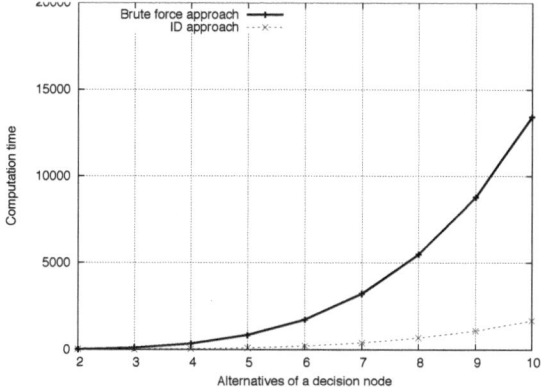

Fig. 8. Computation time VS. Ω_d

When the number of alternatives of the decision nodes is small (i.e., 2), both approaches have similar computation time. When the number of alternatives becomes larger, the dynamic programming approach behaves much better than the brute force approach.

Fig. 9 presents the computation time when the number of alternatives of the chance nodes is varied from 2 to 10. For these experiments, we set the other parameters as follows: the number of the decision nodes is set to be 4. The number of alternatives of decision nodes (D_i) is set to be 4. This means there are four options for all the decision nodes in the ID. The considered period is set to be $t = 2$, i.e., we consider the tenure example for the period during 2012 and 2013. And the number of QoS attributes is set to be 3. From Fig. 9, we can see that both approaches will have polynomial time complexity. But the dynamic programming approach behaves much better than the brute force approach.

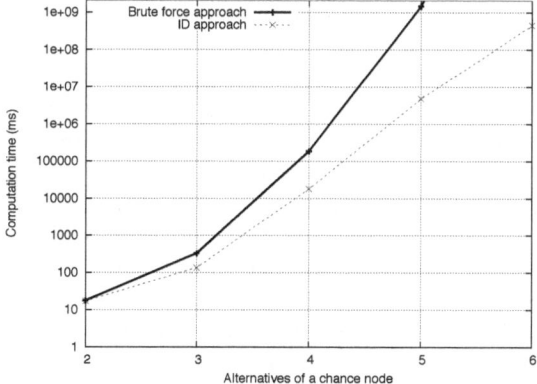

Fig. 9. Computation time VS. Ω_c

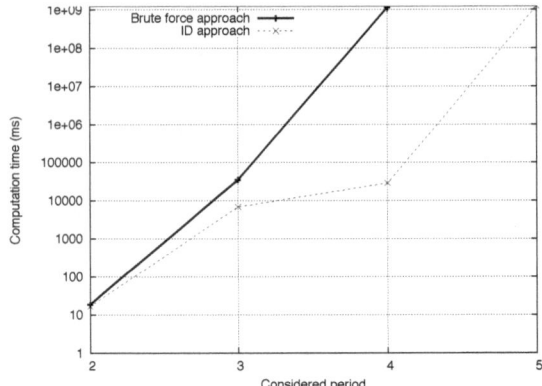

Fig. 10. Computation time VS. t

Fig. 10 presents the computation time when the considered period is varied from 2 to 5. For these experiments, we set the other parameters as follows: the number of the decision nodes is set to be 4. The number of alternatives of decision nodes (D_i) is set to be 4. The number of alternatives of chance nodes ($\Omega_{w_a(t)}$ and $\Omega_{q_a^i(t)}$) is set to be 2. This means there are two options for all the decision nodes and chance nodes in the ID. And the number of QoS attributes is set to be 3. From Fig. 10, we can see that both approaches will have exponential time complexity. When the considered period is short (i.e., 2 years or 3 years), both approaches have similar computation time. When the consider period becomes longer, the dynamic programming approach behaves much better than the brute force approach.

6   Related Work

Service composition is an active research area in service-oriented computing [5]. During the last decade, service composition problem can be categorized into two groups. One group focuses on the functional composability among component services. The other group aims to make optimal decisions to select the best component services based on non-functional properties (QoS).

Functional-driven service composition approaches typically adopt semantic descriptions of services. Examples of automatic approaches include Policy-based approach proposed by [19] and composability model driven approach proposed by [5]. Other functional-driven composition approaches use AI planning methods. Most of them [20] assume that each service is an action which alters the state of the world as a result of its execution. The inputs and outputs parameters of a service act as preconditions and effects in the planning context. Users only need to specify the inputs and the outputs of the desired composite service, a plan (or a composite service) would automatically generated by the AI planners.

Functional-driven service composition approaches mostly do not attempt to find an optimal solution but only to find a solution. However, the non-functional properties (QoS) of resulting composite service is a determinant factor to ensure customer satisfaction. Different users may have different requirements and preferences regarding QoS. Therefore, QoS-aware composition approaches are needed. QoS-aware service composition problem is usually modelled as a Multiple Criteria Decision Making [6] problem. The most popular approaches include integer linear programming and genetic algorithms. An Integer Linear Program (ILP) consists of a set of variables, a set of linear constraints and a linear objective function. After having translated the composition problem into this formalism, specific solver software such as LPSolve [21] can be used. [22] and [23] use Genetic Algorithms (GA) for service composition. Individuals of the population correspond to different composition solutions, their genes to the abstract component services and the possible gene values to the available real services. While GAs do not guarantee to find the optimal solution, they can be more efficient than ILP-based methods (which have exponential worst-case time complexity).

Most of the existing composition approaches are not well suited for cloud environment [23]. They usually consider the qualities at the time of the composition [5]. The proposed composition approach consider the problem from a long-term perspective.

7 Conclusion

This paper proposes a cloud service composition approach to aid end users selecting and composing SaaS providers and IaaS providers in the cloud environment. Compared to traditional service composition framework in SOC, the proposed approach considers service composition from a long-term perspective. Cloud economic models for both end users and cloud service providers are leveraged during the composition. Specially, an influence diagram approach is adopted to solve cloud service composition problems. In future work, discrete QoS model will be extended to continuous model, where each chance node in an ID has infinite alternatives. Besides, machine learning algorithms will be researched on refining the economic model for both end users and cloud service providers to improve the performance.

References

1. Motahari-Nezhad, H., Stephenson, B., Singhal, S.: Outsourcing business to cloud computing services: Opportunities and challenges. IEEE Internet Computing (2009)
2. Youseff, L., Butrico, M., Da Silva, D.: Toward a unified ontology of cloud computing. In: Grid Computing Environments Workshop (2009)
3. Yu, Q., Liu, X., Bouguettaya, A., Medjahed, B.: Deploying and managing web services: issues, solutions, and directions. The VLDB Journal 17(3), 537–572 (2008)
4. Armbrust, M., Fox, A., Griffith, R., Joseph, A., Katz, R., Konwinski, A., Lee, G., Patterson, D., Rabkin, A., Stoica, I., et al.: Above the clouds: A berkeley view of cloud computing. EECS Department, University of California, Berkeley, Tech. Rep. UCB/EECS-2009-28 (2009)

5. Medjahed, B., Bouguettaya, A., Elmagarmid, A.: Composing web services on the semantic web. The VLDB Journal 12(4), 333–351 (2003)
6. Zeng, L., Benatallah, B., Ngu, A., Dumas, M., Kalagnanam, J., Chang, H.: QoS-aware middleware for web services composition. IEEE Transactions on Software Engineering 30(5), 311–327 (2004)
7. Dash, D., Kantere, V., Ailamaki, A.: An economic model for self-tuned cloud caching. In: IEEE 25th International Conference on Data Engineering, pp. 1687–1693 (2009)
8. Kantere, V., Dash, D., Francois, G., Kyriakopoulou, S., Ailamaki, A.: Optimal Service Pricing for a Cloud Cache. IEEE Transactions on Knowledge and Data Engineering (2011)
9. Shachter, R.: Probabilistic inference and influence diagrams. Operations Research, 589–604 (1988)
10. Gelmon, S., Agre-Kippenhan, S.: Promotion, tenure and the engaged scholar. AAHE Bulletin 54(5), 7–11 (2002)
11. Milanovic, N., Malek, M.: Current solutions for web service composition. IEEE Internet Computing, 51–59 (2004)
12. Wu, B., Chi, C., Chen, Z., Gu, M., Sun, J.: Workflow-based resource allocation to optimize overall performance of composite services. Future Generation Computer Systems 25(3), 199–212 (2009)
13. Pinedo, M.: Scheduling: theory, algorithms, and systems. Springer (2012)
14. Baumol, W., Blinder, A.: Economics: principles and policy. South-Western Pub. (2011)
15. Jensen, F.: An introduction to Bayesian networks, vol. 74. UCL Press, London (1996)
16. Shachter, R.: Evaluating influence diagrams. Operations Research 34(6), 871–882 (1986)
17. Tatman, J., Shachter, R.: Dynamic programming and influence diagrams. IEEE Transactions on Systems, Man and Cybernetics 20(2), 365–379 (1990)
18. Elvira, a Java implementation of influence diagram (2005), http://www.ia.uned.es/~elvira
19. Chun, S.A., Atluri, V., Adam, N.R.: Using semantics for policy-based web service composition. Distributed and Parallel Databases 18(1), 37–64 (2005)
20. Wu, D., Parsia, B., Sirin, E., Hendler, J., Nau, D.: Automating DAML-S Web Services Composition Using SHOP2, p. 195 (2003)
21. Berkelaar, M., Eikland, K., Notebaert, P., et al.: lpsolve: Open source (mixed-integer) linear programming system. Eindhoven U. of Technology (2004)
22. Canfora, G., Di Penta, M., Esposito, R., Villani, M.: An approach for QoS-aware service composition based on genetic algorithms. In: Proceedings of the 2005 Conference on Genetic and Evolutionary Computation, pp. 1069–1075 (2005)
23. Ye, Z., Zhou, X., Bouguettaya, A.: Genetic Algorithm Based QoS-Aware Service Compositions in Cloud Computing. In: Yu, J.X., Kim, M.H., Unland, R. (eds.) DASFAA 2011, Part II. LNCS, vol. 6588, pp. 321–334. Springer, Heidelberg (2011)

Cloud Service Selection
Based on Variability Modeling

Erik Wittern[1], Jörn Kuhlenkamp[1], and Michael Menzel[2]

[1] eOrganization Research Group, Karlsruhe Institute of Technology (KIT)
Englerstr. 11, 76131 Karlsruhe, Germany
{Erik.Wittern,Joern.Kuhlenkamp}@kit.edu
http://www.eorganization.de
[2] Research Center for Information Technology
Karlsruhe Institute of Technology (KIT)
Menzel@fzi.de

Abstract. The selection among Cloud services is a recent problem in research and practice. The diversity of decision-relevant criteria, configurability of Cloud services and the need to involve human decision-makers require holistic support through models, methodologies and tools. Existing Cloud service selection approaches do not address all stated difficulties at the same time. We present an approach to capture capabilities of Cloud services and requirements using variability modeling. We use *Cloud feature models* (CFMs) as a representation mechanism and describe how they are utilized for requirements elicitation and filtering within a presented *Cloud service selection process* (CSSP) that includes human decision-makers. Filtering produces a reduced number of valid Cloud service configurations that can be further assessed with current multi-criteria decision making-based selection approaches. We present software tools that we use to demonstrate the applicability of our approach in a use case about selecting among Cloud storage services.

Keywords: Cloud service selection, variability modeling, feature modeling, decision-making.

1 Introduction

Since the dawn of service computing, the problem of how to select software services is omnipresent for IT decision-makers. Service selection, typically, builds upon a) the representation of decision-relevant capabilities of the *candidates* to select among and b) the representation of the *requirements* and *preferences* of the decision-maker (e.g. a person, institution or automated agent). Both representations are matched to determine the candidate that best fulfills the decision-maker's needs. For example, in service-oriented computing, the selection of *Web services* has been addressed similarly: In policy matchmaking, policies capture capabilities and requirements towards Web services and are matched to determine a service to fulfill the request, e.g., in [17].

C. Liu et al. (Eds.): ICSOC 2012, LNCS 7636, pp. 127–141, 2012.
© Springer-Verlag Berlin Heidelberg 2012

Recently, the growing number of *Cloud services* raises the need for dedicated representation of their capabilities as well as requirements and preferences towards them and for corresponding selection methods. Such approaches need to consider the specifics of selecting Cloud services: Cloud services typically hold state, for example, a Cloud storage service persists user data. Because of this and because Cloud service interfaces are not standardized, exchanging them is costly. Thus, Cloud service selection is a relatively long-lasting decision, compared, for example, with Web service selection. It must include strategic considerations like vendor lock-in or legal aspects that require involvement of human decision-makers. Cloud services, especially Infrastructure as a Service, frequently feature *configurability*: consumers can choose among many options on how to consume the service. For example, Amazon's *simple storage solution (S3)* allows consumers to define a preferred geographical location for the servers or to use different pricing schemes[1]. Overall, representations to support Cloud service selection need to be capable of representing the diverse decision-relevant aspects, must support integration of human decision-makers and must reflect Cloud services' configurability.

In this paper, we contribute to Cloud service selection in two ways: First, we present an approach to improve the way that Cloud service capabilities and consumer requirements towards them are represented. We introduce *Cloud feature modeling*, based on variability modeling, to address the presented challenges of representing Cloud services. Second, utilizing *Cloud feature models (CFMs)*, we present a *Cloud service selection process (CSSP)* as a methodology for decision-making. It includes narrowing down the number of service candidates based on stated requirements. Enabling automated support for delimiting the number of candidates is required to keep following decision phases manageable. The process also encompasses selection based on preferences that can make use of previously introduced multi-criteria decision making approaches, e.g. [10].

The remainder of this paper is structured as follows: Section 2 discusses related work from the area of Cloud service selection. Section 3 introduces our approach to model the Cloud service selection problem with Cloud feature modeling. We provide a formalization of the introduced modeling elements to clearly define their usage. Section 4 presents our CSSP, addressing the involved roles and activities. Section 5 presents our prototypical implementation of a modeling tool supporting our approach and discusses a use case to illustrate the approach's applicability. Finally, Section 6 discusses our work and gives an outlook on future research.

2   Related Work

Cloud service selection has recently been addressed in numerous publications: in [12], the authors propose a mechanism to automatically select Cloud storage services. Capabilities of candidate services are expressed in an XML schema and matched with requirements. The usage of *multi-criteria decision making*

---

[1] http://aws.amazon.com/de/ec2/

(MCDM) approaches for the selection of Cloud services has been proposed in multiple papers. In [13], the authors use a combination of a revised wide-band Delphi method to weight attributes and simple additive weighting to determine candidate ranking. In [7] and [10], the authors utilize Analytical Hierarchy Process (AHP) or Analytical Network Process (ANP) to support the selection. The presented hierarchies are designed to address aspects relevant to specific classes of Cloud services, i.e., IaaS, PaaS and SaaS. In [11], the authors present an overview of existing Cloud service selection approaches. They formalize the Cloud service selection problem and propose an approach to determine the similarities between a requirement vector and all candidates' capability vectors to recommend the most suitable candidate.

The presented approaches face certain limitations that we address in this paper. [12] omit support for XML definitions making the approach rather arduous to human decision-makers. It is commonly assumed, e.g. in [13,9,10,7], that representations of the service candidates to choose from are provided as input for the presented MCDM approaches. However, it is not discussed how to derive these representations. In contrast, we present a modeling approach and corresponding methodology to create such representations. The *configurability* that today's Cloud services offer is neglected in existing approaches that focus only on a handful of candidates. By considering configurability, we provide decision-makers with a decision-basis that better reflects actual choices. Many MCDM approaches also base their selection recommendation on preferences only, e.g. [7,10]. In contrast, we consider both requirements and preferences in our CSSP.

Overall, our approach addresses modeling of Cloud service candidates and a holistic approach for selecting among them - both aspects have not yet been addressed in literature.

3   Modeling the Cloud Service Selection Problem

We propose to utilize *variability modeling* as a foundation to model decision-relevant criteria of Cloud services. Variability modeling approaches, such as *feature modeling* [3], are commonly used to capture the commonalities and differences in system families. They enable to represent multiple *configurations* of a system in a single model. Within this section, we introduce our Cloud feature modeling approach.

3.1   Feature Modeling Basics

Our modeling approach builds upon *extended feature modeling* [3,2] to represent the commonalities and differences of Cloud services. We assume the definition of *feature* as a system property that is relevant to some stakeholder, be it a functional or non-functional property of the system [5]. Following this definition, we consider features to be on the right level of abstraction to capture aspects of value for service consumers [15] - and thus also to capture the diverse aspects relevant in Cloud service selection.

As a basis to describe our adaptations, we formalize feature modeling as follows: A *Feature Model (FM)* is represented by a directed graph $G = (V, E)$

with the set of vertices V representing features and the set of edges E representing relationships between features. Each FM contains a single root feature $r \in V$. A relationship $e = \{init(e), ter(e)\}$ is described by the initial vertex $init(e) \in V$ and the terminal vertex $ter(e) \in V$. We distinguish between two types of relationships [8]: In *decomposition relationships* $E^{de} \subseteq E$, we refer to $init(e)$ as p_e and *parent feature* and to $ter(e)$ as c_e and *child feature*. The four sets $E^{mandatory}$, $E^{optional}$, E^{XOR}, $E^{OR} \subseteq E^{de}$ represent relationships that decompose features hierarchically. *Cross-tree relationships* $E^{cr} \subseteq E$ consist of the two sets $E^{requires}$, $E^{excludes} \subseteq E^{cr}$. They restrict the number of configurations represented by a FM. A *configuration* is a valid selection of features from a FM [2] that fulfills all specified relationships (e.g., a mandatory feature needs to be contained in each configuration where its parent feature is also contained). A feature is described by a number of *feature attributes* (FAs). We use the notation $v_i.x$ to refer to the feature attribute x of feature v_i. We capture FAs in a quantitative manner [3]. A quantitative approach enables automatic analysis upon FMs and to capture infinite domains in a clear and concise way [6]. According to [2] no consensus on a notation on FAs exists, but it is agreed on that FAs at least comprise of the basic building blocks *name*, *domain* and *value*. We refer to the basic building blocks by $name(v_i.x)$, $dom(v_i.x)$ and $val(v_i.x)$.

3.2   Cloud Feature Modeling

Despite the described potential of FMs for Cloud service selection (i.e. level of abstraction of features, capability to represent configurability), FMs were neither specifically designed for decision support nor to model Cloud services. Therefore, in this section, we describe how to adapt the model and notation of FMs to support our CSSP presented in Section 4. We refer to an adopted feature model as Cloud feature model (CFM). Figure 1 presents a very simple example of our approach's models and their elements for illustration purposes.

Enriched Feature Attributes. Feature attributes serve different purposes in our modeling approach: they describe quantitative and numeric properties of Cloud service offers and requirements of decision-makers regarding these properties. Feature attributes allow for an automated mapping of configurations to MCDM approaches.

Feature Attribute Types (FAT) are introduced to specify global information regarding multiple feature attributes of the same type. Using them avoids redundant specification of attribute information and allows to provide *standard aggregation strategies (SASs)* for feature attributes. FATs are referenced by the name of a FA. Therefore, two FAs $v_i.x$ and $v_j.x$ reference the same FAT if $name(v_i.x) = name(v_j.x)$ holds. Within a FAT at least the attribute domain and a SAS for a group of feature attributes is specified. We limit our approach to quantitative attribute values. Therefore, attribute domains can be discrete or continuous and finite or infinite. Examples for attribute domains are *integer* and *real*. A *boolean* domain may be represented by 0,1 [8].

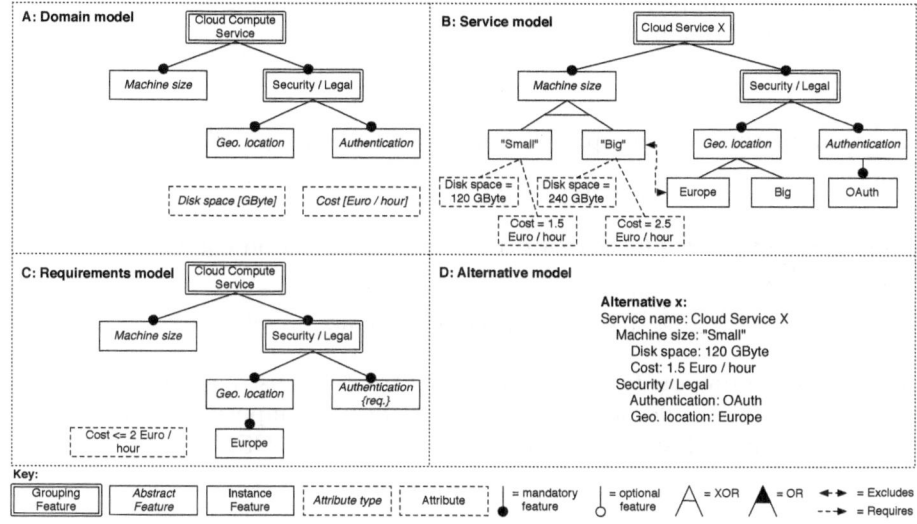

Fig. 1. Exemplary models illustrating model types and modeling elements

Standard Aggregation Strategies (SAS) are used to aggregate all values of FAs with the same FAT for a single configuration. Within literature, approaches exist that aggregate feature attributes [3] or specify global constraints for aggregations of feature attribute values [8]. However, our approach takes an explicit process model, re-usability of models and multiple stakeholders into account. We define a SAS of a FAT abstractly as a closed (binary) function on the attribute domain specified within the FAT. Examples for commutative SASs on the attribute domain *integer* are functions that represent addition and multiplication.

Feature Types. We use feature types to represent additional design constraints, limiting the number of valid modeling choices, and provide additional semantics in contrast to traditional features. Therefore, a number of existing automated analysis approaches for FMs [2] are applicable for resulting CFMs, respectively. We propose to utilize *grouping features*, *abstract features* and *instance features*. Each feature type is represented by a set of features $V^{gr}, V^{ab}, V^{in} \subseteq V$. No additional feature types are included.

$$V \backslash (V^{gr} \cup V^{ab} \cup V^{in}) = \emptyset \tag{1}$$

Furthermore, each feature belongs to a single feature type.

$$V^{gr} \cap V^{ab} = V^{gr} \cap V^{in} = V^{ab} \cap V^{in} = \emptyset \tag{2}$$

Grouping Feature: Grouping features decompose the decision problem, thus helping to organize and structure the CFM. Grouping features contain a set of abstract features which address a similar concern, thus providing a comprehensive view for different stakeholders. For example, all abstract features concerning *security* can be grouped underneath an according grouping feature. The root feature of a CFM is a grouping feature.

$$r \in V^{gr} \tag{3}$$

The parent feature of a grouping feature must be a grouping feature.

$$c_{e_i} \in V^{gr} \rightarrow p_{e_i} \in V^{gr} \forall e_i \in E^{de} \tag{4}$$

Grouping features decompose to abstract features and grouping features and not to instance features.

$$p_{e_i} \in V^{gr} \rightarrow c_{e_i} \in (V^{gr} \cup V^{ab}) \forall e_i \in E^{de} \tag{5}$$

The purpose of grouping features is to solely structure abstract features. Grouping features are only decomposed by mandatory decomposition relationships. Therefore, grouping features do not add variability to a CFM.

$$p_{e_i} \in V^{gr} \rightarrow e_i \in E^{mandatory} \forall e_i \in E^{de} \tag{6}$$

Abstract Feature: An abstract feature defines an abstract capability of a Cloud service that can be instantiated in different ways by Cloud service offers, e.g., "authentication". Therefore, abstract features are to be considered by decision-makers in the CSSP. An abstract feature corresponds to a variability point because it potentially contains multiple instance features, one or some of which can be selected to instantiate the abstract feature.

$$p_{e_i} \in V^{ab} \rightarrow c_{e_i} \in V^{in} \forall e_i \in E^{de} \tag{7}$$

The parent feature of an abstract feature must be a grouping feature.

$$c_{e_i} \in V^{ab} \rightarrow p_{e_i} \in V^{gr} \forall e_i \in E^{de} \tag{8}$$

Instance Feature: An instance feature represents a concrete capability of a single Cloud service offer. For example, "OAuth" can be an instance feature for the abstract feature "authentication". Instance features can be decomposed into instance features and represent additional variability points.

$$p_{e_i} \in V^{in} \rightarrow c_{e_i} \in V^{in} \forall e_i \in E^{de} \tag{9}$$

Model Types. CFMs and their configurations represent artifacts within the Cloud service selection process (CSSP) presented in Section 4. We propose to differentiate distinct model types based on the usage of models in the CSSP. Three of the model types are themselves CFMs, namely *domain model*, *service model* and *requirements model*, whereas the fourth type, the *alternative model*, can be represented by other notations. In the following, for each CFM type, its purpose and formal model within the overall CSSP are presented followed by an example.

Domain Model: The domain model's purpose is to represent all relevant abstract decision aspects of the selection problem, e.g., technical, legal or business ones. The domain model does not state the concrete realization of a Cloud service offer or requirements of a decision-maker, but serves as a common blueprint for both service and requirements models. Service and requirements models must not address all abstract decision aspects stated in the domain model. Therefore, the domain model itself does not require to contain variability. Abstract decision aspects are represented by abstract features and hierarchically structured by grouping features. Therefore, a domain model $G_D = (V_D, E_D, FAT_D)$ only includes a reduced set of features.

$$V_D \backslash (V_D^{gr} \cup V_D^{ab}) = \emptyset \tag{10}$$

A domain model contains a set of feature attribute types FAT to specify the non-functional properties to regard in the CSSP. Furthermore, a domain model does not contain cross-tree relationships.

$$E_D^{cr} = \emptyset \tag{11}$$

By acting as a common basis, the domain model supports aggregation of and comparability between service and requirements models. Our approach uses a single domain model within each CSSP. The example domain model illustrated in figure 1 A describes which aspects to regard and how to structure them for selecting a "Cloud Compute Service". For example, the abstract feature "machine size" can contain each service candidate's machine sizes in the corresponding service models. The grouping feature "Security / Legal" categorizes abstract features addressing this concern. Furthermore, attribute types like "cost" with the unit "Euro / hour" define quantitative aspects to regard.

Service Model: A service model $G_{S_D} = (V_{S_D}, E_{S_D}, FAT_{S_D})$ represents a single concrete Cloud service offer considered in the CSSP. A service model's purpose is to capture how this Cloud service offer concretely realizes the abstract decision aspects defined in the domain model. Service models encompass the configurability of Cloud services with regard to these aspects. Therefore, a single service model represents multiple configurations of a Cloud service. A service model G_{S_D} contains the same grouping and abstract features as the domain model G_D it relates to.

$$V_{S_D}^{gr} \cup V_{S_D}^{ab} = V_D^{gr} \cup V_D^{ab} \tag{12}$$

Additionally, it includes instance features to represent the modeled Cloud service's implementation options. Service models also contain the same attribute types as the domain model they relate to.

$$FAT_{S_D} = FAT_D \tag{13}$$

Therefore, each instance feature can be described by feature attributes that relate to one of the attribute types defined in the corresponding domain model. Service models may also contain cross-tree relationships that limit the number of possible configurations. Ultimately, a service model is a CFM without additional design constraints. An example service model is illustrated in figure 1 B. It describes a specific Cloud compute service called "Cloud Service x". It has, for example, two instance features for "machine size", one of which can be chosen, namely "small" or "big". Attributes attached to the instance features denote the instances' "disk space" and "cost".

Requirements Model: A requirements model $G_{R_D} = (V_{R_D}, E_{R_D}, FAT_{R_D})$ represents the requirements that a decision-maker has with regard to the abstract decision aspects in a CSSP. Similar to service models, requirements models contain the same grouping and abstract features as the domain model they relate to.

$$V_{R_D}^{gr} \cup V_{R_D}^{ab} = V_D^{gr} \cup V_D^{ab} \tag{14}$$

Requirements models also contain the same attribute types as the domain model they relate to.

$$FAT_{R_D} = FAT_D \tag{15}$$

This provides the decision-maker with the same structure of decision-relevant aspects as stated in the domain model, thus guiding the requirements stating. The following requirements statements are possible:

- **Any instance feature required:** This requirement states that an abstract feature needs to be instantiated. It does, however, not matter which specific instance feature is chosen if multiple exist. To capture this requirement in the requirements model, the abstract feature is marked *required* using a dedicated property.
- **Specific instance feature required:** This requirement states that an abstract feature needs to be instantiated by a specific instance feature. To model this requirement, the required instance feature is modeled in the requirements model underneath the corresponding abstract feature.

Within the requirements model, a decision-maker can further state requirements regarding values of attributes. The following statements are possible:

- **Threshold for attribute value:** This requirement states that the attribute value of the chosen alternative needs to conform to the specified threshold. To model this requirement, a subset of the corresponding attribute type's domain $dom(v_i.x)$ is chosen in the requirements model to determine the set of valid instantiation values.
- **Specific numerical value required:** This requirement states that the attribute value of the chosen alternative needs to match the specified value. To model this requirement, a specific value for the corresponding attribute type is chosen in the requirements model to determine the valid instantiation value.

The stated requirements represent *minimum* requirements. This means, for example, that if a required instance feature is contained next to other instance features in a service configuration, the configuration fulfills the stated requirements. An example requirements model is illustrated in figure 1 C. The model states that the attribute "cost" needs to be $< 2 Euro/hour$ for a service (configuration) to be considered in the selection. Further, the abstract feature "geographical location" is marked as *required* and instance feature "Europe" is modeled and thus required.

Alternative Model: An alternative model represents a single valid *configuration* derived from a service model, thus a concrete candidate to be selected. Alternative models are not CFMs. Rather, they are represented in a format that allows to use them in further selection steps (i.e. ranking based on preferences). Because alternative models represent valid configurations of a Cloud service, they might be used as basis to deploy the service. Alternative models list the features contained in the configuration they represent. Further, aggregated values for each attribute type defined in the corresponding domain model are contained. An example alternative model is illustrated in figure 1 D. It represents a valid configuration of the "Cloud Service X" service. The presented alternative model fulfills all requirements stated in the requirements model in figure 1 C.

3.3   Model Type Transitions

The transitions between the different model types are illustrated in figure 2. The domain model is the basis for all other models by defining the structure of grouping and abstract features and the relevant attribute types. Service and requirements models are derived from a domain model by adding instance features. Adding optional instance features increases the configurability of the service or requirements model if compared to the domain model: all configurations of the domain model are possible plus additional configurations in which the instance features are contained. Adding optional instance features thus corresponds to the unidirectional refactoring *add optional node* defined by [1]. Adding mandatory instance features, however, does not increase the configurability because is no longer possible to configure the service model in a way that no instance feature is chosen. Thus, overall the transition from a domain model to a service or requirements model can best be described as an *arbitrary edit* [14]. To denote the move from a completely abstract model to a model containing concrete instance features, we refer to this arbitrary edit as *instantiation*. In our approach, the service models define all possible configurations on how to use a Cloud service. Each configuration is potentially represented by an alternative model. We delimit the set of alternative models by determining only those configurations that

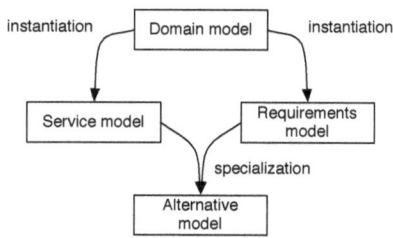

Fig. 2. Transitions between model types

fulfill the constraints stated in the requirements model. Thus, overall the process of deriving alternative models from service models under consideration of the requirements model removes configurations from the service models, which is in literature denoted as *specialization* of a feature model [5].

4   Cloud Service Selection Process (CSSP)

The models and their transitions defined in Section 3 are basis for the CSSP that aims to select Cloud service configurations that fulfill requirements and align best with a decision-maker's objectives. The CSSP involves two roles to execute different tasks and communicate in immediate interactions: Firstly, the role *(human) decision-maker* might be filled by a single or multiple (human) actors. Secondly, the role *decision support tools* presumes software tool implementations of our approach that return Cloud service selection recommendations based on given model inputs. Figure 3 depicts the process and included roles in Business Process Model and Notation (BPMN). The process is triggered by decision-makers that intend to select a Cloud service. Their task is to define multiple models: a domain model, multiple service models and a requirements model. Subsequently, the tool processes the models as input, and generates and evaluates viable Cloud service configurations into a list of recommendations. A detailed description of the activities is given in the following:

 - **Define domain model:** Initially, a domain model must be devised to fix a feature hierarchy for future service and requirements models. The modeling process can be self-contained and repetitive. However, eventually, the human decision-makers who participate must release a CFM in a consent to finish the activity.
 - **Define service models and requirements model:** Given a complete domain model, next, the current Cloud service landscape can be reflected in service models that follow the domain model's structure. In parallel, in a requirements model, constraints on features and attributes can be set.

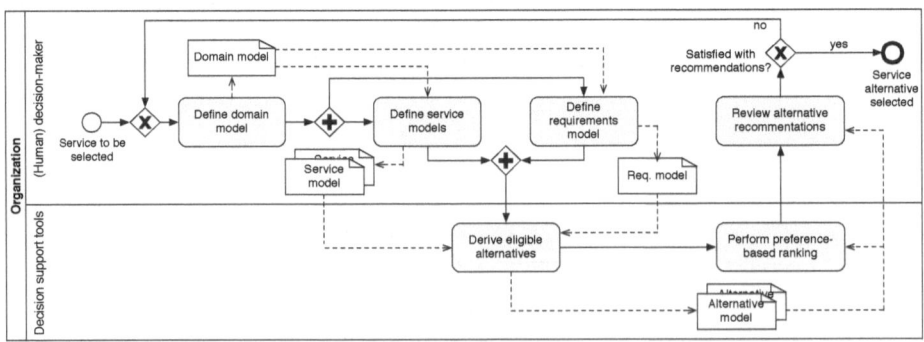

Fig. 3. Cloud Service Selection Process in BPMN

However, some constraints are based on instance features of existing service models (see section 3.2) and, hence, premise a prior modeling of a subset of service models.

- **Derive eligible alternatives:** Based on the set of service models, eligible alternatives can be generated. This can be done by matching the stated requirements of a requirements model with all service models for according node pairs to find viable service configurations, since both models are following the structure of one domain model. Matching can be performed similar to approaches in policies, where name spaces are compared. Alternative models are employed to represent eligible, alternative configurations in a map-like structure.
- **Perform preference-based ranking:** Resulting alternative models can serve as a basis for multi-criteria decision-making (MCDM) methods that allow to obtain a preference-based ranking of the alternatives. Decision criteria can be defined upon the attributes of alternative models derived from service models. Few other Cloud service selection approaches based on MCDM, e.g., the $(MC^2)^2$ framework [10] using an analytic hierarchy process, mention the need for extensive requirements elicitation and filtering. Our approach replaces their alternative definition and simple requirements checks.
- **Retrieve alternative recommendations:** The recommended alternative can subsequently be assessed by a decision-maker. In case of satisfaction, the CSSP stops. Otherwise, further iterations of the process are possible as discussed below.

Our approach allows for cycles to foster evolutionary Cloud service selection. Decision-makers can start with simple models and few requirements and incrementally improve models to strive for more precise results. After reviewing recommendations, a decision-maker can step back and either improve the domain model, service models, or requirements model. However, changes in a model can affect the validity of other models, e.g., an extended domain model requires to change all other models and changing a service model might induce changes in the requirements model. On the other hand, the requirements model allows frequent adjustments to the set of requirements, which is supposed to be common. The process depicted in Figure 3 illustrates the cycle with an optional path from reviewing recommendations back to the start activity (i.e., domain model definition). Entering a new cycle, a decision-maker has the chance to alter models if needed and gain new service recommendations. Dependencies between models have been addressed in Section 3.3 and their management is not automated in our approach yet, and, hence, left to a modeler.

5   Use Case: Cloud Storage Selection

To evaluate the applicability of our modeling approach and subsequent selection process, we applied it to a use case that aims select among *Cloud storage services*. Cloud storage services allow to easily upload data to Cloud data centers, for instance for backup purposes or to share and access data on diverse devices, e.g., mobile phones. The use case is relevant for (technical) decision-makers in search for decision support to select Cloud storage services.

5.1   Implementation

We created a prototypical implementation of a Cloud feature model editor. The implementation builds upon our previous tool suite for service feature modeling [16] and is based on the Eclipse Modeling Framework (EMF)[2]. Our editor provides a graphical interface to model CFMs, including attribute and feature types. We also implemented a reasoning engine that determines the possible configurations for a given CFM and aggregates the attributes based on the standard aggregation strategy defined in the attribute type (see section 3.2). The reasoning engine uses the freely available CHOCO constraint satisfaction problem solver[3], that has also been successfully used by other researchers for such purposes [2]. A requirements matching module determines alternative models in text-form that fulfill the needs stated in the requirements model. The implementation of our tool is publicly available[4].

5.2   Performing the Use Case

We performed the use case with regard to those parts of the CSSP that concern modeling and derivation of alternatives, leaving the preference-based ranking open because it is not focus of this work (for details about this step, see for example [10,11,13]).

Definition of Domain Model: We defined a domain model to specify all aspects to be included in the selection. These aspects are derived from published descriptions of the services in focus[5]. As illustrated in Figure 4 A, we defined two grouping features "safety" and "usability". We used abstract features to denote the aspects whose concrete instantiations we want to assess, e.g., "versioning" and "data encryption". The abstract feature "plans" relates to offered combinations of "data volume" and "price". Attribute types denote quantitative characteristics to regard in the selection, for example, "storage capacity" in GByte and "monthly cost" in Dollar.

Definition of Service Models: Based on the domain model, we created 3 service models that represent a random selection of Cloud storage offers: "Dropbox", "Box.net" and "Wuala". Per service model, we specified concrete capabilities in form of instance features and attributes based on the publicly available service descriptions. Figure 4 B illustrates parts of the service model we created for Drobpox. Instance features are used, for example, to indicate the "data encryption" mechanisms that Dropbox offers. Attributes denote, for example, the "monthly cost" for the "free" plan, which are 0. Dropbox's "user management

---

[2] http://www.eclipse.org/modeling/emf/
[3] http://www.emn.fr/z-info/choco-solver/
[4] https://github.com/ErikWittern/CloudServiceSelection
[5] http://www.dropbox.com, http://www.box.com, http://www.wuala.com

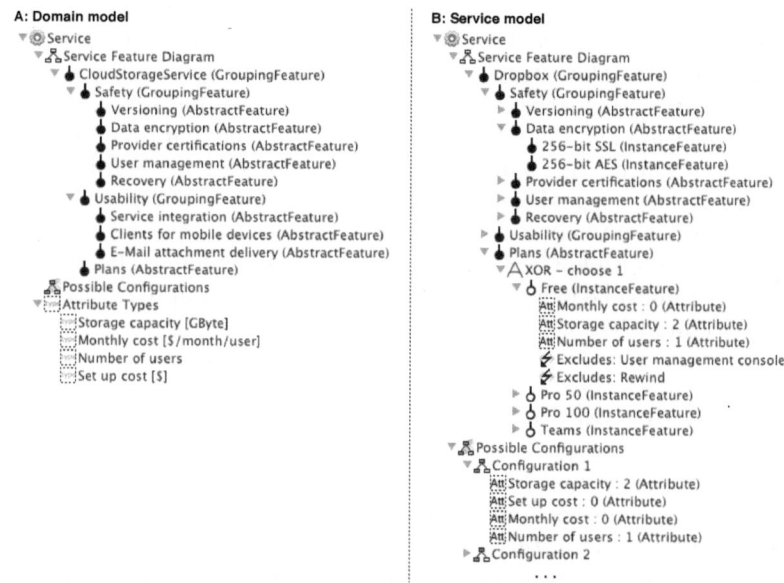

Fig. 4. Domain model and service model for "Dropbox" of the use case; screen shots taken from our prototype CFM tool

console" and "rewind" recovery feature are not part of the free plan and thus excluded using cross-tree relationships.

Definition of Requirements Model: Based again on the domain model, we created a simple requirements model. The model states that any "user management" instantiation is required by setting an according property in the abstract feature. Further, attribute type "storage capacity" ought to be $> 60GByte$, while "monthly cost" should be $< 20.00\$/user/month$.

Derivation of Eligible Alternatives: Having the 3 service models and the requirements model in place, we triggered matching of the models to determine those configurations that fulfill the stated requirements. From the original 45 configurations contained in the 3 service models (4 for Box.com, 12 for Dropbox and 29 for Wuala), 5 fulfilled the stated requirements (1 from Box.com and 4 from Wuala).

5.3   Discussion

The use case shows that our modeling approach is capable to efficiently capture the configurations to select from when consuming a Cloud storage service - the 3 service models contained 45 configurations. The requirements elicitation allows to eliminate configurations that do not meet stated requirements, leading in this case to a reduction of configurations by factor 9. The models produced in this use case are publicly available[6]. Because all 3 service models are based on the same domain model, their resulting configurations are comparable to each other. Hence, configurations allow for a service selection already or, after transferring them into adequate alternative models, they can act as input for further MCDM approaches. The application of the use case indicated multiple theses worth following: first, stating the requirements model for existing service models is easy for human decision-makers compared to the creation of the service models, thus allowing to iteratively adapt it if needed. Second, the reuse of existing service models in multiple CSSPs can greatly reduce modeling effort. Third, the collaboration of multiple experts from different domains improves the quality of created service models.

6   Conclusion and Future Work

In this paper, we addressed human-centered modeling of capabilities of Cloud service offers and requirements towards them with a holistic support consisting of models, a process, and a software tool. We adapt feature modeling to capture diverse aspects and configurations of Cloud services: we introduced extended feature attributes, feature types and model types to enable the resulting CFMs to be used within the also presented CSSP. We demonstrate the applicability of our approach in a use case where we compare overall 45 configurations of 3 Cloud storage services. The large number of configurations illustrates how useful it is to utilize variability modeling to represent Cloud services. By applying requirements filtering we showed that we can effectively delimit the number of alternative models, thus generating suitable input for subsequent selection phases (i.e. preference-based ranking).

In future work, we want to involve multiple stakeholders into the modeling of and selection among Cloud services by providing means for collaboration. To better address the dynamics of Cloud computing, we envision to (automatically) incorporate dynamic attribute values into the CFMs that allow for example to consider up to date benchmark results in the Cloud service selection. Next to selecting single Cloud services, the selection and composition of multiple services, concepts for model reuse and an iterative process should be considered.

Acknowledgment. This work was supported by the COCKPIT project [4].

References

1. Alves, V., Gheyi, R., Massoni, T., Kulesza, U., Borba, P., Lucena, C.: Refactoring Product Lines. In: Proc. of the 5th Int. Conf. on Generative Programming and Component Engineering, GPCE 2006, pp. 201–210. ACM, Portland (2006)
2. Benavides, D., Segura, S., Ruiz-Cortés, A.: Automated Analysis of Feature Models 20 Years Later: A Literature Review. Information Systems 35(6), 615–636 (2010)

---

[6] http://bit.ly/CloudServiceSelectionModels

3. Benavides, D., Trinidad, P., Ruiz-Cortés, A.: Automated Reasoning on Feature Models. In: Pastor, Ó., Falcão e Cunha, J. (eds.) CAiSE 2005. LNCS, vol. 3520, pp. 491–503. Springer, Heidelberg (2005)
4. COCKPIT Project: Citizens Collaboration and Co-Creation in Public Service Delivery (2012), http://www.cockpit-project.eu
5. Czarnecki, K., Helsen, S., Eisenecker, U.: Formalizing Cardinality-based Feature Models and their Specialization. Software Process: Improvement and Practice 10(1), 7–29 (2005)
6. Czarnecki, K., Helsen, S., Eisenecker, U.: Staged Configuration through Specialization and Multilevel Configuration of Feature Models. Software Process: Improvement and Practice 10(2), 143–169 (2005)
7. Godse, M., Mulik, S.: An Approach for Selecting Software-as-a-Service (SaaS) Product. In: Proc. of the 2009 IEEE Int. Conf. on Cloud Computing, CLOUD 2009, pp. 155–158. IEEE, Washington, DC (2009)
8. Karataş, A.S., Oğuztüzün, H., Doğru, A.: Mapping Extended Feature Models to Constraint Logic Programming over Finite Domains. In: Bosch, J., Lee, J. (eds.) SPLC 2010. LNCS, vol. 6287, pp. 286–299. Springer, Heidelberg (2010)
9. Li, A., Yang, X., Kandula, S., Zhang, M.: CloudCmp: Comparing Public Cloud Providers. In: Proc. of the 10th Annual Conf. on Internet Measurement, IMC 2010, pp. 1–14. ACM, New York (2010)
10. Menzel, M., Schönherr, M., Tai, S.: (MC2)2: Criteria, Requirements and a Software Prototype for Cloud Infrastructure Decisions. Software: Practice and Experience (2011)
11. ur Rehman, Z., Hussain, F., Hussain, O.: Towards Multi-Criteria Cloud Service Selection. In: Proc. of the 5th Int. Conf. on Innovative Mobile and Internet Services in Ubiquitous Computing, IMIS 2011, pp. 44–48. IEEE, Perth (2011)
12. Ruiz-Alvarez, A., Humphrey, M.: An Automated Approach to Cloud Storage Service Selection. In: Proc. of the 2nd Int. Workshop on Scientific Cloud Computing, pp. 39–48. ACM, New York (2011)
13. Saripalli, P., Pingali, G.: MADMAC: Multiple Attribute Decision Methodology for Adoption of Clouds. In: Proc. of the 4th Int. Conf. on Cloud Computing, pp. 316–323. IEEE, Washington, DC (2011)
14. Thüm, T., Batory, D., Kastner, C.: Reasoning About Edits to Feature Models. In: Proc. of the 31st Int. Conf. on Software Engineering, ICSE 2009, pp. 254–264. IEEE, Washington, DC (2009)
15. Wittern, E., Zirpins, C.: On the Use of Feature Models for Service Design: The Case of Value Representation. In: Cezon, M., Wolfsthal, Y. (eds.) ServiceWave 2010 Workshops. LNCS, vol. 6569, pp. 110–118. Springer, Heidelberg (2011)
16. Wittern, E., Zirpins, C., Rajshree, N., Jain, A.N., Spais, I., Giannakakis, K.: A Tool Suite to Model Service Variability and Resolve It Based on Stakeholder Preferences. In: Pallis, G., Jmaiel, M., Charfi, A., Graupner, S., Karabulut, Y., Guinea, S., Rosenberg, F., Sheng, Q.Z., Pautasso, C., Ben Mokhtar, S. (eds.) ICSOC 2011. LNCS, vol. 7221, pp. 250–251. Springer, Heidelberg (2012)
17. Wohlstadter, E., Tai, S., Mikalsen, T., Rouvellou, I., Devanbu, P.: GlueQoS: Middleware to Sweeten Quality-of-Service Policy Interactions. In: Proc. of the 26th Int. Conf. on Software Engineering, ICSE 2004, pp. 189–199. IEEE Computer Society, Washington, DC (2004)

Extending Enterprise Service Design Knowledge Using Clustering

Marcus Roy[1,2], Ingo Weber[2,3,*], and Boualem Benatallah[2]

[1] SAP Research, Sydney, Australia
[2] School of Computer Science & Engineering, University of New South Wales
[3] Software Systems Research Group, NICTA, Sydney, Australia
{m.roy,ingo.weber,boualem}@cse.unsw.edu.au

Abstract. Automatically constructing or completing knowledge bases of SOA design knowledge puts traditional clustering approaches beyond their limits. We propose an approach to amend incomplete knowledge bases of Enterprise Service (ES) design knowledge, based on a set of ES signatures. The approach employs clustering, complemented with various filtering and ranking techniques to identify potentially new entities. We implemented and evaluated the approach, and show that it significantly improves the detection of entities compared to a state-of-the-art clustering technique. Ultimately, extending an existing knowledge base with entities is expected to further improve ES search result quality.

1 Introduction

In large-scale software development efforts, such as enterprise Service-Oriented Architectures (SOAs), ESs are commonly developed using service design guidelines – guarded by SOA Governance [13,8,16]. These guidelines may include entities (e.g. Sales Order) and naming conventions used to construct unambiguous ES operation names, referred to as ES signatures. For instance, consider the ES signature "SalesOrderItemChangeRequestConfirmation_In" from SAP's ESR[1]. Although such service design knowledge is largely used to consistently design ES signatures, it can also be utilized for other applications, e.g. tools to automatically generate, duplicate-check and validate compliant ES signatures as well as to search for ESs. We tested the latter in an ongoing, separate stream of work, where we use service design knowledge in an entity-centric keyword search for ESs, with highly encouraging results. However, such service design knowledge can be incomplete, e.g. due to partial modeling, or become outdated as related systems and business requirements evolve over time. Particularly when customers tailor an off-the-shelf enterprise application to their specific need, they may disregard design guidelines when developing new ESs. Therefore, resulting

---

* NICTA is funded by the Australian Government as represented by the Department of Broadband, Communications and the Digital Economy and the Australian Research Council through the ICT Centre of Excellence program.

[1] Enterprise Service Registry: http://sr.esworkplace.sap.com

C. Liu et al. (Eds.): ICSOC 2012, LNCS 7636, pp. 142–157, 2012.

ESs may not fully comply with existing service design guidelines and possibly incorporate new knowledge, i.e. new entities or additions to naming conventions. This knowledge is inherent to ES signatures and may not be reflected in service design knowledge yet. The absence of such knowledge can therefore limit the effectiveness of above mentioned applications, e.g. it strongly affects the precision and recall of search results in an entity-centric search. Hence, there is a need to extract design knowledge from existing ES signatures.

To amend existing knowledge bases, there are a few approaches that can be used such as entity recognition [3,5,9] or clustering techniques [7,23,12,21]. With entity recognition, known entities can be recognized from text, e.g. using entity graphs [3]. The recognition effectiveness hereby also depends on the completeness of the entity graph and becomes uncertain when entities are missing. On the other hand, clustering techniques, e.g. hierarchical agglomerative clustering (HAC) [12,7], can be used to find term clusters from text representing potentially new entities. Although these clusters can be used, e.g. for Web service matchmaking [7], it is not clear how well these clusters represent exact entity names. This is because clustering tries to assign terms to discrete clusters, which does not work well for entities consisting of repetitive terms overlapping with other entities, e.g. "Sales Order" and "Sales Price". Also, clustering assumes potential entities to be statistically independent. In that context, we observed that naming conventions may cause terms of entities to frequently co-occur with each other, which clustering can misunderstand as a cluster.

In this paper, we propose an approach that combines entity recognition and a knowledge base-driven clustering to find names of unknown entities from ES signatures. We hereby aim to improve the accuracy of recognizing new entities by removing known entities from the input to our knowledge base-driven clustering, and by possibly merging newly formed clusters with co-exiting entities. First, we utilize existing service design knowledge to learn existing naming conventions. Second, we reuse naming conventions to recognize known entities in ES signatures. Third, we perform the knowledge base-driven clustering over the remaining, unknown terms and check their co-occurrence with recognized entities. For this, we introduce measures of confidence and cohesion, to describe the quality of (potentially overlapping) term clusters and the strength of their connectivity to co-occurring entities. Finally, resulting clusters are added to the knowledge base, as either new or specialized entities.

We implemented the proposed approach and evaluated the knowledge base-driven clustering compared to the HAC used in [7] on a large-scale repository from SAP with more than 1600 ES signatures. Our evaluation shows that the proposed approach achieves reasonably high precision and recall values of clustered entities and outperforms the HAC. In short, our contributions are as follows:

– Reusing service design knowledge to recognize entities from signatures
– A knowledge base-driven clustering approach, which uses generated (potentially overlapping) term clusters and recognized entities to find new entities.
– An in-depth evaluation using a real-world testbed.

We next describe the knowledge base and challenges in its effective use. In Section 3, we explain the proposed approach, followed by the evaluation in Section 4. Related work is discussed in Section 5, Section 6 concludes the paper.

2   Using Service Design Knowledge

We start by motivating and describing an abstract representation of service design knowledge, followed by open challenges how to effectively use the knowledge.

2.1   A Representation of Service Design Knowledge

Organizations use SOA Governance to better manage their SOA [13], which can be applied to any part of a service life-cycle addressing areas such as service design and development among others. In this work, we only focus on the service design phase [2]. In this phase, enterprises employ service design methodologies to create business-aligned, reusable and long-living ESs [16,8]. Such methodologies typically describe guidelines and best practises providing clear instructions to developers on how to create and name services that comply with agreed-on design principles. These design principles are the basis of our knowledge base, as described in detail in previous work [15]. There we also showed how to derive an abstract representation of this service design knowledge consisting of (i) a graph of entities and (ii) an automaton describing a set of ES signatures. This representation is summarized below.

First, we define a Directed Acyclic Graph (DAG) of typed entities $e \in E_{KB}$ with type $c \in C_{KB}$ in RDF. This DAG captures an abstract view of a data model and related design patterns, stemming from a service design methodology. Fig. 1 shows a partial example DAG, depicting entities e_i as white boxes (i.e. RDF literals) and associated types c_j as grey ovals (i.e. RDF classes). For instance, entity e_{14} : Sales Order is of type c_9 : Business Object; e_{14} belongs to entity e_{15} : Sales Order Processing of type c_{10} : Process Component. We consider such a DAG as a structured vocabulary of typed entities.

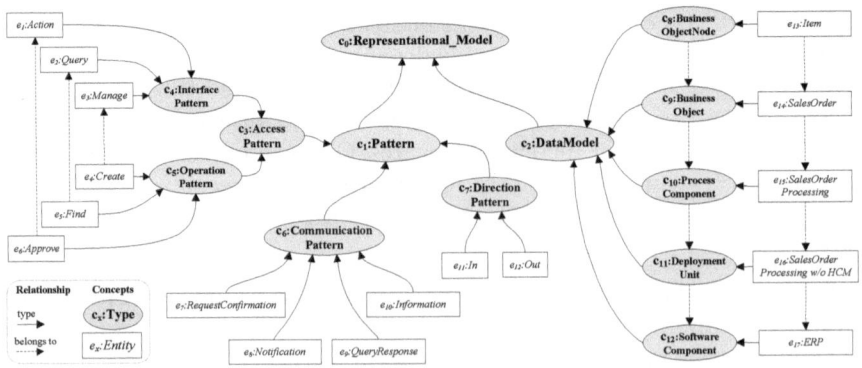

Fig. 1. Example of a typed entity graph representing a structured vocabulary

Second, we define a non-deterministic automata with epsilon moves to capture a (possibly incomplete) set of naming conventions. We defined the automaton on a set of entities, the input alphabet. The set of transitions uses the types of entities. As such, an ES signature $S_i \in S$ is interpreted as a sequence of entities e_i, where each respective type c_j triggers a state transition. A governance-compliant signature is accepted by the corresponding automaton, if it reaches a final state in the automaton after its last entity. Fig. 2 shows an excerpt of an automaton, related to the example DAG in Fig. 1.

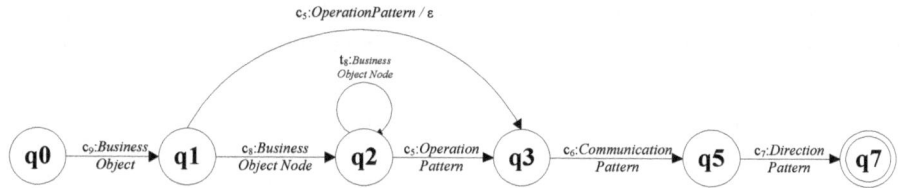

Fig. 2. Example of an automaton describing a subset of ES signatures

The following example ES signature, S_{x_1}, is accepted by the automaton from Figure 2, according to the split into entities of (abbreviated) types shown below.

$$S_{x_1}: \quad \underbrace{\texttt{SalesOrder}}_{c_9:\text{BO}} \underbrace{\texttt{Item}}_{c_8:\text{BON}} \underbrace{\texttt{Change}}_{c_5:\text{OP}} \underbrace{\texttt{RequestConfirmation}}_{c_6:\text{CP}} \underbrace{\texttt{\_In}}_{c_7:\text{DP}}$$

2.2 Challenges of Using Service Design Knowledge

In the previous section we provided an example of an ES signature that completely matched exact entities in the knowledge base and is accepted by a respective automaton. Although these types of ES signatures constitute the majority of cases, there are signatures that can only be matched partially as shown in the example below[2]. Apart from recognized entities, the signature also contains terms (here: `Reporting` and `Bulk`) that cannot be matched to entities. In this context, we refer to terms as single words separated by their camel case notation.

$$S_{x_2}: \quad \underbrace{\texttt{Reporting}}_{?} \underbrace{\texttt{Employee}}_{c_9:\text{BO}} \underbrace{\texttt{Bulk}}_{?} \underbrace{\texttt{Notification}}_{c_8:\text{BON}} \underbrace{\texttt{ByID}}_{c_5:\text{OP}} \underbrace{\texttt{QueryResponse}}_{c_6:\text{CP}} \underbrace{\texttt{\_In}}_{c_7:\text{DP}}$$

Since these terms do not match existing entities, they might be (parts of) entities missing from the KB. Using signature S_{x_2} as an example, we introduce two types of new entities as follows. First, the term `Reporting` alone does not seem to represent an independent entity. Instead, `Reporting` together with the entity following it, i.e. `Employee`, describes a specialization of the existing `Employee`. In contrast, the term `Bulk` is not a specialization of `Notification`, but rather a

---

[2] We used a constructed example of a signature to illustrate two common pitfalls.

general property: `Bulk` is also found in the context of other entities, e.g. `Payment` or `Message`. In the following section, we describe an approach that recognizes known entities, extracts unknown terms and determines whether they are likely a specialization of an existing entity or a separate, new entity.

3   Extending Services Design Knowledge Using Clustering

In this section, we describe the proposed solution to identify unknown entities from ES signatures. We start with an overview, before explaining each step of the approach in detail. The inputs to the approach are a list of ES signatures and a populated entity graph (cf. Section 2). Given this input, the following four phases are executed (see Fig. 3).

Strict Classification recognizes signatures that are completely matched with entities from the knowledge base. For each of these signatures, it extracts the corresponding entity sequence and consolidates all sequences into an automaton using [19].

Approximate Classification uses the automaton from the first step to detect known entities in the remaining signatures. All unknown terms are collected.

Knowledge base-driven Clustering applies two measures to candidate entities: (i) a confidence measure to form term clusters of closely connected unknown terms and (ii) a cohesion measure to merge term clusters with already recognized entities. If predefined thresholds are exceeded, a cluster can be considered as a new entity. In contrast to common clustering methods which only take into account unknown terms, our knowledge base-driven clustering uses the existing KB in addition to the unknown terms.

KB Extension adds new entities to the KB: pure term clusters represent separate new entities; term clusters merged with existing entities represent specialization of these entities.

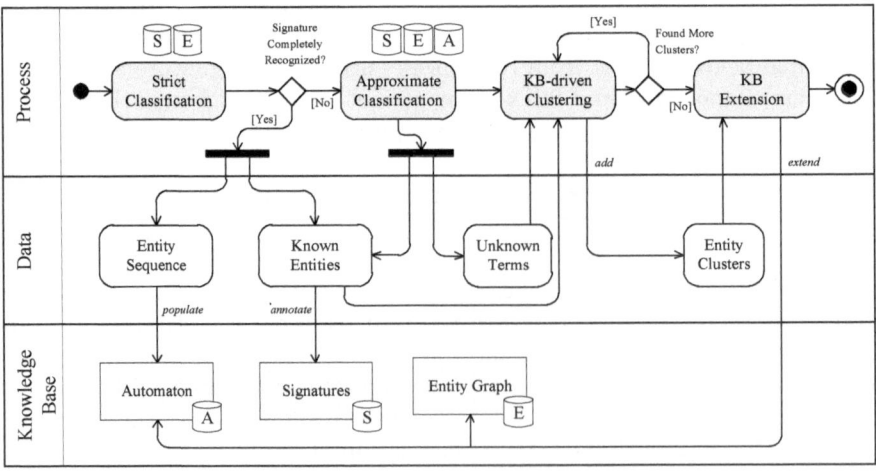

Fig. 3. Overview of the different components of the proposed approach

The strict and approximate classification can be considered as a pre-clustering of signatures $S_i \in S$ into a set of recognized entities $E_i \in E$ and a set of unknown terms $T_i \in T$. In the remainder, we therefore refer to a signature S_i as a 3-tuple of $E_i, T_i,$ and O_i:

$$S_i := (E_i, T_i, O_i) \tag{1}$$

where O_i specifies the order of terms and entities: $O_i = (x_{i_1}, ..., x_{i_m})$ where $x_{i_j} \in E_i \cup T_i$. A pair of signature parts $x_{i_j}, x_{i_k} \in E_i \cup T_i$ is said to be *neighbors in S_i* iff $j = k+1$ or $j = k-1$. A set of signature parts $X = \{x_j, ..., x_k\}$ with $X \subseteq E_i \cup T_i$ is said to be *connected in S_i* iff there is a permutation $X' = (x_{j_1}, ..., x_{j_n})$ of X such that all pairs $(x_{j_l}, x_{j_{l+1}})$ are neighbors in S_i.

3.1   Strict Classification

The goal of this phase is to reverse-engineer approximate naming rules from signatures that can be explained fully and unambiguously. For this, the strict classification uses as input the set of ES signatures (S) and an entity graph (E) as depicted in Figure 3. First, it identifies matches between all parts of a signature and the vocabulary defined in the entity graph. If not every part of a signature matches some entity from the vocabulary, the signature is rejected.

For the remaining signatures, there may be more than one explanation – i.e. more than one set of known entities that together matches all parts of the signature. To reject signatures with unclear explanations, the classification uses the relationships from the entity graph as follows. For the recognized entities, it traverses the ancestors and descendants from the "belongs-to" relationship, and builds sets of *graph-related* entities and types respectively. It then requires that all entities in the signature whose types are graph-related, are themselves graph-related as well. For instance, the signature "SalesOrderItemCreateRequestConfirmation_In" contains the entity "Item" (typed "Business Object Node" (BON)) and the entity "Sales Order" (typed "Business Object"(BO)). Due to BON being graph-related to BO (see Fig. 1), "Item" is also required to be graph-related to "Sales Order" – which is indeed the case. If, for any pair of entities in an explanation, this constraint does not hold, the classification rejects the explanation. Note that this is, in practical terms, very strict indeed: some correct explanations are likely to be rejected. Finally, the strict classification rejects any signature where the number of remaining explanations is not exactly 1.

The result of the strict classification is a set of signatures, each explained by sequence of recognized entities. These entity sequences are then used to build a minimal automaton as described in [19], and annotate related signatures with the recognized entities [15]. Inversely, the automaton transitions are annotated with their respective *popularity*, i.e., the absolute number, of how often a given transition has been used in the strictly classified signatures.

Example 1. Strict Classification result for S_{x_1}:

$S_{x_1} = (E_{x_1}, \emptyset)$

$E_{x_1} = \{\text{SalesOrder, Item, Change, RequestConfirmation, In}\}$

$O_{x_1} = (\text{SalesOrder, Item, Change, RequestConfirmation, In})$

3.2   Approximate Classification

The approximate classification takes as an input the ESs signatures (S), the entity graph (E), and the automaton (A) built in the previous step. For each signature that has been rejected by the strict classification, the approximate classification aims to find known entities that explain parts of it.

As in the previous step, approximate classification has to deal with the challenge of multiple possible explanations for signature parts. For example, the compound term "Sales Order Confirmation" could be considered (a) a single entity (typed BO) or (b) as a concatenation of two independent entities "Sales Order" (typed BO) and "Confirmation" (typed "Communication Pattern" (CP)). The approximate classification therefore uses the automaton to find the most likely explanation amongst multiple possibilities.

This phase starts off like the previous one, by matching neighboring signature parts against entities from the entity graph, to produce a set of possible explanations (if any) for the parts of each signature. For signatures with multiple explanations, the approximate classification filters and ranks the explanations according to their level of match and popularity with the automaton. That is, explanations that are contradictory to the automaton are rejected. For the remaining explanations, the classification computes the sum of the popularity of the transitions taken by this explanation, and ranks the remaining explanations accordingly. It then rejects all but the highest-ranked explanation.

As an example for the filtering, the automaton may denote that a valid signature only contains one CP. Therefore, using the above partial signature example "Sales Order Confirmation", explanation (b) would be rejected if another CP appears later in the signature and explanation (a) is kept. As an example for the ranking, say there was no other CP. Then, say explanation (a) might have a partial popularity of 320, and explanation (b) a partial popularity of $320 + 80 = 400$, the ranking would prefer explanation (b). Finally, we collect recognized entities E_i and remaining unknown terms T_i to be used in the next step.

Example 2. Approximate Classification result for S_{x_2}:

$S_{x_2} = (E_{x_2}, T_{x_2}, O_{x_2})$

$E_{x_2} = \{\text{Employee, Notification, By, ID, QueryResponse, In}\}$

$T_{x_2} = \{\text{Reporting, Bulk}\}$

$O_{x_2} = (\text{Reporting,Employee,Bulk,Notification,By,ID,QueryResponse,In})$

3.3   Knowledge Base-Driven Clustering

The goal of the knowledge base-driven Clustering is to find potential clusters of entities from the set of unknown terms T_i, in the context of existing sets of entities E_i and the order O_i. For this we use a confidence and a cohesion measure, as illustrated in Figure 4. In summary, the clustering first groups terms that co-occur in multiple signatures into term clusters (cf. right dashed bounding box), and computes the *term cluster confidence* score *conf* of the cluster candidates. Second, it merges term cluster candidates that have a high *conf* value with co-occurring entities using the

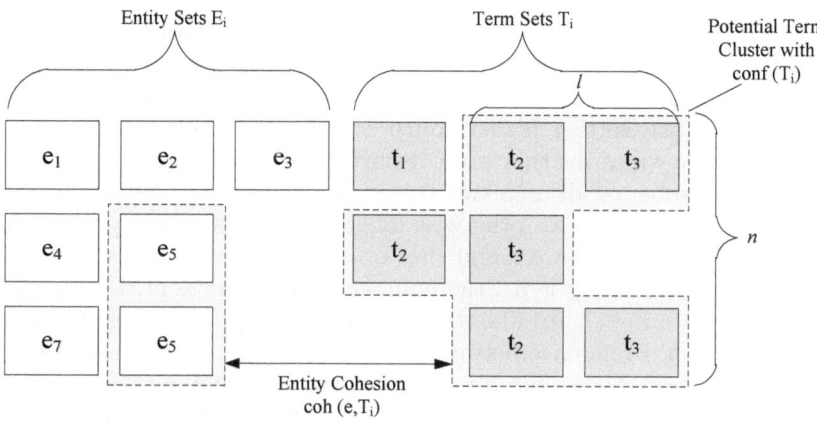

Fig. 4. Schematic clustering example, using Term Confidence and Entity Cohesion. Not shown is the influence of the term/entity order.

entity cohesion score *coh*: the cohesion between term clusters and entities (cf. left and right dashed bounding boxes). We now explain both measures in detail.

Term Cluster Confidence. To identify potential term clusters, we consider any non-empty subset of terms $T_i \subseteq T$, as long as some signature contains this subset (formally: $\exists S_j : T_i \subseteq T_j$) and the terms in T_i are connected in S_j (as per the above definition). We refer to the set of all potential term clusters fulfilling this condition as $\mathcal{T}$. To calculate a confidence value $conf(T_i)$ for an arbitrary, but fixed term cluster T_i, we first define $S_t \subseteq S$ as the set of signatures whose respective term set T_j is a superset of T_i:

$$S_t(T_i) := \{S_j \in S \mid T_i \subseteq T_j, S_j = (E_j, T_j, O_j)\} \tag{2}$$

We further define p_n as the size of S_t (the number of signatures containing T_i), p_l as the size of T_i, and p_r as the average size of the complete term sets contained in S_t:

$$p_n(T_i) := |S_t| \tag{3}$$

$$p_l(T_i) := |T_i| \tag{4}$$

$$p_r(T_i) := \frac{\sum_{j:S_j \in S_t} |T_j|}{p_n(T_i)} \tag{5}$$

Finally, we define the term cluster confidence *conf* for T_i, normalized over all term cluster candidates $\mathcal{T}$ where $a, b \in [1, \infty)$ are decimal values:

$$p_t(T_i) := \ln(p_n(T_i)) \times \frac{p_l(T_i)^a}{p_r(T_i)^b} \tag{6}$$

$$conf(T_i) := \frac{p_t(T_i)}{\max(\{p_t(T_k)|T_k \in \mathcal{T}\})} \tag{7}$$

The fraction p_l/p_r hereby represents the ratio of the sizes of the term cluster vs. the average size of all term sets in the signatures in which T_i occurs.

This fraction can be seen as a signal-to-noise ratio T_i in relation to all unknown terms. We further exponentiate the numerator of the fraction by a and the denominator with b. Intuitively, setting higher values for a prioritizes long term clusters. In contrast, setting higher values for b increases the penalty for long "rests", i.e., unknown terms that are not part of the candidate cluster. Since p_r is the average number of all unknown terms, i.e., the rest as well as the cluster, we recommend setting $a \geq b$ – otherwise longer clusters would in general be penalized. Based on samples, we found that $a = 3$ and $b = 2$ returns best results. The third main factor in p_t is p_n, the number of occurrences of the cluster candidate. To mitigate imbalance due to high variance in p_n, we apply the natural logarithm function. Preference between p_n and p_l/p_r can be expressed with the ratio a/b: the higher, the less important p_n becomes. In summary, the confidence score prioritizes long clusters, appearing often, but with little noise.

Next, we define a threshold tr_{conf}: after calculating the confidence values for all candidate clusters, all term cluster candidates T_i with $conf(T_i) > tr_{conf}$ are added to the set of resulting clusters. This threshold primarily works by allowing *rivaling* explanations of term clusters to get added to the result set *simultaneously*. The whole confidence computation step is run as a *fixpoint algorithm*: term clusters that are added to the result set in one round are removed from the set of unknown terms. This results in a changed set of cluster candidates. For these we re-calculate *conf*, and so on. This is done until no more clusters are found. Since *conf* is normalized among the *current* set of candidates, at least the cluster with maximal confidence is added to the result set.

Finally, we *filter* the term cluster result set with a two-dimensional threshold $tr_f := (tr_{f1}, tr_{f2})$ as follows. tr_{f1} is a relative threshold: clusters in the result set are ranked according to their p_t value, and the lowest-ranked portion of size tr_{f2} are removed – e.g., the last 10%. In contrast, tr_{f2} is an absolute threshold, with respect to p_t: all term clusters T_i with $p_t(T_i) \leq tr_{f2}$ are removed from the result set. The combined threshold works to remove noise from the result set.

Entity Cohesion. As motivated with the example of "Reporting" and "Employee" above, some term clusters (e.g., "Reporting") should not form entities by themselves, but should be merged with other entities to form a specialization of those (e.g., "ReportingEmployee").

To determine which cluster candidates from the previous step should be merged with some entity, we compute a cohesion score *coh* that captures co-occurrences of connected term clusters T_i with entities. For this, we first define the projection $\rho(T_i)$ as the set of entity sets E'_j that (i) co-occur with T_i in some signature E_j, and (ii) contain only entities neighboring with some term from T_i in S_j. We further define the entity set U_c as the union of these entity sets.

$$\rho(T_i) := \{E'_j \mid T_i \subseteq T_j, S_j = (E_j, T_j, O_j), E'_i \subseteq E_j,$$
$$\forall e \in E'_j \; \exists t \in T_i : t, e \text{ are neighbors}\} \tag{8}$$

$$U_c := \bigcup_{E'_j \in \rho(T_i)} E'_j \tag{9}$$

We then define the cohesion $coh(e, T_i)$ between an entity e and a term cluster T_i as the ratio between signatures containing both e and T_i and all signatures containing T_i:

$$coh(e, T_i) := \frac{|\{E'_k \mid e \in E'_k, T_i \subseteq T_j, E'_k \in \rho(T_j)\}|}{p_n(T_i)} \tag{10}$$

Note that coh uses the projection defined above, and thus only counts co-occurrences between e and T_i where e is the neighbor of some term in T_i.

After calculating the cohesion between T_i and all candidate entities e, we decide if and how to combine T_i and the candidates as follows. If each occurrence of T_i is a co-occurrence with e (formally: $coh(e, T_i) = 1$), we merge T_i with e and add the result as a specialization of e. If for each candidate entity e we have $coh(e, T_i) < 1$, a threshold tr_{coh} is applied to determine if the co-occurrence between e and T_i is frequent enough to justify merging. If the cohesion exceeds tr_{coh} merging is justified – however, there must be cases where the term cluster appears without e (else the cohesion would have been 1). Therefore, we add both the term cluster by itself, as a new entity, and term cluster merged with entity to the knowledge base. The merged cluster hereby becomes a specialization of e as well as the new entity. If the cohesion is below the threshold, we only add the original term cluster to the knowledge base as a new entity. The clustering result $C(e, T_i)$ between e and T_i can thus be formally defined as:

$$C(e, T_i) := \begin{cases} e \cup T_i & , \forall e \in U_c : coh(e, T_i) = 1 \\ \{T_i, e \cup T_i\} & , \nexists e' \in U_c : coh(e', T_i) = 1 \\ & \quad \wedge \forall e \in U_c : tr_{coh} < coh(e, T_i) < 1 \\ T_i & , \nexists e' \in U_c : tr_{coh} < coh(e, T_i) \leq 1 \\ & \quad \wedge \forall e \in U_c : coh(e, T_i) < tr_{coh} \end{cases} \tag{11}$$

3.4   Knowledge Base Extension

The outcome of the clustering are cluster sets – independent, new entities and new entities as specializations of existing entities. Depending on the type of cluster, different implications apply regarding the extension of the entity graph and automata with clustered entities as follows.

Adding Entities to the Entity Graph. Term clusters that have not been merged with existing entities only consists of terms and are therefore treated as independent entities. Every independent entity gets assigned a new, specific type, which is added directly under the root node in the entity graph. This is done because there is insufficient information to determine if the new entity should be considered to be of an existing entity type. In contrast, a specialization of an entity is added to the entity graph as a new entity under the same parent as the original entity and gets assigned the same type of the original entity.

Adding Entities to the Automaton. Since the automaton uses entity types as it alphabet, each newly added independent entity requires a new state to be added to the automaton. The corresponding new type is added as a new transition. Figure 5 shows this for our example. Since specialized entities inherit the type of the original entity, the transition already exists and no changes have to be made to the automaton. Note that the update of the automaton is done automatically during the next strict classification using the revised entity graph.

Example 3 (Knowledge Base Extension Example)
Say, term clusters $T_b = \{\texttt{Bulk}\}$ and $T_r = \{\texttt{Reporting}\}$ both exceed given thresholds tr_{conf} and tr_f, and that T_r plus entity $\texttt{Employee}$ exceeds a given tr_{coh}. Therefore, T_b is added to the entity graph as a new entity $e_b = \texttt{Bulk}$ with equally-named type $c_{13} = \texttt{Bulk}$. During the next iteration, e_b will be recognized as an entity and incorporated into the automaton (cf. Figure 5). In contrast, term cluster T_r will be merged with entity $\texttt{Employee}$ and added to the knowledge base as entity $e_r = \texttt{Reporting Employee}$ with the same type as $\texttt{Employee}$, i.e. $c_9 : \texttt{Business Object}$. During the next iteration, e_r will be recognized as an entity supporting the already existing transition based on type c_9.

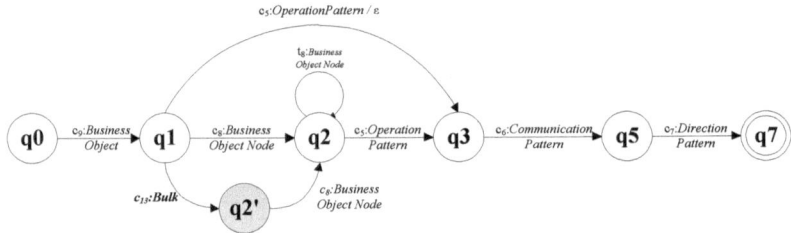

Fig. 5. Extending the example service design automaton from Fig. 2

As a result, the revised automaton also accepts signature S_{x_2} as follows:

$$S_{x_2}: \quad \underbrace{\texttt{Reporting Employee}}_{c_9:\text{BO}} \quad \underbrace{\texttt{Bulk}}_{c_{13}:\text{BULK}} \quad \underbrace{\texttt{Notification}}_{c_8:\text{BON}} \underbrace{\texttt{ByID}}_{} \underbrace{\texttt{QueryResponse}}_{c_6:\text{CP}} \underbrace{\texttt{\_In}}_{c_7:\text{DP}}$$

$$\phantom{S_{x_2}:}\qquad\qquad\qquad\qquad\qquad\qquad\qquad\qquad c_5:\text{OP}$$

4   Evaluation

We implemented the proposed, knowledge base-driven clustering approach $\mathcal{A}_{kb}$. As a baseline, we also implemented the HAC approach $\mathcal{A}_{cl}$ used in [7], and evaluated the performance of both approaches on a real-world testbed.

4.1   Evaluation Setup

The performance evaluation is based on a corpus of 1651 of SAP's (A2X) Enterprise Services, as well as an entity graph (cf. Figure 1) which we extracted from SAP's Enterprise Service Registry. Using the set of signatures and the entity graph as an input, we first performed a strict classification (cf. Section 3.1). The list of completely recognized signatures is from here on referred to as S_t, the set

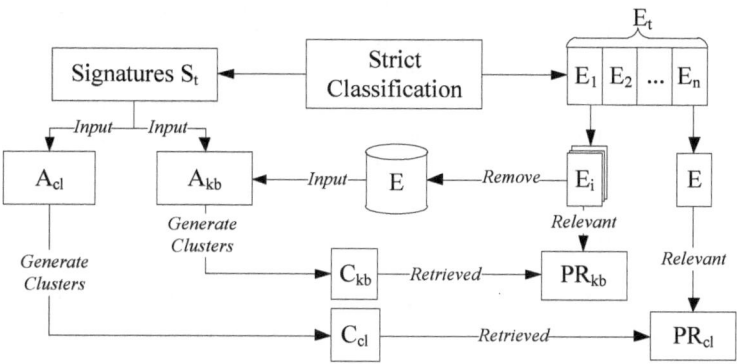

Fig. 6. Evaluation Setup for $\mathcal{A}_{kb}$ and $\mathcal{A}_{cl}$

of contained entities as E_t. We use S_t and E_t as the basis to determine precision, i.e. the fraction of clustered entities that is correct, and recall, i.e. the fraction of correct entities that has been clustered, for $\mathcal{A}_{kb}$ and $\mathcal{A}_{cl}$. Finally, we conducted the evaluation process as shown in Figure 6.

Knowledge Base-Driven Clustering $\mathcal{A}_{kb}$. For $\mathcal{A}_{kb}$, we used the set of signatures S_t and a *shortened version* of the entity graph as an input. The entity graph is reduced by removing a subset of entities from E_t, so that when we fed it into $\mathcal{A}_{kb}$, we can check if it produces clusters that match the entities removed before. By doing so, we can realistically simulate the situation where an incomplete KB has to be extended, while being able to check with certainty which clustering results are correct. For this, we apply a *round robin* strategy to determine equally-sized random subsets of entities $E_i \in E_t$, which are iteratively removed from the entity graph. The so-obtained shortened entity graphs are fed to $\mathcal{A}_{kb}$. For instance, a round robin partition of 3 initiates three different iterations, each having a third of E_t randomly removed from the entity graph and the result fed into $\mathcal{A}_{kb}$. By comparing the outputted clusters from $\mathcal{A}_{kb}$ against the previously removed E_i, we can calculate the average precision and recall PR_{kb} over all partitions. As usually, the F-Measure *F1* is the harmonic mean between PR. Using different numbers of round robin partitions allows us to investigate clustering performance in relation to how much of the entity graph is missing – i.e., how incomplete the KB is to begin with. In our experiment, we used the round robin partitions $RR \in [2, 3, 4, 5, 6, 8, 10, 20]$, which we each executed three times to mitigate randomness-based effects. For each round robin partition, we ran different combinations of the thresholds for confidence $tr_{conf} \in [0.1, \ldots, 0.9]$ and entity cohesion $tr_{coh} \in [0.1, \ldots, 0.9]$. Due to the way in which we created the test cases (all signatures in S_t were completely recognized before removing some entities), there is no noise present in the input signatures S_t. Hence, we switched the noise-filtering off by setting $tr_f = (0, 0)$.

Hierarchical Agglomerative Clustering $\mathcal{A}_{cl}$. For $\mathcal{A}_{cl}$, we used the HAC described in [7], which only requires a list of signatures S_t as an input. As in the strict classification, we split signatures in S_t into terms using their camel case notation. We then ran the term clustering with different values of support $p_s \in [1, \ldots, 10]$ (occurrences of a term – see [7] for details) and confidence $p_c \in [0.1, \ldots, 0.9]$ (co-occurrence of two terms). The outcome is a set of term clusters C_{cl}. As for $\mathcal{A}_{kb}$, we determined precision and recall PR_{cl}, but here based on C_{cl} and the complete set of entities E_t used in S_t.

4.2   Evaluation Results

First, consider the influence of entity cohesion. Figure 7(b) depicts the average F-Measure for various cohesion thresholds tr_{coh}. As shown, the average F-Measure steadily increases until its maximum at $tr_{coh} = 0.7$ and only slightly decreases beyond that. Figure 7(a) shows average F-Measures ($AvgF1$) and maximum F-Measure ($MaxF1$) for $\mathcal{A}_{kb}$ without ($-Coh$) and with cohesion ($+Coh$). With cohesion, $AvgF1$ and $MaxF1$ are continuously higher than without: F-Measure increases with cohesion by $11\% - 21\%$ ($AvgF1$) and by $14\% - 24\%$ ($MaxF1$). The graph also shows that $AvgF1 + tr_{coh}$ steadily increases with growing round robin partitions, as illustrated by the trend line. Therefore, the highest results can be found at $RR = 20$, with an average $F1$ of 0.55 and maximum $F1$ of 0.70.

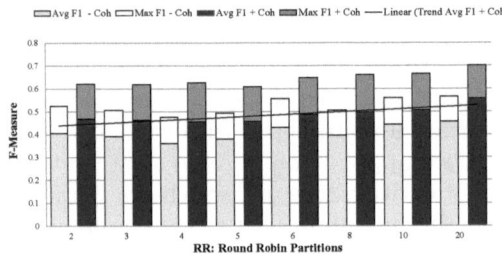 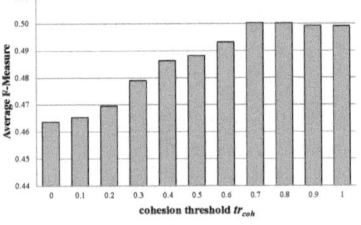

(a) Avg and Max F-Measure for RR (b) Avg F-Measure for tr_{coh}

Fig. 7. Impact of Cohesion and Round Robin Partitions on F-Measure

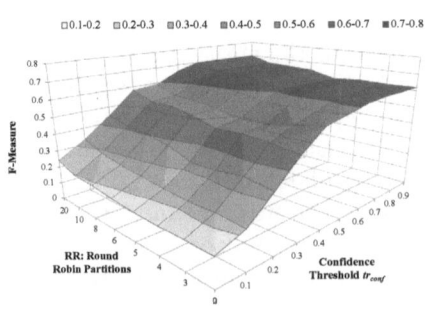 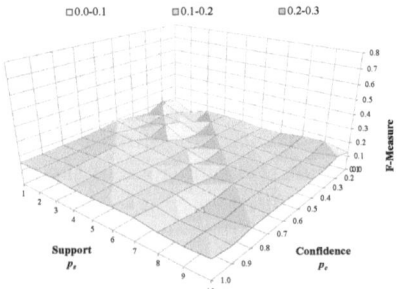

(a) F-Measure for $\mathcal{A}_{kb}$ (b) F-Measure for $\mathcal{A}_{cl}$

Fig. 8. Overall effectiveness of $\mathcal{A}_{kb}$ and $\mathcal{A}_{cl}$ for varying parameters

Figure 8(a) and 8(b) show the F-measure of $\mathcal{A}_{kb}$ and $\mathcal{A}_{cl}$ for combinations of $tr_{conf} \times RR$ (with a fixed $tr_{coh} = 0.7$) and $p_c \times p_s$ respectively. From Figure 8(a), it becomes clear that the term confidence tr_{conf} significantly influences the effectiveness of the $\mathcal{A}_{kb}$ clustering. That is, the F-Measure significantly increases with growing confidence thresholds and plateaus around its maximum of ≈ 0.7 for $tr_{conf} \geq 0.6$. The graph also shows a slightly higher F-Measure with increasing round robin partitions, and reaches a local maximum (relative to tr_{conf}) at $RR = 20$. Hence, we found the globally maximal F-Measure of ≈ 0.7 for $RR = 20$, $tr_{conf} \geq 0.6$ and $tr_{coh} = 0.7$. Figure 8(b) shows the results for the $\mathcal{A}_{cl}$ clustering. The F-Measure here ranges from 0.1 to a maximum of 0.21 ($p_c = 0.2$ and $p_s = 1$). It also shows that the parameters p_c and p_s do not have a significant impact on the overall performance of the clustering. From close observation of the data, we found that, when increasing p_c and p_s, infrequent but relevant terms are ignored, thus affecting both precision and recall. On the other hand, smaller values for p_c and p_s increase the number of terms considered by $\mathcal{A}_{cl}$ to find more term clusters – relevant and irrelevant alike. Therefore, an increase of recall might largely be outweighed by a decrease of precision.

5   Related Work

Since the proposed approach combines entity recognition with clustering, we mainly focus on prior work related to these two areas.

Named Entity Recognition Using Entity Graphs. Although most Named Entity Recognition (NER) references can be found with unstructured text, described recognition techniques, e.g. based on similarity scores [3] might be relevant. For instance, [9,20,3] describe graph based identification of entities using entity (and relationship) similarity measures. In [5], the authors calculate a similarity score of overlapping segments of text with entities from dictionaries. Similar to [4], they use a TF-IDF similarity score [22] and assume statistically independent terms, which is not the case for compact ES signatures where terms appear in a specific order. Moreover, for such structured signatures, a similarity score seems to be less feasible. That is, potential entities are found as exact matches during strict/approx. classification or as new entities during clustering.

Named Entity Recognition Using Supervised Learning. In general, rule-based approaches can be applied to extract named entities from documents, which often requires a significant manual effort. Therefore, supervised machine learning techniques [6,17] and bootstrapping algorithms [1,11] have been proposed to recognize entities or classify, e.g. Web Services [10,14]. For instance, [11] describes a similar approach based on a three level bootstrapping algorithm used with machine learning for regular expressions. The difference to our work is that no upfront naming definitions are required as they are extracted from unambiguous signatures - for multiple entity types. Further, we do not extract entities similar to recognized entities but compliant to recognized naming definitions.

Unsupervised Clustering. Many clustering approaches have been proposed using e.g. document similarity to merge cluster at document level. For instance, single and complete link [18] use the smallest minimum and maximum pairwise similarity distance between two clusters. Word-IC [23] uses a hierarchical agglomerative clustering (HAC) [21] based on the number of intersection terms within documents. Our work differs that we use clustering on operation-level to cluster entities (rather than documents) and thus can better determine the accuracy of intersecting terms relative to their noise. In [7,12] the authors also use HAC, e.g. based on term co-occurrences in operation names [7], to measure the cohesion and correlation within and between term clusters. However, we showed that such clustering performs moderate for entities with overlapping terms whose appearance is not statistically independent (e.g. using naming conventions).

6   Conclusion

In this paper, we presented an approach for amending incomplete knowledge bases of ES design knowledge. The approach only requires a set of ES signatures and an incomplete KB. It first reverse-engineers naming conventions and uses them to filter out unlikely explanations for partially understood signatures. The approach then suggests term clusters from unknown parts of the signature and possibly merges them with co-existing entities to form new entities. We evaluated the approach on a testbed of 1651 ES signatures from SAP. After removing parts of the KB, we tested how successful the approach re-added missing parts. The approach performed reasonably well when half of the KB was removed, and even better when only smaller chunks were missing. Moreover, the approach performed significantly better than a state-of-the-art clustering approach. In future work, we plan to improve our search engine for ESs and extend the current comparative experiment to other clustering techniques.

References

1. Agichtein, E., Gravano, L.: Snowball: Extracting Relations From Large Plain-Text Collections. In: DL 2000, pp. 85–94. ACM, New York (2000)
2. Bennett, S.G., Gee, C., Laird, R., Manes, A.T., Schneider, R., Shuster, L., Tost, A., Venable, C.: SOA Governance: Governing Shared Services On-Premise and in the Cloud. Prentice Hall (2011)
3. Brauer, F., Huber, M., Hackenbroich, G., Leser, U., Naumann, F., Barczynski, W.M.: Graph-Based Concept Identification and Disambiguation for Enterprise Search. In: WWW 2010, pp. 171–180. ACM, New York (2010)
4. Chakaravarthy, V.T., Gupta, H., Roy, P., Mohania, M.: Efficiently Linking Text Documents With Relevant Structured Information. In: VLDB 2006, pp. 667–678 (2006)
5. Chandel, A., Nagesh, P., Sarawagi, S.: Efficient Batch Top-k Search for Dictionary-based Entity Recognition. In: ICDE 2006, p. 28 (April 2006)
6. Chieu, H.L., Ng, H.T.: Named Entity Recognition: A Maximum Entropy Approach Using Global Information. In: COLING 2002, USA, pp. 1–7 (2002)

7. Dong, X., Halevy, A., Madhavan, J., Nemes, E., Zhang, J.: Similarity Search for Web Services. In: VLDB 2004, pp. 372–383. VLDB Endowment (2004)
8. Falkl, J., Laird, R., Carrato, T., Kreger, H.: IBM Advantage for SOA Governance Standards (July 2009), http://www.ibm.com/developerworks/webservices/library/ws-soagovernanceadv/index.html
9. Hassell, J., Aleman-Meza, B., Budak Arpinar, I.: Ontology-Driven Automatic Entity Disambiguation in Unstructured Text. In: Cruz, I., Decker, S., Allemang, D., Preist, C., Schwabe, D., Mika, P., Uschold, M., Aroyo, L.M. (eds.) ISWC 2006. LNCS, vol. 4273, pp. 44–57. Springer, Heidelberg (2006)
10. Heß, A., Kushmerick, N.: Learning to Attach Semantic Metadata to Web Services. In: Fensel, D., Sycara, K., Mylopoulos, J. (eds.) ISWC 2003. LNCS, vol. 2870, pp. 258–273. Springer, Heidelberg (2003)
11. Irmak, U., Kraft, R.: A Scalable Machine-Learning Approach for Semi-Structured Named Entity Recognition. In: WWW 2010, pp. 461–470. ACM, USA (2010)
12. Karypis, G., Han, E.-H., Kumar, V.: Chameleon: Hierarchical Clustering Using Dynamic Modeling. Computer 32(8), 68–75 (1999)
13. Malinverno, P.: Service-oriented architecture craves governance (October 2006), http://www.gartner.com/DisplayDocument?id=488180
14. Oldham, N., Thomas, C., Sheth, A., Verma, K.: METEOR-S Web Service Annotation Framework with Machine Learning Classification. In: Cardoso, J., Sheth, A. (eds.) SWSWPC 2004. LNCS, vol. 3387, pp. 137–146. Springer, Heidelberg (2005)
15. Roy, M., Suleiman, B., Schmidt, D., Weber, I., Benatallah, B.: Using SOA Governance Design Methodologies to Augment Enterprise Service Descriptions. In: Mouratidis, H., Rolland, C. (eds.) CAiSE 2011. LNCS, vol. 6741, pp. 566–581. Springer, Heidelberg (2011)
16. SAP. Governance for Modeling and Implementing Enterprise Services at SAP (April 2007), http://www.sdn.sap.com/irj/sdn/go/portal/prtroot/docs/library/uuid/f0763dbc-abd3-2910-4686-ab7adfc8ed92
17. Saquete, E., Ferrández, O., Ferrández, S., Martínez-Barco, P., Muñoz, R.: Combining Automatic Acquisition of Knowledge With Machine Learning Approaches for Multilingual Temporal Recognition and Normalization. In: IS 2008, pp. 3319–3332 (2008)
18. Voorhees, E.M.: The Effectiveness and Efficiency of Agglomerative Hierarchic Clustering in Document Retrieval. PhD thesis, Ithaca, NY, USA (1986)
19. Watson, B.W.: A New Algorithm for the Construction of Minimal Acyclic DFAs. Science of Computer Programming 48(2-3), 81–97 (2003)
20. Wang, W., Xiao, C., Lin, X., Zhang, C.: Efficient Approximate Entity Extraction With Edit Distance Constraints. In: SIGMOD 2009, pp. 759–770. ACM, USA (2009)
21. Willett, P.: Recent Trends in Hierarchic Document Clustering: A Critical Review. Information Processing and Management 24(5), 577–597 (1988)
22. Witten, I.H., Moffat, A., Bell, T.C.: Managing Gigabytes: Compressing and Indexing Documents and Images. Morgan Kaufmann, San Francisco (1999)
23. Zamir, O., Etzioni, O., Madani, O., Karp, R.: Fast and Intuitive Clustering of Web Documents. In: Knowledge Discovery and Data Mining, pp. 287–290 (1997)

Participatory Service Design through Composed and Coordinated Service Feature Models

Erik Wittern, Nelly Schuster, Jörn Kuhlenkamp, and Stefan Tai

eOrganization Research Group, Karlsruhe Institute of Technology
Englerstr. 11, 76131 Karlsruhe, Germany
{Erik.Wittern,Nelly.Schuster,Joern.Kuhlenkamp,Stefan.Tai}@kit.edu
http://www.eOrganization.de

Abstract. Active participation of diverse stakeholders such as consumers or experts in service engineering is critical. It ensures that relevant aspects of service quality, service acceptance and service compliance are addressed. However, coordination of diverse stakeholder inputs is difficult and their collaborative creation of common design artifacts demands novel engineering solutions. We present a service-oriented approach for engineering design artifacts: service feature models are introduced as compositions of model parts that can be contributed by different stakeholders and software resources acting as services. Our method and tool applies service-orientation to collaborative design, thereby taking participatory service engineering to the level of coordinated service composition.

Keywords: Service engineering, service feature modeling, coordination, collaboration, participatory service design.

1 Introduction

Participatory service engineering is about the involvement of different stakeholders, in the role of service providers and service consumers, into the analysis, design, and development of services [10,11]. In the public sector, for instance, stakeholders include citizens, municipalities, and corporations. Involving different stakeholders into the service engineering life cycle is a non-trivial task; however, participation promises to better meet the interests and needs of all parties involved, to improve customer satisfaction, and to better comply with relevant policies and laws [10].

In service design, stakeholders typically are represented by groups of experts, including software engineers, infrastructure providers, decision-makers, and legal experts. These stakeholders collaborate with each other, contributing specific knowledge. Results of the collaboration are manifested in one or more design artifacts (such as documents or code), which correspondingly address the diversity of relevant service aspects, including technical, business-related or legal ones.

Participatory service design can thus be seen as the process of coordinating a set of stakeholders, where each stakeholder is represented by one or more experts

C. Liu et al. (Eds.): ICSOC 2012, LNCS 7636, pp. 158–172, 2012.
© Springer-Verlag Berlin Heidelberg 2012

and contributes to the creation of design artifacts. Here, we introduce *service feature models (SFMs)* as a modeling approach for service design to create such coordinated, composed design artifacts: SFMs capture design aspects that are contributed by different stakeholders (or even other sources). SFMs include design alternatives (e.g. the set of authentication mechanisms the implementation of a service could use), decisions (e.g. which authentication mechanism to use), and constraints (e.g. that a service has to be delivered electronically). They can be composed to serve as a single design artifact that describes diverse relevant design issues.

This design artifact is a document composed of services: model parts are contributed by human-provided services or by software services. Thus, responsibilities for the specification of design aspects can be delegated to dedicated experts who can work on them in parallel. In addition, data from software services or form resources on the Web can be integrated, which can serve as a base for design decision-making. To manage causal dependencies between model parts and to govern the collaborative composition activities, we define coordination mechanisms that involve a coordinator role along with a set of lightweight coordination rules.

The remainder of this paper is structured as follows: In Section 2 we introduce and discuss service feature modeling as a technique to support service design. We present its methodology in service design, its modeling elements and shortly discuss how we used the approach in the context of the COCKPIT project [6]. In Section 3, we present our approach to compose SFMs of services. For this purpose, we build on our composition and coordination model for document-based collaboration [16] and define (a) a *service composition model* which allows coordinators to delegate modeling tasks to responsible experts based on the modularization of SFMs and (b) a set of *coordination rules* which allow the (semi-)automated management of dependencies between different model parts and activities. The system architecture and proof-of-concept implementation that we used to determine the applicability of our approach is described in Section 4. In Section 5, we discuss related work. Finally, we summarize our work and present an outlook in Section 6.

2   Service Feature Models

To provide a comprehensive view of a participatory service design, design artifacts stemming from experts of different domains or disciplines need to be captured and integrated in one service model. *Service feature modeling* has been designed for this purpose and has been conceptualized in previous work [19]. Service feature modeling builds upon the well-established feature modeling approach from software product line engineering [12]. Therefore, SFMs benefit from efficient modeling methodologies, formalisms and automatic reasoning capabilities designed for standard feature models, e.g., [4,3,7,8,13].

2.1 Methodology

Iterative service design and rapid development of service design alternatives allow to communicate, discuss and assess design alternatives, improving overall service quality. We distinguish two phases in iterative service design: first, a rapid *modeling phase*, second, a detailed *configuration phase*.

In the modeling phase, a SFM is created as a design artifact that represents a number of relevant design aspects. Multiple design alternatives are modeled in this design artifact that represents a set of possible implementations of the service.

In the configuration phase, decisions between design alternatives are made. The resulting artifact of the configuration phase is a *configuration*. In contrast to a SFM, a configuration represents only a single valid service design. A configuration serves as input for service implementation and documents the design decisions made. During the configuration phase, constraints and preferences are specified based on requirements. Requirements are collected from stakeholders, for instance citizens in public service design. Modeling of constraints and preferences improves service design because it reveals trade-offs that result from choosing one design alternative over another.

2.2 Modeling Elements

An exemplary SFM is illustrated in Figure 1. It represents (simplified) the "Access extracts of insurance record in Social Security Organization (GR01)" service that the Greek Ministry of Interior provided as a service scenario in the COCKPIT project. The service's goal is to allow employees to access their insurance record to verify that their employers contributed to the social security insurance.

The *service feature diagram* is the graphical representation of a SFM, in which *features* are decomposed into a tree-structure. Features represent service design

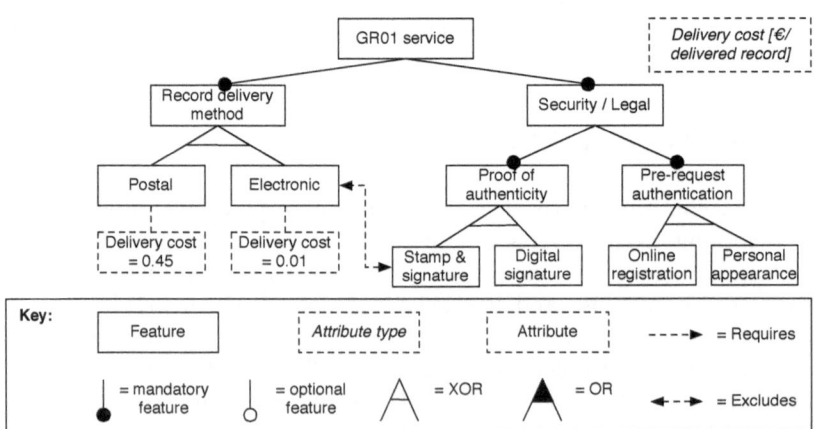

Fig. 1. Exemplary "Access extracts of insurance record in Social Security Organization (GR01)" service modeled (simplified) as SFM

aspects of relevance for a stakeholder, e.g. an access channel, a work-flow variant or a legal aspect. Features can be denoted as *mandatory* or *optional*. This allows service engineers to derive several configurations during the configuration phase. Features can also be grouped in *XOR* or *OR* groups, meaning that for a valid configuration, exactly one or at least one feature from the group needs to be selected. Causal dependencies can be specified through *cross-tree relationships*. They depict that one feature either *requires* or *excludes* another feature to be part of a valid configuration. For example, in Figure 1, if "stamp & signature" is selected, the record delivery method "electronic" cannot be selected and vice versa. *Attributes* describe measurable, non-functional characteristics of features [4]. For example, an attribute can denote the "delivery cost" of a feature representing the delivery method. *Attribute types* capture common characteristics of attributes. For example, in Figure 1, the attribute type "delivery cost" defines the measure for all attributes of that type to be "€/ delivered record".

2.3 Service Feature Modeling in Practice

The COCKPIT EU project aims to enable diverse stakeholders, including e.g. citizens, to participate in the design of public services [6]. We developed service feature modeling in this context to address the necessity of combining diverse service design aspects in a single model. In COCKPIT, service feature modeling was applied to three public service (re-) design scenarios. SFMs were modeled that represent multiple variants of how to provide the public service in question. During the configuration phase, citizens participated by stating their preferences regarding the SFM's attribute types on a deliberation platform. These preferences were, using multi-criteria decision making, applied to the possible service alternatives to determine a ranking of the alternatives. However, we learned in COCKPIT that it is highly desirable not only to enable participation in the configuration but also in the modeling of SFMs to integrate expert knowledge from diverse disciplines at an early stage. This is what motivated our approach for composed and coordinated SFMs.

3 Collaborative Service Feature Modeling

In collaborative service feature modeling, model parts contributed by diverse participants are composed into a single SFM. The structure of the composition is defined by our *service composition model*. *Roles* describe activities that participants perform. *Coordination mechanisms* provide the required coordination of the service composition and modeling activities.

Figure 2 depicts an example where several participants collaborate to create the "GR01" service. As illustrated, responsibilities for the modeling of certain service aspects are separated among several participants: a "service engineer", responsible for the creation of the overall service design, contributes an initial SFM representing the "GR01" service. For the aspect "security / legal", a dedicated SFM is delivered by a "legal expert". On the lower left side, a "cost estimation service" contributes attribute values for two attributes of the type "delivery

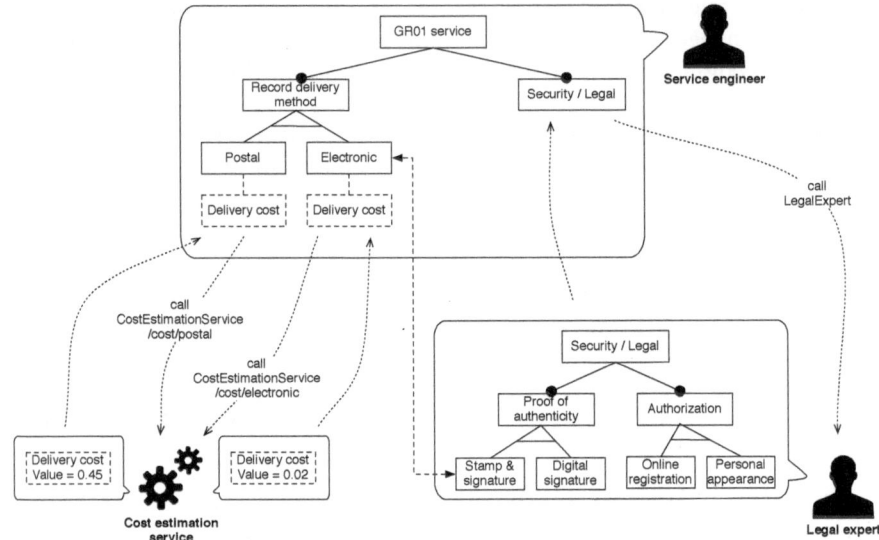

Fig. 2. Example of SFM composed of services

cost". The overall SFM representing the "GR01" service is thus a composition of results contributed by human and non-human service providers.

3.1   Service Composition Model

The service composition model defines how results and services can be composed in order to derive a coherent SFM. The model is illustrated in Figure 3. It is based on and extends previous work [16,17]. Note that *service* does not denote the service to be modeled but the services that contribute results.

The intended outcome of the collaboration, a composed SFM, consists of multiple *results*. We distinguish two specific types of (expected) results:

- **SFMs** are parts of a larger SFM. The *sub result* relationship denotes the potential nesting of SFMs. For example, in Figure 2, the SFM corresponding to the "GR01" service contains another SFM corresponding to the service's "security / legal" aspects. The tree structure of the SFM itself does not

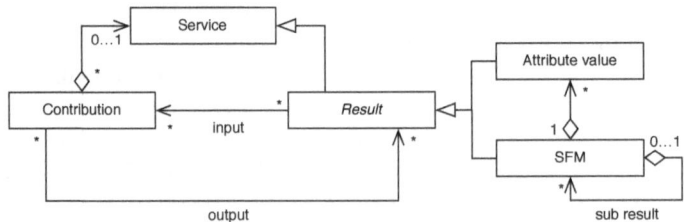

Fig. 3. Service composition model, based on [16]

necessarily correspond to the tree structure of the service composition model. As defined in Section 2.2, SFMs contain features, attribute types, attributes and cross-tree relationships.

 - **Attribute values** are primitive data types (i.e. integer, double or string) representing measurable, non-functional characteristics of a feature. As such, attribute values cannot, in contrast to SFMs, be decomposed further into sub results. In Figure 2, two attribute values are contributed to the "delivery cost" attributes of the "postal" and "electronic" delivery.

Contributions denote the delivery or transformation of results. Results are the output of one or more contributions. A contribution is performed by a dedicated human-based or software service. This service may transform existing results which it gets as input. Separating contributions from results provides the flexibility of having multiple contributions collectively work on a result or of using a single contribution for delivering or transforming multiple results. For example, for a SFM the contributions "create SFM", "validate SFM" and "approve SFM" may exist. In Figure 2, contributions are illustrated as speech bubbles delivered by the services "service engineer", "cost estimation service" and "legal expert". Results themselves are offered as services and can be reused in other SFM modeling projects.

3.2   Roles

During collaboration, participants take different roles. A role describes a set of activities an actor may perform in participatory service design. A single actor may engage in multiple roles at the same time or vary roles over time [18]. We refer to an actor in one of the three following roles by the name of the role:

 - **Modelers** contribute SFMs. They define how to decompose features, which attributes to use to describe properties of features and what attribute types they relate to, and finally what cross-tree relationships exist between features. In general, we assume that human actors hold the role modeler (e.g. a legal expert).
 - **Attribute value providers** provide contributions to attribute values. To account for dynamic changes in attribute values during and after service design as well as for complex calculations of attribute values, we propose to utilize non-human actors, e.g. Web services, for the role of an attribute value provider (e.g. a benchmark service).
 - **Coordinators** have two assigned responsibilities. Firstly, they identify contributions and assign modeling tasks for both SFMs and attribute values. Secondly, coordinators assign services to identified contributions in the role of either modeler or attribute value provider. Coordination activities can be delegated by assigning the coordinator role with respect to a single result. This allows for coordination activities within a different department involved in the collaborative service design (e.g. the legal department).

Modeler and coordinator roles are closely related because the division of labor is performed using the overall SFM structure and requires basic understanding of modeling.

3.3   Coordination Mechanisms for Service Feature Modeling

During service feature modeling, human experts collaborate to construct the SFM according to the component model described in Section 3.1. To start the collaboration, a coordinator defines several required results and contributions. In order to delegate tasks, the coordinator assigns human experts or software services to the contributions. During collaboration, additional results or contributions are added or services assigned. As soon as services are assigned, they are allowed to participate through delivering or transforming respective results.

The challenge in realizing such collaboration is to coordinate interactions of services with the overall SFM in order to avoid inconsistencies due to dependencies between tasks or contributions, e.g., due to cross-tree relationships. To coordinate collaborative service feature modeling, we identified four required types of *coordination mechanisms*.

Coordination of Basic Interactions. In our previous work, we specified and visualized a *service binding protocol* for service assignments [16] allowing the delegation of results to responsible modelers. This protocol is suitable for SFM compositions as well: The binding of a service to a contribution is initiated by the coordinator, asking the service for its commitment to contribute. The service may accept or decline. We expect that, in most cases, the service provider will accept the binding as he was selected based on his expertise for the respective service model part. Software services automatically accept a binding request.

As soon as a service is bound, it can deliver the results related to the assigned contribution, e.g., new SFMs or attribute values. The response of the service is an update of the associated output results. In addition, during collaboration, a bound service can be manually called by a coordinator, for instance, as a reminder to contribute not yet delivered results. The results can be updated by the service until they are approved by a coordinator. This is defined in the *service request / response protocol* [16].

These protocols allow easy integration of human and software services alike as they do not require complex activities. All service providers need to implement the protocols. This hierarchical coordination model is suitable for multidisciplinary service design projects, where experts for different domains as well as responsible service engineers for a SFM exist that are responsible for the delegation of work to experts.

Coordination of Cross-Tree Relationships. Cross-tree relationships denote that one feature either requires or excludes the existence of another feature in a configuration (see Section 2.2). Changing or deleting a feature that is part of a cross-tree relationship can cause inconsistencies in a SFM. Thus, if a cross-tree relationship in a result relates to a feature in another result, a notification to the modeler of the cross-tree relationship should be sent if the feature is changed or deleted.

For the management of such dependencies, we use the event-condition-action (ECA) rule mechanism of [16] and configure it with event types and rules required for collaborative service feature modeling. Events are emitted on changes of results as well as on each transition in the basic interaction protocols presented above. Events are input to rules which might trigger actions, e.g. service calls or the sending of notification messages.

To coordinate cross-tree relationships, we define the events *FeatureUpdated* and *FeatureDeleted* that are emitted on changing or deleting an SFM containing the feature. Additionally, if a cross-tree relationship is specified by a modeler in an SFM and the SFM is updated, a rule is automatically instantiated that triggers adequate measures in reaction to these events. For example, based on the SFM illustrated in Figure 2, as soon as the legal expert identifies the exclude relationship between delivery method "electronic"and "stamp & signature", a rule is created as defined below. If "electronic" is changed to "certified mail", the legal expert is notified to check the excludes dependency to "stamp & signature" for validity and possibly adapt it. (Note: the values "electronic" and "legal expert" in the following rule denote unique, non-changeable IDs of the results or contributions, respectively.)

```
EVERY FeatureUpdated("electronic") OR FeatureDeleted("electronic")
DO notify("legal expert");
```

Coordination of Attribute Type Dependencies. Attribute types allow modelers to define common characteristics of attributes, e.g. the measurement unit for "cost". If an attribute type is changed or deleted, potential inconsistencies can occur with regard to the attributes relating to this type. Thus, a modeler of an attribute should be notified in such cases. Similar to handling cross-tree relationships, attribute type dependencies are coordinated using ECA rules. The dedicated events are *AttributeTypeUpdated* and *AttributeTypeDeleted*. Rules for such attribute type dependencies listen for events denoting a change of the attribute type. The rules are automatically created as soon as an SFM is created or updated including an attribute that relates to an attribute type in another result. As action, notifications are sent to the modelers of SFMs including attributes of this type. For instance, if the measurement unit of an attribute type "delivery cost" is changed from "€/ delivered record" to "€/ month", the modelers of SFMs including an attribute using this attribute type are notified and possibly request the according attribute value providers with updated parameters.

```
EVERY AttributeTypeUpdated("delivery cost")
   OR AttributeTypeDeleted("delivery cost")
DO notify("service engineer")
```

Coordination of Attribute Provisioning Dependencies. Contributions of attribute value providers are useful to include real-time data into the SFM or include complex data that results from a calculation. The invocation of such services should be performed during the configuration phase since currentness of attribute values influences the selection among alternatives. As we can not always count on the automated push of attribute values from external Web services in case they have recent data, we suggest to define new event types which denote the end of the modeling phase and are emitted, for instance, if requested via the modeling tool. The event might then trigger a rule which requests all services delivering an attribute value. Additionally, a rule might request services at certain points in time, e.g., every morning at 8am. Such rules can be manually specified throughout the collaboration by the coordinators of SFMs. Alternatively, we suggest that they are created as soon as attribute value providers are bound to a contribution and deleted if the binding is removed.

```
EVERY ModelingPhaseFinished
DO requestContribution("big machine benchmark");
```

```
AT (timer:8am)
DO requestContribution("big machine benchmark");
```

We believe that the proposed event types and rules are suitable to avoid inconsistencies during service feature modeling. However, we do not claim completeness. As the ECA rules coordination approach is very generic and extensible, additional rules and event types can be specified whenever needed. For example, modelers can specify rules which notify them if a certain result was delivered or updated, using events of type *SFMUpdated* or *SFMDeleted*.

4   Proof of Concept

We designed a system architecture supporting the conceptualized collaboration model and prototypically implemented it. The implementation strongly builds upon and extends the implementation used within the COCKPIT EU project [20].

4.1   Architecture and Components

The architecture is shown in Figure 4. The individual components are presented in the following subsections.

Service Feature Model Designer (SFM Designer): The *SFM designer* provides a user interface for participating experts. It addresses two basic functionalities. First, it provides *modeling* capabilities via graphical UI used to create and adapt SFMs that are provided as results. As such, it acts as a service adapter for these human experts who, as modelers, contribute results. Second, the SFM designer provides *coordination* capabilities. It allows coordinators to define (expected) results and to define which services should contribute the results. Supporting the configuration phase, the SFM designer can determine all possible configurations for a given SFM and aggregates their attributes.

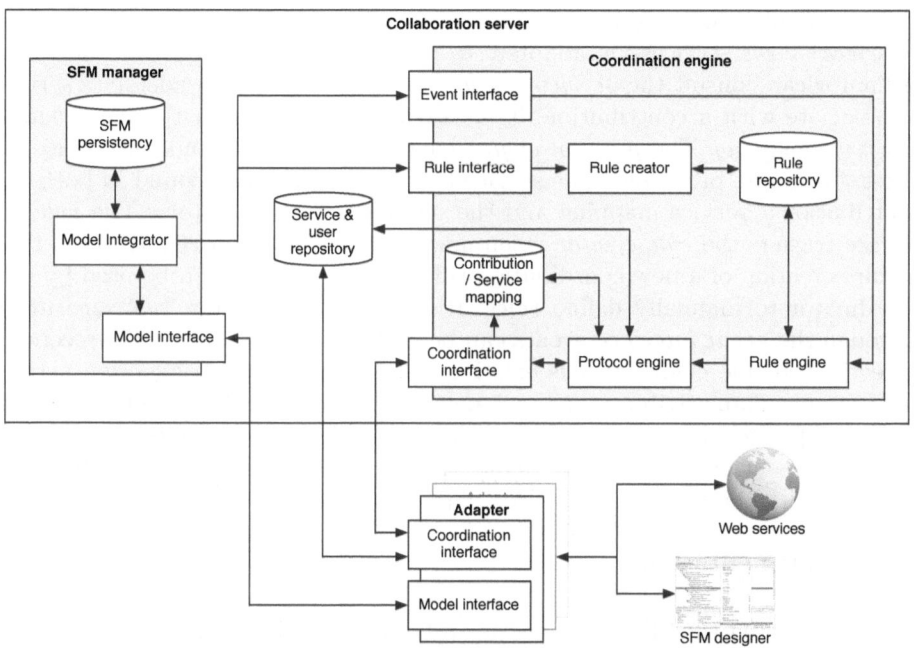

Fig. 4. Architecture of a system for collaborative service feature modeling

Adapters: Our system design foresees numerous adapters that allow services to participate in the collaboration. Adapters ensure compatibility of the service interfaces and our system's interfaces, e.g. they implement the coordination protocols described in Section 3.3. Per service interface, a dedicated adapter is required. Adapters have two interfaces to communicate with our system: via the *coordination interface*, services can be asked for binding and can then be requested to update according results. The *model interface* is used to retrieve existing results of the model in focus and to contribute (create, update, or delete) results.

Collaboration Server: The *collaboration server* handles the coordination required for asynchronous collaboration in service feature modeling. It consists of three components, the *service & user repository*, the *SFM manager* and the *collaboration engine.*

The SFM manager stores the contributed results, namely SFMs and attribute values, in the *SFM persistency* component. Using the *model interface*, any service bound via adapters can create, retrieve, update or delete results - thus, for both SFM and attribute value results, CRUD methods are provided. Results sent or requested pass through the *model integrator*. It checks committed results for a) model elements that require coordination rules to be defined, e.g. attributes relating to attribute types outside of the result, and b) changes w.r.t. model elements that require coordination, e.g. changes to cross-tree relationships. In such cases, the model integrator triggers the *coordination engine* to create rules or throw events. Further, if a result from the collaboration server is requested, the model integrator composes it by integrating all sub results into one coherent SFM.

The coordination engine contains the coordination logic. The *coordination interface* allows services via adapters to participate in the coordination. A coordinator can consult the *service & user repository* to find an adequate service to associate with a contribution. The association is stored in the *contribution / service mapping*. The *protocol engine* controls the binding and the service request / response protocol of the service based on information found in both the contribution / service mapping and the service & user repository. The *rule interface* triggers the *rule creator* when new model elements are contributed that require creation of a new coordination rule. Additionally, it can be used by any coordinator to manually define rules. Rules are stored in the *rule repository*. Through the *event interface* events can be sent to the *rule engine*. On receiving an event the rule engine checks existing rules and possibly triggers an action. For example, if an attribute type is changed, the "AttributeTypeUpdated" event triggers a previously specified rule which notifies all depending modelers. Notifications are sent via the *protocol engine* that communicates via the coordination interface with the respective service adapters.

4.2   Implementation

We implemented the SFM designer as an Eclipse-based rich client on top of the Eclipse Modeling Framework (EMF)[1]. Adapters are built on RESTful design principles utilizing Jersey[2]. Figure 5 shows the user interface of the SFM designer. We implemented our collaboration server based on the Grails Web

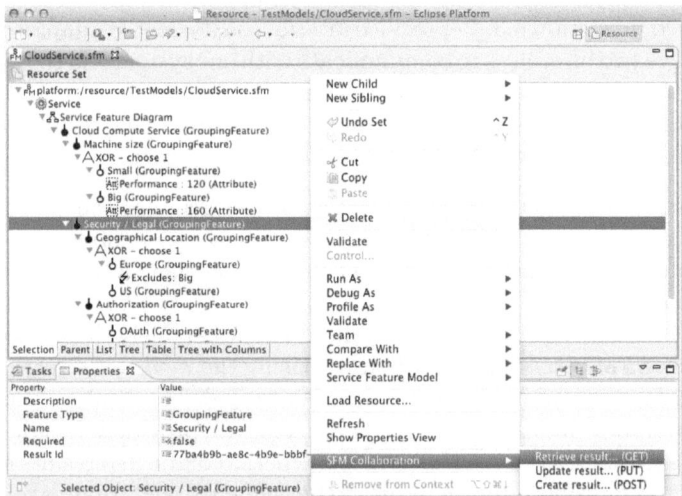

Fig. 5. Screen shot of the SFM designer with exemplary SFM and menu bar entries allowing to coordinate collaboration

---

[1] http://www.eclipse.org/modeling/emf/
[2] http://jersey.java.net/

application framework[3] and RESTful design principles. We built Java and Groovy[4] server libraries. The SFM manager stores SFMs within the SFM persistency in XML format. Service repository, rule repository and contribution/service mapping persist data in a MySQL database. We use ESPER[5] to implement our rule engine. Rules are expressed in the ESPER Event Processing Language (EPL).

Using our prototype implementation, we asserted the functionality of the presented approach. We are able to successfully assign contributions to human-based and Web services. For SFM results, corresponding resources are created, updated, retrieved and deleted by the SFM manager. On updating SFMs, the model integrator triggers the creation of rules and triggers events w.r.t. existing rules as conceptualized in Section 3.3. Notifications are currently send via e-mail. Alternative reactions depend on the implementation and can include, for instance, triggering service calls. Our implementation overall shows the applicability of our approach to enable collaborative creation of SFMs composed of services and thus affirms its ability to foster participatory service design.

5 Related Work

Some approaches to participatory service design exist. For example, [10] presents a high-level methodology for the participatory analysis, design, and optimization of services in the public sector. Our approach is in-line with this methodology and similar works and extends them by contributing a specific modeling notation and corresponding tools.

Regarding collaborative modeling, most of the approaches we found discuss the creation of models in the CAD domain where several experts work together to derive a graphical model of a product. For instance, the authors of [5] present an approach for collaborative editing of a central model maintained on a server, also addressing basic coordination problems, e.g. concurrency and synchronization. They do not consider a human coordinator or the creation of model parts by services. In contrast, we aim to allow a coordinator to split the model into parts to be delegated to responsible experts. We thus provide coordination mechanism on an application level.

Several works address how multiple *feature models* can be combined. [1] proposes to compose feature models that address specific domains, aiming to better deal with rising complexity for large feature models, to foster the model's evolution and also to engage diverse stakeholders into the modeling. In [2], a representation of feature models using description logics and a corresponding configuration method is presented to allow multiple experts to model and configure feature models. Both works focus on how to combine multiple models but do not address the coordinated creation of models or the integration of up-to-date values. Methodologies addressing the modeling of modular feature models

---

[3] http://www.grails.org
[4] http://groovy.codehaus.org/
[5] http://esper.codehaus.org/

are named as an intended future work. In contrast, we focus on the coordination of creating modular feature models collaboratively.

The approach presented in [9] focuses on collaborative modeling in software engineering. It allows software engineers to decompose UML diagrams into fine-grained design model parts that can be modified by distributed participants. The approach has some similarities to our approach, e.g., hierarchically breakdown of models into parts, event-based notifications and coordination mechanisms to manage concurrent access and dependencies between model parts. In [22] a model and tool are presented that enable software architects to collaboratively capture architectural decision alternatives and decision outcomes in a specialized Wiki. In the modeling phase, architects can define dependencies between decisions. Alternatives are used to ensure consistent and correct decision-making during the configuration phase. Despite some similarities, both presented approaches do not (yet) support delegation of modeling parts through a coordinator and do not enable the integration of content provided by software services into the models.

Flexible composition of services through end-users has been discussed in the mashups area [21]. Mashups allow end-users to easily compose and integrate (Web) services into artifacts. In addition, approaches for the integration of human-provided services into collaboration exist [15]. However, we are not aware of any approach that allows participants to create models through a mashup mechanism.

Overall, having analyzed related work in various research areas, we believe that our approach uniquely combines coordination and service-composition concepts to support participation of various experts in service design.

6   Conclusion and Future Work

In this paper, we addressed participatory service design by presenting SFMs as design artifacts capable of integrating various design issues. As we experienced in the COCKPIT project, especially the modeling phase in the SFM methodology allows for discussion and knowledge exchange in an early stage of the service design. Accordingly, we presented a service-composition model which allows participants to delegate responsibilities for model parts to experts who can independently contribute their parts to a central, uniform design artifact. By separating responsibilities based on the model structure, we tackle the challenge of integrating sub-models into a coherent model while still allowing participants to model in parallel [14]. In our approach participants act as human or software services, allowing the integration of dynamic or complex data into SFMs which can be kept up to date automatically. Collaboration activities are coordinated through a) the delegation of work based on the SFM structure and b) interaction protocols and a simple event-condition-action rule mechanism. This mechanism can also be used as a notification mechanism to manage causal dependencies between model parts, for instance cross-tree relationships. We presented the architecture of a system realizing our approach and a proof-of-concept implementation that allowed us to act out the relevant use cases of our approach.

In future work, we plan to address the collaborative configuration of SFMs. Configuration results could be used to incorporate the configuration of a (sub) SFM. It may be noted, however, that the collaborative configuration of feature models is already addressed in numerous works, e.g. [7,13]. Further, we want to investigate means to support consensus-based decisions on model parts, e.g. quorum-based decisions. We also envision the parameterization of service calls from a SFM based on dependent results, which would allow for even more flexible integration of results.

Acknowledgment. This work was supported by the COCKPIT project [6].

References

1. Acher, M., Collet, P., Lahire, P., France, R.: Composing Feature Models. In: van den Brand, M., Gašević, D., Gray, J. (eds.) SLE 2009. LNCS, vol. 5969, pp. 62–81. Springer, Heidelberg (2010)
2. Bagheri, E., Ensan, F., Gasevic, D., Boskovic, M.: Modular Feature Models: Representation and Configuration. Journal of Research and Practice in Information Technology 43(2), 109–140 (2011)
3. Benavides, D., Segura, S., Ruiz-Cortés, A.: Automated Analysis of Feature Models 20 Years Later: A Literature Review. Information Systems 35(6), 615–636 (2010)
4. Benavides, D., Trinidad, P., Ruiz-Cortés, A.: Automated Reasoning on Feature Models. In: Pastor, Ó., Falcão e Cunha, J. (eds.) CAiSE 2005. LNCS, vol. 3520, pp. 491–503. Springer, Heidelberg (2005)
5. Bidarra, R., Berg, E.V.D., Bronsvoort, W.F.: Collaborative Modeling with Features. In: Proc. of the 2001 ASME Design Engineering Technical Conferences, DETC 2001, Pittsburgh, Pennsylvania (2001)
6. COCKPIT Project: Citizens Collaboration and Co-Creation in Public Service Delivery (March 2012), http://www.cockpit-project.eu
7. Czarnecki, K., Helsen, S., Eisenecker, U.: Formalizing Cardinality-based Feature Models and their Specialization. Software Process: Improvement and Practice 10(1), 7–29 (2005)
8. Czarnecki, K., Helsen, S., Eisenecker, U.: Staged Configuration through Specialization and Multilevel Configuration of Feature Models. Software Process: Improvement and Practice 10(2), 143–169 (2005)
9. De Lucia, A., Fasano, F., Scanniello, G., Tortora, G.: Enhancing collaborative synchronous UML modelling with fine-grained versioning of software artefacts. Journal of Visual Languages and Computing 18(5), 492–503 (2007)
10. Hartman, A., Jain, A.N., Ramanathan, J., Ramfos, A., Van der Heuvel, W.-J., Zirpins, C., Tai, S., Charalabidis, Y., Pasic, A., Johannessen, T., Grønsund, T.: Participatory Design of Public Sector Services. In: Andersen, K.N., Francesconi, E., Grönlund, Å., van Engers, T.M. (eds.) EGOVIS 2010. LNCS, vol. 6267, pp. 219–233. Springer, Heidelberg (2010)
11. Holmlid, S.: Participative, co-operative, emancipatory: From participatory design to service design. In: 1st Nordic Conference on Service Design and Service, Oslo, Norway (2009)
12. Kang, K.C., Cohen, S.G., Hess, J.A., Novak, W.E., Peterson, A.S.: Feature-Oriented Domain Analysis (FODA) Feasibility Study. Tech. rep., Carnegie Mellon University (November 1990)

13. Mendonça, M., Cowan, D., Malyk, W., Oliveira, T.: Collaborative Product Configuration: Formalization and Efficient Algorithms for Dependency Analysis. Journal
of Software 3(2) (2008)
14. Renger, M., Kolfschoten, G.L., de Vreede, G.J.: Challenges in Collaborative Modeling: A Literature Review. In: Dietz, J.L.G., Albani, A., Barjis, J. (eds.) CIAO!
2008 and EOMAS 2008. LNBIP, vol. 10, pp. 61–77. Springer, Heidelberg (2008)
15. Schall, D., Truong, H.L., Dustdar, S.: Unifying human and software services in
web-scale collaborations. IEEE Internet Computing 12(3), 62–68 (2008)
16. Schuster, N., Zirpins, C., Scholten, U.: How to Balance between Flexibility and
Coordination? Model and Architecture for Document-based Collaboration on the
Web. In: Proc. on the 2011 IEEE Int. Conf. on Service-Oriented Computing and
Applications (SOCA), pp. 1–9 (2011)
17. Schuster, N., Zirpins, C., Tai, S., Battle, S., Heuer, N.: A Service-Oriented Approach to Document-Centric Situational Collaboration Processes. In: Proc. of the
18th IEEE Int. Workshops on Enabling Technologies: Infrastructures for Collaborative Enterprises, WETICE 2009, pp. 221–226. IEEE Computer Society, Washington, DC (2009)
18. Sonnenwald, D.H.: Communication roles that support collaboration during the
design process. Design Studies 17(3), 277–301 (1996)
19. Wittern, E., Zirpins, C.: On the Use of Feature Models for Service Design: The
Case of Value Representation. In: Cezon, M., Wolfsthal, Y. (eds.) ServiceWave
2010 Workshops. LNCS, vol. 6569, pp. 110–118. Springer, Heidelberg (2011)
20. Wittern, E., Zirpins, C., Rajshree, N., Jain, A.N., Spais, I., Giannakakis, K.: A Tool
Suite to Model Service Variability and Resolve It Based on Stakeholder Preferences.
In: Pallis, G., Jmaiel, M., Charfi, A., Graupner, S., Karabulut, Y., Guinea, S.,
Rosenberg, F., Sheng, Q.Z., Pautasso, C., Ben Mokhtar, S. (eds.) ICSOC 2011.
LNCS, vol. 7221, pp. 250–251. Springer, Heidelberg (2012)
21. Yu, J., Benatallah, B., Casati, F., Daniel, F.: Understanding Mashup Development.
IEEE Internet Computing 12(5), 44–52 (2008)
22. Zimmermann, O., Koehler, J., Leymann, F., Polley, R., Schuster, N.: Managing
Architectural Decision Models with Dependency Relations, Integrity Constraints,
and Production Rules. Journal of Systems and Software 82(8), 1249–1267 (2009)

PerCAS: An Approach to Enabling Dynamic and Personalized Adaptation for Context-Aware Services

Jian Yu[1], Jun Han[1], Quan Z. Sheng[2], and Steven O. Gunarso[1]

[1] Faculty of Information and Communication Technologies,
Swinburne University of Technology,
Hawthorn, 3122, Melbourne, Victoria, Australia
{jianyu,jhan}@swin.edu.au, 7253702@student.swin.edu.au
[2] School of Computer Science,
The University of Adelaide, SA 5005, Australia
qsheng@cs.adelaide.edu.au

Abstract. Context-aware services often need to adapt their behaviors according to physical situations and user preferences. However, most of the existing approaches to developing context-aware services can only do adaptation based on globally defined adaptation logic without considering the personalized context-aware adaptation needs of a specific user. In this paper, we propose a novel model-driven approach called PerCAS to developing and executing *personalized context-aware services* that are able to adapt to a specific user's adaptation needs at runtime. To enable dynamic and personalized context-aware adaptation, user-specific adaptation logic is encoded as rules, which are then weaved into a base process with an aspect-oriented mechanism. At runtime, the active user-specific rule set will be switched depending on who is using/invoking the service. A model-driven platform has been implemented to support the development and maintenance of personalized context-aware services from specification, design, to deployment and execution. Initial in-lab performance experiments have been conducted to demonstrate the efficiency of our approach.

Keywords: Context-aware services, web services, personalized adaptation, model-driven development, aspect-oriented methodology, business rules.

1 Introduction

Context awareness refers to the system capability of both sensing and reacting to situational changes, which is one of the most exciting trends in computing today that holds the potential to make our daily life more productive, convenient, and enjoyable [7,14,10]. Recently, with the rapid development of service-oriented computing paradigm, Web services have become a major technology for building distributed software systems and applications over the Internet [21]. Through the

C. Liu et al. (Eds.): ICSOC 2012, LNCS 7636, pp. 173–190, 2012.

use of context, a new generation of *smart* Web services is currently emerging as an important technology for building innovative context-aware applications [27,29].

To date, how to build context-aware Web services (CASs in short) that are able to dynamically change its adaptation logic is still a major challenge [13]. Although CASs are meant to be aware of and adaptive to context change, in most existing approaches context-awareness logic is usually tightly coupled with the main functionality of a service and thus not able to change at runtime [26,23]. Another issue that hinders the usability of CASs is that existing context-aware systems and services usually define the context-awareness logic based on a specific *context* instead of a specific *user*, which may lead to system behavior that is not in accord with this user's preference. For example, in a context-aware travel booking system, one of the context-awareness features is that if the weather forecast in the destination is `rainy` when the customer arrives, then a pickup service will be arranged. Such context-awareness logic may be suitable for Alice, but may not be suitable for Bob, who wants to have a rent-car service instead. Because user's long tail of needs can never be exhausted [1], CASs that are able to do context-aware adaptation according to user's personalized needs are highly desirable.

To tackle the above-mentioned challenges, in this paper, we present a novel approach called PerCAS to developing and executing a type of dynamically adaptive CASs that are able to automatically switch context-awareness logic at runtime according to a user's unique adaptation needs. We call such CASs the *personalized CASs*. We have designed and implemented a model-driven development approach to facilitate the modeling of personalized context-aware adaptation logic and the automatic generation of executable service code. A high-level business rule language is proposed to facilitate the specification of a user's personalized context-aware adaptation logic, and an aspect-oriented mechanism is used to integrate the adaptation logic into the main functionality. A runtime environment that integrates both a rule engine and a Web service process engine is implemented to support the dynamic switching between personalized adaptation logic and the execution of personalized context-aware services.

The rest of the paper is organized as follows. Section 2 introduces a motivating scenario that will be referred to throughout the paper. Section 4 describes the PerCAS approach in detail. Section 4 introduce the PerCAS model-driven development platform. Section 5 discusses the execution environment architecture and demonstrates how dynamic and personalized adaptation is achieved in this architecture. In this section, we also discuss an initial performance evaluation of the execution environment. Section 6 is related work discussion and we conclude our paper in Section 7.

2   A Motivating Scenario

In this section, we present a context-aware travel booking service as a motivating scenario. It is worth noting that part of this scenario is borrowed from the case study used in [13].

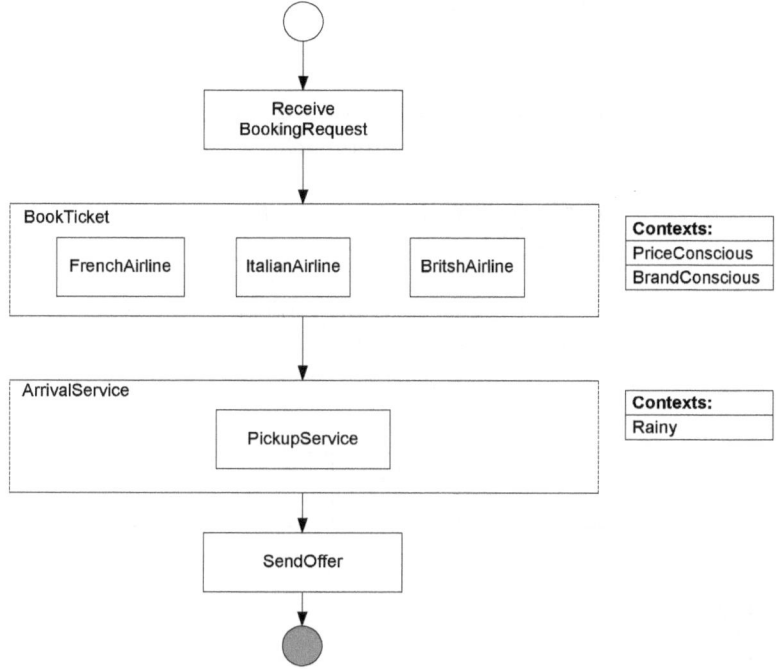

Fig. 1. The travel booking scenario

Figure 1 is the main process of the travel booking service. As we can see, the travel booking service is started when a customer issues a booking request. When the request is received, the service invokes three ticket booking services provided by three different airlines. After that, according to the weather forecast, if it is rainy at the destination when the customer arrives, a pickup service is invoked. Finally the offer is sent to the customer.

The context-awareness features of the travel booking service are as following: 1) if the customer is PriceConscious, then the lowest quote from the three airlines will be used; 2) if the customer is BrandConscious, then only one airline service needs to be invoked instead of three; 3) if it is forecasted to be rainy at the destination, a pickup service will be invoked.

At runtime, it is highly desirable that this context-aware travel booking service can dynamically change its context-awareness logic to suit the personalized needs of customers. For example, if a customer Alice happens to be RegionConscious, which means she prefers to fly airlines from a certain region because of her food preference, how can we introduce this new context and its associated context-awareness logic to the service? Furthermore, the other customer Bob may want to use a rent car service instead of the pickup service if it rains, while Alice still wants to use the pickup service. How can we solve this conflict by providing personalized context-awareness logic unique to individual customers?

3   The PerCAS Approach

3.1   Overview

In this section, we briefly introduce the PerCAS approach and discuss several key principles used in the design of this approach.

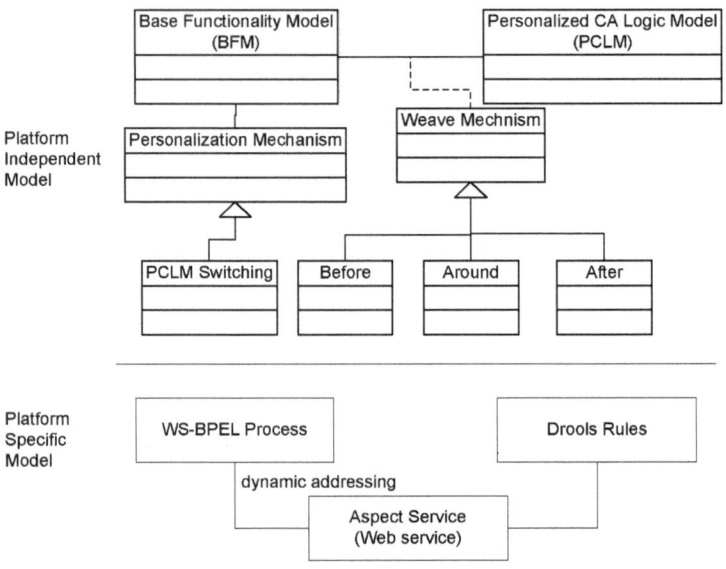

Fig. 2. Overview of the PerCAS approach

As illustrated in Figure 2, PerCAS is a model-driven approach that contains a Platform Independent Model (PIM) and a Platform Specific Model (PSM). In the PIM, the main components include a *Base Functionality Model* (BFM in short) that represents the core functionality of the service, a *Personalized Context-Awareness Logic Model* (PCLM in short) that represents the personalized context-awareness logic of the user, a *Weave Mechanism* that integrate the above two models using an aspect-oriented technique, and a *Personalization Mechanism* for switching context-awareness logic between individual users. Because dynamically adaptive systems are generally difficult to specify due to its high complexity and variability [30,20], we adopt the *separation of concerns* principle [15] to manage complexity and variability: the context-awareness logic that needs to be changed is separated from the main functionality. The BFM represents the relatively stable processing procedure of a service; while the PCLM represents the variable context-awareness logic. A process language adapted from BPMN (Business Process Modeling Notation)[1] has been designed as the modeling language for the BFM. As to the PCLM, we have designed a natural language-like high-level rule language as its modeling language. We adopt

---

[1] http://www.bpmn.org/

a rule language to specify the PCLM because: i) Business-level rules are easier to be used by technically non-experienced users because of their atomic and declarative nature [25,5]. In our case, the user may use our rule language to define his/her personalized context-awareness rules. ii) Context-awareness rules as a type of business rules are one of the core components in specifying requirements. Keeping rules in the design model instead of translating them into complex conditional branches of a process not only prevents the paradigm shift from declarative rules to procedural processes but also maintains the modularity and traceability of rules. We adopt an aspect-oriented approach to integrate the BFM and the PCLM using the Weave Mechanism. This approach ensures the modularity of the BFM and the PCLM so that they can evolve independently. If we directly translate rules into process structures and insert them into a process, both modularity and traceability of the rules are lost. Based on the aspect-oriented methodology [8], context-awareness rules can be applied *before*, *after* a service, or *around* it to replace this service. Finally, a personalization mechanism is applied to the BFM for switching between personalized context-awareness rules that are encapsulated in PCLM.

In the PSM, WS-BPEL (BPEL in short) [9], the de facto industry standard for service composition, is used as the process execution language, and Drools[2] is used as the rule execution language. Accordingly, the BFM is transformed to a BPEL process and the PCLM is translated to Drools rules. An aspect service that encapsulates the invocation logic to Drools rules is used as the communication bridge between the BPEL engine and the Drools rule engine. At runtime, the aspect service takes the unique URL to the Drools rule file (corresponding to a unique PCLM, or user) to switch aspects containing personalized context-awareness rules.

3.2   The Base Functionality Model

The BFM captures the main processing logic of a service, excluding all the context-awareness logic. Mainly we reuse the language constructs defined in BPMN for its popularity. To make the BFM and PCLM semantically interoperable, we have extended the **Business Activity** element of BPMN with semantic annotations.

As illustrated in Figure 3, the BFM modeling language in general has two types of elements: the *Flow Object* and the *Connecting Object*, where flow objects are processing entities and connecting objects specify the flow relations between flow objects. There are three types of flow objects: the *Business Activity*, the *Event*, and the *Parallel Gateway*. Business activities represent the main processing unit of a service. Events have the common meaning as defined in BPMN: they are happenings that affect the execution of a process, for example start events and exceptions. Gateways also have the common meaning as defined in BPMN: they determines forking and merging of paths. It is worth noting that although context-awareness logic usually can be specified as static

---

[2] http://www.jboss.org/drools/

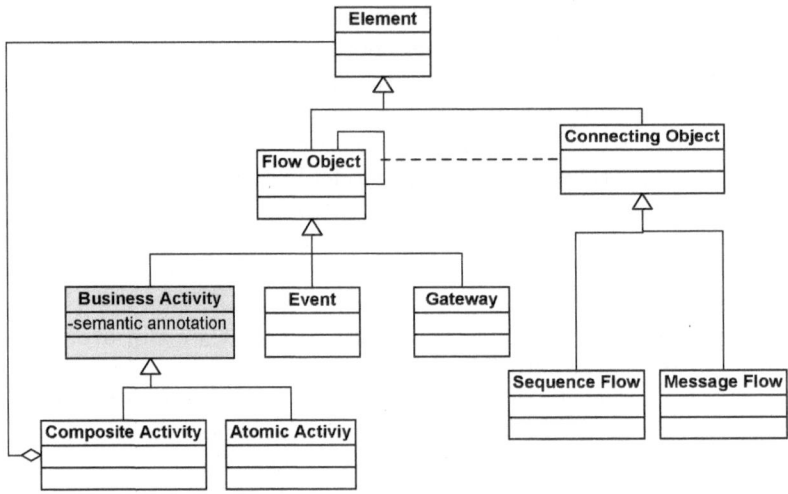

Fig. 3. The BFM language structure

gateway structures, but in our approach, such logic must not be specified in BFM, instead, they should be specified in PCLM.

The detailed definition of the Business Activity is given as follows. A business activity is a tuple of *name*, *inputs*, and *outputs*: $t = <name: \mathcal{N}ame, \mathcal{I}: \mathcal{N}ame \times \mathcal{C}, \mathcal{O}: \mathcal{N}ame \times \mathcal{C}>$, where $\mathcal{N}ame$ is a finite set of names; $\mathcal{C}$ is a finite set of types, and every input or output of a business activity has a name and a type. The type of an input or output parameter is a concept or property defined in an ontology. As we know, an ontology provides a shared vocabulary, which can be used to model a domain—that is, the type of objects and concepts that exist, and their properties and relations [2]. The purpose that we associate an I/O parameter with an ontology concept or property is twofold: first, the ontology serves as the common ground between the BFM and the PCLM and thus makes these two models semantically interoperable; second, the semantics attached to business activities later can be used to semantically discover services that implement business activities. For example, suppose the `BookTicket` activity needs to use the customer information as an input parameter, then we may use an ontology concept `Customer` that has properties such as `firstName`, `lastName`, and `passportNumber`, to give a semantic meaning to this input parameter.

Figure 4 shows the BFM of the motivating example. It only contains two business activities: `BookTicket` and `SendOffer`. We do not include the arrival service in it because the arrival service is part of the context-awareness logic, and such logic needs to be defined in the PCLM instead.

Fig. 4. The BFM of the motivating scenario

3.3 The Personalized Context-Awareness Logic Model

The PCLM captures the context-awareness logic. Usually there are more than one PCLM defined for one BFM. PCLMs can be defined either at design time or runtime, and a specific user can choose one of the PCLM or dynamically defines a new PCLM as his/her PCLM.

A PCLM is composed of a set of rules, and each rule r is defined as a 3-tuple: $r = < type, condition, action >$. Type is defined based on the context related to a PCLM. For example, two contexts `PriceConscious` and `BrandConscious` have the same context type `TicketingPreference`. Rules having the same type can be switched dynamically at runtime. The definition of *condition* and *action* follows the typical event-condition-action (ECA) pattern but the *event* part is specified in the weave mechanism (see the next subsection for details) because the triggering of rules is determined by point cuts in the aspect.

We have designed a natural-language-like high-level rule language to facilitate the specification of PCLM. This language is defined based on the propositional logic based constraint languages such as WSCoL [3] and JML [4], . The syntax of this rule language is defined as follows:

```
<rule>        ::= <type>, <cond> , <action>

<type>        ::= <concept>

<cond>        ::= not <cond> | <cond> and <cond> |
                  <cond> or <cond> | <term> <relop> <term>
<term>        ::= <property> | <term> <arop> <term> |
                  <const> | <fun> (<term> <term>*)
<property>    ::= <concept>(_<n>)?(.<obj_prop>)*.
                  <datatype_prop>
<relop>       ::= less than | less than or equal to |
                  equal to | greater than or equal to |
                  greater than
<arop>        ::= + | - | * | /
<n>           ::= 1 | 2 | 3 |...

<fun>         ::= <predef> | <usrdef>
<predef>      ::= abs | replace | substring | sum | avg
                  | min | max | ...

<action>      ::= (<activity>) | (<property> | <concept>(_<n>)?
                  = <term> | <activity>))*
```

As we can see, ontology concepts and properties are used in the specification of a PCLM rule. Because of the *atomic* feature of rules, in many situations, only one instance (or variable) of the same concept/type is involved in the definition of a rule. In such cases, the name of an ontology concept is directly used to represent one of its instances to bring certain convenience to the rule author. For example, to define the condition "*if the customer is price conscious*", we can just write the following natural-language-like condition expression: "*Customer.PriceConscious equal to true"*, in which the ontology concept `Customer` actually means a specific customer in the context of the rule. If more than one instance of the same concept is needed in a rule expression, number subscriptions, such as `Customer_1`, `Customer_2`, are used to identify a specific instance. Based on Web Ontology Language (OWL) [19], an ontology concept could be a complex structure having both *object properties* and *datatype properties*, where an object property navigates to another concept in the ontology and a datatype property has a specific primitive data type such as *integer, boolean,* or *string.* For example, suppose the `Customer` concept has an object property `contact` whose range is the concept `Contact`, and `phoneNumber` is a *string* datatype property of `Contact`. Finally, for the action part, we can either assign the result of a term expression to a variable, or assign the result of the invocation of a business activity to a variable.

The following are examples of three PCLM rules:

$\mathcal{R}_1$: *If a customer is brand conscious, use the airline with the specified brand.*

```
[type]      TicketingPreference
[Cond]      Customer.Preference.brandConscious  equal  to
    "true"
[Action]    BookTicket(Customer.Preference.brand).
```

$\mathcal{R}_2$: *If it rains at the arrival airport, use the pickup service:*

```
[type]      Weather
[Cond]      ArrivalAirport.weatherCondition  equal  to  "
    Rainy"
[Action]    Pickup(Customer).
```

$\mathcal{R}_3$: *If it rains at the arrival airport, use the rent-car service:*

```
[type]      Weather
[Cond]      ArrivalAirport.weatherCondition  equal  to  "
    Rainy"
[Action]    RentCar(Customer).
```

The user can dynamically put rules into his/her own PCLM. For example, Alice's PCLM is composed of two rules R_1 and R_2: $PCLM_1 = \{R_1, R_2\}$, while Bob's PCLM contains one rule R_3 only: $PCLM_2 = \{R_3\}$. It is worth noting that because the rule type is used for dynamic switching between rules, rules with the same type are not allowed to be put in the same PCLM to achieve deterministic selection.

3.4   The Weave Mechanism and Personalization Mechanism

The weave mechanism connect PCLM rules to BFM business activities based on the concept of *aspect*: each aspect *asp* weaves a type of PCLM rules to a BFM activity: $asp \in \{Before, Around, After\} \times \mathcal{T} \times R.Type$, where $\mathcal{T}$ is the set of

BFM business activities and $R.Type$ is the set of PCLM rule types. Similar to AspectJ [11], we also identify three types of aspect: *before aspects*, *around aspects*, and *after aspects*. An aspect is always associated with a business activity. Both before aspects and around aspects are executed before the execution of the associated activity, but if an activity has an around aspect, the execution of this activity will be skipped after the execution of the around aspect. In another word, the around aspect *replaces* its associated activity. From the perspective of the ECA pattern, $event \in \{Before, Around, After\} \times \mathcal{T}$ becomes the triggering event of a PCLM rule.

PCLM rules are associated with an aspect based on their types. So it is a type (or set) of PCLM rules that are associated with a BFM activity instead of a single PCLM rule. For example, we can define two context-awareness aspects for the travel booking service discussed in Section 2:

$$asp_1 = \{Around, BookTicket, TicketingPreference\}$$
$$asp_2 = \{After, ArrivalService, Weather\}$$

In asp_2, Because R_2 and R_3 belong to the same type `Weather`, they can be dynamically switched and applied to the `ArrivalService` activity.

It is worth noting that the interoperability between an BFM activity and its associated PCLM rules is established through the predefined ontology. For example, the input parameters of the `BookTicket` activity must contain two parameters having semantic annotation `DepartureAirport` and `ArrivalAirport`, so that the associated rule (for example R_2) can use these properties in its definition.

Finally the personalization mechanism is used to associate a user to a PCLM, for example $PCLM_1.user = Alice$, so that at runtime when it is identified that the invocation is from this user, his/her specific PCLM will be used, and rules will be selected from this PCLM to apply to the corresponding BFM. If a context-awareness aspect is defined while there is no rule can be used (based on the rule type) in the specific PCLM, then this aspect will be ignored. For example, suppose Bob's PCLM has no rule with type $TicketingPreference$, then asp_1 will be ignored when Bob invokes the travel booking service.

4   The PerCAS Development Platform

We have implemented a model-driven platform for graphically specifying the PerCAS PIM models and for automatic transformation of these models to executable PSM code.

4.1   The Graphical Development Interface

Figure 5 shows the main graphical development interface of the PerCAS platform. There are totally three tabs: the left tab is an OWL viewer used for users to explore ontology concepts defined in OWL; the middle tab, as shown in Figure 5, is the main environment for defining PerCAS models; the right tab is for

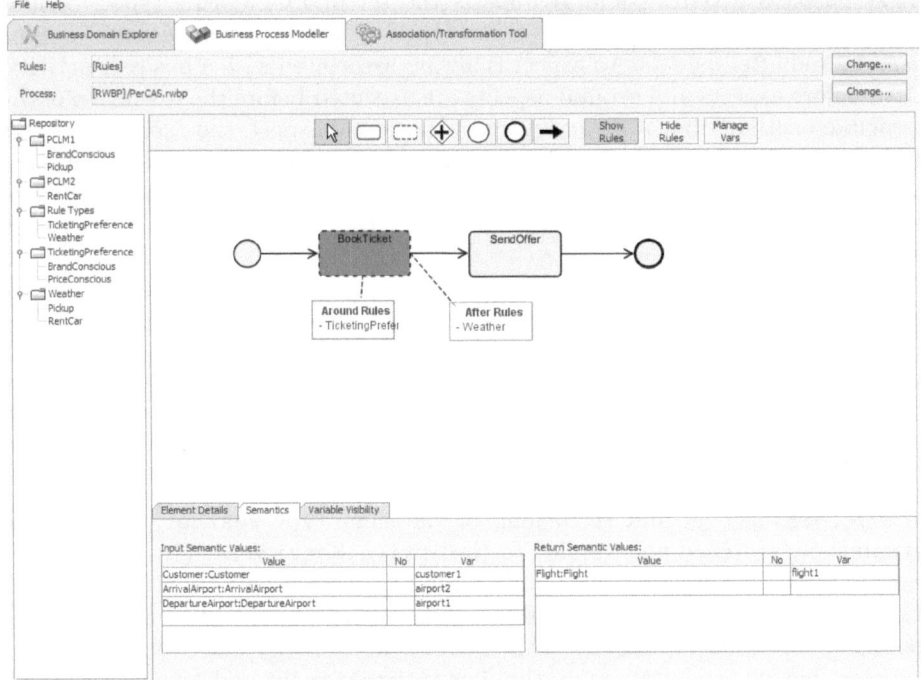

Fig. 5. Snapshot of the PerCAS Platform

transforming models to executable code. For space limitation, we only introduce
the main graphical environment (the middle tab). As we can see, the left pane
displays the structure of the PCLM rule repository: there are two PCLMs defined: one contains the `BrandConscious` rule (R_1) and the `Pickup` rule (R_2), and
the other contains the `RentCar` rule (R_3). As discussed in Section 3.4, $PCLM_1$
may be used by Alice, and $PCLM_2$ by Bob. In the rest of the structure, two rule
types: `TicketingPreference` and `Weather` are defined, with each type contains
two rules.

The middle pane is the main canvas for composing a PerCAS service. BFM
language constructs are displayed as a list of buttons on top of the canvas. When
the user creates a BFM activity, its semantics can be specified in the bottom
pane. If we select a concept or datatype property from the drop-down menu
that contains all the concepts and datatype properties in the domain ontology
as the type for a parameter, a variable is automatically created to represent this
parameter. As shown in the snapshot, the `BookTicket` activity has three input
parameters with type `Customer`, `DepartureAirport` and `ArrivalAirport`, and
one output parameter with type `Flight`.

After the BFM model is created, the user may drag-n-drop one of the rule
types from the left pane to an activity in the middle canvas. The platform then
will ask the user whether weave the rule type *before*, *around*, or *after* the
activity. As shown in the figure, the `TicketingPreference` type is weaved as an

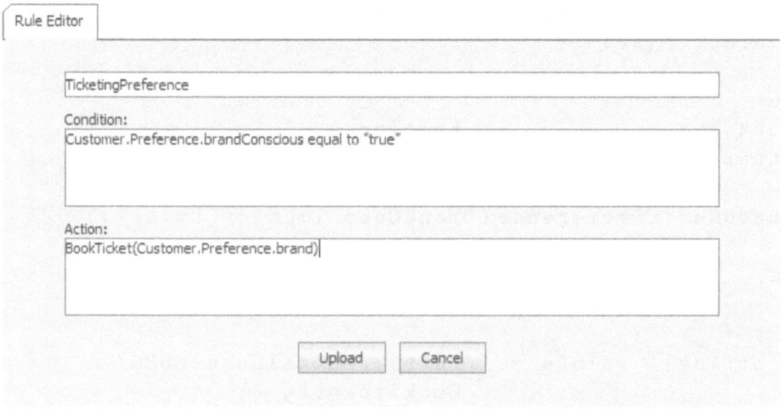

Fig. 6. The PCLM Rule Editor

around aspect, and the `Weather` type is weaved as an after aspect. It is worth noting that if a BFM activity is attached with PCLM rules, then the solid line of its shape becomes the dash line to indicate that it is context-dependent and adaptive.

A new PCLM rule can be created in the "Rule Editor" dialog box, which will appear if we right-click one of the folder icons in the left rule repository pane and select "New Rule" from the pop-up menu. As shown in Figure 6, the rule editor uses the concepts in the domain ontology to define the *condition* and *action* components of a rule. It is worth noting that all the I/O parameter variables in the base model that are visible to a rule will be automatically bound to the corresponding concepts or properties in the rule.

4.2 Transformation

Before we can transform the defined PerCAS PIM to executable code, we need to associate each BFM activity with a Web service. This can be done in the "Association and Transformation" tab of the graphical interface.

Each PCLM rule is automatically transformed to an executable Drools rule. Figure 7 shows the generated Drools rule code for rule $\mathcal{R}_1$ discussed in Section 3.3. In order to keep the invocation of Web services associated with activities defined within rules self-contained, service information for Web services associated with activities defined within rules are encoded directly into the rule code. First, the bindings for ontology classes used in the rule as well as an *enabler* helper-class are defined (Lines 5-6), followed by the *condition* statement as translated into Drools syntax (Lines 8). If the condition is evaluated as true, the Web service associated with the *BookTicket* will be invoked, using the *enabler* helper class (Lines 12-25).

The weaved BFM model is transformed to a BPEL process. Constructs such as *Start Event* and *Activity* that does not have aspects are translated directly into their corresponding BPEL constructs (in this case, *receive* and *invoke*).

```
1  rule "BrandConscious"
2    dialect "java"
3
4  when
5    $enabler            : Enabler()
6    $Customer           : Customer()
7
8    Customer((Preference(brandConscious == "true"))
9
10 then
11
12   try {
13     String[] wsInfo = { "http://localhost:8080/
14                         BookTicket",
15                         "bookTicket", "BookTicketService",
16                         "ContactServicePort",
17                         "http://localhost:8080/
18                         BookTicketService/BookTicketService
                           ?
19                         wsdl"};
20
21     String[][] varInfo  = {{ $Customer.getBrand()}};
22     String[][] varNames = { { "CustomerBrand" }};
23
24     $enabler.runService(wsInfo, varInfo, varNames);
25   } catch (Exception e) { e.printStackTrace() };
26
27 end
```

Fig. 7. Drools rule code corresponding to Rule $\mathcal{R}_1$

For activities that have aspects, we use a special Web service called *aspect service* as the communication bridge between the BPEL process and the rules running on the Drools rule engine. An aspect service will be invoked before invoking an activity if it has *before* and/or *around* aspects, and another aspect service will be invoked after invoking an activity if it has *after* aspects. To achieve dynamic switching between PCLMs, each PCLM is translated to a Drools rule file, and the aspect service takes as input a URI to the Drools rule file, along with the values and ontology class names of all variables involved in the aspect. When a user invokes a PerCAS service, his/her unique PCLM URL will be used as an parameter to the aspect service. The aspect service returns two Boolean values corresponding to abort and skip evaluation outcomes, as well as the values of all variables that may have been updated based on rule evaluation. Finally, conditional constructs are inserted around the activity invocation to handle abort and skip actions based on the return of the aspect service.

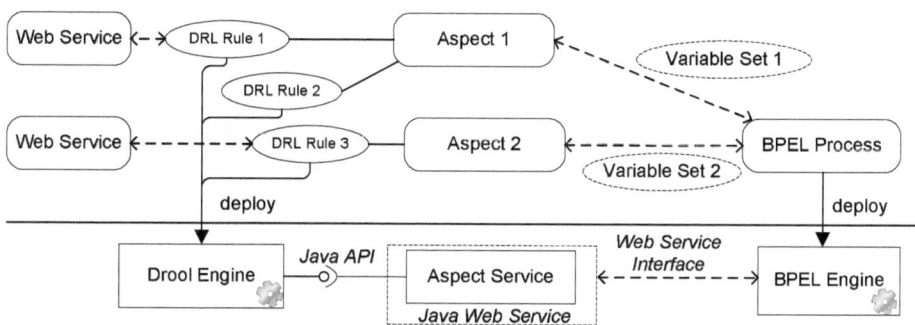

Fig. 8. The architecture of the PerCAS runtime environment

5   The Runtime Environment

We have implemented the PerCAS runtime environment based on Riftsaw-2.3.0 open source BPEL engine [3] and Drools-5.0 rule engine. Both engines are running inside the JBoss Application Server-7.0.

Figure 8 is the architecture of the PerCAS runtime environment. The bottom level of the anatomy includes the main components of the runtime environment: a *Drool engine*, a *BPEL engine*, and a *generic aspect service* that encapsulates the rule invocation logic. The aspect service is written in Java and exposed as a Web service for the BPEL process to invoke. Every time when an aspect in the process is reached for execution, the aspect service is invoked and corresponding variables (including the IO parameters of its associated activity and user selected variables) are passed from the process to it; these variables are used in the execution of the rules of the aspect. After all the rules in the aspect are executed, these variables are updated and passed back to the process.

Next we use this architecture and the motivating scenario to briefly demonstrate how dynamic and personalized adaptation is achieved in PerCAS. Suppose Alice is using the travel booking service, then the url to $PCLM_1$ (defined in Section 3.3) will be used as an parameter to the aspect service, and because asp_1 (defined in Section 3.4) is an around aspect to the `BookTicket` service, this aspect will select a rule with type `TicketingPreference` from $PCLM_1$, which is R_1. Similarly, when Bob is invoking the service, $PCLM_2$ will be used and R_2 will be selected and executed instead. Because the BFM process and the PCLM rules are separately deployed, it is possible to change the PCLM rules while the process is still running. For example, when the `BookTicket` service is still running, Alice may change the rules defined in $PCLM_1$, e.g., change her arrival service preference from `Pickup` to `RentCar`. If the modified $PCLM_1$ is successfully deployed before asp_2 (the *after* aspect) is executed, the new rule will be used in asp_2.

---

[3] http://www.jboss.org/riftsaw/

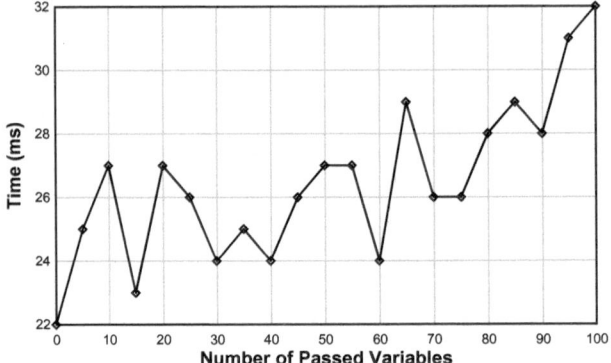

Fig. 9. Execution time of a single aspect service w.r.t. the number of passed variables

According to the above discussed architecture, we can see that the main performance impact of this runtime environment lies in the aspect service, which is responsible for executing the context-awareness logic outside the BPEL engine. We have conducted an initial experiment to test the impact of invoking a single aspect service with various number of randomly generated primitive type variables passed. Every setting is tested five times and the average execution time of an empty aspect service w.r.t. the number of passed variables is shown in Figure 9. As we can see, it costs 22 ms to invoke an empty aspect service without passing any variables and costs 32 ms to invoke an empty aspect service with 100 variables passed to it. This result shows that the variable exchange between the Riftsaw BPEL server and the Drools server is very fast, and there is only 10 ms increase from passing no variable to passing 100 variables. The reason could be that these two servers are two components that both run inside the same JBoss application server.

6   Related Work

The PerCAS approach presented in this paper is closely related to two categories of research work: one is model-driven development of context-aware services, and the other is dynamic context-aware process adaptation. In the rest of this section, we discuss related work from these two perspectives.

As mentioned by Kapitsaki et al. [16], the model-driven approach is a popular approach to developing context-aware services because of its strong support to the development process. ContextServ [26] is a platform that uses UML[4] to model contexts, context-awareness, and services, and then transforms the model to an executable context-aware Web service. Composite contexts can be modeled by composing atomic contexts using UML state diagrams. The main context-awareness features that can be modeled by ContextServ include *context binding*, which binds a context to the input parameter of a service, and

---

[4] http://www.uml.org/

context triggering, which modifies the output of a service to suit a specific context. CAMEL (Context Awareness ModEling Language) and its associated development tools [12,28] combine model-driven development and aspect-oriented design paradigms so that the design of the application core can be decoupled from the design of the adaptation logic. In particular, CAMEL categorizes context into state-based which characterizes the current situation of an entity and event-based which represents changes in an entity's state. Accordingly, state constraints, which are defined by logical predicates on the value of the attributes of a state-based context, and event constraints, which are defined as patterns of event, are used to specify context-aware adaptation feature of the application. CAAML (Context-aware Adaptive Activities Modeling Language) [17] aims at modeling context-aware adaptive learning activities in the E-learning domain. This language focuses on modeling two classes of rules - rules for context adaptation and rules for activity adaptation - to support pedagogical designing. The above approaches mainly focus on how to specify context-awareness features of a single service or software component at *design time*. The focus of the PerCAS approach instead is on making the context-awareness features changeable at *runtime* based on user preferences. Also, PerCAS supports to do context-aware adaptation on a process instead of a single service, which is the reason that we adopt BPMN instead of UML as the base modeling language.

In terms of dynamic context-aware process adaptation, Apto [13] is a model-driven approach for generating the process variants that corresponding to the changes in requirements and context. Necessary changes to a process is modeled as *evolution fragments* using UML, and a process variant can be created by applying an evolution fragment to the base process. Dynamic adaptation is achieved by first generating a new process variant, then transforming the process variant to a BPEL process, and then re-deploying this new BPEL process. Although both Apto and PerCAS can achieve the same goal of creating dynamic and personalized context-aware services, Apto clearly needs more professional experience to create a correct evolution fragment as it needs full understanding of both the process logic and the process language constructs, while PerCAS advocates to use natural language-like rules to define context-awareness logic. There are quite a few works aiming at extending the dynamic adaptability of BPEL processes using aspects and rules. AO4BPEL [6] is an aspect-oriented extension to BPEL that supports dynamic weaving of aspects in BPEL processes. Although they also advocate to use rules in an aspect, a rule engine is not integrated in their approach and rules are manually mapped to BPEL conditionals. Marconi et al. [18] also proposed a set of constructs and principles for embedding the adaptation logic within a flow language specification and showed how BPEL can be extended to support the proposed constructs. Rosenberg and Dustdar [24] proposed a runtime environment where both a BPEL engine and a rule engine are connected to a service bus. Dynamic adaptation is achieved through intercepting the messages exchanged between the process and a partner service and invoking business rules running on the rule engine before and after the execution of the partner service. This approach may not be able to implement the *around* aspect as rules are inserted before and after the invocation of a partner services while the partner service cannot be disabled or replaced. Paschke and Teymourian [22] discussed a rule based business process execution environment where a rule engine is deployed on an ESB (Enterprise Service Bus) and exposed as Web services. Dynamic adaptation is achieved by explicitly defining and integrating Rule Activities, which invoke the rule service, in the BPEL process, and rules can be modified and applied without re-deploying the process. The above works mainly focus on the execution language and environment, while PerCAS is a systematic engineering approach with a graphical modeling language and development platform.

7   Conclusion

In this paper, we have presented PerCAS, a model-driven approach for developing dynamic and personalized context-aware services using aspects and rules. We have introduced the models and methodology of separating the context-awareness logic from the base functionality logic of a service, as well as weaving the context-awareness logic to the base process. A natural language-like rule language is proposed for specifying context-awareness logic and personalized rules can be dynamically switched at runtime. We have also developed a development platform to support the graphical modeling and transformation of such services, and a runtime environment that integrates both a BPEL engine and a Drools rule engine for their execution. In the future, we plan to apply this approach in more real-life case studies to validate its effectiveness. We also plan to investigate runtime validation techniques that can be used to check the consistency of context-awareness logic switching.

References

1. Anderson, C.: The Long Tail: Why the Future of Business is Selling Less of More. Hyperion Books (2006)
2. Arvidsson, F., Flycht-Eriksson, A.: Ontologies I (2008),
   http://www.ida.liu.se/~janma/SemWeb/Slides/ontologies1.pdf
3. Baresi, L., Guinea, S.: Self-Supervising BPEL Processes. IEEE Transaction on Software Engineering 37(2), 247–263 (2011)
4. Burdy, L., Cheon, Y., Cok, D.R., Ernst, M.D., Kiniry, J.R., Leavens, G.T., Leino, K.R.M., Poll, E.: An Overview of JML Tools and Applications. Int'l J. Software Tools for Technology Transfer 25(3), 40–51 (2005)
5. Charfi, A., Mezini, M.: Hybrid Web Service Composition: Business Processes Meet Business Rules. In: Proc. of the 2nd International Conference on Service Oriented Computing (ICSOC 2004), pp. 30–38 (2004)
6. Charfi, A., Mezini, M.: AO4BPEL: An Aspect-oriented Extension to BPEL. World Wide Web 10, 309–344 (2007)
7. Dey, A.K., Mankoff, J.: Designing Mediation for Context-aware Applications. ACM Trans. on Computer-Human Interaction 12(1), 53–80 (2005)
8. Elrad, T., Filman, R.E., Bader, A.: Aspect-Oriented Programming: Introduction. Commun. ACM 44(10), 29–32 (2001)

9. Evdemon, J., Arkin, A., Barreto, A., Curbera, B., Goland, F., Kartha, G., Khalaf, L., Marin, K., van der Rijn, M.T., Yiu, Y.: Web Services Business Process Execution Language Version 2.0. BPEL4WS Specifications (2007)
10. Ferscha, A.: 20 Years Past Weiser: What's Next? IEEE Pervasive Computing 11, 52–61 (2012)
11. Gradecki, J.D., Lesiecki, N.: Mastering AspectJ: Aspect-Oriented Programming in Java. Wiley (2003)
12. Grassi, V., Sindico, A.: Towards Model Driven Design of Service-Based Context-Aware Applications. In: Proc. of the International Workshop on Engineering of Software Services for Pervasive Environments: In Conjunction with the Sixth ESEC/FSE Joint Meeting, pp. 69–74 (2007)
13. Jaroucheh, Z., Liu, X., Smith, S.: Apto: A MDD-based Generic Framework for Context-Aware Deeply Adaptive Service-based Processes. In: Proc. of the 2010 IEEE International Conference on Web Services (ICWS 2010), pp. 219–226 (2010)
14. Julien, C., Roman, G.C.: EgoSpaces: Facilitating Rapid Development of Context-Aware Mobile Applications. IEEE Trans. on Software Engineering 32(5), 281–298 (2006)
15. Kambayashi, Y., Ledgard, H.F.: The Separation Principle: A Programming Paradigm. IEEE Software 21(2), 78–87 (2004)
16. Kapitsaki, G.M., et al.: Context-Aware Service Engineering: A Survey. J. Syst. Software (2009)
17. Malek, J., Laroussi, M., Derycke, A., Ben Ghezala, H.: Model-Driven Development of Context-aware Adaptive Learning Systems. In: Proc. of the 10th IEEE International Conference on Advanced Learning Technologies (ICALT 2010), Washington, DC, USA, pp. 432–434 (2010)
18. Marconi, A., Pistore, M., Sirbu, A., Eberle, H., Leymann, F., Unger, T.: Enabling Adaptation of Pervasive Flows: Built-in Contextual Adaptation. In: Baresi, L., Chi, C.-H., Suzuki, J. (eds.) ICSOC-ServiceWave 2009. LNCS, vol. 5900, pp. 445–454. Springer, Heidelberg (2009)
19. Mcguiness, D.L., van Harmelen, F.: OWL Web Ontology Language Overview. W3C Recommendation (February 2004), http://www.w3.org/TR/owl-features/
20. Morin, B., Barais, O., Nain, G., Jezequel, J.M.: Taming Dynamically Adaptive Systems using Models and Aspects. In: Proc. of the 31st International Conference on Software Engineering (ICSE 2009), pp. 122–132 (2009)
21. Papazoglou, M.P., Traverso, P., Dustdar, S., Leymann, F.: Service-Oriented Computing: State of the Art and Research Challenges. Computer 40(11), 38–45 (2007)
22. Paschke, A., Teymourian, K.: Rule Based Business Process Execution with BPEL+. In: Proc. of I-KNOW 2009 and I'SEMANTICS 2009, pp. 588–601 (2009)
23. Prezerakos, G.N., Tselikas, N., Cortese, G.: Model-Driven Composition of Context-Aware Web Services Using ContextUML and Aspects. In: Proc. of the IEEE International Conference on Web Services 2007 (ICWS 2007), pp. 320–329 (2007)
24. Rosenberg, F., Dustdar, S.: Usiness Rules Integration in BPEL - a Service-Oriented Approach. In: Proc. of the 7th IEEE International Conference on E-Commerce Technology, pp. 476–479 (2005)
25. Ross, R.G.: Principles of the Business Rules Approach. Addison-Wesley (2003)
26. Sheng, Q.Z., Pohlenz, S., Yu, J., Wong, H.S., Ngu, A.H.H., Maamar, Z.: ContextServ: A Platform for Rapid and Flexible Development of Context-Aware Web Services. In: Proc. of the 31st International Conference on Software Engineering (ICSE 2009), pp. 619–622 (2009)
27. Sheng, Q.Z., Yu, J., Dustdar, S. (eds.): Enabling Context-Aware Web Services: Methods, Architectures, and Technologies. CRC Press (2010)

28. Sindico, A., Grassi, V.: Model Driven Development of Context Aware Software Systems. In: Proc. of the International Workshop on Context-Oriented Programming (COP 2009), New York, NY, USA, pp. 7:1–7:5 (2009)
29. Truong, H.L., Dustdar, S.: A Survey on Context-Aware Web Service Systems. International Journal of Web Information Systems 5(1), 5–31 (2009)
30. Zhang, J., Cheng, B.H.C.: Model-Based Development of Dynamically Adaptive Software. In: Proc. of the 28th International Conference on Software Engineering (ICSE 2006), pp. 371–380 (2006)

A Method for Assessing Influence Relationships among KPIs of Service Systems

Yedendra Babu Shrinivasan, Gargi Banerjee Dasgupta, Nirmit Desai,
and Jayan Nallacherry

IBM Research, Bangalore, India
{yshriniv,gaargidasgupta,nirmit.desai,
jayan.nallacherry}@in.ibm.com

Abstract. The operational performance of service systems is commonly measured with *key performance indicators (KPIs)*, e.g., time-to-resolve, SLA compliance, and workload balance. The assumption is that healthy KPIs lead to healthy business outcomes such as customer satisfaction, cost savings, and service quality. Although the domain experts have an intuitive understanding of the causal relationships among the KPIs, the degree of influence a cause KPI has on the effect KPI is difficult to estimate based on intuition. Also, the intuitive understanding could be wrong. Further, we show how the causal relationships are intricate with aspects such as the *rate* of influence and *conditionality* in measurements. As a result, although crucial, it is nontrivial to estimate the degree of influence. Without the degree of influence, prediction of business outcomes and decisions based on them tend to be *ad hoc*. This paper presents a novel method for validating the intuitive direction and the polarity of a causal relationship provided by domain experts. Further, the method also estimates the degree of influence based on the measure of Pearson's correlation. Using the degree of influence and least squares regression, the method predicts values of effect KPIs. The method is evaluated by applying it on 10 widely used KPIs from 29 real-life service systems. We find that the method validates 8 of the 15 intuitive relationships and estimates the degree of influence for each of the validated relationships. Further, based on the degrees of influence and the regression model learned from the 29 service systems, the method could estimate the values of the effect KPIs with an average root-mean-squared error (RMSE) of 1.2%, in 9 additional service systems.

1 Introduction

A *Service System (SS)* is an organization composed of (a) the resources that support, and (b) the processes that drive service interactions so that the outcomes meet customer expectations [1,18,15]. SS are labor intensive due to the large variation in the tasks and skills of service workers (SWs) required to address service requests from multiple customers. A service provider would typically need multiple SS to support its customers. Given that the problem solving and other activities in the SS vary greatly with customers, processes are rarely supported by workflow engines and manually executed by the SWs. Hence, the KPI data availability is limited to coarse-grained and high-level measures.

Although we refer to the examples in the IT services domain, the ideas and the approach presented later apply to SS in general. To achieve service quality in the domain

C. Liu et al. (Eds.): ICSOC 2012, LNCS 7636, pp. 191–205, 2012.

of IT services, the service providers adopt standardized process frameworks such as ITIL [1], COBIT [2], and Lean [2] Six Sigma [3]. Such frameworks also define the KPIs to enable performance assessment of each of the processes. For example, an incident management process maybe measured by the MTTR (mean time to resolve) as well as incidents resolved within SLA target time. Similarly, a work assignment process maybe measured by the mean waiting time for an incident and mean utilization of SWs. Such KPIs are widely used by service providers in making business decisions. Naturally, a poorly performing KPI attracts attention and the service provider invests in improving the underlying process.

However, the service delivery processes are inter-related in an intricate manner. For example, the KPIs of the incident management process maybe impacted by the KPIs of the work assignment process. We say that the *direction* of this causal relationship is from the work assignment process KPI to the incident management process KPI. Additionally, an increase in one KPI may imply a decrease in another. In such cases, We say that the *polarity* of the causal relationship is negative. Further, the *degree* of influence one KPI has on another varies — some KPIs are independent implying no influence. Lastly, the influences among KPIs do not occur instantaneously, the performance of one process influences another with a certain latency. We say that each causal relationship has a *rate* of influence associated with it. Sometimes, the validity of the method of measuring a KPI is conditional to assumptions about performance levels of other KPIs it is dependent on, e.g., optimal staffing level maybe computed by assuming that the work assignment process is at its best performance level and the work execution process is performing as-is on the ground. We say that the effect KPI of a causal relationship is *conditional* on the assumption that the performance level of the cause KPI is best, as-is, or worst. These attributes of causal relationships may also evolve over time, e.g., incident management may be automated in future, making it independent of the work assignment process. Given that such changes are rare, this paper assumes that the SS are in a steady state.

In both of the above examples, an investment in the improvement of the incident management process maybe misplaced without having predicted the impact it would have on the business outcomes such as cost savings. Assessing the direction, polarity, and degree of influence among the KPIs is a prerequisite to predicting their impact to the business outcomes. As an added benefit, if the degree and rate influence of causal relationships can be assessed, a system dynamics simulation model can be created, which can answer questions such as the feasibility and cost of reaching a performance goal across multiple KPIs [11].

A possible approach is to gather KPI data to assess each of the above attributes for all pairs of KPIs to guide the decisions. However, because the KPIs involved in a relationship may come from multiple processes, inferring causality from data is difficult at best [17]. Though the domain experts can intuitively identify the cause and effect in a KPI relationship based on their knowledge of implicit temporal or data flow

---

[1] http://www.itilofficialsite.com/home/home.aspx

[2] http://www.isaca.org/Knowledge-Center/cobit

[3] http://asq.org/learn-about-quality/six-sigma/overview/overview.html

dependencies involved, the intuition may not hold in reality. For example, it is intuitive that SLA performance influences customer satisfaction. However, it has been shown that consistently meeting customer SLAs does not have any impact on customer satisfaction [10]. Hence, there needs to be a validation of the intuitive causal relationships and a method for estimating the degree of influence for validated relationships.

Hence, this paper (1) assumes that the intuitive direction, conditionality, and the polarity of the causal relationships among KPIs (including KPIs representing business objectives) is given by domain experts; then it proposes a method for (2) validating the direction and the polarity of a causal relationship, (3) estimating the degree of influence of a causal relationship based on a measure of correlation, and (4) predicting the values of effect KPIs for new SS by applying linear regression. We defer the assessment of the rate of influence to future work. The conditionality of a causal relationship does not need validation as it simply reflects how the KPIs are measured on the ground.

We validate this method by applying it to 3 inter-related processes and 10 KPIs used by a large IT services provider. One of the KPIs is the business outcome of *staffing deficit*. Equipped with data on these KPIs from 38 real-life SS and a set of intuitive causal relationships, we apply our method to 29 SS and find that 8 of the 15 intuitive relationships are validated and the remaining are found to be invalid. Based on the interviews of the domain experts, these results match the skepticism they expressed about the invalidated relationships and a confidence about the validated ones. Further, based on the data from the same 29 SS, we estimate the degree of influence for each of the validated relationships based on the measure of Pearson's correlation. We express the relationships as a set of linear equations and apply least squares linear regression to predict the values of effect KPIs of the remaining 9 SS. We find that the average RMSE in the estimated values is quite low at 1.2%.

Business process KPIs and their influence relationships have received significant attention. In the area of SOA, it is mostly focused on measures that are collected automatically during process executions and relate to individual process instances [21,20]. These data help construction of models that detect risky situations within a process instance and adapt its course towards desirable outcomes. This paper focuses on separating the process expertise from the method user by clearly defining the information that process experts provide and the results that the method user produces. This helps make the method generally applicable in the services domain. Further, we predict high-level business objectives based on coarse-grained KPIs which are not available at a process instance level and hence harder to learn from. Also, the influence relationships validated by the method are not process or SS specific and hold for any SS in the domain of IT services. Approaches to KPIs in the management science area study the influence relationships only at a conceptual level and do not lead to prediction of effect KPI values [7,6,16]. Also, these approaches do not consider the important notion of *internal performance* of KPIs.

The rest of the paper is organized as follows. Section 2 presents our general method. Section 3 describes the IT service processes, the KPIs, and the intuitive causal relationships provided by the domain experts. Section 4 describes the application of the method to the IT service KPIs and the results. We summarize the related works in Section 5 and conclude in Section 6.

2   Method: Influence Estimation

Based on KPI data from multiple SS, the goal of the method is to validate the direction and polarity of the intuitive relationships provided by the domain experts, estimate the degree of influence for the validated relationships, and construct a regression model to predict the effect KPIs for new SS. The basic measure of influence we employ is that of the Pearson's correlation coefficient [4]. Before describing the steps of our method, we introduce the notations used in the following.

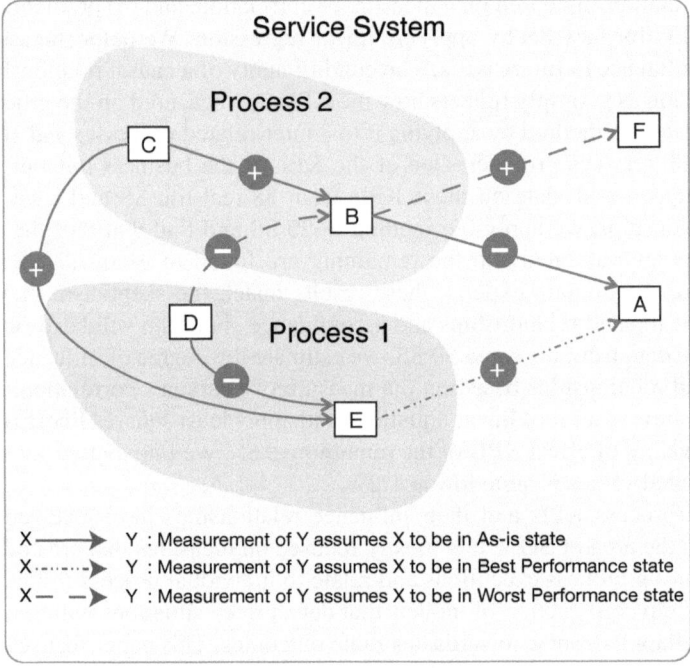

Fig. 1. Example of intuitive relationships among KPIs provided by the domain experts

Figure 1 shows an example of the relationships provided by the domain experts for a SS. KPIs B and C measure the performance of $Process_2$ whereas KPIs D and E measure the performance of $Process_1$. KPIs A and F measure performance of the SS as a whole and are not associated with any particular process. We call such process independent KPIs *business outcomes*. The direction of the edges among the KPIs indicate the direction of the causality and the signs on the edges indicate the polarity of the relationship. For example, higher the value of C higher the value of B whereas lower the value of D higher the value of B. We write these as $C \xrightarrow{+} B$ and $D \xrightarrow{+} B$, respectively. The conditionality of the relationships is indicated by the line type: as-is indicated by a solid line, **best** by a dotted line, and **worst** by a dashed line.

---

[4] http://en.wikipedia.org/wiki/Pearson_product-moment_correlation_coefficient

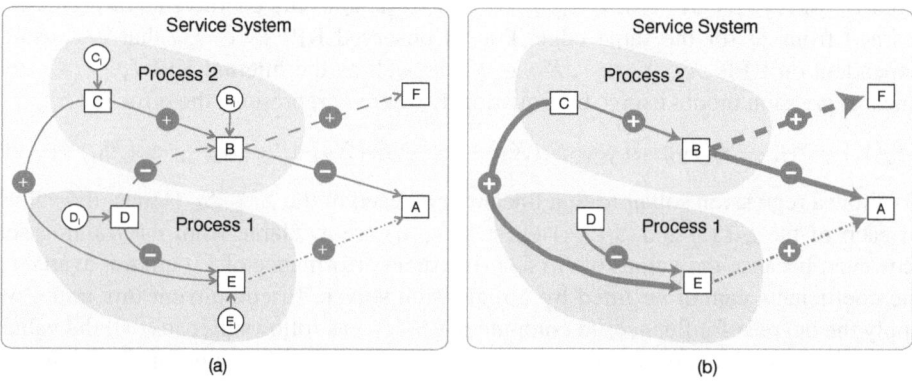

Fig. 2. (a) Influence relationships with internal performance (shown as circles) (b) Validated influence relationships among KPIs where the thickness of the edges denotes the degree of influence in relationships

2.1 Internal and Observed KPIs

The value of an effect KPI is not completely defined by the cause KPIs. This is because an effect KPI may have an associated process that influences the observed measurement of the KPI. For example, although a work assignment process influences the mean-time-to-resolve (MTTR), the process of problem resolution itself significantly determines the value of MTTR. Hence, we distinguish between KPIs reflecting the *internal* performance of the associated process alone and those reflecting the *observed* performance that factors in all the causal dependencies. The internal KPIs are shown as circles whereas the observed KPIs are shown as squares. For example, in Figure 2(a), B_i is the internal measure whereas B is observed. Each observed KPI K is associated with an internal KPI K_i having a causal relationship to K with a positive polarity and **as-is** conditionality. Note that A and F do not have associated internal KPIs because they are not associated with a process and are classified as business outcomes as described earlier. Intuitively, the value of observed KPI would be same as that of the internal KPI if the observed KPI were causally dependent on no other KPI. This distinction implies that an observed KPI can be expressed in terms of the associated internal KPI as well as the other observed KPIs on which the KPI is causally dependent on.

2.2 Problem Formulation: KPI Value Prediction

Here, we formulate the problem of predicting the value of an effect KPI via linear regression. Let $\mathcal{K}$ be the set of all KPIs in the relationships provided by the domain experts. If $\mathcal{K}_o$ is the set of observed KPIs and $\mathcal{K}_i$ is the set of internal KPIs, then $\mathcal{K} = \mathcal{K}_o \cup \mathcal{K}_i$ and $\mathcal{K}_o \cap \mathcal{K}_i = \phi$. Let $\mathcal{S}$ denote the set of all SS with $\mathcal{S}_l$ being the set of SS in the training set and $\mathcal{S}_t$ being the test set, $\mathcal{S} = \mathcal{S}_l \cup \mathcal{S}_t$ and $\mathcal{S}_l \cap \mathcal{S}_t = \phi$.

Value of a KPI K in SS S_j is indicated by $S_j(K)$ and takes the values $[0, 1]$. Whereas $\gamma_{K_i K_j} \in [-1, 1]$ denotes the degree of influence measured by our method for the edge from K_i to K_j (K_i, $K_j \in \mathcal{K}$), $\alpha_{K_i K_j} \in [-1,1]$ denotes the coefficients of regression learned from S_l for the same edge. For an observed KPI $Y \in \mathcal{K}_o$ that is causally dependent on KPIs $X_1, X_2, \ldots, X_n \in \mathcal{K}_o$ as well as the internal KPI $I_Y \in \mathcal{K}_i$, the linear regression model is give by Equation 1, where ϵ_i represents the error for S_i.

$$S_i(Y) = \alpha_{I_Y Y} \cdot S_i(I_Y) + \alpha_{X_1 Y} \cdot S_i(X_1) + \alpha_{X_2 Y} \cdot S_i(X_2) + \ldots + \alpha_{X_n Y} \cdot S_i(X_n) + \epsilon_i \quad (1)$$

To allow a regression solver to fit a linear curve, each of the $S_i \in S_l$. Hence, the values of each of the $S_i(Y)$ and $S_i(X_j)$ ($1 < j < n$) are available from the training set. However, because the values of $S_i(I_Y)$ (internal performance of Y) are not available, the coefficients cannot be fitted by a regression solver. To circumvent this issue, we apply the degree of influences to compute the $S_i(I_Y)$ as follows. Because all the values on the RHS of Equation 2 are known, we directly derive the value of $S_i(I_y)$ for all $S_i \in S_l$.

$$S_i(I_Y) = S_i(Y) - \gamma_{X_1 Y} \cdot S_i(X_1) - \gamma_{X_2 Y} \cdot S_i(X_2) - \ldots - \alpha_{X_n Y} \cdot S_i(X_n) \quad (2)$$

The γ terms represent the degree of influences computed via our method that is described next and show in Table 1.

Table 1. Rules for the validation of intuitive relationships and estimating the degree of influence

State of cause KPI assumed by the effect KPI	Intuitive polarity of relationship (p)	Cause KPI performance State	Correlation between cause and effect KPIs	Sign of Observed Correlation	Validation test	Degree of influence
Best performance state	+	Healthy	a	+	Valid	$p \cdot \frac{(|a|+|b|)}{2}$, only if valid
				-	Invalid	
		Weak	b	+	Invalid	
				-	Valid	
	-	Healthy	a	+	Invalid	
				-	Valid	
		Weak	b	+	Valid	
				-	Invalid	
Worst performance state	+	Healthy	a	+	Invalid	$p \cdot \frac{(|a|+|b|)}{2}$, only if valid
				-	Valid	
		Weak	b	+	Valid	
				-	Invalid	
	-	Healthy	a	+	Valid	
				-	Invalid	
		Weak	b	+	Invalid	
				-	Valid	
As-is performance state	+	All states	a	+	Valid	$p \cdot |a|$, only if valid
				-	Invalid	
	-	All states	a	+	Invalid	
				-	Valid	

2.3   Steps

Step M_0. From domain experts, gather the set of observed KPIs $\mathcal{K}_o$ and the direction, polarity, and conditionality of the intuitive causal relationships among them. The output of this step would look like Figure 2(a).

Step M_1. Measure the values of each of the observed KPIs for a long enough period in a large enough set of SS, depending on the inherent variation and rate of change in the processes involved. Aggregate the KPIs collected over time with a suitable measure of central tendency, e.g., mean, median, or mode. The output of this step would be the value $S_i(X_j)$ for KPI X_j and SS S_i in $[0, 1]$, where 0 indicates the best performance and 1 indicates the worst performance.

Step M_2. For each cause KPI, decide the threshold of performance level such that values better than this level reflect healthy performance and values worse than this level reflect weak performance (better would be lower and worse would be higher values). Based on these thresholds, decide the performance state of the cause KPI.

Step M_3. Compute the Pearson's correlation coefficient for the pair of KPIs having a causal relationship. If the conditionality is either best or worst, compute the coefficient of correlation a between KPI values from SS having only healthy performance in the cause KPI and b between KPI values from SS having only weak performance. This is because if the measurement of an effect KPI assumes the cause KPI to be in the best state, then for the SS where the cause KPI is in the healthy state, the cause KPI's influence would be limited. However, a positive correlation is expected because the healthier the cause KPI, the healthier the effect KPI. On the other hand, if the cause KPI is in the weak state, it has a higher negative influence on the the effect KPI.

Step M_4. For each intuitive causal relationship from M_0, look up the row from Table 1 that matches the conditionality, the polarity, the performance state of cause KPI, and the sign of the correlation coefficient computed from M_3. The "Validation test" column provides the validation result of the intuitive relationship. The "Degree of influence" column provides the estimated degree of influence γ_{XY} for validated relationship between each KPI pair X and Y from M_0. The output of this Step looks like Figure 2(b).

Step M_5. From Equation 2, compute the estimated internal performance measure iY_i for each S_i in the training set. Using these iY_i, feed the Equation 1 to a regression solver to estimate the coefficients of regression α_{XY} for the validated relationship between each KPI pair X and Y from M_4.

Step M_6. For each $S_i \in \mathcal{S}_t$, and each effect KPI involved in a validated causal relationship, apply Equation 1 to estimate the value of the effect KPI $S_i(Y)$. Compute RMSE based on the difference between the estimated and the actual values.

3   Case Study: IT Services

This section describes the case study from the domain of IT services. In this domain, the customers own data centers and other IT infrastructures supporting their business.

The size, complexity, and uniqueness of the technology installations drive outsourc-ing of the management responsibilities to specialized service providers. The service providers manage the data-centers from remote locations called *delivery centers* where groups of SWs skilled in specific technology areas support corresponding SRs.

Each SW has an associated skill level (discreet skill levels) and usually works on issues equal or below her skill-level. Customers submit SRs along with its associated priority. The work also arrives as internal SRs corresponding to all the internal work that goes on such as proactive fixes, preparing reports, and attending meetings. Each SR is routed to a queue manager who assesses the minimum skill-level required to service the SR. The SR is then queued up in the corresponding skill-level priority queue, where the priority may be the same as the one assigned by the customer or a modified priority based on factors such as earliest deadline or shortest service time. A resource allocator follows two alternative models: (a) as soon as an SR is queued up, it is pushed to the *best* SW and queued in the work queue of the SW, or (b) the SR waits in the skill-level queue until it reaches the head of the queue and a SW with a matching skill level becomes available and pulls it.

In some cases a work assignment policy may assign work to a appropriately skilled SW, but a *swing policy* can overrule it by utilizing a higher skilled SW for servicing a SR with lower skill-level requirement. Typically, this is to control the growth of a lower-skill queue. A SW would service the SR by carrying out necessary work which consumes time. This time is referred to as service time with distributions that vary by the priority of a SR as well as the minimum skill-level required to service it [5]. Once a SW is done with an SR, it exits the system. A *preemption policy* may specify that a SR with higher priority preempts those with lower priority. For each customer and priority there are contractual SLA targets defined representing the SR resolution time deadlines and the percentage of the all SRs that must be resolved within this deadline within a month. For example, the contractual agreement $(customer_1, High) = \langle 4, 95 \rangle$, means that 95% of all SRs from $customer_1$ with priority=High in a month must be resolved within 4 hours. Also, the SWs work in shifts that specifies the working times as well as days. The aim is to cover the business hours of each of the customers by deploying shifts with a consummate staffing levels.

3.1   KPIs in IT Services

We consider three processes of work assignment, work execution, and proactive check-ing. Each process is further measured by several KPIS as shown in Table 2. Staffing deficit is a KPI that is a business outcome because it is measured for the entire SS and cannot be tied to any particular process. We estimate the optimal staffing, on which the measurement of staffing deficit depends, using the recently proposed and widely adopted simulation optimization framework [3,14,5]. The framework essentially mini-mizes the staffing requirement such that the SLA targets are met, the SR queues are not growing unbounded, and SWs do not work overtime.

3.2   Intuitive KPI Relationships

The intuitive KPI relationships are shown in Figure 3. We explain the intuition behind each of the relationships in the following.

Table 2. KPIs and their measurements

Work Assignment	$(1 - p)$ **where** p **is:**
A. Central Assignment: SRs should be centrally assigned to SWs	Fraction of SRs dispatched via dedicated dispatchers.
B. Workload distribution: Achieve even distribution of workload among SWs in each skill group.	Proximity among utilizations of all SWs of all skill groups.
C. Planned Up-skilling: SRs are assigned to SWs with lower skills in a planned manner to up-skill them.	Fraction of higher-skill SRs assigned to lower-skilled SWs as per skill plan.
D. Skill Under-Utilization: SRs are assigned to SWs with higher skills to control backlogs.	Fraction of low-skill SRs assigned to higher-skilled SWs.
E. Cross Customer work SWs should work on SRs from multiple customers.	Fraction of SWs working for multiple customers.
Work Execution	$(1 - p)$ **where** p **is:**
F. Rework: Number of attempts to required to resolve SRs.	Fraction of SRs resolved in the first attempt.
Proactive checking	$(1 - p)$ **where** p **is:**
G. Workload Complexity: Majority of SRs are of low complexity.	Fraction of SRs requiring the lowest skill level.
H. Customer coverage: Proactive checking covers all customers.	Fraction of customers proactively checked in the last 60 days.
I. Issues Identified: Issues found via proactive checking.	1 if at least one issue identified per week, 0 otherwise.
Business Outcomes	**Measured as:**
J. Staffing Deficit:	optimal staffing minus current staffing divided by current staffing (optimal staffing described later).

1. Centralized Assignment (A) $\xrightarrow{-}$ Staffing Deficit (J): Lower the value of A more the work in the SS being centrally assigned. Hence, greater are the chances of it being timely assigned to the right skilled workers, which should lower the staffing requirement leading to lower current staffing. Because the measurement of J assumes A to be in the **best** state, J does not vary based on the actual performance in A. Hence, the staffing deficit increases, which accounts for the negative influence.

2. Skills Underutilization (D) $\xrightarrow{+}$ Staffing Deficit (J): Higher skilled people are more expensive than their lower skilled counterparts. Higher the value of D, more the skill underutilization level, which should increase the staffing requirement. Because the measurement of J assumes D to be in the **worst** possible state, J does not vary based on the actual performance in D. Hence the staffing deficit increases. This accounts for the positive influence.

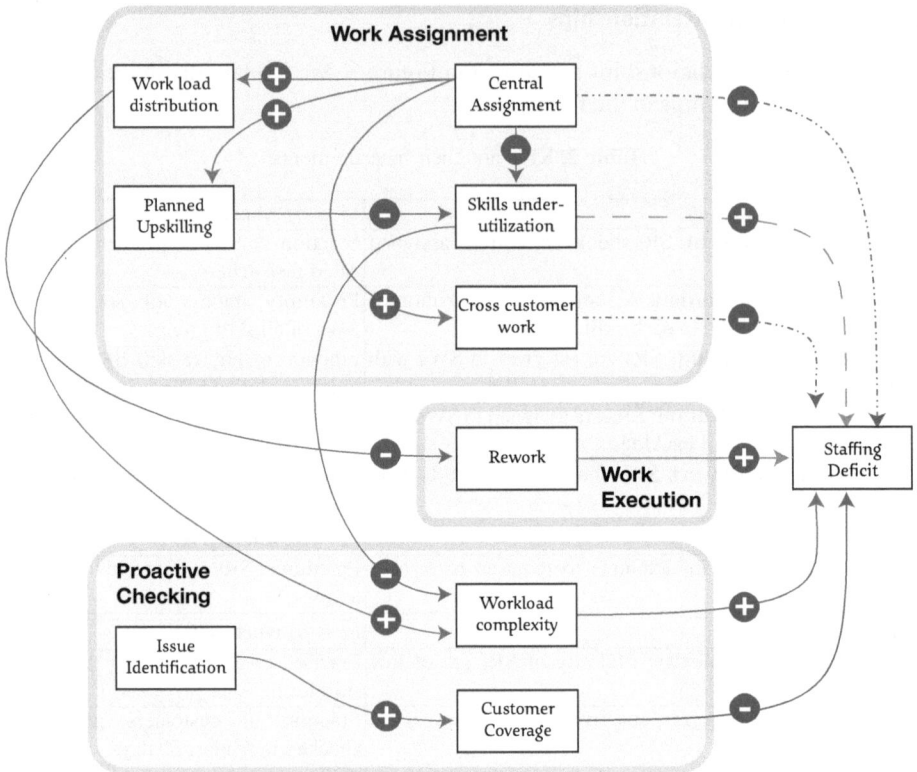

Fig. 3. Hypothetical KPIs relationship model of a SS

3. Cross Customer Work (E) $\xrightarrow{-}$ Staffing Deficit (J): Lower the value of E more workers in the SS are able to work across accounts. Hence, greater is the flexibility in
work assignment which should lower the staffing requirement leading to lower current staffing. Because the measurement of J assumes E to be in the **best** state, J does
not vary based on the actual performance in E. Hence, the staffing deficit increases,
which accounts for the negative influence.

4. Rework (F) $\xrightarrow{+}$ Staffing Deficit (J): Higher the value of F, more rework is required.
Hence higher is the workload which increases the staffing requirement. Because
the measurement of J assumes F to be in the **as-is** state, J should be higher, when
F is higher. Hence the staffing deficit increases which accounts for the positive
influence.

5. Workload Complexity (G) $\xrightarrow{+}$ Staffing Deficit (J): Higher the value of G, more is the
work complexity, which increases the staffing requirement. Because the measurement of J assumes G to be in the **as-is** state, J should be higher when G is higher.
Hence the staffing deficit increases which accounts for the positive influence.

6. Customer Coverage (H) $\xrightarrow{-}$ Staffing Deficit (J): Lower the value of H, more proactive checks are triggered for customers. This translates to additional work, which
increases workload and hence increases the staffing requirement. Because the

measurement of J assumes H to be in the **as-is** state, J should be higher, when H is lower. Hence the staffing deficit increases which accounts for the negative influence.

7. Central Assignment (A)$\xrightarrow{+}$ Workload Distribution (B): More the work in the SS is centrally assigned, the greater are the chances of it being distributed evenly among the workers.

8. Central Assignment (A)$\xrightarrow{+}$ Planned Up-skilling (C): More the work in the SS is centrally assigned, the greater are the chances of a Up-skilling plan being followed.

9. Central Assignment (A)$\xrightarrow{+}$ Cross-customer work (E): More the work in the SS is centrally assigned, the greater are the chances of it assigning multiple customers' work to a worker.

10. Central Assignment (A)$\xrightarrow{-}$ Skill under-utilization (D): More the work in the SS is centrally assigned, the lower are the chances of a high skilled worker being assigned low skilled work.

11. Skills under-utilization (D)$\xrightarrow{-}$ Workload Complexity (G): Higher the workers' skills under-utilization, lower are the chances of having repeatable less complex work in the SS.

12. Issues Identified (I)$\xrightarrow{+}$ Customer Coverage (H): Higher the number of issues identified in time, greater the chances of the proactive checks being triggered for every customer.

13. Planned Up-skilling (C)$\xrightarrow{+}$ Work Complexity (G): Higher the number of high skill requests assigned to low skilled workers to up-skill them, the complexity of the work in the SS becomes higher.

14. Planned Up-skilling (C)$\xrightarrow{-}$ Skills under-utilization (D): Higher the number of high skill requests assigned to low skilled workers to up-skill them, the number of high skilled workers doing low skilled work becomes lower.

15. Workload Distribution (B)$\xrightarrow{-}$ Rework (F):More evenly is the work distributed among the workers, lower are the chances that rework may be needed.

4   Method Validation: IT Services

We use the method proposed in Section 2 to analyze real data from a major IT services provider and validate/revisit the intuitive relationships.

We found that only 8 out of the 15 intuitive relationship hold. Table 3 provides the results of validation study and the estimated degree of influence for validated relationships based on data from 29 SS. Figure 4 shows these validated relationships along with their degree of influence. Also, the RMSE on prediction of each of the effect KPI values are shown in Table 4 with the average RMSE of 1.2%. The fact that some intuitions got invalidated implies that this method is valuable. However, if an edge was missed by an expert, our method would not discover it, which is a limitation of our method. The fact that we can predict staffing deficit so accurately means that it is possible to apply this method to predict high-level business outcomes based on KPI data.

Table 3. Influence relationship validation summary

#	Effect	Cause	Assumed state of cause	Intuitive polarity	Population	Expected Polarity	Observed Correlation	Validation	Influence
1	Staffing deficit	Central Assignment	Best	-	Healthy	-	-0.187	Valid	-0.11
					Weak	+	0.034	Valid	
2	Staffing deficit	Cross Customer Work	Best	-	Healthy	-	0.22	Invalid	
					Weak	+	-0.012	Invalid	
3	Staffing deficit	Skills under-utilization	Worst	+	Healthy	-	-0.095	Valid	0.05
					Weak	+	-0.058	Invalid	
4	Staffing deficit	Rework	As-is	+	All	+	0.289	Valid	0.29
5	Staffing deficit	Workload complexity	As-is	+	All	+	0.053	Valid	0.05
6	Staffing deficit	Customer Coverage	As-is	-	All	-	-0.035	Valid	-0.04
7	Work load distribution	Central Assignment	As-is	+	All	+	0.931	Valid	0.93
8	Planned Up-skilling	Central Assignment	As-is	+	All	+	-0.243	Invalid	
9	Skills under-utilization	Central Assignment	As-is	-	All	-	0.865	Invalid	
10	Skills under-utilization	Planned Up-skilling	As-is	-	All	-	-0.361	Valid	-0.36
11	Cross customer work	Central Assignment	As-is	+	All	+	-0.131	Invalid	
12	Rework	Work load distribution	As-is	-	All	-	0.761	Invalid	
13	Workload complexity	Skills under-utilization	As-is	-	All	-	0.738	Invalid	
14	Workload complexity	Planned Up-skilling	As-is	+	All	+	-0.375	Invalid	
15	Customer Coverage	Issue Identification	As-is	+	All	+	0.608	Valid	0.61

5   Related Work

Over the last few years, industry has witnessed increased focus on attaining excellence in service systems in many verticals. Current days of service systems have been highly IT oriented and there have been studies around the need of measurement frameworks especially for IT services [9]. A fair amount of research is also focusing on service quality [16] that measures wellness of meeting the customer expectations. It has been widely discussed and adopted by delivery frameworks [7] that the operational processes and their KPIs are inter-related to each other and they influence the business outcomes of the service systems.

Human provided services especially in the areas of IT Services are highly people-intensive and complex. Service system performance and KPIs are measured generally at a coarse-grained level rather than at process instance level and also gathering such KPI metrics is highly manual. While our work is dealing with such service systems, we found that similar studies in the areas of BPM and Service Oriented Architecture (SOA) deal with automated processes and instance level KPIs [4]. One such study [20] proposes a framework for monitoring and automatically managing dependency trees using machine learning. Further work [21] observed in this area is also about preventing KPI violations based on decision tree learning and proactive runtime adaptation.

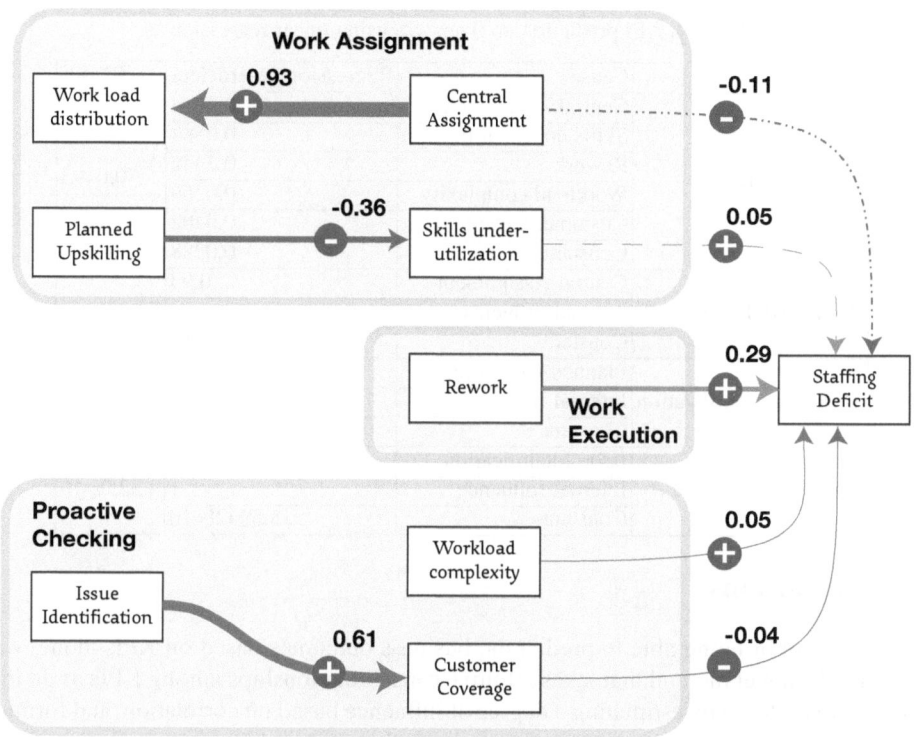

Fig. 4. Validated influence relationships among KPIs based on 29 Service Systems. The thickness of the edges denotes the degree of influence in relationships.

Additional studies in the similar area [11] use intuitive models to develop the relations of KPI and apply cognitive mapping cluster analysis. These are complementary because this paper uses real data from SS to validate such intuitive models. Other related studies [8] discuss developing intuitive models but use them for simulation to develop new processes rather than methods to validate the same with real SS. More studies exist [13,19,12], however we did not find them to be proposing a method to validate the relationships of KPIs.

The main difference between the above works and this paper is that, this paper focuses on the separating the process expertise from the application of the method for process KPI analysis. This is done by clearly defining the information that process experts provide and the results that the method users produce. This helps make the method generally applicable in the services domain because it does not assume any process insights. Further, we predict high-level business objectives based on coarse-grained KPIs which are not available at a process instance level and hence harder to learn from. Also, the influence relationships validated by the method are not process or SS specific and hold for any SS in the domain of service systems.

Table 4. KPI prediction on 9 new SS using linear regression

Effect	Cause	Regression co-efficient	RMSE
Staffing deficit	Central Assignment	-0.2124	0.0495
	Skills under- utilization	-0.0584	
	Rework	0.3346	
	Workload complexity	-0.0259	
	Customer Coverage	0.0402	
	Constant	-0.0288	
Work load distribution	Central Assignment	0.93	5.487E-11
	Internal Influence	1	
	Constant	5.25616E-11	
Skills under- utilization	Planned Up-skilling	-0.36	2.188E-10
	Internal Influence	1	
	Constant	1.04131E-10	
Customer Coverage	Issue Identification	0.61	2.333E-10
	Internal Influence	1	
	Constant	3.5942E-10	

6 Conclusions

With the aim of being able to predict the business outcomes based on KPIs alone, we presented a novel method that takes intuitive causal relationships among KPIs as an input, validates them by estimating a degree of influence based on correlation, and formulates a linear regression model based on training that can predict the business outcome. The evaluation of the method on 38 real-life SS from the IT services domain shows that the method is able to validate or invalidate the intuitive relationships as well as predict the business outcome of staffing deficit with an RMSE of only 1.2%. A limitation of our method is that if a process expert missed a causal relationship, our method has no way of discovering it. However, because the prediction is based on regression, a few missing edges may simply cause a different fit in the regression and may increase the RMSE. Hence, the prediction is more robust against missing edges.

References

1. Alter, S.: Service system fundamentals: Work system, value chain, and life cycle. IBM Systems Journal 47(1), 71–85 (2008)
2. Apte, U.M., Goh, C.H.: Applying lean manufacturing principles to information intensive services (2004)
3. Banerjee, D., Dasgupta, G., Desai, N.: Simulation-based evaluation of dispatching policies in service systems. In: Winter Simulation Conference (2011)
4. Cardoso, J., Sheth, A.P., Miller, J.A., Arnold, J., Kochut, K.: Quality of service for workflows and web service processes. Journal of Web Semantics 1(3), 281–308 (2004)
5. Diao, Y., Heching, A.: Staffing optimization in complex service delivery systems. In: CNSM, pp. 1–9 (2011)
6. Elbashir, M.Z., Collier, P.A., Davern, M.J.: Measuring the effects of business intelligence systems: The relationship between business process and organizational performance. International Journal of Accounting Information Systems 9(3), 135–153 (2008)

7. Grembergen, W.V., Haes, S.D.: Cobit's management guidelines revisited: The kgis/kpis cascade. Information Systems Control Journal 6(1), 1–3 (2005)
8. Han, K.H., Kang, J.G., Song, M.: Two-stage process analysis using the process-based performance measurement framework and business process simulation. Expert Systems with Applications 36(3, Part 2), 7080–7086 (2009)
9. Lepmets, M., Ras, E., Renault, A.: A quality measurement framework for it services by marion lepmets. In: SRII Global Conference (2011)
10. Lin, S.P., Chen, L.F., Chan, Y.H.: What is the valuable service quality gap for improving customer satisfaction? In: ICSSSM, pp. 242–247 (2009)
11. Linard, K., Fleming, C., Dvorsky, L.: System dynamics as the link between corporate vision and key performance indicators. In: System Dynamics Conference, pp. 1–13 (2002)
12. Motta, G., Pignatelli, G., Barroero, T., Longo, A.: Service level analysis method - SLAM. In: Proceedings of ICCSIT, pp. 460–466 (2010)
13. Nor, R., Nor, H., Alias, R.A., Rahman, A.A.: The ICTSQ-PM model in the context of mus: consideration of KPI and CFS. In: UTM Postgraduate Annual Research Seminar, pp. 1–5 (2008)
14. Prashanth, L.A., Prasad, H.L., Desai, N., Bhatnagar, S., Dasgupta, G.: Stochastic Optimization for Adaptive Labor Staffing in Service Systems. In: Kappel, G., Maamar, Z., Motahari-Nezhad, H.R. (eds.) ICSOC 2011. LNCS, vol. 7084, pp. 487–494. Springer, Heidelberg (2011)
15. Ramaswamy, L., Banavar, G.: A formal model of service delivery. In: SCC, pp. 517–520 (2008)
16. Schneider, B., White, S.S.: Service Quality: Research Perspectives (Foundations for Organizational Science). Sage Publications (2003)
17. Silverstein, C., Brin, S., Motwani, R., Ullman, J.: Scalable techniques for mining causal structures. Data Mining and Knowledge Discovery 4, 163–192 (2000)
18. Spohrer, J., Maglio, P., Bailey, J., Gruhl, D.: Steps toward a science of service systems. Computer 40(1), 71–77 (2007)
19. Strasunskas, D., Tomasgard, A.: A method to assess value of integrated operations. In: AMCIS, p. 459 (2010)
20. Wetzstein, B., Leitner, P., Rosenberg, F., Brandic, I., Dustdar, S., Leymann, F.: Monitoring and analyzing influential factors of business process performance. In: Proceedings of EDOC. IEEE Computer Society (2009)
21. Wetzstein, B., Zengin, A., Kazhamiakin, R., Marconi, A., Pistore, M., Karastoyanova, D., Leymann, F.: Preventing kpi violations in business processes based on decision tree learning and proactive runtime adaptation. Journal of Systems Integration 3(1), 3–18 (2012)

Dynamic Performance Management in Multi-tenanted Business Process Servers Using Nonlinear Control

Tharindu Patikirikorala[1], Indika Kumara[1], Alan Colman[1], Jun Han[1],
Liuping Wang[2], Denis Weerasiri[3], and Waruna Ranasinghe[3]

[1] Swinburne University of Technology, Australia
[2] Royal Melbourne Institute of Technology, Australia
[3] WSO2 Inc, Palo Alto, CA

Abstract. The methodologies to develop multi-tenanted architectures have been investigated in the recent literature due to the popularity of cloud computing. A number of challenges need to be overcome if multi-tenanted architectures are to be effective and efficient. Among the challenges is the management of performance properties while effectively sharing the limited resources between the tenants. This work presents an approach to design such a management system for a multi-tenanted business process server. This approach not only enables performance to be maintained at different levels for different tenants depending on their priorities, but also autonomously detects the overloads of aggressive tenants and dynamically changes the control objectives to safeguard the business operations of other tenants. The novelty of the proposed approach is the use of the nonlinear feedback control. The experiment results indicate that the proposed nonlinear control approach achieves the objectives much better compared to the existing fixed and linear control techniques.

1 Introduction

With the popularity of the cloud computing, multi-tenanted architectures are becoming important to realize economies of scale in a flexible manner. In such architectures, pools of resources are shared by multiple tenants/customers thereby raising many challenges for the practitioners. These challenges include enabling *tenant-specific* customizations, data isolation, security isolation and performance management while effectively achieving high resource utilization and sharing. However, these objectives are often competing with each other.

Researchers from SAP present three implementation and deployment options for multi-tenanted software systems in [12] with different levels of trade-offs. 1) *Shared infrastructure*: The tenant specific application instance is deployed in individual virtual machine (VM) instances. This option enables customizations to be provided as per tenant requirements, data and performance isolation [7]. The main drawbacks of this approach are the under-utilization of resources and requirement of a significantly large number of VMs to cater a larger number

C. Liu et al. (Eds.): ICSOC 2012, LNCS 7636, pp. 206–221, 2012.

of tenants [7]. 2) *Shared Middleware*: In this option, the application instances of many tenants share a single middleware instance with the view of having a dedicated middleware instance for each tenant. Consequently, higher resource utilization, tenant consolidation and customizability can be achieved compared to the first option. However, effective performance and resource management techniques have to be provided by the multi-tenanted middleware provider. 3) *Shared application*: In previous two options the application is unaware of the tenants. In this option, tenant management techniques have to be integrated and, in the ideal case, any application instance can serve requests of any tenant. This option enables higher resource utilization and consolidation, but the monolithic application makes customizability and runtime isolation more problematic.

Although the shared infrastructure mechanism can be enabled by the well established virtualization technology to share hardware resources, it is evident that the shared middleware option provides many advantages to the stake-holders. However, as mentioned the issues related to multi-tenancy such as i) data, security and execution isolation, ii) performance and resource management, iii) overload detection and protection, iv) scaling the tenant application instance have to be considered in the development of the multi-tenanted middleware compared to the traditional middleware.

This paper presents a middleware platform which takes into account the first three requirements[1]. Work in [14] has implemented a multi-tenanted Business Process Server (BPS) which enables business process deployments for multiple tenants with the capabilities of data, security and execution isolation. Here, we extend the same BPS and focus on the implementation of performance and overload management. To maintain the performance properties of tenants at acceptable levels depending on the business objectives or priorities in a multi-tenanted environment effective resource management is required at runtime [12,4]. In order to achieve these control objectives this work uses a relative management scheme [9], which also provides facilities to adjust the tenant priority levels at runtime. However, the novelty of our approach compared to the existing approaches (e.g., [9,13]) is that we take into account the nonlinear dynamics of the system and design compensators to reduce the impact of the nonlinearities on the management system, which enables the control system to operate in a wider operating range. Furthermore, the management system is also equipped with a novel overload management mechanism, to detect and react efficiently by degrading the priority of the aggressive tenant workloads in order to safeguard the business operations of the rest of the tenants. The experiment results conducted by deploying the BPS and control system in a VM environment and under instantaneous and real-world workload settings indicate that the proposed nonlinear control methodology achieves the management objectives significantly better compared to the existing fixed resource partitioning and linear control schemes.

---

[1] Scaling includes migration of the specific application to another middleware instance or starting new middleware instances [12]. This is out of the scope of this paper.

2 Background

WSO2 BPS: WSO2 Stratos Business Process Server[2] is a multi-tenanted work-flow engine which executes business processes compliant with WS-BPEL standard, and is built on top of WSO2 Carbon platform[3]. WSO2 Stratos BPS also supports data and execution isolation [14]. Figure 1a) shows its high level architecture. A user of a tenant can consume a business process via a business process endpoint, which is a standard web service endpoint. *WSO2 Stratos Identity Server (IS)* provides security services such as authentication and authorization of tenants and users. *WSO2 Stratos Manager* is used to provision and manage tenants including tenant subscriptions and billing. Business process artifacts for each tenant are kept in *WSO2 Stratos Governance Registry* which is a multi-tenanted governance tool that follows the shared database and shared schema multi-tenanted data architecture pattern defined in [2]. WSO2 Stratos BPS uses Apache ODE[4] as its BPEL execution run-time environment. The ODE-Axis2 Integration Layer encapsulates the tenant-ware business process executions. In the current multi-tenanted BPS instance, a single ODE process engine is shared by multiple tenants. Therefore, a workload of each tenant is treated equally, which does not maintain the performance at required priorities or does not detect and avoid interference between tenants under the overload situations.

Relative Guarantee Scheme: Maintaining absolute values for the performance properties at runtime is difficult due to the workload characteristics of software systems [9]. As a result, maintaining the performance properties of multiple classes (or in other words tenants) at different priorities levels using relative performance management scheme has been identified as a promising alternative [20,9]. In the relative management scheme, the performance properties of the classes are maintained proportional to the performance differentiation factors derived from the business or system design requirements. Let Q_i, P_i be the actual performance property value of interest and the specified differentiation factor respectively of a class $i = 0,\dots n\text{-}1$, out of n number of classes. Between the pair of classes i and j, the objective of the relative management scheme is to maintain $\frac{Q_j}{Q_i} = \frac{P_j}{P_i}$ ($i = 0 \dots n - 1, i \neq j$) at runtime under varying workload conditions. For instance, $\frac{P_1}{P_0} = 2$ means that the performance attribute of $class_1$ has to be maintained twice as of $class_0$. However, the main challenge to maintain the performance differentiation ratio in a shared resource environment is to compute the dynamic resource allocation ratio $\frac{S_j}{S_i}$ (where S_i and S_j, are the resource caps for i and j classes respectively). Lu et al. in [9] proposed a linear feedback control algorithm to automate relative performance and resource management.

---

[2] http://wso2.com/products/business-process-server/
[3] http://wso2.com/products/carbon/
[4] http://ode.apache.org/

3   Related Work

Much of the work related to multi-tenanted systems has been done in the last few years including work on maturity levels [2], data isolation [18,19], enabling customizations [11] and tenant placement [3,6].

A survey of the application of control engineering approaches to build self-adaptive software system can be found in [15]. The relative performance management scheme combined with linear model based feedback control is applied to manage the connection delay in web servers [9,10] and database processing delay in database servers [13]. In addition, Ying et al. analyze the nonlinearities and the related issues of relative management scheme in [10]. These existing control approaches use linear models to represent the inherently nonlinear behavior of the software system. Such models are insufficient to capture the nonlinearities exist in the relative management scheme as shown in this paper.

Feedback control has been also applied for the case of multi-tenanted software system in [8]. Their work is based on adjusting the thread priorities of different tenants depending on their level of importance. Consequently, this approach cannot provide finer grain performance differentiations depending on the business requirements because they rely on thread priority scheduling of the underlying environment. SPIN [7] implements a performance isolation technique by detecting aggressive tenants and reacting to reduce the negative effect on other tenants. However, this work does not consider typical performance variables such as response time in the management solution and the solution depends on highly stochastic workload rates, which are hard to measure or predict accurately.

In this paper we focus on the performance management of a multi-tenanted BPS. In particular, compared to general linear control approaches, we integrate a nonlinear control mechanism proposed in [16] to implement a relative management scheme and a novel overload detection method to achieve the performance objectives of the multi-tenanted BPS. To the best of our knowledge this is the first approach that provides data, security and execution isolation and performance management together in a multi-tenanted BPS.

4   Problem Overview and Analysis

In this section we present an overview of the performance management problem of a BPS serving multiple tenants.

4.1   Assumptions

For the purposes of this paper we have made a number of working assumptions:

1) The number of tenants (say n) placed in a single BPS instance is known at the design time.

2) The number of concurrent process instances (or worker threads) is considered as the shared and main bottlenecked resource as mentioned in [12]. This is because the hardware resources such as CPU and memory cannot be controlled in the granularity of the tenants at the middleware level.

3) When a tenant has overloaded the BPS, a portion of the workload will be rejected to avoid instabilities due to unbounded growth of the queues. Alternatively, tenant migration or scaling out can be done, which are out of the scope of this paper.

4) BPS profiling has been done, and the number of concurrent process instances that could exist in the BPS is determined (say S_{total}) based on the response time requirements of the tenants. This property is important to constrain the total resources and concurrent number of process worker threads affecting the response time of the BPS.

4.2   Performance Management Problem Definition

The main control objective is to share the available S_{total} process instances in an effective way to maintain the response time at levels that are acceptable or depending on the tenant's priority levels, with low interference between 0, 1, ..., n tenants. In addition, the unpredictable overload situations of an aggressive tenant have to be automatically detected and resource allocation decisions have to be made to protect the performance of other tenants.

To achieve these performance objectives we adopt a hybrid of fixed and flexible resource management mechanisms as recommended in [4] to increase resource sharing and utilization. That is, some amount of process instances (say, $S_{i,min}$, where $i = 0, 1, ... n$) need to be reserved for each tenant during the entire period of operations in order to avoid starvation of resources, however under unpredictable workloads the discretionary resources $s_{total} - \sum_{i=0}^{n-1} s_{i,min}$ are shared between the tenants depending on the demands. To enable the flexible resource partitioning $s_{total} - \sum_{i=0}^{n-1} s_{i,min} > 0$. With these settings, the control objectives are now specified based on the relative performance and resource management scheme as follows.

Control objectives: According to the business requirements let us say differentiation/priority factors for n classes are set statically or dynamically as $P_i(k), i = 0 \ldots n - 1$. Then, the control objective according to the relative management scheme becomes maintaining the response time ratio of $(i - 1)^{th}$ and $(i)^{th}$ classes $\frac{R_i(k)}{R_{i-1}(k)}$, around $\frac{P_i(k)}{P_{i-1}(k)}$ while computing the process instance caps $S_i(k), i = 0, 1 \ldots n - 1$. Furthermore, the management system should honor the following constraints, related to total resource availability and per-tenant resource reservations at all times.

$$S_i(k) \geq S_{i,min}, \qquad \sum_{i=0}^{n-1} S_i(k)) = S_{total} \qquad (1)$$

Example: Let us consider a BPS instance with two tenants, 0 and 1. $R_0(k)$ and $R_1(k)$ are the response times of two tenants respectively at the kth sample. Furthermore, the process instance caps are $S_0(k)$ and $S_1(k)$ where $S_0(k) + S_1(k) = S_{total} = 20$ and $S_{0,min}, S_{1,min} = 4$. According to [9] the manipulated variable is $u = \frac{S_0(k)}{S_1(k)}$ and the controlled variable is $y = \frac{R_1(k)}{R_0(k)}$.

4.3 Analysis of Nonlinearity

Input nonlinearity: When the above requirements are embedded in the design, the manipulated variable $u = \frac{S_0(k)}{S_1(k)}$ can only take certain discrete values. By choosing $S_0 = 4, 5, \ldots, 16$, with $S_{total} = 20$ the manipulated variable $u = \frac{S_0}{S_1}$ takes value at $\frac{4}{16}, \frac{5}{15}, \ldots, \frac{15}{5}, \frac{16}{4}$. When these data points are plotted, one of the observations is that the operating points that the controller can take are unequally spaced. If we take the nominal operating point as when both tenants get equal number of process instances, $\frac{10}{10}$, the spacing increases towards the right side and spacing decreases towards the left side of the nominal point. Such, unequally spaced operating points exhibit the characteristics of *static input nonlinearities*, which could adversely affect the management of a linear controller.

Output nonlinearity: The controlled variable y ($\frac{R_1}{R_0}$) of the system exhibits the similar behavior to the u because of the division operation, however it cannot be predetermined. This is because R_0 and R_1 can take a large range of values, causing the $\frac{R_1}{R_0}$ ratio to have a large set of values. For example, when R_1 increases the $\frac{R_1}{R_0}$ increases at a high rate. In contrast, when R_0 increases the $\frac{R_1}{R_0}$ decays at a high rate. The divider operator in the output creates an asymmetric behavior leading to this nonlinearity. Such output nonlinear behavior may also cause performance degradation in a linear controller.

From this analysis it is evident that the above nonlinearities have to be taken in to account in the design of relative performance management system.

5 Approach

This section presents the methodology to design the management system that takes into account the requirements formulated in Sections 4.

Firstly, a set of major modifications was done to WSO2 BPS, in order to enable the performance and resource management capabilities. In particular, tenant-aware queues, response time monitors/sensors for each tenant and resource partition scheduler were integrated. Figure 1a) shows the architecture of the BPS after these modifications. The *Tomcat transport layer* receives the requests from the users of tenants, and forwards the requests to *Axis2 message handler chain*. Upon processing the request in the handler chain, an Axis2 message context is created, and the information about the tenant (so-called tenant domain) in the request is used to identify the corresponding BPEL process. When *ODE-Axis2 Integration Layer* receives an Axis2 message context, the message context is classified based on the available tenant information and put to the message queue corresponding to that tenant. The thread that processed the request waits until a notification of the result is available, in order to send back the response to the client. The management system informs the *Scheduler* via the actuator about the process instance caps for each tenant. The scheduler is implemented based on the algorithm specified in [9]. In addition, the average response time of requests is calculated in a 2 seconds sample window by the sensor for each tenant (R_i, $i = 0, 1, \ldots n$) and sent to the management system.

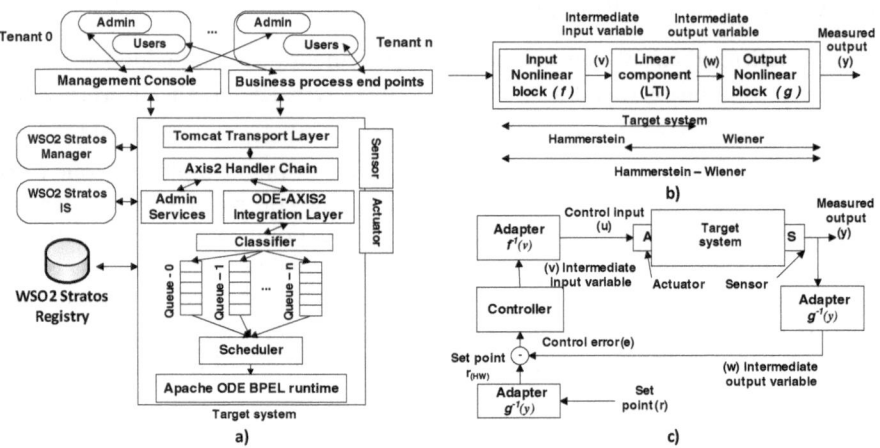

Fig. 1. Block diagram of a) WSO2 BPS, b) Hammerstein-Wiener model and c) Proposed control system

According to the analysis in Section 4.3, the control system designer must consider the aforementioned dominant input and output nonlinear dynamics of the system. A possible way to compensate these nonlinearities is by estimating the existing nonlinearities and then design compensators. Hammerstein-Wiener block structure model is well known in control literature to characterize input and output nonlinearities [16]. As shown in Figure 1b), the Hammerstein-Wiener model has a linear block surrounded by two nonlinear blocks. The entire model can be divided in to two segments called Hammerstein and Wiener block structures. The Hammerstein model has a nonlinear component preceding a linear component. In contrast, the Wiener model has a linear component followed by a nonlinear component. The nonlinear blocks capture the static nonlinearities in the system, while the linear block captures the rest of the dynamics of the system. u and y denote the input and output of the Hammerstein-Wiener model respectively. The intermediate variables v and w are, in general, not measurable.

In this work we use Hammerstein-Wiener model to formally estimate the nonlinear dynamics of the system, followed by their inverse functions to design compensators, which will effectively remove or reduce the impact of nonlinearities on the control system. The novelty of the proposed management system design compared to the linear control system architecture is the integration of the pre-input and post-output compensator as shown in Figure 1c). In this work, the approach proposed in [16] is utilized to design a Hammerstein-Wiener control system. The following subsections present the design details of the control system briefly together with the new overload management method.

5.1   Input Nonlinear Block Design

From the example analyzed in Section 4.3, the discontinuous operating points (u) may induce significant static input nonlinearity. If we implement equally spaced operating points, a linear controller may provide better performance in the entire operating region. Such a conversion mechanism can be implemented by using the input nonlinear component of Hammerstein-Wiener model, transforming the input (u) into the intermediate input (v) with equal spaces.

Firstly, in order to compute the possible operating points (range of u) for the controller in the original system, we can utilize equation (1) and calculate a point for each $s_0 \in \{s_{0,min}, s_{total} - \Sigma_{j=0}^{n-1}(s_{j,min})\}$. Here, we have computed the operating points for a controller of the first pair of tenants, assuming that the rest of the tenants are guaranteed the required minimum allocation $S_{i,min}$. Let us represent these $p > 1$ number of operating points as $u = \{u_1, u_2, \ldots u_p\}$. Then, select an arbitrary $v_{min} \leq v \leq v_{max}$ for the intermediate input variable v^5. With δv defined as $\delta v = \frac{v_{max} - v_{min}}{p-1}$, the intermediate input variable takes its own operating points as $v_1 = v_{min}, v_2 = v_1 + \delta v, \ldots, v_{l+1} = v_l + \delta v, \ldots, v_p = v_{max}$. Thirdly, map the individual values u_l and v_l in the u and v sets to create data pairs, where $l = 1, 2 \ldots, p$. These data pairs can be used to approximate a polynomial $v = f^{-1}(u)$ of order m using curve fitting. After estimation of the f^{-1} function, it is used to implement the pre-input compensator and then integrated to the BPS as shown in Figure 1c). The same compensation is done for each controller, managing the class pair $i - 1$ and i according to the relative management control scheme (see, [9]).

5.2   Output Nonlinear Block Design

The output nonlinearity described in Section 4.3 cannot be estimated using the similar methodology in Section 5.1 because the output nonlinearity cannot be analytically defined. In [16], a method is proposed to estimate the output non-linearity of the relative management scheme based on the Wiener model. We can use the same estimation approach because after the integration of the pre-input compensator the system can be treated as a Wiener model.

Firstly, the possible values of v are applied as a sinusoidal input signal to gather output data, after applying suitable workloads for the first pair of tenants for a sufficient amount of time. The gathered data is then input to the *nlhw* command in the *Matlab: system identification toolbox*, which provides algorithms to estimate the Wiener model. Afterwards, following the procedure in [16] data for w is computed and then $(w - y)$ data pairs are used to estimate the coefficients in the inverse output nonlinearity with a suitable function using the least squares approach. In this work we use a *log* function. Upon the estimation of the inverse output nonlinearity, the $w = g^{-1}(y)$ function is implemented as a component and integrated to each control system managing class pair $i - 1$ and i as shown in Figure 1c).

---

[5] The simulation results in [17] indicate the values selected for v_{min} and v_{max} has less/no effect on the performance of the control system

5.3   Linear Model Design

The next step is to derive the linear component of the Hammerstein-Wiener model to capture the rest of the dynamics in the system. For this purpose a linear autoregressive exogenous input (ARX) model can be estimated similar to the existing work [9,13] by conducting a system identification [5] experiment. However, the transformed variables v and w have to be used in this experiment because of the integration of the compensators into the system.

5.4   Controller Design

By integrating the nonlinear compensators, the system can be assumed to be linear. Consequently, even though the nonlinearities are explicitly considered we can still use a linear controller and the well-established formal design methodologies, which is an added advantage of this proposed nonlinear control approach. We implement a Propositional Integral (PI) controller, which is one of the widely adopted controllers due to their robustness, disturbance rejection capabilities and simplicity [15]. The control equation of the PI controller is shown in equation (2) for the case of Hammerstein-Wiener model. The controller calculates v(k) for $k \geq 0$, given $v(0)$, which is then converted to $u(k)$ using $f^{-1}(v(k))$. $e(k)$ represents the *control error*, computed by $g^{-1}(y) - g^{-1}(r)$, where r is the set point of the original system. K_p (propositional gain) and K_i (integral gain) are called gains of the PI controller. Upon calculation u(k),the algorithm presented in [9] can be used to compute the individual process instance caps $(S_i(k), i = 0, 1 \ldots, n - 1)$ implemented in the BPS.

$$v(k) = v(k - 1) + (K_p + K_i)e(k) - K_p e(k - 1) \tag{2}$$

5.5   Overload Detection and Adaptation

A typical behavior observed during a persistent overload caused by a single tenant is the unbounded growth of the request queue of that tenant [1]. As a consequence, the average response time of that tenant will increase substantially leading to system instabilities or failures. In such situations, if a single queue was implemented without the tenant-aware queuing, the requests of less aggressive tenants will also be rejected while significantly degrading their performance. Therefore, tenant-aware queuing and admission control mechanisms have to be implemented to reject a portion of the workloads in order to limit the response time and to maintain the performance isolation. Furthermore, because of the unpredictable overloads of different tenants, the management system should self-adapt at runtime after detecting the overloads.

An approach to detect server overloads by setting threshold on the queue length was proposed in [1] for a single queue based web server. In this work, we use a similar approach, however for multiple queues. We set queue limits $(q_{len,i}, i \epsilon\ 0, 1, \ldots n - 1)$ for each tenant as a configuration parameter, where the incoming requests will be rejected with a SOAP fault message when the queue limit is reached. With the effective resource management the portion of workload rejected can be reduced avoiding the overloads of one tenant affecting the others. To detect the overload, we set a threshold on the queue $q_{Thresh,i}(\leq q_{len,i}, i\epsilon\ 0, 1, \ldots n - 1)$ for each tenant. Then, the queue length $(q_i(k))$ signal of each tenant is evaluated against the $q_{Thresh,i}$. If $q_i(k)$ stays above the threshold for T_{window} number of consecutive time samples, we say that the tenant i has overloaded the system. Similarly, to detect the end of an overload, $q_i(k)$ must stay below the threshold for T_{window} number of consecutive samples.

When an overload is detected, the system self-adapts by triggering a change to the specified priority levels of the tenants in the control system. When there is no overload by any tenant we assume that all the tenants placed in the BPS have equal priorities. Then, when an overload is detected, say, by tenant i, less priority is given to the requests of tenant i compared to other tenants. This can be implemented using the relative performance management scheme simply by adjusting the differentiation factor P_i dynamically (see Section 2). Afterwards, these differentiation settings can be implemented as simple rules in the management system. As a result, under overload situations our approach maintains the response times of each tenant according to the priority levels specified in the rules, with no human interventions.

6 Experimentation

This section provides the details of the experiments. A BPS with two tenants $(n = 2)$ is considered. The BPS and database was deployed in a VM with two 2.67 GHz CPUs and 3 GB memory. We used the LoanProcess[6] as the deployed business process for each tenant, which invokes three partner services sequentially. The workload generators and partner web services were deployed in two VMs each with a 2.67 GHz CPU and 2 GB memory. After initial profiling the maximum concurrent process instances S_{total} was set to 20. Although higher S_{total} increases the throughput, the response time was significantly affected as well (e.g., $S_{total} = 30$ increased response time around 100 ms). In addition, $S_{1,min}, S_{2,min} = 4$. Furthermore, BPS can handle 75 to 80 requests/sec workload without any overload.

6.1 System Modeling and Controller Design

This section gives the design details of the control system. Firstly, to design the pre-input compensator the possible operating points for u were calculated as $\frac{4}{16}, \ldots, 1, \ldots, \frac{16}{14}$. Then, the points of the intermediate variable v were selected as values $-6, -5, \ldots -1, 0, 1 \ldots 5, 6$ by setting $\delta v = 1$, $v_{min} = -6$ and $v_{max} = 6$. Following the design process in Section 5.1, a fourth order polynomial was used to represent the inverse input nonlinear function (see equation (3)).

$$u = f^{-1}(v) = 0.0003828 * v^4 + 0.003445 * v^3 + 0.01722 * v^2 + 0.1857 * v + 1.006 \quad (3)$$

---

[6] It is sample BPEL process available at `https://svn.wso2.org/repos/wso2/branches/carbon/3.2.0/products/bps/2.1.2/modules/samples/product/src/main/resources/bpel/2.0/LoanProcess/`

Similarly, following the design process in Section 5.2, a sinusoidal signal was designed with the possible values of v and then 40 requests/sec workloads were applied for each tenant to gather output data for 500 sample periods. Subsequently, the output inverse nonlinear function was represented by the equation (4). For the linear model estimation an experiment with a pseudo random input signal and 35 requests/sec workload for each tenant were used. The estimated ARX model is given in equation (5).

The final step is to implement the *Hammerstein-Wiener control system* (called as HWCS) using the ARX model and pole-placement design method [5]. The finalized parameters after placing poles at 0.7 are $K_p = 0.47$, $K_i = 0.16$ and $v(0) = 0$. In order to compare the management provided by the HWCS we also implemented a *linear control system* (called as LCS), with the same setting used in HWCS implementation. The parameters of LCS are $K_p = 0.64$, $K_i = 0.25$ and $u(0) = 1$.

$$w = g^{-1}(y) = 7.48 log(y) - 0.08 \qquad (4)$$
$$w(t+1) = \quad 0.79w(t) + 0.58v(t) \qquad (5)$$

6.2   Experiment Results

This section compares the management capabilities of LCS and HWCS. Due to the variability of the operating conditions, each experiment was conducted 10 times and the average statistics of Sum of Square Error (SSE) are compared in Table 1.

6.2.1   High Workload Separately

This experiment compares the performance of LCS and HWCS when the total workload from two tenants is under the system capacity, however each tenant increases its workload to a high level requiring more resources than the other at separate time periods. Till the 20th sample workloads of 25 requests/sec was applied for $tenant_0$ and $tenant_1$. Then, at the 20th sample $tenant_0$ workload increases to 60 requests/sec. This could be a scenario where a high resource demand for $tenant_0$, while $tenant_1$ is at a lower workload rate. Afterwards, at the 90th sample $tenant_0$ workload reduces to 25 requests/sec. Then, at the 120th sample, $tenant_1$ workload increases to 60 requests/sec from 25 requests/sec. The set point ($\frac{P_1}{P_0}$) is fixed at 1, where both classes are treated equally. The output and control signals of the LCS and HWCS are shown in Figure 2.

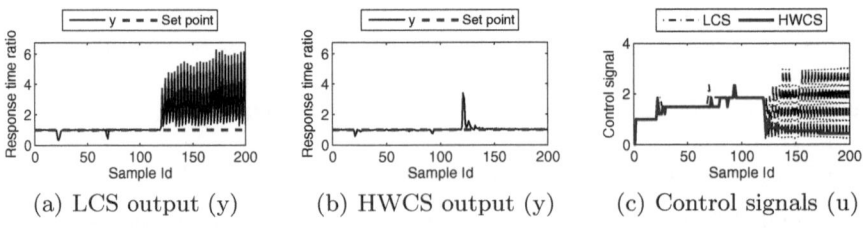

(a) LCS output (y)   (b) HWCS output (y)   (c) Control signals (u)

Fig. 2. Results of the LCS and HWCS under high workloads separately

First, let us analyze the performance of the control systems in region where tenant$_0$ gets more resources (between 20th and 90th samples). The settling times and overshooting of the LCS is higher than HWCS. This is because of the output nonlinearity, the variations in the output signal are damped out so that the linear controller takes time to reject the workload disturbance and adjust the resource caps. In contrast, the output nonlinearity compensated HWCS rejects the disturbance much efficiently compared to LCS. Then, after settling down, both control systems provide similar steady state behavior, achieving the set point with small errors. At the 120th sample when tenant$_1$ increases its workload demanding more resources. LCS shows a highly oscillatory/unstable behavior with large steady state errors (see Figure 2(a)). The control signal (resource allocation decisions) of LCS illustrated in Figure 2(c), shows a highly oscillatory behavior, which led to this unstable behavior at the output. The reason for this behavior is the issue of input nonlinearity discussed in Section 4.3. The smaller gaps between the operating points when tenant$_1$ requires more resources affect the LCS under noisy workload conditions making the LCS to jump between several resource allocation points without settling down. This is an indication that the LCS cannot provide effective performance and resource management when the workload of tenant$_1$ is high. However, the performance in this region can be improved by reducing the aggressiveness (gains) of the controller. This adversely affects the performance when the workload of tenant$_0$ is high. Consequently, LCS fails to achieve effective performance management in the entire operating region under aforementioned nonlinearities. In contrast, the pre-input compensator of the HWCS reduces the impact of input nonlinearity by maintaining the control signal at a steady state (see Figure 2(c)), providing highly satisfactory steady state performance after the disturbance at the 120th sample without affecting the stability. The statistics in Table 1 show significant improvements in the case of HWCS compared to LCS.

6.2.2 Different Priority Levels between Tenants

This section compares the performance differentiation capabilities of the control systems when the set point is $\frac{P_1}{P_0} = 1.5$, making tenant$_0$ more important than tenant$_1$. For this case 25 and 55 requests/sec were applied for tenant$_0$ and tenant$_1$ respectively. Table 1 shows the results of two control systems.

The performance of LCS is similar to what was observed in the previous section. In particular, due to high workload of tenant$_1$, LCS has to operate in the region where the input nonlinearity is severe. Consequently, LCS produces highly oscillatory outputs and unstable behavior in the system. In contrast, the nonlinearity compensated HWCS provides significantly better steady state behavior compared to LCS. The statistics from Table 1 shows a significant reduction in SSE statistics for the case of HWCS.

6.2.3 Overload Detection and Adaptation

In this case we evaluate the overload detection and adaptation capabilities of the proposed control approach. The parameters related to overload detection, i.e. $q_{len,i}$, $q_{Thresh,i}$ and T_{window} were set to 30, 20 and 4 respectively. As the

Table 1. The SSE statistics of LCS and HWCS

Section	LCS	HWCS
6.2.1	602.43	12.41
6.2.1	994.71	16.71

Table 2. The total number of requests rejected from each tenant

Tenant	FCS	LCS	HWCS
0	4262	2296	1968
1	4012	5095	1859

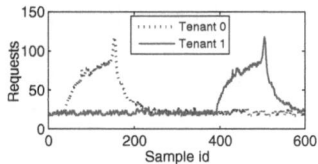

Fig. 3. Workload settings extracted from 1998 world cup website workload traces

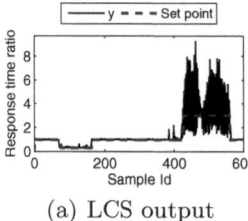
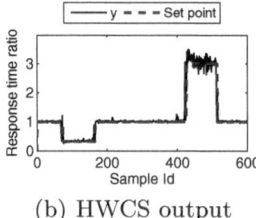
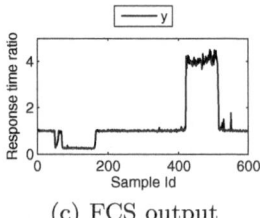

(a) LCS output   (b) HWCS output   (c) FCS output

Fig. 4. Results of the control systems under persistent overloading by tenants

adaptive rules, we set $P_0 : P_1 = 1{:}3$ when tenant$_1$ overloads the system, while $P_0 : P_1 = 3{:}1$ when tenant$_0$ overloads the system. If both tenants are running below the system capacity or overload the system at the same time $P_0 : P_1$ set to $1 : 1$. In this experiment the workload settings extracted from 1998 football world cup workload traces[7] were used. However, the workload rates have to be scaled to fit the requirements of this experiment. Figure 3 shows the workload rates applied on the BPS for two tenants, which overloads the system in separate time periods. In addition to LCS and HWCS, we also provide the results of a fixed partition controller (FCS) that sets $S_0(k) : S_1(k) = 10{:}10$. Figure 4 shows the results of these control systems.

In order to analyze the overload detection capabilities let us investigate the behavior of the set point signal implemented by the management systems (see Figures 4(a), 4(b)). Initially, the set point is at 1 indicating both workloads are running below the system capacity, therefore both tenants are equally treated. However, when tenant$_0$ overloads the system, the proposed control solution has detected the overload around the 60th sample and dynamically changed the set point to be $\frac{1}{3}$. Consequently, the overload of the aggressive tenant$_0$ has not degraded the performance of tenant$_1$ during the overload, maintaining its response time approximately 3 times less than tenant$_0$'s. Similarly, the control system has detected the overload of tenant$_1$ when it overloads the system, and has changed the set point to 3, giving high priority to tenant$_0$. Therefore, it is evident that the proposed overload detection and adaptation mechanism can implement effective performance management and isolation under heavy overload and varying workload conditions.

---

[7] http://ita.ee.lbl.gov/html/contrib/WorldCup.html

When LCS is compared with HWCS, it is clear that the nonlinearities have affected the performance of LCS when $tenant_1$ overloads the system and demands more resources after the 420th sample. Thereby leading to oscillations at the output and affecting the performance of the less aggressive tenant at that time period. The total requests rejected during the experiment listed in Table 2 indicates significantly larger workload rejections for $tenant_1$ and moderate workload rejections for $tenant_0$, in the case of LCS compared to HWCS. When FCS is compared to HWCS, it is evident that the response time of the overloaded tenant has significantly degraded compared to HWCS. For instance, the response time ratio is around $\frac{1}{4}$ and 4 when $tenant_0$ and $tenant_1$ overload the system respectively. Further, the request rejection statistics in Table 2 indicate significantly larger rejections compared to HWCS as well. The reason for this observation is that the resources are not shared or utilized efficiently in FCS, where some resources reserved for one tenant are wasted, while the other requires more resources than are allocated. Therefore, the proposed overload detection and self-adaptive priority adjustment mechanism coupled with HWCS achieves the performance and resource management objectives of the multi-tenanted BPS significantly better compared to the existing fixed partition and linear control methods.

7 Conclusions and Discussion

In this work we have implemented a BPS that can manage performance and resource under unpredictable workload conditions of different tenants. The priority levels of the performance variables are enforced by using the relative performance management scheme, while resource management was done using a hybrid of resource reservation and flexible resource partitioning scheme. In order to automate the management a nonlinear control technique was presented based on the Hammerstein-Wiener model. From the experiment results in Section 6.2, it is evident that the input and output nonlinearities in the relative management scheme significantly affects the performance of a linear control mechanism, consequently leading to instabilities in the system. In contrast, Hammerstein-Wiener model based nonlinear control system, which compensates the nonlinearities, improves the management capabilities compared to linear control. In addition, the proposed overload detection and self-adaptive mechanism shows accurate detection and stable adaptation under unpredictable overloads of different tenants.

Threats to Validity: Although the approach presented in Section 5 is generalized for system with n tenants, the experiment presented in this paper limits the number of tenants to 2. This is because only two tenants could be placed to effectively share the resources depending on the resource availability of the VM and number of the process threads that can run concurrently in the BPS without affecting the response time (see [14] for profiling results). In addition, the number of process instances used was limited to 20 to maintain the performance isolation with the increase of concurrent process worker threads. Further evaluation results are presented for the cases of more than two tenants and large number of resources based on a shared application multi-tenanted system in the technical report [17]. Furthermore, the proposed approach is validated using a

220   T. Patikirikorala et al.

business process executes in short time periods. However, some real world scenarios may have long running business processes (may be days) which may affect the experiment results.

References

1. Abdelzaher, T.F., Bhatti, N.: Web content adaptation to improve server overload behavior. Comput. Netw. 31(11-16), 1563–1577 (1999)
2. Chong, F., Carraro, G.: Architecture strategies for catching the long tail. MSDN (2006)
3. Fehling, C., Leymann, F., Mietzner, R.: A framework for optimized distribution of tenants in cloud applications. In: International Conference on Cloud Computing (CLOUD), pp. 252–259 (2010)
4. Guo, C.J., Sun, W., Huang, Y., Wang, Z.H., Gao, B.: A framework for native multi-tenancy application development and management. In: Conference on Enterprise Computing, E-Commerce, and E-Services, pp. 551–558 (2007)
5. Hellerstein, J.L., Diao, Y., Parekh, S., Tilbury, D.M.: Feedback Control of Computing Systems. John Wiley & Sons (2004)
6. Kwok, T., Mohindra, A.: Resource Calculations with Constraints, and Placement of Tenants and Instances for Multi-tenant SaaS Applications. In: Bouguettaya, A., Krueger, I., Margaria, T. (eds.) ICSOC 2008. LNCS, vol. 5364, pp. 633–648. Springer, Heidelberg (2008)
7. Li, X.H., Liu, T.C., Li, Y., Chen, Y.: SPIN: Service Performance Isolation Infrastructure in Multi-tenancy Environment. In: Bouguettaya, A., Krueger, I., Margaria, T. (eds.) ICSOC 2008. LNCS, vol. 5364, pp. 649–663. Springer, Heidelberg (2008)
8. Lin, H., Sun, K., Zhao, S., Han, Y.: Feedback-control-based performance regulation for multi-tenant applications. In: International Conference on Parallel and Distributed Systems, pp. 134–141 (2009)
9. Lu, C., Lu, Y., Abdelzaher, T.F., Stankovic, J.A., Son, S.H.: Feedback control architecture and design methodology for service delay guarantees in web servers. IEEE Trans. Parallel Distrib. Syst. 17, 1014–1027 (2006)
10. Lu, Y., Abdelzaher, T., Lu, C., Sha, L., Liu, X.: Feedback control with queueing-theoretic prediction for relative delay guarantees in web servers. In: IEEE Real-Time and Embedded Technology and Applications Symposium, p. 208 (2003)
11. Mietzner, R., Unger, T., Titze, R., Leymann, F.: Combining different multi-tenancy patterns in service-oriented applications. In: Enterprise Distributed Object Computing Conference, pp. 131–140 (2009)
12. Momm, C., Krebs, R.: A qualitative discussion of different approaches for implementing multi-tenant saas offerings. In: Software Engineering (Workshops), pp. 139–150 (2011)
13. Pan, W., Mu, D., Wu, H., Yao, L.: Feedback control-based qos guarantees in web application servers. In: IEEE International Conference on High Performance Computing and Communications, pp. 328–334 (2008)
14. Pathirage, M., Perera, S., Kumara, I., Weerawarana, S.: A multi-tenant architecture for business process executions. In: IEEE International Conference on Web Services, pp. 121–128 (2011)
15. Patikirikorala, T., Colman, A., Han, J., Wang, L.: A systematic survey on the design of self-adaptive software systems using control engineering approaches. In: Symposium on Software Engineering for Adaptive and Self-Managing Systems (2012)

16. Patikirikorala, T., Wang, L., Colman, A., Han, J.: Hammerstein-wiener nonlinear model based predictive control for relative qos performance and resource management of software systems. Control Engineering Practice 20(1), 49–61 (2011)
17. Patikirikorala, T., Wang, L., Colman, A., Han, J.: A nonlinear feedback control approach for differentiated performance management in autonomic systems. Technical report (2011)
18. Wang, Z.H., Guo, C.J., Gao, B., Sun, W., Zhang, Z., An, W.H.: A study and performance evaluation of the multi-tenant data tier design patterns for service oriented computing. In: Conference on e-Business Engineering, pp. 94–101 (2008)
19. Weissman, C.D., Bobrowski, S.: The design of the force.com multitenant internet application development platform. In: International Conference on Management of Data, pp. 889–896 (2009)
20. Zhou, X., Wei, J., Xu, C.-Z.: Quality-of-service differentiation on the internet: A taxonomy. Journal of Network and Computer Applications 30(1), 354–383 (2007)

An Optimized Derivation of Event Queries to Monitor Choreography Violations

Aymen Baouab, Olivier Perrin, and Claude Godart

Loria - Inria Nancy - Université de Lorraine - UMR 7503,
BP 239, F-54506 Vandoeuvre-les-Nancy Cedex, France
{aymen.baouab,olivier.perrin,claude.godart}@loria.fr

Abstract. The dynamic nature of the cross-organizational business processes poses various challenges to their successful execution. Choreography description languages help to reduce such complexity by providing means for describing complex systems at a higher level. However, this does not necessarily guarantee that erroneous situations cannot occur due to inappropriately specified interactions. Complex event processing can address this concern by analyzing and evaluating message exchange events, to the aim of checking if the actual behavior of the interacting entities effectively adheres to the modeled business constraints. This paper proposes a runtime event-based approach to deal with the problem of monitoring conformance of interaction sequences. Our approach allows for an automatic and optimized generation of rules. After parsing the choreography graph into a hierarchy of *canonical* blocks, tagging each event by its block ascendancy, an optimized set of monitoring queries is generated. We evaluate the concepts based on a scenario showing how much the number of queries can be significantly reduced.

Keywords: web-service choreography, cross-organizational processes, event processing, business activity monitoring.

1   Introduction

The ability of linking cross-organizational business processes is receiving increased attention in an ever more networked economy [1]. Indeed, collaborative computing grows in importance and processes have to deal with complicated transactions that may take days or weeks to complete across wide ranging geographies, time zones, and enterprise boundaries.

Building complex distributed processes, without introducing unintended consequences, represents a real challenge. Choreography description languages help to reduce such complexity by providing means for describing complex systems at a higher level. The birth of a service choreography is often determined by putting together external norms, regulations, policies, best practices, and business goals of each participating organization. All these different requirements have the effect of constraining the possible allowed interactions between a list of partners. However, this does not necessarily guarantee that erroneous situations cannot

C. Liu et al. (Eds.): ICSOC 2012, LNCS 7636, pp. 222–236, 2012.

occur due to inappropriately specified interactions. Indeed, runtime verification must be taken into consideration, to the aim of checking if the actual behavior of the interacting entities effectively adheres to the modeled business constraints.

Run-time monitoring of services composition have been a subject of interest of several research efforts [2–8]. Todays business process monitors mostly use complex event processing (CEP) to track and report the health of a process and its individual instances. During the last ten years, CEP was a growing and active area for business applications. Business activity monitoring (BAM) was one of the most successful areas where CEP has been used. Based on key performance indicators (KPIs), BAM technology enables continuous, near real-time event-based monitoring of business processes. Most commercial BPM software products (e.g. Oracle BAM, Nimbus, Tibco and IBM Tivoli) include BAM dashboard facilities for monitoring, reporting violations of service level agreements (SLAs), and displaying the results as graphical meters. However, such products are typically limited to internal processes that are under control, i.e., intra-organizational setting.

Providing an easy, real-time way to monitor cross-organizational processes, i.e., when each step is executed by a different company in a collaborative network, represents a complicated task. This is due to the fact that monitors have to deal with huge volumes of unstructured data coming from different sources. Moreover, errors may propagate and failures can cascade across partners. By managing aggregations of various alerts, CEP might give business administrators a better visibility, provide accurate information about the status and results of the monitored processes, and help to automatically respond immediately when problems occur.

In this paper, we address the problem of monitoring conformance of interaction sequences with normative cross-organizational process models. We have chosen to take the choreography description as a basis for the generation of rules. We first define a notification event structure by specifying which data it should contain. After parsing the choreography graph into a hierarchy of *canonical* blocks, tagging each event by its block ascendancy, an optimized set of monitoring queries is generated. Derived queries can be directly used in a complex event processing environment. Further, we evaluate the concepts based on a scenario showing how much the number of queries can be significantly reduced.

The rest of the paper is organized as follows. *Section 2* presents a motivating example. *Section 3* illustrates our approach and *Section 4* presents some evaluation results. *Section 5* outlines some implementation guidelines, *Section 6* discusses related work, and *Section 7* summarizes the contribution and outlines future directions.

2 Scenario and Motivation

To illustrate the concepts of our work, we adopt the scenario of a business-to-business choreography involving a customer (C), a supplier (S) and two shippers $(S1$ and $S2)$. In this cross-organizational choreography, the customer first interacts with a supplier by sending a request for a quote (message M1) and receiving an

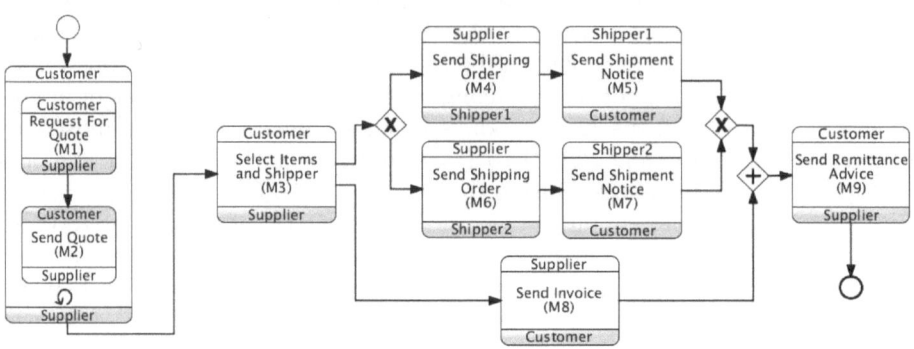

Fig. 1. Cross-organizational choreography example (BPMN 2.0 Diagram)

answer (M2). This step (M1, M2) can be repeated until the customer gets its final decision by selecting items for purchase and the preferred shipper (M3). Then, the supplier transmits a shipping order (M4 or M6) to the selected shipper and sends, in parallel, an invoice to the customer (M8). After finishing the shipment phase, the shipper sends a shipment notice (M5 or M7) to the customer. Finally, the customer proceeds to the payment phase by sending a remittance advice to the supplier (M9) indicating which payables are scheduled for payment. *Figure* 1 shows how to model such a choreography using the BPMN 2.0 notation [9].

During the execution phase, many choreographies shared between different business partners may be instantiated. Indeed, each organization may have multiple external interactions associated with different choreographies instances. Here, there is a need to check the consistency of all incoming and outgoing calls with respect to the current step in each choreography that an organization is participating to. The set of allowed service calls at any given point in time should be dynamic and minimal. Thus, ability to derive instant insights into the cross-organizational interactions is essential. That is, companies should be able to create intelligent agents that monitor their message exchange with the external world in real-time, and automate analysis to detect unusual interaction sequences that fall outside choreography patterns. For instance, a call that is not associated with any current expected step of the instantiated choreographies should be reported to the monitoring applications as a potential violation. Controlling incoming calls at earlier stage may reduce some of common attacks (e.g. DoS attack). Furthermore, it represents a crucial requirement to prevent any malicious peer from exploiting external flow authorizations.

3   Complex Event Queries to Monitor Choreographies

Before we dive headfirst into our approach, we briefly formalize some basic notions . *Section* 3.1 gives background information on Complex Event Processing

(CEP). *Section* 3.2 introduces some formal definitions of a choreography. Afterward, we present the conceptual architecture and we describe the detailed procedure of our approach.

3.1 Complex Event Processing (CEP)

Monitoring business in a highly distributed environment is critical for most enterprises. In the SOA world, CEP can play a significant role through its ability to monitor and detect any deviations from the fixed process models [10]. Indeed, such a technology enables the real time monitoring of multiple streams of event data, allows to analyze them following defined event rules, and permits to react upon threats and opportunities, eventually by creating new derived events, or simply forwarding raw events.

To support real time queries over event data, queries are stored persistently and evaluated by a CEP system as new event data arrives. An *event processor* is an application that analyzes incoming event streams, flags relevant events, discards those that are of no importance, and performs a variety of operations (e.g. reading, creating, filtering, transforming, aggregating) on events objects.

Event processing tools allow users to define patterns of events and monitors are supposed to detect instances of these patterns. Event patterns become more and more sophisticated and queries more complicated. Thus, there is a need to assist the administrator by a semi-automatic generation of event pattern rules from any process model. To identify non-trivial patterns in event sequences and to trigger appropriate actions, CEP techniques to encode the control flow of a process model as a set of event queries have been introduced [11, 12]. Following this strategy, violations can be detected when defined anti-patterns are matched by the CEP engine.

3.2 Formal Foundation (Choreography)

A choreography defines re-usable common rules that govern the ordering of exchanged messages, and the provisioning patterns of collaborative behavior, as agreed upon between two or more interacting participants [13]. In this paper, we perceive a choreography as a description of admissible sequences of send and receive messages between collaborating parties. Our approach focuses on the global behavior of the choreography. Only ordering structures (sequence, parallel, exclusiveness, and iteration) and interaction activities (message exchange activities) are considered. In other words, it is outside the scope of this paper to specify internal activities (e.g. assign activities, silent activities) since they do not generate message exchanges. For the sake of simplicity, we also omit assignment of global variables. We use "participant" and "partner" interchangeably.

We formalize the semantics of a choreography as follows.

Definition 1 (Choreography). *Formally, a choreography C is a tuple (P, I, O) where*

- P *is a finite set of participants,*
- I *is a finite set of interactions,*

– $\mathcal{O}$ is a finite set of ordering structures defining constraints on the sequencing of interactions.

An interaction is the basic building block of a choreography, which results in an exchange of information between parties. Every interaction $I \in \mathcal{I}$ corresponds to a certain type of message (e.g. XML Schema), and is associated with a direction of communication, i.e., a source and a destination of the exchanged message. Let $\mathcal{M}_T$ be the set of message types. Formally, an interaction is defined as follows.

Definition 2 (Interaction). *An interaction $I \in \mathcal{I}$ is a tuple (Iid,s,d,m_t) where Iid is a unique identifier of the interaction, s,d $\in \mathcal{P}$ are the source and the destination of the message, and $m_t \in \mathcal{M}_T$ is the type of the message.*

The sequencing of interactions is typically captured by four major types of ordering structures:

Sequence.   The sequence ordering structure restricts the series of enclosed interactions to be enabled sequentially, in the same order that they are defined.
Exclusiveness.   The exclusiveness ordering structure enables specifying that only one of two or more interactions should be performed.
Parallel.   The parallel ordering structure contains one or more interactions that are enabled concurrently.
Iteration.   An iteration (loop) structure describes the conditional and repeated execution of one or more interactions.

3.3   Approach Overview

Our approach relies only on choreography state changes, i.e., when a global message is sent or received, monitoring only the interactions between the peers in an unobtrusive way, i.e., the exchanged messages are not altered by the monitors and the peers are not aware of the monitors.

Figure 2 provides an overview of the approach. We assume that events that reflect occurrences of message exchanges are provided by one or multiple external

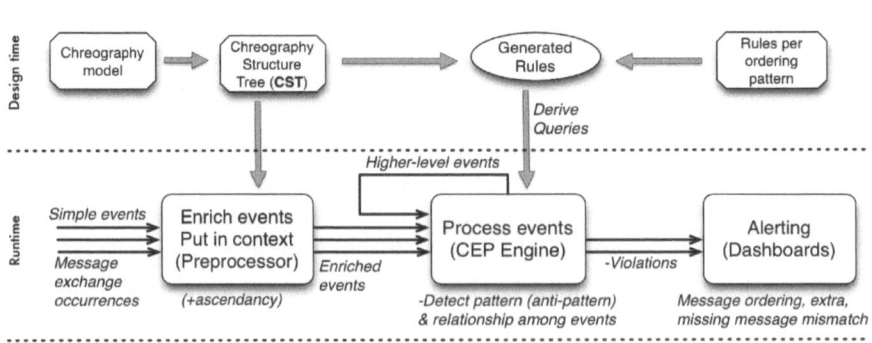

Fig. 2. Conceptual Architecture

components, i.e., event producers. Before being forwarded to a CEP engine, these basic events are enriched by their ascendancy nodes in the structure tree that is derived from the choreography model. Afterwards, the event processor executes predefined complex event queries over the enriched event stream in order to target behavioral deviations during the execution of each choreography. These queries are derived, during design time, from a pre-generated set of rules. Detected violations are sent to be shown in dashboards.

3.4 Basic-Level Events Generation

Most agree, an event is just a fact of something occurring. In the context of a choreography of services, events occur when messages are sent and received. In our case, for each exchanged message, a new notification event is generated. In other words, notification events are generated as transitions occur in the choreography interaction graph. Each notification event is correlated to a choreography message and is generated in order to inform about the occurrence of that message. We define a notification event as follows.

Definition 3 (Notification Event). *A notification $n \in \mathcal{N}$ is a tuple*

$$event = (Eid,\ Cid,\ Iid,\ TS)$$

where Eid is a unique identifier of the event, Cid is a unique identifier for the choreography instance (used for correlation), $Iid \in \mathcal{I}$ is the identifier of the interaction associated to the observed choreography message, and TS is the timestamp of generation).

The field Cid is required to correlate events to the different choreography instances. During the execution phase, we may have several instances of different defined choreography models. Obviously, we need to correlate notification events belonging to the same instance. The most common solution [14] to deal with this issue is to define two identifiers that have to be contained in each message (e.g. included in the SOAP header): The choreography ID (a unique identifier for each choreography model) and the choreography instance ID (a unique identifier for each choreography instance). An additional component along the boundary of each participant may be adapted to include and read the identifier whenever a choreography message is exchanged.

The field TS represents the time at which the choreography message is recorded by the event producer. Timestamping events allows for a local ordering through a sequential numbering which is required to analyze the acquired monitoring data.

In this paper, we assume the asynchronous communications among the partners to have an exactly-once in-order reception, i.e., exchanged messages are received exactly once and in the same order in which they are sent. Although this assumption seems to be strong, it is feasible through the adoption of reliable messaging standards (e.g. *WS-ReliableMessaging* [15]).

3.5 Causal Behavioral Profiles

To pinpoint conformance violations during runtime, event rules need to be generated from the fixed interaction-ordering constraints. Following the concept of causal behavioral profiles, [11] proposes to generate a rule between each couple of interaction. As introduced in [16], a causal behavioral profile provides an abstraction of the behavior defined by a process model. It captures behavioral characteristics by relations on the level of activity pairs. That is, a relation is fixed between each couple of activities indicating whether they should be in strict order, in interleaving order, or exclusive to each other. In a choreography, an interaction can be seen as the basic activity. Thus, the same type of relation might be used. For instance, in the model presented in *figure* 1, interactions (M_1) and (M_2) are in strict order. Interactions (M_4) and (M_7) are exclusive to each other. However, interactions (M_5) and (M_8) are in interleaving order. Interleaving order can be seen as the absence of an ordering constraint. Therefore, this relation is not considered when monitoring choreography execution.

Following this approach, in a given choreography with n interactions, the number of rules is equal to n^2. This may overhead the the number of generated queries by extra overlapping ones. For instance, if we have two constraints stating that M_1 should occur before M_2 and M_2 before M_3, then there is no need to fix an additional constraint stating that M_1 should occur before M_3, because this can be deduced automatically. This can be justified by the fact that ordering constraints are transitive. Moreover, when an interaction is performed at an unexpected stage, generated queries may result in multiple redundant alerts. Then, additional queries have to be added in order to identify the root cause for the set of violations as it is done in [11].

Instead of fixing a constraint between each couple of interaction, our approach consists on fixing constraints only between neighbor interactions. To do that, a structural fragmentation of the choreography model is needed.

3.6 Choreography Structure Tree

Until now, we have defined what constitutes a basic level event. In order to reduce the number of constraints, and thus the number of event queries, we provide a decomposition that is inspired from the refined program structure tree (R-PST) of business processes defined in [17] which is a technique for parsing and discovering the structure of a workflow graph. R-PST is proposed as a hierarchical decomposition of a process model into single-entry / single-exit (SESE) *canonical* blocks. A block F is *non-canonical* if there are blocks X,Y,Z such that X and Y are in sequence, $F = X \cup Y$, and F and Z are in sequence; otherwise F is said to be *canonical* [18]. It has been proved that such a SESE decomposition is unique, modular, and can be computed in linear time [17]. In fact, derived blocks never overlap, i.e., given two blocks either one block is completely contained in another block or these blocks are disjoint.

Following this approach, we parse the choreography graph into a hierarchy of SESE *canonical* blocks. *Figure* 3 illustrates *canonical* blocks of our motivating

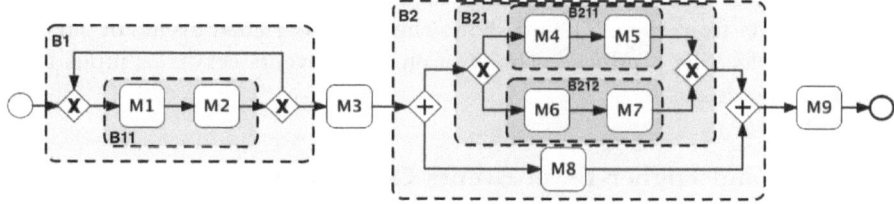

Fig. 3. Fragment decomposition

example. The result of such a decomposition can be represented as a tree that we name Choreography Structure Tree (CST). The largest block that contains the whole graph is the root block of the generated tree. The child blocks of a sequence are ordered left to right from the entry to the exit. *Figure* 4(a) shows the generated CST of our motivation example. We concretize the internal tree nodes by annotating them with the type of ordering pattern, i.e., sequence, parallel, exclusiveness, loop, relating direct descendants. As such, we explicitly establish the structural relation between them.

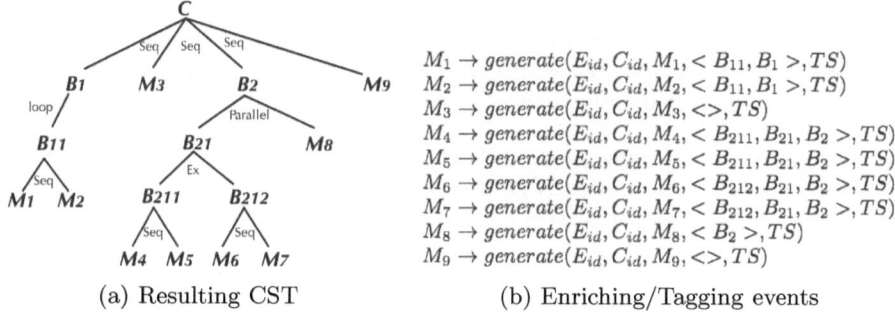

$M_1 \to generate(E_{id}, C_{id}, M_1, < B_{11}, B_1 >, TS)$
$M_2 \to generate(E_{id}, C_{id}, M_2, < B_{11}, B_1 >, TS)$
$M_3 \to generate(E_{id}, C_{id}, M_3, <>, TS)$
$M_4 \to generate(E_{id}, C_{id}, M_4, < B_{211}, B_{21}, B_2 >, TS)$
$M_5 \to generate(E_{id}, C_{id}, M_5, < B_{211}, B_{21}, B_2 >, TS)$
$M_6 \to generate(E_{id}, C_{id}, M_6, < B_{212}, B_{21}, B_2 >, TS)$
$M_7 \to generate(E_{id}, C_{id}, M_7, < B_{212}, B_{21}, B_2 >, TS)$
$M_8 \to generate(E_{id}, C_{id}, M_8, < B_2 >, TS)$
$M_9 \to generate(E_{id}, C_{id}, M_9, <>, TS)$

(a) Resulting CST   (b) Enriching/Tagging events

Fig. 4. Enriching basic level events

3.7   Enriching Events

After generating the CST, we propose to enrich each basic level event by adding a new field called *ascendancy* containing the list of all superior blocks of the observed message. For instance, the event related to the message (M4) in our motivating example (Figure 3) is tagged by the sequence $< B_{211}, B_{21}, B_2 >$ as it belongs, respectively, to the blocks B_{211}, B_{21} and B_2. This is a kind of tagging each incoming event in order to put it in context, i.e., its supposed location in the CST. After the enrichment step, each basic-level event is transformed into the following structure:

$$event = (Eid, Cid, \text{Iid}, < ascendancy >, TS)$$

This step might be performed by a preprocessor component handling basic event filtering and enrichment. Upon reception of each new basic event, the preprocessor fetches in the CST the ascendancy of the related interaction, and includes the result as a list of blocks identifiers. *Figure* 4(b) exemplifies how to generate enriched events from the CST and shows the newly enriched events of our motivating example. The produced stream of enriched events serves as input to the main event processor.

3.8   Rules and Higher-Level Events Generation

After enriching events by their superior blocks, rules can be applied to fix block ordering. By doing so, the number of rules decreases exponentially from a level to its higher. Here, we need a generation of higher level events at the end of execution of each block. These newly generated events, indicates the block termination – we note $End(B)$. In the CEP world, a high level event is an event that is an abstraction of other events called its members. In our case, events members are those related to interactions contained in the same block.

   To specify these rules, two types of constraints are defined:

- The strict order constraint, denoted by the function $Seq(B_1, B_2)$, holds for two messages M_1 and M_2, respectively tagged with B_1 and B_2, if M_2 never occurs before $End(B_1)$ and M_1 never occurs after M_2.
- The exclusiveness constraint, denoted by the function $Ex(B_1, B_2)$, holds for two messages M_1 and M_2, respectively tagged with B_1 and B_2, if they never occur together within the same choreography instance.

Depending on the ordering patterns, i.e., sequence, parallel, exclusiveness, and iteration, rules are automatically defined to fix when to generate block termination events. *Figure* 5 illustrates the rules for each type of pattern.

Sequence Block. When we have a sequential enactment of n interaction blocks $B_1, ..., B_n$, we can simply enforce the order between each two consecutive blocks, i.e., $Seq(B_i, B_{i+1})$, $i \in \{1..n-1\}$. The completion of the final block in the list induces the generation of the whole block termination event, i.e., $End(B_n) => Generate(End(B))$.

Parallel Block. In case of parallel enactment of n interactions blocks $B_1, ..., B_n$, a violation can only be detected by the absence of one of the internal blocks. Thus, such a violation materializes only at the completion of the whole block B. The completion event is generated only after the termination of all child blocks, i.e, $End(B_1)\&...\&End(B_n) => Generate(End(B))$.

Exclusiveness Block. This choreography construct models the conditional choice. Here, one enactment of only one of the branches is allowed. The decision about which of the branches is enacted is taken internally by one of the participants. In case of n branches of interactions blocks $B_1, ..., B_n$, exclusiveness constraint between each possible couple is generated, i.e., $Ex(B_i, B_j)$, $i \neq j$, $i, j \in \{1..n\}$. The completion event is generated after the termination of one of child blocks, i.e, $End(B_1)$ *or*...*or* $End(B_n) => Generate(End(B))$.

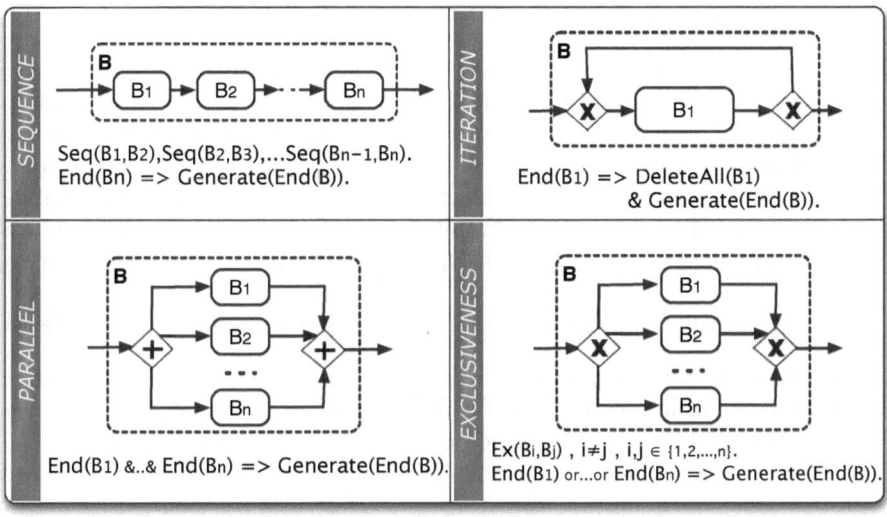

Fig. 5. Rules for each pattern

Iteration Block. In a choreography, an iteration (also called *loop*) activity B specifies the repeated enactment of a branch B_1, which is said to be the body of the iteration. To allow for the repetition of the body's interactions without raising other violations, we need to erase a part of the event history at the end of each iteration and generate the whole block termination event in order to allow the following block to be executed, i.e., $End(B_1) => DeleteAll(B_1)$ & $Generate(End(B))$. Here, $DeleteAll(B_1)$ deletes from the history all events containing B_1 in their *ascendancy* field.

Following this four basic rules and a level per level exploring of the CST, specific rule instances can be automatically generated after the definition of any choreography model. For instance, *table* 1 shows the generated rules from the choreography model presented in *figure* 3. We use the character ';' as a separator between them. The level number represents the depth in the CST.

Table 1. Generated Rules

Level	Generated rules
1	$Seq(B_1, M_3)$; $Seq(M_3, B_2)$; $Seq(B_2, M_9)$; $M_9 \Rightarrow generate(End(C))$
2	$End(B_{11}) \Rightarrow deleteAll(B_{11})$ & $generate(End(B_1))$; $End(B_{21})$ & $M_8 \Rightarrow generate(End(B_2))$
3	$Seq(M_1, M_2)$; $M_2 \Rightarrow generate(End(B_{11}))$; $Ex(B_{211}, B_{212})$; $End(B_{211})$ or $End(B_{212}) \Rightarrow generate(End(B_{21}))$
4	$Seq(M_4, M_5)$; $M_5 \Rightarrow generate(End(B_{211}))$; $Seq(M_6, M_7)$; $M_7 \Rightarrow generate(End(B_{212}))$

3.9   Runtime Pattern Matching

In order to detect violations, rules need to be automatically formulated into event processing queries. Indeed, a generated event query has to match a negation of a rule pattern. For instance, the constraint $Seq(B_1, B_2)$ is violated if and only if the event processor matches any event belonging to the block B_2 that is followed by another event belonging to the block B_1 or simply followed by the high level event $End(B_1)$. However, the constraint $Ex(B_1, B_2)$ is violated when it matches two events, respectively tagged with B_1 and B_2, occur together within the same instance.

When executing the event queries, three types of violation can be detected:

Message ordering mismatch. This violation occurs when the order of messages is not in line with the defined behavior. As an example, when considering the model presented in *figure* 3, let $< M_1, M_2, M_4, M_8, M_3, M_5, M_9 >$ be the sequence of recorded events for one choreography instance. Referring to the generated rules in *table* 1, $Seq(M_3, B_2)$ is twice violated because two messages (M_4 and M_8 that are tagged with B_2) have occurred before M_3.

Extra message mismatch. This violation is detected by the presence of an extra message. It can be matched by a joint occurrence of two exclusive messages. For instance, let $< M_1, M_2, M_4, M_8, M_6, M_5, M_9 >$ be the sequence of recorded events. Here, M_6 is an extra message. $Ex(B_{211}, B_{212})$ is twice violated because two messages (M_4 and M_5 that are tagged with B_{211}) have occurred together with M_6 (that is tagged with B_{212}) within the same instance.

Missing message mismatch. This violation is detected by the absence of a message. This can be materialized only at the competition of the smallest block containing the message. In fact, when the End event of this block is not generated, the following sequence is violated. For instance, let $< M_1, M_2, M_3, M_8, M_4, M_9 >$ be the sequence of recorded events. As we can see, M_5 is missing after M_4. Here, $End(B_{211})$, and thus $End(B_{21})$ and $End(B_2)$ are not generated. As M_9 occurred before $End(B_2)$, $Seq(B_2, M_9)$ is then violated.

4   Evaluation

As we can see in *table* 1, we have 14 generated rules. To these rules we may add 9 other rules $Ex(M_i, M_i)$, $i \in \{1..9\}$ in order to indicate that each message should occur only once. Note that this does not affect the messages inside the loop block as their events are deleted at the end of each iteration. These additional rules bring the total number out to 23 (instead of 9x9=81 using the classic behavioral profile approach [11]). Clearly, the benefit of our approach depends on the topology of the CST, e.g., the average number of interactions per blocks, the types of ordering patterns.

For instance, *figure* 6 shows a case where two blocks B_1 and B_2, containing respectively N and M messages in sequence, are exclusive to each other.

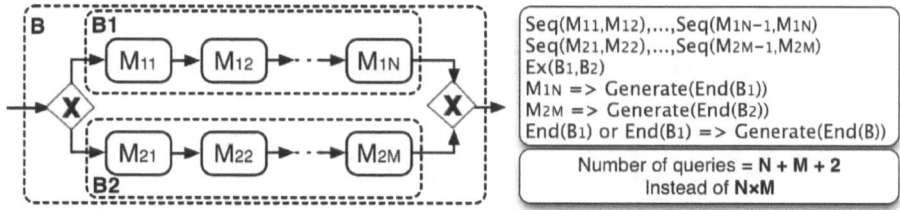

Fig. 6. Special case : Exclusiveness

Here, the total number of generated rules is equal to $N+M+2$ instead of NxM. Clearly, when N and M increase, the difference increases also. For instance, when $N=M=5$, the number of rules is equal to 12 instead of 25 (48%). However, when $N=M=10$, the number of rules is equal to 22 instead of 100 (22%). This is one case, among others, that illustrates how our approach can significantly reduce the number of needed queries.

5   Implementation

To execute the queries, we assume the utilization of a CEP engine, coupled with SOAP handlers in order to capture events. First, an input stream and a window to store incoming events on the input stream are created. Queries might be encoded in any dedicated query language that provides pattern definitions. Typical patterns are conjunction, disjunction, negation, and causality. To show the feasibility of our approach, we have chosen to encode the generated queries of our motivating example using the *Esper Processing Language* [19] as it is a commercially proven system and available as open source. This language is a SQL-like language used for querying the inbound event streams. Here, event objects are used instead of specifying tables in which to pull data. The defined queries are registered within the Esper engine in form of event patterns. Then, incoming events are continuously analyzed and processed against these patterns. When matching results are found, defined actions can be undertaken.

Figure 7 shows three queries of our motivating example written in Esper. The first matches if the rule $Seq(M_1, M_2)$ is violated. It detects if a message M_1 is not preceded by a message M_2 that belongs to the same choreography instance $(e2.Cid = e1.Cid)$. The second query matches if the rule $Ex(B_{211}, B_{212})$ is violated. It detects any two messages having respectively B_{211} and B_{212} as substrings in their *ascendancy* field and belonging to the same choreography instance. However, the third query matches if the rule $Seq(B_1, M_3)$ is violated. In other words, it detects any message of type M_3 that is not preceded by the generated event $End(B_1)$.

```
 // Matching Seq(M1,M2) violations :
"@Name('Seq M1 M2') select * from pattern "
    + "[ (e2=MsgEvent(e2.iid=2) and not e1=MsgEvent(e1.iid=1))] where e1.cid=e2.cid" ,

 // Matching Ex(B211,B212) violations :
"@Name('Ex B211 B212') select * from pattern "
    + "[ e1=MsgEvent(e1.ascendancy like '%B211,%') and "
    + "e2=MsgEvent(e2.ascendancy like '%B212,%')] where e1.cid=e2.cid",

 // Matching Seq(B1,M3) violations :
"@Name('Seq B1 M3') select * from pattern "
    + "[ e3=MsgEvent(e3.iid=3) and not b1=MsgEvent(b1.endOf like 'B1')] "
    + "where e3.cid=b1.cid",
/*...*/
```

Fig. 7. Coding event queries using Esper

6   Related Work

Run-time monitoring of services composition have been a subject of interest of several research efforts. In this section we want to outline some of the most relevant contributions with the aim to provide a distinction to our work.

Subramanian et al. [20] presented an approach for enhancing BPEL engines by proposing a new dedicated engine called "SelfHealBPEL" that implements additional facilities for runtime detection and handling of failures. Barbon et al. [21] proposed an architecture that separates the business logic of a web service from the monitoring functionality and defined a language that allows for specifying statistic and time-related properties. However, their approach focus on single BPEL orchestrations and do not deal with monitoring of choreographies in a cross-organizational setting. Ardissono et al. [2] presented a framework for supporting the monitoring of the progress of a choreography in order to ensure the early detection of faults and the notification of the affected participants. The approach consists on a central monitor which is notified by each participant whenever he sends or receives a message.

In case of decentralized processes within the same organization (or within a circle of trust), Chafle et al. [7] have modeled a central entity as a status monitor which is implemented as a web service. On each partition, a local monitoring agent captures the local state of the composite service partition and periodically updates the centralized status monitor. The status monitor maintains the status of all the activities of the global composite service. In [8], the authors introduce the concept of monitor-based messenger (MBM), which processes exchanged messages through a runtime monitor. Each local monitor stamps its outgoing messages with the current monitor state to prevent desynchronizations, provide a total ordering of messages, and offer protection against unreliable messaging.

Regarding event-centric perspectives, process monitoring solutions focus on intra-organizational processes and are mostly based on Business Activity Monitoring (BAM) technology [22]. To the best of our knowledge, only two event-centric approaches deal with monitoring cross-organizational choreographies.

The first one [23] uses a common audit format which allows processing and correlating events across different BPEL engines. The second approach [14] introduces complex event specification and uses a choreography instance identifier (ciid) to deal with event correlation (which is not supported in [23]).

In contrast to the previously mentioned works, we rather focus on providing an approach for the automated generation of an optimized set of monitoring queries from any choreography specification. These queries are then directly used in a CEP environment. Weidlich *et al.* [11] proposes a formal technique to derive monitoring event-based queries from a process model. Following the concept of causal behavioral profiles [16], authors propose to generate a rule between each couple of interaction. Then, additional queries have to be added in order to identify the root cause for the set of violations. Instead of fixing a constraint between each couple of interaction, our approach consists on fixing constraints only between neighbor blocks of interactions.

7 Conclusion and Future Work

In this paper, we have proposed an approach for monitoring message exchange deviations in cross-organizational choreographies. Our contribution is a formal technique to generate event-based monitoring queries that match message ordering violations. We have demonstrated that after parsing the choreography graph into a hierarchy of *canonical* blocks, and tagging each event by its block ascendancy, our approach allows to significantly reduce the number of needed queries. Furthermore, we have shown how can these queries be directly used in a CEP environment by providing implementation guidelines.

As future work, we plan to investigate the efficiency of our approach for different types of choreographies. Moreover, we aim to enhance it by providing additional monitoring features to address some quality of service concerns. For instance, it would be interesting to deal with delays in message exchanges. To this end, time constraints violations might be calculated by fixing timeouts and expected time to elapse between messages.

References

1. Grefen, P.: Towards dynamic interorganizational business process management. In: Enabling Technologies: Infrastructure for Collaborative Enterprises (2006)
2. Ardissono, L., Furnari, R., Goy, A., Petrone, G., Segnan, M.: Monitoring choreographed services. In: Innovations and Advanced Techniques in Computer and Information Sciences and Engineering, CISSE 2006, pp. 283–288 (2006)
3. Francalanza, A., Gauci, A., Pace, G.: Runtime monitoring of distributed systems (extended abstract). Technical report, University of Malta, WICT (2010)
4. Moser, O., Rosenberg, F., Dustdar, S.: Event Driven Monitoring for Service Composition Infrastructures. In: Chen, L., Triantafillou, P., Suel, T. (eds.) WISE 2010. LNCS, vol. 6488, pp. 38–51. Springer, Heidelberg (2010)
5. Baouab, A., Fdhila, W., Perrin, O., Godart, C.: Towards decentralized monitoring of supply chains. In: 19th IEEE International Conference on Web Services, ICWS (2012)

6. Baouab, A., Perrin, O., Godart, C.: An event-driven approach for runtime verification of inter-organizational choreographies. In: 2011 IEEE International Conference on Services Computing, SCC (2011)
7. Chafle, G.B., Chandra, S., Mann, V., Nanda, M.G.: Decentralized orchestration of composite web services. In: Proceedings of the 13th International World Wide Web Conference, WWW Alt. 2004. ACM, New York (2004)
8. Halle, S., Villemaire, R.: Flexible and reliable messaging using runtime monitoring. In: 13th Enterprise Distributed Object Computing Conference Workshops, EDOCW 2009 (September 2009)
9. OMG: Business process model and notation (bpmn), version 2.0 (2011)
10. Etzion, O., Niblett, P., Luckham, D.: Event Processing in Action. Manning Pubs. Co Series. Manning Publications (2010)
11. Weidlich, M., Ziekow, H., Mendling, J., Günther, O., Weske, M., Desai, N.: Event-Based Monitoring of Process Execution Violations. In: Rinderle-Ma, S., Toumani, F., Wolf, K. (eds.) BPM 2011. LNCS, vol. 6896, pp. 182–198. Springer, Heidelberg (2011)
12. Weidlich, M., Polyvyanyy, A., Desai, N., Mendling, J., Weske, M.: Process compliance analysis based on behavioural profiles. Inf. Syst. 36(7) (November 2011)
13. Kavantzas, N., Burdett, D., Ritzinger, G., Fletcher, T., Lafon, Y., Barreto, C.: Web services choreography description language version 1.0. W3C (2005)
14. Wetzstein, B., Karastoyanova, D., Kopp, O., Leymann, F., Zwink, D.: Cross-organizational process monitoring based on service choreographies. In: Proceedings of the 2010 ACM Symposium on Applied Computing, SAC 2010 (2010)
15. Fremantle, P., Patil, S., Davis, D., Karmarkar, A., Pilz, G., Winkler, S., Yalçinalp, U.: Web Services Reliable Messaging (WS-ReliableMessaging). OASIS (2009)
16. Weidlich, M., Polyvyanyy, A., Mendling, J., Weske, M.: Efficient Computation of Causal Behavioural Profiles Using Structural Decomposition. In: Lilius, J., Penczek, W. (eds.) PETRI NETS 2010. LNCS, vol. 6128, pp. 63–83. Springer, Heidelberg (2010)
17. Polyvyanyy, A., Vanhatalo, J., Völzer, H.: Simplified Computation and Generalization of the Refined Process Structure Tree. In: Bravetti, M., Bultan, T. (eds.) WS-FM 2010. LNCS, vol. 6551, pp. 25–41. Springer, Heidelberg (2011)
18. Vanhatalo, J., Völzer, H., Leymann, F.: Faster and More Focused Control-Flow Analysis for Business Process Models Through SESE Decomposition. In: Krämer, B.J., Lin, K.-J., Narasimhan, P. (eds.) ICSOC 2007. LNCS, vol. 4749, pp. 43–55. Springer, Heidelberg (2007)
19. EsperTech: Esper - Complex Event Processing (2011), http://esper.codehaus.org
20. Subramanian, S., Thiran, P., Narendra, N., Mostefaoui, G., Maamar, Z.: On the enhancement of bpel engines for self-healing composite web services. In: International Symposium on Applications and the Internet, SAINT 2008 (2008)
21. Barbon, F., Traverso, P., Pistore, M., Trainotti, M.: Run-time monitoring of instances and classes of web service compositions. In: IEEE International Conference on Web Services (2006)
22. Dahanayake, A., Welke, R.J., Cavalheiro, G.: Improving the understanding of bam technology for real-time decision support. Int. J. Bus. Inf. Syst. 7 (2011)
23. Kikuchi, S., Shimamura, H., Kanna, Y.: Monitoring method of cross-sites' processes executed by multiple ws-bpel processors. In: CEC/EEE 2007 (2007)

Dynamic Service Selection with End-to-End Constrained Uncertain QoS Attributes

Rene Ramacher and Lars Mönch

Chair of Enterprise-wide Software Systems,
Univerity of Hagen, 58084 Hagen, Germany
{Rene.Ramacher,Lars.Moench}@FernUni-Hagen.de

Abstract. Services and service compositions are executed in an uncertain environment with regard to several aspects of quality. Static service selection approaches that determine the entire service selection prior to the execution of a service composition are extensively discussed in the literature. Nevertheless, the uncertainty of quality aspects has been not well addressed in the service selection phase so far, leading to time-consuming and expensive reconfiguration of service compositions at their execution time. Due to the uncertain and dynamic nature of the execution environment, a dynamic service selection approach is highly desirable. In a dynamic service selection, the services are selected during the execution of a service composition taking into account the conditions caused by already executed services. A dynamic service selection contributes to implement robust service compositions to support reliable business processes, where robustness is measured in terms of fulfilling quality constraints of a service composition. In this paper, we examine a dynamic service selection approach based on a Markov decision process. The service selection is considered from a cost minimizing point of view with an end-to-end constrained execution time. A simulation study demonstrates that the dynamic service selection outperforms an optimal static service selection in an uncertain environment with respect to robustness of the service compositions and cost minimizing.

Keywords: Dynamic Service Selection, Uncertain QoS, Markov Decision Process.

1 Introduction

Complex business functionality is implemented by the composition of already existing services in Service-oriented Architectures (SOAs) [7]. Process models are used to formulate the business or application logic of a service composition. A task within a process model represents certain functionality associated with functional requirements. These requirements have to be provided by a service to execute the corresponding service composition. Therefore, for each task a certain service has to be selected from a set of appropriate services which is known as the service selection problem (SSP). Taken into account the principle of loose coupling, the service selection for each task can be postponed until its execution,

C. Liu et al. (Eds.): ICSOC 2012, LNCS 7636, pp. 237–251, 2012.
© Springer-Verlag Berlin Heidelberg 2012

i.e., late binding. The quality of a service (QoS) and its cost are considered to distinguish between services providing an identical or a similar functionality [10]. A service selection aims for optimizing certain QoS attributes of a service composition while other QoS attributes are end-to-end constrained [13,14].

Service compositions are executed in an uncertain environment with regard to several QoS aspects. For example, the response time of a service depends on the utilization of the service itself and the underlying network. Because the value of an uncertain QoS attribute is unknown until the service is executed, estimated values are taken into account when a service selection is determined. The actual QoS value will often deviate from the estimated one. The deviation of a QoS value may cause a violation of end-to-end constraints or the deterioration of QoS attributes to be optimized. When end-to-end constraints are exceeded, the execution of the entire service compositions fails.

Most of the approaches for the SSP discussed in the literature deal with a static service selection [4,11,14]. The services for all tasks are selected prior to the execution of the composition in a static service selection. Those approaches are not able to react on unforeseen events like the deviation of QoS values during the execution of a service composition. An apparent approach to deal with deviations is to adjust the service selection for unexecuted tasks in a reconfiguration step taking into account the conditions caused by already executed services [1]. Because the reconfiguration of a service composition considering the entire set of services leads to a high computational and communication effort [5], several efficient reconfiguration approaches based on heuristics are proposed in the literature [5,6]. Due to the uncertainty of several QoS attributes, the execution of a service composition is dynamic and hard to predict. Therefore, a dynamic service selection that takes into account the uncertainty inherent to estimated QoS attributes is appropriate. In contrast to a static service selection, in a dynamic service selection the services are determined individually for each task considering the conditions caused by formerly executed tasks. Although the service selection is carried out locally for each task using an appropriate decision model, a dynamic service selection is able to account for end-to-end constrained QoS attributes.

In this paper, we propose a dynamic service selection approach for sequential service compositions. The SSP is modeled as a Markov Decision Process (MDP) that is able to capture the uncertainty of the QoS attributes. Solving the MDP, we obtain a service selection strategy that is used to drive the dynamic service selection at the execution time. We study the proposed dynamic service selection model for a cost minimizing service selection considering an end-to-end constrained execution time. Its performance is compared to an optimal static service selection approach with reconfiguration by means of randomly generated problem instances. We show that the dynamic service selection ensures robust service compositions fullfiling their end-to-end constraints with lower costs compared to an optimal static service selection approach when an uncertain environment is assumed.

The rest of the paper is organized as follows. The service composition model is formalized in Section 2. The MDP formalism is briefly summarized in Section 3. Furthermore, it is described how the dynamic service selection is modeled as an MDP. The design of the computational experiments and the results are presented in Section 4. Related work is discussed in Section 5. Finally, Section 6 concludes the paper summarizing the major findings and motivating future research.

2 Service Composition Model

The process or business logic, i.e., control and data flow, of a service composition is formulated using a process model. We consider abstract process models based on tasks. A task t_i represents a certain functionality with associated functional requirements. An approach to formulate and execute abstract process models is proposed in [2]. The set of services, a service class, that fulfills the functional requirements of a task t_i is denoted with S_i. A service from S_i offered by a provider j is denoted as $s_{ij} \in S_i$. Each task t_i has to be bound to a service s_{ij} to execute the corresponding service composition. The binding of the service s_{ij} to the task t_i is indicated by $t_i \leftarrow s_{ij}$. For abbreviation, we denote the service s_{ij} for which $t_i \leftarrow s_{ij}$ holds with s_i. In this paper, we consider sequential process models with n tasks. The predecessor of the task t_{i+1} is the task t_i, $i = 1, \ldots, n - 1$. The task t_{i+1} can only be started after the processing of t_i is completed, i.e., the service s_{i+1} is invoked after the service s_i has been terminated.

The cost of a service and its response time are considered as non-functional attributes. The cost of a service s_{ij}, assumed to be known in advance, is denoted with $c(s_{ij})$. In contrast to the cost, the response time of a service s_{ij} can only be estimated prior to the execution of s_{ij}. We distinguish between the actual response time $p(s_{ij})$, the expected response time $E[p(s_{ij})]$, and the variance of the response time $Var[p(s_{ij})]$ of a service s_{ij}. The quantities $E[p(s_{ij})]$ and $Var[p(s_{ij})]$ can be determined using a monitoring system for gathering execution-related information.

We consider the total cost $c(sc)$ and the total execution time $p(sc)$ for a given service composition sc. The cost of a service composition is the sum of costs $c(s_i)$ of the services s_i bound to the tasks:

$$c(sc) = \sum_{i=1}^{n} c(s_i).$$

(1)

Since we consider sequential service compositions, the total execution time $p(sc)$ is the sum of the response times of the services bound to the tasks:

$$p(sc) = \sum_{i=1}^{n} p(s_i).$$

(2)

The total execution time of a service composition is restricted to a predefined value $R > 0$. The execution of a service composition is feasible if $p(sc) \leq R$ holds. Otherwise, the execution of sc is failed. When penalty costs for failed service compositions are known, e.g. due to an Service Level Agreement, we denote them by c^p.

3   Dynamic Service Selection

3.1   Markov Decision Processes

An MDP can be used to model decision processes containing uncertainty. Formally, an MDP is represented as a four-tuple (Γ, A, T, R) where Γ is the set of states the decision process consists of and A is the set of possible actions. The mapping $T : \Gamma \times A \times \Gamma \to [0,1]$ provides for $\gamma_1, \gamma_2 \in \Gamma$ and $a \in A$ the probability $T(\gamma_1, a, \gamma_2)$ that the process moves to state γ_2 when action a is performed in state γ_1. The mapping $R : \Gamma \times A \times \Gamma \to \mathbb{R}$ is the reward function. The value of $R(\gamma_1, a, \gamma_2)$ is for $\gamma_1, \gamma_2 \in \Gamma$ and $a \in A$ the expected utility when action a is performed in state γ_1 and the process moves to state γ_2. Solving an MDP results in a strategy $\pi : \Gamma \to A$ that maps each state $\gamma \in \Gamma$ to an appropriate action $a \in A$ such that the expected total reward of the entire process is maximized.

A dynamic service selection based on an MDP requires an appropriate modeling of states and actions as well as determining the transition probabilities and choosing an appropriate reward function. For the researched problem, states are used to represent the task currently to be processed and a time interval in which the processing of a task will be started. The processing of a task t_i is modeled as an action. The state model with the corresponding actions, the state transitions probability, and the cost function as negative reward function are formulated in Subsection 3.2. Based on the proposed state model, Subsection 3.3 describes the probability model used to define the state transition function.

3.2   State Model

The execution of a service composition requires the selection of a service $s_{ij} \in S_i$ that is invoked to execute the task t_i. With regard to a constrained execution time, the service selection for a certain task has to be driven by the time already consumed by previously executed services. The difference of the consumed time and the execution time restriction R determines the time that is still available to execute the remaining tasks. For this reason, we propose a state model that captures the already consumed time. A set of states Γ_i is used for each single task t_i. The state $\gamma_{ik} \in \Gamma_i$ is associated with a time interval $[l_{ik}, u_{ik}]$. The processing of task t_i cannot start before l_{ik} and not later than u_{ik} in state γ_{ik}.

We distinguish m_i states with disjunct time intervals for each task t_i, $i = 2, \ldots, n$. The task t_1 is represented by the single state γ_{11} with $l_{11} = 0$ and $u_{11} = 0$. Moreover, two final states $\gamma_{n+1,1}$ and $\gamma_{n+1,2}$ are introduced. The interval boundaries of these states are set to $l_{n+1,1} = 0$ and $u_{n+1,1} = R$ as well as $l_{n+1,2} = R$ and $u_{n+1,2} = \infty$, respectively. The complete state model consists of $\sum_{i=1}^{n+1} m_i + 3$ states. The set of all states is $\Gamma = \bigcup_{i=1}^{n+1} \Gamma_i$.

The interval boundaries of the states in Γ_i with $i = 2, \ldots, n$ are determined taking into account the earliest time $(\underline{p_i})$ and the latest time $(\overline{p_i})$ at which the processing of task t_i can be started. These quantities are calculate as:

$$\underline{p_i} = \sum_{a=1}^{i-1} \min\{E[p(s_{aj})] | s_{aj} \in S_a\}. \tag{3}$$

$$\overline{p_i} = \sum_{a=1}^{i-1} \max\{E[p(s_{aj})] | s_{aj} \in S_a\}. \tag{4}$$

Taking into account $\underline{p_i}$ and $\overline{p_i}$, the interval boundaries l_{ik} and u_{ik} of each state $\gamma_{ik} \in \Gamma_i$ are determined as:

- state γ_{i1}: $l_{i,1} = 0$ and $u_{i1} = \underline{p_i}$
- state γ_{ik}, $k = 2, \ldots, m_i - 1$: $l_{ik} = \underline{p_i} + (k-2)\Delta$ and $u_{ik} = \underline{p_i} + (k-1)\Delta$, where $\Delta := \left(\overline{p_i} - \underline{p_i}\right) / (m_i - 2)$
- state γ_{i,m_i}: $l_{i,m_i} = \overline{p_i}$ and $u_{i,m_i} = \infty$.

The quantities m_i are parameters of the approach. Note that because of our choice of Δ the model requires $m_i > 2$.

The set of actions A_i that can be performed in each state $\gamma_{ik} \in \Gamma_i$ is derived from the service class S_i. Note that each $\gamma_{ik} \in \Gamma_i$ represents the task t_i. An action $a_{ij} \in A_i$ corresponds to the invocation of the service $s_{ij} \in S_i$. The final states in Γ_{n+1} are associated with the empty action set $A_{n+1} = \emptyset$. The set of all actions is $A = \bigcup_{i=1}^{n+1} A_i$.

The state transitions of the MDP reflect the sequential processing of the tasks of a service composition. The selection of an action $a_{ij} \in A_i$ in state $\gamma_{ik} \in \Gamma_i$ corresponds to the invocation of the service $s_{ij} \in S_i$ to process the task t_i. The invocation of the service s_{ij} terminates with a certain probability in the time interval of each state $\gamma_{i+1,y} \in \Gamma_{i+1}$ in which either the processing of the task t_{i+1} can be started for $i < n$ or the processing of the service composition is completed for $i = n$. Accordingly, the decision process moves from γ_{ik} to each state $\gamma_{i+1,y} \in \Gamma_{i+1}$ with a certain probability when a_{ij} is selected for γ_{ik}. The probability $T(\gamma_{ik}, a_{ij}, \gamma_{i+1,y})$ of moving to $\gamma_{i+1,y} \in \Gamma_{i+1}$ depends on the response time of service s_{ij} that is associated with a_{ij} and the time interval represented by γ_{ik}. Details on calculating the probability $T(\gamma_{ik}, a_{ij}, \gamma_{zy})$ are discussed in Subsection 3.3.

A state model for a simple service composition consisting of three tasks and $m_1 = m_2 = 3$ is shown in Figure 1. For each state except of γ_{11}, the associated time interval is plotted on the horizontal axis. The state γ_{11} is associated with the degenerated interval 0. For the sake of simplicity, some state transitions are only indicated by a dashed line.

The cost function C maps each state transition to the cost $c(s_{ij})$ resulting from the invocation of the service associated with the action a_{ij} and a penalty value p that is applied when the decision process moves to an undesired state. We obtain:

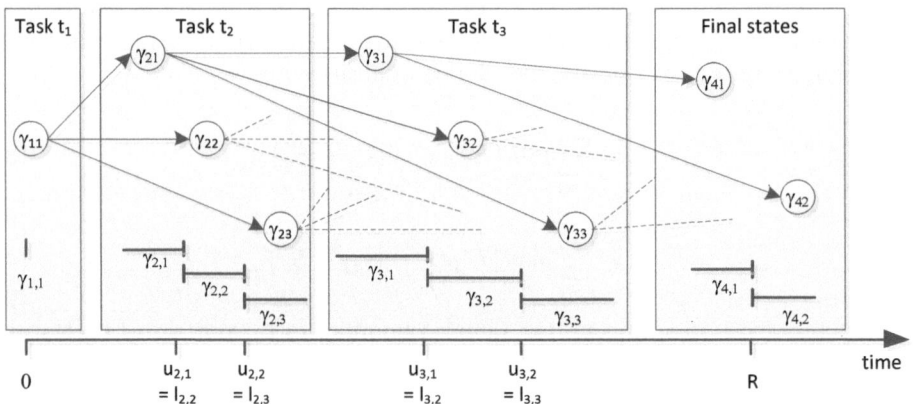

Fig. 1. State model of a service composition consisting of three tasks and $m_1 = m_2 = 3$

$$C(\gamma_{ik}, a_{ij}, \gamma_{zy}) = c(s_{ij}) + p. \qquad (5)$$

The decision process contains only the single undesired state $\gamma_{n+1,2}$. This is the state the process is moved to when the execution time restriction R is exceeded. Therefore, p is 0 for all states γ_{zy} with $z \neq n+1$ and $y \neq 2$. When penalty costs are available (cf. Section 2), then p is set to c^p. Otherwise, the value of p is calculated dependening on a risk factor rf as:

$$p = rf \sum_{i=1}^{n} \left(\max\{c(s_{ij}) | s_{ij} \in S_i\} - \min\{c(s_{ij}) | s_{ij} \in S_i\} \right). \qquad (6)$$

Modeling the dynamic service selection as an MDP requires that the Markov condition is fulfilled. It states that the optimality of an action does not depend on the sequence of actions already performed. Based on the proposed state model, the Markov condition is fulfilled because the consequences of already performed actions are summarized in the time interval of a certain state. Therefore, the optimality of an action in a certain state only depends on the state and the expected costs of the states the process is supposed to move to.

3.3   State Transition Probability Model

The quantity $T(\gamma_{ik}, a_{ij}, \gamma_{zy})$ is the probability that the process moves to γ_{zy} when the action a_{ij} is performed in γ_{ik}. Because of the sequential processing of the service composition, $T(\gamma_{ik}, a_{ij}, \gamma_{zy})$ is 0 for all $\gamma_{zy} \in \Gamma_z$ with $z \neq i+1$. To determine $T(\gamma_{ik}, a_{ij}, \gamma_{i+1,y})$, we assume that the processing of task t_i starts at some point $\beta_{ik} \in [l_{ik}, u_{ik}]$. Thus, the service s_{ij} that is associated with the action a_{ij} is invoked at time β_{ik}. $T(\gamma_{ik}, a_{ij}, \gamma_{i+1,y})$ is the probability that the invocation of s_{ij} terminates at some point in the time interval $[u_{i+1,y}, l_{i+1,y}]$ represented by $\gamma_{i+1,y}$.

We assume that β_{ik} is uniformly distributed on the interval $[l_{ik}, u_{ik}]$, i.e. $\beta_{ik} \sim U[l_{ik}, u_{ik}]$. The assumption is reasonable when the intervals $[l_{ik}, u_{ik}]$ are small which is ensured by an appropriate selection of m_i. The response time of a service s_{ij} is modeled as a random variable ρ_{ij}. We assume that the distribution information of ρ_{ij} is available either in closed form or in form of an empirical distribution function. The later one can be derived using information from a monitoring system. When the service s_{ij} is invoked in the interval $[l_{ik}, u_{ik}]$ then the time at which the invocation of s_{ij} terminates is a random variable Ψ_{ijk}, with $\Psi_{ijk} = \beta_{ik} + \rho_{ij}$. Accordingly, $T(\gamma_{ik}, a_{ij}, \gamma_{i+1,y})$ is the probability that $\Psi_{ijk} \geq l_{i+1,y}$ and $\Psi_{ijk} \leq u_{i+1,y}$ holds. We obtain:

$$T(\gamma_{ik}, a_{ij}, \gamma_{i+1,y}) = (1 - F(l_{i+1,y}))F(u_{i+1,y}), \tag{7}$$

where $F(x) = P(\Psi_{ijk} \leq x)$ is the probability distribution of Ψ_{ijk}. The distribution F can be calculated as a convolution of β_{ik} and ρ_{ij} because the two random variables are independent. When the convolution of β_{ik} and ρ_{ij} is not available in closed form, then F has to be numerically evaluated by sampling $\beta_{ik} + \rho_{ij}$.

In this paper, we assume that the response time of a service s_{ij} follows a normal distribution with $\mu_{ij} = E[p(s_{ij})]$ and $\sigma_{ij}^2 = Var[p(s_{ij})]$, i.e., we have $\rho_{ij} \sim N(\mu_{ij}, \sigma_{ij}^2)$. A closed form expression can be derived for the density function of Ψ_{ijk} in this specific situation. Figure 2 shows the density function of Ψ_{ijk} for an action a_{ij} that is performed in state γ_{ik}. The integral of the shaded area (b) represents the state transition probability $T(\gamma_{ik}, a_{ij}, \gamma_{i+1,y})$. The probability density of the equal distribution is depicted as the shaded area (a).

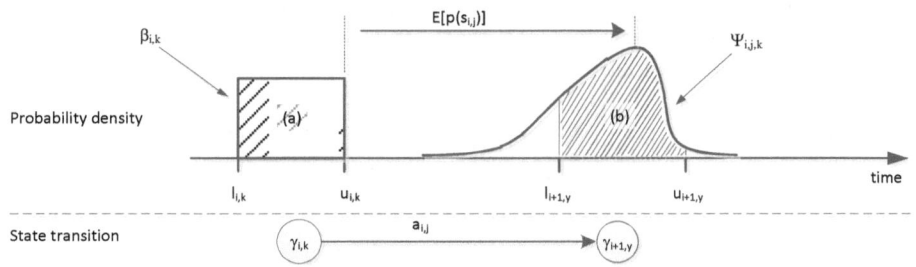

Fig. 2. State transition probability $T(\gamma_{ik}, a_{ij}, \gamma_{i+1,y})$ when $\rho_{ij} \sim N(\mu_{ij}, \sigma_{ij}^2)$

3.4 Algorithm

A strategy $\pi : \Gamma \to A$ determines the action $\pi(\gamma) \in A$ that is chosen in the state $\gamma \in \Gamma$. An optimal solution of the dynamic SSP is a strategy π that minimizes the expected cost of a service composition. Algorithms to solve an MDP are based on the expected costs $V(\gamma)$ for each state $\gamma \in \Gamma$. With regard to the dynamic service selection, the expected cost $V(\gamma_{ik})$ for a state $\gamma_{ik} \in \Gamma_i$ represents the immediate cost associated with γ_{ik}, i.e. invocation of a service and penalty costs if an undesired state is reached, and the cost $V(\gamma_{zy})$ of the states γ_{zy} the process is expected to move to. For $z < n$ the cost of each γ_{zy} consists of the sum of costs resulting from the invocation of services to process the remaining tasks $t_z, \ldots, t_n$ and the penalty costs that occur when an undesired state is reached. Therefore, the expected cost of a state $\gamma \in \Gamma$ is calculated recursively as:

$$V(\gamma) = \min_{a \in A} \sum_{\gamma' \in \Gamma} T(\gamma, a, \gamma') \left\{ C(\gamma, a, \gamma') + \lambda V(\gamma') \right\}, \tag{8}$$

where $C(\gamma, a, \gamma')$ represents the immediate cost when action a is performed in γ and the process is moved to γ' (cf. Subsection 3.2). The sum of the immediate costs and the expected costs of a subsequent state γ' is weighted with the probability $T(\gamma, a, \gamma')$ that the process is moved to γ'. Note that the cost of a service associated with the action a is considered in total because the probabilities $T(\gamma, a, \gamma')$ sum up to 1. The penalty cost included in $C(\gamma, a, \gamma')$ when an undesired state γ' is reached is considered only as a fraction depending on the probability that the process is moved to γ'. The equation (8) is known as the Bellman update. The parameter λ in expression (8) represents the impact of the costs expected for future states on the costs of earlier states. A standard algorithm to calculate the expected costs for each state $\gamma \in \Gamma$ is given by the backward value iteration. Here, the Bellman update is applied iteratively where convergence of the scheme is ensured by choosing $0 \leq \lambda < 1$.

The dynamic SSP is formulated as a finite MDP with non-stationary expected costs and due to the sequential processing, each strategy π is guaranteed to be a proper strategy, i.e. it ends in a finite state of the MDP. Therefore, it turns out that the special case of additive costs, i.e. $\lambda = 1$, is approved without losing the convergence property of the backward value iteration algorithm [8]. Hence, based on the expected cost for each state, the action $a \in A$ chosen in a state $\gamma \in \Gamma$ is determined as follows:

$$\pi(\gamma) = \arg\min_{a \in A} \sum_{\gamma' \in \Gamma} T(\gamma, a, \gamma') \left\{ C(\gamma, a, \gamma') + V(\gamma') \right\}. \tag{9}$$

4   Performance Study

A simulation study is conducted to evaluate the performance of the dynamic service selection. The MDP approach described in Section 3 is compared with an optimal static service selection approach with reconfiguration. The average cost of a service composition and the number of failed service compositions are considered as performance indicators. Furthermore, we examine the computational effort required to evaluate the service selection strategy at the execution time of a service composition. Randomly generated problem instances are used. The experimental design is described in Subsection 4.1. Subsection 4.2 elaborates on the optimal static service selection approach with reconfiguration. The results of the computational experiments are presented and discussed in Subsection 4.3.

4.1   Generation of Problem Instances

A problem instance consists of n tasks. A set of m services is generated for each task. The services are distinguished into the *gold*, *silver*, and *bronze* categories with respect to their prices and response times. These categories mimic the assumption that a service of a higher price is also expected to have a higher quality, i.e. a lower response time.

The price of a service depends on the categorie the service belongs to and the factor m_{class} that represents the ratio between the price and the quality of the services in different categories. We consider $c_{silver}^{ref} = 100r$, $c_{gold}^{ref} = m_{class} \cdot c_{silver}^{ref}$, and $p_{bronze}^{ref} = 1/m_{class} \cdot p_{silver}^{ref}$ as reference prices for each service category, where r is a realization of a random variable $X \sim U[0,1]$. Moreover, we consider $p_{gold}^{ref} = 10$, $p_{silver}^{ref} = 50$, and $p_{bronze}^{ref} = 90$ as reference response times for the different service categories.

The price and the expected response time of a service s_{ij} that belongs to the service category $cat \in \{gold, silver, bronze\}$ is chosen as:

$$c(s_{ij}) = c_{cat}^{ref} + (r - 0.5) c_{cat}^{ref}, \tag{10}$$

and

$$E[p(s_{ij})] = p_{cat}^{ref} + (r - 0.5) p_{cat}^{ref}, \tag{11}$$

where r is a realization of an random variable $X \sim U[0,1]$. The variance of the response time is selected depending on the factor m_σ as follows:

$$Var[p(s_{ij})] = m_\sigma E[p(s_{ij})]. \tag{12}$$

Because our comparison approach likewise the majority of existing reconfiguration approaches does not consider penalty costs, we exclude the evaluation of the effects caused by penalty costs from the experimentation. Instead, we evaluate the influence of the risk factor rf (see equation (6)) on the performance of the dynamic service selection. The factors and their levels are summarized in Table 1.

Table 1. Factors used to generated problem instances

Factor	Level	Count
Number of tasks	$n \in \{5, 10, 15, 20\}$	4
Number of providers per task	$m \in \{5, 10, 15\}$	3
Expected price difference	$m_{class} \in \{1, 3, 5, 6\}$	4
Variance in response time	$m_\sigma \in \{0.1, 0.15, 0.2, 0.25\}$	4
Risk factor	$rf \in \{0.3, 0.5, 0.7\}$	3

4.2   Comparison Approach

We use a Mixed Inter Programming (MIP)-based service selection with reconfiguration as an optimal service selection approach. The approach is based on the MIP shown in (13) - (16). The MIP determines a cost minimizing service selection taking into account an end-to-end constrained execution time. In addition to the price $c(s_{ij})$ of a service s_{ij} and its expected processing time $E[p(s_{ij})]$, the MIP contains two parameters α and β. These parameters are required to use the MIP in a reconfiguration setting. The quantities α and β represent the current progress of a service composition. The parameter $\alpha = 1, \ldots, n-1$ identifies the task that is to be processed next. The value of β represents the time, passed since the start of processing the service composition.

The MIP contains the binary decision variables z_{ij}. The value of z_{ij} is 1, if the service s_{ij} is used to execute the task t_i, otherwise 0. The MIP model is formulated as follows:

$$\min \sum_{i=\alpha}^{n} \sum_{j=1}^{m} c(s_{ij}) z_{ij} \tag{13}$$

subject to:

$$\sum_{j=1}^{m} z_{ij} = 1, \forall i : i = \{\alpha, \ldots, n\} \tag{14}$$

$$\sum_{i=\alpha}^{n} E[p(s_{ij})] z_{ij} \leq R - \beta \tag{15}$$

$$z_{ij} \in \{0,1\}, \forall i, j : i = \{1, \ldots, n\}, j = \{1, \ldots, m\}. \tag{16}$$

The objective function (13) minimizes the costs resulting from the services used to execute the tasks. The equations (14) force that exactly one service s_{ij} is selected for each task t_i. The inequality (15) ensures that the expected amount of time to process the remaining tasks t_k, $k = \alpha, \ldots, n$ is smaller than the difference of the execution time restriction R the time β already passed. The constraints (16) make sure that the decision variables are binary.

Instead of using the reconfiguration in a heuristic manner, i.e. only by exceeding a threshold, the reconfiguration is invoked after the processing of each task.

4.3   Simulation Results

The execution of a service composition is simulated using the discrete-event simulation engine SLX. The response time of each service s_{ij} follows a normal distribution $N(E[p(s_{ij})], Var[p(s_{ij})])$. The MIP is implemented and solved by ILOG OPL 6.3 and CPLEX solver 12.3, respectively.

The influence of the number of states used in the MDP approach is evaluated. Therefore, each problem instance is solved with $m_i = 10, 20$, and 40 states for each $i = 2, \ldots, n+1$, respectively. The corresponding approaches are denoted by $MDP(10)$, $MDP(20)$, and $MDP(40)$.

For each approach $A \in \{MIP, MDP(10), MPD(20), MDP(40)\}$, 100 invocations are simulated for each problem instance. The simulation records the average cost c^A per successfully executed service composition and the percentage of requests v^A that are successfully executed for each approach A. Moreover, the simulation keeps tracks of the average computation time ct^A, required by the approach A to determine the service selection of all tasks at the execution time of the service composition.

Figure 3 shows an evaluation of the MIP and the MDP(40) approach with respect to the uncertainty expressed through the factor m_σ. Different values of the risk factor rf are considered for MDP(40). The average cost per service composition is summarized in Figure 3 a). In general, the results state that the MIP is outperformed by the MDP approaches with respect to costs. The advantage of the MDP approaches increases with increasing uncertainty. The lowest average cost are observed for $MDP(40)$ with $rf = 0.3$ independently of m_σ. The average costs observed for the MDP approaches increase with an increasing risk factor.

Results with repect to v are shown in Figure 3 b). The data reveals that the MIP leads to a large fraction of failed service compositions, i.e., a low value of v. The value of v decreases from 87 percent for $m_\sigma = 0.1$ to 81 percent for $m_\sigma = 0.25$. For $m_\sigma = 0.1$ and $m_\sigma = 0.15$, a value close to 100 percent of successfully executed service compositions is observed for all MDP approaches. For the remaining values of m_σ, it can be concluded that a higher risk factor leads to a higher value of v. The execution time restriction is fulfilled in 99 percent for $rf = 0.7$.

An evaluation of c^A with respect to different values of m_{class} is shown in Figure 4 a). The data reveals that in the case of homogenous costs, i.e. $m_{class} = 1$, a similar performance is observed for all approaches. The MIP leads to the minimal average cost per service composition for $m_{class} = 1$. However, the costs determined by the MDP approaches are lower than the cost of the MIP for the remaining values of m_{class}. The results point out that a larger number of states

a)
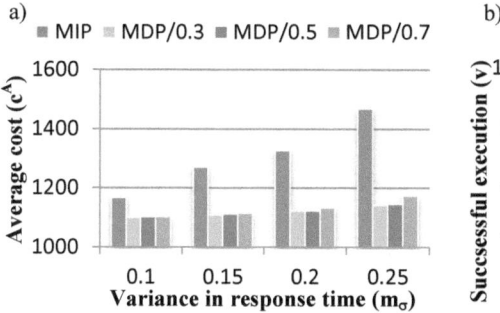

b)
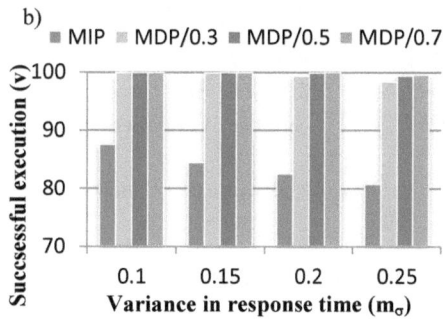

Fig. 3. a) Average cost depending on m_σ for MIP and MDP(40) with different rf values b) percentage of succesfully executed service compositions depending on m_σ.

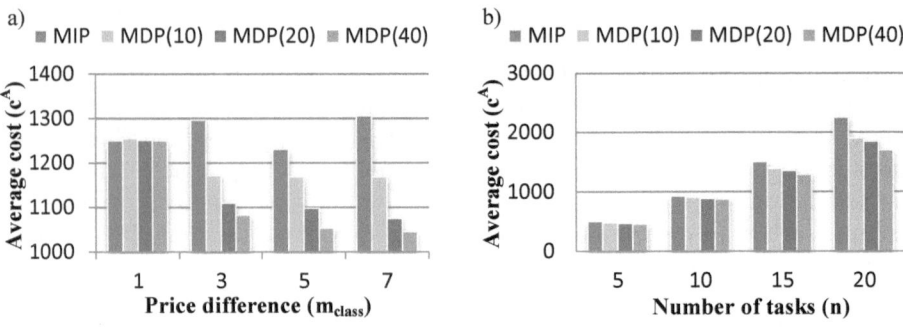

Fig. 4. Average cost per service composition depending on m_{class} (a) and on n (b)

improves the performance of the MDP. The lowest values for c^A are obtained for $MDP(40)$. Results of a sensitive analysis with respect to the number of tasks are shown in Figure 4 b). The performance gap of the MIP compared to the MDP increases with an increasing number of tasks.

Figure 5 presents the results of an sensitive analysis of v for different values of m and n. It can be observed that v is close to 100 percent for all MDP approaches, independently from n and m. The values of v observed for the MIP point out that an increasing number of tasks as well as an increasing number of providers lead to a higher fraction of failed service compositions. Taken into account the number of tasks, the fraction of failed service compositions increases from 9 percent for $n = 5$ tasks up to more than 30 percent for $n = 20$ tasks.

The computation time ct^A required to evaluate the service selection strategy varies from 0.4 seconds for the MDP(40) approach on average for $n = 15$ to less than 0.03 seconds on average for the MDP(10) approach for $n = 5$.

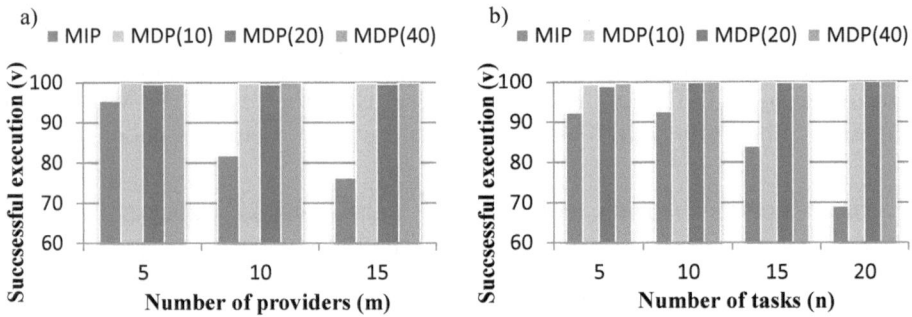

Fig. 5. Percentage of succesful executions for different m (a) and n (b)

5   Related Work

The service selection with uncertain QoS values has been tackled by researchers in the recent years. The majority of the existing work is devoted to the recon-figuration of service compositions. A reconfiguration is required when services fail [12] or the QoS values deviate from the original specification [1,5,6]. Service breakdowns are addressed by Yu and Lin [12]. Two algorithms are proposed to reconfigure the service compositions which are already in execution and to provide a backup service selection that is used by future requests of a service composition, respectively. Both algorithms are offline approaches, i.e., the service reconfiguration as well as the backup path are determined simultaneously with the initial service selection. Both approaches are restricted to a single service failure. A failure of several services can neither be handled by the reconfiguration nor by the backup service selection. The violation of end-to-end constrained QoS values due to the deviation of QoS values is not considered at all.

Canfora et al. [1] consider the reconfiguration of end-to-end constrained service compositions with uncertain QoS attributes. An approach for an online reconfiguration of service compositions is presented. Reconfiguration regions are identified taking into account conditional branches, parallelizing operators, and loops. A reconfiguration region consists of all unexecuted tasks that will be reselected to avoid the violation of the end-to-end constraints. The reselection is performed by a common static service selection approach e.g. an Integer Programming-based [14] or Genetic Algorithm-based [4] service selection.

Another reconfiguration approach is discussed by Lin, Zhang, and Zhai [6]. The efficiency of the reconfiguration is addressed. A heuristic is proposed that restricts the size of the reconfiguration regions using a distance measure [6]. The distance is increased iteratively until a reconfiguration region is identified that is of a sufficient size to successful reconfigure the service composition. In addition to restricting the size of a reconfiguration region, Li et al. [5] propose a restriction of the number of tasks considered by the reconfiguration. Supplement services are identified during the initial service selection. The reconfiguration of each task is then narrowed to the set of supplement services to improve the efficiency of the reconfiguration.

Each of the reconfiguration approaches discussed so far has to be regarded as a static service selection. Gao et al. [3] propose an approach for a dynamic service selection based on MDP. The uncertainty with respect to the availability of services is taken into account. The service selection aims for the optimization of a single QoS attribute, e.g. the total cost of a service composition or their execution time.

A further MDP-based dynamic service selection approach for the adaption of processes with inter-process dependencies is discussed by Verma et al [9]. The process execution is affected by exogenous factors. The corresponding implications require an adaption of the service selection at the execution time. The combination of services is restricted by the inter-process dependencies i.e. the combination of services used for different tasks has to be coordinated. As exogenous factor they consider a delayed delivery that requires a decision to wait for the delayed delivery or to place a new order at a different service provider.

End-to-end constrained QoS attributes are neither considered in [3] nor in [9]. Therefore, both approaches are not suitable for a dynamic service selection with an end-to-end constrained execution time. Although delays are considered in [9], the approach is only based on the information that a delay occurs but the delay itself is not quantified. However, the quantification of the actual delay is mandatory with regard to an end-to-end constrained processing time to drive the service selection for the tasks to be executed.

6 Conclusion

Services and service compositions are executed in an uncertain environment with respect to several aspects of quality. The uncertainty is not addressed sufficiently by existing static service selection approaches leading to expensive and time-consuming reconfigurations at the execution time of a service composition. Anticipating deviations resulting from estimated QoS values improve the overall quality of service compositions and their robustness, measured in terms of violated end-to-end constraints.

A dynamic service selection approach modeled as an MDP is proposed in this paper. Modeling the service selection decision as an MDP allows for explicating the uncertainty inherent to several QoS attributes within the decision model. The performance of the proposed approach is studied for a cost minimizing service selection with an end-to-end constrained execution time. An extensive simulation study reveals that in an uncertain environment the dynamic service selection outperforms a static service selection approach with reconfiguration with respect to robustness of the service compositions and to costs. Furthermore, it is shown that the approach is efficient with respect to the computational burden resulting from the service selection decision at the execution time of a service composition.

There are several directions for future research. Although the proposed approach allows for taking into account arbitrary distributed response times, the experiments conducted in this paper are based on the assumption that the response times of the serivces are normally distributed. The normal dsitribution assumption for response times might be violated in a real-world environment. Therefore, further experiments should be performed to assess the performance of the proposed dynamic service selection approach when arbitrary distributions are considered. It should also be evaluated whether the normal distribution assumption represents a sufficient approximation to deal with arbitrary distributed response times or not.

Furthermore, the decision model proposed in this paper is based on sequential process models. Although the sequential process model is a fundamental service composition pattern and serves as a basis for many other service composition patterns with regard to an QoS optimizing service selection [11], a further direction for future research is to extend the model proposed in this paper to more complex process models including conditional branches and parallelizing operators.

References

1. Canfora, G., Di Penta, M., Esposito, R., Villani, M.L.: QoS-aware replanning of composite web services. In: Proceedings of the IEEE International Conference on Web Services, pp. 121–129 (2005)

2. Casati, F., Ilnicki, S., Jin, L., Krishnamoorthy, V., Shan, M.-C.: Adaptive and Dynamic Service Composition in eFlow. In: Wangler, B., Bergman, L.D. (eds.) CAiSE 2000. LNCS, vol. 1789, pp. 13–31. Springer, Heidelberg (2000)
3. Gao, A., Yang, D., Tang, S., Zhang, M.: Web Service Composition Using Markov Decision Processes. In: Fan, W., Wu, Z., Yang, J. (eds.) WAIM 2005. LNCS, vol. 3739, pp. 308–319. Springer, Heidelberg (2005)
4. Jaeger, M.C., Mühl, G.: QoS-based selection of services: The implementation of a genetic algorithm. In: Proceedings of the KiVS Workshop 2007: Service-Oriented Architectures und Service Oriented Computing (SOA/SOC), pp. 359–370. VDE (2007)
5. Li, J., Ma, D., Mei, X., Sun, H., Zheng, Z.: Adaptive QoS-aware service process reconfiguration. In: Proceedings of the 2011 IEEE International Conference on Services Computing, SCC 2011, pp. 282–289. IEEE Computer Society, Washington, DC (2011)
6. Lin, K.-J., Zhang, J., Zhai, Y.: An efficient approach for service process reconfiguration in SOA with end-to-end QoS constraints. In: Proceedings of the 11th International Conference on Commerce and Enterprise Computing, pp. 146–153 (2009)
7. Papazoglou, M.P., Traverso, P., Dustdar, S., Leymann, F.: Service-oriented computing: a research roadmap. International Journal of Cooperative Information Systems 17(02), 223–255 (2008)
8. Russell, S.J., Norvig, P.: Artificial Intelligence: A Modern Approach, 3rd edn. Prentice-Hall, Inc., Upper Saddle River (2009)
9. Verma, K., Doshi, P., Gomadam, K., Miller, J., Sheth, A.: Optimal adaptation in web processes with coordination constraints. In: Proceedings of the IEEE International Conference on Web Services, pp. 257–264 (2006)
10. Wang, S.G., Sun, Q.B., Yang, F.C.: Towards web service selection based on QoS estimation. International Journal of Web Grid Services 6(4), 424–443 (2010)
11. Yu, T., Lin, K.-J.: Service selection algorithms for web services with end-to-end QoS constraints. In: Proceedings of the IEEE International Conference on E-Commerce Technology, pp. 129–136. IEEE Computer Society (2004)
12. Yu, T., Lin, K.-J.: Adaptive algorithms for finding replacement services in autonomic distributed business processes. In: Proceedings of the International Symposium on Autonomous Decentralized Systems, pp. 427–434 (2005)
13. Yu, T., Zhang, Y., Lin, K.-J.: Efficient algorithms for web services selection with end-to-end QoS constraints. ACM Transactions on the Web (TWeb) 1(1) (2007)
14. Zeng, L., Benatallah, B., Dumas, M., Kalagnanam, J., Sheng, Q.Z.: Quality driven web services composition. In: Proceedings of the 12th International Conference on World Wide Web, pp. 411–421. ACM (2003)

A Constraint-Based Approach to Quality Assurance in Service Choreographies[*]

Dragan Ivanović[1], Manuel Carro[1,2], and Manuel V. Hermenegildo[1,2]

[1] School of Computer Science, T. University of Madrid (UPM), Spain
idragan@clip.dia.fi.upm.es, {mcarro,herme}@fi.upm.es
[2] IMDEA Software Institute, Spain

Abstract. The knowledge about the quality characteristics (QoS) of service compositions is crucial for determining their usability and economic value; the quality of service compositions is usually regulated using Service Level Agreements (SLAs). While end-to-end SLAs are well suited for request-reply interactions, more complex, decentralized, multi-participant compositions (service choreographies) typically need multiple message exchanges between stateful parties and the corresponding SLAs thus involve several cooperating parties with interdependent QoS. The usual approaches to determining QoS ranges structurally (which are by construction easily composable) are not applicable in this scenario. Additionally, the intervening SLAs may depend on the exchanged data. We present an approach to data-aware QoS assurance in choreographies through the automatic derivation of composable QoS models from participant descriptions. Such models are based on a message typing system with size constraints and are derived using abstract interpretation. The models obtained have multiple uses including run-time prediction, adaptive participant selection, or design-time compliance checking. We also present an experimental evaluation and discuss the benefits of the proposed approach.

Keywords: Service Compositions, Quality of Service, Quality Assurance, Constraints, Abstract Interpretation.

1 Introduction

Service-Oriented Computing (SOC) is a widely-accepted paradigm for the development of highly dynamic, flexible, and distributed Service-Based Applications (SBAs). Service compositions allow putting together several specialized, loosely coupled, and platform-independent service components in order to perform complex and/or inter-organizational tasks [10]. In such scenarios, many of those components may be provided and controlled by third parties [22].

The Quality of Service (QoS) properties of service components and compositions are critical for their usability. Service Level Agreements (SLAs) are a means

---

[*] The authors were partially supported by Spanish MINECO project 2008-05624/TIN *DOVES* and Community of Madrid project P2009/TIC/1465 *PROMETIDOS-CM*.

C. Liu et al. (Eds.): ICSOC 2012, LNCS 7636, pp. 252–267, 2012.
© Springer-Verlag Berlin Heidelberg 2012

for defining permissible values for QoS attributes that are relevant in some scenario or for a particular purpose (such as execution time, monetary cost, or availability) and that a service (composition) provider is expected to deliver to a client. SLAs are commonly specified under the assumption that each interaction between the client and the service is viewed as a single session, and, accordingly, such end-to-end SLAs correspond to a request-reply message exchange pattern between the two parties. However, many business processes involve more complex message exchange patterns between two or more stateful participants, where several interactions may belong to the same session and build upon each other, and where the data that is exchanged may significantly affect the behavior of the participants in terms of QoS, including the number of messages exchanged.

For such complex, multi-participant choreographies, a coherent support for QoS assurance which includes negotiation, prediction, and QoS-driven adaptation [16] is relevant both theoretically and practically. While several types of run-time adaptation aimed at avoiding or mitigating SLA violations have been proposed [10,12,21], these are often only applicable to the request-response message exchange pattern and/or to acyclic control structures. Several prediction and run-time adaptation approaches based on machine learning [15], online testing [19], and model checking [20], well suited for orchestrations with centralized control flow, have been proposed.

In this paper, we propose a constraint-based approach for supporting QoS assurance for service choreographies that involve multiple, stateful participants and complex message exchanges. The proposed approach can be applied both at design time and at run time to support QoS negotiation, prediction, and QoS-driven adaptation. This work extends [14] for the case of service compositions with interconnected constraint models of stateful, interacting choreography participants, combining the derivation of QoS constraints with static analysis techniques.

We first present a motivational example (Section 2), then describe our approach (Section 3), review several examples of its application (Section 4), and finish with some conclusions (Section 5).

2   Motivation

Figure 1 shows a simplified example of a choreography for purchasing goods or services in a large organization where the procurement function is centralized. It uses the BPMN notation [17] with swim lanes delimiting participants, and dashed lines showing the flow of messages between them.

Participant A is the procurement process, which starts by receiving a procurement request (a_0), and continues by sending the list of specifications to the agent (a_3) and retrieving budget line information for this purchase (a_2), in parallel. Participant B is the agent which receives the list of specifications (a_{13}) and performs a loop (a_{14}) for each item from the specification list. For each item, B looks into the supplier catalogs (a_{15}) to find out alternative purchasing options; since that can depend on the choice of earlier items, specifications are processed sequentially. If only one alternative is found, it is automatically chosen (a_{19}), but

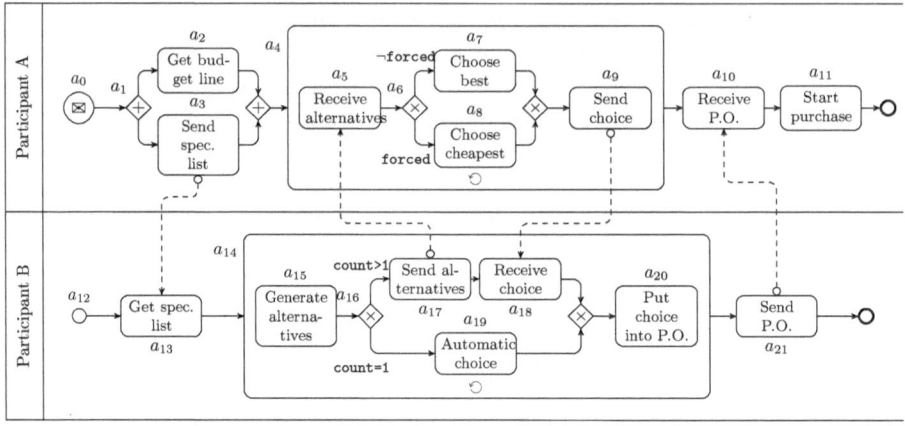

Fig. 1. An example choreography for purchase ordering

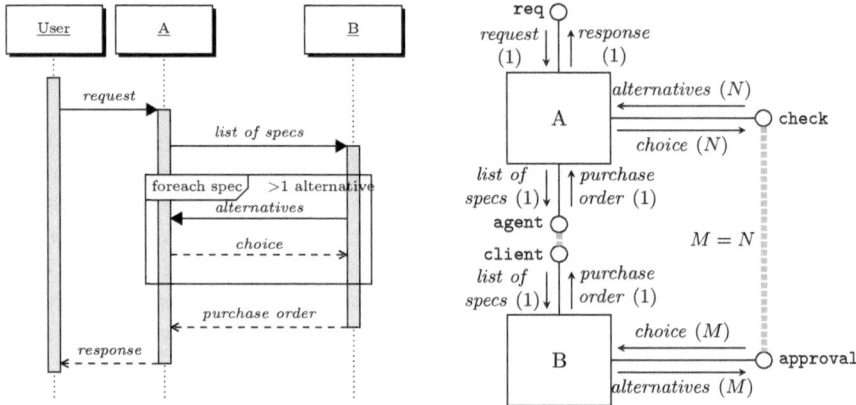

Fig. 2. Message exchange sequence and a component model for a choreography session

if two or more alternatives exist, B asks A to chose among them (a_{17}) and waits for the answer (a_{18}). The choice is added to the purchase order (a_{20}). After processing all specifications, agent B returns the final purchase order document to A (a_{21}). Whenever A is asked to choose between alternatives (a_5), it acts based on the budget line restrictions: if forced, it uses the cheapest option; otherwise it tries to chose the best solution. After answering all choice queries, A receives the purchase order from B (a_{10}) and starts the purchase (a_{11}), which provides the return notification to the requester, to whom the purchased goods and services will be delivered directly.

Figure 2 abstracts away the logic of the participants from Figure 1, and concentrates only on the exchange of messages. The left-hand side of the figure shows a sequence diagram for message exchanges in a session involving the initiating user and the participants A and B. The right-hand side of the figure shows A and B as components with connector links (**req**, **agent**, and **check** for A, **client** and approval for B), with messages sent and received over these links. The number of message of each kind within a single session is shown in parentheses. Wiring between the connectors is shown with thick dotted lines. For each wire, both the kind and the cardinality of messages in both directions must match.

The end-to-end QoS characteristics of A (such as, e.g., its execution time) depend on several factors. Firstly, if the number of specification items n is > 0, there can be between 0 and n callbacks from B to A in the *foreach* loop. Secondly, the behavior of A for each callback from B depends on whether it is forced to choose the cheapest alternative, which is known at the exit of a_2. Some of these factors are controlled by the user (n), some by third parties (a_2 which sets the forced flag for a_6, a_{15} which generates alternatives), and some on the implementation of A (the logic and complexity of determining the best choice in a_7). With respect to the quality assurance issues illustrated by this example, we are interested in tackling the following problems:

- *Automatically deriving a QoS model of the choreography for a given input request or a class of input requests.* Such a model can be used as an input for determining SLA offerings from the service provider to the users.
- *Using the QoS model of the choreography to predict SLA violations at runtime,* at different points in execution. E.g., greater accuracy of prediction can be obtained when the forced flag becomes known after a_2.
- *SLA compliance checking of choreography participants at design-time for a given class of input requests.* This is the basis for adaptive dynamic selection (binding) of service components.

3   Constraint-Based QoS Modeling for Choreographies

The proposed constraint-based approach to modeling QoS for service choreographies is implemented in two main phases. The first one focuses on the creation of QoS models for the choreography participants as Constraint Satisfaction Problems [7,1] (CSP). We will show how to generate a model of the QoS metrics under consideration (Section 3.1), capture the view of each participant regarding the effective QoS at every moment in the execution (Section 3.2), and how to automatically derive these models (Section 3.3). The model is enriched with information about the shape and size of messages, inferred using static analysis techniques, in order to increment its accuracy and the precision of the prediction (Section 3.4).

The second phase of the approach consists of connecting the models for the different participants and solving them as a whole (Section 3.5). Note that when deriving QoS models for choreographies, joining the different sub-models is done following the structure of the composition. In the present case, the overall structure may not lend itself to structural analysis and participants take a prominent role. Therefore determining the overall QoS characteristics is done by joining per-partner models (Section 3.5) mimicking the topology of the choreography.

3.1   Modeling Cumulative QoS Metrics

Execution time, availability, reputation, bandwidth consumed, and cost are some of the most common QoS attributes. In this work we focus on attributes that can be numerically quantified using some measurement scale, or QoS metric: e.g., execution time can be measured using time units. QoS metrics do not need to have a fixed origin (a "true zero" value), but one unit of distance needs to express the same variation in the attribute everywhere on the scale. This requirement excludes, for instance, ordinal voting-based reputation ranking between services, where the unit difference in ranking does not carry information about the difference in votes received.

We additionally require QoS metrics to be cumulative and non-negative: QoS values of activities in a sequence add up to give the QoS value for the sequence, and this value should never decrease by adding more activities. Some QoS metrics, such as availability (expressed in terms of probabilities), that do not use addition to calculate aggregation in a sequence, can be converted into additive metrics using a suitable transformation. For instance, the availability p of n sequential activities with availabilities p_i is $p = \Pi_{i=1}^{n} p_i$ and can be converted into $\lambda = \Sigma_{i=1}^{n} \lambda_i$ with the transformation $\lambda = -\log p$.

Cumulative QoS metrics allow us to represent the QoS of a service composition at any point in execution as a sum of two components: the *previously accumulated* QoS up to that point, and the *pending* QoS for the remainder of the execution. Non-negativity guarantees that the pending QoS can only decrease as the execution proceeds. While the accumulated QoS can be estimated empirically (by measuring elapsed time, network traffic, or accumulated monetary cost), the pending QoS for the remainder of the execution is in our approach modeled as a CSP over variables that represent QoS values for composition activities and control constructs. Solving this CSP gives a prediction of the pending QoS.

3.2   QoS Models of Participants and Continuations

Service choreographies provide a "global view" of a multi-participant, stateful message exchange within some logical unit of work. There are several possibilities to provide both abstract and executable descriptions of choreographies. On the more abstract side BPMN (as in Figure 1) or WS-CDL [24], which is a high-level specialized choreography language, can be used. On the more executable side, we can use choreography extensions of standard process (orchestration) languages, such as BPEL 4Chor [8]. In our approach, we assume that the implementation details of the participants are essentially private and that the participants can be viewed as communicating components that conform to the protocol (as in Figure 2). Conformance, compatibility, and realizability of choreographies has been studied using formal methods such as Petri Nets [23], session types [9], and state machines [3].

As mentioned before, we proceed by developing a separate QoS model for each participant in the choreography. Each participant is seen as a component with a number of connector links (or channels, in WS-CDL terminology). Each link

$$
\begin{aligned}
S \ := \quad & \texttt{send}(c, E) \mid \texttt{recv}(c, v) \mid \texttt{invoke}(c, E, v) && (\textit{send/receive messages}) \\
\mid \ & \texttt{let } v = E && (\textit{variable assignment}) \\
\mid \ & [S, S, ..., S] && (\textit{sequence of } n \geq 0 \textit{ activities}) \\
\mid \ & (\texttt{if}(E) \rightarrow S \; ; \; S) && (\textit{if-then-else}) \\
\mid \ & S \texttt{ and } S && (\textit{parallel "and" split/join}) \\
\mid \ & \texttt{foreach}(v : E) \texttt{ do } S && (\textit{iterate over list elements}) \\
\mid \ & \texttt{foreach}(\texttt{recv}(c, v)) \texttt{ do } S && (\textit{iteratively receive multiple messages}) \\
\mid \ & \texttt{stream}(c) \texttt{ do } S && (\textit{send multiple messages}) \\
\mid \ & \texttt{relax} && (\textit{do nothing}) \\
c, v \ := \quad & \langle \textit{identifier} \rangle \\
E \ := \quad & \langle \textit{expression} \rangle
\end{aligned}
$$

Fig. 3. Abstract syntax of the participant continuation language.

c is bi-directional, and each direction (in/out) is characterized by a triplet of the form $\langle N_{\text{in/out}}(c), \bar{q}_{\text{in/out}}(c), \Delta \bar{q}_{\text{in/out}}(c) \rangle$, where N is multiplicity of in/out messages, $\bar{q}$ are QoS values corresponding to the first in/out message, and $\Delta \bar{q}$ are increments of QoS values for the successive messages (for N>1). For example, for the case of execution time, $T_{\text{in}}(c)$ is the time when the first message was received over link c and $\Delta T_{\text{in}}(c)$ is the time interval between the successive messages. N, $\bar{q}$ and $\Delta \bar{q}$, as well as other variables in the constraint QoS models developed in this section, are not numeric constants, but represent intervals of possible numeric values for all legal execution cases, whose upper and lower bounds are inferred from the constraint model.

We build the QoS model of a participant by looking at its current point in execution. To stay close to the executable specifications, we follow the same approach as in our previous work on run-time prediction for orchestrations [14]. We use the notion of a *continuation* which describes the current state of the participant and the remainder of the computation until its end [18]. At the beginning, the continuation is the entire process and it is gradually reduced by eliminating the completed activities as the execution proceeds. The continuation information is always implicitly present in the state of the engine which executes the participant, and, in principle, can be obtained either by inspecting its internal state or by observing the process events from the outside. The latter is less robust since missed events or run-time composition modifications can invalidate the information inferred through external observation.

We represent continuations using an abstract language for the participant processes (Figure 3). It is based on a prototypical process language implementation that provides the continuation information explicitly at each execution step [14]. The participant state is kept in variables whose types are described in Section 3.4. Variable values are assigned using the `let` construct or received over some link with `recv`. The standard sequential operator, *if-then-elses*, and AND-parallel splits/joins are supported. For simplicity, we present only two `foreach` looping constructs: one over elements of a list and another one over messages received over some channel. The `send` and `recv` messaging constructs can be combined into an `invoke`; note that *request-reply* patterns are not enforced (this is left to the protocol). Participants use the `stream` construct to send a series of messages within the same session which can be received with a `recv`-based `foreach`.

3.3 Automatic Derivation of the QoS Constraint Model for a Participant

The constraint QoS model for a participant is inferred automatically from the continuation and the previously accumulated QoS, using the structural approach of [14], where QoS values for complex constructs are derived from their components. A separate constraint QoS model is derived for each QoS metric of interest. Due to space constraints, we will present here only on the derivation of execution time. More details and treatment of other metrics, such as availability, can be found in [14].

```
1   recv(req,request),
2   (    invoke(budget,
                 request,line)
3   and send(agent,
                 request/specs)
4   ),
5   foreach(recv(check,alts)) do
6   [ (   if(not(line/forced))
7       -> invoke(best,alts,choice)
8       ; let choice=first(alts)
9       ),
10      send(check,choice)
11  ],
12  recv(agent,po),
13  send(req,po)
```

$T_1^- = \max(T_A, T_{\text{in}}(\text{request})), \; T_4^+ = T_1^-, \; N_{\text{in}}(\text{req}) = 1 \,;$
$T_4^+ \leq T_2^+ \leq T_4^-, \; T_{\text{out}}(\text{budget}) = T_2^+ + t_{\text{send}},$
$T_2^- = T_{\text{in}}(\text{budget}), \; N_{\text{in/out}}(\text{budget}) = 1$
$T_4^+ \leq T_3^+ \leq T_4^-,$
$T_3^- = T_{\text{out}}(\text{agent}) = T_3^+ + t_{\text{send}}, \; N_{\text{out}}(\text{agent}) = 1$
$\max(T_2^- - T_2^+, T_3^- - T_3^+) \leq T_4^- - T_4^+ \leq (T_2^- - T_2^+) + (T_3^- - T_3^+)$
$T_5^+ = \max(T_4^-, T_{\text{in}}(\text{check}),) \; k_5 = N_{\text{in}}(\text{check}) \geq 0$
$T_6^+ = T_7^+ = T_8^+, \; c_6 \in \{0, 1\}, \; L_5 = \max(T_{10}^- - T_6^+, \Delta T_{\text{in}}(\text{check}))$
$T_7^- = T_7^+ + \Delta T_{\text{best}}$
$T_8^- = T_8^+ + t_{\text{expr}}$
$(c_6 = 1 \wedge T_6^- = T_7^-) \vee (c_6 = 0 \wedge T_6^- = T_7^-)$
$N_{\text{out}}(\text{check}) = k_5, \; T_{\text{out}}(\text{check}) = T_{10}^+ = T_6^-, \; \Delta T_{\text{out}}(\text{check}) = L_5$
$T_5^- = T_5^+ + k_5 \times L_5$
$T_{12}^- = \max(T_5^-, T_{\text{in}}(\text{agent})), \; N_{\text{in}}(\text{agent}) = 1$
$T_{13}^+ = T_{12}^-, \; N_{\text{out}}(\text{req}) = 1, \; T_{13}^- = T_{\text{out}}(\text{req}) = T_{13}^+ + t_{\text{send}}$

Fig. 4. Structurally derived QoS constraint model for participant A

Figure 4 shows the automatically derived QoS constraint model for the execution time for participant A at its start, i.e., when the continuation consists of the entire participant process. The code for the participant A is shown on the left-hand side in the abstract syntax, and the generated constraints appear on the corresponding lines to the right. For an activity on line i, we denote its starting time with T_i^+ and its end time with $T_i^-, T_i^- \geq T_i^+$. T_A represents the execution time at the current execution point (here at the start), and is an input to the model.[1] The code communicates over channels `req`, `agent`, and `check` (Figure 2), plus an additional channel `budget` which is used to invoke the budget line information service a_2 from Figure 1.

The execution of participant A is a sequence of commands, and the metric for the execution time is cumulative. Therefore for a sequence $S = [S_1, S_2, ..., S_n]$

---

[1] Remember (Section 3.2) that these variables actually contain admissible ranges.

we have $T^+ = T_1^+$, $T^- = T_n^-$, and for adjacent activities S_i and S_{i+1} we have $T_i^- = T_{i+1}^+$. For clarity of presentation, here we ignore the internal time used by the process engine between steps, which needs to be taken into account in real applications (see [14]).

The reception of a single message with recv(c, v) (lines 1 and 12) finishes at time $T_i^- = \max(T_j^-, T_{in}(c))$, where T_j^- is the finish time of the previous activity, and $T_{in}(c)$ is the time at which the message arrives on the channel c. Since in our case messages are received over the same channel at a single place in code, the recv construct also sets $N_{in}(c) = 1$. The command send(c, E) (lines 3, 10, 13) delivers a message to the mailbox on the other side of the channel, for which it takes some time marked with t_{send}, which is also a constrained variable and considered an input to the model. $T_{out}(c)$ is equated with the finish time T_i^- of the send construct. Outside a loop (lines 3 and 12), $N_{out}(c)$ is set to 1, and $\Delta T_{out}(c)$ is not constrained, because it is not applicable. The invoke construct in line 2 is treated as a send-recv sequence.

The timing for the AND-parallel flow (ending in line 4) depends on the particular process engine implementation, and can vary between real parallelism and sequential execution of the two activities. Without a more detailed knowledge of the implementation details, the duration of the parallel flow $T_4^- - T_4^+$ may vary between the maximum and the sum of durations of the two "parallel" activities.

The recv-based loop (line 5) starts when both the preceding activity has finished (T_4^-) and the first message on the check channel has become available $(T_{in}(\text{check}))$. The number of iterations of the loop (k_5) equals the number of messages arriving through the channel, $N_{in}(\text{check})$. Since every loop iteration can start only upon message reception, the effective length of a loop iteration L_5 is the maximum between the actual duration of the loop iteration $(T_{10}^- - T_6^+)$ and the interval between incoming messages $\Delta T_{in}(\text{check})$. Sending a message in each iteration of the loop (line 10) equates the multiplicity of outgoing messages $N_{out}(\text{check})$ to the number of loop iterations k_5, and the interval between messages $\Delta T_{out}(\text{check})$ to the effective iteration length L_5. The *if-then-else* construct (line 6) introduces a binary constraint variable c_6 which captures the truth value of the condition, and a disjunctive constraint (line 9) which covers the *then* and the *else* cases. Finally, the internal operations, such as the expression evaluation (line 8) and a call to an internal procedure best (line 7), simply add the corresponding time intervals (resp. Δt_{expr} and Δt_{best}).

3.4   Analysis of Message Types with Size Constraints

The constraint QoS models whose derivation we described above include a number of internal structural parameters, such as the number of loop iterations and condition truth values (k_5 and c_6 in Figure 4) that depend on data that is received by these services. There are several ways in which the information about shape of the data can be organized and used to further constrain the values of these structural parameters and, therefore, make the constraint models more precise. One possibility would be to apply *computational cost analysis* techniques to an appropriate abstraction of the participant processes in order to obtain an

$$
\begin{aligned}
\tau := \ & \texttt{any} \mid \texttt{none} & \textit{(some unspecified value and no value)} \\
& \mid \texttt{bool}(a..b) & \textit{(Boolean between } a \textit{ and } b, \ a,b \in \{0,1\}, \ a \le b) \\
& \mid \texttt{number}(a..b) & \textit{(number between } a \in \mathbb{R} \cup \{-\infty\} \textit{ and } b \in \mathbb{R} \cup \{+\infty\}, \ a \le b) \\
& \mid \texttt{string}(a..b) & \textit{(string with finite size between } a \in \mathbb{N} \textit{ and } b \in \mathbb{N} \cup \{+\infty\}, \ a \le b) \\
& \mid \texttt{list}(a..b, \tau) & \textit{(list with finite size between } a \in \mathbb{N} \textit{ and } b \in \mathbb{N} \cup \{+\infty\}, \ a \le b) \\
& \mid \{ x_1 : \tau, \ x_2 : \tau, \ ..., x_n : \tau \} & \textit{(record with named fields } x_1, ..., x_n, \ n \ge 0)
\end{aligned}
$$

Abbrev.: $\texttt{bool} \equiv \texttt{bool}(0..1)$, $\texttt{number} \equiv \texttt{number}(-\infty..+\infty)$, $\texttt{string} \equiv \texttt{string}(0..+\infty)$, $\texttt{list}(\tau) \equiv \texttt{list}(0..+\infty, \tau)$

Fig. 5. A simple typing system for messages with size constraints

analytic functional relationship between the size of input data (number magnitudes, list lengths, etc.) and the upper and lower bounds of possible values for the structural parameters [13]. Another possibility, which we discuss in this subsection, is to use a simple form of type analysis which is directly applicable to the abstract representations of continuations used in our approach.

Figure 5 shows a simple type system with size constraints which includes Booleans, numbers, strings, lists, and records with named fields. Each type τ in this system has a denotation $[\![\tau]\!]$ which is the set of all values that belong to it. For instance, $[\![\texttt{number}(0..1)]\!] = \{ x \in \mathbb{R} \mid 0 \le x \le 1 \}$. By definition, we take $[\![\texttt{none}]\!] = \emptyset$. We write $\tau_1 \sqsubseteq \tau_2$ as a synonym for set inclusion $[\![\tau_1]\!] \subseteq [\![\tau_2]\!]$. The set of all types with size constraints together with the relation $\sqsubseteq$ forms a *complete lattice* [6] with **any** as the top element, and **none** as the bottom element, i.e., $\texttt{none} \sqsubseteq \tau \sqsubseteq \texttt{any}$ for arbitrary τ. We introduce the *least upper bound* operation $\sqcup$ on types, where $\tau_1 \sqcup \tau_2 = \tau$ means that τ is the smallest type (w.r.t. $\sqsubseteq$) such that $\tau_1 \sqsubseteq \tau$ and $\tau_2 \sqsubseteq \tau$. For example, $\texttt{number}(0..10) \sqcup \texttt{number}(8..100) = \texttt{number}(0..100)$, $\texttt{list}(1..5, \texttt{number}) \sqcup \texttt{list}(9..9, \texttt{bool}) = \texttt{list}(1..9, \texttt{any})$, and $\texttt{none} \sqcup \tau = \tau \sqcup \texttt{none} = \tau$.

The lattice structure of types from Figure 5 provides a domain for the application of abstract interpretation-based analysis techniques [4] to obtain a combination of type and size analysis for data in the participant processes before constructing the QoS model. This kind of analysis is well suited for our case in which looping is done by iterating over list elements and streams of messages, where the size range of the list type directly translates into the range of loop iterations. We enrich the link (channel) descriptions by adding input and output message types, $\tau_{\text{in}}(c)$ and $\tau_{\text{out}}(c)$.

For instance, in Figure 4, we start with $\tau_{\text{in}}(\texttt{req}) = \{\texttt{specs} : \texttt{list}(a..b, \tau_{\text{spec}}), \ \texttt{userId} : \texttt{number}\}$ where $a \ge 1$ and we derive that $\tau_{\text{out}}(\texttt{budget}) = \texttt{number}$ and $\tau_{\text{in}}(\texttt{budget}) \sqsubseteq \{\texttt{forced} : \texttt{bool}\}$. Also, in participant B, $\tau_{\text{out}}(\texttt{agent}) = \texttt{list}(a..b, \tau_{\text{spec}}) = \tau_{\text{in}}(\texttt{client})$. The result of the analysis for B is shown in Figure 6. From it, we infer that $A.N_{\text{in}}(\texttt{check}) = B.N_{\text{out}}(\texttt{approval})$ is between 0 and $\max(a, b)$.

3.5 Centralized and Distributed Processing of QoS Constraints

Solving a constraint model involves finding one (or several) set(s) of values for the constrained variables that satisfy the set of constraints, or determining that the set of constraints is unsatisfiable. Constraint solvers sometimes need to give an

1	`recv(client,specs),`	$\tau_{\mathrm{in}}(\text{client}) = \text{list}(a..b, \tau_{\mathrm{spec}}), 1 \le a \le b$
2	`let po = [],`	$\text{po} : \text{list}(0..0, \text{none})$
3	`stream(approval) do`	
4	`  foreach(spec:specs) do [`	$a \le k_4 \le b$
5	`    invoke(gen,spec,alts),`	$\tau_{\mathrm{out}}(\text{gen}) = \tau_{\mathrm{spec}},\ \tau_{\mathrm{in}}(\text{gen}) = \text{list}(1.. + \infty, \tau_{\mathrm{alt}})$
6	`    ( if(count(alts)>1)`	
7	`    -> invoke(approval,`	$\tau_{\mathrm{out}}(\text{approval}) = \text{list}(1.. + \infty, \tau_{\mathrm{alt}}),$
	`          alts,choice)`	$0 \le N_{\mathrm{out}}(\text{approval}) \le \max(a, b)$
8	`    ; let choice=first(alts)`	
9	`    ),`	$\text{choice} : \tau_{\mathrm{alt}}$
10	`    let po = po + [choice]`	$\text{po}_{\mathrm{before}} : \text{list}(n..m, \tau) \Rightarrow$
		$\Rightarrow \text{po}_{\mathrm{after}} : \text{list}(n + 1..m + 1, \tau \sqcup \tau_{\mathrm{alt}})$
11	`  ],`	$\text{po} : \text{list}(a..b, \tau_{\mathrm{alt}})$
12	`send(client,po)`	$\tau_{\mathrm{out}}(\text{client}) = \text{list}(a..b, \tau_{\mathrm{alt}})$

Fig. 6. Analysis of types with size constraints for participant B

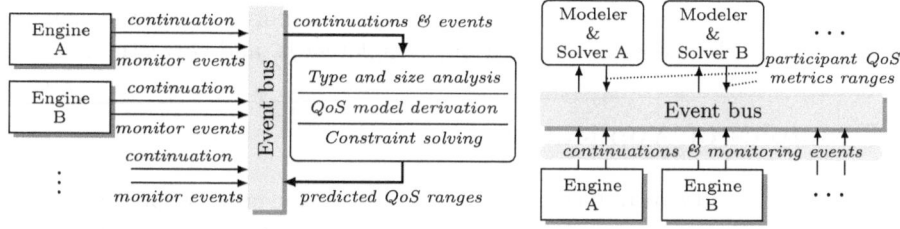

Fig. 7. Centralized (left) and distributed (right) processing of choreography QoS constraints.

approximation of the actual solutions. These approximations are always complete (no solution is discarded), but maybe not correct (they may contain values that are not part of any solution [7]). Some constraint solvers are better suited for some classes of constraints than others. E.g., if the generated constraints are linear, a linear constraint solver is likely to detect inconsistencies and to narrow down the value sets closer to the actual answers, compared to a more general one. The constraint models generated using our approach in general involve non-linear integer and real arithmetic constraints, as well as disjunctions of constraints.

The constraint QoS models for each participant can be, in principle, derived and analyzed for the different message types separately, and the models obtained in that way can be composed together by connecting the appropriate input/output links and solving the resulting integrated model centrally. This architecture is shown on the left-hand side of Figure 7. Different participants may, in general, execute on different nodes (process execution engines) in a Service-Oriented System. They publish participant continuations and the related monitoring events (which can be used for establishing the previously accumulated QoS) to an event bus. An aggregated feed of continuations is read from the event bus and processed by a single component that performs the analysis, modeling, and constraint solving of the integrated participant models, and publishes the (updated) QoS metrics ranges for the entire choreography. An advantage of the centralized approach is that it offers integrated information about the behavior of the participants and QoS for the choreography. However, it may not scale well, since it requires global streaming of continuations, monitoring events and results to and from a single processing component. Besides, it can be undesirable in some settings since data regarding execution characteristics may need to be sent from their administrative domains to a central, external point.

A decentralized approach aimed at alleviating somehow these issues is shown on the right-hand side of Figure 7. Here, continuations and monitoring events published by process engines are processed by modules which can be close in the network topology to the engines, and (optionally) inside their administrative boundaries. These modules perform a per-participant QoS analysis that updates the ranges for $\langle \tau_{\text{out}}, N_{\text{out}}, \bar{q}_{\text{out}}, \Delta\bar{q}_{\text{out}} \rangle$ for each outgoing channel using the corresponding ranges for $\langle \tau_{\text{in}}, N_{\text{in}}, \bar{q}_{\text{in}}, \Delta\bar{q}_{\text{in}} \rangle$ that are produced by the modelers/solvers for participants at the other end. The updates are communicated to the connected participant models and the process is repeated until a stable solution is reached. This can be achieved using distributed constraint solving algorithms [11], which ensure termination, completeness, and correctness.

4   Examples of Application

In this section, we illustrate how the proposed constraint-based approach can be of benefit in providing answers to the questions posed at the end of Section 2, using the motivating example. The aim of the approach is to be fully automated and supported by tools. Currently, our prototype executes processes written in the continuation language (Section 3.2), transmits continuations, and formulates and solves the QoS constraint models.

4.1   Supporting SLA Negotiation for Classes of Input Data

A constraint-based QoS model can be used at design time to help the providers of the participating processes in a choreography develop realistic SLA offers that can be used to negotiate with their users. In such a case, participant providers (e.g., the provider for participant A from Figure 1) can use the derived models, along with assumptions and empirical assessments of the behavior of the environment (network latency, component behavior, etc.) to develop reasonable SLA offers to the end users.

We illustrate this application with an experiment on an SLA addressing execution time. Assuming that participant A receives the request of some user at time $T_{\text{in}}(\texttt{req}) = 0$, we are interested in knowing which guarantees can be offered to the user with respect to $T_{\text{out}}(\texttt{req})$ for a given class of input data. Besides the data, the participant QoS models for A and B depend on several internal activity parameters: t_{send} is the time needed by a participant to deliver the message to a participant mailbox, t_{budget} is the time needed to retrieve budget line information in activity a_3, and t_{best} is the time required by activity a_7 to find the best choice among the alternatives offered.

Table 1. Experimental inputs and outputs of the execution time model

Ranges for internal activity parameters		
Parameter name	Confidence interval 99% parameter range [ms]	Confidence interval 90% parameter range [ms]	Confidence interval 80% parameter range [ms]
a_3: t_{budget}	500 .. 1 500	642 .. 1 167	673 .. 1 094
a_7: t_{best}	100 .. 700	195 .. 509	215 .. 468
a_{15}: t_{gen}	200 .. 500	247 .. 404	257 .. 384
t_{send}	25 .. 150		

Case 1: Varying confidence intervals for participants A and B		
Spec. list size	Confidence interval 99% $T_{out}(\text{req})$ range [ms]	Confidence interval 90% $T_{out}(\text{req})$ range [ms]	Confidence interval 80% $T_{out}(\text{req})$ range [ms]
1 .. 10	274 .. 17 100	322 .. 14 868	332 .. 14 376
11 .. 20	2 274 .. 32 100	2 797 .. 27 970	2 912 .. 27 057
21 .. 50	4 274 .. 77 100	5 272 .. 67 273	5 492 .. 65 103
50 .. 100	10 074 .. 152 100	12 450 .. 132 780	12 972 .. 128 512
101 .. 200	20 274 .. 302 101	25 069 .. 263 793	26 128 .. 255 330

Case 2: Varying confidence intervals for A and B with **force=true**		
Spec. list size	Confidence interval 99% $T_{out}(\text{req})$ range [ms]	Confidence interval 90% $T_{out}(\text{req})$ range [ms]	Confidence interval 80% $T_{out}(\text{req})$ range [ms]
1 .. 10	274 .. 10 100	322 .. 8817	332 .. 8535
11 .. 20	2 274 .. 18 100	2 797 .. 15 867	2 912 .. 15 376
21 .. 50	4 274 .. 42 100	5 272 .. 37 017	5 492 .. 35 900
50 .. 100	10 074 .. 82 100	12 450 .. 72 268	12 972 .. 70 106
101 .. 200	20 274 .. 162 100	25 069 .. 142 768	26 128 .. 138 518

The ranges of values for these parameters are normally empirically established by monitoring. Such empirical data is effectively a sample (or a collection of samples) of the "true population" set from which the QoS metric values are drawn and whose exact bounds are generally unknown. We can use well-known techniques of descriptive statistics on these samples to estimate the parameters of central tendency (mean, median) and dispersion (standard deviation) for the whole population of values. In that way, we can define intervals whose bounds include the QoS values with some level of confidence. This level will be < 100%, since, in general, total confidence is not attainable. Note that the choice of the confidence level is generally a matter of heuristics. A 99% confidence interval, for instance, is wider (and thus safer) than a 90% one, but, depending on the distribution of values, it may lead to overly conservative predictions and SLA offers to the clients that are safer, but too pessimistic, unattractive, and uncompetitive. The top part of Table 1 lists the ranges of the mentioned component execution time across three experimental confidence levels: 99%, 90% and 80%, with a common range for t_{send}.

The central part of Table 1 shows the ranges for $T_{out}(\text{req})$ obtained by solving the model for each confidence interval in the experiment. In general, for each class of input data sizes, the range of $T_{out}(\text{req})$ contracts, and its maximum, which can be offered as an element of the SLA, decreases when using smaller confidence intervals. To further refine the SLA offer, the provider for participant A can look at the branch condition in a_6, and offer more attractive "fast-track" conditions (with circa 40% reduction in the upper execution time bound) when it becomes known that the force flag will be set to true, as shown in the lower part of Table 1.

We used the ECL^iPS^e constraint logic programming system [2] which has native support for integer and real non-linear arithmetic constraints, including disjunctions of constraints, that are used in the derivation of the model. Deriving the constraint models with our pilot implementation and solving them with a centralized solver took on average around 260 ms on an i86_64 laptop computer with 4GB of RAM running Mac OS X 10.7.3.

4.2 Predicting SLA Violations at Run Time

The constraint-based QoS model can be used for predicting SLA violations at runtime. Since the participant SLA is always related to some event that happens in one of the participants (such as sending the reply in activity a_{11} of our sample choreography), we can apply a variation of the constraint-based prediction method for orchestrations [14]. In that method, we make predictions at each point

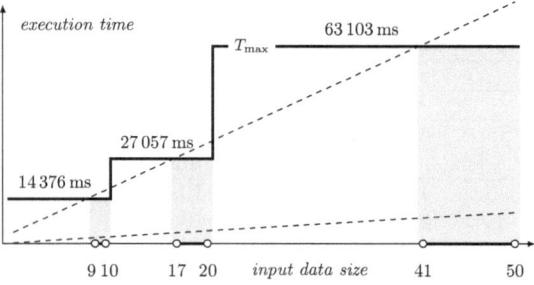

Fig. 8. An example of SLA failure prediction zones

in execution of the participant processes for which we have the continuation and the monitoring data describing the previously accumulated QoS metrics. In the case of execution time, the imminent failure condition for participant A is predicted when the constraint $T_{out}(\text{req}) \leq T_{max}$ is proven unsatisfiable in the constraint QoS model, i.e., when SLA compliance cannot possibly be achieved.

Using the experimental settings from the previous subsection, we predict SLA violations for a running choreography with fixed input data size (known at run time), by taking T_{max} to be the upper bound of $T_{out}(\text{req})$ for the 80% confidence interval in each input data class from Table 1. The thick black line in Figure 8 shows T_{max} for input data sizes in the range 1..50. The dashed lines show the upper and lower bound of $T_{out}(\text{req})$ for a 99% confidence interval. SLA violations are possible in the gray zones that correspond to data size intervals 9..10, 17..20, and 41..50. In those intervals, imminent SLA violation can be predicted between 175 ms and 325 ms ahead of T_{max}. For other input data sizes (in ranges 1..8, 11..16, and 21..40), the predictor is able to predict SLA conformance at the very start. In both cases, the percentage of correctly predicted cases is typically very high, between 94% and 99% [5].

4.3 SLA Compliance Checking, Dynamic Binding and Adaptation

We now turn to a situation where there exist several implementations for a participant role in a choreography, that are known to be compatible with the communication protocol, message data types, and message cardinalities. We now want to see how the knowledge about participant QoS models can help us rule out some combinations of participant implementations (or promote others) at design time.

For instance, let us take participant A from Figure 1, and assume that there are two implementations that can take the role of B and which differ only in the method for generating alternatives in activity a_{15}: while B_1 can generate one or more alternatives, B_2 always generates at least two. Although the ranges for all participant model variables of B_2 are subsets of the corresponding ranges for B_1, the combination of A with B_2 is illegal for some SLAs and input data sizes for which A with B_1 may work. E.g., for $T_{\max} = 18\,000$ ms, the constraint model predicts that the combination of A and B_2 is guaranteed to fail for input data sizes of 50 and above when `forced=false` in A. Since A does not control `forced`, for such data sizes it should rule out B_2, and choose B_1 which has a chance to meet the SLA.

This kind of analysis can be performed by checking that every internal structural parameter of A in the constraint QoS model for the choreography (such as the condition in a_6 and the number of iterations of a_4) augmented with condition $T_{\text{out}}(\text{req}) > T_{\max}$ has at least one value for which the condition $T_{\text{out}}(\text{req}) \leq T_{\max}$ is satisfiable for the given range of input data sizes. Alternatively, the same check can be used for dynamic binding

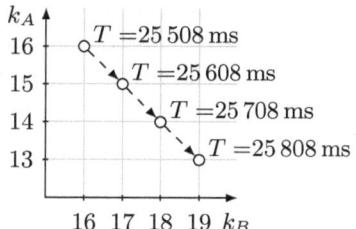

Fig. 9. Adaptation need detection in B.

at run-time to select an implementation for the role of B for the known size of the particular input request. Such dynamic binding provides a finer-grained per-request selection, at the cost of additional run-time analysis.

However, selecting B_1 does not guarantee $T_{\text{out}}(\text{req}) \leq T_{\max}$: if at run time each invocation of a_{15} happens to return more than one alternative (thus behaving in the same way as B_2), the SLA will be violated for some input data sizes. Participant B can use its QoS model to detect such a situation and to adapt by forcing a_{15} to start returning single items. At the beginning of each iteration in loop a_{14} from Figure 1, B can test whether the execution of a_{15}, if it generates multiple alternatives, can lead to an SLA violation. If so, it can coerce a_{15} to produce a single item and so enforce the SLA. The earliest points in time when that can happen for input data sizes in the range 17..20 and $T_{\max} = 27\,057$ ms (the central gray zone in Figure 8), are shown in Figure 9. k_B stands for the previous number of iterations of a_{14}, and k_A stands for the previous number of times when more than one alternative was generated in a_{15}.

5   Conclusions

The constraint-based approach to QoS assurance for service choreographies presented is based on the automatic derivation of QoS constraint models from abstract descriptions of multiple participating processes that can engage in complex, stateful conversations. The QoS attributes that can be modeled include execution time, availability, monetary cost, the quantity of data transferred, and any others that can be mapped onto cumulative, non-negative numerical metrics. For greater precision, the model derivation is augmented with an analysis of message types with size constraints, and the resulting models are data sensitive. The participant models can be derived, integrated, and solved centrally, or in a distributed fashion. The approach can be used at design-time, for classes of input data, and also at run time, with the actual data, whenever the information about the current point in execution is provided for the participants. The resulting models can be used to support SLA negotiation, SLA violation prediction, design-time SLA conformance for classes of input data, dynamic binding of participants, and SLA-driven run-time adaptation.

Based on our prototype implementation, our future work will aim at the development of the supporting tools and systems, and interfacing them with the service infrastructure components, such as the execution engines and service buses, and with choreography design tools. We will also aim at evaluating the quality of QoS prediction offered by the constraint-based models in distributed settings and when used with incomplete or inaccurate information about the QoS properties of the service environment and components.

References

1. Apt, K.R.: Principles of Constraint Programming. Cambridge University Press (2003)
2. Apt, K.R., Wallace, M.G.: Constraint Logic Programming Using ECLIPSE. Cambridge University Press (2007)
3. Basu, S., Bultan, T., Ouederni, M.: Deciding choreography realizability. In: Proceedings of the 39th Annual ACM SIGPLAN-SIGACT Symposium on Principles of Programming Languages, POPL 2012, pp. 191–202. ACM, New York (2012)
4. Cousot, P., Cousot, R.: Abstract Interpretation: a Unified Lattice Model for Static Analysis of Programs by Construction or Approximation of Fixpoints. In: Proc. of POPL 1977, pp. 238–252. ACM Press (1977)
5. Ivanović, D., Carro, M., Hermenegildo, M.: Exploring the impact of inaccuracy and imprecision of qos assumptions on proactive constraint-based QoS prediction for service orchestrations. In: Proceedings of the 4th International Workshop on Principles of Engineering Service-Oriented Systems, PESOS 2012, pp. 931–937. IEEE Press (June 2012)
6. Davey, B.A., Priestley, H.A.: Introduction to Lattices and Order, 2nd edn. Cambridge University Press (2002)
7. Dechter, R.: Constraint Processing. Morgan Kauffman Publishers (2003)
8. Decker, G., Kopp, O., Leymann, F., Weske, M.: BPEL4Chor: Extending BPEL for Modeling Choreographies. In: ICWS, pp. 296–303 (2007)

9. Dezani-Ciancaglini, M., de'Liguoro, U.: Sessions and Session Types: An Overview. In: Laneve, C., Su, J. (eds.) WS-FM 2009. LNCS, vol. 6194, pp. 1–28. Springer, Heidelberg (2010)
10. Di Nitto, E., Ghezzi, C., Metzger, A., Papazoglou, M., Pohl, K.: A journey to highly dynamic, self-adaptive service-based applications. Automated Software Engineering 15, 313–341 (2008), doi:10.1007/s10515-008-0032-x
11. Faltings, B., Yokoo, M. (eds.): Artificial Intelligence Journal: Special Issue on Distributed Constraint Satisfaction, vol. 161. Elsevier Science Publishers Ltd., Essex (2005)
12. Hielscher, J., Kazhamiakin, R., Metzger, A., Pistore, M.: A Framework for Proactive Self-adaptation of Service-Based Applications Based on Online Testing. In: Mähönen, P., Pohl, K., Priol, T. (eds.) ServiceWave 2008. LNCS, vol. 5377, pp. 122–133. Springer, Heidelberg (2008)
13. Ivanović, D., Carro, M., Hermenegildo, M.: Towards Data-Aware QoS-Driven Adaptation for Service Orchestrations. In: Proceedings of the 2010 IEEE International Conference on Web Services, ICWS 2010, Miami, FL, USA, July 5-10, pp. 107–114. IEEE (2010)
14. Ivanović, D., Carro, M., Hermenegildo, M.: Constraint-Based Runtime Prediction of SLA Violations in Service Orchestrations. In: Kappel, G., Maamar, Z., Motahari-Nezhad, H.R. (eds.) ICSOC 2011. LNCS, vol. 7084, pp. 62–76. Springer, Heidelberg (2011)
15. Leitner, P., Michlmayr, A., Rosenberg, F., Dustdar, S.: Monitoring, prediction and prevention of sla violations in composite services. In: ICWS, pp. 369–376. IEEE Computer Society (2010)
16. Metzger, A., Benbernou, S., Carro, M., Driss, M., Kecskemeti, G., Kazhamiakin, R., Krytikos, K., Mocci, A., Di Nitto, E., Wetzstein, B., Silvestril, F.: Analytical Quality Assurance. In: Papazoglou, M.P., Pohl, K., Parkin, M., Metzger, A. (eds.) Service Research Challenges and Solutions. LNCS, vol. 6500, pp. 209–270. Springer, Heidelberg (2010)
17. Object Management Group. Business Process Modeling Notation (BPMN), Version 1.2 (January 2009)
18. Reynolds, J.C.: The discoveries of continuations. LISP and Symbolic Computation Journal 6, 233–247 (1993)
19. Sammodi, O., Metzger, A., Franch, X., Oriol, M., Marco, J., Pohl, K.: Usage-based online testing for proactive adaptation of service-based applications. In: COMPSAC 2011 – The Computed World: Software Beyond the Digital Society. IEEE Computer Society (2011)
20. Schmieders, E., Metzger, A.: Preventing Performance Violations of Service Compositions Using Assumption-Based Run-Time Verification. In: Abramowicz, W., Llorente, I.M., Surridge, M., Zisman, A., Vayssière, J. (eds.) ServiceWave 2011. LNCS, vol. 6994, pp. 194–205. Springer, Heidelberg (2011)
21. Stein, S., Payne, T.R., Jennings, N.R.: Robust execution of service workflows using redundancy and advance reservations. IEEE T. Services Computing 4(2), 125–139 (2011)
22. Tselentis, G., Dominigue, J., Galis, A., Gavras, A., Hausheer, D.: Towards the Future Internet: A European Research Perspective. IOS Press, Amsterdam (2009)
23. van der Aalst, W.M.P., Dumas, M., Ouyang, C., Rozinat, A., Verbeek, H.M.W.: Choreography Conformance Checking: An Approach based on BPEL and Petri Nets. In: The Role of Business Processes in Service Oriented Architectures, Dagstuhl Seminar Proceedings (2006)
24. World Wide Web Consortium. Web Services Choreography Description Language Version 1.0 (November 2005)

Structural Optimization of Reduced Ordered Binary Decision Diagrams for SLA Negotiation in IaaS of Cloud Computing[*]

Kuan Lu[1], Ramin Yahyapour[1], Edwin Yaqub[1], and Constantinos Kotsokalis[2]

[1] Gesellschaft für wissenschaftliche Datenverarbeitung mbH Göttingen, Germany
[2] IT & Media Center of Dortmund University of Technology, Germany
{kuan.lu,ramin.yahyapour,edwin.yaqub}@gwdg.de,
constantinos.kotsokalis@tu-dortmund.de

Abstract. In cloud computing, an automated SLA is an electronic contract used to record the rights and obligations of service providers and customers for their services. SLA negotiation can be a time-consuming process, mainly due to the unpredictable rounds of negotiation and the complicated possible dependencies among SLAs. The operation of negotiating SLAs can be facilitated when SLAs are translated into Reduced Ordered Binary Decision Diagrams (ROBDDs). Nevertheless, an ROBDD may not be optimally structured upon production. In this paper, we show how to reduce the number of 1-paths and nodes of ROBDDs that model SLAs, using ROBDD optimization algorithms. In addition, we demonstrate the reduction of 1-paths via the application of Term Rewriting Systems with mutually exclusive features. Using the latter, ROBDDs can be generated accurately without redundant 1-paths. We apply the principles onto the negotiation of IaaS SLAs via simulation, and show that negotiation is accelerated by assessing fewer SLA proposals (1-paths), while memory consumption is also reduced.

Keywords: Cloud computing, IaaS, SLA negotiation, Term rewriting, ROBDD structural optimization.

1 Introduction

Recent years have witnessed wide adoption of utility computing for service provisioning, in favor of more adaptive, flexible and simple access to computing resources. Utility computing has enabled a pay-as-you-go consumption model for computing similar to traditional utilities such as water, gas or electricity [1]. As a realization of utility computing [2], cloud computing provides computing utilities that can be leased and released by the customers through the Internet in an on-demand fashion. More recently, from the perspective of service type, three service delivery models are commonly used, namely, *Software-as-a-Service*

---

[*] The research leading to these results is supported by Gesellschaft für wissenschaftliche Datenverarbeitung mbH Göttingen (GWDG) in Germany.

C. Liu et al. (Eds.): ICSOC 2012, LNCS 7636, pp. 268–282, 2012.

(SaaS), *Platform-as-a-Service* (PaaS) and *Infrastructure-as-a-Service* (IaaS) [5]. Automated negotiation may be used to accommodate a customer's heterogeneous requirements against a service provider's capabilities and acceptable usage terms. The result of such a negotiation is a Service Level Agreement (SLA), an electronic contract that establishes all relevant aspects of the service. SLA negotiation can be *time-consuming*, mainly due to the unpredictable rounds of negotiation and the possible complicated dependencies among SLAs. For instance, an SaaS provider negotiates with one or more IaaS providers for computing resources to host her applications. Thus, a SaaS SLA could have dependencies with one or more IaaS SLAs. Establishing an SLA might need one or more rounds of negotiation until both sides agree with the stipulation of the contract.

In our previous work [20], SLAs were canonically represented as Reduced Ordered Binary Decision Diagrams (ROBDDs), aiming to *facilitate* SLA negotiation. A BDD diagram includes some decision nodes and two terminal nodes (0-terminal and 1-terminal). A path from the root node to the 1-terminal represents a variable assignment for which the Boolean function is true. Such a path is called "1-path". A 1-path can also be treated as an SLA proposal. Nevertheless, ROBDDs may be suboptimal in structure. Firstly, the ROBDDs should be maintained throughout the whole life cycle of SLAs, so diagrams with too many nodes may waste a lot of memory. Secondly, an ROBDD may have semantically redundant 1-paths that improperly reflect a customer's requirements; as a result, SLA negotiation may slow down.

In this paper, we propose that by applying BDD node optimization algorithms, the number of nodes for the ROBDDs can be decreased efficiently. Thus, SLAs occupy less memory space. Additionally, the size and number of paths (especially as regards 1-paths) can be reduced by eliminating those that are semantically redundant via BDD path optimization algorithms. Consequently, the SLA negotiation is accelerated by assessing fewer SLA proposals (1-paths). Furthermore, a novel alternative solution for reducing semantically redundant 1-paths during construction is introduced. We argue that all the options of an SLA term are mutually exclusive. Thus, customizing an SLA term is rewritten as correctly selecting an option for this term. This process can be treated as an implementation of an SLA *Term Rewriting System*.

The remainder of this paper is structured as follows. In Section 2, we discuss related work. Section 3 describes how an SLA can be modeled as an ROBDD. In Section 4, we present how the structure of an initial ROBDD can be optimized. In order to validate our mechanisms, in Section 5, we simulate the SLA negotiation by transforming IaaS SLAs into ROBDDs and optimizing the initial ROBDDs. Finally, we conclude the paper in Section 6.

2   Related Work

In cloud computing, SLAs are used to ensure that service quality is kept at acceptable levels [8]. An SLA management component may consist of several components: discovery, (re-)negotiation, pricing, scheduling, risk analysis, monitoring, SLA enforcement and dispatching [7], where SLA negotiation determines the cardinality of parties involved, their roles, the visibility of the offers exchanged and so on [30]. Furthermore, Ron et al. in [9] define the SLA life cycle in three phases: creation phase, operation phase and removal phase. Our focus is on IaaS SLA negotiation during the SLA creation phase.

Based on [7], our framework [3] [4] [20] (developed in the SLA@SOI EU Integrated Project [29]) covers the features for multi-round negotiation with counteroffers customer and service provider. In general, apart from IaaS, the framework can be easily extended to other scenarios (e.g., SaaS, PaaS) as well in which automated SLA management is considered. In our scenario, virtual resources are created and provisioned through Open Cloud Computing Interface (OCCI) [25] and OpenNebula [26]. The VMs are compute instances, connected with OS image and network instances. The storage pool is formed by several images, which means that customers are able to upload their own images.

The service provider can abstract the services in perspicuous terms, e.g., the instances of Amazon EC2 [21]. Thus, non-technical customers can mainly focus on the service as a whole rather than considering the service in too much detail. However, the service provider would best allow customers with flexibility and adaptability [22]. Chandra et al. [23] suggest that fine-grained temporal and spatial resource allocation may lead to substantial improvements in capacity utilization. Therefore, in IaaS, this means that customers are free to customize the VM configuration. Namely, the granularity of customizing VMs evolves from setting the number of predefined VM to the detailed specification of each term in a VM. In this paper, the SLA terms that can be customized (see Table 1), the ROBDD structural optimization in Section 4 and the simulation in Section 5 are based on the cloud infrastructure provided by the GWDG for its customers and scientific communities.

Service availability is one of the most important Quality of Service (QoS) metrics with respect to IaaS. In [24], authors outline that the service availability

Table 1. SLA terms and descriptions

SLA term	Option	Variable
Service_name	[service name]	$[x_1]$
Business_hours	[09:00-17:00]	$[x_2]$
VM_number	[1]	$[x_3]$
CPU_core	[1, 2, 4]	$[x_4, x_5, x_6]$
CPU_speed	[2.4 GHz, 3.0 GHz]	$[x_7, x_8]$
Memory	[1 GB, 2 GB]	$[x_9, x_{10}]$
Network	[Net-1, Net-2]	$[x_{11}, x_{12}]$
Storage_image	[Private, OS-1, OS-2]	$[x_{13}, x_{14}, x_{15}]$
Service_availability	[99.99%, 99.9%]	$[x_{16}, x_{17}]$

guaranteed by three large cloud providers (Amazon, Google and Rackspace Cloud) is more than 99.9% in order to obtain good reputation in todays competitive market. Therefore, we propose to provide a basic service availability of 99.9% and an advanced availability of 99.99%. The later one implies that the service provider has to pay special attention (e.g., extra resources) on the service during SLA monitoring phase in order to avoid SLA violation.

At the moment, many representations of SLAs, e.g., WS-Agreement [16], WSLA [17] and the SLA model in [19], focus on enabling interoperability between independent agents. However, our focus is on a system-internal representation that is able to efficiently support decision-making during SLA negotiation. In [20], we presented a novel application of ROBDD, for representing, managing and facilitating the construction of SLAs. During BDD construction, although pushing all facts and conditions to the top of the diagram provides a possibility for optimizing the BDD, there could still be lots of semantically redundant 1-paths. Furthermore, this kind of ordering does not reduce the total number of decision nodes, which waste memory space.

In order to optimize the structure of the ROBDD, we studied Term Rewriting Systems (TRS) for Boolean functions [14] [15] that could be applied in SLA terms selection to reduce the number of redundant 1-paths of an ROBDD. In mathematics, rewriting systems cover a wide range of methods of transforming terms of a formula with other terms. In TRS, a term can be recursively defined to a constant c, or a set of variables $x_1 ... x_n$, or a function f [15]. The terms are composed of binary operators logical conjunction "$\wedge$", logical disjunction "$\vee$" and unary operator "$\neg$". In IaaS, an SLA term contains one or more variables, namely the options. We make an effort to rewrite the set of SLA terms while customizing SLA templates in a way that depicts the customer's request precisely.

Alternatively, the existing BDD optimization algorithms in [10] [12] [28] [31] provide us with the theoretical foundation to reduce the size of ROBDD. Furthermore, JavaBDD [13], a Java library for manipulating BDDs, is the tool we chose for setting up the BDD handling and programming environment.

3   Modeling SLA with ROBDD

An SLA is essentially a set of facts and a set of rules. Facts are globally (with respect to the contract) applicable truths, such as parties involved, monetary unit, etc. Rules include:

- the conditions that must hold for a certain clause to be in effect;
- the clause, typically describing the expected result that the customer wishes to receive and which is usually referred to as Service Level Objective (SLO);
- a fall-back clause in the case that the aforementioned clause is not honored.

As an example, for the condition "time of day is after 08:00", the clause could be "service availability $\geq$ 99.9%", and the fall-back clause could be an applicable penalty. This kind of format actually reflects real-life contracts and their if-then-else structure.

BDDs, based on Shannon's decomposition theorem [6], are well-known in the domain of Computer Aided Design (CAD) for Very Large Scale Integrated (VLSI) circuits. They can represent Boolean functions as rooted, directed and acyclic graphs, which consist of decision nodes and two terminal nodes called 0-terminal and 1-terminal. Each decision node is labeled by a Boolean variable and has two child nodes called low child and high child. A path from the root node to the 1-terminal represents a variable assignment for which the Boolean function is true. Such a path is also called "1-path". Compared to other techniques to represent Boolean functions, e.g., truth tables or Karnaugh maps, BDDs often require less memory and offer faster algorithms for their manipulation [10].

A BDD, with all variables occurring in the same order on all paths from the root, is said to be ordered (OBDD). Furthermore, if all identical nodes are shared and all syntactically redundant paths are eliminated, the OBDD is said to be reduced, shortly termed ROBDD [12]. For example, Eq. (1) is a disjunction Boolean function with 3 variables. Its corresponding ROBDD is illustrated in Fig. 1 (a), including 3 decision nodes (x_1, x_2, x_3) and 3 1-paths ($x_1 = $ true, $x_2 = $ false, $x_3 = $ false), ($x_1 = $ false, $x_2 = $ true, $x_3 = $ false) and ($x_1 = $ false, $x_2 = $ false, $x_3 = $ true). As already mentioned, ROBDDs are useful for modeling SLAs due to their capability to provide canonical representations generated on the grounds of if-then-else rules. Especially, ROBDDs can express SLAs unambiguously. Equivalent SLAs, which are structurally different, are eventually represented by the same ROBDD. On the contrary, using formats developed for on-the-wire representation such as WS-Agreement [16] does not guarantee this property. Hence, ROBDDs can be used internally in systems that have to manage SLAs.

$$f(x_1, x_2, x_3) = x_1 \lor x_2 \lor x_3 \tag{1}$$

An SLA could have dependencies with one or more sub-SLAs. The SLA manager has to parse the SLA request into an ROBDD and analyze all of its 1-paths. A 1-path is a potential SLA proposal that satisfies the customer's requirements. Nevertheless, an ROBDD may have semantically redundant 1-paths that reflect the customer's requirements improperly and reduce the time efficiency of the negotiation process. Moreover, the SLA manager should maintain the ROBDDs throughout the whole life cycle of SLAs. Accordingly, the size of 1-path and node of ROBDDs for SLAs ought to be simplified and controlled.

4   ROBDD Structural Optimization

4.1   SLA Term Rewriting System with Mutual Exclusiveness in ROBDD

According to the canonicity Lemma in [12], by reducing all the syntactically redundant paths, there is exactly one ROBDD with n basic variables in the order of $x_1 < x_1 < ... < x_n$. In this unique ROBDD, all variables of a disjunction function are mutually exclusive. Based on the truth table, e.g., a disjunction function is true when all its variables are true. However, such an assignment does not exist in ROBDD; as the ROBDD checks these variables one after another, the first true variable already ensures this function to be true and that leaves the rest of the variables not evaluated. For instance, as we explained in Section 3, the ROBDD (Fig. 1 (a)) of Eq. (1) has 3 decision nodes and 3 1-paths and its structure can't be simplified anymore. Therefore, if the inputs of a disjunction function are the basic variables, they are mutually exclusive and the ROBDD contains no redundant nodes and 1-paths. In contrast, when the inputs are not basic variables, despite the mutually exclusive feature among the inputs (only one of the inputs will be selected), the ROBDD of this disjunction function might have redundant nodes and 1-paths. *Semantically, options of most SLA terms are mutual exclusive, which means the customer can only choose one of them and this term must be represented as a combination of all the options with binary operators "logical conjunction" (∧), "logical disjunction" (∨) and unary "negation" (¬).* While constructing an ROBDD, using Table 1, a simple SLA (see Eq. (2)) can be customized by specifying SLA term "Network" with 2 mutually exclusive options "x_{11}" and "x_{12}" and SLA term "Service_availability" with 2 mutually exclusive options "x_{16}" and "x_{17}". This SLA indicates that inputs "$x_{11} \wedge x_{16}$" and "$x_{12} \wedge x_{17}$" both are acceptable for the customer.

$$SLA = (x_{11} \wedge x_{16}) \vee (x_{12} \wedge x_{17}) \tag{2}$$

Its ROBDD (see Fig. 1 (b)) includes 6 decision nodes and 4 1-paths. However, two of those paths, namely (x_{11} = true, x_{12} = true, x_{16} = false, x_{17} = true) and (x_{11} = true, x_{12} = true, x_{16} = true), are not correct, since x_{11} and x_{12} cannot be true concurrently. In IaaS, selecting both "Net-1" and "Net-2" as network is an illogical clause. Therefore this inaccurate SLA representation creates two unrealistic semantically redundant 1-paths and such paths should be eliminated at the very beginning.

Consequently, we propose that specifying an SLA term (t) with 2 options (α_1 and α_2) can be rewritten as illustrated in Formula (3).

$$t \to (\alpha_1 \wedge \neg\alpha_2) \vee (\neg\alpha_1 \wedge \alpha_2) \to \alpha_1 \oplus \alpha_2 \tag{3}$$

Mutual exclusiveness cannot be simply represented as a combination of all the options with the exclusive disjunction "⊕", when there are more than 2 options in an SLA term. Because the output is true when the number of "true" variables is odd and the output is false when the number of "true" variables is even [27]. For example, all-true assignment makes the expression $\alpha_1 \oplus \alpha_2 \oplus \alpha_3$ true, which is however not what we expect. Thus, when an SLA term (t) contains n ($n \geq 3$) options ($\alpha_1,...,\alpha_n$), we have the following assumptions:

$$N = \{1, ..., n\} \tag{4}$$

$$A \cup B = N \tag{5}$$

$$A \cap B = \emptyset \tag{6}$$

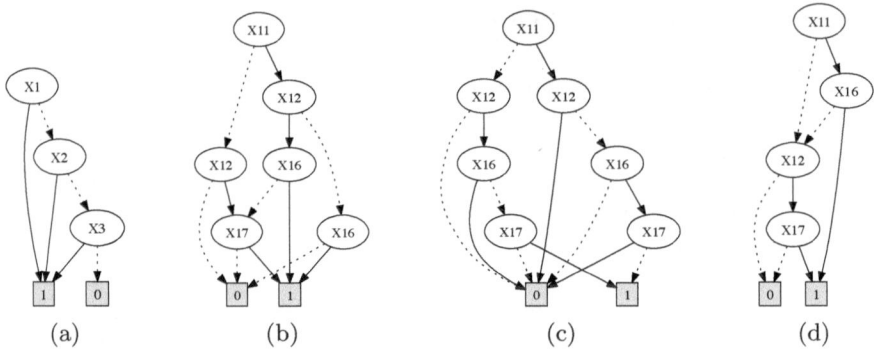

Fig. 1. (a) The ROBDD of disjunction function, (b) Mutual exclusiveness of disjunction function but with semantically redundant 1-path in ROBDD, (c) Mutual exclusiveness of disjunction function without semantically redundant 1-path in TRS ROBDD, (d) ROBDD after path optimization

$$A \neq \emptyset, B \neq N \tag{7}$$

From Eq. (4) to (6), N is a set of sequential numbers of all options. N can be further divided into 2 disjoint subsets. Options that concern a customer are put into A and indifferent ones are in B. Eq. (7) means that the customer should select at least one option. Thereby specifying an SLA term (t) with n $(n \geq 3)$ options can be rewritten as Eq. (8).

$$t \rightarrow \bigvee_{l \in A} \left(\left(\bigwedge_{k \in A} \neg \alpha_k \right) \wedge \alpha_l \right) \wedge \left(\bigwedge_{m \in B} \neg \alpha_m \right), l \neq k \neq m \tag{8}$$

For SLA term t, $\bigcup_{l \in A} a_l$ is a set of options that the customer is flexible with and the rest of the options in A ($\bigcup_{k \in A} a_k$) should be denied *explicitly* with "$\neg$". In the meanwhile, the unconcerned options in N, namely set B, should also be negated with "$\neg$" in order to not conflict with other SLA option(s) from the same customer. Therefore, when $n = 3$, Eq. (8) can be specified as Eq. (9), in this case the set B is empty, which means the customer is flexible with any option of $\alpha_1, \alpha_2, \alpha_3$.

$$(\alpha_1 \wedge \neg \alpha_2 \wedge \neg \alpha_3) \vee (\neg \alpha_1 \wedge \alpha_2 \wedge \neg \alpha_3) \vee (\neg \alpha_1 \wedge \neg \alpha_2 \wedge \alpha_3) \tag{9}$$

Based on above concepts, Eq. (2) can be written as Eq. (10) with 7 decision nodes and 2 1-paths in its TRS ROBDD (see Fig. 1 (c)). The number of redundant 1-paths is reduced efficiently although the node size increases by 1.

$$(x_{11} \wedge x_{16} \wedge \neg x_{12} \wedge \neg x_{17}) \vee (x_{12} \wedge x_{17} \wedge \neg x_{11} \wedge \neg x_{16}) \tag{10}$$

In summary, the above term rewriting concepts can be set into a dictionary and updated dynamically according to the use case, whereby the semantically redundant 1-paths can be eliminated efficiently. This also reduces the complexity of planning and optimization processes for SLA management. However, the shortcoming is that perhaps this approach might introduce extra decision nodes.

4.2   ROBDD Variable Swap and Sifting Algorithm

Alternatively, structural optimization algorithms can be applied to reduce the size of ROBDD. Here, the size means the number of nodes or paths. The algorithms make use of basic techniques such as variable swaps and the sifting algorithm. As approved in [10], *a swap of adjacent variables in a BDD only affects the graph structure of the two levels involved in the swap, leaving the semantic meaning of Boolean function unchanged.*

Algorithm 1. Sifting algorithm [11]

---

sort level numbers by descending level sizes and store them in array sl;
for $i = 1 \to n$ do
  if $sl[i] = 1$ then
    $sift\_down(i, n)$; // the BDD size is recorded in $sift\_down()$;
  else if $sl[i] = n$ then
    $sift\_up(i, 1)$; // the BDD size is recorded in $sift\_up()$;
  else if $(sl[i] - 1) > (n - sl[i])$ then
    $sift\_down(i, n)$;
    $sift\_up(n, 1)$;
  else
    $sift\_up(i, 1)$;
    $sift\_down(1, n)$;
  end if
  $sift\_back()$;
end for

Based on the variable swap, the classical sifting algorithm is described in Algorithm 1, where the levels are sorted by descending level sizes. The largest level contains the most nodes and is considered first. Then, the variable is moved downwards until the terminal nodes and upwards from the initial position to the top. In the previous steps, the BDD size resulting from every variable swap is recorded. In the end, the variable is moved back to the position, which led to a minimal BDD size. Here, the size could be the number of nodes or the 1-paths.

4.3   Node Optimization

The sifting algorithm, based on the efficient exchange of adjacent variables, is able to dynamically reorder the structure of BDD in a way to change the number of decision nodes. While the sifting algorithm is executing, we record the BDD node size for each variable swap. In the meanwhile, we also store all the $<$ *node*, $1 - path >$ pairs into a $<$ *node*, $1 - path >$ array, which can further be used in Section 4.5 for determining the optimal $<$ *node*, $1 - path >$ pair. In the end, a BDD with minimum number of decision nodes is derived.

In Section 4.1, we strive to define the TRS ROBDD accurately enough so that no semantically redundant 1-paths exist. Thereby, we say *the quantity and semantic meaning of 1-path of TRS ROBDD do not vary with the changes of variable ordering of TRS ROBDD.* As we showed that a TRS ROBDD might introduce extra decision nodes, we can further use node optimization to reduce its node size. Clearly, in this case node optimization only improves the node size and leaves the 1-path unchanged.

In-memory, each decision node requires an index and pointers to the succeeding nodes [28]. Since each decision node in an ROBDD has two pointers, the memory size required to represent an ROBDD is given by Eq. (11).

$$Memory(ROBDD) = (1 + 2) \times nodes(ROBDD) \tag{11}$$

4.4 Path Optimization

Apart from the BDD node optimization, another criterion –namely, the number of 1-paths– for BDD optimality is also considered. As the variable ordering heavily influences the number of nodes of a BDD, the sifting algorithm can be modified to minimize the number of 1-paths instead of the node size of a given BDD. After each swap of two adjacent variables, i.e. after processing all nodes in the two levels, changes are only propagated from those two levels down to the terminal nodes. During modified sifting no upper limit on the number of 1-paths is used to stop the swapping operations [10].

Similarly, we record the 1-paths number of BDD for each variable swap. In the meanwhile, we also store all the $< 1 - path, node >$ pairs into a $< 1 - path, node >$ array, which can further be used in Section 4.5 for determining the optimal $< 1 - path, node >$ pair. In the end, a BDD with minimum number of 1-paths is derived.

Although for Eq. (2), the 1-paths number can be reduced from 4 to 3, path (x_{11} = true, x_{12} = true, x_{16} = false, x_{17} = true) still exists (see Fig. 1 (d)), where x_{11} and x_{12} are true at the same time. Path optimization relieves the work of SLA management, but it does not eliminate the semantically redundant 1-paths completely. Thus, the SLA manager still needs to evaluate the validity of each 1-path despite the partial reduction of 1-paths.

4.5 Multicriteria Optimization Problem

As it is demonstrated in [10], the number of paths can be significantly reduced for some benchmarks. At the same time, the number of nodes does not necessarily increase and may even be reduced.

The path optimization algorithm re-constructs an ROBDD with the minimal number of 1-paths, but not necessarily the minimal number of decision nodes. Similarly, node optimization algorithm re-constructs the ROBDD with the minimal number of decision nodes, but not necessarily the minimal number of 1-paths. As Lemma 5.5 in [10], for all Boolean functions of two or three variables there exists a BDD that is minimal both in size and the number of 1-paths. This is however not true for functions of more than three variables. Therefore, this becomes a multicriteria optimization (MCO) problem for gaining a minimal number of decision nodes and 1-paths (see Algorithm 2).

Algorithm 2. Calculate optimal (node, path) pair

---

store node and 1_path size of *node_minimization*() into *n_nopti* and *p_nopti*;
store node and 1_path size of *path_minimization*() into *n_popti* and *p_popti*;
if *n_nopti* = *n_popti* **then**
   return (*n_popti*, *p_popti*);
else if *p_nopti* = *p_popti* **then**
   return (*n_nopti*, *p_nopti*);
else
   return *node_path_pair_selection*();
end if

In Algorithm 2, if the node size of an ROBDD after executing the path optimization is equal to that after executing the node optimization, the result of the path optimization will be taken. An analogous statement holds if the path size of an ROBDD after executing the node optimization is equal to that after executing the path optimization, thus we take the result of the node optimization. These two situations mean we can get minimal size of paths and decision nodes at the same time. Otherwise, we can't have an optimized ROBDD in both ways. A compromise between the two measures should be considered in *node_path_pair_selection*(). Here, end users have to specify it according with their requirements. For example, the customer may only concern the number of 1-paths regardless of number of nodes or the other way around. A sample solution based on geometric distance [32] for this MCO problem could be resolved by Eq. (12). Selection of a point that is closest to the Optimal Point (OP). A preference is given to the point with the smallest number of 1-paths, when multiple points have the same distance to the OP.

$$Distance\_to\_OP = \sqrt{(n\_opti)^2 + (p\_opti)^2} \tag{12}$$

5   Experimental Verification

Based on the SLA template (Table 1), we assume that a customer starts an SLA negotiation for service "IaaS-1", given that business hours are between 09:00 and 17:00. The customer needs one VM with 2 or 4 CPU cores, CPU speed is either 2.4 GHz or 3.0 GHz, memory size is 2 GB, network is 10 Gb/s Net-1, either OS-1 or OS-2 is selected and customer's private image is uploaded, service availability must be 99.99% or higher; Or a VM with 1 CPU core, CPU speed must be 2.4 GHz, memory size is 1 GB, network is 10 Gb/s either Net-1 or Net-2, either OS-1 or OS-2 is selected, no private image is uploaded, service availability is at least 99.9% or higher.

Table 2 illustrates the set of facts and clauses that we will use for this use case scenario. It is straightforward to see that these facts and clauses can be considered as Boolean variables, which evaluate to true or false. The SLA can also be correctly evaluated if it is modeled according to the following equations.

$$f_1 = x_1 \wedge x_2 \tag{13}$$

Table 2. Example clauses of an SLA template

Variable	Proposition	Proposition Type
x_1	Service_name = "IaaS-1"	Fact
x_2	Business_hours = 09:00 - 17:00	Fact
x_3	VM = "1"	Clause
$x_5 \vee x_6$	CPU_core = "2" or "4"	Clause
$x_7 \vee x_8$	CPU_speed = "2.4 or 3.0" GHz	Clause
x_{10}	Memory = "2 GB"	Clause
x_{11}	10 Gb/s Network = "Net-1"	Clause
x_{13}	Storage = "Private image"	Clause
$x_{14} \vee x_{15}$	Storage = "OS-1 image" or "OS-2 image"	Clause
x_{16}	Service_availability $\geq$ 99.99%	Clause
x_3	VM = "1"	Clause
x_4	CPU_core = "1"	Clause
x_7	CPU_speed = "2.4 GHz"	Clause
x_9	Memory = "1 GB"	Clause
$x_{11} \vee x_{12}$	10 Gb/s Network = "Net-1" or "Net-2"	Clause
$\neg x_{13}$	Storage != "Self image"	Clause
$x_{14} \vee x_{15}$	Storage = "OS-1 image" or "OS-2 image"	Clause
x_{17}	Service_availability $\geq$ 99.9%	Clause

$$f_2 = x_3 \wedge (x_5 \vee x_6) \wedge (x_7 \vee x_8) \wedge x_{10} \wedge x_{11} \tag{14}$$

$$f_3 = x_{13} \wedge (x_{14} \vee x_{15}) \wedge x_{16} \tag{15}$$

$$f_4 = x_3 \wedge x_4 \wedge x_7 \wedge x_9 \wedge (x_{11} \vee x_{12}) \tag{16}$$

$$f_5 = \neg x_{13} \wedge (x_{14} \vee x_{15}) \wedge x_{17} \tag{17}$$

$$SLA = f_1 \wedge ((f_2 \wedge f_3) \vee (f_4 \wedge f_5)) \tag{18}$$

This SLA request is firstly transformed to an initial ROBDD with 29 decision nodes and 40 1-paths. Memory requirement is 87 indices and pointers. By applying the term rewriting, the number of 1-paths of the initial ROBDD is reduced to be 12, however, the decision nodes are increased by 2 (31 decision nodes).

As already mentioned in Section 4.3, we can further optimize this ROBDD by using the node optimization. There will be 30 decision nodes in this ROBDD (see Fig. 2 (a)). Memory requirement is 90 indices and pointers. Alternatively, by applying the path and node optimization, the initial ROBDD is optimized to be with 21 decision nodes and 12 1-paths. Memory requirement is 63 indices and pointers. (see Fig. 2 (b)). Eventually, we attempted to simulate the similar SLA negotiation above for 1000 times to compare the performance of three approaches. We reused our planning and optimization algorithms in [3] to balance the price, profit and failure rate. Each time, the SLA template was customized randomly by selecting different combinations of options for all the SLA terms. Each SLA template was first transformed into an initial ROBDD using the approach in [20]. Then we rewrote the same initial ROBDD using TRS, and following that we used BDD node optimization to reduce the nodes of TRS ROBDD by the greatest extent. Finally, we optimized the initial ROBDD by using BDD optimization algorithms. All the decision nodes and 1-paths for each approach were aggregated and compared with each other. Additionally, we assumed that each round of negotiation starts when the customer submits the SLA template to SLA manager and stops when the SLA manager sends an offer or a counter-offer back to the customer. The total negotiation time of each approach

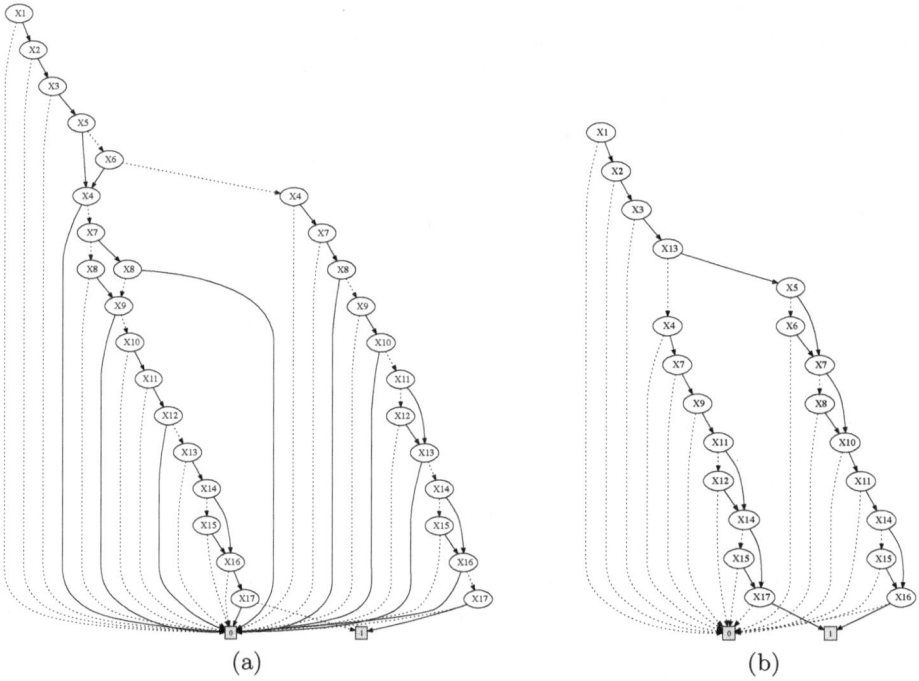

(a)   (b)

Fig. 2. (a) The ROBDD with 30 decision nodes and 12 1-paths by applying term rewriting and node optimization. (b) The ROBDD with 21 decision nodes and 12 1-paths by applying path and node optimization

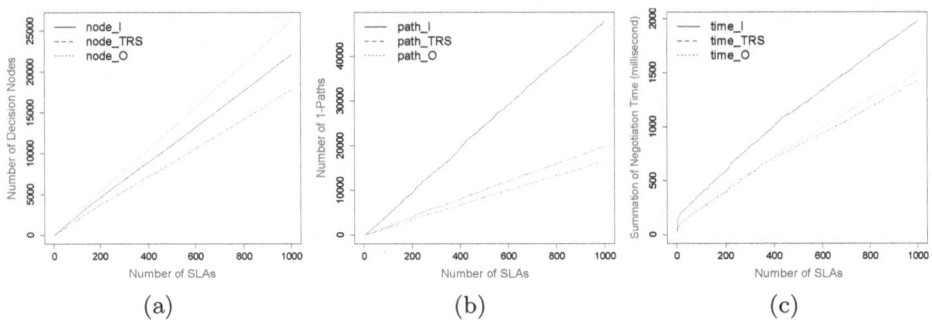

Fig. 3. The number of nodes (a), 1-paths (b) and negotiation time (c) statistics of the initial ROBDD (blue), the TRS ROBDD (red) and the ROBDD after running BDD optimization algorithms (green)

was counted. Thus, the whole simulation took approximately 13521 seconds on a 1.8 GHz processor. Initial ROBDDs had 22123 decision nodes ($node\_I$) and 47880 1-paths ($path\_I$) and the negotiation time ($time\_I$) was 1982 milliseconds (ms). Fig. 3 (a) illustrates that the number of decision nodes increased proportionally in all approaches. The TRS ROBDDs had the most decision nodes ($node\_TRS$=26421), because the least number of 1-path ($path\_TRS$=16554) in Fig. 3 (b) and the least negotiation time ($time\_TRS$=1432 ms) in Fig. 3 (c) were realized at the cost of nodes. *Eclectically*, BDD optimization algorithms not only reduced the number of decision nodes ($node\_O$=17838) and redundant 1-paths ($path\_O$=19804) efficiently, but also showed their time saving ($time\_O$=1505 ms) feature. The TRS approach accurately represented the requirements of the customer, therefore all its 1-paths were valid paths. By setting $path\_TRS$ as a benchmark, the differences between $path\_TRS$ and the 1-path number of other approaches were semantically redundant 1-paths. Thus, the $time\_I$ and $time\_O$ were greater than the $time\_TRS$, since they had to use an extra algorithm to verify the invalid 1-paths during the SLA negotiation. Experimentally, it was proved that after running 1-path verification, the rest 1-paths of the initial ROBDD and the ROBDD by applying path and node optimization was exactly the same as the one of the TRS ROBDD with respect to quantity and semantic meaning.

In summary, the TRS/node optimization led to the most reduction in number of 1-paths (65.43%) and negotiation time (27.75%), although the number of decision nodes had an increase of 19.43%. Furthermore, BDD node/path optimizations led to the most reduction in number of decision nodes, which was 19.37%. Moreover, they had reduction in number of 1-paths (58.64%) and negotiation time (24.07%), but it may still not completely eliminate all the semantically redundant 1-paths, for which reason, the SLA manager requires more time to verify 1-paths during the negotiation. However, it could be a good eclectic approach. From another standpoint, for example, at 1000 ms of the SLA negotiation, the respective SLA number of three approaches were $SLAs\_I$=397, $SLAs\_TRS$=650 and $SLAs\_O$=605. Therefore, the TRS approach had the most SLAs and potentially led to more profits and higher customer satisfaction.

6   Conclusions and Future Work

The negotiation of SLAs in service computing overall, and cloud computing in specific, can be supported by the modeling of SLAs as ROBDDs. Nevertheless, ROBDDs may be suboptimal in structure. In this paper, we show that by applying the BDD node optimization, the number of nodes can be decreased efficiently. Thus, SLAs occupy less memory space. Additionally, the size of semantically redundant 1-paths can be eliminated through the BDD path optimization. Consequently, the SLA negotiation is accelerated by assessing fewer SLA proposals (1-paths). Furthermore, we build on the observation that the options of an SLA term may be mutually exclusive. Thus, an SLA term is rewritten as correctly selecting an option for this term. This process can be treated as an implementation of an *SLA term rewriting system*. Hence, the approach above can eliminate the number of semantically redundant 1-paths at BDD creation phase. Finally, we discuss the strengths and weaknesses of the approaches with an IaaS use case.

In the future, we wish to apply TRS to SLA translation. Furthermore, a suitable representation and transformation would need to be defined to be able to use term rewriting into our scenario. Besides, there is a gap in using the canonical form of the structure for outsourcing and decision-making, related to matching paths from different BDDs and finding out whether they are equivalent so that the outsourced requirements match the available services from sub-contractors.

References

1. Vázquez, T., Huedo, E., Montero, R.S., Llorente, I.M.: Evaluation of a Utility Computing Model Based on the Federation of Grid Infrastructures. In: Kermarrec, A.-M., Bougé, L., Priol, T. (eds.) Euro-Par 2007. LNCS, vol. 4641, pp. 372–381. Springer, Heidelberg (2007)
2. Zhang, Q., Cheng, L., Boutaba, R.: Cloud computing: state-of-the-art and research challenges. Journal of Internet Services and Applications, 7–18 (2010)
3. Lu, K., Roeblitz, T., Chronz, P., Kotsokalis, C.: SLA-Based Planning for Multi-Domain Infrastructure as a Service. In: 1st International Conference on Cloud Computing and Services Science, pp. 343–351. Springer (2011)
4. Lu, K., Roeblitz, T., Yahyapour, R., Yaqub, E., Kotsokalis, C.: QoS-aware SLA-based Advanced Reservation of Infrastructure as a Service. In: Third IEEE International Conference on Coud Computing Technology and Science (CloudCom 2011), pp. 288–295. IEEE Computer Society (2011)
5. Antonopoulos, N., Gillam, L.: Cloud Computing: Principles, Systems and Applications. Springer (2010)
6. Shannon, C.E.: A symbolic analysis of relay and switching circuits. AIEE (57), 713–723 (1938)
7. Wu, L.L., Buyya, R.: Service Level Agreement (SLA) in Utility Computing Systems. Architecture, 27 (2010)
8. Chazalet, A.: Service Level Checking in the Cloud Computing Context. In: IEEE 3rd International Conference on Cloud Computing, pp. 297–304 (2010)
9. Ron, S., Aliko, P.: Service level agreements. Internet NG project (2001)
10. Ebendt, R., Drechsler, R.: Advanced BDD Optimization. Springer (2005)

11. Rudell, R.: Dynamic variable ordering for ordered binary decision diagrams. In: IEEE/ACM International Conference on Computer-Aided Design, pp. 8–15. IEEE Computer Society Press, Los Alamitos (1993)
12. Andersen, H.R.: An Introduction to Binary Decision Diagrams, pp. 8–15. Citeseer (1999)
13. JavaBDD (2007), http://javabdd.sourceforge.net/
14. Klop, J.W.: Term Rewriting Systems. Stichting Mathematisch Centrum, Amsterdam (1990)
15. Baader, F., Nipkow, T.: Term Rewriting and All That, pp. 1–2, 34–35. Cambridge University Press (1999)
16. Open Grid: Web Services Agreement Specification (2007), http://www.ogf.org/
17. Keller, A., Ludwig, H.: Specifying and Monitoring Service Level Agreements for Web Services. Journal of Network and Systems Management, 57–81 (2003)
18. Christensen, E., Curbera, F., Meredith, G., Weerawarana, S.: Web Services Description Language (WSDL) 1.1 W3C Note, World Wide Web Consortium (2001)
19. Kearney, K.T., Torelli, F., Kotsokalis, C.: SLA*: An abstract syntax for Service Level Agreements. In: GRID, pp. 217–224 (2010)
20. Kotsokalis, C., Yahyapour, R., Rojas Gonzalez, M.A.: Modeling Service Level Agreements with Binary Decision Diagrams. In: Baresi, L., Chi, C.-H., Suzuki, J. (eds.) ICSOC-ServiceWave 2009. LNCS, vol. 5900, pp. 190–204. Springer, Heidelberg (2009)
21. Amazon EC2 Cloud (2012), http://aws.amazon.com/ec2/
22. Bartlett, J.: Best Practice for Service Delivery. The Stationery Office (2007)
23. Chandra, A., Goyal, P., Shenoy, P.: Quantifying the benefits of resource multiplexing in on-demand data centers. In: 1st ACM Workshop on Algorithms and Architectures for Self-Managing Systems (2003)
24. Machado, G.S., Stillerm, B.: Investigations of an SLA Support System for Cloud Computing. In: Praxis der Informationsverarbeitung und Kommunikation (2011)
25. Open Cloud Computing Interface Specification (2012), http://occi-wg.org/about/specification/
26. Opennebula (2012), http://opennebula.org/
27. 74LVC1G386, 3-input Exclusive-Or gate, Data Sheet, NXP B.V. (2007)
28. Prasad, P.W.C., Raseen, M., Senanayake, S.M.N.A., Assi, A.: BDD Path Length Minimization Based on Initial Variable Ordering. Journal of Computer Science (2005)
29. SLA@SOI (2011), http://sla-at-soi.eu/
30. Yaqub, E., Wieder, P., Kotsokalis, C., Mazza, V., Pasquale, L., Rueda, J., Gomez, S., Chimeno, A.: A Generic Platform for Conducting SLA Negotiations. In: Wieder, P., Butler, J., Yahyapour, R. (eds.) Service Level Agreements For Cloud Computing, Part 4, pp. 187–206. Springer (2011)
31. Drechsler, R., Guenther, W., Somenzi, F.: Using lower bounds during dynamic BDD minimization. IEEE Trans. on CAD, 50–57 (2001)
32. Ehrgott, M.: Multicriteria Optimization, 2nd edn., pp. 171–195. Springer (2005)

A Service Composition Framework Based on Goal-Oriented Requirements Engineering, Model Checking, and Qualitative Preference Analysis[*]

Zachary J. Oster[1], Syed Adeel Ali[2], Ganesh Ram Santhanam[1],
Samik Basu[1], and Partha S. Roop[2]

[1] Department of Computer Science, Iowa State University, Ames, Iowa 50011, USA
{zjoster,gsanthan,sbasu}@iastate.edu
[2] Department of Electrical and Computer Engineering,
The University of Auckland, New Zealand
{sali080,p.roop}@auckland.ac.nz

Abstract. To provide an effective service-oriented solution for a business problem by composing existing services, it is necessary to explore all available options for providing the required functionality while considering both the users' preferences between various non-functional properties (NFPs) and any low-level constraints. Existing service composition frameworks often fall short of this ideal, as functional requirements, low-level behavioral constraints, and preferences between non-functional properties are often not considered in one unified framework. We propose a new service composition framework that addresses all three of these aspects by integrating existing techniques in requirements engineering, preference reasoning, and model checking. We prove that any composition produced by our framework provides the required high-level functionality, satisfies all low-level constraints, and is at least as preferred (w.r.t. NFPs) as any other possible composition that fulfills the same requirements. We also apply our framework to examples adapted from the existing service composition literature.

1 Introduction

Service-oriented architectures [8] have become increasingly popular as a way to support rapid development of new applications. These applications may be implemented as *composite services* (also known as *compositions*) that are formed from existing services. The process of developing a composite service that satisfies a given set of user requirements is called *service composition* [16].

Requirements for a service composition may be divided into three main types: functional requirements, behavioral constraints, and non-functional properties. *Functional requirements* describe *what* actions or capabilities are to be provided; for instance, an e-commerce composite service must have a component that handles online payment options. These include both high-level requirements (e.g.,

---

[*] This work is supported in part by U.S. National Science Foundation grants CCF0702758 and CCF1143734.

the composition must process online payments) and more detailed low-level requirements (e.g., the composition shall verify the identity of credit-card users). *Behavioral constraints* describe *how* the functionality must be provided by specifying required interactions and/or ordering of the component services. For example, the e-commerce composite service must be composed so that the shipping service is not invoked before the payment is confirmed and an address is verified.

Non-functional properties (NFPs) may include quality of service (QoS), cost, scalability, or other desirable properties that are not necessary for the composition to perform the required tasks. Ideally, a composition would satisfy the entire set of NFPs, but in practice trade-offs between NFPs must often be considered. For example, some users might prefer the increased security of locally-hosted services over the greater scalability of cloud-based services. A service composition framework must consider preferences and trade-offs between NFPs in order to identify a composition that satisfies all functional requirements and behavioral constraints while fulfilling an *optimal* set of NFPs.

The Driving Problem. While there exist a number of service composition frameworks and algorithms associated with them (many of which are surveyed in [16]), very few of them consider all of these aspects in a single framework. These existing methods often have one or more other important drawbacks:

- They frequently treat all functional requirements as mandatory, choosing between several versions of the same low-level functionality instead of considering diverse low-level implementations of the same high-level functionality.
- They typically do not focus on verifying low-level behavioral constraints.
- They often consider only NFPs that affect the QoS of the composition but ignore other important NFPs, especially those that are not easily quantified.
- They typically require that the names and/or structures of a service's accepted inputs and available outputs exactly match those of other services.

Our Solution. The *contribution* of our work is a service composition framework that addresses the above shortcomings in the following fashion:

- A **Goal Model** (as used in the Goal-Oriented Requirements Engineering (GORE) [5] methodology) is used to describe the functional requirements for a composite service. Non-functional properties are associated with the nodes of the goal model to indicate how satisfaction of each requirement by an existing service contributes to the satisfaction of the NFPs.
- A **Conditional Importance Preference Network** (CI-net) [3] is used to formally describe qualitative preferences and trade-offs between non-functional properties. We claim that it is more intuitive to express preferences over NFPs in qualitative terms because not all trade-offs may be naturally quantifiable (e.g., it may be difficult or even impossible to describe to what extent locally hosted services are preferred to cloud-based services).
- **Model Checking** is used to automatically construct a composition that satisfies behavioral constraints specified in Computation Tree Logic (CTL) [7]. The final composite service is chosen from a set of preferred candidate compositions that satisfy the overall functional requirements. Structural mismatches between input/output data types are also resolved in this step.

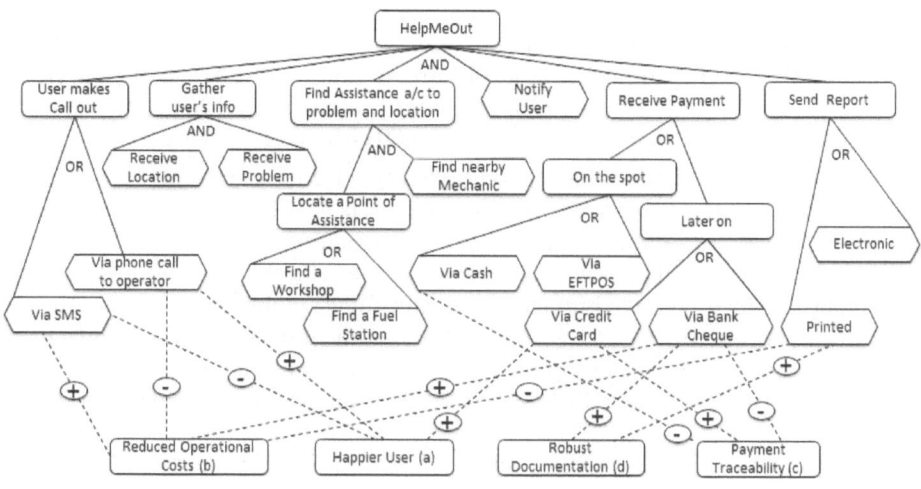

Fig. 1. *HelpMeOut* goal model

We formally *prove the correctness* of the results computed by our framework. We also show our framework's *practical feasibility* by applying it to produce a correct composite service that solves a non-trivial service composition problem.

This work advances the state of the art in service composition by considering high-level functional requirements, low-level behavioral specifications [1], and NFPs [14] all at once, which allows the search space for candidate compositions to be effectively reduced (relative to considering these aspects separately). Although a few existing techniques provide such integrated solutions, our framework handles a wider range of problems than those techniques.

Organization. Section 2 introduces the example used to demonstrate our approach. Section 3 describes the existing concepts that form the basis of our composition framework. Section 4 presents our framework in detail and proves its correctness. Section 5 describes our implementation and results from three case studies. Section 6 discusses related work on similar problems in service composition. Section 7 concludes the paper and discusses future avenues for research.

2 Illustrative Example

We motivate our composition approach using the example of *HelpMeOut*, a proposed service composition (taken and modified from [1]) that makes it easier for a vehicle's driver to call for assistance in case of an emergency.

Functional Requirements. Figure 1 presents the functional requirements for the *HelpMeOut* system using a goal model (AND-OR graph). They include collecting the vehicle's location and problem, searching for a nearby point of assistance, locating a mechanic that can visit the user, receiving payment, and reporting the event. Intermediate requirements appear in round-edged boxes, while basic requirements that may be realized from available services are shown in hexagons. The graph illustrates dependencies between the requirements. For instance, the root (level 0) describes the overall functional requirement, which is realizable if all of the requirements at level 1 are satisfied (**AND-decomposition**). In contrast, the requirement *Receive Payment* is satisfied if either of the requirements *On the Spot* or *Later On* is satisfied (**OR-decomposition**).

Preferences and Trade-offs. Along with functional requirements, Figure 1 captures dependencies between NFPs and services. These are represented in boxes which are connected to functional requirements via edges annotated with "+" or "-". The "+" annotation represents the satisfaction of the functional requirement having a positive impact on the non-functional property, while the "-" annotation represents a negative impact. For instance, satisfying the requirement that the users can contact an operator via a phone call may result in a happier user (positive impact) but will have a negative impact on reducing operational cost.

It may not be possible to consider a set of basic requirements such that (a) they have only positive impacts on the NFPs, (b) all NFPs are considered, and (c) the root-level requirement is satisfied following the traditional semantics of "and" and "or". Therefore, preferences and trade-offs over NFPs are important for identifying a preferred set of basic requirements that result in satisfying the root-level requirement. Consider the following preference statements:

1. If robust documentation is used, payment traceability is more important than reducing operational costs.
2. If costs are reduced at the expense of customer satisfaction, then using robust documentation takes precedence over ensuring payment traceability.

Behavioral Constraints. While functional requirements describe the necessary functionalities, behavioral constraints ensure correct low-level interaction or ordering of the services participating in the composition. For example, *Help-MeOut* requires that if the *EFTPOS* or the *Cash* service is used for payment on the spot, then a printed report should be sent instead of an electronic report.

Annotated Service Repository. Suppose there is a repository of services that are available for use in the composition. Each service is specified using a standard service specification language such as WSDL [4], which describes the service's high-level functionality (semantics) as well as its inputs, outputs, and low-level behavior. From this complete specification, a *labeled transition system* (LTS), which captures the dynamics of the service, is extracted manually.

LTSs for the services in our repository are depicted in Figure 3. Because the *PhoneCall* and *SMS* services serve only as interfaces between a user and the system, their LTSs are not shown to avoid complexity.

3   Preliminaries

3.1   Goal Model: Decomposition of Functional Requirements

The overall functionality of the composition Θ can be decomposed into a Boolean combination of individual functionalities θ [14]. The relationships between θs in this Boolean combination can be represented graphically as an *AND-OR* graph $\mathcal{G}^\Theta$ such as the one for the *HelpMeOut* service in Figure 1. The basic functional requirements that can be realized from available services are optionally associated with NFPs to denote their positive or negative impact. This combination of decomposition of functional requirements and associations to NFPs is known as a *goal model*. Goal models are key to the Goal-Oriented Requirements Engineering [5] methodology, where they are used for the same purposes.

3.2   CI-Nets: Expressing NFP Preferences

In our framework, the user specifies preferences between different sets of NFPs in a qualitative preference language called *Conditional Importance Networks* (CI-nets) [3]. A CI-net P is a collection of statements of the form $S^+, S^- : S_1 > S_2$, where S^+, S^-, S_1, and S_2 are pairwise disjoint subsets of NFPs. Each statement specifies that if there are two outcomes (two candidate services satisfying all functional requirements) where both satisfy S^+ and none satisfy S^-, then the outcome that satisfies S_1 is preferred to the one that satisfies S_2. The preference order induced by the CI-net follows the semantics of these statements as well as a monotonicity rule, which ensures that an outcome satisfying a set Γ of NFPs is preferred to outcomes that satisfy the set $\Gamma' \subset \Gamma$ (all else being equal).

The semantics of CI-nets is given formally in terms of a *flipping sequence* [3]. Given two outcomes γ and γ', γ' is preferred to γ (denoted by $\gamma' \succ \gamma$) if and only if there exists a sequence of outcomes $\gamma = \gamma_1, \gamma_2, \ldots, \gamma_n = \gamma'$ such that for each $i \in [1, n-1]$, one of the following is true:

- γ_{i+1} satisfies one more NFP than γ_i.
- γ_{i+1} satisfies $S^+ \cup S_1$ and does not satisfy S^-; γ_i satisfies $S^+ \cup S_2$ and does not satisfy S^-; and there exists a CI-net statement $S^+, S^-; S_1 > S_2$.

Deciding whether one outcome is preferred to another (with respect to the CI-net semantics) is referred to as *dominance testing*. It relies on generating an *induced preference graph* (IPG), which represents the partial order between outcomes based on the preference semantics, and then verifying reachability of one outcome from another: γ' is reachable from γ if and only if an improving flipping sequence exists from γ to γ'. In [13], we have presented a model checking-based approach for dominance testing based on preferences expressed in CI-nets.

Example 1. Consider the preferences given in Section 2. The first preference can be expressed as CI-net statement

$$\{Robust\ Documentation\}; \{\} : \\ \{Payment\ Traceability\} > \{Reduced\ Operational\ Costs\} \tag{1}$$

The second preference can be expressed as CI-net statement

$$\{Reduced\ Operational\ Costs\}; \{Happier\ User\} : \\ \{Robust\ Documentation\} > \{Payment\ Traceability\} \tag{2}$$

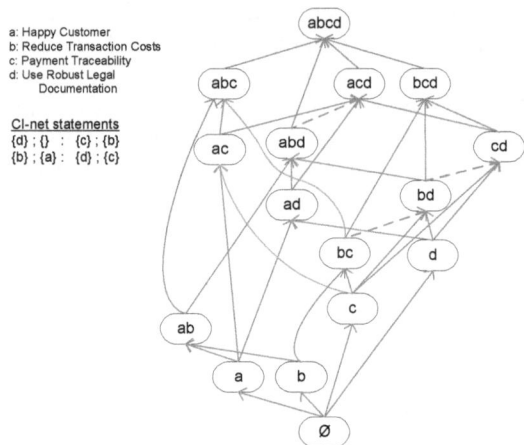

Fig. 2. Induced preference graph for CI-net statements 1 and 2

Figure 2 shows the IPG corresponding to the preferences expressed by these CI-net statements for the illustrative example in Section 2. Each directed edge in the graph represents a "flip" from a less-preferred set of NFPs to a more-preferred set. Solid edges (e.g., from $\{c\}$ to $\{bc\}$) indicate *monotonicity flips*; here, the set $\{Reduced\ Operational\ Costs,\ Payment\ Traceability\}$ is preferred because it has one more NFP than the set $\{Payment\ Traceability\}$. Dashed edges (e.g., from $\{bc\}$ to $\{bd\}$) indicate *importance flips*, which are induced by a CI-net statement (in this case, by statement 2 above). Figure 2 shows that the set of all NFPs is most preferred, while the empty set (no NFPs satisfied) is least preferred.

3.3   Service Representations and Composition

Labeled transition systems (LTS) [7] represent the low-level behaviors of services in our system. An LTS is a digraph where nodes model states and edges represent transitions. It is given by a tuple: $(S, s_0, \Delta, I, O, AP, L)$, where S is the set of states, $s_0 \in S$ is the start state, $\Delta \subseteq S \times (I \cup O) \times S$ is the set of transitions where each transition is labeled with an input action $\in I$ or an output action $\in O$, AP is the set of atomic propositions, and L is a labeling function which maps each state $\in S$ to a set of propositions $\subseteq AP$. The labeling function describes configurations or states of the LTS. We use the notation $s \xrightarrow{!a} s'$ (resp. $s \xrightarrow{?a} s'$) to denote output (resp. input) action a when the system moves from s to s'.

Figure 3 illustrates the LTSs of available services that can be used to realize the composite service discussed in Section 2. With $AP = \{t_0, t_1, t_2, t_3, t_4\}$ and $S = \{s_0, s_1, s_2, s_3, s_4\}$, the LTS for the *Vehicle* service moves from the start state s_0 to state s_1 after the action `Location`: $s_0 \xrightarrow{\text{Location}} s_1$. The state s_1 moves to state s_2 when the service outputs the `Problem` description. This is followed by the input `MechCntct`, which contains the contact information for the mechanic,

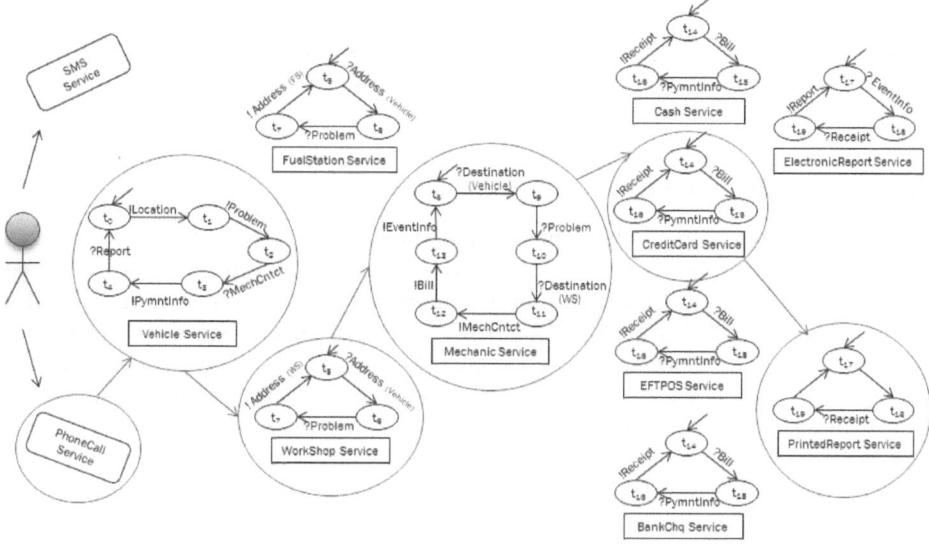

Fig. 3. *HelpMeOut* services. Circled services constitute the final composition.

and then by the output `PymntInfo`. Finally, the system moves back from state s_4 to state s_0 with the output of a `Report` of the incident.

Formally, given $\text{LTS}_i = (S_i, s_{0i}, \Delta_i, I_i, O_i, AP_i, L_i)$ where $i \in \{1, 2\}$ and $AP_1 \cap AP_2 = \emptyset$, the synchronous parallel composition $\text{LTS}_1 \times \text{LTS}_2$ is defined as $(S, s_0, \Delta, \tau, AP, L)$, such that $S \subseteq S_1 \times S_2$, $s_0 = (s_{01}, s_{02})$, $AP = AP_1 \cup AP_2$, $L((s_1, s_2)) = L(s_1) \cup L(s_2)$, and $\Delta \subseteq S \times [\tau]S$: $(s_1 s_2) \xrightarrow{\tau} (s_1' s_2') \Leftarrow s_1 \xrightarrow{!a} s_1' \wedge s_2 \xrightarrow{?a} s_2'$. In other words, a parallel composition of LTSs representing services describes all possible behaviors exhibited by the services via exchange of messages (output from one is consumed by input to another).

3.4 Behavioral Constraints

We use an expressive temporal logic named Computation Tree Logic (CTL) [7] to describe the behavioral constraints. A CTL formula φ is described over a set of atomic propositions AP as follows:

$$\varphi \rightarrow AP \mid \textbf{true} \mid \neg\varphi \mid \varphi \wedge \varphi \mid \textbf{E}(\varphi\textbf{U}\varphi) \mid \textbf{AF}\varphi$$

The semantics of a CTL formula, denoted by $[\![\varphi]\!]$, is given in terms of the sets of states where the formula is satisfied. AP is satisfied in all states which are labeled with the propositions in AP, `true` is satisfied in all states, $\neg\varphi$ is satisfied in states which do not satisfy φ, and $\varphi_1 \wedge \varphi_2$ is satisfied in states which satisfy both φ_1 and φ_2. $\textbf{E}(\varphi_1\textbf{U}\varphi_2)$ is satisfied in states from which there exists a path to a state satisfying φ_2 along which φ_1 is satisfied in all states. Finally, $\textbf{AF}\varphi$ is satisfied in states from which all paths eventually end in a state satisfying φ.

Example 2. Recall the behavioral constraint specified in Section 2, which stated that if either the *EFTPOS* or the *Cash* service is used for payment *On the Spot*, then a printed report should be sent instead of an electronic report. This can be expressed by the CTL statement $\mathtt{AG}((EFTPOS \vee Cash) \Rightarrow \mathtt{AX}(PrintedReport))$.

3.5   Data Mismatches

A data mismatch occurs when the input and output actions of two services that can potentially communicate do not match. Data mismatches can be classified as systemic, syntactic, structural, and semantic [15]. Systemic level mismatches are no longer a problem due to standardized network protocols like IP, TCP, and UDP. Syntactic mismatches are automatically resolved by using a standard service description language such as WSDL (Web Service Description Language [4]).

A semantic mismatch occurs when communicating services refer to the same piece of information with different names. For example, in Figure 3 the vehicle's location is sent via an output `Location`, while *FuelStation* and *Mechanic* services expect to consume the location information via input actions `Address` and `Destination` respectively. We address this problem using a data dictionary [1]. The dictionary elements — expressing distinct concepts — are grouped as sets of synonyms, resulting in a collection of meaningfully linked words and concepts.

A structural mismatch occurs when the data received by a service is found in other-than-expected order, style or shape. Differences in number or order of XML tags of interacting services are examples of structural mismatches. We utilize the graph-theoretic solution introduced in [1] to address this problem.

4   Service Composition Framework

Our service composition framework takes as input the entire set of functional requirements, the preferences and trade-offs over non-functional properties, the given behavioral constraints, and a repository of available services. Given these inputs, our framework automatically constructs a composite service that is most preferred (optimal) with respect to the users' non-functional property preferences and that satisfies the functional requirements and all behavioral constraints.

4.1   Specifying the Service Composition Problem

The inputs to the service composition framework are:

Θ A goal model, which shows a Boolean (AND/OR) combination of functional requirements θ and their impact on non-functional properties.

P A preference relation specified using a CI-net, which forms a partial order over the powerset of all NFPs under consideration.

Ψ A set of Computation Tree Logic (CTL) statements ψ that formally describe the behavioral constraints as temporal properties of the composition.

R A repository of services, which are each specified in a standard description language (e.g., WSDL) from which a corresponding LTS has been extracted.

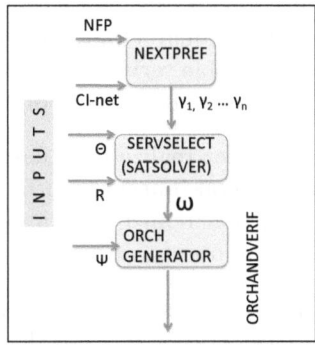

Fig. 4. Overview of framework

The Composition Problem. The objective is to solve the following problem: Does there exist a composition C of services $\in R$ such that

$$[C \text{ satisfies } \Theta \wedge \Psi] \text{ and} \\ \forall \text{ composition } C' \text{ of services} \in R : [C' \text{ satisfies } \Theta \wedge \Psi \Rightarrow C' \not\succ C] \quad (3)$$

In other words, our objective is to identify a composition C such that (1) C satisfies all functional requirements and behavioral constraints and (2) no other composition C' that satisfies these requirements/constraints is preferred to C.

4.2   Selecting, Creating, and Verifying a Composition

Figure 4 illustrates the proposed framework for addressing this problem. The **first module** NEXTPREF uses the non-functional properties NFP and the CI-net statements describing the preferences and trade-offs over them to compute an ordered sequence $\gamma_1, \gamma_2, \ldots, \gamma_n$. Each γ_i in the sequence represents a subset of NFP where $\gamma_{i+1} \not\succ \gamma_i$ with respect to the CI-net statements. In other words, the sequence of γ_is forms a total order consistent with the partial order of the induced preference graph. Based on the techniques proposed in [13], this module represents the induced preference graph (see Figure 2) as an input model of a standard model checker (specifically, NuSMV [6]) and identifies sequence $\gamma_1, \gamma_2, \ldots, \gamma_n$ by verifying carefully selected temporal properties of the IPG.

Example 3. Consider the IPG in Figure 2. To conserve space, let $a = Happier$ *User*, $b = Reduced Operational Costs$, $c = Payment Traceability$, and $d = Robust Documentation$. Clearly $\gamma_1 = \{a, b, c, d\}$ is the most preferred set of NFPs. Next, consider all sets of NFPs with edges pointing to $\{a, b, c, d\}$. Figure 2 contains no edges between three of these sets, which means that none of them are strictly preferred to each other; however, the graph does contain an edge from $\{a, b, d\}$ to $\{a, c, d\}$, which is induced by CI-net statement 1. Therefore, we assign $\gamma_2 = \{a, b, c\}$, $\gamma_3 = \{b, c, d\}$, and $\gamma_4 = \{a, c, d\}$ (although these sets could be in any order). We then assign $\gamma_5 = \{a, b, d\}$, as it is strictly less preferred than γ_4 according to Figure 2. This process continues until all sets of NFPs (including the empty set) have been placed into the sequence.

The **second module** is SERVSELECT. This module takes into account the goal model representing the overall functional requirement Θ and its relationship with the NFPs, the repository R of available services, and the sequence of γ_is in order of preference starting from γ_1. For each γ_i, the module identifies

- the set of services (say X_i^+) that realize functional requirements which have *only* positive impacts on the non-functional properties in γ_i; and
- the set of services (say X_i^-) that realize functional requirements which have *some* negative impacts on the non-functional properties in γ_i.

Example 4. Consider the NFP set γ_4 in Example 3 and the goal model in Figure 1. Based on the dependencies between services that satisfy functional requirements (hexagons in Figure 1) and the NFPs that each service satisfies, SERV-SELECT identifies $X_4^+ = \{PhoneCall,\ CreditCard,\ PrintedReport\}$ and $X_4^- = \{SMSCall,\ Cash,\ BankChq\}$. Services in X_4^+ have only positive impacts on the NFPs in γ_4, while services in X_4^- have a negative impact on some NFP in γ_4.

Next, SERVSELECT solves the satisfaction problem and identifies the set $\mathcal{W}$ of all sets of services Y such that the composition of all services in Y realizes a set of functional requirements which, when satisfied, result in satisfaction of Θ. Note that the presence of OR-nodes in the graph allows Θ to be satisfied in many different ways. Finally, SERVSELECT verifies $X_i^+ \subseteq Y$ and $X_i^- \cap Y = \emptyset$. Satisfaction of these conditions ensures that Y is the most preferred set of services that satisfy Θ and the non-functional properties in γ_i. If the conditions are not satisfied by any assignment Y, the module considers γ_{i+1} from the sequence of γ_is. This is repeated until a suitable service set Y is obtained. In the worst case, the least-preferred (empty) NFP set γ_n will be used; when this occurs, $X_n^+ = X_n^- = \emptyset$, making the above conditions vacuously true. Therefore, a non-empty set Y will always be obtained.

Example 5. Initially, SERVSELECT uses the goal model in Figure 1 and the repository of services that includes all services in Figure 3 to identify all possible compositions of available services that may satisfy the overall functional requirement Θ. Recall the sequence of NFP sets identified in Example 3. Observe in Figure 1 that there exists no combination of low-level functionalities that leads to satisfaction of γ_1 (all NFPs), γ_2, or γ_3. Fortunately, the set of services $Y = \{PhoneCall,\ Vehicle,\ WorkShop,\ Mechanic,\ CreditCard,\ PrintedReport\}$ satisfies the required conditions for γ_4: $X_4^+ \subseteq Y$ and $X_4^- \cap Y = \emptyset$.

The **third module**, ORCHANDVERIF, takes as input the set $\mathcal{W}$ of sets of services Y from the SERVSELECT module and the set of behavioral constraints Ψ expressed in CTL. This module verifies whether there exists an orchestration of services $\in Y$ that satisfies Ψ; it also considers data mismatches when composing services (see Section 3.5). The core of the verification technique is a tableau algorithm which takes services in Y and constructs their orchestration in a goal-directed fashion, possibly including interleaving of services; details of the technique are available in [1]. If the verification fails, a different Y is selected

Algorithm 1. Driver Program

1: **procedure** VERICOMP(Θ, NFP, P, Ψ, R)
2:     $\langle \gamma_1, \gamma_2, \ldots, \gamma_n \rangle :=$ NEXTPREF(NFP, P)
3:     **for** $i = 1 \to n$ **do**
4:         $\mathcal{W} :=$ SERVSELECT(Θ, γ_i, R)
5:         **for all** $Y \in \mathcal{W}$ **do**
6:             $C :=$ ORCHANDVERIF(Y, Ψ, R)
7:             **if** $C \neq \emptyset$ **then**
8:                 **return** C
9:     **return false**
---

from $\mathcal{W}$ and the process is repeated until a suitable Y is identified (*success*) or all elements of $\mathcal{W}$ have been considered (*failure*). Successful termination of the process results in a set of services which (1) satisfies the functional requirements Θ, (2) satisfies all behavioral constraints Ψ, and (3) is most preferred with respect to CI-net preferences over the set of NFPs.

Example 6. Figure 5 presents the successfully generated orchestration of the most preferred set of services (given in Example 5) that fulfills the behavioral constraints (given in Example 2). Recall that the *PhoneCall* service serves as an interface only, so it is omitted from Figure 5 to avoid complexity.

The entire process is presented in the procedure VERICOMP in Algorithm 1. Line 2 invokes NEXTPREF. Lines 3–8 iterate over the sequence of γ_is where SERVSELECT in Line 4 identifies a set $\mathcal{W}$, and ORCHANDVERIF is iteratively invoked in Lines 5–8 to identify the most preferred orchestration C.

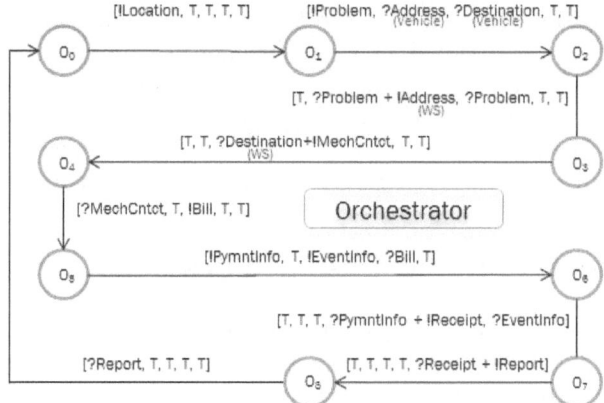

Fig. 5. States and transitions of the synthesized orchestrator. Services are ordered as: [*Vehicle, WorkShop, Mechanic, CreditCard, PrintedReport*].

4.3 Theoretical Properties

Theorem 1 (Soundness & Completeness). *Given an AND-OR combination of functional requirements Θ, a set of behavioral constraints Ψ in terms of temporal properties in CTL, a set of non-functional properties NFP, preferences and trade-offs in CI-nets, and a repository of services R,* VERICOMP *returns a composition C if and only if C satisfies the condition in (3).*

Proof. The SERVSELECT module identifies all sets of services Y such that if the services in Y can be composed, the resulting composition satisfies Θ. Further, given Ψ and a set of services Y as input, the ORCHANDVERIF module returns a composition C if and only if the services in Y can be composed in a way that satisfies all behavioral constraints in Ψ; this follows directly from results in [1].

It remains to prove that for any composition C returned by our framework and for all other compositions C' that satisfy both Θ and Ψ, $C' \not\succ C$. Suppose in contradiction that $C' \succ C$, i.e., C' satisfies a more preferred set of NFPs than C, but our framework returns C. Let γ_C and $\gamma_{C'}$ be the sets of NFPs satisfied by C and C' respectively. By Theorem 1 in [13], $\gamma_{C'}$ precedes γ_C in the sequence returned by NEXTPREF; therefore, our framework attempts to compose and verify C' before considering C. Because C' satisfies both Θ and Ψ, ORCHANDVERIF succeeds in creating and verifying C'. As a result, our framework returns C', contradicting our earlier assumption.   □

Complexity. Let n be the number of leaf-level functional requirements in Θ, let k be the maximum number of services in R satisfying any requirement $\theta \in \Theta$, and let p be the number of NFPs considered. Algorithm 1 (VERICOMP) iterates up to 2^p times over the outer loop (lines 3–8), once per subset of NFP. The largest number of possible compositions returned by SERVSELECT is k^n if all non-leaf nodes in $\mathcal{G}^\Theta$ are AND nodes and if the composition has up to n services. The inner loop (lines 5–8) calls ORCHANDVERIF at most k^n times (once for each possible composition that satisfies the NFP set γ), taking $O(2^n 2^{|\Psi|})$ time per call (where $|\Psi|$ is the number of CTL formulae to be satisfied). The worst-case complexity of our framework, given an AND-OR tree with only leaf and AND nodes, is therefore $O(2^p k^n 2^n 2^{|\Psi|})$. However, we expect k and p to be small in most practical applications. Additionally, each OR node in $\mathcal{G}^\Theta$ improves the worst-case complexity by reducing the number of leaf-level requirements to verify.

5   Implementation and Case Studies

We have implemented our framework as a Java-based tool that is based on existing components. The SERVSELECT module is derived from the goal-model analysis tool in [13], the ORCHANDVERIF module is based on the composition tool in [1], and the NEXTPREF module is built on the NuSMV [6] model checker.

Table 1 displays results from applying our service composition and verification framework to three case studies adapted from the existing literature. These

Table 1. Results of Applying Our Implementation to Three Case Studies

Case Study	High-Level Functions	Services	NFPs	CI-net Rules	Orchestrator States	Orchestrator Trans	Total Run Time (s)	Preference Reasoning Time (s)	Orch. and Verif. Time (s)
HelpMeOut [1]	9	12	4	2	9	9	2.69	1.44	1.25
Online Bookseller [13]	5	9	4	3	16	16	3.00	1.59	1.41
Multimedia Delivery [14]	8	15	3	2	9	10	2.03	0.84	1.19

results were obtained by running our tool on a machine running Windows 7 Professional (32-bit) with 2 GB of RAM and an Intel Core 2 Duo processor running at 1.83 GHz. Each time shown is the mean of the times observed for 10 runs of that operation on that case study. The preference reasoning and orchestration/verification modules each take time on the order of seconds, while service selection (satisfiability analysis) requires minimal time. This is because the semantics of CI-nets requires exploration of the entire induced preference graph, while the behavioral constraints must be verified with respect to all possible executions of the composite service. These results show the feasibility of our composition framework for real-world applications.

More information on our implementation and on the case studies used in this evaluation is available at http://fmg.cs.iastate.edu/project-pages/icsoc12/.

6   Related Work

All service composition frameworks are designed to produce composite services that satisfy users' functional requirements. Some also account for low-level behavioral constraints or non-functional properties, but very few integrate all three in a unified way. The TQoS algorithm [9] provides one such framework. TQoS considers both transactional and QoS properties when composing services, selecting services that have locally optimal QoS for each part of the desired functionality. Additionally, TQoS guarantees by construction that composite services it produces satisfy a standard set of transactional constraints. Our framework goes beyond TQoS in two ways: (1) it more accurately represents users' true preferences between sets of NFPs by using CI-nets instead of a weighted-average method, and (2) it can verify that a composition satisfies *any* behavioral constraint that can be specified using CTL, not just a small fixed set of properties.

The composition method presented in [18] is representative of many techniques that consider both functional and non-functional properties. [18] models the entire problem as an integer linear programming problem, employing simple syntactic matching of inputs and outputs to form the composite service and utilizing quantitative preference valuations for NFPs. In contrast, [17] uses qualitative NFP valuations to select services to compose based on a set of preferences expressed by the user in a different language for qualitative preferences, namely tradeoff-enhanced conditional preference networks (TCP-nets). Our framework's strategy for handling NFP preferences is inspired in part by [17].

In [2], ter Beek et al. focus on verification of functional requirements in a scenario similar to our example in Section 2. The service-oriented architecture in [2]
is modeled as a set of state machines illustrated as UML-like diagrams. Temporal
constraints representing functional requirements and behavioral constraints are
specified in the temporal logic UCTL (an extension of CTL) and verified over the
diagrams using an on-the-fly model checking tool. Though [2] does not consider
NFPs, it shows that model checking is feasible in an industrial-scale service-
oriented computing scenario. Our framework employs model checking for both
verifying behavioral constraints and reasoning over users' NFP preferences to
construct a service composition that truly satisfies the users' needs.

The matching of I/O variable names or types, known as semantic or concept-
based similarity matching, is typically performed using a data dictionary. Liu et
al. [10] used the lexical database WordNet [12] to perform concept-based similarity matching, while we use our own universal dictionary [1] for the same purpose. Another data-related operation, data flow (without handling mismatches),
is performed via routing the data among the ports of Web services. An example
of this is the ASTRO approach [11], where data flow requirements are collected
in a hypergraph called a *data net*, which is then transformed into a State Transition System to become part of a planning domain for composition. Because
neither semantic matching nor data routing are complete data solutions due to
the complex XML schema associated with Web service data types, we proposed
a graph-theoretic solution [1] that bridges these gaps by addressing the problem
at the XML schema level; this is incorporated into the framework in this paper.

7 Conclusions and Future Work

We have presented a framework for service composition that takes into account
high-level functionalities, low-level behaviors, and non-functional properties in
order to identify and create the most preferred service composition that provides
the required functionality (if such a composition exists). Our framework makes
use of user-friendly representations for specifying functional requirements and
non-functional properties, but it also uses model checking to obtain guarantees
that a composition will satisfy specified low-level temporal properties. We proved
that our composition algorithm is sound, complete, and weakly optimal with
respect to the user's non-functional property preferences, and we presented initial
results obtained from a prototype implementation of our framework.

The next steps for this work are to refine our current proof-of-concept implementation and empirically compare our tool's performance to similar algorithms
such as [2] and [9]. Our future work includes allowing partial satisfaction of
NFPs as in [5], automating translation of WSDL service specifications to LTSs,
exploring different approaches to dominance testing and different semantics for
expressing preferences, and applying our approach for service composition to the
related problems of service substitution and adaptation.

References

1. Ali, S.A., Roop, P.S., Warren, I., Bhatti, Z.E.: Unified management of control flow and data mismatches in web service composition. In: Gao, J.Z., Lu, X., Younas, M., Zhu, H. (eds.) SOSE, pp. 93–101. IEEE (2011)
2. ter Beek, M.H., Gnesi, S., Koch, N., Mazzanti, F.: Formal verification of an automotive scenario in service-oriented computing. In: ICSE, pp. 613–622. ACM, New York (2008)
3. Bouveret, S., Endriss, U., Lang, J.: Conditional importance networks: A graphical language for representing ordinal, monotonic preferences over sets of goods. In: International Joint Conference on Artificial Intelligence, pp. 67–72 (2009)
4. Chinnici, R., Moreau, J.J., Ryman, A., Weerawarana, S.: Web services description language version 2.0 part 1: Core language. W3C Recommendation, World Wide Web Consortium (June 2007), http://www.w3.org/TR/wsdl20/
5. Chung, L., Nixon, B., Yu, E., Mylopoulos, J.: Non-Functional Requirements in Software Engineering. Kluwer Academic (2000)
6. Cimatti, A., Clarke, E., Giunchiglia, E., Giunchiglia, F., Pistore, M., Roveri, M., Sebastiani, R., Tacchella, A.: NuSMV 2: An OpenSource Tool for Symbolic Model Checking. In: Brinksma, E., Larsen, K.G. (eds.) CAV 2002. LNCS, vol. 2404, pp. 359–364. Springer, Heidelberg (2002)
7. Clarke, E., Grumberg, O., Peled, D.: Model Checking. MIT Press (January 2000)
8. Erl, T.: SOA: Principles of Service Design. Prentice Hall (2008)
9. Haddad, J.E., Manouvrier, M., Rukoz, M.: TQoS: Transactional and QoS-aware selection algorithm for automatic web service composition. IEEE T. Services Computing 3(1), 73–85 (2010)
10. Liu, X., Huang, G., Mei, H.: A user-oriented approach to automated service composition. In: ICWS, pp. 773–776. IEEE Computer Society (2008)
11. Marconi, A., Pistore, M.: Synthesis and Composition of Web Services. In: Bernardo, M., Padovani, L., Zavattaro, G. (eds.) SFM 2009. LNCS, vol. 5569, pp. 89–157. Springer, Heidelberg (2009)
12. Miller, G.A.: WordNet: A lexical database for English. Communications of the ACM 38(11), 39–41 (1995)
13. Oster, Z.J., Santhanam, G.R., Basu, S.: Automating analysis of qualitative preferences in goal-oriented requirements engineering. In: Alexander, P., Pasareanu, C.S., Hosking, J.G. (eds.) ASE, pp. 448–451. IEEE (2011)
14. Oster, Z.J., Santhanam, G.R., Basu, S.: Identifying optimal composite services by decomposing the service composition problem. In: ICWS, pp. 267–274. IEEE Computer Society (2011)
15. Ouksel, A.M., Sheth, A.: Semantic interoperability in global information systems. SIGMOD Rec. 28, 5–12 (1999)
16. Pessoa, R.M., da Silva, E.G., van Sinderen, M., Quartel, D.A.C., Pires, L.F.: Enterprise interoperability with SOA: a survey of service composition approaches. In: van Sinderen, M., Almeida, J.P.A., Pires, L.F., Steen, M. (eds.) EDOCW, pp. 238–251. IEEE Computer Society (2008)
17. Santhanam, G.R., Basu, S., Honavar, V.G.: TCP−Compose* – A TCP-Net Based Algorithm for Efficient Composition of Web Services Using Qualitative Preferences. In: Bouguettaya, A., Krueger, I., Margaria, T. (eds.) ICSOC 2008. LNCS, vol. 5364, pp. 453–467. Springer, Heidelberg (2008)
18. Yoo, J.W., Kumara, S.R.T., Lee, D., Oh, S.C.: A web service composition framework using integer programming with non-functional objectives and constraints. In: CEC/EEE, pp. 347–350. IEEE (2008)

WCP-Nets: A Weighted Extension to CP-Nets for Web Service Selection

Hongbing Wang[1,*], Jie Zhang[2], Wenlong Sun[1],
Hongye Song[1], Guibing Guo[2], and Xiang Zhou[1]

[1] School of Computer Science and Engineering, Southeast University, Nanjing, China
[2] School of Computer Engineering, Nanyang Technological University, Singapore
hbw@seu.edu.cn

Abstract. User preference often plays a key role in personalized applications such as web service selection. CP-nets is a compact and intuitive formalism for representing and reasoning with conditional preferences. However, the original CP-nets does not support fine-grained preferences, which results in the inability to compare certain preference combinations (service patterns). In this paper, we propose a weighted extension to CP-nets called WCP-nets by allowing users to specify the relative importance (weights) between attribute values and between attributes. Both linear and nonlinear methods are proposed to adjust the attribute weights when conflicts between users' explicit preferences and their actual behaviors of service selection occur. Experimental results based on two real datasets show that our method can effectively enhance the expressiveness of user preference and select more accurate services than other counterparts.

1 Introduction

User preference often plays a key role in personalized and AI applications [5] such as web service selection [15,20] in order to support automatic decision making [11,10]. Basically, it can be represented in two ways: quantitative ("I prefer Thai Airline at the level of 0.7") or qualitative ("I prefer Qantas Airline to Thai Airline"). In addition, it can be expressed unconditionally ("No matter what time it is, I always prefer Qantas Airline to Thai Airline") or conditionally ("If time is late, I prefer Qantas Airline to Thai Airline"). However, it is generally agreed that users feel more comfortable and natural to express their preferences in a qualitative and conditional manner [4].

CP-nets [4] is a compact and intuitive formalism for representing and reasoning with conditional preferences under the *ceteris paribus* ("all else being equal") semantics. It has attracted much attention in the literature [3,6,9,7,16,17]. However, it suffers from two inherent issues: 1) users are unable to express their fine-grained preferences. More specifically, they cannot specify the level of their preferences between attribute values or between attributes; 2) due to the limited expressiveness [21], many *service patterns*, each of which is defined as a

---

* This work is supported by NSFC project titled with "System of Systems Software Mechanisms and Methods based on Service Composition" and JSNSF(BK2010417).

C. Liu et al. (Eds.): ICSOC 2012, LNCS 7636, pp. 298–312, 2012.
© Springer-Verlag Berlin Heidelberg 2012

combination of attribute values for all attributes, are incomparable. It is critical and essential for web service selection to effectively reason and represent user preference. Therefore, the expressiveness of CP-nets and the ability to compare service patterns have important impacts on web service selection. To solve these problems, some approaches attempt to enhance the expressiveness by relaxing the *ceteris paribus* semantics of CP-nets and defining a logical framework [21], or by adding relative importance in statements [6], etc. Some others focus on the comparison of service patterns such as using a utility function [3]. However, none of them can well solve these two problems at the same time.

In this paper, we propose a weighted extension to CP-nets called *WCP-nets* by allowing users to express their preferences in a fine-grained manner. More specifically, user preference can be delineated at multiple levels as described in [22]. For example, an attribute value x_0 can be preferred to another attribute value x_1 equally at level 1, or mildly at level 2, ..., or extremely at the maximum level. In addition, the relative importance (weight) between attributes can be explicitly specified as well, reflecting the extent to which an attribute is more important than another. We also propose a new measurement for the degree of preference of any given service pattern, which can be calculated both in linear or nonlinear methods. In this way, not only the expressiveness of WCP-nets is high, but all service patterns can also be compared. Experimental results based on two real datasets demonstrate that WCP-nets outperforms other approaches. In addition, the results also indicate that linear method can converge faster but nonlinear method achieves better accuracy.

2 Background and Related Work

To begin with, we will introduce the basic principles and the concerned problems of CP-nets. Then we will detail the major variants of CP-nets in the literature proposed to enhance the expressiveness of user preference and the effectiveness in comparisons between service patterns. Finally, we will review several recent studies based on CP-nets or its variants for web service selection.

2.1 CP-Nets

CP-nets [4] is a graphical model for representing and reasoning with conditional preference in a compact, intuitive and structural manner. It consists of two parts, namely directed dependence graph (DDG) and conditional preference tables (CPTs). DDG contains a set of attributes $V = \{X_1, ...X_n\}$ represented as nodes, where each node X_i is associated with a finite domain $D(X_i) = \{x_{i1}, ..., x_{in}\}$. A child node X_i is dependent on a set of directed parent nodes $Pa(X_i)$. They are connected by arcs from $Pa(X_i)$ to X_i in the graph. Under the semantics of ceteris paribus ("all else being equal"), the values of X_i is only dependent on the values of $Pa(X_i)$. Thus, a *service pattern* can be defined as a combination of attribute values for all attributes represented in CP-nets, i.e. $sp = x_1x_2 ... x_n$, where $x_i \in D(X_i)$ for $i = 1 ... n$ represents a specific value on attribute X_i.

In addition, each node X_i is annotated with a CPT denoted by $CPT(X_i)$, which expresses user preferences over the attribute values of X_i. A preference between two attribute values x_{i1} and x_{i2} can be specified by the relation $\succ$ given the conditions of the values of $Pa(X_i)$. For example, the preference $x_{11} :$ $x_{21} \succ x_{22}$ indicates that attribute value x_{21} is preferred to another value x_{22} for attribute X_2 if its parent node X_1 has the value x_{11}.

A typical CP-nets is illustrated in Figure 1(a, b). It describes the data storage and access service of a company which consists of three attributes with respect to the quality of service (QoS), namely A : Platform, B : Location and C : Provider. Figure 1(e) shows that each attribute has two specific values. Specifically, data can be stored in either a file system a_1 or a database a_2 which can be located in New York b_1 or Beijing b_2 and can be accessed publicly c_1 or privately c_2. The user has an unconditional preference on Platform that a file system is always preferred to a database. But for the preference of the others, it depends on the choices of previous attributes. For example, if the database is chosen for data storage, then the location in New York is preferred to Beijing. In that case, users prefer data to be accessed publicly rather than privately. Note that this example will be used throughout the rest of this paper.

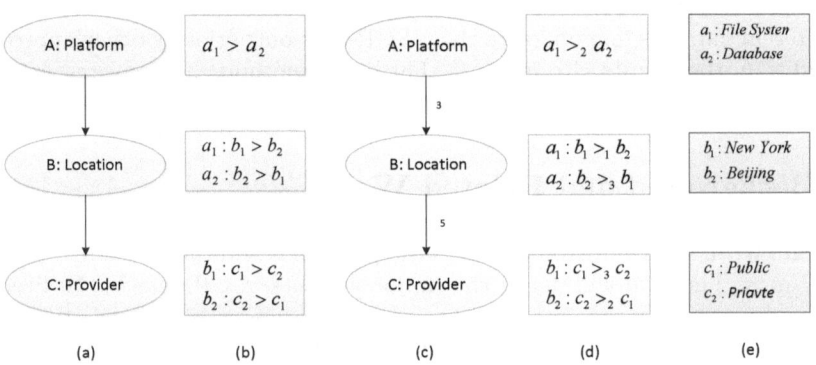

Fig. 1. (a, b) CP-nets; (c, d) WCP-nets; (e) Attribute Values

2.2   Problems of CP-Nets

Although CP-nets is an effective tool to represent and reason with conditional preference, it suffers from two inherent issues. The first is that users are unable to represent more fine-grained preference. For example, in Figure 1(b), the user can only specify that a_1 is preferred to a_2 (i.e. $a_1 \succ a_2$), but not able to indicate to what extent the preference would be. The user may indeed desire to express that a_1 is strongly preferred to a_2.

Another concern is regarding the relative importance between attributes. The dependence relationship in CP-nets merely indicates that parent nodes are more important than their children nodes. This fact usually results in that many service patterns are non-comparable. Take the service patterns $a_2b_2c_2$ and $a_1b_2c_1$ in

Figure 1(a, b) as an example. Although $a_2b_2c_2$ has preferred values on attributes B and C and only violates on attribute A, it is difficult to compare with $a_1b_2c_1$ that has only one preferred value on attribute A but two violations on attributes B and C. The reason is that multiple violations on lower priority (children) attributes may not be preferred to a single violation on a higher priority (parent) attribute.

2.3   Extensions and Variants of CP-Nets

In order to overcome the aforementioned issues, a number of approaches to date have been proposed to extend the original CP-nets in the literature. Some other variations for different purposes (e.g. cyclic preference [9], uncertainty in preference [7]) are not considered in this paper.

Wilson [21] relaxes the ceteris paribus semantics of the CP-nets and proposes a logical framework for expressing conditional preference statements. Specifically, it allows conditional preference statements on the values of an attribute and a set of attributes can vary while interpreting the preference statement. Although this method indeed increases the expressiveness of the CP-nets, it changes the basic reasoning foundations which is different from our proposal.

Boutilier et al. [3] propose a quantitative formalism UCP-nets by enabling users to apply a utility value to each value of attributes other than preference orderings. Service patterns can be compared based on the summed utility value of all attributes. The utility function is a GAI (Generalized Additive Independent) [2] which relies on the structure of CP-nets. Therefore, it is difficult for users to identify a well-suited utility function that can also guarantee the satisfaction of the principles of CP-nets.

Another noticeable extension to CP-nets is proposed by Brafman et al. [6], called Tradeoff CP-net (TCP-nets). It strengthens preference statements by adding relative (qualitative) importance to different attributes. In addition, it maintains the structures and ceteris paribus semantics of CP-nets. Although the expressiveness of TCP-nets is increased to some extent, it is demonstrated in [21] that the expressiveness of TCP-nets is still limited.

In this paper, we propose another significant extension to CP-nets by adding relative importance (weights) between attribute values and between attributes. We name this variant weighted CP-nets, or WCP-nets. The intuition behind is that users may have multiple levels of preference for one state over another [22]. Hence, users are able to express fine-grained preference at multiple preference levels. The concept of *Violation Degree* is introduced to measure the extent to which a service pattern is preferred. In this way, all service patterns can be compared based on this computed value. In addition, we provide two (one linear and another non-linear) methods to flexibly adjust attribute weights such that the measured violation degree well matches users' true preferences.

2.4 CP-Nets in Web Service Selection

There have been a number of studies that model users' qualitative preferences based on CP-nets in order to provide them with personalized web service recommendations. A typical problem for qualitative preference is that users may not express their preferences in detail and some of them could be unspecified. Wang et al. [18] propose that user's missing qualitative preferences could be complemented based on the preferences of similar users, that is, a collaborative filtering method. Wang et al. [19] also indicate that effective web service selection could be done in the absence of complete user preference. Our work does not attempt to elicit more preferences from users, but allow them to express more fine-grained preferences through which web services could be correctly selected.

In addition to CP-nets, other approaches or variants have also been applied to model qualitative preference for web service selection. For example, Santhanam et al. [15] represent user preference by means of TCP-nets through which a set of composite services can be returned. García et al. [8] propose an ontology-based method that transforms user preference modeling to an optimization problem. However, Wang et al. [17] point out that using a qualitative or quantitative approach alone cannot completely handle user preference of web services. Instead, they present user preference by adopting both qualitative and quantitative approaches. In particular, users' qualitative preferences are described by TCP-nets while quantitative preferences are specified by arbitrary positive numbers. Inspired by these studies, we propose to represent user preference in a qualitative way (WCP-nets) and base web service selection on a quantitative method to compute violation degree, i.e. the extent to which a service pattern is preferred.

3 WCP-Nets: A Weighted Extension

In this section, we first describe in detail how to extend CP-nets and how to compare service patterns using the relative importance (weights) based on the concept of violation degree. The weights can be further adjusted linearly or nonlinearly to resolve conflicts between user preference and user behavior. An intuitive example will be presented to exemplify the detailed procedure in the end of this section.

Table 1. The Level of Relative Importance

Level	Definition	Description
1	Equally important	Two values are equally preferred
2	Moderately importance	The first value is mildly preferred to the second
3	Quite importance	The first value is strongly preferred to the second
4	Demonstrably important	The first value is very strongly preferred to the second
5	Extremely important	The first value is extremely preferred to the second

3.1 Adding Weights to Conditional Preference

We adopt the concept of multiple levels of relative importance in [22] but use different level scales, as shown in Table 1. Five-level importance is utilized ranging from level 1 "Equally important" to level 5 "Extremely important". This semantics can be applied to both the relative importance between attribute values and the relative importance between attributes. Formally, we use $\succ_k$ instead of $\succ$ to represent the preference relations in the CPTs, where k refers to the level of relative importance. In addition, the importance level between attributes is assigned and tapped to the arcs in the DDG. The WCP-nets of the previous example is illustrated in Figure 1(c, d). It can be explained that value a_1 is mildly preferred to value a_2 on attribute A which is more important than attribute B at the level of 3. This explanation also holds for the rest.

Since the level of relative importance between attributes is known and the summation of all weights should be 1, the computation of the weights of attributes is trivial. In Figure 1(c), we know $w_B/w_A = 1/3$ and $w_C/w_B = 1/5$, where w_A, w_B, and w_C denote the weight of A, B and C, respectively. Since $w_A + w_B + w_C = 1$, we can easily yield the values of all attribute weights. These computed weights are regarded as the initial attribute weights in our work.

3.2 The Concept of Violation Degree

WCP-nets bases the comparison between service patterns on the concept of violation degree whose definition is given as follows.

Definition 1. *Violation Degree of an Attribute refers to the level of relative importance if the attribute value selected is not preferred for an attribute of a service pattern according to the corresponding CPT. Formally, it is denoted as $V_X(sp)$, where X represents an attribute of a service pattern sp.*

For the attribute A in Figure 1(d), given the preference $a_1 \succ_2 a_2$, if value a_2 is selected in a service pattern (e.g. $a_2b_2c_2$) rather than value a_1 (i.e. the preference is *violated*), then the violation degree V of attribute A is 2, denoted as $V_A(a_2b_2c_2) = 2$. Similarly, given the service pattern $a_1b_1c_2$, we can get the violation degree of attribute C is 3, i.e. $V_C(a_1b_1c_2) = 3$. Generally, the greater the violation degree of an attribute is, the less preferred is the attribute value.

Definition 2. *Violation Degree of a Service Pattern refers to the combination of violation degrees of all attributes for a service pattern, taking into consideration the weights of all attributes. Formally, it is denoted as $V(sp)$ and calculated by*

$$V(sp) = F(w_X, V_X(sp)) \tag{1}$$

where F is an aggregation function, taking into account attribute weights w_X and attribute violation degrees $V_X(sp)$.

There could be different methods to define specific functions for F to calculate the violation degree of a service pattern, linearly or nonlinearly. A simple linear method is a weighted summation of violation degrees of all attributes and the attribute weights. And artificial neuron network (ANN) is used as a nonlinear implementation for the aggregation function F. We will discuss it later in detail. Intuitively, a service pattern is more preferred if it has a smaller violation degree.

3.3   Adjusting Initial Attribute Weights

Although users express their preference explicitly, it does not guarantee that what services they select is consist with what are claimed they would like. Conflicts between user behavior and stated preference could occur in real life. O'Sullivan et al. [14] also confirm that explicit preferences are not always consistent with implicit user behaviors in the filed of recommendations. In this paper, we propose to flexibly adjust attribute weights such that the measured violation degree based on users' explicit preferences well matches users' actual behaviors. Two models are utilized to adjust the attribute weights in line with the two methods (linear and nonlinear) to calculate violation degree of a service pattern. In particular, the Lagrangian model [13] is used for linear adjustment and artificial neuron network (ANN) is for the nonlinear. The basic principle is to adjust the attribute weights of a service pattern when it is selected by a user rather than the one with the smallest violation degree. Given different applications and real constrains, other linear and nonlinear methods may be more suitable since we focus on how to adjust attribute weights in general rather than optimization.

3.3.1   Lagrangian Linear Weight Adjustment
We apply the Lagrangian model [13] to adjust the attribute weights of a selected service pattern if it does not have the smallest violation degree. Luenberger and Ye [13] contend that this method is clear in meaning, simple and practical to change the constrained optimization into unconstrained problems.

Assume that sp' is the best service pattern calculated using the initial attribute weights and sp is the service pattern that a user actually selects. Let w'_k be the initial weight of attribute k, and w_k be the adjusted weight of the same attribute. To be expected, users select the service pattern with the smallest violation degree, i.e. $V(sp) \le V(sp')$. Ideally when the selected service pattern is exactly the computed best service pattern, it can be re-written as

$$\sum_{k=1}^{m} \Big(V_k(sp') - V_k(sp) \Big) w_k = 0 \qquad (2)$$

where m is the number of attributes for the service and $\sum_{k=1}^{m} w_k = 1$. The weights that minimize the summed square of weight variations are the optimal. Aiming to obtain the optimal attribute weights, we construct a single objective optimization model as follows:

$$\begin{cases} \min F(w) = \sum_{k=1}^{m} (w_k - w'_k)^2; \\ \sum_{k=1}^{m} \big(V_k(sp') - V_k(sp) \big) w_k = 0; \\ \sum_{k=1}^{m} w_k = 1. \end{cases} \qquad (3)$$

The Lagrangian model will linearly aggregate constrains in (3) as

$$\sum_{k=1}^{m}(w_k - w_k')^2 + \lambda_1 \sum_{k=1}^{m}(V_k(sp') - V_k(sp))w_k + \lambda_2 \sum_{k=1}^{m} w_k = 1 \qquad (4)$$

Then take the partial derivative of variables to obtain

$$\begin{cases} \frac{\partial L}{\partial w_1} = 2(w_1 - w_1') + (V_1(sp\prime) - V_1(sp\prime)) + \lambda_2 = 0 \\ \vdots \\ \frac{\partial L}{\partial w_m} = 2(w_m - w_m') + (V_m(sp\prime) - V_m(sp)) + \lambda_2 = 0 \\ \sum_{k=1}^{m}(V_k(sp') - V_k(sp))w_k = 0 \\ \sum_{k=1}^{m} w_k = 0 \end{cases} \qquad (5)$$

Finally, we can determine the optimal weights

$$w_k = w_k' - [\delta_k - \frac{\sum_{n=1}^{m} \delta_n}{m}] * \frac{\sum_{n=1}^{m} \delta_n * w_n'}{\sum_{n=1}^{m} \delta_n^2 - \frac{[\sum_{n=1}^{m} \delta_n]^2}{m}} \qquad (6)$$

where $\delta_n = V_n(sp') - V_n(sp)$.

3.3.2   BP-ANN Nonlinear Weight Adjustment

Back propagation (BP) is a supervised learning algorithm which is often used to learn the best weights for the neurons (attributes) in the artificial neural networks (ANNs). ANN is well-suited for learning without a specific mathematical model and able to perform accurate non-linear fit [12]. A typical BP-ANN is shown in Figure 2. The first layer consists of n input units. Each input unit is fully connected to all h hidden units in the middle layer which results in m outputs in the last layer using the same connectivity. One of the advantages of ANN is that it can effectively approximate any complex nonlinear functions which correspond to the nonlinear combination functions in our case.

BP attempts to minimize the *Mean Square Error* (MSE) between the actual outputs and the desired ones. A set of training data is iteratively imported into the network until the learning is converged and the adjusted weights are kept stable. The training data is usually in the form of $< x_1, \ldots, x_n, d_1, \ldots, d_n >$, where x_i represents the initial input and d_i is the desired output.

In our case, the inputs of the network are the violation degrees of attributes of the selected service pattern, and the outputs are those of the calculated best service pattern. The strength of the links between the first and second layers is the initial attribute weights of the selected service pattern. We normalize the attribute weights to be in $[0, 1]$.

Using the initial attribute weights, a number of service patterns, including the computed best service pattern and some random service patterns that are ordered by the violation degrees, will be returned to users and they may make a decision to select the most preferred one. If users choose some random service pattern instead of the expected best one, the adjustment process will be

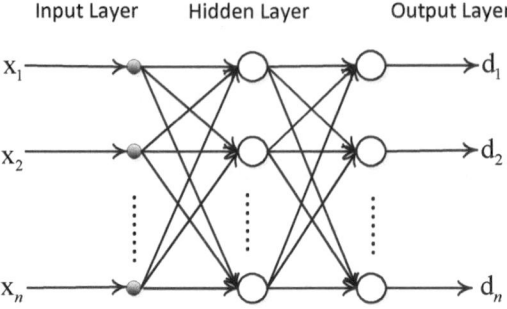

Fig. 2. A Typical BP Artificial Neural Network

activated. Then we assign the violation degree of the best service patten to the selected pattern. After the adjustment, BP algorithm is applied to retrieve another set of service patterns again and allow users to select again. This process will be continued until the best computed service pattern is selected by users, that is, the weight adjustment has converged.

3.4   Example

This section is introduced here to exemplify how WCP-nets works step by step. Since the relative importance between attributes is $w_A/w_B = 3, w_B/w_C = 5$ while the summation of all weights is $w_A + w_B + w_C = 1$, we can determine the initial attribute weights: $w_A = 0.7143, w_B = 0.2381, w_C = 0.0476$. There are eight service patterns, i.e. $(sp_1, sp_2, sp_3, sp_4, sp_5, sp_6, sp_7, sp_8) = (a_1b_1c_1, a_1b_1c_2, a_1b_2c_1, a_1b_2c_2, a_2b_1c_1, a_2b_1c_2, a_2b_2c_1, a_2b_2c_2)$. If we use linear method to calculate the violation degrees of service patterns, the values of them are 0, 0.1428, 0.1190, 0.2381, 2.1429, 2.2857, 1.5238, 1.4286, respectively. Thus the ranking sequence of service patterns is

$$sp_1 > sp_3 > sp_2 > sp_4 > sp_8 > sp_7 > sp_5 > sp_6 \qquad (7)$$

To select the proper services, we first find out if there are any web services in the database that are in line with the best preferred service pattern sp_1. If so, we recommend these web services to a user Bill, otherwise we return those that satisfy the next best service pattern sp_3. This process repeats until some services are returned. However, the problem is that in practice the service Bill selects may conflict with his aforementioned preferences due to some reasons like preference drifting over time. Assume his real preference ranking of service patterns is

$$sp_1 > sp_6 > sp_2 > sp_3 > sp_4 > (sp_5 = sp_8) > sp_7 \qquad (8)$$

To solve this issue, we need to adjust the initial attribute weights to obtain accurate violation degree of a service pattern. To show the adjustment process, we do not generate web services in the database that meet the description of

sp_1. Now we detail the adjustment process. Considering preference sequence (7), we return 4 web service patterns (here every service pattern responses to a unique web service) to Bill, including the computed best service pattern $sp3$ and three random service patterns (sp_6, sp_4, sp_7). He then selects the most preferred service pattern in the light of real sequence (8), i.e. sp_6 rather than sp_3. Since the conflict occurs, the adjustment process is subsequently activated. Applying the Lagrangian method described in Section 3.3.1 to adjust the weights, we can obtain a new set of attribute weights based on which a new preference sequence is produced as below.

$$sp_1 > sp_2 > sp_4 > sp_3 > sp_7 > sp_8 > sp_5 > sp_6 \qquad (9)$$

At this iteration, Bill will select his most preferred service pattern among the retrieved 4 patters, say (sp_2, sp_4, sp_3, sp_7). According to Bill's real preference sequence (8), sp_2 will also be selected, hence there is no need to alter any attribute weights. We may continue this adjustment process to judge whether sp_2 is the most preferred available service pattern.

An alternative weight adjustment method is nonlinear and conducted by BP-ANN. The first step is to initialize a BP-ANN. Specifically, the violation degrees and weights of attributes of a service pattern will be imported into the network. And the eight outputs derived from the network will be ordered. Suppose after a few iterations of training, the violation degrees of eight service patterns are (113.5641, 117.3781, 92.0738, 108.8373, 49.4641, 87.3097, 58.6806, 143.2908). The best computed service pattern sp_5 together with three randomly selected patterns sp_6, sp_8, sp_2 are returned for further selection. According to sequence (8), Bill is likely to select sp_6 and hence the conflict happens. For weight adjustment, we assign the violation degree of sp_5 to sp_6. These new values of four service patterns will be regarded as the desired outputs for next iterative training. We continue this adjustment process until the attribute weights are stable.

4   Experimental Validation

The major concern we would like to verify for WCP-nets is threefold: 1) how good it is to distinguish service patterns compared with CP-nets and TCP-nets[1]? 2) how accurate the retrieved service patterns would be? 3) what is the distinction between linear and nonlinear weight adjustments?

4.1   Data Acquisition

For the experiments, we use two real datasets: $Adult$[2] and QWS [1]. The former is obtained form the UCI Machine Learning Repository, consisting of 32,561 records. Each record is regarded hereafter as a concrete dating service that contains 14 attributes. The latter contains 2507 real web services which stem from

---

[1] UCP-nets is excluded in our experiments because it is essentially a quantitative approach for CP-nets rather than a CP-nets extension.

[2] http://archive.ics.uci.edu/ml/datasets/Adult

public sources on the web including *Universal Description, Discovery, and Integration* (UDDI) registries, search engines, and service portals. Each web service contains nine attributes. All experiments are conducted using an IBM server with 8 CPUs of 2.13 GHz and a RAM of 16 GB.

4.2   Performance Analysis

The performance of WCP-nets is measured by the percent of comparable service patterns (CSPs) and the accuracy of returned web services. The difference between linear and nonlinear weight adjustment methods is also distinguished.

4.2.1   The Percent of Comparable Service Patterns

The first concern is the ability of WCP-nets in comparing different service patterns (CSPs) relative to CP-nets and TCP-nets. Specifically, for each experiment, we vary the number of attributes from 3 to 11 with step 2 and record the percents of service patterns that are comparable using three different methods. We conduct in total four experiments where the number of attribute values is taken from $\{2, 4, 6, 8\}$, respectively. In each case, 1000 CP-nets are randomly generated (for both dependency graphs and CPTs) to represent users' preferences. Based on CP-nets, TCP-nets is constructed by adding relative qualitative importance, and WCP-nets is built by adding relative quantitative importance between attributes. Each experiment is executed 1000 times and the average of the percent of CSPs is computed. The results are illustrated in Figure 3, where (a) - (d) represents the results when the number of attribute values is 2, 4, 6, 8 respectively.

Consistent results are obtained in four experiments, showing that WCP-nets outperforms CP-nets and TCP-nets in comparing different service patterns. In particular, since the relative quantitative importance between attributes is added to the CP-nets, the expressiveness of TCP-nets is better than CP-nets. But there are still a number of service patterns that cannot be comparable. On the contrary, WCP-nets are always able to compare all services patterns in terms of the computed violation degree.

4.2.2   The Accuracy of Retrieved Web Services

Another batch of experiments are conducted to investigate the accuracy of the web services (WSs) that are retrieved by three different methods, i.e. WCP-nets, TCP-nets and CP-nets. The experiments are based on the aforementioned two real datasets. Specifically, we randomly choose 3, 5, 7, 9, 11 attributes from the dataset and apply three methods to model user preference and retrieve the suitable WSs as required. A pre-processing is utilized to convert continuous attribute value to three sections. For example, the value of the attribute *Response time* in QWS is continuous from 0 to the maximum 4207.5ms which is then uniformly segmented into three parts. Finally, the three parts are symbolized as three attribute values of *Response time*. CP-nets is generated randomly as well as TCP-nets and WCP-nets. Generally, the best WS pattern is retrieved if it

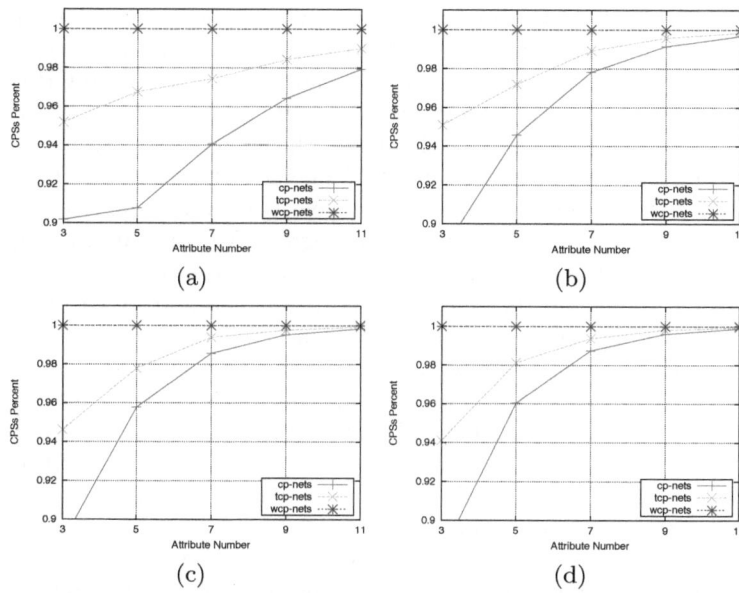

Fig. 3. The Percent of Comparable Service Patterns (CSPs)

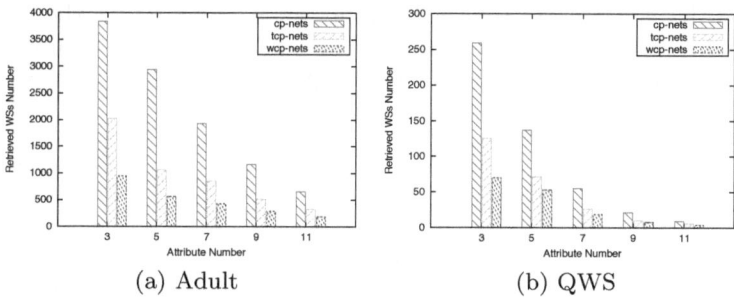

Fig. 4. The Accuracy of the Retrieved Web Services (WSs)

meets user preference expressed in (W, T)CP-nets. Otherwise, the second best WS pattern will be returned. All experiments are repeated 1000 times and the results of the average performance are delineated in Figure 4.

We count the number of retrieved WSs as the measurement of accuracy. The intuition is that the more accurate user preference is, the less number of retrieved WSs is. Clearly, TCP-nets show its strength relative to CP-nets whereas WCP-nets achieves the best accuracy. Theoretically, TCP-nets covers more aspects that are unknown to CP-nets, while WCP-nets expresses not only more but also fine-grained user preference that is not available in the others.

4.2.3   Linear vs. Nonlinear Weight Adjustments

The purpose of this subsection is to investigate the distinctions between linear and nonlinear weight adjustment methods and give readers guides on how to select suitable adjustment method for their own applications. The comparison will be focused on the efficiency and effectiveness for weight adjustments.

The experiments are based on the real datasets. A set of WCP-nets with 3, 5, 7, 9, 11 attributes are generated randomly, and 8 services are randomly selected in each time from the real datasets. The same preprocessing is used for continuous attribute value as Section 4.2.1. The adjustment of attribute weights is activated when conflicts occur, i.e. users select a random service rather than the expected one with minimum violation degree. We continue the adjustment process for at least 30 times even when users do select the computed best service. The purpose is to reduce the selection due to chance and avoid local optimal values. For the nonlinear method, three hidden layers are used in the BP-ANN. The violation degrees of attribute values are used as inputs and the weights of attributes as the weights of inputs. The number of neurons in hidden layer is empirically set 75% of the number of inputs. The training function we utilize is *traingd*, the transfer function between hidden layers is *tansig* and the transfer function of output layer is *purelin*. All experiments is repeated 1000 times and the average performance is adopted.

The efficiency is measured as the number of interactions required before convergence. The effectiveness is reflected by the accuracy of the retrieved WSs using different methods. A web service will be labeled *accurate* if it meets user preference which is simulated by a random function. A set of accurate WSs are selected as the benchmark. Hence the accuracy is computed as the percentage of retrieved WSs over the benchmark. The results shown in Figures 5 and 6 represent the efficiency and effectiveness, respectively.

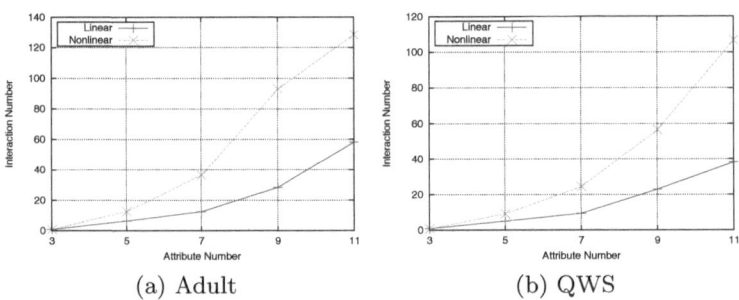

(a) Adult   (b) QWS

Fig. 5. The Efficiency of Linear and Nonlinear Methods

Figure 5 shows that the linear method consistently converges much faster than the nonlinear one as the number of interactions required by the former is greatly less than the latter. However, Figure 6 indicates that the latter achieves much better accuracy than the former. A conclusion can be drawn that, for those who require fast convergence, the linear method is more preferred and for those who seek best accuracy, the nonlinear method should be adopted.

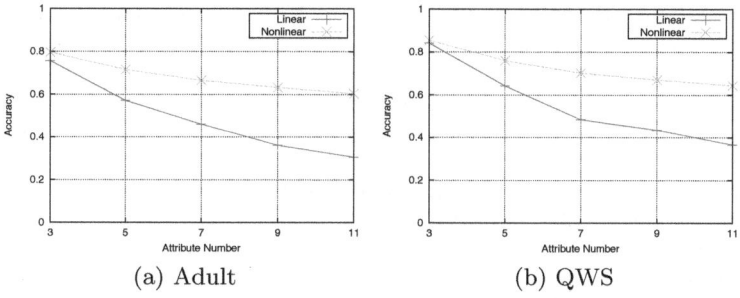

(a) Adult   (b) QWS

Fig. 6. The Accuracy of Linear and Nonlinear Methods

5   Conclusion

We proposed a weighted extension to CP-nets called WCP-nets, aiming to solve
the issues of CP-nets described in Section 2.2. More specifically, the relative importance (weights) between attribute values and that between attributes were
added to the original CP-nets to allow users to express more fine-grained preference. The concept of violation degree was introduced to measure the extent to
which a service pattern is preferred. Both linear and nonlinear methods were presented to adjust users' initial weights when conflicts between stated preference
and actual choices occur. Experiments on two real datasets were conducted and
the results showed that our method can not only increase the expressiveness of
user preference, but also select more accurate services than other counterparts.

References

1. Al-Masri, E., Mahmoud, Q.: Discovering the best web service. In: Proceedings of
   the 16th International Conference on World Wide Web, pp. 1257–1258 (2007)
2. Bacchus, F., Grove, A.: Graphical models for preference and utility. In: Proceedings of the Eleventh Conference on Uncertainty in Artificial Intelligence, pp. 3–10.
   Morgan Kaufmann Publishers Inc. (1995)
3. Boutilier, C., Bacchus, F., Brafman, R.: Ucp-networks: A directed graphical representation of conditional utilities. In: Proceedings of the Seventeenth Conference
   on Uncertainty in Artificial Intelligence, pp. 56–64 (2001)
4. Boutilier, C., Brafman, R., Domshlak, C., Hoos, H., Poole, D.: Cp-nets: A tool for
   representing and reasoning with conditional ceteris paribus preference statements.
   J. Artif. Intell. Res. (JAIR) 21, 135–191 (2004)
5. Brafman, R., Domshlak, C.: Preference handling-an introductory tutorial. AI Magazine 30(1), 58 (2009)
6. Brafman, R., Domshlak, C., Shimony, S.: On graphical modeling of preference and
   importance. Journal of Artificial Intelligence Research 25(1), 389–424 (2006)
7. Châtel, P., Truck, I., Malenfant, J., et al.: Lcp-nets: A linguistic approach for
   non-functional preferences in a semantic soa environment. Journal of Universal
   Computer Science 16(1), 198–217 (2010)

8. García, J., Ruiz, D., Ruiz-Cortés, A., Parejo, J.: Qos-aware semantic service selection: An optimization problem. In: Proceedings of 2008 IEEE Congress on Services-Part I, pp. 384–388 (2008)
9. Gavanelli, M., Pini, M.: Fcp-nets: extending constrained cp-nets with objective functions. In: Constraint Solving and Constraint Logic Programming, ERCIM (2008)
10. Koriche, F., Zanuttini, B.: Learning conditional preference networks. Artificial Intelligence 174(11), 685–703 (2010)
11. Lamparter, S., Ankolekar, A., Studer, R., Grimm, S.: Preference-based selection of highly configurable web services. In: Proceedings of the 16th International Conference on World Wide Web, pp. 1013–1022. ACM (2007)
12. Liu, J., Chang, H., Hsu, T., Ruan, X.: Prediction of the flow stress of high-speed steel during hot deformation using a bp artificial neural network. Journal of Materials Processing Technology 103(2), 200–205 (2000)
13. Luenberger, D., Ye, Y.: Linear and nonlinear programming, vol. 116. Springer (2008)
14. O'Sullivan, D., Smyth, B., Wilson, D., Mcdonald, K., Smeaton, A.: Improving the quality of the personalized electronic program guide. User Modeling and User-Adapted Interaction 14(1), 5–36 (2004)
15. Santhanam, G.R., Basu, S., Honavar, V.G.: TCP−Compose* – A TCP-Net Based Algorithm for Efficient Composition of Web Services Using Qualitative Preferences. In: Bouguettaya, A., Krueger, I., Margaria, T. (eds.) ICSOC 2008. LNCS, vol. 5364, pp. 453–467. Springer, Heidelberg (2008)
16. Sun, X., Liu, J.: Representation and realization of binary-valued cp-nets in single-branch tree. In: Proceedings of the 2010 Seventh International Conference on Fuzzy Systems and Knowledge Discovery, FSKD, vol. 4, pp. 1908–1911 (2010)
17. Wang, H., Liu, W.: Web service selection with quantitative and qualitative user preferences. In: Proceedings of IEEE/WIC/ACM International Conferences on Web Intelligence and Intelligent Agent Technology, vol. 1, pp. 404–411 (2011)
18. Wang, H., Zhang, J., Tang, Y., Shao, S.: Collaborative approaches to complementing qualitative preferences of agents for effective service selection. In: Proceedings of the 2011 IEEE International Conference on Tools with Artificial Intelligence, ICTAI, pp. 51–58 (2011)
19. Wang, H., Zhang, J., Wan, C., Shao, S., Cohen, R., Xu, J., Li, P.: Web service selection for multiple agents with incomplete preferences. In: Proceedings of the 2010 IEEE/WIC/ACM International Conference on Web Intelligence and Intelligent Agent Technology, WI-IAT, pp. 565–572 (2010)
20. Wang, H., Zhou, X., Zhou, X., Liu, W., Li, W., Bouguettaya, A.: Adaptive Service Composition Based on Reinforcement Learning. In: Maglio, P.P., Weske, M., Yang, J., Fantinato, M. (eds.) ICSOC 2010. LNCS, vol. 6470, pp. 92–107. Springer, Heidelberg (2010)
21. Wilson, N.: Extending cp-nets with stronger conditional preference statements. In: Proceedings of the National Conference on Artificial Intelligence, pp. 735–741 (2004)
22. Xu, H., Hipel, K., Marc Kilgour, D.: Multiple levels of preference in interactive strategic decisions. Discrete Applied Mathematics 157(15), 3300–3313 (2009)

WS-Finder: A Framework for Similarity Search of Web Services

Jiangang Ma[1], Quan Z. Sheng[1], Kewen Liao[1],
Yanchun Zhang[2], and Anne H.H. Ngu[3]

[1] School of Computer Science, The University of Adelaide, Australia
{jiangang.ma,michael.sheng,kewen.liao}@adelaide.edu.au
[2] School of Engineering and Science, Victoria University, Australia
yanchun.zhang@vu.edu.au
[3] Department of Computer Science, Texas State University, USA
angu@txstate.edu

Abstract. Most existing Web service search engines employ keyword search over databases, which computes the distance between the query and the Web services over a fixed set of features. Such an approach often results in incompleteness of search results. The Earth Mover's Distance (EMD) has been successfully used in multimedia databases due to its ability to capture the differences between two distributions. However, calculating EMD is computationally intensive. In this paper, we present a novel framework called WS-Finder, which improves the existing keyword-based search techniques for Web services. In particular, we employ EMD for many-to-many partial matching between the contents of the query and the service attributes. We also develop a generalized minimization lower bound as a new EMD filter for partial matching. This new EMD filter is then combined to a k-NN algorithm for producing complete top-k search results. Furthermore, we theoretically and empirically show that WS-Finder is able to produce query answers effectively and efficiently.

1 Introduction

Similarity search of Web services (WSs) is a crucial task in many practical applications such as services discovery, service composition and Web applications like incorporating Google Maps to locate businesses [1–6]. In addition, because WSs have become one of the standard technologies for sharing data and programs on the Web, and also because new paradigm of the pay-per-use is adopted by the recent Cloud Computing, a number of enterprises are developing large-scale software applications by wrapping their data, business processes, and databases applications into WSs. These WSs can be further composed to new services that provide value-added functionalities. For example, according to a recent statistics[1](accessed on 07/05/2012), there are 28,606 WSs available on the Web, provided by 7,739 different providers. As a result, searching desired services is described to be akin to looking for a needle in a haystack [7].

---

[1] http://webservices.seekda.com

C. Liu et al. (Eds.): ICSOC 2012, LNCS 7636, pp. 313–327, 2012.
© Springer-Verlag Berlin Heidelberg 2012

Currently, most existing WSs search engines employ simple keyword search on WSs descriptions in databases. This is based on the fact that WSs are syntactically described by Web Services Description Language (WSDL), which makes it feasible to index these WSDL files through using keywords strategy [5].

However, the simple keyword search strategy adopted by these search engines suffer from a limitation. The exact keyword search may miss many relevant search results. This is because exact keyword-based search approaches compute the distance between the query and the services over a fixed set of features. That is, most existing Web-based search engines [1, 4] compute a similarity score by matching each keyword in the query against the keyword at corresponding position in the WSs descriptions in database, not considering the impact of the similarity of the neighboring keywords. We refer to this type of search as one-to-one search. The limitation of this approach is that one-to-one search may not return all relevant results. For example, consider a typical keyword searching query WHOLESALE issued against the service database. In this case, WSs whose function descriptions contain keyword SALE may not be returned because the keyword WHOLESALE in the query are not present in the WSs description, which results in *incompleteness* of search results. However, we can see that there is some partial similarity between WHOLESALE and SALE.

One potential approach to capture the partial similarity is to integrate the neighboring keywords into the similarity computation by using the term partial match techniques such as the Earth Mover's Distance (EMD)[8]. EMD has been successfully used in multimedia databases due to its ability to capture the differences between two distributions. However, calculating EMD is computationally intensive. Another possible method is to describe services capabilities by using the Semantic Web. For example, some research [9] uses ontology to annotate the elements in WSs for finding common semantic concepts between the query and services advertisements. As we here focus on similarity search of WSs from the point of view of algorithms, Semantic Web is beyond the scope of this paper and will not be discussed further.

To address the challenges involved in similarity search for WSs, in this paper, we have designed and implemented a novel framework called WS-Finder, which improves the existing keyword-based search techniques for WSs. In particular, we employ EMD for many-to-many partial matching between the contents of the query and the service attributes. To facilitate search of WSs in an efficient manner, we design a new WS model. We also develop a generalized minimization lower bound as a new EMD filter for partial matching in order to overcome the complexity of computing EMD. This new EMD filter is then combined to a k-NN algorithm for producing complete top-k search results. Furthermore, we theoretically and empirically show that WS-Finder is able to produce query answers effectively and efficiently. Our key contributions are as the following:

- We propose a novel WS model that incorporates WS architecture information into *records* stored in databases. Such model could not only be searched in WS entries but also mined by the optimization algorithm proposed in the paper.

- We develop a *generalized independent minimization lower bound* (LB_{GIM}) extended from the LB_{IM} lower bound in [10] as a new EMD filter for partial matching. The filter is then incorporated into a *k-NN algorithm* for producing top-k results. To the best of our knowledge, LB_{GIM} is the first effective and easy-to-compute lower bound for the *general* EMD. In particular, it is flexible and suitable for keyword-based content searches where words are always compared with different lengths. Whereas almost all other lower bound filters [8, 10, 11] are only developed for *special* EMD with equal total weights. For this reason, LB_{GIM} also has great potential to be used in other application domains. We compute LB_{GIM} by proposing a *unified greedy algorithm*.
- We conduct an extensive experimental evaluation over a set of real datasets of WSs. Our experimental results show that WS-Finder produces query answers with high recall and precision and low response time.

The remainder of this paper is organized as follows. In Section 2, we describe a Web service model and the WS-Finder architecture and in Section 3, we discuss an EMD-based optimization algorithm. In Section 4, we present experimental results to show the effectiveness and efficiency of our approach. Section 5 is dedicated to related work, and finally, Section 6 concludes the paper and discusses some future research directions.

2 Web Service Model and WS-Finder Architecture

In this section, we briefly describe a model to represent Web services and the architecture of the WS-Finder system.

2.1 Web Service Model

As one of key factors resulting in an effective similarity search of WSs is how WSs are stored [5], we first introduce a new model to represent WSs. The model incorporates WSs' architecture information such as functional and non-functional requirements (FRs and NFRs). The FR attributes of a WS are name, category, function and description while NFR attributes include QoS such as response time (RT), availability (AVA), reliability (REL) and etc. Specifically, we model WSs as *records* stored in a database, where each WS usually has a record with some attributes and values to describe the basic structured information of the entry. Such records could not only be searched in WS entries but also mined by algorithms. Thus, all these records form a WS database **DB**.

Definition 1. *A Web service record $r \in$ **DB** is represented by a tuple $r = \langle n^r, c^r, f^r, d^r, \mathbf{QoS}^r \rangle$, where n^r, c^r, f^r and d^r contain the content of the attribute name, category, function , description, and $\mathbf{QoS}^r = \{QoS_1^r, QoS_2^r, \ldots\}$ contains an ordered set of numerical NFR contents respectively.* □

The examples of WS records are shown in Table 1.

Table 1. Web service records

	FR Attributes				NFR Attributes		
ID	Name	Category	Function	Description	RT (s)	AVA (%)	REL (%)
1	B.S. Stillwell Ford	New cars	getCarPrice	Finance facilities at competitive rates	1.2	86	88
2	City Holden	Used cars	getCarColor	Minimise the hassle of a second hand vehicle	0.8	92	80

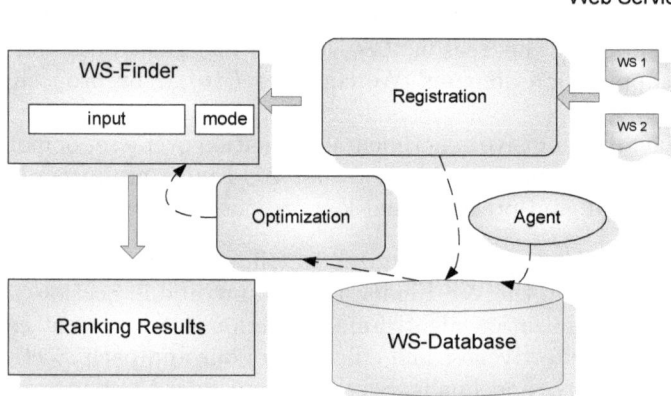

Fig. 1. WS-Finder Architecture

2.2   WS-Finder Architecture

The proposed architecture consists of three main components (see Figure 1). The registration component deals with the registration of WSs. Service providers can register their WSs through this component. The registered WSs are pre-processed to remove common terms and stopwords by using word stemming and the stopwords removing approaches. Then the processed WSs are stored in service database in terms of records, with the techniques and approaches introduced in this paper for enabling similarity search. The registration process can be performed offline.

The optimization component handles the query optimization for similarity search. It enables effective and efficient search by using EMD techniques. In this paper, we mainly concentrate on this optimization component.

3   EMD-Based Optimization Algorithm

In this section, we discuss an EMD-based optimization algorithm to support similarity search. Formally, given a database **DB** containing WS records and a query q, similarity search returns all records $r \in \mathbf{DB}$, such that $dis(q, r) \leq \varepsilon$, where $dis(q, r)$ is a distance function, and ε the specified similarity threshold. We use EMD as a measure for the distance $dis_{EMD}(q, r)$ between a keyword and an attribute word sequences $\mathbf{kw}^q$ and $\mathbf{aw}^{r,M^q}$ from a query q and a record r, which describes their similarity. The problem we focus on here is the design of efficient computing EMD methods that will minimize the total number of actual EMD computations.

3.1 Earth Mover's Distance

The Earth Mover's Distance was first introduced in computer vision for improving distance measure between two distributions. As it can effectively capture the differences between two distributions and allow for partial matching, EMD is successfully exploited for various applications like phishing detection [12], document retrieval [13], and databases [10, 14].

Traditional distance measure in computer vision is based on computing the similarity between histograms of two objects. Given two objects histograms x=$\{x_i\}$ and $y = \{y_i\}$, the L_p distance, defined as $L_p(x, y) = (\sum_{i=0}^{n} |x_i - y_i|^p)^{\frac{1}{p}}$, is used to compute the distance of the histograms. Due to its rigid binning distance measure, a small shift of bins in the histograms often results in a large distance in L_P. To overcome the limitation of bin-by-bin approach, EMD incorporates information cross bins into the definition of the distances between two objects. This can be achieved with the help of the solution of solving transporting problem, where the distribution of one object is regarded as a mass of earth with quality W and the other as a collection holes with a given limited capacity U. Mathematically, the EMD involves in the solution of transportation problem in linear programming.

3.2 Defining EMD

EMD describes the normalized minimum amount of work required to transform one distribution to the other. Computing the exact EMD requires solving the famous *transportation problem* [8] in operations research.

In our context, the *subtask* is to find EMD between a keyword and an attribute word sequences $\mathbf{kw}^q$ and $\mathbf{aw}^{r,M^q}$ from a query q and a record r, which describes their similarity. For simplicity, let any subtask to involve two word sequences $\mathbf{kw}$ and $\mathbf{aw}$ instead of $\mathbf{kw}^q$ and $\mathbf{aw}^{r,M^q}$, where $|\mathbf{kw}| = n_1$ and $|\mathbf{aw}| = n_2$. Finding the minimum work of the subtask to transform $\mathbf{kw}$ to $\mathbf{aw}$ through the flow $\mathbf{f} = \{\forall 1 \le i \le n_1, 1 \le j \le n_2 : f_{ij}\}$ is equivalent to computing the optimal solution to the following linear program (LP) with variable f_{ij}:

$$
\begin{aligned}
&\text{minimize} : \sum_{i=1}^{n_1} \sum_{j=1}^{n_2} f_{ij} d_{ij} \\
&\text{subject to} : \\
&\forall 1 \le i \le n_1 : \sum_{j=1}^{n_2} f_{ij} \le w_{kw_i} \quad &(1.1) \\
&\forall 1 \le j \le n_2 : \sum_{i=1}^{n_1} f_{ij} \le w_{aw_j} \quad &(1.2) \\
&\forall 1 \le i \le n_1, 1 \le j \le n_2 : f_{ij} \ge 0 \quad &(1.3) \\
&\sum_{i=1}^{n_1} \sum_{j=1}^{n_2} f_{ij} = \min \left(\sum_{i=1}^{n_1} w_{kw_i}, \sum_{j=1}^{n_2} w_{aw_j} \right) \quad &(1.4)
\end{aligned}
$$
(1)

where $\mathbf{d} = \{\forall 1 \le i \le n_1, 1 \le j \le n_2 : d_{ij}\}$ is the ground distance matrix between $\mathbf{kw}$ and $\mathbf{aw}$; $\mathbf{w_{kw}}$ and $\mathbf{w_{aw}}$ are weight vectors of keywords and attribute words respectively. These distances and weights are necessary *input values* to LP

(1) that will be defined later. Furthermore, constraint (1.1) restricts the total outgoing flow from any keyword not to exceed the corresponding weight; (1.2) limits the total incoming flow to any attribute word to be no larger than the weight; (1.3) ensures the positiveness of all flows; (1.4) defines the amount of total flow which is equal to the minimum of keyword and attribute word sequences' total weights. Note that unlike in [10, 14, 15], the flow system we consider here is more general, which means the total weights of word sequences may not be equal. Therefore, the system can be modeled as a directed *complete bipartite graph* with n_1 keyword nodes and n_2 attribute word nodes as two parts. For simplicity, let the total number of nodes $n = n_1 + n_2$ and total number of edges (representing flows) $m = n_1 \times n_2$.

Now if we assume the optimal flow $\mathbf{f}^*$ is found for the above LP, the EMD is then the corresponding work *normalized* by the amount of total flow:

$$EMD\,(\mathbf{kw},\,\mathbf{aw}) = \frac{\sum_{i=1}^{n_1} \sum_{j=1}^{n_2} f_{ij}^* d_{ij}}{\sum_{i=1}^{n_1} \sum_{j=1}^{n_2} f_{ij}^*}$$

which has the capability to avoid favoring shorter queries in our partial words matching context.

3.3   Web Service Query Processing

WS-Finder processes queries in a multi-step manner. In particular, there are two processing paths depending on the query type: *basic* or *advanced*. On both paths, content filtering is the main technique for efficient query computation.

EMD-Based Query Processing without Filter. For each query q and its k required answers, WS-Finder is able to operate the search process in database with a *boolean function* $\phi^{q,k}: r \to \{0, 1\}$, where $\phi^{q,k}(r) = 1$ if $EMD\,(\mathbf{kw}^q,\,\mathbf{aw}^{r,M^q}) \leq$ $\mathbf{EMDs}^{q,\mathbf{DB}}(k)^2$. EMD function computes EMD between keyword and attribute word sequences, and the *ascendingly sorted* set of all EMD values is defined as : $\mathbf{EMDs}^{q,\mathbf{DB}} = \left\{\forall r \in \mathbf{DB} : EMD\,(\mathbf{kw}^q,\,\mathbf{aw}^{r,M^q})\right\}^+$. This process can then be translated into the following SQL query:

$$SELECT \; * \; FROM \; \mathbf{DB}$$
$$WHERE \; \phi^{q,k}(r)$$
$$ORDER \; BY \; E\bar{M}D$$

where $\phi^{q,k}(r)$ is a boolean predicate in SQL and $E\bar{M}D$ denotes the extra created attribute name storing contents of $\mathbf{EMDs}^{q,\mathbf{DB}}$.

EMD-Based Query Processing with Filter. Because generating the set $\mathbf{EMDs}^{q,\mathbf{DB}}$ may take too long for a large number of exact EMD computations, we use LB_{GIM} filter for basic query uses $E\hat{M}D$ function to approximate EMD, and computes the

---

^{2} The k-th element in the set $\mathbf{EMDs}^{q,\mathbf{DB}}$.

set : $\mathbf{E\hat{M}Ds}^{q,\mathbf{DB}} = \left\{ \forall r \in \mathbf{DB} : E\hat{M}D \left(\mathbf{kw}^q, \mathbf{aw}^{r,M^q} \right) \right\}^+$ in a much shorter time. This set together with range and top-k queries is able to generate a filtered set $\mathbf{DB}' \subseteq \mathbf{DB}$ for processing the final top-k query. Therefore, the boolean function which describes the search process is revised to be : $\phi^{q,k} \colon r \in \mathbf{DB}' \to \{0, 1\}$, where $\phi^{q,k}(r) = 1$ if $EMD \left(\mathbf{kw}^q, \mathbf{aw}^{r,M^q} \right) \leq \mathbf{EMDs}^{q,\mathbf{DB}'}(k)$.

3.4 Defining Input Values

Before computing the EMD, we need to decide the input values $\mathbf{w_{kw}}$, $\mathbf{w_{aw}}$ and $\mathbf{d}$. Intuitively, the weight of a word can be calculated by its length, so $\mathbf{w_{kw}}$ and $\mathbf{w_{aw}}$ can be easily computed. Note that $\mathbf{w_{aw}}$ is computed offline while $\mathbf{w_{kw}}$ is online. However, the ground distance is not so obvious because it needs to reflect the similarity between a pair of words with possibly different lengths. Assume the words to compare are kw_i and aw_j with lengths w_{kw_i} and w_{aw_j} respectively, our first adopted distance metric SED compares them character-wise[3] in $O\left(\min\left(w_{kw_i}, w_{aw_j}\right)\right)$ time and gets the number of different characters $diff$. The value of SED is therefore:

$$SED\left(kw_i, aw_j\right) = diff + \left| w_{kw_i} - w_{aw_j} \right|$$

For example, $SED\left(\text{``CAR''}, \text{``CITY''}\right) = 2 + 1 = 3$. The advantage of this metric is the linear time complexity and no required extra space. However it is not robust enough to capture the distance between words having similar structures. For instance, $SED\left(\text{``SALE''}, \text{``WHOLESALE''}\right) = 9$, but these two words have the similar suffixes. Our second chosen metric LD [16] instead represents the *edit distance* between two words. LD is a classical distance metric that has been used in many important applications such as spell-checkers, Unix diff command and DNA sequence alignment. The following definition explains LD in our context.

Definition 2. *The edit distance (LD) between a keyword and an attribute word is the least total number of character insertions, deletions and substitutions required to transform one to the other.* □

LD can be computed in $O\left(w_{kw_i} w_{aw_j}\right)$ time using dynamic programming (dp) to solve an equivalent sequence alignment problem. Also, there is an efficient way in maintaining the dp table that only requires $O\left(\min\left(w_{kw_i}, w_{aw_j}\right)\right)$ space. For the details, refer to the Hirschberg's algorithm [17]. Adopting this metric, $LD\left(\text{``SALE''}, \text{``WHOLESALE''}\right) = 5$ since a minimum of five insertions are required. Despite that LD provides more robustness than SED in partial matching between words, its computation takes quadratic time and requires linear extra space which is more expensive. In Section 4, we also empirically compare the impacts of SED and LD on the performance of WS-Finder.

---

[3] Compare capitalized characters at the same index.

3.5   The EMD Filter: LB_{GIM}

We now discuss the generation of the EMD filter LB_{GIM} for word sequences partial matching. We will prove that LB_{GIM} lower bounds the general EMD and is suitable for EMD computation with unequal total weights case.

There are many ways in computing exact EMD with *arbitrary* distance metric. The streamlined approach we adopted is the transportation-simplex method [18] due to its supercubic (between $\Omega\left(n^3\right)$ and $O\left(n^4\right)$) empirical performance [8, 19]. Also, this algorithm exploits the special structure of the transportation problem and hence runs fast in practice.

Even though the algorithms for calculating the exact EMD are deemed to be efficient, as the amount of WS contents continue to increase, the framework's response time for top-k queries may be increased quickly. Hence we use the filtering idea similar to [8, 10, 11] to minimize the total number of actual EMD computations. However, their lower bound filters are only for EMD with equal weights ($\sum_{i=1}^{n_1} w_{kw_i} = \sum_{j=1}^{n_2} w_{aw_j}$ in our case), which is clearly not suitable for the comparison of word sequences that requires solving the general EMD (including the unequal total weights case). For this reason, we develop the LB_{GIM} filter generalized from LB_{IM} in [10] for word sequences partial matching. We will also see in the next subsection how this filter is incorporated into the k-NN algorithm for producing the final results.

Our LB_{GIM} is a *conditional lower bound* depending on three cases of LP (1): 1)$\sum_{i=1}^{n_1} w_{kw_i} < \sum_{j=1}^{n_2} w_{aw_j}$; 2)$\sum_{i=1}^{n_1} w_{kw_i} > \sum_{j=1}^{n_2} w_{aw_j}$; 3) $\sum_{i=1}^{n_1} w_{kw_i} = \sum_{j=1}^{n_2} w_{aw_j}$. In particular, case 3) is the same as LB_{IM}. For cases 1) and 2), we develop new lower bound LPs (3) and (2) respectively in the following and LB_{GIM} can be either of their normalized optimal solutions.

$$
\begin{aligned}
&\text{minimize } \sum_{i=1}^{n_1} \sum_{j=1}^{n_2} f_{ij} d_{ij} \\
&\text{subject to } \forall 1 \le i \le n_1 : \sum_{j=1}^{n_2} f_{ij} = w_{kw_i} \quad (2.1) \\
&\qquad\qquad \forall 1 \le i \le n_1, 1 \le j \le n_2 : f_{ij} \le w_{aw_j} \quad (2.2) \\
&\qquad\qquad \forall 1 \le i \le n_1, 1 \le j \le n_2 : f_{ij} \ge 0 \quad (2.3)
\end{aligned}
\tag{2}
$$

$$
\begin{aligned}
&\text{minimize } \sum_{i=1}^{n_1} \sum_{j=1}^{n_2} f_{ij} d_{ij} \\
&\text{subject to } \forall 1 \le i \le n_1, 1 \le j \le n_2 : f_{ij} \le w_{kw_i} \quad (3.1) \\
&\qquad\qquad \forall 1 \le j \le n_2 : \sum_{i=1}^{n_1} f_{ij} = w_{aw_j} \quad (3.2) \\
&\qquad\qquad \forall 1 \le i \le n_1, 1 \le j \le n_2 : f_{ij} \ge 0 \quad (3.3)
\end{aligned}
\tag{3}
$$

Theorem 1. LB_{GIM} *lower bounds the general EMD.*

Proof. For case 3), the theorem holds as the proof in [10] states that LB_{IM} lower bounds the EMD with equal total weights. For case 1), the constraint (1.4) in LP (1) immediately becomes constraint (2.1) that also subsumes constraint (1.1). Also, constraint (2.2) provides a more relaxed search space of f_{ij} than (1.2), since satisfying (1.2) $\Rightarrow$ satisfying (2.2) but not vice versa. So LP (2) will attain the same or a smaller optimal solution than LP (1). After being normalized by the amount of total flow, we obtain LB_{GIM} as a lower bound. Finally, because case 2) with LP (3) is similar to the situation of case 1) we analyzed, we have LB_{GIM} lower bounds the general EMD in all cases.

Although LB_{GIM} seems to involve 3 cases, we can still provide a fast *unified greedy algorithm* to resolve this. Moreover, the algorithm enables us to avoid explicitly solving these LPs which take much longer time. The main idea for developing the greedy algorithm is to look at LB_{GIM} from the point of view of algorithms rather than restricting ourselves to its mathematical view (the LP formulations). The algorithmic view of the problem is explained by Figure 2. In this problem, we are asked to find the minimum cost flow subject to the constraints in LPs. If case 1) happens (the upper figure), we can consider each of keyword *in turn* due to the relaxed constraint (2.2). For each keyword, we first ascendingly sort all its edges by distances. Then the *greedy strategy* is always trying to assign a *larger flow* value along the edge with the *shorter distance* until constraint (2.1) is fulfilled. Afterwards the unassigned edges associated with the keyword will have zero flow value. LB_{GIM} can then be easily calculated from assigned flows and edge distances. If case 2) happens (the lower figure), without loss of generality, we can reverse the direction of flow, consider each attribute word in turn instead and do the same thing as case 1). Finally, if case 3) happens, we consider both case 1) and case 2) and take the larger LB_{GIM} value which is closer to the exact EMD value.

For example, as shown in Figure 3, **kw**={ *"HOLDEN", "CAR", "SERVICES"*} and **aw**={ *"CITY", "HOLDEN"*}. Also, for simplicity if we use SED as the distance metric, then $\mathbf{d} = \begin{pmatrix} 6\ 0 \\ 3\ 6 \\ 8\ 8 \end{pmatrix}$, $\mathbf{w_{kw}} = \{6, 3, 8\}$ and $\mathbf{w_{aw}} = \{4, 6\}$ and the problem falls into the case 2) of LB_{GIM}. So we reverse the flow direction with $\mathbf{d}^T = \begin{pmatrix} 6\ 3\ 8 \\ 0\ 6\ 8 \end{pmatrix}$ and follow the greedy algorithm to get the total cost of assigned flows $TC = 3 \times 3 + (4 - 3) \times 6 + 6 \times 0 = 15$, where the total flow is $TF = 4 + 6 = 10$. Hence $LB_{GIM} = \frac{TC}{TF} = 1.5$. In the following, we also provide the greedy algorithm's optimality proof and the runtime complexity analysis.

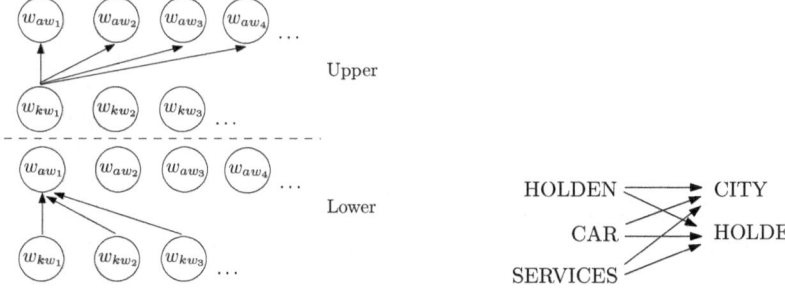

Fig. 2. Algorithmic view of LB_{GIM} **Fig. 3.** An example of computing LB_{GIM}

Lemma 1. *The unified greedy algorithm obtains the normalized optimal solutions of LPs, i.e. the LB_{GIM}, and it runs in $O\left(n^2 \log n\right)$ time.*

Proof. The optimality of the algorithm is quite clear, since the relaxed constraints (2.2) and (3.1) enable us to treat either keywords or attribute words independently. Therefore the local greedy optimal choices for the words will combine to the global optimal choice. In terms of the runtime complexity, for every independent keyword/attribute word, in the worst case the algorithm needs to compare it with all attribute words/keywords, which takes $O\left(n^2\right)$ in total. However, we need to sort every word's associated distances first, which totally takes $O\left(n^2 \log n\right)$ that dominates the runtime.

3.6   Top-k Records Retrieval

In this section, we would like to study how this filter is incorporated into the k-NN algorithm for producing the final results. There are two common query types in any retrieval systems, namely the *range query*, and the *top-k query* that is also known as the k nearest neighbor (k-NN) query. A range query is associated with a specified *metric* and a *threshold*. The answer to this query is the set of all objects within the threshold after measuring by the metric. On the other hand, a top-k query is more flexible, since the threshold which is sometimes hard to decide is not needed anymore. Instead, it requires an input k that specifies the *cardinality* of the result set. In our problem, the two metrics are EMD and its lower bound filter, which are calculated by the EMD and $E\hat{M}D$ functions respectively as introduced in Section 3.3. Continuing from that section, we then define the queries in our framework as follows:

Definition 3. *A* range query q *to a domain* $\mathbb{D} \subseteq \mathbf{DB}$ *with metric c and a threshold* ϵ *asks for a* range set *of records* $\mathbf{RS}_{c,\epsilon}^{q,\mathbb{D}} = \left\{ \forall r \in \mathbb{D} \mid c\left(\mathbf{kw}^q, \mathbf{aw}^{r,M^q}\right) \leq \epsilon \right\}$, *where c is either EMD or $E\hat{M}D$.*   □

Definition 4. *A* top-k query q *to a domain* $\mathbb{D} \subseteq \mathbf{DB}$ *with metric c asks for a* top-k *set of records* $\mathbf{TKS}_{c}^{q,\mathbb{D}} = \left\{ \forall r \in \mathbb{D} \mid c\left(\mathbf{kw}^q, \mathbf{aw}^{r,M^q}\right) \leq \epsilon' \right\}$, *where c is either EMD or $E\hat{M}D$, and* $\epsilon' = \mathbf{EMDs}^{q,\mathbb{D}}(k)$.   □

The *domain* $\mathbb{D}$ for a query in our framework is either $\mathbf{DB}$ or its subset and $\mathbf{EMDs}^{q,\mathbb{D}}(k)$ was defined similarly in Section 3.3. A *range set* of records are returned for a range query and a *top-k set* of records for a top-k query. Now, in order to correctly utilize an $E\hat{M}D$ filter to reduce the number of exact EMD calculations in the framework, it is necessary to combine range and top-k queries together as shown in Algorithm 1. In the algorithm, step 1 and 2 issue a top-k query to $\mathbf{DB}$ with $E\hat{M}D$ as the metric. In the framework, assume we use LB_{GIM} with LD for $E\hat{M}D$ and there are totally R records in domain $\mathbf{DB}$, then for a query these two steps take $O\left(RN^2 \log N + R \log R\right)$ time where N is the maximum number of words ($\geq$ any n) contained in a pair of matching word sequences. Step 3 and 4 then computes the exact EMDs for the set of k records obtained in step 2, and set the maximum one as the threshold to issue a range query to $\mathbf{DB}$ with $E\hat{M}D$ as the metric. These steps take $O\left(kN^3 \log N + R\right)$ time. Finally, step 5 and 6 issue another top-k query to the remaining records

---

Algorithm 1. k-NN Algorithm with LB_{GIM}

Input: query q with $\mathbf{kw}^q$ and M^q, input number k
Output: set $\mathbf{TKS}^{q,\mathbf{DB}}_{EMD}$.

1. $\forall r \in \mathbf{DB}$: compute $E\hat{M}D\left(\mathbf{kw}^q, \mathbf{aw}^{r,M^q}\right)$.
2. Construct the set $\mathbf{I} = \mathbf{TKS}^{q,\mathbf{DB}}_{E\hat{M}D}$.
3. $\forall r \in \mathbf{I}$: compute $EMD\left(\mathbf{kw}^q, \mathbf{aw}^{r,M^q}\right)$. Set $\epsilon = \max_r EMD\left(\mathbf{kw}^q, \mathbf{aw}^{r,M^q}\right)$.
4. Construct the set $\mathbf{DB}' = \mathbf{RS}^{q,\mathbf{DB}}_{E\hat{M}D,\epsilon}$.
5. $\forall r \in \mathbf{DB}'$: compute $EMD\left(\mathbf{kw}^q, \mathbf{aw}^{r,M^q}\right)$.
6. Construct the result set $\mathbf{TKS}^{q,\mathbf{DB}'}_{EMD}$ which will be proved to be the same as the required output $\mathbf{TKS}^{q,\mathbf{DB}}_{EMD}$.

($\mathbf{DB}'$ obtained in step 4) with EMD as metric for getting the result set. Assuming there are total R' records left after filtering in step 3 and 4, the final steps then take $O\left(R'N^3 \log N + R' \log R'\right)$ time. Note that following Algorithm 1, we first show an important property of the $E\hat{M}D$ metric w.r.t. range queries.

Lemma 2. *Range sets obtained from domain* $\mathbb{D}$ *satisfy* $\mathbf{RS}^{q,\mathbb{D}}_{E\hat{M}D,\epsilon} \supseteq \mathbf{RS}^{q,\mathbb{D}}_{EMD,\epsilon}$.

The last thing left is to verify the *completeness* of the result set $\mathbf{TKS}^{q,\mathbf{DB}'}_{EMD}$, i.e. this set does not lose any actual k-NN records from $\mathbf{DB}$ using EMD as the metric. This is shown through the following lemma.

Lemma 3. *Top-k set* $\mathbf{TKS}^{q,\mathbf{DB}'}_{EMD}$ *produced from Algorithm 1 guarantees no false drops of the actual k-nn records.*

The proofs of Lemma 2 and 3 are omitted due to the constraint of the space.

4 Experiments

4.1 Experimental Setting

Dataset and preprocessing. The experiments were conducted over four datasets which were synthetically generated from the two publicly accessible WS data colletions[4,5] The WS data in these collections are gathered from real world service sites. Also, they are classified into different categories which are suitable for our requirements of the empirical study. Our created datasets include contents of both FR and NFR attributes (as described in Section 2.1) for query processing of our framework. Each dataset contains 139, 218, 315 and 404 WS

---

[4] http://www.uoguelph.ca/~qmahmoud/qws/dataset
[5] http://www.andreas-hess.info/projects/annotator/ws2003.html.

records respectively that covers different WS categories. In particular, we focus on **business**, **communication** and **countryInfo** categories. The raw WSs information is then preprocessed, transforming from datasets into formatted WS records in the database of our framework.

Implementation. We used C++ programming language to implement the algorithms described in Section 3.6. All of our experiments were conducted on a low to middle sized laptop computer running Windows Vista with 3GB RAM and 1.66GHz Intel(R) Core(TM)2 Duo CPU.

Similarity Search Measure. In order to evaluate the effectiveness of EMD for similarity search of WSs, we use the widely adopted standards in information retrieval: *recall* and *precision* to measure the overall performance of the framework. In particular, given a query q, let C be the total number of retrieved services, A be the total number of relevant services in the service collection and B be the number of relevant services retrieved. The recall and precision of WS search are defined as Recall=B/A and Precision=B/C respectively. Both recall and precision values are in the range between 0 and 1. The higher value of the measure indicates the more effective search results.

Variable Parameters. We identify 3 variable parameters in the experiment and investigate their impact on the experimental results. These parameters are the size of WS database, value of k in top-k queries, and the ground distance used in computing EMD which is either SED or LD.

4.2   Experimental Results

We conducted 3 groups of experimental studies. The first two explored the effectiveness of our EMD approach according to the recall and precision measurements respectively. The last group demonstrates the efficiency of similarity search using EMD and the lower bound filter LB_{GIM}.

Measuring Recall. We measured the recall of EMD-based similarity search against two variable parameters: the DB size and the ground distance. For a test query, we fixed the other variable parameter k to be the total number of relevant services in the respective database. We also compared recalls on three chosen WS categories as mentioned in the dataset description. For instance, for a query q if we know there are total p relevant service records from the business category in a database with size s, then k is fixed to be p for q searching against this particular database's business category. Therefore, for queries q's against different categories and databases with different sizes, we need to measure different p's in order to determine respective values of k.

   Figure 4 shows the impact of DB sizes and ground distances. Overall, the impact of DB size on the recall of EMD-based WS search is not significant, which indicates a good property of EMD approach. Recall values in both diagrams are well above 0.6 for all DB sizes. For the impact of ground distances chosen for EMD, LD in general outperforms SED, especially in the case of larger DB sizes.

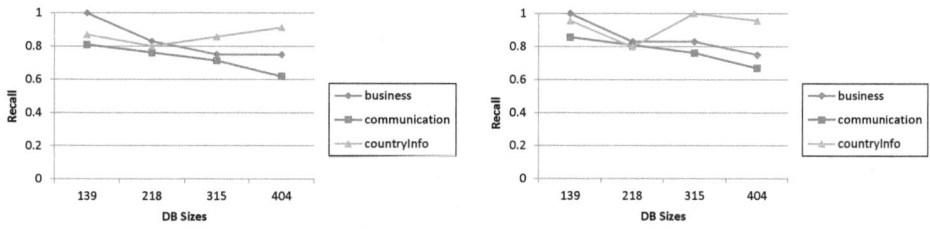

Fig. 4. EMD recall (left with SED, right with LD) v.s. DB Sizes

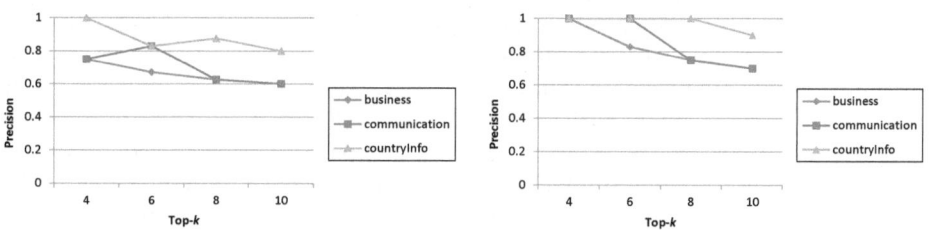

Fig. 5. EMD precision (left with SED, right with LD) v.s. Top-k queries

Measuring Precision. For a top-k query, the precision measures the value $\frac{p}{k}$ where p is the number of relevant services retrieved out of k services. Therefore this experiment is irrelevant to the parameter of DB size, but relevant to the other two parameters: k and the ground distance. For k, we chose the value of 4, 6, 8 and 10 to see its impact. The ground distance has still two choices: SED or LD. For simplicity, we again focused on the `business`, `communication` and `countryInfo` categories for retriving WSs and measuring the respective precisions.

Figure 5 presents the results from the precision measurements. Regarding the ground distances, LD outperforms SED significantly. Most noticeably, for the category `countryInfo` values of precisions are ones for $k = 4, 6, 8$. LD also provides much higher precision than SED for matching individual words having similar structures. For the impact of k, we can generally conclude that the precision decreases as the value of k increases. Nevertheless, even for top-10 queries precision values in both diagrams are still well above 0.6.

5 Related Work

Dong et al. [2] put forward a valuable similarity search approach to find Web services based on the keyword strategy. With the help of the co-occurrence of the terms appearing in service inputs and outputs, names of operation and description in services, the similarity search approach employs the agglomerative clustering algorithm to match WSs. There are also a number of work focusing on services matching and selection based on information retrieval (IR), which analyses the one-to-one relationship between keywords. A very recent work [4] has proposed a QoS aware search engine for WSs. Although these approaches work well in searching WSs, they ignore many-to-many similarity and partial matching. Our work shares some flavour with the optimal WSs matching search proposed in [20]. However, our work differs from these works in that we employ EMD to capture partial similarity for searching WSs.

EMD is first proposed in [8] to model similarity measure between two distributions. Because of its various advantages such as allowing for partial matching and matching human perception better than other simiarity measures, it is widely exploited for various applications like phishing detection [12], document retrieval [13], and databases [10, 14]. However, the computation cost of EMD is expensive because of its principle based on linear programming. For this reason, there are a number of research [10] focusing on designing effective lower bound on EMD to improve the efficiency of computing EMD. Nevertheless, their lower bound filters are only for EMD with equal weights ($\sum_{i=1}^{n_1} w_{kw_i} = \sum_{j=1}^{n_2} w_{aw_j}$ in our case), which is clearly not suitable for the comparison of word sequences that requires solving the general EMD (including the unequal total weights case). For this reason, we develop the LB_{GIM} filter generalized from LB_{IM} in [10] for word sequences partial matching.

6   Conclusions

In this paper, we propose a new EMD-based approach for effective Web services search. The proposed EMD filter is the first effective and fast-to-compute lower bound for the general EMD. Our approach is flexible and suitable for keyword-based content searches where words with different lengths are compared. We conducted experiments over a set of real datasets of Web services and the experimental result show that WS-Finder produces query answers with high recall and precision.

The proposed approach and techniques open up some interesting directions for future research. For example, by integrating with Semantic Web technique, we can perform similarity serach for distinguishing words such as *post* and *mail*. To further improve the perfromance of EMD search, we can leverage various index structures such as inverted lists, signature files or R Tree.

References

1. Platzer, C., Dustdar, S.: A vector space search engine for web services. In: Proceedings of the 3rd European IEEE Conference on Web Services (ECOWS 2005), pp. 14–16. IEEE Computer Society Press (2005)
2. Dong, X., Halevy, A., Madhavan, J., Nemes, E., Zhang, J.: Similarity search for web services. In: Proceedings of the Thirtieth International Conference on Very Large Data Bases (VLDB 2004), pp. 372–383. VLDB Endowment (2004)
3. Ma, J., Zhang, Y., He, J.: Efficiently finding web services using a clustering semantic approach. In: Proceedings of the 16th International Workshop on Context Enabled Source and Service Selection, Integration and Adaptation: Organized with the 17th International World Wide Web Conference (WWW 2008). ACM (2008)

4. Zhang, Y., Zheng, Z., Lyu, M.: Wsexpress: a qos-aware search engine for web services. In: Proceedings of the IEEE International Conference on Web Services (ICWS 2010), pp. 91–98. IEEE (2010)

5. Al-Masri, E., Mahmoud, Q.: Investigating web services on the world wide web. In: Proceeding of the 17th International World Wide Web Conference (WWW 2008), pp. 795–804. ACM (2008)

6. Ma, J., Zhang, Y., He, J.: Web services discovery based on latent semantic approach. In: Proceedings of the IEEE International Conference on Web Services (ICWS 2008), pp. 740–747. IEEE (2008)

7. Garofalakis, J., Panagis, Y., Sakkopoulos, E., Tsakalidis, A.: Web service discovery mechanisms: Looking for a needle in a haystack? In: Proceedings of the International Workshop on Web Engineering (2004)

8. Rubner, Y., Tomasi, C., Guibas, L.: The earth mover's distance as a metric for image retrieval. International Journal of Computer Vision 40(2), 99–121 (2000)

9. Paolucci, M., Kawamura, T., Payne, T.R., Sycara, K.: Semantic Matching of Web Services Capabilities. In: Horrocks, I., Hendler, J. (eds.) ISWC 2002. LNCS, vol. 2342, pp. 333–347. Springer, Heidelberg (2002)

10. Assent, I., Wenning, A., Seidl, T.: Approximation techniques for indexing the earth mover's distance in multimedia databases. In: Proceedings of the 22nd International Conference on Data Engineering (ICDE 2006), pp. 11–22. IEEE (2006)

11. Ljosa, V., Bhattacharya, A., Singh, A.K.: Indexing spatially sensitive distance measures using multi-resolution lower bounds. In: Proceedings of the 10th International Conference on Advances in Database Technology (EDBT 2006), pp. 865–883. ACM (2006)

12. Fu, A., Wenyin, L., Deng, X.: Detecting phishing web pages with visual similarity assessment based on earth mover's distance (emd). IEEE Transactions on Dependable and Secure Computing, 301–311 (2006)

13. Wan, X.: A novel document similarity measure based on earth mover's distance. Information Sciences 177(18), 3718–3730 (2007)

14. Xu, J., Zhang, Z., Tung, A., Yu, G.: Efficient and effective similarity search over probabilistic data based on earth mover's distance. Proceedings of the VLDB Endowment 3(1-2), 758–769 (2010)

15. Assent, I., Wichterich, M., Meisen, T., Seidl, T.: Efficient similarity search using the earth mover's distance for large multimedia databases. In: Proceedings of the 24th International Conference on Data Engineering (ICDE 2008) (2008)

16. Navarro, G., Raffinot, M.: Flexible pattern matching in strings: practical on-line search algorithms for texts and biological sequences. Cambridge Press (2002)

17. Hirschberg, D.S.: A linear space algorithm for computing maximal common subsequences. Communications of ACM 18, 341–343 (1975)

18. Hillier, F., Liberman, G.: Introduction to mathematical programming. McGraw-Hill, New York (1991)

19. Ling, H., Okada, K.: An efficient earth mover's distance algorithm for robust histogram comparison. IEEE Transactions on Pattern Analysis and Machine Intelligence, 840–853 (2007)

20. Srivastava, U., Munagala, K., Widom, J., Motwani, R.: Query optimization over web services. In: Proceedings of the 32nd International Conference on Very Large Data Bases (VLDB 2006), pp. 355–366. VLDB Endowment (2006)

A Framework for Trusted Services

Icamaan da Silva and Andrea Zisman

Department of Computer Science, City University London, United Kingdom
icamaan.silva.1@city.ac.uk, a.zisman@soi.city.ac.uk

Abstract. An existing challenge when selecting services to be used in a service-based system is to be able to distinguish between good and bad services. In this paper we present a trust-based service selection framework. The framework uses a trust model that calculates the level of trust a user may have with a service based on past experience of the user with the service and feedback about the service received from other users. The model takes into account different levels of trust among users, different relationships between users, and different levels of importance that a user may have for certain quality aspects of a service. A prototype tool has been implemented to illustrate and evaluate the work. The trust model has been evaluated in terms of its capacity to adjust itself due to changes in user ratings and its robustness.

Keywords: Trust model, direct interaction, and recommended feedback.

1   Introduction

Despite the advances in the area, service selection is still a challenging problem for service-oriented computing. Several approaches have been developed to support the selection of services based on one, or a combination of, functional, behavioural, quality, and contextual aspects [3][17][18][26]. However, given the large number of existing (similar) services and the open characteristics of SOC in which anyone can freely publish services, it is necessary to have mechanisms to distinguish between "*good*" and "*bad*" services.

The use of QoS information supplied by service providers [8], or even behavioural information as assumed in certain approaches [17][23], is not enough to distinguish between good and bad services during the selection process. (After all, this information can be inaccurate or exaggerated by service providers.) The use of service level agreements (SLAs) to guarantee certain quality aspects of a service does not assist with the selection process (SLAs are created after services have been selected). In addition, SLA requires extra cost and time to establish and monitor the agreement between the involved parties. As outlined in [9][22], it is important to use mechanisms for service selection that rely on feedback from consumers such as *trust* and *reputation* approaches. Furthermore, in recent years, we have experienced increasing use of SOC for business-to-consumer interactions in which provision of support for the needs and demands of consumers and applications is required. Service providers need to consider the reputation of their services to improve them and make a difference in a competitive environment.

C. Liu et al. (Eds.): ICSOC 2012, LNCS 7636, pp. 328–343, 2012.

Trust and reputation have been the focus of research in several open systems such as e-commerce, peer-to-peer, and multi-agent systems [5][10][15][16]. Some trust and reputation approaches have been suggested for web-service systems [8][19][22]. In general, web-services based approaches are limited and immature [22]. For example, the majority of these approaches present one or more of the followings issues: (i) assume that information given by service providers can be trusted; (ii) assume that feedbacks provided can always be trusted; (iii) give the same importance for feedbacks provided by different users; and (iv) demand a large number of interactions or non-intuitive information from users.

In this paper we describe a trust-based service selection framework to support the selection of services based on the level of trust a user may have with a service. More specifically, the framework uses a trust model that we have developed to calculate the level of trust a user may have with a service based on past experience of the user with the service (viz. *direct interactions*), and feedback about the service received from other users (viz. *recommended feedback*). Unlike existing approaches and models [1][4][5][24], the trust model that we describe in this paper considers different levels of importance that a user may have for the various quality aspects of a requested service, different levels of trust among users, and different relationships between users. For a user U, the approach considers three groups of related users, namely (a) *trusted group*, composed by people that U trusts; (b) *non-trusted group*, composed by people that U does not trust; and (c) *unknown group*, composed by people that U does not know and cannot say anything about the level of trust with them. The different types of relationships will interfere on how the recommended feedbacks are used during the computation of the trust values. The framework also supports the identification of malicious users.

The remainder of this paper is structured as follows. In Section 2 we describe an overview of the framework. In Section 3 we present the trust model used in the framework. In Section 4 we discuss implementation and evaluation aspects of our work. In Section 5 we give an account of related work. Finally, in Section 6 we discuss concluding remarks and future work.

2   Overview of the Framework

Figure 1 shows an overview of the architecture of trust-based service selection framework with its main components, interactions, and different types of data used as input or generated as output by the main components.

The framework supports a service selection process in which a service requester (consumer) creates a query to be executed by the service discovery component. The service discovery component searches for services that can fulfil the query and provides a list of candidate services. This list of services is used by the trust manager component to calculate trust values associated with the services in the list and to generate a ranked list of services. The consumer receives the ranked list of services, decides on the service to use, and provides his/her own rating for the service after using the service. This rating is stored in the rating repository and will be used by the trust manager in future computations of trust values for the service.

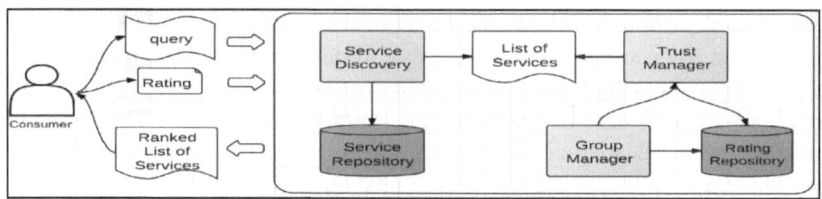

Fig. 1. Overview of trust-based service selection framework

The *service discovery* component identifies candidate services for a service request (query). The framework uses the service discovery component that was developed by one of the authors of this paper to identify services that match functional, behavioural, quality, and contextual aspects of a query. Details of this component are out of the scope of this paper and can be found in [18][26].

The *trust manager* component is responsible to calculate trust values of services based on a trust model that we have developed (see Section 3). The trust value of a service S is calculated by considering the past experiences that the consumer had with S, the level of trust that the consumer has with other users, the feedbacks about S from other users, and the level of importance the consumer may give for quality aspects of S. All feedbacks about S are stored in the *rating repository*.

The *group manager* component assists the framework with the concepts of groups associated with a user; i.e., trusted, non-trusted, and unknown groups. It decides on the group to which a user should be allocated and when a user should move from one group to another. For a user U, the groups of trusted, non-trusted, and unknown users associated with U are defined based on the level of trust that U has with these other users. The level of trust is calculated by comparing the ratings provided by U and the ratings provided by the other users for the services. The framework assumes valid and invalid ratings provided for a service S. More specifically, for two users U and U' and a service S, a rating for S provided by U' is valid when the rating matches the rating for S given by U, and it is invalid otherwise. When the rating is valid, the level of trust between U and U' increases; when the rating is invalid, the level of trust between U and U' decreases. It is possible to move a user U' from one group to another group of users associated with U, depending on the level of trust between U and U'. For a service S, the feedbacks of the users in the non-trusted group are ignored during the calculation of the trust value of S.

The *rating repository* stores ratings provided by the users, the level of importance of the quality aspects for a service, the levels of trust associated with the users, and information about the various groups.

3   Trust Model

As described before, the trust value that a user U_i has for a service S is based on direct interaction of user U_i with service S, and recommended feedback from other users for service S, given by the function below:

$$T_{Ui}(S) = w_d D_{Ui}(S) + w_f F_{Ui}(S) \tag{1}$$

where:

- $T_{Ui}(S)$: is the final trust value calculated for a service S for user U_i;
- $D_{Ui}(S)$: is a score for service S based on past interactions of user U_i with S;
- $F_{Ui}(S)$: is a score for service S based on recommended feedback from other users considering the relationships that U_i has with these users (i.e., trusted group, non-trusted group, and unknown group);
- w_d, w_f: associated weights, with $w_d + w_f = 1$.

In the case where a user did not have a past interaction with the service, or there are no feedback from other users for the service, these respective values are not considered to calculate the trust value.

Direct Interaction. The score given for the **direct interaction** with a service ($D_{Ui}(S)$) is calculated based on the work proposed by Josang *et al.* [6] that uses multinomial Dirichlet probability distribution. In this case, a user provides continuous rating values between 0 and 10, which are mapped to one of the following five categories, namely (i) *mediocre*, (ii) *bad*, (iii) *satisfactory*, (iv) *good*, and (v) *excellent*. The rationale for using Dirichlet distribution is to allow support for several category values with a solid statistical foundation, and to be able to represent discrete ratings as a function of a continuous rating.

In the model, the mapping of a rating c [0,10] into a discrete 5-component variable (v_1, v_2, ..., v_5) representing the categories (i) to (v) above is based on the calculation of the level of membership of c for each v_i variable according to the function presented in [6]. The levels of memberships are represented as a vector $\vec{V}$ of size five (viz. *membership* vector) and c is a rating provided by the user divided by 10. The sum of the values of the v_i representing c in vector $\vec{V}$ is equal to 1. For example, in the situation in which a user gives rating 7.0 for a service S, the values for categories (i) to (v) above (represented as v_1, v_2, v_3, v_4, v_5) are $\vec{V} = [0, 0, 0.2, 0.8, 0]$, respectively[6].

Our approach considers membership vectors for all the past ratings for a service S provided by user U_i, as well as the level of importance that U_i gives for different quality aspects of S. When a user requests a particular service, the user can specify the importance of the service quality aspects by using different weights for each of the aspects. For example, it is possible to use the weights *2: most important aspect; 1: less important aspect*; and *0: non-important aspect*. A rating given by a user is associated with the service as a whole. The weights given for each of the quality aspects are used to measure the level of similarity between different interactions with the service and to support distribution of ratings with the various quality aspects.

In order to illustrate, consider the scenario in Table 1 in which user U_1 had two past interactions with service S (i_1 and i_2), with ratings 7.0 ($c=0.7$) and 8.0 ($c=0.8$) respectively. For this scenario, assume the quality aspects of cost, availability, and response time with their respective importance for U_1 as shown in the table. Suppose i_3 the current interaction of the user. The direct interaction score will be calculated based on the similarities that exist between the quality aspects considered in interaction i_3 and the other interactions.

Table 1. Scenario for past interactions

U$_r$/S	Rating	c	Cost	Availability	Response Time
i_r/S	7.0	0.7	1	1	0
i_r/S	8.0	0.8	2	0	1
i_r/S			2	1	1

In the model, the similarity between the different interactions is calculated by:

$$d_l = 1 - \frac{\sum_x |(p_{l,x} - p'_x)|}{10} \tag{2}$$

where:

- d_l: is the similarity distance between the current and the l-th previous interactions;
- $p_{l,x}$: is the weight associated with each service quality aspect x in the l-th previous interaction;
- p'_x: is the weight associated with each service quality aspect x in the current interaction.

The score for a service S based on past interactions of user U_i with S is calculated by the function below:

$$D_{Ui}(S) = \sum_{j=1}^{k} \rho_j \delta_j \quad \text{with} \quad \rho_j = \frac{(j-1)}{(k-1)} \quad \delta_j = \frac{\vec{R}[j]+C}{\sum_{m=1}^{k}(\vec{R}[m]+C)} \quad \vec{R} = \sum_{l=1}^{n} d_l \vec{V}_l \, \alpha^{\Delta t} \tag{3}$$

where:

- $\vec{R}$: is the aggregated vector calculated by the weighted sum of all the vectors $\vec{V}_l$;
- $\vec{V}_l$: is the membership vector for a past interaction of U_i;
- n: is the total number of past interactions of Ui;
- k: is the total number of categories ($k=5$);
- d_l: is the similarity value for the various quality aspects of S calculated as in (2);
- ρ_j: is a value assigned to each category $v_1,\dots,v_k$ to provide a value in an interval;
- C: is a constant used to ensure that all values in the elements of vector $\vec{R}$ are greater than 0, to allow a posterior analysis of the Dirichlet distribution;
- $\alpha^{\Delta t}$ is the aging factor, where α is a constant and Δt is the difference between the time of a user's request and the time of past interactions with S.

Consider the scenario in Table 1. In this case, the membership vectors for each interaction i_1 and i_2 are: $V_1 = \{0, 0, 0.2, 0.8, 0\}$ and $V_2 = \{0, 0, 0, 0.8, 0.2\}$; the similarity distances are calculated as in (2), with $d_1 = 0.8$ and $d_2 = 0.9$; the aggregated vector $\vec{R} = \{0, 0, 0.16, 1.36, 0.18\}$; and $D_{Ui}(S) = 0.625$.

In the model, the number of past interactions of a user with a service S interferes with the calculation of $D_{Ui}(S)$. In order to demonstrate this consider an evaluation of the trust model in which there is an increase in the number of past interactions from a user from 0 to 200 interactions. For this evaluation, suppose the same weights associated with $D_{Ui}(S)$ and $F_{Ui}(S)$ ($w_d = w_f = 0.5$), and $C=0.4$ (see function (3)). For each of these past interactions assume the ratings provided by the user as (a) 10.0, (b)

6.0, and (c) 2.0. In all the cases (a) to (c), the evaluation assumes the same level of importance for the service quality aspects (cost = availability = response time = 1).

Figure 2 shows the results of the experiments for the cases (a), (b), and (c) executed in a prototype of the trust model that we have developed. As shown in the figure, when there are no past interactions, the value of $D_{Ui}(S)$ is 0.5, given that there is a 50% of chance of trusting a non-previously used service. We also observed that for rating values that are more distant than the medium rating value (5.0), it is necessary to consider a larger number of past interactions to reach an associated score for $D_{Ui}(S)$ that is closer to the rating. For example, for a rating of 10.0 (case (a)), $D_{Ui}(S)$ =1 after approximately 50 interactions; while for a rating of 6.0 (case (b)), $D_{Ui}(S)$ =0.6 after approximately 15 interactions; and for a rating of 0.2 (case (c)), $D_{Ui}(S)$ =0.2 after approximately 30 interactions. This is expected since in practice a higher level of trust is achieved with more opportunities of interactions (e.g., the level of trust between individuals usually increases with time).

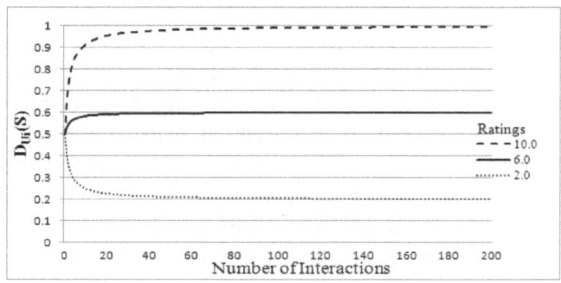

Fig. 2. Experiment results

Recommended Feedback. The score calculated based on **recommended feedback** from other users ($F_{Ui}(S)$) uses an associated level of trust between a user U_j and user U_i, and a score for service S calculated based on past interactions of U_j with S ($D_{Uj}(S)$). User U_j is classified in one of the three groups (trusted, non-trusted, and unknown) depending on the level of trust between U_j and Ui. The associated level of trust for a user U_j is calculated based on the Beta distribution given below:

$$t_{Ui,Uj} = \frac{\alpha + 1}{(\alpha + \beta + 2)} \qquad (4)$$

where

- U_j : is a user in one of the groups;
- α: is the number of "valid" recommended feedback provided by U_j;
- β: is the number of "invalid" recommended feedback provided by U_j.

The calculation of the score of recommended feedback from other users ($F_{Ui}(S)$) is given by the function below. In this case, the approach considers users classified in the trusted and unknown groups.

$$F_{Ui}(S) = \frac{\sum_{j=1}^{n} t_{Ui,Uj} D_{Uj}}{\sum_{j=1}^{n} t_{Ui,Uj}} \qquad (5)$$

where

- $D_{Uj}(S)$: is the score for service S calculated based on past interactions of user U_j with service S (see function (3))
- $t_{Ui,Uj}$: is the associated level of trust for a user U_j;
- n: is the total number of users in the trusted and unknown groups.

Table 2. Scenario for recommended feedback

User	Group	Previous Interactions	Interaction Results	$t_{Ui,Uj}$	D_{Ui}
U_2	TG	12	10V, 2I	0.79	0.82
U_3	TG	20	16V, 4I	0.77	0.75
U_4	UG	2	1V, 1I	0.5	0.88
U_5	TG	0	0	0.78	0.65
U_6	UG	0	0	0.5	0.31

In order to illustrate the computation of $F_{Ui}(S)$, consider the scenario shown in Table 2. In the table *TG* and *UG* represent trusted and unknown groups; *V* and *I* represent valid and invalid feedbacks. In this case, the level of trust for users U_4 and U_5 are calculated as the average of the level of trusts for the other users in their respective groups. For this scenario, $F_{Ui}(S) = 0.70$. Considering the scenarios shown in Tables 1 and 2, with $w_d = w_f = 0.5$, the trust value for service S is $T_{Ui}(S) = 0.66$.

In the model, the number of users in a certain group interferes with the calculation of $F_{Ui}(S)$. To demonstrate how the number of users in a group influences the value of $F_{Ui}(S)$, consider an evaluation of the trust model in which there is (a) an increment in the number of users in the trusted group from 0 to 100 with a fixed number of five users in the unknown group, and (b) an increment in the number of users in the unknown group from 0 to 100 with a fixed number of five users in the trusted group. For each above case we analysed the values of the calculated recommended feedback with ratings provided by users as 10.0 and as 0.0. Suppose the same weights associated with $D_{Ui}(S)$ and $F_{Ui}(S)$ ($w_d = w_f = 0.5$), and $C = 0.4$ (see function (3)). Figure 3 shows the results of the evaluation for the cases (a) and (b) for ratings of value 10.0. As shown in the figure, the users in the trusted group have a higher influence in the recommended feedback value than the users in the unknown group (the line in the graph for the trusted group is always above the one representing the unknown group). A similar situation occurs when the rating is 0.0.

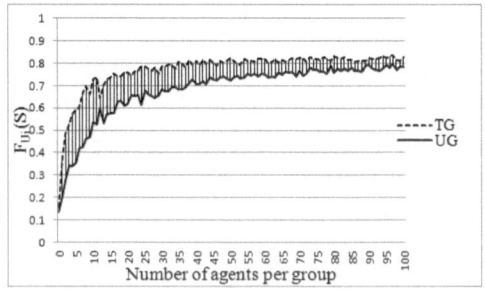

Fig. 3. Results of experiment

We also analysed how the different service quality aspects used in the model may influence the trust values computed by the model and, therefore, the selection of a service that best matches the request of a user. In this analysis we considered cost, response time, and availability service quality aspects. We executed an experiment in a scenario for 60 units of time (time-steps) with one main user requesting a service with a different importance for a quality aspect in each set of ten time-steps. Table 3 summarises the relevant quality aspects for the user in the different sets of time-steps.

We considered three services S1, S2, and S3 with similar functionalities, and 30 other users interacting with one of the three services and providing ratings accordingly to their satisfaction with respect to a service and certain quality aspects. Table 4 summarises the ratings provided by the various users for a service and the respective quality aspect considered for each case in the experiment.

Table 3. Quality aspects with respect to the time-steps

Time-steps	1-10	11-20	21-30	31-40	41-50	51-60
Quality aspects	cost	resp. time, availability	cost, resp. time, availability	Cost	resp. time, availability	cost, resp. time, availability

Table 4. Ratings provided by the various users

Experiments	Users	Service	Rating	Quality aspects
C.a	u1, ... ,u10	S2	8.8	cost, response time, availability
C.b	u11, ... , u20	S1	8.5	cost
C.c	u21, ... , u30	S3	9.0	response time, availability

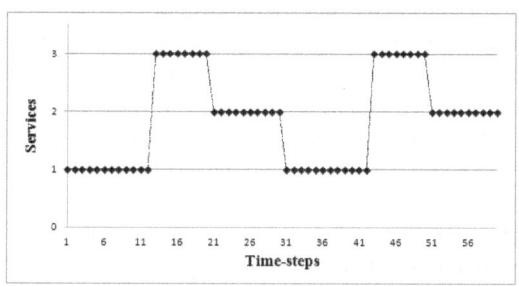

Fig. 4. Services selected in each time-step

Figure 4 shows the services that were selected in each time-step for the above scenario. In this case the services were selected taking into consideration the quality aspects of the services and the user requests, and not necessarily the service with the highest rating provided by the users (S3 in this scenario).

4   Implementation Aspects and Evaluation

A prototype tool of the framework has been implemented. The trust manager and group manager components were implemented in Java (J2SE), and the rating repository was implemented in MySQL database. The service discovery component was also implemented in Java and is exposed as a web service using Apache Axis2. To simulate the different behaviours of the users in the evaluation, we implemented a simulator in Java for requests and ratings provided by different users.

The work was evaluated in terms of Case (1): *the time required by the trust model to adjust trust values due to changes in user ratings*; and Case (2): *the robustness of the trust model against unfair ratings,* as described in the following.

Case (1): This case is concerned with the level of match that exists between the trust value of a service S and user ratings given for this service. More specifically, we measure the time that it takes the trust model to adjust itself with respect to changes in the ratings provided by users, so that the trust value of S matches the rating values received by users of S. The matching levels (ML) are in a scale of 0.0 to 1.0, where a full match has a matching level of 1.0, and are calculated using the function below:

$$ML = 1 - |(\mu_{Ur}(S) - T(S))| \qquad (6)$$

where:

- $\mu_{Ur}(S)$ is the expected value for the user ratings for service S, calculated based on rating intervals;
- $T(S)$ is the trust value for service S.

This type of evaluation is important to analyse how our model responds to changes in the quality of the services (reflected in the user ratings). These changes in service quality can be caused due to modifications in the services by service providers, in order to satisfy new requirements and demands, or new rules and regulations. The changes in the service quality can also be caused due to deviations in the expectations of the users of a service. For example, users are always demanding faster responses for their online requests, or expecting to pay less for a service.

The evaluation was executed in a scenario in which one main user requests the trust value of a service S and 100 other users interact with S and provide ratings for S, within a certain interval of values, for a certain moment of time. In the evaluation we considered 90 units of time (time-steps). We also assumed that for each interval of 30 time-steps there is a change in the ratings provided by the users. We considered aging factor of $\alpha=0.5$ (see function (3)), and the times for the user requests and past iterations as the values of the time-steps. We executed the experiments for four different cases with respect to the interval of ratings provided by the users in each time-step (C1.1, C1.2, C1.3, and C1.4). In each case, we started with the highest rating interval (values [10.0, 8.0]) for the first set of 30 time-steps; dropped the ratings for the second set of 30 time-steps to intervals of [0.0, 2.0[, [2.0, 4.0[, [4.0, 6.0[, and [6.0, 8.0[, respectively; and raised the rating values within the interval of [10.0, 8.0] again in the third set of 30 time-steps, to provide different values across the range of possible ratings. The ratings within each of the intervals are randomly generated, by using a module that we have implemented, based on uniform distribution.

Figure 5 shows graphs with the results of the experiments for the four cases above. As shown in the figure, the matching level of the trust values with the ratings given by the users in each case drops after each 30 time-steps (when there is change in the rating). The results also show that the approach takes between four and seven time-steps for a full match between the interval of the trust value and the interval of the ratings given by the users, depending on the variation level in the rating intervals. For example, in the case of interval ratings between [0.0, 2.0[(case C1.1), the approach takes seven time-steps to achieve a match between the trust value and the rating. In the case of interval ratings between [6.0, 8.0[(case C1.4), the approach takes four time-steps to achieve the match. Similarly, in the cases C1.2 and C1.3 the approach takes five and six time-steps to achieve the match, respectively.

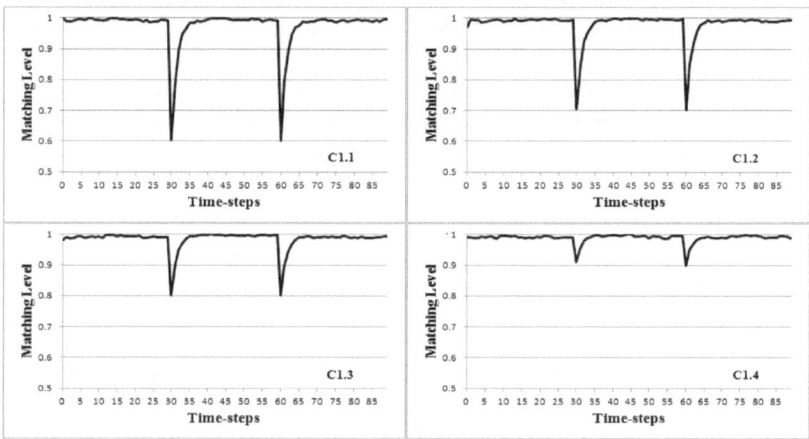

Fig. 5. Matching levels with respect to time-steps with aging factor

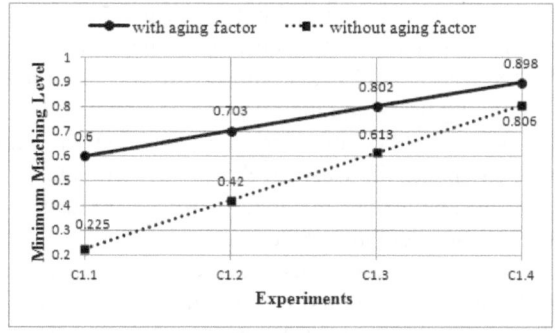

Fig. 6. Minimum Matching levels according to the rating variation

Figures 5 and 6 show the minimum values achieved for the match between the trust and rating interval values. As shown in Figure 6, these values grow linearly with respect to the reduction in the difference of the rating intervals (continuous line in the figure). More specifically, the drops in the matching values are 0.60 in the case C1.1; 0.703 in the case C1.2; 0.802 in the case C1.3; and 0.898 in the case C1.4.

Based on the experiments, we also noticed that the use of an aging factor influences the amount of time it takes for the trust value to reach a match with a given rating interval. This was observed by executing the above experiments (C1.1, C1.2,

C1.3, C1.4) without taking into account the aging factor for past rating values and, therefore, considering the same importance for all rating values throughout all time-steps ($\Delta t=0$ in function (3)). Table 5 summarises the number of time-steps for each case in the experiment when the trust values match the respective interval of the rating values. The minimum values achieved for the match between the trust and rating values are shown in Figure 6 (dashed line). These values are smaller when compared to the situation in which an aging factor is used. However, they are still linear with respect to the rating variation values.

The above results are expected given that when using an aging factor, older past ratings have very little importance when compared to more recent past ratings for a certain time-step. Contrary, in the case in which the aging factor is considered, the older past ratings have the same level of importance than the most recent ones, requiring more user iterations for the trust values to match the rating values.

Table 5. Number of time-steps needed to reach a full matching level without the aging factor

Cases	C1.1	C1.2	C1.3	C1.4
Number of Time-steps	240	183	124	60

Case (2): This case is concerned with the robustness of the trust model with respect to unfair ratings provided by malicious users. By robustness we mean the capacity of the model to provide trust values that are not influenced by unfair ratings. In the approach, this is achieved by identifying unfair ratings and not considering them in the calculation of the trust values. Unfair ratings are a major challenge to approaches based on users' feedbacks since it is possible to have users providing ratings to either promote or discredit a particular service according to their interests.

In our approach, the trust model deals with possible unfair ratings by considering different trust levels among users and the non-trusted group of users. As described in Section 2, the feedbacks provided by users are classified as valid or invalid. This classification is used to update the trust level among users and to move users to the non-trusted group, when applicable. Feedbacks from users in the non-trusted group are ignored during the trust calculation process.

As in the Case (1), the evaluation was executed in a scenario in which one main user requests a particular service S, and considering 90 units of time with 100 users providing ratings for S in each time-step. We assumed service S with *excellent* quality level; i.e.; fair feedback ratings for S are in the interval [10.0, 8.0]. We considered unfair feedback ratings for S as values in the interval [0.0, 4.0]. We also considered that the main user requesting service S provides a fair feedback rating for S. The 100 users in the experiments are divided into two sets with 50 users in each set. We assumed users in the first set always providing fair feedback ratings, and users in the second set giving unfair ratings (malicious users).

We executed the experiments for five different cases (C2.1 to C2.5) with respect to the percentage of unfair ratings provided by the 50 users in the second set. In the case

C2.1, 100% of the ratings provided by the 50 users in the second set were unfair ratings (values between [0.0, 4.0]); while in the cases C2.2, C2.3, C2.4, and C2.5, 80%, 60%, 40%, and 20%, respectively, of the provided ratings by the users in the second set were unfair. The rating values within each of the situations considered in the experiments are randomly generated, for the interval of fair and unfair ratings. In time-step 0 of the experiment, we considered that there has been no feedback ratings provided for service S and assumed an initial default trust value for this service as 0.5.

We analysed the robustness of the model by considering situations in which the concept of the different groups are used and when the concept of groups are not used. We considered that a user moves to the non-trusted group when the associated level of trust between this user and the user requesting the service is less than 0.3 (see Section 3); furthermore, we considered that a user in the non-trusted group moves out of this group (becomes a trusted user) when the associated level of trust is greater or equal to 0.7. The use of a high value for the associated level of trust to remove a user from the non-trusted group is to reflect the fact that, in general, when an individual looses trust with someone else, it is necessary to have more evidence of *good* attitude to restore trust between the individuals.

Figure 7 shows the results of the experiments for the cases C2.1 to C2.5, respectively, with and without the existence of the groups. As shown in Figure 7, when using the concept of groups, for the case C2.1 the model reaches the trust value of 0.9 for S faster than in the cases C2.2 and C2.3. In the case C2.1 this happens because the approach quickly identifies malicious users and moves them to the non-trusted group. For the cases C2.2, and C2.3, the same happens, although it takes the model more time to identify the non-trusted users. In the cases C2.4 and C2.5, the model never reaches the value of 0.9, given the low percentage of unfair ratings provided by the users in the second set, not allowing the approach to move a large number of users to the non-trusted group. Table 6 shows a summary of the number of users that are moved to and from the non-trusted group for each case.

The results in Figure 7 also show that when the concept of groups are not used, the approach takes a long time for reaching the trust value of 0.9 for S (case C2.1), or never reaches this value (all the other cases in the experiments). In these situations, the concepts of valid and invalid feedbacks are considered to calculate the trust value. The graphs also show that in the cases C2.1 and C2.2, the differences in the trust values for using and not using the concept of groups start bigger and are reduced with time, while in the cases C2.3 and C2.4; these differences are more constant since the beginning. This is because the reduction in the number of unfair ratings given by the users in the second group (reflected in the various percentages) makes it more difficult to distinguish between malicious and non-malicious users. For the case C2.5, there is no difference when using or not the concept of groups. This is because the low number of unfair rates (20%) yields on few users moving to the non-trusted group and a high percentage of those users to leave the group (see Table 6).

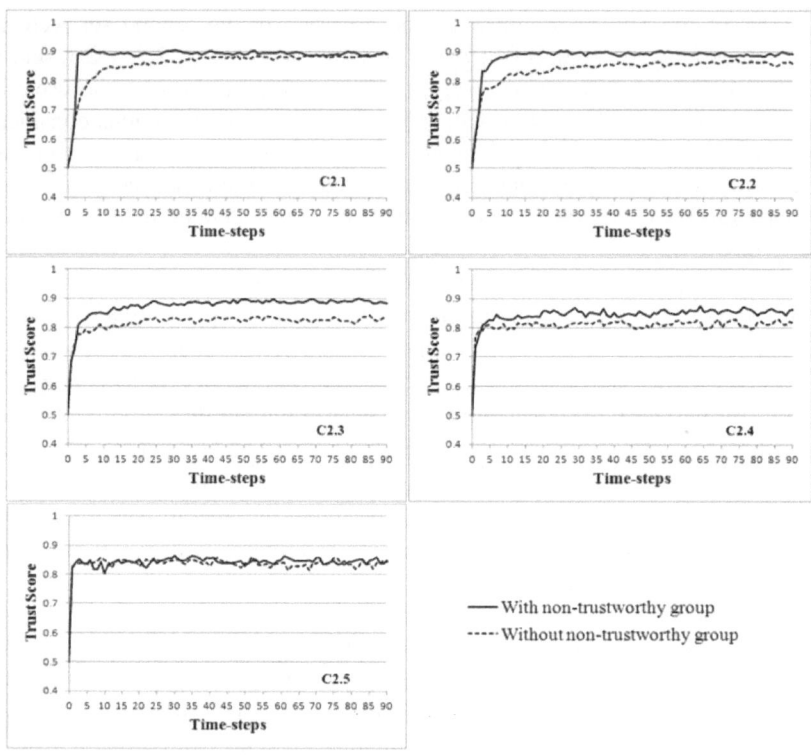

Fig. 7. Trust scores according to unfair ratings with and without the non-trusted group

The above results demonstrate that the concept of groups provide better results than when not using the groups for the majority of the cases, or the same result when there is a low percentage of unfair ratings. Moreover, the approach supports the identification of the majority of malicious users (all of them for the cases C2.1, C2.2, and C2.3). The way the approach considers the notion of valid and invalid ratings also contributes to the results achieved by the approach.

Table 6. Number of users moved from and to the non-trusted group

Cases	C2.1	C2.2	C2.3	C2.4	C2.5
Users that moved to	50	50	50	28	9
Users that moved from	0	0	0	1	6

5   Related Work

Several approaches have been proposed to support service selection, trust, and reputation management systems [5][10][15][16]. Some of these approaches propose different ways to combine feedbacks from users of services in order to calculate appropriate reputation scores [5][13][14][11][20]. Many of these approaches are concerned with only reputation management aspects and do not consider QoS attributes and different levels of trust between users, as in the case of our work.

Existing trust models can be classified as (i) Bayesian models [5][13], when trust values are calculated based on probabilistic distribution; (ii) belief models [4][24], that associates degrees of belief to the possible output supported by the model; and (iii) discrete models [1], that associate discrete categories to determine the level of trust with other users or services. The reputation model in [5] is based on beta distribution and considers direct experience as well as feedback from other users to model the behavior of a system. The belief model in [4] uses metrics called *opinion* to describe belief and disbelief about a proposition, as well as the degree of uncertainty regarding probability of an event. The discrete model in [1] takes into account the perception a user has from another user. The trust model described in this paper is based on the combination of concepts from Bayesian and discrete models. More specifically, we extend the approach in [5] to support the calculation of trust values considering different levels of importance for quality aspects of a requested service and different relationships between users (group concept). Similar to our model, in [5] the model supports different levels of trust between users. However, our model calculates these levels of trust based on a beta distribution, while in [5] this are calculated based on opinion. The concepts of discrete model used in our approach are represented by the notion of groups.

A large number of works have been proposed to support service selection in which more than one feedback from users are considered [2][25][19][12][11][21][7]. However, the majority of these approaches fail to provide a good reputation management system as they consider the available feedbacks in the same way when calculating trust values [2][25][19][12][11]. This causes a significant drawback given that these approaches are not able to distinguish between malicious users and do not provide proper importance to users' feedback with a good history of past interactions. Furthermore, some of these approaches usually demand a large amount of information from the service consumers [2][25][19][11][12]. In some cases these approaches even demand non-intuitive information such as graphs curves to calculate the trust values, or several parameters to be configured in order to achieve a good performance [21].

The work in [2] proposes a framework for quality of service management based on user expectations. The users are responsible for providing ratings and expectation values on QoS attributes. The approach described in [25] uses a reputation manager to calculate reputation scores and assumes that service consumers will provide QoS requirements, weights to be associated to the reputation score, QoS scores, and ratings to assess the services. This approach considers the most recent rating of each user and assumes that all users provide non-malicious and accurate ratings.

In [19] the authors describe an approach to service selection based on the user's perception of the QoS attributes rather than the actual attribute values. In order to identify the most appropriate values for each QoS attribute, the approach requires several interactions with the users. The proposal to mitigate this issue is based on the presentation of non-intuitive curves. The work in [12] does not have any mechanism to prevent malicious feedback and does not provide ways of checking whether the same feedback in different websites is used more than once. The framework in [11] uses an ontology-based approach to assist providers to advertise their services and consumers to express their preferences and ratings.

The QoS-based service selection and ranking solution in [21] supports prediction of future quality of web services. The authors introduce a mechanism to avoid unfair ratings based on statistical analysis of the reports from users. The success of the proposed methodology depends on the selection of an optimal configuration for the design parameters. On another example, in [7] a method to calculate reputation based on users' ratings, service compliance, and verity is described. Compliance refers to performance history with respect to delivering the agreed level of qualities. Verity represents the success of a web service or service provider in meeting the agreed quality levels and is calculated based on the variance of the compliance levels. No mechanism to avoid malicious users and unfair feedbacks is provided.

The framework and trust model described in this paper complement existing service selection reputation approaches. It differs from existing approaches by providing a model to calculate trust values of services based on different trust levels between users of the services, level of importance of service quality aspects, and weighted recommended feedback. The approach also considers the notion of valid and invalid feedbacks when calculating the trust values of the services.

6   Conclusion and Future Work

In this paper we presented a framework for trust-based service selection. It uses a trust model to calculate the trust value of a service based on past experience of the user of the service and feedback ratings about the service received from other users. The trust model also considers the level of trust among users, and level of importance for different quality aspects of the services. The users can be classified in three groups, namely trusted, non-trusted, and unknown users. This classification is considered when using feedback ratings from users to calculate trust values. The approach also supports identification of malicious users based on the comparison of rating values.

We are currently extending the trust model to consider different types of more fine-grained relationships between users, or group of users, and how these relationships could influence the level of trust in the recommended feedback from other users. For example, a user U can have different levels of trust with a friend or a relative, although they can both be in the trusted group of U. We are also considering transitive relationship between users. We are extending the model to provide more fine-tuned values for the trust levels between a user requesting a service and users in the unknown group, based on past interactions with common services between the users. Other areas for future work are concerned with the development of mechanisms to decompose feedback and rating of service compositions to specific services in the composition, bootstrapping, and analysis of the impact of changes in the values of constant C (see function 3) for the calculation of the trust values.

References

[1]   Abdul-Rahman, A., Hailes, S.: Supporting Trust in Virtual Communities. In: HCISS (2000)
[2]   Deora, V., Shao, J., Gray, W.A., Fiddian, N.J.: A Quality of Service Management Framework Based on User Expectations. In: Orlowska, M.E., Weerawarana, S., Papazoglou, M.P., Yang, J. (eds.) ICSOC 2003. LNCS, vol. 2910, pp. 104–114. Springer, Heidelberg (2003)

[3]   Hausmann, J., Heckel, R., Lohmann, M.: Model-based Discovery of Web Services. In: Intl. Conference on Web Services (2004)

[4]   Josang, A.: A Logic for Uncertain Probabilities. International Journal of Uncertainty, Fuzziness and Knowledge-Based Systems 9(3), 279–311 (2001)

[5]   Josang, A., Haller, J.: Dirichlet Reputation Systems. In: 2nd International Conference on Availability, Reliability and Security (ARES 2007), Vienna (April 2007)

[6]   Josang, A., Luo, X., Chen, X.: Continuous Ratings in Discrete Bayesian Reputation Systems. In: Proceedings of the IFPIM 2008 (2008)

[7]   Kalepu, S., Krishnaswamy, S., Loke, S.W.: Reputation = f(User Ranking, Compliance, *Verity*). In: Proc. of the IEEE International Conference on Web Services (2004)

[8]   Liu, Y., Ngu, A., Zheng, L.: QoS computation and policing in dynamic web service selection. In: Proc. of World Wide Web Conference (2004)

[9]   Malik, Z., Bouguettaya, A.: Reputation Bootstrapping for Trust Establishment among Web Services. IEEE Internet Computing 13(1) (2009)

[10] Matsuo, Y., Yamamoto, H.: Community gravity: Measuring bidirectional effects by trust and rating on online social networks. In: World Wide Web Conference (2009)

[11] Maximillen, E.M., Singh, M.P.: Multiagent System for Dynamic Web Services Selection. In: Proc. 1st Workshop on Service-Oriented Computing and Agent-Based Engineering (2005)

[12] Meng, L., Junfeng, Z., Lijie, W., Sibo, C., Bing, X.: CoWS: An Internet-Enriched and Quality-Aware Web Services Search Engine. In: Intl. Conference on Web Services (2011)

[13] Mui, L., Mohtashemi, M., Halberstadt, A.: A computational Model of Trust and Reputation. In: Proc. of the 35th Hawaii International Conference on System Science (2002)

[14] Nguyen, H.T., Zhao, W., Yang, J.: A Trust and Reputation Model Based on Bayesian Network for Web Services. In: IEEE International Conference on Web-Services, Miami (2010)

[15] Ruohomaa, S., Kutvonen, L.: Trust Management Survey. In: Herrmann, P., Issarny, V., Shiu, S.C.K. (eds.) iTrust 2005. LNCS, vol. 3477, pp. 77–92. Springer, Heidelberg (2005)

[16] Schafer, J.B., Frankowski, D., Herlocker, J., Sen, S.: Collaborative Filtering Recommender Systems. In: Brusilovsky, P., Kobsa, A., Nejdl, W. (eds.) The Adaptive Web. LNCS, vol. 4321, pp. 291–324. Springer, Heidelberg (2007)

[17] Shen, Z., Su, J.: Web Service Discovery Based on Behavior Signature. In: IEEE SCC (2005)

[18] Spanoudakis, G., Zisman, A.: Discovering Services during Service-based System Design using UML. IEEE Transactions of Software Engineering 36(3), 371–389 (2010)

[19] Srivastava, A., Sorenson, P.G.: Service Selection based on customer Rating of Quality of Service Attributes. In: IEEE International Conference on Web Services (2010)

[20] Tan, L., Chi, C., Deng, J.: Quantifying Trust Based on Service Level Agreement for Software as a Service. In: Proc. of Intl. Computer Software and Applications Conf. (2008)

[21] Vu, L., Hauswirth, M., Aberer, K.: QoS-based Service Selection and Ranking with Trust and Reputation Management. In: Proc. of the Cooperative Information System Conf. (2005)

[22] Wang, Y., Vassileva, J.: Towards Trust and Reputation Based Web Service Selection: A Survey. International Transaction Systems Science and Applications 3(2) (2007)

[23] Wang, X., Vitvar, T., Kerrigan, M., Toma, I.: A QoS-Aware Selection Model for Semantic Web Services. In: Dan, A., Lamersdorf, W. (eds.) ICSOC 2006. LNCS, vol. 4294, pp. 390–401. Springer, Heidelberg (2006)

[24] Wang, Y., Singh, M.P.: Evidence-Based Trust: A Mathematical Model Geared for Multiagent Systems. ACM Transactions on Autonomous and Adaptive Systems (2010)

[25] Xu, Z., Martin, P., Powley, W., Zulkernine, F.: Reputation-Enhanced QoS-based Web Services Discovery. In: IEEE International Conference on Web Services (2007)

[26] Zisman, A., Spanoudakis, G., Dooley, J.: A Framework for Dynamic Service Discovery. In: Int. Conf. on Automated Software Engineering (2008)

Configuring Private Data Management as Access Restrictions: From Design to Enforcement

Aurélien Faravelon[1], Stéphanie Chollet[2], Christine Verdier[1], and Agnès Front[1]

[1] Laboratoire d' Informatique de Grenoble,
220, rue de la chimie, BP 53 F-38041 Grenoble Cedex 9
{aurelien.faravelon,christine.verdier,agnes.front@imag.fr}@imag.fr
[2] Laboratoire de Conception et d'Intégration des Systèmes
F-26902, Valence cedex 9, France
stephanie.chollet@lcis.grenoble-inp.fr

Abstract. Service-Oriented Computing (SOC) is a major trend in designing and implementing distributed computer-based applications. Dynamic late biding makes SOC a very promising way to realize pervasive computing, which promotes the integration of computerized artifacts into the fabric of our daily lives. However, pervasive computing raises new challenges which SOC has not addressed yet. Pervasive application relies on highly dynamic and heterogeneous entities. They also necessitate an important data collection to compute the context of users and process sensitive data. Such data collection and processing raise well-known concerns about data disclosure and use. They are a brake to the development of widely accepted pervasive applications. SOC already permits to impose constraints on the bindings of services. We propose to add a new range of constraints to allow data privatization, *i.e.* the restriction of their disclosure. We extend the traditional design and binding phases of a Service-Oriented Architecture with the expression and the enforcement of privatization constraints. We express and enforce these constraints according to a two phases model-driven approach. Our work is validated on real-world services.

Keywords: Access restriction, SOA, workflow, private data.

1 Introduction

Service-Oriented Computing (SOC) is a major trend in designing and implementing distributed computer-based applications. Applications are implemented by composing already existing functionalities called services which exposed over networks such as the Internet. Services are loosely coupled and SOC thus promotes the distinction between the design of the composition and its execution. Indeed, the application is designed without knowing which services will actually be available. The application is then executed by invoking and binding the necessary services among the set of available services.

Dynamic late biding makes SOC a very promising way to realize pervasive computing, a new paradigm which promotes the integration of computerized

C. Liu et al. (Eds.): ICSOC 2012, LNCS 7636, pp. 344–358, 2012.
© Springer-Verlag Berlin Heidelberg 2012

artifacts into the fabric of our daily lives. Pervasive computing relies on distributed and highly heterogeneous and dynamic entities. Sensors, softwares or devices are such entities. Their composition is crucial to build efficient and innovative applications. Pervasive applications have to be flexible and adaptive. Exposing functionalities as services, distinguishing the application's design from its execution and realizing the application by binding the actual services meet these requirements.

However, pervasive computing raises new challenges which SOC has not addressed yet. Pervasive computing necessitates an important data collection. Collecting the location of users who interact with the application, for instance, is necessary to identify their contexts of use. Using pervasive computing thus means sharing data which flow in the application - such as medical files or credit application - and disclosing data about the users of the composition. As sensitive data can be derived from seemingly inoffensive pieces of data, these two groups of people can be modeled in details. Such a possibility raises well-known concerns about data disclosure and use. They are a brake to the development of widely accepted pervasive applications. As a result, there must exist a mechanism to constraint data disclosure.

SOC already permits to impose constraints on the bindings of services. We propose to add a new range of constraints to allow data privatization, *i.e.* the restriction of their disclosure. Privatization constraints bear on what an observer external to the composition can deduce from the binding of services, on what a client can ask a service provider about and on what a service provider can ask a client about.

We extend the traditional design and binding phases by allowing the expression and the enforcement of privatization constraints. We express and enforce these constraints according to a two phases model-driven approach:

- At design level, we extend a composition language with a platform independent privatization language to express privacy constraints which must be enforced at binding time. Privacy designers can use this language to express privatization constraints.
- At binding time, automatic model-to-text transformations inject the appropriate code to enforce privatization constraints in a Service-Oriented Architecture (SOA). We modify the SOA to store the information necessary to enforce access restriction.

The paper is structured as it follows. In Section 2, we introduce a global overview of our approach. We detail our design level in Section 3 and the execution level in Section 4. Eventually, we validate our approach in Section 5 before discussing the works related to ours in Section 6 and concluding in Section 7.

2   Global Approach

Our goal is to ease the design and implementation of privacy-aware pervasive applications realized as compositions of heterogeneous and dynamic services.

We propose a model-based approach where security properties related to private data management as access restriction are specified at design time. These properties are realized through code generation at binding time depending on the available services.

Because of the inherent heterogeneity and dynamism of services, access restriction is a problem throughout the entire application's life-cycle. Services that are actually used at runtime are generally not known at design time. Their access restrictions capabilities cannot be predicted or relied on. Furthermore, design time involves non-technical stackeholders who cannot make sense of technical minutes.

We have designed and connected two platform-independent views, a service composition one and an access restriction one. From these views and their relationships, we automatically generate an executable privacy-aware service composition as shown on Figure 1.

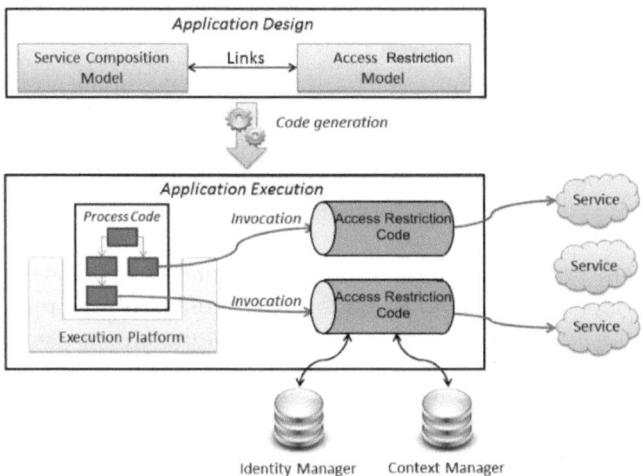

Fig. 1. Background of our proposition

Composition and access restriction are specified at design time. We are driven by two principles: abstraction and separation of concerns. Modeling allows us to abstract away technical details and separation of concerns permits to accommodate different viewpoints of the same application. Privacy experts can design the privacy policy.

At binding time, the application is realized as a service orchestration. Access restriction features are injected through the generation of a proxy for each service instance. We have also developed an identity manager which deals with users privileges and a context manager which handles contextual information retrieval and processing.

3   Design Level

Figure 2 displays the service composition and the access restriction metamodels and their relationships.

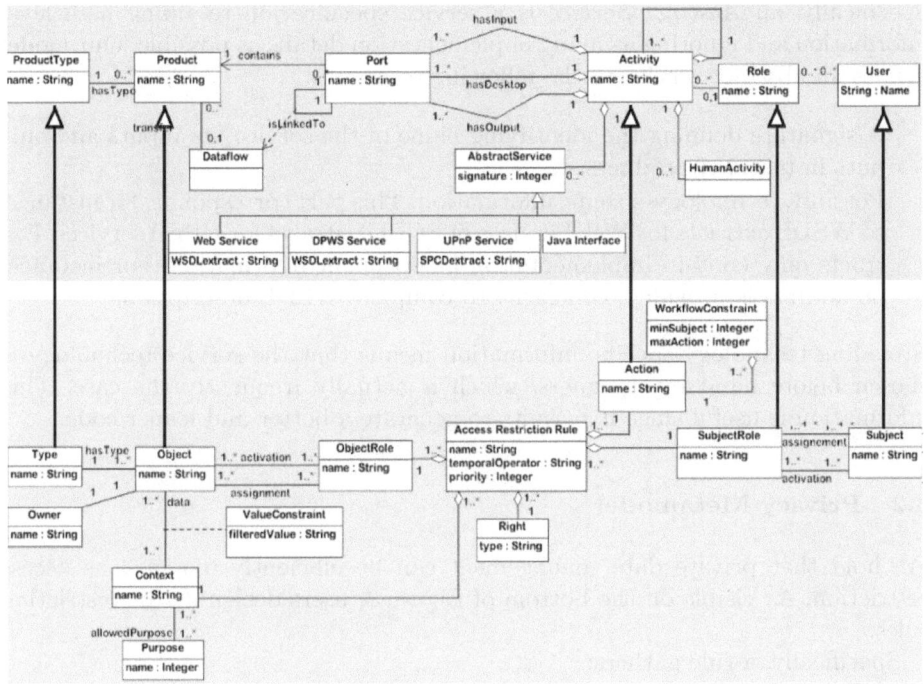

Fig. 2. Relations between Service Composition and Access Control Metamodels

3.1   Service Composition Metamodel

Our approach regarding service composition builds on the Abstract Process Engine Language (APEL) [5]. As visible at the top of Figure 2, APEL is a high level process definition language. We chose APEL because it natively supports any type of service when other process languages, such as WS-BPEL, are dedicated to a specific technology. It contains a minimal set of concepts sufficient to specify a process:

– An *Activity* is a step in the process that results in an action, realized by a human or a computer. Activities can be made of sub-activities; they are then said to be composite. An activity has *Ports* representing communication interfaces. An *Activity* must be realized by a *User*.

- A *Product* is an abstract object that flows between activities. *Dataflows* connect output ports to input ports, specifying which product variables are being transferred between activities.
- An *Abstract Service* can be attached to an activity. It represents a type of service to be called in order to achieve the activity.

Specifically, an *Abstract Service* is a service specification retaining high level information and ignoring as many implementation details as possible. Our model defines an abstract service in the following terms:

- A signature defining the identifying name of the service, its inputs and outputs in terms of products.
- Possibly, technology-specific information. This part corresponds, for instance, to WSDL extracts for Web Services or SCPD extracts for UPnP services. Extracts only contain implementation-independent information. For instance, no address is provided, contrarily to complete WSDL descriptions.

Providing technology-specific information means that the service technology is chosen before hand by designers, which is actually frequently the case. This information is useful since it permits to generate a better and leaner code.

3.2   Privacy Metamodel

We hold that private data management can be efficiently modeled as access restriction. As visible on the bottom of Figure 2, users design access restriction rules.

Specifically, a rule gathers:

- A *Subject i.e.* a user or a software agent that acts in the application. *Subject* are categorized in *SubjectRoles* according to their position in an organization.
- An *Object i.e.* any entity a *Subject* can affect. *Objects* can be categorized according to their functionalities for instance according to *ObjectRoles*. Each *Object* has an owner and a type. The owner is responsible for managing the access to their data.
- An *Action i.e.* an access mode to an *Object*.
- A *Right i.e.* the modality of a *Subject*'s relation to an *Action*. *Rights* are divided into permissions, obligations and prohibitions, they apply to *SubjectRoles* and *ObjectRoles*.

Several *Access Control Rules* may apply to the same set of *Actions*, *ObjectRoles* and *SubjectRoles*. *Access Control Rules* are conditioned by:

- *Context i.e.* a situation defined by a constraint over the values of a set of *Objects*. The *Context* entity captures the specificity of pervasive access restriction. A *Context* indicates for which purpose the access restriction rule is satisfied. A purpose is the reason why an *Action* is performed.

– The satisfaction of a workflow security patterns. We accomodate two of them, separation and binding of duties. Both of them restrict the number of *Subjects* that can intervene in a group of *Action* and the number of *Action* each *Subject* can perform. We gather these constraints under the name *Workflow Constraints*. They are defined by the maximum amount of *Actions* a set of *Subjects* can perform in a group of *Actions*.

Managing rules conflict is important to ensure the consistency of the privacy policy. Each rule is associated with a priority level. The rules with the highest priority win over the ones with lowest levels. When several *Access Control Rules* apply to the same set of *Actions*, *ObjectRoles* and *SubjectRoles*, these rules cannot share the same conditions. Eventually, when a permission or an obligation and a prohibitions are conflicting, the prohibition always takes the precedence.

3.3   Logical Semantics

Having described the basis of our access restriction model, we now integrate them in order to allow the computation of privatization policies.

We have focused on **Compositions** as a temporally ordered flow of **Activities**, *i.e.* the activation of **Roles** by **Subjects**. This can be seen as a model of Computational Tree Logic CTL, [6]. CTL relies on a tree-like structure suitable for workflows where a moment can lead to several others. For example, from an **Activity**, another **Activity**, or an error can follow, leading to two different ends of the process.

Quantifiers to express that an access restriction rule bears on a single moment or on all of them are thus needed. We note **A** if all the moments are involved and **E** if only one of them is. CTL relies on temporal operators to indicate that a clause must be *always* (noted $\Box$), or *sometime* (noted $\Diamond$) true or that it must be true *until the next moment* (noted $\bigcirc$) or *until a moment in general* (noted u). Past CTL, PCTL [9], adds S, *since*, X^{-1}, *previous* and N, *from now on*.

We have previously emphasised three modalities of **Rights**. We note the **Permission** of doing something **P** and the Obligation **O**.

The syntax of our logical language in BNF, with ϕ and ψ, two access restriction policies is as follows:

$$\phi, \psi := \neg\phi|p|\phi \wedge \psi|(\mathbf{A}|\mathbf{E})\Box\phi|(\mathbf{A}|\mathbf{E})\Diamond\phi|(\mathbf{A}|\mathbf{E}) \bigcirc \phi|(\mathbf{A}|\mathbf{E})\phi u\psi|S\phi|X^{-1}\phi|N\phi|$$
$$\mathbf{P}\phi|\mathbf{O}\phi$$

Computability. At binding time, evaluating the access restriction policy to determine a user's right, can be seen as a model-checking problem. We specify access restriction rules and **Flow Constraints** with logical propositions that are built as Kripke structures [11]. We define a satisfaction relation $\models$ between the policies ϕ and ψ and a **Composition** C. A **Composition** can be run, *i.e.* a set of **Activities** can be performed by a set of **Subjects** on a set of **Resources** under a certain **Context**, if and only if $C \models \phi, \psi$.

Let $C = (a_0, a_1, ..., a_n)$ where each a_i is an action, *i.e.* a tuple of the form $<context, right, subject, object>$. Then, $C \models \phi$ if and only if $(C, |C|) \models \phi, \psi$. C is defined by structural induction on ϕ and ψ as:

$(C, i) \models p$ iff $p \in a_i$

$(C, i) \models \neg\phi$ iff $(C, i) \not\models \phi$

$(C, i) \models \phi \wedge \psi$ iff $(C, i) \models \phi$ and $(C, i) \models \psi$

$(C, i) \models \mathbf{E} \bigcirc \phi$ iff $(C, i + 1) \models \phi$

$(C, i) \models \mathbf{E}\phi u \psi$ iff there exists $k \geq 0$ s.t. $(C, i + k) \models \phi$
         and $(C, i + j) \models \psi$ for all $k > i \geq 0$

$(C, i) \models \mathbf{A}\phi u \psi$ iff for all a_n there exists $k \geq 0$ s.t. $(C, i + k) \models \phi$
         and $(C, i + j) \models \psi$ for all $k > i \geq 0$

$(C, i) \models X^{-1}\phi$ iff $n > 0$ and $(C, i - 1) \models \phi$

$(C, i) \models \phi S \psi$ iff there exists $k \geq n$ s.t. $(C, k) \models \phi$
         and $(C, i) \models \psi$ for all $k < i \leq 0$ $(C, i) \models N\phi$ iff $a_n \models \phi$

3.4 Linking Service Composition and Access Control Views

When designing an application from multiple points of view, three problems must be addressed [16]. First, the metamodels must be related in order to build complete specifications. Then, views must be synchronized *i.e.* a mechanism must be provided to preserve coherency between views at execution. Relationships between the service composition and the access restriction metamodels are displayed on Figure 2.

Two points are of foremost interest: the classes to link in each metamodel, and the cardinalities of their relations. In the access restriction view, we define an *Action* as an access mode to an *Object*. In the process view, we define an *Activity* as an operation on a *Product*. In order to compose the two views, we thus express that an *Action* is a specific type of *Activity* constrained by access restriction rules. The *Action* class thus inherits from *Activity*. The same stands for *Objects* in the process view, that are specific *Products* to which access is restricted.

Views are designed in conformity with their metamodel. Views are then composed according to the inheritance defined between the metamodels: each activity in the process specification is refined into several possible actions constrained with access restriction rules defined in the access restriction view.

4 Execution Level

At runtime, available services cannot be trusted because they may not enforce access restriction. We secure an heterogeneous and dynamic composition in two steps:

- Before execution, orchestration code and access restriction insertion code are generated from each view's specifications. To synchronize the view, insertion points of access restriction code in the orchestration are identified.

- At execution time, the access restriction code is inserted between the orchestrator and the available services.

Figure 3 displays the execution of a pervasive orchestration secured by access restriction. When a new service is discovered by the execution machine, a secured proxy is generated and registered in the registry. Thus, the registry only contains secured Web-Services and the orchestrator cannot directly access unsecured services. Consequently, the composition cannot be executed without access restriction enforcement.

Access restriction enforcement relies on three components. The *Decision Point* evaluates the access restriction policy for a user and a given context. The *Context Manager* stores the path to contextual information sources such as users' smartphones or the composition's log file. The *Identity Manager* stores the roles of users and their identity.

When a secured proxy is invoked, it calls the access restriction *Decision Point*. The proxy provides the *Decision Point* with the current user's name and the current *Activity*'s name. The *Decision Point* retrieves the user's privileges from the *Identity Manager* and the necessary contextual information from the *Context Manager*. It then checks the access restriction policy according to the retrieved information and provides the secured proxy with a decision. The access restriction policy is composed of the global access restriction policy defined at the level of the composition and the restriction imposed by the concerned data owners. If the user is allowed to access the current activity, the secured proxy invokes the available service it protects. Otherwise, it rejects the invocation. Each communication between the proxy and the other components is secured with authentication.

Generating an Executable Access Control Policy. The *Decision Point* checks an executable access restriction policy derived from a process specification and its associated access restriction requirements. We generate the access restriction rules that apply to each *Action* and their temporal ordering from the designer's specifications. We gather all these information into an executable access restriction policy represented as an XML file. The access restriction policy is expressed according to the following grammar represented in Backus-Normal form, where S is a *Subject*, SR a *Subject Role* defined by a set of *Constraints* Cs. OR an *Object Role* defined by a set of *Constraints* Co and O an *Object*. SRA refers to the activation of a *Subject Role* by S, and ORA, the activation of an *Object Role* by O.

$$SR := Cs^+$$
$$OR := Co^+$$
$$SRA := (SasSR)^+ \ ORA := (OasOR)^+$$

An *Action* A, performed by a *Subject* S, playing the *Role* SR, on the *Object* O, playing the *Role* OR, under the *Context* Ctx with the *Right* R is represented in BNF as:

$$A := Ctx\,(R\,(SRAORA))$$

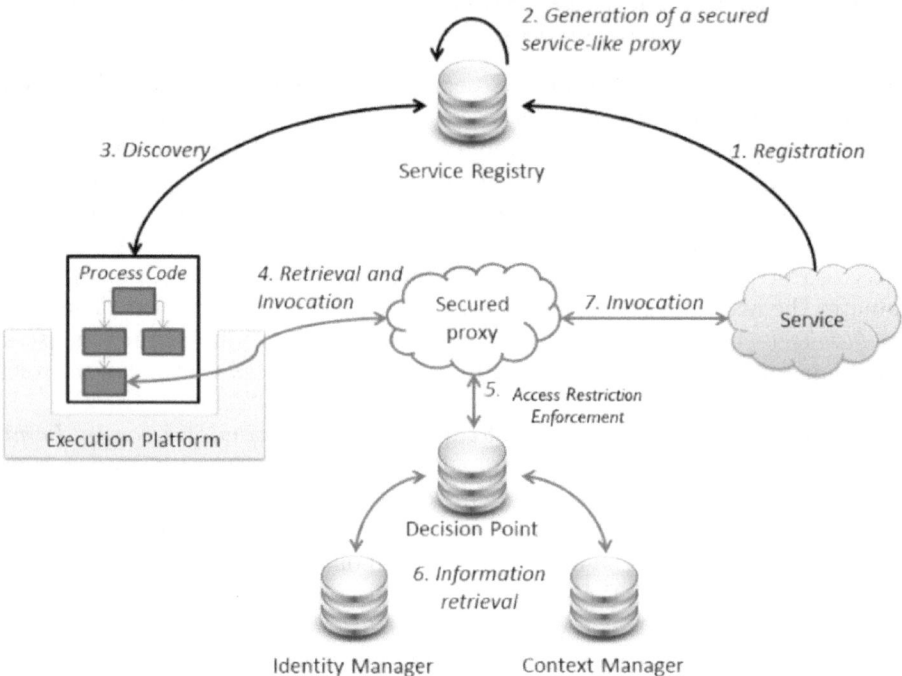

Fig. 3. Execution of a Secured Composition of Services

A *Process* consists in a temporally ordered flow of *Activities*. A *Process P* is represented in BNF as:

$$P := A^+$$

One or several *Workflow Constraint P, i.e. Separation of Duties* and *Binding of Duties* can be added to the composition. Such a constraint is represented by the following boolean constraint where *MaxS* is the maximal amount of *Subjects* allowed to perform *MinA*, a minimal number of Activities:

$$P \rightarrow MaxS \text{ and } MinA$$

We see a *Process* as a temporally ordered flow of *Activities, i.e.* the activation of *Roles* by *Principals*. This can be seen as a model of Computational Tree Logic CTL, [6], an executable logic which holds a tree-like structure of time. Each node of the three is an action and we can specify the lifetime of its associated access restriction rules according to five temporal operators, *until the next activity, until an activity in general, since an activity, since the previous activity* and *from now on.*

Identifying Insertion Points and Enforcing Access Control at Execution. At execution, each *Activity* is realized by a service. Each available service is secured as it registers to the service registry by a proxy. This step is comparable to the compilation of the access restriction and the composition model for a specific platform. The proxy is built at runtime according to the target service through code generation from a template. Each template is parametrized by a set of variables such as the endpoint to call or the service's implementation. Each variable is set with values from the actual service to protect. We rely on Java Emitter Templates (JET) to perform code generation. Figure 4 shows a snippet of a JET for a secured proxy implemented as a Web Service.

```
...
DecisionPointService dp = new DecisionPointServiceLocator();
try {
        DecisionPoint portToDecisionPoint = dp.getDecisionPoint();
        //Test: Is the user allowed to access the current activity?
        right = portToDecisionPoint.makeDecision(userName, activity, sessionID);
        if (!right.equalsIgnoreCase("DENIED")) { // Calls the protected service if the user is allowed to do so
                <%=serviceName%> port = portToService.<%=getServicePortMethod%>();
                <%if (!returnType.equals("void")){%><%=returnType%> resultat=<%}%>port.<
                %=methode.getName()%>(<% numParam=0; for (Class c:
                parametresMethode) {numParam++;%><%=nomParam+numParam%><%if (numParam<
                (parametresMethode.length)){%><%=", "%><%}%>%><%}%>);
                <%if (!returnType.equals("void")){%>return resultat;<%}%>
} catch (ServiceException e) {
        e.printStackTrace();
}
} catch (RemoteException e) {
        e.printStackTrace();
}
...
```

Fig. 4. Extract of the proxy.javajet file

The proxy is itself a Web-Service and is thus transparent for the composition. As a consequence, our approach is independent from a specific platform or specific service type. The proxy acts as an access restriction enforcement point. To do so, Figure 4 shows that the proxy intercepts the invocation and asks the *Decision Point* to check if the current user is allowed to access the current activity. If and if only so, it invokes the service it protects.

We have adopted a centralized approach: the orchestrator is a centralized entity. However, for scalability reasons, the identify manager, the context manager and the decision point can be replicated.

5   Validation

In order to validate our approach, we have developed an environment to model and execute a privacy-aware service composition secured by access restriction. This tool is a significative extension of the FOCAS orchestrator [5]. In this Section, we present its use and the results of our approach.

5.1   Design Level: Modeling Environment

The first part of the tool is dedicated to modeling compositions from multi-ple points of views. Functional experts can outline composition as processes by drawing activities, the links between them and the products that flow from one activity to another. The tool can also be used by privacy designers to visualize the data flow in the composition and the context-sensitivity of each activity in order to restrict data disclosure.

For each activity, access restriction rules can be defined. Figure 5 shows a snapshot of our tool for the alert management process.

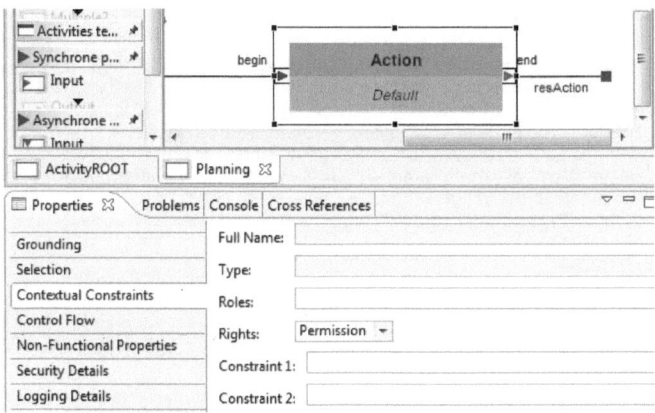

Fig. 5. Snapshot of our modeling environment

Each activity is associated to a set of property tabs which permit to edit its functional properties and the access restriction properties. Our tool permits the synthesis and the abstraction of process and access restriction views. Security experts and data owners can thus restrict object flows. We represent the exe-cution of access restriction as a composition of dedicated services. Data owners can thus restrict the access to contextual data necessary to compute and access restriction decision.

Our tool allows several stakeholders to work together at various points of the composition's lifecycle. Moreover, it has two major advantages. First, as all models instantiate our domain specific modeling language and their links, specifications are *de facto* valid and coherent. Then, the tool provides a global view on the composition while allowing to define access restriction rules at service level. Temporal logic is hard to handle, especially when users are not familiar with such languages. Our tool presents time ordering of activity as a process, an intuitive representation. Temporal operators are derived from the process structure.

5.2   Binding Time: Execution Environment

At runtime, we add computation time dedicated to proxy generation and access restriction enforcement. We analyze this extra cost for four services in our service composition. We have constrained four activities with privatization constraints and we have secured a service for each activity. Services 1, 2 and 3 can only be accessed if the user is in a specific location and possesses a specific role. Service 4 is constrained with the same properties to which we had a constraint on the hours shifts it can be accessed. The client requesting the access to Service 4 must be on duty. The client's work schedule must thus be checked. Figure 6 displays, for each service, the duration of the service call, of the proxy generation and of access restriction enforcement.

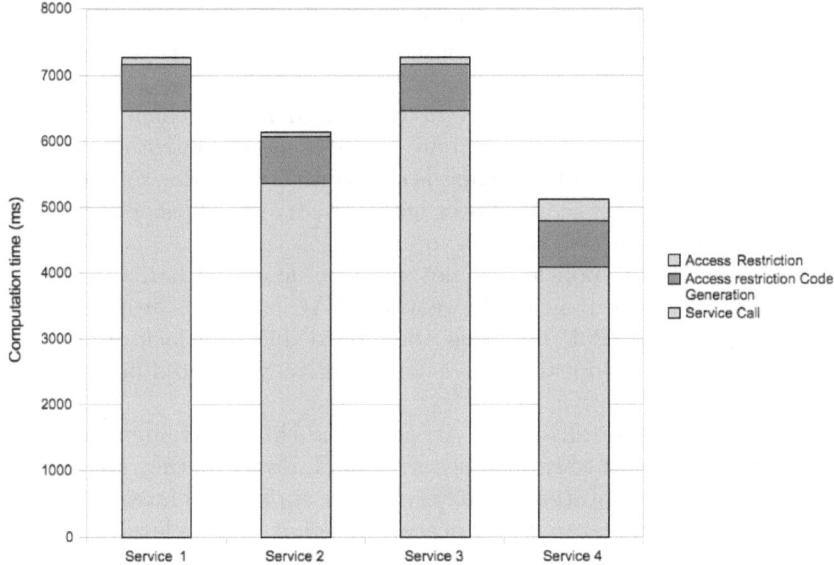

Fig. 6. Overhead Entailed by our approach

The proxy generation time is stable. It is caused by the parsing of the description of the unsecured service (such as a WSDL file) and the generation of the proxy with the JET template. The generation only happens once when the service registers to the service registry.

This analysis shows that access restriction enforcement takes at least 1% and at most 8% of the execution time of a service secured by our method. This time encompasses the retrieval of contextual data and, the processing of an access restriction decision and its enforcement. In formal terms, verifying a rule entails a small cost of $O(|C| * |\phi|)$ where $|C|$ is the size of the current achieved composition and $|\phi|$ the access restriction rule's size, *i.e.* the number of literals and operators in a rule. As a result, we can expect access restriction enforcement time to remain small throughout the execution of a secured composition.

6   Related Works

In [4] [14], the authors propose to specify security properties such as audit or encryption at design time and enforce them at runtime. In comparison, we focus on modeling and enforcing private data management as access restriction.

Privacy-oriented languages, such as the Enterprise Privacy Authorization Language (EPAL) and the Platform for Privacy Preferences (P3P) use access control concepts. Most access control models rely on the notions of *Principals, Categories, Actions* and *Permissions* [1]. *Principals* gather users, software agents and resources. They may belong to several *Categories*, that can be composed to refine them, and the *Permissions* are granted to these *Categories* for the performance of a set of *Actions*. The Role-Based Access Control (RBAC) model [7], for instance, categorizes *Users* according to *Roles* which express jobs or positions in an organisation. *Permissions* are attributed to *Roles*, which are stable *i.e.* organizational categories. The Attribute-Based Access Control model (ABAC) is another promising way of modeling access control. In order to obtain Rights, a User must exhibit a set of attributes with the correct values. This approach is suitable for pervasive access control.

However, the ABAC policies are not as readable as the RBAC ones as roles clearly architecture the policies. Moreover, EPAL is only a proposition and is not widely supported. P3P has been abandoned due to a lack of support and accessibility by non-technical users. A usable privacy-oriented language is thus yet to come.

Languages, such as the eXtensible Access Control Markup Language (XACML) or the WS-Policy permit to express access control. However, they are specific to a type of service implementation, Web Services for application integration. Several works use these languages to model access control at process level. [17] annotate process specifications with access control constraints from which they generate access control code. However, [17] proposes to generate XACML access code without addressing its execution when access control is known to influence the architecture of an application [13]: XACML, for instance, relies on a dedicated architecture. In contrast, we implement specific components to maintain the data related to access restriction enforcement.

Many works which focus on securing an executable application or service composition [3] [15] [10] [2] are dedicated to a service implementation or make strong assumptions on the access control capabilities or the availability of services. Heterogeneity is then still a brake to the development of service compositions secured by access control. The UPnP standard, for instance, defines no access control mechanism for UPnP aware devices. The dynamism of services is another challenge. Several works extend the Business Process Execution Language (BPEL) with access control features [12] [8]. Thus, they suppose they already know the service to invoke. It is not necessarily the case in a pervasive environment.

In contrast, we promote a platform-independent specification of access control and service composition. High level concepts can be easily grasped by non technical people. We automatically transform this specification into an executable secured process at runtime, according to the available service. We also investigate in depth the impact of access control on the composition's architecture by building components dedicated to access control enforcement.

7 Conclusion

In this paper, we have addressed the issue of designing and executing privacy-aware service compositions for pervasive applications. We have introduced a model-driven approach to the production of such compositions. We have understood privacy-awareness as private data management throughout the composition. We have provided a high-level language to privatize data, *i.e.* to express this management as access restriction. The validation on real world services shows that access restriction can be captured at design time in an abstract way. At runtime, the extra computation time entailed by access restriction enforcement remains reasonable.

Late code generation addresses the heterogeneity and the dynamism of actual services. Our experience shows that metamodeling is a demanding task. Identifying the necessary concepts to specify access restriction, for instance, is long and cumbersome. The same can be said of the creation of templates for each target service technology. However, the benefits of our approach overstep these difficulties. Metamodeling and building up templates allow knowledge capitalization. It also permits to obtain generic specifications, what is important in a highly heterogeneous envrionment. Focusing on non-technical concepts permits to integrate a wide range of stakeholders to an application's lifecycle and to build up early a coherent and extensive access restriction policy.

Finally, our approach calls for several future works. First, in term of access restriction, we have posited that a single designer designed the entire policy. For legal reasons, we may need data subjects to express their privacy preferences. As a result, we are currently exploring the distributed administration of the privacy policy. Second, our work is going to be validated in the frame of the INNOSERV project by the French research agency. Then, the spirit of our approach can be applied to other non-functional properties. When the metamodels of non-functional properties do not overlap with the composition metamodel, the adequacy of our proposition remains. Our future works will be dedicated to adding extra non-functional properties to service compositions.

References

1. Barker, S.: The next 700 access control models or a unifying meta-model? In: Proceedings of the 14th ACM Symposium on Access Control Models and Technologies, SACMAT 2009, pp. 187–196. ACM, New York (2009)

2. Basin, D., Doser, J., Lodderstedt, T.: Model Driven Security: from UML Models to Access Control Infrastructures. ACM Transactions on Software Engineering and Methodology 15, 39–91 (2006)
3. Carminati, B., Ferrari, E., Hung, P.: Security Conscious Web Service Composition. In: International Conference on Web Services (ICWS), pp. 489–496. IEEE Computer Society, Los Alamitos (2006)
4. Chollet, S., Lalanda, P.: Security specifcation at process level. In: SCC 2008: Proceedings of the 2008 IEEE International Conference on Services Computing, pp. 165–172. IEEE Computer Society, Washington, DC (2008)
5. Dami, S., Estublier, J., Amiour, M.: APEL: A Graphical Yet Executable Formalism for Process Modeling. Automated Software Engg. 5(1), 61–96 (1998)
6. Emerson, E.A.: Temporal and modal logic. In: van Leeuwen, J. (ed.) Handbook of Theoretical Computer Science, vol. B, pp. 995–1072. MIT Press (1990)
7. Ferraiolo, D.F., Kuhn, D.R.: Role-based access controls. In: Proceedings of the 15th National Computer Security Conference, pp. 554–563 (1992)
8. Garcia, D.Z.G., de Toledo, M.B.F.: Ontology-based security policies for supporting the management of web service business processes. In: ICSC, pp. 331–338 (2008)
9. Laroussinie, F., Schnoebelen, P.: Specification in ctl + past for verification in ctl. Inf. Comput. 156, 236–263 (2000)
10. Orriëns, B., Yang, J., Papazoglou, M.P.: Model Driven Service Composition. In: Orlowska, M.E., Weerawarana, S., Papazoglou, M.P., Yang, J. (eds.) ICSOC 2003. LNCS, vol. 2910, pp. 75–90. Springer, Heidelberg (2003)
11. Pnueli, A.: The temporal logic of programs. In: Proceedings of the 18th Annual Symposium on Foundations of Computer Science, pp. 46–57. IEEE Computer Society, Washington, DC (1977)
12. Rodríguez, A., Fernández-Medina, E., Piattini, M.: A BPMN Extension for the Modeling of Security Requirements in Business Processes. IEICE - Transactions on Information and Systems E90-D(4), 745–752 (2007)
13. Samarati, P., de Capitani di Vimercati, S.: Access Control: Policies, Models, and Mechanisms. In: Focardi, R., Gorrieri, R. (eds.) FOSAD 2000. LNCS, vol. 2171, pp. 137–196. Springer, Heidelberg (2001)
14. Souza, A.R.R., Silva, B.L.B., Lins, F.A.A., Damasceno, J.C., Rosa, N.S., Maciel, P.R.M., Medeiros, R.W.A., Stephenson, B., Motahari-Nezhad, H.R., Li, J., Northfleet, C.: Incorporating Security Requirements into Service Composition: From Modelling to Execution. In: Baresi, L., Chi, C.-H., Suzuki, J. (eds.) ICSOC-ServiceWave 2009. LNCS, vol. 5900, pp. 373–388. Springer, Heidelberg (2009)
15. Srivatsa, M., Iyengar, A., Mikalsen, T.A., Rouvellou, I., Yin, J.: An Access Control System for Web Service Compositions. In: International Conference on Web Services (ICWS), pp. 1–8. IEEE Computer Society, Los Alamitos (2007)
16. Vallecillo, A.: On the Combination of Domain Specific Modeling Languages. In: Kühne, T., Selic, B., Gervais, M.-P., Terrier, F. (eds.) ECMFA 2010. LNCS, vol. 6138, pp. 305–320. Springer, Heidelberg (2010)
17. Wolter, C., Schaad, A., Meinel, C.: Deriving XACML Policies from Business Process Models. In: Weske, M., Hacid, M.-S., Godart, C. (eds.) WISE Workshops 2007. LNCS, vol. 4832, pp. 142–153. Springer, Heidelberg (2007)

Modeling User's Non-functional Preferences for Personalized Service Ranking

Rozita Mirmotalebi[1], Chen Ding[1], and Chi-Hung Chi[2,3]

[1] Department of Computer Science, Ryerson University, Toronto, Canada
{rozita.mirmotalebi,cding}@ryerson.ca
[2] School of Software, Tsinghua University, Beijing, China
[3] Intelligent Sensing and Systems Laboratory – CSIRO, Hobart, Australia
chihungchi@gmail.com

Abstract. Modeling users' online behavior has great benefit for many e-Commerce web sites and search engines. In the context of software service selection, if we could understand users' personal preferences, we could rank the services in a more satisfactory way. Many users have some general preferences on the desired values of non-functional properties (e.g. provider history, service popularity, etc.) of services, even if they may not explicitly define them. In this paper, we propose to build user profiles on these non-functional preferences, and then use them to personalize the ranking results for individual users. Our experiment showed that personalized ranking could promote the services matching with the user preferred non-functional values to higher positions, making it easier for users to identify their desired services. We also tested how different factors impact the degree of improvement on the ranking accuracy.

Keywords: Service Ranking, Service Selection, Non-functional Preference, User Modeling, Personalization.

1 Introduction

When more and more providers publish and host their software services in the cloud, it becomes a challenge for users to find their desired services. Although cloud service directories, or service search engines such as Seekda[1] can provide the searching function over users' functional requirements, they often lack the support for the further selection among a list of functionally similar services. If this list is long, users are still overwhelmed by the amount of information they need to process.

When multiple services implement a same function, users often select them based on their non-functional properties, such as service cost, reputation of the provider, reliability of the service, etc. Although users may have explicit requirements (e.g. cost < \$15/month) guiding the selection process, their implicit general preferences also play a key role in this process. For instance, one user may always choose the service from a provider with a good reputation, another user may normally choose the service

---

[1] http://webservices.seekda.com

C. Liu et al. (Eds.): ICSOC 2012, LNCS 7636, pp. 359–373, 2012.
© Springer-Verlag Berlin Heidelberg 2012

with the highest reliability, and yet another user may balance between the cost and the response time. Personalized search could provide personalized ranking results to individual users based on their profiles, and it is a well accepted solution to deal with the information overload problem on the web [8]. For software service selection, if we could create users' personal profiles based on their non-functional preferences, these profiles can be used to build a personalized ranking list of candidate services. Here, we use the term non-functional preferences to refer to properties users have concerns on and the types of values they prefer (e.g. higher/lower values) on these properties.

There have been many research efforts on non-functional property based service selection. In these studies, users are normally required to specify their non-functional requirements for every single query. However, sometimes users may not want to spend time on defining them, or don't know how to define them, plus there are default requirements which always apply (e.g. always prefer a service with lower cost). In this paper, we propose to model users' general non-functional preferences for service selection. Since a personal profile is built for every user, there is no need to type in the general non-functional requirement each time any more. If the user has a different requirement for a query, he could always specify it explicitly, which would overwrite the one in his profile. In the paper, we assume there are existing matchmaking algorithms we can use so that we focus our study on the personalized ranking part. Also we only focus on the selection system which interacts with a human user instead of a software agent. This setting makes the profiling process feasible and meaningful.

People make their decisions based on various criteria. For service selection, there are some common criteria which are important to almost everyone, and there are also specific criteria which are only important to individual users or domains. It is definitely impossible to include every single criterion in the user model. However, our algorithm and the system design are generic enough so that we could always expand or tailor our user model for a particular domain or a user group. In the paper, we choose some common selection criteria whose values we could find in our dataset.

User preferences can be captured either explicitly or implicitly. We have carefully-designed user interfaces to elicit users' non-functional preferences explicitly. When the explicit profile is missing, we have the implicit profile with user's non-functional preferences inferred by checking the values of the non-functional properties of the services a user has invoked in the past. The profile could evolve over time by asking users to update their profiles or by observing the changing invocation patterns.

There are two major contributions of the paper. First, to the best of our knowledge, user modeling on their non-functional preferences for software service selection is a very new idea. Standard recommender systems cannot accomplish this task without major modifications. We also propose an approach which could implicitly infer user preferences based on their invocation histories. Second, personalized ranking based on users' general interests and preferences has been successfully used for web search, while it hasn't been applied to software service selection yet. In many existing personalized service ranking algorithms, personalization is not achieved through the long-term user profiles and not many properties are considered. Ours is unique in its focus on users' long-term preferences on multiple non-functional service properties.

The rest of the paper is organized as follows. We show a very simple motivating example in Section 2. Then we discuss the user modeling process in Section 3. Our personalized service ranking algorithm is explained in Section 4. In Section 5, we explain how we design the experiment and build a proper dataset to validate the importance of the personalized ranking. In Section 6, we review the related work. Finally in Section 7 we conclude the paper and list the future work.

2   A Motivating Example

Assume that *Bob* and *Dave* have registered in our service selection system and used our system for a while. When registration, *Bob* explicitly specified his non-functional preferences as: (provider name: *P*, service availability: high), which means he prefers services from a provider named *P*, and also services with high availability. *Dave* didn't specify any personal preferences. But his invocation history shows that out of 20 services he invoked, 18 services have high ratings, and 15 services are from well-established providers. So the system concludes his preferences as: (provider history: long, service rating: high). We also assume that all preferences are equally important to users.

Now both of them are searching for a report generating service. 4 services are returned and part of their non-functional property values are listed in Table 1.

Table 1. Non-functional property values of 4 services

	Provider Name	Provider History	Service Availability	Service Rating
s_1	P	< 1 year	90%	4
s_2	P	< 1 year	95%	3
s_3	Q	5 years	99%	4
s_4	R	2 years	70%	5

By checking two users' non-functional preferences, the system generates a different personalized ranking list for *Bob* and *Dave* (the detailed steps are explained later). The former is: s_2, s_1, s_3, s_4, and the latter is: s_3, s_4, s_1, s_2. With this personalized result, both users could find their desired services easily. Although this is an over-simplified example, it shows the benefit of the personalized ranking. In the real scenario when there are more services returned, the benefit would be more obvious.

3   Modeling User's Non-functional Preferences

3.1   Defining Non-functional Preferences

Non-functional property based software service selection is similar to the consumer purchase decision process [4]. There are many factors affecting this process. In this paper we are not aiming at identifying and defining them systematically. We just pick a few common purchase criteria (e.g. preference on a certain provider because of the brand loyalty) which we could find their values in our dataset and divide them into two categories: provider related, and service related. For the latter, a significant group is QoS (Quality of Service) properties [12]. Due to the restriction of our dataset, we only choose two of them (i.e. availability, response time) in this paper. Normally when a user has a preference on a property, it is not one single fixed number, and instead, it could be a range of values expressed using some fuzzy linguistic terms, e.g. a service with a *good* reliability, a service with a *low* cost, or it could be a set of preferred values, e.g. a service from a few well-known providers *A*, *B* and *C*. Based on this observation, all of the non-functional preferences defined below are either sets or fuzzy values. The first four are provider related and the rest are service related.

- **PN** (Provider Names): the names of the user preferred providers (a set value). The provider name is either a company's legal name, or the top level domain name of the hosting web site. Users could have multiple preferred providers.
- **PL** (Provider Locations): the preferred locations of the providers (a set value). The location is the geographical location of either the company or the hosting web site. It could be further categorized into two types: **PCT** (Provider Continent) and **PCY** (Provider Country). Users could have preferences on one of them or both.
- **PH** (Provider History): the preferred history of the providers. The provider history is defined as the number of years the provider has been established. Preference on this property is usually defined as a fuzzy value such as short, medium and long.
- **PP** (Provider Popularity): the preferred level of popularity of the providers (a fuzzy value). The provider popularity is measured by the ratio of the number of invocations of services from the provider over the total number of invocations.
- **SL** (Service Languages): preferred languages of the service outputs (a set value).
- **SH** (Service History): the preferred history of the services (a fuzzy value). The service history is defined as the number of years the service has been offered.
- **SF** (Service Freshness): the preferred level of freshness of the services (a fuzzy value). The service freshness is measured by its latest update time. If a service is regularly maintained and updated, it is considered fresh.
- **SP** (Service Popularity): the preferred level of popularity of the services (a fuzzy value). It is measured by the ratio of the number of invocations of the service over the total number of invocations of all functionally equivalent services.
- **SR** (Service Rating): the preferred ratings of the services (a fuzzy value). The rating of a service is the average of all received ratings on the service.
- **SC** (Service Cost): the preferred cost level of the services (a fuzzy value). The cost of a service is the fee a user needs to pay in order to use the service.
- **SD** (Service Documentation): the preferred level of documentation of the services (a fuzzy value). It measures how much documentation a service provides to its users and its fuzzy values are none, partial and good.
- **SA** (Service Availability): the preferred availability of the services (a fuzzy value). Service availability measures the probability a service is operating normally and can be accessed by users successfully.
- **SRT** (Service Response Time): the preferred response time of the services (a fuzzy value). The response time of a service is the time from the end of the service request to the beginning of the response.

This list is far from complete. However, we can always include more properties when necessary because our framework is generic and extensible. Also right now we only consider 2 types of preferences. It is possible to extend our system to include more types, such as dislike preferences, composite preferences, as specified in [3].

3.2 Data Collection for User Modeling

To understand how our system collects the user data and generates the personalized ranking result, we first explain its architecture model as shown in Figure 1. This architecture model is an extension to our previous work [15]. We use the user-side proxy to collect the service usage data for individual users. If a user fills the required preference forms, the explicit user profiling component will generate the user model. If the user does not fill the forms or leave some values undefined, the implicit user profiling component will check the services the user invoked in the past on their non-functional properties to see whether any general patterns can be observed, which will then be saved in the user model. In the selection stage, the personalized ranking component will rank the matching services based on the generated user profile.

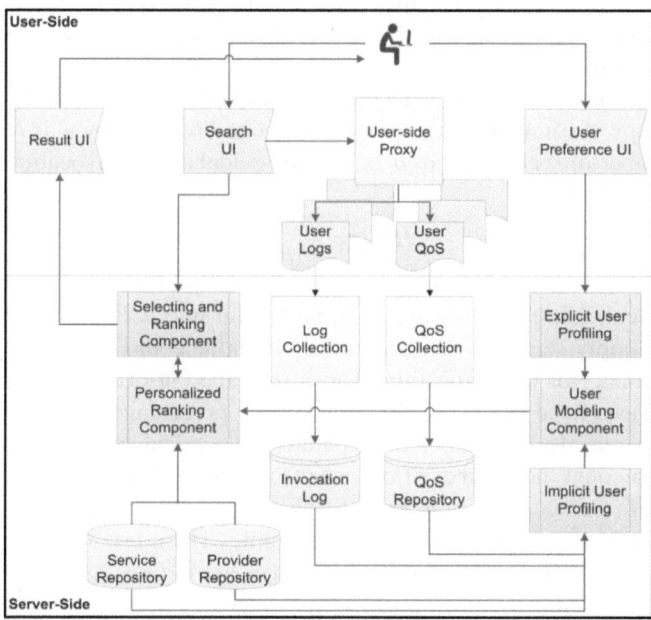

Fig. 1. Architecture of our personalized service ranking system

3.3 Implicit User Modeling

Below we list the notations we use to represent providers, services and users.

- P: the set of all the providers in the repository.
- p_i: the i-th software service provider in P. It has 4 properties – name, location, history, and popularity, and their values can be found in the provider repository. We use $p_i.n$, $p_i.l$, $p_i.h$, $p_i.p$ to represent these properties, and furthermore $p_i.ct$ and $p_i.cy$ for its continent and country.

- S: the set of all the services in the repository.
- s_i: the i-th software service in S. It has 9 properties – language, history, freshness, popularity, rating, cost, documentation, availability, and response time, and their values can be found in the service repository. We use $s_i.l$, $s_i.h$, $s_i.f$, $s_i.p$, $s_i.r$, $s_i.c$, $s_i.d$, $s_i.a$, $s_i.rt$ to represent these properties and $s_i.pd$ to refer to its service provider.
- U: the set of all the users of the system.
- u_i: the i-th user of our system. The user profile includes user's login information such as user id and password, user's non-functional preferences on 4 provider-related and 9 service-related properties, as well as the other useful information such as services invoked by this user. To refer to his preferences, we use $u_i.PN$, $u_i.PL$ ($u_i.PCT$, $u_i.PCY$), $u_i.PH$, $u_i.PP$, $u_i.SL$, $u_i.SH$, $u_i.SF$, $u_i.SP$, $u_i.SR$, $u_i.SC$, $u_i.SD$, $u_i.SA$, and $u_i.SRT$ respectively.

The non-functional preferences can be categorized into two groups based on their data types. The first group includes PN, PL, SL, and their values are all sets, e.g. $u_i.PN = \{A, B\}$ where A, B are provider names. The second group includes all of the rest, and they all have fuzzy values, e.g. $u_i.PH =$ long. Each group has its own way of calculating the implicit preference values.

In the first group, we use PN as an example, and other preferences follow the same calculation steps. Assume that the number of invoked services by u_i is NI_i, and among them, the number of services from p_j is NI_{ij}, we calculate the invocation frequency of provider p_j by user u_i as:

$$IFP_{ij} = \frac{NI_{ij}}{NI_i} \tag{1}$$

Then we compare the result with a predefined threshold T_{IF}, and if it is above the threshold, we consider p_j as user preferred and add it into $u_i.PN$. It is possible that we may have an empty set for $u_i.PN$. The threshold value could be chosen based on the statistical summary of the invocation history (e.g. the cut-off value to get top k providers), or set as a fixed value, e.g. 50% (a majority percentage).

For PL, we consider PCT and PCY separately. To calculate its invocation frequency, we need to count the number of services from a provider of a certain continent or country. For SL, we count the number of services in a certain language.

In the second group, we use PH as the example. There are 3 fuzzy values for the provider history. In our system, their value ranges are defined as: short (≤ 1.5 years), medium (>1.5 years and ≤ 3 years), and long (> 3 years). The choice of these values is based on the dataset we have. It could be redefined for different datasets. Also the number of fuzzy values can be redefined.

For all the services u_i has invoked, we find their corresponding providers. Then for each provider p_j, if $p_j.h$ is in the range of short history (i.e. ≤ 1.5 years), the value of $NI_i(s)$ will be incremented by 1. The invocation frequency of providers with a short history by user u_i is defined as:

$$IFH_i(s) = \frac{NI_i(s)}{NI_i} \tag{2}$$

$IFH_i(m)$ and $IFH_i(l)$ for medium and long histories can be calculated similarly. Among these three, we choose the one with the largest value and then compare it with a threshold T_{IFH}. If it is above the threshold, the corresponding history range (short, medium, or long) is considered as user preferred. Otherwise, $u_i.PH$ will be "no preference". We could set the threshold as 50% to make sure this preference is considered only when a dominating pattern exists.

For other preferences in this group, the basic calculation steps are the same. However, the number of fuzzy values and their ranges might be different. We define PH, PP, SH, SF, SP, SC, SD to have 3 fuzzy values, and SR, SA, SRT to have 5.

After the implicit user modeling step, a user profile on his non-functional preferences is set up for every user.

4   Personalized Service Ranking

In our system, when a user submits a query, after the service discovery and matchmaking step, the personalized ranking component ranks all the matching services based on the user profile. The ranking step is essentially the similarity calculation between user's non-functional preferences and services' non-functional property values. Services with higher matching scores with the user's profile are ranked higher in the result list. To calculate the overall similarity score for the complete profile, we need to first define how to measure the similarity for individual properties. Again we divide them into two groups based on their data types.

In the first group, to calculate the similarity between a matching service s_k and a user u_i's non-functional preference on provider names, we use the following formula:

$$sim_{PN}(u_i, s_k) = \begin{cases} 1 & if\ u_i.PN = \emptyset \\ 1 & if\ s_k.pd.n \in u_i.PN \\ 0 & if\ s_k.pd.n \notin u_i.PN \end{cases} \quad (3)$$

When $u_i.PN$ is empty, it means the user has no preference on providers, any provider is considered as a match, and thus the similarity score is 1. When $u_i.PN$ is not empty, if $s_k.pd$ is in the user preferred list, the similarity score is 1, and otherwise, the score is 0. Similar steps are used for SL. In our current implementation, we only get Boolean similarity values. Later, if want to get a numeric similarity score, we could consider different degrees of preference on different providers.

To calculate the similarity on provider locations, because the location property has two sub-properties: continent and country, there are different scenarios we need to consider. When the service provider's country is one of user preferred countries, it is considered as a perfect match and the similarity score is 1. If only the continent matches, it is a partial match and the score is 0.5. The formula is as below:

$$sim_{PL}(u_i, s_k) = \begin{cases} 1 & if\ u_i.PL = \emptyset \\ 1 & if\ s_k.pd.cy \in u_i.PCY \\ 0.5 & if\ s_k.pd.ct \in u_i.PCT\ and\ s_k.pd.cy \notin u_i.PCY \\ 0 & if\ s_k.pd.ct \notin u_i.PCT\ and\ s_k.pd.cy \notin u_i.PCY \end{cases} \quad (4)$$

In the second group, if a user has no preference on the property, the similarity score is always 1. Otherwise, the following steps are taken. First, the user preferred fuzzy value on the property is converted to a scale number. For instance, if the fuzzy values are short, medium, long, their corresponding scale numbers are 0, 1, and 2. Then, each matching service is assigned with a scale number on the property based on the range definition of the scales. For instance, if a service provider has been established for just one year, the provider history falls into the range for the fuzzy value "short", and its scale number is 0 (for short history). We adopt the method proposed in [14] to calculate the similarity between two scale numbers. For 3-scale preferences, we use the matrix below to get the similarity score. The left column represents user preferences and the top row represents service property values.

$$
u_i \begin{matrix} & & & s_k & \\ & & 2 & 1 & 0 \\ 2 \\ 1 \\ 0 \end{matrix} \begin{bmatrix} 1 & 0.7 & 0 \\ 0.7 & 1 & 0.7 \\ 0 & 0.7 & 1 \end{bmatrix} \tag{5}
$$

For 5-scale preferences, we use a different matrix.

$$
u_i \begin{matrix} & & & & s_k \\ & 4 & 3 & 2 & 1 & 0 \\ 4 \\ 3 \\ 2 \\ 1 \\ 0 \end{matrix} \begin{bmatrix} 1 & 0.7 & 0.2 & 0 & 0 \\ 0.7 & 1 & 0.3 & 0 & 0 \\ 0.2 & 0.3 & 1 & 0.3 & 0.2 \\ 0 & 0 & 0.3 & 1 & 0.7 \\ 0 & 0 & 0.2 & 0.7 & 1 \end{bmatrix} \tag{6}
$$

After we get the similarity scores for all the properties, we could combine them to get an overall score for the matching service using the formula as shown below:

$$
sim(u_i, s_k) = \sum_{h=1}^{n} \alpha_h * sim_{a_h}(u_i, s_k) \tag{7}
$$

where n is the number of non-functional preferences, a_h refers to the h-th preference, α_h is the coefficient on a_h, which measures how important the similarity score on the h-th property is to the overall score, the sum of the coefficients should be 1, and $sim_{a_h}(u_i, s_k)$ measures the similarity of user u_i's profile and service s_k on the h-th property. In our current implementation, we use equal weights for all properties. Finally all the matching services can be ranked on their overall scores.

5   Experiments

5.1   Experiment Design

To the best of our knowledge, there is no publicly available dataset on service invocation histories. It is also difficult to collect an adequate amount of user data if we don't run a service selection system which is used by a lot of users. Due to these constraints, in our experiment, we didn't test the implicit user modeling component, and we only focused on the personalized ranking component. We developed a Windows-based prototype system using Java 1.6 with Eclipse IDE. We used MySQL Workbench 5.2 to build the provider and service repositories as well as the user profiles.

We wanted to demonstrate that for a registered user who has entered his personal preferences on non-functional service properties explicitly through the user interface, our system could generate a personalized ranking result for him. We also ran a simulator to generate user profiles with different combinations of preferences to test how different factors would affect the ranking accuracy.

Seekda is a publicly available web service search engine. It contains a good number of web services published online. It also maintains useful information of each service, such as its origin country, the provider information, a link to its WSDL file, tags, its availability, a chart of its response time in the past, a user rating, its level of documentation, etc. For most of the non-functional properties we consider in our system, we could find their values from either Seekda or the original hosting sites, except the provider popularity, the service popularity and the service cost. In the experiment, we excluded them from the similarity calculation.

We built our dataset by collecting web service data from Seekda during a six-month period (December, 2010 to May, 2011). There were 7739 providers and 28606 services stored in Seekda (as of August 2, 2011). Since some data were manually collected, such as the established time of a provider or the average response time of a service, we were not able to get all the services in Seekda. We followed a few different ways to get services: 1) for each continent, find some representative countries, and then for each country, find some representative providers, and get all the services published by these providers; 2) based on the tag cloud, choose tags with a large/medium/small number of matching services, and get all of these services; 3) follow the links provided by Seekda, get the most used services and the recently found services. After removing the services with expired URLs, we finally got 1208 services from 537 providers, and each provider contains at least one service. Since Seekda started crawling and monitoring web services from 2006, the oldest service in our dataset was published in 2006. We extracted the information we need and saved them into the provider repository and the service repository.

There are 287 service tags saved in our dataset, of which we chose 30 of them together with their matching services for our experiment. These tags are categorized into three groups based on the number of matching services. Group 1 has 10 tags and each tag has less than 50 matching services, group 2 has 10 tags with the number of services per tag between 50 and 100, and group 3 has 10 tags with more than 100 services per tag. In the experiment, each tag was used as a searching keyword to be submitted to our selection system. After the functional matching step, the relevant services were retrieved. Then the personalized ranking result could be generated based on the user profile.

We simulated 60 users. They are divided into 6 groups. For users in each group, they have preferences on a same number of properties (not necessarily same properties): 1, 2, 4, 6, 8, and 10 respectively, and for the rest of the properties, they have no preference on their values. For instance, one group may have preferences on 2 non-functional properties, and no preferences on the others. Users in this group could have preferences on different non-functional properties. User A from this group has preferences on service rating and service languages, and user B from the same group has preferences on provider names and provider history.

5.2   User Preference Forms and An Illustrating Example

In order to solicit user preferences, after a user registers to our system, he is required to specify his preferences on various non-functional properties. He could also update his profile later when necessary. There are two forms a user needs to fill. Figure 2 shows the first one. QoS related properties such as *SA*, *SRT* are included in another form, which is not shown in the paper due to the page limitation.

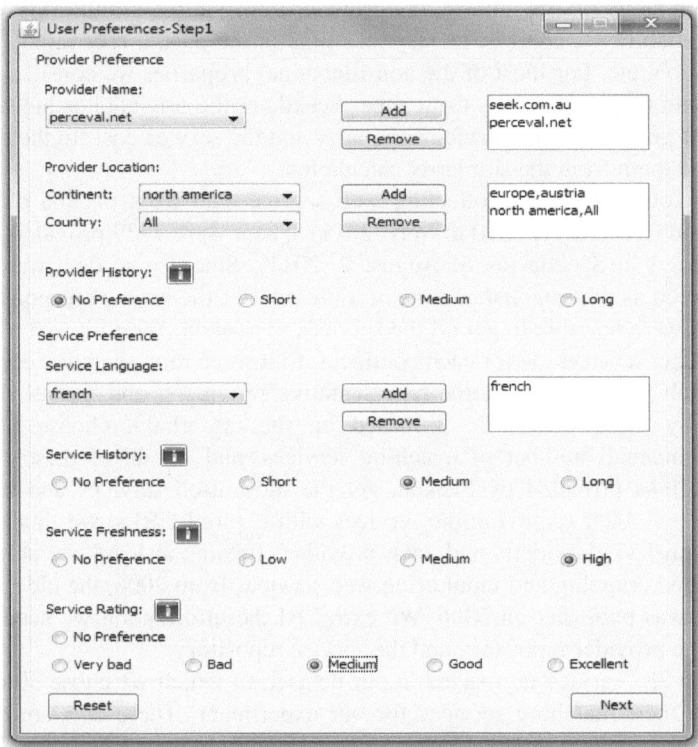

Fig. 2. User Preference Form 1

For properties with fuzzy values (e.g. provider history), there are information icons beside them. When a user clicks on an icon, the value range of the property will be displayed. Table 2 lists value ranges for all of these properties. Our system could handle multiple scales. But for the simplicity reason, we only use two scales here: 3 and 5, which are the common choices for fuzzy values. For history related properties, we use 3 scales because most services in our dataset are relatively new and the value span is small. For other properties, we use 5 scales.

After the user fills the forms, his profile will be built. Assume a user named *Dave* has the following profile: (*PH*: long, *SD*: good, *SA*: excellent). When *Dave* submits a query "Finance" to our system, the personalized ranking result is generated based on this profile. Table 3 shows the top 10 results, together with their original rankings and their related non-functional property values.

Table 2. Properties and their value ranges

Property	Ranges of its fuzzy values
PH (year)	short: <=1.5, medium: >1.5 and <=3, long: >3
SH (year)	short: <=1.5, medium: >1.5 and <=3, long: >3
SF (month)	low: <=6, medium: >6 and <=12, high: >12
SR (0~5)	very bad: <=1, bad: >1 and <=2.5, medium: >2.5 and <=3.5, good: >3.5 and <=4.5, excellent: >4.5
SA (%)	very bad: <=50, bad: >50 and <=70, medium: >70 and <=80, good: >80 and <=95, excellent: >95
SRT (ms)	very bad: >=790, bad: <790 and >=770, medium: <770 and >=750, good: <750 and >=700, excellent: <700

Table 3. Top 10 services with their original rankings and property values

Rank	Service Name	PH	SD	SA	Original Rank
1	DelayedStockQuote	4.30	good	99.50	3
2	ForeignExchangeRates	4.10	good	99.70	4
3	XigniteQuotes	4.30	good	99.81	8
4	XigniteHelp	4.09	good	99.73	17
5	LeadStatusQuery	3.41	good	98.63	18
6	AffiliateServices	3.17	good	99.25	22
7	XigniteGlobalQuotes	2.83	good	99.67	6
8	XigniteMoneyMarkets	2.83	good	99.38	12
9	XigniteFundHoldings	2.83	good	99.38	15
10	FinanceService	2.41	good	97.26	23

By checking the results, we can see that services satisfying user preferred non-functional values are promoted to higher positions. For instance, the original rankings for the 3rd and 4th services are 8 and 17, but since they have a long provider history, a good documentation and an excellent availability, their positions are promoted.

5.3 Factors Influencing the Result Accuracy

Since to the best of our knowledge, no similar work has been done before, in this experiment, we focus on evaluating the degree of improvement from the personalized ranking, as well as the impacts of different factors on this improvement. We mainly tested two factors: the number of functionally matching services, and the number of non-functional properties on which users have defined their preferences. According to a study on web users' searching behavior [7], the ranking order is really important because users normally only check the top N results (a common value for N is 10). So in this paper we use the ranking improvement to measure the system benefit. We take the top 10 results from the personalized ranking list, check their non-functional property values making sure they satisfy user preferred values (if not, remove them), and then check the ranking positions of these services in the original ranking list. If they are ranked very high in the original list, it means our algorithm does not improve the ranking very much. If they are originally ranked very low, it means our algorithm can promote these services to better positions, and therefore our personalized ranking is beneficial. Here we measure the benefit using the Mean Average Precision (MAP) [7]. We take the personalized ranking results as the reference and check the precision of the original results. A lower value means a bigger loss in accuracy and thus a higher benefit. The following formula is used for each query q:

$$MAP_q = \frac{\sum_{i=1}^{R}(P(i)*rel(i))}{\min(R,10)} \tag{8}$$

where R is the number of functionally matching services, $P(i)$ measures the precision in the i-th position [7], $rel(i)$ is 1 if the i-th result is one of the top 10 services in the personalized result and 0 otherwise, $min(.)$ is to get a lower value between R and 10.

For each of the 60 users we simulated, we also generated some random service requests. Each user submitted 30 queries using 30 selected tags. Then we measured the MAP value for each query. Here we chose 3 tags from each group to discuss the results. The 9 selected tags are *charter flight, telecommunication, traffic, travel, government, finance, bioinformatics, tourism,* and *university.* Their corresponding numbers of services are 7, 21, 38, 70, 76, 97, 120, 140 and 169 respectively.

Figure 3 shows the average MAP values for these 9 keywords. The result is averaged on all 60 users. Since we listed the keywords in the ascending order of their numbers of matching services, from this figure, we can tell the relationship between the number of services and the MAP value. Initially when there are only 7 services (for *charter flight*), its MAP value is over 0.8, which shows the personalized ranking gets similar results as the original one and the benefit is not very obvious. When the number of services gets bigger, the benefit becomes higher. The slope is sharp when the number of services is below 50, and becomes fairly even after 50. The average MAP value when the number of services is above 50 is 0.11, which means that many of the top results from the personalized ranking are not in the original top list. It clearly shows the importance of the user modeling and the personalization, especially when there are many functionally matching services.

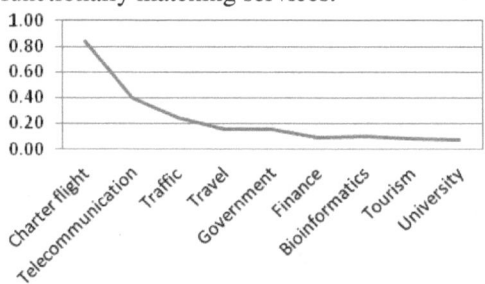

Fig. 3. Average MAP for 9 queries

Figure 4 shows the average MAP values for users with different numbers of preferences. The result is averaged on 10 users in each group and on all the 9 queries. In this figure, we could see that when users have preferences on more non-functional properties, the MAP value is getting smaller. So the personalized ranking could help more when users have more preferences. The curve here is not very sharp compared to Figure 3. It shows that the impact from the number of preferences is less than that from the number of services. When the number of preferences is above 4, there is no big difference in the result.

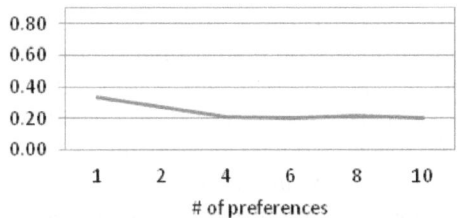

Fig. 4. Average MAP for different number of preferences

In general, based on these experiment results, we could conclude that the personalized ranking could benefit the service selection system to satisfy individual requirements, especially when there are a lot of functionally similar services and users have preferences on more than one non-functional property.

6 Related Work

Personalized service ranking or service recommendation based on user preferences has attracted research attention in recent years. In [11], previous interactions between service providers and requestors were modeled as a social network, and then results from the social network analysis were fed into a Bayesian classifier to rank services. In [9], personal profiles were built using the collaborative filtering technique to find similar users based on their invocation histories and the association rule mining to identify service dependencies based on the past composition transactions of these similar users. User similarity in [16] was measured by the similarity between the rankings of their observed QoS values on commonly invoked services, and then the personalization was implemented using the past experiences from similar users. The work in [2] collected the service invocation data and used it for the later discovery. However it only focused on the functional query part. In the above work, QoS data was included in the ranking process in [11] [16], but not the other two. All of them used the past usage data, mainly invocation histories to get the personalized results.

There are also systems relying on the explicit user ratings for the service ranking. Item-based collaborative filtering was used in [6] to predict the user rating on a service and the services were then ranked based on the predicted ratings. In [1], the score of a service was calculated based on ratings on this service from similar users and ratings on similar queries. In [14], service selection was based on both objective and subjective QoS values. A fuzzy inference system can handle the objective QoS factors (e.g. latency), and the collaborative filtering was used on subjective QoS factors (e.g. user ratings). The approach proposed in [5] was based on user experiences on given services, as well as their preferences, which provided contexts for the experiences and made the personalization more accurate. Personalization in [13] was achieved by considering different user factors, such as user preferences on different QoS properties, user-defined comparisons on QoS values, and user's confidence level on the reputation mechanism used in the selection process.

Compared to these papers, our paper is unique because it emphasizes on building user models to capture their long-term non-functional preferences. Some papers also built user profiles. However, their profiles only considered users' functional interests [2], or the invocation frequencies on services [9]. The profile in [13] was a little similar to ours. But it puts too much workload on users by asking them to compare values for each QoS property. In our work, users only need to pick a fuzzy value or choose from a list of possible values, and we also have a more thorough definition on non-functional preferences and an implicit user data collection mechanism.

Non-functional preferences have been used for service selection and ranking in some work, e.g. [3] [10]. In [3], an expressive and user-friendly preference model was proposed, which considers both qualitative and quantitative preferences, as well as atomic and composite preferences. In [10], qualitative preferences can be defined using the TCP network, which can handle the conditional preferences and relative importance of various non-functional properties, and quantitative preferences can be defined as utilities using the UCP network. Currently our paper only considers 2 types of user preferences and does not consider the relative importance of different properties. In the future, we could extend our work based on [3] and [10].

7   Conclusions

In this paper, we proposed a user modeling approach to build user profiles on their non-functional preferences. Then a personalized ranking algorithm could be applied to the service selection process to identify user desired services. In the user modeling stage, the system could collect the user data explicitly through user forms, or implicitly by analyzing the past usage data. In the selection stage, after the functionally matching services are identified for the user query, they are ranked based on how well they could match with the user preferred values on the specified non-functional properties. Experiment results showed that the personalized ranking has largely improved the result accuracy for individual users.

There are a few directions we would like to work on in the future. First, we could set up a service community such as the one in [2] to collect the real usage data in order to evaluate our implicit user modeling algorithm. We would also like to conduct a user study to evaluate our system. Second, we would like to implement and test other more complex profiling and similarity calculation algorithms to see whether we could further improve the system performance.

Acknowledgements. This work is partially sponsored by Natural Science and Engineering Research Council of Canada (grant 299021-2010).

References

1. Averbakh, A., Krause, D., Skoutas, D.: Recommend me a Service: Personalized Semantic Web Service Matchmaking. In: Proceedings of the 17th Workshop on Adaptivity and User Modeling in Interactive Systems (2009)
2. Birukou, A., Blanzieri, E., D'Andrea, V., Giorgini, P., Kokash, N.: Improving Web Service Discovery with Usage Data. IEEE Software 24(6), 47–54 (2007)
3. García, J.M., Ruiz, D., Ruiz-Cortés, A.: A Model of User Preferences for Semantic Services Discovery and Ranking. In: Aroyo, L., Antoniou, G., Hyvönen, E., ten Teije, A., Stuckenschmidt, H., Cabral, L., Tudorache, T. (eds.) ESWC 2010, Part II. LNCS, vol. 6089, pp. 1–14. Springer, Heidelberg (2010)
4. Howard, J.A., Sheth, J.N.: The Theory of Buyer Behavior. John Wiley & Sons (1969)
5. Klan, F., König-Ries, B.: A Personalized Approach to Experience-Aware Service Ranking and Selection. In: Greco, S., Lukasiewicz, T. (eds.) SUM 2008. LNCS (LNAI), vol. 5291, pp. 270–283. Springer, Heidelberg (2008)
6. Manikrao, U.S., Prabhakar, T.V.: Dynamic Selection of Web Services with Recommendation System. In: Proceedings of the International Conference on Next Generation Web Services Practices, pp. 117–121 (2005)
7. Manning, C.D., Raghavan, P., Schütze, H.: Introduction to Information Retrieval. Cambridge University Press (2008)
8. Qiu, F., Cho, J.: Automatic Identification of User Interest for Personalized Search. In: Proceedings of the 15th International Conference on World Wide Web, pp. 727–736 (2006)
9. Rong, W., Liu, K., Liang, L.: Personalized Web Service Ranking via User Group combining Association Rule. In: Proceedings of the 7th International Conference on Web Services, pp. 445–452 (2009)
10. Schröpfer, C., Binshtok, M., Shimony, S.E., Dayan, A., Brafman, R., Offermann, P., Holschke, O.: Introducing Preferences over NFPs into Service Selection in SOA. In: Di Nitto, E., Ripeanu, M. (eds.) ICSOC 2007. LNCS, vol. 4907, pp. 68–79. Springer, Heidelberg (2009)
11. Shafiq, M.O., Alhajj, R., Rokne, J.: On the Social Aspects of Personalized Ranking for Web Services. In: Proceedings of the IEEE International Conference on High Performance Computing and Communications, pp. 86–93 (2011)
12. Tran, V.X., Tsuji, H., Masuda, R.: A New QoS Ontology and its QoS-based Ranking Algorithm for Web Services. Simulation Modeling Practice and Theory 17(8), 1378–1398 (2009)
13. Vu, L.H., Proto, F., Aberer, K., Hauswirth, M.: An Extensible and Personalzied Approach to QoS-enabled Service Discovery. In: Proceedings of the 11th International Database Engineering and Applications Symposium, pp. 37–45 (2007)
14. Wang, H.C., Lee, C.S., Ho, T.H.: Combining Subjective and Objective QoS Factors for Personalized Web Service Selection. Expert Systems with Applications 32(2), 571–584 (2007)
15. Zhang, Q., Ding, C., Chi, C.H.: Collaborative Filtering Based Service Ranking using Invocation Histories. In: Proceedings of the IEEE Internation Conference on Web Services, pp. 195–202 (2011)
16. Zheng, Z., Zhang, Y., Lyu, M.R.: CloudRank: A QoS-Driven Component Ranking Framework for Cloud Computing. In: Proceedings of the 29th IEEE International Symposium on Reliable Distributed Systems, pp. 184–193 (2010)

An Adaptive Mediation Framework for Mobile P2P Social Content Sharing

Chii Chang[1], Satish Narayana Srirama[2], and Sea Ling[1]

[1] Faculty of Information Technology, Monash University, Australia
{chii.chang;chris.ling}@monash.edu
[2] Institute of Computer Science, University of Tartu, Estonia
srirama@ut.ee

Abstract. Mobile Social Network in Proximity (MSNP) represents a new form of social network in which users are capable of interacting with their surroundings via their mobile devices in public mobile peer-to-peer (MP2P) environments. MSNP brings opportunity to people to meet new friends, share device content, and perform various social activities. However, as the fundamental topology of MSNP is based on public MP2P network, many challenges have arisen. Existing related works restrict the MP2P social network to operate in specific platforms and protocols. Enabling MSNP in a dynamic public MP2P requires a more flexible solution, which can adapt its behaviour to comply with environment. Hence, we propose a mobile device-hosted service-oriented workflow-based mediation framework for MSNP. The fundamental portion of the framework is based on the Enterprise Service Bus architecture which supports changes in runtime resources without the need to re-launch the application. In order to adapt to different situations, our workflow tasks adjust the execution behaviour at runtime. The workflow engine dynamically selects the best approach to complete the mobile user's request based on the cost and performance, calculated by combining fuzzy set and cost performance index. The developed prototype is discussed along with detailed performance.

1 Introduction

The evolved mobile technologies provide users convenient ways to participate in various virtual online social networks (OSN) such as Twitter [32], Facebook[13]. In the past few years, researchers [36,25,31,28,27,17] have tried to leverage OSN with short range mobile communication technologies (e.g., Bluetooth [6], Wi-Fi Direct [35]) to bring OSN activities into mobile peer-to-peer (MP2P) network. These new breeds of mobile social network (MSN) applications encourage users to socialise with people in proximity via their smart mobile devices, and potentially bring opportunities to make new friends. We use the term — Mobile Social Network in Proximity (MSNP) to illustrate such an environment in which participants are capable of performing various generic OSN activities with proximal users. A typical activity in MSNP is content (e.g., text, images, music, etc.) sharing and mashup [19].

C. Liu et al. (Eds.): ICSOC 2012, LNCS 7636, pp. 374–388, 2012.
© Springer-Verlag Berlin Heidelberg 2012

Mashup is a content-driven composition technique used to compose content derived from various sources into a single customisable presentation. In MSNP, participants may generate various content from their smart mobile device and post/synchronise to different social websites (e.g., Twitter, Facebook, etc.) or cloud storages (e.g., Dropbox [12]). Let us call these participants *content providers*. A *content provider* may intend to share his/her new content to public proximal mobile users in order to bring more visitors/readers to his/her own web pages or potentially establish connection with new friends. The content provider's MSNP application may generate a metadata and advertise it to other MSNP participants' devices based on their preference. Meanwhile, some MSNP participants may also intend to perform a location-based content mashup from proximal content providers to retrieve their interested information. MSNP is useful for attendees to fast share information in the high population event such as Comiket [9] without establishing a centralised system in the venue.

Considering the resource limitations of mobile devices and the dynamic nature of MP2P environment, communication becomes a crucial challenge to both content provider and content consumer. In order to enhance the overall performance of MSNP communication, some tasks such as semantic service/content matchmaking process may be distributed to remote Cloud services (e.g., Google App Engine (GAE) [14], Amazon EC2 [2] etc.). However, distributing tasks to Cloud is not always an efficient solution, because utilising Cloud service consumes extra costs such as network latency, price of using the service etc. In some cases, remaining the communication within local wireless network is more efficient when both performance and cost are considered, especially when there are only a few MSNP peers involved. On the other hand, when there are many MSNP peers involved, it may be more efficient to distribute more tasks to more powerful Cloud services. Hence, there is a need to design a framework which is capable of dynamically change its approach at runtime to adapt to different situations, while the MSNP peer is performing MP2P social network activities.

In this paper, we propose AMSNP: an **A**daptive **M**ediation framework for service-oriented mobile **S**ocial **N**etwork in **P**roximity. The contributions consist of:

- A workflow-controlled Web service-oriented mediation framework for mobile devices to easily leverage heterogeneous service resources automatically.
- An adaptation scheme, which can automatically decide what services should be used to complete the workflow tasks. The decision making is based on a cost-performance index scheme.
- A prototype implementation, evaluated on a real mobile device.

The remainder of this paper is structured as follows: In Section 2, we summarise the foundation of MSNP, followed by our proposed framework, and the adaptiation strategy. Section 3 provides an example of how the MSNP activity can be modelled using workflow. Section 4 describes the prototype implementation and the evaluation results. In Section 5, we describe the difference between our work and related works. Section 6 provides the conclusion and future research direction.

2   System Design

2.1   Overview of MSNP

In an MSNP environment, each mobile device is a mobile Web service
consumer and also a provider [29].
When two peers join the same wireless network, they utilise standard
communication technologies such as
DPWS [22], or Zeroconf [15] to exchange their service description metadata (SDM). We expect each peer has
its own backend Cloud storage to synchronise its IP address as a small text
file in its Cloud storage (or alternatively utilising public DNS servers if

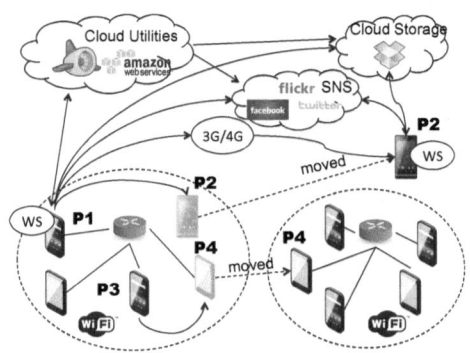

Fig. 1. MSNP architecture

available). The URL of the text file is described in a peer's SDM. Hence, when
a peer (e.g., Fig.1, P2 and P4) moves out from the current network, the other
peers (e.g., Fig.1, P1 and P3) in its previous network can still interact with it
via mobile Internet.

Since P1 and P3 have previously exchanged their SDM with P2 and P4, they
have cached the SDM of P2 and P4 in either their local memory or synchronised
to their Cloud storages. When P1 and P3 receive requests from other peers in the
same network that are performing service discovery, P1 and P3 can also provide
P2 and P4's SDM to these peers. Instead of having the SDM directly send to
the peers by P1 and P3, P1 and P3 can synchronise the cached SDM to their
Cloud storages, and simply provide the URL link to the other peers. Similar
concept is applied to content sharing and mashup, say for example, P1 intends
to mashup the content provided by P2 and P3. When P1 invokes P2 and P3 for
the content, P2 and P3 will simply reply the corresponding metadata documents,
which contain the description about where the content can be retrieved from the
Internet.

Taking into account that mobile devices usually have limited processing power,
it is reasonable for a MSNP peer to delegate the processes to its backend Cloud
utility service (CloudUtil). In Fig. 1 for example, P1 utilises its backend CloudU-
til for semantic service discovery. Furthermore, CloudUtil can be used to directly
access the content uploaded by other MSNP peers in Social Network Services
(SNS) to discover useful content for P1's mashup (if the content has been described in Really Simple Syndication (RSS) feed format).

A content provider in MSNP can also actively push recommendation to other
participants based on the participant's service preference. Due to privacy concerns, MSNP peers may prefer not to share their private information. However,
when a list of available services (described semantically) is provided to the participant, the participant can simply reply which service type it is interested in.

This process can be done automatically by applying context-aware prefetching scheme, which has been described in our previous work [7].

2.2   AMSNP Framework

The framework design is based on the Enterprise Service Bus (ESB) architecture [26]. ESB is a software infrastructure that can easily connect resources by combining and assembling services to achieve a Service Oriented Architecture (SOA). Fig. 2 illustrates the architecture and main components of AMSNP. The architecture consists of four parts:

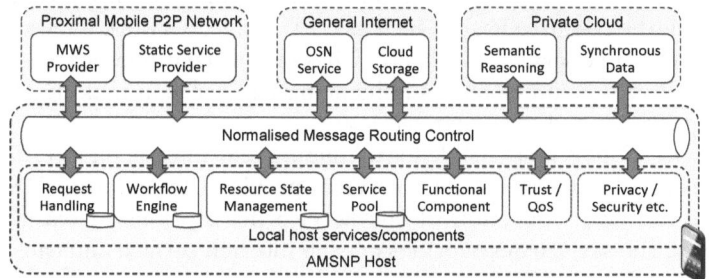

Fig. 2. Architecture of AMSNP Framework

- Proximal Mobile P2P Network — It represents the other MSNP peers within the same network. Depending on the developer's preference, an AMSNP host can support various network communication protocols such as XMPP [30], UPnP [33], Bonjour [4], etc.
- General Internet — Basically, the content generated by the MSNP peers are updated to their OSN services such as SNSs (e.g., Facebook, Twitter) or their Cloud storages. In our design, the Cloud storage services play an important role in MSNP. As mentioned previously, each MSNP peer synchronises its current IP address to its Cloud storage in order to resolve the dynamic IP issue of mobile P2P network.
- Private Cloud — MSNP peer can utilise a number of backend Cloud utility services for distributing tasks in order to reduce the resource usage of the device and also improve the overall performance. For example, the semantic service discovery process requires the MSNP peers to process a number of semantic metadata and matchmaking. Such a task can be distributed to its Cloud utility services. Additionally, an MSNP peer can also synchronise some data to its private Cloud, possibly in the form of cached service description metadata documents.
- AMSNP Host — It represents an MSNP peer with embedded AMSNP framework. An AMSNP host is built based on ESB architecture. Each component of AMSNP is a service, and can be launched/terminated at runtime. A function can be performed by a local service within the AMSNP host, or it can be performed by an external service such as a private Cloud utility service

depends on the definitions of corresponding workflow pattern. AMSNP system is controlled by the WS-BPEL [21] workflow engine. When the user's application submits a request to AMSNP, the request will be handled by the *Request Handling* component, and a corresponding workflow pattern will be selected. The selected workflow pattern will then be passed to the workflow engine for execution via the message routing control component. Each workflow task is managed by a *Task Agent*. The *Task Agent* will decide how to perform the task after analysing the cost-performance scheme, which is described in the next section.

The AMSNP host contains the following main components:

⋄ *Resource State Management* service is responsible for continually monitoring the resource usages such as CPU usage, network bandwidth usage, Cloud utility service usage, etc. These resource usages are cost intensive, and are the main elements influencing the decision making of the adaptation scheme in the next section.

⋄ *Service Pool* is responsible for managing information on internal services, private Cloud services, and services provided by external MSNP peers. It contains a collection of the service descriptions of external MSNP peers, the service descriptions of each internal service and each accessible private Cloud utility service.

⋄ *Functional Components* are miscellaneous utility components such as semantic metadata matchmaking component, calculation component (for calculating the CPI value in next section), message parsing, and so on.

⋄ *Trust/QoS* and *Privacy/Security* are additional components needed to improve the quality of service and security requirements. They are not within the scope of this paper. We will consider them in our future work.

2.3 Adaptive Approach Selection Based on CPI Model

As we mentioned in the previous section, each request received by the *Request Handler*, is to be processed by triggering a corresponding business process workflow pattern. In a basic workflow pattern document (e.g., WS-BPEL), the endpoint (either a single service or a composite service) for processing each task/activity has been pre-defined in the document. Considering the dynamic nature of mobile P2P environment, the pre-defined endpoint may not be the best selection for the task. For example, a workflow is launched when the network has only 10 or less peers in existence. The workflow defines that the task for service discovery will be fully performed by a local host service of the device without using external distributed services. However, once the workflow is launched, the situation can change, there can be 50 more peers suddenly joining the network. Such a change can make the pre-defined approach no longer feasible. On the other hand, distributing tasks to external service (such as a service deployed on GAE) is not always the best approach because in many cases, performing tasks in local host is more efficient. This concern leads us to apply the dynamic adaptation technique, which is capable of identifying the best approach for each workflow task at runtime.

In this section, we propose an adaptation scheme that can decide which approach should be chosen for each workflow task at runtime based on the latency (timespan) of the approach, and costs. In order to clarify the terminologies used in this scheme, we first provide following definitions:

Definition 1: *Approach* — A. $A = \{a_j \in A : 1 \leq j \leq N\}$. Each $a_j \in A$ consists of a performance value (p), and a set of cost element values (E). Where $E^{a_j} = \{e_k^{a_j} \in E^{a_j} : 1 \leq k \leq N\}$.

The approach for a task is selected at runtime after the workflow is launched, and the decision is made based on the cost and performance.

Definition 2: *Workflow pattern.* A workflow pattern defines a goal and a set of sequential or parallel abstract tasks — T, where $T = \{t_i \in T : 1 \leq i \leq N\}$. Each $t_i \in T$ can be completed by numerous pre-defined approaches.

For example, a set of services — S ($S = \{s_i \in S : 1 \leq i \leq N\}$) has been discovered that can provide the content requested. The task of invoking each $s_i \in S$ to retrieve content, can be either performed by approach — a_1: using a localhost component to retrieve all content, or it can be performed by approach — a_2: distribute the process to a cloud service and then synchronise the result to user's mobile device.

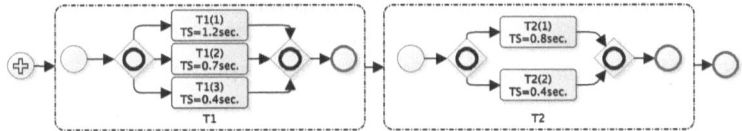

Fig. 3. Workflow path selection based on timespan

Fig. 3 shows a sample workflow which has two tasks. For task $T1$, there are three selective approaches, and for task $T2$, there are two selective approaches. Each approach consumes different timespan. In order to achieve the goal effectively, the system needs to identify the shortest path to reach the goal. Initially, the shortest path can be obtained by (1).

$$path_x = min \left\{ \sum_{i \in T, j \in A_i} p_j^i \right\} \tag{1}$$

Where p_j^i denotes the timespan of approach j of task i.

However, the shortest timespan may not mean the approach selection is the most efficient when the cost is considered. Hence, we propose a *cost-performance index* (CPI) scheme to enable our workflow system to analyse and select the most efficient approach at runtime. The scheme combines fuzzy set [38] and the *weight of context* [11]. The reason to choose fuzzy set approach is because the explicit purpose is to compare the performance and cost between approaches instead of static values. Hence, fuzzy set appeared to be a feasible solution.

Let D^{t_x} be a set of timespan value for the selective approaches (A_{t_x}) of task — t_x, where D is a finite set, and $D = \{d_i \in D : 1 \leq i \leq |A|\}$, in which d_i represents the timespan of a_i, $a_i \in A$. Let L be the longest timespan in D, where $L = max\{d_i \in D\}$. The performance value of each approach — R_i is computed by (2):

$$R_i = \begin{cases} 1 & \text{iff } d_i \equiv L \\ (L+1) - d_i & \text{otherwise} \end{cases} \qquad (2)$$

Let $\tilde{A}$ be the fuzzy set of A. $\tilde{A} = \{\tilde{a}_j \in \tilde{A} : 1 \leq j \leq |A|\}$. We need the normalised fuzzy number of the ranking values. Hence, the fuzzy number of an approach's ranking value (denoted by $\tilde{a}_x$) will be: $\tilde{a}_x = R_x / \sum_{a_j \in A} R_j$. Where R_x is the performance value of a_x derived from (2), and $\tilde{a}_x$ is the normalised fuzzy number of the performance value of a_x, in which $0 \leq \tilde{a}_x \leq 1$.

At this stage, we assume there is a mechanism that can measure the timespan for each approach at runtime based on our previous work [8]

Definition 3: *Cost element* — E^{a_j} is a finite set, where $E^{a_j} = \{e_k \in E^{a_j} : 1 \leq k \leq N\}$. An a_j contains an E^{a_j}, and the value of e_k is denoted by v_{e_k}.

The cost element set is comparable between different related approaches. If approach a_1 for task t_1 — $E_{a_1}^{t_1}$ contains the value of "battery cost", then the approach a_2 for task t_1 — $E_{a_2}^{t_1}$ must also contain such a value. Based on this concept, the overall CPI between different approaches can be compared.

Since we are comparing the cost element between different approaches, the normalised value of a cost element — $\tilde{v}_{e_x}$ can be computed from $\tilde{v}_{e_x} = \frac{v_{e_x}}{\sum_{e_k \in E} v_{e_k}}$, and the average value of the total cost of a_j — $CV_{a_j}^{t_i}$ can be computed from $CV_{a_j}^{t_i} = \frac{\sum_{e_k \in E_{a_j}} \tilde{v}_{e_k}}{|E_{a_j}|}$. By applying the basic CPI model, the cost-performance value — δ of an approach — a_j will be:

$$\delta_{a_j}^{t_i} = \frac{\tilde{a}_j}{CV_{a_j}^{t_i}} \qquad (3)$$

However, the importance of weight of an e_k is different for different users. For example, when the device battery-life remains 50%, the user may consider that saving the battery life of his/her mobile device is more important than spending money on using Cloud services for computational needs. In this case, the weight of the battery life cost element will be higher than the weight of the bandwidth cost of the Cloud service. Therefore, the normalised value of an e_k needs be refined as $\tilde{v}_{e_k} \cdot w_{e_k}$, where w_{e_k} denotes the weight of e_k, and the cost will be refined as follow:

$$\hat{C}_{a_j}^{t_i} = \frac{\sum_{e_k \in E} \tilde{v}_{e_k} \cdot w_{e_k}}{\sum_{e_k \in E} w_{e_k}}, w_{e_k} \geq 1 \qquad (4)$$

Finally, the cost-performance value of a_j will be refined as:

$$\delta_{a_j}^{t_i} = \frac{\tilde{a}_j}{\hat{C}_{aj}^{ti}} \qquad (5)$$

3   Example

In this section, we use an example to show how the workflow system can be applied to an MSNP scenario. In the scenario, a MSNP peer (*PeerX*) intends to advertise content recommendation metadata (*CRM*; describing the URIs of the recommended content/service) to other MSNP peers. Fig. 4(a) illustrates the conceptual workflow of the content advertising process, and Fig. 4(b) describes the workflow in Business Process Modelling Notation (BPMN) [34]. BPMN has been chosen to describe the workflow process because it can be mapped to WS-BPEL [23], and WS-BPEL has been used in our prototype to control the processes. In this example, the workflow consists of two parallel tasks operated asynchronously (see Fig. 4(b)):

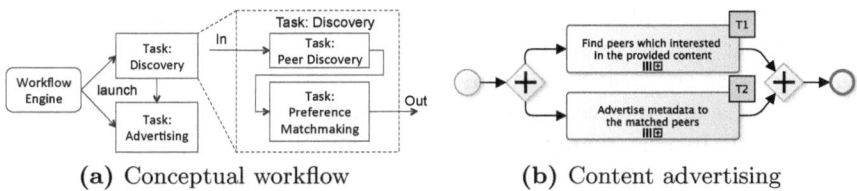

(a) Conceptual workflow   (b) Content advertising

Fig. 4. Content advertising workflow

- *discovery* (T1) — discovers peers which are interested in the content. T1 consists of two sub-tasks: *Peer Discovery* and *Preference Matchmaking*. *Peer Discovery* denotes the process of discovering physical peers in MSNP environment and retrieving the content/service preference metadata from the peer. The result of *Peer Discovery* will be sent to *Preference Matchmaking* for determining whether the peer is interested in the provider's content/service or not. The result of *Preference Matchmaking* will be represented as the result of T1, and will be sent to T2.
- *advertising* (T2) — sends *CRM* to the matched peers.

Each task is managed by a task agent and the basic task handling workflow is described in Fig. 5. When a task is launched, the first step (S1 in Fig. 5) defines a feasible approach based on the CPI scheme described in the previous section. In step 2 (S2), an *event gateway* is placed. The task agent will enter the standby

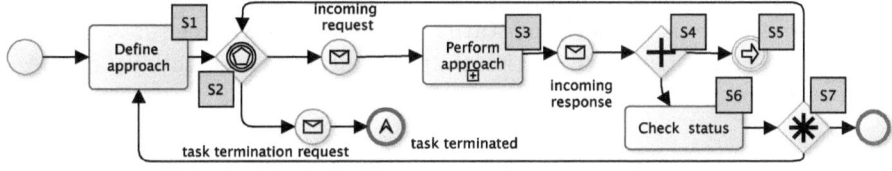

Fig. 5. Generic task

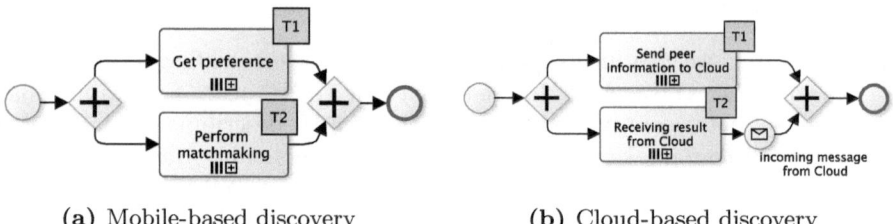

(a) Mobile-based discovery   **(b)** Cloud-based discovery

Fig. 6. Approaches

mode to receive the incoming messages. There are two kinds of requests sent to the task agent: (1) the general request for the task; or (2) the termination request, which informs the task agent to terminate its task state. If the task involves activating a localhost service, when the termination request is received, the task agent will terminate the launched service, and inform the workflow engine to release the task agent from memory.

If the task agent receives an incoming request, it will perform the selected approach (S3). In this example, two approaches have been defined for task 1 (see T1 in Fig. 4), which are mobile-based discovery (Fig. 6(a)) and cloud-based discovery (Fig. 6(b)). Each is a sub-workflow and consists of two parallel tasks. For the approach in Fig. 6(a), the task agent will perform a sub-process (Fig. 6(a) — T1) to retrieve the service preference metadata from each MSNP peer in the network. The response message received by Fig. 6(a) — T1 will be passed to Fig. 6(a) — T2 for service matchmaking process. As for Fig. 6(b), which is the cloud-based approach, the mobile host will send a request to its Cloud utility service (CloudUtil) when an MSNP peer is found (see Fig. 6(b) — T1). The request message contains the basic information about the peer (e.g, the URL to retrieve its current IP address), the CloudUtil will retrieve and process the service preference metadata from each MSNP peer to find out which peer is interested in the content provided by the *PeerX*. The parallel task (Fig. 6(b) — T2) is launched at the same time as Fig. 6(b) — T1 to receive result from the CloudUtil.

The result of Fig. 6(a) — T2 or Fig. 6(b) — T2 will be sent to the original workflow (see "incoming response" in Fig. 5). When the original workflow receives the response, it reaches the *parallel gateway* (see S4 in Fig. 5) in which two activities will be performed. The first is to forward the response message to the next task (S5). In this example, the result from service matchmaking will be sent to the task agent which manages the advertisement task (Fig. 4 — T2). The second activity is to check the status by interacting with the *Resource State Management* component (see Section 2.2). The status check activity can result three possible condition:

- If the current status has changed (e.g., a large number of peers have joined the network, or the device battery life has reached a specific level), the task agent will perform the "define approach" step again.

- If the task is completed (e.g., the task has been defined that the advertisement will be only pushed to 50 peers and there are 50 peers which have been discovered), the task will be terminated.
- if the previous two conditions were not met, the task state will remain, and the task agent will continue to perform the same approach when it receives the incoming request.

4   Prototype

A prototype has been implemented using Objective-C and has been installed and tested in an *iPod Touch 4th generation* [3]. Currently, the prototype's workflow process component can process $< sequence >$ and $< flow >$ of WS-BPEL 2.0 documents. We simulate the other MSNP peers by deploying different number of Web service provider peers in a Macbook (2008), and each peer is published in a Bonjour network as a Web service provider. In this test case, each peer has a back-end Cloud storage using Dropbox, and the peer's current IP address is continually synchronising to its Cloud storage, and is retrievable from a static URL address using HTTP GET request. Moreover, since each peer is a Web service provider, the communication does not rely on the common Web service request/response process. Instead, when two peers initiate the communication, they exchange their basic description metadata, which contains the information of which URL provides the peer's current IP address. By doing so, a requester does not wait for the response when it send out the query, instead the request query contains a specific ID. When the provider complete the request, it invokes the requester node and sends the result (with the specific ID contained in the requester's query) to the requester.

4.1   Evaluation

The evaluation aims to show how the adaptation mechanism changes its approach at runtime based on the cost and performance. The test case was based on the scenario described in Section 3 previously.

At the start of the test case, 10 MSNP peers have been found. After the workflow is executed, more peers have joined the network. Hence, the system needs to perform the calculation to identify whether the approach should change or not, based on the CPI values of approaches.

In the experiment, three cost elements have been considered: CPU usage of mobile device, network bandwidth cost of mobile device, network bandwidth of the Cloud utility service. In a networked system, CPU usage and network transaction costs are two of the main elements that consume the most battery-life of a mobile device. The Cloud bandwidth cost has been considered because it is one of the limitations of GAE. Note that the cost element of the Cloud in this evaluation was only used to show how the system behaves based on the proposed CPI scheme. In reality, the cost of a Cloud utility service such as the application that has been deployed on GAE or Amazon EC2 can involve other factors such as instance creating platform, hardware performance, time of usage, etc.

Mobile devices have limited processing capacity. In the test, tasks were performed asynchronously. Our experiment involved 250 MSNP peers and the total cost of using GAE is within its free usage plan limitation. If there were more than 250 MSNP peers involved, the device is unable to handle its tasks efficiently within an acceptable timespan. Hence, we did not consider the pure cost elements of Cloud like those in Amazon EC2. In the following discussion, Approach 1 represents a workflow consisting of T1A1, and T2; Approach 2 represents a workflow consisting of T1A2, and T2. T1 and T2 are parallel tasks and their sessions will remain until the workflow is terminated. For example, the entire process can be set for a specific period, and it will terminate when the period expired.

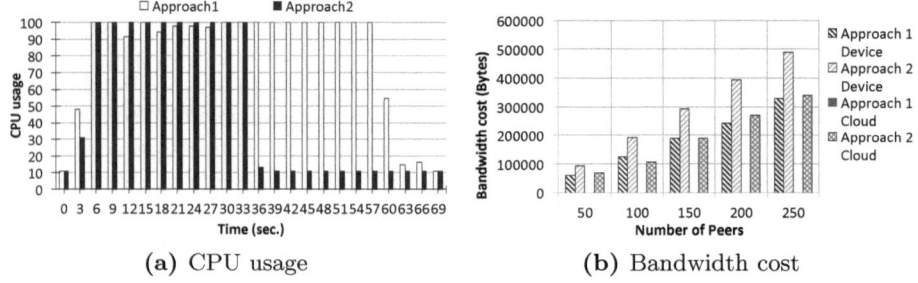

(a) CPU usage   (b) Bandwidth cost

Fig. 7. Cost records

Fig. 7(a) illustrates the recorded CPU usage of the two approaches. The figure shows that while the application is running, it consumes around 11% of CPU usage. This is because the device is running a Web server and has joined Bonjour network, in which the device needs to continually communicate with the router to update the Bonjour service list. At the 3 second mark, the workflow has been triggered, so the CPU usage goes to 100%. For Approach 1, the CPU usage over 90% for 51 seconds. On the other hand, for Approach 2, the CPU usage over 90% was 27 seconds. The CPU usage cost element of our experiment was based on how long the CPU usage stays at over 90%. In Fig. 7(a), Approach 1 costs 24 more seconds than Approach 2. Fig. 7(b) illustrates the bandwidth cost recorded for both device-side and the Cloud utility service-side for different member of MSNP peers in the network. 'Device' denotes the bandwidth cost of the *MCP*'s device. 'Cloud' denotes the bandwidth cost of the Cloud utility service. Since Approach 1 does not use Cloud utility service, the cost value of 'Approach 1 Cloud' is always zero.

Fig. 8(a) illustrates the process timespan recorded for each approach influenced by the number of MSNP peers. As the figure shows, with fewer the number of peers, Approach 2 (which distributes the matchmaking process to Cloud) does not improve the performance much. Fig. 8(b) illustrates the CPI values of both approaches influenced by the number of peers. In this case, the weight of each cost element has been set equally to 1. As the number of peers increases,

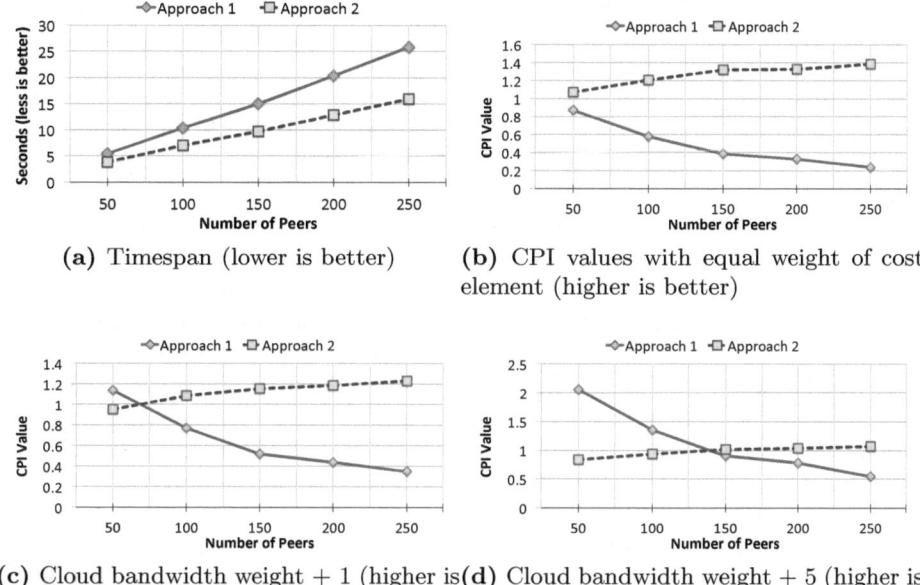

(a) Timespan (lower is better)

(b) CPI values with equal weight of cost element (higher is better)

(c) Cloud bandwidth weight + 1 (higher is better)

(d) Cloud bandwidth weight + 5 (higher is better)

Fig. 8. Cost performance index testing result

the CPI value of Approach 1 is reduce. In the next case, we assume the system intends to reduce the Cloud bandwidth usage because the available bandwidth deserving the free-of-charge period is getting low. Hence, the weight of Cloud bandwidth is increased by 1. The result (Fig. 8(c)) shows that when the number of peers is 50, the CPI value of Approach 1 is higher than Approach 2. Hence, the workflow remains in Approach 1. In the final case (Fig. 8(d)), we assume that the available bandwidth of free-of-charge period is nearly reach the end. Hence, the weight of the Cloud bandwidth is increased by 5. In this case, the workflow engine only selects Approach 2 when there are 150 peers or more.

5   Related Works

In recent years, a number of works have been proposed to enable proximal-based MP2P social network. However, existing decentralised MSNs are still in their early stages. Works such as [37,25,36] were focused on how to enable the OSN activities in mobile P2P networks. Within decentralised MSN, two works have focused on how content can be shared. The authors in [1] have modelled the user's interest profiles, and also introduced a formal mathematical scheme to decide how the content can be proactively pushed to the friends/contacts with potential interest in the content. The authors in [16] have proposed ontology-based formal semantic models to enable content sharing using semantic content matchmaking scheme. The approach enables the user-interests-based content routing in decentralised MSN by analysing the similarity of user profiles. A common limitation in existing decentralised MSN solutions is that they were tightly-coupled solutions with limited flexibility and scalability. The AMSNP framework proposed in this paper is a service-oriented solution based on ESB architecture design and standard technologies, which allows fundamental resources used in the participants' interaction to be changed dynamically at runtime.

Workflow management systems (WfMS) enable autonomous processes, which can highly reduce user's interference in content mashup and content advertisement scenarios. Researchers [18,20] in MP2P area usually apply WfMS in specialised purpose scenarios such as field-work, rescue operations or disaster events, in which the involved mobile nodes are manageable, and collaborate for the same goal. Workflow adaptation schemes in these works focused on failure recovery or resource allocation. This is understandable because MP2P systems (in particular: mobile ad hoc network — MANET) deal with special purpose scenarios rather than general-purpose scenario [10] like in MSNP. Few works have been done on proposing workflow systems for MP2P content mashup. In [24], the authors have proposed a workflow system based on a Java API — AmbientTalk for mashup in MP2P environment. The work mainly focused on how to implement workflow tasks on-top of AmbientTalk. In [5], an adaptive workflow scheduling scheme has been presented for mobile ad hoc network in disaster scenario. These works have been designed for similar MP2P environments such as MSNP. However, they did not address issues raised in this paper. In this paper, the adaptivity of workflow mainly focuses on how to select the most feasible approach to complete the task of content mashup process based on performance (e.g., timespan of the approach) and costs (bandwidth, battery, transaction-load etc.).

6   Conclusion and Future Work

In this paper, we have proposed a workflow-based adaptive mediation framework for service-oriented MSNP. The framework enables a MSNP participating device to dynamically change its behaviour to adapt to different situations when it receives a user's request. The adaptation mechanism utilises the proposed CPI scheme to support the device to automatically select a feasible approach for each task within a request handling process by comparing the dynamically changed cost and performance of the approaches.

Workflow systems provide flexibility and scalability of MSNP processes. The adaptation scheme introduced in this paper enables the system to select a feasible approach to complete the workflow task. It also potentially brings a new form of MSNP communication. For example, an active peer in a MSNP environment can provide a recommended routing approach (described in WS-BPEL) to a new peer joining the network. The new peer can automatically execute the WS-BPEL workflow process to perform service discovery or content retrieval without the need for user's manual control.

In the future, we will model different types of mobile P2P communication protocols in WS-BPEL and develop a more advanced MSNP environment simulator to evaluate our framework. Moreover, we intend to distribute more workflow tasks to different Cloud services to compare the cost and performance of different MSNP approaches.

References

1. Allen, S.M., Colombo, G., Whitaker, R.M.: Uttering: social micro-blogging without the internet. In: The 2nd Int. Workshop on Mobile Opportunistic Networking, pp. 58–64. ACM (2010)
2. Amazon: Amazon Elastic Compute Cloud, http://aws.amazon.com/ec2/
3. Apple: iPod Touch, http://www.apple.com/ipodtouch/
4. Apple: Open Source: Bonjour, https://developer.apple.com/opensource/
5. Avanes, A., Freytag, J.C.: Adaptive workflow scheduling under resource allocation constraints and network dynamics. Proc. VLDB Endow. 1(2), 1631–1637 (2008)
6. Bluetooth: Bluetooth, http://www.bluetooth.com/Pages/Bluetooth-Home.aspx
7. Chang, C., Ling, S., Krishnaswamy, S.: Promws: Proactive mobile web service provision using context-awareness. In: PerCOM Workshops 2011, pp. 69–74 (2011)
8. Chang, C., Srirama, S.N., Krishnaswamy, S., Ling, S.: Proactive web service discovery for mobile social network in proximity. MENERVA, JNIT (to be published, 2012), http://dl.dropbox.com/u/59860036/service_discovery.pdf
9. Comiket: Official Comic Market Site, http://www.comiket.co.jp/index_e.html
10. Conti, M., Giordano, S.: Multihop ad hoc networking: The reality. IEEE Communications Magazine 45(4), 88–95 (2007)
11. Delir Haghighi, P., Krishnaswamy, S., Zaslavsky, A., Gaber, M.M.: Reasoning about Context in Uncertain Pervasive Computing Environments. In: Roggen, D., Lombriser, C., Tröster, G., Kortuem, G., Havinga, P. (eds.) EuroSSC 2008. LNCS, vol. 5279, pp. 112–125. Springer, Heidelberg (2008)
12. Dropbox: Dropbox, http://www.dropbox.com/
13. Facebook: Facebook, http://www.facebook.com/
14. Google Inc.: Google App Engine, https://developers.google.com/appengine/
15. IETF: Zero Configuration Networking (Zeroconf), http://www.zeroconf.org/
16. Li, J., Wang, H., Khan, S.: A semantics-based approach to large-scale mobile social networking. In: Mobile Networks and Applications, pp. 1–14 (2011)
17. Lubke, R., Schuster, D., Schill, A.: Mobilisgroups: Location-based group formation in mobile social networks. In: 2011 IEEE Int. Conf. on Pervasive Computing and Communications Workshops, pp. 502–507 (March 2011)
18. Mecella, M., Angelaccio, M., Krek, A., Catarci, T., Buttarazzi, B., Dustdar, S.: Workpad: an adaptive peer-to-peer software infrastructure for supporting collaborative work of human operators in emergency/disaster scenarios. In: Int. Symposium on Collaborative Technologies and Systems, pp. 173–180 (May 2006)
19. Merrill, D.: Mashups: The new breed of web app. IBM developerWorks (2006), http://public.dhe.ibm.com/software/dw/xml/x-mashups-pdf.pdf
20. Neyem, A., Franco, D., Ochoa, S.F., Pino, J.A.: An Approach to Enable Workflow in Mobile Work Scenarios. In: Shen, W., Yong, J., Yang, Y., Barthès, J.-P.A., Luo, J. (eds.) CSCWD 2007. LNCS, vol. 5236, pp. 498–509. Springer, Heidelberg (2008)
21. OASIS: WS-BPEL 2.0 (2007), http://docs.oasis-open.org/wsbpel/2.0/wsbpel-v2.0.html
22. OASIS: DPWS (2009), http://docs.oasis-open.org/ws-dd/ns/dpws/2009/01

23. Ouyang, C., Dumas, M., ter Hofstede, A.H.M., van der Aalst, W.M.P.: From bpmn process models to bpel web services. In: ICWS 2006, pp. 285–292 (2006)
24. Philips, E., Carreton, A.L., Joncheere, N., De Meuter, W., Jonckers, V.: Orchestrating nomadic mashups using workflows. In: The 3rd and 4th Int. Workshop on Web APIs and Services Mashups, pp. 1:1–1:7. ACM (2010)
25. Pietiläinen, A.K., Oliver, E., LeBrun, J., Varghese, G., Diot, C.: Mobiclique: middleware for mobile social networking. In: The 2nd ACM Workshop on Online Social Networks, pp. 49–54 (2009)
26. Robinson, R.: Understand Enterprise Service Bus scenarios and solutions in Service-Oriented Architecture, Part 1,
    http://www.ibm.com/developerworks/webservices/library/ws-esbscen/
27. Sapuppo, A.: Spiderweb: A social mobile network. In: The 2010 European Wireless Conference, pp. 475–481. IEEE (2010)
28. Schuster, D., Springer, T., Schill, A.: Service-based development of mobile real-time collaboration applications for social networks. In: The 8th IEEE Int. Conf. on Pervasive Computing and Communications Workshops, pp. 232–237. IEEE (2010)
29. Srirama, S., Jarke, M., Prinz, W.: Mobile web service provisioning. In: Int. Conf. on Internet and Web Applications and Services, pp. 120–125 (2006)
30. The XMPP Standards Foundation: XMPP, http://xmpp.org/
31. Tsai, F.S., Han, W., Xu, J., Chua, H.C.: Design and development of a mobile peer-to-peer social networking application. Expert Syst. Appl. 36, 11077–11087 (2009)
32. twitter: twitter, http://www.twitter.com/
33. UPnP Forum: Universal Plug and Play, http://www.upnp.org/
34. White, S.A.: Introduction to BPMN,
    http://www.omg.org/bpmn/Documents/Introduction_to_BPMN.pdf
35. Wi-Fi Alliance: Wi-Fi Direct^{TM},
    http://www.wi-fi.org/discover-and-learn/wi-fi-direct%E2%84%A2
36. Xing, B., Seada, K., Venkatasubramanian, N.: Proximiter: Enabling mobile proximity-based content sharing on portable devices. In: PerCOM 2009, pp. 1–3. IEEE Computer Society (2009)
37. Yang, G., Liu, Z., Seada, K., Pang, H.Y., Joki, A., Yang, J., Rosner, D., Anand, M., Boda, P.P.: Social proximity networks on cruise ships. In: MIRW, pp. 105–114. ACM (2008)
38. Zadeh, L.: Fuzzy sets. Information and Control 8(3), 338–353 (1965),
    http://www.sciencedirect.com/science/article/pii/S001999586590241X

Socially-Enriched Semantic Mashup of Web APIs

Jooik Jung and Kyong-Ho Lee

Department of Computer Science
Yonsei University
Seoul, Republic of Korea
jijung@icl.yonsei.ac.kr, khlee@cs.yonsei.ac.kr

Abstract. As Web mashups are becoming one of the salient tools for providing composite services that satisfy users' requests, there have been many endeavors to enhance the process of recommending the most adequate mashup to users. However, previous approaches show numerous pitfalls such as the problem of cold-start, and the lack of utilization of social information as well as functional properties of Web APIs and mashups. All these factors undoubtedly hinder the proliferation of mashup users as locating the most appropriate mashup becomes a cumbersome task. In order to resolve the issues, we propose an efficient method of recommending mashups based on the functional and social features of Web APIs. Specifically, the proposed method utilizes the social and functional relationships among Web APIs to produce and recommend the chains of candidate mashups. Experimental results with a real world data set show a precision of 86.9% and a recall of 75.2% on average, which validates that the proposed method performs more efficiently for various kinds of user requests as compared to a previous work.

Keywords: Web api, mashup recommendation, functional semantics, social relationship.

1 Introduction

In the past few years, Web mashups have attracted tremendous interest from both service developers and end-users. These applications exhibit the ability to combine existing service functionalities with a minimal development effort and thus making them a powerful tool for providing composite services that satisfy users' requests [5]. However, the explosive growth of Web APIs (hereafter, when we use the term "API", it refers to a "Web API") raises challenging problems of how to enforce the adequacy of the mashups and the ways to accelerate the discovery of the component APIs. Moreover, current mashup composition methods manually search and select the component services and thus aggravating the overall mashup generation process [1]. Hence, many of the researches have tried to exploit various social or functional features of APIs as a solution to the aforementioned issues. Despite the effort, most of the contemporary approaches utilize these social and semantic features separately or exhibit the problem of cold-start where APIs that have no history of being selected for mashup composition are never selected in future compositions.

C. Liu et al. (Eds.): ICSOC 2012, LNCS 7636, pp. 389–403, 2012.
© Springer-Verlag Berlin Heidelberg 2012

In this paper, we propose a novel technique for recommending mashups from natural language requests as well as exploiting both functional and social features of Web APIs and their corresponding ontologies in the process. To elaborate, we first present a systematic approach for extracting functional semantic descriptors from a user request, which are required to facilitate the discovery and composition processes of APIs. We then represent the functional and social features of candidate APIs with graph-based network models. Finally, the assessments of the candidate mashup chains are computed for the purpose of recommendation. As for the social features, we exploit the popularity, collaboration and ratings of APIs to augment the social richness of the proposed method. Furthermore, the executability of a candidate mashup is computed by exploiting the connectivity between the input/output parameters of the participating APIs.

To evaluate the performance of the proposed approach, 20 different natural language requests, each with varying complexity, were used. The experimental results showed a precision of 86.9% and a recall of 75.2% on average. Particularly, it is worth mentioning that as the complexity of a natural language query increased, the precision of the proposed algorithm on that specific request also depicted an increase.

The remaining sections are organized as follows. In Section 2, we present a brief survey of related work. Section 3 describes, in detail, the proposed hybrid method for recommending Web API mashups. The results and analysis of our experimentation are presented in Section 4. We conclude this paper and discuss our plans for future work in Section 5.

2   Related Work

Given the proliferation of Web-based services like Web APIs, there have been many researches on how to compose them efficiently and accurately. The following papers discuss various approaches for discovering and composing APIs, and recommending the resulting mashups.

In [2, 3] a keyword-based search approach which integrates social information is proposed for the purpose of selecting mashup components. First, the authors build an API functional taxonomy, which is used to locate the APIs that match the desired functionalities, using the descriptions of APIs. The description-based technique is enhanced by combining social ranking measures to rank each API. However, the method neglects the functional features of APIs such as their input/output parameters and thus the executability of the resulting mashup is not guaranteed.

The authors in [4] propose a mechanism to specify the functional semantics of Web services based on action and data ontologies. Composite Web services are represented by a graph which describes the relations among the component services in terms of input and output parameters and their functional semantics. We concur with this approach of assigning each Web service, or API in our case, with its corresponding functional semantics to accelerate the service discovery process. However, this particular work lacks the utilization of social information which has the potential to enhance the mashup formation process.

In [21] a method which combines semantics and collective knowledge to assign component descriptors to each Web API is introduced. The author states that this hybrid technique ultimately accelerates the speed of API selection process by manipulating these component descriptors. Here, the technique does not exploit any of the past historical information of APIs.

The majority of works in the area of mashup composition have utilized the tags of mashups and APIs for the purpose of recommendation. In [6] the authors propose a social technique to mine the tags of mashups and APIs for recommendation purposes. However, there is a pitfall to this approach since API developers do not necessarily reuse the same tags to describe APIs. In [7, 8] tag-based clustering approaches are proposed for computing the similarity between tag clouds, where the services corresponding to a specific tag are grouped together. In these researches, the usefulness of mining tags in discovering candidate APIs cannot be judged due to insufficient experiments.

In [9] a faceted classification of Web APIs and an algorithm which ranks those APIs are proposed. By using this approach, the authors argue that the API retrieval process can be improved. Although the technique provides a coarse-grain mechanism for API discovery, the semantic descriptions of APIs are not taken into consideration.

Some of the works [10, 11, 12, 13] are launched to exploit the social networks of mashup developers for constructing mashups. To improve the composition process, the authors in [10] suggest that developers should consider the social networks or collaborative environments of users. Some of the information extractable from social networks are users' past experiences [11, 13] related to the services that they have used. By exploiting the social networks and this "extra" information, the authors in [12] propose that the recommendation of component services is possible from the perspectives of mashup developers.

We strongly believe that the exploitation of social networks has the potential to impact the discovery and composition process of Web APIs and thus we aim to integrate this feature with our approach. ProgrammableWeb[1] is a popular online repository of APIs and mashups [14, 15]. In our work, we utilize this repository for building our data set, which are to be exploited for discovering APIs and constructing their corresponding social and connectivity graphs.

3   The Proposed Mashup Recommendation Algorithm

In this section, we present the proposed mechanism to combine the Web API discovery via functional semantics and the corresponding mashup chain composition based on the social elements and input/output connectivity of candidate APIs. The mechanism consists of the following four major phases: (3.1) extraction phase, (3.2) discovery phase, (3.3) chaining phase, and (3.4) selection phase. Furthermore, the chaining phase is divided into two sub-phases: chaining based on input/output connectivity graph and chaining based on social graph, and the selection phase is also composed of two sub-phases: connectivity analysis and social analysis. The general overview of our approach is illustrated in Figure 1.

---

[1] http://www.programmableweb.com/

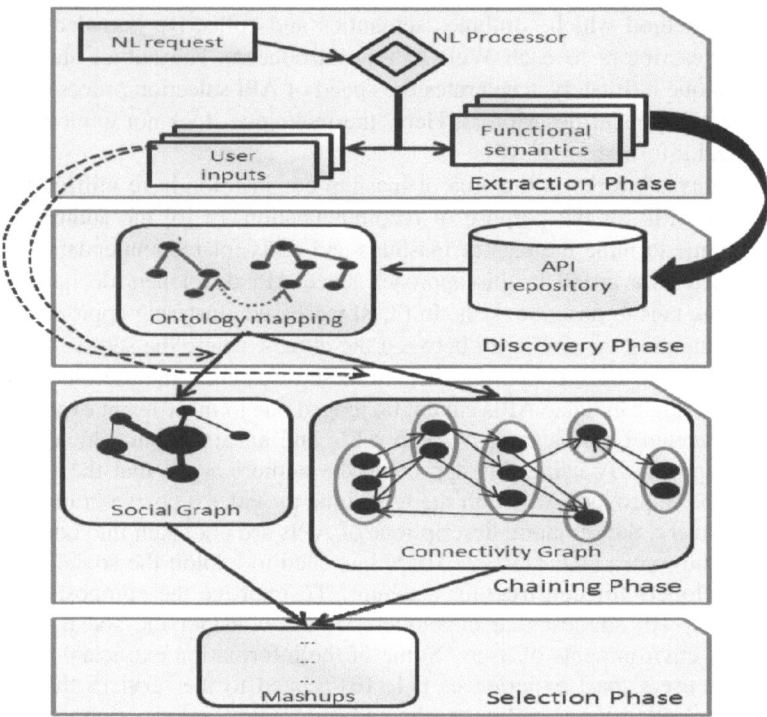

Fig. 1. Overview of the proposed approach

3.1   Extraction Phase

In the extraction phase, we gather the necessary information, namely the functional semantics and user inputs of the requested mashup operations from a user request, which are to be utilized in the next phase. In order to demonstrate this process, we begin by extracting the functional semantics and user inputs from a natural language request as shown in Figure 2. We have particularly selected our input language to be in the form of a natural language request from all other possible choices, as it would be sufficient for ontology mapping.

Before digging into the details of the proposed method, we first define the terms: functional semantics and user inputs. Functional semantics consist of two components, action and object. These two elements combined describe the kinds of services that a particular mashup service offers. As an example, for a functional semantic pair { *rent, movie* }, *rent* and *movie* correspond to the action and object components respectively. User inputs represent various input parameters exploitable by the operations of the mashup service. Unlike the Web services discussed in [4], the current Web APIs do not provide their functional semantics explicitly, and the descriptions of their operations and input/output parameters do not follow any form of a rigid guideline. Thus, it is worth noting that our dataset of Web APIs and proposed ontologies are constructed manually by our team through analysis of APIs available from the ProgrammableWeb directory.

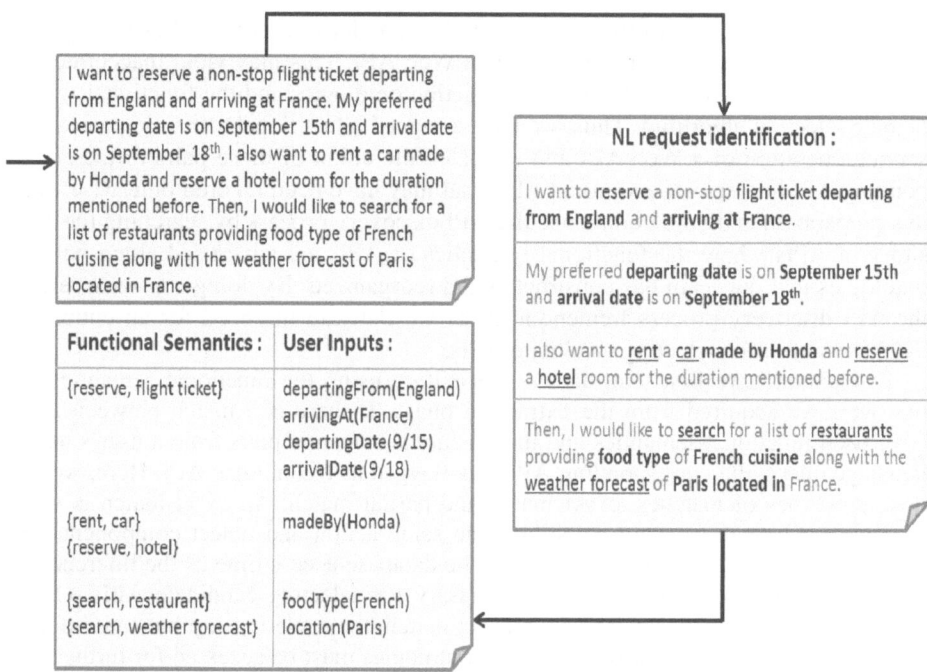

Fig. 2. An example of a natural language request and the proposed extraction method

To initiate the extraction phase, the proposed method divides a natural language request into sentence blocks similar to the work of Lim and Lee [16]. Each of these sentence blocks are then processed by a natural language processor known as the RASP system [17]. Specifically, a natural language query is checked for main verbs, which may represent the action component of the functional semantics to be extracted, and nouns, which may describe the object component of the functional semantic and possibly user inputs. The diagram on the right hand side of Figure 2 shows the result from applying a natural language processor to the natural language description illustrated on the top left hand side of the figure. The action and object components of the functional semantics are indicated by underlined texts, and the user inputs are depicted by bolded texts.

In order to finalize the extraction process, the identified verbs and nouns are extracted and categorized into functional semantics and user inputs. Main verbs and nouns are classified as functional semantic pairs whereas auxiliary verbs and nouns are categorized as user inputs. The final outcome of the extraction phase is illustrated in the bottom left hand side of Figure 2.

3.2 Discovery Phase

Once functional semantic pairs have been extracted and user inputs have been obtained, the discovery phase initiates. The purpose of this phase is to locate all APIs whose functional semantics conform to the functional semantics of a user's natural language request. It is worth mentioning that previous researches have assigned a single pair of functional semantics to each Web API. This may yield inaccurate data due to the imperfection of the object and action ontologies and the functional semantic pair selection algorithm. Thus, we have assigned a functional semantic pair to each service operation of a Web API and allocated the union of those pairs to the corresponding API to discover additional APIs that may have been ignored otherwise. Once this preparation ends, we commence the API discovery process by searching the repository of APIs where the functional semantics of APIs are advertised along with the ontologies that our team has constructed and reorganized. By doing so, we accelerate the API discovery process tremendously as we mitigate the need for an entire API database search for selecting candidate APIs.

To elaborate, we first scan the API repository using the functional semantic pairs that we have acquired from the extraction phase. If there is a match between APIs' advertised functional semantics and the functional semantic pairs from a user's natural language query, the corresponding API gets flagged as a candidate API. Here, we propose two types of matches: exact match and partial match. An exact match is where any two functional semantic pairs have the same action and object components. For this particular case, we can save much of the database access time as the inference via object and action ontologies are not necessary for selecting candidate APIs. On the other hand, if two concepts are not an exact match, their relationship must be inferred. In this case, therefore, the action or object ontologies must be accessed for further verification.

For the partial match cases, (1) is revised from the work of Li et al. [18] to compute a similarity value between two ontology concepts. The equation involves two key elements, the height of the matching parent, denoted as *parHeight* and distance to the parent, denoted as d, which determine the similarity between two different ontology concepts. The rationale behind this equation is that the similarity between two ontology concepts must increase as the height of their intersecting parent concept increases and as the distance to that parent from two concepts decreases.

$$ConceptSim(C_1, C_2) = \frac{parHeight(C_1, C_2)}{(d(C_1) + d(C_2)) \, / \, 2} \tag{1}$$

where parHeight(C_1,C_2) =   height of   matching parent concept of concept C_1 and C_2,
$d(C_n)$ = concept C_n's distance to the matching parent concept

Here, we describe the process of mapping the concepts from object and action ontologies to the object and action components of the functional semantic pairs extracted from the previous phase. This process is a revised version of the work of Klusch et al. [19]. As mentioned earlier, this mapping process is targeted for the candidates which fall into the partial match category as these APIs may still be selected if their values from (1) are above a threshold. Continuing with our example of the natural language request described previously, we have picked {*reserve, hotel*} for a demonstration. Figure 3 illustrates the action and object ontologies for a Web API named TourCMS[2]

---

[2] http://www.tourcms.com/

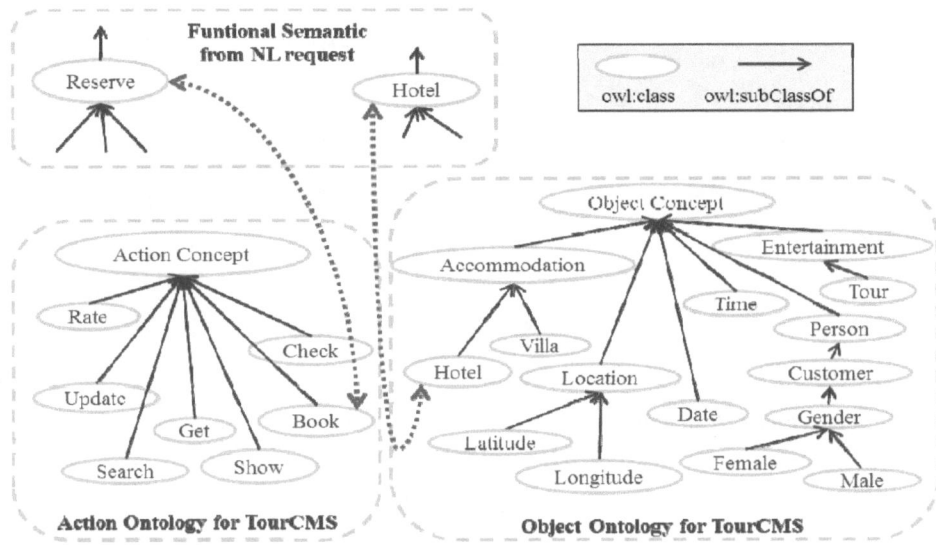

Fig. 3. An example of mapping concepts using action/object ontologies

and how the functional semantic pair, {*reserve, hotel*}, gets mapped to the corresponding ontology concepts in the case of a partial match. It is also worth noting that the threshold is adjustable by the users of this system.

3.3   Chaining Phase

The next step involves the composition of the candidate APIs obtained from the previous phase to yield mashup chains [20]. This mashup chain construction process depends on the proposed I/O connectivity graphs and social graphs. In addition, the user inputs and the functional semantic pairs from the extraction phase are utilized for further pruning.

Chaining Based on Connectivity Graph
Here, we exploit the user inputs and the functional semantic pairs obtained from the extraction phase to construct an I/O connectivity graph. An I/O connectivity graph is a graph depicting the collaboration relationships between various APIs at the operation level. In other words, this graph takes into account that APIs are in fact bridged by the connectivity of their operations. The construction of the graph is based on the mappings of the candidate APIs' input/output parameters within the I/O ontology. Moreover, Figure 4 shows a simplified version of the I/O connectivity graph containing arbitrarily generated APIs for illustration purposes. In this figure, the enclosing nodes and the enclosed nodes represent the APIs and their operations respectively. Also, the direction of the edges between two enclosed nodes dictates the dataflow. That is, the operation where the arrow points to can at least take one output of the

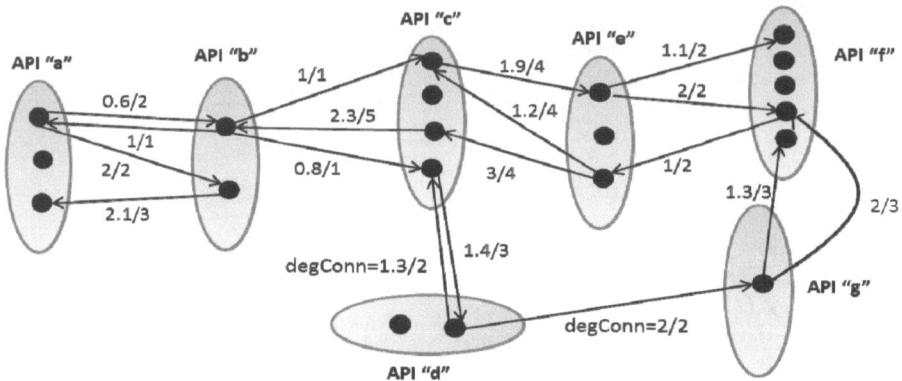

Fig. 4. A simplified version of the proposed I/O connectivity graph

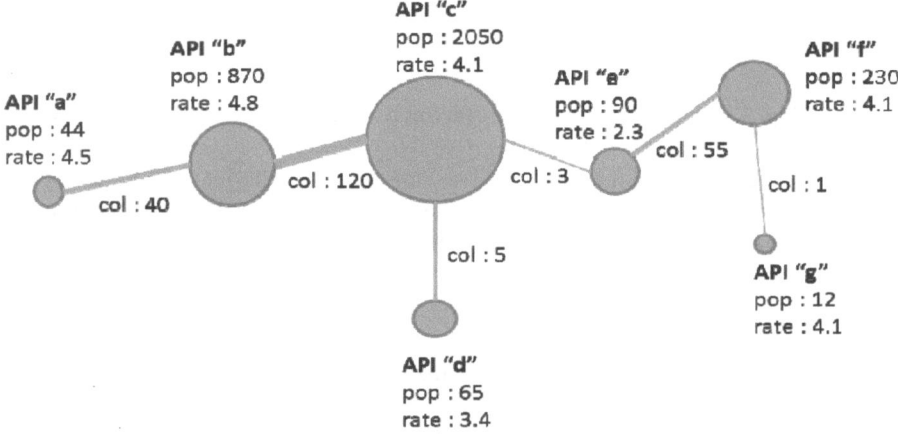

Fig. 5. A simplified social graph version of Figure 4

preceding operation as its input. The edge weight representing the degree of connectivity, denoted as *degConn*, then becomes the following:

$$degConn(u \rightarrow v) = \frac{|ExactMatch| + \alpha \cdot |PartialMatch|}{total\ number\ of\ v's\ inputs} \qquad (2)$$

where *degConn*(u →v) = *degree of connectivity from operation u to v*,
|*ExactMatch*| = *number of concepts matching exactly,*
|*PartialMatch*| = *number of concepts matching partially,*
α = *weight for partial match,*
$0 \leq degConn(u \rightarrow v) \leq 1$

This equation is essentially the ratio of the total number of inputs of the target operation that are provided by the preceding operation to the total number of inputs of the target operation. Furthermore, it is worth mentioning that the value of the weight for partial match can be selected by the users to alter the degree of emphasis on partial match cases.

Once the I/O connectivity graph illustrating the candidate mashup chains is obtained, we then try to reduce the search space even further. For this purpose, we deploy two pruning methods which facilitate the successive reduction of the search space: pruning via functional semantics and pruning via user inputs. First, we reduce the search space by pruning the mashup chains whose combined functional semantics do not contain all of the functional semantics extracted from a natural language description. This is due to the fact that any of the candidate chains may be connected simply by their input/output parameters. If so, the resulting candidate mashup chains may be inadequate for satisfying the user request and are removed as a consequence. After that, we execute another pruning method which exploits the user inputs. That is, we reduce the search space further by pruning the mashup chains whose APIs' operations do not utilize all of the user inputs as their operation parameters. In other words, the operations of the APIs composing the mashup chains must take all of the user inputs as their input parameters.

Chaining Based on Social Graph

Once an I/O connectivity graph has been revised to yield various mashup chains satisfying a user request, a social graph for these finalized candidate mashup chains is constructed. A social graph is a graph portraying the relationships between APIs by capturing various social elements such as the rating and popularity of an API, and the collaboration of two APIs. Figure 5 illustrates a simplified version of the social graph for the APIs contained in the I/O graph generated from the previous section. This graph is similar to the API collaboration network proposed in the work of Tapia et al. [2], with the addition of API ratings to enhance the social richness of our approach. In this figure, nodes and edges represent APIs and their collaborations in existing mashups respectively. In addition, the popularity, denoted as *pop*, is the number of times that a particular API is used in the formation of mashups. It is important to note that the size of a node is dependent on its popularity value. The collaboration, denoted as *col*, describes the number of times that two adjacent APIs are used concurrently in the composition of mashups. This factor also indicates how thick the edges should be in a social graph. Lastly, the rating, denoted as *rate*, is the averaged user rating value of a particular API.

3.4   Selection Phase

In this section, we describe how an I/O connectivity graph and a social graph are exploited in recommending the finalized candidate mashup chains satisfying a user request.

Connectivity Analysis

For every I/O connectivity sub-graph corresponding to each of the finalized candidate mashups, we calculate the connectivity rank using the degree of connectivity values. Recall that the degree of connectivity, denoted as *degConn*, represents the ratio of how many of the required inputs of a particular operation are satisfied by its preceding

J. Jung and K.-H. Lee

operation in their collaboration. To elaborate, the total degree of connectivity for a particular mashup signifies the executability of that mashup. By taking advantage of I/O connectivity of APIs, the newly created APIs are given an opportunity to be utilized and hence alleviating the cold-start problem. The following formula describes the connectivity rank calculation for a candidate mashup chain:

$$ConRank(I) = \frac{\sum_{u,v}^{q} degConn(u \rightarrow v)}{q} \tag{3}$$

where ConRank(I) = connectivity rank for mashup chain I,
degConn(u →v) = degree of connectivity from operation u to v,
q = total number of connectivity relationships in the mashup chain,
0 ≤ ConRank(I) ≤ 1

Social Analysis

Once all of the candidate mashup chains have been assigned with their corresponding connectivity rank values, we then evaluate the social ranks of those chains. As mentioned above, we have three social factors in our social graph namely the popularity, collaboration, and user rating, denoted as *pop*, *col* and *rate* respectively. To calculate the social rank values of a candidate mashup, we use (4), which is based on the fact that the popularity of a single Web API is greater than or equal to the total collaboration of that API. Thus, the first segment of the equation computes how many of the existing collaboration relationships are remaining in the newly constructed social graph. As this number increases, the candidate mashup chain is assigned a higher social rank value. Moreover, the second segment of (4) is simply normalizing the ratings of the participating APIs.

$$SocRank(I) = \frac{\sum col(i)}{\sum pop(i)} \cdot \frac{\sum rate(i)}{MaxRating \cdot |i|} \tag{4}$$

where SocRank(I) = social rank for mashup chain I,
col(i) = collaboration for API i,
pop(i) = popularity for API i,
rate(i) = rating for API i,
MaxRating = 5,
0 ≤ SocRank(I) ≤ 1.

Once the connectivity and social ranks for every candidate mashup chain have been obtained, we then determine the final assessment values of those chains. Here, we refer to the final assessment as the recommendation assessment, denoted by *recAssess*. The computation of *recAssess* value utilizes both the social rank and connectivity rank as described in (5).

$$recAssess(I) = \beta \cdot SocRank(I) + (1 - \beta) \cdot ConRank(I) \tag{5}$$

where recAssess(I) = recommendation assessment of mashup chain I,
β = weight,
0 ≤ recAssess(I) ≤ 1

Table 1. A Portion of the Natural Language Queries along with their Extracted Functional Semantics and User Inputs

	Request17	Request10	Request8	Request3
Extracted functional semantics	{reserve,flight ticket} {rent,car} {reserve,hotel} {search,restaurant} {search,weather}	{show,house} {search,person} {inform,time} {compute,radius}	{search,menu} {search,price} {inform,friend} {view,photo}	{search,car} {rent,car} {show,map}
Extracted user inputs	departFrom(England) arriveAt(France) departDate(9/15) arriveDate(9/18) madeBy(Honda) foodType(French) location(Paris)	city(Vancouver) firstName(Sam) lastName(Lee) longitude(123,06) latitude(49,13)	foodType(Japanese) restaurantName(Guu) city(London)	minPrice(0) maxPrice(8500) carType(SUV)

4   Experimental Results

In order to evaluate the performance of our approach, we have manually built a Web API repository based on a well-known real world API database, Programmable-Web.com. To elaborate, we have extracted and parsed 614 APIs along with their data such as name, popularity, rating, description, and category. Then, we have analyzed APIs' description manuals available on the Web to obtain all of their operations and input/output parameters. As a result, we ended up with 777 operations and 7128 input/output parameters. Thereafter, we have extracted the functional semantics from each operation and also constructed action/object/input/output ontologies for those APIs using Protege[3], an open-source ontology editor.

Once our API database was established, 20 different natural language requests with varying complexity were manually created for test purposes. Table 1 illustrates a small portion of the natural language queries and the outcomes obtained from the extraction phase. Moreover, a connectivity graph and a social graph were constructed for each request, and various factors required for the computation of recommendation assessment values were also calculated. Finally, the candidate mashup chains with higher recommendation assessment values than the optimal threshold were selected for recommendation.

To verify whether a candidate mashup chain is a valid one or not, we had our teams of mashup experts compose mashup services for a comparison with the automatically generated candidate mashup chains. If a particular mashup service executes successfully and produces a sound outcome as expected by a given request, then that mashup chain is considered to be valid.

As for the precisions of the resulting mashups from all 20 requests, the outcome ranged from minimum of 77.8% precision to maximum of 93.6% precision. In addition, the values of recall ranged from 72.5% to 87.5%. Figure 6 illustrates the precision and recall values of final mashups recommended from all of the natural language requests. Particularly, the natural language query described earlier in the paper,

---

[3] http://protege.stanford.edu/

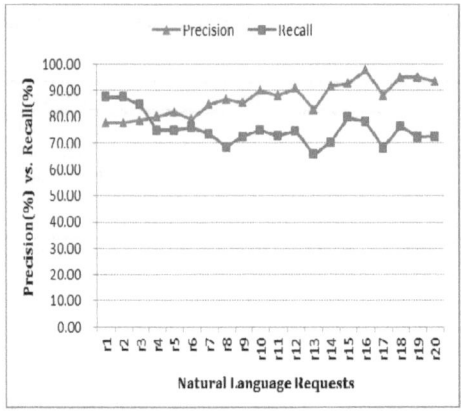

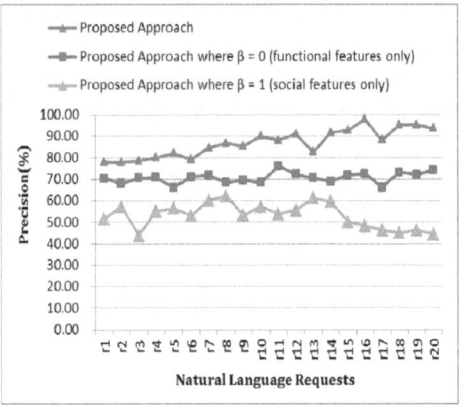

Fig. 6. A precision vs. recall graph of the proposed approach

Fig. 7. A precision graph for three different versions of the proposed method

request17 from Table 1, yielded a precision of 86.7% and a recall of 68.4%. Overall, the experimental results depicted an average precision of 86.9% and an average recall of 75.2%.

In addition, Figure 7 depicts three different precision graphs of the resulting mashups obtained using different versions of our proposed method. The first line from the bottom represents the precision of the recommended mashups where β, from Equation (5), was set to be 1. By assigning so, the proposed method only considered the social features of APIs and ignored the functional features such as the I/O connectivity of API operations. This particular version of the proposed method exhibited an average precision of 53.1% which was significantly lower than the proposed method which exploited both the social and functional features of APIs.

On the other hand, the middle line in Figure 7 illustrates the precision of the recommended mashups, where β, from Equation (5), was set to be 0. This particular graph represents the version of our proposed method which only utilizes the functional features of APIs. For this approach, the precision was observed to be 70.7% on average. This value was still lower than the precision of the proposed approach which integrates both the functional and social features of Web APIs. Also, we have included, at the top, the precision graph of the original version of our method from Figure 6 in Figure 7 to facilitate easy comparison. It is worth mentioning that for this particular graph line, we have used 0.41, which was found to exhibit relatively high precision after several experiments, for the value of β.

In comparison with the experimental results from the work of Gomadam et al. [9], our algorithm exhibited a significant improvement in performance. As for the experimental setup, Gomadam et al. have also exploited the Web APIs from ProgrammableWeb.com and tested with 5 different user queries. In their work, the average precision was found to be around 77% and the average recall was approximately 70%. These numbers indicate that our approach has shown 9.9% and 5.2% improvements in the precision and recall respectively.

Nevertheless, the proposed algorithm yielded 13.1% of erroneous results on average for those 20 natural language queries. From all of the recommended mashups,

13.1% of them were either not executable or did not satisfy the user requests due to the following reasons. First, due to the fact that ontologies are human-constructed, they may contain insufficient information required for concept mapping and inference engines. For example, a functional semantic pair, {*rent, Mustang*}, extracted from a user request may not be able to infer that Mustang is a car after ontology concept mapping. Consequently, an incorrect service was discovered and regarded as a candidate API service.

Second, an error in the extraction of functional semantic pairs and user inputs from the test queries was unavoidable. To elaborate, the proposed algorithm accepts a user query that is composed in natural language. By forming the queries in natural language, mashup users are able to diminish the formality of query generation compared to other querying techniques. However, as these users gain more expressive power when constructing queries, it becomes harder for a natural language processor to capture all of their intentions. As a consequence, the extracted functional semantic pairs and user inputs may vary from what the users expect. In this case, the proposed approach selected an incorrect service which is not consistent with the intention of our test queries.

5   Conclusions and Future Work

In this paper, we have presented a hybrid approach which combines both the social and functional features of APIs to enhance the API discovery and composition processes. Moreover, we have introduced new algorithms for computing the rankings of the resulting candidate mashup chains to assist mashup users. We have first extracted the functional semantic pairs and user inputs from a natural language request. Then, we have selected the corresponding Web APIs that match the extracted functional semantic pairs. After that, a connectivity graph and a social graph between the candidate APIs have been constructed based on ontology mapping. Finally, the candidate mashup chains have been examined in order to recommend the ones that are adequate for satisfying a user's request.

Overall, the proposed algorithm performed efficiently for a number of different natural language queries, each with varying complexity. The experimental results showed an average precision of 86.9% and an average recall of 75.2%, which implies a significant improvement from a previous work. In addition, our experimental results demonstrated that the combination of social and functional features exhibited a significantly better precision than these exploited separately.

Although our current database of Web APIs contains a sufficient amount of data to conduct valid experiments, we believe that there is a necessity for an exhaustive experiment with a more large volume of APIs. In addition, we are looking to adjust or possibly move away from formatting our input in natural language form as this particular technique exhibits a fair amount of noise compared to other query techniques. So, we will be researching on other various query techniques to enhance the quality of our work. Furthermore, we strongly believe that the exploitation of wisdom of crowds through crowdsourcing techniques is an area that has the potential to enhance the API composition process as stated in Section 2. Therefore, we will also be investigating different ways to leverage on this aspect for its integration with our approach.

Acknowledgment. The research was supported by Basic Science Research Program through the National Research Foundation of Korea (NRF) funded by the Ministry of Education, Science and Technology (2011-0026423).

References

1. Elmeleegy, H., Ivan, A., Akkiraju, R., Goodwin, R.: Mashup advisor: a recommendation tool for Mashup development. In: IEEE International Conference on Web Services, ICWS, pp. 337–344 (2008)
2. Tapia, B., Torres, R., Astudillo, H.: Simplifying mahsup component selection with a combined similarity- and social-based technique. In: 5th International Workshop on Web APIs and Service Mashups, MASHUPS (2011)
3. Torres, R., Tapia, B., Astudillo, H.: Improving Web API Discovery by leveraging social information. In: IEEE International Conference on Web Services, ICWS, pp. 744–745 (2011)
4. Shin, D.H., Lee, K.-H., Suda, T.: Automated generation of composite web services based on functional semantics. Journal of Web Semantics 7(4), 332–343 (2009)
5. Maximilien, E.M., Wilkinson, H., Desai, N., Tai, S.: A Domain-Specific Language for Web APIs and Services Mashups. In: Krämer, B.J., Lin, K.-J., Narasimhan, P. (eds.) ICSOC 2007. LNCS, vol. 4749, pp. 13–26. Springer, Heidelberg (2007)
6. Goarany, K., Kulczycki, G., Blake, M.B.: Mining social tags to predict mashup patterns. In: 2nd International Workshop on Search and Mining User-Generated Contents, SMUC, pp. 71–78 (2010)
7. Bouillet, E., Feblowitz, M., Feng, H., Liu, Z., Ranganathan, A., Riabov, A.: A folksonomy-based model of web services for discovery and automatic composition. In: IEEE International Conference on Services Computing, SCC, pp. 389–396 (2008)
8. Fernandez, A., Hayes, C., Loutas, N., Peristeras, V., Polleres, A., Tarabanis, K.: Closing the Service Discovery Gap by Collaborative Tagging and Clustering Techniques. In: 7th International Semantic Web Conference, ISWC, pp. 115–128 (2008)
9. Gomadam, K., Ranabahu, A., Nagarajan, M., Sheth, A.P., Verma, K.: A faceted classification based approach to search and rank web apis. In: IEEE International Conference on Web Services, ICWS, pp. 177–184 (2008)
10. Schall, D., Truong, H.L., Dustdar, S.: Unifying Human and Software Serivces in Web-Scale Collaborations. IEEE Internet Computing 12(3), 62–68 (2008)
11. Maaradji, A., Hacid, H., Daigremont, J.: Towards a Social Network Based Approach for Services Composition. In: IEEE International Conference on Communications, ICC, pp. 1–5 (2010)
12. Maaradji, A., Hacid, H., Skraba, R.: Social Web Mashups Full Completion via Frequent Sequence Mining. In: IEEE World Congress on Services, SERVICES, pp. 9–16 (2011)
13. Maaradji, A., Hacid, H., Skraba, R., Lateef, A., Daigremont, J., Crespi, N.: Social-based Web services discovery and composition for step-by-step mashup completion. In: IEEE International Conference on Web Services, ICWS, pp. 700–701 (2011)
14. Yu, S., Woodard, C.J.: Innovation in the Programmable Web: Characterizing the Mashup Ecosystem. In: Feuerlicht, G., Lamersdorf, W. (eds.) ICSOC 2008. LNCS, vol. 5472, pp. 136–147. Springer, Heidelberg (2009)
15. Wang, J., Chen, H., Zhang, Y.: Mining user behavior pattern in mashup community. In: 10th IEEE International Conference on Information Reuse & Integration, IRI, pp. 126–131 (2009)

16. Lim, J.H., Lee, K.-H.: Constructing composite web services from natural language requests. Journal of Web Semantics 8(1), 1–13 (2010)
17. Briscoe, T., Carroll, J., Watson, R.: The second release of the RASP system. In: Proc. of the COLING/ACL Conference, pp. 77–80 (2006)
18. Li, Y., Bandar, Z.A., McLean, D.: An Approach for Measuring Semantic Similarity between Words Using Multiple Information Sources. IEEE Transactions on Knowledge and Data Engineering 15(4), 871–882 (2003)
19. Klusch, M., Fries, B., Sycara, K.: OWLS-MX: A hybrid Semantic Web service matchmaker for OWL-S services. Journal of Web Semantics 7(2), 121–133 (2009)
20. Roy Chowdhury, S., Daniel, F., Casati, F.: Efficient, Interactive Recommendation of Mashup Composition Knowledge. In: Kappel, G., Maamar, Z., Motahari-Nezhad, H.R. (eds.) ICSOC 2011. LNCS, vol. 7084, pp. 374–388. Springer, Heidelberg (2011)
21. Melchiori, M.: Hybrid Techniques for Web APIs Recommendation. In: 1st International Workshop on Linked Web Data Management, LWDM, pp. 17–23 (2011)

Application of Business-Driven Decision Making to RESTful Business Processes

Qinghua Lu[2,1], Xiwei Xu[1,2], Vladimir Tosic[1,2], and Liming Zhu[1,2]

[1] NICTA, Australian Technology Park, Sydney, NSW, Australia
[2] University of New South Wales, Sydney, NSW, Australia
{Qinghua.Lu,Xiwei.Xu,Vladimir.Tosic,Liming.Zhu}@nicta.com.au

Abstract. Runtime adaptability is a desired quality attribute in business processes, particularly cross-organizational ones. Past work showed that designing and implementing business processes following the REpresentational State Transfer (REST) principles increases runtime adaptability. However, the past solutions for RESTful business processes (RESTfulBP) were limited to manual selection of process fragments to be composed at runtime. Therefore, we have now integrated into the RESTfulBP system an extended version of our MiniZnMASC middleware to enable concurrent selection of different RESTfulBP process fragments for different classes of user at runtime. This selection maximizes overall business value, while satisfying all given constraints. We also extended the RESTfulBP runtime engine with a process fragment processor, a constraint processor, a process fragment repository, and several types of monitoring resources. Experiments with prototype implementations showed that our solutions are feasible, functionally correct, business beneficial, with relatively low performance overhead, and with satisfactory scalability.

Keywords: REST, business-driven IT management, middleware, Web service composition management, decision support, middleware, autonomic computing.

1   Introduction

To improve adaptability of business processes, we previously designed an architecture style "RESTful business processes (RESTfulBP)" [1] that adapts the REpresentational State Transfer (REST) principles [2] to business process design, implementation and execution. Compared with the traditional business process using flow-based languages (e.g., BPEL), RESTfulBP has two significant characteristics: 1) at the process level, RESTfulBP models business processes in a declarative style at design time and allows reusable process fragments to be bundled, unbundled and re-bundled flexibly and rapidly at runtime; 2) RESTfulBP can fully utilize the mechanisms of the HTTP protocol to provide a lightweight adaptable infrastructure supporting business process execution and adaptation. In RESTfulBP, decision making points are where process fragments can be bundled, unbundled, and re-bundled. When several process fragments can be used at a decision making point, it is necessary to determine which one to use. Since the affected RESTfulBP users can have different characteristics, one

C. Liu et al. (Eds.): ICSOC 2012, LNCS 7636, pp. 404–419, 2012.

single selection of a process fragment for all users can rarely achieve best business value for the RESTfulBP owner organization. It is often necessary to concurrently examine selection of process fragments for all affected users. In past work [1], this decision is made manually by a "knowledge worker", who is authorized to manage business process instances. However, it is hard for humans to have entire knowledge about the runtime RESTfulBP states and understand multifaceted interdependencies between diverse components and metrics at various levels of abstraction. It is also difficult for knowledge workers to manually calculate business value that each process fragment leads to and decide which process fragment to execute taking into account business strategies of the RESTfulBP owner organisation. Therefore, a business-driven decision making support tool is needed to assist knowledge workers in the process fragment selections at runtime.

Based on the past studies on autonomic business-driven IT management [3, 4], we previously designed MiniZnMASC [5, 6] that is an autonomic business-driven decision making middleware for adaptation of Web service compositions. In this paper, we extend MiniZnMASC with new algorithms and build it into RESTfulBP to provide runtime decision making support in the process fragment selections at each decision making point of RESTfulBP. The adapted version of MiniZnMASC first examines all available process fragments at each decision making point and selects different groups of process fragments for different classes of users, in ways that satisfy the business value constraints and other constraints (e.g., resource limitations). The use of MiniZnMASC can be fully automatic, when it selects and invokes the combination of process fragments (one process fragment per class of user) that maximizes business value. However, a more realistic use scenario is semi-automatic, when a knowledge worker examines MiniZnMASC advices and selects the final combination of process fragments based on own knowledge and experience. The new architecture of RESTfulBP with built-in MiniZnMASC introduces a process fragment processor, a constraint processor, a process fragment repository, and several kinds of monitoring resources for process fragment processing. The recorded monitored data are sent to MiniZnMASC in an XML file and are used in adaptation decision making. The adaptation actions decided by MiniZnMASC are invoked by sending a HTTP request.

The remainder of this paper is organized as follows. Section 2 introduces a motivating example for this work. Section 3 examines related work and summarizes our past work on RESTfulBP and MiniZnMASC. Section 4 discusses in detail how we integrated the extended MiniZnMASC into RESTfulBP. Section 5 evaluates the proposed solutions. The last section concludes the paper.

2   Motivating Example

The motivating example illustrating the usefulness of our solutions is the loan approval process from the Lending Industry XML Initiative (LIXI) [7]. It is a human-intensive process that largely depends on the knowledgeable human for guidance. Thus, the software is used to assist the human to direct the process rather than completely automate the process execution. As outlined in the upper part of Fig. 1, this is a complicated business process, where entities are from different businesses and entities of the same type can differ. Thus, the lending institution classifies its users into three classes according to their credit history and previous loan records: gold, silver, and bronze. It also offers different service levels, which have different guaranteed technical QoS, prices per invocation, and penalties if the guarantees are not met.

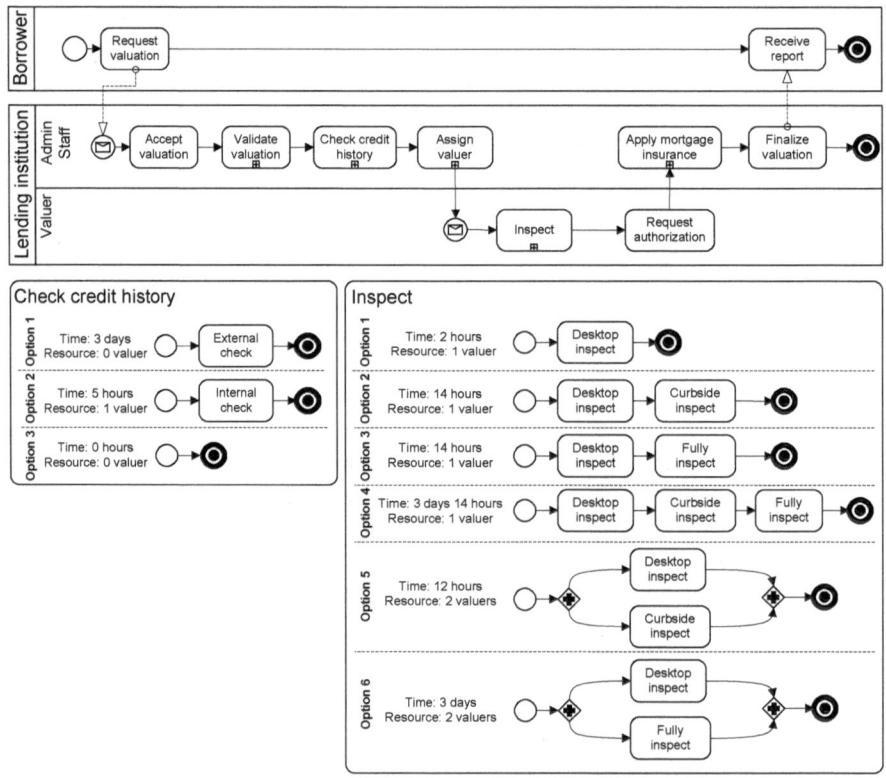

Fig. 1. A loan approval process with possible process fragments

There are many decision making points in the loan approval process where advanced decision making is necessary. Due to space limitations, we only discuss the decision making of the "Inspect" sub-process, for which the lower-right part of Fig. 1 outlines possible process fragments and corresponding time/resource constraints. (The lower-left part of Fig. 1 shows another sub-process, "Check credit history", as an illustration that there are many decision making points, but we do not have space to describe this sub-process here.) There are three types of property inspection: desk-top, curbside, and full. Desk-top inspection estimates the property value based on the existing data repository – it has a negligible cost and can be completed by 1 valuer within 2 hours. Curbside inspection includes the outside inspection (without entering the property) and requires 0.5 day for 1 valuer to complete. Full inspection includes both inside and outside inspections and may take 3 days or more to be completed, because the valuer has to make an appointment with the property owner. The possible process fragments at the "Inspect" decision making point are shown in the expanded "Inspect" sub-process. The initiation of the inspection is very flexible in terms of the number of the inspections and the sequence of the chosen inspections. MiniZnMASC filters the process fragments depending on the constraints and monitored data and sorts them based on business value. However, there are some knowledge and runtime situations that are hard to capture in predefined policies, so a knowledge worker might be required to make the final decision among the filtered process fragments.

For one example runtime situation at the "Inspect" sub-process, the Table 1 shows the number of currently running loan approval process instances in each class of user and the calculated business value and cost of each adaptation option per instance. Further, the lending institution has 6 valuers and the completion time limit for the "Inspection sub-process" is 4 days. Two other constraints limit the overall business value to at least $6000 and the overall cost to at most $2000. Domain experts provide information that helps determine business values, costs, and various constraints for decision making. The advices produced by MiniZnMASC are in the last line of Table 1.

Table 1. Business value (V) and cost (C) (AU$) of different adaptation alternatives for different classes of user at the "Inspect" decision making point

Class of user	Gold	Silver	Bronze
Number of instances	2	3	5
Option 1	V: 500; C:50	V: 300; C: 50	V: 100; C: 50
Option 2	V: 400; C: 100	V: 600; C: 100	V: 200; C: 100
Option 3	V: 400; C: 150	V: 400; C: 150	V: 200; C: 150
Option 4	V: 300; C: 200	V: 400; C: 200	V: 600; C: 200
Option 5	V: 1000; C: 100	V: 400; C: 100	V: 200; C: 100
Option 6	V: 800; C: 150	V: 400; C: 150	V: 200; C: 150
Selected adaptation	Option 5 or Option 6	Option 2	Option 4

Section 4 explains how our extended MiniZnMASC middleware makes such decisions based on policies specified in the WS-Policy4MASC language. We have used the described example for evaluation of our solution (cf. Section 5).

3   Related Work and Background

3.1   Related Work

Process fragment is not a new concept and it has been shown previously that that dividing business process into process fragments can improve the flexibility and dynamic evolution [1, 8]. For example, the process fragment concept in our work is similar to a worklet from [8] – a small, self-contained, complete workflow process that handles one task in a larger, composite process. It can be also regarded as a process-level continuation in distributed business processes. A similar concept has been used in [9], but this approach is aimed to overcome the bottleneck of centralized process and improve the performance, while our work has significantly broader scope. A novelty of RESTfulBP is that it utilizes the existing Web infrastructure to provide a light-weight architecture for the execution of process fragments. RESTfulBP also inherits good characteristics of REST, such as loose coupling and interoperability. Although REST [2] and Resource-Oriented Architecture [10] principles are well established, their application to Web-based business process systems has not been well understood. Several proposals to bring REST to business processes have emerged from the industry and research community. Most of them extend SOA standards with RESTful interfaces [10, 11] or impose selected REST constraints on business process implementation [12-15]. However, these have several limitations, which RESTfulBP overcomes. Firstly, the methods for introducing additional constraints focus only on two constraints: uniform interfaces and "hypermedia as the engine of application state". They ignore other useful mechanisms of the Web infrastructure: content negotiation, rich metadata, and transfer of process fragments to enable truly distributed and localized process execution. There are very few style implementation guidelines and associated methodologies. Secondly, there is a lack of full support for workflow patterns. Finally, confusion arises when different and sometimes conflicting additional constraints are proposed without a clear definition of the new style and associated methodology for implementing it.

On the other hand, there are many publications on particular types of adaptation of business processes. We provided a classification and a relatively detailed analysis of many additional related works in [16]. While in industry practice adaptation decision making is still mainly done by human administrators, the vast majority of research focuses on adaptation with minimal help from humans. However, the past adaptation decision making algorithms predominantly choose adaptation that maximizes technical metrics (e.g., [17, 18]), while maximization of business metrics is still an open research area [4, 16]. While [19] is not directly on adaptation of business processes, some of its solutions could be reused in our context. It presented a system for maximization of business metrics that schedules the triggered management policies by minimizing the penalty specified in service level agreements (SLAs), but it did not examine resolution for conflicting policies, which is a critical problem in policy-based management. Different adaptation triggers often require different monitoring, decision making, and adaptation execution. For example, if a management system does not monitor business-related events, it will not be able to recognize the adaptation needs they cause, so it will not be able to react and adapt appropriately. However, the vast majority of past works (e.g., [17, 20]) researching adaptation of business processes focused on adaptations triggered by technical reasons, while only a few research projects (e.g., [21, 22]) examined the impact of business causes (but without addressing them completely). In particular, [21] identified three types of adaptation causes: exceptions, business policy changes, and business model changes. There are many other additional causes that were not addressed, such as infrastructure updates, business strategy changes, and business customer changes. Adaptation of a business process instance could change various aspects of system configuration and execution:

structure of the implemented business process type (e.g., replacing one block of activities with another for all instances) [17], Web services used for the implementation (e.g., replacing a faulty service) [23], execution of the instance (e.g., rolling back to a checkpoint) [24], or contracts with customers (e.g., changing SLAs) [25]. There is a lot of research literature presenting support for individual types of change, but a comprehensive support for all these types of change was first provided in the WS-Policy4MASC language and the MASC middleware [23], which is the predecessor of the research presented in this paper. Our work is different from traditional solutions of optimization problems in business processes. We focus on the runtime decision making support for concurrent adaptation of multiple RESTful business process instances with consideration of business value for the process owner.

3.2   Background

3.2.1   The RESTfulBP Architecture Style

The RESTfulBP architectural style is a set of architectural constraints [1] that aims to establish communication and coordination mechanisms among participants in a business process from a peer-to-peer and distributed point of view. Small pieces of workflow logic, called "process fragments", are defined within each endpoint and can be transferred to other endpoints at runtime. RESTfulBP models four types of business process entities (process, instance, task, and state) as resources identified by declarative URIs [10]. The entity resources are manipulated through a set of uniform methods, resembling the standard HTTP methods (GET, PUT, POST, and DELETE). The process entity resources are connected through a Microformat [21]. The Microformat-based messages are used to communicate routing information at runtime. RESTfulBP uses content negotiation and authentication mechanisms provided by the Web infrastructure to choose an appropriate representation of an entity resource for the role-based requester. A server can estimate the desired representation format according to the ACCEPT request header, which indicates the preferred media type. The current media type is extended to indicate the role of the requesting participant. RESTfulBP communicates exception information in the message header. The HTTP protocol is extended with an optional header field "Exception" to denote the type of exception, so that the requestor can get sufficient information from the message header only. The tool support for RESTfulBP includes: an annotation tool based on the Eclipse project BPMN Modeler [22], a programming API that facilitates implementation of RESTful process-aware systems, and a runtime engine that powers the programming API.

3.2.2   The MiniZnMASC Middleware

In complex long-running business processes, changes happen often (e.g., business goal changes, service performance changes). When such changes occur during runtime, the affected Web service compositions should be adapted. This adaptation can be usually done in several ways and advanced decision making is needed to determine how to proceed. MiniZnMASC [5] is a runtime autonomic decision making middleware for adaptation of Web service compositions. It implements novel decision-making algorithms that can concurrently make different adaptation decisions for different classes of instance in a way that achieves maximum overall business value while satisfying all given constraints. A "class of instance" is a group of Web service composition instances that share a combination of characteristics that warrants adaptation in the same way. The most important characteristics are: the implemented business process type, the executed Web service composition, the current position/state within the running Web service composition, and the class of consumer. The decision-making algorithms in MiniZnMASC use information specified as policy assertions in WS-Policy4MASC. WS-Policy4MASC [4, 23] is a policy language that can describe various adaptations and all information necessary for decision making. WSPolicy4MASC extends the WS-Policy industry standard and defines five new types of policy assertions: 1) goal policy assertions (GPA) prescribe conditions to be met (e.g., desired response time), 2) action policy assertions (APA) list adaptation actions to be performed in particular situations, 3) utility policy assertions (UPA) specify business values for particular situations, 4) probability policy assertions (PPA) specify probabilities of occurrence, and 5) meta policy assertions (MPA) describe how to select among alternative adaptation decisions to maximize business value.

4   Extending MiniZnMASC and Integrating It into RESTfulBP

To provide business-driven decision making support for the runtime RESTfulBP process fragment selection, we extend the MiniZnMASC middleware with new decision making algorithms. The new decision making algorithms concurrently select different combinations of process fragments (addressing all classes of user) at a decision making point. The selections found by MiniZnMASC satisfy all given business value (e.g., cost) constraints and other constraints (e.g., resource limitations) and depend on business metrics and business strategies, plus operational conditions (e.g., current number of users in each class). The selected combinations of process fragments can be provided as an advice for knowledge workers who make final decisions. Alternatively, when knowledge workers completely trust the specified WS-Policy4MASC policies, MiniZnMASC can automatically select and invoke the combinations that it determines optimal from the business viewpoint, similarly to [4, 5].

While these algorithms are based on the autonomic MiniZnMASC algorithms described in [4, 5], the main differences are in the constraint programming model: 1) the new model can select more than one process fragments for each class of RESTfulBP user while the original model can only select one adaptation action for each class of Web service composition instance; 2) the new model handles various constraints including business value constraints (e.g., discarding a process fragment that leads to business value smaller than the minimal acceptable one), time constraints, and resource constraints, while the original model had a business value optimisation objective and primarily worked with cost constraints. The new constraint programming model makes MiniZnMASC more suitable for integration into RESTfulBP as a decision making support tool. The novel integration of MiniZnMASC with RESTfulBP enables semi-automatic business-driven adaptations in complex, multi-user RESTfulBP with minimal help from human knowledge workers.

There were four challenges to integrate MiniZnMASC into RESTfulBP: 1) tailor the previous automatic decision making algorithms to semi-automatic decision making algorithm and tailor the previous modelling in MiniZnMASC to describe the selection of process fragments in RESTfulBP; 2) design external monitoring mechanism in RESTfulBP that can send real-time data to MiniZnMASC; 3) externally execute the adaptation actions; 4) design the overall architecture of the integrated system.

4.1   The Constraint Programming Model for Decision Making Algorithms

In this subsection, we describe our solution to the first challenge identified above, while our solutions to the other three challenges are presented in the next subsection. We represent our decision making model in constraint programming and code it in the constraint programming language MiniZinc [25]. The *Policy Conflict Resolution* module (cf. Fig. 2) of MiniZnMASC contains the MiniZinc solver, which instantiates the model with values from WS-Policy4MASC files and runtime monitoring data and solves this instantiated model for the new MiniZnMASC optimization algorithm.

We use the following notation. Unless noted otherwise, the listed variables are specified in WS-Policy4MASC files. N is the number of classes of user. X_n $(n=1,..., N)$ is the current number of instances in class n and it is determined from runtime monitoring data. M_n $(n=1,..., N)$ is the number of process fragment options (at the examined decision point) for a user in class n. $A_{n,i}$ $(n=1,..., N; i=1,..., M_n)$ is the i-th process fragment option for class n. K is the number of business value types [4] that can be reasoned about. $V_{k,n,i}$ $(k=1,..., K; n=1,..., N; i=1,..., M_n)$ is the summary business value of type k for process fragment option $A_{n,i}$. It is calculated by our algorithm, summarized in [4], for calculation of summary business metrics from the values in WS-Policy4MASC utility and probability policy assertions. (The probabilities specify uncertainties and risks.) The algorithm is implemented in MiniZnMASC as Java code, so in this constraint programming model we just use its result $V_{k,n,i}$. We also derived a precise mathematical formula showing how $V_{k,n,i}$ is calculated, but this is not crucial for this paper. W_k $(k=1,..., K)$ is the weight of business value type k. These weights are specified in WS-Policy4MASC meta policy assertions and are usually in the interval [-1,1] (negative values are for costs).

The summary business value of all used business value types for a process fragment option $A_{n,i}$ is calculated as: $B_{n,A_{n,i}} = \sum_{k \in UsedBVTs} W_k * V_{k,n,i}$ $(k=1,..., K; n=1,..., N; i=1,..., M_n)$. The set *UsedBVTs* contains all business value types deemed relevant (as specified in the used WS-Policy4MASC meta policy assertion) for comparing business worth of process fragment options. This feature addresses the fact that in different business situations different sets of business value types are relevant.

The problem of finding the globally optimal set of process fragments can be represented in constraint programming as the task to find the set of N process fragments $J_n \in \{A_{n,1}, ..., A_{n,M_n}\}$ $(n=1,..., N)$ that satisfy all given constraints and have the highest summary business value. We use j_n to denote i of the chosen $A_{n,i}$, that is $J_n = A_{n,i} \Leftrightarrow j_n = i$. The most important are business value constraints describing business situations when a process fragment option should be discarded because it

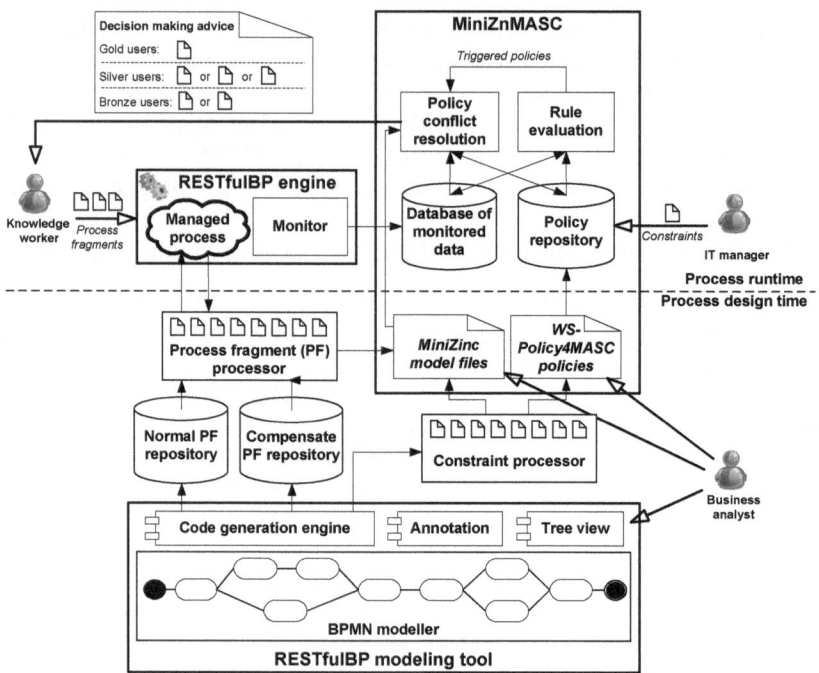

Fig. 2. Architecture of RESTfulBP with integrated MiniZnMASC

leads to business value that is smaller than the acceptable minimum. These constraints are modeled as: $\sum_{n=1}^{N} X_n * B_{n,j_n} \geq MinBusinessValue$. Cost constraints describe common business situations when a process fragment option should be discarded because its short-term costs are higher than available funds. They are modeled similarly to: $\left|\sum_{n=1}^{N}(X_n * \sum_{k \in CostBVTs} W_k * V_{k,n,j_n})\right| \leq CostLimit$. Here, the set *CostBVTs* contains all business value types representing relevant costs (as specified in the used WS-Policy4MASC meta policy assertion). Resource constrains are another constraint type important in practice. Resources (e.g., memory, processor time, bandwidth, energy, etc.) are often limited and this is one of the main reasons why decisions of concurrent instances should be considered together instead of separately. WS-Policy4MASC enables definition of non-financial business value types that represent resource usage and use appropriate units. For example, it is possible to define that all non-financial costs with attribute *Cause="Memory"* represent memory usage and have unit *"GB"*. Then, a memory limit can be modelled similarly to: $\left|\sum_{n=1}^{N}(X_n * \sum_{k \in MemoryBVTs} W_k * V_{k,n,j_n})\right| \leq MemoryLimit$, where the set *MemoryBVTs* contains all business value types that represent memory usage. Time constraints are yet another important constraint type, because time (both calendar time for completion of a task/sub-process and time that can be spent actively working on a task/sub-process) is often limited in business processes. Time constraints often depend on characteristics of a business process instance (e.g., gold class usually has lower time limits than bronze class). $P_{n,i}$ *(n=1,..., N; i=1,..., M_n)* is the number of tasks/sub-processes in $A_{n,i}$ and $Y_{n,i,p}$ *(n=1,..., N; i=1,..., M_n; p=1,..., $P_{n,i}$)* is a particular task/sub-process in $A_{n,i}$. Thus, time constraints can be modeled similarly to: $WorkTime(Y_{n,i,p}) \leq WorkTimeLimit(Y_{n,i,p})$ and $CalendarTime(Y_{n,i,p}) \leq CalendarTimeLimit(Y_{n,i,p})$. WS-Policy4MASC and MiniZnMASC can also support additional constraint types, but they are not very common in practice.

4.2   Architecture of RESTfulBP That Adds the Extended MiniZnMASC

Fig. 2 shows the architecture of RESTfulBP with integrated MiniZnMASC middleware. The dash line in the middle separates the components at design time and runtime in perspective of the produced business process. At design time, the business process is defined by business analysts using BPMN with RESTfulBP annotations. The purpose of modeling is to identify the tasks in the business process at different levels of abstraction, the roles of the process participants, the control dependencies between the tasks (e.g., sequencing, parallel), and various constraints. Besides, the constraint programming models and management policies which provide the basis for MiniZnMASC are also defined by the business analyst according to all relevant RESTfulBP models and other business information, e.g., process fragments, constraints, business strategies, and operational conditions. At runtime, the RESTfulBP engine is used to execute the produced processes. RESTfulBP is designed for the human-intensive processes. Thus, a knowledge worker is usually required to drive the process execution, and MiniZnMASC is used to assist the knowledge worker in making more suitable decisions from a group of available process fragments. (As mentioned above, MiniZnMASC can make decisions without human involvement, but humans have to fully trust them and this might not be realistic in complex situations.)

4.2.1   Process Design Time

The *RESTfulBP modeling tool* is built on the basis of the Eclipse platform and several existing Eclipse projects. BPMN modeler is an Eclipse-based business process diagram editor. It realizes Business Process Modeling Notation (BPMN) [24] specification. The *Annotation* plug-in is implemented on top of the BPMN modeler by utilizing the extension mechanisms of Eclipse. It builds upon several extension points provided by the BPMN modeler and the Eclipse platform. The *Annotation* plug-in allows the developers to annotate various elements of BPMN diagrams with RESTfulBP information, which is essential for the *Code Generation Engine* to generate code. The *Code Generation Engine* can extract useful information from the diagram and generate process skeletons and constraints for certain tasks or sub-process. It consists of four modules: workflow pattern detector, constraints detector, code generation wizard, and code generation template. The workflow pattern detector can recognize which workflow pattern a certain task belongs to, by referring to its pre-and-post tasks. The identified workflow pattern is used by the code generation template to create tasks and process fragments. Developers can configure the generated project using the code generation wizard, e.g. by choosing the path of the dependent library. Then, the code generation engine combines the information from both the template and the wizard forms to create an executable process. The process fragments extracted from the normal process are the normal process fragments, while the process fragments extracted from the compensation process are the compensate process fragments used for exception handling. The information is stored in an XML file as an input of the *Process Fragment Processor*. The *Process Fragment Processor* extracts the identification number of each process fragment and stores it for different decision making points and possible exception points. The output of the process fragment processor includes some of the information required by MiniZinc models, e.g. the number of available process fragments. The constraints detector can extract the constraints for the tasks. The information is stored in an XML file as an input of the *Constraint Processor*. The *Constraint Processor* treats all received constraints and stores them for different constraint types. The *Tree Viewer* organizes the tasks and corresponding process fragments into a tree construct. All tasks are children of the root node. A task can contain an arbitrary number of process fragments as its children.

4.2.2   Process Runtime

During process execution, RESTfulBP provides a runtime environment that allows process fragments to be exchanged between process participants. The process is driven by a knowledge worker, who is responsible for selecting (based on own knowledge) the most suitable process fragment to execute from a group of process fragments. MiniZnMASC can assist the knowledge worker by selecting for different classes of user smaller groups of process suitable fragments that satisfy given constraints. The selections made by MiniZnMASC are based on monitored data from the runtime execution and according to policies in WSPolicy4MASC [4, 23]. If changes happen in the operational environment, IT managers may update the constraints and relevant policies in the *Policy Repository* at runtime. MiniZnMASC is used not only to assist the knowledge worker to make decisions in normal process execution, but also to provide an exception handling mechanism (e.g., when a server is down).

For process monitoring, the *Monitor* module of RESTfulBP uses a set of monitoring resources to provide monitoring functionality. The monitoring resource on the top-level is addressed by a URI, e.g. "{processURI}/monitoring/". It has a set of sub-resources, each of which represents a type of runtime data to be monitored. For example, "{processURI}/monitoring /responsetime" represents the response time metric, while "{processURI}/monitoring/availability" represents the availability metric. These QoS metrics can be used to measure different service levels of process entities, which are also represented by sub-resources of QoS metric resources. For example, response time of a certain process instance can be accessed trough the resource "{processURI}/monitoring/responsetime/{instanceId}". Similarly, response time of a certain task of the same process instance is represented by "{processURI}/monitoring/responsetime/{instanceId}/{taskId}". The monitoring resources record all relevant runtime data automatically at runtime. The monitored data is stored in the *Database of Monitored Data*, which includes both technical metric data (e.g., measured response time) and business metric data (e.g., paid prices and penalties).

5   Evaluation

5.1   Feasibility, Functional Correctness, and Business Benefits

We implemented prototypes of the extended MiniZnMASC middleware and the new RESTfulBP system containing MiniZnMASC and performed with it a number of diverse tests, using the motivating example from Section 2 and other examples. The new MiniZnMASC prototype was built by extending the prototype discussed in [5], so it was also implemented in Java and uses the PostgreSQL database. The new prototypes show that implementation of our solutions is feasible.

We first tested functional correctness of the MiniZnMASC by comparing results calculated by the prototypes and by hand, in various scenarios. Since we found no differences, these results indicate that the new algorithms do not have functional errors. We then comprehensively tested the new overall RESTfulBP system that includes the extended MiniZnMASC. After debugging minor errors, we found no further problems with the prototype implementation of our core solutions.

For the motivating example we also calculated summary business value (incl. possible revenue and relevant costs) for different possible decisions, some of which are shown in Table 2. These results confirm that using the new MiniZnMASC algorithms for automatic selection of process fragments to be executed leads to business benefits. The combination of these tests of functional correctness and business benefit shows that the developed algorithms and middleware will select process fragments best from the business viewpoint, according to the information specified in policies.

Table 2. Total business value (V) and cost (C) is AU$ of different decisions

Decision	Business benefits
Single Selection of Option 1	V: 2400; C:500
Single Selection of Option 2	V: 3600; C: 1000
Single Selection of Option 3	V: 3000; C: 1500
Single Selection of Option 4	V: 4800; C: 2000
Single Selection of Option 5	V: 4200; C: 1000
Single Selection of Option 6	V: 3800; C: 1500
Selections by MiniZnMASC	V: 6400~6800; C: 1500~1600

5.2 Performance and Scalability

For the evaluation of performance and scalability, we used a Hewlett-Packard laptop model HP EliteBook6930p with Intel Core 2 Duo CPU T900 2.53GHz processor and 4.00 GB of RAM memory, running 32-bit Windows Vista operating system. This configuration is near the lower end of environments in which the RESTfulBP system with MiniZnMASC might be run in practice. The fact that we found performance satisfactory in this low-end environment gives us confidence that performance will not be a problem in practical use of our solutions. To minimize the impact of noise (e.g., background operating system processes that we were not able to switch off), we repeated tests hundreds of times at different times of day and averaged their results.

Table 3. Performance of decision making (DM) and conflict resolution algorithm (CRA), with increasing number of conflicting action policy assertions (APAs) and utility policy assertions (UPAs)

Test case	Execution time of DM	Execution time of CRA
3 APAs, each with 2 UPAs	Average: 250 ms Range: 234-266 ms	Average: 16 ms Range: 15-32 ms
10 APAs, each with 32 UPAs	Average: 905 ms Range: 889-936 ms	Average: 31 ms Range: 16-32 ms
100 APAs, each with 64 UPAs	Average: 12309 ms Range: 12262-12449 ms	Average: 140 ms Range: 140-156 ms

In one set of performance and scalability tests, we increased the complexity of decision making in a decision point. We simultaneously increased two aspects of this complexity: 1) the number of available process fragments (represented through conflicting WS-Policy4MASC action policy assertions - APAs); 2) the complexity of calculating summary business value for each process fragment (represented through the number of WS-Policy4MASC utility policy assertions - UPAs). Using the Java "System.currentTimeMillis()" call, we measured the execution time of whole MiniZnMASC business-driven decision making (DM) and the execution time of only the Confliction Resolution Algorithm (CRA) that is core to this decision making. Table 3 shows the measured results of the range and average of the execution time for some test scenarios. The overall execution time of decision making in MiniZnMASC rises because the execution time of the summation of business values for each conflicting action policy assertion increases with increasing number of conflicting action policy assertions and utility policy assertions. The last test case (100 conflicting action policy assertions, 64 utility policy assertions) is much more complicated than realistic scenarios in practice, so 12.3 sec is not an issue. It is important to note that in realistic application scenarios of MiniZnMASC to RESTfulBP the number of conflicting action policy assertions will be low, while the overall number of action policy assertions can be huge. We also checked that the number of additional non-conflicting action policy assertions in the MiniZnMASC Policy Repository has no significant effect on performance, even when there are hundreds of action policy assertions.

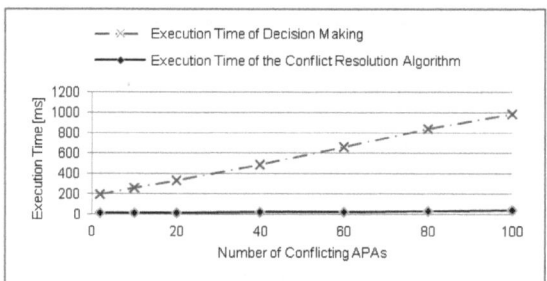

Fig. 3. Performance results with increasing number of conflicting action policy assertions (APAs), each with 2 utility policy assertions (UPAs)

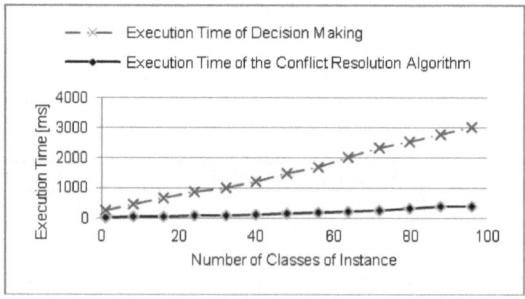

Fig. 4. Performance results with increasing number of classes of instance

Fig. 3 shows the performance measurement results when we increased the number of action policy assertions, while Fig. 4 shows the performance measurement results when we increased the number of classes of user. In both figures, the upper line is for the execution time of the overall MiniZnMASC business-driven decision making, while the lower line is for the execution time of the Conflict Resolution Algorithm. Both lines show linearity, which is good. In our application of MiniZnMASC to RESTfulBP, the decision making component first decides the action policy assertions triggered by events received from the external monitoring modules and finds utility policy assertions and probability policy assertions for the relevant action policy assertions. Then, if the number of action policy assertions is more than one, the new MiniZnMASC integrated into RESTfulBP runs the Conflict Resolution Algorithm to select among the conflicting action policy assertions. The results in Fig. 4 show that the majority of the execution time of the overall decision making is spent on deciding triggered action policy assertions and setting utility policy assertions and probability policy assertions, and not on the Conflict Resolution Algorithm.

6   Conclusion

The past solution for RESTfulBP was limited to manual selection of process fragments to be composed at runtime. Therefore, in this paper, we extended our MiniZn-MASC middleware with new decision making algorithms to enable semi-automatic concurrent selection of different RESTfulBP process fragments for different classes of user at runtime. The selections suggested by MiniZnMASC take into consideration business metrics, business strategies, and operational conditions (e.g., the current number of users in each class). These selections maximize overall business value while satisfying all given constraints. The new algorithms required several extensions of the constraint programming models and the MiniZnMASC middleware.

We also proposed new architecture of RESTfulBP that integrates MiniZnMASC middleware. In particular, we introduced a process fragment processor, a constraint processor, a process fragment repository, and several types of monitoring resources into the RESTfulBP runtime engine to automatically record values of different technical and business metrics. The monitored runtime data is passed to MiniZnMASC in an XML file, which is used in the decision making. MiniZnMASC results are usually provided as a decision making advice for knowledge workers who make final decisions (although it is also possible for MiniZnMASC to select and invoke process fragments without human intervention). New prototypes were implemented using Java, PostgreSQL database, and the MiniZinc solver. Experiments with the prototypes showed that our solutions are feasible, functionally correct, business beneficial, with relatively low performance overhead, and with satisfactory scalability.

Acknowledgments. NICTA is funded by the Australian Government as represented by the Department of Broadband, Communications and the Digital Economy and the Australian Research Council through the ICT Centre of Excellence program.

References

1. Xu, X., Zhu, L., Kannengiesser, U., Liu, Y.: An Architectural Style for Process-Intensive Web Information Systems. In: Chen, L., Triantafillou, P., Suel, T. (eds.) WISE 2010. LNCS, vol. 6488, pp. 534–547. Springer, Heidelberg (2010)
2. Fielding, R.: Architectural Styles and the Design of Network-based Software Architectures. Universityof California, Irvine (2000)
3. Bartolini, C., Sahai, A., Sauve, J.P.: Proceedings of the Second IEEE/IFIP Workshop on Business-Driven IT Management. IEEE (2007)
4. Tosic, V.: Autonomic Business-Driven Dynamic Adaptation of Service-Oriented Systems and the WS-Policy4MASC Support for Such Adaptation. Intl. J. of Systems and Service-Oriented Eng. (IJSSOE) 1, 79–95 (2010)
5. Lu, Q., Tosic, V.: Support for Concurrent Adaptation of Multiple Web Service Compositions to Maximize Business Metrics. In: Proc. of IM 2011, pp. 241–248. IEEE (2011)
6. Lu, Q., Tosic, V., Bannerman, P.L.: Support for the Business Motivation Model in the WS-Policy4MASC Language and MiniZnMASC Middleware. In: Kappel, G., Maamar, Z., Motahari-Nezhad, H.R. (eds.) ICSOC 2011. LNCS, vol. 7084, pp. 265–279. Springer, Heidelberg (2011)
7. LIXI (Lending Industry XML Initiative). Web resource, http://www.lixi.org.au/
8. Adams, M., ter Hofstede, A.H.M., Edmond, D., van der Aalst, W.M.P.: Worklets: A Service-Oriented Implementation of Dynamic Flexibility in Workflows. In: Meersman, R., Tari, Z. (eds.) OTM 2006. LNCS, vol. 4275, pp. 291–308. Springer, Heidelberg (2006)
9. Yu, W.: Consistent and Decentralized Orchestration of BPEL Processes. In: Proc. of SAC 2009, pp. 1583–1584. ACM (2009)
10. Richardson, L., Ruby, S.: RESTful Web Services. O'Reilly Media (2007)
11. Overdick, H.: Towards Resource-Oriented BPEL. In: Emerging Web Services Technology, vol. II, pp. 129–140. Springer (2008)
12. Pautasso, C.: BPEL for REST. In: Dumas, M., Reichert, M., Shan, M.-C. (eds.) BPM 2008. LNCS, vol. 5240, pp. 278–293. Springer, Heidelberg (2008)
13. Webber, J., Parastatidis, S., Robinson, I.: How to GET a Cup of Coffee. Web resource, http://www.infoq.com/articles/webber-rest-workflow
14. zur Muehlen, M., Nickerson, J., Swenson, K.: Developing Web Services Choreography Standards–The case of REST vs. SOAP. Decision Support Systems 40, 9–29 (2005)
15. Rest-client. Web resource, http://github.com/caelum/rest-client
16. Baker, M.: Hypermedia Workflow. Web resource, http://www.markbaker.ca/2002/12/HypermediaWorkflow/
17. Chafle, G., Dasgupta, K., Kumar, A., Mittal, S., Srivastava, B.: Adaptation in Web Service Composition and Execution. In: Proc. ICWS 2006, pp. 549–557. IEEE (2006)
18. Tong, H., Zhang, S.: A Fuzzy Multi-attribute Decision making Algorithm for Web Services Selection Based on QoS. In: Proce. of APSCC 2006, pp. 51–57. IEEE (2006)
19. Lu, Q., Tosic, V.: MiniMASC: A Framework for Diverse Autonomic Adaptations of Web Service Compositions. In: Proc. of UIC/ATC (Worksh. ANS) 2010, pp. 460–468. IEEE (2010)
20. Aib, I., Boutaba, R.: Business-Driven Optimization of Policy-Based Management Solutions. In: Proc. of IM 2007, pp. 254–263. IEEE (2007)
21. Microformat. Web resource, http://microformats.org/
22. BPMN Modeler. Web resource, http://www.eclipse.org/bpmn/

23. Tosic, V., Erradi, A., Maheshwari, P.: WS-Policy4MASC - A WS-Policy Extension Used in the Manageable and Adaptable Service Compositions (MASC) Middleware. In: Proc. of ICWS 2007, pp. 458–465. IEEE (2007)
24. Business Process Model and Notation (BPMN) 1.1. Web resource, http://www.omg.org/spec/BPMN/1.1/
25. Nethercote, N., Stuckey, P.J., Becket, R., Brand, S., Duck, G.J., Tack, G.: MiniZinc: Towards a Standard CP Modelling Language. In: Bessière, C. (ed.) CP 2007. LNCS, vol. 4741, pp. 529–543. Springer, Heidelberg (2007)

Declarative Choreographies for Artifacts*

Yutian Sun[1], Wei Xu[2,**], and Jianwen Su[1]

[1] Department of Computer Science, UC Santa Barbara, USA
[2] School of Computer Science, Fudan University, China

Abstract. A choreography models a collaboration among multiple participants. Existing choreography specification languages focus mostly on message sequences and are weak in modeling data shared by participants and used in sequence constraints. They also assume a fixed number of participants and make no distinction between participant type and participant instances. Artifact-centric business process models give equal considerations on modeling both data and control flow of activities. These models provide a solid foundation for choreography specification. This paper makes two contributions. First, we develop a choreography language with four new features: (1) Each participant type is an artifact schema with (a part of) its information model visible to choreography specification. (2) Participant instance level correlations are supported and cardinality constraints on such correlations can be explicitly defined. (3) Messages have data models, both message data and artifact data can be used in specifying choreography constraints. (4) The language is declarative based on a mixture of first order logic and a set of binary operators from DecSerFlow. Second, we develop a realization mechanism and show that a subclass of the choreography specified in our language can always be realized. The mechanism consists of a coordinator running with each artifact instance and a message protocol among participants.

1 Introduction

Collaborative business processes (CBPs) are a necessity for businesses to stay competitive [8,11]. A recent study reports that an overwhelming majority of eCommerce volume is associated with B2B collaboration [13]. CBPs involve multiple participants, and multiple resources spread over multiple administrative domains. Typically CBPs are complex in terms of process logic, relationships among participants and resources, distributed execution, and semantic mismatches between participant data, ontologies, and behaviors. Such complexity is the source of many technical difficulties in design, analysis, realization, execution, and management of CBPs. Tools and support for CBPs continue to be a major challenge in current and future enterprise [13].

CBPs can be divided into two classes. An *orchestrated* CBP uses a designated "mediator" to communicate and coordinate with all participating BPs (business processes). Although this approach is widely used in practice (e.g., for cross-organizational workflows), it loses autonomy of participating BPs and does not scale well. The *choreography* approach specifies global behaviors among participating BPs but otherwise leaves

---

* Supported in part by NSF grant IIS-0812578 and grants from IBM and Bosch.
** Part of work done while visiting UCSB.

C. Liu et al. (Eds.): ICSOC 2012, LNCS 7636, pp. 420–434, 2012.

the BPs to operate autonomously and communicate in the peer-to-peer fashion. Technical difficulties for this approach include the lack of suitable choreography specification language(s) and mechanisms to coordinate among participating BPs in absence of a central control point. This paper develops a language for CBP choreography specification and addresses the coordination issue.

A choreography models a collaboration among multiple participants. A choreography may be specified as a state machine representing message exchanges between two parties [9] or permissible messages sequences among two or more parties with FIFO queues [2], or as a process algebra expression with sequence, parallel, conditional, and loop constructs [3,4]. It may be specified in individual pieces using patterns [24], as a composition of message interactions [19], or implicitly through participants behaviors [6]. WS-CDL proposes an XML-based package for specifying choreography through a conventional set of control flow constructs over messaging activities. Existing choreography languages focus mostly on specifying message sequences and are weak in modeling data shared by participants and used in choreography constraints. WS-CDL models data through variables that only implicitly associated with participants that produce data. A tightly integrated data model with message sequence constraints would allow a choreography to accurately constrain execution. Also, these languages assume a fixed number of participants and makes no distinction between a participant *type* and a participant *instance*. For example, an *Order* process instance may communicate with **many** *Vendor* process instances; this cannot be effectively captured without the type vs. instance distinction. Therefore, a choreography language should be able to model correlations between process instances. Existing languages either do not support such correlations, or lack the ability to reference instance correlations in a choreography.

In recent BPM research, artifact-centric BP models [17] have attracted increasing attention. An artifact-centric BP model includes (*i*) an information model for business data, (*ii*) a specification of lifecycle that defines permitted sequences of activities, and (*iii*) a data model for keeping track of runtime status and dependencies. Artifact-centric BP models provide a technical foundation for choreography specification.

This paper focuses on choreography specification and realization, and makes the following two technical contributions. **First**, we develop a choreography language with four distinct and new features: (1) Each participant type is an artifact schema (BP model) with a selected sub-part of its *information model* visible to choreography specification. (2) Correlations between participant types and *instances* are explicitly specified, along with *cardinality constraints* on correlated instances (e.g., each *Order* instance may correlate with exactly one *Payment* instance and multiple *vendor* instances). In particular, Skolem notations are used to reference correlated participant instances. (3) Messages can include data; both message data and artifact data can be used in specifying choreography constraints. Also, Skolem notations are used to manipulate dependencies among messages and participant instance created by messages. (4) Our language is declarative and uses logic rules based on a mix of first-order logic and a set of binary operators from DecSerFlow [22]. **Second**, we formulate a distributed algorithm that realizes a subclass of the choreography in our language. This subclass contains choreographies allowed by most existing languages including conversation protocols [21]. Specifically, a choreography is translated to an equivalent finite state machine. Based on this global state machine, our distributed algorithm coordinates participant instances using a simple protocol. We show that the set of global behaviors of coordinated execution of participant instances by our algorithm coincides with the set of behaviors permitted by the choreography. Furthermore, the total number of messages in each successful run is at most twice the number of messages needed for the collaborative process execution plus the number of participants.

This paper is organized as follows. A motivating example is provided Section 2. The choreography language and the realization results are presented in Sections 3 and 4 (resp.). Related work is discussed in Section 5. Conclusions are in Section 6.

2 Motivating Example

This section illustrates with an example concepts including artifact-centric BPs and motivates the need for specification of correlations among process instances and choreographies with data contents.

Consider an online *store* where items are available at *vendor*s. A vendor may use several *warehouses* to store and manage its inventory. Once the customer completes shopping, she initiates a payment process in her *bank* that will send a check to the store on her behalf. Meanwhile, the store groups (1) the items in her cart by warehouses and sends to each warehouse for fulfillment, and (2) the items by vendors and requests each vendor to complete the purchase. The vendors inform warehouses upon completion of the purchases. After the store receives the payment and vendors' completion of purchases, the store asks warehouses to proceed with shipments.

In this example, four types of participants (*store, vendor, warehouses,* and *bank*) are involved and each type has its own BP. Although *store* and *bank* have only one process instance each for a single shopping session, there may be multiple instances of *vendor* and of *warehouse*. In artifact-centric modeling, an artifact instance encapsulates a running process. For example, *store* initiates an "Order" (artifact) instance. Fig. 1 shows a part of the structured data in an Order instance. The structure contains attributes ID, (shopping) Cart, etc., where Cart is a relation-typed attribute (denoted by "*") that may include 0 or more tuples with four nested attributes: Inv(entory)_ID, (item) Name, Quan(tity), and Price. Similarly, other participant BPs are also artifact instances: Purchase instances represent order processing at vendors, Fulfillment instances are packing and delivery processes at warehouses, and a Payment instance is initiated upon a customer request to make a payment to the online *store*.

Consider specifying a choreography for the CBP in this example, there are two major difficulties. First, existing languages do not support multiple participant instances, and thus the fact that multiple vendor/warehouse instances cannot be easily represented and included in specifying behaviors. Some process algebra based languages allow instantiation of new instances from sub-expressions in a choreography [3,4], but it is not clear how it is related to multiple participant instances. Second, behaviors often depend on data contents. For example, when an order request is received with total amount $\geqslant 10$, the order processing should proceed as described in the above; for orders with amount <10, the processing may be optional. Such conditions on data cannot be easily expressed in most languages. WS-CDL may express this through copying messages to variables, but copying adds unnecessary data manipulations.

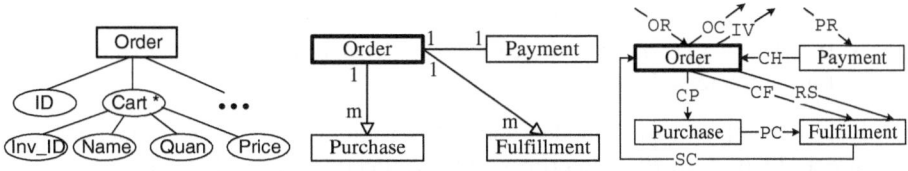

Fig. 1. Data structure   **Fig. 2.** Correlation diagram   **Fig. 3.** Message diagram

3   A Declarative Choreography Language

This section introduces a declarative language for defining choreographies. In this language, a choreography assumes participant BPs are modeled as artifacts and consists of correlations between artifacts and instances, messages, and a set of choreography constraints based on first-order linear temporal logic. §3.1 defines "collaborative schemas" containing correlations and messages, and choreography constraints are defined in §3.2.

3.1   Correlations of Artifacts, Messages, and Collaborative Schemas

Artifacts represent participant BPs, the notion of an "artifact interface" captures an artifact with "visible" data contents for choreography specification.

Definition: An *artifact (interface)* is a pair (v, Att), where v is a (distinct) name and Att a set of attribute names (or attributes) whose values may be hierarchically structured.

The attributes in an artifact interface can be accessed in choreography. Each artifact interface always contains the attribute "ID" to hold a unique identifier for each artifact "instance". The data type of an attribute can be hierarchical or another artifact interface; in the latter case, values of the attribute are identifiers of the referenced instance.

Given an artifact interface $\alpha = (v, Att)$, an *artifact instance* I of α is a partial mapping from Att to the corresponding domains such that I.ID is defined and unique.

We now define an important notion of a "correlation graph". Intuitively, such a graph specified whether instances of two BPs are correlated and whether the correlation is one instance of a BP correlating to one or many instances of the other BP. Similar to WS-CDL, only a pair of correlated instances may exchange messages in our model.

Definition: A *correlation graph* G is a tuple (V, ρ, E, C, λ), where
- V is a nonempty set of artifact interfaces closed under references (through attributes). We may call artifact interfaces in V "nodes" (of the graph),
- $\rho \in V$ is the *primary* artifact interface (the root),
- $E \subseteq V \times V$ is symmetric denoting correlations (undirected edges) among artifact interfaces such that (V, E) is connected and contains no self-loops,
- $C \subseteq E$ is asymmetric denoting creation relationships among artifact interfaces such that (i) for each $v \in V$ there exists at most one pair $(u, v) \in C$ (can only be created once), (ii) (V, C) is acyclic (no cyclic creations), (iii) there is no $v \in V$ such that $(v, \rho) \in C$ (primary instances can only be created by external messages), and
- λ is a partial mapping from $E \times V$ to $\{1, m\}$ (cardinality of correlations) such that
  - $\lambda((u, v), v') \in \{1, m\}$ iff v' is an end node of $(u, v) \in E$,
  - for each $(\rho, v) \in E$, $\lambda((\rho, v), \rho) = 1$ (single primary instance),

- for each $(u, v) \in C$, then $\lambda((u, v), u)$ is 1 (no multiple creation), and
- for each $(u, v) \in (E - C)$ where $(v, u) \notin C$, $\lambda((u, v), u) = \lambda((v, u), u)$ (consistency for undirected edges).

Intuitively, a correlation graph models correlations among artifacts and artifact instances. More precisely, if two artifact interfaces are correlated (connected by an edge), it indicates that some instances of these two artifact interfaces are correlated. The mapping λ indicates the type of cardinality of instances (1-to-1, 1-to-*many*, *m*-to-1, *m*-to-*m*). Fig. 2 shows a correlation graph for the example in Section 2 with 4 nodes and 3 edges (2 directed and 1 undirected) with cardinality constraints. The artifact interface Order is primary. The directed edges indicate creation of instances, e.g., an Order instance would create multiple Purchase instances and multiple Fulfillment instances.

If there is an edge (α_1, α_2) in a correlation graph for two artifact interfaces α_1 and α_2, correlations of their instances can be represented by a binary relation *Corr*. *Corr* may change at runtime, but it must always satisfy cardinality constraints in a correlation graph. Given an identifier (ID) y of an artifact instance of α_2, the notation $\alpha_1\langle y \rangle$ denotes the set $\{x \mid \exists y Corr(x, y)\}$ in the current "system state" (details provided in §3.2).

Example 31. Consider the example in Fig. 2, if o is the ID of a Purchase instance, the expression "Order$\langle o \rangle$" is the ID of the correlated Order instance. ∎

The relation *Corr* changes when one instance creates another (a directed edge in a correlation graph). In Fig. 2, the instance level correlations between Order and Purchase (Fulfillment) are created at runtime. If two artifacts are connected by an undirected edge, their correlated identifier pairs are assumed to exist in *Corr*. In our running example, the instance level correlation between Order and Payment may be specified by the customer using, e.g., the Order ID submitted to the bank.

In addition to correlations specified in a correlation graph, there may be correlations that are "derived" from existing correlations. For example, a Purchase instance is correlated with a Fulfillment instance if they have a common item in their correlated Order instance. Derived correlations will be defined with rules that use "path expressions" and the "intersection" predicate.

Path expressions (with the "dot" operator) are used to access hierarchical data [5]. Technically, given an artifact interface $\alpha = (v, Att)$, a path expression of α is of form "$v.A_1.A_2.\cdots.A_n$", where $A_1 \in Att$ and each A_{i+1} ($i \in [1..(n-1)]$) is an attribute nested in A_i.

Example 32. Continue with the example in Section 2, a path expression could be "Order.Cart.Inv_ID", which corresponds to the structure shown in Fig. 1. ∎

If a path expression e returns an identifier of an instance, $e.A$ will return the value of attribute A in the instance. In general a path expression may return a set of values, similar to XPATH expressions.

We use a (binary) *intersection* predicate "$\sqcap$" to check if two input sets have nonempty overlap. We also apply the predicate on individual values treating a value as a singleton set. The predicate is conveniently generalized to more than 2 inputs.

Example 33. If a Purchase instance I_P (identifier) and a Fulfillment instance I_F correlate to the same Order instance, "Order$\langle I_P \rangle \sqcap$ Order$\langle I_F \rangle$" is true. ∎

An *atomic condition* is an intersection condition applied to path expressions. Here we use interface name to denote the identifier of an arbitrary instance of the interface. A *correlation condition* is a set (conjunction) of atomic conditions.

Definition: Given a correlation graph $G = (V, \rho, E, C, \lambda)$, and two artifact interfaces $\alpha_1, \alpha_2 \in V$ where $(\alpha_1, \alpha_2) \notin E$, a *correlation rule* of α_1 and α_2 is of form "$\text{COR}(\alpha_1, \alpha_2) :$ c", where c is a correlation condition.

Given artifact interfaces α_1 and α_2, a correlation rule $\text{COR}(\alpha_1, \alpha_2) : c$, and two instance IDs I_1 of α_1 and I_2 of α_2, I_1 is *correlated* with I_2 if c is true on I_1 and I_2.

Example 34. The rule below defines correlation between `Fulfillment` and `Purchase`:

COR(Purchase, Fulfillment): (Order⟨Purchase⟩ ⊓ Order⟨Fulfillment⟩) ∧

(Purchase.item.inventory_ID ⊓ Fulfillment.item.inventory_ID)

Note that `Purchase` (`Fulfillment`) in the above represents an arbitrary instance. ∎

Once a rule $\text{COR}(\alpha_1, \alpha_2) : c$ is defined, the notation $\alpha_1 \langle \alpha_2 \rangle$ (or $\alpha_2 \langle \alpha_1 \rangle$) can be used in the same way as other correlations. Derived correlations do not have cardinality constraints specified.

A rule $\text{COR}(\alpha_1, \alpha_2) : c$ *depends on* another rule $\text{COR}(\alpha_3, \alpha_4) : c'$, if the condition c contains $\alpha_3 \langle \alpha_4 \rangle$ or $\alpha_4 \langle \alpha_3 \rangle$.

We now define the messages among the artifacts, using "ext" to denote the external environment (as the sender or receiver).

Definition: Given a correlation graph $G = (V, \rho, E, C, \lambda)$ and a correlation rule set Γ, a *message type m* wrt G, Γ is a tuple $(M, \nu_s, \nu_r, \pi, \phi)$, where
- M is a name;
- ν_s and ν_r are distinct artifact interfaces denoting the sender and receiver (resp.) such that at most one of them can be "ext", and if both are in V, they must be correlated (via an edge in G or by a correlation rule in Γ);
- π is a set of attributes (holding a payload);
- ϕ is "+" (the sending instance creates an instance of the receiving artifact upon arrival of each message instance) or "−" (no creation).

Fig. 3 shows a message diagram, each edge represents a message type with the edge direction indicates the message flow.

Example 35. Continue with the example in Section 2, "CP(Order, +Purchase) [*OrderID, Amount,...*]" defines a message type from `Order` to `Purchase`. (We use a slightly modified syntax for readability.) The "+" symbol indicates that a new receiving instance will be created by each arriving message. The attributes inside "[...]" denote message contents. "PR(ext, +Payment) [*OrderID, Amount...*]" is a message type whose messages are from the external environment. ∎

A *message instance* of a message type $(M, \nu_s, \nu_r, \pi, \phi)$ is of form $M(id_m, id_s, id_r, \mu)$, where id_m is a unique message ID, μ is a mapping from π to the corresponding domains, and id_s and id_r are the IDs of instances of α_s and α_r (resp.) such that if ν_s (ν_r) is "ext" id_s (resp. id_r) is also "ext".

Definition: A *collaboration schema* is a tuple (G, Γ, Msg), where G is a correlation graph; Γ is a set of correlation rule of G whose rule dependencies are acyclic, and Msg is a set of message types wrt G, Γ.

Roughly, a collaboration schema defines the correlations among artifact interfaces (participant types) and among instances (participants), and the message types.

3.2 Choreography Constraints

Roughly, a specification consists of "choreography constraints", each stating a temporal property on message occurrences and may also contain conditions on data in related artifact instances and the messages.

In the technical discussions, we make the following assumptions concerning identifiers. For each artifact interface or message type (name), there is a countably infinite set of artifact or message (resp.) instance IDs; furthermore, these ID sets are pairwise disjoint. Let $\mathbf{ID}_A$ ($\mathbf{ID}_M$) be the union of all artifact (resp., message) instance ID sets. We further assume the existence of three countably infinite sets: an irreflexive *artifact correlation* set $\mathbf{CORR} \subseteq \mathbf{ID}_A^2$, a *message-artifact dependency* set $\mathbf{MA} \subseteq \mathbf{ID}_M \times \mathbf{ID}_A$, and an irreflexive *message-message dependency* set $\mathbf{MM} \subseteq \mathbf{ID}_M^2$.

The correlation set $\mathbf{CORR}$ captures correlations among artifact instances. The message-artifact dependency set $\mathbf{MA}$ holds dependencies of an arriving message ID that causes creation of an artifact ID. The message dependency set $\mathbf{MM}$ represents the relationships between messages, e.g., one message may depend another based on contents, or simply request-response. For example, an invoice message may respond to an order request.

For executable languages, it is necessary to define how the sets $\mathbf{CORR}, \mathbf{MA}, \mathbf{MM}$ are created and maintained at runtime. However, a choreography language provides only a specification, i.e., conditions that must be satisfied by every execution. Due to this reason we do not specify how these sets are created and maintained, instead, we assume that they are predetermined and fixed. Conditions will be provided to ensure consistency of the sets and runtime correlations/dependencies among artifact/message instances.

We now define "system states" that represent snapshots at time instants. Note that we require all artifact instances in a system state must be correlated directly or indirectly. This restriction allows us to focus on a single collaboration instance.

Definition: For a collaboration schema $C = (G, \Gamma, Msg)$, a *system (s-)state* of C is a triple $(S, \overline{M}, m)$, where S is a set of artifact instances for G, $\overline{M}$ a finite set of message IDs, m a message instance of a message type M in Msg such that (1) the ID of m is in $\overline{M}$, (2) if m's sender is not "ext", the sender instance is in S, (3) if M is artifact creation, m's receiver ID is not in S and the message and receiver IDs are in $\mathbf{MA}$, (4) if M is not creation, either m's receiver is "ext" or has ID in S, (5) if neither sender or receiver is "ext", they are correlated according to $\mathbf{CORR}$, (6) for each correlation rule in Γ and each pair of artifact instance IDs in S, if the IDs satisfy the rule condition, they are correlated in $\mathbf{CORR}$, letting S' be the set of all artifact IDs in S or m, (7) the graph $(S', \mathbf{CORR})$ is connected and satisfies all cardinality conditions in G, and (8) the graphs $(\overline{M} \cup S', \mathbf{MA})$ and $(\overline{M}, \mathbf{MM})$ encode functions (each node has $\leqslant 1$ outgoing edge).

An s-state is *initial* if S is empty, $\overline{M}$ a singleton set, m is from "ext" to the primary artifact interface.

An s-state is a snapshot of artifact instances, past message IDs, the current message sent. Conditions (2)(4) demand that the sender and receiver are existing artifact instances if not external for non-creation message types. Conditions (3)(5)(6) concern correlations and dependencies. The connectivity and cardinality condition (7) requires that each pair of artifact instance IDs is correlated via one or more correlations and all cardinality constraints in the correlation graph hold. Finally condition (8) ensures that each message creates at most one artifact and/or depends on at most one message.

Let $(S, \overline{M}, m)$ be an s-state and S' all artifact IDs in S or m. If an artifact instance I in S' is correlated to instances $I_1, ..., I_n$ in S' of artifact interface α according to CORR, the notation $\alpha\langle I\rangle$ denotes the set $\{I_1, ..., I_n\}$ in the s-state. For each message ID μ in $\overline{M}$ if $(\mu, I_1) \in$ MA where I_1 is the ID of an instance of artifact interface α and in S', the notation $\alpha[\mu]$ denotes I_1 in the s-state. And if $(\mu, \mu') \in$ MM for $\mu, \mu' \in \overline{M}$ and the message type of μ is M, $M[\mu']$ has the value μ (a reply to μ') in the s-state.

For a collaboration schema $C = (G, \Gamma, Msg)$, a *system (s-)behavior* of C is a finite sequence $\sigma_1\sigma_2\cdots\sigma_n$ of s-states of C such that σ_1 is initial, messages in σ_i's have distinct IDs, and for each $i \in [1..(n-1)]$, the following conditions all hold for $\sigma_i=(S_i, \overline{M}_i, m_i)$ and $\sigma_{i+1}=(S_{i+1}, \overline{M}_{i+1}, m_{i+1})$: every artifact ID in S_i is in S_{i+1} and every artifact ID in S_{i+1} is either in S_i or the receiving ID of m_i, and $\overline{M}_{i+1} = \overline{M}_i \cup \{m_{i+1}\}$ (m_{i+1} denotes its ID).

Intuitively, an s-state advances by consuming the current message (instance) and producing the next message. If the receiving ID does not correspond to an artifact instance, a new instance is created. The changes of data contents of artifact instances are the responsibility of participant processes and thus not captured in s-state transitions. Also, message-message dependency is not required, creating such dependencies is also done by individual participant BPs.

We now focus on "choreography constraints". Roughly, we apply (non-temporal) "message formulas" to s-states which examines message type and contents as well as the contents of sending/receiving artifact instances. Each constraint then uses a temporal operator to connect two message formulas. Individual LTL operators are not expressive enough, therefore we use binary operators from DecSerFlow [22].

Let C be a collaboration schema. Each message type (name) is a ternary *message predicate*. For each s-state σ, and a message type M, $M(\mu, a, b)$ is *satisfied* in σ if μ, a, b are the IDs of the message instance, its sending and receiving artifact (resp.) in σ. Note that Skolem notations can be used to indicate dependencies. For example, $M(M[\mu], a, b)$ is true in s-state σ the response message of type M to the message μ is sent from a to b. For notational convenience, we will abbreviate "$M(M[\mu], a, b)$" as "$M[\mu](a, b)$".

Starting from artifact/message IDs, path expressions can be used to access attribute values, hierarchically organized values, and other artifacts whose IDs are stored as attribute values. Built-in relational comparisons can be used to test results of path expressions. Given an s-state, satisfaction of *data conditions* with path expressions is defined in the standard manner. If an attribute value is not defined, a guarded approach such as in [10] can be used. Data conditions are used in conjunction with message predicates.

Example 36. The formula "$CP(\mu, I_O, I_P) \wedge \mu.cart.price > 100$" checks if the message μ from Order instance I_O to Purchase instance I_P has an item with price > 100. ∎

Our logic language includes variables ranging over ID_A and ID_M and message predicates, data conditions with variables. Given a collaboration schema C, a *message formula of C* is of form $\Phi \wedge (\bigwedge_{i=1}^{n} \varphi_i)$, where Φ is a message predicate and for each φ_i is a data condition with path expressions and Skolem notions built from variables in Φ.

Let C be a collaboration schema. a *choreography constraint of* C is an expression of form $\Psi_1 \Theta \Psi_2$ where Ψ_i's are message formulas and Θ is one of the following temporal operators from DecSerFlow [22]: exist, co-exist, normal response, normal precedence, normal succession, alternative response, alternative precedence, alternative succession, immediate response, immediate precedence, and immediate succession.

Variables in a choreography constraint are universally quantified and range restricted to the types and the current s-state. We use examples to illustrate the constraints in the remainder of the section. Operators in DecSerFlow can be translated into LTL [22]. The semantics for choreography constraints are rather technical and omitted here. Roughly, choreography constraints can be expressed in first order logic with LTL.

Example 37. Consider the restriction on message sequences for the example in Section 2: For each order-request (OR), with amount greater than 10, sent to a (new) `Order` instance, there is a corresponding create-purchase (CP) message in the future sent by the order instance to all correlated `Purchase` instances, and vice versa. The choreography constraint defining the restriction is

$$\forall x \in \text{Order OR}(\mu, \text{ext}, x) \wedge \mu.\text{amount} > 10 \ (succ) \rightarrow \text{CP}[\mu](x, \text{Purchase}[\mu])$$

Here $\text{CP}[\mu]$ and $\text{Purchase}[\mu]$ denote the CP message instance and the `Purchase` artifact instance caused by μ. The operator "$p \ (succ) \rightarrow q$" is normal succession that means: each p is followed by a q (possibly not immediate) and each q is preceded by a p (possibly not immediate). ∎

Example 38. Consider the restriction that for each order, if there is an item with price is > 100, then no ready-to-ship (RS) message is sent until all purchase-complete (PC) messages have been sent. This can also be expressed using normal succession:

$$\forall x \in \text{Fulfillment} \forall y \in \text{Purchase}\langle x \rangle \text{PC}(\mu, y, x) \wedge y.\text{cart.price} > 100(succ) \rightarrow \text{RS}[\mu](\text{Order}\langle x \rangle, x)$$

Here $\text{Order}\langle x \rangle$ denotes the correlated `Order` artifact instance of x. Similarly, $\text{RS}[\mu]$ denotes an RS message depending on μ. ∎

Definition: A *choreography (specification)* is a pair (C, κ) where C is a collaboration schema and κ a set of choreography constraints over C.

"Satisfaction" of a choreography $\mathcal{S} = (C, \kappa)$ by an s-behavior of C is defined based on the above discussions. The *semantics* of of $\mathcal{S}$ is the set of all s-behaviors of C that satisfy all constraints in κ.

4   Realizability

In this section, we show that a subclass of choreographies defined in Section 3.2 can be realized. This is accomplished in two stages, we first translate a choreography into a "guarded conversation protocol" that is a conversation protocol of [1] extended with data contents and conditions. We then present a distributed algorithm that runs along with execution of each artifact, and show that an s-behavior is a possible execution with the algorithm iff it satisfies the choreography.

4.1 Guarded Conversation Protocols

A choreography $S = (C, \kappa)$ is *one-to-one* (or *1-1*) if the correlation graph in C only has 1-1 correlations. The class of 1-1 choreographies roughly corresponds to choreographies definable in most existing languages, with a possible exception of BPEL4Chor [6,12]. We focus on 1-1 choreographies in this section.

Definition: A *guarded (conversation) protocol* is a tuple (T, s, F, M, C, δ), where (i) T is a finite set of states, $s \in T$ is the initial state, $F \subseteq T$ is a set of final states; (ii) M is a finite set of messages type names, (iii) C is a set of data conditions, and (iv) $\delta \subseteq T \times M \times C \times T$ is a set of transitions.

A guarded protocol extends conversation protocol of [7] with data conditions on messages (and associated artifacts). The semantics of a guarded protocol is standard except that the data condition must be satisfied when making a transition.

Example 41. Fig. 4 shows an example guarded protocol with four states: t_2 is initial and t_2, t_4 are the final states. Two message types are involved, X and Y. C_X and C_Y are data conditions. The transition from t_2 to t_3 can be made if the condition C_X is true and message X is sent. An edge labeled with "else" stands for a collection of transitions other than the specified one(s) leaving the same state. An edge labeled with "*" represents all possible transitions leaving the state.   ∎

Given an s-behavior B (of a correlation schema), and a guarded protocol τ, the notion of τ *accepting B* is defined in the standard way.

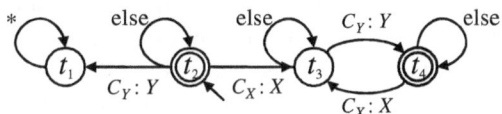

Fig. 4. A guarded conversation protocol example

Theorem 42. Let S be a 1-1 choreography. One can effectively construct a guarded conversation protocol τ such that each s-behavior B satisfies S iff it is accepted by τ.

Since temporal operators in choreography constraints are operators in DecSerFlow that is contained in LTL [22], one can use a general technique to obtain Büchi automaton [23]. Guarded protocols can then be constructed. However, we use a simpler approach: translating each choreography constraint to a guarded protocol and then construct a product state machine for all constraints. Fig. 4 shows a guarded protocol for constraint "$X \wedge C_X(succ) \rightarrow Y \wedge C_X$", where X, Y are message predicates and C_X, C_Y data conditions.

Example 43. Fig. 5(a) shows a part of the guarded protocol translated from Example 38, where c_1 is "Payment.balance > CH.amount" and c_2 is "CP.items ≠ null". Since each participant can have at most one instance (1-1 choreography) type level notation is used here. The initial state is t_1, the final states are t_4 and t_6 (in the original guarded protocol, they are not final states but we make them final to show a complete example). Only two sequences of messages can be accepted in this example: either (1) CP CH PC, or (2) CH CP. Note that this is not realizable in [7].   ∎

The only-if direction of Theorem 42 fails if 1-1 condition on choreography is removed. This is because different instances of the same interface may progress in different paces and a guarded protocol cannot capture such situations.

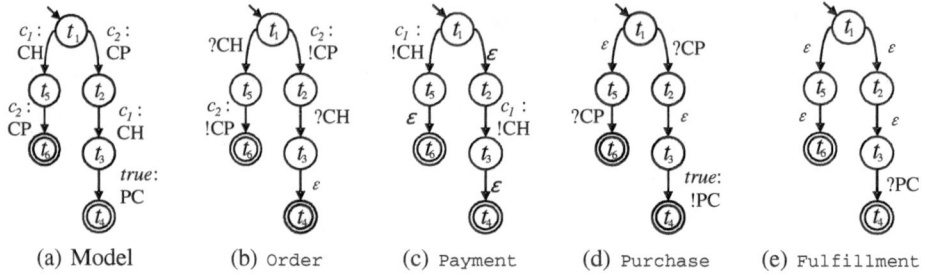

(a) Model   (b) Order   (c) Payment   (d) Purchase   (e) Fulfillment

Fig. 5. A translated guarded protocol and project to artifacts

4.2   Guarded Peers

Guarded automaton was introduced in [7] to represent a state machine for a participant. We modify the notion to allow message predicates and data conditions. The following defines a projection of a guarded protocol to a participant.

Definition: Given a guarded conversation protocol $\tau = (T, s, F, M, C, \delta)$ and an artifact type α, a *guarded peer for* α wrt τ is a tuple $(T, s, F, M', C', \delta_s, \delta_r, \delta_\varepsilon)$, where (1) $M' \subseteq M$ such that each message in M' has α as a sender or receiver, (2) $C' \in C$ contains a condition c if there exists $t, t' \in T$ and a message m in M', where m is sent by α and $(t, c, m, t') \in \delta$, (3) $\delta_s \subseteq T \times C' \times M' \times T$ (sending transitions) contains elements (t, c, m, t') if $(t, c, m, t') \in \delta$ and m is sent by α, (4) $\delta_r \subseteq T \times M' \times T$ (receiving transitions) contains elements (t, m, t') if there exists $c \in C$, $(t, c, m, t') \in \delta$ and the receiver of m is α, and (5) $\delta_\varepsilon \subseteq T \times \{\varepsilon\} \times T$ (empty transitions) contains elements (t, ε, t') if there exists $c \in C$, $m \in M$, $(t, c, m, t') \in \delta$ and α is neither the receiver or sender of m.

Example 44. Fig. 5(b)–(e) show four guarded peers (Order, Payment, Purchase, and Fulfillment) projected from Fig. 5(a). The "?" mark denotes receiving a message, the "!" mark denotes sending a message.   ∎

An artifact (instance) sends or receives messages according to its guarded peer, i.e., each guarded peer is autonomous. If all guarded peers start from their initial states, make their transitions autonomously, the composition terminates when every guarded peer reaches a final state. Our composition model is basically the same as [7], except that FIFO queues are not used.

Example 45. Consider the sequence of messages "CH CP" that is accepted by the guarded protocol in Fig. 5(a) (Example 43). The projected peers are shown in Fig. 5(b)–(e). Payment can send a CH to Order. Then Payment follows an empty transition into its final state t_6 and Payment is now in t_5. Later on, Order sends a CP to Purchase and both of them can reach their final states (t_6). While for Fulfillment, it sends or receives nothing and follows two empty transitions to t_6.   ∎

Naturally, given a guarded protocol τ, if a sequence of transitions is accepted by τ, the sequence is also accepted by all guarded peers of τ. In general, the other direction may not necessarily hold [2].

Example 46. Continue with Examples 43 and 44. Suppose Payment sends a CH through edge (t_1, t_5) and ends at final state t_6. Then Order sends a CP, receives the CH sent by Payment, and reaches final state t_4. Correspondingly, Purchase receives the CP from Order and reaches final state t_4 by sending Fulfillment a PC. Finally, Fulfillment receives the PC and ends at t_4 as well.

Clearly, the above sequence of messages "CH CP PC" allows all guarded peers to reach their final states but cannot be accepted by the original guarded protocol.   ∎

The *realizability problem* is to ensure that the collective transitions for all guarded peers are equivalent to transitions for the original guarded protocol. While this problem has not been investigated, a closely related problem of "realizability checking problem" [2] which tests if a conversation protocol can be restored from the product of its projected peers has been studied extensively (see [21]).

4.3   A Realization Mechanism

Instead of checking if a guarded protocol is the product of its guarded peers, we take a different approach. We develop a protocol (algorithm) that in addition to the original messages, it also adds a small number of "synchronization" messages to aid participants (peers) in their autonomous execution. We show that the synchronized execution generates equivalent behaviors as the original guarded protocol and that in every successful execution, the total number of synchronization messages is bounded by the sum of the number of messages in the guarded protocol and the number of guarded peers.

A naïve protocol simply broadcasts every message to all. However, this approach requires as many as $N^* \times (k-1)$ messages during the process, where N^* is the number of message instances (needed for the collaboration), and k is the number of peers.

To reduce synchronization messages, an improvement is developed that employs a "token passing" method: only the participant who owns a "token" can make a transition. Once a transition is conducted (or equivalently, a message is sent), the "token" will be passed to the next sender and this process repeats.

Given a guarded protocol $\tau = (T, s, F, M, C, \delta)$, we augment τ with a new message type named *sync* without any data attributes. We also introduce two functions, *Flag* and *State*. The function *Flag* maps message (including sync) instances to the set $\{SND, RCV, FIN\}$ such that if μ is an instance of sync, $Flag(\mu) \in \{SND, FIN\}$. Intuitively, SND is the token, RCV means the message that is regular, FIN instructs the receiver to terminate. The function *State* maps each message instance to T to indicate the current (global) state. Each message is sent along with its *Flag* and *State* values.

To implement the framework, a coordinator is used for each peer (instance) to help on transition decisions. Once a coordinator receives the token carried by a message, it makes a transition for its peer by sending a message with an appropriate *Flag*, and possibly passes the token to the next sender if different (via a flagged sync message).

As mentioned at the beginning of this section, once (the coordinator of) a sender sends a message with the flag RCV, it passes the token to (the coordinator of) the next sender through a message with the flag SND. In order to know who will be the possible sender, a concept "*sender set*" is defined first.

Given a guarded protocol $\tau = (T, s, F, M, C, \delta)$, the *sender set* of a state $t \in T$, denoted as $sdr(t)$, is a set containing all artifact interfaces α that is the sender of m where $(t, c, m, t') \in \delta$ for some $t' \in T$, $c \in C$, and $m \in M$. In Fig. 5(a), the sender sets for t_1 to t_6 are {Order, Payment}, {Payment}, {Purchase}, $\varnothing$, {Order}, and $\varnothing$, resp.

Sender sets are known at design time, the current sender can choose the next sender from the corresponding sender set of the current state at runtime. The initial sender should be delegated externally by, e.g., the environment. These steps are repeated until a peer (with the token) reaches a final state. This peer then informs all other peers to end the execution by sending messages of flag FIN. Alg. 1 accomplishes the coordinator that runs on individual peers.

Algorithm 1. Coordinator for Peer p

Input: $sdr, p = (T, s, F, M, C, \delta_s, \delta_r, \delta_\varepsilon)$

```
1:  loop
2:      Wait for the next message m
3:      if Flag(m) = SND then
4:          if ∃c ∈ C, ∃m' ∈ M, ∃t ∈ T,
                (State(m), c, m', t) ∈ δₛ then
5:              Send m' (flag: RCV, state: t);
6:              randomly select s from sdr(t);
7:              Send to s a sync message
                (flag: SND, state: t);
8:          end if
9:      else if Flag = RCV then
10:         if State(m) ∈ F then
11:             Boardcast sync message
                (flag: FIN, state: State(m))
12:             Terminate
13:         end if
14:     else
15:         Terminate {"FIN" case}
16:     end if
17: end loop
```

Example 47. The following describes a possible execution. The user chooses and sends to Order (in the sender set for t_1). Order sends a CP (flag: RCV) to Purchase and inform Payment to be the next sender (through a sync message with flag SND) since $sdr(t_2) = $ {Payment}. After Payment sends a CH to Order, it will pick Purchase from $sdr(t_3)$. Finally, Purchase sends a PC to Fulfillment. Once the Fulfillment reaches its final state t_4, FIN messages will be broadcast. ∎

Theorem 48. Given a guarded conversation protocol τ, each sequence of ground messages, is accepted by τ iff it is generated by Alg. 1 running for guarded peers of τ.

Remark 49. Denote by N^* the number of regular messages that should be sent, and $\hat{N}$ as the number of regular and synchronization messages sent according to Alg. 1. It is easy to see that $\hat{N} < 2N^* + (k - 1)$, where k is the number of peers. Furthermore, if FIN messages are not needed, the bound is reduced to $\hat{N}/N^* < 2$.

5 Related Work

The choreography approach to modeling and analysis BP or service interactions has been studied for a decade. A survey for formal models and results is provided in [21].

A WS-CDL choreography constrains message exchanges based on conditions that may involve information types, variables and tokens. Message contents need be copied to variables to be used in conditions. There is no data model for participants in a collaboration, nor direct support for multi-instances of a participant (type).

Let's Dance [24] provides a set of sequencing constraint primitives to allow a choreography to be specified in a graphical language. It lacks a clearly support for data or information models. Earlier work on conversations was reported in [9]. In the conversation model, BP systems collaborate with each other via generic asynchronous message exchanging. The information model in the conversation is limited.

BSPL [19] models messages with input and output parameters and compose the messages into protocols where constraints on message sequences are derived from the input/out parameters such that each parameter is defined exactly once in execution. A realization mechanism is reported in [20].

Recent work in [6,12] extend BPEL to support choreographies with a bottom-up approach to build a choreography from specified participant behaviors. BPEL4chor supports service interaction patterns, e.g., one-to-many send, one-from-many receive, one-to-many send/receive patterns through aggregation. Similar work on BPMN was reported in [18]. However, neither BPEL nor BPMN's extensions directly include data in their conceptual models and instance level correlation support is much weaker.

Artifact-centric choreography [14] extends existing artifact-centric BP models with agents and locations. BPs can access artifacts from their locations with the help of agents. Petri-Net is used to specify artifact internal behaviors and external interactions. The model has no artifact data attributes.

There have been work done on testing if a choreography is realizable. In [15,16], a choreography is defined wrt a set of peers forming a collaboration. The notions of completed, partial and distributed realizability of choreography were defined and studied. It was shows that partial realizability is undecidable whereas distributed and complete realizability are decidable. [2,1] focused on the realizability problem of global behavior of interaction services. Sufficient conditions are given for realizability.

6 Conclusions

This paper proposes a declarative choreography language that can express correlations and choreographies for artifact-centric BPs in both type and instance levels. It also incorporate data contents and cardinality on participant instances into choreography constraints. Furthermore, a subclass of the rule-based choreography is shown to be equivalent to a state-machine-based choreography.

References

1. Conversation protocols: a formalism for specification and verification of reactive electronic services. Theo. Comp. Sci. 328(1-2), 19–37 (2004)
2. Bultan, T., Fu, X., Hull, R., Su, J.: Conversation specification: a new approach to design and analysis of e-service composition. In: Proc. Int. Conf. on World Wide Web, WWW (2003)
3. Busi, N., Gorrieri, R., Guidi, C., Lucchi, R., Zavattaro, G.: Choreography and Orchestration Conformance for System Design. In: Ciancarini, P., Wiklicky, H. (eds.) COORDINATION 2006. LNCS, vol. 4038, pp. 63–81. Springer, Heidelberg (2006)
4. Carbone, M., Honda, K., Yoshida, N., Milner, R., Brown, G., Ross-Talbot, S.: A theoretical basis of communication-centred concurrent programming (2006)
5. Cattell, R., Barry, D.: The Object Data Standard: ODMG 3.0. Morgan Kaufmann (2000)
6. Decker, G., Kopp, O., Leymann, F., Weske, M.: BPEL4Chor: Extending BPEL for Modeling Choreographies. In: Proc. 5th Int. Conf. on Web Services, ICWS (2007)

7. Fu, X., Bultan, T., Su, J.: Analysis of interacting BPEL web services. In: Proc. Int. Conf. on World Wide Web, WWW (2004)
8. Hammer, M., Champy, J.: Reengineering the Corporation: A Menifesto for Business Revolution. Harper Business Press, New York (1993)
9. Hanson, J., Nandi, P., Kumaran, S.: Conversation support for business process integration. In: Proc. Int. Conf. on Enterprise Distributed Object Computing, EDOC (2002)
10. Hull, R., Llirbat, F., Simon, E., Su, J., Dong, G., Kumar, B., Zhou, G.: Declarative Workflows that Support Easy Modification and Dynamic Browsing. In: Proc. Int. Joint Conf. on Work Activities Coordination and Collaboration, WACC (1999)
11. Katila, R., Mang, P.Y.: Exploiting technological oppurtonities: The timing of collaborations. Research Policy 32(2), 317–332 (2003)
12. Kopp, O., Engler, L., van Lessen, T., Leymann, F., Nitzsche, J.: Interaction Choreography Models in BPEL: Choreographies on the Enterprise Service Bus. In: Fleischmann, A., Schmidt, W., Singer, R., Seese, D. (eds.) S-BPM ONE 2010. CCIS, vol. 138, pp. 36–53. Springer, Heidelberg (2011)
13. Liu, C., Li, Q., Zhao, X.: Challenges and opportunities in collaborative business process management: Overview of recent advances and introduction to the special issue. Information Systems Frontiers 11(3), 201–209 (2009)
14. Lohmann, N., Wolf, K.: Artifact-Centric Choreographies. In: Maglio, P.P., Weske, M., Yang, J., Fantinato, M. (eds.) ICSOC 2010. LNCS, vol. 6470, pp. 32–46. Springer, Heidelberg (2010)
15. Lohmann, N., Wolf, K.: Realizability Is Controllability. In: Laneve, C., Su, J. (eds.) WS-FM 2009. LNCS, vol. 6194, pp. 110–127. Springer, Heidelberg (2010)
16. Lohmann, N., Wolf, K.: Decidability Results for Choreography Realization. In: Kappel, G., Maamar, Z., Motahari-Nezhad, H.R. (eds.) ICSOC 2011. LNCS, vol. 7084, pp. 92–107. Springer, Heidelberg (2011)
17. Nigam, A., Caswell, N.S.: Business artifacts: An approach to operational specification. IBM Systems Journal 42(3), 428–445 (2003)
18. Pfitzner, K., Decker, G., Kopp, O., Leymann, F.: Web Service Choreography Configurations for BPMN. In: Di Nitto, E., Ripeanu, M. (eds.) ICSOC 2007. LNCS, vol. 4907, pp. 401–412. Springer, Heidelberg (2009)
19. Singh, M.: Information-driven interaction-oriented programming: BSPL, the blindingly simple protocol language. In: Proc. Int. Conf. on Autonomous Agents and Multiagent Systems (AAMAS), pp. 491–498 (2011)
20. Singh, M.: LoST: Local state transfer. In: Proc. Int. Conf. on Web Services, ICWS (2011)
21. Su, J., Bultan, T., Fu, X., Zhao, X.: Towards a Theory of Web Service Choreographies. In: Dumas, M., Heckel, R. (eds.) WS-FM 2007. LNCS, vol. 4937, pp. 1–16. Springer, Heidelberg (2008)
22. van der Aalst, W.M.P., Pesic, M.: DecSerFlow: Towards a Truly Declarative Service Flow Language. In: Bravetti, M., Núñez, M., Zavattaro, G. (eds.) WS-FM 2006. LNCS, vol. 4184, pp. 1–23. Springer, Heidelberg (2006)
23. Vardi, M., Wolper, P.: Reasoning About Infinite Computations. Inf. Comput. 115(1) (1994)
24. Zaha, J.M., Barros, A., Dumas, M., ter Hofstede, A.: Let's Dance: A Language for Service Behavior Modeling. In: Meersman, R., Tari, Z. (eds.) OTM 2006. LNCS, vol. 4275, pp. 145–162. Springer, Heidelberg (2006)

Managing Resource Contention in Embedded Service-Oriented Systems with Dynamic Orchestration

Peter Newman and Gerald Kotonya

Computing Department, Lancaster University
Lancaster LA1 4WA, UK
{p.newman,gerald}comp.lancs.ac.uk

Abstract. As embedded systems become increasingly complex, not only are dependability and timeliness indicators of success, but also the ability to dynamically adapt to changes in the runtime environment. Typically, they operate in resource-constrained environments and often find application in isolated locations, making them expensive to manage with small resource changes in their operating environment having a significant impact on system quality. The service-oriented model of deployment offers a possible solution to these challenges; however, resource contention between services and resource saturation can result in significant Quality of Service (QoS) degradation. This *emergent QoS* is difficult to anticipate before deployment as changes in QoS are often dynamic. This paper presents *EQoSystem*, a runtime, resource-aware framework that combines monitoring with dynamic workflow orchestration to mediate resource contention within the orchestration environment. The results from a medium-sized case study demonstrate the efficacy of *EQoSystem*.

Keywords: Emergent Service Properties, Runtime Architecture, Quality Assurance, Service-oriented Systems, Embedded.

1 Introduction

The prevalence of embedded systems has seen them deployed in a number of domains, including consumer devices, robotics, sensor networks, and communication systems [1].They are typically long lived, have stringent space, power and weight requirements, and commonly find application in difficult to access locations, resulting in most operating on resource-constrained platforms [2][3]. As such, they are expensive to manage and even small resource changes in their operating environment can have a significant impact on system quality [4]. Furthermore, as they are commonly deployed in safety and mission critical domains, it is essential that modifications are performed without stopping the system.

The Service-oriented Architecture (SOA) paradigm offers a potential solution to these challenges as it allows software systems to be dynamically composed and reconfigured using services discoverable on a network [5]. However, resource contention between services and resource saturation in the orchestration platform can result in significant performance degradation and service outages.

C. Liu et al. (Eds.): ICSOC 2012, LNCS 7636, pp. 435–449, 2012.

As this is a dynamic problem, such contentions are difficult to anticipate before deployment, making it challenging to specify the correct system environment in advance.

A number of research initiatives are investigating effective ways to manage the quality of embedded service-oriented systems at runtime, with many proposing resource management through the use of pre-determined degraded Quality of Service (QoS) policies; they are however, generally based on static quality properties [6]. Current quality management schemes for service-oriented systems are inadequate for addressing quality challenges posed by embedded systems for the following reasons:

- *Poor support for monitoring system resources.* Current service monitoring initiatives focus largely on static service properties and lack the ability to recover from problems caused by changes in system resources [7].
- *Static service orchestration.* Existing quality assurance approaches for service-oriented systems are based on static service orchestration which does not take into account the status of the service and changes in system resources [8]. This can result in an application that is inefficient and performs poorly.
- *Poor support for mitigating resource contention.* Ensuring quality is particularly problematic for service-oriented systems that operate in resource-constrained environments [3]. Not only must a service provide an acceptable QoS, but it must also be compatible with the resource constraints of the service consumer.

Building upon our previous work [9], we propose a runtime resource-aware framework that combines resource monitoring with dynamic workflow orchestration to mediate resource contention between services deployed within the orchestration environment. Our primary aim is to improve system performance through efficient resource utilisation, and to lower power consumption as a side-effect of this. We use a medium-sized case study deployed on an embedded system to demonstrate the efficacy of our framework.

2   Related Work

Current initiatives explore a number of resource monitoring and quality management strategies within the service-oriented and embedded domains. Our discussion is representative rather than exhaustive.

Robinson and Kotonya review a number of quality management initiatives for service-oriented systems and propose a self-managing architecture that combines service monitoring, negotiation, and vendor reputation as a way to manage runtime quality [8]. The quality management framework supports different SOAs such as Apache River[1] and web services. However, it is not concerned with resource contentions in the orchestration environment, and is aimed at desktop computers rather than embedded systems.

---

[1] Previously known as Jini (http://river.apache.org/)

Moser *et al.* focus on the monitoring and runtime configuration of services [10]. The authors describe a system named *VieDAME* that allows BPEL processing to be monitored according to a specified QoS profile. It also allows existing services to be replaced with semantically similar services using a specified replacement policy. However, as VieDAME is designed to support web services and web service protocols, it is inappropriate for SOAs designed to support resource-constrained systems.

Wolff *et al.* propose μSOA, a connector concept designed to handle heterogeneous communication channels while reducing the processing demands for parsing XML messages [11]. This approach reduces the message size and parsing overhead of intercepted SOAP messages bound to the embedded system and translating them into μSOA messages. Although it presents a way to reduce the overhead of SOAP messages within the embedded domain, it does not address the contention of resources between services encountered during runtime.

Workflow orchestration is a central concept to service orientation, and in resource constrained systems, this scheduling of tasks takes on added importance. Reichert and Dadam propose a framework called ADEPT for the support of *ad hoc* structural changes to workflows [12]. Central to their framework is a formal graph-based model which supports a number of flow elements and control structures including: branch statements, task elements, and loop structures. Various operations to this model are achievable through the framework, including the addition and removal of tasks within the workflow. However, these operations are not automated and must be manually applied.

Sharma *et al.* discuss the implementation of *Smartware*, a differentiated QoS framework [13] capable of both static and dynamic prioritisation of service requests. In their approach, web service requests are queued by the framework based on their priority and the current scheduling policy. The scheduling policies are based on a number of classes which determine request priority; these classes include *Application, Device,* and *Client* Level priority. Each request is scored against a combination of the priority class values to calculate the overall priority level of the request. Although the work presented is limited to web services, potentially the approach could be applied to other SOA protocols.

3   Framework - EQoSystem

EQoSystem (Emergent QoS System) is comprised of two components; a client that is deployed on the embedded platform and a service that is deployed on a remote server. The client is responsible for monitoring resources and effecting changes to the orchestration of services while the service is responsible for selecting and executing resource management policies based on periodic readings from the client. *EQoSystem* is implemented in Java and uses Apache River for the discovery and acquisition of services, although its architecture is not tied to a particular SOA implementation. Services obtained using Apache River can be acquired either as a proxy of the service object or the service object itself, which provides greater flexibility in service implementation as it allows services to maintain state locally.

Dynamic workflow orchestration is achieved through a selection of pluggable, runtime resource management policies, which determine if (and what) changes need to be made to the orchestration. These resource management policies are selected by comparing current resource usage patterns against pre-defined resource usage signatures (i.e. *Activation Patterns*) at runtime. Figure 1 shows a high-level architectural view of our framework and how it fits within the *publish-find-bind* model [14].

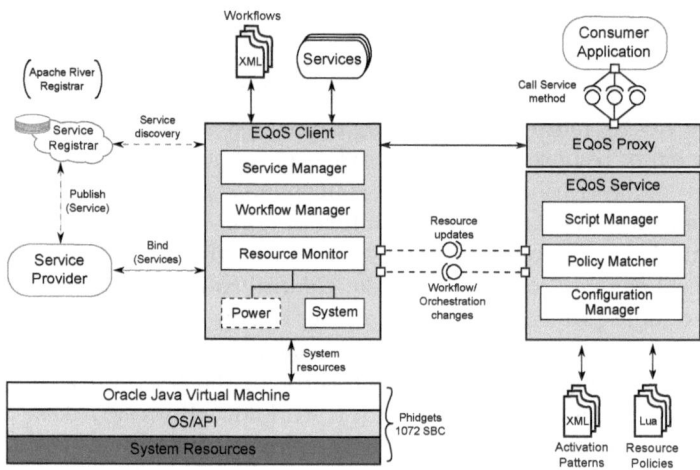

Fig. 1. Framework software architecture

EQoSystem is composed of a number of software components which are described below.

- The *Configuration manager* is responsible for the configuration of both the *EQoS client* and *EQoS service* and specifies configuration information such as the level of resources required for policy matching to start.
- The *Resource monitor* monitors the resources of the embedded platform and uses the builder pattern to insulate it against platform-specific resource access APIs.
- The *Script manager* performs the execution of resource policy scripts.Any workflow and service changes made by the scripts are conferred to both the *EQoS client* and *EQoS service* so that future changes can be made based on the current status of the *Consumer application.*
- The *Policy Matcher* matches resource usage levels against *activation patterns* specified in the framework configuration file. The decision is based on a minimum match percentage and a number of pattern annotations (including the *consequence* of invoking the policy). Once matched, the *Script manager* invokes the associated resource policy script.

– The *Service manager* is an extensible component which is responsible for the acquisition, invocation and orchestration of services. Services are acquired when the *Consumer application* attempts to bind to a service via the *EQoSystem* framework and are maintained and invoked on behalf of the *Consumer application*. Should a resource management policy require changes to be made to the orchestration of services, these are also effected by the *Service manager*.
– The *Workflow manager* maintains a list of all sequences available for execution within the framework and is responsible for the alteration and removal of these sequences at runtime. Workflow changes will only affect the sequences that require changes and will be executed only when a sequence is inactive.
– The EQoS proxy is a lightweight object proxy and is responsible for providing an interface to services bound by the *Consumer application*, with service calls being intercepted by an associated invocation handler. The service call is then passed to the *Workflow manager*, with any matching sequence being invoked by the framework and the returned value from that sequence passed to the caller. Otherwise, the original service call is invoked normally.

4   Resource Management

A resource management policy defines a strategy for resolving or managing system resource contention. Pluggable resource management is supported, allowing for different resource management policies to be used. The framework's current resource policies have been informed by the work of Kircher and Jain, who proposed a number of resource policy patterns [15].

4.1   Resource Policies

Our approach for resource management focus on addressing resource contention through workflow management and service orchestration. The strategies currently implemented are briefly discussed below.

– *Service Unbinding* removes a service currently bound within the framework and is based on the *evictor pattern*. Over time, services may continue to be bound despite not being called by the application. Preemptively unbinding these services can reduce the memory load of the service consumer platform. Services are rebound when required by the application.
– *Service call Removal* removes a task from the workflow. This strategy relies on the scenario where performing the task is less important than the uninterupted operation of the application. The removal of a task requires the ability to reflect on the requirements of the application [16].
– *Service call Replacement* swaps a task within a workflow for another predetermined one. In the case of selecting a task with lesser computational complexity, this strategy assumes that in some circumstances, the requirement to perform the task is weaker when compared with maintaining the operation of the application. Swapping a computationally expensive task for

one that consumes less CPU time might still satisfy the initial requirements albeit at a lower QoS [16].

These resource policy strategies have been implemented in the Lua[2] scripting language, allowing them to be pluggable at runtime. Lua was chosen primarily for its relatively fast execution time.

4.2 Policy Activation and Invocation

Each resource management policy has a trigger defined by a pattern of resource usage (i.e. activation pattern) that the platform must exhibit before the resource policy script is executed. When any of the trigger values are reached, the policy matcher determines the resource management policy that best fits the resource usage pattern. Listing 1.1 shows a simple example of an activation pattern.

Listing 1.1. Resource policy activation pattern.

```
 1 <xsi:preference_set>
 2     <xsi:preference_set_name>
 3         cpu-load_management.lua
 4     </xsi:preference_set_name>
 5     <xsi:preference>
 6         <xsi:type>pattern</xsi:type>
 7         <xsi:name>cpu_load</xsi:name>
 8         <xsi:value>upper:80</xsi:value>
 9     </xsi:preference>
10     <xsi:preference>
11         <xsi:type>annotation</xsi:type>
12         <xsi:name>consequence</xsi:name>
13         <xsi:value>qos_downgrade:cpu_load_decrease</xsi:value>
14     </xsi:preference>
15 </xsi:preference_set>
```

The execution of resource management policies can often result in resource trade-offs. For example, unbinding a service that caches data will release physical memory, however CPU load and network bandwidth are likely to increase in order to re-acquire the previously cached data. To allow for automated distinction between similar resource management policies, policy descriptions include system quality and resource trade-off information.

5 Workflow Management

As defined by Sommerville, a workflow shows the sequence of tasks in a process along with their inputs, outputs and dependencies [14]. The *EQoS client* parses and modifies workflows as a method of resource management. Before any changes are made, they are validated to ensure that the return type of a branch is correct and that data and flow dependencies are not violated. A simple XML-based workflow language has been developed to aid in the evaluation of the framework. The workflow document is parsed by the *EQoS Service*, with workflow elements being created and transmitted to the *EQoS Client* for processing.

---

[2] Lua scripting language homepage http://www.lua.org/

5.1   Workflow Composition and Specification

The XML workflow language supports a number of flow elements and control structures including: branch statements, task elements, and loop structures, which can be annotated to provide contextual information for the resource management decisions made by the *EQoSystem* framework. Each element within a workflow has a number of associated dependencies, representing the elements to follow the execution of the current element. Once loaded, the workflow manager interprets the XML document as a control-data flow graph. Briefly, the elements supported by the *EQoSystem* framework include:

- *Sequence* elements, which specify a number of task and conditional elements sequencially.
- *Task* elements, which contain information regarding the service to be called and what parameters are required. Within the mark-up of the XML document, it is also possible to annotate a task with additional meta-data and whether the task requires semantic adaptation.
- *Variable Task* elements, which contain a primary task as well as a number of replacement *task* elements and a list of elements it depends on. It acts as a task within the workflow but allows for any of the contained tasks to replace it during workflow management.
- *Conditional* elements, which allow for different branches of a sequence to be performed based on a condition.
- *Loop* elements, which allow for sections of a sequence to be performed multiple times based on a condition.

In addition to conditional branching, *parallel branching* is also supported; this is where the workflow branches unconditionally between two or more sequences. Separate workflow agents handle sequences in parallel branches, allowing for the *tasks* to be processed concurrently.

The *EQoSystem* workflow specification also supports semantic adaptation, which may include: the conversion of parameter types, the number of parameters passed to the service call or filtering of the parameter values. Adapters are generated with the workflow and loaded into the Java classloader on system initialisation. Should the workflow indicate that semantic adaptation for a task is required, the invocation of that task is preempted by the invocation of the associated adapter. Once the adapter has been invoked and the new parameters have been returned, execution continues as normal.

6   Case Study - Asset Tracker

We have developed a case study to visualise framework processes and to evaluate system quality at runtime. The system consists of a wireless *asset tracker* deployed on a pocket-sized Single Board Computer (SBC) developed by *Phidgets*[3]. A visualisation interface is deployed on the *EQoS Service* platform to monitor system resources in realtime. Figure 2 the shows the system in operation.

---

[3] Powered by a 400MHz ARM920T processor, 64MB of RAM and a number of digital and analog IO ports. http://www.phidgets.com/

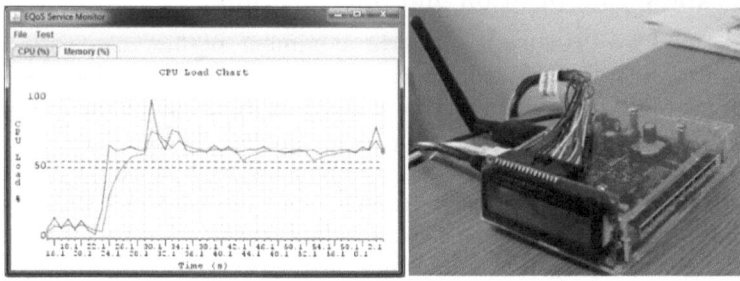

Fig. 2. Framework deployed on Phidgets 1072 SBC

The *asset tracker* is a device designed to aid the computer-system engineers in maintaining assets distributed around Lancaster University campus. Examples of assets include computers, printers, scanners, networking hardware, and other such devices. The application guides the engineers around campus, notifying them in real-time of the location of pending maintenance work and the shortest path to the asset. The device also provides a short description of the asset and the reported fault and utilises the wireless network to access this information. Because of their sensitive nature and cost, it is preferable that data regarding asset location is encrypted. The *asset tracker* is composed of eight services (which have various computational and memory requirements) that are deployed on a number of remote, virtual machines. These services are:

- *The XML parsing service*, which is used to read XML-based map data related to the environment the application is running.
- *The tree-based traversal service*, which provides search and manipulation utilities for tree-based data received from the *XML parsing service.*
- *The map generation service*, which allows for structural objects of the map-data to be added and composed into a digraph. Once generated, it is then divided into map-blocks containing a set number of connected vertices (interesections), their edges (roads, and the location of buildings distributed around campus.
- *The map caching service*, which is used for caching map-blocks recently received from the *map generation service.*
- *The navigation service*, which provides location based services, such as finding a route from the current location to a requested destination.
- *The asset database service*, which provides access to the database that stores data regarding assets such as their location and maintenance reports.
- *The asset caching service*, which is used for caching data recently received from the *asset database service.* Asset data is stored in a directory structure, allowing for both child and parent data to be annotated.
- *The encryption service*, which is used for encrypting data sent and received from the *asset database service.* The currently supported encryption algorithms are RSA, AES, and DES.

6.1 Methodology

We employed a number of resource-doping mechanisms to artificially constrain system resources to ensure that the orchestration platform operated closer to its maximum resource load. Physical memory was constrained by allocating memory to a different process operating on the device whilst CPU usage was doped by a utility we developed to maintain CPU usage at specific levels of load.

The memory usage of the services was monitored using a Java instrumentation agent called *Classmexer*[4], capable of performing deep memory inspection on objects during runtime. When system resources were polled, the memory usage of each service was measured and the aggregate was then used to calculate the overall memory-load of the platform. A number of operation scenarios were devised, representing situations that the framework might have to deal with during normal operation. These are captured in five simulation scripts designed to reflect both normal and extreme usage patterns and are briefly described below.

- *Short patrol* is a small list of 7 randomly chosen destinations located within the east-end of campus.
- *Perimeter patrol* comprises of a list of 11 destinations located around the periphery of the university campus. They are ordered by proximity.
- *Backtrack patrol* is similar to the perimeter patrol, however only contains half of the destinations and these destinations are revisited in reverse order.
- *Scatter patrol* is a list of 17 locations that work from one end of the campus to the other. They are ordered by proximity.
- *Complete patrol* visits all 51 locations around campus randomly.

Locations and assets are unevenly distributed across the university campus and as such some map blocks are likely to contain more assets and locations.

6.2 Resource Benchmarking

To best inform the activation patterns used during the case study, it was important to understand the performance of the application and its relationship with the underlying system resources [17]. As such, we performed resource benchmarking experiments on the *Phidget SBC* to determine the effect constrained resources can have on the execution of tasks.

Figure 3 shows the response-time delay of the CPU when performing the benchmark test at certain CPU loads. The level of each CPU load interval is averaged over 20 samples. As shown on the chart, the critical threshold is roughly at 90% of CPU load; this is where the delay from process context switching starts to have serious implications for performance. The performance impact of physical memory contention can vary depending on the configuration of the platform. If swap space has been allocated, there is likely to be a significant response-time delay when memory usage approaches 100% as processes are moved from physical

---

[4] Java instrumentation agent homepage `http://www.javamex.com/classmexer`

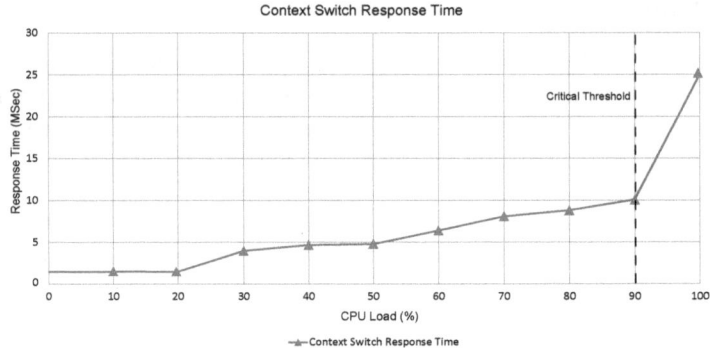

Fig. 3. Mean response time vs. CPU load

memory to swap space and *vice versa*. Because our platform does not have swap partition, reaching 100% of physical memory load is likely to cause unexpected behaviour, such as the application to ceasing to function (i.e. *hang*). As such, it is desirable to maintain memory load significantly below 100%.

7   Results

We evaluated our framework on the *asset tracker* using different operation scenarios, running in different resource priority configurations. Where used, the activation pattern for CPU resource management was set to activate at 85% of CPU load (i.e. slightly below the critical threshold). Similarly, memory policy management was set to activate at 85% of physical memory load to ensure physical memory usage never reaches 100% load.

7.1   Normal Operational Scenarios

Table 1 shows the average and peak CPU load, and execution time (i.e. performance) for the normal operation scenarios.

The results show a marked decrease in overall CPU load when the application is running in the *CPU management* configuration as compared with the *No management* configuration. The graph in Figure 4 shows a sample of the CPU usage exhibited by the *Asset Tracker* during the operation of the *Complete Patrol* simulation with different policy management configurations. As expected, the *Mixed Management* and *CPU Management* configurations demonstrate the best load reduction and performance. When CPU load surpasses the specified resource threshold (85%) after roughly 18 seconds, both configurations demonstrate a significant drop in CPU load thereafter. This decrease can be attributed to cryptography-based tasks being swapped for less computationally intensive cryptographic methods.

Table 1. CPU load of normal operation scenarios (%)

Configuration	Policy Type		Scenario	CPU Load (%)		Execution Time (sec)
	CPU	Mem		Average	Peak	
No management	x	x	Short	79.08	100	113
			Perimeter	65.21	100	265
			Backtrack	46.07	100	362
			Scatter	46.27	100	444
			Complete	24.73	100	1007
Memory management	x	✓	Short	78.00	94	114
			Perimeter	66.59	100	259
			Backtrack	47.39	100	349
			Scatter	58.16	100	549
			Complete	53.33	100	1446
CPU management	✓	x	Short	69.03	90	107
			Perimeter	47.28	92	210
			Backtrack	33.01	92	310
			Scatter	30.75	93	377
			Complete	16.33	100	880
Mixed management	✓	✓	Short	70.80	96	96
			Perimeter	49.03	96	227
			Backtrack	33.45	97	289
			Scatter	37.50	100	429
			Complete	24.62	100	921

Key : x Disabled ✓ Enabled

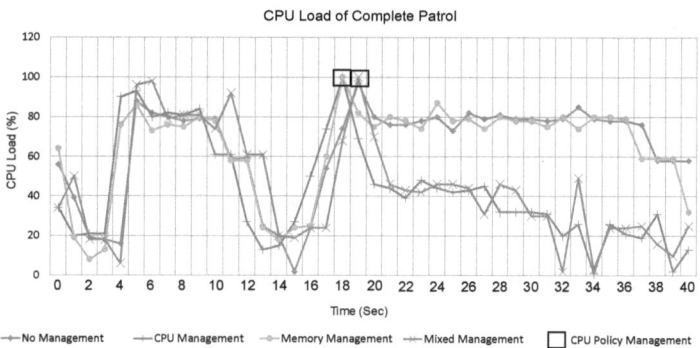

Fig. 4. CPU load of Complete patrol

Figure 5 shows the memory consumption of services for the *Asset Tracker* in the *Complete Patrol* and *Scatter Patrol* scenarios for all configurations. It is important to note that the memory usage of the overall system differed slightly between each test iteration because the resolution of the memory doping tool was only accurate to 100Kb. As illustrated, both *CPU management* and *No management* configurations show the unaltered memory consumption of the application whereas the *Memory management* and *Mixed management* configurations show a marked reduction. This reduction is attributed to the unbinding of services until they are needed.

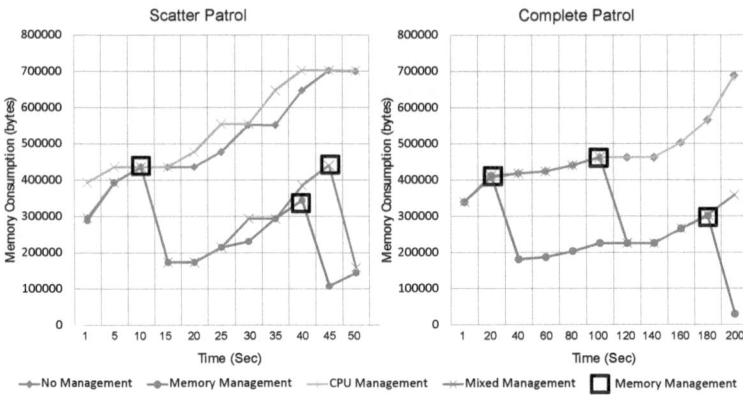

Fig. 5. Service memory consumption of simulations

When the application is running solely in the *Memory management* configuration, the average CPU load, peak CPU load and execution time are higher than that of any of the other management configurations. This is due to the nature of the services being unbound by the resource policy script. The two highest memory consuming services within the case study are caching services and as such when they are unbound and then later rebound, the consumer application needs to reacquire previously obtained map blocks.

As can be seen, a number of resource management changes are invoked to maintain physical memory below the level specified in the activation patterns. This demonstrates the framework's ability to continually make adjustments during runtime.

7.2   Power Management Scenario

The aim of this scenario was to establish whether our framework using workflow orchestration could affect the consumption of power in a deployment environment powered by battery. To this end, analog current and voltage sensors were attached to the Phidget to measure power consumption at real-time, while the *Complete patrol* was executed and repeated to put the system under continuous load. For the purpose of the test, another activation pattern was added to the framework configuration that would trigger a *power consumption* strategy when the supplied voltage was lower than 10; more specifically, the strategy would invoke workflow elements responsible for turning off the backlight of the LCD display. Early results of the power consumption experiment are illustrated in Figure 6.

The results of using the *Power consumption* configuration demonstrate that the battery life is significantly greater (roughly 30 minutes) than the scenario using the *No management* configuration.

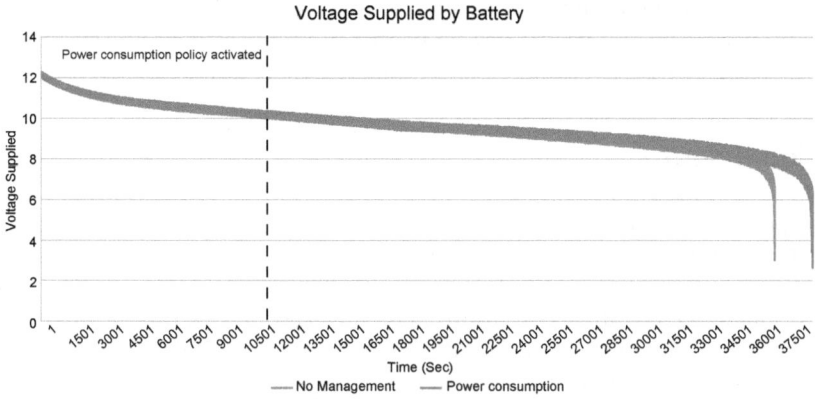

Fig. 6. Battery-life/Power consumption of Phidget

7.3 Resource Instability Scenario

The aim of this scenario was to establish whether our framework could support a platform where resource usage was highly variable with a number of resource policies conflicting to maintain a resource equilibrium. An additional activation pattern was added to the framework configuration, which would trigger a *service call replacement* strategy once CPU load was below 30%; this level was chosen as average CPU load settles below it once a task had been replaced with a less CPU intensive one. Once invoked, this *service call replacement* strategy would attempt to upgrade the QoS of the application by replacing existing service calls for higher fidelity tasks.

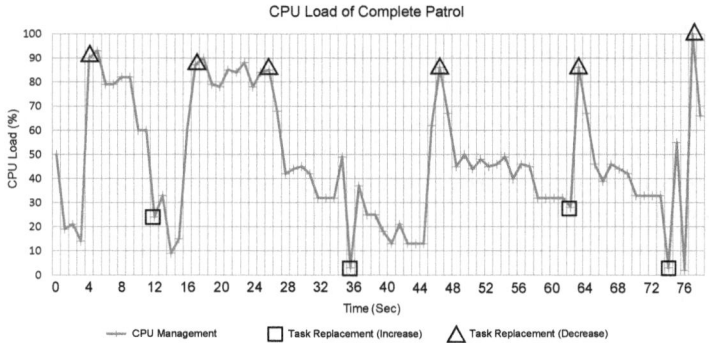

Fig. 7. Thrashing of CPU management policy

Figure 7 illustrates that the application continues to execute as multiple, repeated resource management changes occur. This shows that the number of resource management changes made does not affect the uninterrupted execution of the framework or the underlying application. However, the execution time of the complete patrol in this scenario was 24 seconds greater than the closest normal scenario, suggesting that rapid resource management impacts performance.

8   Conclusions

This paper has presented a runtime framework that combines resource monitoring with dynamic workflow orchestration to mediate resource contention through swappable resource management policies, allowing them to be matched at runtime to changing resource conditions. Outside the orchestration environment, our approach assumes the availability of a service monitoring and negotiation approach such as the work of Robinson and Kotonya [8] to ensure the provision is in accordance with the SLA. We have recently started to investigate the impact of the *EQoSystem* framework on the power consumption of the Phidgets SBC running the Asset Tracker using Phidgets current and voltage sensors. Initial results show a significant drop in the rate of power consumption for the SBC when the system is configured for *Power consumption* management.

Our solution has gone a considerable way towards addressing the three key limitations identified in Section 1. By providing support to monitor dynamic service properties (i.e. systems resources) and adapting to them at runtime, we address the *poor support for monitoring system resources*. Through our resource strategies, we are able to achieve service management and workflow orchestration based on resource utilisation at runtime, thus achieving dynamic service orchestration rather than *static service orchestration*. Finally, we provide a viable option to mitigate resource contention by managing services bound to the orchestration environment, addressing the *poor support for mitigating resource contention* limitation.

Although the framework addresses a number of resource management challenges in embedded service-oriented systems, several improvements are required if it is to be deployed in large-scale systems. As such, we are exploring ways to improve the performance of our framework to better suit a wider class of embedded system. Finally, it was found that multiple resource management policies can intersect, compete, and conflict with each other, necessitating more intelligent ways of combining resource management with context-awareness to provide better trade-off analysis and decision support.

References

1. Rellermeyer, J.S., Alonso, G.: Concierge: A Service Platform for Resource-constrained Devices. SIGOPS Oper. Syst. Rev. (3), 245–258 (2007)
2. Crnkovic, I.: Component-based Software Engineering for Embedded Systems. In: Proceedings of the 27th International Conference on Software Engineering, ICSE 2005, pp. 712–713 (May 2005)
3. Milanovic, N., Richling, J., Malek, M.: Lightweight Services for Embedded Systems. In: WSTFEUS 2004, pp. 40–44 (2004)

4. Seceleanu, C., Vulgarakis, A., Pettersson, P.: REMES: A Resource Model for Embedded Systems. In: 2009 14th IEEE International Conference on Engineering of Complex Computer Systems, pp. 84–94 (June 2009)

5. Chen, Y., Bai, X.: On Robotics Applications in Service-Oriented Architecture. In: 28th International Conference on Distributed Computing Systems Workshops, ICDCS 2008, pp. 551–556 (June 2008)

6. Menascé, D.A., Ruan, H., Gomaa, H.: QoS Management in Service-oriented Architectures. Perform. Eval. 64(7-8), 646–663 (2007)

7. Gross, H.-G., Mayer, N., Riano, J.P.: Assessing Real-Time Component Contracts Through Built-in Evolutionary Testing. In: Atkinson, C., Bunse, C., Gross, H.-G., Peper, C. (eds.) Component-Based Software Development. LNCS, vol. 3778, pp. 107–122. Springer, Heidelberg (2005)

8. Robinson, D., Kotonya, G.: A Runtime Quality Architecture for Service-Oriented Systems. In: Bouguettaya, A., Krueger, I., Margaria, T. (eds.) ICSOC 2008. LNCS, vol. 5364, pp. 468–482. Springer, Heidelberg (2008)

9. Newman, P., Kotonya, G.: A Runtime Resource-Management Framework for Embedded Service-Oriented Systems. In: Proceedings of the 2011 Ninth Working IEEE/IFIP Conference on Software Architecture, WICSA 2011, pp. 123–126. IEEE Computer Society, Washington, DC (2011)

10. Moser, O., Rosenberg, F., Dustdar, S.: Non-intrusive Monitoring and Service Adaptation for WS-BPEL. In: Proceedings of the 17th International Conference on World Wide Web, WWW 2008, pp. 815–824. ACM, New York (2008)

11. Wolff, A., Michaelis, S., Schmutzler, J., Wietfeld, C.: Network-centric Middleware for Service Oriented Architectures across Heterogeneous Embedded Systems. In: EDOC Conference Workshop, EDOC 2007, pp. 105–108 (2007)

12. Reichert, M., Dadam, P.: A Framework for Dynamic Changes in Workflow Management Systems. In: Proceedings, 8th Int'l Conference on Database and Expert Systems Applications (DEXA 1997), pp. 42–48. IEEE Computer Society Press (1997)

13. Sharma, A., Adarkar, H., Sengupta, S.: Managing QoS Through Prioritization in Web Services. In: Proceedings of the Fourth International Conference on Web Information Systems Engineering Workshops, pp. 140–148 (2003)

14. Sommerville, I.: Software Engineering, 9th edn. International computer science series. Addison-Wesley, Harlow (2010)

15. Kircher, M., Jain, P.: Pattern-Oriented Software Architecture. Patterns for Resource Management, vol. 3. Wiley (June 2004)

16. Bencomo, N., Whittle, J., Sawyer, P., Finkelstein, A., Letier, E.: Requirements Reflection: Requirements as Runtime Entities. In: Proceedings of the 32nd ACM/IEEE International Conference on Software Engineering, ICSE 2010, vol. 2, pp. 199–202. ACM, New York (2010)

17. Heo, J., Zhu, X., Padala, P., Wang, Z.: Memory Overbooking and Dynamic Control of Xen Virtual Machines in Consolidated Environments. In: Integrated Network Management, IM 2009, pp. 630–637 (June 2009)

Semantic Service Composition Framework for Multidomain Ubiquitous Computing Applications

Mohamed Hilia, Abdelghani Chibani, Karim Djouani, and Yacine Amirat

Paris-Est Créteil University (UPEC)
Signals Images & Intelligent Systems Laboratory
mohamed.hilia@evidian.com,
{chibani,djouani,amirat}@upec.fr
http://www.lissi.fr

Abstract. In this paper we propose a semantic framework based on constructive description logic. The main innovative aspect of our work consists in the formalization of a composition in the form of e-contract semantic statements where the semantic and logic correctness/soundness are formally checked. The e-contract model is based on cooperation ontology and includes control rules. This model improves on the one hand the common understanding between heterogeneous domains, and on the other hand, it ensures an efficient control of each service from remote requester and preserves the confidentiality of the know-how and the privacy of the local domains. In the conclusion of this paper we present a health care scenario that demonstrates the feasibility of our framework and the demonstration statements of the e-contract in $\mathcal{BCDL}_0$.

Keywords: Collaborative Provisioning Process, Service Composition, Constructive Description Logics, Theorem Proving.

1 Introduction

Several frameworks and middleware have been proposed for performing service composition in pervasive computing in order to comply with the evolving needs of users and organizations, and to take into account the changes of the execution environment. Most of these approaches facilitate the composition task by offering high level abstractions by using web services and semantic web technologies. However, the composed services can involve the cooperation of services belonging to different domains. Enabling this cooperation poses several heterogeneity issues that concerns the semantics of the operations and their control policies.

Leveraging such issues requires semantic framework that provides composition tools along the formal verification of the semantic soundness and the correctness of the composed service regarding what is requested [16].

During the recent years, several approaches were proposed in the state of the art to provide semantic management tools for using description logics and semantic web ontologies such as WSDL-S, DAML-S, WSMO, SWSL, SAWSDL

C. Liu et al. (Eds.): ICSOC 2012, LNCS 7636, pp. 450–467, 2012.

[19]. The most adopted language for building semantic description of web services is OWL-S [10], the successor of DAML-S. In fact, OWL-S is a high-level ontology that allows the description of semantic web services behavior characteristics using business processes and workflow, and the grounding using web service technical specification language such as WSDL. Services described using OWL-S ontology can be even simple or complex service that corresponds to the composition of a set of simple services. The semantic description of services using OWL-S can be published in a declaratory way, on top of standard directory such as UDDI, to facilitate their discovery by software agents running Description Logics based ontology matchmaker algorithms. Describing complex services capabilities and effects using ontologies and composition languages (e.g. BPEL, OWL-S) to build any cooperative provisioning systems implies the existence of a common understanding on the semantics of provisioning services capabilities of each domain, their associated messaging dialogs and their usage control policies. Description Logics is considered as a powerful tool offering a high expressiveness to formalize semantics, and is associated with decidable inference procedures for reasoning on them.

Beyond representation and expressiveness concerns using DL to describe the composition of multi domain heterogeneous services, an important issue that should be treated is how we can prove the correctness of the resulting composition according to the model theory and the objective of the cooperation. Bozzato et al. proposed a formal framework of service composition calculus that assures that any composite service specification (i.e. the service profile) can be verified according to its semantic and logic correctness/soundness by verifying the applicability conditions of the flow control rules used in the composition using the basic constructive description logic, called $\mathcal{BCDL}_0$ [4]. In this paper, we present a formal framework that deals with main issues of services composition formalization for multi domain environments. Concretely our framework reuses $\mathcal{BCDL}_0$ logics and extends the work initiated in [8] with additional control flows and methodology for service composition. The main innovative aspect in our work consists in the formalization of a composition according to formal cooperation e-contract statements that can be proved. The e-contract is specified using the instantiation and extension of the cooperation ontology. The latter describes the cooperation of both business and provisioning operations of the services of each domain and their corresponding control rules. The combination of the cooperation ontology with e-contract statements improves on one hand the common understanding between heterogeneous domains. On the other hand it insures an efficient control of services execution by remote requester and preserves the confidentiality of the know-how and the privacy of the local domains.

The rest of this paper is organized as follows. Section 2 describes the semantic framework architecture. Section 3 overviews the constructive logic $\mathcal{BCDL}$ and its subsystem $\mathcal{BCDL}_0$. Section 4 details the $\mathcal{BCDL}_0$-based multi-domain cooperation ontology specification. Section 5 presents the proposed integrated model. A use case of the proposed model is studied in section 6 and section 7 presents the related work. Section 8 gives the conclusion and the ongoing work.

2   Semantic Cooperation Framework

2.1   Framework Overview

Our framework is built using the following specification components : e-contract, cooperation ontology and the abstraction views (see Figure.1). The abstraction views provide high-level definition of the interfaces required to invoke local services of each domain involved in the cooperation. Each view is defined according to the following formula : $SV(Si) :: Pcond(I) \implies Post(O)$, where SV is the service view label, Si service interface, $Pcond$ are the preconditions over the input parameters I, and $Post$ are the postcondition over the output parameters O. Note that the effects are defined with postconditions. Our approach is not intrusive and does not imply the modification of local services. So local services can be invoked in the same manner and under the same constraints by local or remote applications. Each interface is formalized as set of preconditions and their corresponding effects. For each service we consider two views: view on the provisioning operations and a view on the business operations. The provisioning operations concerns the configuration of any nonfunctional parameters needed for the execution of the business service. For instance, the provisioning of QoS parameters that should be done before, during and after the use of a business service such as a camera based monitoring service that requires the provisioning of the following QoS parameters: codec, data transfer rate and security credentials. Many efforts have been undertaken to define ontologies of quality of service concepts. In our work we define upper concepts that can be mapped into these ontologies.

The e-contract defines the workflow for orchestrating the invocation of services and the rules for controlling their invocation. We consider two types of rules: flow control rules and usage control rules (including QoS conrtol). Each service invocation is formalized as a message exchanged between two domains. This message is represented in $\mathcal{BCDL}$ according to the following semantic quadruple (Speech act, service view, source domain, destination domain). The content of each message is specified according to the concepts of the cooperation ontology. The latter is composed of three blocks. The first block provides an upper ontology that describes the concepts used to describe the workflow messages templates, and imports the external QoS ontologies to deal with QoS consideration [21]. For instance, an action execution message is different from notification message. The second block provides common sense ontology the application domain concepts that are used within speech acts, and describes the concepts used to define control rules. The third block describes the concepts used to define global QoS and usage rules regarding the execution of the multi domain composition such as execution time, cost, energy, etc. The cooperation ontology and e-contract formalization are respectively detailed in sections 4, and 5.

Until today, two main approaches have been adopted to build cross-organizational (i.e. multi domain) cooperative systems, namely : bottom-up and top-down approaches. In the bottom-up approach [9,20] we start by enumerating the existing services as a starting point to define the cooperation possibilities in order to get at the final stage a composite service (i.e. collaborative workflow) that satisfies a set of mutual agreement rules. Conversely, the top-down approaches [6,1] start by specifying a set of common objectives that correspond to a global workflow. According to these objectives, each partner implements local processes that represent a part of the global workflow. Unfortunately, these approaches do not deal with cooperation and control of provisioning management processes. On the one hand, the bottom-up approaches listed above offer no control for the interactions model, and the specification lacks of semantic aspects to ensure the workflows interoperability, and on the other hand, top-down approaches respect neither, the existing workflow nor the design flexibility of the control and the cooperation.

In our framework we propose a hybrid approach that allows domain managers to define the composition according to the steps methodology, depicted in (Figure 1).

1. *Abstraction*: Each domain manager defines local abstract views on the services that are used to build the multi domain composite service. Concretely, this leads to create view on local workflow. The abstraction of the inputs and outputs of this workflow view corresponds to the definition of an atomic service profile. The view is described using interfaces and execution point that allow to invoke a specific process in an internal workflow. The advantage of using abstract views is preserving the confidentiality.

2. *Consistency Checking*: In this step, the managers check the consistency of the cooperation ontology after the refinement of the upper ontology concepts with the specific concepts needed for the cooperation. This is performed by using an automatic consistency checker of ontology such as Pellet.

3. *E-Contract*: The domain managers of the participating domains define the cooperation process which defines the cooperation goals. Afterward, they define the atomic processes involved, and they define the flow control between them. The cooperation process is defined by using abstraction views formalized in Section 5.1. Based on the cooperation process definition with semantic concept, the managers set the list of the obligations, authorizations, and prohibitions, and also temporal constraints.ie deadlines. The cooperation ontology model is detailed in Section 4

4. *Formal Verification*: After the definition of the flow control, and usage control rules in $\mathcal{BCDL}_0$ formalism, we use an interactive theorem prover to prove the soundness of the composite service.

5. *Views Creation*: We generate services invocation interfaces. These interfaces represent atomic provisional tasks that should be handled by the participating domains. A provisional task is any process that can change the environment or effect the running way of business services, such as request for an account creation, task approval, permission assignment, role delegation, notification, etc. The behavioral flow control of the cooperation is also managed through interfaces that must be implemented or mapped with internal process interfaces.

6. *Mapping*: This step consists of creating the mapping between tasks of internal processes view and those generated in the previous step. In this step, we must check the compliancy of the internal security policy with the cooperation defined rules. This step make reuse of the existing processes.

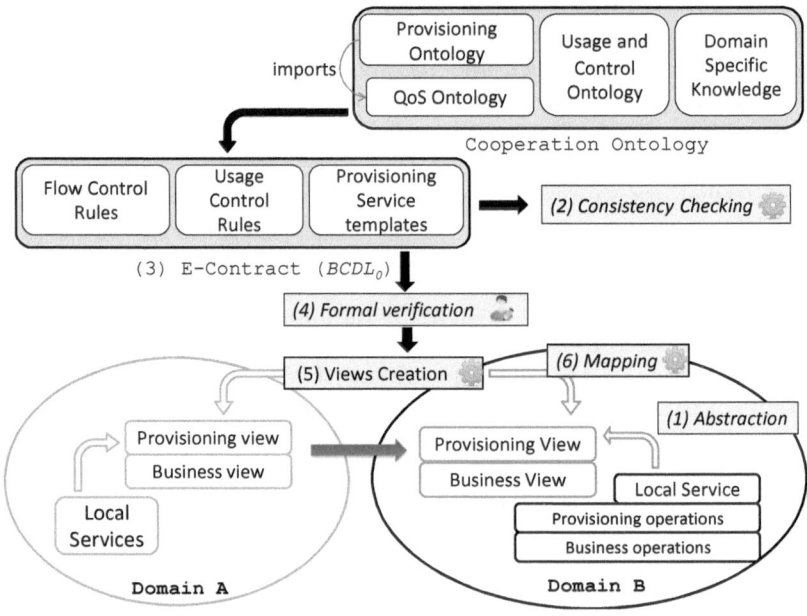

Fig. 1. Global architecture schema of the semantic composition framework

3   Basic Constructive Description Logic ($\mathcal{BCDL}$)

3.1   Towards Constructive Description Logics

Building successfully a cooperative provisioning framework requires the representation of the shared resources (i.e. services, exchanged data) by ensuring the common interpretation and semantic interoperability between the participating domains. Description logics [2] are a family of knowledge representation languages which can be used to represent knowledge of an application domain in a structured and formal way. However, their semantics are restricted to classical reading of description for concepts and individuals [3]. Furthermore, Constructive Description Logics (CDL) has emerged to give new interpretations of DL formulas. CDL aim at modeling knowledge domain and problems that can hardly be treated in the context of classical semantics. This is deeply discussed in [18]. Recently, Ferrari et al. in [5] have proposed $\mathcal{BCDL}$, a constructive description logic based on information terms semantics. This logic allows a constructive interpretation of $\mathcal{ALC}$ formulas. A constructive analysis allows us to exploit the computational properties of its formulas and proofs. $\mathcal{BCDL}_0$ is a subsystem of $\mathcal{BCDL}$ [4].

The constructive interpretation of $\mathcal{BCDL}_0$ is based on the notion of *information term* [5]. Intuitively, an information term α for a closed formula K is a structured object that provides a justification for the validity of K in a classical model.

3.2 $\mathcal{BCDL}_0$: Syntax and Semantics

Let define the language $\mathcal{L}$ for $\mathcal{ALC}$ based on the following sets : NC a set of *Concepts names*, NR set of *Roles names*, NI a set of *Individual names*, and Var a set of *Individual Variables names*. $\mathcal{BCDL}_0$ grammar is defined as follows : $C, D := A \mid\neg C \mid C \sqcup D \mid C \sqcap D \mid \exists R. C \mid \forall R. C$. Where C, $D \in$ NC, $R \in$ NR, and A an atomic concept. The $\mathcal{BCDL}_0$ grammar is the same as $\mathcal{ALC}$. The generated concepts by the latter, enable the construction of the following $\mathcal{BCDL}_0$ formulas K, such that : $K := \perp \mid t \ : \ C \mid A \sqsubseteq C \mid \ (s, \ t) : R$, where s,t $\in$ NI $\cup$ Var.

Let $\mathcal{N} \subseteq NI, \mathcal{L}_N$ be the list of formulas generated by the finit subset $\mathcal{N}$. An *Interpretation (Model)* $\mathcal{M}$ for $\mathcal{L}_N$ is the pair $(\mathcal{D}^{\mathcal{M}}, \ .^{\mathcal{M}})$. $\mathcal{D}^{\mathcal{M}}$ defines the domain, corresponding to an not empty set, and $.^{\mathcal{M}}$ is a valuation function such that : for every $c \in \mathcal{N}$, $c^{\mathcal{M}} \in \mathcal{D}^{\mathcal{M}}$, for every $A \in$ NC, $A^{\mathcal{M}} \subseteq \mathcal{D}^{\mathcal{M}}$, and for every $R \in$ NR, $R^{\mathcal{M}} \subseteq \mathcal{D}^{\mathcal{M}} \times \mathcal{D}^{\mathcal{M}}$.

3.3 $\mathcal{BCDL}_0$ Computational Interpretation

The constructive interpretation of $\mathcal{BCDL}_0$ is based on *information terms*. Formally, given $\mathcal{N} \subseteq NI$ and a closed formula K of $\mathcal{L}_N$, the set of information terms $IT_\mathcal{N}(K)$ can be defined by induction on K :

$$IT_\mathcal{N}(K) \qquad = \{tt\} \text{, iff K is a } \textit{closed formula}$$
$$IT_\mathcal{N}(c : C_1 \sqcap C_2) = \{(\alpha, \beta) | \alpha \in IT_\mathcal{N}(c : C_1) \text{ and } \beta \in IT_\mathcal{N}(c : C_2)\}$$
$$IT_\mathcal{N}(c : C_1 \sqcup C_2) = \{(k, \alpha) | k \in 1, 2 \text{ and } \alpha \in IT_\mathcal{N}(c : C_k)\}$$
$$IT_\mathcal{N}(c : \exists R.C) \ = \{(d, \alpha) | d \in \mathcal{N} \text{ and } \alpha \in IT_\mathcal{N}(d : C)\}$$
$$IT_\mathcal{N}(c : \forall R.C) \ = \{\phi : \mathcal{N} \to \bigcup_{d \in \mathcal{N}} IT_\mathcal{N}(d : C) | \ \phi(d) \in IT_\mathcal{N}(d : C)\}$$
$$IT_\mathcal{N}(A \sqsubseteq C) \ = \{\phi : \mathcal{N} \to \bigcup_{d \in \mathcal{N}} IT_\mathcal{N}(d : C) | \ \phi(d) \in IT_\mathcal{N}(d : C)\}$$

$\mathcal{BCDL}$ reasoning technique is compatible with the realizability relation of K formula by a given information term. The realizability relation is defined as follows:

Realizability: Let $\mathcal{M}$ be a Model for $\mathcal{L}_N$, K a closed formula and $\eta \in IT_\mathcal{N}(K)$. The *realizability* relation is defined as $M \triangleright \langle \eta \rangle K$ by induction on the structure of K.

$\mathcal{M} \triangleright \langle tt \rangle K$ iff $\mathcal{M} \vDash K$

$\mathcal{M} \triangleright \langle (\alpha, \beta) \rangle c : C_1 \sqcap C_2$ iff $\mathcal{M} \vDash \langle \alpha \rangle c : C_1$ and $\mathcal{M} \vDash \langle \beta \rangle c : C_2$

$\mathcal{M} \triangleright \langle (k, \alpha) \rangle c : C_1 \sqcup C_2$ iff $\mathcal{M} \vDash \langle \alpha \rangle c : C_k$

$\mathcal{M} \triangleright \langle (d, \alpha) \rangle c : \exists R.C$ iff $\mathcal{M} \vDash (c : d) : R$ and $\mathcal{M} \vDash \langle \alpha \rangle d : C$

$\mathcal{M} \triangleright \langle \phi \rangle c : \forall R.C$ iff $\mathcal{M} \vDash c : \forall R.C$, and, for every $d \in \mathcal{N}, \mathcal{M} \vDash (c, d) : R$ implies $\mathcal{M} \vDash \langle \phi(d) \rangle d : C$

$\mathcal{M} \triangleright \langle \phi \rangle A \sqsubseteq C$ iff $\mathcal{M} \vDash A \sqsubseteq C$, and, for every $d \in \mathcal{N}$ if $\mathcal{M} \vDash \langle tt \rangle d : A$ then $\mathcal{M} \vDash \langle \phi(d) \rangle d : C$

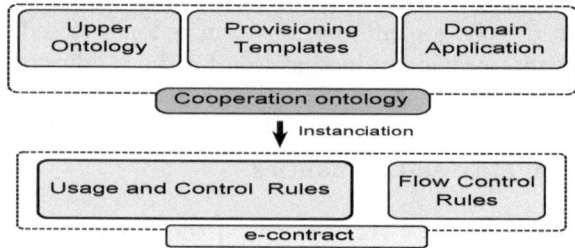

Fig. 2. Semantic model for multi-domain service composition

Definition (Theory) : A theory T consists of $TBox$ and $ABox$. A $TBox$ is a finit set of formulas of the form $A \sqsubseteq C$. An $ABox$ is a set of role assertions and concept assertions :

- *Role assertion* is a formula of the kind $(c, d){:}R$, with $c, d \in$ NI and $R \in$ NR
- *Concept assertion* is a formula of the kind $t : C$, with $t \in$ NI and $C \in$ NC

The theories defined by $\mathcal{BCDL}_0$ are sound with the respect of information term semantics. In [4], the authors have shown the natural deduction calculus $\mathcal{ND}$ as the proof calculus for $\mathcal{BCDL}_0$, and gives the soundness theorem according to realizability relation and the natural deduction proofs of $\mathcal{ALC}$ formulas.

Theorem 1 (Soundness) : Let $\mathcal{N}$ be a finit subset of NI and let $\pi :: \Gamma \vdash K$ be a proof of $\mathcal{ND}$ over $\mathcal{L}_\mathcal{N}$ such that the formulas K in Γ are closed. Then :

- $\Gamma \vDash K$
- For every model $\mathcal{M}$ and $\gamma \in IT(\Gamma)$, $\mathcal{M} \rhd \langle \phi \rangle \, \Gamma$ implies $\mathcal{M} \rhd \langle \phi_N^\pi(\gamma) \rangle \, K$

4   Cooperation Ontology Specification

In this section, we specify the main components of the multi-domain cooperation ontology (see Figure 2). This ontology is divided into three ontologies, which are respectively, provisioning ontology, usage and control ontology, and the domain specific ontology . Each ontology is specified by using constructive description logics formulas.

4.1   Provisioning Ontology Specification

This ontology described by its $TBox$ (see Table 1) expresses the provisioning part of the multi-domain cooperation ontology. The main concept in this theory, is the *ProvisioningTask*. It represents the atomic unit of work in a provisioning process. This concept is generalized by the concept $Task$ which is related to three concepts, namely, the target runtime domain, *Domain*, a *Hook* to be plugged-in into a specific abstract view interface, and a list of states represented by the concept, *TaskState*.

Table 1. Provisioning Ontology

$Add \sqsubseteq ProvisioningMessage$	$AutomaticTask \sqsubseteq ProvisioningTask$
$AutomaticTask \sqsubseteq \neg ManualTask$	$Delete \sqsubseteq ProvisioningMessage$
$Lookup \sqsubseteq ProvisioningMessage$	$ManualTask \sqsubseteq ProvisioningTask$
$ManualTask \sqsubseteq \neg AutomaticTask$	$Modify \sqsubseteq ProvisioningMessage$
$ProvisioningAction \sqsubseteq Action$	$ProvisioningTask \sqsubseteq Task$
$ProvisioningTask \sqsubseteq \exists executedBy\ Domain$	$\sqcap \exists hasHook\ Hook \sqcap \exists hasState\ TaskState$
$Search \sqsubseteq ProvisioningMessage$	$\exists assignedTo\ Thing \sqsubseteq Action$
$\exists executedBy\ Thing \sqsubseteq Task$	$\top \sqsubseteq \forall executedBy\ Domain$
$\exists hasProvisioningMessage\ Thing \sqsubseteq ProvisioningAction$	$\exists hasPerformer\ Thing \sqsubseteq ManualTask$
$\top \sqsubseteq \forall hasPerformer\ Role$	$\exists hasState\ Thing \sqsubseteq Task$
$\top \sqsubseteq \forall hasProvisioningMessage\ ProvisioningMessage$	$\exists hasHook\ Thing \sqsubseteq Task$
$\top \sqsubseteq \forall hasState\ TaskState$	$\exists hasTargetObject\ Thing \sqsubseteq ProvisioningAction$

We note that, each task is performed by a physical atomic action represented by the concept *Action*. An *Action* is the physical operation assigned to a *Task*. The *ProvisioningTask* is managed by executing the provisioning message described by the concept *ProvisioningMessage* on a specific object (e.g Service, Resource). This provisioning action can be classified as *AcceptedAction* if the domain validates the request, otherwise as *RefusedAction*. For example : adding an access account *Object* for the subject *Cardiology Doctor* on the monitoring service Policy. A provisioning task can be either automatically triggered by provisioning management system, or manually performed by a user with the requested role *Role*.

4.2 Control Access and Usage Rules Ontology Specification

Table 2 gives the control rules to access the shared resources. These rules, inspired from XACML standard, are based on deontic logic formalization of the *Prohibition*, *Obligation* and *Permission*.

The *Policy* concept has an access effect which is an authorization (*Permit* concept $\top$) or a prohibition (*Deny* concept $\bot$) . It is applicable on a Target. The policy is a set of rules *Rule* and propositional formula specified as a *Condition*. Each rule is defined by a domain on a target *Target*. A target is a set of simplified conditions for the provisioning action.

4.3 Domain Specific Ontology Specification

In this ontology, we express the domain specific concepts and their relations to model the knowledge of this domain. This ontology is used to add additional concepts to the cooperation ontology that are used for the data conversion from a domain to another during the cooperation execution. For instance, the concept *Account* as a specific *Object* in a domain. We note the following formula, *Account* $\sqsubseteq$ *Object*. This refinement permit to specify the local concepts such as security concepts without disclosing any information neither about their internal structures nor their content. In such way, we preserve the privacy and the confidentiality of the shared information which is an important issues in multi-domain applications.

Table 2. Usage and Control Rules Ontology [13]

$ABACPolicy \sqsubseteq AccessControlPolicy$	$Access \sqsubseteq Action$
$AccessControlPolicy \sqsubseteq SecurityPolicy$	$Action \sqsubseteq Event$
$Agent \sqsubseteq Resource$	$Agent \sqsubseteq \neg Object$
$Attribute \sqsubseteq Descriptor$	$Attribute \sqsubseteq \neg Time$
$Attribute \sqsubseteq \neg Location$	$Location \sqsubseteq Descriptor$
$Location \sqsubseteq \neg Time$	$Location \sqsubseteq \neg Attribute$
$Object \sqsubseteq Resource$	$Object \sqsubseteq \neg Agent$
$Parameter \sqsubseteq Attribute$	$Person \sqsubseteq Agent$
$PersonalData \sqsubseteq Object$	$Time \sqsubseteq Descriptor$
$Time \sqsubseteq \neg Location$	$Time \sqsubseteq \neg Attribute$
$\exists assignedTo\ Thing \sqsubseteq Permission$	$\top \sqsubseteq \forall assignedTo\ SecurityAttribute$
$\exists controledBy\ Thing \sqsubseteq Action$	$\top \sqsubseteq \forall controledBy\ SecurityPolicy$
$\exists hasAttribute\ Thing \sqsubseteq ABACPolicy$	$\exists grants\ Thing \sqsubseteq Permission$
$\exists hasDescriptor\ Thing \sqsubseteq Condition$	$\exists describedBy\ Thing \sqsubseteq Resource$
$\exists hasParameter\ Thing \sqsubseteq Action$	$\top \sqsubseteq \forall describedBy\ Descriptor$
$\exists hasValidity\ Thing \sqsubseteq SecurityAttribute$	$\top \sqsubseteq \forall controls\ Action$
$\exists identifies\ Thing \sqsubseteq PersonalData$	$\exists controls\ Thing \sqsubseteq SecurityPolicy$
$\exists isAssignedTo\ Thing \sqsubseteq SecurityAttribute$	$\top \sqsubseteq \forall grants\ Action$
$\exists managesBy\ Thing \sqsubseteq SecurityPolicy$	$\exists has\ Thing \sqsubseteq SecurityPolicy$
$\exists on\ Thing \sqsubseteq Access$	$\exists specifies\ Thing \sqsubseteq SecurityPolicy$
$\exists performedBy\ Thing \sqsubseteq Event$	

5   E-Contract Modeling

5.1   Service Specification

A service specification is an expression of the form $p(x) :: P \Longrightarrow Q$ where: p is a label that identifies the service; x is the input parameter of the service (to be instantiated with an individual name from $\mathcal{N}$); P and Q are concepts over $\mathcal{L}_N$. P is called the service precondition, denoted by $Pre(p)$, and Q the service postcondition, denoted by $Post(p)$. The service implementation is modeled as a function : $\Phi_p : \bigcup_{t \in \mathcal{N}} IT_{\mathcal{N}}(t : P) \rightarrow \bigcup_{t \in \mathcal{N}} IT_{\mathcal{N}}(t : Q)$. We denote by the pair $(p(x) :: P \Longrightarrow Q, \Phi_p)$ (or with (p, Φ_p)) a service definition over $\mathcal{L}_N$. The service specification provides the formal description of the behavior of the service in terms of pre- and post- conditions. The function p represents a formal description of service implementation (i.e. of the input/output function). Note that the service definition is based on multi-domain cooperation ontology.

5.2   Provisioning Service Modeling

In this section, we provide an example of atomic service specification that constitutes the atomic provisioning action.

Request : The request provisioning service is a query for action execution. It is an action with a destination domain *Domain*, and it requests for an action execution represented by *RequestAction* concept. The postconditions or effects of this action are answers from the target domain. The latter, can accept the requested action, *AcceptedAction*, or refuse it,*RefusedAction*, with the associated explanation message, *Message*. This provisioning service is formalized in Table 3.

Table 3. Request action specification

$Request(action)$ ::
$RequestAction \ \sqcap \ \exists \ hasTargetDomain.Domain \ \sqcap$ $\Longrightarrow AcceptedAction \ \sqcup \ (RefusedAction \ \sqcup \ \exists \ hasMessage.Message)$

The notion of correctness of implementation with respect to the process specification is modeled as follows :

Uniform Resolvability Let define $\mathcal{L}_{\mathcal{N}}$ as language over $\mathcal{N}$, a service definition $(p(x) \ :: \ P \Longrightarrow Q, \Phi_p)$ over $\mathcal{L}_{\mathcal{N}}$ and a model $\mathcal{M}$ for $\mathcal{L}_n$. Φ_p *uniformly solves* $p(x) :: P \Longrightarrow Q$ iff , for every individual name $t \in \mathcal{N}$, and every $\alpha \in IT_{\mathcal{N}}(t : P)$ such that $\mathcal{M} \triangleright \langle \alpha \rangle \, t : P, \ \mathcal{M} \triangleright \langle \Phi_p(\alpha) \rangle \, t : Q$

In the rest of this section, we propose a list of provisioning services for the provisioning management in multi-domain environment. As we have mentioned, each functionality is specified by using a single speech act, which represent an atomic service. In our framework we establish a list of predefined actions. As example of these actions : request for action execution, approval of requested action, delegate an action, assign an action to a domain.

Uniform Resolvability Definition. Let *action* be an individual name which represent the input of *Request* speech act. In our setting, the service implementation correspond to function mapping information terms for the precondition into information terms for the postcondition. This function formalizes the behavior of the effective implementation of the web services. In particular let us consider the implementation $\Phi_{Request}$ of the request service. Let *action* be the individual name representing an *RequestAction*. The input of request is any information term for $\alpha \in IT_{\mathcal{N}}(action : Pre(Request))$. *action* can be seen as a reference to a database record providing the information required by the service pre-condition and can be seen as a structured representation of such information. Let assume that α has the following form : $\alpha = (tt, (domainA, tt))$; this information term means that *action* is a request action with the target domain *domainA*. Now, let $\beta = \Phi_{Request}(\alpha) \in IT(action : Post(Request))$. If $\beta = (1, tt)$, this classify *action* as accepted. Otherwise β could be $(2, (tt, (refusal\_message, tt)))$ which classifies *action* as refused and specifies that there is a message *message* to comment this refusal. To conclude, we remark that the intended model $\mathcal{M}$ we use to evaluate the correctness of the system is implicitly defined by the knowledge base of the system. Indeed, *action* : Pre(Request) is valid in $\mathcal{M}$ if and only if in our system *action* effectively codify a request and *domainA* is classified as a target Domain.

In this case, since $\Phi_{Request}$ uniformly solves the service specification, we know that *action* : Post(Request) is valid in $\mathcal{M}$, this trivially corresponds to the fact that, looking at its knowledge base, the domain can generate its acceptance.

5.3   Service Composition Calculus $\mathcal{PC}$

A *service composition* is the process that combines the existing services to build a new process called the composite process. A composite service in an environment $E = \{\mathcal{L}_{\mathcal{N}}, T, \eta, (p_1, \Phi_1), ..., (p_n, \Phi_n)\}$ is defined as follows :

$$\frac{p\,(x) :: P \Longrightarrow Q}{\begin{array}{l} \Pi_1 : p_1\,(x) :: P_1 \Longrightarrow Q_1 \\ \Pi_2 : p_2\,(x) :: P_2 \Longrightarrow Q_2 \end{array}}\;rule$$

$$...$$

$$\Pi_n : p_n\,(x) :: P_n \Longrightarrow Q_n$$

Where

- $p\,(x) : P \Longrightarrow Q$ is a service specification over E
- *rule* is one of the rules of the service composition calculus $\mathcal{PC}$
- For every $i \in \{1, ..., n\}, \Pi_i : p_i(x) :: P_i \Longrightarrow Q_i$ is a service composition over E that meets the applicability conditions of rule

5.4   Control Flow Rules and Composition Process

The atomic provisioning management processes presented above can be combined to express the cooperative provisioning process by using the flow control rules expressed in constructive description logic. These rules are inspired from the basic control flow pattern [15]. They define the basic modeling patterns of business processes behavior. Furthermore, They have been widely used to evaluate the features of existing workflows systems [14].

The control flow rules are detailed below as well as the applicability conditions (*AC*). The proof of these applicability conditions implies the correctness of the composition.

Sequence: It expresses the fact that a task is performed after the completion of another one in the same process.

Parallel Split: It expresses the splitting of a task into multiple parallel tasks

Synchronization: It represents the convergence of two or more tasks into a single synchronization point. The outgoing task is enabled after the execution of all the incoming tasks.

Exclusive Choice: Based on the truth of fulfilled condition, the flow selects a single ongoing task.

Simple Merge: It consists of the convergence of two or more tasks into a single task. The outgoing tasks are performed when an incoming task is triggered.

Table 4. Flow control rules

$\dfrac{p\,(x)::P\Rightarrow Q}{\begin{array}{l}\Pi_1:p_1\,(x)::P_1\Longrightarrow Q_1\\ \Pi_2:p_2\,(x)::P_2\Longrightarrow Q_2\\ \quad\vdots\\ \Pi_n:p_n\,(x)::P_n\Longrightarrow Q_n\end{array}}$	*Sequence*	$AC=\begin{cases}T,x:P\;\vdash_{\overline{\mathcal{BCDL}_0}}\;x:P_1\\ T,x:Q_{k-1}\;\vdash_{\overline{\mathcal{BCDL}_0}}\;x:P_k,\text{for }k\in\{2,\dots,n\}\\ T,x:Q_n\;\vdash_{\overline{\mathcal{BCDL}_0}}\;x:Q\end{cases}$
$\dfrac{p\,(x)::P\Rightarrow Q}{\begin{array}{l}\Pi_1:p_1\,(x)::P_1\Longrightarrow Q_1\\ \Pi_2:p_2\,(x)::P_2\Longrightarrow Q_2\\ \quad\vdots\\ \Pi_n:p_n\,(x)::P_n\Longrightarrow Q_n\end{array}}$	*Parallel Split*	$AC=\begin{cases}T,x:P\;\vdash_{\overline{\mathcal{BCDL}_0}}\;x:P_k,\text{for }\;k\in\{1,\dots,n\}\\ T,x:Q_1\sqcap\;\dots\;\sqcap Q_n\;\vdash_{\overline{\mathcal{BCDL}_0}}\;x:Q\end{cases}$
$\begin{array}{l}p\,(x)::P\Longrightarrow Q\\[4pt] \dfrac{}{\begin{array}{l}\Pi_1:p_1\,(x)::P_1\Longrightarrow Q_1\\ \Pi_2:p_2\,(x)::P_2\Longrightarrow Q_2\\ \quad\vdots\\ \Pi_n:p_n\,(x)::P_n\Longrightarrow Q_n\end{array}}\end{array}$	*Synchronization*	$AC=\begin{cases}T,x:P_1\sqcap\;\dots\;\sqcap P_n\;\vdash_{\overline{\mathcal{BCDL}_0}}\;x:P\\ T,x:Q_k\;\vdash_{\overline{\mathcal{BCDL}_0}}\;x:Q,\;\text{for }\;k\in\{1,\dots,n\}\end{cases}$
$\begin{array}{l}p\,(x)::P\Longrightarrow Q\\[4pt] \dfrac{}{\begin{array}{l}\Pi_1:p_1\,(x)::P_1\Longrightarrow Q_1\\ \Pi_2:p_2\,(x)::P_2\Longrightarrow Q_2\\ \quad\vdots\\ \Pi_n:p_n\,(x)::P_n\Longrightarrow Q_n\end{array}}\end{array}$	*Exclusive Choice*	$AC=\begin{cases}T,x:P\;\vdash_{\overline{\mathcal{BCDL}_0}}\;x:P_1\sqcup\;\dots\;\sqcup P_n\\ T,x:Q_k\;\vdash_{\overline{\mathcal{BCDL}_0}}\;x:Q,\text{for }\;k\in\{1,\dots,n\}\end{cases}$
$\begin{array}{l}p\,(x)::P\Longrightarrow Q\\[4pt] \dfrac{}{\begin{array}{l}\Pi_1:p_1\,(x)::P_1\Longrightarrow Q_1\\ \Pi_2:p_2\,(x)::P_2\Longrightarrow Q_2\\ \quad\vdots\\ \Pi_n:p_n\,(x)::P_n\Longrightarrow Q_n\end{array}}\end{array}$	*Simple Merge*	$AC=\begin{cases}T,x:P\;\vdash_{\overline{\mathcal{BCDL}_0}}\;x:P_k,\;\text{for }k\in\{1,\dots,n\}\\ T,x:Q_1\sqcup\;\dots\;\sqcup Q_n\;\vdash_{\overline{\mathcal{BCDL}_0}}\;x:Q\end{cases}$

6   Scenario : Healthcare Monitoring

In this section, we present a scenario under implementation of platform for the tele-rehabilitation of patients at home. This complex platform is defined according to the requirements and discussions with clinical physicians at UPEC university hospital. The platform is specified as a service composition using several atomic services involving three main domains: the hospital (domainA), the patient home (Domain B) and the emergency agency (Domain C), see Figure 3. The tele-rehabilitation coaching platform allows physicians to order and monitor any rehabilitation program. The latter is composed as a plan of physical activities along with medications that should be undertaken by the patient under the control of the system and the physician. The home is equipped with set of smart devices such as mobile robot equipped with smart display, ip camera, and wearable sensors such as accelerometers and vital sensors that allows on one hand, to monitor the progress of the rehabilitation, and on the other hand, triggering alarms to prevent any damages when an incident happens. Putting such critical service partly under the control of a system requires that the rehabilitation program and its corresponding provisioning tasks requires the verification of the consistency and the correctness of the composite service. The figure 3 depicts the main services that are used to define the composite service. We denote two provisioning tasks. The first one concerns the creation of an account for a physician to monitor the rehabilitation devices and sensors at the patient's home and the second task concerns the provisioning of the rehabilitation program inside the memory of the robot, which will schedule the program according to the approval of the patient. If the patient refuses the program the coach is notified and can in this case postpone the program or communicate with patient through the robot smart display. If an incident happens during the execution of the rehabilitation program a notification is sent to the emergency agency (domain C) that will check the notification and order the intervention of an ambulance first aid officer at the patient home

Note that to allow the emergency agency checking the situation, temporal credentials are given in the notification message that allow an officer to control remotely the robot and its camera.

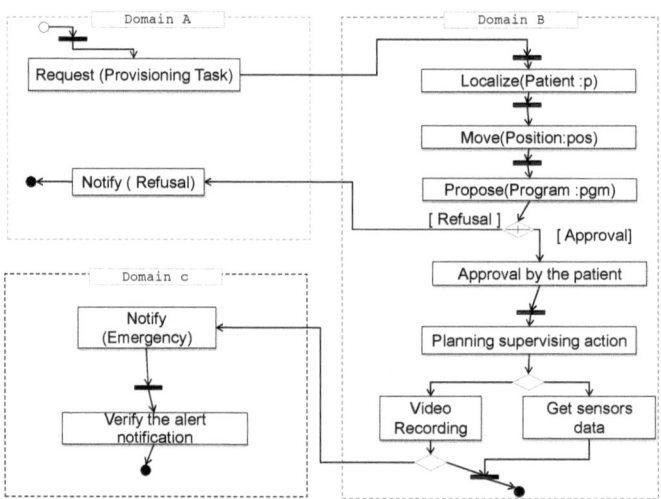

Fig. 3. Service access provisioning process

Let define the required services to successfully build this cooperation, Let's follow the methodology of our framework described in section 2.1. The fist step consists of adding the concepts to the upper ontology to meet the required view definition concepts. We have implemented the ontology by using the ontology editor *protégé*, and we have used its embedded pellet consistency checker. The workflow of the multidomain service composition is defined as follows :

1. The Request corresponds to the provisioning operation of uploading the rehabilitation plan in the robot memory. This request describes the environment criteria and the ambient conditions in which the request will be performed

2. The Robot receives the request and updates the list of the patient daily activities by adding the requested program. When the program time arrives, the robot starts the execution of these task :

   (a) Use localization service to localize the patient in the house by using the RFID identification
   (b) Move to the patient
   (c) Propose the Provisioned Task for performing the activity with the different information
   (d) If the patient refuse, we notify the Coach. Otherwise, the robot must plan for the exercise supervising
   (e) When the patient finishes his activities, the recorded data about These activities are serialized, afterwards, these data are sent to the coach to analyze them and propose other activities

For the lack of space, the steps concerning the e-contract formalization, the creation of services views and the formal validation are detailed in the appendix.

The next step corresponding to the service invocation. According to the approach we defined above the provisioning messages that are grounded using Service Provisioning Markup Language (SPML). SPML is dedicated to service provisioning and combined with web services. It allows to define provisioning operations such as Add, Delete, modify in both synchronous and asynchronous manner. The objects of the provisioning are generated using the mapping with cooperation ontology to XML data structures defined according DSML. For example, the SPML operation with the DSML profile for adding an account is as follows :

Example of SPML Add User Request

```
<spml:addRequest requestID="0123456789">
    <spml:data>
        <dsml:attrname="objectclass">
                <dsml:value>User</dsml:value>
        </dsml:attr>
        <dsml:attrname="ID">
                <dsml:value>Hubert Staub</dsml:value>
        </dsml:attr>
        <dsml:attrname="Organization">
                <dsml:value>DomainB</dsml:value>
        </dsml:attr>
    </spml:data>
</spml:addRequest>
```

The last step of our work consists of service specification that is grounded as web service specification. For instance, interfaces defined in service views are grounded according to the SPML web service standard in the case of provisioning operations, while business operation are grounded into SOAP web services.

7   Related Work

In the recent years, services composition is a hot research topic especially in ubiquitous computing and ambient intelligence. Most of the proposed approaches have tackled services composition from two view point: (i) composition or assembly of new application functionalities using planning or workflow approaches and (ii) modeling and matchmaking users and services specifications using description logics and semantic web ontologies such as SA-WSDL, DAML-S/OWL-S, WSMO, SWSL, etc. These ontologies provides composition applications with the capability of discovering and invoking services automatically. These works are discussed in several surveys [19,17]. Unfortunately, most of these approaches is based on semantic representation that give no way to verify correctness of the composition. Theorem proving based techniques are used to prove soundness and correctness. [12] introduces a method for automatic composition of semantic Web services using Linear Logic theorem proving for DAML-S services description. In this approach, services are expressed by extra-logical axioms. Linear Logic, as a resource conscious logic, enables people to define attributes of Web services formally (including qualitative and quantitative values of non-functional attributes). In addition, Linear Logic has close relationship with π-calculus, which is the formal foundation of many Web service composition languages. This idea of this work has motivated the work recently presented in[11]. This approach is based on the proofs-as-processes paradigm originally introduced by Abramsky, Bellin and Scott. In comparison to the work of [12], they preserved the original theory of Bellin and Scott by using CLL in conjunction with the standard polyadic π-calculus syntax. With respect to the application of $\mathcal{BCDL}$ in service composition, [4] proposed $\mathcal{BCDL}_0$ formalization to proof the correctness of the composition with regards to the service request. The Correctness can be checked directly by verifying the applicability conditions of the composition rules. However, using only the rules proposed in this work is insufficient in the case of multi domain service composition. For instance, the lack of flow control operators such as synchronization or simple merge makes impossible to formalize most of the provisioning services. In our work we have extended their model theory by adding the missing rules.

8   Conclusion and Future Work

In this paper, we proposed semantic framework for the multi-domain cooperative provisioning services. This framework offers an integrated formalization model that allows to specify services composition semantics and their corresponding cooperation policy for multi domain environment. The model is built using the basic constructive description logic $\mathcal{BCDL}$. This logic is characterized by its correctness and soundness properties. In this paper, we exploit their computational properties to proof the correctness of the cooperative provisioning services with the regards to the established e-contact. The ongoing work, we are implementing the proposed model by using ISABELLE theorem prover to automate the verification of cooperation e-contract.

References

1. Ayed, S., Boulahia, N.C., Cuppens, F.: Deploying access control in distributed workflow. In: Proceedings of the Sixth Australasian Conference on Information Security, AISC 2008, vol. 81, pp. 9–17 (2008)
2. Baader, F.: The Description Logic Handbook: Theory, Implementation, and Applications. Cambridge University Press (2003)
3. Bozzato, L.: Kripke Semantics and Tableau Procedures for Constructive Description Logics. PhD thesis, Università Degli Studi Dell'inubria (2009)
4. Bozzato, L., Ferrari, M.: A note on semantic web services specification and composition in constructive description logics. Journal of Syntax and Semantics (2010)
5. Ferrari, M., Fiorentini, C., Fiorino, G.: BCDL: Basic constructive description logic. Journal of Automated Reasoning 44(4), 371–399 (2010)
6. Hafner, M., Breur, M., Breu, R., Nowak, A.: Modelling inter-organizational workflow security in a peer-to-peer environment. In: IEEE International Conference on Web Services, pp. 533–540 (2005)
7. Hilia, M.: Methodology steps (2012),
https://dl.dropbox.com/u/12278812/icsoc/appendix/scenario_proof.pdf
(accessed July 30, 2012)
8. Hilia, M., Chibani, A., Amirat, Y., Djouani, K.: Cross-organizational cooperation framework for security management in ubiquitous computing environment. In: Proceedings of the 23rd International Conference on Tools with Artificial Intelligence, pp. 464–471 (2011)
9. Lin, D., Ishida, T.: Interorganizational workflow collaboration based on local process views. In: Asia-Pacific Services Computing Conference, pp. 789–794. IEEE Computer Society, Los Alamitos (2008)
10. Martin, D., Burstein, M., Mcdermott, D., Mcilraith, S., Paolucci, M., Sycara, K., Mcguinness, D., Sirin, E., Srinivasan, N.: Bringing semantics to web services with owl-s. Journal of World Wide Web Internet and Web Information Systems 10(3), 243–277 (2007)
11. Papapanagiotou, P., Fleuriot, J.: A theorem proving framework for the formal verification of web services composition. In: Proceedings of the 7th International Workshop on Automated Specification and Verification of Web Systems, pp. 1–16 (2011)
12. Rao, J., Küngas, P.: Logic-based web services composition: From service description to process model. In: Proceedings of the International Conference on Web Services (ICWS), pp. 446–453 (2004)
13. Reul, Q., Zhao, G., Meersman, R.: Ontology-based access control policy interoperability. In: Proc. 1st Conference on Mobility, Individualisation, Socialisation and Connectivity, MISC (2010)
14. Roman, D., Toma, I.: A CTR-based approach to service composition patterns. In: Third International Conference on Next Generation Web Services Practices, NWeSP, pp. 13–18 (October 2007)
15. Russell, N., Ter Hofstede, A., Mulyar, N.: Workflow controlflow patterns: A revised view (2006)
16. Sheng, Q., Benatallah, B., Maamar, Z., Ngu, A.: Configurable composition and adaptive provisioning of web services. Journal of IEEE Transactions on Services Computing 2, 34–49 (2009)
17. Stavropoulos, T., Vrakas, D., Vlahavas, I.: A survey of service composition in ambient intelligence environments. Journal of Artificial Intelligence Review, 1–24 (2011)

18. Troelstra, A.: Aspects of constructive mathematics. Journal of Studies in Logic and the Foundations of Mathematics 90, 973–1052 (1977)
19. Urbieta, A., Barrutieta, G., Parra, J., Uribarren, A.: A survey of dynamic service composition approaches for ambient systems. In: Proceedings of the First International Conference on Ambient Media and Systems, pp. 1–8 (2008)
20. Weigand, H., van den Heuvel, W.J.: Cross-organizational workflow integration using contracts. Decision Support Systems 33(3), 247–265 (2002)
21. Zhou, C., Tien Chia, L., Sung Lee, B.: DAML-QOS ontology for web services. In: Proceedings of the IEEE International Conference on Web Services, ICWS 2004, pp. 472–479 (2004)

Appendix: Methodology Steps

Given the cooperation environment $E_{Cooperation}$ defined by the services, and the flow control rules of $\mathcal{PC}$. We define the new process $CoachingAndMonitoring$ as the composition Π of the states specifications. The behavior of this process is defined as follows: The coaching platform domain uses the $Request$ service (Service Composition Π_1), to query the provisioning target (The Robot) to localize the patient and then to move until his position. It first invokes the $Request$ service, then he proceeds for localizing the patient by using $Localise$ service, Afterwards, he moves into the patient by calling $Move$ service. The service $ProposeActivity$ proposes to the patient to requested Request. The answer of the sequence composition of these services is then combined by $ProposeActivity$ service (Service Composition Π_4) which propose the activity to the patient. Then $ProcessActivity$ (Π_5) by means of an Exclusive Choice rule of two services. The proposed action is then refused, or it is accepted. In the last case, an accepted proposal action is generated and the rehabilitation program is added to the patient daily activities. The program is then processed by the $ProcessPlanningSupervision$ (Π_7) service. This service triggers the parallel execution of the $VideoRecording$ service and the $SensorsDataRetreival$ service. The latter produces a recording data of the specified target. These services must be synchronized before doing the rest of the composite service. Thus, the $DoActivitySynthesis$ (Π_8) is specified by using synchronization flow control rule. This service serializes and protects these data and notifies the coach with the successful end of the request process. Then this data is notified to the coach by using the service $ProcessRecordingData$ (Π_9).

Now let discuss how the composite process computes information terms by explaining a sample execution. Let $action$ be a coach request represented by the concept $CoachRequest$ with the associated provisioning action $prvg\_action$.

Π :: $CoachingAndMonitoring$ $Service$ Then, a call to the $CoachingAndMonitoring$ service over $action$ has as input information term :

$$\alpha_1 = (tt, (prvg\_action, tt)) \in IT_{\mathcal{N}}(x : Pre(CoachingAndMonitoring))$$

Following the composition Π, the execution of $CoachingAndMonitoring$ service starts with the sequence rule, and the first invoked service is :

Π_1 : $Request\,(Provisioning\,Action : action)$ ::
$Coach\,Request \; \sqcap \; \exists \, has\,Provisioning\,Action.Provisioning\,Action$
$\Longrightarrow (Accepted\,Provisioning\,Action \; \sqcap \; \exists \, has\,Program.Program) \sqcup \; Refused\,Action$

Π_1 : *Request Service* This service process the information term α_1. Let suppose that the *domainB* accepts the provisioning request and produces the program *program* for the patient *patient$_1$*. The provisioning action is codified in the information term :

$\beta_1 = \Phi_{Request}(tt, (prvg\_action, tt)) \in IT_{\mathcal{N}}(x : Post(Request))$. Let us assume that β_1 has the following form : $\beta_1 = (2, (tt, (program_1, (tt, (program\_person_1, tt)))))$. Where $program\_person_1$ represents the concerned person or (Target) by the program. The execution of the *Request* service is forwarded by the *Localize* service execution.

Π_2 : $Localize(Object)$ ::
$Localization\,Action \; \sqcap \; \exists \, is\,Localizable.Object \Longrightarrow Target \sqcap \; \forall \, has\,Location.Position$

This service performs a localization action, it needs a target to be localized. As result, it generates the objects target with its associated position.

Π_2 : *Localize Service.* According to the applicability conditions of the Sequence rule, we have the proof : $\pi_1 :: T_{Cooperation}, x : Post(Request) \vdash_{\overline{BCD\mathcal{L}_0}}$ $x : Pre(Localize)$. The corresponding operator $\phi_{\mathcal{N}}^{\pi_1}$ allows us to extract from β_1 the information term α_2 such that :

$\alpha_2 = (tt, (program\_person_1, tt)) \in IT_{\mathcal{N}}(x : Pre(Localize))$. The Localize service consists of generating the position of the specified target, In this case, the target is the patient. The position of this target is codified in the information term : $\beta_2 = \Phi_{Localize}((tt, (program\_person_1, tt)) \in IT_{\mathcal{N}}(x : Post(Localize))$. Let assume that β_2 has the following form : $\beta_2 = (tt, (position\_program\_person_1, tt))$.

Now, let consider the applicability condition of the sequence rule, in particular :
$\pi_2 :: T_{Cooperation}, x : Post(Localize) \vdash_{\overline{BCD\mathcal{L}_0}} x : Pre(Move)$. The corresponding operator $\phi_{\mathcal{N}}^{\pi_2}$ allow us to extract from β_2 the information term α_3 such that:
$\alpha_3 = (tt, (position\_program\_person_1, tt)) \in IT_{\mathcal{N}}(x : Pre(Move))$. After that, the execution of the *Move* service is occurred. For the lack of space, the rest the formal validation is detailed in [7].

Sparse Functional Representation
for Large-Scale Service Clustering

Qi Yu

College of Computing and Information Science,
Rochester Institute of Technology
qi.yu@rit.edu

Abstract. Service clustering provides an effective means to discover
hidden service communities that group services with relevant functionalities. However, the ever increasing number of Web services poses key
challenges for building large-scale service communities. In this paper,
we address the scalability issue in service clustering, aiming to discover
service communities over very large-scale services. A key observation is
that service descriptions are usually represented by long but very sparse
term vectors as each service is only described by a limited number of
terms. This inspires us to seek a new service representation that is economical to store, efficient to process, and intuitive to interpret. This new
representation enables service clustering to scale to massive number of
services. More specifically, a set of anchor services are identified that allow to represent each service as a linear combination of a small number
of anchor services. In this way, the large number of services are encoded
with a much more compact anchor service space. We conduct extensive
experiments on real-world service data to assess both the effectiveness
and efficiency of the proposed approach. Results on a dataset with over
3,700 Web services clearly demonstrate the good scalability of sparse
functional representation.

1 Introduction

Service oriented computing holds tremendous promise by exploiting Web services
as an efficient vehicle to deliver and access various functionalities over the Web.
The past few years have witnessed a fast boost of Web services due to the
wide adoption of service-oriented computing in both industry and government.
The proliferating services have formed a functionality-centric repository, through
which key computing resources can be conveniently accessed via the standard
Web service interface. However, the ever increasing number of Web service poses
key challenges to discover services with user required functionalities. A rigorous
and systematic methodology is in demand for efficiently and accurately searching
user desired services from a large and diverse service repository.

Universal Description Discovery and Integration (UDDI) provides a standard
registry service to publish and discover Web services. To make a service search-
able, the service provider needs to first publish its service in the UDDI registry.
Nonetheless, as service providers are autonomous in nature, it is infeasible to enforce them to publish their services in the registry. In fact, most service vendors

C. Liu et al. (Eds.): ICSOC 2012, LNCS 7636, pp. 468–483, 2012.
© Springer-Verlag Berlin Heidelberg 2012

choose to directly advertise their services via their own web sites. Furthermore, when change occurs to a published service, the service entry in the UDDI may need to be updated to ensure consistency. This gives rise to additional maintenance cost for service providers. Recent statistics show that more than 50% services in the public UDDI registries are invalid.

Service search engines have gained increasing popularity by automatically collecting service descriptions using crawlers. Service descriptions are then indexed and matched against user's searching keywords. One key impediment towards the wide adoption of service search engines has been the poor search quality resulted from simple keyword matching. While keyword matching may perform reasonably well on regular Web pages, it suffers from service descriptions, which are usually generated from application programs using Web service deployment tools. Many service descriptions are comprised of very limited number of terms, most of which are not proper words. Therefore, there is a low chance for a service description to match a searching keyword even though the service may provide the exact user-desired functionality.

Clustering techniques have been adopted to improve the quality of service discovery [5,16,3]. Service clustering computes the similarity among services to group together relevant services into homogeneous service communities. Clustering enables services to be discovered by exploiting the proximity to other services. Consider two similar services, S_1 and S_2, where S_1 contains the searching keyword while S_2 does not. Through service clustering, both S_1 and S_2 will be returned as they are deemed to provide similar functionality desired by the user. In this way, the search quality can be dramatically improved. Furthermore, service discovery can be directed to only relevant service communities so that more efficient performance is achieved.

As the number of services keeps increasing, building service communities over large-scale Web services arises as a central challenge. Following traditional document clustering, each service description $\mathbf{s}_i$ is denoted by a term vector, in which $\mathbf{s}_i(j)$ is set to the normalized frequency (or other metrics such as TF/IDF) of $\mathbf{t}_j$ if $\mathbf{t}_j \in \mathbf{s}_i$ and 0 otherwise. The length of $\mathbf{s}_i$ is equal to the size of the term dictionary, which consists of the distinct terms over all service descriptions. Most service descriptions are generated from program source codes, where various naming conventions may be used by different developers. This results in a large number of distinct terms especially when scaling to a massive number of services. For example, in one of the real service dataset used in our experiments [18], we extract around 17,000 distinct terms from over 3,700 service descriptions. However, each service description only consists of 20 distinct terms on average. Therefore, the term vector $\mathbf{s}_i$ will be very large and extremely sparse (density is around 0.1% in our dataset) when dealing with large-scale services.

Simple clustering algorithms, such as K-means, scales well with the number of services. The similarity between two term vectors is usually computed based on the number of terms that co-occur in these two vectors. However, directly applying these algorithms to large-scale service clustering usually leads to poor clustering quality because the term vectors for service descriptions are extremely sparse and hence less likely to share common terms. Advanced algorithms, such as matrix factorization based ones (e.g., SVD co-clustering [17] and NMTF [4]), have been demonstrated to be more effective in dealing with limitations of service descriptions and generate high-quality service communities. However, it remains unclear how these algorithms can handle extremely large and sparse term vectors. In addition, the high computational cost also prohibits them from scaling to a massive number of services.

In this paper, we address the scalability issue in service clustering, aiming to discover service communities over very large-scale services. The central idea is that instead of using a large and highly diverse dictionary of terms, we seek a much more succinct representation of service descriptions. Inspired by recent works on sparse coding [8,19], we devise a novel strategy to learn a set of "anchor" services, which form a new dictionary to encode the service descriptions. This allows each service to be represented as a linear combination of a small number of anchor services. In general, the number of anchor services is smaller than the number of distinct terms with several orders of magnitude. Hence, the large number of services are encoded with a much more compact dictionary of anchor services. The new representation is essentially a projection onto the anchor service space. Similarity between services is determined based on how they are related to a small number of anchor services. Simple clustering algorithms, like K-means, can then be applied to this compact representation to efficiently and accurately cluster large-scale services. We demonstrate the effectiveness of the proposed algorithm via extensive experiments on two real-world service datasets.

The remainder of the paper is organized as follows. We discuss some related works in Section 2, which provide a background overview of the proposed approach. We present the details of sparse functional representation in Section 3. We use a concrete example to explain how sparse functional representation works and provide intuitive justifications of its effectiveness. We also propose a novel clustering scheme that integrates information from both the anchor service space and the term vector space. We apply sparse functional representation to two real-world service datasets and assess its effectiveness in Section 4. We conclude the paper and provide some future directions in Section 5.

2   Related Work

Service clustering and related technologies have been increasingly adopted to facilitate service discovery [5] or other key tasks in service computing, such as service composition [10] and service ontology construction [13].

Clustering has been a central technique to improve the accuracy of service search engines. Woogle, a Web service search engine, performs term clustering to generate a set of high-level concepts, which are then used to facilitate the matching between users' queries and the service operations [5]. Similarly, term clustering is also used in [10] to facilitate service discovery and composition. Basic K-means algorithms are usually used and the similarity between terms are evaluated based on their co-occurrence in the service descriptions. Quality

Threshold (QT) clustering is employed to cluster Web services in [6] to bootstrap the discovery of Web services. WSDL descriptions are carefully parsed and important components are extracted, which include content, types, messages, ports, and name of the Web service. Weights are assigned to each component when similarity between two services is evaluated. More complicated algorithms, such as Probabilistic Latent Semantic Analysis (PLSA), have also been applied to service clustering and discovery [12]. A SVD based algorithm is adopted to achieve the co-clustering of services and operations in [17]. Co-clustering exploits the duality relationship between services and operations to achieve better clustering quality than one-side clustering.

Given the limitations of the WSDL service descriptions, some recent proposals seek to explore external information sources, such as Wordnet [1] and Google, to improve service clustering and discovery [9,1]. In [16], matrix factorization and the semantic extensions of service descriptions have been integrated for service community discovery. The integration has the effect of placing the extended semantics into the context of the service, which more effectively leverages the extended semantics to benefit community discovery. As Web services usually consist of both WSDL and free text descriptors, novel approaches have been developed in [13] to integrate both types of descriptors for effective bootstrapping of service ontologies. Another important piece of information that is complementary to service descriptions is the service tags that users use to annotate services. A novel approach, referred to as WTCluster, is developed in [3] that exploits both WSDL documents and service tags for Web service clustering.

3 Sparse Functional Representation for Service Clustering

Sparse functional representation aims to seek a compact dictionary of anchor services to succinctly represent large-scale services. Consider a set of services $\mathcal{S} = \{\mathbf{s}_1, ..., \mathbf{s}_m\}$, where each $\mathbf{s}_i \in \mathbb{R}^n$ is denoted as a term vector and n is the size of the term dictionary that is comprised of all distinct terms extracted from the services in $\mathcal{S}$. By mapping terms into rows and services into columns, $\mathcal{S}$ is conveniently represented by a two dimensional service matrix $\mathbf{X} \in \mathbb{R}^{n \times m}$. Each entry $\mathbf{X}_{ij} \in \mathbf{X}$ is set to the normalized frequency of term $\mathbf{t}_i$ in service $\mathbf{s}_j$ and zero if $\mathbf{t}_i \notin \mathbf{s}_j$. Table 1 provides a quick reference to a set of symbols that are commonly used in the paper.

As discussed in Section 1, due to the diverse naming conventions used in service descriptions, the size of the term dictionary increases dramatically with the number of services in $\mathcal{S}$. This will result in a huge and extremely sparse matrix $\mathbf{X}$. For example, in our experiments, a $16,884 \times 3,738$ matrix is constructed from a real-world service dataset with $3,738$ services. $\mathbf{X}$ consists of approximately 6.3×10^8 entries, among which only 0.1% are nonzero, implying a 99.9% sparsity ratio. This poses a set of key challenges for clustering large-scale services. First,

---

[1] http://wordnet.princeton.edu/

Table 1. Symbols and Descriptions

Symbol	Description
S	set of services
s_j, t_i	the jth service and i^{th} term
X, A, W, Z	matrices
X'	the transpose of matrix X
X_{ij}	the element at the ith row and j^{th} column of matrix X
x_j	the j-th column vector of matrix X
$x_j(i)$	the i-th element of x_j
x_i^T	the i-th row vector of matrix X

scalability arises as a significant challenge for storing and processing a large service matrix whose size grows quickly with the number of services. Second, the highly sparse term vectors are a key impediment for applying many clustering algorithms to generate high-quality clusters as sparse vectors are less likely to share common terms.

3.1 Sparse Functional Representation

The above observation implies that a large and diverse term dictionary does not provide a suitable representation for large-scale service clustering. Instead, concepts with coarser granularity may be more instrumental to produce a compact and cohesive service representation. Hence, we aim to seek a new service representation that is economical to store, efficient to process, and intuitive to interpret. This new representation will enable service clustering to scale to massive number of services. Inspired by recent advances in sparse coding [8,19], we devise a novel sparse functional representation (SFR) strategy to discover a set of so called "anchor services". The anchor services are expected to capture the high-level functionalities of services while significantly compressing the original term vector space. More specifically, SFR seeks a matrix $A = \{a_1, ..., a_k\}$, where each $a_i \in \mathbb{R}^n$ denotes an anchor service and is a linear combination of a set of term vectors (or columns of X):

$$A = \{a_1, ..., a_k\} = XW \tag{1}$$

$$a_i = Xw_i = \sum_{j=1}^{m} W_{ij}x_j, \forall i = 1, ..., k \tag{2}$$

where $W = \{w_1, ..., w_k\} \in \mathbb{R}^{m \times k}$ is a weight matrix. Each entry W_{ij} denotes how much service s_j contributes to anchor service a_i. It is worth to note that W_{ij} may take a negative value, meaning that s_j related information is removed from a_i. Hence, a negative entry in W serves as the "de-noise" purpose to generate an anchor service with purer functionality or concept.

In practice, we have $k \ll n$. Hence, the anchor services provide a compact way to represent large-scale services. The desired anchor services are expected to capture high-level concepts or functionalities of the service space. Thus, we should be able to recover the original services by using the anchor services. Meanwhile, as most services are designed with specific purposes, it is common for a single service to provide focused and limited functionalities. In another word, a service is expected to be only related to a small subset of anchor services that cover its functionalities. Therefore, a desired anchor service set should optimize the following objection function:

$$\min_{\mathbf{A}, z_i \geq 0} J_0 = \sum_{i=1}^{m} ||\mathbf{x}_i - \mathbf{A}\mathbf{z}_i||^2 + \lambda ||\mathbf{z}_i||_0 \qquad (3)$$

$$\text{subject to } ||\mathbf{a}_j||^2 \leq c, \forall j = 1, ..., k$$

where $\mathbf{z}_i \in \mathbb{R}_+^k$ is the coefficient vector with $\mathbf{z}_i(j)$ signifying the correlation between $\mathbf{x}_i$ and anchor service $\mathbf{a}_j$. $||\mathbf{z}_i||_0$ is the L_0 norm of $\mathbf{z}_i$ that counts the number of nonzero elements in $\mathbf{s}_i$. Since each service is expected to correlate with only a small subset of anchor services, $\mathbf{z}_i$ with many nonzero elements will be penalized and λ is the penalty parameter. Therefore, the second term of Eq. (3) corresponds to a sparsity constraint on $\mathbf{z}_i$. The norm constraint on the size of the anchor service, i.e., $||\mathbf{a}_j||^2 \leq c$, avoids arbitrarily large anchor services that keep $\mathbf{A}\mathbf{z}_i$ unchanged while making $\mathbf{z}_i$ arbitrarily close to zero.

It is worth to note that $\mathbf{z}_i$ is non-negative, which allows more intuitive interpretation of the proposed sparse functional representation. More specifically, the functionality of each service is represented as an additive combination of functionalities encoded by a small number of anchor services.

3.2   Relaxation of the Objective Function

It has been proved that finding $\mathbf{A}$ and $\mathbf{s}_i$ that optimize objective function in Eq. (3) is NP-hard [19]. Therefore, instead of directly solving Eq. (3), we tackle the following optimization problem with a relaxed constraint:

$$\min_{\mathbf{W}, \mathbf{S} \geq 0} J_1 = ||\mathbf{X} - \mathbf{X}\mathbf{W}\mathbf{Z}||_F^2 + \lambda \sum_{i=1}^{m} ||\mathbf{z}_i||_1 \qquad (4)$$

$$\text{subject to } ||\mathbf{X}\mathbf{w}_j||^2 \leq c, \forall j = 1, ..., k$$

where $||\mathbf{Y}||_F = \sum_{ij} \sqrt{\mathbf{Y}_{ij}}$ stands for Frobenius norm; $\mathbf{z}_i$ is the i-th column of $\mathbf{Z} \in \mathbb{R}^{k \times m}$; $||\mathbf{z}_i||_1 = \sum_{j=1}^{k} |\mathbf{Z}_{ji}|$ is the L_1 norm of $\mathbf{z}_i$. We replace $\mathbf{A}$ and $\mathbf{a}_j$ by $\mathbf{X}\mathbf{W}$ and $\mathbf{X}\mathbf{w}_j$, respectively, due to Equations (1) and (2).

The first term of J_1 is equivalent to the first term of J_0 reformulated in the matrix form. The key difference between J_0 and J_1 is the change from the L_0 norm of $\mathbf{z}_i$ to the L_1 norm. The relaxed optimization is in essence to minimize a quadratic function with a L_1 norm constraint on $\mathbf{z}_i$ and a L_2 norm constraint on $\mathbf{a}_j$. The optimization problem in the form of Eq.(4) is commonly known as *basis pursuit*, which has been demonstrated to be effective in finding sparse coefficient vectors (i.e., $\mathbf{z}_i$'s). Therefore, the solution of J_1 is expected to provide a good approximation to the optimal solution of J_0. Furthermore, the relaxed optimization problem is computational attractive, which can be efficiently tackled by iteratively solving a L_1 regularized least squares problem and L_2 regularized least square problem to obtain $\mathbf{Z}$ and $\mathbf{W}$, respectively [8].

3.3   An Illustrating Example

In what follows, we use a simple example to further illustrate the key ideas of SFR as presented above. We randomly choose six services from a real-world service dataset, in which three services are from the travel domain and the other three are from the medical domain. Processing the service descriptions results in 12 distinct terms. Hence, a 12×6 service matrix $\mathbf{X}$ is constructed. The transpose of $\mathbf{X}$ is given in Eq. (5) for the convenience of presentation, in which each row denotes a service and each column denotes a distinct term. Each entry corresponds to a term frequency and each row vector is further normalized to have L_2 norm equal to 1.

$$
\mathbf{X}' = \begin{pmatrix}
0.29 & 0.29 & 0.86 & 0.29 & 0.096 & 0 & 0 & 0 & 0 & 0 & 0 & 0 \\
0.26 & 0.26 & 0.61 & 0.26 & 0.088 & 0.61 & 0.18 & 0 & 0 & 0 & 0 & 0 \\
0.33 & 0.33 & 0.33 & 0.33 & 0.11 & 0 & 0 & 0.33 & 0.66 & 0 & 0 & 0 \\
0 & 0 & 0 & 0 & 0.092 & 0 & 0 & 0 & 0 & 0.55 & 0.83 & 0 \\
0 & 0 & 0 & 0 & 0.092 & 0 & 0 & 0 & 0 & 0.55 & 0 & 0.83 \\
0 & 0 & 0 & 0 & 0.092 & 0 & 0 & 0 & 0 & 0.55 & 0 & 0.83
\end{pmatrix}
\tag{5}
$$

It is clear from Eq. (5) that even for a small service set with just six services, the service matrix $\mathbf{X}$ is already very sparse. There are around 60% (42 out of 72) zero entries. The sparsity ratio will increase dramatically when the set scales to a large number of services.

We set the number of anchor services as 4 (i.e., $k = 4$) and solve the relaxed optimization problem in Eq. (4), which leads to:

$$
\mathbf{W} = \begin{pmatrix}
-0.12 & 0.4 & 0.37 & 0.14 \\
-0.13 & 0.39 & 0.35 & 0.15 \\
-0.14 & 0.31 & 0.34 & 0.17 \\
0.55 & -0.17 & 0.26 & 0.098 \\
0.32 & -0.12 & -0.19 & 0.44 \\
0.3 & -0.12 & -0.2 & 0.44
\end{pmatrix},
\mathbf{Z} = \begin{pmatrix}
0 & 0 & 0 & 0.24 & 0.22 & 0.21 \\
0.23 & 0.23 & 0.2 & 0 & 0 & 0 \\
0.27 & 0.26 & 0.24 & 0.13 & 0.0087 & 0.0054 \\
0.26 & 0.26 & 0.26 & 0.26 & 0.42 & 0.42
\end{pmatrix}
$$

$$\tag{6}$$

The i-th column of $\mathbf{Z}$ (i.e., $\mathbf{z}_i$) corresponds to the new representation of the i-th service (i.e., i-th row of $\mathbf{X}'$ in Eq. (5)) in the anchor service space. As expected, $\mathbf{Z}$ has a sparse structure, which justifies the effectiveness of L_1 norm approximation of the original optimization problem. The first three columns of $\mathbf{Z}$ imply that the first three services are only relevant to the last three anchor services. In contrast, the other three services, which correspond to the last three columns of $\mathbf{Z}$, are tightly coupled with the first and last anchor services (the third entries of these three columns are close to zero). All entries in $\mathbf{Z}$ are non-negative, which allows functionality of each service to be represented as an additive combination of functionalities encoded by a small number of relevant anchor services.

Some interesting observations are also revealed from the weight matrix $\mathbf{W}$. These observations demonstrate that the interplay between the weight matrix $\mathbf{W}$ and the coefficient matrix $\mathbf{Z}$ helps achieve the effectiveness of SFR. For example, the first three entries of $\mathbf{w}_1$ (i.e., the first column of $\mathbf{W}$) take negative values. These negative entries imply that information related to the first three services are removed from the first anchor service $\mathbf{a}_1$. Therefore, a negative entry $\mathbf{W}_{ij}$ has the effect of "decoupling" the i-th service from j-th anchor service. In contrast, a positive entry $\mathbf{W}_{ij}$ signifies the "addition" of the i-th service's functionality to the j-th anchor service. The decoupling and addition mechanism helps discover cohesive concepts or service functionalities that are captured by the anchor services. It also leads to unambiguous service-to-anchor service relationships. For example, $\mathbf{z}_1^T$, the first row of the coefficient matrix $\mathbf{Z}$, consists of three zero and three nonzero entries. This implies that the first three services are completely irrelevant to anchor service $\mathbf{a}_1$ whereas the last three are tightly coupled with $\mathbf{a}_1$. In fact, the three zero entries are resulted from the first three entries in $\mathbf{w}_1$, which decouple the first three services from $\mathbf{a}_1$. The three nonzero entries are due to the last three entries of $\mathbf{w}_1$ that add the functionalities of the last three service into $\mathbf{a}_1$. Similarly, the second row of $\mathbf{Z}$ shows that the first three services are relevant to anchor service $\mathbf{a}_2$ while the last three service are irrelevant to it.

3.4   Clustering in Anchor Service Space

By optimizing objection function J_0 or its relaxed version J_1, we aim to find an anchor service set $\mathbf{A}$ and a new sparse representation $\mathbf{z}_i$ to best approximate $\mathbf{x}_i$:

$$\mathbf{x}_i \approx \mathbf{A}\mathbf{z}_i = \sum_{j=1}^{k} \mathbf{a}_j \mathbf{Z}_{ji} \qquad (7)$$

Therefore, the new representation $\mathbf{z}_i$ can be regarded as the projection of $\mathbf{x}_i$ onto the anchor service space $\mathbf{A} = \{\mathbf{a}_1, ..., \mathbf{a}_k\}$. The coefficient vector $\mathbf{z}_i$ captures the relevance between the i-th service and all the k anchor services. The sparsity constraint on $\mathbf{z}_i$ leads to clear-cut relationships between a service and anchor services. Hence, services can be easily separated based on their distinct relationships with the anchor services using sparse functional representation.

Figure 1 provides a schematic view of service clustering in the anchor service space. Since each service is only related to a small subset of anchor services, the similarity between two services can be easily computed based on how they are related to the anchor services. More specifically, two services are similar if they are related to a similar set of anchor services. Therefore, the anchor services serve as a bridge to relate different services. Since the anchor services capture the high-level concepts of the services, projection onto the anchor service space provides a better way to assess the similarity between services than using terms. The sparsity constraint on the coefficient vectors provides a clear separation between services, which significantly facilitates service clustering. Any simple clustering

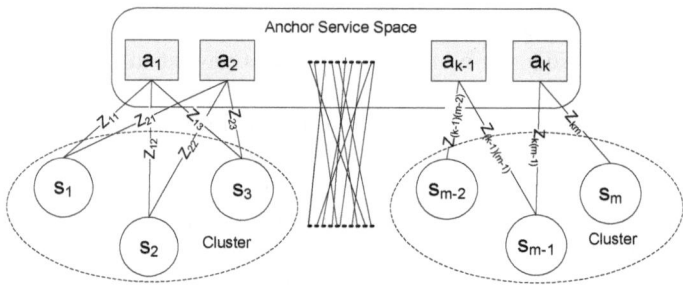

Fig. 1. Clustering in Anchor Service Space

algorithms, such as K-means, may be directly applied to the coefficient matrix **Z** to generate service clusters. Meanwhile, the anchor service space has a much low dimensionality than the term vector space (i.e., $k \ll n$), clustering in the anchor service space can easily scale to a massive number of services.

3.5   Term Vector and Anchor Service Integration

Sparse functional representation is formed by projecting term vectors $\mathbf{x}_i$'s onto an anchor service space. Service clustering is then performed on the projected representation, which is independent on the original term vector space. In this section, we present a new clustering scheme that integrates information from both the anchor service space and the term vector space.

One piece of information in the term vector space that can be leveraged is the term vectors that share a decent number of distinct terms. If two term vectors have a reasonable number of common terms, it means that they share similar high-level concept and hence should be clustered together. This useful information can be incorporated into anchor space clustering in a semi-supervisory manner to improve the overall clustering quality. More specifically, we construct a neighborhood graph G, in which each vertex corresponds to a term vector $\mathbf{x}_i \in \mathbf{X}$. Two vertices $\mathbf{x}_i$ and $\mathbf{x}_j$ are connected in G if the similarity between $\mathbf{x}_i$ and $\mathbf{x}_j$ is no less than a threshold value. The similarity can be simply computed by using cosine similarity. Assume that $\mathbf{B}$ is the incidence matrix of G. Therefore, $\mathbf{B}_{ij} = 1$ if $\mathbf{x}_i$ and $\mathbf{x}_j$ are connected in G (i.e., similar to each other) and 0 otherwise. We expect $\mathbf{B}$ to be sparse as it is less likely for most term vectors to share many common terms.

Consider any pair of term vectors $\mathbf{x}_i$ and $\mathbf{x}_j$ and their corresponding sparse functional representations $\mathbf{z}_i$ and $\mathbf{z}_j$. If $\mathbf{x}_i$ and $\mathbf{x}_j$ are similar, we expect $\mathbf{z}_i$ and $\mathbf{z}_j$ to be similar as well. In contrast, if $\mathbf{z}_i$ and $\mathbf{z}_j$ significantly deviate from each other, $||\mathbf{z}_i - \mathbf{z}_j||^2 \mathbf{B}_{ij}$ will be large as $\mathbf{B}_{ij} = 1$ when $\mathbf{x}_i$ and $\mathbf{x}_j$ are close in the term vector space. Therefore, we can use $||\mathbf{z}_i - \mathbf{z}_j||^2 \mathbf{B}_{ij}$ as a penalty term and incorporate it into objection function J_1, which leads to

$$\min_{\mathbf{W}, \mathbf{S} \geq 0} J_2 = ||\mathbf{X} - \mathbf{X}\mathbf{W}\mathbf{Z}||_F^2 + \lambda \sum_{i=1}^{m} ||\mathbf{z}_i||_1 + \gamma \sum_{i=1}^{m} \sum_{j=1}^{m} ||\mathbf{z}_i - \mathbf{z}_j||^2 \mathbf{B}_{ij} \quad (8)$$

subject to $||\mathbf{X}\mathbf{w}_j||^2 \leq c, \forall j = 1, ..., k$

where γ is the penalty parameter. It is worth to note that if $\mathbf{x}_i$ and $\mathbf{x}_j$ are not evaluated to be similar, we have $\mathbf{B}_{ij} = 0$. In this case, the term $||\mathbf{z}_i - \mathbf{z}_j||^2 \mathbf{B}_{ij}$ is set to 0 and will not affect the objective function J_2.

4   Experimental Study

We apply the proposed SFR to two real-world service datasets. To evaluate its effectiveness in service clustering, we will compare our approach with a set competitive service clustering algorithms. As both clustering quality and efficiency are important evaluation metrics, we will report both clustering accuracy and CPU times in our experimental results.

4.1   Service Dataset Description

We include two real-world service datasets: one middle scale dataset with 452 services [7] and one large-scale dataset with 3,738 services [18]. We describe the properties of each dataset in what follows:

- **Dataset_1**: The first service dataset consists of 452 WSDL descriptions of services from 7 different application domains. More specifically, the services are distributed as follows: communication (42), education (139), economy (83), food (23), medical (45), travel (90), and weapon (30). The domain information provides labels of the service clusters, which will be used to evaluate the accuracy of the clustering algorithms in our experiments.
- **Dataset_2**: The second service dataset consists of WSDL descriptions of 3,738 services located in more than 20 countries. The services are more diverse and complicated, coming from a large number of domains varying from government to academia and industry. Unlike **Dataset_1**, no cluster labels are available in this dataset.

4.2   Metrics for Clustering Quality

For **Dataset_1**, the service domains will serve as the ground truth to evaluate the clustering quality. More specifically, we adopt two metrics to measure the service clustering quality: ACcuracy (i.e., AC) and Mutual Information (i.e., MI). Both AC and MI are widely used metrics to assess the performance of clustering algorithms [15,2]. For **Dataset_2**, since no true service cluster labels are available, we cannot use the above two metrics to evaluate clustering quality. Instead, we choose to use the Silhouette Value (i.e., SV), which is a commonly used metric for clustering quality evaluation when no ground truth is available.

- **Accuracy:** For a given service $\mathbf{s}_i$, assume that its cluster label is c_i and its domain label is d_i based on the domain information. The AC metric is defined as follows:

$$AC = \frac{\sum_{i=1}^{m} \delta(d_i, map(c_i))}{m} \tag{9}$$

where m is the total number of Web services in the service dataset. $\delta(x, y)$ is the delta function that equals to one if $x = y$ and equals to zero if otherwise. $map(c_i)$ is the permutation mapping function that maps each assigned cluster label to the equivalent domain label. The best mapping between the two sets of labels is achieved by the Kuhn-Munkres algorithm [11].

– **Mutual Information:** Let $\mathcal{D}$ be the set of application domains obtained from the service dataset and $\mathcal{C}$ be the service clusters obtained a service clustering algorithm. The mutual information metric $MI(\mathcal{D}, \mathcal{C})$ is defined as follows:

$$MI(\mathcal{D}, \mathcal{C}) = \sum_{d_i \in \mathcal{D}, c_j \in \mathcal{C}} p(d_i, c_j) \log_2 \frac{p(d_i, c_j)}{p(d_i)p(c_j)} \tag{10}$$

where $p(d_i)$ and $p(c_j)$ are the probabilities that a randomly selected service from the service set belongs to domain d_i and cluster c_j, respectively. $p(d_i, c_j)$ is the joint probability that the randomly selected service belongs to both domain d_i and cluster c_j.

– **Silhouette Value:** The silhouette value for service $\mathbf{s}_i$ measures how similar that $\mathbf{s}_i$ is to the services in its own cluster compared to services in other clusters, and ranges from -1 to +1. More specifically, SV is defined as the average over the silhouette values of all services:

$$SV = \frac{\sum_{i=1}^{m} SV_i}{m} \tag{11}$$

$$SV_i = \frac{(b_i - a_i)}{\max(a_i, b_i)} \tag{12}$$

where SV_i is the silhouette value for the i-th service $\mathbf{s}_i$; a_i is the average distance from $\mathbf{s}_i$ to the other services in the same cluster as $\mathbf{s}_i$, and b_i is the minimum average distance from $\mathbf{s}_i$ to services in a different cluster, minimized over clusters. Therefore, SV essentially measures the "cohesiveness" of the clusters.

4.3   Clustering on Dataset_1

Before running any service clustering algorithms, we need to preprocess the service descriptions in **Dataset_1**. We apply a standard text processing procedure that includes tokenization, stopword removal, and stemming to extract distinct terms from the service descriptions. As a result, 803 distinct terms are extracted. Thus, a 803×452 service matrix $\mathbf{X}$ is constructed. We compare the proposed SFR based clustering with the following service clustering algorithms:

– **NMTF**: Non-negative matrix tri-factorization based approach to simultaneously cluster services and operations offered by the services [4].
– **NMTFS**: Extending service descriptions by including semantically similar terms to address the sparsity issue and then applying NMTF to the extended service descriptions [16].

Table 2. Clustering Results on **Dataset_1**

Algorithms	Quality			Performance
	Accuracy (%)	Mutual Information (%)	Silhouette Value	CPU time (s)
NMTF	51.1	48.0	0.28	17.9
NMTFS	56.6	46.5	0.28	19.0
KmeanS	42.7	21.2	-0.1	33.0
SVDC	45.3	36.3	0.22	**0.9**
SFR	**60.4**	**56.6**	**0.7**	19.1

- **KmeanS**: Applying K-means clustering to the semantically extended service descriptions.
- **SVDC**: Applying Singular Value Decomposition (SVD) to co-cluster services and operations they offers [17].

We set the number of anchor services as 30, i.e., $k = 30$. The two penalty parameters λ and γ in objection function J_2 are set to 1 and 0.1, respectively. These will be used as default parameter values in our experiments unless specified otherwise. It is worth to note that a wide range of values work reasonably well for these parameters. We will investigate the impact of different parameters in Section 4.5.

Table 2 reports both clustering quality and CPU times from all the algorithms under comparison. The clustering quality is evaluated using all the three evaluation metrics described in Section 4.2. SFR clearly outperforms all other competitors in terms of clustering quality. It achieves 60.4% in clustering accuracy, which is 7% better than the second highest accuracy achieved by NMTFS. In terms of mutual information, it is 17.9% better than second best, NMTF. The results on silhouette value are pretty much consistent with those on accuracy and mutual information. SFR achieves a silhouette value at 0.7, which is much higher than all other algorithms. This demonstrates that sparse functional representation provides good separation between similar services and dissimilar ones, which makes service clustering much easier. A higher silhouette value signifies that the generated clusters are more cohesive.

In terms of performance, the CPU time used by SFR is similar to other matrix factorization based clustering algorithms, including NMTF and NMTFS. This is reasonable for a middle scale service dataset especially when the number of distinct terms are relatively small. It is worth to note that the time for SFR includes both finding the anchor service set and performing clustering in the anchor service space. In fact, most time is spent on former as clustering in SFR is just applying K-means to a compact sparse functional representation of the service space. SVDC achieves a very fast response time, which is only 0.9 second. This is because it computes a service-operation correlation matrix in order to perform co-clustering. Since the number of operations is much less than the number of terms, SVDC actually works on a much smaller matrix, which justifies its fast performance. Nonetheless, the poor clustering quality of SVDC implies that the service-operation correlation matrix does not provides a good representation for service clustering.

Table 3. Clustering Results on **Dataset_2**

Algorithms	Quality	CPU time (s)	
	Silhouette Value	Construction	Clustering
NMTF	0.05	-	359.9
PKmeans	0.31	-	3.97
Kmeans	0.21	-	3.23
SVDC	NaN	-	1131.3
SFR	**0.38**	367.3	2.7

4.4   Clustering on Dataset_2

We adopt the same standard text processing procedure to process the $3,738$ service descriptions in **Dataset_2**, which results in $16,884$ distinct terms. Therefore, a $16,884 \times 3,738$ service matrix $\mathbf{X}$ is constructed. Each term vector has a dimensionality of $16,884$. Before applying any clustering algorithms on such high dimensional data, a common practice is to first reduce the dimensionality. Thus, we employ Principle Component Analysis (PCA) to reduce the dimensionality to 64. It is also worth to note that algorithms, such as NMTFS and KmeanS, require to perform semantic extensions on each distinct term. This will lead to a huge term dictionary for a large service set, like **Dataset_2**. The resultant service matrix will be several orders larger than $\mathbf{X}$. To avoid prohibitive computational cost, we are not including NMTFS and KmeanS for comparison. Instead, we add another two algorithms into the mix:

- **Kmeans**: Directly applying Kmeans clustering to the terms vectors in $\mathbf{X}$.
- **PKmeans**: Applying Kmeans after PCA dimensionality reduction.

Since there are no cluster labels for **Dataset_2**, we only use silhouette value to evaluate clustering quality. We set the number of clusters to 30. The number of anchor services is set to 128 and all other parameters take their default values for SFR.

Table 3 reports the clustering result on **Dataset_2**. In terms of clustering quality, SFR achieves the highest silhouette value among all the algorithms. This is consistent with the results from **Dataset_1**. It is also worth to note that SVDC fails to converge after spending over $1,000$ seconds, so no silhouette value is computed. For the CPU times, we record both the construction time that is used to discover the anchor services and the clustering time for SFR. Even though SFR uses relatively long time (which is similar to the clustering time used by NMTF) for anchor service discovery, it achieves the best clustering time. The fast clustering performance of SFR further justifies that sparse functional representation indeed makes clustering easier. Once the anchor space is discovered, it can be stored and reused. Therefore, for large-scale service clustering, anchor services can be first discovered offline and then service clustering can be performed in realtime to meet different user requirements on number of clusters, distance metrics, clustering algorithms, and so on.

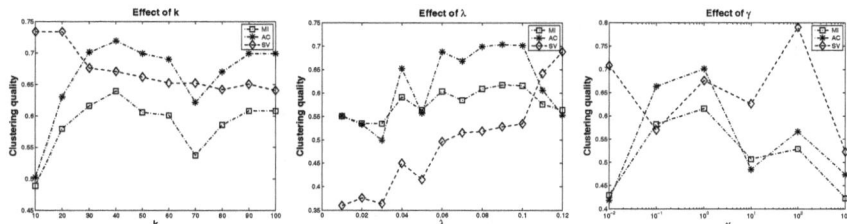

Fig. 2. Impact of Parameters

4.5 Impact of Parameters

We investigate the impact of different parameters in this section, including the number of anchor services (i.e., k), and the two penalty parameters (i.e., λ and γ). We vary one of these three parameters while keeping the other two fixed at their default values. Figure 2 shows how different parameters affect the clustering quality in **Dataset_1**.

Accuracy and mutual information always vary in a similar way with the changes of parameters. Both accuracy and mutual information reach their respective highest values when $k = 40, \lambda = 0.1$, and $\gamma = 1$, respectively. The silhouette value, on the other hand, varies differently with accuracy and mutual information. First, the SV value decreases as k increases. Recall that in SFR, services are clustered based on their relationships with the anchor services. The sparsity constraint forces services to be only related to a small subset of the anchor services. Therefore, when k is small, the sparse representation of a service will "concentrate" on a small number of anchor services. This will lead to very compact and cohesive clusters. Therefore, SV will decrease as k increases. Similar explanation is applied to the impact of λ, which enforces the sparsity constraint. Increasing λ will make $\mathbf{z}_i$'s more sparse, which has the effect of moving services closer to the relevant anchor services and further away from less relevant ones. This will also produce more cohesive clusters. Therefore, SV increases as λ increases. Instead of monotonically decreasing or increasing as with the increase of k and λ, the SV value reaches it peak value when γ is 100 and then decreases when γ increases further. In contrast, accuracy and mutual information reach their peak values when $\gamma = 1$. The discrepancy may be due to that the domain definition of the service set is not in line with the cohesiveness of the service clusters. For example, some services may be cross-domain in nature but assigned to a domain that is inconsistent with the clustering result.

The results on **Dataset_2** show very similar patterns as those of **Dataset_1** (in term of SV values because only SV values are reported for **Dataset_2**). Therefore, we skip the presentation of the results to avoid repetition.

5   Conclusion and Future Directions

We present Sparse Functional Representation (SFR), a novel service representation scheme, which is economical to store, efficient to process, and intuitive to interpret. SFR projects long and sparse term vectors onto an anchor service space, which consists of a small number of anchor services. The similarity between services is encoded by their proximity to the anchor services. The sparsity constraints enforce that each service is only related to a small subset of anchor services. This has the effect of moving services closer to the relevant anchor services and further away from irrelevant ones. These key features significantly facilitate large-scale service clustering. Comprehensive experiments on two real-world service datasets clearly demonstrate the effectiveness of SFR and its ability to scale to a large number of services. An interesting future direction is to further improve the construction performance of SFR. We plan to apply the recently developed low-rank approximation techniques, such as Colibri [14], to filter nearly duplicate or linearly dependent term vectors from the service matrix $\mathbf{X}$. Low-rank approximation allows SFR to work on a much smaller service matrix, from which anchor services are expected to be discovered more efficiently.

References

1. Bose, A., Nayak, R., Bruza, P.: Improving Web Service Discovery by Using Semantic Models. In: Bailey, J., Maier, D., Schewe, K.-D., Thalheim, B., Wang, X.S. (eds.) WISE 2008. LNCS, vol. 5175, pp. 366–380. Springer, Heidelberg (2008)
2. Cai, D., He, X., Han, J.: Document clustering using locality preserving indexing. IEEE Trans. Knowl. Data Eng. 17(12), 1624–1637 (2005)
3. Chen, L., Hu, L., Zheng, Z., Wu, J., Yin, J., Li, Y., Deng, S.: WTCluster: Utilizing Tags for Web Services Clustering. In: Kappel, G., Maamar, Z., Motahari-Nezhad, H.R. (eds.) ICSOC 2011. LNCS, vol. 7084, pp. 204–218. Springer, Heidelberg (2011)
4. Ding, C.H.Q., Li, T., Peng, W., Park, H.: Orthogonal nonnegative matrix t-factorizations for clustering. In: KDD, pp. 126–135 (2006)
5. Dong, X., Halevy, A., Madhavan, J., Nemes, E., Zhang, J.: Similarity search for web services. In: VLDB 2004: Proceedings of the Thirtieth International Conference on Very Large Data Bases, pp. 372–383. VLDB Endowment (2004)
6. Elgazzar, K., Hassan, A.E., Martin, P.: Clustering wsdl documents to bootstrap the discovery of web services. In: ICWS, pp. 147–154 (2010)
7. Klusch, M., Fries, B., Sycara, K.: Automated semantic web service discovery with owls-mx. In: AAMAS, pp. 915–922. ACM, New York (2006)
8. Lee, H., Battle, A., Raina, R., Ng, A.Y.: Efficient sparse coding algorithms. In: NIPS, pp. 801–808 (2006)
9. Liu, F., Shi, Y., Yu, J., Wang, T., Wu, J.: Measuring similarity of web services based on WSDL. In: ICWS, pp. 155–162 (2010)
10. Liu, X., Huang, G., Mei, H.: Discovering homogeneous web service community in the user-centric web environment. IEEE T. Services Computing 2(2), 167–181 (2009)
11. Lovasz, L.: Matching Theory (North-Holland mathematics studies). Elsevier Science Ltd. (1986)
12. Ma, J., Zhang, Y., He, J.: Efficiently finding web services using a clustering semantic approach. In: CSSSIA 2008: Proceedings of the 2008 International Workshop on Context Enabled Source and Service Selection, Integration and Adaptation, pp. 1–8. ACM, New York (2008)
13. Segev, A., Sheng, Q.Z.: Bootstrapping ontologies for web services. IEEE Transactions on Services Computing 5, 33–44 (2012)

14. Tong, H., Papadimitriou, S., Sun, J., Yu, P.S., Faloutsos, C.: Colibri: fast mining of large static and dynamic graphs. In: KDD, pp. 686–694 (2008)
15. Xu, W., Liu, X., Gong, Y.: Document clustering based on non-negative matrix factorization. In: Proceedings of the 26th Annual International ACM SIGIR Conference on Research and Development in Informaion Retrieval, SIGIR 2003, pp. 267–273. ACM, New York (2003)
16. Yu, Q.: Place Semantics into Context: Service Community Discovery from the WSDL Corpus. In: Kappel, G., Maamar, Z., Motahari-Nezhad, H.R. (eds.) ICSOC 2011. LNCS, vol. 7084, pp. 188–203. Springer, Heidelberg (2011)
17. Yu, Q., Rege, M.: On service community learning: A co-clustering approach. In: ICWS, pp. 283–290 (2010)
18. Zhang, Y., Zheng, Z., Lyu, M.R.: Wsexpress: A qos-aware search engine for web services. In: ICWS, pp. 91–98 (2010)
19. Zheng, M., Bu, J., Chen, C., Wang, C., Zhang, L., Qiu, G., Cai, D.: Graph regularized sparse coding for image representation. IEEE Transactions on Image Processing 20(5), 1327–1336 (2011)

Updatable Process Views for User-Centered Adaption of Large Process Models

Jens Kolb, Klaus Kammerer, and Manfred Reichert

Institute of Databases and Information Systems
Ulm University, Germany
{jens.kolb,klaus.kammerer,manfred.reichert}@uni-ulm.de
http://www.uni-ulm.de/dbis

Abstract. The increasing adoption of process-aware information systems (PAISs) has resulted in large process model collections. To support users having different perspectives on these processes and related data, a PAIS should provide personalized views on process models. Existing PAISs, however, do not provide mechanisms for creating or even changing such process views. Especially, changing process models is a frequent use case in PAISs due to changing needs or unplanned situations. While process views have been used as abstractions for visualizing large process models, no work exists on how to change process models based on respective views. This paper presents an approach for changing large process models through updates of corresponding process views, while ensuring up-to-dateness and consistency of all other process views on the process model changed. Respective update operations can be applied to a process view and corresponding changes be correctly propagated to the underlying process model. Furthermore, all other views related to this process model are then migrated to the new version of the process model as well. Overall, our view framework enables domain experts to evolve large process models over time based on appropriate model abstractions.

1 Introduction

Process-aware information systems (PAISs) provide support for business processes at the operational level. A PAIS strictly separates process logic from application code, relying on explicit *process models*. This enables a separation of concerns, which is a well established principle in computer science to increase maintainability and to reduce costs of change [1]. The increasing adoption of PAISs has resulted in large process model collections. In turn, each process model may refer to different domains, organizational units and user groups, and comprise dozens or even hundreds of activities [2]. Usually, the different user groups need customized views on the process models relevant for them, enabling a personalized process abstraction and visualization [3]. For example, managers rather prefer an abstract process overview, whereas process participants need a detailed view of the process parts they are involved in. Hence, providing personalized process views is a much needed PAIS feature. Several approaches for

C. Liu et al. (Eds.): ICSOC 2012, LNCS 7636, pp. 484–498, 2012.

creating process model abstractions based on process views have been proposed [4,5,6]. However, these proposals focus on creating and visualizing views, but do not consider another fundamental aspect of modern PAISs: change and evolution [1,7]. More precisely, it is not possible to change a large process model through editing or updating one of its view-based abstractions. Hence, process changes must be directly applied to the core process model, which constitutes a complex as well as error-prone task for domain experts, particularly in connection with large process models. To overcome this limitation, in addition to view-based process abstractions, users should be allowed to change large process models through updating related process views.

In the *proView*[1] project, we address these challenges by not only supporting the creation and visualization of process views, but additionally providing change operations enabling users to modify a process model through updating a related process view. In this context, all other views associated with the changed process model are migrated to its new version as well. Besides view-based abstractions and changes, *proView* allows for alternative process model representations (e.g., tree-based, form-based, and diagram-based) as well as interaction techniques (e.g., gesture- vs. menu-based) [8,9,10]. Overall goal is to enable domain experts to "interact" with the (executable) process models they are involved in.

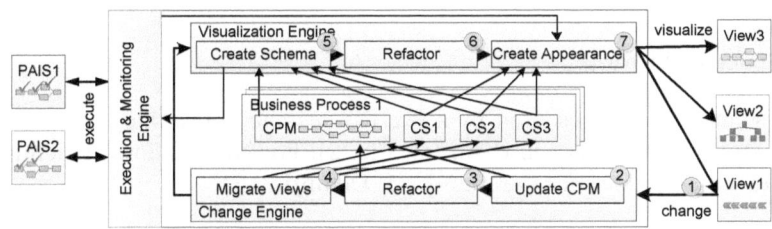

Fig. 1. The proView Framework

Fig. 1 gives an overview of the *proView* framework: A *business process* is captured and represented through a *Central Process Model (CPM)*. In addition, for a particular CPM, so-called *creation sets (CS)* are defined. Each creation set specifies the schema and appearance of a particular process view. For defining, visualizing, and updating process views, the *proView* framework provides engines for *visualization, change,* and *execution & monitoring.*

The *visualization engine* generates a process view based on a given CPM and the information maintained in a creation set CS, i.e., the CPM schema is transformed to the view schema by applying the corresponding *view creation operations* specified in CS (Step ⑤). Afterwards, the resulting view schema is *simplified* by applying well-defined *refactoring operations* (Step ⑥). Finally, Step ⑦ customizes the visual appearance of the view (e.g., creating a tree-, form-, or activity-based visualization [5,8]). Section 2 provides insights into these steps.

---

[1] http://www.dbis.info/proView

When a user updates a view schema, the *change engine* is triggered (Step
①). First, the view-based model change is propagated to the related CPM using
well-defined change propagation algorithms (Step ②). Next, the schema of the
CPM is simplified (Step ③), i.e., behaviour-preserving refactorings are applied
to foster model comprehensibility (e.g., by removing surrounding gateways not
needed anymore). Afterwards, the creation sets of all other views associated with
the CPM are migrated to the new CPM schema version (Step ④). This becomes
necessary since a creation set may be contradicting with the changed CPM
schema. Finally, all views are recreated (Steps ⑤-⑦) and presented to users.
Section 3 presents the view update operations and migration rules required to
change business processes through editing and updating process views. Section
4 then discusses related work and Section 5 summarizes the paper.

2   Fundamentals on Process View Creation

Section 2.1 defines the notion of *process model* and useful functions. Section
2.2 then discusses how *process views* can be created and formally represented
in *proView* (i.e., Step ⑤, Fig. 1). Section 2.3 introduces behaviour-preserving
process model refactorings enabling *lean* and *comprehensible* process views.

2.1   Process Model

A process model is represented by a *process schema* consisting of *process nodes*
and the *control flow* between them (cf. Fig. 2). For control flow modeling, *gateways* and *control flow edges* are used (cf. Definition 1).

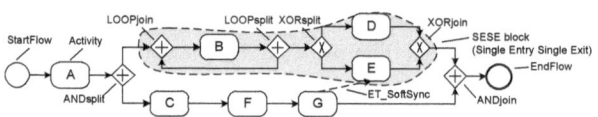

Fig. 2. Example of a Process Model

Definition 1 (Process Model). *A process model is defined as a tuple* $P =
(N, E, EC, NT, ET)$ *where*

- *N is a set of nodes (i.e., activities and gateways),*
- *$E \subset N \times N$ is a precedence relation ($e = (n_{src}, n_{dest}) \in E$ with $n_{src} \neq n_{dest}$),*
- *$EC : E \rightarrow Conds \cup \{\text{TRUE}\}$ assigns transition conditions to control edges,*
- *$NT : N \rightarrow \{StartFlow, EndFlow, Activity, ANDsplit, ANDjoin, XORsplit,
  XORjoin, LOOPsplit, LOOPjoin\}$ assigns a node type $NT(n)$ to each node $n \in
  N$; N is divided into disjoint sets of activity nodes A ($NT = Activity$) and gate-
  ways S ($NT \neq Activity$), i.e., $N = A \cup S$, and*
- *$ET : E \rightarrow \{ET\_Control, ET\_SoftSync, ET\_Loop\}$ assigns a type $ET(e)$ to each
  edge $e \in E$.*

Definition 1 can be used for representing the schemas of both the *Central Process Model (CPM)* and its associated *process views*. Note that this definition focuses on control flow. In particular, it can be applied to existing activity-oriented modeling languages, but is not restricted to a specific one. This paper uses BPMN as notation due to its widespread use. We further assume that a process schema is *well-structured*, i.e., sequences, branchings (of different semantics), and loops are specified as blocks with well-defined start and end nodes having the same gateway type. These blocks—also known as SESE blocks (cf. Definition 2)—may be arbitrarily nested, but must not overlap (like, e.g., blocks in BPEL). To increase expressiveness, *sync edges* are supported, which allow for a *cross-block* synchronization of parallel activities (as BPEL links do). For example, in Fig. 2, activity E must not be enabled before G is completed.

Definition 2 (SESE). *Let $P = (N, E, EC, NT, ET)$ be a process model and $X \subseteq N$ be a subset of activity nodes (i.e., $NT(n) = Activity$, $\forall n \in X$). Then: Subgraph P' induced by X is called* SESE *(Single Entry Single Exit) block iff P' is connected and has exactly one incoming and one outgoing edge connecting it with P. Further, let $(n_s, n_e) \equiv MinimalSESE(P, X)$ denote the start and end node of the minimum SESE comprising all activities from $X \subseteq N$.*

How to determine SESE blocks is described in [11]. Since we presume a well-structured process schema, a minimum SESE can be always determined.
To determine the predecessor and successor of a single node or SESE block within a process model $P = (N, E, EC, NT, ET)$, operations $n_p = pred(P, N')$ and $n_s = succ(P, N')$ with $N' \subseteq N$ are provided. Thereby n_p is the only node having exactly one outgoing edge $e_p = (n_p, n) \in E$, $n \in N'$. In turn, since N' represents a SESE, e_p is the only incoming edge of any node in N' connecting it with P. Similarly, $succ(P, N')$ returns the node directly succeeding set N'.

2.2   Process View Creation

To create a process view on a process model, the latter has to be *abstracted*. For this, *proView* provides *elementary view creation operations*. In turn, these may be combined to realize *high-level view creation operations* (e.g., *show all my activities and their precedence relation*) in order to support users in creating process views easily [12]. At the elementary level, two categories of operations are required: *reduction* and *aggregation*. An elementary *reduction* operation hides an activity of the original process model in the process view created. For example, operation $RedActivity(V, n)$ removes node n together with its incoming and outgoing edges, and inserts a new edge linking the predecessor of n with its successor in view V (cf. Fig. 3a). A formal definition can be found in [12,13].

An *aggregation* operation, in turn, takes a set of activities as input and combines them into an abstracted node in the process view. For example, operation $AggrSESE(V, N')$ removes all nodes of the SESE block, containing activities from set N' (including their edges), and inserts an abstract activity in the resulting process view instead (cf. Fig. 3b). Furthermore, elementary operation

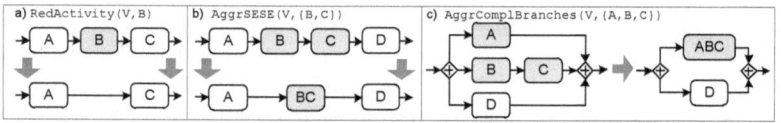

Fig. 3. Examples of Process View Creation Operations

AggrComplBranches(V, N′) aggregates complete branches of an XOR/AND block to a branch with one abstracted node. *N′* must contain the activities of these branches (i.e., activities between split and corresponding join gateway) that shall be replaced by a single branch with one aggregated node (cf. Fig. 3c). Generally, a process view can be created through the consecutive application of elementary operations on a process model. Remember that this process model represents a particular business process and is denoted as *Central Process Model (CPM)*. A particular CPM may have several associated views. Note that the presented view operations consider other process perspectives (e.g., data elements and data flow) as well; due to lack of space we omit further details.

Definition 3 (Process View). *Let CPM be a process model. A process view V(CPM) is described through a creation set $CS_V = (CPM, Op, PS)$ with:*

- *CPM $= (N, E, EC, NT, ET)$ is the process model underlying the view and denoted as Central Process Model,*
- *Op $= \langle Op_1, \ldots, Op_n \rangle$ is the sequence of elementary view creation operations applied to CPM: $Op_i \in \{RedActivity, AggrSESE, AggrComplBranches\}$,*
- *PS $= (PS_1, \ldots, PS_m)$ is a tuple of parameters and corresponding parameter values defined for a specific view.*

Definition 3 expresses that a process view can be created through the consecutive application of the operations contained in the corresponding creation set. In this context, configuration parameters (shortly: *parameter*) are required to describe how high-level operations shall be mapped to elementary view creation operations depending on the selected nodes in the CPM (see [12] for details). Section 3 will show that these parameters are required to enable automatic change propagation from a view to its underlying CPM.

A *view node n* either directly corresponds to node *n* of the CPM or it abstracts a set of CPM nodes. *CPMNode(V, n)* reflects this by returning either node *n* or a node set N_n of *CPM* $= (N, E, EC, NT, ET)$, depending on the creation set $CS_V = (CPM, Op, PS)$ with $Op = \langle Op_1, \ldots, Op_k \rangle$.

$$CPMNode(V, n) = \begin{cases} n & n \in N \\ N_n & \exists Op_i \in Op : N_n \xrightarrow{Op_i} n \end{cases}$$

2.3   Refactoring Operations

When creating process views, unnecessary control flow structures might result due to the generic nature of the view creation operations applied, e.g., single branches of a parallel branching might be empty or a parallel branching only

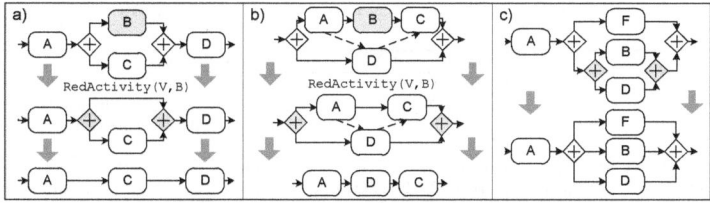

Fig. 4. Examples of View Refactoring Operations

have one remaining branch. In such cases, gateways can be removed in order to obtain a more comprehensible schema of the process view. For example, the view in Fig. 4a is created by reducing activity B. Afterwards, an AND block only surrounding activity C remains. In this case, the surrounding AND gateways can be removed without losing the predecessor/successor relations of the view activities (i.e., behaviour is preserved). Fig. 4b shows another example reducing activity B within a sequence. Afterwards, the synchronizing relationships become obsolete and hence can be removed. Fig. 4c shows an example of nested AND gateways which may be combined to simplify the model.

The *pro View* framework offers a set of operations for refactoring the schema of process views, without affecting the dependencies of activities within the view and hence without changing behavioural semantics [13].

3   Changing Processes through Updatable Process Views

Process views are not only required for enabling personalized process visualization through abstracting the underlying CPM. They also shall provide the basis for changing large process models based on appropriate abstractions. Section 3.1 describes how updates of a process view can be accomplished and then propagated to the underlying CPM. Section 3.2 presents migration rules for updating all other process views associated with the changed CPM as well.

3.1   Updating Process Views

When allowing users to change a business process model based on a personalized process view, it has to be ensured that this change can be automatically propagated to the underlying CPM without causing syntactical or semantical errors. Hence, well-defined view update operations are required guaranteeing for a proper propagation of view updates to the corresponding CPM. Table 1 gives an overview of the view update operations supported by *pro View.*

Propagating view changes to the underlying CPM is not straightforward. In certain cases, there might be ambiguities regarding the propagation of the view change to the underlying CPM. For example, it might not be possible to determine a unique position for inserting an activity in the CPM due to the abstractions applied when creating the view (cf. Fig. 5).

Consider the example from Fig. 5. Inserting activity Y in view $V1$ and propagating this change to the underlying CPM results in a unique insert position, i.e.,

Table 1. Update Operations for Process Views

Operation	Parameter & Value	Description
$InsertSerial(V, n_1, n_2, n_{new})$	InsertSerialMode = { **EARLY**, LATE, PARALLEL}	Inserts activity n_{new} between n_1 and n_2 in view V. The parameter describes the propagation behaviour of this insertion.
$InsertParallel(V, n_1, n_2, n_{new})$ $InsertCond(V, n_1, n_2, n_{new}, c)$ $InsertLoop(V, n_1, n_2, n_{new}, c)$	InsertBlockMode = { **EARLY_EARLY**, EARLY_LATE, LATE_EARLY, LATE_EARLY}	Inserts activity n_{new} as well as an AND/XOR/Loop block surrounding the SESE block defined by n_1 and n_2 in view V. The first (last) part of the parameter value before (after) the underline specifies the propagation behaviour of the split (join) gateway.
$InsertBranch(V, g_1, g_2, c)$	InsertBranchMode = { **EARLY**, LATE}	Inserts an empty branch between split gateway g_1 and join gateway g_2 in view V. In case of conditional branchings or loops, a condition c is required.
$InsertSyncEdge(V, n_1, n_2)$	-	Inserts a sync edge from n_1 to n_2 in V, where n_1 and n_2 belonging to different branches of a parallel branching.
$DeleteActivity(V, n_1)$	DeleteActivityMode = { **LOCAL**, GLOBAL}	Deletes activity n_1 in view V. The parameter decides whether the activity is deleted *locally* (i.e., reduced in the view) or removed from the CPM (i.e., *global*).
$DeleteBranch(V, g_1, g_2)$	-	Deletes an empty branch between gateways g_1 and g_2 in view V.
$DeleteSyncEdge(V, n_1, n_2)$	-	Deletes a sync edge between activities n_1 and n_2 in view V.
$DeleteBlock(V, g_1, g_2)$	DeleteBlockMode={ **INLINE**, DELETE}	Deletes an AND/XOR/Loop block enclosed by gateways g_1 and g_2 in view V. The parameter describes whether elements remaining in the block shall be *inlined* or *deleted*.

this view update can be automatically propagated to the CPM without need for resolving any ambiguity. By contrast, inserting activity X in view $V1$ allows for several insert positions in the related CPM. More precisely, there are ambiguities in how to transform the view change into a corresponding CPM change, i.e., X may be inserted directly after activity A or directly before activity C. Note that this ambiguity is a consequence of the reduction (i.e., deletion of B) applied when creating the view. However, when propagating view updates to a CPM, users should not be burdened with resolving such ambiguities. Hence, to enable automated propagation of view updates to a CPM, *proView* supports parameterizable propagation policies. Hereafter, we introduce parameterizable view update operations that can be configured differently to automatically propagate view updates to a CPM resolving ambiguities if required (cf. Table 1).

For example, consider view update operation *InsertSerial* in Fig. 5. Here, parameter *InsertSerialMode* defines whether X is inserted directly after A (i.e., *InsertSerialMode=EARLY*) or directly before C (i.e., *InsertSerialMode=LATE*). Each configuration parameter has a default value (printed in bold in Table 1), but can be set specifically for any view and stored in *parameter set PS* of creation set CS (cf. Section 2.2). We exemplarily provide algorithms for operations *InsertSerial* and *InsertParallel* to indicate how a view change can be transformed into a corresponding CPM change taking such parameterizations into account.

Table 2. View Update Operation: InsertSerial

Algorithm 1: InsertSerial(V, n_1, n_2, n_{new})
Pre $n_1' = last(CPMNode(V, n_1)), \ n_2' = first(CPMNode(V, n_2))$
Post $if(succ(CPM, n_1') == n_2')$ $\quad InsertNode(CPM, n_1', n_2', n_{new}, Activity)$ $\quad else \ switch(InsertSerialMode):$ $\quad\quad EARLY: InsertNode(CPM, n_1', succ(CPM, \{n_1'\}), n_{new}, Activity)$ $\quad\quad LATE: \ InsertNode(CPM, pred(CPM, \{n_2'\}), n_2', n_{new}, Activity)$ $\quad\quad PARALLEL: (n_s, n_j) = MinimalSESE(CPM, \{n_1', n_2'\})$ $\quad\quad\quad InsertNode(CPM, pred(CPM, \{n_s\}), n_s, g_s, ANDsplit)$ $\quad\quad\quad InsertNode(CPM, n_j, succ(CPM, \{n_j\}), g_j, ANDjoin)$ $\quad\quad\quad InsertEdge(CPM, g_s, g_j, ET\_Control)$ $\quad\quad\quad InsertNode(CPM, g_s, g_j, n_{new}, Activity)$ $\quad\quad\quad InsertEdge(CPM, n_1', n_{new}, ET\_SoftSync)$ $\quad\quad\quad InsertEdge(CPM, n_{new}, n_2', ET\_SoftSync)$

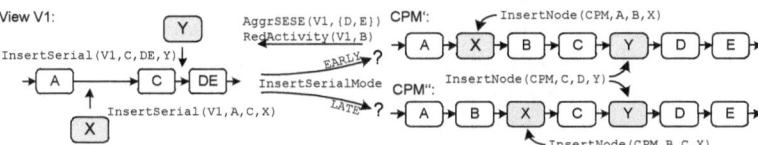

Fig. 5. Ambiguity when Propagating View Changes to the CPM

InsertSerial. As shown in Fig. 5, $InsertSerial(V, n_1, n_2, n_{new})$ adds an activity to the schema of process view V. Activity n_1 describes the node directly *preceding* and n_2 the node directly *succeeding* the activity n_{new} to be added to process view V. Algorithm 1 (cf. Table 2) shows how a view change described by operation *InsertSerial* can be transformed into a schema change of the related CPM. First of all, the nodes of the CPM corresponding to n_1 and n_2 are determined. If one of these nodes is an aggregated one, *CPMNode* returns a set of nodes. In this case, *first/last* returns the first/last node within this set (regarding control flow). When applying this change, it is checked whether nodes n_1' and n_2' (i.e., corresponding CPM nodes of n_1 and n_2) are direct neighbours. In this case, n_{new} can be directly inserted between these two nodes by applying the basic change operations *InsertNode* and *InsertEdge* to the CPM (cf. Table 3). In turn, if n_1' and n_2' are no direct neighbours in the CPM[2], it must be decided where to insert the activity, taking the value of parameter *InsertSerialMode* into account. As shown in Table 2, when setting this parameter to *EARLY*, the activity is directly inserted after n_1' (cf. Table 3). In turn, when choosing value *LATE*, it is inserted directly before n_2'. Finally, parameter value *PARALLEL* determines the minimum SESE block containing activities n_1' and n_2'. This is followed by adding an AND block surrounding the SESE block. The latter is accomplished by adding an *ANDsplit* and *ANDjoin* gateway as well as an empty branch between them. Finally, n_{new} is added to this empty branch. To ensure that the same

---

[2] e.g., when creating the view, the CPM might have been reduced by deleting activities or gateways due to refactorings of the view schema.

Table 3. Basic Process Model Change Operations

Algorithm 2: InsertNode(P, n_1, n_2, n_{new}, node_type)
Pre $succ(P, n_1) = n_2, \{n_1, n_2\} \subseteq N, P = (N, E, EC, NT, ET)$
Post $NT(n_{new}) = node\_type$
$\quad N' = N \cup \{n_{new}\}$
$\quad e_1 = (n_1, n_{new}), e_2 = (n_{new}, n_2)$ with $ET(e_1) = ET(e_2) = ET\_Control$
$\quad E' = E \setminus \{(n_1, n_2)\} \cup \{e_1, e_2\}$
Algorithm 3: InsertEdge(P, n_1, n_2, edge_type)
Pre $\{n_1, n_2\} \subseteq N, P = (N, E, EC, NT, ET)$
Post $e_{new} = (n_1, n_2), ET(e_{new}) = edge\_type$
$\quad E' = E \cup \{e_{new}\}$

precedence relations as for the process view are obeyed, sync edges from n_1' to n_{new} and from n_{new} to n_2' are inserted as well.

We now show that the transformation of a view update (as defined by *InsertSerial*) to a corresponding change of the underlying CPM, followed by the recreation of this view, results in the same view schema as one obtains when directly inserting this activity in the view. We consider this as a fundamental quality property of our view update propagation approach. For this purpose, we introduce the notion of *dependency set* (cf. Definition 4).

Definition 4 (Dependency Set). *Let* $P = (N, E, EC, NT, ET)$ *be a process model. Then:* $\mathbb{D}_P = \{(n_1, n_2) \in N \times N | n_1 \preceq n_2, NT(n_1) = NT(n_2) = Activity\}$ *is denoted as dependency set. It reflects all direct control flow dependencies between two activities.*

For example, the dependency set of the *CPM* depicted in Fig. 5 is $\mathbb{D}_{CPM'} = \{(A, X), (X, B), (B, C), (C, Y), (Y, D), (D, E)\}$.

Theorem *(InsertSerial Equivalence) Let CPM be a central process model and* $\mathbb{D}_{CPM}$ *be the corresponding dependency set. Further, let V be a view on CPM with creation set $CS_V = (CPM, Op, PS)$ and corresponding dependency set $\mathbb{D}_V$. Then: Inserting n_{new} in V can be realized by applying InsertSerial(V, n_1, n_3, n_{new}). Concerning the dependency set, propagating this change operation to the CPM results in the same view schema than one obtains when inserting n_{new} directly in V.*

As shown, *RedActivity* and related refactorings may cause ambiguities. Hence, their influence on the dependency set has to be discussed. Applying *RedActivity* (V, n_2) with $(n', n_2), (n_2, n'') \in E$ to a process schema with dependency set $\mathbb{D}$ results in $\mathbb{D}' = \mathbb{D} \setminus \{(n', n_2), (n_2, n'')\} \cup \{(n', n'')\}$, $n', n'' \in N$.

Proof: Inserting n_{new} directly in view V results in dependency set $\mathbb{D}_V' = \mathbb{D}_V \cup \{(n_1, n_{new}), (n_{new}, n_3)\} \setminus \{(n_1, n_3)\}$. When inserting n_{new} in the CPM, we have to distinguish four cases:

Case 1: No activity is reduced between n_1 and n_3, i.e., no parameter is required and $\mathbb{D}_{CPM}' = \mathbb{D}_{CPM} \cup \{(n_1, n_{new}), (n_{new}, n_3)\} \setminus \{(n_1, n_3)\} = \mathbb{D}_V'$.

Case 2-4: An activity (activity set) is reduced between n_1 and n_3, i.e., ambiguities occur and parameter *InsertSerialMode* becomes relevant.

Case 2: InsertSerialMode=EARLY results in $\mathbb{D}'_{CPM} = \mathbb{D}_{CPM} \cup \{(n_1, n_{new}), (n_{new}, n_2)\} \setminus \{(n_1, n_2)\}$ and $RedActivity(n_2) \in Op$ with $\{(n_1, n_2), (n_2, n_3)\} \subset \mathbb{D}_{CPM}$. Without loss of generality, we may assume that just one activity is reduced between n_1 and n_3. Next, view V is recreated with $RedActivity(n_2)$; this results in $\mathbb{D}'_V = \mathbb{D}'_{CPM} \setminus \{(n_{new}, n_2), (n_2, n_3)\} \cup \{(n_{new}, n_3)\} = \mathbb{D}_{CPM} \cup \{(n_1, n_{new}), (n_{new}, n_2)\} \setminus \{(n_1, n_2)\} \setminus \{(n_{new}, n_2), (n_2, n_3)\} \cup \{(n_{new}, n_3)\} = \mathbb{D}'_V$.

Case 3: InsertSerialMode=LATE: similar to EARLY, whereby n_{new} is inserted directly before n_3.

Case 4: InsertSerialMode=PARALLEL: results in $\mathbb{D}'_{CPM} = \mathbb{D}_{CPM} \cup \{(n_1, n_{new}), (n_{new}, n_3)\}$ and $RedActivity(n_2) \in Op$ with $\{(n_1, n_2), (n_2, n_3)\} \subset \mathbb{D}_{CPM}$. Next, V is recreated with $RedActivity(n_2)$; this results in $\mathbb{D}'_V = \mathbb{D}'_{CPM} \setminus \{(n_1, n_2), (n_2, n_3)\} \cup \{(n_1, n_3)\}$. At this point, the parallel branching is still remaining in the graph, i.e., one branch containing n_{new} and an empty branch due to reductions. Finally, refactorings remove unnecessary branchings: $\mathbb{D}'''_V = \mathbb{D}''_V \setminus \{(n_1, n_3)\} = \mathbb{D}'_V$.

InsertParallel. When inserting an activity in parallel to existing activities by applying *InsertParallel* to a view, again the transformation of this change to a corresponding CPM change might raise ambiguities regarding the positions the ANDsplit and ANDjoin gateways shall be inserted. Fig. 6a illustrates this. To deal with this ambiguity, parameter *InsertBlockMode* must be set. It allows configuring the positions at which the ANDsplit (i.e., $EARLY\_*$, $LATE\_*$) and ANDjoin respectively (i.e., $*\_EARLY$, $*\_LATE$) shall be inserted.

Table 4 provides a detailed view of the *InsertParallel* operation: n_1/n_2 denotes the start/end of the SESE block to which activity n_{new} shall be added in parallel. When transforming this view update to a corresponding CPM change, it must be decided where to add the ANDsplit and the ANDjoin gateways in

Table 4. View Update Operation: InsertParallel

Algorithm 4: InsertParallel(V, n_1, n_2, n_{new})
Pre (n_1, n_2) *is SESE in view V* $\quad n'_1 = last(CPMNode(V, n_1)),\ n'_2 = first(CPMNode(V, n_2))$
Post $if(pred(V, last(CPMNode(V, n_1)))! = last(CPMNode(V, pred(V, n_1))))$ $\quad switch(InsertBlockMode)$ $\quad\quad EARLY\_* : n'_1 = succ(CPM, CPMNode(V, pred(n_1)))$ $\quad\quad LATE\_* : \quad n'_1 = last(CPMNode(V, n_1))$ $\quad if(pred(V, last(CPMNode(V, n_2)))! = last(CPMNode(V, pred(V, n_2))))$ $\quad switch(InsertBlockMode)$ $\quad\quad *\_EARLY : n'_2 = first(CPMNode(V, n_2))$ $\quad\quad *\_LATE : \quad n'_2 = succ(CPM, CPMNode(V, pred(V, n_2)))$ $\quad (n_s, n_j) = MinimalSESE(CPM, \{n'_1, n'_2\})$ $\quad InsertNode(CPM, pred(CPM, \{n_s\}), n_s, g_s, ANDsplit)$ $\quad InsertNode(CPM, n_j, succ(CPM, \{n_j\}), g_j, ANDjoin)$ $\quad InsertEdge(CPM, g_s, g_j, ET\_Control)$ $\quad InsertNode(CPM, g_s, g_j, n_{new}, Activity)$

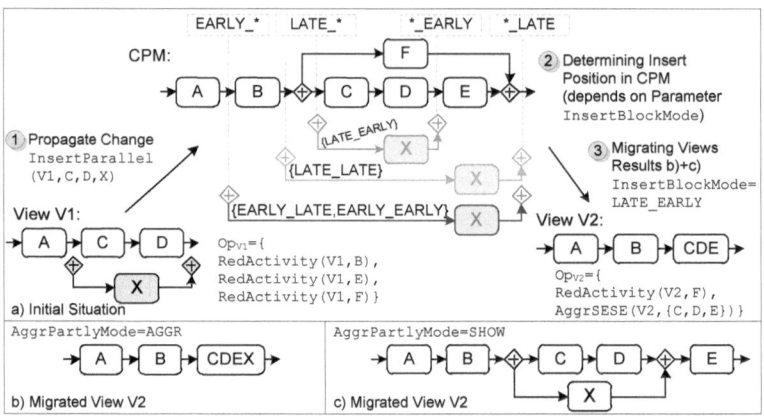

Fig. 6. Updating the CPM after a View Change

case of ambiguities. Regarding the ANDsplit, for example, it is checked whether the direct predecessor of n_1 in the CPM is the same as in view schema V. If this is not the case, parameter *InsertBlockMode* is used to decide whether to position the ANDsplit at the earliest or latest possible location in the CPM. The same procedure is applied in respect to the ANDjoin. After determining the corresponding insert positions in the CPM, a minimum SESE block is determined to properly insert the surrounding AND block with a branch containing n_{new}. Fig. 6a shows an example illustrating how different insert positions depending on the parameter value are chosen. Note that, independent of the concrete parameter value and insert position respectively, the user of view V always gets the same model when re-applying the view creation and refactoring operations on the CPM. Similar to *InsertParallel*, the propagation of a change expressed in terms of operations *InsertConditional* or *InsertLoop* can be accomplished. In addition to insert join/split gateways, branching condition c has to be set to guarantee proper process execution (cf. Table 1).

3.2   Migrating Process Views to a New CPM Version

When changing a CPM through updating one of its associated views, all other views defined on this CPM must be updated as well. More precisely, it must be guaranteed that all process views are up-to-date and hence users always interact with the current version of a process model and related views respectively. To ensure this, after propagating a view change to a CPM, the creation sets of all other process views must be migrated to the new CPM version (cf. Definition 3). Note that in certain cases this creation set will contradict to the CPM, e.g., an activity might be inserted in a branch, which is aggregated through an AggrComplBranches operation. In this case, the operation has to be adapted including the new activity. Table 5 provides *migration rules* required to migrate creation sets of associated views after updating the CPM.

Table 5. Process View Migration Rules

Migration Rule M1:
$\exists AggrSESE/AggrComplBranches(V, N_a) = Op_1 : N_a \supset \{pred(V, N_c), succ(V, N_c)\},\ Op_1 \in Op$
$\Rightarrow$ AggrComplMode=SHOW: $Op' = Op \setminus Op_1$
AggrComplMode=AGGR: $Op' = Op \setminus Op_1 \cup \{AggrSESE/AggrComplBranches(V, N_a \cup N_c)\}$
Migration Rule M2:
$\exists AggrSESE/AggrComplBranches(V, N_a) = Op_1 : pred(V, N_c) \in N_a \oplus succ(V, N_c) \in N_a$
$\Rightarrow$ AggrPartlyMode=SHOW: $Op' = Op \setminus Op_1$
AggrPartlyMode=AGGR: $Op' = Op \setminus Op_1 \cup \{AggrSESE/AggrComplBranches(V, N_a \cup N_c)\}$
Migration Rule M3:
$\exists RedActivity(V, pred(V, N_c))) = Op_1 \wedge RedActivity(V, succ(V, N_c)) = Op_2,\ Op \supset \{Op_1, Op_2\}$
$\Rightarrow$ RedComplMode=SHOW: no action required
RedComplMode=RED: $Op' = Op \cup Op_N,\ Op_N = \{n \in N_c | RedActivity(V, n)\}$
Migration Rule M4:
$\exists RedActivity(V, pred(V, N_c))) = Op_1 \oplus RedActivity(V, succ(V, N_c)) = Op_2,\ Op \supset \{Op_1, Op_2\}$
$\Rightarrow$ RedPartlyMode=SHOW: no action required
RedPartlyMode=RED: $Op' = Op \cup Op_N,\ Op_N = \{n \in N_c | RedActivity(V, n)\}$

Regarding migration rule *M1*, N_c denotes the set of nodes added to the CPM. If the direct predecessor and successor of this node set are both aggregated to the same abstract node (i.e., both are element of set N_a, which is aggregated through AggrSESE or AggrComplBranches), the migration rule will be applied. In this case, there exist two options: either node set N_c is included in the aggregation or this aggregation is removed and the change is shown to the user. This can be expressed by parameter *AggrComplMode* for each view: parameter value *SHOW* suggests removing the aggregation operations in the creation set, while value *AGGR* (default) extends the aggregated node set by the new nodes in N_c. If only one of the nodes (i.e., the predecessor or successor of N_c) is included in an aggregation, migration rule *M2* is applied. In this case, parameter *AggrPartlyMode* expresses whether the aggregation shall be expanded (i.e., *AGGR*) or resolved (i.e., *SHOW*). Fig. 6bc present examples of this operation.

Migration rules *M3* and *M4* handle changes within reduced node sets. Analogous to the handling of aggregation operations, migration rule *M3* is applied if both the predecessor and successor of node set N_c are removed due to a reduction. In turn, *M4* is applied if exactly only one of these two nodes is reduced. In this case, parameter *RedComplMode* (or *RedPartlyMode*) and its values (*SHOW* or *RED* (default)) determine whether node set N_c is visible or reduced in the view.

After migrating all creation sets belonging to a CPM, the corresponding views are recreated (cf. Fig. 1). Applying a change to the CPM and recreating the process views afterwards allows us to guarantee that all views are up-to-date.

Since the recreation of a process view is expensive, several optimization techniques are applied. First, instead of recreating all process views, this is only accomplished for those views affected by the change. Second, when changing the creation set, the visualization engine exactly knows which parts of the process view have changed and respective parts are then recreated.

4   Related Work

In the context of cross-organizational processes, views have been applied for creating abstractions of partner processes hiding private process parts [6,14,15,16].

However, process views are manually specified by the process designer, but do not serve as abstractions for changing large process models as in *proView*.

An approach providing predefined process view types (i.e., human tasks, collaboration views) is presented in [4]. As opposed to *proView*, this approach is limited to these pre-specified process view types. In particular, these views are not used as abstractions enabling process change. In turn, [17] applies graph reduction techniques to verify structural properties of process schemas. The *proView* project accomplishes this by enabling aggregations that use high-level operations. In [18] SPQR-tree decomposition is applied when abstracting process models. This approach neither takes other process perspectives (e.g., data flow) nor process changes into account.

The approach presented in [19] determines semantic similarity between activities by analyzing the schema of a process model. The similarity discovered is used to abstract the process model. However, this approach neither distinguishes between different user perspectives on a process model nor provides concepts for manually creating process views.

An approach for creating aggregated process views is described in [20]. It proposes a two-phase procedure for aggregating parts of a process model not to be exposed to the public. However, process view updates to evolve or adapt processes are not considered.

View models serving monitoring purpose are presented in [21,22]. Focus is on the run-time mapping between process instances and views. Further, the views have to be pre-specified manually by the designer.

In turn, [23] aligns technical workflows with business processes. It allows detecting changes through behavioural profiles and propagating them to change regions of the corresponding technical model. These regions indicate the schema region to which the change belongs. Automatic propagation is not supported. Similarly, [24] describes a mapping model between a technical workflow and a business process. An automatic propagation of changes is not supported.

For defining and changing process models, various approaches exist. [25] presents an overview of frequently used patterns for changing process models. Further, [7] summarizes approaches enabling flexibility in PAISs. In particular, [26] presents an approach for adapting well-structured process models without affecting their correctness properties. Based on this, [27] presents concepts for optimizing process models over time and migrating running processes to new model versions properly. None of these approaches takes usability issues into account, i.e., no support for user-centered changes of business processes is provided.

The *proView* framework provides a holistic framework for personalized view creation. Further, it enables users to change business processes based on their views and guarantees that other views of the process model are adapted accordingly. None of the existing approaches covers all these aspects and is based on rigid constraints not taking practical requirements into account.

5   Conclusion

We introduced the *proView* framework and its formal foundation; *proView* supports the creation of personalized process views and the view-based change of business processes, i.e., process abstractions not only serve visualization purpose, but also lift process changes up to a higher semantical level. A set of update operations enables users to update their view and to propagate the respective schema change to the underlying process model representing the holistic view on the business process. Parameterization of these operations allows for automatically resolving ambiguities when propagating view changes; i.e., the change propagation behaviour can be customized for each view. Finally, we provide migration rules to update all other process views associated with a changed process model. Similar to the propagation, per view it can be decided how much information about the change should be displayed to the user.

The *proView* framework described in this paper is implemented as a client-server application to simultaneously edit process models based on views [28]. The implementation proves the applicability of our framework. Furthermore, user experiments based on the implementation are planned to test the hypothesis that view-based process changes improve the handling and evolution of large process models. Overall, we believe such view-based process updates offer promising perspectives to better involve process participants and domain experts in evolving their business processes.

References

1. Weber, B., Sadiq, S., Reichert, M.: Beyond Rigidity - Dynamic Process Lifecycle Support: A Survey on Dynamic Changes in Process-Aware Information Systems. Computer Science - Research and Development 23(2), 47–65 (2009)
2. Weber, B., Reichert, M., Mendling, J., Reijers, H.A.: Refactoring Large Process Model Repositories. Computers in Industry 62(5), 467–486 (2011)
3. Streit, A., Pham, B., Brown, R.: Visualization Support for Managing Large Business Process Specifications. In: van der Aalst, W.M.P., Benatallah, B., Casati, F., Curbera, F. (eds.) BPM 2005. LNCS, vol. 3649, pp. 205–219. Springer, Heidelberg (2005)
4. Tran, H.: View-Based and Model-Driven Approach for Process-Driven, Service-Oriented Architectures. TU Wien, Dissertation (2009)
5. Bobrik, R., Bauer, T., Reichert, M.: Proviado – Personalized and Configurable Visualizations of Business Processes. In: Bauknecht, K., Pröll, B., Werthner, H. (eds.) EC-Web 2006. LNCS, vol. 4082, pp. 61–71. Springer, Heidelberg (2006)
6. Chiu, D.K., Cheung, S., Till, S., Karlapalem, K., Li, Q., Kafeza, E.: Workflow View Driven Cross-Organizational Interoperability in a Web Service Environment. Information Technology and Management 5(3/4), 221–250 (2004)
7. Reichert, M., Weber, B.: Enabling Flexibility in Process-aware Information Systems - Challenges, Methods, Technologies. Springer (2012)
8. Kolb, J., Reichert, M., Weber, B.: Using Concurrent Task Trees for Stakeholder-centered Modeling and Visualization of Business Processes. In: Oppl, S., Fleischmann, A. (eds.) S-BPM ONE 2012. CCIS, vol. 284, pp. 237–251. Springer, Heidelberg (2012)
9. Kolb, J., Rudner, B., Reichert, M.: Towards Gesture-based Process Modeling on Multi-Touch Devices. In: Proc. 1st Int'l Workshop on Human-Centric Process-Aware Information Systems (HC-PAIS 2012), Gdansk, Poland, pp. 280–293 (2012)

10. Kolb, J., Hübner, P., Reichert, M.: Automatically Generating and Updating User Interface Components in Process-Aware Information Systems. In: Proc. 10th Int'l Conf. on Cooperative Information Systems (CoopIS 2012) (to appear, 2012)
11. Johnson, R., Pearson, D., Pingali, K.: Finding Regions Fast: Single Entry Single Exit and Control Regions in Linear Time. In: Proc. Conf. on Programming Language Design and Implementation (ACM SIGPLAN 1994) (1993)
12. Reichert, M., Kolb, J., Bobrik, R., Bauer, T.: Enabling Personalized Visualization of Large Business Processes through Parameterizable Views. In: Proc. 26th Symposium on Applied Computing (SAC 2012), Riva del Garda (Trento), Italy (2012)
13. Bobrik, R., Reichert, M., Bauer, T.: View-Based Process Visualization. In: Alonso, G., Dadam, P., Rosemann, M. (eds.) BPM 2007. LNCS, vol. 4714, pp. 88–95. Springer, Heidelberg (2007)
14. Chebbi, I., Dustdar, S., Tata, S.: The View-based Approach to Dynamic Inter-Organizational Workflow Cooperation. Data & Know. Eng. 56(2), 139–173 (2006)
15. Kafeza, E., Chiu, D.K.W., Kafeza, I.: View-Based Contracts in an E-Service Cross-Organizational Workflow Environment. In: Casati, F., Georgakopoulos, D., Shan, M.-C. (eds.) TES 2001. LNCS, vol. 2193, pp. 74–88. Springer, Heidelberg (2001)
16. Schulz, K.A., Orlowska, M.E.: Facilitating Cross-Organisational Workflows with a Workflow View Approach. Data & Knowledge Engineering 51(1), 109–147 (2004)
17. Sadiq, W., Orlowska, M.E.: Analyzing Process Models Using Graph Reduction Techniques. Information Systems 25(2), 117–134 (2000)
18. Polyvyanyy, A., Smirnov, S., Weske, M.: The Triconnected Abstraction of Process Models. In: Dayal, U., Eder, J., Koehler, J., Reijers, H.A. (eds.) BPM 2009. LNCS, vol. 5701, pp. 229–244. Springer, Heidelberg (2009)
19. Smirnov, S., Reijers, H.A., Weske, M.: A Semantic Approach for Business Process Model Abstraction. In: Mouratidis, H., Rolland, C. (eds.) CAiSE 2011. LNCS, vol. 6741, pp. 497–511. Springer, Heidelberg (2011)
20. Eshuis, R., Grefen, P.: Constructing Customized Process Views. Data & Knowledge Engineering 64(2) (2008)
21. Shan, Z., Yang, Y., Li, Q., Luo, Y., Peng, Z.: A Light-Weighted Approach to Workflow View Implementation. In: Zhou, X., Li, J., Shen, H.T., Kitsuregawa, M., Zhang, Y. (eds.) APWeb 2006. LNCS, vol. 3841, pp. 1059–1070. Springer, Heidelberg (2006)
22. Schumm, D., Latuske, G., Leymann, F., Mietzner, R., Scheibler, T.: State Propagation for Business Process Monitoring on Different Levels of Abstraction. In: Proc. 19th ECIS, Number Ecis, Helsinki, Finland (2011)
23. Weidlich, M., Weske, M., Mendling, J.: Change Propagation in Process Models using Behavioural Profiles. In: Proc. 6th IEEE Int'l Conf. Services Comp., pp. 33–40 (2009)
24. Buchwald, S., Bauer, T., Reichert, M.: Bridging the Gap Between Business Process Models and Service Composition Specifications. In: Service Life Cycle Tools and Technologies: Methods, Trends and Advances, pp. 124–153. IGI Global (2011)
25. Weber, B., Reichert, M., Rinderle, S.: Change Patterns and Change Support Features - Enhancing Flexibility in Process-Aware Information Systems. Data & Knowledge Engineering 66(3), 438–466 (2008)
26. Reichert, M., Dadam, P.: ADEPTflex - Supporting Dynamic Changes of Workflows Without Losing Control. Journal of Intelligent Inf. Sys. 10(2), 93–129 (1998)
27. Rinderle, S., Reichert, M., Dadam, P.: Flexible Support of Team Processes by Adaptive Workflow Systems. Distributed and Par. Databases 16(1), 91–116 (2004)
28. Kolb, J., Kammerer, K., Reichert, M.: Updatable Process Views for Adapting Large Process Models: The proView Demonstrator. In: Proc. of the Business Process Management 2012 Demonstration Track, Tallinn, Estonia (to appear, 2012)

Management-Based License Discovery for the Cloud

Minkyong Kim, Han Chen, Jonathan Munson, and Hui Lei

IBM T.J. Watson Research Center, 19 Skyline Drive, Hawthorne, NY 10532
{minkyong,chenhan,jpmunson,hlei}@us.ibm.com

Abstract. Enterprise software is typically licensed through contracts that require organizations to monitor their own usage of the software and purchase the number or amount of licenses required by the vendor's terms and conditions for that software. Vendors reserve the right to audit an organization's use of their software, and if an organization is under-licensed, costly back-payments may be required. For this reason, organizations go to great expense to maintain a complete and accurate inventory of their software so that they know their license obligations. The cloud, as an environment offering both greater flexibility in, and a higher degree of control over, an enterprise's computing infrastructure, presents both new challenges for license compliance as well as new opportunities. In this paper, we introduce a new approach to producing accurate software inventories based on capturing the knowledge that is present in cloud management systems at the time of software provisioning and installation. We also demonstrate new capabilities for rule-based alerting and enforcement that are made possible by our approach.

1 Introduction

Enterprise software is typically licensed through contracts that require organizations to monitor their own usage of the software and purchase the number of licenses required by the vendor's terms and conditions for that software. Vendors reserve the right to audit an organization's use of their software, and if an organization is under-licensed, costly back-payments may be required, in addition to civil fines and legal fees. Recently, one software vendor demanded $9 million in back payments [6]. In addition to the vendors themselves, organizations such as the Business Software Alliance police this space, with many lawsuits resulting in $11 and $13 million settlements [10].

To protect themselves from such incidents, organizations may employ a variety of tools, including license management tools that enable them to keep track of the licenses they have purchased, as well as scanning tools that scan the computers on their network for software and generate reports describing what software is installed. These reports are then used to determine what licenses are required. This technology has inherent limitations, which we describe below, and as a result, much manual effort is required to ensure the organization is compliant.

The cloud, as an environment offering both greater flexibility in, and a higher degree of control over, an enterprise's computing infrastructure, presents both new challenges for license compliance as well as new opportunities. The level of automation that clouds provide enables application deployers to provision and deprovision virtual machines (VMs) quickly, and stop them and start them even more quickly. These dynamics are

C. Liu et al. (Eds.): ICSOC 2012, LNCS 7636, pp. 499–506, 2012.

not well-matched with current scanning technology, which relies on machines being idle and available on a regular schedule.

However, the same automated management of infrastructure that presents challenges also provides an opportunity to dramatically change the way software discovery is performed. Software instances are created through machine provisioning and software installation, which, in a modern cloud environment, can be performed under automated control. During such operations, the information needed to determine required licensing—precise software identifiers, characteristics of the VMs, on which the software will run, even the purposes to which the software is being put—are knowable.

In this paper, we describe a new approach to license management for cloud environments, based on our experience with both public clouds and enterprise license management. We present a Management-based License Discovery (MLD) system that taps into a cloud's infrastructure management processes to automatically discover license usage and support the license compliance process. We also demonstrate new capabilities for rule-based alerting and enforcement that are made possible by our approach. We present the architecture of MLD and its interaction with other components in the cloud. We describe the implementation of the prototype of the system briefly. We will then discuss the user interface (at the web font-end) in detail; this provides visualization of our system's capabilities.

2 Background

The problem of determining what an enterprise's license obligations are is surprisingly complex. A large enterprise may have hundreds of thousands of software instances to account for, and the license required for any given instance may be determined by many factors, including not only the characteristics of the machine on which the software is installed, but also what other software it may be a component of, what contract this particular instance was purchased under, and what purpose this instance is used for (e.g., production or test).

The first part of this license compliance process is to generate a complete and accurate software inventory, annotated with the various factors above. This is called *software discovery*. In conventional infrastructures this is normally performed by agent-based computer scanning tools that are guided by a catalog of software "signatures"—fingerprints, as it were, that indicate if a particular software is installed. Signatures may be based on what files are present, or may be based on what processes are running.

The discovery process reports the precise software version installed as well as the characteristics of the machine it is installed on (number of cores, clock speed, RAM, etc.). It may also attempt to make certain judgments that are designed to avoid over-counting. One of these is that, when multiple instances of a single software "family" (e.g. Adobe Acrobat; Reader and Pro) are identified, only one will be reported. The definition of a family is determined by the software catalog guiding the discovery.

The discovery technology may also attempt to determine (if the discovery catalog is sufficiently rich) whether a software instance is part of a larger software installation. Many IBM products contain within them middleware products such as an application server and a database server. Normally, these products are licensed separately, but when bundled as components, they do not require separate licenses. Because bundle relationships cannot be known simply based on knowledge of disk or process-table contents, scanning tools will only suggest them.

In the last phase of the discovery step, the software inventory is checked and additional information is added to it (e.g., whether an instance is used for production or test). This phase is typically labor-intensive and depends on knowledge and data held by the IT staff responsible for software asset management. It typically consists of: identifying any software instances that were reported but for which there is no corresponding machine (software orphans); identifying machine instances for which there is no reported software (machine orphans); removing software instances that are the result of known identification problems; confirming probable bundles identified by the scanning tools; identifying known bundles that the scanning tools cannot detect; applying the results of software-specific tools or scripts that identify instances that were missed or correct identifications that were incomplete.

3   Motivation

Scanning-based discovery has several drawbacks, especially when it is used in a self-service, rapid provisioning Infrastructure-as-a-Service (IaaS) cloud environment. One is that it puts a high burden on the host computer. The time it takes to finish the scanning process is directly proportional to the storage volume size, unless we make the assumption about standard software installation locations, but this assumption increases the risk of missed discovery. Although CPU resource consumption may be limited in modern multicore computers, the impact on disk I/O bandwidth can be significant, which could lead to potentially adverse performance impact on the actual workload. This is especially true in a cloud computing environment, where disks are virtualized and multiple virtual machines share a limited number of physical disk spindles on the hypervisor.

Due to the high overhead mentioned above, the scanning can typically only be scheduled at a relatively low frequency, for example, once a week or even once a month. The rapid provisioning nature of cloud means that many workloads can be relatively short lived and thus may be missed entirely by the periodic scans.

Scanning technology is only as accurate as the discovery catalog is complete and up-to-date. New software products or versions can be missed if they are not first cataloged. Complex software products such as databases have many editions and optional features, and it is difficult for scanning technology to identify which editions are installed and which features are in use. These, however, may strongly affect licensing.

Once the list of software products has been discovered, the inventory needs to go through a manual process to be ready for the next step, *reconciliation*. License reconciliation is the process of matching each software instance that requires a license with a license owned by the enterprise, and ensuring that there are a sufficient number of licenses, or license units, owned. Although this manual step is necessitated in part by the accuracy problems inherent in scanning technology, it is also used to add licensing-relevant information beyond what scanning can provide, such as what contract software was purchased under; whether it is used in production, or test, or development; whether it is used as on a primary node or only in backup capacity; or whether it is used in a client or a server capacity.

4   Management-Based License Discovery

As discussed in Section 2, in the last phase of software discovery, the enterprise applies, in a labor-intensive process, its knowledge of the context of the software in its inventory, such as bundle relationships, contracts, and the kind of workloads served by the software. In this section, we describe Management-based License Discovery (MLD) wherein this kind of knowledge is encoded in structures that are accessed in the management system workflows that are used to provision VM images and install software bundles. In this way, an accurate software inventory may be maintained at all times. MLD also maintains data on the licenses an enterprise owns, and is thus able to offer services such as warning when an under-licensing situation may exist. Because the system is integrated with the cloud management system, it has access to not only the image and bundle catalogs, telling it what software is included in each image and bundle, but also has the knowledge of the characteristics of each virtual machine, and so can generate the software inventory records completely and accurately using this information. It therefore avoids all the issues that scanning technology has in a cloud deployment.

4.1   Design

To tack the license usage, users need to provide the information on the licenses that they own. This information typically includes software name, software version, license types, license dates, etc. Users also need to specify whether the licenses can be applied at the general software level or at the specific version level.

Through the license management web front-end, users can specify a set of rules. There are pre-action rules that are applied before the service action is executed and the post-action rules that are applied after the action has been taken. One of the important pre-action rules is whether to *enforce* the license compliance or to *inform* the status of the license usage. If a user chooses the enforcement option, the user must own the required licenses in order for the action (such as provisioning or installation) to succeed.

The post-action rules include those related to alerts. Users can specify under what condition they want to receive an alert message. For example, a rule can be if the current usage reaches 90% or above of the licenses that a user owns, send an alert message to a specific e-mail account.

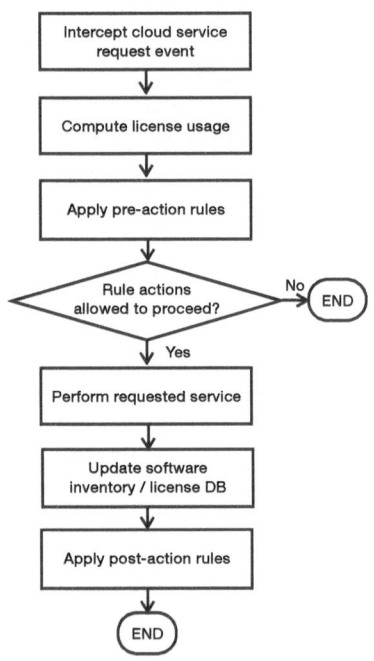

Fig. 1. MLD main flow

In addition to pre-action and post-action rules, there are other rules associated with the events that are not triggered by individual service request. For example, report generation is triggered periodically by a timer. Users can specify the period at which the reports should be generated and the level of details that reports should include.

Once the rules are defined, the license manager is ready to update license usage upon the arrival of cloud service requests. As the cloud service requests arrive through the web-based front-end, our license management engine taps into these events and computes the license usage. Our license manager can either enforce the license compliance or only detect the potential problems and generate warnings. In case of enforcement, the license manager will see whether the user owns appropriate licenses to proceed with the action. If the user indeed has the required license, the cloud management layer will execute the action. Once the action completes successfully, our license manager updates the software inventory and the license DB. The last step is to check whether there are post-action rules such as sending the alerts based on the current license usage. Figure 1 shows the main flow of the license manager as the individual cloud service request arrives at the system.

4.2 Persisted Data

There are three main sets of data that need to be persisted for license management: information on available licenses, rules and license usage. In our prototype system, we use IBM DB2 to persist our data. Here are the three data sets: First, MLD keeps track of the licenses that users own. The information on each license includes the details on the software, effective dates, and license type. Second, MLD persists the rules that users enter through the web front-end. A rule is typically associated with an account (user) and has the start and end dates, during which it is affective. The rules include those describing the condition for alerts and the period for generating reports. Third, MLD persists license usage information by tracking the software instances that are running. Information for each software instance includes the start and end time of the software instance, ID of VM instance that contains this software instance and license type. Whenever a cloud service event changes the number of running software instances, MLD updates the number of required licenses and generates alerts based on the alert rules. Beside these three main sets of data, MLD also persists alert messages in database and generated reports in the file system, with the link to the file system location in database.

4.3 Interaction with the Other Components in Cloud

MLD assumes that certain information can be retrieved from the existing cloud components. When a provisioning request arrives at the cloud, it typically contains VM image ID, but does not contain the list of software components that come with the VM image. We assume that the cloud has the meta-data that describes the list of software components in VM images. Our current prototype has been tested for IBM SmartCloud Enterprise (SCE) [5] environment, in which a meta-data file (called *topology* file) in the XML format lists the software components in VM images.

After a VM instance has been started, users can install additional software. We assume that users go through the management process to do so. When software components are installed in the form of software *bundle*, which consists of multiple software components, the list of software components again can be retrieved from the exiting cloud components. We assume that given the software bundle ID, MLD can easily retrieve this information.

5   Prototype

We have implemented a prototype system of MLD on IBM's SCE [5], an IaaS cloud offering. MLD receives the events from the cloud management layer that are relevant to software license management, including VM provisioning, VM deprovisioning, software bundle installation and uninstallation. In addition to license discovery, the system also implements additional value-added services, such as visualization, usage alerts and reports. The account administrator accesses the system via a Web-based user interface. Once logged in, the administrator has access to three main sections of the application: Dashboard, Limits and Reports.

Dashboard. The dashboard page provides a high level overview of software license usage. After the administrator enters a query date range in the query section and clicks the "Go" button, the section below is refreshed to show an *overview table*. Each row represents a single software product, the type (e.g., PVU, Cores, MIPs) of license that is applied to it, the entitlement value and the peak usage value during the query range.

From the *overview table*, the administrator can click on a particular product and obtain a *detailed view* of all VM instances that are alive during the query range (Figure 2), which explains the license usage value that is presented in the *overview table*. At the bottom of this *detailed view* page, we also present a graphic visualization of the license consumption, with time as x-axis and licenses as y-axis (Figure 3). The administrator also has the ability to save the query result as a report, which will be described later.

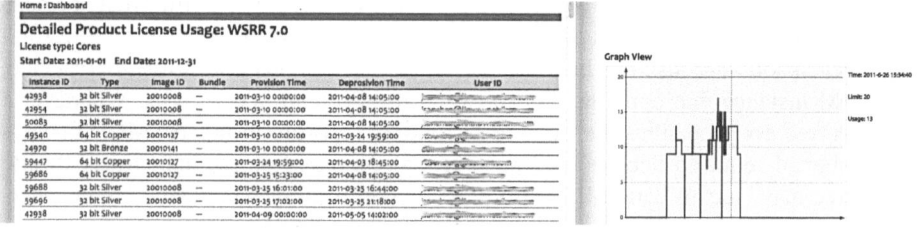

Fig. 2. Prototype: Per-software Detailed View   **Fig. 3.** License Usage

Limits. The second main section of the application is the Limits and Alerts page. Each row in the table represents a single software product. By clicking on the hot links in the license type and entitlement columns, an administrator can configure the license type and entitlement value for the selected software product. The entitlement values are used by an alert rule engine that can generate notification e-mails based on current license consumption situation with respect to its configured limit.

By clicking on the "Edit alert rules" link from the page, the administrator can manage the alert rules for his account. An alert rule consists of condition (above, below, equal), threshold (expressed as a percentage of the entitlement value), message severity, notification e-mail address, and the set of software products to which it is applied. After an alert rule is applied to a software product, its license consumption value is monitored by the system. When the test condition is met, for example, usage is over 95% of the entitlement value, a notification e-mail is sent to the pre-configured e-mail address in the alert rule, so that the responsible stakeholder can take appropriate actions.

Reports. The third main section of the application contains a list of all archived reports for the account. There are two ways to generate reports. First, an administrator can manually create a report based on the query result obtained from the dashboard page. Second, reports can be generated automatically according to rules. The administrator can manage the report generation rules in a separate page accessible from the main report page. A report generation rule specifies the frequency of the generation (daily, monthly, quarterly), start date, and time of date at which the report is to be created.

Users can choose the level of details that the report should include. A typical report contains the maximum number of software instances that were running for each software product during the period that the report includes and the number of licenses that the user owns for each product. It may also include alert messages that are generated during the corresponding reporting period.

Once a report is created, it is listed in the main report list. The administrator can download the report as an XML format for further downstream process or as a PDF format for human viewing. After reviewing the report content, the administrator has the option to sign the report with additional comments for audit and compliance purposes.

6   Related Work

There has been a limited amount of work on license management within the research community. To best of our knowledge, our work is the first to address how automation of license discovery can be achieved in a managed cloud environment.

One approach for automating license management is to develop a model to capture the business process and license requirements. Giblin *et al.* [3] developed a meta-model that can capture free-form passages describing the license requirements and regulations. Liu *et al.* [8] presented a modeling method for both business process and compliance rules. Once both are presented as models, process models can be verified against compliance rules by means of model-checking technology, which is automated. This thread of work is orthogonal to our work in management-based discovery but can complement it by providing information in a semantic-rich, machine-friendly manner. However, our approach does not require a model, as we implicitly collect semantically-rich information by tapping into the management process.

There have been some efforts on managing license compliance for free and open source software development. Gangadharan *et al.* [2] presents a way to implement clauses of open source software license in a machine interpretable way and describes a novel algorithm that analyzes compatibility between multiple free and open source licenses. Another example that shows developers' interest in license terms of open source software is Google's Advanced Search [4], which provides an option of filtering out search according to the different degrees of license obligations (e.g., "free to use or share," "free to use, share, or modify").

There are some less relevant efforts, but still consider licenses. LASS [1] presents a service selection problem with the license specification as one of the factors during the selection process. There have been other papers [7,9] on service selection, but these do not consider the license specification. While these papers focus on the service selection, the focus of our paper is license management.

7   Conclusion and Future Work

License management is an important problem in the enterprise world, as the costs of non-compliance are severely high. Avoiding these penalties has been a costly process for enterprises. The scanning-based approach has well known drawbacks, and the labor necessary to prepare software inventories for license reconciliation is extensive.

In this paper, we presented management-based license discovery (MLD), which takes advantage of a cloud's managed environment. MLD taps into a cloud's infrastructure management processes to automatically discover license usage and support the license compliance process. We also demonstrated new capabilities for rule-based alerting and enforcement that are made possible by our approach. We presented our initial prototype that has been intended for IBM's SCE. We believe that our automated system can significantly reduce the cost of license management.

While we believe that our prototype system demonstrates the value of our management-based discovery approach, we are aware that it does not fully address all the requirements an enterprise may have for preparing an inventory for license reconciliation. There is a need to capture the usage context of software, such as whether an instance is used in development or production. However, the precise context that matters may differ from enterprise to enterprise. We need to be able to allow the enterprise to indicate which context attributes should be captured when software is installed, and to extend the standard software inventory with those attributes. We are now extending our system in order to do that.

References

1. Gangadharan, G.R., Comerio, M., Truong, H.-L., D'Andrea, V., De Paoli, F., Dustdar, S.: LASS – License Aware Service Selection: Methodology and Framework. In: Bouguettaya, A., Krueger, I., Margaria, T. (eds.) ICSOC 2008. LNCS, vol. 5364, pp. 607–613. Springer, Heidelberg (2008)
2. Gangadharan, G., D'Andrea, V., Paoli, S., Weiss, M.: Managing license compliance in free and open source software development. Information Systems Frontiers 14, 143–154 (2012)
3. Giblin, C., Muller, S., Pfitzmann, B.: From regulatory policies to event monitoring rules: Towards model driven compliance automation. Technical report
4. Google. Advanced Search, http://www.google.com/advanced_search?hl=en
5. IBM. IBM Smart Cloud, http://www.ibm.com/cloud-computing/us/en/
6. Kanaracus, C.: SAP, Rent-a-Center in Battle Over Millions in Fees. CIO (2011), http://www.cio.com/article/686832/SAP_Rent_a_Center_in_Battle_Over_Millions_in_Fees
7. Lamparter, S., Ankolekar, A., Studer, R.: Preference-based selection of highly configurable web services. In: Proc. of the 16th Int. World Wide Web Conference, pp. 1013–1022. ACM Press (2007)
8. Liu, Y., Muller, S., Xu, K.: A static compliance-checking framework for business process models. IBM Systems Journal 46(2), 335–361 (2007)
9. Reiff-Marganiec, S., Yu, H.Q., Tilly, M.: Service Selection Based on Non-functional Properties. In: Di Nitto, E., Ripeanu, M. (eds.) ICSOC 2007. LNCS, vol. 4907, pp. 128–138. Springer, Heidelberg (2009)
10. Rosenberg, S.D.: Software License Compliance: Myth vs. Reality. E-Commerce Times (2008), http://www.ecommercetimes.com/story/64465.html

Ensuring Well-Formed Conversations between Control and Operational Behaviors of Web Services

Scott Bourne, Claudia Szabo, and Quan Z. Sheng

School of Computer Science
The University of Adelaide, SA 5005, Australia
{scott.bourne,claudia.szabo,michael.sheng}@adelaide.edu.au

Abstract. Despite a decade's active research and development, Web services still remain undependable. Designing effective approaches for highly dependable Web service provisioning has therefore become of paramount importance. Our previous work proposes a novel model that separates the service behavior into operational and control behaviors for flexible design, development, and verification of complex Web services. In this paper, we further this research with a set of conversation rules to facilitate the verification of rich conversations between control and operational behaviors. The rules are specified as temporal logic formulas to formally check rich conversation patterns. The proposed approach is realized using state-of-the-art technologies and experiments show its feasibility and benefits.

1 Introduction

Web services have been the focus of active research in the past decade [1–4]. Unfortunately, techniques on Web services design and deployment have not fully matured yet. Recent statistics show that only 28,600 Web services exist on the Web[1], and many have serious issues such as timeout, dependability and unexpected behavior, due to market pressures that require ad-hoc deployment without proper quality assurance. An important challenge remains verifying the soundness and completeness of a Web service at *design time*. This permits developers to identify major design flaws before costly development and will further the quality of the developed Web service [3, 5, 6].

Towards the verification of Web services at design time, our earlier work has proposed a novel model that separates the service behavior into *control* and *operational* behaviors, allowing for flexible design, development, and verification of complex Web services [3]. The control behavior guides the execution of the system and maintains a transactional state, while the operational behavior defines the underlying business logic. The conversation between control and operational behavior is formed by messages that direct the operational behavior and report events to the control behavior. The verification of the Web service can be

---

[1] http://webservices.seekda.com

C. Liu et al. (Eds.): ICSOC 2012, LNCS 7636, pp. 507–515, 2012.

thus translated into verifying that the control and operational behavior contain conversations that are well-formed.

In this paper, we define well-formed conversations between our proposed operational and control behaviors as conversations that start and end properly and for which several syntactic and semantic properties are met. This provides high flexibility and facilitates the definition and validation of rich conversations between operational and control behavior, at design time, before the Web service is developed. In particular, we propose to ensure well-formed conversations between control and operational behavior by defining a set of *conversation rules*, which ensure that (i) a conversation starts and ends correctly, and (ii) sequences of message exchange that may lead to deadlock and other undesired properties are not permitted. The main contributions of our work are as follows:

- A set of conversation rules to facilitate the verification of complex Web services.
- A service verification approach based on model checking that extracts temporal logic properties from a set of pre-defined rules.
- A prototype implementation that extends our existing set of tools with a conversation verifier to facilitate the automated verification of Web service design.

The remainder of this paper is organized as follows. Section 2 presents an overview of our Web service model for separating operational and control behaviors. Section 3 presents the conversation rules. We show how these rules are transformed to LTL properties in Section 4 and present an example in Section 5. Finally, we discuss related work and conlude in Section 6.

2   Background

In this section, we briefly overview our Web service behavior model presented in [3]. Our model enables a richer description of Web services by abstracting and separating a Web service's behavior into control and operational behaviors. The control behavior is an application-independent model of the state of the Web service from a transactional point of view, while the operational behavior represents the business logic that underpins the functionalities of the service. The execution of the operational behavior is guided by the control behavior, while events in the operational behavior influence the actions taken by the control behavior. Interested readers are referred to [3] for more details of this model.

We model the service behaviors using statecharts [7]. Figure 1(a) and (b) show the control and operational behavior models of WeatherWS, a weather information retrieval service. The operational behavior states are given meaningful names to reflect the underlying operations.

To enable inter-behavior communication, we propose a set of *message types*. These message types are classified as *initiation* messages and *outcome* messages. Initiation messages are sent from the control behavior for the purpose of directing the operational behavior, while outcome messages are replies that indicate the

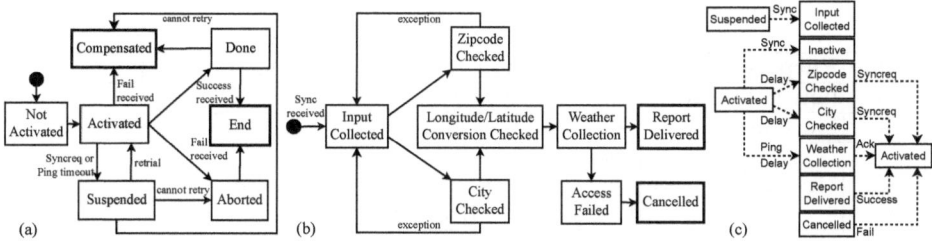

Fig. 1. Control (a) and operational behavior (b) of WeatherWS, with interactions (c).

current state of the operational behavior. The set of initiation messages include Sync, Delay, and Ping. Sync is used to trigger the execution of the operational behavior, Delay forces a response following an unacceptable delay, and Ping tests the liveness of an operational behavior state, triggering a timeout situation when no acknowledgement is received. Our outcome messages include Success, Fail, Syncreq, and Ack. Success and Fail indicate the commitment or abortion of the service. Syncreq requests another Sync to attempt forward recovery following an internal failure. Ack is used to respond to Ping and confirm the liveness of a state. The intra-behavior transition labels in Figure 1(c) shows the inter-behavior messages required for WeatherWS, while their effect is shown in (a) and (b).

However, guidance is still needed to produce a set of messages that ensure reliable and semantically correct conversations. We propose a set of rules to apply to behavior conversations to serve this purpose, as detailed in the following sections.

3   Conversation Rules

Our message types form conversations describing the execution of a Web service. However, there is a potential for invalid sequences, deadlocking situations, or incomplete sessions. We propose a list of conversation rules to ensure that behavior conversations are *well-formed*. We define well-formed conversations as sequences of messages that are correct, free of deadlock, and express the behavior of a service from invocation to termination. Our conversation rules specify correct sequences of message types, and ensure that a service is invoked and terminated correctly.

3.1   Conversation Sessions

Our proposed conversation rules apply to sequences of inter-behavior messages called *conversation sessions*. A conversation session is the ordered sequence of inter-behavior messages sent from the invocation of a service until both behaviors reach a termination state, i.e. the End or Compensated state in the control behavior.

A conversation session can be defined as a sequence of message types of length n. Each message is expressed as $m(t)$ where $m \in [Sync, Success, Fail, Syncreq, Delay, Ping, Ack]$ and t denotes the order such that $t \in [1, ..., n]$. For example:

Table 1. Conversation Rules

Name	Purpose	Conversation Rule
CR1	Initial Message	$\exists m \in [Sync], m(1)$
CR2	Final Messages	$\exists m \in [Success, Fail, Ping, Syncreq], m(n-1)$
CR3	Message Sequence	$\forall m_i \in [Sync, Ack],$ $\exists m_j \in [Success, Fail, Delay, Syncreq, Ping],$ $\forall t \in [0, ..., n-1], m_i(t) \Rightarrow m_j(t+1)$
CR4	Message Sequence	$\forall t \in [0, ..., n-1],$ $\exists m \in [Sync, Syncreq, Delay, Ping, Ack], m(t)$
CR5	Message Sequence	$\forall t \in [0, ..., n-2], Syncreq(t) \Rightarrow Sync(t+1)$
CR6	Message Sequence	$\exists m_j \in [Success, Fail, Syncreq],$ $\forall t \in [0, ..., n-1], Delay(t) \Rightarrow m_j(t+1)$
CR7	Message Sequence	$\exists m_j \in [Sync, Ack], \forall t \in [0, ..., n-1], Ping(t) \Rightarrow m_j(t+1)$
CR8	Message Sequence	$\forall m_i \in [Sync, Success, Fail, Ack, Delay, Syncreq],$ $\exists m_j \in [Sync, Success, Fail, Syncreq, Delay, Ping],$ $\forall t \in [0, ..., n-1], m_i(t) \Rightarrow m_j(t+1)$

- `Sync(1).Syncreq(2).Sync(3).Fail(4)` is a *well-formed* conversation session. It expresses a complete and deadlock-free execution of the service where each message logically follows the previous.

However, a lack of rules to ensure well-formed conversation sessions can lead to deadlocking states or incomplete sessions.

- `Sync(1).Syncreq(2).Delay(3)` is a deadlocking conversation session. The operational behavior is waiting for a `Sync` message before if can continue, while the control behavior is suspended until it receives a reply to `Delay`.
- `Sync(1).Ping(2).Ack(3).Ping(4).Ack(5)` is an incomplete conversation session, as the execution of the service has not fully terminated.

3.2   Conversation Rule Formalisms

We propose a set of conversation rules to enforce completeness of conversation sessions and logical message sequences, as shown in Table 1. The message sequence rules can be expressed as a series of `if-then` conditions as follows:

$$\forall m_i \in \mathcal{I}, \exists m_j \in \mathcal{J}, \forall t \in \mathcal{T}, m_i(t) \Rightarrow m_j(t+1)$$

where $\mathcal{I}, \mathcal{J} \subseteq [Sync, Success, Fail, Syncreq, Delay, Ping, Ack]$ and $\mathcal{T} \subseteq [1, ..., n-1]$. The set $\mathcal{I}$ identifies a set of message types, and $\mathcal{J}$ defines those that can immediately follow. This revises the formula presented in [3] by allowing rules to apply to several message types.

Rule CR1 specifies that all conversation sessions must begin with `Sync`, and CR2 defines the valid final messages for conversation sessions, ensuring that the control behavior does not enter a termination state before the operational behavior has completed. `Ping` can be the final message of a conversation session following an unrecoverable time-out, while `Syncreq` can be the final message when another `Sync` message cannot be sent (such as once a retrial limit has been exceeded).

Rule CR3 defines the set of valid messages to follow a `Sync` or `Ack` message. Once either of these message types are received, the operational behavior begins or resumes execution until completion or encountering a problem. This rule ensures that the control behavior does not send additional `Sync` messages while the operational behavior is executing.

Rule CR4 prevents the incorrect use of `Success` and `Fail` by specifying they cannot be used before the final message of the conversation session.

Rules CR5 and CR6 refer to messages that follow `Syncreq` and `Delay` messages respectively. A `Syncreq` message must only be replied with a `Sync` message (therefore it is impossible for `Syncreq` to be sent at $n - 1$, as a session cannot end with `Sync`). Similarly, a `Delay` message must be immediately followed by a `Success`, `Fail` or `Syncreq` message.

Rule CR7 indicates that only a `Sync` or `Ack` message may follow a `Ping` message. We recall that when a `Ping` message is sent, either an `Ack` message is returned to confirm the liveness of an operational state, or a time-out situation occurs. In the case of a time-out, a `Sync` message can be sent to retry the process. This rule prevents sequences such as `Ping(t).Success(t+1)`, where the operational behavior has completed successfully, but the control behavior is still waiting for an acknowledgement and cannot proceed. Rule CR8 is also needed to ensure that `Ack` can only follow `Ping`.

The conversation rules also imply other desirable properties, such as preventing the same message type to be sent consecutively, and ensuring every `Sync` message eventually receives an outcome message (`Success`, `Fail` or `Syncreq`), excepting a time-out. By defining initial messages, final messages, and valid message sequences, our proposed rules set can ensure complete and correct conversation sessions.

4 From Conversation Rules to Temporal Logic

To formally verify a service design against our conversation rules, we explore the use of model checking [8] to ensure conformance to pre-defined temporal properties describing our proposed rules. We use Linear Temporal Logic (LTL) [9] for this purpose. LTL expresses properties of a system model over a linear and discrete timeline by using *temporal operators* over model variables.

While our conversation rules can be applied to a simple sequence of message types, the LTL properties must apply to a complete service model. This poses two challenges when producing LTL transformations. Firstly, the complexity of the service model can cause state delays between certain inter-behavior messages. Secondly, there is a need to extract the state of the conversation session from the service model. To address these issues, the LTL properties consider potential message delays where appropriate and use a set of proposed conversation variables.

Table 2. Conditions for Message Processing

Message	Processed Condition
Sync	The operational behavior begins or resumes execution.
Success, Fail	The control state transitions from the Activated state.
Syncreq	A Sync message is sent in reply or a termination state is entered.
Delay	A Success, Fail or Delay message is sent in reply.
Ping	An Ack message is sent in reply.
Ack	Automatically processed in the following state.

Table 3. LTL Transformations of Conversation Rules

CR1	$(IM = nil \wedge OM = nil) \cup (IM = Sync \wedge IP = FALSE \wedge OM = nil)$
CR2	$\Box((((IM = Sync \vee IM = Delay) \wedge IP = FALSE) \vee (OM = Ack \wedge OP = FALSE))$ $\rightarrow \Diamond((OM \neq Ack \wedge OP = FALSE) \vee (IM \neq Sync \wedge IM \neq Delay \wedge IP = FALSE)))$
CR3	$\Box(((IM = Sync \wedge IP = FALSE) \vee (OM = Ack \wedge OP = FALSE))$ $\rightarrow \bigcirc ((IP = TRUE \wedge OP = TRUE) \vee$ $((IP = FALSE \wedge (IM = Ping \vee IM = Delay)) \vee$ $(OP = FALSE \wedge (OM = Success \vee OM = Fail \vee OM = Syncreq)))))$
CR4	$\Box((OM = Success) \rightarrow \bigcirc (OM = Success \wedge OP = TRUE \wedge IP = TRUE))$ $\Box((OM = Fail) \rightarrow \bigcirc (OM = Fail \wedge OP = TRUE \wedge IP = TRUE))$
CR5	$\Box((OM = Syncreq \rightarrow \bigcirc(OM = Syncreq \wedge OP = TRUE \wedge IP = TRUE)) \vee$ $((OM = Syncreq \wedge OP = FALSE) \rightarrow \bigcirc((OM = Syncreq \wedge OP = FALSE) \vee$ $(OP = TRUE \wedge IM = Sync \wedge IP = FALSE))))$
CR6	$\Box((IM = Delay \wedge IP = FALSE) \rightarrow \bigcirc((IP = Delay \wedge IP = FALSE \wedge OP = TRUE) \vee$ $(IP = TRUE \wedge OP = FALSE \wedge (OM = Fail \vee OM = Success \vee OM = Syncreq))))$
CR7	$\Box((IM = Ping \wedge IP = FALSE)$ $\rightarrow \bigcirc ((IP = FALSE \wedge OP = TRUE \wedge (IM = Sync \vee IM = Ping)) \vee$ $(OM = Ack \wedge OP = FALSE \wedge IP = TRUE)))$
CR8	$\Box((OM = Ack \wedge OP = FALSE) \rightarrow (IM = Ping \wedge IP = TRUE))$ $\Box((OP = FALSE) \rightarrow \bigcirc \neg(OM = Ack \wedge OP = FALSE))$

The LTL transformations of our conversation rules utilize temporal operators over four proposed variables to express the conversational state. Initiation and outcome message are denoted by the variables IM and OM respectively. Both variables are initialized at nil. We also propose two boolean variables, IP and OP to indicate when their corresponding message is active or processed. Their values are set to FALSE upon sending and TRUE after processing. The processing conditions for each message type is shown in Table 2. We employ the following operators over these conversation variables: $\bigcirc$ for the next state, $\Diamond$ for at least one future state, $\Box$ for all states, and $\cup$ for one property to hold until another is met.

Table 3 shows the LTL transformations of the conversation rules. The transformations of some rules, CR1 and CR4, are straightforward. We enforce CR2 by ensuring at least one valid final message always follows a non-final message.

Delays of several states can potentially occur following `Sync`, `Ping`, `Syncreq`, and `Ack`. Therefore, the transformations of rules CR3, CR5, CR6 and CR7 allow unchanged conversational states as one valid *next* state. Rule CR8 requires two LTL properties to express; one to ensure that `Ping` is the initiation message to precede `Ack`, and another to prevent outcome messages between `Ping` and `Ack`.

These LTL properties can be used to verify a complex service designed as control and operational behaviors, by ensuring it only produces well-formed conversation sessions. A service design can be checked against the rules by creating a model that contains our message variables and using a model checking tool to verify that none of the rules are violated.

5   System Implementation and Validation

We implemented the approach proposed in this paper by extending our existing prototype system for the design and verification of Web services. Our system is implemented in Java and uses state-of the art technologies such as XML, SOAP, WSDL, and model checking. Users can access the system via the user interface shown in Figure 2, to compose, verify and execute complex services as interacting control and operational behaviors. The NuSMV model checker [10] is used to verify service designs within this system. The prototype enables a service design to be transformed into the input language of NuSMV, and then verified for conformance to the LTL transformations of our conversation rules. The prototype is an extension of the system in [3].

To evaluate our proposed approach, we conducted experiments using the implemented prototype and the WeatherWS example shown in Figure 1. The control behavior, operational behavior, and inter-behavior conversations were modeled in SMV, the input language of NuSMV. We applied the NuSMV model

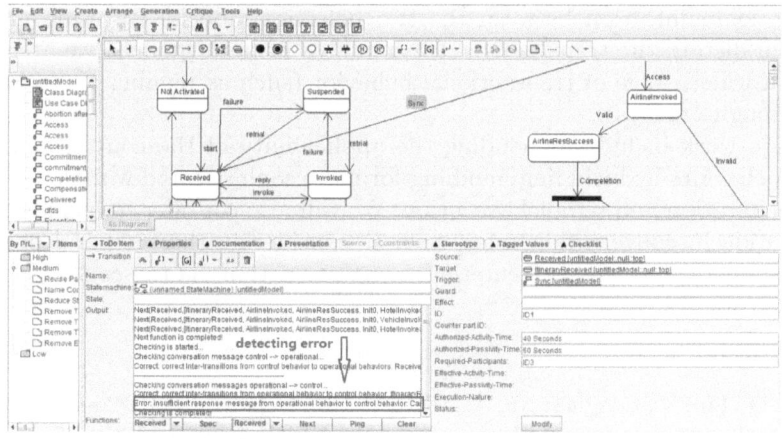

Fig. 2. Specifying Service Behaviors

checker to verify that the conversational behavior of this model does not violate any of the LTL properties produced in Section 4. We verified ten testcases with artificially introduced errors. If any of the properties are violated by the model, NuSMV produces a state sequence that leads to the contradiction. Our SMV transformation of WeatherWS as it appears in Figure 1 satisfied the set of conversation rules.

6 Discussion and Conclusion

The verification of Web service behavior remains an important challenge despite active research and development over the last decade. Our work facilitates the flexible verification of Web services at design time by modeling Web service behavior as a conversation between an operational behavior that defines the underlying business logic of the system, and an application-independent control behavior that guides the execution of the operational behavior. We propose a set of conversation rules that are specified as temporal properties and verify using a model checker.

Most existing work on Web service conversation modeling has focused on the interactions between a deployed service and a client. Technical specifications have been proposed to express the conversational requirements of a complex service as part of an interface [4, 11]. In contrast, we apply temporal logic and model checking to ensure that all possible conversations follow a set of rules for correctness and completeness. In a similar effort, Kova et al. [12] study the mapping between the control and operational behaviors and also propose to verify the conversations using LTL properties and the NuSMV model checker. In their approach, the behaviors are merged into a single model that express the possible flow of control states. Model checking is used to verify that the transitions between operational states do not violate transitions defined in the control behavior model. Our work differs by defining message types and rules for the communication between the two behavior models. By using messages that can dictate the transitions between states in both models, we are able to model a wider range of transactional behavior (such as pinging operations and responding to delays).

Future work includes expanding the applicability of the control and operational behaviors by including handling for more sophisticated workflow patterns such as iteration and parallel execution. We will also consider to include context information in conversation rules, such as considering the temporal properties of failed operations when attempting corrective action via the control behavior.

References

1. Yu, Q., Liu, X., Bouguettaya, A., Medjahed, B.: Deploying and Managing Web Services: Issues, Solutions, and Directions. The VLDB Journal 17(3), 537–572 (2008)
2. Vieria, M., Laranjeiro, N., Madeira, H.: Benchmarking the Robustness of Web Services. In: Proceedings of the 13th International Symposium on Pacific Rim Dependable Computing (2007)

3. Sheng, Q., Maamar, Z., Yahyaoui, H., Bentahar, J., Boukadi, K.: Separating Operational and Control Behaviors: A New Approach to Web Services Modeling. IEEE Internet Computing 14(3), 68–76 (2010)
4. Benatallah, B., Casati, F., Toumani, F.: Web Service Conversation Modeling: A Cornerstone for E-Business Automation. IEEE Internet Computing 8(1) (2004)
5. Bhiri, S., Perrin, O., Godart, C.: Ensuring Required Failure Atomicity of Composite Web Services. In: Proceedings of the 14th International World Wide Web Conference, pp. 138–147. ACM (2005)
6. Liu, A., Li, Q., Huang, L., Xiao, M.: FACTS: A Framework for Fault-tolerant Composition of Transactional Web Services. IEEE Transactions on Services Computing 3(1), 46–59 (2010)
7. Harel, D., Naamad, A.: The STATEMATE Semantics of Statecharts. ACM Transactions on Software Engineering and Methodology 5(4), 293–333 (1996)
8. Clarke, E.M.: Model Checking. In: Ramesh, S., Sivakumar, G. (eds.) FST TCS 1997. LNCS, vol. 1346, pp. 54–56. Springer, Heidelberg (1997)
9. Emerson, E.: Temporal and Modal Logic. In: Handbook of Theoretical Computer Science, vol. 2, pp. 995–1072 (1990)
10. Cimatti, A., Clarke, E., Giunchiglia, E., Giunchiglia, F., Pistore, M., Roveri, M., Sebastiani, R., Tacchella, A.: NuSMV 2: An OpenSource Tool for Symbolic Model Checking. In: Brinksma, E., Larsen, K.G. (eds.) CAV 2002. LNCS, vol. 2404, pp. 359–364. Springer, Heidelberg (2002)
11. Ardissono, L., Goy, A., Petrone, G.: Enabling Conversations with Web Services. In: Proceedings of the Second International Joint Conference on Autonomous Agents and Multiagent Systems, pp. 819–826. ACM (2003)
12. Kova, M., Bentahar, J., Maamar, Z., Yahyaoui, H.: A Formal Verification Approach of Conversations in Composite Web Services using NuSMV. In: Proceedings of the Conference on New Trends in Software Methodologies, Tools and Techniques, pp. 245–261. IOS Press (2009)

Variability in Service-Oriented Systems: An Analysis of Existing Approaches

Holger Eichelberger, Christian Kröher, and Klaus Schmid

Software Systems Engineering, University of Hildesheim
Marienburger Platz 22, 31141 Hildesheim, Germany
{eichelberger,kroeher,schmid}@sse.uni-hildesheim.de

Abstract. In service-oriented systems services can be easily reused and shared without modification. However, there are business situations where a variation of services is needed to meet the requirements of a specific customer or context. Variation of software systems has been well researched in product line engineering in terms of Variability Implementation Techniques (VITs). While most VITs focus on the customization of traditional software systems, several VITs have been developed for service-oriented systems. In this paper, we discuss the problem of service customization and provide an overview of different VITs for service variability. For this purpose, we will define four dimensions to describe, characterize and analyze existing VITs: the *technical core idea*, the *object of variation*, the *forms of variation*, and the *binding time*.

1 Introduction

Customization of software systems is current practice in industry to meet the requirements of customers in a qualitative and timely manner. The most frequent reasons for customization are: novel functionality [10], optimization for quality of service aspects [8], and seamless integration into existing infrastructures [5]. Companies face ever-increasing demands on customization due to growing numbers of requirements and rising complexity of software systems.

In Service-oriented Computing (SoC) a typical approach to satisfy varying requirements is to add, remove, or replace services. However, there are situations where the customization of existing services is needed. This could be realized by implementing a completely new variant of a service, but it is more appropriate from a business point of view to customize the service implementation as needed. This will lower the development effort and increase reusability. However, SoC does not provide for the customization of services in terms of tailoring individual aspects of a single service.

An industry best practice to achieve tailor-made systems with low effort and high quality are Software Product Line Engineering (SPLE) methods [9]. The key idea of SPLE with respect to customization is to focus on the differences (called *variabilities*) among similar systems instead of repeating the development. A *variability model* represents all variabilities on an abstract level (including constraints among them) and is used to derive a valid product configuration for instantiation. A *Variability Implementation Technique* (VIT) is an approach to realize variability according to a

C. Liu et al. (Eds.): ICSOC 2012, LNCS 7636, pp. 516–524, 2012.
© Springer-Verlag Berlin Heidelberg 2012

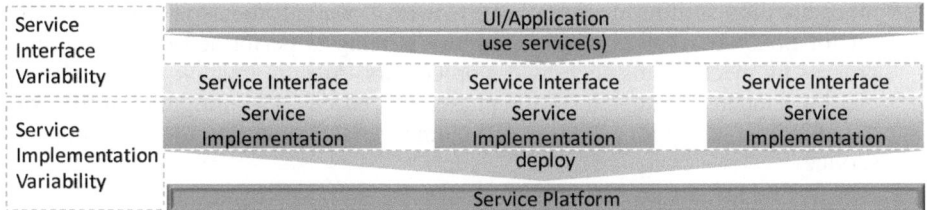

Fig. 1. The role of variability in services

configuration. As the problem of customization is also relevant for SoC, there is a need for approaches that integrate VITs with service-oriented technologies.

In this paper, we will provide a classification of VITs for SoC. The scope of this paper is on service variability including variability of interfaces and implementations. Other forms, like variabilities in business processes, service compositions, or service platforms are out of scope due to space restrictions.

The paper is organized as follows: in the next section, we detail the dimensions to analyze and characterize VITs. Section 3 will describe the approach of the literature study we carried out to identify VITs. The results of the analysis will be presented in Section 4. In Section 5, we will draw conclusions and point out future challenges.

2   Characterizing Variability Implementation

The combination of services with VITs forms the problem space of this work. In this section, we identify dimensions for analyzing and characterizing VITs for SoC. We will use these dimensions to classify the results of our analysis in Section 4 as they provide a good basis for selecting a specific variability technique in practice.

D1. *Technical core idea*: The VITs described in literature are at the heart of our analysis. For each VIT we will discuss the technical core idea, the individual prerequisites, and the provided capabilities.
D2. *Variability object*: We differentiate between service interface and service implementation variability as shown in Fig. 1 due to the scope of this paper. *Service interface variability* allows customizing the interface of a service. Typically, this also requires *service implementation variability*. Service implementation variability enables the customization of the implementation of a service (and thus its behavior).
D3. *Form of the variation*: *Optional*, *alternative*, and *multiple selection* are well known forms of variation in SPLE [9]. *Extension* as a form of variation is particularly relevant to SoC as it supports variability without a predefined range of possible variations. Further functionality may extend an existing service (without creating a new service). Extensions are unknown at development time but may be introduced later (this is a typical open-world scenario). Further forms are mentioned in SPLE literature, but as we could not identify these as part of our analysis, we will not list these here.
D4. *Binding time*: The binding time determines when a decision is made about a variability. This may be either made once and cannot be altered afterwards (*permanent*) or rebinding for a new variation is possible (*volatile*). Different binding

times are discussed in literature [14]. However, we will focus on a representative set for SoC. At *compile time*, variability binding is performed during the build process by mechanisms such as pre-processors. At *initialization time*, variability binding happens during the startup phase, e.g., based on a configuration file. *Runtime* binding subsumes all cases of binding variability during the execution of a service.

3 Literature Study

We performed a literature study in order to systematically survey existing VITs and to classify them according to the dimensions introduced in Section 2. We defined a strategy based on the guidelines for systematic reviews by Kitchenham and Charters [7] in order to structure our survey. However, our goal is not an evidence-based analysis, but to ensure completeness and correctness of the identified literature. In this section, we will briefly describe our strategy.

We performed our literature search using the most prominent search engines as publication sources[1]. For the search queries, we used six different search strings (combinations of service or SOA and variability, product-line, or SPLE) to cover the entire range of available literature on that topic. We used these search strings with each search engine. The individual searches yielded more than two thousand papers from which we selected about two hundred to be relevant, that discuss variability in SoC (based on reading the title and the abstract). After eliminating duplicates, we applied a set of inclusion and exclusion criteria (topicality and maturity of the approach, focus of the approach, etc.) yielding the final set of relevant papers.

As a result, the literature study revealed 20 VITs in total, which are in principle relevant to service-oriented computing. However, due to space restrictions we decided to focus in this paper exclusively on service variability as discussed in Section 2.

4 Analysis of Variability Implementation Techniques

In this section, we will present the results of our analysis. Please note, that we introduce descriptive names for the VITs for clear identification and ease of reading. The next sections below follow the sequence of dimensions defined in Section 2.

4.1 Technical Core Ideas

A VIT describes a specific way of realizing variability. In this section, we introduce the identified VITs, their technical core idea, and the addressed service technologies. These are summarized in Table 1[2].

---

[1] ACM Digital Library: http://dl.acm.org/, IEEE Computer Society: http://www.computer.org, Google Scholar: http://scholar.google.com/, and Citeseer: http://citeseerx.ist.psu.edu/

[2] Realization approaches and SOAP/WSDL are derived from the VITs; OSGi and REST are representative examples of service technologies (marked as optional if concluded to be applicable).

Table 1. Realization approaches and service technologies required by VITs

m: mandatory, o: optional		PP	CbSi	FOPbR	CW	ASW
Realization Approach	Component-based	-	m	-	-	-
	Aspect-oriented	-	o	-	-	m
	Interception	-	-	-	-	m
	Feature-oriented	-	o	m	m	-
	Generative	m	-	-	-	-
Service Technology	OSGi	o	o	o	o	-
	SOAP / WSDL	o	o	m	o	m
	REST	o	o	o	o	-

The *Pattern Plugin* (*PP*) approach [12] is a generative approach, i.e. service variants are generated from a variant-enabled design model. The design model is an extension of UML, and includes common and variable parts (as variation points) of a Service-Oriented Architecture (SOA). A variant is expressed as a stereotyped model element (variation model) which holds the information on the actual variation. A SOA variant is defined by selecting appropriate variants. The variation models of the variants are composed into the primary design model via pattern plugins. A pattern plugin describes an individual variant. The composed model can finally be transformed into code artifacts. The encapsulation of variability in variation models and related plugins allows to arbitrarily selecting the service technology (marked as optional in Table 1).

Component-based Service Implementation (*CbSI*) [10] adds a component layer as a refinement of services and realizes variability on the component level. The approach is rather generic and more a conceptual framework than a single approach. For example, a service can be implemented as an optional component (service implementation). Other VITs like aspects, features, etc. are possible (optional in Table 1). *CbSI* provides variability of the implementation, while the service layer is variation-free (with respect to service implementation variability). Thus, this VIT does not require a specific service technology (optional in Table 1).

The *FOP-based Refinement* (*FOPbR*) approach [1] relies on Feature-Oriented Programming (FOP). A feature represents an increment in functionality, which affects one or multiple services simultaneously. *FOPbR* encapsulates the code of a feature into a feature module. A feature module consists of a set of refinements for a service's base code which are enacted by joining the base and the feature code. As a prerequisite, FOP needs to be available for the implementation language, such as for Java [4] or WSDL [2] (mandatory in Table 1). The use of other service technologies is unclear, but we expect this to be optional.

The *Class Wrapper* (*CW*) approach [13] also applies FOP techniques to SoC. In contrast, *CW* uses Java HotSwap to update bytecode in place using the same class identity. HotSwap is required to add features in terms of base classes and wrappers to the service implementation (plain Java code). Base class code updates only internal algorithms without affecting the class schema. Wrappers are used to introduce new elements such as additional methods. In order to invoke the functionality provided by the wrapper, HotSwap is used to update all object references of the changed class.

Table 2. Variability objects addressed by VITs

x: supported		PP	CbSI	FOPbR	CW	ASW
Variability	Service Interface	x	-	x	-	-
Objects	Service Implementation	x	x	x	x	x

While *CW* is conceptually similar to *FOPbR*, however, it would also allow the volatile rebinding at runtime as we will discuss in Section 4.4. The customization of arbitrary Java code yields service technology-independence (optional in Table 1).

The *Aspect Service Weaver* (*ASW*) approach [11] relies on Aspect-Oriented Programming (AOP) and message interception. *ASW* intercepts existing service message chains (based on SOAP) between service consumer and provider. If a message includes a request for a method that the service does not support, advice services are required. An advice service implements additional code (the variability) that can be woven into existing services. The *ASW* tool [3] supports this for SOAP and Web services (marked as mandatory in Table 1).

4.2   Variability Objects

A variability object is an element of a SoC that is supposed to vary. As discussed in Section 1 we restrict our scope to services, i.e. services interface variability and service implementation variability. In this section, we describe which variability objects can be supported by which VIT (cf. Table 2) and how variation is realized.

The *PP* approach supports interface and implementation variability. The basic service, which is supposed to vary, is described by a service operation description and it's in- and outputs. Each variant is given as a variation model. In case of an interface variant, the model specifies the modified interface, the affected in- and outputs as well as a variant description. For an implementation variant, the model lists the affected operations, in- and outputs. The variation models are associated with the basic service model. Given a specific selection of the variants for a basic service, a code generator produces the service interfaces and the related service implementation variants.

In *CbSI*, implementation variability is enabled by the component layer. Each service implementation is realized by at least on component. The selection of the components for the implementation makes up the variability. Thus, the same service may provide different functionality based on the selected components. However, there is no mechanism that ensures that the in- and outputs of the service interface (service layer) and the service implementation (component layer) match. This must be done on a more abstract level, e.g. in the variability model which controls the customization.

FOPbR supports both, interface and implementation variability. An interface variant is a refinement of a WSDL interface definition [2] that includes the affected service methods. An implementation variant is realized as a class refinement introducing new and/or modified functionality. The set of related interface and class refinements represents a feature, which can be applied to the service's base implementation.

The *CW* approach only supports implementation variability. The base program is given as plain Java. Each feature consists of a set of classes and wrappers. A class

Table 3. Forms of variation supported by VITs

x: supported		PP	CbSI	FOPbR	CW	ASW
Form of Variation	Optional	x	x	x	x	x
	Alternative	x	x	x	x	x
	Multiple Selection	-	x	(x)	(x)	(x)
	Extension	-	-	(x)	(x)	(x)

may introduce new functionality, while a wrapper refines one of the base classes in terms of altered methods. The wrapper class therefore holds an object of the wrappee class, which enables the wrapper to call the basic methods of the base class first and then manipulate the results by calling additional methods introduced by the wrapper.

The *ASW* only supports implementation variability. A functional variant, e.g. a specific method, is encapsulated as an advice service. If this functionality is requested by a service call, the *ASW* weaves the code of the advice service into the base service. Joinpoints identify the functionality which should be modified in the service base code [6]. The advice service can then be woven before, after or around this joinpoint.

4.3   Forms of Variation

Form of variation describes how specific variants can be selected. In this section, we discuss the support of the VITs for the forms of variation (cf. Table 3).

The *PP* approach supports optional and alternative forms of variation. Typically, each variant provides functionality describing a service implementation or a service interface variant. Thus, the selection is either optional or an alternative, but there is no support for selecting multiple variants or the explicit modeling of extensions.

In *CbSI* a component may be optional, an alternative, or combined with other components (multiple selection) to implement a service. However, components cannot be added after development time (extension) as the components are linked to specific services in the service layer and later (re-)linking of components is not supported.

The other VITs support optional, alternative, and multiple selection as well as extension in principle. In *FOPbR* and *CW* the use of refinements or wrappers is optional. Multiple refinements or wrappers which affect the same functionality of a service will override previously applied variants. Extensions to the base implementation after development time can be applied by refinements and wrappers. As both VITs need access to the service code, we put extension in Table 3 in brackets. Similar for multiple selection as it is not directly supported by the technique, but can be simulated.

In *ASW* an advice service may or may not be woven into an existing service (optional). It may also be possible to select one or multiple advice services as long as the advice services will not affect the same joinpoint (cf. Section 4.2). This will also result in overriding previously applied variants as in *FOPbR* and *CW*. Introducing new functionality, which was unknown at development time, requires the joinpoints of a service to be accessible. As again some support for extension is given, but no full support we put this in brackets in Table 3. Similar for multiple selection.

Table 4. Binding times supported by VITs

p: permanent, v: volatile		PP	CbSI	FOPbR	CW	ASW
Binding Time	Compile Time	p	p	p	-	(v)
	Initialization Time	-	-	-	(v)	(v)
	Runtime	-	-	-	v	v

4.4   Binding Times

The binding time defines when a decision for a specific variant must be made. In this section, we describe the binding times supported by the individual VITs (cf. Table 4).

PP, *CbSI*, and *FOPbR* only support permanent compile time binding. In *PP*, customization is realized by replacing existing or adding additional variants. This must be done before the generation process and, thus, at the latest at compile time. Replacing variants in the design model after the generation will not affect the generated code (permanent binding). In *CbSI*, the components of a service implementation are instantiated and composed at compilation time. In *FOPbR* the features are handled by the compiler which applies them to the corresponding base code. Thus, the selection of variants must be done at compile time and cannot be changed afterwards.

CW supports volatile runtime binding via Java HotSwap which enables class (re-) binding. While the authors do not explicitly propose to use this approach at initialization time, this is, however, also possible (marked with brackets in Table 4).

Typically, AOP approaches are capable of compile time binding through static weaving and (some form of) runtime binding by dynamic weaving [6]. *ASW* explicitly supports volatile binding at runtime but may also be applied at initialization or compilation time (again marked with brackets in Table 4). Further, *ASW* allows reweaving code of advice services (volatile binding).

5   Conclusion

Customization of SoC is typically done by adding, removing or exchanging services. However, there are situations where variations of the characteristics of services are needed. We presented an overview of existing VITs for services and characterized them with respect to core idea, variability object, form of variation, and binding time.

In our analysis, we also identified gaps and challenges. The characterized VITs support only WSDL-based web services explicitly. There is no explicit proof-of-concept for other service technologies like OSGi or REST. While the variability objects are well supported, none of the VITs provides guidance to ensure that modifications to service interfaces also match the related implementation. As the modifications are also local to a service, there is no guarantee that the interfaces on caller as well as on callee side are customized. Regarding the form of variation, the VITs do not support the open-world scenario, i.e. extension of existing services with functionality which was unknown at development time (unless the code is accessible). Further, all binding times are (partially) supported but only one VIT supports all binding times. Ideally, customization should be possible to perform at all binding times.

The most obvious result of our analysis is that no VIT supports all dimensions in a comprehensive manner. Each approach focuses on a subset of elements of the dimensions and, thus, provides specific mechanisms for these elements. However, in SoC, we need integrated solutions that support all aspects of service variability appropriately. An integrated solution will enable the customization of service (and SoC in general) across technology and business boundaries with low effort and high quality.

In future work, we will focus on such an integrated VIT for SoC. For this purpose, we will consider already analyzed VITs for variability objects such as service platforms, service deployment, service composition, and business processes.

Acknowledgments. This work is partially supported by the INDENICA project, funded by the European Commission grant 257483, area Internet of Services, Software & Virtualisation (ICT-2009.1.2) in the 7th framework programme.

References

1. Apel, S., Kaestner, C., Lengauer, C.: Research Challenges in the Tension Between Features and Services. In: 2nd Intern. Workshop on System Development in SOA Environments, pp. 53–58 (2008)
2. Apel, S., Lengauer, C.: Superimposition: A Language-Independent Approach to Software Composition. In: Pautasso, C., Tanter, É. (eds.) SC 2008. LNCS, vol. 4954, pp. 20–35. Springer, Heidelberg (2008)
3. Baligand, F., Monfort, V.: A Concrete Solution for Web Services Adaptability Using Policies and Aspects. In: 2nd Intern. Conference on Service Oriented Computing, pp. 134–142 (2004)
4. Batory, D., Sarvela, J.N., Rauschmayer, A.: Scaling Step-Wise Refinement. In: 25th Intern. Conference on Software Engineering, pp. 187–197 (2003)
5. Istoan, P., Nain, G., Perrouin, G., Jézéquel, J.-M.: Dynamic Software Product Lines for Service-Based Systems. In: 9th Intern. Conference on Computer and Information Technology, vol. 2, pp. 193–198 (2009)
6. Kiczales, G., Lamping, J., Mendhekar, A., Maeda, C., Lopes, C., Loingtier, J.-M., Irwin, J.: Aspect-Oriented Programming. In: Aksit, M., Auletta, V. (eds.) ECOOP 1997. LNCS, vol. 1241, pp. 220–242. Springer, Heidelberg (1997)
7. Kitchenham, B., Charters, S.: Guidelines for Performing Systematic Literature Reviews in Software Engineering. Technical Report EBSE-2007-01, School of Computer Science and Mathematics Keele University, Staffs ST5 5BG, UK (2007)
8. Li, Y., Zhang, X., Yin, Y., Wu, J.: QoS-Driven Dynamic Reconfiguration of the SOA-Based Software. In: Intern. Conference on Service Sciences, pp. 99–104 (2010)
9. van der Linden, F., Schmid, K., Rommes, E.: Software Product Lines in Action - The Best Industrial Practice in Product Line Engineering. Springer (2007)
10. Medeiros, F.M., de Almeida, E.S., Meira, S.R.L.: Towards an Approach for Service-Oriented Product Line Architectures. In: 3rd Workshop on Service-Oriented Architectures and Software Product Lines (2009)
11. Monfort, V., Hammoudi, S.: Towards Adaptable SOA: Model Driven Development, Context and Aspect. In: Baresi, L., Chi, C.-H., Suzuki, J. (eds.) ICSOC-ServiceWave 2009. LNCS, vol. 5900, pp. 175–189. Springer, Heidelberg (2009)

12. Narendra, N.C., Ponnalagu, K., Srivastava, B., Banavar, G.S.: Variation-Oriented Engineering (VOE): Enhancing Reusability of SOA-Based Solutions. In: 5th IEEE Intern. Conference on Services Computing, pp. 257–264 (2008)
13. Siegmund, N., Pukall, M., Soffner, M., Köppen, V., Saake, G.: Using Software Product Lines for Runtime Interoperability. In: Workshop on Reflection, AOP and Meta-Data for Software Evolution, pp. 1–7 (2009)
14. Svahnberg, M., van Gurp, J., Bosch, J.: A Taxonomy of Variability Realization Techniques. Software – Practice and Experience 35(8), 705–754 (2005)

A Symbolic Framework for the Conformance Checking of Value-Passing Choreographies*

Huu Nghia Nguyen[1], Pascal Poizat[1,2], and Fatiha Zaïdi[1]

[1] LRI; Univ. Paris-Sud, CNRS, Orsay, France
[2] Univ. Évry Val d'Essonne, Evry, France
{huu-nghia.nguyen,pascal.poizat,fatiha.zaidi}@lri.fr

Abstract. Checking choreography conformance aims at verifying whether a set of distributed peers or local role specifications match a global specification. This activity is central in both top-down and bottom-up development processes for distributed systems. Such systems usually collaborate through information exchange, thus requiring value-passing choreography languages and models. However, most of the conformance checking techniques abstract value-passing or bound the domains for the exchanged data. As an alternative, we propose to rely on symbolic models and an extension of the symbolic bisimulation equivalence. This enables one to take into account value passing while avoiding state space explosion issues. Our framework is fully tool supported.

Keywords: choreography, specification, conformance, symbolic transition systems, symbolic branching bisimulation, tools.

1 Introduction

Context and Issues. A *choreography* is the description with a global perspective of *interactions* between *roles* played by *peers* (services, organizations, humans) in some collaboration. One key issue in choreography-based development is checking the *conformance* of a set of local descriptions wrt. the choreography global specification. This issue naturally arises both in bottom-up and in top-down development processes [1], and is also a cornerstone for realizability checking. The definition of conformance should not be too strict. It should support *choreography refinement, e.g.*, with peers and interactions being added in the implementation by the service architect in order to enforce the specification. Finally, entities in a distributed system usually exchange information, *i.e.*, data, while interacting. Consequently, *data should be supported* in choreography specifications, in the descriptions of the local entities, and in the conformance relation.

Related Work. In Table 1, we compare related conformance checking approaches. Columns 2 and 3 focus on data support. Some approaches [2–4] *abstract data away*. This is known to yield over-approximation issues, *e.g.*, false

---

* This work is supported by the PIMI project (ANR-2010-VERS-0014-03) of the French National Agency for Research.

C. Liu et al. (Eds.): ICSOC 2012, LNCS 7636, pp. 525–532, 2012.

Table 1. Choreography conformance approaches

	Data & Value-Passing		Expressiveness		Conformance	
	supported	treatment	loops	assignment	global	relation (based on)
[2]			yes	no	yes	Trace equivalence
[3]	no	-	yes	no	yes	Weak bisimulation
[4]			yes	no	yes	Strong bisimulation
[5]		closure	yes	yes	no	Weak bisimulation
[6]	yes	closure	no	yes	yes	Branching bisimulation
[7]		bound data	yes	no	yes	Branching bisimulation
this paper		symbolic	yes	limited	yes	Branching bisimulation

negatives in the verification process. Data can be supported by working on *closed implementation-level systems* where sent messages contain only ground data [5, 6]. In such a case, the state space explosion of the system model is limited. However, this is not adequate when working on abstract specifications where there are no such ground sent messages but only free variables and constraints on their values. Another solution is to *bound data domains*. The issue is that conformance may not yield outside the bounds. Defining bounds in order to avoid false positives in the verification process can be difficult. In our framework, data is supported using a *symbolic approach* and conformance may be checked for whole data domains.

Columns 4 and 5 are relative to choreography *expressiveness*. Having both loops and assignments may yield state space explosion if one does not close the system or bound data domains. In this work, we do support loops and a limited form of assignment through message reception.

The last two columns are relative to the kind of conformance being supported and the behavioural equivalence being used. *Global conformance* is important in conformance checking since one wants not only to know if each peer is conform to its role, *i.e.*, *local conformance*, but also if the peers altogether have a behaviour that is conform to the choreography. Local conformance does not implies global conformance. Weak and branching bisimulations are able to support internal actions and hiding (formally, τ actions). This is important, *e.g.*, if one has to deal with messages added to make some choreography realizable. Branching bisimulation [8] has been preferred over weak bisimulation in the last years since it is a congruence, hence supports compositional reasoning.

Symbolic bisimulations, defined on Symbolic Transition Graphs (STGs), have been introduced in [9] with both early and late semantics. In this work, we use a late semantics. STGs have then been extended to STGs with assignments (STGAs) in [10, 11]. These works mostly concentrate on strong and weak bisimulation. Symbolic branching bisimulation has not yet received much attention. As a consequence, there is tool support for symbolic strong bisimulation [12] but not for symbolic branching bisimulation.

Contributions. Our contributions are the following. Based on process algebras for choreography [2, 13], we propose *a specification and description language* addressing both the *global* (choreography) and the *local* (peers description, role requirements) perspective over distributed systems. Our language supports

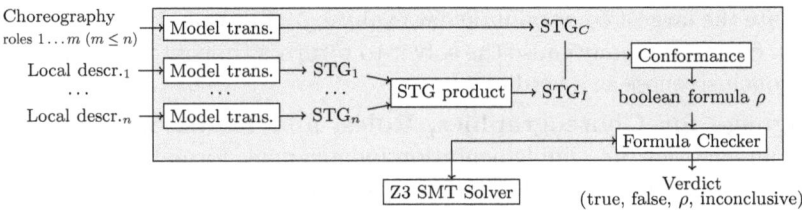

Fig. 1. Architecture of our framework

information exchange and data-related constructs (conditional and loop constructs). We give a *fully symbolic semantics* to this language using a model transformation into STGs, thus avoiding data abstraction and over-approximation, restriction to manually bound data domains, and limitation to implementation-level closed descriptions. Accordingly, we build on branching bisimulation [8] and on a symbolic extension of weak bisimulation [11] to develop a specific *symbolic version of branching bisimulation* dedicated at *checking the conformance* of a set of local entities wrt. a choreography specification. Our equivalence enables one to check conformance in presence of choreography *refinement*, *i.e.*, where new peers and/or interactions may be added wrt. the specification. Going further than a *true* vs. *false* result for conformance, our approach supports the generation of the *most general constraint over exchanged information* in order to have conformance. Finally, our framework is *fully tool supported*[1].

In the sequel, we present the principles of our approach (technical detail can be found in [14]) and we end with conclusions and perspectives of our work.

2   Architecture of the Framework

In this section, we introduce our framework for choreography conformance checking. We also present some of the experiments we have made to evaluate it. The architecture of our framework is given in Figure 1. We take as input a choreography global specification C, with m roles. We also take an implementation description I, given as $n \geq m$ entity local descriptions. These may correspond either to peer descriptions or to role requirements. The case when $n > m$ denotes, *e.g.*, an implementation where some peers have been added to make a choreography realizable. All inputs are first transformed into STGs. The product of STGs and the restriction to actions in C are used to retrieve a unique STG for I, thus yielding two STGs to compare: one for C ($\mathcal{C}$) and one for I ($\mathcal{I}$). We then check if $\mathcal{I}$ conforms to $\mathcal{C}$, which generates the largest boolean formula ρ such that the initial states of $\mathcal{I}$ and $\mathcal{C}$ are conformance related. Finally, this formula is analysed using the Z3 SMT solver[2] in order to reach a conformance verdict. This can be "always true" or "always false", "always" meaning whatever the data values exchanged between peers are. However, sometimes we can have conformance only for a subset of these values. Going further than pure true/false conformance, our framework thus allows

---

[1] Our tool is freely available at `http://www.lri.fr/~nhnghia/sbbc/`

[2] `http://research.microsoft.com/en-us/um/redmond/projects/z3/`

to compute the largest constraint on data values, ρ, that would yield conformance. Complex constraints may cause the solver to return a timeout. In such a case, we emit inconclusiveness as a verdict.

A Language for Choreographies, Roles, and Peers. Since we are interested in an abstract, *i.e.*, implementation independent, formal choreography language, we choose an interaction-based model [15] and the usual τ actions can be ignored [16]. Our specification language, inspired by [2, 13], is used to specify distributed systems with a global perspective, *i.e.*, *choreographies*, to define local requirements, *i.e.*, *roles*, and to describe the pieces of a distributed implementation, *i.e.*, *peers*. Due to this multi-purpose objective, it is first presented in terms of an abstract alphabet, A. We then explain how A can be realized for the different purposes. The syntax of our specification language, $L(A)$, is given by:

$$ L ::= \mathbf{1} \ \mid \ \alpha \ \mid \ L;L \ \mid \ L+L \ \mid \ L|L \ \mid \ L{\triangleright}L \ \mid \ [\phi] \triangleright L \ \mid \ [\phi] * L $$

A basic activity is either termination ($\mathbf{1}$) or a regular activity $\alpha \in A$. Structuring is achieved using sequencing (;), non deterministic choice ($+$), parallelism ($|$), and interruption ($\triangleright$). Furthermore, we have data-based conditional constructs, namely guards ($\triangleright$) and loops ($*$), where ϕ is a boolean expression.

The basis of an interaction-model choreography description is the interaction. Let us denote an interaction c from role a to role b by $c^{[a,b]}.x$, where x is a variable that represents the information exchanged during interaction (x is omitted when there is none). We stress out that x can be structured, *e.g.*, to denote a multiple data exchange as done in Web services with XML message types. A *choreography specification* for a set of roles R, a set of interactions Ch, and a set of variables V, is an element of $L(A)$ with $A = \{c^{[a,b]}.x \mid c \in Ch \wedge a \in R \wedge b \in R \wedge a \neq b \wedge x \in V\}$.

The events of a local entity a (peer or role) can be abstracted as sending and reception events, denoted respectively with $c^{[a,b]}!x$ and $c^{[b,a]}?x$, where b is another entity, *i.e.*, $a \neq b$, and x is the information exchanged during interaction (x is omitted when there is none). An *entity description* for an entity a, a set of roles R with $a \in R$, a set of interactions Ch, and a set of variables V, is an element of $L(A)$ with $A = \{c^{[a,b]}!x, \ c^{[b,a]}?x \mid c \in Ch \wedge b \in R \wedge a \neq b \wedge x \in V\}$.

Example 1. Let us suppose a shipping choreography between two roles: c (client) and s (shipper). The client first requests shipping by providing the weight of goods to be sent. If this is less than 5 kgs then the goods will be sent for free. Otherwise, the shipping has to be paid. This can be described as follows:

$$ Shipping ::= \mathbf{Request}^{[c,s]}.x_1; ([x_1 < 5] \triangleright \mathbf{FreeShip}^{[s,c]} + [x_1 \geq 5] \triangleright \mathbf{PayShip}^{[s,c]}) $$

A tentative to implement the shipping choreography is that the client sends the weight to the shipper and then waits for either free or paid shipping, while it is the shipper that checks the weight in order to decide which shipping is used:

$$ Client\ c ::= \mathbf{Request}^{[c,s]}!y_1; (\mathbf{FreeShip}^{[s,c]}? + \mathbf{PayShip}^{[s,c]}?) $$
$$ Shipper\ s ::= \mathbf{Request}^{[c,s]}?z_1; ([z_1 < 5] \triangleright \mathbf{FreeShip}^{[s,c]}! + [z_1 \geq 5] \triangleright \mathbf{PayShip}^{[s,c]}!) $$

Symbolic Transition Graph. An STG [9] is a transition system where a set of variables, possibly empty, is associated to each state and where each transition

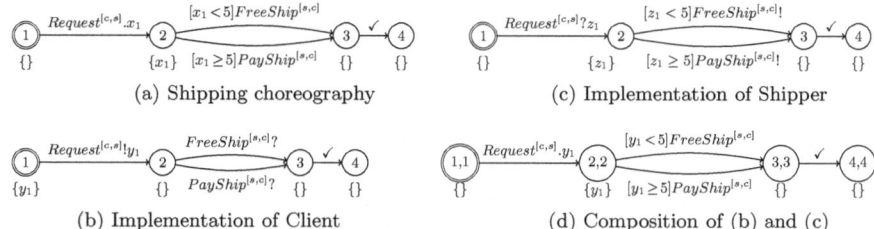

(a) Shipping choreography

(c) Implementation of Shipper

(b) Implementation of Client

(d) Composition of (b) and (c)

Fig. 2. STGs for Example 1

may be guarded by a boolean expression ϕ that determines if the transition can be fired or not. Actions labelling transitions will correspond in our work to the elements of the alphabets we have seen earlier on. We also add a specific event, $\checkmark$, to denote activity termination. A transition from state s to s' with a guard ϕ and labeled by an action α takes the form $s \xrightarrow{[\phi] \, \alpha} s'$. We use STGs as a formal model to give semantics to our language. The product of STGs is used to give a semantics to a set of interacting local entities. We assume that the STGs use disjoint sets of variables which can be achieved using, *e.g.*, indexing by the name of the entity. The rule-based of model transformations and our algorithm for the product of STGs can be found in a technical report extension of this paper [14].

Example 2. The STGs for the choreography, the client and shipper in Example 1 are shown in Figure 2(a-c). Figure 2(d) presents the product of the STGs in Figure 2(b) and Figure 2(c). The free variables of the states are given below them, *e.g.*, $\{x_1\}$ for state 2 in the choreography STG.

Choreography Conformance. Since our semantic models are STGs, we define conformance over two STGs, $\mathcal{I}$ (implementation) and $\mathcal{C}$ (choreography). We choose branching bisimulation [8] as a basis since it supports equivalence in presence of τ actions that result from the hiding of interactions added in implementations wrt. specifications, *i.e.*, refinement. However, branching bisimulation is defined over ground terms (no variables), while STGs may contain free variables. In [6, 7], this issue is considered by introducing at each state an evaluation function that maps variables to values, thus reducing open terms to ground ones. This may lead to state space explosion when domains of the variables are big. Alternatively, we base our work on (late) symbolic extensions of bisimulations, introduced in [9–11], that directly support open terms.

To make implementation and specification comparable, we remind the reader that we assume the two STGs have disjoint sets of variables which can be achieved using, *e.g.*, indexing. We also assume that a local entity has the same identifier than the corresponding role in the choreography. This constraint could be lifted using a mapping function. Additional interactions may have been introduced in the implementation wrt. the specification during refinement, *e.g.*, to make it realizable. In order to compare the STGs, we have to hide these interactions.

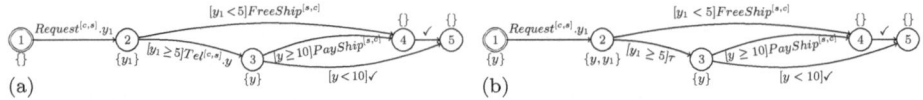

Fig. 3. A refinement (a) for the STG in Figure 2(d) and its restriction (b)

Example 3. We give a refinement example in Figure 3(a) where the client specifies the maximum (s)he agrees to pay for the shipping (y). This influences the sequel of the implementation since the non-free shipping costs \$10: if the user requires to pay less, no shipping is done. The restriction of this STG to the set of actions used in the choreography specification, $\{Request^{[c,s]}, FreeShip^{[s,c]}, PayShip^{[s,c]}\}$, yields the STG in Figure 3(b) where *Tel* has been hidden.

Conformance Computation. Our algorithm for the computation of the conformance relation between two STGs [14] is a modification and simplification of the one proposed in [11] that computes symbolic weak bisimulation. Simplification was made possible since there may be τs in $\mathcal{I}$ (after hiding) but not in $\mathcal{C}$. The algorithm outputs a set of boolean formulas ρ_{s_1,s_2} relative to pairs of states (s_1, s_2), s_1 being in $\mathcal{I}$ and s_2 in $\mathcal{C}$. ρ_{s_1,s_2} denotes the conditions under which s_1 and s_2 are conformance related. In the algorithm, these boolean formulas are encoded as a Predicate Equation Systems (PES) [10], *i.e.*, a set of functions each of which contains a boolean expression, *e.g.*, $R(x) ::= (x \geq 0)$.

Example 4. Applying the algorithm on the STGs in Figure 3(b) (implementation) and in Figure 2(a) (specification), we retrieve the following PES:

$$R_{1,1}() \qquad ::= \forall Z_0 \; R_{2,2}(Z_0, Z_0)$$
$$R_{2,2}(y_1, x_1) ::= (((x_1 \geq 5 \Rightarrow y_1 \geq 5 \wedge R_{3,2}(y_1, x_1)) \wedge (y_1 \geq 5 \Rightarrow x_1 \geq 5 \wedge R_{3,2}(y_1, x_1)))$$
$$\wedge((x_1 < 5 \Rightarrow y_1 < 5 \wedge R_{4,3}) \wedge (y_1 < 5 \Rightarrow x_1 < 5 \wedge R_{4,3}))) \wedge (\neg(y < 10))$$
$$R_{3,2}(y_1, x_1) ::= ((x_1 \geq 5 \Rightarrow y \geq 10 \wedge R_{4,3}) \wedge (y \geq 10 \Rightarrow x_1 \geq 5 \wedge R_{4,3}))$$
$$\wedge((\neg(y < 10)) \wedge (\neg(x_1 < 5)))$$
$$R_{4,3}() \qquad ::= true$$

Indeed, it can be simplified into $\{R_{1,1} ::= y \geq 10, R_{2,2} ::= y \geq 10, R_{3,2} ::= y \geq 10 \wedge Z_0 \geq 5, R_{4,3} ::= true\}$ but this demonstrates the need for an automatic PES satisfiability checking procedure as defined below.

PES Satisfiability and Conformance Verdict. The PES resulting from the conformance computation algorithm has to be analyzed in order to reach a conformance verdict. We realize this step with the Z3 SMT Solver by translating the PES into the Z3 input language as demonstrated in Listing 1.1 for the PES in Example 4. Each predicate equation in the PES is translated as a boolean function (using *define-fun*) and each free variable is translated as an integer function (using *declare-fun*). We then check R1_1 in order to conclude on conformance. For this, the **check-sat** Z3 command is run as following. If R1_1 asserted *false* (as in Listing 1.1) yields an *unsat* response then there is no interpretation such that $R_{1,1}$ is false, hence we can conclude directly that conformance is *true*. Otherwise, we have to retry with R1_1 asserted to *true* to reach a verdict. The result may then be *unsat*, *sat*, or *timeout* corresponding respectively to the conformance being *false*, *may be* (ρ), or *inconclusive*.

Listing 1.1. Translation into the Z3 language of the PES in Example 4

```
1  (set-option :print-warning false)
2  (declare-fun y () Int)
3  (define-fun R4_3 () Bool true)
4  (define-fun R3_2 ((y_1 Int)(x_1 Int)) Bool (and (and (implies (>= x_1 5)
     (and (>= y 10) R4_3)) (implies (>= y 10) (and (>= x_1 5) R4_3))) (and (
     not (< y 10)) (not (< x_1 5)))))
5  (define-fun R2_2 ((y_1 Int)(x_1 Int)) Bool (and (and (and (implies (>=
     x_1 5) (and (>= y_1 5) (R3_2 y_1 x_1))) (implies (>= y_1 5) (and (>=
     x_1 5) (R3_2 y_1 x_1)))) (and (implies (< x_1 5) (and (< y_1 5) R4_3))
     (implies (< y_1 5) (and (< x_1 5) R4_3)))) (not (< y 10))))
6  (define-fun R1_1 () Bool (forall ((Z_0 Int)) (R2_2 Z_0 Z_0)))
7  (assert (= R1_1 false))    ; uncomment for step 1, comment for step 2
8  ; (assert (= R1_1 true))   ; comment for step 1, uncomment for step 2
9  (check-sat)
```

Table 2. Experimental results

Id	Name [Reference]	#Peers/Roles	Implementation		Specification		Verdict	Duration
			#Int.	#Trans./States	#Int.	#Trans./States	Orig./Ours	(seconds)
01	Shipping [n/a]	2/2	3	4/4	3	4/4	-/YES	0.069
		2/2	4	5/5	3	4/4	-/YES	0.084
	Example 4 →	2/2	4	6/5	3	4/4	-/ρ	0.102
04	Market [6]	4/4	8	9/10	8	10/10	YES/NO	0.118
		8/4	16	27/26	8	10/10	YES/NO	0.201
06	RFQ [7]	3/3	6	8/7	6	8/8	NO/NO	0.078
07	Booking [4]	4/4	8	12/11	8	12/11	YES/YES	0.096

Experiments. We have experimented our framework, including on examples from the literature (Tab. 2). For the implementations and the specifications, we respectively give the numbers of peers, roles, interactions, and transitions and states in the corresponding STGs. We also give the conformance verdicts in the paper the example is taken from and with our approach. Finally, we give the execution time (Mac Book Air with OS 10.7, 4 GB RAM, core i5 1.7 GHz) for the process described in Figure 1 (but for the time to parse the input files). Rows 1 to 3 correspond to the specification STG in Figure 2(a) and, respectively, to the implementations STGs in Figures 2(d) (row 1), 3(a) (row 2), and 3(b) (row 3). Rows 4 and 5 correspond to the example and mutation in [6]. The difference in the verdict comes from the fact the we distinguish between an STG ending with ✓ (successful termination) or not, hence an implementation deadlocking after achieving all interactions of a specification will not conform to it: the specification may do ✓ while the implementation may not. Row 6 corresponds to a negative example in [7] and row 7 to a positive one in [4].

3 Conclusion

In this paper, we have proposed a formal framework for checking the conformance of a set of role requirements or peer descriptions with reference to a choreography specification. Symbolic models and equivalences enable us to check conformance in presence of data without suffering from state space explosion and without bounding data domains. Going further than strict conformance, we are able to give the most general constraint over data exchanged between peers in order to achieve conformance. Our approach is fully tool supported[1].

We advocate that once a choreography projection function supporting data is defined, then our framework could be used not only for conformance checking but also for realizability checking. This is our first perspective. A second perspective is to extend our framework with non-limited assignment and asynchronous communication. Our last perspective is to integrate the extensions of our tools as a verification plugin for the BPMN 2.0 Eclipse editor. A BPMN 2.0 to STG model transformation is ongoing, based on our BPMN to LTS (no data) one [17].

References

1. Poizat, P.: Formal Model-Based Approaches for the Development of Composite Systems. Habilitation thesis, Université Paris Sud (November 2011), http://www.lri.fr/~poizat/documents/hdr.pdf
2. Qiu, Z., Zhao, X., Cai, C., Yang, H.: Towards the Theoretical Foundation of Choreography. In: Proc. of WWW 2007 (2007)
3. Basu, S., Bultan, T.: Choreography Conformance via Synchronizability. In: Proc. of WWW 2011 (2011)
4. Salaün, G., Bultan, T.: Realizability of Choreographies Using Process Algebra Encodings. In: Leuschel, M., Wehrheim, H. (eds.) IFM 2009. LNCS, vol. 5423, pp. 167–182. Springer, Heidelberg (2009)
5. Li, J., Zhu, H., Pu, G.: Conformance Validation between Choreography and Orchestration. In: Proc. of TASE 2007 (2007)
6. Busi, N., Gorrieri, R., Guidi, C., Lucchi, R., Zavattaro, G.: Choreography and Orchestration Conformance for System Design. In: Ciancarini, P., Wiklicky, H. (eds.) COORDINATION 2006. LNCS, vol. 4038, pp. 63–81. Springer, Heidelberg (2006)
7. Kazhamiakin, R., Pistore, M.: Choreography Conformance Analysis: Asynchronous Communications and Information Alignment. In: Bravetti, M., Núñez, M., Zavattaro, G. (eds.) WS-FM 2006. LNCS, vol. 4184, pp. 227–241. Springer, Heidelberg (2006)
8. Van Glabbeek, R., Weijland, W.: Branching Time and Abstraction in Bisimulation Semantics. Journal of the ACM 43(3) (1996)
9. Hennessy, M., Lin, H.: Symbolic Bisimulations. Theoretical Computer Science 138(2), 353–389 (1995)
10. Lin, H.: Symbolic Transition Graph with Assignment. In: Sassone, V., Montanari, U. (eds.) CONCUR 1996. LNCS, vol. 1119, pp. 50–65. Springer, Heidelberg (1996)
11. Li, Z., Chen, H.: Computing Strong/Weak Bisimulation Equivalences and Observation Congruence for Value-Passing Processes. In: Cleaveland, W.R. (ed.) TACAS 1999. LNCS, vol. 1579, pp. 300–314. Springer, Heidelberg (1999)
12. Basu, S., Mukund, M., Ramakrishnan, C.R., Ramakrishnan, I.V., Verma, R.: Local and Symbolic Bisimulation Using Tabled Constraint Logic Programming. In: Codognet, P. (ed.) ICLP 2001. LNCS, vol. 2237, pp. 166–180. Springer, Heidelberg (2001)
13. Bravetti, M., Zavattaro, G.: Towards a Unifying Theory for Choreography Conformance and Contract Compliance. In: Lumpe, M., Vanderperren, W. (eds.) SC 2007. LNCS, vol. 4829, pp. 34–50. Springer, Heidelberg (2007)
14. Nguyen, H.N., Poizat, P., Zaïdi, F.: A Symbolic Framework for the Conformance Checking of Value-Passing Choreographies. Long version, in P. Poizat Webpage
15. Decker, G., Kopp, O., Barros, A.P.: An Introduction to Service Choreographies. Information Technology 50(2), 122–127 (2008)
16. Kopp, O., Leymann, F.: Do We Need Internal Behavior in Choreography Models? In: Proc. of ZEUS 2009 (2009)
17. Poizat, P., Salaün, G.: Checking the Realizability of BPMN 2.0 Choreographies. In: Proc of SAC 2012 (2012)

Service Composition Management Using Risk Analysis and Tracking

Shang-Pin Ma and Ching-Lung Yeh

Department of Computer Science and Engineering, National Taiwan Ocean University,
Keelung, Taiwan
{albert,19957009}@ntou.edu.tw

Abstract. How to effectively and efficiently monitor, manage, and adapt web services is becoming a significant issue to address. In this paper, we argue that only solving emerging service faults at deployment time or runtime is not enough; on the contrary, we believe that prediction of service faults is equivalently important. We propose a risk-driven service composition management process including four main phases: preparation, planning, monitoring and reaction, and analysis. By applying the proposed approach, risky component services can be removed earlier, and the fault source can be tracked and identified more easily when any failure occurs. We believe the proposed risk-driven approach can effectively and efficiently ensure the robustness of an SOA-based system.

Keywords: service management, risk management, service composition.

1 Introduction

Service-Oriented Architecture (SOA) has become an important trend in software engineering for developing loosely-coupled applications and integrating legacy and modern systems. Accordingly, how to effectively and efficiently monitor, manage, and adapt web services is also becoming a significant issue to address. Today, many mechanisms [1, 2, 4, 5, 10, 12] are available to perform service monitoring and management for improving various types of QoS (Quality of Service), such as availability and reliability.

In this paper, we argue that only solving emerging service faults at deployment time or runtime is not enough; on the contrary, we believe that prediction of service faults is equivalently important. Risk analysis is an approach which is commonly used in project management domain [9]. The potential problems which may hinder the development of project are called risk. If the problems occur, the project will to be mired in difficulties. Therefore, the risk should be reduced before the project executing. At present, the risk management techniques are used in a variety of domains, such as electricity [7] and wireless security [6]. The risk concept is also applied to enhance the service-oriented design process to select appropriate business partners [8]. In this study, we bring the risk notion into the web service management mechanism to foresee possible problems or weak points in an SOA-based system.

C. Liu et al. (Eds.): ICSOC 2012, LNCS 7636, pp. 533–540, 2012.

Our proposed risk-driven service composition management process includes four main phases: preparation, planning, monitoring and reaction, as well as analysis. In preparation phase, the risk probability and the risk impact of each component service in a composite service are calculated based on historical QoS data. If any component service is too risky, another interface-compatible service will take over the risky one. Besides, a service dependency graph is also produced in this phase for tracking the fault source at runtime. In planning phase, a monitoring plan is generated based on the service dependency graph and the risk analysis result. In the monitoring and reaction phase, the composite service is monitored according to the monitoring plan. If any service failure occurs or a component service becomes too risky (i.e. risk exposure is larger than a given threshold), a fault tracking path is built immediately and automatically based on the service dependency graph, and appropriate reaction actions, such as re-invocation or service substitution, are chosen and performed in the light of the monitoring plan. Finally, in the analysis phase, all service execution logs are cumulated and analyzed to update the historical QoS database for further processing. By applying the proposed approach, risky component services can be removed earlier, and the fault source can be tracked and identified more easily when any failure occurs. We believe the proposed risk-driven approach can effectively and efficiently ensure the robustness of an SOA-based system.

The structure of the paper is as follows. Section 2 describes the details of the proposed service composition management approach, including core concepts and the proposed management process. Final section concludes this study.

2   Approach Descriptions

This section describes the proposed approach in detail, including the core concepts and the process of risk-driven service composition management.

2.1   Core Concepts for the Proposed Approach

For establishing the proposed service composition management mechanism, we introduce the significant concepts first by utilizing the UML class diagram and representing each concept as a class (shown in Figure 1). Composite service is the aggregation of multiple component services which are described by service profiles. The service profile is to obtain and store significant attributes of a component services, including service name, service interface, service type, service input, service output, and service provider. A Service Dependency Graph (SDG) can be produced based on the flow of a composite service to ease service fault tracking. The component service risk is consisting of risk impact and risk probability, which are calculated according to the composite service flow structure and the historical QoS (Quality of Service) data. Component service risk can be mitigated by performing replication or substitution actions for component services. The composite service risk is estimated by cumulating values of all component service risks.

A service flow instance is instantiated when the service requester utilizes a composite service. When any service failure occurs during execution of the service flow instance, we can track the Fault Tracking Path (FTP), which is consisting of a service fault source, intermediate nodes, and a service failure occurrence point, to find the cause of faults and to perform appropriate reaction actions. FTP is automatically generated based on the built SDG. Four reaction strategies are included in this study: Substitution, Compensation, Re-invoke, and Re-start. Substitution is a strategy that tries to select another service with the same service interface as the faulty one. The corresponding service interface of a service component is recorded in the service profile. Compensation is used to restore correct object states which were correct, in case these were affected by a fault. Re-invoke is re-executing the same service invocation with exactly the same parameters and contracts. Re-start is stopping and starting the web service server so that service may become available.

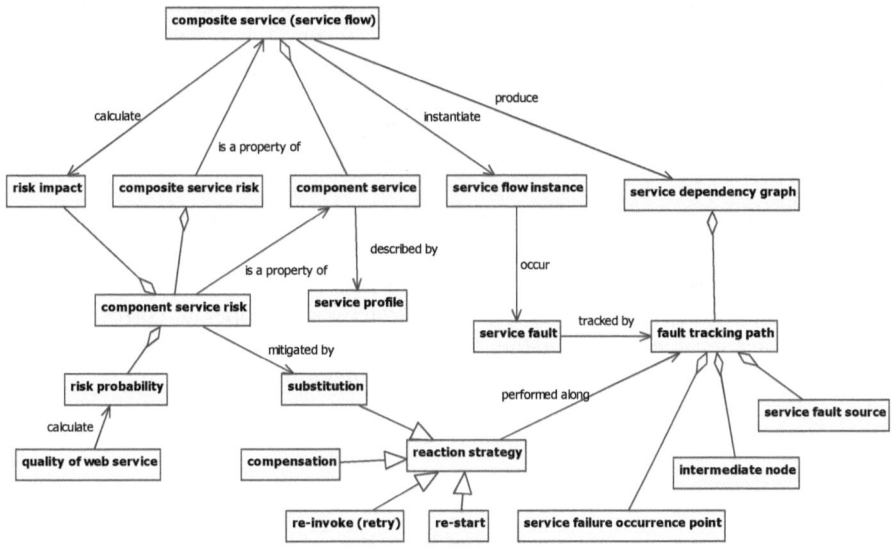

Fig. 1. Conceptual Model

Service Risk. Risk is the potential that may lead to damage. In our proposed approach, we bring the notion of risk to predict possibility faults or QoS decline by calculating risk exposure by equation (1).

$$Risk = Probability \times Impact \tag{1}$$

At preparation phase, difference mitigation actions, such as service replication or service substitution, will be executed according to the risk exposure level. At runtime, the risk exposure level is also an important indicator to carry out reaction strategies. Two elements of risk, risk probability and risk impact, are described as following.

Table 1. The Rating of Availability & Reliability

Rating	Detail
0.2	Both Availability and Reliability are more than 99.999%
0.4	Availability or Reliability is between 99.999% and 99.9%
0.6	Availability or Reliability is between 99.9% and 99%
0.8	Availability or Reliability is between 99% and 90%
1.0	Availability or Reliability is between 90% and 0%

Risk probability. Risk probability is a value to estimate the stability of a component service. We adopt the QoS value of the component service in historical data to calculate by equation (2):

$$P = \left[(1 - w_p) \times T + w_p \times AR \right] \tag{2}$$

Where w_p is a weight value to represent the importance of AR value, AR is the rating of Availability & Reliability as showing in Table 1, and T is a value calculating by equation (3) for evaluating the stability of service response time.

$$T = \frac{Standard\ Deviation}{Arithmetic\ Mean} \tag{3}$$

Risk impact. Risk impact is a value to indicate the possible damage when a component service in composite service becomes malfunctional. In this study, risk impact is calculated by extending the method proposed in [11] since if a component service is more important, the damage is larger if this service cannot operate correctly. In this study, risk impact value is aggregating by the importance score assigned by the user and analysis results of execution path analysis by equation (4).

$$I = \frac{(1 - w_i) \times I_e + w_i \times I_u}{I_{max}} \tag{4}$$

Where I_u is the score assigned by users (i.e. W_u value in [11]), I_e is the score calculated by execution path analysis (i.e. W_p value in [11]), w_i is the weight to represent importance of I_u in this equation, and I_{max} is the maximum of I values for all component services. Notably, through execution path analysis, we can assert that some of the component services play more important roles than others since these services emerged in more execution paths.

2.2   Risk-Driven Service Composition Management Process

Based on above concepts, we devise a management process, called Risk-Driven Service Composition Management (RDSCM), including four sub-processes: Preparation, Planning, Monitoring & Reaction, and Analysis. Differ from [2], we additionally define the preparation phase to prepare artifacts that can be leveraged when faults occur in following phases.

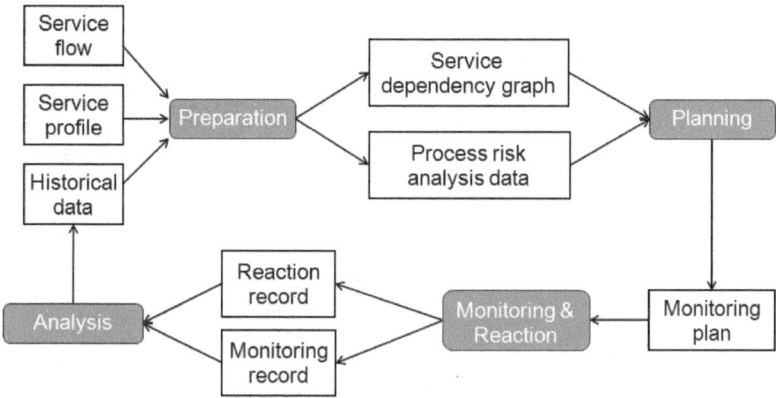

Fig. 2. Risk-Driven Service Composition Management Process

As shown in Figure 2, in preparation phase, RDSCM calculates the risk impact of each component service based on the service flow, and computes the risk probability of each component service according to historical QoS data. The risk exposure values can be determined by aggregating impact and probability data. Besides, RDSCM also analyzes the service flow and service profiles of all component services in the flow to generate the SDG (service dependency graph). In the planning phase, RDSCM produces a monitoring plan based on SDG and process risk analysis data. In the monitoring & reaction phase, RDSCM monitors the composite service according to the monitoring plan. If any fault occurs, RDSCM selects appropriate reaction actions specified in the monitoring plan. Finally, in the analysis phase, RDSCM analyzes all execution records and update the historical QoS data, which will influence risk analysis results of other instances of the same composite service or other composite services.

Preparation Process. As afore-mentioned, in the preparation phase, the risk of the component services which in the composite service are analyzed. If the risk of a component service is higher than a given threshold, RDSCM will try to select another service with the same service interface to replace the faulty one. The substitute strategy, such as selecting the service with best QoS or selecting the service used most frequently, can be decided in advance. If the risk of the substitute service is still too high, RDSCM will stop the process and show alert message.

In the preparation phase, SDG will be built. In opposite to the service flow showing the execution sequence, the SDG represents the dependency relationship among component services for a composite service. For constructing the dependency graph, we extract the data flow among component services, i.e. the source and the target of service data, and invert the service flow. For example, a process which has input and output data is shown in the left-hand side of Figure 3, and the dependency graph of this process is shown in the right-hand side. Due to the service S_2 accepts the input data o_1 from service S_1, we can assert S_2 depends on S_1, and the edge representing this dependency relationship in SDG is connected from source S_2 to target S_1. Following above graph construction rules, an SDG can be generated automatically.

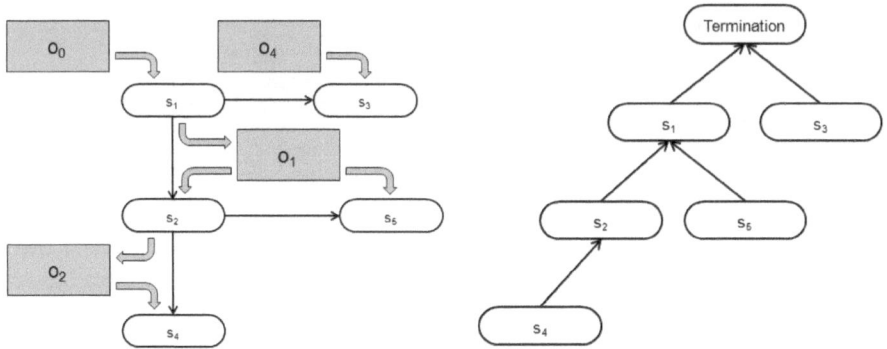

Fig. 2. Example: Building the Service Dependency Graph

Planning Process. In this phase, RDSCM automatically produces a monitoring plan in XML format, which can be modified by the manager. The plan includes four parts (1) Monitoring Attribute: to specify the QoS attributes which the manager plans to monitor; (2) Monitoring Threshold: to set the threshold of the high risk. (3) Monitoring Frequency: to arrange the monitoring frequency, i.e. the cycle time of QoS probing, for services with medium and low risk; and (4) Substitution Policy: to determine the procedure to swap the faulty or risky service. Available substitution policies include choosing the most used services, choosing the service with best QoS, and choosing the service with lowest risk.

Monitoring and Reaction Process. In this phase, RDSCM monitors the execution of the composite service based on the monitoring plan. This phase has two main tasks: first is collecting execution data with all service instances or additional service probing records according to the monitoring frequency setting; and second is detecting and recovering service faults.

   If an instance reveals faults, RDSCM bases the SDG to produce a FTP (fault tracking path), and selects reaction strategies as well as performs recovery actions for component services which are in the fault tracking path. Following the error chain paradigm, a FTP includes the failure occurrence point, the fault source, zero or more intermediate services. Besides, zero or more non-failure services are preceding the fault source in the service flow. For example, as shown in Figure 3, if service S_4 is the failure occurrence point which reveals the fault, the possible longest FTP $\{S_4S_2S_1\}$ is established first due to any of these three services may be the fault source. If the service S_1 is confirmed as the fault source, the final FTP is also $\{S_4S_2S_1\}$ and service S_2 is assigned as an intermediate service since S_2 is either the failure occurrence point nor the fault source. If the service S_2 is determined as the fault source, the FTP is $\{S_2S_1\}$ without intermediate service.

   When the FTP is produced, RDSCM can carry out the service recovery process to fix the process instance. RDSCM increases the risk of the fault source (and updates the value into database) first, and derives the service type of all services in the FTP for further processing. In this study, the service type can be identified from two view-points: Retriable and Compensable (this notion is borrowed from [3]). If a component service guarantees a successfully termination after a finite number of invocations, it is Retriable (R); otherwise it is not retriable. If the component service which supports compensable transactions, it is Compensable (C); on the other hand, if this component service execution does not affect the state of the service, it is Non-compensatory (N). Depending on the type, RDSCM can fulfill appropriate reaction actions to recover the all services in the FTP. In the proposed recovery process, the fault source needs to recover first. For example, if the service type of the fault source is CR, RDSCM compensates this service at first, and then re-invokes it and tests if the service is workable. If the service is still malfunctioned, RDSCM selects another interface-compatible service according to the substitution policy to take over the faulty service. Next, RDSCM may compensate intermediate services or the failure occurrence point first (if the service is compensable) since the incorrect data may affect the business state of these services, and then re-invokes the service (if the service is retriable). Notably the reaction strategy of service substitution is unnecessary for non-fault-source services since these services are not malfunctional. Following above steps, all services in the FTP are recovered along the inverse sequence of the FTP and then the faulty composite service is recovered accordingly.

3   Conclusions

This paper presents a risk-driven approach to manage composite web services. The goal of this study is reduce the probability and damage of service faults occurring and further ensure the robustness of the SOA-based system, with the following key contributions:

- Bring the notion of risk management into web service management.
- Devise a method to calculate the service risk exposure for estimating the possible faults which reside in a service composition.
- Devise a method to construct the service dependency graph (SDG) and the fault tracking path (FTP) to efficiently track service faults and recover the faulty composite service.

Acknowledgements. This research was sponsored by National Science Council in Taiwan under the grant NSC 100-2221-E-019-037.

References

[1] Baresi, L., Guinea, S., Nano, O., Spanoudakis, G.: Comprehensive Monitoring of BPEL Processes. IEEE Internet Computing 14(3), 50–57 (2010)
[2] Calinescu, R., Grunske, L., Kwiatkowska, M., Mirandola, R., Tamburrelli, G.: Dynamic QoS Management and Optimization in Service-Based Systems. IEEE Transactions on Software Engineering 37(3), 387–409 (2011)

[3] El Haddad, J., Manouvrier, M., Ramirez, G., Rukoz, M.: QoS-Driven Selection of Web Services for Transactional Composition. In: 2008 IEEE International Conference on Web Services, ICWS 2008 (2008)

[4] Erradi, A., Maheshwari, P., Tosic, V.: WS-Policy based Monitoring of Composite Web Services. In: The Fifth European Conference on Web Services, pp. 99–108. IEEE Computer Society (2007)

[5] Friedrich, G., Fugini, M., Mussi, E., Pernici, B., Tagni, G.: Exception Handling for Repair in Service-Based Processes. IEEE Transactions on Software Engineering 36(2), 198–215 (2010)

[6] Hsin-Yi, T., Yu-Lun, H.: An Analytic Hierarchy Process-Based Risk Assessment Method for Wireless Networks. IEEE Transactions on Reliability 60(4), 801–816 (2011)

[7] Kettunen, J., Salo, A., Bunn, D.W.: Optimization of Electricity Retailer's Contract Portfolio Subject to Risk Preferences. IEEE Transactions on Power Systems 25(1), 117–128 (2010)

[8] Kokash, N.: Risk Management for Service-Oriented Systems. In: Baresi, L., Fraternali, P., Houben, G.-J. (eds.) ICWE 2007. LNCS, vol. 4607, pp. 563–568. Springer, Heidelberg (2007)

[9] Kwan, T.W., Leung, H.K.N.: A Risk Management Methodology for Project Risk Dependencies. IEEE Transactions on Software Engineering 37(5), 635–648 (2011)

[10] Lee, J., Ma, S.-P., Lee, S.-J., Wu, C.-L., Lee, C.-H.L.: Towards a High-Availability-Driven Service Composition Framework. In: Service Life Cycle Tools and Technologies: Methods, Trends and Advances, pp. 221–243. IGI Global (2012)

[11] Ma, S.-P., Kuo, J.-Y., Fanjiang, Y.-Y., Tung, C.-P., Huang, C.-Y.: Optimal service selection for composition based on weighted service flow and Genetic Algorithm. In: 2010 International Conference on Machine Learning and Cybernetics, ICMLC (2012)

[12] Moser, O., Rosenberg, F., Dustdar, S.: Non-intrusive monitoring and service adaptation for WS-BPEL. In: The 17th International Conference on World Wide Web, pp. 815–824. ACM, Beijing (2008)

Assisting Business Process Design by Activity Neighborhood Context Matching

Nguyen Ngoc Chan, Walid Gaaloul, and Samir Tata

Information Department, TELECOM SudParis
UMR 5157 CNRS Samovar, France

Abstract. Speeding up the business process design phase is a crucial challenge in recent years. Some solutions, such as defining and using reference process models or searching similar processes to a working one, can facilitate the designer's work. However, recommending the whole process can make the designer confused, especially in case of large-size business processes. In this paper, we introduce the concept of activity neighborhood context in order to propose an approach that fasten the design phase regardless the size of business process. Concretely, we recommend the designer the activities that are close to the designing process from existing business processes. We evaluate our approach on a large collection of public business processes. Experimental results show that our approach is feasible and efficient.

1   Introduction

The advantages of business process design have involved many industrial and research contributions on facilitating the business process design, which is the initial and key step that impacts the completeness and success of a business process. In this paper, we present an original approach to help to facilitate the design phase by recommending business process designers a list of relevant activities to the ongoing designed process. Consider a scenario where a business process designer is designing a "train-reservation" process to provide a booking service (Fig. 1): whenever the train operating company receives a reservation request, it searches trains according to the request details, presents possible alternatives to the customer and waits for a response. If it receives a cancel request, the process will be terminated; otherwise, it will ask the customer for the credit card information, then process the payment and send back the customer the reservation confirmation with the payment details.

The "train-reservation" process in Fig. 1 can achieve the required business goal. However, the process design could not stop at that point as the preliminary design requirements could evolve. He might want to: (i) add new functionalities in the preliminary process, (ii) design a new variant of the preliminary process respecting new business constraints or contexts, or (iii) find alternative activities in order to better handle activity failure or exception.

To help the designer achieve his goals, instead of recommending business processes, we propose to recommend activities that have similar neighborhood context with a selected one. This context is defined as a business process fragment

C. Liu et al. (Eds.): ICSOC 2012, LNCS 7636, pp. 541–549, 2012.

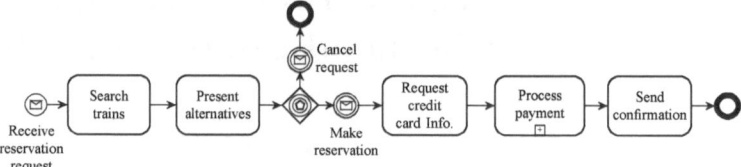

Fig. 1. Train reservation process

around an activity, including the associated activity and connection flows connecting it and its neighbors. For a selected activity, we match its neighborhood context with the neighborhood contexts of other activities. A matching between two neighborhood contexts is scored by a similarity value. Then, base on the similarity values, we present for the business designer N activities that have highest similarity values.

For example, if the designer selects activities: "Search trains", "Request credit card Info." and "Process payment" for recommendations, our approach recommends him relevant activities as given in Fig. 2.

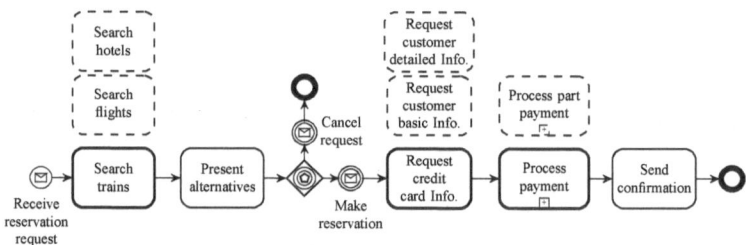

Fig. 2. Recommendations for the train reservation process

The recommendations given by our approach do not make the designer confused since they do not recommend the whole business structure. In contrast, short lists of recommended activities can help the designer easily open his view to improve the working process. For example, those recommendations, the designer is supposed to have ideas to improve the "train-reservation" process by such ways that: he can either add the "Request customer basic Info." activity for future customer services or improve the current process to achieve a traveling service, which combines activities in the "train-reservation" and "hotel-reservation" processes (Fig. 3).

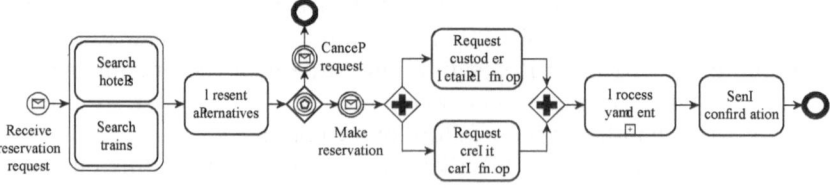

Fig. 3. New traveling process improved from the train reservation process

This paper is organized as following: the next section presents the related work. Details of the approach are elaborated in section 3. Section 4 shows our implementation and experiments. Finally, we conclude our work in section 5.

2   Related Work

Some existing approaches [1,2,3] target to fasten the design phase by retrieving similar process to the current designed process from repositories. They proposed either to rank existing business process models for similarity search [1,4], or to measure the similarity between them [2,3,5] for creating new process models. In our approach, we focus partially on the business process and take into account only the activity neighborhood context for recommendations instead of matching the whole business process.

R. Dijkman et. al. [6] used Levenshtein distance to compare the activity labels; graph edit distance and vector space model to determine the similarity between business process structures. They also proposed the ICoP framework [7] to identify the match between parts of process models using these metrics. Different from them, we focused on activity neighborhood contexts with layers and zones. We compute the similarity between neighborhood contexts based on the matching of connection flows in zones with zone weight consideration instead of matching activity labels or matching virtual documents.

S. Sakr et. al. [8] proposed a query language which takes into account the partial process models to manage business process variants. They, however, retrieve parts of processes based on strictly mapping to a structured input without considering the activity similarity. In our work, we retrieve the relevant activities based on the similarity values which are computed based on a tree structure mapping (section 3.2).

A search framework that aims at retrieving process segments was proposed by M. Lincoln et. al. [9]. In their work, they defined the object grouping model (OGM) which includes the relationship between a primary object and others in a process segment. Different from them, we take into account the sequence of connection flow elements instead of the repetition of edges and we match connection flows in zones to infer the similarity instead of using TF-IDF for the OGM-segment matching.

3   Activities Neighborhood Context Matching

This section elaborates our proposal to recommend activities for a business process. To achieve recommendations, we firstly present activities' contexts using graph theory (section 3.1). Secondly, we compute the similarities between activity neighborhood contexts (section 3.2). Finally, for a chosen activity, we recommend a list of activities and their involved neighborhood contexts based on the computed similarity values (section 3.3). To demonstrate our approach, we assume that there exists a 'flight-reservation' process (Fig. 4) and we are going to compute the similarity between the "Search trains" (Fig. 1) and "Search flights" (Fig. 4) activities based on their neighborhood contexts.

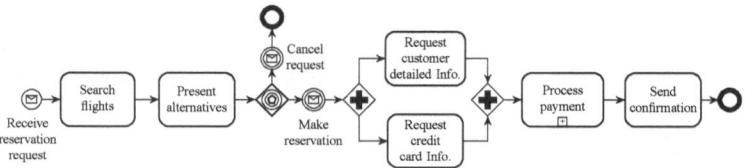

Fig. 4. Flight & hotel reservation processes

3.1 Graph-Based Activity Neighborhood Context

We choose graph theory to present a business process and an activity neighbor-hood context because the structure of a business process can be mapped to a graph. Without loss of generality, we select and use BPMN in our approach as it is one of the most popular business process modeling language. In our work, we define an activity or a start event or an end event as a vertex, and the sequence of *connection elements* (gateways, messages, transitions, events) that connect two vertexes as an edge (or a *connection flow*).

Definition 1 (k^{th}-layer neighbor). *A kth-layer neighbor of an activity a_x is an activity connected from/to a_x via k connection flows ($k \geq 0$). The set of kth-layer neighbors of an activity a_x in a business process $\mathcal{P}$ is denoted by $N_{\mathcal{P}}^k(a_x)$. $N_{\mathcal{P}}^0(a_x) = \{a_x\}$;*

Definition 2 (k^{th}-zone flow). *A kth-zone flow of an activity $a_x \in \mathcal{P}$ is a con-nection flow which connects an activity in $N_{\mathcal{P}}^{k-1}(a_x)$ and an activity in $N_{\mathcal{P}}^k(a_x)$. Set of all k^{th}-zone flows of an activity $a_x \in \mathcal{P}$ is denoted by $Z_{\mathcal{P}}^k(a_x)$. $Z_{\mathcal{P}}^0(a_x) = \emptyset$ and $|Z_{\mathcal{P}}^k(a_x)|$ is the number of connection flows in the kth connection zone of a_x.*

A path in a business process graph is called as a *connection path*. A connec-tion path from a_i to a_j in a business process $\mathcal{P}$ is *indirected* and denoted by $CP_{\mathcal{P}}(a_i, a_j)$. The *length* of a connection path $CP_{\mathcal{P}}(a_i, a_j)$ is denoted by $Len(CP_{\mathcal{P}}(a_i, a_j))$ and the *shortest connection path* between a_i and a_j is de-noted by $SP_{\mathcal{P}}(a_i, a_j)$.

Definition 3 (Activity neighborhood context graph). *Let $V_{\mathcal{P}}$ is the set of vertexes, $L_{\mathcal{P}}$ is the set of connection element names, and $E_{\mathcal{P}} \subseteq V_{\mathcal{P}} \times V_{\mathcal{P}} \times L_{\mathcal{P}}$ is the set of edges (connection flows) in the process $\mathcal{P}$. An edge $e = < a_x, a_y, P_{\mathcal{P}}(a_x, a_y) > \in E_{\mathcal{P}}$ is considered to be directed from a_x to a_y. $P_{\mathcal{P}}(a_x, a_y)$ is the string of the connection flow from a_x to a_y in $\mathcal{P}$.*

The neighborhood context graph of an activity $a_x \in \mathcal{P}$ is a labeled directed graph $G_{\mathcal{P}}(a_x) = (V_{\mathcal{P}}(a_x), L_{\mathcal{P}}(a_x), E_{\mathcal{P}}(a_x))$ where:

1. *$V_{\mathcal{P}}(a_x) = V_{\mathcal{P}}$*
2. *$L_{\mathcal{P}}(a_x) = L_{\mathcal{P}}$*
3. *$E_{\mathcal{P}}(a_x) \subseteq E_{\mathcal{P}} \times N$,*
   $E_{\mathcal{P}}(a_x) = \{e_t^x, e_t^x = (e_t, z_t(a_x)) : e_t = < a_i, a_j, P_{\mathcal{P}}(a_i, a_j) > \in E_{\mathcal{P}}, z_t(a_x) = Min(Len(SP_{\mathcal{P}}(a_i, a_x)), Len(SP_{\mathcal{P}}(a_j, a_x))) + 1, a_i, a_j \in V_{\mathcal{P}}\}$

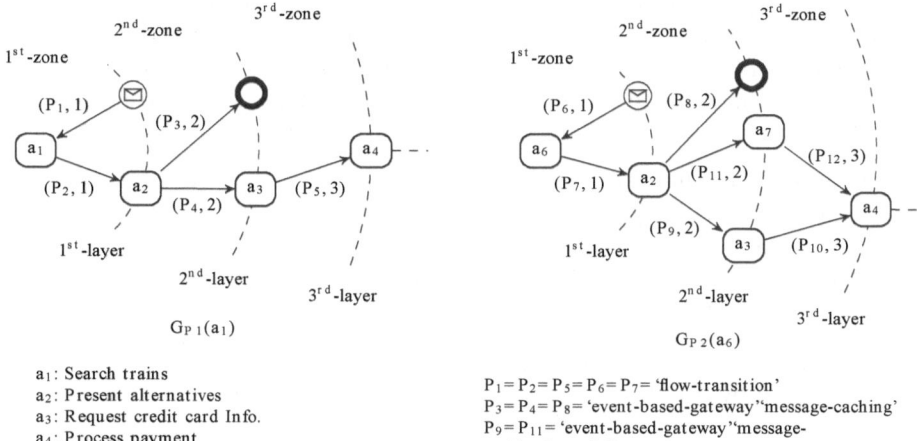

a1: Search trains
a2: Present alternatives
a3: Request credit card Info.
a4: Process payment
a6: Search flights
a7: Request customer detailed Info.

$P_1 = P_2 = P_5 = P_6 = P_7 =$ 'flow-transition'
$P_3 = P_4 = P_8 =$ 'event-based-gateway''message-caching'
$P_9 = P_{11} =$ 'event-based-gateway''message-caching''parallel'
$P_{10} = P_{12} =$ 'parallel'

Fig. 5. Example: activity neighborhood context graph

For example, an excerpt of the "Search trains" neighborhood context graph created from "train-reservation" process (Fig. 1) and an excerpt of the "Search flights" neighborhood context graph created from "flight-reservation" process (Fig. 4) are represented in Fig. 5.

3.2 Neighborhood Context Matching

In our work, we aim at *exploiting the relation between activities* to find activities that have similar neighborhood contexts with the context of a selected activity. We propose to *match all connection flows that belong to the same connection zone and have the similar ending activities.*

Connection Flow Matching. To compute the similarity between activity neighborhood contexts, we propose to match all the connection flows connect them to/from their neighbors. Since each connection flow is a sequence of connection elements which can easily be mapped to a sequence of characters, we propose to use the Levenshtein distance [10] to compute the matching between two connection flows. Concretely, given two connection flows $P(a_i, a_j) = p_1 p_2 \ldots p_n$ and $P'(a_{i'}, a_{j'}) = p'_1 p'_2 \ldots p'_m$, their pattern matching is given by Eq. (1).

$$M_p(P, P') = 1 - \frac{LevenshteinDistance(P, P')}{Max(n, m)} \qquad (1)$$

In our example, $M_p(P_1, P_6) = M_p(\text{'flow-transition', 'flow-transition'}) = 1$; $M_p(P_4, P_9) = M_p(\text{'event-based-gateway''message-caching', 'event-based-gateway''message-caching''parallel'}) = 0.67$ and so on.

Activity Neighborhood Context Matching. The neighborhood context matching between two activities is synthesized from the matchings of associated connection flows. Besides, the behavior of an activity is stronger reflected by the connection flows to its closer neighbors. Therefore, we propose to assign a weight (w_k) for each kth connection zone, so called *zone-weight* and inject this weight into the similarity computation: $w_z = \dfrac{k+1-z}{k}$, where z is the zone number $(1 \leq z \leq k)$ and k is the number of considered zones around the activity.

Consequently, suppose that $e = (< a_x, a_y, P_{\mathcal{P}m}(a_x, a_y) >, z)$ is the edge connecting a_x and a_y by the connection flow $P_{\mathcal{P}m}(a_x, a_y)$ belongs to zone z in the activity neighborhood context graph $G_{\mathcal{P}m}(a_i)$, $e \in V_{\mathcal{P}m}(a_i)$. Similarly, $e' = (< a_{x'}, a_{y'}, P_{\mathcal{P}n}(a_{x'}, a_{y'}) >, z') \in V_{\mathcal{P}n}(a_j)$. The activity neighborhood context matching of a_i and a_j within k connection zones with the direction consideration is given by Eq. 2.

$$M_{\mathcal{P}m,\mathcal{P}n}^{k}(a_i, a_j) = \frac{2}{k+1} \times \sum_{z=1}^{k} \frac{\sum\limits_{e.z=e'.z'=z} \frac{k+1-z}{k} \times M^*(e,e')}{|Z_{\mathcal{P}m}^{z}(a_i)| - |Z_{\mathcal{P}m}^{z-1}(a_i)|} \qquad (2)$$

where:

- $M^*(e, e') = M_p(P_{\mathcal{P}m}(a_x, a_y), P_{\mathcal{P}n}(a_{x'}, a_{y'}))$ if :
  ① $(z = z' = 1) \wedge ((a_x = a_i \wedge a_{x'} = a_j \wedge a_y = a_{y'}) \vee (a_x = a_{x'} \wedge a_y = a_i \wedge a_{y'} = a_j))$
  ② $(1 < z = z' \leq k) \wedge (a_x = a_{x'}) \wedge (a_y = a_{y'})$
- $M^*(e, e') = 0$ in other cases.
- $|Z_{\mathcal{P}m}^{z}(a_i)| - |Z_{\mathcal{P}m}^{z-1}(a_i)|$ is the number of connection flows in the zth connection zone of $G_{\mathcal{P}m}(a_i)$ (see Definition 2).

Return to the illustrated example, neighborhood context matching computed within three zones[1] between a_1 and a_6 (Fig. 5) is: $M_{\mathcal{P}1,\mathcal{P}2}^{1}(a_1, a_6) = \frac{2}{3+1} \times$ $(\frac{\frac{3}{3} \times M_p(P_1,P_6) + \frac{3}{3} \times M_p(P_2,P7)}{2} + \frac{\frac{2}{3} \times M_p(P_3,P_8) + \frac{2}{3} \times M_p(P_4,P_9)}{2} + \frac{\frac{1}{3} \times M_p(P_5,P_{10})}{1}) = 0.78.$

3.3   Activity Recommendation

The activity neighborhood context graph presents the interactions between the associated activity and its neighbors in layers. It infers the associated activity's behavior. Therefore, the matching between their neighborhood context graphs exposes the similarity between associated activities in terms of their behaviors. In our approach, the higher the matching values are, the more similar the corresponding neighborhood contexts are. For each activity in a business process, we compute its neighborhood context graph matching with others. Then, we sort the computed matching values in descending order and pick up top-N activities which have the highest matching values for the recommendation. For instance, the recommendations for the selected activities are shown in Fig. 2.

---

[1] The zone number can be tuned by the process designer, the more details he wants, the greater zone number is.

4   Experiments

In our experiments, we aim at assessing the number of activities that have similar neighborhood contexts retrieved from a large collection of real business processes. Our goal is to two fold: (i) to show that we can find similar activity neighborhood contexts based on our proposed matching solution to prove that our approach is feasible in real use-cases and (ii) to analyze the parameters that impact the context matching computation and show the usefulness of our approach. Details of the dataset and experiments are given as following.

4.1   Dataset

The dataset used for validating our approach is a shared collection of business process models which has been used for the experiments reported in [11]. In statistics, the collected dataset consists of 850 BPMN processes with 2203 start events, 2727 end events, 4466 activities (including 406 subprocesses), 13498 gates and 33885 sequence flows. On average, there are 8.2 activities, 2.6 start events, 3.21 end events, 39.87 interactions per process, and 5.24 gates per one connection flow. Among 4466 activities, there are 1561 activities' names existing in more than one BPMN process.

4.2   Experiments

In the first case, we set k^{th}-zone $= 1$ and match the activity neighborhood context graphs of all activities in the repository using the proposed computation. In results, 4373/4466 activities in the repository (97.92%) have matching values with others greater than 0, in which 1889 activities (43.20%) have matching values greater than 0.5 and 168 activities (3.84%) have matching values belonging to $[0.9,1.0]$.

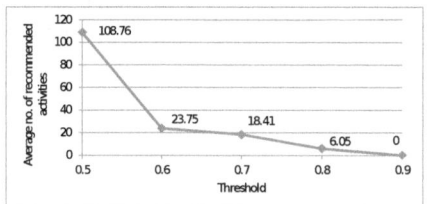
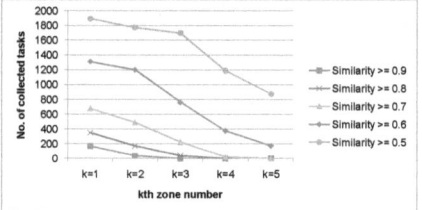

(a) Average number of recommended activities with different thresholds

(b) Number of activities having similarity $>= 0.5$ within 5 zones

Fig. 6. Experiments on activities recommendation

In another experiment we compute, for each activity, within three zones the average number of recommended activities that have similarity values greater than a given threshold. With 0.8 as threshold, for each activity, our approach recommends on average 6.05 activities that have similar neighborhood contexts.

We can notice that this average number of recommended activities decreases when the threshold increases as showing Fig. 6a. We noticed also the same behavior if we fix the threshold and tune the the zone number, i.e. the average number of recommended activities decreases when the zone number increases.

In the second case, we increase the kth-zone value to extend our evaluation to the further layers. We get experiments with $k = \overline{1..5}$. We retrieved 4446 activities in the second zone, 4372 activities in the third zone, 4254 activities in the forth zone and 4072 activities in the fifth zone that have similarity values greater than 0. Fig. 6b shows only cropped data with the accumulated numbers of activities having similarity values greater than 0.5. These numbers decrease when k increases because our algorithm matches only the connection flows connecting two similar activities in the greater zone numbers. When k increases, the number of unmatched neighbors generally increases faster than the matched neighbors. This yields the number of unmatched connection flows increases fast and causes the reduction of similarity values in further zones.

In general, the experiments show that our approach is feasible in retrieving activities that have the similar neighborhood context in real use-cases. Based on the computed similarity, business process recommendation strategies can be run to assist the business process designer to facilitate his (re)design.

5 Conclusion

In this paper, we propose an original approach that captures the activity neighborhood context to assist business process designers with recommendations. Based on the recommended activities, the designer can easily improve or expand the process to achieve more business goals. In addition, our solution can help to create more business process variants.

In our future work, we intend to investigate the co-existence of connection flows in business processes, as well as the number of time that an activity is used in oder to refine our matching algorithm. We also aim at extending our approach to use event logs to infer the business processes for the approach's input.

References

1. Yan, Z., Dijkman, R., Grefen, P.: Fast Business Process Similarity Search with Feature-Based Similarity Estimation. In: Meersman, R., Dillon, T.S., Herrero, P. (eds.) OTM 2010, Part I. LNCS, vol. 6426, pp. 60–77. Springer, Heidelberg (2010)
2. van der Aalst, W.M.P., Alves de Medeiros, A.K., Weijters, A.J.M.M.: Process Equivalence: Comparing Two Process Models Based on Observed Behavior. In: Dustdar, S., Fiadeiro, J.L., Sheth, A.P. (eds.) BPM 2006. LNCS, vol. 4102, pp. 129–144. Springer, Heidelberg (2006)
3. Li, C., Reichert, M., Wombacher, A.: On Measuring Process Model Similarity Based on High-Level Change Operations. In: Li, Q., Spaccapietra, S., Yu, E., Olivé, A. (eds.) ER 2008. LNCS, vol. 5231, pp. 248–264. Springer, Heidelberg (2008)

4. Dijkman, R., Dumas, M., García-Bañuelos, L.: Graph Matching Algorithms for Business Process Model Similarity Search. In: Dayal, U., Eder, J., Koehler, J., Reijers, H.A. (eds.) BPM 2009. LNCS, vol. 5701, pp. 48–63. Springer, Heidelberg (2009)
5. Ehrig, M., Koschmider, A., Oberweis, A.: Measuring similarity between semantic business process models. In: APCCM 2007, pp. 71–80 (2007)
6. Dijkman, R., Dumas, M., van Dongen, B., Käärik, R., Mendling, J.: Similarity of business process models: Metrics and evaluation. Inf. Syst. 36(2), 498–516 (2011)
7. Weidlich, M., Dijkman, R., Mendling, J.: The ICoP Framework: Identification of Correspondences between Process Models. In: Pernici, B. (ed.) CAiSE 2010. LNCS, vol. 6051, pp. 483–498. Springer, Heidelberg (2010)
8. Sakr, S., Pascalau, E., Awad, A., Weske, M.: Partial process models to manage business process variants. IJBPIM 6(2), 20 (2011)
9. Lincoln, M., Gal, A.: Searching Business Process Repositories Using Operational Similarity. In: Meersman, R., Dillon, T., Herrero, P., Kumar, A., Reichert, M., Qing, L., Ooi, B.-C., Damiani, E., Schmidt, D.C., White, J., Hauswirth, M., Hitzler, P., Mohania, M. (eds.) OTM 2011, Part I. LNCS, vol. 7044, pp. 2–19. Springer, Heidelberg (2011)
10. Levenshtein, V.I.: Binary Codes Capable of Correcting Deletions, Insertions and Reversals. Soviet Physics Doklady 10, 707 (1966)
11. Fahland, D., Favre, C., Jobstmann, B., Koehler, J., Lohmann, N., Völzer, H., Wolf, K.: Instantaneous Soundness Checking of Industrial Business Process Models. In: Dayal, U., Eder, J., Koehler, J., Reijers, H.A. (eds.) BPM 2009. LNCS, vol. 5701, pp. 278–293. Springer, Heidelberg (2009)

Adaptive Case Management in the Social Enterprise

Hamid Reza Motahari Nezhad, Claudio Bartolini, Sven Graupner, and Susan Spence

Services Research Lab, Hewlett Packard Laboratories
Palo Alto, California, USA
{hamid.motahari,claudio.bartolini,sven.graupner,
susan.spence}@hp.com

Abstract. In this paper, we introduce SoCaM, a framework for supporting case management in social networking environments. SoCaM makes case entities (cases, processes, artifacts, etc.) first class, active elements in the social network and connects them to people. It enables social, collaborative and flexible definition, adaptation and enactment of case processes among people. It also offers mechanisms for capturing and formalizing feedback, from interactions in the social network, into the case, process and artifact definitions. We report on the implementation and a case management scenario for sales processes in the enterprise.

Keywords: Case Management, Ad-hoc Processes, Enterprise Social Networks.

1 Introduction

Case management accounts for a large proportion (>90%) of process-centric activities in the enterprise, where knowledge workers are involved in domains such as customer relationship management, IT service management, health, legal, financial, government and telecommunications [4]. A case consists of a set of artifacts, actors (human or systems), tasks – planned and unplanned - and the coordination of the tasks to achieve a certain goal [5]. Adaptive case management (ACM) refers to managing all of the work needed to handle a specific case in a flexible manner by adhering to the principles of planning-by-doing and accommodating changes in the environment [3, 4]. Managing cases often involves a mix of automated work (emails, communication, document and partly workflow management applications) and human work. The main inefficiency in today's case management comes from the fact that the people, information systems, process definitions and enactment tools are isolated and disconnected.

Social media and in particular social networks are emerging as the main communication and interaction platforms for people. Social networks have been deployed in the enterprise (e.g., platforms such as Yammer, Jive Engage, SocialText, Salesforce Chatter, and HP WaterCooler[1]). However, their use is limited to information sharing among employees and they have not been linked to and used as

---

[1] WaterCooler is an internal HP social networking platform [6].

C. Liu et al. (Eds.): ICSOC 2012, LNCS 7636, pp. 550–557, 2012.

productivity tools in the enterprise. This is reflected in their low adoption in the enterprise. For example, less than 5% of employees are active users of HP WaterCooler [6, 14] even though it has been deployed in HP for more than five years.

In this paper, we present SoCaM, a framework for flexible case management centered on an extended notion of an enterprise social network that consists of people and things. The main contributions are as follows:

- We define *process*, *task* and *artifact* as first class entities in the social network of people and things.
- We define a *case* as a first class entity in the social network. A case may include one or more processes as the basis for the enactment of the case.
- We support the adaptive enactment of best practice processes for case management applications by offering a wide range of flexibility features including adaptive tasks, adaptive case templates and partially fulfilled tasks, and the addition of at-will ECA (event-condition-action) rules.
- We enable process, task and artifact to become active entities to subscribe to a case that uses them, so they are informed about and can identify the changes made to their definitions during case enactment.
- We report on a use case of this technology in the domain of sales processes in the HP Enterprise Services organization.

The paper is structured as follows. In Section 2, we present the requirements for adaptive case management in a social context. In Section 3, we present SoCaM, the proposed framework for social case management. Section 4 presents the architecture, the implementation of a prototype SoCaM framework and the case study. We discuss related work in Section 5 and conclude with future work in Section 6.

2   Requirements of ACM in the Social Enterprise

We conducted a case study on sales case management within the HP Enterprise Services business. We focused on how people in a sales team collaborate within and across teams, and how they define, enact and coordinate their activities for a sales case. We found that there are best-practice process definitions that provide guidelines on the sales process. Sales teams decide on the actual activities that they perform in a specific sales case. A key observation is that the work is defined around artifacts of the case. Tasks define work stages on the artifacts, what input(s) are needed and what output(s) are generated. The case may use one or more process templates, and tasks in the case either belong to a process template or are added in an ad-hoc manner. There is a need for flexibility in *task execution order*. Many of the tasks are *optional* by definition. Many of the tasks may be completed after several rounds of execution (so there is a need for support for *partial fulfillment*) where, in each round, the tasks work on the same set of artifacts as input/output. Finally, *process definition configurability* is important for tasks and templates to enable the process to be adapted for the case as more contextual information on the case becomes available.

Adding the perspective of an enterprise social network, we see the need for making *process, artifact and task active* in the social network so that, like other entities in the network (such as people), they should also be capable of emitting and consuming events. Beyond representation, the ability for these entities to subscribe to information about their usage and to analyze feedback is also important. Entities can use such information to enhance their representation and to adjust their behavior in the network (in terms of the events that they emit).

3   SoCaM: The Social Case Management Framework

The Social Case Management (SoCaM) framework is designed for the definition and enactment of best practice processes in an enterprise social network environment. SoCaM represents process, task, artifact and case as first class entities in the social network. In this approach, each best practice process is registered in the network environment. Each individual task of a process may be also registered as a first class entity. This enables the sharing of reusable tasks across several processes, and also the receiving of finer granularity feedback from the network at the task level. The profile of the task includes a description of how the task needs to be performed, the roles that are involved in the task, input and output artifacts, task variances (based on configurable parameters such as deal type, size, geography and sales region), and the list of supporting resources. The process (template) profile then includes a description, a list of tasks and the precedence of tasks which can be represented as a dependency graph or a list view.

When a new case is created in the SoCaM environment, the case manager may choose a number of configuration parameters. In the context of the Services Sales domain, the configurable parameters are: region, industry, size of the deal, and deal type. SoCaM prepares the list of compatible processes and a recommended set of process templates are presented to the user. The user may choose to include one or more of the process templates in the case. Examples of process templates are pursuit management, solution management, customer management, etc. These will be added to the task space of the cases, using each process as a way to group tasks. Note that tasks in the added process templates may have dependencies (based on their input/output). These dependencies will be automatically established by the SoCaM engine. The user may define additional precedence constraints on the tasks across templates.

3.1   The SoCaM Data Model

The SoCaM data model is depicted in Fig. 1. A case consists of a set of tasks and a set of artifacts. A case may be associated with one or more process definition templates. A process (template) represents the definition of a best practice in the organization. A process consists of a set of inter-related tasks. The task relationships capture their recommended precedence. Artifacts are documents and they are first class entities in case management. We define an artifact template such that an artifact is an instance of a template. An artifact template is independent of any case, while an artifact, on the other hand, is an instantiation of a template for a specific case.

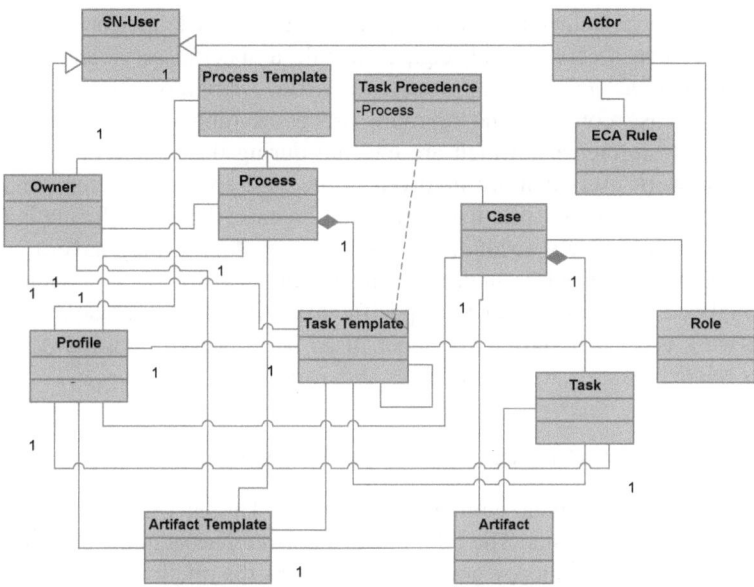

Fig. 1. The conceptual data model for representing case entities in a social network environment.

Task. A task has a profile, an owner, a set of attributes, including state, and a set of roles associated with it. Having a profile means that the task can be followed by the social network users. We represent a task template as a tuple *tt=<name, state, roles, artifacts-templates, permission, owner, followers>*. The *state=<Ready, Assigned, Pending, Completed>*, and this list can be updated by the task owner. The possible set of *roles=<Accountable/Approver, Responsible, Follower>*. An actor may be assigned as Accountable/Approver (as somebody who is eventually accountable, and optionally can be mandated to approve the task before it is declared as completed), Responsible (the person who performs the task), or Follower (somebody, assigned at execution time, who is interested in being informed of the status of the task during execution in a case). The *followers* list, on the other hand, refers to network users who follow updates to the definition of this task. The *owner* is a user in the social network who has edit authority on the task. The *permission* specifies the view and edit access permissions on the task. By default, the view access is set to case actors, and the edit access is set to responsible/accountable actors. These permission settings and those for comments/updates on the task can be expanded to include followers, all social network users or specific external users (through their email). We use the term *task* to refer to the instantiation of a template. A task has a set of *actors* associated with it.

Process. A process is composed of a set of tasks that are inter-related. We define a process template as *pt=<name, tasks, tpgraph, artifact-templates, owner, permission, followers>*.The variable *tpgraph* refers to the task precedence graph, which is a graph that shows the recommended relationships among tasks, based on the dependencies among their input/outputs. The *tpgraph* may represent a multi-level graph for a process in which some tasks may include a *tpgraph* for the set of their subtasks. We use term *process* to refer to the instantiation of a template for a specific case.

Case. A case is a container for a collection of adaptive tasks performed on a set of artifacts to achieve a certain goal, e.g., to handle a specific service engagement. A case is defined as *c=<name, processes, tasks, artifacts, actors, permission, followers>*. A case contains one or more processes (and references to associated process template references) which are enacted during the course of case handling. The social network users that are involved in the case are called actors, and may be assigned to one of an extensible list of roles in the case. The default role is the *case-manager* who is ultimately accountable for the case. A case may have a number of followers, who receive public updates from the case. An actor is a social network user who takes a role in a case or in a specific task. An actor (and also an owner, as a social network user) may define a number of ad-hoc (Event-Condition-Action) rules on events related to cases, tasks, processes and artifacts.

3.2   Flexible Process Enactment for Case Management

The SoCaM case management engine adopts the WS-HumanTask framework [12] for the definition of human tasks. The relationships between tasks in the context of a case are modeled using a dependency graph that maintains the relationships between cases, actors, tasks, artifacts and processes. This graph can dynamically change during the course of case handling. In addition to the flexibility features such as adding a task, skipping a task, and removing a task, we also support:

Adaptive tasks: tasks that adapt to the context of the case. The model allows parametric modeling and configuration of tasks, that enables them to be enacted differently in different contexts; for example, Service deals may be characterized by parameters such as the size of the deal, the solution complexity, and different geographical regions.

Adaptive process templates: The system adapts the order and number of tasks in a case process template based on changes in the contextual parameters of the case.

Partially fulfilled tasks: identifying tasks that can be partially fulfilled and completed during several rounds of execution, often based on the acceptance/review conditions. The important aspect is that, in each iteration, the task will act on the same artifacts.

Social tasks: tasks that are open to all social network users or selected external users through permission settings and get completed based on some conditions such as minimum number of contributions, etc. This enables the soliciting of contributions to the case through crowdsourcing practices, by engaging all enterprise employees, or from external users such as customers.

3.3   Supporting Cases in a Social Network

The case profile names it, describes its purpose, presents its current status and provides pointers to related entities including people and tasks. A case profile is a container and aggregator of activities around the case, and these activities are posted to the activity pages of actors and followers of the case. Fig. 2 shows a sample case

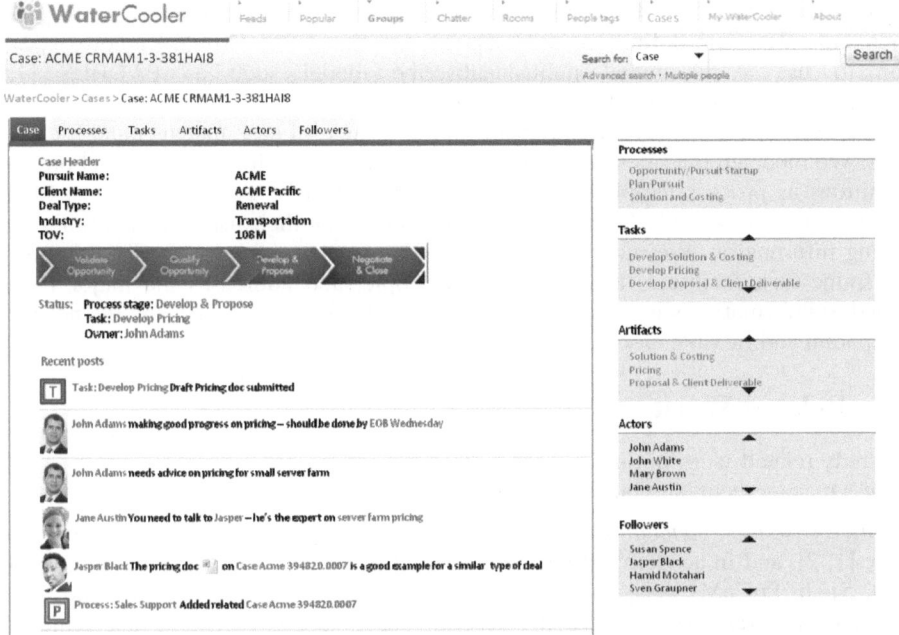

Fig. 2. The case elements in a social network environment

profile in HP WaterCooler. A social network user can explore the description and composition of the case to see what best practice guidelines it enacts, and which process templates it uses, and view the current status of the case and choose to follow the case.

A social network user who is a case actor can also view a list of past and current activities on the case, tailored to their role, participate in discussions by commenting e.g. associated with a process or task, to justify an action such as skipping a task, which will both form a part of the record for this case history and be reflected back to the process usage history in the process template. Each case has an email address. Users can include the case in the email exchanges. The emails are posted to the case profile on behalf of the sender. This feature addresses information lock-in among enterprise employees since, today, a lot of information related to the case or individual tasks are locked in emails, or spread across multiple communication channels such as email and IM.

3.4   Implementation and Case Study

We have developed SoCaM on top of HP WaterCooler (see [14]). We extended the data model of WaterCooler by creating nodes for entities (process, task, case and artifact) and related information in a graph database. For the data model, we have extended Neo4J (neo4j.org/), a scalable graph database, to represent and store information about cases, and to relate cases to people and other entities in WaterCooler. The template manager module supports the definition of process, task and artifact templates and maps them into the graph node representation. The task definitions are based on the WS-HumanTask framework implementation from jBoss (jbpm.org). The rule definitions are mapped into the jBPM Drools framework. We plan to use a distributed publish/subscribe model such as PADRES [13] (padres.msrg.org) that suits the social network environment.

As a case study, we have used SoCaM in the context of case management for sales cases. We modeled the sales processes which include hierarchical, multi-level process definitions as process templates in SoCaM, and their tasks as task templates. Many sales people were already familiar with WaterCooler but their use of it was limited to sharing information. We received very supportive and encouraging feedback on how this framework facilitates the job of sales people, and addresses the major issues related to information silos, broken and fragmented communications, and the need for transparent and flexible case management in social network environments.

4   Related Work

We study related work in three categories: adaptive case management, artifact-centric process management, and business process management in social networks.

Adaptive case management. Case management is a hot topic in research and practice today [1, 2], and in academia it has been studied in various contexts including health [3, 4, 5]. In SoCaM, we adopt the same basic principles as in [3] and could use a similar formal framework to formally describe our model. The main advances include that our framework supports extra flexibility features such adaptive tasks, adaptive templates and social tasks for opening up tasks to actors outside the system, and also enables actors to define ad-hoc personal rules to manage the case.

Artifact-centric business processes. The artifact-centric approach for business processes represents a class of approaches [9, 10] in which the state changes and evolution of business artifacts are considered as the main driver of the business process. While we share the same observation that business artifacts are the center of attention in case management applications, we take a hybrid approach in SoCaM where object lifecycle (as input or outcome of tasks or cases) is important, but the model contains tasks that define activities over artifacts and some control flow level actions to take the case forward.

Social BPM. Recently the topic of social BPM has received a lot of interest in academia and practice [7, 8]. Most approaches by BPM vendors or research offer extensions for business process models to represent tasks that can be exposed in social networks (e.g., for voting, ranking, etc). [7] offers a model driven approach for generating code for tasks in popular social networks such as Facebook and LinkedIn and also an extended business process management engine. Current effort focuses on supporting traditional workflow applications in the social network environment. We go beyond and support the enactment of ad-hoc processes in the context of adaptive case management in enterprise social networks.

5   Conclusions and Future Work

We have presented SoCaM, a framework for social case management. We provide a technology solution for flexible case management in the social network environment that represents case elements as first class entities in the social network, and includes provision for collecting and analyzing feedback about the usage of process, task and artifact entities. The benefits of case management using SoCaM include the ease of capturing and enabling the exploration of relationships between people and entities, offering a context for sharing and keeping a record of knowledge about cases, processes, tasks and artifacts and also the ability to use notifications, based on a publish/subscribe model, to communicate changes and updates. Research to support case management applications in a social network environment is in its early stages. We plan to make our research prototype more scalable in a production environment, specifically w.r.t. distributing and propagating changes and subscribing to events.

References

1. Singularity, Case Management: Combining Knowledge with Process (July 2009), http://www.bptrends.com/publicationfiles/07-09-WP-CaseMgt-CombiningKnowledgeProcess-White.doc-final.pdf
2. de Man, H.: Case Management: A Review of Modeling Approaches (January 2009), http://www.bptrends.com/publicationfiles/01-09-ART-%20Case%20Management-1-DeMan.%20doc-final.pdf
3. van der Aalst, W.M.P., Weske, M., Grünbauer, D.: Case handling: a new paradigm for business process support. Data Knowl. Eng. 53(2), 129–162 (2005)
4. Burns, E.V.: Case Management 101. In: Swenson, K.D., Palmer, N., Silver, B., Fischer, L. (eds.) Taming the Unpredictable. Future Strategies Inc. (2011)
5. Palmer, N.: BPM and ACM (Adaptive Case Management). In: Swenson, K.D., Palmer, N., Silver, B., Fischer, L. (eds.) Taming the Unpredictable. Future Strategies Inc. (August 2011)
6. Brzozowski, M.: WaterCooler: Exploring an Organization Through Enterprise Social Media. In: Proc. the ACM International Conference on Supporting Group Work, pp. 219–228 (2009)
7. Fraternali, P., Brambilla, M., Vaca, C.: A Model-driven Approach to Social BPM Applications. In: Fischer, L. (ed.) Social BPM. Future Strategies Inc. (May 2011)
8. Fischer, L.: Social BPM. Future Strategies Inc. (May 2011)
9. Kumaran, S., Liu, R., Wu, F.Y.: On the Duality of Information-Centric and Activity-Centric Models of Business Processes. In: Bellahsène, Z., Léonard, M. (eds.) CAiSE 2008. LNCS, vol. 5074, pp. 32–47. Springer, Heidelberg (2008)
10. Bhattacharya, K., Gerede, C., Hull, R., Liu, R., Su, J.: Towards Formal Analysis of Artifact-Centric Business Process Models. In: Alonso, G., Dadam, P., Rosemann, M. (eds.) BPM 2007. LNCS, vol. 4714, pp. 288–304. Springer, Heidelberg (2007)
11. Salesforce, Sales process management and workflow (2012), http://www.salesforce.com/crm/sales-force-automation/workflow/
12. OASIS, Web Services – Human Task (WS-HumanTask) Specification Version 1.1 (November 2009), http://docs.oasis-open.org/bpel4people/ws-humantask-1.1-spec-cd-06.pdf
13. Wun, A., Jacobsen, H.-A.: Modelling performance optimizations for content-based publish/subscribe. In: Proceedings of the 2007 Inaugural International Conference on Distributed Event-Based Systems (DEBS 2007), pp. 171–179. ACM, USA (2007)
14. Graupner, S., Bartolini, C., Motahari-Nezhad, H., Mirylenka, D.: Social Media Meet the Enterprise – Analysis, Conclusions and Advancing to the Next Level. In: The Proceedings of EDOC 2012, China (September 2012)

Automating Form-Based Processes through Annotation*

Sung Wook Kim[1], Hye-Young Paik[1], and Ingo Weber[1,2],**

[1] School of Computer Science & Engineering, University of New South Wales
[2] Software Systems Research Group, NICTA, Sydney, Australia
{skim,hpaik,ingo.weber}@cse.unsw.edu.au

Abstract. Despite all efforts to support processes through IT, processes based on paper forms are still prevalent. In this paper, we propose a cost-effective and non-technical approach to automate form-based processes. The approach builds on several types of annotations: to help collect and distribute information for form fields; to choose appropriate process execution paths; and to support email distribution or approval for filled forms. We implemented the approach in a prototype, called *EzyForms*. We conducted a user study with 15 participants, showing that people with little technical background were able to automate the existing form-based processes efficiently.

1 Introduction

Business Process Management Systems (BPMS) enable organisations to automate and continuously improve business processes in order to achieve better performance. Although the benefits of BPMS have been widely recognised, there is still a large portion of business processes that are not adequately addressed by these systems. These types of processes make up the so-called long tail of processes, i.e. highly customised processes that are unique to individual organisations, or concern a small number of workers.

In this paper, we particularly focus on the long tail of processes that consists of form documents. Forms provide a low-tech, quick and flexible way to manage processes. However, they impose a good deal of manual labour on the end users, such as searching/downloading required forms, entering the same information repeatedly, printing/faxing forms and so on.

A typical form-based processes exhibit the following characteristics. First, a form-based process consists of one or more paper-based forms which are eventually to be submitted to an administration unit to trigger an organisational process (e.g., a trip request). Second, a form-based process is initiated and executed by a single user (e.g., a trip requestor), and the user is normally responsible for finding information about the process (e.g., reading instructions on a web page, searching/downloading forms). Third, a form-based process involves obtaining

---

* This work is supported by SDA Project, Smart Services CRC, Australia
** NICTA, http://www.nicta.com.au/about/

C. Liu et al. (Eds.): ICSOC 2012, LNCS 7636, pp. 558–565, 2012.

zero or more approvals on completed forms, which could mean the user having to write multiple email requests and coordinating the chain of approval manually. Although there are other types of form-based processes (e.g., a process involving more than one user), our current work focuses on this model initially.

Our approach is to enable the form users to model and deploy their *existing* form-based processes into a service-enabled framework without requiring technical knowledge or the cost of re-engineering. The key concept of our proposal is in various types of annotations on forms and effective applications of such information during the modelling and execution phases of form-based processes. Our contributions in this paper are:

- a prototype named *EzyForms*, a framework that supports the whole life-cycle of form-based process management. It includes the following novel aspects:
  - identification of different types of annotation for simple, implicit modelling and execution of form-based processes,
  - smart applications of the annotations to support basic data flows and execution patterns in form-based processes,
  - a WYSIWYG-fashion integration of forms in every stage of the process life-cycle, from form service creation through to modelling and execution.
- evaluation of such a framework through user studies.

Note that a full version of the paper is available at [1].

2   Proposed Approach

We aim to enable form owners to automate the form-based processes themselves, and allow end users to execute the process efficiently. This approach consists of four steps: form upload, form annotation, process modelling, and process execution.

2.1   Form Upload

In order to fill-in the forms electronically, we convert a form into a Web service. This is done by our previous work, FormSys [2], through which PDF forms[1] are uploaded to the central FormSys repository. Formally, we define $\mathcal{F} := \{F_1, F_2, \ldots\}$ as the set of all forms in the system, where each form has a set of fields $\mathcal{G}(F_i) := \{f_1, f_2, \ldots, f_n\}$.

2.2   Form Annotation

We recognise the fact that, to remove the need of BPM/IT professionals' involvement, the system must ascertain necessary information by itself as much as possible (e.g., which form is relevant for process X, which fields in form A are duplicated in form B). This is, of course, not always feasible or accurate. To bridge the gap, we introduce the form annotation step which is an act of adding metadata to the form. Due to its informality and flexibility in use, annotation

---

[1] We use AcroForm, a PDF sub-standard, which contains interactive form elements.

has been widely accepted by users for assisting Web browsing or searching, and utilised in many systems like Flickr, Delicious, and Youtube [3,4]

There are two types of annotations, each assisting different aspects of process automation: annotation for process modelling and for process execution. Also, the annotation is defined on two levels: the form-library level (i.e., the annotation is defined on the form generically, without regards to the processes in which the form is involved) and the process level (starting from the form-library level, the annotation can be refined within the context of a process – see Sect. 2.3).

Annotation for Modelling. This annotation is used to help form owners when modelling a new process.

- *Form description tag*: these are descriptive or representative tags that can describe the form. For example, the travel reimbursement form in our usage scenario may have form descriptions tags like `travel`, `reimbursement`, `travelcost`. We formalize the system-wide set of form description tags as $\mathcal{T} := \{t_1, t_2, \ldots\}$, and the annotation function $T : \mathcal{F} \mapsto 2^{\mathcal{T}}$ as a mapping from the forms to the description tags which apply to this form: $T(F_i) = \emptyset$ or $T(F_i) = \{t_{i_1}, \ldots, t_{i_k}\}$ for $F_i \in \mathcal{F}$ and $t_{i_1}, \ldots, t_{i_k} \in \mathcal{T}$ where k corresponds to the number of form description tags added to the form. These tags contribute to the search and discovery of forms.
- *Input field tag*: these are synonyms, alias or any descriptive tags for an input field in a form. For example, name field in the travel reimbursement form may have tags such as `name`, `staffname`, `fullname`. Formally, we write $\mathcal{I} := \{i_1, i_2, \ldots\}$ for the set of input field tags available in the system. The respective annotation function $I : \mathcal{G} \mapsto 2^{\mathcal{I}}$ is defined as a mapping from the form fields to the field tags: $I(f_j) = \emptyset$ or $I(f_j) = \{i_{j_1}, \ldots, i_{j_k}\}$ for $f_j \in \mathcal{G}$ and $i_{j_1}, \ldots, i_{j_k} \in \mathcal{I}$ where k corresponds to the number of tags added to the input field. These tags contribute to ascertain simple data flow between forms. That is, by comparing the tags associated with input fields from each form, as well as their respective text labels, we can postulate if any given two input fields share the same input data.

Annotation for Execution

- *Condition*: This type of annotation specifies conditions under which the form should be used. We define the system-wide set of conditions as $\mathcal{C} := \{c_1, c_2, \ldots\}$, and the condition annotation function $C : \mathcal{F} \mapsto 2^{\mathcal{C}}$ as a mapping from the forms to the conditions which apply to this form: $C(F_i) = \emptyset$ or $C(F_i) = \{c_{i_1}, \ldots, c_{i_k}\}$ for $F_i \in \mathcal{F}$ and $c_{i_1}, \ldots, c_{i_k} \in \mathcal{C}$ where k corresponds to the number of conditions associated with the form. The conditions on a form are a template for conditions in a process. Process-level conditions determine if the form should be filled by a particular end user at process execution stage. Details on all execution aspects are given below.
- *Approver*: This annotation type describes the names and email addresses of people who are responsible for approving some form (e.g., travel requests may need approval from the Head of School), and used when dispatching approval request emails. Formally, we write $\mathcal{A} := \{a_1, a_2, \ldots\}$ for the set

of approvers stored in the system, and $A : \mathcal{F} \mapsto 2^{\mathcal{A}}$ is a function mapping from the forms to the approvers which apply to this form: $A(F_i) = \emptyset$ or $A(F_i) = \{a_{i_1}, \ldots, a_{i_k}\}$ for $F_i \in \mathcal{F}$ and $a_{i_1}, \ldots, a_{i_k} \in \mathcal{A}$ where k corresponds to the number of approvers associated with the form.

- *Email Template*: This annotation type specifies email templates for creating email content to be sent to approvers, where the filled-in form gets attached. The email templates available in the system are formally referred to as $\mathcal{E} := \{e_1, e_2, \ldots\}$, and the email annotation function as $E : \mathcal{F} \times A \mapsto \mathcal{E}$, a mapping from the forms and their respective approvers to the email template which should be sent to this approver for this form: $E(F_i, a_j) = e_k$ iff $a_j \in A(F_i)$, else undefined.

Note that the collected annotations on different forms by different form owners are centrally managed and shared via *EzyForms* Knowledge Base (KB). Also, adding annotations is an activity separate from process modelling tasks and it is possible that annotation and modelling are done by different people.

2.3   Process Model

The process model is designed based on the following characteristics of form-based processes:

- they are purely form-to-form processes, that is, it is possible to describe the processes as multiple steps of fill-form activities
- they are a single sequential flow where conditions are used to determine optional part of the flow (i.e., which form is relevant for the current user).

In this section, we describe the the formal model for the association between form annotation and the process model.

Process Definition. The annotations associated with the form documents in a process are translated into the process model. A *process model* is defined as a 6-tuple $p := (\mathcal{F}|_p, C|_p, A|_p, E|_p, I|_p, O)$, such that:

- $\mathcal{F}|_p \subseteq \mathcal{F}$ is a projection from the set of all forms to its subset used in p.
- $C|_p : \mathcal{F}|_p \mapsto 2^{\mathcal{C}}$ is a function mapping from the forms in p to the conditions which apply to this form: $C|_p(F_i) = \emptyset$ or $C|_p(F_i) = \{c_{i_1}, \ldots, c_{i_k}\}$ for $F_i \in \mathcal{F}|_p$ and $c_{i_1}, \ldots, c_{i_k} \in \mathcal{C}$.
- $A|_p : \mathcal{F}|_p \mapsto 2^{\mathcal{A}}$ is a function mapping from the forms in p to the approvers which apply to this form: $A|_p(F_i) = \emptyset$ or $A|_p(F_i) = \{a_{i_1}, \ldots, a_{i_k}\}$ for $F_i \in \mathcal{F}|_p$ and $a_{i_1}, \ldots, a_{i_k} \in \mathcal{A}$.
- $E|_p : \mathcal{F}|_p \times A \mapsto \mathcal{E}$ is a function mapping from the forms in p and their respective approvers to the email template which should be sent to this approver for this form: $E|_p(F_i, a_j) = e_k$ iff $a_j \in A(F_i)$, else undefined.
- $I|_p : \mathcal{G}(F_k) \mapsto \{\mathcal{I}, \bot\}$ is defined as a mapping from a form field to zero or one field tag: $I|_p(f_j) = \bot$ (no field tag) or $I|_p(f_j) = i_j$, where $f_j \in \mathcal{G}(F_k)$, the form belongs to p: $F_k \in \mathcal{F}|_p$, and $i_j \in \mathcal{I}$.

– O specifies the order of the forms in p, and thus is an ordered permutation of $\mathcal{F}|_p : O = (F_{i_1}, \ldots, F_{i_k})$ where k corresponds to the number of elements in $\mathcal{F}|_p$, and $i_j \neq i_l$ for any $j, l \in \{1, \ldots, k\}$.

Almost all process-specific annotations are projections of their respective forms-library level counterparts. The exception is the field tags: where on the form library level sets of field tags can be annotated, on the process-specific level at most one field tag can be assigned to each field. Note that we do not require the annotations on the process level to be subsets of the library level.

2.4   Process Execution

We now explain how a process model in our approach is executed. When an end user starts an instance of some process model $p = (\mathcal{F}|_p, C|_p, A|_p, E|_p, I|_p, O)$, the approach first asks the user to determine the truth of all conditions used in the process (if any), as a set union: $\bigcup_{F_i \in \mathcal{F}|_p} C|_p(F_i)$. This means that conditions which are shared between forms are only evaluated once. The user selects whether the condition applies to her case, i.e., is true for this instance, or not.

Next, the forms without conditions, or whose conditions all were marked to be true, are executed. That is, a form F_i is only shown to the user if $C|_p(F_i) = \emptyset$ or c_j is true for all $c_j \in C|_p(F_i)$. The execution takes place in the order specified by O. Form execution here means that each form is shown to the user, who can enter values for the fields. The user can go back and forth between the forms.

The process-level field tags (zero or one per field) are hereby interpreted as data mapping: all fields tagged with the same tag are set to the same value. For a fixed but arbitrary $i \in \mathcal{I}$, this set of fields is $\{f \in \mathcal{G}(F) \mid F \in \mathcal{F}|_p, I|_p(f) = i\}$. This value equality is applied whenever the value for a field in this set is changed.

After filling all desired values into the forms, the user can trigger the next step in the process, where all filled forms can be downloaded in their original format. Finally, all approval emails are sent out for each form F_i without annotated conditions ($C|_p(F_i) = \emptyset$) or where all conditions $C|_p(F_i)$ are true.

3   *EzyForms* Implementation

A prototype (Fig. 1) has been implemented and its screencast is available at http://www.cse.unsw.edu.au/~hpaik/ezyforms/.

Form Upload and Annotation. The forms and their matching Web services are stored in the repository in *FormSys Core Component*. `Matcher` and `Form Annotation Manager` components are responsible for managing tag library and tag recommendations. We use Apache Lucene[2] to create indices on the form's title text, file name, text content as well as the annotation tags.

Process Modelling and Execution. `Input Field Mapper` generates mapping candidates for any selected input fields amongst forms during the modelling

---

[2] http://lucene.apache.org/

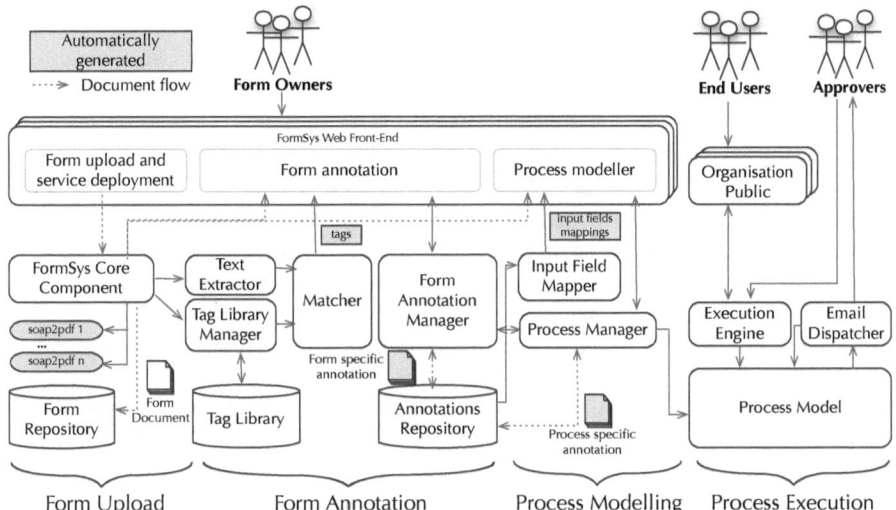

Fig. 1. *EzyForms* Architecture

process. **Process Manager** stores and manages all processes created by the form owners. When an end user instantiates a process, **Execution Engine** first, interacts with the end user to evaluate any conditions in the process, determines forms to be filled-in, presents the forms for input and executes the form services. Finally, it interacts with **Email Dispatcher** to send the forms according to the approval chain generated.

Approval Chains. From the approver annotations, we auto-generate an approval chain model that supports a multi-level hierarchy (e.g., supervisor, then Head of School, then the Dean) as well as "parallel-splits" (e.g., signed by two supervisors). From the approval chain model, *EzyForms* dispatches approval request emails to appropriate approvers and collate the responses.

Recommendation for Adding Tags. For form owners, manually creating tags for a form (e.g., for input fields) can be time-consuming and tedious. To assist, our system includes recommendation algorithms for suggesting tags. For example, the algorithm for recommending form description tags will consider elements such as title text of the form, or free text appearing after the title (which is normally a description/instruction about the form) to derive potentially relevant terms. The details of the tag recommendation algorithms and evaluation results are explained in [5].

Candidate Generation for Mappings. For form owners, the mapping task in form-based process modelling involves identifying input fields that share the same value across forms. To assist, we automatically generate a suggested list for mapping candidates in the chosen forms. We take the tags in an input field with those appearing in other input fields. We then calculate the number of common tags between any two input fields. Based on the common tags, we generate a ranked list of mapping candidates.

4   User Study

In this section, we present a summarised version of our user study results. A full version is available at [1]. The study included 15 participants. The main goals of the study were to evaluate whether: i) our form annotation approach can be applied to people with little technical background (especially in BPM) to automate processes and ii) end users find the automated execution of a form-based process convenient.

The task scenario was based on a university student activity grant application process. The participants were given two paper forms[3] and asked to observe the forms and the process instructions. Then, using our tool, the participants were asked to execute form annotation and process modelling tasks as if they were the form owners. For the form annotation task, they first identified the form fields that they thought would frequently appear across other forms, and annotated those fields with descriptive tag names. For the process modelling task, the participants used the two form services to create an application process.

We categorised 7 participants into 'experienced users' and 8 participants into 'novice users'. All fifteen participants were able to use the tool and complete the given set of tasks designed for the form owner's role – without any extra help, regardless of their respective category. The questionnaire results on the tasks showed the tool was easy to use and intuitive (scoring well over 4 in a 5-point scale in all questions). Overall, we believe our proposed approach to automating the form-based process (and its implementation in *EzyForms*) is applicable to both groups and not bound to any process modelling experience.

All participants were able to complete the tasks given for the second role, form end user. Figure 2(a) shows the scores on the questionnaires which asked to rate the amount of improvement they saw at each steps of the form-based process, compared to the manual ones. All participants commented that *Ezy-Forms* allowed them to conduct the process in more efficient manner. This is largely due to the fact that most manual work was either completely removed or significantly reduced (e.g., identifying which forms to fill-in, downloading forms to fill-in). Finally, each participant selected three favourite features from our approach without specific order. It shows that the most popular point was that they no longer had to fill-in same information repeatedly, closely followed by the point that they did not have to identify required forms by themselves (the conditions annotation in our tool automates that aspect) (Fig. 2(b)).

5   Conclusion and Future Work

In this paper, we have presented a pragmatic approach for automating form-based processes. In our approach, the form-based process model and execution

---

[3] www.arc.unsw.edu.au/get-involved/clubs-and-societies/
club-forms-and-policy

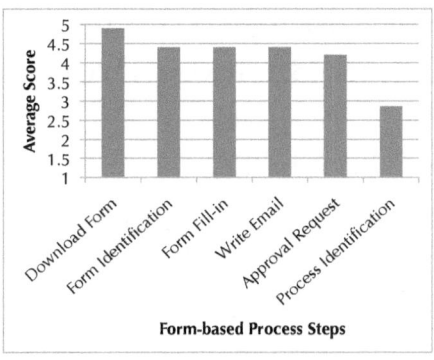

(a) Process execution steps (end user experience)

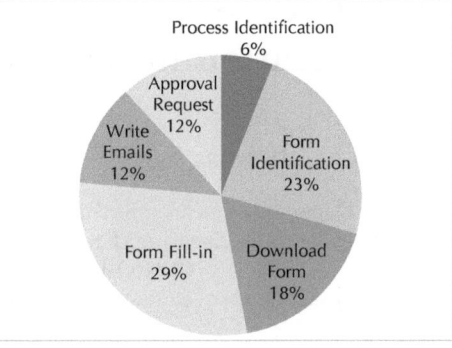

(b) Favourite features

Fig. 2. Form annotation user study evaluation

are deliberately kept plain so that deriving their definitions for automation is attainable through tags and other simple form of annotations by the form owners. So far in this work, we have identified the types of annotations that can be used to support the end-to-end life-cycle of form-based processes. We have developed a fully working prototype named *EzyForms* as proof of concept. Our preliminary evaluation revealed that form annotation approach for automating form-based processes are applicable to people with little or no technical background, and that automated form-based processes significantly improved the overall user experience especially for form fill-in, form identification and form download tasks.

In future work, we plan to explore the process data management issue so that *EzyForms* can deal with process specific data (e.g., id number of the project that will fund the travel) and sharing of such data between users. We will improve the tooling features including more complex input fields mapping (e.g., concatenating two strings or manipulating dates) and attaching files to the forms.

References

1. Kim, S.W., Paik, H.Y., Weber, I.: Automating Form-based Processes through Annotation. Technical Report 201221, School of Computer Science and Engineering, The University of New South Wales (2012),
   ftp://ftp.cse.unsw.edu.au/pub/doc/papers/UNSW/201221.pdf
2. Weber, I., Paik, H.Y., Benatallah, B., Gong, Z., Zheng, L., Vorwerk, C.: FormSys: Form-processing Web Services. In: WWW 2010, pp. 1313–1316 (2010)
3. Cattuto, C., Loreto, V., Pietronero, L.: Semiotic Dynamics and Collaborative Tagging. Proceedings of the National Academy of Sciences 104, 1461–1464 (2007)
4. Golder, S.A.: Usage Patterns of Collaborative Tagging Systems. Journal of Information Science 32, 198–208 (2006)
5. Kim, S.W.: Form annotation framework for long tail process automation. In: Workshop on User-Focused Service Engineering, Consumption and Aggregation (to be published in 2012) (2011)

PASOAC-Net: A Petri-Net Model to Manage Authorization in Service-Based Business Process

Haiyang Sun[1], Weiliang Zhao[2], and Surya Nepal[3]

[1] Department of Computing, Macquarie University, Sydney, Australia
[2] Faculty of Engineering, University of Wollongong, Wollongong, Australia
[3] CSIRO ICT Centre, Sydney, Australia
haiyang.sun@mq.edu.au, wzhao@uow.edu.au, Surya.Nepal@csiro.au

Abstract. A successful execution of a Business Process (BP) is possible only if the proper coordination exists between (1) BP's execution policy, (2) BP's authorization policy, and (3) the authorization policies of BP's resources. Hence, there is a need of an effective authorization model that brings all types of policies together for a BP executing successfully without breaking any authorization and business rules. This paper proposes a Petri-Net process model, Process-Aware Service-Oriented Authorization Control Net (PASOAC-Net). PASOAC-Net is developed based on the conceptual model PASOAC, an extension of Role Based Access Control (RBAC), which takes both resources and users into account. A set of authorization constraints is designed in PASOAC to coordinate the user access and the resource support in a process environment.

1 Introduction

For a successful execution, a Business Process (BP) must be able to satisfy authorization policies of resources to receive their supports. The interactions between the BP and its users are also imperative. Users need to satisfy the process authorization policies before accessing to the specific process functions. Execution policies are used to manage the sequence of task invocations within a BP, i.e., business logic. Without an appropriate coordination on these policies, a BP may not be able to perform properly. Therefore, how to manage the user accesses and the resource supports in a BP in a distributed environment, e.g., web service domain, becomes a challenging task. We will discuss this point further through a motivating example.

1.1 Motivating Example

In Fig. 1, we illustrate an execution sequence of Financial Lease BP. Each operation (also known as task) of BP is depicted as a rectangle in the process. A User table is used to illustrate three types of users, and their associated access policies on operations. Four types of resources are illustrated in Resource table in Fig. 1. The sequence of interactions among users, resources, and operations of BP is numbered in Fig. 1. The requirements for accessing and supporting Financial Lease are stated below,

C. Liu et al. (Eds.): ICSOC 2012, LNCS 7636, pp. 566–573, 2012.

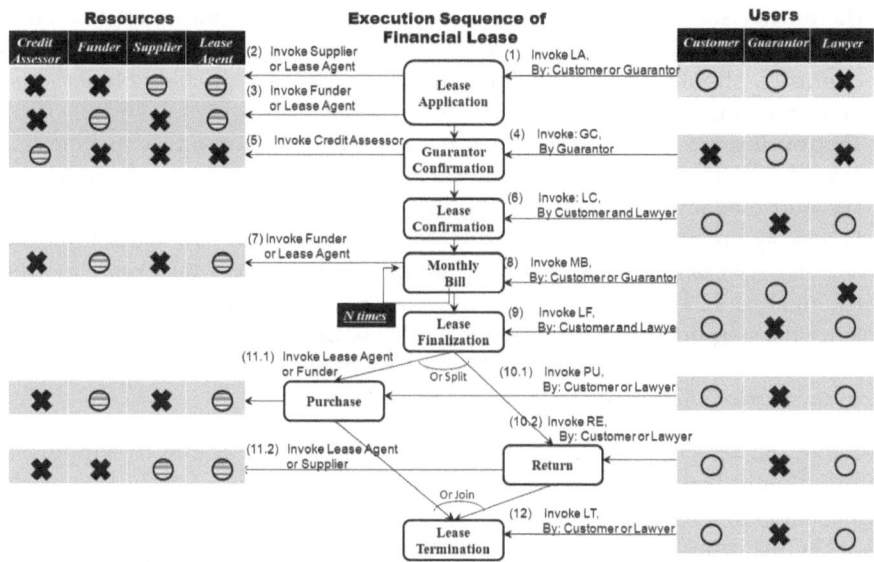

Fig. 1. Execution Sequence of Financial Lease

– **User:** (1) Customer should be able to access all operations. (2) The operation *Guarantor Confirmation* can only be made by Guarantor. Guarantor can start the lease on behalf of the Customer and help to repay the rental. (3) Lawyer after lease finalization stage can deal with any rest activities on behalf of its client. Furthermore, Lawyer is necessary to involve in operations of *Lease Confirmation* and *Lease Finalization* with Customer.

– **Resource:** (1) Funder is used to provide financial support. (2) Supplier is the product provider. (3) Lease Agent can provide both product and fund to Financial Lease, since the Lease Agent will seek its own Funder and Supplier. (4) Credit Assessor can evaluate the credit histories of Guarantor and Customer.

We can observe from the above example that the user accesses and the resource supports are not only regulated by their specific authorization policies, but also need to be restricted by the business constraints enacted during the execution of BP. Otherwise, authorization issues can be raised to cease process execution. These business constraints can be categorized as follows,

– **Synchronization:** The sequence of the user accesses and resource supports should be synchronized with the execution sequence of the operations in BP. When an operation is ready to execute in a process instance, the relevant users and resources that can access and support the operation should be invoked. Once the operation finishes, the permissions assigned to the user and resource to access and support the operation should be revoked immediately. For example, when the operation *Guarantor Confirmation* starts,

the authorization to access the operation should be granted to `Guarantor`. When the operation finishes, the authorization of `Guarantor` access to the operation should be revoked immediately to avoid repeated submissions of guarantor information.
- **Dependency**: A user access of (or a resource support on) a specific operation in a BP may depend on another user access (or resource support). In the above example, operation *Monthly Bill* can be supported by `Funder` or `Lease Agent` and accessed by `Customer` or `Guarantor`. To avoid fraudulent activity, a `Guarantor` can pay the rental on behalf of the `Customer` to access the operation *Monthly Bill* only if a `Funder` issues the bill. This constraint is used when an entity can play as both `Lease Agent` and `Guarantor`. Obviously, if the entity pays the bill issued by itself, it may eventually do harm to `Customer`'s interest.

Therefore, an effective authorization model is highly desirable to support the coordination of the user accesses and resource supports in a BP. In this work, a conceptual model named Process-Aware Service-Oriented Authorization Control (PASOAC) is proposed to manage authorization of business process by considering both user access and resource support. Two types of authorization policies, (1) Authorization Synchronization Policies and (2) Authorization Dependence Policies, are included in the conceptual model to deal with the above business security requirements. Authorization flow (i.e, sequences of user accesses and resources supports with associated authorization policies) is modeled by a Petri-Net based process model PASOAC-Net.

The rest of paper is organized as follows. Section 2 describes the conceptual model PASOAC. Authorization policies are also defined in this section. The specification of PASOAC-Net is described in Section 3. Section 4 overviews some related work. Concluding remarks are provided in Section 5.

2   Conceptual Model-PASOAC

In this section, we specify the PASOAC conceptual model by using the notation of **Entity-Relationship (E-R) Diagram**. In Fig. 2, rectangles represent elements and diamonds represent relationships. We define Role (**R**) as a type of user that requires to access the operations (**Op**) of BP. Resource type (**ReT**) is defined as a type of resource that can provide support on the operation (**Op**). Their associated relationships, *access* and *support*, are all many-to-many.

In Fig. 2, there are two types of authorization policies, *Synchronization* and *Dependency*. A sequence of role accesses on operations of BP can be called as *role-flow*; while a sequence of resource type support on operations of BP can be called as *resource type-flow*. An authorization flow consists of role-flow and resource type-flow, and must be executed consistently with the control flow of BP. In Fig. 2, three red arrows are used to represent the sequence of role access (role-flow), business logic of BP (control-flow), and the sequence of resource type support (resource type-flow) respectively. Authorization Synchronization Policy

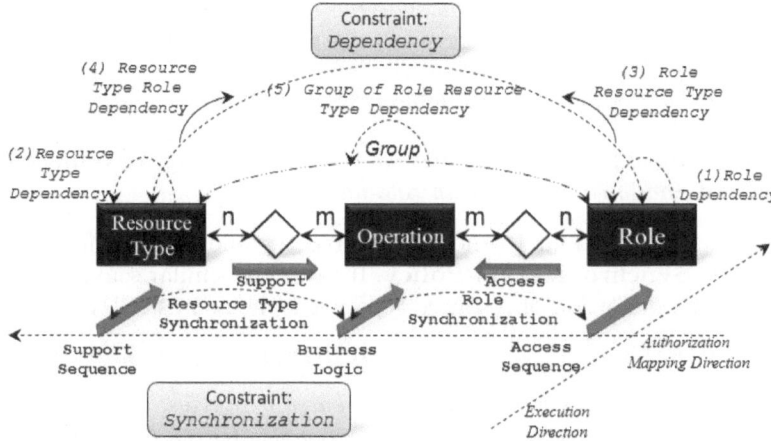

Fig. 2. Process-Aware Service-Oriented Authorization Control

is therefore divided into two types, (1) Role Synchronization Policy and (2) Resource Type Synchronization Policy. Authorization Dependency Policies restrict that a role or a resource type is not able to access or support the operations, until the other role or the other resource type has already accessed or supported specific operations. Authorization Dependency Policies are separated into 5 categories, (1) between roles, (2) between resource types, (3) between roles and resource types, (4) between resource types and roles, and (5) between groups of role and resource type (See Fig. 2).

3 Specification of PASOAC-Net

PASOAC-Net is a Petri-Net process model divided into three parts, role-net, resource type-net, and constraint-net, respectively.

3.1 Structure of PASOAC-Net

Role-Net is used to model role-flow and enforce the **Role Synchronization Policy**. In role-net, we use each transition (the black rectangle) to represent a role access on specific operation. We use token that flows between the transitions in role-net to represent the operations. When the transition consumes one token, it means that the operation (token) has been accessed by the role (the transition). The new generated tokens by this transition will represent the next operation that need to be accessed according to the business logic of BP. Role-Net is formally defined as follows,

Definition 1 *Role-Net is a tuple* $\mathcal{H} = (P^r, T^r, F^r, i^r, o^r)$

- P^r is a set of places, graphically represented as circles,
- T^r is a set of transitions, graphically represented as black bars to represent role accesses on specific operations in role-net. $T^e \subset T^r$ is a set of empty transitions as or-split, or-join, and-split, or and-join,
- $F^r = (P^r \times T^r) \cup (T^r \times P^r)$,
- i^r and o^r are input place and output place respectively, to initially deposit token and finally collect token in role-net.

Resource Type-Net is used to model resource type-flow and enforce the **Resource Type Synchronization Policy**. It bears the similar semantics as Role-Net. The formal definition of resource type-net is defined as follows,

Definition 2 *Resource Type-Net is a tuple $\mathcal{G} = (P^{ret}, T^{ret}, F^{ret}, i^{ret}, o^{ret})$,*

- P^{ret} is a set of places graphically represented as circles,
- T^{ret} is a set of transitions, graphically represented as black bars to represent resource type supports in resource type-net. $T^e \subset T^{ret}$ is a set of empty transitions as or-split, or-join, and-split, or and-join,
- $F^{ret} = (P^{ret} \times T^{ret}) \cup (T^{ret} \times P^{ret})$,
- i^{ret} and o^{ret} are input place and output place respectively, to initially deposit token and finally collect token in resource type-net.

Constraints-Net is used to enforce the five **Authorization Dependency Policies**. Each transition in constraint-net is linked from one transition in role-net or resource type-net and points to another transition in role-net or resource type-net. Hence, without token movement through the transition in constraints-net, the relevant role-net or resource type-net which is pointed by the transition in constraints-net can not accumulate enough tokens to fire, according to the basic execution policy of Petri-Net. We can use this method to realize the dependency between roles, between resource types, even between role and resource type. The group dependency policy is different from the other dependency polices, in that the depending role and resource types can be executed individually, but can not be both executed if the depended role and resource type are not both executed. The formal definition of constraint-net is defined as follows,

Definition 3 *Constraints-Net is a tuple $C = (P^c, T^c, F^c, W, Count)$, Where:*

- P^c is a set of places graphically represented as circles,
- T^c is a set of transitions, graphically represented as black bars to represent constraints in between roles, between resource types, and between role and resource type. For group dependency policy, transitions are separated as follows,
  - $T^e \subset T^c$ is a set of empty transitions as and-split to simultaneously split the token movement pathes to $T_x \subset T^c$ and $T_y \subset T^c$.
  - $T_x \subset T^c$ represents an indictor to show, when Group B depends Group A, if a role or a resource type in group B has already been used to deal with specific operation.
  - $T_y \subset T^c$ represents an indictor to show if both role and resource type in group A have been executed.

- $F^c = (P^c \times T^c) \cup (T^c \times P^c) \cup (T^{ret} \times P^c) \cup (P^c \times T^{ret}) \cup (T^r \times P^c) \cup (P^c \times T^r)$, where, $T_x \bullet \times T^r$ and $T_x \bullet \times T^{ret}$ $(T_x \bullet = \{p \in P^c | (T_x \times p) \in F^c\})$ can be **weak relation** or **normal relation** depending on the amount of tokens in $T_x \bullet$. (1) If no token is deposited in $T_x \bullet$, then the relation between $T_x \bullet$ and the transition in role-net or resource type-net becomes a weak relation that will not affect the execution of the linked transition. (2) When at least one token is deposited in $T_x \bullet$, the relation between $T_x \bullet$ and the transition in role-net or resource type-net becomes normal relation that affects the execution of the linked transition.

- $W : F^c \rightarrow IN$ is a weight function on the relation between place and transition. It reflects how many tokens are needed to pass the relation (IN represents Integer). For example, $W:(\bullet T_y, T_y) \rightarrow 2$ $(\bullet T_y = \{p \in P^c | (p, T_y) \in F^c\})$, $W:(T_x \bullet, T_r) \rightarrow 2$ and $W:(T_x \bullet, T_{ret}) \rightarrow 2$. The weights of all other relations are 1.

- $Count : P^c \rightarrow IN$ is a function to calculate the amount of tokens at each place. The result of this function on specific place can be used to decide if the relation between transition and this place is weak relation or normal relation.

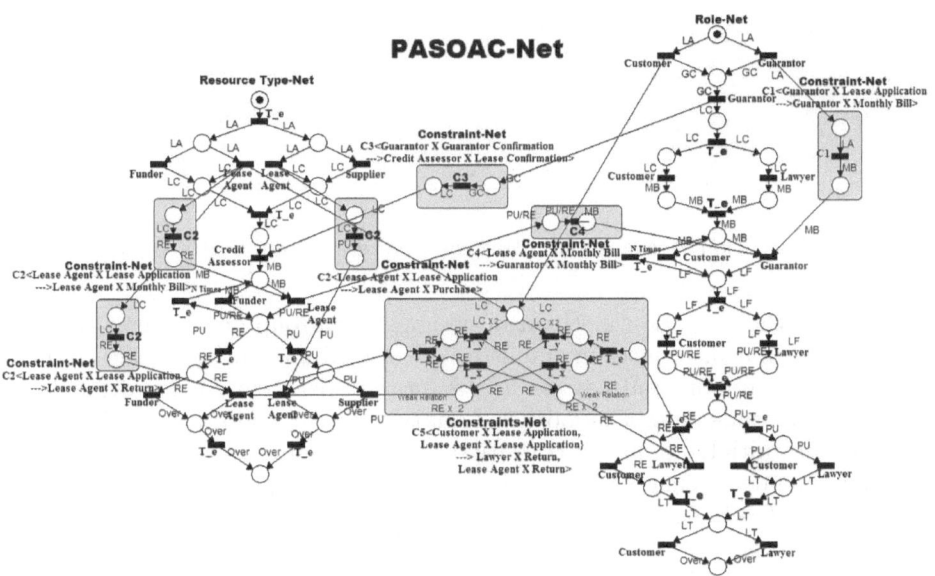

Fig. 3. PASOAC-Net

In Fig. 3, a comprehensive view of PASOAC-Net based on the motivating example is presented, where both role-net and resource type-net are illustrated as well as each category of constraint-net.

3.2   Execution of PASOAC-Net

The token movement in PASOAC-Net is regulated by its execution mechanism. The PASOAC-Net execution complies with the general execution policy of Petri-Net. At beginning, two tokens are deposited at each initial place of role-net and resource type-net. Once the tokens reach the final place of each net, we believe that the BP is successfully executed by complying with all authorization policies.

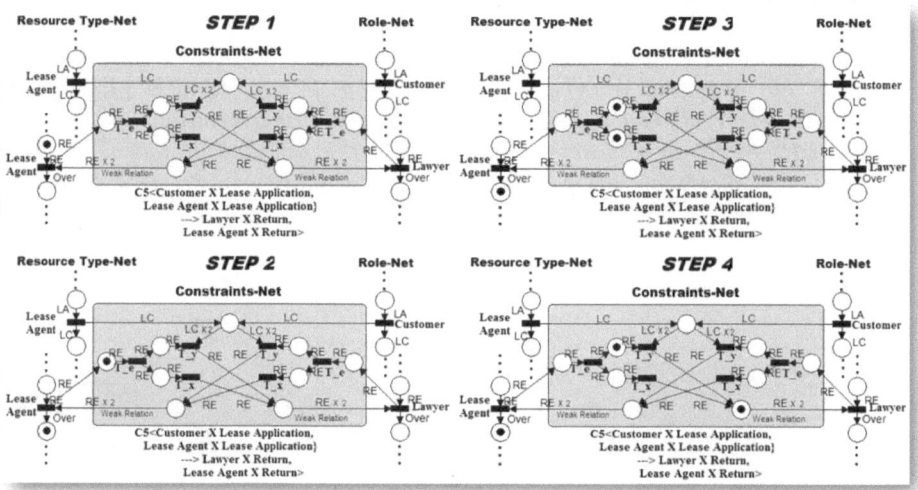

Fig. 4. Execution Mechanism of Constraint-Net for Group Dependency Policy

However, the execution mechanism designed for group dependency policy is complicated that introduces in details here. For example, in Fig. 4, the group of **Lease Agent** support and **Lawyer** access on the operation *Return* depends on the group of **Lease Agent** support and **Customer** access on the operation *Lease Application*. Initially, only the transition (**Lease Agent** support on *Return*) in resource type-net is enabled by a token arrival in its pre-place. There is no token deposited in $T_x\bullet$ in constraint-net. The relation between $T_x\bullet$ and the transition (**Lease Agent** support on *Return*) is weak relation, that will not affect the fire of this transition (**See Step 1 in Fig. 4**). After firing, one token is passed to T_e in constraint-net and the other one is moved into the post-place of this transition in resource type-net (**See Step 2 in Fig. 4**). The token in pre-place of T_e in constraint-net is split into $\bullet T_y$ and $\bullet T_x$ after T_e firing (**See Step 3 in Fig. 4**). At this time, T_x can be enabled and fired to deposit one token from $\bullet T_x$ to $T_x\bullet$. When Count$(T_x\bullet)$=1, the relation between $T_x\bullet$ and the transition (**Lawyer** access on *Return*) in role-net becomes normal relation that affects the fire of the transition. Since W:$T_x\bullet\times T_r$=2 and W:$T_x\bullet\times T_{ret}$=2, one token in $T_x\bullet$ now is not enough to enable the normal relation with weight 2. Therefore, even if the pre-place of the transition (**Lawyer** access on *Return*) in role-net has accumulated enough token, the transition still can not be fired, since its pre-place ($T_x\bullet$) in constraints-net has not accumulated enough tokens to pass the relation with weight 2. The group dependency policy is enforced to restrict the Lawyer access on *Return* before the group of Lease Agent support and Customer access on the operation *Lease Application* have both been executed (**See Step 4 in Fig. 4**).

4   Related Work

Role based access control (RBAC) [1, 2, 3] is a widely accepted approach on BP authorization. In [4], the authors proposed a workflow authorization model (WAM) and an authorization template (AT) to realize the synchronization of role-flow with workflow. In [5], the authors propose a constrained workflow system where local and global cardinality constraints as well as SoD and BoD are enforced. However, all above authorization models in workflow environment, that deal with resources within the same security domain as workflow, can not be used directly as ready solutions for authorization of service based BP, since resources in web service domain spread across organizational boundary. The authorization dependency policies are also missing in the existing models.

5   Conclusion and Future Work

In this paper, we propose an authorization conceptual model PASOAC for managing user access and resource support in business processes. Two types of authorization constraints, *Synchronization* and *Dependency*, are considered in PASOAC. A Petri-Net based process model PASOAC-Net is developed based on PASOAC as a formal infrastructure to ensure the successful execution of BP by enforcing various types of synchronization and dependency policies.

References

[1] Sandhu, R.S., Coyne, E., Feinstein, H., Youman, C.: Role-based Access Control Models. IEEE Computer 29(2), 38–47 (1996)
[2] Ahn, G., Sandhu, R.: Role-Based Authorization Constraints Specification. ACM Transactions on Information and System Security (TISSEC) 3(4), 207–226 (2000)
[3] Ferraiolo, D., Sandhu, R., et al.: Proposed NIST Standard for Role-Based Access Control. TISSEC 4(3), 224–274 (2001)
[4] Atluri, V., Huang, W.-K.: An Authorization Model for Workflows. In: Martella, G., Kurth, H., Montolivo, E., Bertino, E. (eds.) ESORICS 1996. LNCS, vol. 1146, pp. 44–64. Springer, Heidelberg (1996)
[5] Tan, K., Crampton, J., Gunter, C.A.: The consistency of task-based authorization constraints in workflow. In: IEEE Workshop of Comp. Security Foundations (2004)
[6] Wonohoesodo, R., Tari, Z.: A Role Based Access Control for Web Services. In: Proceedings of SCC, pp. 49–56 (2004)
[7] Fischer, J., Majumdar, R.: A Theorey of Role Composition. In: Proceedings of ICWS, pp. 49–56 (2008)

WSTRank: Ranking Tags to Facilitate Web Service Mining

Liang Chen[1], Zibin Zheng[2], Yipeng Feng[1], Jian Wu[1], and Michael R. Lyu[2]

[1] Zhejiang University, China
[2] The Chinese University of Hong Kong, China

Abstract. Web service tags, terms annotated by users to describe the functionality or other aspects of Web services, are being treated as collective user knowledge for Web service mining. However, the tags associated with a Web service generally are listed in a random order or chronological order without considering the relevance information, which limits the effectiveness of tagging data. In this paper, we propose a novel tag ranking approach to automatically rank tags according to their relevance to the target Web service. In particular, service-tag network information is utilized to compute the relevance scores of tags by employing HITS model. Furthermore, we apply tag ranking approach in Web service clustering. Comprehensive experiments based on 15,968 real Web services demonstrate the effectiveness of the proposed tag ranking approach.

1 Introduction

Web service[1] has become an important paradigm for developing Web applications. Especially the emergence of cloud infrastructure offers a powerful and economical platform to greatly facilitate the development and deployment of a large number of Web services [13]. Based on the most recent statistics[2], there are 28,593 Web services being provided by 7,728 distinct providers over the world and these numbers keep increasing in a fast rate.

WSDL (Web Service Description Language) document and extra description given by service providers are two major kinds of data to be utilized for Web services mining [8]. Despite the abundance of extra service description for most current Web services, limited semantic information can be obtained from the XML-based description document, i.e., WSDL document. The fast growing number and limited semantic information of Web services pose significant challenges to Web service mining, e.g., Web service clustering, Web service searching, etc.

---

[1] In this paper, we focus on non-semantic Web services. Non-semantic Web services are described by WSDL documents while semantic Web services use Web ontology languages (OWL-S) or Web Service Modeling Ontology (WSMO) as a description language. Non-semantic Web services are widely supported by both the industry and development tools.

[2] http://webservices.seekda.com

C. Liu et al. (Eds.): ICSOC 2012, LNCS 7636, pp. 574–581, 2012.
© Springer-Verlag Berlin Heidelberg 2012

In recent years, tagging, the act of adding keywords (tags) to objects, has become a popular mean to annotate various Web resources, e.g., Web page bookmarks, online documents, and multimedia objects. Tags provide meaningful descriptions of objects, and allow users to organize and index their contents. Tagging data was proved to be very useful in many domains such as multimedia, information retrieval, data mining, and so on [1][12]. In Web service domain, some Web service search engines, such as SeekDa!, also allow users to annotate tags to Web services. Recently, Web service tags are being treated as collective user knowledge for Web service mining, and attract a lot of attention. Some research work have been conducted to employ tagging data for Web service clustering[6], Web service discovery[3][9], Web service composition [5], etc.

Fig. 1. Two exemplary Web services from SeekDa!

However, existing studies reveal that many tags provided by SNS (Social Network System) users are imprecise and there are only around 50% tags actually related to the target object [10]. Furthermore, the relevance levels of tags can't be distinguished from current tag list, where tags are just listed in a random order or chronological order without considering the relevance information. Figure 1 shows two exemplary Web services[3] from SeekDa! and their tags annotated by users. Take the *USWeather* Web service as an example, its most relevant tag, i.e., "weather", can not be discovered from the order of tag list directly. Similarly, the most relevant tag to *XigniteQuotes* Web service is "stock quote", while its position in the tag list is the 7th. Furthermore, there are some imprecise tags annotated to Web services, such as "unknown","format", etc.

Relevance-independent tag list and imprecise tags limit the effectiveness of tags in Web service mining, or even produce negative effects. In this paper, we propose a novel tag ranking approach named *WSTRank*, to automatically rank tags according to their relevance to the target Web service. In *WSTRank*,

---

[3] http://webservices.seekda.com/providers/webservicex.net/USWeather
http://webservices.seekda.com/providers/xignite.com/XigniteQuotes

we employ HITS [11] model to obtain the relevance score of tag based on a service-tag network.

To demonstrate the effectiveness of tag ranking approach for Web service mining, we apply *WSTRank* into one classical application, i.e., Web service clustering, which is usually used to cluster the Web services with the same or similar functionality to handle the low recall of Web services search.

In particular, the main contribution of this paper can be summarized as follows:

1. This paper identifies the critical problem of tag ranking for Web service mining and proposes a hybrid approach named *WSTRank* to rank tags of Web services. To the best of our knowledge, *WSTRank* is the first tag ranking approach for Web services.
2. Extensive real-world experiments are conducted to study the tag ranking performance of *WSTRank*. The experimental results demonstrate the effectiveness of *WSTRank*. Further, we evaluate the impact of tag ranking to Web service clustering.
3. We publicly release our Web service tag dataset to promote future research, which includes 15,968 real-world Web services and their tags. The released dataset makes our experiment reproducible.

2   Web Service Tag Ranking

In this section, we introduce the computation of HITS based tag authority, which is treated as the relevance score of tag. Hyperlink-Induced Topic Search (HITS) (also known as hubs and authorities) is a link analysis algorithm that rates Web pages, developed by Jon Kleinberg. It is a precursor to PageRank. The idea behind Hubs and Authorities stemmed from a particular insight into the creation of Web pages when the Internet was originally forming. In this section, we propose to obtain the authority of tag in the service-tag network, which could reflect the importance of tag. In the following, we first introduce how to build the service-tag network, and then present a HITS-based algorithm for tag authority computation.

2.1   Service-Tag Network Building

Service-tag network can be modeled as a weighted directed graph G, where node s_i means a service and node t_i means a tag. For each node in G, it has two values, i.e., hub and authority. There are three kinds of directed edges in G:

1. Edge from service node to tag node. Given a service s_1 annotated with three tags t_1, t_2, and t_3, then there is a directed edge from s_1 to t_1, t_2, and t_3, respectively. In particular, the weight of this kind of edge is 1.
2. Edge from service node to service node. Given two services s_1 and s_2, if there is one or more than one common tags annotated to these two services, we create one directed edge from s_1 to s_2 and one directed edge from s_2 to s_1.

These two edges have the same weight, which is depended on the common tags, i.e., $weight = \frac{t_{s_1} \bigcap t_{s_2}}{t_{s_1} \bigcup t_{s_2}}$, where t_{s_1} and t_{s_2} mean the set of tags annotated to s_1 and s_2, respectively.

3. Edge from tag node to tag node. Given two tags t_1 and t_2, and these two tags are annotated to one or more than one services. Similarly, we create one directed edge from t_1 to t_2 and one directed edge from t_2 to t_1. The weight of edge is also depended on the common services, i.e., $weight = \frac{s_{t_1} \bigcap s_{t_2}}{s_{t_1} \bigcup s_{t_2}}$, where s_{t_1} and s_{t_2} mean the set of services contain t_1 and t_2, respectively.

In this way, we obtain the service-tag network by building a weighted directed graph.

2.2   Tag Authority Computation

HITS based algorithm is a kind of iterative algorithm. We consider two types of updates as follows:

– **Authority Update.** For each node p in G, we update the authority of node p to be:

$$Auth(p) = \sum_{i=1}^{n} Hub(p_i) \times w(p_i, p), \qquad (1)$$

where $p_i (i = 1, \ldots, n)$ means the node that points to p, and $w(p_i, p)$ is the weight of edge from p_i to p. That is, the authority of node p is the sum of all the weighted hub values of nodes that point to p.

– **Hub Update.** For each node p in G, we update the hub value of p to be:

$$Hub(p) = \sum_{i=1}^{n} Auth(p_i) \times w(p, p_i), \qquad (2)$$

where $p_i (i = 1, \ldots, n)$ means the node that p points to, and $w(p, p_i)$ means the weight of edge from p to p_i.

Algorithm 1 shows the detailed HITS based computation process. As the initialization, we set the authority value and hub value of each node in G as 1 (line 1-3). K in line 4 means the number of iterations. Empirically, we set $K = 50$ in the experiments. The parameter *norm* is used for normalization, and is initialized as 0 (line 5). According to the Authority Update rule, we compute the authorities of all nodes in G, and then normalize them by using parameter *norm* (line 6-16). Similarly, hub values of nodes can be computed by employing Hub Authority rule (line 18-29). After K iterations, we return the authorities of all tag nodes (line 30-32).

3   Experiment

In this section, we first give a brief description of dataset and experiment setup, and then compare the performance of different tag ranking approaches in terms of NDCG.

Algorithm 1. Tag Authority Computation Algorithm
___
    Input: G:service-tag network; K: number of iterations
    Output: Auth(t): authority of tag node
 1: **for all** node p in G **do**
 2:    Auth(p)=1,Hub(p)=1
 3: **end for**
 4: **for** iteration from 1 to K do **do**
 5:    norm=0
 6:    **for all** node p in G **do**
 7:       Auth(p)=0
 8:       **for all** node p_i which points to p **do**
 9:          Auth(p)+=Hub(p_i) $\times weight(p_i, p)$
10:       **end for**
11:       norm+=square(Auth(p))
12:    **end for**
13:    norm=sqrt(norm)
14:    **for all** node p in G **do**
15:       Auth(p)=Auth(p)/norm
16:    **end for**
17:    norm=0
18:    **for all** node p in G **do**
19:       Hub(p)=0
20:       **for all** node p_i that p points to **do**
21:          Hub(p)+=Auth(p_i) $\times weight(p, p_i)$
22:       **end for**
23:       norm+=square(Hub(p))
24:    **end for**
25:    norm=sqrt(norm)
26:    **for all** node p in G **do**
27:       Hub(p)=Hub(p)/norm
28:    **end for**
29: **end for**
30: **for all** tag node t in G **do**
31:    return Auth(t)
32: **end for**
___

3.1   Dataset Description and Experiment Setup

To evaluate the performance of *WSTRank*, we employ the dataset consists of 15,968 real Web services crawled form the Web service search engine Seekda!. For each Web service, we can obtain the information of service name, WSDL document, tags, availability, and the name of service provider.

For each service, each of its tags is labeled as one of the five levels: Most Relevant (score 5), Relevant (score 4), Partially Relevant (score 3), Weakly Relevant (score 2), and Irrelevant (score 1). As the manual creation of ground truth costs a lot of work, we select 98 Web services from the dataset and distinguish the following categories: "Email", "Stock", "Tourism", "Weather", "Calculation", and "Linguistics". Specifically, There are 11 Web services in "Email"category,

18 Web services in "Stock" category, 20 Web services in "Tourism" category, 14 Web services in "Weather" category, 18 Web services in "Calculation" category, and 17 Web services in "Linguistics" category. Due to the space limitation, we don't shows the detailed information of these Web services.

It should be noted that all experiments are implemented with JDK 1.6.0-21, Eclipse 3.6.0. They are conducted on a Dell Inspire R13 machine with an *2.27 GHZ Intel Core I5 CPU* and *6GB RAM*, running *Windows7 OS*.

3.2 Performance Evaluation of Tag Ranking

To study the performance of tag ranking, we first compute the NDCG vaule of Baseline (i.e., original tag lists), and then compare the performance of the following approache:

- **WSTRank**. In this approach, linking relationship in the service-tag network is employed to rank tags. In this experiment, we choose HITS model to represent the linking relationship.

To evaluate the performance of Web service tag ranking, we employ the Normalized Discounted Cumulative Gain (NDCG) [2] metric, which is widely accepted as the metric for ranking evaluation in information retrieval. Table 1 and Table 2 show the ranking performance of above 4 approaches, respectively employing NDCG@3 and NDCG@5 as the evaluation metric. NDCG@k indicates that only the ranking accuracy of the top-k tags is investigated. Given one category of Web services, we compute the NDCG@k value of each Web service, and set the average value as the NDCG@k value of this category. For each column in the Tables, we have highlighted the best performer among all approaches. The values shown in the bottom row are the performance improvements achieved by the best methods over the Baseline.

Table 1. NDCG@3 performance of tag ranking

Method	Tourism	Weather	Calcu	Lingu	Stock	Email	Average
Baseline	0.756	0.862	0.602	0.621	0.806	0.869	0.753
WSTRank	**0.797**	**0.917**	**0.962**	**0.771**	**0.935**	**0.911**	**0.882**
	5.42%	6.38%	59.8%	24.15%	16.00%	4.83%	17.1%

Table 2. NDCG@5 performance of tag ranking

Method	Tourism	Weather	Calcu	Lingu	Stock	Email	Average
Baseline	0.714	**0.892**	0.709	0.787	**0.877**	**0.901**	0.813
WSTRank	**0.781**	0.855	**0.917**	**0.788**	0.862	0.874	**0.846**
	9.38%	-4.32%	29.34%	0.13%	-1.74%	-3.09%	4.06%

From above two Tables, it can be observed that our proposed *WSTRank* approach largely improves the accuracy of tag ranking. Compared with the Baseline, the improvement brought by *WSTRank* achieves 59.8% at the highest point, and achieves -4.32% in the worst case. In addition, we can also find that the improvement caused by *WSTRank* always decreases when the value of k increases from 3 to 5.

4   Related Work

With the popularity of SNS, tagging data, which is annotated by users and provides meaningful descriptions, is widely employed in many research domains such as mutlimedia, information retrieval, data mining, etc [1]. Recently, tagging data oriented technologies are also employed in service oriented computing. Eric *et al.* propose a folksonomy-based model for Web service discovery and automatic composition, in which tags are utilized as semantic information [5]. In our premise work, we utilize both WSDL documents and tags to cluster Web services, based on the notion that combining users' knowledge and service providers' knowledge [6]. Tagging data is also employed in Web service discovery [7]. To handle the problem of limited tags, Zeina *et al.* propose to employ machine learning technology and WordNet synsets to automatically annotate tags to Web services [4].

5   Conclusion

In this paper, we propose to rank Web service tags to facilitate Web service mining. In our proposed *WSTRank* approach, we utilize the linking relationships in service-tag network to obtain the relevance scores of tags. In particular, HITS model is employed to compute the authority of tag in service-tag network. The experimental results based on real Web services demonstrate the effectiveness of *WSTRank* approach.

In our future work, we plan to expand the scale of tag dataset by inviting volunteers and employing automated tagging approaches. Moreover, *WSTRank* will be applied in applications of Web service mining, e.g., Web service clustering, Web service search and Web service recommendation, to verify the effectiveness of tag ranking in Web service mining.

Acknowledgements. This research was partially supported by the National Technology Support Program under grant of 2011BAH15B05, the National Natural Science Foundation of China under grant of 61173176, Science and Technology Program of Zhejiang Province under grant of 2008C03007, National High-Tech Research and Development Plan of China under Grant No. 2009AA110302, National Key Science and Technology Research Program of China (2009ZX01043-003-003).

References

1. Ames, M., Naaman, M.: Why we tag: Motivations for annotation in mobile and online media. In: Proc. of the SIGCHI Conference on Human Factors in Computing Systems (CHI), pp. 971–980 (2007)
2. Arvelin, K.J., Kekalainen, J.: Cumulated gain-based evaluation of IR techniques. ACM Transactions on Information Systems 20(4), 422–446 (2002)
3. Averbakh, A., Krause, D., Skoutas, D.: Exploiting User Feedback to Improve Semantic Web Service Discovery. In: Bernstein, A., Karger, D.R., Heath, T., Feigenbaum, L., Maynard, D., Motta, E., Thirunarayan, K. (eds.) ISWC 2009. LNCS, vol. 5823, pp. 33–48. Springer, Heidelberg (2009)
4. Azmeh, Z., Falleri, J.-R., Huchard, M., Tibermacine, C.: Automatic Web Service Tagging Using Machine Learning and WordNet Synsets. In: Filipe, J., Cordeiro, J. (eds.) WEBIST 2010. LNBIP, vol. 75, pp. 46–59. Springer, Heidelberg (2011)
5. Bouillet, E., Feblowitz, M., Feng, H., Liu, Z., Ranganathan, A., Riabov, A.: A folksonomy-based model of web services for discovery and automatic composition. In: IEEE International Conference on Services Computing, pp. 389–396 (2008)
6. Chen, L., Hu, L., Zheng, Z., Wu, J., Yin, J., Li, Y., Deng, S.: WTCluster: Utilizing Tags for Web Services Clustering. In: Kappel, G., Maamar, Z., Motahari-Nezhad, H.R. (eds.) ICSOC 2011. LNCS, vol. 7084, pp. 204–218. Springer, Heidelberg (2011)
7. Ding, Z., Lei, D., Yan, J., Bin, Z., Lun, A.: A web service discovery method based on tag. In: International Conference on Complex, Intelligent and Software Intensive Systems, pp. 404–408 (2010)
8. George, Z., Athman, B.: Web service mining. Springer (2010)
9. Hou, J., Zhang, J., Nayak, R., Bose, A.: Semantics-Based Web Service Discovery Using Information Retrieval Techniques. In: Geva, S., Kamps, J., Schenkel, R., Trotman, A. (eds.) INEX 2010. LNCS, vol. 6932, pp. 336–346. Springer, Heidelberg (2011)
10. Kennedy, L.S., Chang, S.F., Kozintsev, I.V.: To search or to label?: predicting the performance of search-based automatic image classifiers. In: Proc. of the 8th ACM International Workshop on Multimedia Information Retrieval, pp. 249–258 (2006)
11. Li, L., Shang, Y., Zhang, W.: Improvement of hits-based algorithms on web documents. In: Proc. of the 11th International World Wide Web Conference, pp. 527–535 (2002)
12. Sigurbjörnsson, B., van Zwol, R.: Flickr tag recommendation based on collective knowledge. In: Proc. of the 17th International Conference on World Wide Web (WWW), pp. 327–336 (2008)
13. Zheng, Z., Ma, H., Lyu, M.R., King, I.: Wsrec: A collaborative filtering based web service recommender system. In: Proc. of the 7th International Conference on Web Services (ICWS), pp. 437–444 (2009)

Maintaining Motivation Models (in BMM) in the Context of a (WSDL-S) Service Landscape

Konstantin Hoesch-Klohe, Aditya K. Ghose, and Hoa Khanh Dam

Decision Systems Lab (DSL),
School of Computer Science and Software Engineering,
University of Wollongong.
{khk789,aditya,hoa}@uow.edu.au

Abstract. The ever-changing business context requires organisations to constantly adapt their motivation and service representations. While there has been work focusing on the relation between the motivation- and service level, very little work has been done in providing machinery for handling (propagating) changes at the motivation level and identifying the resulting impact on the service landscape. In this paper, we propose a novel framework which addresses this problem.

1 Introduction

A motivation model (e.g. represented as a Business Motivation Model[1]) is an important artefact in an organizational context, as it encodes organizational intent and guides the maintenance of its service capabilities and ultimately all service capabilities of an organisation should be traceable back to (and justified by) elements in the motivation model.

The ever-changing business context requires organisations to constantly adapt their motivation and service representations. For example, an organisation may change its vision in terms of modifying its goals (which may render existing service capabilities superfluous) or may have to give up (or adopt) services, e.g. to remain compliant with changing regulations (which may result in unrealized organisation motivation). A *manual* adaption can be a time-consuming and error-prone exercise. For example, we might overlook inconsistencies or commit to sub-optimal modifications (often simply because of human cognitive limits on the space of alternative modifications we can explore). Formally (semi-)automated machinery is therefore desirable.

Existing work however focuses on identifying and verifying the functional relationship between the motivation- and service level (e.g. [2], [3], [4]), or techniques for handling changes at the service level (e.g. [5], [6]). Little work has been done in providing means to identify the consequent impact of changes made at the motivation level to the service level. Previous work (e.g. [7], [8]) has been done in providing formal machinery for dealing with changes at the motivation level. Formal requirement engineering approaches such as KAOS [9] and FormalTropos[10] focus on verification. Zowghi et al. [7] provides an operator which maps one goal model (represented by a default theory) to another, but does not consider

C. Liu et al. (Eds.): ICSOC 2012, LNCS 7636, pp. 582–590, 2012.

hierarchical relationships among goals nor their relation to services. Ernst et al.
[8] address the above, but in their formalization goals are required to be atomic
statements (as opposed to formulas in an arbitrary language, as is the case in
our work[1]). which does not permit the kind of analysis we provide.

In this paper, we propose a novel framework for handling changes at the motivation level and highlighting consequent impacts to the service level. Section 2 covers
preliminaries and introduces a running example. Section 3 introduces a motivation-
service (F-hyper-) graph and introduces a hierarchical entailment relation with the
graph. Section 4 formalize a change operator which is recommended for (but is not
restricted to) changes driven by compliance, i.e. where a motivation model needs to
be adapted to meet compliance obligations. This is important in the service context, since non-compliant motivation models give rise to non-compliance at the
service level. Finally, we conclude and outline future work in section 5.

2   Preliminaries

Business Motivation Model: A Business Motivation Model (BMM)[1], as
standardized by OMG, is a hierarchical representation of organisational *motivation*. In a BMM model the *vision* is the most abstract element and attained
via a set of goals. A *goal* is a statement about a state or motivation the organisation seeks to maintain or bring about. A *strategy* represents an accepted
course of action to achieve the ends (i.e. the goals and vision). Strategies, are
implemented via *tactics*, which are narrower in scope. Figure 1 (left side) shows
some examples of a vision, strategy, goal and tactic and their hierarchical representation in a BMM (right side). In the BMM of Figure 1 (right side), the

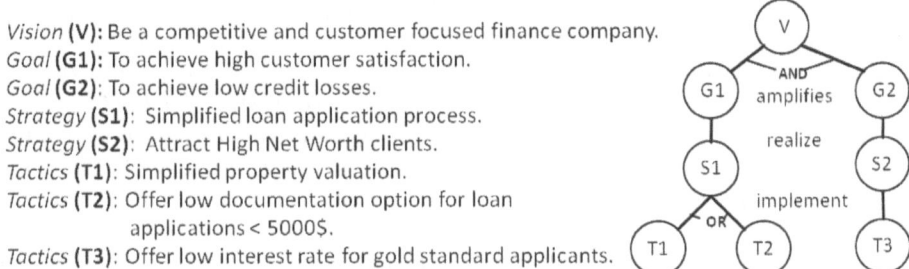

Fig. 1. A Business Motivation Model (right) and its description (left)

"AND" connection between goals "G1" and "G2" relating them to parent vision
"V" indicates that *both* goals need to be realized to bring about the vision; the
"OR" connection between tactics "T1" and "T2", and strategy "S1" denotes that
either of the tactics can be pursued to implement the strategy.

Service Representation: Semantic service description standards like WSDL-S
and OWL-S enforce a degree of rigour and detail in how services are modelled,

---

[1] We only require a finitely generated formal language with an associated entailment
relation (⊨) relating sentences in the language.

which in turn supports more sophisticated analysis. Most of these standards
support the specification of pre- and post-conditions, which we leverage in our
framework. Our current work leverages WSDL-S, but, as noted above, other
semantic service standards could equally well be used. For simplicity of exposition, we use the syntax of classical logic in representing pre- and post-conditions
(effects) in the following. Service descriptions are maintained in a *service catalogue*. In our running example will refer to the following services in the service catalogue of a hypothetical organisation (for brevity we only provide their
name and effect): *Simplified Property Valuation* (Se1): PropertyValued ∧ Sim-
plifiedPropertyValuation; *Small Loan Service* (Se2): LoanApplicationHandled ∧
LowDocumentation; *Premium Loan Service* (Se3): IncomeStatementReceived ∧
LoanApplicationHandled ∧ GoalStandardDiscount.

3   Formal Representation

We now describe a formal representation of BMM models and service cata-
logues that permits the application of (semi-) automated machinery for managing change of various kinds. The formal representation is based on a *motivation
library* and *Motivation-Service graph*, which are described in detail as follows.

Motivation Library: A motivation library is a domain specific collection of
feasible motivations, i.e., motivational elements which are feasible to realize[2].
All elements of an organisation's BMM are part of the library, but the library
may contain additional elements. We require each motivational element to be
represented by a formal assertion of the language $\mathcal{L}$. In other words, the library
is simply a set LIB of assertions, such that $LIB \subseteq \mathcal{L}$. The assertions provide
a (machine understandable) description of the respective motivation element.
Within the motivation library, we refer to the motivational elements that an
organisation desires to (i.e. would like to) adopt to its BMM as $LIB^{des} \subseteq LIB$.
The motivational elements the organisation is actually *committed to*, is given by
the elements (denoted by their formal assertion) of the BMM model. Naturally,
an organisation should be committed to all desired motivations. However, this
may not always be possible. An organisation may not commit to bring about a
desired motivation m, because m may be *inconsistent* with other (desired) motivations, which have been accorded higher preference, or m may be *infeasible* to
pursue with other desired motivations (e.g. doing so would cause a compliance
violation). Maintaining a motivation library has several advantages: it supports
reuse and avoids unnecessary loss of information (this has also been pointed
out by e.g. [7]). In other words, motivations which are currently infeasible, inconsistent, not desired or justified (by a desired element), are retained in the
library in anticipation of future situations where these might be adopted (e.g.
when they become feasible again, or the source of inconsistency goes away due
to other changes).The list below provides the assertions for the respective BMM

---

[2] Note that some states of affairs might be highly desirable for an organization, but
not feasible to achieve.

elements of Figure 1, as well as the strategy S3 and the tactic T4 (which do not appear in the current BMM, but might have appeared in a previous one), as part of the library. Note that the assertions may be arbitrarily detailed, but are kept simple for ease of exposition.

V: `Competitive` ∧ `CustomerFocused`	G1: `HighCustomerSatisfaction`
G2: `LowCreditLoss`	S1: `SimplifiedLoanProcessing`
S2: `HighNumberOfHighNetWorthClients`	T1: `SimplifiedPropertyValuation`
T2: `LowDocumentation`	T3: `GoldStandardDiscount`
S3: `StrictCreditAssessment`	T4: `IncomeStatementRecevied`

Motivation-Service Graph: We use an acyclic F-hypergraph to represent an Motivation-Service Graph. An *F-hypergraph* (given by a set of vertices V and edges E) is a generalization of a simple (directed) graph, which allows edges with a single source vertex but (potentially) more than one target vertices. An F-hypergraph is acyclic, iff there does not exist a path in the graph for which the "start"- and "end-" vertex are the same. A formal definition can be found in [11]. A *Motivation-Service-graph* (MS-graph) is a *labelled* acyclic and F-hypergraph representation of the BMM elements, services (from a service catalogue) and their hierarchical relationships. In an *MS-graph*, each vertex is either associated with an element of the motivation library or the service catalogue. Hereafter, we will also assume the ability to refer to the type of each element of the motivation library (via the type associated vertex). Vertices associated with services will refer to the service post-conditions. We use edges $e = (x, Y)$ to denote an AND-relation between a vertex x and a set of sub-vertices Y (note that edges represent *refinement* relationships between BMM elements or *realization* relationships between BMM tactics and services). For example, the edge "e1" of the MS-graph in Figure 2 (left hand side) is an AND-relation. In an OR-relation we use edges $e = (x, Y)$ and $e' = (x, Y')$ to denote that the sets of vertices $Y \subset V$ and $Y' \subset V$ are distinct refinements or realizations of x. For example, the edge "e4" and "e5" of the MS-graph in Figure 2 (left hand side) are two distinct relations. Note that, if we had defined the relationship between a goal and each of its refinements (realizations) individually (as we would be obliged to do in a simple graph), we would not have been able to distinguish between goals belonging to alternative refinements (realizations). We believe that our formalization addresses many of the deficiencies in the way AND/OR (goal) graphs are formalized (most ignore the fact that such graphs are in fact hypergraphs and that AND edges are in fact F-hyperedges).

In addition, a *background knowledge base* $\mathcal{KB} \subseteq \mathcal{L}$ is used as an encoding of domain and organisation specific knowledge (which for example could be represented in RuleML). The $\mathcal{KB}$ may contain the knowledge that a low loan processing time results in high customer satisfaction (e.g LowLoanProcessingTime → HighCustomerSatisfaction), or that accepting credit applications with low documentation (i.e. without an income statement, etc.) is considered not to be a strict credit assessment (e.g. LowDocumentation → ¬ StrictCreditAssessment). The following rules are also considered in our example: HighCustomerSatisfaction

$\rightarrow$ CustomerFocused, StrictCreditAssessment $\rightarrow$ LowCreditLoss, LowCreditLoss $\rightarrow$ Competitive, LowDocumentation $\rightarrow$ SimplifiedLoanProcessing, SimplifiedPropertyVal- uation $\rightarrow$ SimplifiedLoanProcessing, HighNumberOfHighNetWorthClients $\rightarrow$ LowCred- itLoss, GoldStandardDiscount $\rightarrow$ HighNumberOfHighNetWorthClients, IncomeState- mentReceived $\rightarrow$ StrictCreditAssessment.

Although we acknowledge that maintaining a formal representation of domain knowledge can be laborious, it should be emphasized that such an exercise has advantages beyond this paper (e.g. it forces stakeholders to make precise their knowledge, assumptions and terminology and thereby helps to highlight potential inconsistencies and their resolution by coming to a shared understanding).

Wellformed Motivation-Service Graph: We refer to an MS-graph that does not contain alternative refinements (or decompositions) as an *AND-MS-graph*. Any *general MS-graph* (which may contain alternative refinements), can be rep- resented as a set of distinct AND-MS-graphs. We use the function $\Delta_{AND}(G)$ to denote all maximal AND-MS-graphs that are sub-graphs of a given MS-graph G. For example, the MS-graph of Figure 2 (left hand side) has *two* AND-MS- (sub) graphs (one includes T1 and Se1, the other includes T2 and Se2). In the following, we refer to a vertex v as a root vertex, iff there does not exist a (hyper-) edge e in the MS-graph, such that v is an element of the targets of e. An AND-MS-graph as wellformed if it satisfies the following properties.

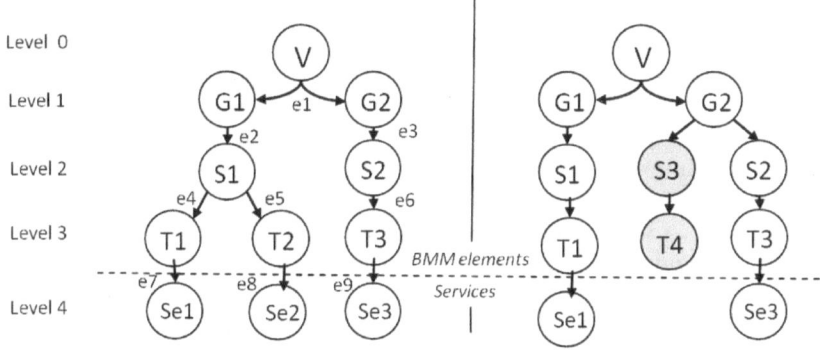

Fig. 2. The original MS-graph (left side) and its modification (right side)

(1) All root vertices are *desired*, of type "vision" and can only point to vertices of type "goal", which can only point to vertices of type "goal" or "strategy". A vertex of type "strategy" can only point to vertices of types "strategy" and "tactic", which can only point to vertices of types "tactic" and "service".
(2) The conjunction of the assertions associated with all vertices must be consistent with the domain knowledge base, since the organisation intends to concurrently realize all of them (i.e. there is no sequencing knowledge encoded that might suggest that one should be achieved before another).

(3) All target vertices of any edge must *minimally entail* the source vertex of the respective edge. We have adapted this property from [9]. Observe that in our running example the effects of service Se1, Se1 and Se3 respectively entail the tactics T1, T2 and T3 and are hence part of the MS-graph.

A *general MS-graph* is well-formed iff all $\mathcal{G} \in \Delta_{AND}(G)$ are well-formed. In our example, the strategy S3 and tactic T4 (part of the motivation library) do not participate in the MS-graph of Figure 2 (left hand side), as doing so would result in a derivable AND-MS-graph which is not wellformed (i.e. inconsistent) and the organisation has given precedence to the other elements.

k-Level Entailment: We now define a hierarchical entailment relation for MS-graphs, called k-level entailment. k-level entailment permits us to answer whether a particular assertion is derivable (or not derivable) from a particular level onwards in the MS-graph. We define *k-level vertices* as a subset of MS-graph vertices, such that for each element v, there exists a path of length k from *a* root vertex to v, *or* v is a leaf vertex and there exists a path from a root vertex to v with a length less than k. The root vertices themselves are 0-level vertices. For example, Figure 2 indicates the level of each vertex.

For an *AND-MS-graph* $\mathcal{G}$, an assertion α is k-entailed, iff all k-level vertices together with the $\mathcal{KB}$ entail the assertion and there does not exist a lower level (lower in terms of the value of k) in the MS-graph for which this is the case, i.e. k is the "earliest" (i.e. lowest) level at which the assertion is entailed. We use $\mathcal{G} \models_k \alpha$ to say that $\mathcal{G}$ k-entails an assertion α. For example the assertion LowDocumentation is entailed at level 3. From the definition of a wellformed MS-graph if follows that, if an assertion α is k-level entailed, than α is entailed in all levels i that follow after k. We refer to to this as α being *i-consequence*. For a general MS-graph G an an assertion α is *strongly k-entailed* (denoted by $G \models_k^{str} \alpha$) iff all AND-MS-graphs derivable from G have α as an i-consequence and $k \leq i$. Conversely, we say that a general MS-graph G *does not entail* an assertion α (denoted by $G \not\models^{str} \alpha$) iff there does not exist an AND-MS-graph derivable from G that entails α at any k.

4   Maintaining Motivation-Service Graphs

In this section, we show how to maintain an organisation's motivation model (i.e. the BMM) and service capabilities (i.e. the catalogue) in their conjoint MS-graph representation. There can be many change drivers. Organizations change their motivations to respond to dynamic business contexts, e.g., by the addition of motivation elements (via an *add-vertex* operator) or the removal of motivations (via a *remove-vertex* operator[3]) . An MS-graph may have to be modified to meet compliance obligations, e.g., to ensure that an assertion is entailed by the graph (via an *entail-assertion* operator) or isn't (via a *not-entail-assertion* operator). Due to space constraints, we only describe the "not-entail-assertion"

---

[3] The modification of a motivation can be viewed as a removal of the prior version followed by the addition of its modified version.

operator, which is also the most complex of the four types mentioned above). The properties of the *not-entail-assertion* operator are inspired by the AGM logic of theory change [12] and belief contraction postulates. A key insight from this framework is the need to minimize change to a body of knowledge encoded in an artefact such as an MS-graph We therefore require means to assess the extent of change, which might be encoded in a notion of proximity between two MS-graphs.

Motivation-Service Graph Proximity: Given MS-graphs G, G' and G'' we say that $G' <_G G''$ if G' is "closer" to G than G''. There relation $<_G$ may be defined in various ways. From a *graph theoretic* perspective, we may view G' to be closer to G if it has more vertices and edges in common with G. This intuition places an equal weighting on all elements of the graph. However, this is not sensible for MS-graphs, since some vertices justify others and hence should be given precedence (e.g., a strategy is justified by the goal it aims to bring about). We prefer an MS-graph that preserves the original graph up to level $k + 1$ over one that preserves the original graph up to level k. On the basis of this argument, one possible intuition for defining $<_G$ could be k *level set intersection cardinality*. MS-graph G' is preferred over G'' if G' shares more vertices with the original MS-graph G at level 0. In case of a tie, G' is preferred over G'' if it shares more vertices with G at level $k + 1$, and so on.

"Not Entail Assertion" Operator: The "not entail assertion" operator (denoted by $\ominus$) minimally modifies an MS-graph to obtain one where an assertion is strongly not derivable. A key application is in compliance management. In the running example, if new regulations require that each loan must be backed up by sufficient documentation, the organisation must ensure that the assertion $\alpha =$ LowDocumentation is not derivable from the MS-graph (in the example α corresponds to a single assertion but may in general be a consequence of a set of assertions). Our formalization can handle this. We offer the following normative properties for the "not entail assertion" operator.

1. *Wellformedness:* For a wellformed MS-graph G, $G \ominus \alpha$ is wellformed.
2. *Success:* For a wellformed MS-graph G where $G \ominus \alpha = G'$, $G' \not\models^{str} \alpha$.
3. *Vacuity:* For a wellformed MS-graph G where $G \not\models^{str} \alpha$, $G \ominus \alpha = G$.
4. *Desire-inclusion:* For a wellformed MS-graph G where $G \not\models^{str} \alpha$, there does not exist a desired goal in the library, such that if it were to be added to G the resulting MS-graph would satisfy the properties 1-3 (i.e. the resulting MS-graph should include as many desired goals as possible)
5. *Minimal-change:* For a wellformed MS-graph G where $G \ominus \alpha = G'$, there does not exist a G'' which satisfies the 4 properties above and $G'' <_G G'$. In other words, the operation should return the MS-graph which satisfies the above conditions and is closest to the original graph.

Definition 1. *Given a wellformed MS-graph G and an assertion α, let the operation $G - \alpha$ return a set, such that each $G' \in (G - \alpha)$ satisfies the properties (1)-(5). We define $G \ominus \alpha = s(G - \alpha)$, where s is a selection function which returns an element in $G - \alpha$.*

$\ominus$ represents a class of operators, parameterized by the proximity relation $<_G$ and the selection function s. The removal of a element from G might permit the addition of previously inconsistent desired motivations from the library to G. In our example, the vertices T2 and Se2 of the MS-graph make α derivable, which might lead to their removal. This may permit the inclusion of the previously inconsistent library elements S3 and T4 to the MS-graph.

The MS-graph in Figure 2 (right side) denotes the outcome of the "not entail assertion" (with $\alpha = $ LowDocumentation) operator (instantiated by k-level intersection cardinality) with respect to the original MS-graph (right side)[4]. Tactic T4 can be included in the MS-graph but it is not realized by a service (or combination of services). This would have to be flagged to the user, who could then decide to adopt the required functionality, drop the unrealized options from MS-graph, or leave the model unchanged. Furthermore, the service Se2 is not part of the MS-graph any more (and flagged as such to the user) since it is part of the service catalogue, but does not contribute to bringing about any organisational motivation.

5   Conclusion and Future Work

In this paper, we have proposed a formal framework to deal with changes at the motivation level and assessing their impact to the service landscape. An operator class (the "not entail assertion" operator) for compliance driven changes was introduced. We have developed a prototype implementation of the operator (using A* search technology) for propositional logic, which suggests the feasibility of our approach. Future work would involve investigating the scalability of our approach and the deployment of local search versus global search techniques in real world scenarios. Formalizing additional operator classes which capture other situations of change is also part of our future work.

References

1. OMG: Bmm, http://www.omg.org/spec/BMM/1.1/PDF (2010)
2. Jokhio, M.S.: Goal-based testing of semantic web services. In: ASE, pp. 707–711 (2009)
3. Chopra, A.K., Dalpiaz, F., Giorgini, P., Mylopoulos, J.: Modeling and Reasoning about Service-Oriented Applications via Goals and Commitments. In: Pernici, B. (ed.) CAiSE 2010. LNCS, vol. 6051, pp. 113–128. Springer, Heidelberg (2010)
4. Lu, Q., Tosic, V., Bannerman, P.L.: Support for the Business Motivation Model in the WS-Policy4MASC Language and MiniZnMASC Middleware. In: Kappel, G., Maamar, Z., Motahari-Nezhad, H.R. (eds.) ICSOC 2011. LNCS, vol. 7084, pp. 265–279. Springer, Heidelberg (2011)
5. Andrikopoulos, V., Benbernou, S., Papazoglou, M.: On the evolution of services. IEEE Transactions on Software Engineering (2011)

---

[4] In our example all elements in the motivation library are desired, and recall that the desire inclusion property has primacy over the minimal change property.

6. Hibner, A., Zielinski, K.: Semantic-based dynamic service composition and adaptation. In: 2007 IEEE Congress on Services, pp. 213–220 (2007)
7. Zowghi, D., Ghose, A.K., Peppas, P.: A Framework for Reasoning About Requirements Evolution. In: Foo, N.Y., Göbel, R. (eds.) PRICAI 1996. LNCS, vol. 1114, pp. 157–168. Springer, Heidelberg (1996)
8. Ernst, N., Borgida, A., Jureta, I.: Finding incremental solutions for evolving requirements. In: RE (2011)
9. Darimont, R., Van Lamsweerde, A.: Formal refinement patterns for goal-driven requirements elaboration. ACM SIGSOFT Software Engineering Notes 21(6) (1996)
10. Fuxman, A., Liu, L., Mylopoulos, J., Pistore, M., Roveri, M., Traverso, P.: Specifying and analyzing early requirements in Tropos. Requirements Engineering 9(2) (2004)
11. Gallo, G., Longo, G., Pallottino, S., Nguyen, S.: Directed hypergraphs and applications. Discrete Applied Mathematics 42(2-3), 177–201 (1993)
12. Alchourrón, C., Gärdenfors, P., Makinson, D.: On the logic of theory change: Partial meet contraction and revision functions. The Journal of Symbolic Logic 50(2) (1985)

Ontology-Learning-Based Focused Crawling for Online Service Advertising Information Discovery and Classification

Hai Dong[1], Farookh Khadeer Hussain[2], and Elizabeth Chang[1]

[1] School of Information Systems, Curtin University of Technology, Australia
[2] School of Software, University of Technology, Sydney, Australia

Abstract. Online advertising has become increasingly popular among SMEs in service industries, and thousands of service advertisements are published on the Internet every day. However, there is a huge barrier between service-provider-oriented service information publishing and service-customer-oriented service information discovery, which causes that service consumers hardly retrieve the published service advertising information from the Internet. This issue is partly resulted from the ubiquitous, heterogeneous, and ambiguous service advertising information and the open and shoreless Web environment. The existing research, nevertheless, rarely focuses on this research problem. In this paper, we propose an ontology-learning-based focused crawling approach, enabling Web-crawler-based online service advertising information discovery and classification in the Web environment, by taking into account the characteristics of service advertising information. This approach integrates an ontology-based focused crawling framework, a vocabulary-based ontology learning framework, and a hybrid mathematical model for service advertising information similarity computation.

1   Introduction

It is well recognized that the information technology has a profound effect on the conduct of the business, and the Internet has become the largest marketplace in the world. Innovative business professionals have realized the commercial applications of the Internet for their customers and strategic partners. They therefore turn the Internet into an enormous shopping mall and a huge catalogue [1]. In the service industry, Internet advertising is also popular among small and medium enterprises, due to the advantages of low cost, high flexibility, and ease of publishing. Nevertheless, many service consumers find it difficult to quickly and precisely retrieve service advertising information from the Internet, not only owing to the lack of specialized service information registration and retrieval platforms, but also because of the following features of service advertising information.

Ubiquity. Service advertisements can be registered by service providers through various business information registries [2]. These business information registries are geographically distributed over the Internet, yet there is no particular approach or application being designed to quickly and precisely locate the service information from these registries.

C. Liu et al. (Eds.): ICSOC 2012, LNCS 7636, pp. 591–598, 2012.

Heterogeneity. Given the diversity of services in the real world, many schemes have been proposed to classify services from various perspectives. Nevertheless, there is not a publicly agreed scheme available for classifying service advertising information over the Internet.

Ambiguity. Most of service advertising information does not retain a consistent format or standard. They are described by natural languages and embedded in vast Web information, the content of which is sometimes ambiguous for service consumers to understand.

Service (information) discovery is not a fresh topic in the academia. Many theories and applications have been developed so far. Nevertheless, at present few studies have been carried out in the research area of service advertising information discovery, by taking into account the above features of service advertising information.

In order to address this research issue, in this paper, we propose a novel ontology-learning-based focused crawling approach for service advertising information discovery and classification. The proposed approach is the integration of a semantic focused crawling framework, an ontology-learning framework, and a hybrid service advertising information similarity model. The semantic focused crawling framework is to address the issues of service advertising information for service information discovery; the ontology learning framework is to solve the limitations of ontology-based focused crawling; and the hybrid model is to measure the relatedness of service advertising information from the perspectives of text similarity and statistics.

2   Related Work

A semantic focused crawler is a software agent that is able to traverse the Web, and retrieve as well as download related Web information for specific topics, by means of semantic Web technologies [3], [4]. The goal of semantic focused crawlers is to precisely and efficiently retrieve and download relevant Web information by understanding the semantics underlying the Web information and the semantics underlying the predefined topics. According to a survey conducted by Dong et al. [5], the limitation of the semantic focused crawlers is that their crawling performance crucially depends on the quality of ontologies. This eventual consequence of this problem could be reflected in the gradually descending curves in the performance of semantic focused crawlers.

In order to solve the above issue, researchers start to pay their attention to enhancing semantic focused crawling technologies by integrating them with ontology learning technologies. The goal of ontology leaning is to semi-automatically extract facts or patterns from corpus or data and turn facts and patterns into machine-readable ontologies [6]. A few studies have been conducted in this field as follows:

Zheng et al. [7] proposed a supervised ontology-learning-based focused crawler that aims to maintain the harvest rate of the crawler in the crawling process.

The main idea of this crawler is to construct an artificial neural network (ANN) model to determine the relatedness between a Web page and an ontology.

Su et al. [8] proposed an unsupervised ontology-learning-based focused crawler in order to compute the relevance scores between topics and Web pages. Given a specific domain ontology and a topic represented by a concept in this ontology, the relevance score between a Web page and the topic is the weighted sum of the occurrence frequencies of all the concepts of the ontology in the Web page. This crawler makes use of reinforcement learning, which is a probabilistic framework for learning optimal decision making from rewards or punishments [9], in order to train the weight of each concept. The learning step follows an unsupervised paradigm which uses the crawler to download a number of Web pages and learn statistics based on these Web pages.

From the above survey, we found that none of the two crawlers is able to really evolve ontologies by enriching their contents, namely their vocabularies. When numerous unpredictable new terms outside the scope of the vocabulary of an ontology emerge in Web pages, these approaches cannot determine the relatedness between the new terms and the topic, and cannot make use of the new terms for the relatedness determination, which could result in the decline in their performance.

3   System Functions and Framework

The proposed ontology-learning-based focused crawler primarily consists of three components based on the functionalities, i.e., a storage component - the *service knowledge base*, a processing component - the *crawling and processing* module, and a computing component - the *service advertising information classification and ontology learning* module (Fig. 1).

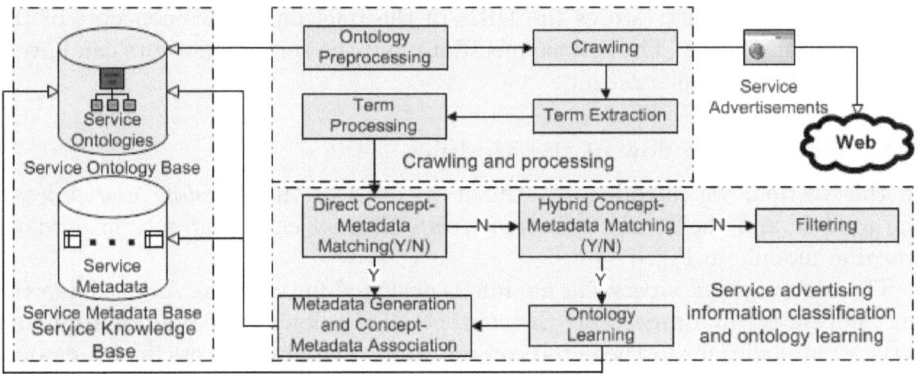

Fig. 1. Framework of the proposed ontology-learning-based focused crawler

3.1   Service Knowledge Base

The *service knowledge base* consists of a *service ontology base* and a *service metadata base*. The former is designed with the purpose of storing the machine-readable representation of domain-specific service knowledge, i.e., service ontologies. The latter is used to store semantically annotated service advertising information, i.e., service metadata.

For the service ontologies stored in the *service ontology base*, it is reasonable to make use of hierarchical ontologies for service advertising information discovery and classification, in which service concepts are linked by the *class/subclass* relationship. We define that each service concept contains the following elementary properties:

- A *conceptDescription* property is used to store the textual descriptions of a service concept, which consists of one or more phrases or sentences. Each phrase or sentence is a description or definition of a service concept, which is defined by domain experts. This property will be used in the process of service metadata classification (Section 3.2).
- A *learnedConceptDescription* property has a similar purpose to the *conceptDescription* property, which is automatically learned from service advertising information through the proposed crawler (Section 3.2).
- A *linkedMetadata* property is used to associate a service concept and a relevant service metadata. This property is used to classify and filter the generated service metadata by means of the concepts in a service ontology.

A service metadata is the semantic descriptions of a service entity, which consists of the following elementary properties:

- A *serviceDescription* property stores the textual description, e.g., a phrase or a sentence, regarding a service entity. The content of this property is automatically extracted from the crawled service advertising information by the proposed crawler (Section 3.2).
- A *linkedConcept* property is the inverse property of the *linkedMetadata* property. This property stores the URIs of the relevant service concepts of the service metadata. The service metadata and the service concepts can have a many-to-many relationship.

3.2   System Workflow of the Modules

In this section, we introduce the functionalities of the *crawling and processing* module and the *service advertising information classification and ontology learning* module in Fig. 1.

The *crawling and processing* module is designed for crawling service advertising information and processing the contents of the downloaded information and service ontologies for forthcoming computation. The first process in this module is *preprocessing*, which processes the contents of the *conceptDescription* property of each concept in a service ontology, before the crawler starts crawling. This process is realized by using Java WordNet Library[1] to implement tokenization,

---

[1] http://sourceforge.net/projects/jwordnet/

part-of-speech tagging, nonsense word filtering, stemming, synonym searching, and term weighting. The term weighting is to measure the particularity of each term in the service ontology. Here we make use of the inverse document frequency (IDF) model for the weight calculation. For a term (t) in a concept description $(CD_{j,h})$ of a service ontology (O), the weight of the term is

$$W(t) = log\frac{\{|C||\forall C \in O\}}{\{|C_\alpha||[t \in \delta(CD_\beta)] \bigcap (\exists CD_\beta \in C_\alpha) \bigcap (\forall C_\alpha \in O)\}} \qquad (1)$$

where $|C|$ is the number of concepts in the ontology, $|C_\alpha|$ is the number of the concepts that contain the term, and $\delta(CD_\beta)$ is the set of sysnoyms of the terms in a concept description.

The missions of the *crawling* and *term extraction* processes are to download a service advertisement from the Internet at one time, and to extract the required service advertising information from the downloaded advertisement, according to the service metadata schema defined in Section 3.1, in order to prepare the properties to generate service metadata and service provider metadata. These two processes are realized by the semantic focused crawlers designed in our previous work [3], [4], in which the extraction rules and templates are defined by observing common patterns in HTML codes.

The *term processing* process is to process the contents of the *serviceDescription* property of the service metadata, which is similar to the *preprocessing* process. The major difference is that the former does not need the function of synonym searching. Similarly, the terms in the *serviceDescription* property also need a weight to indicate their particularity. Here, a term matching function is designed for passing the weights of ontological terms obtained in the *preprocessing* process, in order to reduce the computing cost in this real-time process. If no term in a service ontology matches a term in the *serviceDescription* property, the term will be regarded as a new term and assigned the maximum valid weight for its particularity, i.e., *log (number of concepts in the ontology)*.

The procedure of the *service advertising information classification and ontology learning* module is described as follows: first, the *direct string matching* process examines whether or not the content of the *serviceDescription* property of a service metadata is included in the *conceptDescription* and *learnedConceptDescription* properties of a service concept. If the answer is yes, then the concept and the metadata are considered as relevant. By means of the *etadata generation and association* process, the metadata can then be generated and stored in the *service metadata base* as well as associated to the concept. If the answer is no, a *hybrid concept-metadata matching* process will be invoked to check the relatedness between the metadata and the concept (Section 4). If the *serviceDescription* property of the metadata is related to any phrases in the *conceptDescription* property of the concept, the metadata and the concept are considered as relevant, and the contents of the *serviceDescription* property of the metadata can be regarded as a new phrase for the *learnedConceptDescription* property of the concept; otherwise the metadata is deemed as non-relevant to the concept. The above process is repeated until all the concepts in the service ontology are compared to the metadata. If none of the concepts is relevant to the metadata, this metadata is then regarded as non-relevant to the service domain represented by the ontology and will be filtered.

4   Hybrid Concept-Metadata Matching Models

In this *hybrid concept-metadata matching* process, the extents of relatedness between the service description and the concept descriptions are assessed by a text-based concept-metadata matching (TCM) model and a probability-based concept-metadata matching (PCM) model. The results of the two models are then aggregated by a trained support vector machine (SVM) model. The eventual output of the hybrid model is the binary relatedness (relevant/non-relevant) between the service description and the concept descriptions.

The key idea of the TCM model is to measure the text similarity between a concept description of a service concept ($CD_{j,h}$) and a service description (SD_i) of a service metadata, by means of a weighted Dice's coefficient model and WordNet. The weighted Dice's coefficient model is mathematically expressed as follows:

$$sim_T(CD_{j,h}, SD_i) = \frac{\sum_{\forall u \in SD_i : u \in \delta(CD_{j,h})} w(u) + \sum_{\forall v \in CD_{j,h} : \exists \delta(v) \in SD_i} w(v)}{\sum_{\forall s \in SD_i} w(s) + \sum_{\forall t \in CD_{j,h}} w(t)}$$

(2)

where $\delta(CD_{j,h})$ is the set of synonyms of the terms in the concept description, and $\delta(v)$ is the set of synonyms of a single term in the concept description.

The PCM model is a complementary solution for measuring the relevance between a concept description ($CD_{j,h}$) and a service description (SD_i) by measuring their co-occurrence frequencies in the crawled service advertisements, based on a probabilistic model. The PCM model is mathematically expressed as follows:

$$maxSim_P(CD_{j,h}, SD_i) = \max_{CD_{j,\theta} \in C_j} [P(CD_{j,\theta}|CD_{j,h}) \cdot P(CD_{j,\theta}|SD_i)]$$
$$= \max_{CD_{j,\theta} \in C_j} [\frac{n_{j,h}^{j,\theta}}{n_{j,h}} \cdot \frac{n_i^{j,\theta}}{n_i}]$$

(3)

where $CD_{j,\theta}$ is a concept description of C_j, $n_{j,h}^{j,\theta}$ is the number of service advertisements that contain both $CD_{j,\theta}$ and $CD_{j,h}$, $n_{j,h}$ is the number of service advertisements that contain $CD_{j,h}$, $n_i^{j,\theta}$ is the number of service advertisements that contain both $CD_{j,\theta}$ and SD_i, and n_i is the number of service advertisements that contain SD_i.

The SVM classifier for each concept is designed to best aggregate the results of TCM model and the PCM model in order to decide on the semantic relatedness between a concept description and a service description, through a supervised training paradigm. This classifier provides a binary classification function (*relevant/non-relevant*), which is characterized by a hyperplane in a given feature space. For more details on SVM, we refer interested readers to the examples in [10].

5   System Implementation and Evaluation

We implement a prototype of the proposed ontology-learning-based focused crawler, and compare the performance of this crawler with the existing work reviewed in Section 2, i.e., Zheng et al.'s and Su et al.'s crawler, in the context of service advertising information discovery and classification, based on harvest rate, precision, and recall.

The overall framework of this crawler is built in Java within the platform of Eclipse 3.7.1[2]. The libSVM[3] Java library is utilized for the implementation of the SVM classifiers. For the purpose of comparatively analyzing our work and the two crawlers, we implement a prototype for each crawler in Java, in which the ANN model used by Zheng et al.'s crawler is built in Encog[4]. Next, we use a previously designed transport service ontology, which represents the domain knowledge in the transport service domain. The details of the transport service ontology can be referenced from [3].

In order to evaluate our crawler and the two crawlers in an open and heterogeneous Web environment, we choose two mainstream transport service advertising websites - Australian Yellowpages[5] (abbreviated as Yellowpages below) and Australian Kompass[6] (abbreviated as Kompass below), as the experimental data source. There are around 4400 downloadable transport-related service or product advertisements registered in Yellowpages, and around 10000 similar advertisements registered in Kompass, all of which are published in English. Since Zheng et al.'s crawler and the proposed crawler both need a supervised training process, and Su et al.'s crawler needs an unsupervised training process, we label the advertisements from Yellowpages, and use these advertisements as the training data set for all of these crawlers. Subsequently, we use the unlabeled advertisements from Kompass as the test data source.

The performance of the proposed crawler, Su et al.'s crawler, Zheng et al.'s crawler on the metrics of harvest rate, precision, and recall is shown in Table 1. Since Zheng et al.'s crawler does not have the function of classification, we only obtain its performance data on harvest rate.

Table 1. Overall performance of the ontology-learning-based focused crawlers

	Proposed crawler	Su et al.'s crawler	Zheng et al.'s crawler
Harvest rate	18.00%	6.80%	40.80%
Precision	88.03%	50.51%	N/A
Recall	55.55%	23.72%	N/A

It can be seen that the proposed crawler outperforms Su et al.'s crawler on all of the three parameters, only falling behind Zheng et al.'s crawler on the harvest

---

[2] http://www.eclipse.org/
[3] http://www.csie.ntu.edu.tw/~cjlin/libsvm/
[4] http://code.google.com/p/encog-java/
[5] http://www.yellowpages.com.au/
[6] http://au.kompass.com/

rate. However, harvest rate only concerns the capability of crawling Web pages but not the capability of crawling *right* Web pages. It is found that only around 25% of advertisements (Web pages) in the test data source are real transport-service-related advertisements. The harvest rate of the proposed crawler is closer to this ratio than the other two crawlers, which can partly prove the capability of the proposed crawler on crawling *right* service advertising information in a heterogeneous environment.

6   Conlusion

In conclusion, in the above experiments the proposed ontology-learning-based focused crawler shows the competitive performance, in comparison with the existing research work, in a simulated heterogeneous Web environment. This test primarily proves the feasibility of the proposed crawling framework for service advertising information discovery and classification.

References

1. Wang, H., Lee, M.K.O., Wang, C.: Consumer privacy concerns about Internet marketing. Commun. ACM 41, 63–70 (1998)
2. Dong, H., Hussain, F.K., Chang, E.: A service search engine for the industrial digital ecosystems. IEEE Trans. Ind. Electron. 58, 2183–2196 (2011)
3. Dong, H., Hussain, F.K.: Focused crawling for automatic service discovery, annotation, and classification in industrial digital ecosystems. IEEE Trans. Ind. Electron. 58, 2106–2116 (2011)
4. Dong, H., Hussain, F.K., Chang, E.: A framework for discovering and classifying ubiquitous services in digital health ecosystems. J. of Comput. and Syst. Sci. 77, 687–704 (2011)
5. Dong, H., Hussain, F.K., Chang, E.: State of the Art in Semantic Focused Crawlers. In: Gervasi, O., Taniar, D., Murgante, B., Laganà, A., Mun, Y., Gavrilova, M.L. (eds.) ICCSA 2009, Part II. LNCS, vol. 5593, pp. 910–924. Springer, Heidelberg (2009)
6. Wong, W., Liu, W., Bennamoun, M.: Ontology learning from text: A look back and into the future. ACM Computing Surveys X (2011) (to appear)
7. Zheng, H.-T., Kang, B.-Y., Kim, H.-G.: An ontology-based approach to learnable focused crawling. Inform. Sciences 178, 4512–4522 (2008)
8. Su, C., Gao, Y., Yang, J., Luo, B.: An efficient adaptive focused crawler based on ontology learning. In: Proceedings of the Fifth Int. Conf. on Hybrid Intelligent Syst. (HIS 2005), pp. 73–78. IEEE Computer Society, Rio de Janeiro (2005)
9. Rennie, J., McCallum, A.: Using reinforcement learning to spider the Web efficiently. In: Bratko, I., Dzeroski, S. (eds.) Proceedings of the Sixteenth Int. Conf. on Mach. Learning (ICML 1999), pp. 335–343. Morgan Kaufmann Publishers Inc., Bled (1999)
10. Boser, B.E., Guyon, I.M., Vapnik, V.N.: A training algorithm for optimal margin classifiers. In: Proceedings of the Fifth Annual Workshop on Computational Learning Theory, pp. 144–152. ACM, Pittsburgh (1992)

A Learning Method for Improving Quality of Service Infrastructure Management in New Technical Support Groups

David Loewenstern[1], Florian Pinel[1], Larisa Shwartz[1], Maíra Gatti[2], and Ricardo Herrmann[2]

[1] IBM TJ Watson Research Center
Hawthorne, NY 10532 USA
{davidloe,pinel,lshwart}@us.ibm.com
[2] IBM Research - Brazil
São Paulo, SP, 04007-900 Brazil
{mairacg,rhermann}@br.ibm.com

Abstract. Service infrastructure management requires the matching of tasks to technicians with a variety of expert knowledge in different areas. Most Service Delivery organizations do not have a consistent view of the evolution of the technician skills because in a dynamic environment the creation and maintenance of a skill model is a difficult task, especially in light of privacy regulations, changing service catalogs and worker turnover. In addition, as services expand, new technical support groups for the same type of services are created and also new technicians may be added, either into a new group or into existing groups. To tackle this problem we evolve a method for ranking technicians on their expected performance according to their suitability for receiving the assignment of a service request. This method makes use of similarities between the technicians and previous tasks performed by them. We propose a strategy for incorporating new technicians and delivery team reorganizations into the method and we present experimental results demonstrating the efficacy of the strategy. Applying this strategy to new teams yields on average acceptable accuracy within 4 hours, though with a wide variation across teams for the first 12 hours. Accuracy and its variability approach the quality of accuracy on older teams over 24 hours.

Keywords: service management, service quality, machine learning, ticket dispatching, request fulfillment

1 Introduction

Composition of atomic services for building more complex and useful services has in recent years become a popular approach to delivering customer defined services. The paradigm of composing and arranging atomic services into complex services is generally a bottom-up approach. From a providers perspective, bottom-up composition of atomic services into complex services is important,

C. Liu et al. (Eds.): ICSOC 2012, LNCS 7636, pp. 599–606, 2012.
© Springer-Verlag Berlin Heidelberg 2012

particularly with regards to cost-effectiveness. Overall process costs can be reduced by late binding to a service supplier depending on the performance of the service suppliers preceding this step. Cost of staff significantly outweighs infrastructure cost, and the difference is increasing. A large portion of service delivery costs is associated with human effort. It is no longer common to have dedicated technical support groups for a particular type of service or even a customer. To minimize overhead and benefit from economy of scale, service providers use cross-account support groups with skills in a specific technical area or layer.

In this paper these technical support groups are known as pools. A typical pool could support for example UNIX platforms, database services or application services. Customers requests are managed as tickets. Tickets are routed to pools through an initial evaluation outside the scope of this paper. Each pool contains a dispatcher who routes tasks (tickets or work orders) to appropriate technicians within the pool.As the number of industries that utilize computing services grows, the volume of information needed by supporting staff has become great and will continue to increase. Although information technology tools have become indispensable, we continue to rely heavily on human experts for problem resolution requiring deep understanding of existing services and their underlying technology. In a sample study it was found that the most qualified technician resolved an issue better (with respect to SLA metrics) than other people in 75% of cases. Dispatching service requests to the best technician takes a significant fraction of the time required to process the request [1].

Because of these factors, dispatching within service delivery is a good candidate for software to assist the manual process or automate it completely. Skills and availability of these resources are an important property of the service, and ideally they need to be included in the service definition or the service delivery system. In actual practice, however, most organizations do not have a consistent view of this information, due to privacy concerns and volatile nature of this information. Some existing work [2] describes a method for finding an appropriate technician to work on tasks by making use of similarities between the technicians and previous tasks performed by them. As services expand, new pools for the same type of services are created. This means that there are pools with no historical data on pool performance, even though some of the technicians could have some history from their assignments in pools they were part of previously. In addition, new technicians may be added, either into a new pool or into existing pools. The central problem to be addressed by this paper is therefore how to rank a set of new technicians in a new pool according to their suitability for receiving the assignment of a request.

This paper focuses on quickly making use of historical data as it becomes available. Our approach starts by examining what the method in [2] builds in lieu of an explicit skill model. The method builds a model composed of a weighted set of features in which neither the features nor the weights encode any information about individual technicians or their skills. Instead, the weights model the judgment of a dispatcher or group of dispatchers (in a service line) about what features of any technician history and of a request are relevant to determining how to assign each request in that pool to a technician. Because the features are not specific to a particular pool, but only to the technician history, reassigning existing technicians to existing pools is not an issue. The problem of handling new pools can then be reduced to two smaller problems: how to make use of existing weights from the new pool service line until there is enough data from the new pool to calculate weights normally, and how to determine features for technicians with no history in any pool.

Our results show that for mature pools, with a lookback of 1 day, the technician chosen by the dispatcher was in the top quarter of the predicted ranked list 90% of the time. For new pools the results show that most pools processing smaller numbers of requests show greater variation for the first 12 hours, but this narrows after 12 hours. Average differences are good by the fourth hour, and converge toward zero over the course of the run.

The remainder of this paper has this structure: Section 2 presents related work. Section 3 discusses our method in some detail. Section 4 describes the experiments used to validate the method and presents the results of the experiments. Finally, Section 5 discusses conclusions and future work.

2 Related Work

Related to the work presented in this paper, [3] reviews staff scheduling and rostering problems, and the methods reported in the literature for their solution. More recently, the workflow community has been emphasizing the use of machine learning mechanisms. [4] presents an approach to automatically suggest staff assignment for activities in a workflow. Using assignments of previously completed activities as features, a number of supervised machine learning algorithms are applied to the workflow event log and compared to achieve the best accuracy. [5] is a complementary work proposed as a solution to allocate the most proficient set of employees for a whole business process based on workflow event logs. Furthermore, in [6], a staff assignment decision tree is built for a given workflow activity using a skill data model; assignment rules are then derived from the trees. By contrast, the service requests we work with are individual tasks, and we cannot rely on previously completed workflow activities to build feature vectors. As explained in Section 1, maintaining a skill model is also impossible.

In the IT Service Management domain, [7] examines problem tickets that need to be routed among various expert groups. The authors analyze the contents of incoming tickets to identify a set of semantically relevant past tickets, and then create a weighted Markov model from the resolution sequences of these tickets to generate routing sequence recommendations. This is different from our work, as we want to assign a single resolver to each problem.

In [2], the authors present a solution for the problem of assigning an individual technician in the absence of an explicit skill model. Suitability for assignment of a new work order to a technician is inferred by taking into account the similarity of the work order to previous assignments and the outcomes of the previous assignments (such as whether the work order had to be reassigned). The measure itself is composed of dynamic work order features calculated from a work order and a continually updating history, and weights computed from historical data using Support Vector Machine (SVM)^{rank} [8].When applied to the steady state problem of existing pools of technicians with sufficiently long histories of prior assignments, the technician that has actually been assigned to the work order by the human dispatcher is ranked among the top quarter of candidate technicians by the algorithm, the Top-Quarter Percentage (TQP), 90% of the time. The following section details methods for modifying the solution for non-steady state cases, with new technicians with no history of prior assignments for calculating feature vectors, or new pools with no training set for inferring the feature weights.

3   Method

Let us call the algorithm presented in [2] as described in Section 2 the **base** algorithm. In a linear ranking SVM such as **base**, ranking is performed by evaluating the target function $F(x) = \omega \cdot x - b$ where ω is a weight vector, x is a feature vector, and b is a bias. In the technician assignment problem, $x(u, r)$ represents the features of a technician w_u with respect to a request r and is defined by $f_{i,j,k}(w_u, r)$, for all i, j, k, and $F(x(u))$ is a real-valued score such that $F(x(u, r)) > F(x(v, r))$ when technician w_u should be ranked better than w_v for handling request r. Because the target functions are only meaningful when compared with each other, we can ignore the bias and normalize the weights so that $\omega \cdot \omega = 1$. Doing this allows us to mix target functions so long as they are defined on the same set of features.

In the case of a new pool, we cannot calculate $F(x)$ initially since there is no training data. However, we can substitute another target function, $F'(x) = \omega' \cdot x - b'$ that had been calculated from some data we do have. Reasonable sources of data for calculating F' include all of the other pools in the same service line as the new pool, or even all other pools processing the same types of service requests. One would expect using F' in place of F would reduce the accuracy of the proposed technician assignments to a degree depending on how similar the new pool is to the pools used to calculate F'. Once the new pool has processed a sufficient number of service requests, it will become possible to calculate F for the new pool.

We would like a smooth transition from F' to F as the new pool processes requests and so generates training data. We propose a **mixture** algorithm, mixing F' and F over a "breaking-in" period. During this period, we use for the new pool a mixed target function $F_{mix}(x) = (\Delta \omega' + (1 - \Delta)\omega) \cdot x$, where $\Delta = (t - t_0)/(t_B - t_0)$, t is the time the request is assigned, t_0 is the time the new pool commenced operations, and t_B is the time the new pool is considered to have finished its breaking-in period. In practice, it is not necessary to recalculate F_{mix} for every request if the pools used to train F' are similar to the new pool.

We define the **hourly** and **daily** methods as implementations of the **mixture** algorithm, with $F_{mix}(x)$ recalculated in one hour segments. The alternative weights ω' are calculated over all other pools in the same service line as the new pool. In **daily** the ω' are calculated once, from the 24 hours before the start of the experiment, while in **hourly** they are recalculated at the beginning of each one hour segment from the previous 24 hours.

New technicians pose a more difficult problem than new pools do. The features of **base** are calculated from requests previously handled by a given technician; in effect, the feature vector $x(u, r)$ represents the recent work history of technician w_u with respect to a new request r. If w_u is a new technician then $x(u, r)$ cannot be calculated at all. If we could match w_u to some existing technician w_v based on static information about their capabilities, we could use a mixture method similar to the one discussed in the previous section, creating a $x_{\mathrm{mix}}(u, r)$ from $x(u, r)$ and the recent work history $x(v, r)$ of w_v. However, the motivation for **base** is to avoid creating and maintaining such information, so there is no way to match w_u to w_v. In recognition of this, the **mixture** algorithm, like the **base** algorithm, does not recommend technicians without histories. Requests must be assigned to new technicians through some policy outside the scope of this paper, for example according to a mentoring or cross-training policy or on a round-robin basis, until all technicians in the pool have sufficient history. Instead, Section 4 will explore how much history is sufficient.

Another method, **flat**, which extends **base**, is evaluated to gauge the value of using the **mixture** algorithm against a non-mixture alternative. Instead of using a mixture, **flat** uses a flat distribution across all features ($\omega' = 1$) for the first segment and subsequently the unmixed weight vector ω calculated each segment from whatever data is available in the "new" pool.

It is also common for dispatchers to group together similar requests and assign them to a single technician, a process known as *batching*. For these cases, we devised **batch**, which draws requests from the fifteen minutes prior to the new request, since batched requests appear as a set of individual requests with very similar features (including technician assignment) in a short time span. It's expected that the method works very well with very little history for new technicians: indeed, the ideal amount of history for determining whether to add a given request to a batch is just the time from when its first element was assigned until the time the current element is processed by the dispatcher. Batches are identified by matching all the values from their pool, priority, classification, account and work type features. Technicians are then ranked by the higher number of requests that were assigned to them in the period, if any.

4   Experimental Results

The methods from Section 3 were tested using the data from [2]. To simulate the effect of creating a new pool with new technicians, features and SVM weights were calculated for each pool separately using a fixed protocol:

- Each test ran over the course of 24 hours, divided into 24 hourly segments, with data collected at the end of each segment.

- SVM weights were calculated for each segment using only data dating from the beginning of the day until just prior to the beginning of the segment.
- Features were calculated for each work order using only data dating from the beginning of the day until just prior to the assignment of the work order.

The 24 hour test run was chosen based on the results reported in [2]: although longer look-back windows improved performance, a one day look-back window performed adequately and was used as the baseline for most tests. The data was collected once per hour as a reasonable compromise: more frequent, shorter segments marginally improved accuracy but greatly increased computation time, while less frequent, longer segments obscured differences in accuracy among the methods. Each method was run on seven consecutive days, with the results averaged to smooth out weekly variation in workload.

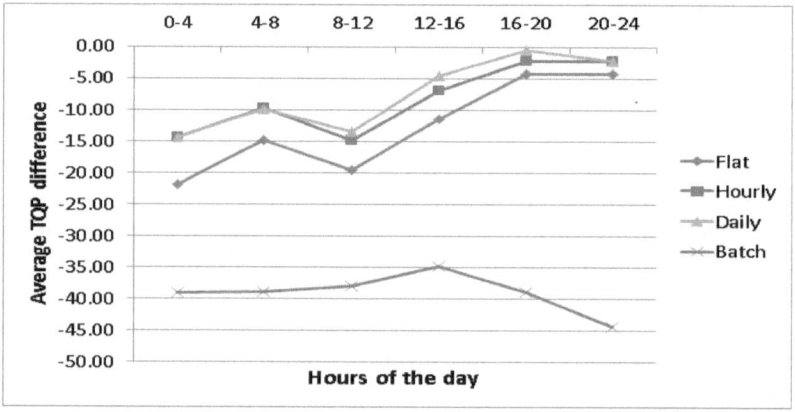

Fig. 1. Average differences in Top-Quarter Percentage (TQP) between several methods applied to "new" pools and **reference**, the reference algorithm applied to the corresponding established pools. See text for details.

Figure 1 presents the results of four separate methods using the same data set as described in the previous section and averaged over 7 one-day runs. Their performance is measured by subtracting their TQP from that of the **reference** method, defined as the **base** algorithm using a 24 hour lookback window ending just prior to the beginning of the run for SVM training and a 24 hour lookback window ending just before each individual work order for feature calculation, thereby treating the same pool as an established pool. The results for each segment then are grouped into 4-hour blocks to simplify the graph.

The **flat, hourly** and **daily** methods all start off with lower accuracy than **reference** and asymptotically approach it over the course of each run, with **flat** starting out substantially worse but also converging, indicating both the value of using the **mixture** algorithm and the resilience of the underlying **base** algorithm. Even over the first hours of each run, all three methods perform fairly well. The relatively good performance of **flat** led to the hypothesis that it and therefore all of the methods exploit batches as described in Section 3. The **batch** method directly tests this hypothesis, demonstrating TQP better than chance but worse than the other methods, indicating the exploitability of batch information but also indicating that batching alone does not explain the success of the other methods.

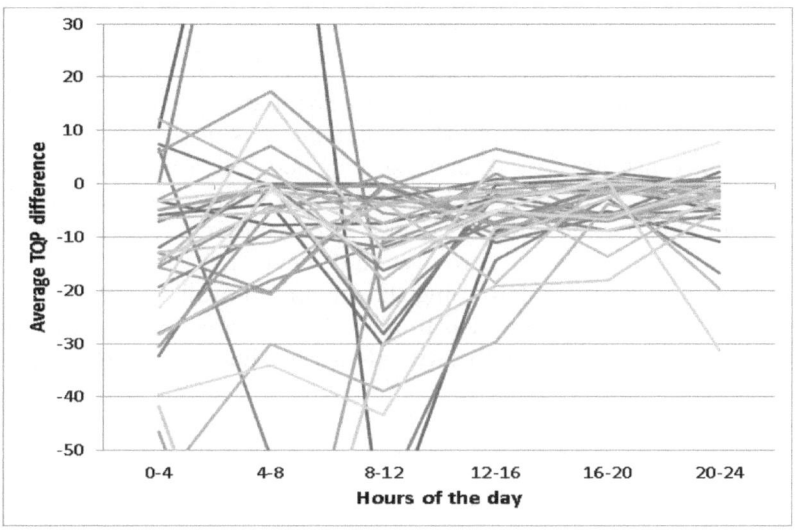

Fig. 2. Average difference in TQP between the **daily** and **reference** methods, broken out per pool. See text for details.

Figure 2 plots the difference between the TQP per pool for the **daily** experiment and the results from the reference method averaged across all runs for pools processing at least 300 requests over the seven days of the experiment (meaning less than two requests per hour). As expected considering the results shown by figure 1, the trend is from lower TQP to higher, with the difference converging on zero over the run. In the first twelve hours, some pools showed wide swings in TQP relative to the reference method; this can be traced to the effect of one or two requests in each pool per run. The number of requests varies over the course of each run, peaking in mid-afternoon (segments 16-20) and falling off at night (segments 0-4 and 20-24); this tends to increase the effect of outlying requests.

5 Discussion

This paper provides a method for ranking technicians on their expected performance by making use of similarities between the assignees and previous tasks performed by them. The central problem that we addressed is how to rank a set of technicians according to their suitability for receiving the assignment of a request without maintaining an explicit skill model describing which skills are possessed by each technician, in particular for a new pool containing either new technicians or technicians from other pools. Our method builds a model composed of a weighted set of features in which neither the features nor the weights encode any information about individual technicians or their skills. Instead, the weights model the judgment of a dispatcher or group of dispatchers (in a service line) about what features of any technicians history and of a request are relevant to determining proper assignments. Because the features are not specific to a particular pool, but only to the technicians history, reassigning existing technicians to existing pools is not an issue. For mature pools, with a lookback of 1 day, the technician chosen by the dispatcher was in the top quarter of the predicted ranked list 90% of the time. For new pools the results show that most pools processing smaller numbers of requests show greater variation for the first 12 hours, but this narrows after 12 hours. Average differences are good by the 4th hour, and converge toward zero over the course of the run.

In future work we will explore using the amount of available history to adjust the length of the breaking-in period to allow faster convergence where the data permits. We will also look for alternatives to service lines as a method for finding similar pools.

References

1. dos Santos, C.R.P., Granville, L.Z., Cheng, W., Loewenstern, D., Shwartz, L., Anerousis, N.: Performance management and quantitative modeling of IT service processes using mashup patterns. In: Proceedings of the 7th International Conference on Network and Service Management, CNSM 2011 (2011)
2. Loewenstern, D., Pinel, F., Shwartz, L., Gatti, M., Herrmann, R., Cavalcante, V.: A learning feature engineering method for task assignment. In: Proceedings of the IEEE/IFIP Network Operations and Management Symposium, NOMS 2012 (2012)
3. Ernst, A., Jiang, H., Krishnamoorthy, M., Sier, D.: Staff scheduling and rostering: A review of applications, methods and models. European Journal of Operational Research 153, 3–27 (2004)
4. Liu, Y., Wang, J., Yang, Y., Sun, J.: A semi-automatic approach for workflow staff assignment. Comput. Ind. 59, 463–476 (2008)
5. Yang, H., Wang, C., Liu, Y., Wang, J.: An Optimal Approach for Workflow Staff Assignment Based on Hidden Markov Models. In: Meersman, R., Tari, Z., Herrero, P. (eds.) OTM 2008 Workshops. LNCS, vol. 5333, pp. 24–26. Springer, Heidelberg (2008)
6. Ly, L.T., Rinderle, S., Dadam, P., Reichert, M.: Mining Staff Assignment Rules from Event-Based Data. In: Bussler, C.J., Haller, A. (eds.) BPM 2005. LNCS, vol. 3812, pp. 177–190. Springer, Heidelberg (2006)
7. Sun, P., Tao, S., Yan, X., Anerousis, N., Chen, Y.: Content-Aware Resolution Sequence Mining for Ticket Routing. In: Hull, R., Mendling, J., Tai, S. (eds.) BPM 2010. LNCS, vol. 6336, pp. 243–259. Springer, Heidelberg (2010)
8. Joachims, T.: Training linear svms in linear time. In: Proceedings of the 12th ACM SIGKDD International Conference on Knowledge Discovery and Data Mining, KDD 2006, p. 217 (2006)

Adaptive Service-Oriented Mobile Applications: A Declarative Approach*

Gianpaolo Cugola, Carlo Ghezzi, Leandro Sales Pinto,
and Giordano Tamburrelli

DeepSE Group @ DEI - Politecnico di Milano, Italy
{cugola,ghezzi,pinto,tamburrelli}@elet.polimi.it

Abstract. Modern society increasingly relies on mobile devices and on distributed applications that use them. To increase development efficiency and shorten time-to-market, mobile applications are typically developed by composing together ad-hoc developed components, services available on-line, and other third-party mobile applications. To cope with unpredictable changes and failures, but also with the various settings offered by the plethora of devices, mobile applications need to be adaptive. We address this issue by proposing a declarative approach. The advantages of the proposed solution are demonstrated through an example inspired by an existing worldwide distributed mobile application.

1 Introduction

Mobile applications, commonly referred to as *apps*, are small-sized, efficient, modular and loosely coupled aggregates of software components developed with specific programming frameworks that depend on the target mobile platform. Their development imposes several challenges to modern software engineering. In particular, to achieve the desired efficiency in terms of development time and to exploit existing well established software solutions, apps are typically developed by composing together: (1) ad-hoc developed components, (2) existing services available on-line, (3) third-party apps, and (4) platform-dependent components to access device-specific hardware (e.g., camera, GPS, etc.).

The typical approach to develop such heterogeneous software artifacts follows a three step approach. Developers first start by conceiving the list of needed functionalities and they organize them in a suitable workflow of execution. Secondly, they evaluate the trade-offs between implementing such functionalities directly or resorting to existing services or third-party apps. Finally, they implement the app by integrating all the components together. Building apps as orchestrations of components, services and/or other third-party applications, however, introduces a direct dependency of the system with respect to external software artifacts which may evolve over time, fail, or even disappear, thereby compromising the application's functionality. Moreover, differently from traditional software

---

* This research has been funded by the EU, Programme IDEAS-ERC, Project 227977-SMScom and FP7-PEOPLE-2011-IEF, Project 302648-RunMore.

C. Liu et al. (Eds.): ICSOC 2012, LNCS 7636, pp. 607–614, 2012.

systems, the development of mobile apps is characterized by an increased explicit dependency with respect to hardware and software settings of the deployment environment. Indeed, even if developed for a specific platform (e.g., Android, iPhone, etc.), apps may be deployed on a plethora of different mobile devices characterized by heterogeneous hardware and software configurations (e.g., available sensors, firmware version, etc.). To cope with these peculiarities apps need to be *adaptive* [8] with respect to the heterogeneous deployment environments and with respect to the services and external apps they rely upon. The traditional way to achieve this goal is by explicitly programming the needed adaptations by heavily using exception handling techniques to manage unexpected scenarios when they occur. This is quite hard per-se and cannot be done by inexperienced users. This paper precisely address this issue by proposing a different approach. We abandon the mainstream path in favor of a strongly declarative alternative, called *SelfMotion*[1], which allows apps to be modeled in terms of the abstract functionalities they provide and the overall goal they have to met. SelfMotion apps are then executed by a middleware that leverages automatic planning techniques to elaborate, at run-time, the best sequence of activities to achieve the goal. Whenever a change happens in the external environment (e.g., a service becomes unavailable), which prevents successful completion of the execution, the middleware tries to find an alternative path toward the goal and continues executing the app, which results in a nice and effective self-healing behavior.

2   A Motivating Example: The ShopReview App

Let us now introduce *ShopReview* (SR), the mobile app we will use throughout the paper to explain our approach. SR is inspired by an existing application (i.e., ShopSavvy[2]). It allows users to share data concerning a commercial product or query for data shared by others. Users may use SR to publish the price of a product they have found in a certain shop (chosen among those close to their current location). In response, the app provides the users with alternative, nearby places where the same product is sold at a more convenient price. The unique mapping between the price signaled by the user and the product is obtained by exploiting the product barcode. In addition, users may share their opinion concerning the shop and its prices on a social network such as Twitter.

As introduced in the previous section, the development process for an app like SR starts by listing the needed functionalities and by deciding which of them will be implemented through an ad-hoc component and which will be implemented by re-using existing solutions. For example, the communication with social networks may be delegated to a third party app, while geo-localization of the user may be performed by a ad-hoc component which exploits the GPS sensor on the device.

Table 2 illustrates the abstract components uses as the main building blocks for the SR app. For the `BarcodeReader`, consider we decide to implement its code as for the original ShopSavvy app, which runs an ad-hoc developed component in

---

[1] Self-Adaptive Mobile Application.
[2] http://shopsavvy.mobi/

Table 1. ShopReview Components

Name	Description
BarcodeReader	Allows the user to insert the barcode of the product
GetProductName	Translates the barcode into the product name
GetPosition	Retrieves the current user location
LocalSearch	Retrieves other shops in the neighborhood which offer the product at a more convenient price
SharePrice	Shares the price of a product on a given shop on Twitter
InputPrice	This component collects from the user the product's price

```
if ( manager. hasSystemFeature ( PackageManager. FEATURE_CAMERA_AUTOFOCUS) {
    //Run local barcode recognition
}else{ //Invoke remote service with blurry decoder algorithm }
//....
Location location = null;
if ( manager. hasSystemFeature ( PackageManager. FEATURE_LOCATION_GPS) {
    LocationProvider provider = LocationManager. GPS_PROVIDER;
    try{
        //Return null if the GPS signal is currently not available
        location = locationManager. getLastKnownLocation ( provider );
    }catch ( Exception e){ location = null; }
}
if ( location==null){
    //Device whitout GPS or an excpetion was raised invoking it. We show up a map
    //to allow the user to indicate its location manually
    showMap ();
}
```

Listing 1.1. Adaptive Code Example

charge of acquiring a picture of the barcode from the mobile camera. Since such component may execute correctly only on devices with an autofocus camera and does not work properly on other devices, our choice would limit the usability of our app. To overcome this limitation and allow a correct barcode recognition also on devices with fixed focus cameras, SR needs to provide a form of adaptivity. Indeed, it has to detect if the camera on the current device is autofocus and, if not, it has to invoke an external service to process the acquired image with a special blurry decoder algorithm. A similar approach can be used to get the user location (i.e., GetPosition component), which requires a GPS sensor[3]. To execute SR on devices without GPS we may offer a different implementation, which shows a map to the user for a manual indication of the current location.

The code snippet reported in Listing 1.1 describes a possible implementation of the described adaptive behavior for the Android platform. Although this is just a small fragment of the SR app, which is by itself quite a simple example, it is easy to see how convoluted and error prone the process of defining all possible alternative paths may turn out to be. Things become even more complex considering run-time exceptions, like an error while accessing the GPS or invoking an external service, which have to be explicitly managed through ad-hoc code. We argue that the main reason behind these problems is that the mainstream platforms for developing mobile applications are based on traditional imperative languages in which the flow of execution must be explicitly programmed. In this setting, the adaptive code—represented in our code fragment by all the *if-else* branches—is intertwined with the application logic, reducing the overall readability and maintainability of the resulting solution, and hampering its fu-

---

[3] Network Positioning System is not precise enough for our needs.

ture evolution in terms of supporting new or alternative features, which requires additional branches to be added to the implementation.

3 The SelfMotion Approach

The SelfMotion approach comprises activities at design-time as well as at run-time. Initially, at design time, it requires the intervention of domain experts and software engineers, while at run-time it executes autonomously. Design-time activities are supported by a *declarative language*, while at run-time activities are supported by a *middleware*. At design time, domain experts and engineers must declare the following elements: (1) the app's *Goal*, expressed as a set of facts that are required to be true at the end of the app's execution; (2) the *Initial State*, which models the set of facts one can assume to be true at app invocation time; (3) a set of *Abstract Actions*, which models the primitive operations that can be executed to achieve the goal; (4) A set of *Concrete Actions*, one or more for each abstract action. Concrete actions map abstract ones to executable snippets that define the actual steps required for realizing them, e.g., by invoking an external service. At run-time, the SelfMotion middleware comes into play to actually execute the app. It comprises two distinct components: a *Planner* and an *Interpreter*. The Planner analyzes the goal, the initial state, and the abstract actions to build an *Abstract Execution Plan*, which lists the logical steps to reach the goal. The Interpreter is in charge of enacting this plan by associating each step (i.e., each abstract action) with the concrete action to execute, possibly invoking external components where specified. If something goes wrong (e.g., an external service returns an exception), the Interpreter first tries a different concrete action for the abstract action that failed. If no alternative action can be found or all alternatives have been tried unsuccessfully, it invokes the Planner again to build an alternative plan. From a deployment viewpoint the Interpreter is installed on the mobile device, since it is in charge of actually executing the app. The Planner, instead, may be deployed either locally or remotely.

3.1 The SelfMotion Declarative Language

Abstract Actions. Abstract actions are high-level descriptions of the primitive actions used to accomplish the app's goal. They represent the main building blocks of the app. Listing 1.2 illustrates the abstract actions for the SR reference example: they correspond to the high level components listed in Table 2. In some cases, the same functional component may correspond to several abstract actions, depending on some contextual information (e.g., if the device has a camera with autofocus or not). For example, we split the GetPosition functionality into two abstract actions getPosWithGPS and getPosManually. We also introduced an enableGPS abstract action, which encapsulates the logic to activate the sensor. Similarly, the blurryDecoder abstract action represents a remote component in charge of recognizing barcodes from pictures taken with fixed focus cameras. Together with the blurryBarcodeReader action it can read the barcode when an autofocus camera is not available.

```
action barcodeReader          action blurryBarcodeReader    action enableGPS          action inputPrice(Name)
pre:   hasAutoFocusCamera      pre:   hasFixedFocusCamera     pre:   ~isGPSEnabled      pre:   prodName(Name)
post:  barcode(prodBarcode)    post:  image(blurryImage)      post:  isGPSEnabled       post:  price(prodPrice)

action blurryDecoder(Image)   action getProdName(Barcode)    action localSearch(Barcode, Pos)
pre:   image(Image)            pre:   barcode(Barcode)        pre:   barcode(Barcode), position(Pos)
post:  barcode(prodBarcode)    post:  prodName(name)          post:  listOfLocalPrices

action getPosWithGPS          action getPosManually          action sharePrice(Name, Price)
pre:   hasGPS, isGPSEnabled    pre:   true                    pre:   prodName(Name), price(Price)
post:  position(gpsPos)        post:  position(manualPos)     post:  sharedPrice
```

Listing 1.2. SR Abstract Actions

```
goal (listOfLocalPrices and sharedPrice and position(gpsPos)) or
     (listOfLocalPrices and sharedPrice and position(userDefinedPos))

start (hasFixedFocusCamera and hasGPS and ~isGPSEnabled)
```

Listing 1.3. SR Goal and Initial State

Abstract actions are modeled with an easy-to-use, logic-like language, in terms of: (1) *signature*, (2) *precondition*, and (3) *postcondition*. Signatures include a name and a list of arguments. For instance, the `localSearch` action has the following signature: `localSearch(Barcode, Pos)`. The precondition is expressed as a list of facts that must be true in the current state for the action to be enabled. For `localSearch` we use the expression `barcode(Barcode), position(Pos)` to denote the fact that the `Barcode` parameter is a product barcode, while the `Pos` parameter represents the user's position. The postcondition models the effects of the action on the current state of execution by listing the facts to be added to and the ones to be removed from the state. In our example, when `inputPrice` is executed the fact `price(prodPrice)` is added to the state, while no facts are deleted (deleted facts, when present, are designed by using the "~" symbol). Facts are expressed as propositions, characterized by a name and parameters, which represent relevant objects of the domain. Parameters that start with an uppercase letter denote *unbound objects*, which must be bound to instances, whose name starts with a lowercase letter, to generate an execution plan. For instance, if at any point the fact `position(gpsPos)` is added to the state, the object `gpsPos` becomes available to be bound to the `Pos` parameter in the `localSearch` action.

Goal and Initial State. Besides abstract actions, the goal and initial state are also needed to build and execute apps. The goal specifies the desired state after executing the app. It may actually include a set of states, which reflect all the alternatives to accomplish the app's goal, listed in order of preference. As an example, in the SR app (see Listing 1.3) we have two alternative goals. The first one requires the GPS sensor and the second relies on the user input to retrieve the location. The initial state complements the goal by asserting the facts that are true at app invocation time. It is partially generated at run time by the SelfMotion Middleware, which detects the features of the mobile device in which it has been installed. In our example, assuming the device has a fixed-focus camera and a disabled GPS, it generates the initial state shown in Listing 1.3. Developers may add application specific facts to this auto-generated initial state, if needed. By relying on abstract actions, goal, and initial state, the Planner can build an Abstract Execution Plan. The Planner starts trying to build an Abstract Execution Plan to satisfy the first goal; if it does not succeed

```
1:  blurryBarcodeReader              5:  getProdName(prodBarcode)
2:  enableGPS                        6:  inputPrice(name)
3:  blurryDecoder(blurryBarcodeImage) 7:  localSearch(prodBarcode, gpsPos)
4:  getPosWithGPS                    8:  sharePrice(name, price)
```

Listing 1.4. A Possible Abstract Execution Plan

```
@Action(name="getProdName", priority=1)          @Action(name="getProdName", priority=2)
public String getProdNameViaService(Barcode barcode){   public String getProdNameFromUser(Barcode barcode){
  String barcodeValue = barcode.getValue();        String barcodeValue = barcode.getValue();
  //Use remote Web service (e.g., searchupc.com)   //Ask the user for the product name
  String productName = ...;                         String productName = ...;
  return productName;                               return productName;
}                                                 }
```

Listing 1.5. getProdName Concrete Actions

it tries to satisfy the second goal, and so on. Listing 1.4 reports a possible plan of the SR example for a device without autofocus (i.e., hasFixedFocusCamera is set to true) and with a GPS sensors available but not enabled (i.e., hasGPS set to true, isGPSEnabled set to false). This Abstract Execution Plan is a list of abstract actions that lead from the initial state to a state that satisfies the goal. Notice that: (1) when several sequences of actions could satisfy the goal, the Planner chooses one non-deterministically; (2) although the plan is described as a sequence of actions, the middleware is free to execute them in parallel, as soon as the respective precondition becomes true.

Concrete Actions. Concrete actions are the executable counterpart of abstract actions. Currently, concrete actions are implemented through Java methods. We use the annotation @Action to refer to the abstract actions they implement. In general, several concrete actions may be bound to the same abstract action. This way, if the currently bound concrete action fails (i.e., it returns an exception) the SelfMotion middleware has other options to accomplish the app's step specified by the failed abstract action. For example, the getProdName abstract action may have two concrete actions: one which exploits a Web service (e.g., searchupc.com) to map the barcode value to the product name, and another which asks it to the user. Listing 1.5 reports the code used to define the concrete actions. Notice that, in presence of multiple concrete actions for the same abstract action, it is possible to specify a preferred ordering through the priority attribute.

3.2   Advantages of the SelfMotion Approach

Decoupled Design. SelfMotion achieves a clear separation among different aspects of the app: from the more abstract ones, captured by goals, initial state, and abstract actions, to those closer to the implementation, captured by concrete actions. In defining abstract actions developers may focus on the features they want to introduce in the app, ignoring how they are implemented (e.g., ad-hoc developed components, services, or third party apps). This choice is delayed until run-time binding. Consider the GetProductName component of the SR app. In the inception phase of the app, developers only focus on the features it requires – the preconditions – and the features it provides – the postconditions. Later on, they can implement a first prototype that leverages an ad-hoc component (i.e., manual input of the product name). This solution may gradually evolved, by adding other alternative concrete actions.

Enable Transparent Adaptation. By separating abstract and concrete actions and supporting one-to-many mappings we solve two typical problems of mobile apps: (1) how to adapt to the plethora of devices available, and (2) how to cope with failures happening at run-time. As an example of problem (1), consider the implementation of component `GetPosition` of Listing 1.1 with its SelfMotion counterpart, which relies on several abstract actions with different preconditions (see Listing 1.2). The former requires to explicitly hard-code the various alternatives (e.g., to handle the potentially missing GPS), and any new option introduced by new devices would increase the number of possible branches. Conversely, SelfMotion just requires a separate abstract (or concrete) action for each option, leaving to the middleware the duty of selecting the most appropriate ones, considering the current device capabilities and the order of preference provided by the app's designer. As for problem (2), consider the example of `GetProductName`, which is implemented in SelfMotion by a single abstract action mapped to two different concrete actions (Listing 1.5). The middleware initially tries the first concrete action that invokes an external service: if this returns an exception, the second concrete action is automatically tried. Furthermore, if none of the available concrete actions succeeds, SelfMotion may rely on its *re-planning* mechanism to build an *alternative plan* at run-time. As an example, consider the case in which the middleware is executing the plan reported in Listing 1.4 and assume that the GPS sensor fails to retrieve the user location, throwing an exception. The middleware automatically catches the exception and recognizes the `getPosWithGPS` as faulty, which has no alternative concrete actions. Thus, the Planner is invoked to generate a new plan that avoids the faulty step. The new plan would include the `getPosManually` abstract action.

Improve Code Quality. SelfMotion promotes a clean modularization of the app's functionality into a set of abstract actions and their concrete counterparts and avoids contorted code through cascaded *if-elses* and exception handling constructs. As a result, code is easy to read, maintain, and evolve. By encapsulating all the features in independent actions and by letting the actual flow of execution to be automatically built at run-time by the middleware, SelfMotion increases reusability, since the same actions can be reused across different apps.

4   Related Work

Many existing works focus on the effective and efficient development of mobile applications, as summarized in [5,11]. They cover a wide range of approaches: from how to achieve context-aware behavior (e.g., [6]) to how to apply agile methods in the mobile domain (e.g., [1]).

Context-aware frameworks aim at supporting the development of mobile applications that are sensitive to their deployment context (e.g., the specific hardware platform) and their execution context (e.g., user location). For example, the EgoSpaces middleware [6] can be used to provide context information extracted from data-rich environments to applications. Another approach to mobile computing middleware is presented in [3], which exploits the principle of reflection to support adaptive and context-aware mobile capabilities. In general these approaches provide developers with abstractions to query the current context and detect context changes; i.e., they directly support context-dependent behavior as first-class concept. In the same direction, approaches like [2,10] provide specific context-aware extensions to the Android platform. The aforementioned approaches do not directly compete with ours, but rather they can be viewed as orthogonal. SelfMotion may benefit from their ability to detect context information, for example, to generate plans whose initial state depends on the surrounding context. The added value of SelfMotion is instead its ability to automatically build an execution flow based on the context and the overall design approach it promotes. Last, we would like to mention the foundational work on a three-layer architecture for software adaptation, described in [7,9], which shares with our work the motivation to provide sound architectural principles to the development of adaptive systems.

5   Conclusions and Future Work

SelfMotion is part of a long running research stream on declarative languages [4]. Future work includes building an IDE, possibly integrated in a widely adopted tool such as Eclipse, to further simplify the definition of abstract/concrete actions and goals. As for the SelfMotion middleware, while the current prototype is operational and publicly available, there is still space to further improve performance and robustness.

References

1. Abrahamsson, P., Hanhineva, A., Hulkko, H., Ihme, T., Jäälinoja, J., Korkala, M., Koskela, J., Kyllönen, P., Salo, O.: Mobile-D: An Agile Approach for Mobile Application Development. In: OOPSLA 2004 (2004)
2. Appeltauer, M., Hirschfeld, R., Rho, T.: Dedicated Programming Support for Context-Aware Ubiquitous Applications. In: UBICOMM 2008 (2008)
3. Capra, L., Emmerich, W., Mascolo, C.: CARISMA: Context-Aware Reflective mIddleware System for Mobile Applications. IEEE Trans. Software Eng. (2003)
4. Cugola, G., Ghezzi, C., Sales Pinto, L.: DSOL: a declarative approach to self-adaptive service orchestrations. Computing (2012)
5. Dehlinger, J., Dixon, J.: Mobile application software engineering: Challenges and research directions. In: Workshop on Mobile Software Engineering (2011)
6. Julien, C., Roman, G.C.: Egospaces: Facilitating rapid development of context-aware mobile applications. IEEE Trans. Software Eng. (2006)
7. Kramer, J., Magee, J.: Self-managed systems: an architectural challenge. In: FOSE 2007 (2007)
8. McKinley, P.K., Sadjadi, S.M., Kasten, E.P., Cheng, B.H.C.: Composing adaptive software. Computer (2004)
9. Sykes, D., Heaven, W., Magee, J., Kramer, J.: From goals to components: a combined approach to self-management. In: SEAMS 2008 (2008)
10. van Wissen, B., Palmer, N., Kemp, R., Kielmann, T., Bal, H.: Contextdroid: an expression-based context framework for android. In: PhoneSense 2010 (2010)
11. Wasserman, T.: Software engineering issues for mobile application development. In: FoSER 2010 (2010)

Algorithmic Aspects of Planning under Uncertainty for Service Delivery Organizations

Sreyash Kenkre[1], Ranganath Kondapally[2,*], and Vinayaka Pandit[1]

[1] IBM India Research Laboratory
{srekenkr,pvinayak}@in.ibm.com
[2] Computer Science Dept., Dartmouth College, Hanover, USA
rangak@cs.dartmouth.edu

Abstract. Remote delivery of services using geographically distributed service delivery locations has emerged as a popular and viable business model. Examples of services delivered in this manner are software services, business process outsourcing services, customer support centers, etc. The very nature of services and the fragile nature of the business environments in global delivery locations accentuates the role of uncertainty in planning for business continuity. We model the problem of critical service contingency planning based on *recourse actions*. We present an $O(\log n)$-approximation algorithm, generalizations to other planning problems under uncertainty, and present preliminary empirical results.

1 Introduction

Business continuity is an important aspect of service delivery. This entails service provider's commitment of continuity of business operations to the service seeker. The service provider could be IT enabled service provider, governance body delivering services to its citizens, public utility serving the citizens, etc. In this paper, we present examples from IT-enabled service delivery. But, the concepts are applicable much more broadly.

Recently, countries like India, China, Brazil, etc. have emerged as popular destinations to deliver software services, back-office services, remote infrastructure management, etc. due to the investor friendly policies and access to talent. Typically, the delivery centers and the consumers of the delivery are geographically separated. Such service delivery is enabled by setting up of large-scale, geographically distributed IT infrastructures consisting of heterogenous resources. Although this model is attractive, it also faces the challenges of heightened uncertainties in the operating environments of these geographies. We review the relevant issues taking example of a hypothetical organization X.

Operational Setting: Let us say X is an organization that delivers software services (ex: support, maintenance, testing, feature developments, etc.) to a large number of customers worldwide. X delivers its services from multiple countries, with multiple campuses in each country which allows it to tap into appropriate

---

* The work was done when the author was visiting IBM Research - India

C. Liu et al. (Eds.): ICSOC 2012, LNCS 7636, pp. 615–622, 2012.

workforce with required skills. Furthermore, it deploys a complex infrastructure of servers, communication networks, buildings, utilities, transportation logistics, etc. Each customer is treated as a customer account (or project) and is characterized by the combination of resources it requires. For instance, a customer account could be characterized by the physical security feature of the workplace it requires (ex: seats with secure badge access), the cyber security features of the WANs and LANs it uses, power requirements, and access features to the client environment. Therefore, enabling the service delivery for a customer account essentially involves making available the right combination of the resources. One of the reasons for the feasibility and profitability of X is the fact that there is lot of similarity in the services it delivers to different accounts. Hence, it can achieve economies of scale for resources that are commonly used across accounts (one example of such an infrastructure element is "Wide Area Network"). See [4] to understand why service providers prefer this model.

Motivation for Contingency Planning: Customers sourcing such global service delivery would naturally be worried about the uncertain business environment of the emerging geographies. Therefore, they put in place stringent SLAs on the continuity of service delivery. Typically, the customer identifies a subset of the procured services as "critical" and demands that the service provider provide round the clock continuity for at least the critical services. Examples of critical services in case of X could be "fix all high priority bugs", "fix bugs reported on security features of the product", and so on. See [7] for a client perspective of global sourcing of services. Even for the service provider, a strong commitment to business continuity not only helps meet the SLAs, but also build brand reputation for future business. Therefore, service delivery organizations are increasingly making contingency planning an integral part of overall operations.

Disruptions and Rerouting: Majority of the disruptions that arise in emerging geographies are local to a city, suburban area, etc. Examples of such disruptions are strikes, societal unrest, urban flooding, natural disasters, below par supply of utilities, etc. When a disruption happens at a location, the part of the organization's infrastructure located there is unavailable. Therefore, one of the most popular techniques that companies like X use is to deliver the services out of multiple locations in the geography [3,10,4]. Moreover, at each location, X ensures that there is sufficient residual capacities of different resource types, so that, during a crisis, some of the service delivered from the affected locations can be rerouted to unaffected locations. When X reroutes the services for a customer account from one location to another, it has to ensure that the right combination of the resources are available in the rerouted location. Such a reroute action is called "recourse". See [5,6] for elaboration on the importance and implications of "recourse aware" decision making in business operations resiliency.

Critical Services Contingency Planning Problem: As explained, for each customer account, X has to allocate an appropriate combination of resources, all co-located to enable service delivery. We consider the problem of contingency management plans for the critical services being delivered by the service provider. We assume that the organization has identified a set of challenging scenarios (each scenario is defined by a set of unavailable locations) and a probability distribution on their likelihood. For each critical service, we are given a set of locations from where it can be delivered (based on the availability of the right combination of services). The contingency management of critical services has to : (i) compute a default assignment of the services to the locations for delivery during normal conditions and (ii) compute a scenario specific assignment of the services to the locations under each scenario. The goal is to compute the assignments in such a way that the expected total cost of the normal and contingency operations.

Broader Applicability: The concept of recourse based handling of contingency, as described here, can be applied in other settings like city governance, network design for internet service providers, utilities in the power sector, etc. In our setting, the effect of an incident is local; for example, flooding in an office building only affects the infrastructure situated in the building. In contrast, the effect of an incident could be global. A classic example of this phenomena is the way cascades spread in power grids. The contingency analysis in such networks need more global formulations than ours and can be seen in [1,8].

2   Critical Service Contingency Planning (CSCP)

Location Mapping: As mentioned in the introduction, each project has a requirement in terms of the resource types it requires. Each location in the service delivery infrastructure has a set of available resources. One way to formulate the problem would be to capture all the details of the resources in the problem definition itself, as done in [5,6]. Note that the resource requirements of the critical services and resource availability results in the mapping of each critical service to a possible set of locations that it can be assigned to (as done in [5,6]). But, for simplicity of presentation, we assume that the mapping is itself part of the input. Therefore, in our setting, there is a set of locations, a set of critical tasks, and associated with each critical service is a set of locations to which it can possibly be assigned.

No Capacity Constraints: Capacity constraints are an important consideration and have been modeled in [5,6]. However, it is a well known fact that the critical services form a small fraction of the overall services delivered by the organization. Often, it is in the range 5-10% of the overall work. But, from the point of view credibility of the business operations and client satisfaction it is the most important part of the work and always gets highest priority. Therefore, even when there are capacity constraints, non-critical services are de-prioritized and capacity is made available to the critical tasks. Therefore, we assume that there are no capacity limits at the locations for assigning the critical tasks.

Cost Considerations: When a location is assigned a set of critical services for normal operational setting, it incurs *set up cost*. The set up cost could cover special requirements of critical services, transportation of people, and other procurements. However, suppose a locations has not been assigned any critical service during normal operations and has to suddenly make arrangements for critical services during a disruption, it incurs *recourse cost*. Typically, recourse cost is much higher than the set up cost as the required arrangements (and the implied procurements) have to be carried out at a short notice.

Scenarios: The uncertainty in the service delivery manifests in the form of disruptions in normal operations. We model disruption (also called scenario) as an event which disables the delivery of services from a set of affected locations. In most service delivery organizations, there are domain experts who can model the relevant set of scenarios for the organization. They could take into account aspects like bottlenecks in the infrastructure (example: suppose there is just one mail server for the entire organization, one must consider the disruption which disables the location of the mail server) or external parameters of the locations (example: if some locations are vulnerable to flooding, then, one must consider a scenario which affects such locations). We assume that a domain expert provides the set of scenarios for contingency planning. We further assume that a probability distribution on the likelihood of the scenarios is given.

Problem Formulation: Let the set of locations be specified by the set $L = \{S_1, S_2, \ldots, S_m\}$. Let the set of projects in the service delivery organization be given by $\mathcal{P} = \{P_1, P_2, \ldots, P_t\}$. Let the set of critical tasks across the different projects be given by the set $T = \{v_1, v_2, \ldots v_n\}$. Associated with a critical task v_i is a subset of locations, $\Gamma(v_i) \subseteq L$, which denotes the set of locations to which v_i can potentially be assigned. Given this, one can also define the set of services that can be defined from a location S_i as $CT(S_i) = \{v_i | S_i \in \Gamma(v_i)\}$. The set of scenarios modeled by the domain expert is given by $\mathcal{S} = \{E_1, E_2, \ldots E_k\}$ where $E_i \subseteq L$ is the set of locations affected in the ith scenario. The probability distribution on the likelihood of the scenarios is given by the mapping $\mu : \mathcal{S} \to [0,1]$ such that $\sum_{E_i \in \mathcal{S}} \mu(E_i) = 1$. The set up cost and recourse cost of $S_i \in L$ is given by $c(S_i$ and $r(S_i)$ respectively. The CSCP problem requires us to compute an assignment R of critical services to the locations that is to be followed during normal operations and a set of recourse assignments F_{E_j} for each $E_j \in \mathcal{S}$. Let $Sites(R)$ denote the set of locations that are used in the assignment R and $Sites(F_{E_j})$ denote the set of locations that are used in the assignment F_{E_j}. The goal is to minimize the expected cost of the normal and contingency operations, i.e,

minimize $\left(\left(\sum_{S_i \in Sites(R)} c(S_i) \right) + \left(\sum_{E_j \in \mathcal{S}} \mu(E_j) \cdot \left(\sum_{S_i \in Sites(F_{E_j})} r(S_i) \right) \right) \right)$.

3   Algorithm, Proof, and Generalization

We now present an algorithm for the CSCP problem with a provable approximation ratio. In other words, our algorithm always returns a solution whose cost with respect to the optimal solution is bounded by the approximation ratio.

We first begin by showing the equivalence of our problem to the *Stochastic Set Cover* problem. Set Cover is one of the fundamental problems in combinatorial optimization and approximation algorithms [9] and is the following: given a universe U and a family of sets, $\mathcal{X} = \{X_1, \ldots, X_q\}$ where all the X_is are subsets of U, and a weight function $w : \mathcal{X} \to \mathbb{R}$, the goal to pick a subset $R \subseteq \mathcal{X}$

such that $\cup_{X_i \in R} X_i = U$ and the weight $\sum_{X_i \in R} w(X_i)$ is minimized. Let us consider the problem of just assigning all the critical tasks to one of the sites. The universe is the set of all the critical tasks. Each site is a set which contains the critical tasks that can be assigned to it. The weight function associated with the sites is their set up cost. The task of computing an assignment is now equivalent to the minimum cost set cover of the universe of critical tasks by the sets corresponding to the sites weighted by their set up cost. Let us now consider the CSCP problem. Essentially, it is a two stage stochastic problem. We first want to pick an assignment which acts as the set cover during normal operations. At the second stage, one of the scenarios is revealed by the nature according to the probability distribution on $\mathcal{S}$. At that stage, we have to pick new sites for the critical services that were assigned to the affected locations. In the second stage, we have to incur the recourse cost at the new sites. Essentially, we want to pick a two stage set cover which minimizes the expected cost.

$$\text{Minimize} \sum_{S_j \in L} c(S_j) y_{S_j} + \sum_{E_l \in \mathcal{S}} \mu(E_l) \cdot \left(\sum_{S_j \in L} r(S_j) \cdot y_{S_j}^l \right)$$

$$\sum_{S_j \in \Gamma(v_i)} y_{S_j} \geq 1 \quad \forall v_i \in V \qquad\qquad \text{(Normal Covering)}$$

$$\sum_{j \in L \setminus E_l} y_{S_j} + y_{S_j}^l \geq 1 \quad \forall E_l \in \mathcal{S} \qquad\qquad \text{(Cover } E_l\text{)}$$

$$y_{S_j} \in \{0,1\} \quad \forall S_j \in L$$

$$y_{S_j}^l \in \{0,1\} \quad \forall S_j \in \mathcal{L} \text{ and } E_l \in \mathcal{S} \qquad\qquad \text{(LP)}$$

We present the integer linear programming formulation for the CSCP (See (LP)). Here, y_{S_i}s are decision variables that indicate whether set up cost is incurred in the first stage at S_is and $y_{S_i}^l$ are decision variables that indicate whether recourse cost is incurred in the second stage at S_i in the scenario E_l. The integer linear program is self-explanatory. We present it because it helps us to present generalizations of our result.

Our algorithm is as shown in Algorithm 1. The main idea is to not take any anticipatory decisions in the first stage and use any approximation algorithm for the set cover at both first and second stage. In the second stage, an appropriate set cover instance is created depending on the set of "failed" critical services corresponding to the scenario. Details are presented in the algorithm itself. The main result is the following theorem.

Theorem 1. *Suppose the deterministic algorithm $\mathcal{A}$ in Algorithm 1 has an approximation ratio of α for the Set Cover problem, then, the approximation ratio of the Algorithm 1 is $\left(1 + \max_{S_i \in L} \frac{r(S_i)}{c(S_i)}\right) \alpha$ for the CSCP problem.*

Proof. Due to space considerations, we present just the overview of the proof. Let $(R, F_{E_1}, \ldots, F_{E_k})$ denote the solution computed by the algorithm. Let $(R^*, F_{E_1}^*, \ldots F_{E_k}^*)$ denote the optimal solution of cost:

---

input : Critical Tasks T, Locations L, Critical Task Mapping $\Gamma()$, set up costs
       $c(S_i)$s, recourse costs $r(S_i)$s, and scenarios $\mathcal{S}$
output: First stage assignment R and second stage assignments F_{E_i}s
1 Employ a deterministic algorithm $\mathcal{A}$ for the set cover problem with T as the
   universe, $CT(S_i)$s as the sets, and $c(S_i)$s as the weights. Assign tasks to any of
   the selected sites to which they can be mapped. This gives R and $Sites(R)$. ;
2 **for** $E_j \in \mathcal{S}$ **do**
3   Let $affected = \{v_i \in T | R(v_i) \in E_j\}$, i.e, tasks which are assigned by R to
     an affected location in the scenario E_j ;
4   If any of $affected$ nodes can be assigned to $R \setminus E_j$, then, assign them. Let
     $failed$ be the set of remaining nodes ;
5   Employ $\mathcal{A}$ on $failed$ as the universe, $CT(S_i)$ for $S_i \notin E_j$ as the sets, and
     $r(S_i)$ for $E_j \notin E_j$ as the costs. Assign tasks as in Step 1 to get F_{E_j} and
     $Sites(F_{E_j})$.
6 **end**
7 Output $R, F_{E_1}, \ldots, F_{E_k}$.

Algorithm 1. The Main Algorithm

$$OPT = (\sum_{S_i \in Sites(R^*)} c(S_i) + \sum_{E_j \in \mathcal{S}} \mu(E_j) \cdot (\sum_{S_i \in Sites(F^*_{E_j})} r(S_i)))$$

Clearly, $\sum_{S_i \in Sites(R)} c(S_i) \le \alpha \sum_{S_i \in Sites(R^*)} c(S_i)$ (due to the approximation
property of $\mathcal{A}$). Now consider a scenario E_j. Let $R^*_{1,j}$ be the sites from R^* that
are used by the optimal solution and $R^*_{2,j}$ be the sites with recourse cost used
in the second stage. Note that $\sum_{S_i \in R^*_{1,j}} c(S_i) + \mu(E_j) \sum_{S_i \in R^*_{2,j}} r(S_i) \le OPT$.
Clearly, $R^*_{1,j} \cup R^*_{2,j}$ is candidate for F_{E_j} at step 5 of the algorithm and its recourse
cost is at most $\max_{S_i \in R^*_{1,j} \cup R^*_{2,j}} \frac{r(S_i)}{c(S_i)} \cdot OPT$. Therefore, the algorithm $\mathcal{A}$ at step
5 picks a solution F_{E_j} of cost at most $(\alpha \max_{S_i \in R^*_{1,j} \cup R^*_{2,j}} \frac{r(S_i)}{c(S_i)} \cdot OPT)$ – this is
due to the approximation property of $\mathcal{A}$. Since this applies for every $E_j \in calS$,
we get the approximation ratio claimed in the theorem.

The greedy heuristic of picking the set with best coverage (least cost per element covered) at every step is an $O(\log n)$ approximation where n is the size of
the universe and is asymptotically tight under the assumption of P $\neq$ NP [9].
Therefore, we get an approximation ratio of $(1 + \max_{S_i \in L} \frac{r(S_i)}{c(S_i)}) \log |T|$ and it is
asymptotically the best possible.

3.1 Generalization

We present a generalization of our result to a family of stochastic planning
problems (applicable to service delivery). The proofs will be included in longer
version. Consider any planning problem which has to meet a fixed demand set T.
The demand has to be met by setting up a required structure R by choosing from
a universe options U. There is a set of scenarios $\mathcal{S}$ with a probability distribution

on them and each scenario mentions a subset of U that is not available. We want to build a stochastic solution for the structure R which minimizes the expected cost of building the structure. For example, an internet service provider might want to build Steiner Tree [9] on a set of demand points and the universe consists of the different edges (pairs of end-points) that can be included in the tree. Scenarios are sets of edges that can fail. We can prove the following. Suppose we can write an integer linear program for the problem of computing R and if there is an α approximation for the non-stochastic version of the problem, our algorithmic framework gives an approximation ratio of $(1 + \beta)\alpha$ where β is the worst ratio of the recourse cost to the set up cost of the elements in U.

Finally, we end with a comment on the complexity added by the stochastic part. Consider the problem of constructing Minimum Spanning Tree (MST) of a graph. This is solvable in polynomial time. But, the problem of computing the optimal two stage MST solution to the stochastic version as considered in this paper becomes NP-Complete via a reduction from the Hamiltonian Cycle Problem [2].

4 Experimental Evaluation

The insights obtained from this work have been used in contingency planning problems in service delivery organizations within IBM. However, data from real-life service delivery scenarios are sensitive and difficult to share in public.Therefore, we conduct our experiments on randomly generated instances of the CSCP problem. The random instances were generated by varying the number of sites, number of critical services, relative costs of $c(S_i)$ and $r(S_i)$. We generated up to 50 sites and 1000 services. These are realistic numbers as organizations typically have only tens of sites and hundreds of projects.

We consider following heuristics. P refers to the organizational procedure which the organization may follow for allocation of the critical service to various sites using business rules (state of the art today). We modeled P by simple business rules such as assign to the nearest site, load balance the allocations, etc. P is important because it can capture certain rules that are hard to encode into the CSCP formulation. Heuristic P+P refers to the case when the organizations procedure is used both for the initial allocation as well as drawing up the contingency plan. A refers to the greedy set cover heuristic, which provides α approximation where $\alpha = \log|T|$. Heuristic A+A refers to the case where the procedure A is used both for the initial allocation as well as the drawing up of the contingency plan. In heuristic P+A, we make the initial allocation using P and do the contingency planning using procedure A.

Due to space considerations, we present just a sample of the experimental results in Table 1. We experimented with different probability distributions. Since our theoretical results hold irrespective of the distribution, we present the results on the uniform distribution on scenarios, i.e, no special knowledge other than the list of scenarios is known. The (A+A) solution is consistently the solution of least cost. But, there could be a practical problem in using it since

Sites	Services	P+P	A+A	P+A
20	100	385	120	300
20	200	430	190	370
40	300	613.33	466.66	526.66
40	500	906.66	520	673.33
50	1000	1356.66	780	1326.66

Fig. 1. Comparison Of Heuristics

both the stage solutions are computed without contextual business knowledge. The (P+A) solution is much lower than the (P+P) solution and it may be easier to use effectively. This is because the first stage solution, which is used during normal operations is computed taking organizational constraints into account. The second stage solution computed using the greedy heurisitc can be easily adapted to fit into organizational constraints as the number of affected critical services is much lower than the total number of critical services.

References

1. Choi, J., Mount, T., Thomas, R.: Transmission expansion planning using contingency criteria. IEEE Transactions on Power Systems 22(4), 2249–2261 (2007)
2. Garey, M., Johnson, D.: Computers and Intractability: A Guide to the Theory of NP-Completeness. Freeman (1979)
3. Graham, J., Kaye, D.: A Risk Management Approach to Business Continuity. Rothstein Associates Inc. (2006)
4. Jalona, S., Chandrakar, A.: Evolution of IT services delivery model (2008) Infosys White Paper available at
   http://www.infosys.com/global-sourcing/white-papers/pages/index.aspx
5. Karthik, S., Kenkre, S., Narayanam, K., Pandit, V.: Recourse aware resource allocation for contingency planning in distributed service delivery. In: IEEE Conference on Services Operations, Logistics, and Information, SOLI (2012)
6. Karthik, S., Kenkre, S., Narayanam, K., Pandit, V.: Resiliency analytics framework for service delivery organizations. In: Proc. of the Global Conference of Service Research Innovation Institute, SRII (2012)
7. Keane White Paper. Going global with application outsourcing (2011), Report is available at http://www.keane.com/resources/pdf/WhitePapers/WP-GGAO.pdf
8. Street, A., Oliveira, F., Arroyo, J.M.: Contingency-constrained unit commitment with n-k security criterion: A robust optimization approach. IEEE Transactions on Power Systems 26(3), 1581–1590 (2011)
9. Vazirani, V.: Approximation Algorithms. Springer (2001)
10. Wipro Report. Wipro Business Continuity - "Plan B", Report is available
    http://www.wipro.com/documents/Wipro_Business_Continuity.pdf

A Dynamic QoS-Aware Semantic Web Service Composition Algorithm

Pablo Rodriguez-Mier, Manuel Mucientes, and Manuel Lama

Centro de Investigación en Tecnoloxías da Información (CITIUS)
Universidade de Santiago de Compostela, Spain
{pablo.rodriguez.mier,manuel.mucientes,manuel.lama}@usc.es

Abstract. The aim of this work is to present a dynamic QoS-aware semantic web service composition algorithm that finds the minimal solution graph that satisfies the composition request considering multiple QoS criteria and semantic input-output message structure matching restrictions. Our proposal starts computing an initial solution by selecting only those services from the dataset that are relevant to the user request and meet the semantic restrictions. Then, an optimal QoS-aware composition is calculated using Dijkstra shortest path algorithm. Once the solution is obtained, the number of services is minimized using the optimal aggregated QoS value calculated in the previous step as a bound to prune the state space search. Moreover, a set of extensive experiments with five different datasets from the Web Service Challenge 2009-2010 is presented to prove the efficiency of our proposal.

Keywords: Automatic composition, Shortest Path, QoS optimization, Semantic Web Services.

1 Introduction

QoS-Aware web service composition has attracted a lot of attention from different fields in recent years. In [6], the authors distinguish two different types of composition algorithms: static and dynamic algorithms. Static algorithms require a predefined workflow with abstract processes. Each abstract process can be implemented by a wide variety of web services with different QoS measures that meet the functionality requirements of the process. The goal is to select the best services for each abstract process that fulfills the QoS constraints imposed by the user. Thus, these algorithms are only focused on service selection based on QoS and therefore are more related to the service discovery field. Relevant examples of this category are [10,9,2]. None of these approaches generate composite web services by combining different atomic services automatically. Dynamic algorithms, on the other hand, are more focused on calculating the overall composition structure, satisfying the global QoS. Within this category, the most interesting proposals are [5,8,1,3]. However, most of them can maximize only one QoS attribute and do not consider service minimization, leading to huge solutions with redundant services.

C. Liu et al. (Eds.): ICSOC 2012, LNCS 7636, pp. 623–630, 2012.
© Springer-Verlag Berlin Heidelberg 2012

This paper addresses the problem of the dynamic QoS-Aware semantic web service composition considering multiple QoS attributes and minimizing the total number of services from the composition result. The novelties of our proposal are: 1) A multi-objective Dijkstra-based label setting algorithm that finds the optimal QoS composition (minimizing the total response time and maximizing the throughput) and 2) a combinatorial search algorithm that minimizes the number of services from a solution, keeping the optimal QoS. The algorithm uses the optimal values calculated in the previous phase to effectively reduce the search space size.

The rest of the paper is organized as follows: Sec. 2 introduces the basis of the semantic web service composition and explains the QoS model used to compute the global QoS. Sec. 3 illustrates the proposed algorithm for web service composition. Sec. 4 analyzes the algorithm with five different repositories and section 5 concludes the paper.

2   QoS-Based Semantic Composition Model

We define a web service by a 3-Tuple $S = \{I_S, O_S, Q_S\}$ where $I_S = \{I_S^1, I_S^2, ...\}$ is the set of inputs consumed by the service, $O_S = \{O_S^1, O_S^2, ...\}$ is the set of outputs retrieved when the service is invoked and $Q_S = \{Q_S^1, Q_S^2, ..., Q_S^n\}$ is the set of quality attributes of the service. Inputs and outputs of a service are semantically annotated by concepts that are defined in an ontology. Although concepts from an ontology can be related to each other by different types of relations in our approach we only use the subclass/superclass relationship, so we consider that an output of a service o_{S1} matches the input of other service i_{S2} when o_{S1} is equal or a subclass of i_{S2} ($o_{S1} \subseteq i_{S2}$).

A web service can be invoked only if all their inputs are matched. Given a request $R = \{I_R, O_R\}$, and given a web service $S = \{I_S, O_S, Q_S\}$, the web service S can be invoked only if $I_R \subseteq I_S$ (all inputs matched), i.e., for each input $i_s \in I_S$ there exists an input $i_r \in I_R$ such that $i_r \subseteq i_s$. Also, O_R will be satisfied only if $O_S \subseteq O_R$, i.e., for each output $o_r \in O_R$ there exists an output $o_s \in O_S$ such that o_s is equal or subclass of o_r ($o_s \subseteq o_r$).

2.1   QoS Computation Model for DAG Compositions

Considering the previous description, the QoS-aware composition problem tackled in this paper can be formulated as the automatic construction of a directed acyclic graph (DAG) that models the dependencies among the different web services involved in the composition with a global optimal value of QoS. The DAG contains two special nodes, *Source* (without incoming edges) and *Sink* (without outgoing edges), which provides the requested inputs and consumes the requested outputs respectively. Each directed edge is an ordered pair of two connected vertex (services) (S_i, S_j) of the graph and represents a semantic matching between S_i and S_j (i.e., one or many outputs from S_i match one or many inputs from S_j).

The calculation of the global value of QoS for a composite web service depends directly on the DAG structure. We consider the two quality QoS attributes defined in the Web Service Challenge 2009-2010: response time, which should be minimized, and throughput, which should be maximized. The total QoS value of a composite service corresponds with the aggregated QoS of the $Sink$ node of the composition DAG. To compute the best QoS of a composite service, we define a recursive function for each QoS attribute over the service domain ($QN_R(S)$, $QN_T(S)$):

- Resp. time: $QN_R(S_i, \{S_i^1, ..., S_i^n\}) = Max\{QN_R(S_i^1), ..., QN_R(S_i^n)\} + R(S_i)$
- Throughput: $QN_T(S_i, \{S_i^1, ..., S_i^n\}) = Min\{QN_T(S_i^1), ..., QN_T(S_i^n), T(S_i)\}$

Where $\{S_i^1, ..., S_i^n\}$ are the direct predecessors from the service node S_i and $R(S_i), T(S_i)$ are the functions that returns the response time and the throughput respectively associated to the service S_i. $QN_R(Sink)$ returns the total QoS of a composite service. Note that $R(Source), R(Sink) = 0$ and $T(Source), T(Sink) = \infty$ since $Source$ and $Sink$ are not real services.

3   Algorithm Description

The problem tackled in this paper consists of generating the best composition from the point of view of the QoS and cost (number of services) given a semantic request provided by an user. The steps followed by our proposal are: 1) Discover relevant services for the query; 2) Construct a matching digraph representing all possible matchings between these services; 3) Find the composition DAG with the optimal QoS value using a Dijkstra-shortest path algorithm over the matching digraph and 4) minimize the number of services of the solution using a backward search.

Finding the web service composition with the minimal cost has been proved to be NP-Complete [4]. However, in most cases the optimal QoS can be used as a bound to prune effectively the search space, discarding all those states that worsen the optimal value. In these section, we explain these steps in detail.

3.1   Service Filtering

The first step before calculating the composition is to filter all those services from the repository that are relevant to the request, discarding the rest. The filtering technique is explained in detail in [7]. Given a user request $R_{user} = \{I_R, O_R, W_R\}$ a matching digraph with the relevant services and all the matching relations among their inputs and outputs is generated layer by layer. Each layer contains those services whose required inputs are generated in previous layers. First and last layers contain the virtual services $Source = \{\emptyset, I_R, \{0, \infty\}\}$ and $Sink = \{O_R, \emptyset, \{0, \infty\}\}$, respectively, where $Source$ provides the inputs of the request and $Sink$ receives the outputs specified in the request. The calculation of the layers stops when there are no more services to add. When the process completes, the resultant graph contains all relevant services with their input/output concept matching relationships. The services contained in each layer are:

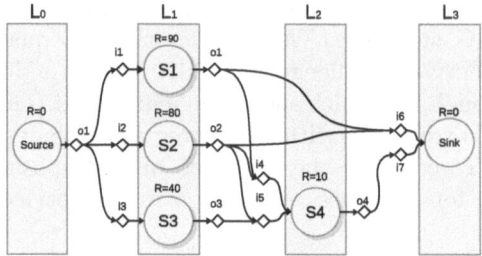

Fig. 1. A matching digraph representing the relations between the filtered (relevant) services for a request. Circles are services and diamonds are concepts (inputs and outputs). A directed edge between two concepts ($c1$, $c2$) represents a $c1 \subseteq c2$ relationship. Note that services from subsequent layers can provide inputs to services from previous layers, and therefore cycles are allowed.

- $L_0 = \{Source\}$, $L_N = \{Sink\}$
- $L_i = \{S_i : S_i \notin L_j(j < i) \land I_{Si} \cap O_{i-1} \neq \emptyset \land I_{Si} \subseteq I_R \cup O_0 \cup \ldots \cup O_{i-1}\}$

3.2   Optimal QoS-Aware Composition

The matching digraph represented in Fig. 1 has two type of nodes: services and concepts. Concepts are the traditional OR-nodes in a directed graph. Each incoming edge to a concept node represents a different path to obtain that concept. Thus, the optimal cost of a concept is determined by the best value among all their incoming paths. Conversely, services are a special type of nodes (AND-nodes) as they are unreachable until all their inputs are matched. The cost to reach a service node is calculated using the worst value among all their concepts. If a concept of a service has not been resolved (has a cost of ∞) then the cost to reach the service (and hence the cost of their outputs) is ∞ too. As our algorithm is multi-objective (minimizes response time and maximizes throughput) both QoS attributes have to be scaled and combined properly using the weights assigned to the request. The normalization of the QoS attributes is described in detail in [10] so is omitted here.

To find the optimal providers for each concept, we define a Dijkstra-based label setting algorithm that minimizes the objective function by exploring the service graph from the *Source* to the *Sink* node. The objective function of a composition is defined as $Global_{QoS}(R, T) = w1 * R + w2 * (1 - T)$, where R and T are the total response time and total throughput (scaled between [0,1]) of the composition and $w1, w2 \in [0, 1] \land w1 + w2 = 1$.

The pseudocode of the Dijkstra algorithm is shown in Alg. 1. The algorithm starts adding the *Source* service to the queue. Then, services in the queue are analyzed in order of increasing cost. The cost of each service S_i is their aggregated value of QoS. This value is calculated as $aggregatedQoS(S_i) = Global_{QoS}(QN_R(S_i, Pred), QN_T(S_i, Pred))$. $Pred = \{S_i^1, ..., S_i^n\}$ is the set of the optimal predecessors for each input of S_i, i.e., $Pred = \{i_1.op, ..., i_j.op\}$ ($i.op$

Algorithm 1. Optimal QoS-Aware Service Composition

1: #Services are ordered in queue by their $aggregatedQoS(Service)$ value
2: $queue \leftarrow (0, Source)$ #0 = best cost, 1 = worst cost
3: **while** $queue \neq \emptyset$ **do**
4:     $S_A \leftarrow queue$ #Extract lower cost service
5:     $newAggregatedQoS = aggregatedQoS(S_A)$
6:     **for all** S_B $matched\_by$ S_A **do**
7:       $inputsMatched = \{i_m : i_m \in (O_{S_A} \cap I_{S_B}) \wedge i_m \in I_{S_B})\}$
8:       **for all** $i_m \in inputsMatched$ **do**
9:         **if** $newAggregatedQoS < i_m.aggregatedQoS$ **then**
10:           $i_m.aggregatedQoS = newAggregatedQoS$
11:           $i_m.op = S_A$ #op means optimalPredecessor
12:         **end if**
13:       **end for**
14:       $newCost = aggregatedQoS(S_B)$
15:       $queue \leftarrow (newCost, S_B)$ #(Re)order the neighbor in queue
16:     **end for**
17: **end while**

---

is the optimal predecessor that provides the input i) where $\{i_1, ..., i_j\} \in I_{S_i}$. If optimal predecessors have not been determined yet, then $aggreatedQoS(S_i) = \infty$.

3.3 Service Minimization

The reconstruction of the optimal QoS-Aware service composition using the optimal providers leads, in most cases, to inefficient compositions with redundant services, which increases the cost of the final composition. For example, following Alg. 1, we obtain that the best compositions contains the services $\{S2, S3, S4\}$ as they are the best providers for each input. However, as the best $aggregatedQoS$ for $S4$ is determined by the worst cost (input $i4$), $S3$ can be removed without affecting the global value of QoS (input $i5$ can be provided by $S2$ with a cost of 80 ms). Thus, we develop a state space search algorithm that finds the composition with the minimum number of services using Dijkstra backwards (from $Sink$ to $Source$), keeping the optimal QoS value calculated previously. The algorithm navigates state by state, selecting in each transition the best combination of services that provides the required inputs for each state, using the optimal QoS as a bound to discard all those actions that worsen the optimal value of QoS.

The search space is the set of all reachable states from the initial state by any sequence of actions. We define the minimization problem as a backward search over the state space. The elements that conform the search space problem are:

- $State$: is defined as a 2-tuple $\{I, O\}$ where $I = \{i_1, ..., i_n\}$ is the set of required inputs and $O = \{o_1, ..., o_n\}$ is the set of the provided outputs.
- $Initial\ state$: $\{I_{Sink}, \emptyset\}$ where I_{Sink} are the required inputs by the $Sink$ node.
- $Goal\ state$: $\{\emptyset, O_{Source}\}$ where O_{Source} are the outputs provided by the $Source$ service.

- *Action*: $A = \{S_1, ..., S_n\}$ is the set of services that provides the required outputs.
- $\phi(A)$: operator function that collects all outputs generated by an *Action*.
- $\gamma(A)$: operator function that collects all inputs required by an *Action*.
- *Transition function*: $f : State_A \times Action \rightarrow State_B$. The resulting state is defined as $State_B = \{\gamma(Action), \phi(Action)\}$.
- *Path cost function* $\delta(S)$: function that returns the size of the path $P = A_1 \cup A_2, ..., \cup A_N$ where P is the union set of all actions from initial state to S. Note that P contains all the different services selected from the initial state to S. The problem is to reach the goal state with the minimum cost.

Given a state $S = \{I, O\}$, the possible actions that can be applied to S are all those combinations of services from the matching digraph that covers the inputs $I \in S$, i.e., $\phi(A) \subseteq I$. Since we know the best aggregated QoS value of the composition, we can filter all those actions that exceed the bound. Consider the example in Fig. 1 and suppose that Alg. 1 determined that the best providers for all inputs are $(Source, S2, S3, S4, Sink)$. The global QoS of the composite service using these services is $QN_R(Sink) = Max(80, 90) = 90$. The initial state can be defined as $S_I = \{\{i6, i7\}, \emptyset\}$. The possible actions that can be applied to this state are $A_1 = \{S1, S4\}$ and $A_2 = \{S2, S4\}$. Although $S1$ is not considered by the algorithm as the best provider for $i6$, $S1$ can replace $S2$ without affecting the global QoS. The resulting states after applying actions A_1 and A_2 are $S_{A_1} = \{\{i1, i5\}, \{o1, o4\}\}$ and $S_{A_2} = \{\{i2\}, \{o2, o4\}\}$ Note that in the next iteration, S_{A_2} reach the solution with the minimum path cost, so the optimal solution consists only of services $S2$ and $S4$. Using Dijkstra to traverse the graph, we can guarantee the optimality of the solutions found.

4   Experiments

In order to prove the validity and efficiency of our algorithm in different situations, we carried out some experiments using five datasets from Web Service Challenge 2009-2010. Table 1 shows the results obtained for each dataset using different weights for response time (w1) and throughput (w2).

The minimization of the services for each solution can be done by searching over the entire service graph (global minimization, *GM*) or considering only the optimal providers obtained for each input (local minimization, *LM*). When the *LM* is performed, instead of considering all alternatives for each input, the algorithm prunes all those optimal redundant services from the original result that are not necessary to obtain the best aggregated value of QoS.

Column #I. Serv shows the initial services obtained before applying the minimization. These services are the optimal providers for each input found with the Alg.1. Column #S. (LM/GM) shows the minimum number of services obtained using local or global minimization. Columns #Rt.(LM/GM) and #Th.(LM/GM) present the results for the response time and the throughput of the composite service. Note that results obtained for response time when $w_1 = 0$ and for the throughput when $w_2 = 0$ are not relevant, as the algorithm does not minimize/maximize the attributes weighted with 0. The last column shows the time elapsed (in milliseconds) between the initial user request and the delivery of the composition result (results are not translated to BPEL, they are provided as DAGs).

4.1 Results Discussion

Table 1 shows the results of the algorithm describing all the characteristics defined in the Web Service Challenge 2009-2010. All tests were executed in a Intel Core 2 Quad Q9550 2.83 GHz with 8 GB RAM, under Ubuntu 10.04 64-bit, with a time limit of 30 seconds for each test (results marked with a dash are those that took more than 30 seconds). The quality of the results is evaluated measuring the best response time, the best throughput and the number of services. Since we do not generate BPEL code, we cannot measure the total composition length.

An important difference between the solutions of the participants from the Web Service Challenge 2009-2010 and our solutions is that they do not minimize both quality attributes (they use the same algorithm to minimize each QoS attribute independently). Thus, their results should be compared with our solutions when $w_1 = 0, w_2 = 1$ or $w_1 = 1, w_2 = 0$, as they cannot provide intermediate solutions. In all cases we obtained the same best solutions as the winners, with less number of services for datasets 4 and 5. Note that the performance of our algorithm is slightly worse due to the minimization process. Solutions for the dataset 4 with the global service minimization cannot be obtained in a reasonable period of time due to the combinatorial explosion. However, local minimization can be used efficiently when the priority is to obtain good quality solutions in a short time.

Table 1. Results obtained by our algorithm

Dataset			Optimal QoS solution			
WSC-2009'01	w1/w2	#I. Serv.	#S. (LM/GM)	Rt.(LM/GM)	Th.(LM/GM)	Time (ms) (LM/GM)
	1.0/0.0	13	5/5	500/500	3000/3000	274/389
	0.5/0.5	7	5/5	760/760	15000/15000	277/291
	0.0/1.0	7	5/5	930/930	15000/15000	270/298
WSC-2009'02	1.0/0.0	25	20/20	1690/1690	3000/2000	868/1988
	0.5/0.5	24	20/20	1800/1770	6000/6000	860/3103
	0.0/1.0	24	20/20	1970/2000	6000/6000	117/7530
WSC-2009'03	1.0/0.0	11	10/10	760/760	2000/4000	1071/1545
	0.5/0.5	33	10/10	840/760	4000/4000	1069/1533
	0.0/1.0	31	18/11	1780/1110	4000/4000	1101/5249
WSC-2009'04	1.0/0.0	50	40/-	1470/-	2000/-	4399/-
	0.5/0.5	73	64/-	3540/-	4000/-	4586/-
	0.0/1.0	72	62/-	3840/-	4000/-	4506/-
WSC-2009'05	1.0/0.0	41	32/32	4070/4070	1000/1000	2646/2801
	0.5/0.5	41	32/32	4280/4200	4000/4000	2667/2680
	0.0/1.0	41	32/30	5470/4750	4000/4000	2657/10953

5 Conclusions

In this paper we have presented a dynamic QoS-Aware semantic web service composition that finds optimal compositions minimizing the total response time and maximizing the throughput. We also presented a method to effectively reduce the total number of services from a composition without affecting the global value of QoS. This technique can also perform a local or a global search to minimize the total services depending on time requirements. Moreover, a full validation has been done using five different datasets from the Web Service Challenge 2009-2010, showing a good performance as in all cases the best solutions with the best values of QoS and the minimum number of services were found.

Acknowledgement. This work was supported by the Spanish Ministry of Economy and Competitiveness (MEC) under grant TIN2011-22935. Pablo Rodríguez-Mier is supported by the Spanish Ministry of Education, under the FPU national plan. Manuel Mucientes is supported by the Ramón y Cajal program of the MEC.

References

1. Aiello, M., Khoury, E.E., Lazovik, A., Ratelband, P.: Optimal QoS-Aware Web Service Composition. In: IEEE CEC 2009, pp. 491–494 (2009)
2. Ardagna, D., Pernici, B.: Adaptive Service Composition in Flexible Processes. IEEE Trans. on Soft. Eng. 33(6), 369–384 (2007)
3. Jiang, W., Zhang, C., Huang, Z., Chen, M., Hu, S., Liu, Z.: QSynth: A Tool for QoS-aware Automatic Service Composition. In: IEEE ICWS 2010, pp. 42–49 (2010)
4. Oh, S.C., Lee, D., Kumara, S.R.T.: Effective Web Service Composition in Diverse and Large-Scale Service Networks. IEEE Trans. on Soft. Eng. 1(1), 15–32 (2008)
5. Oh, S.C., Lee, J.Y., Cheong, S.H., Lim, S.M., Kim, M.W., Lee, S.S., Park, J.B., Noh, S.D., Sohn, M.M.: WSPR*: Web-Service Planner Augmented with A* Algorithm. In: IEEE CEC 2009, pp. 515–518 (2008)
6. Rao, J., Su, X.: A Survey of Automated Web Service Composition Methods. In: Cardoso, J., Sheth, A.P. (eds.) SWSWPC 2004. LNCS, vol. 3387, pp. 43–54. Springer, Heidelberg (2005)
7. Rodriguez-Mier, P., Mucientes, M., Lama, M.: Automatic web service composition with a heuristic-based search algorithm. In: IEEE ICWS 2011, pp. 81–88 (2011)
8. Yan, Y., Xu, B., Gu, Z., Luo, S.: A QoS-Driven Approach for Semantic Service Composition. In: IEEE CEC 2009, pp. 523–526 (2009)
9. Yu, T., Lin, K.-J.: Service Selection Algorithms for Composing Complex Services with Multiple QoS Constraints. In: Benatallah, B., Casati, F., Traverso, P. (eds.) ICSOC 2005. LNCS, vol. 3826, pp. 130–143. Springer, Heidelberg (2005)
10. Zeng, L., Benatallah, B., Ngu, A.H.H., Dumas, M., Kalagnanam, J., Chang, H.: QoS-Aware Middleware for Web Services Composition. IEEE Trans. on Soft. Eng. 30(5), 311–327 (2004)

IT Incident Management by Analyzing Incident Relations

Rong Liu and Juhnyoung Lee

IBM Research
19 Skyline Drive, Hawthorne, NY 10532, USA
{rliu,jyl}@us.ibm.com

Abstract. IT incident management aims to maintain high levels of service quality and availability by restoring normal service operations as quickly as possible and minimizing business impact. Enterprises often maintain many applications to support their business. It is a significant challenge to diagnose incidents at application level due to complicated causes often aggregated from the shared IT environment, network, hardware, software, and changes. In this paper, we present a new approach to diagnosing application incidents by effectively searching for relevant co-occurring and reoccurring incidents. These relevant incidents reveal patterns of application failures and provide insights into incident resolution and prevention. This paper also provides a case study where we implement this approach and evaluate its performance in terms of search accuracy.

Keywords. Incident management, IT service management, incident relation, co-occurrence, reoccurrence, text analytics.

1   Introduction

The objective of the *IT Incident Management* is to restore normal service operations quickly to minimize business impact, thus ensuring high levels of service quality and availability [4]. An incident is any event which is not part of the standard operation of a service and which causes, or may cause, an interruption to or a reduction in the quality of that service. Incidents are the result of failures or errors in IT infrastructure. Incident management becomes more important as IT's contribution to business is ever growing. It also faces increasing challenges because an enterprise often maintains many applications in a shared IT environment composed of thousands of interdependent IT components, e.g. network, hardware, software etc. Incident diagnosis often requires investigation on complicated causes aggregated from this environment. Thus a sophisticated analytical platform is needed to aggregate events from multiple sources, detect suspected causes, suggest resolution, and predict potential failures.

In this paper, we present a new IT incident management approach to diagnosing incidents by effectively searching for relevant *co-occurring* and *reoccurring* incidents. Co-occurring incidents happen at different IT components concurrently and are possibly caused by the same root causes. Reoccurring incidents repeat over time with similar symptoms or features. These relevant incidents together can reveal patterns of application incidents, helping subject matter experts (SMEs) to reason about root

C. Liu et al. (Eds.): ICSOC 2012, LNCS 7636, pp. 631–638, 2012.
© Springer-Verlag Berlin Heidelberg 2012

causes of incidents and accelerate incident resolution. This paper also presents a case study where we implemented and tested this approach. Since our approach is developed based on a generic incident data structure, it can be applied in similar scenarios in incident management, for example, IT help desk support. The rest of this paper is structured as follows. Section 2 describes a motivating real-world case. In Section 3, we discuss the technical details of the proposed approach. Section 4 describes the implementation and reports evaluation results. Section 5 compares this approach with related work. Finally, Section 6 concludes this paper with future work outlined.

2   Case Study

A large corporation in the IT industry has over a thousand applications to support its business ranging from large-scale packaged applications (e.g. SAP) to small proprietary systems, which run in a shared, dynamic IT infrastructure.   A critical objective is to maintain high-level application availability and reduce outages. It is challenging to diagnose incidents at the application level, because those incidents are often aggregated effects from problems in other lower layers. For example, the enterprise had a recent incident that blocked online orders for software. Meanwhile, another application supporting software downloading also failed. An exhaustive investigation led to a highly suspected cause that a dependent application for authenticating customers failed because of a storage area network outage happened in another geographic area.

Although this company has an integrated system for reporting and managing all IT incidents, relevant incidents could not be easily discovered for a few reasons. First, IT components are often managed by workgroups organized by expertise and by geography in a matrix structure. Due to this separation, relevant incidents may not be well communicated across workgroups. Second, the entire IT platform involves extreme complicated *dependencies* among IT components. Without deep knowledge about such dependencies, it would be impossible to scope relevant ones out of a huge number of incidents. Moreover, such dependencies are under constant evolution as the platform changes (e.g., provisioning new servers). Finally, useful information about an incident, such as affected IT components, symptoms, diagnosis results, is often recorded as *free-form text*. A typical incident is shown in Table 1. Another phenomenon is the frequent use of *ambiguous acronyms*. For example, depending on the context, "HRS" may mean "Hostname Resolution System" (an application name) or "Hours". Searching incidents only by keywords without considering their context is often deficient. Next, we propose a new search method to overcome these challenges.

3   Search for Relevant Incidents

As illustrated by the case study, an incident is often not an isolated event. It can be diagnosed by finding relevant co-occurring and reoccurring incidents and consolidating them to discover insights regarding how it happened and how it can be fixed. Our search algorithm consists of three steps: classifying incidents, searching incident by keywords, and calculating relevancy score and ranking search results.

3.1   Incident Classification

A common practice in IT Incident Management is to classify incidents by proper categories [4,8]. For example, we classify the incidents in the case study by keywords from these facets [6]: application, server, middleware, infrastructure, and symptom. It is often feasible to obtain decent vocabulary for these facets. For instance, companies usually maintain lists of applications, servers and middleware as part of their asset portfolio. Such lists become good dictionaries. One can also gather a list of frequently used terms as a dictionary, for instance, for symptom facet. With these dictionaries, keywords can be extracted from incident text by using text analysis software, for instance, IBM Context Analytics (ICA) [3]. Synonyms and annotation patterns are used to improve the accuracy of extraction. For example, MQ is a synonym of MQSeries. After classification, an incident can be represented by a bag of keywords. For instance, incident IN1 in Table 1 is classified by keywords as shown in Figure 1. These keywords are referred to as *classification keywords* in this paper.

Table 1. An Example of Application Incidents

Attributes	Value
Incident ID	IN1
Problem Abstract	ServerXYZ Issue: MQ connectivity has been reported lost.
Problem Description	Ticket#: Sev1; Application: SomeApp; Server/URL: ServerXYZ Issue: MQ connectivity has been reported lost. ITD (InternetService) team should verify and "run mustGather and recycle SomeApp (on ServerXYZ and ServerXYZ 2 as needed; Duty manager needed or not (not at this time); if so, impact: No revenue impact. Business impact is to some of the SomeApp (software service) orders (but not all); Team to be engaged: InternetService
Problem Result	SomeApp recycled
Occurred Time	2011-12-25 08:28:00
Solved Time	2011-12-25 09:25:40
Account ID	SomeAccount
Resolver Group	SomeGroup

After classification, a critical step is to validate the accuracy of each extracted keyword and assign an appropriate accuracy weight that can be used for discovering relevant incidents later. This validation is to ensure (1) an acronym is semantically correct, and (2) the combination of extracted keywords for an incident is valid against proper domain knowledge. For example, we need to check if acronym "HRS" indeed means "Hostname Resolution System". We first check if its full name can be found in the incident text. If it cannot be found, we rely on other extracted keywords or attributes to infer the meaning as in (2). For the example shown in Figure 2, we have learned that "SomeApp" is hosted in server "ServerXYZ" and requires middleware "MQSeries". With this application architecture information, we can confirm that the combination of keywords {SomeApp, ServerXYZ, mqseries} is correct. In case domain knowledge is not available, we can learn it dynamically by checking co-occurrence of keywords [1]. For example, if the joint probability of keyword

"SomeApp" and "ServerXYZ2" is higher than a certain level, we can infer that "ServerXYZ2" may be a hosting server of "SomeApp". After validation, we assign an accuracy weight w_1 to each extracted keyword to indicate the level of confidence on its validity.

Application:	*SomeApp*
Server:	*serverXYZ, ServerXYZ2*
Middleware:	*mqseries*
Symptom:	*mqseries connectivity*

Fig. 1. Classification of Example 1

3.2   Relevant Incident Search

After classification, we structure incident information out of the free-form text. Then we design a hybrid search engine integrating both faceted search and free text search to discover *co-occurring* and *re-occurring* incidents. To simplify its use, the search engine requires only an incident ID as an input, and automatically decides appropriate *search keywords* and ranks returned results by relevancy from high to low.

To find reoccurring incidents, the search engine uses classification keywords as search terms. For example, Figure 1 shows all search keywords for finding reoccurring incidents of IN1 (see Table 1). It takes additional consideration to find co-occurring incidents. First, co-occurring incidents happen about the same time. Hence, a mandatory time constraint is placed to limit the search scope to recent incidents. Second, co-occurring incidents may be reoccurring events. Therefore, classification keywords are also taken. Moreover, co-occurring incidents may indicate dependencies among involved IT components. Hence, we also add keywords representing dependent components as search terms. We refer to these keywords as *dependency keywords*. Taking the same example of IN1, to find co-occurring incidents, two dependent applications, "DepApp1" and "DepApp2", are added. A boosting weight (w_2) can be assigned to each search keyword based on its impact. Our search engine assigns a default weight for each dependency keyword, for instance, $w_2 = 2$.

With search keywords defined, incidents that satisfy any of the search keywords and mandatory time constraints are returned to achieve a high recall rate. For instance, to search for co-occurring incidents for IN1, its search keywords and time constraints are represented as a query shown in Figure 2. This query consists of both structured and unstructured portions. The structured query searches for incidents by using the incident classification keywords and structured fields in database tables. The unstructured part handles the need for free text search, for example, incident symptoms. The final search result is the union of those returned from the two queries.

Structured:
(*application* in ("*SomeApp*", "*DepApp1*", "*DepApp2*") or *server* in ("*ServerXYZ*", "*ServerXYZ2*") or *middleware* in ("*mqseries*")) and *occurred_time* between ("*12/22/2011*", "*12/25/2011*")   )
Unstructured:
+mq +connectivity date>="2011-12-22" date<="2011-12-25"

Fig. 2. Formulate Search Keywords as Queries

With a large number of results returned from search, we adapt vector-space model [7] slightly to calculate the similarity score for returned incidents. Based on this model, a document is represented as a vector of keywords $v = (x_1, x_2, ..., x_n)$ in a n-dimensional vector space, where x_i is the weight of keyword i. $|v|^2 = \sum_n x_i^2$ is the length of the vector. The similarity between (v_1, v_2) is the cosine of the angle θ between them, i.e., $s = \cos(\theta) = \frac{v_1 \cdot v_2}{|v_1| |v_2|}$, where $v_1 \cdot v_2 = \sum_n x_{1i} x_{2i}$. The vector space in our case contains the classification keywords of incidents. The vector of an incident contains all of its classification keywords, and conditionally the dependency keywords. When a dependency keyword is found in a returned incident, it is added to the vector to boost the similarity score. The weight of a keyword is $x = w_1 w_2$, where w_1 is the accuracy weight and w_2 is the boosting weight. Note that in a regular vector-space model, keyword frequency is often an important factor for weight. However, here incident text is often dominated by technique specification or message logs. For instance, a server name appears many times in a log. Frequency-based weights may favor incidents with lengthy messages and have negative impact on search precision.

To illustrate, consider two relevant incidents IN2 (v_2) and IN3 (v_3) for incident IN1 (v_1) as shown in Table 2. v_1 has five classification keywords (w_1=1) and two dependency keywords ($w_2 = 2$). v_2 matches three of the classification keyword (i.e., $v_1 \cdot v_2 = 3$). The similarity score between v_1 and v_2 is $\frac{3}{\sqrt{5}*\sqrt{3}} = 0.77$. v_3 matches one classification keyword and one dependency keyword. Thus, $v_1 \cdot v_3 = 1*1+2*2=5$ and the length of v_1 is $5 + 2^2 = 9$. The similarity score between v_1 and v_3 is $\frac{5}{\sqrt{9}*\sqrt{5}} = 0.75$.

The similarity score considers whether two incidents are similar to each other in terms of classification keywords, but it may not be sufficient for finding truly relevant incidents. Take a query with two keywords {"db2", "SomeApp"} as an example. This query may return a large number of incidents because db2 is a widely used component. Among them, many incidents are about general DB2 issues irrelevant to specific applications. However, since these incidents are classified by only "DB2" keyword, their similarity score $\frac{1}{\sqrt{2}*1} = 71\%$ is actually pretty high.

Table 2. Calculating Similarity Score

Incident		Keyword Vector						$v_1 \cdot v_2$ (or v_3)	$|v_1|*|v_2|$ (or $|v_3|$)	Similarity
		SomeApp	ServerXYZ	ServerXYZ2	mq	mq conn.	dependent app			
							DepApp1	DepApp2			
v_1	IN1	1	1	1	1	1		2			
v_2	IN2	1	1		1				3	$\sqrt{5} * \sqrt{3}$	0.77
v_3	IN3		1					2	5	$\sqrt{9} * \sqrt{5}$	0.75

In order to filter irrelevant results, we use attributes other than the classification keywords to infer a broad context. In the IT incident management domain, an account is a well-accepted concept representing an organization unit responsible for the resolution of incidents in a particular business area. In general, each account involves general-purpose support workgroups, such as Network Support team, and specialized support team, e.g. Internet Service support team. The technology configuration of an account thus can be inferred from the specialized workgroups. We plot a diagram among accounts and specialized workgroups, where each node is either a workgroup or an account and the link between an account and a workgroup indicates the workgroup is called for the account's incidents. An example is shown in Figure 3(a). This diagram illustrates the technology configuration and similarity among accounts by technology configuration. For example, account A1 engages workgroup G1-5, while A2 involves workgroups G3-5 and G7. Using the same vector-space model, the similarity between A1 and A2 is estimated to be 67%, as shown in Figure 3(b). We use this similarity to estimate context relevancy (w_3) because shared workgroups indicate technology dependencies and compatibility between each other. For each incident returned from a search, the final relevancy score $r = f(s, w_3)$. For instance, a simple function we use is $r = \alpha * w_3 + (1- \alpha)*s$, where $0< \alpha <1$. Given that three incidents in Table 2 belong to account A1, A2, and A3 respectively, with $\alpha=0.5$, we can get the final relevancy score for v_2 and v_3 are 0.72 and 0.48 respectively.

3.3   Root Cause Analysis Using Relevant Incidents

Continuous analysis on a group of relevant incidents often provides insights for SMEs to diagnose root causes and define proactive actions to prevent similar incidents. First, we can summarize commonalities of relevant incidents. These commonalities allow SMEs to pinpoint exact problems and exclude other suspected causes. For example, incident IN1 and its reoccurring incidents share common keywords: "ServerXYZ" and "mqseries", suggesting SMEs to focus on MQSeries installed on ServerXYZ server. As another example, if a group of re-occurring incidents all depend on an infrastructure component, this component is a highly suspected cause. Also, extracting common keywords from the resolution description of a group of reoccurring incidents can provide useful insights into resolution strategies. Second, a group of co-occurring incidents may disclose a causal event chain. Chaining these incidents along their occurrence times may disclose potential application dependencies. More advanced analysis can be conducted to correlate a group of relevant incidents with other data, for example, maintenance schedule, resource usage, and change events (i.e., application fix, upgrade). With the correlation, prediction rules can be configured to predict potential problems. For example, incident IN1 has been diagnosed in this way to find its root cause. A finding is that IN1 and its reoccurring incidents are highly correlated with messages alerting lost MQSeries connections after a server rebooted for regular maintenance. With this discovery, a rule is configured to alert SMEs when a server maintenance event is scheduled.

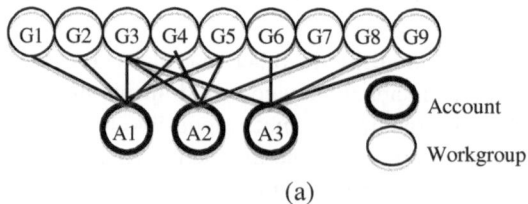

	A1	A2	A3
A1		67%	20%
A2	67%		45%
A3	20%	45%	

(a)   (b)

Fig. 3. Account Configuration & Similarity

4   Search Engine Implementation and Evaluation

Figure 4 shows the implemented architecture of our search engine. This engine has two types of flows: front-end (solid line) and backend (dotted line). At the backend, incidents data are extracted and fed into the IBM Context Analytics (ICA). Classification keywords are extracted, validated, and stored in a database as consolidated incident data. At the front-end, a user issues a query to the search engine and the search engine transforms this query into two sub-queries, one for structured search to the database and the other to ICA for free text search. Search results are consolidated and ranked. Since a large portion of the query is handled as a database query, the search is efficient. Our pilot test shows on average it takes less than a minute to complete a search for co-occurring/reoccurring incidents from about 140,000 incident records.

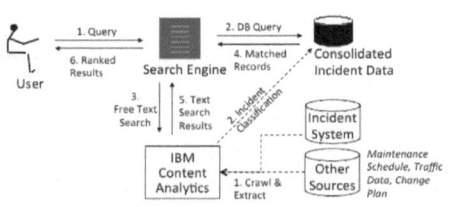

Fig. 4. System Architecture

Table 3. Evaluation Result

Testing Cases	Result			
	Success	Partial Success	Failure	Unknown
Reoccurring	15	1		
Non-reoccurring	3	1	1	2
Total	18	2	1	2

This new search engine is evaluated by SMEs in a pilot test. SMEs carefully chose 23 incidents as testing cases. We designed a new evaluation metric combining both recall and precision rates. For each testing case, at maximum 20 relevant incidents are returned. SMEs rated each testing case: success, partial success, failure, or unknown. A testing case was rated success only if all SME-recognized relevant incidents (usually less than 20) were returned. A result was rated as "unknown" if it cannot be confirmed. Table 4 summarizes the result. The testing result is reasonably positive (78% success rate). Those testing cases rated "partial success" and "failure" are primarily caused by ambiguous acronyms or insufficient information disclosed in incidents.

5   Related Work

In the area of IT Service Management (ITSM), Information Technology Infrastructure Library (ITIL) provides a set of practices that focuses on aligning IT services with the needs of business [4,8]. The work presented in this paper concerns mostly about the investigation and diagnosis of incidents in ITSM using text mining and statistical methods. Recently, there is growing interest in using statistical analytics to analyzing and managing incidents. In [9], an ensemble of Tree-Augmented Bayesian Network models is provided to correlate workload metrics with service level objectives. A service Delivery Portal introduced in [5] provides a set of technologies to help system administrators (SA) to diagnose and manage incidents. This platform aggregates various incident data sources and allows SA to search for relevant events based on keywords or incident attributes. Our approach improves the search accuracy by considering domain knowledge and incident context during search.   Another broad domain related to this work is text mining [1,6] and machine learning [2]. A comprehensive survey of techniques in this domain is provided by [1]. In our work, we adapted Vector Space Model to calculate relevancy score between incidents. Another technique used by our work is co-occurrence networks, which represent the collective interconnection of terms based on their paired presence within a specified unit of text [1]. We apply this concept to automatically learn keyword dependency as domain knowledge.

6   Concluding Remarks and Future Work

IT incident management, which ensure high levels of service quality and availability, is a significant challenge primarily because enterprises often maintain many applications in shared dynamic IT environments. In this paper, we present a new approach to diagnosing application incidents by effectively searching for relevant co-occurring and reoccurring incidents. We designed a hybrid search engine that finds relevant incidents in both structured and unstructured formats. These relevant incidents together reveal underlying patterns of incidents and then provide SMEs insights into incident causes and resolution. We implemented this approach and evaluated its performance in terms of search accuracy. The pilot test shows that this approach is reasonably effective in discovering relevant incidents. Our future work is to develop predictive modeling capability based on relevant incidents discovered. We also plan to enhance its root cause analysis capability with a richer set of test data and test cases.

References

1. Berry, M.W., Castellanos, M.: Survey of Text Mining I: Clustering, Classification, and Retrieval, 2nd edn. Springer (2007)
2. Bishop, C.: Pattern Recognition and Machine Learning. Springer (2006)
3. IBM Content Analytics with Enterprise Search, http://www-01.ibm.com/software/ecm/content-analytics/bundle.html
4. ITIL Incident Management - The ITIL Open Guide, http://www.itlibrary.org/index.php?page=Incident_Management
5. Lenchner, J., Rosu, D., Velasquez, N.F., Guo, S., Christiance, K., DeFelice, D., Deshpande, P.M., Kummamuru, K., Kraus, N., Luan, L.Z., Majumdar, D., McLaughlin, M., Ofek-Koifman, S., Deepak, P., Perng, C.-S., Roitman, H., Ward, C., Young, J.: A service delivery platform for server management services. IBM Journal of Research and Development 53(6), 792–808 (2009)
6. Rodriguez-Castro, B., Glaser, H., Carr, L.: How to *Reuse* a Faceted Classification and Put It on the *Semantic* Web. In: Patel-Schneider, P.F., Pan, Y., Hitzler, P., Mika, P., Zhang, L., Pan, J.Z., Horrocks, I., Glimm, B. (eds.) ISWC 2010, Part I. LNCS, vol. 6496, pp. 663–678. Springer, Heidelberg (2010)
7. Salton, G., Wong, A., Yang, C.S.: A Vector Space Model for Automatic Indexing. Communications of the ACM 18(11), 613–620 (1975)
8. Van Bon, J., Verheijen, T.: Frameworks for IT Management. Van Haren Publishing (2006) ISBN 9789077212905
9. Zhang, S., Cohen, I., Goldszmidt, M., Symons, J., Fox, A.: Ensembles of models for automated diagnosis of system performance problems. In: DSN 2005, Yokohama, Japan (2005)

An Association Probability Based Noise Generation Strategy for Privacy Protection in Cloud Computing

Gaofeng Zhang[1], Xuyun Zhang[2], Yun Yang[3,1,*], Chang Liu[2], and Jinjun Chen[2]

[1] Faculty of Information and Communication Technologies
Swinburne University of Technology, Hawthorn, Melbourne, Australia 3122
{gzhang,yyang}@swin.edu.au
[2] Faculty of Engineering and Information Technology
University of Technology, Sydney, Broadway, NSW, Australia 2007
(Xuyun.Zhang,Chang.Liu,Jinjun.Chen)@uts.edu.au
[3] School of Computer Science and Technology, Anhui University, Hefei 230039, China

Abstract. Cloud computing allows customers to utilise IT services in a pay-as-you-go fashion to save huge cost on IT infrastructure. In open cloud, 'malicious' service providers could record service data from a cloud customer and collectively deduce the customer's privacy without the customer's permission. Accordingly, customers need to take certain actions to protect their privacy automatically at client sides, such as noise obfuscation. For instance, it can generate and inject noise service requests into real ones so that service providers are hard to distinguish which ones are real. Existing noise obfuscations focus on concealing occurrence probabilities of service requests. But in reality, association probabilities of service requests can also reveal customer privacy. So, we present a novel association probability based noise generation strategy by concealing these association probabilities. The simulation comparison demonstrates that this strategy can improve the effectiveness of privacy protection significantly from the perspective of association probability.

Keywords: Cloud service, Privacy protection, Noise generation, Association probability.

1 Introduction

Cloud computing is positioning itself as a promising and market-oriented service platform for delivering information infrastructures and resources [1]. Customers can use these services in a pay-as-you-go fashion while saving huge capital investments on their own IT infrastructures. However, cloud customers may concern about their privacy since they do not have much direct control inside the cloud [2]. So, privacy protection about service is critical as one of the most important research issues in cloud computing.

In cloud environments, there are many organisations which operate under various regulations to protect their customers' privacy. Meanwhile, many 'malicious' and

---

* Corresponding author.

C. Liu et al. (Eds.): ICSOC 2012, LNCS 7636, pp. 639–647, 2012.
© Springer-Verlag Berlin Heidelberg 2012

unknown service providers could exist in these open and virtualised environments. Such service providers may collect service data from customers, and then deduce customers' privacy for unauthorised utilisation. And openness and virtualised features make it hard to distinguish them from these complex processes, especially in automated service compositions [3].

Therefore, cloud customers have to take certain technical actions to protect their privacy automatically at client sides without involving service providers. Compared to existing service-side privacy protection approaches [4, 5], noise obfuscation can match the scenario in this paper. It can inject noise service data into real service data automatically to conceal real data on customers' own, such as service requests, communication logs and so on. A historical probability based noise generation strategy (*HPNGS*) can improve the efficiency of noise obfuscation by past occurrence probabilities [6]. And time-series patterns [7] can improve the effectiveness of privacy protection based on *HPNGS*. In general, current noise obfuscation primarily focuses on concealing occurrence probabilities, and the goal of existing noise obfuscation is that the variance of all occurrence probabilities is as small as possible.

But in reality, privacy is of different varieties. In cloud, there could be various kinds of sensitive data which can be deduced from service data as customer privacy, for example, not only 'real' service requests in noise injected service request queues, but also association rules among 'real' service requests. If two requests are associated by association rules: after one request sent by one customer, then the other has a high probability to be sent sequentially. It could be a distinctive behaviour pattern of this customer, and customers' behaviour patterns or their identities could be revealed accordingly. Hence, it is a serious privacy risk.

In this paper, the main goal of noise obfuscation is that the variance of all association probabilities among service requests is as small as possible. So, we need to analyse association probabilities of past real service requests, and generate noise service requests which can conceal association rules by making association probabilities about the same, and these 'novel' noise service requests can protect customers' privacy as an improvement of privacy protection. Based on this, we present a novel association probability based noise generation strategy (*APNGS*).

The remainder of the paper is organised as follows. In Section 2, we present the association probability based noise generation strategy (*APNGS*). Then, in Section 3, we perform a simulation to demonstrate that *APNGS* can improve the effectiveness of privacy protection significantly. Finally in Section 4, we conclude our contributions and point out future work.

2   Novel Association Probability Based Noise Generation Strategy

Concealing association probabilities is the goal of privacy protection in this paper, and *APNGS* focuses on how to model, analyse and conceal these association probabilities. In this section, we firstly discuss association probability based noise injection model to support *APNGS*. Then, we present association probability model for noise generation. After that, we discuss two key issues of noise generation—noise generation probabilities and noise injection intensity. Lastly, we propose *APNGS*.

2.1   Association Probability Based Noise Injection Model

The noise injection model is based on other existing representative noise injection models [6-8] with some modifications to support *APNGS* as depicted in Fig. 1.

Q_R: queue of customer's real service requests to be protected.

Q_N: queue of 'noise' service requests to be injected in Q_R.

Q_S: queue of final service requests composing of Q_R and Q_N.

Q : a common set of Q_R, Q_S and Q_N. And $Q=\{q_1,q_2,...,q_i...,q_n\}$.

ε: probability for injecting Q_N into Q_R, $\varepsilon \in [0,1]$. It is the noise injection intensity.

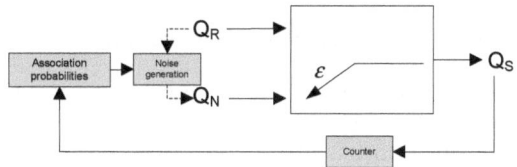

Fig. 1. Association probability based noise injection model

'Association probabilities': they are the basis of this strategy and guide noise generations. 'Noise generation': its function is to generate Q_N. We use 'Association probabilities' and 'Counter' to get noise generation probabilities in *APNGS*.

The overall working process of the model is to inject Q_N into Q_R based on ε, and Q_S is the result. The model can be described as follows: the customer generates a real service request queue Q_R to be sent. The noise service request queue Q_N is generated by *APNGS*. To obtain Q_S, a switch function is: the next service request in Q_S comes from Q_N on the probability of ε, and from Q_R on the probability of 1-ε. Suppose q_i is an item of Q and $P(Q_R=q_i)(t)$, $P(Q_N=q_i)(t)$ and $P(Q_S=q_i)(t)$ are occurrence probabilities of q_i in Q_R, Q_N and Q_S at time t, respectively.

2.2   Association Probability Model for Noise Generation

In this part, we investigate how to obtain association probabilities from service request queues in this association probability model for noise generation.

To define these association probabilities, we have:

$$AP = f_{AP}(Q_R) \tag{1}$$

In equation (1), *AP* denotes association probabilities, and it is an $n \times n$ matrix. Each item in this matrix *AP[i,j]* is association probability between q_i and q_j.

Sliding window is the key and widely used approach to analyse information in a data stream or queue [9]. In this paper, we use a minimised and fixed sliding window to generate association probabilities. As a basic form of sliding windows, a minimised and fixed sliding window can aid to analyse data streams in terms of basic features. So, we obtain the association probability model for noise generation:

$$AP[i, j] = \frac{Con^{i,j}(Q_R)}{t-1} \tag{2}$$

In equation (2), $Con^{i,j}(Q_R)$ is the number of events that q_i and q_j are sent together in Q_R. Under minimised and fixed sliding windows, this event is that q_j is immediately next to q_i as a consequential relation in Q_R. And we use time length t-1 as the denominator to normalise the equation. In some specific privacy protection situations, sliding window can be dynamic to withstand some specific privacy risks, such as side channel knowledge on it, or particular timestamps in request queues. In other words, sliding window is the changing key in noise obfuscation to protect privacy in cloud environments. And as a basic form, minimised and fixed sliding windows adopted in this paper can be easily modified to match specific noise obfuscations.

2.3   Association Probability Based Noise Generation

In this part, we discuss two key issues in noise generation—noise generation probabilities and noise injection intensity. Suppose noise generation probabilities are $P(Q_N = q_i)(t), \forall i \in [1,n]$ which means that for $\forall q_i \in Q$, probabilities of Q_N being q_i at time t, respectively. Noise injection intensity is ε which is introduced earlier.

1)   Noise generation probabilities

In *HPNGS* [6], noise generation probabilities are:

$$\forall i, P(Q_N = q_i) = \frac{M - P(Q_R = q_i)}{n \times M - 1} \tag{3}$$

From equation (3), in $\forall i, P(Q_R = q_i)$, the highest one is $M = MAX\{P(Q_R = q_i), \forall i\}$, which is historical and accumulative data from past Q_R in practice as depicted in Fig. 1, just like $P(Q_R=q_i)$. And n is the number of q_i.

Besides, from Section 1 and [6], existing strategies have the same noise generation goal: $\forall i, P(Q_S = q_i) = 1/n$. So, on the basis of equation (2), we get the noise generation goal in *APNGS*:

$$\forall i, j, t, P(Q_S, t+1, i, j) = P[(Q_S = q_i)(t+1) \mid (Q_S = q_j)(t)] = 1/n \tag{4}$$

In equation (4), the noise generation goal is a family of conditional probabilities to express the probability of Q_S being q_i at time t+1, on the precondition of Q_S being q_j at previous time t. Besides, we have $i, j \in [1,n]$ and $t \in [1,T]$, and T is the time length of the overall process.

To realise equation (4), we can utilise new noise generation probabilities in equation (5) on the basis of equation (3):

$$P[(Q_N = q_i)(t+1) \mid (Q_S = q_j)(t)] = \frac{M(t, j) - P(Q_R, t, i, j)}{n \times M(t, j) - 1} \tag{5}$$

In equation (5), we have two components: equation (6) and equation (7):

$$P(Q_R, t+1, i, j) = P[(Q_R = q_i)(t+1) \mid (Q_S = q_j)(t)] \tag{6}$$

$$M(t+1, j) = MAX\{P[(Q_R = q_i)(t+1) \mid (Q_S = q_j)(t)], \forall i\} \tag{7}$$

In equation (6), $P(Q_R, t+1, i, j)$ is a family of conditional probabilities to express the probability of Q_R being q_i at time $t+1$, on the precondition of Q_S being q_j at time t.

In equation (7), $M(t+1, j)$ is the highest value, for every i, in a family of conditional probabilities to express the probability of Q_R being q_i at time $t+1$, on the precondition of Q_S being q_j at previous time t.

It is clear that equation (6) is the basis of equation (7). So, we only need to focus on equation (6) for association probabilities among service requests introduced before.

To obtain equation (6), we design a process on the basis of equation (2): this is an accumulative process. 3-dimension matrix *Matrix(i,j,t)* has three parameters: t is time parameter, i is from $(Q_R = q_i)(t+1)$ which means an event that the *ith* request in the set Q will appear in Q_R at time $t+1$, j is from $(Q_S = q_j)(t)$ which means an event that the *jth* request in Q appears in Q_S at time t. So, *Matrix(i,j,t)* means all past association relations among service requests q_i and q_j at time t. At a specific time, 2-dimension array *C[i][j]* can replace *Matrix(i,j,t)*. We should collect all requests from time *1* to time t, and get accumulative *C[i][j]*. So, $P(Q_R, t, i, j) = Matrix(i,j,t)/SUM$, Where *SUM* is the number of all association relations among past requests. This presents the implementation of association probability model.

2) Noise injection intensity

According to the association probability based noise injection model defined earlier, to operate noise injection processes, ε is a necessary parameter.

From noise injection model and [6], we can get the relation among Q_S, Q_N and Q_R:

$$P(Q_S, t, i, j) = (1 - \varepsilon) \times P(Q_R, t, i, j) + \varepsilon \times P(Q_N, t, i, j) \tag{8}$$

There are two components in equation (8): $P(Q_N, t, i, j)$ and $P(Q_R, t, i, j)$. So, we have equation (9) based on equations (6) and (4):

$$\forall i, j, t, P(Q_N, t+1, i, j) = P[(Q_N = q_i)(t+1) \mid (Q_S = q_j)(t)] \tag{9}$$

In equation (9), it is clear that the conditional probability of Q_S being q_i at time $t+1$ on the precondition of Q_S being q_j at previous time t is decided by the conditional probability of Q_R being q_i at time $t+1$ on the precondition of Q_S being q_j at previous time t, the conditional probability of Q_N being q_i at time $t+1$ on the precondition of Q_S being q_j at previous time t, and ε. So, we get ε by equations (8) and (4):

$$\varepsilon(t+1) = \frac{\dfrac{1}{n} - P(Q_R, t+1, i, j)}{\dfrac{M(t+1, j) - P(Q_R, t+1, i, j)}{n \times M(t+1, j) - 1} - P(Q_R, t+1, i, j)} = 1 - \frac{1}{n \times M(t+1, j)} \tag{10}$$

It is obvious that equation (5) and equation (10) can make the whole strategy to reach its goal—equation (4). It can address the serious risk identified in Section 1.

2.4   Association Probability Based Noise Generation Strategy

Title: Association probability based noise generation strategy
Input: Q_R is the queue of real service requests
Output: Q_S is the queue of final service requests

Step 1: Collect data and compute association probabilities
Initialise n*n+1 counters: $C[1][1],\ldots\ldots,C[1][n]\ldots\ldots C[n][1],\ldots\ldots C[n][n]$, S to record numbers of associations among each service data item and the sum;
Receive service data from all past Q_R, update the correspondent $C[i][j]$++ and the sum S++;
Compute previous association probabilities :
$$P(Q_R,t+1,i,j) = P[(Q_R = q_i)(t+1) | (Q_S = q_j)(t)] = \frac{C[i][j]}{S}$$

Step 2: Compute noise generation probabilities
Generate noise generation probabilities by equation (5): $P[(Q_N = q_i)(t+1)|(Q_S = q_j)(t)] = \frac{M(t,j) - P(Q_R,t,i,j)}{n \times M(t,j) - 1}$
by $P(Q_R,t,i,j)$ and $M(t,j) = MAX\{P(Q_R,t,i,j),\forall i\}$;

Step 3: Compute noise injection intensity
Compute equation (10): $\varepsilon(t+1) = 1 - \frac{1}{n \times M(t,j)}$ to get the noise injection intensity;
We have noise requests queue
$Q_N\{P[(Q_N = q_i)(t+1)|(Q_S = q_j)(t)],\varepsilon(t+1)\}$;

Step 4: Noise injection process
Generate a noise N by:
$Q_N\{P[(Q_N = q_i)(t+1)|(Q_S = q_j)(t)],\varepsilon(t+1)\}$
Inject N into Q_R on the probability of ε to get Q_S ;
Update $P(Q_R,t,i,j)$ with counters.

Algorithm 1. *APNGS*: Association probability based noise generation strategy

In this part, we present *APNGS*. In Algorithm 1, we utilise $n \times n+1$ counters to record the matrix and the sum of association relations among requests in Step 1. From equation (5), we can generate noise generation probabilities in Step 2. About noise injection intensity, equation (10) can obtain it in Step 3. At last, we can execute the noise injection processes in Step 4.

In summary, we can find out that the major improvement between *APNGS*'s noise generation goal updating: replacing $\forall i, P(Q_S = q_i) = 1/n$ by $\forall i, j, t, P(Q_S, t, i, j) = 1/n$. Hence, *APNGS* can perform better in privacy protection situations considering association probabilities than existing noise generation strategies.

3   Evaluation

In this section, we perform an experimental simulation in our cloud simulation system called SwinCloud [10]. The simulation process is primarily to compute and compare the effectiveness of privacy protection between *APNGS* and *HPNGS* directly, and we discuss comparisons about other existing strategies: *TPNGS* [7] and random generation [8], too. Before the simulation, we generate a service queue as the real service queue from a set with a size of 10 randomly to operate two strategies.

We use a function: *Var_Ass(Strategy, t)* to express the main effectiveness of privacy protection on noise obfuscation to compare two strategies. And *Var_Ass(Strategy, t)* means that the variance of association probabilities in Q_S under *Strategy* protected at time *t*. In other words, time *t* can express the size of Q_R. Besides, we also use *Var(Strategy, t)* to denote the variance of occurrence probabilities in Q_S

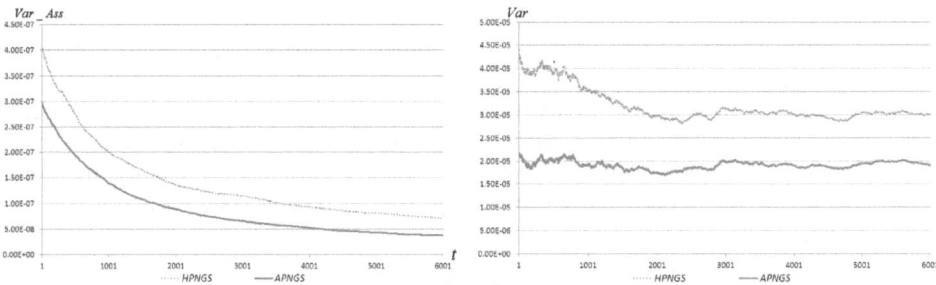

Fig. 2. Effectiveness comparison on association probability between *HPNGS* and *APNGS*

Fig. 3. Effectiveness comparison on occurrence probability between *HPNGS* and *APNGS*

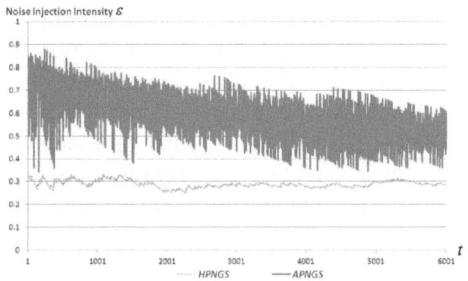

Fig. 4. Comparison on noise injection intensity between *HPNGS* and *APNGS*

with *Strategy* operating at time t. It denotes another aspect of the effectiveness of privacy protection.

In Fig. 2, the horizontal coordinate is time t, and t has a range of [1, 6001]; the vertical coordinate is *Var_Ass*. And if *Var_Ass* is lower, the effectiveness of privacy protection is better, so customer privacy is better kept. We can find out the overall trend being: with time passing, both of them keep on decreasing. Obviously, *Var_Ass(APNGS,t)* is about ¼ to ½ of *Var_Ass(HPNGS,t)*. So, *APNGS* achieves a significant improvement on the effectiveness of privacy protection on noise obfuscation over *HPNGS*, in terms of association probability.

In Fig. 3., we find out that *Var(APNGS,t)* can keep within a low level of about 2.00e-05, and is lower than *Var(HPNGS,t)* which is about 3.00e-05. So, *APNGS* has better effectiveness of privacy protection on noise obfuscation in terms of occurrence probability than *HPNGS*. That is because association probabilities can consider more details of data queues than occurrence probabilities to keep service requests balance.

At last, the cost of noise obfuscation should also be considered by the noise injection intensity. In Fig. 4, ε of *APNGS* is about 1.5 to 1 times more than ε of *HPNGS* with time passing. It means that *APNGS* costs more than *HPNGS*. So, to obtain better effectiveness of privacy protection, customers have to pay more. It is a trade-off depending on customers' demands.

About other typical noise generation strategies, such as random generation [8] and *TPNGS* [7], *APNGS* also performs well: *HPNGS* has already improved efficiency of privacy protection from random generation with similar effectiveness. *TPNGS* still focuses on fluctuations of occurrence probabilities, and association probabilities are not incorporated.

In summary, *APNGS* can significantly improve the effectiveness of privacy protection on noise obfuscation in terms of association probability over existing representative strategies, with good effectiveness of privacy protection on noise obfuscation in terms of occurrence probability, at a reasonable extra cost.

4   Conclusions and Future Work

In this paper, we focused on privacy protection and noise obfuscation in cloud computing. To withstand some malicious service providers which are interested in association information among service requests, we analysed association probabilities in request queues and concealed them by noise obfuscation. Hence, we proposed a novel association probability based noise generation strategy (*APNGS*). The evaluation demonstrated that *APNGS* could significantly improve the effectiveness of privacy protection on noise obfuscation in terms of association probabilities, at a reasonable extra cost, in comparison to existing representative strategies.

Based on our current work, we plan to further investigate how to protect privacy in multiple malicious providers.

References

1. Buyya, R., Yeo, C.S., Venugopal, S., Broberg, J., Brandic, I.: Cloud Computing and Emerging IT Platforms: Vision, Hype, and Reality for Delivering Computing as the 5th Utility. Future Generation Computer Systems 25(6), 599–616 (2009)
2. Ryan, M.D.: Cloud Computing Privacy Concerns on Our Doorstep. Communications of the ACM 54(1), 36–38 (2011)
3. Ren, K., Liu, X., Chen, J., Xiao, N., Song, J., Zhang, W.: A QSQL-based Efficient Planning Algorithm for Fully-automated Service Composition in Dynamic Service Environments. In: 2008 IEEE International Conference on Service Computing (SCC 2008), pp. 301–308. IEEE Press (2008)
4. Evfimievski, A., Gehrke, J., Srikant, R.: Limiting Privacy Breaches in Privacy Preserving Data Mining. In: 22nd ACM SIGMOD-SIGACT-SIGART Symposium on Principles of Database Systems (PODS 2003), pp. 211–222. ACM, Madison (2003)
5. Bu, Y., Fu, A., Wong, R., Chen, L., Li, J.: Privacy Preserving Serial Data Publishing by Role Composition. In: 34th Internationasl Conference on Very Large Data Bases (VLDB 2008), pp. 845–856 (2008)
6. Zhang, G., Yang, Y., Chen, J.: A Histrotical Probability based Noise Generation Strategy for Privacy Protection in Cloud Computing. Journal of Computer and System Sciences 78(5), 1374–1381 (2012)
7. Zhang, G., Yang, Y., Liu, X., Chen, J.: A Time-Series Pattern based Noise Generation Strategy for Privacy Protection in Cloud Computing. In: 12th IEEE/ACM International Symposium on Cluster, Cloud and Grid Computing (CCGrid 2012), pp. 458–465. IEEE Press, New York (2012)

8. Ye, S., Wu, F., Pandey, R., Chen, H.: Noise Injection for Search Privacy Protection. In: 2009 International Conference on Computational Science and Engineering (CSE 2009), pp. 1–8. IEEE Press, New York (2009)
9. Babcock, B., Babu, S., Datar, M., Motwani, R., Widom, J.: Models and Issues in Data Stream Systems. In: 21st ACM SIGMOD-SIGACT-SIGART Symposium on Principles of Database Systems (PODS 2002), pp. 1–16. ACM, Madison (2002)
10. Liu, K., Jin, H., Chen, J., Liu, X., Yuan, D., Yang, Y.: A Compromised-time-cost Scheduling Algorithm in SwinDeW-C for Instance-intensive Cost-constrained Workflows on a Cloud Computing Platform. International Journal of High Performance Computing Applications 24(4), 445–456 (2010)

ARIMA Model-Based Web Services Trustworthiness Evaluation and Prediction

Meng Li[1,2], Zhebang Hua[1,2], Junfeng Zhao[1,2,*],
Yanzhen Zou[1,2], and and Bing Xie[1,2]

[1] Software Institute, School of Electronics Engineering and Computer Science,
Peking University, Beijing 100871, China
[2] Key Laboratory of High Confidence Software Technologies, Ministry of Education,
Beijing 100871, China
{limeng09,huazb12,zhaojf,zouyz,xiebing}@sei.pku.edu.cn

Abstract. As most Web services are delivered by third parties over unreliable Internet and are late bound at run-time, it is reasonable and useful to evaluate and predict the trustworthiness of Web services. In this paper, we propose an ARIMA model-based approach to evaluate and predict Web services trustworthiness. First, we evaluate Web services trustworthiness with comprehensive trustworthy evidences collected from the Internet on a regular basis. Then, the cumulative trustworthiness evaluation records are modeled as time series. Finally, we propose an ARIMA model-based multi-step Web services trustworthiness prediction process, which can automatically and iteratively identify and optimize the model to fit the trustworthiness series data. Experiments conducted on a large-scale real-world data set show that our method can effectively evaluate and predict the trustworthiness of Web services, which helps users to reuse Web services.

1 Introduction

There are more and more reusable Web services available on the Internet. However, as most Web services are provided and/or hosted by third parties over unreliable Internet, it is useful to evaluate and predict the trustworthiness of Web services [1]. Many approaches have been proposed to evaluate the trustworthiness of Web services.

There are several problems with previous approaches. First, there are two kinds of trustworthy evidences: namely objective trustworthy evidences (e.g. QoS attributes) and subjective trustworthy evidences (e.g. reputation) [2, 3]. Most of previous approaches rely on only one kind of evidences, while it is more reasonable to take both kinds into consideration [3–5]. Second, while most previous approaches focus on the current or past trustworthiness of a service, it is reasonable and useful to evaluate and predict the trustworthiness of Web services in the (near) future [6, 7]. Third, previous prediction approaches like [8,

---

* Corresponding Author

C. Liu et al. (Eds.): ICSOC 2012, LNCS 7636, pp. 648–655, 2012.

9] adopt collaborative filtering methods to make prediction, which are based on centralized portals to collect users' usage information. However, without proper incentive schemes, users are not motivated to provide feedbacks, and centralized portals like UDDI repositories are shut down or seldom updated [5].

In this paper, basing on classic time series theory, we propose an ARIMA model-based approach to evaluate and predict the trustworthiness of Web services. First, we evaluate Web services trustworthiness with comprehensive trustworthy evidences collected from the Internet on a regular basis. Then, the cumulative trustworthiness evaluation records are modeled as time series. Finally, we propose an ARIMA model-based multi-step Web services trustworthiness prediction process, which can automatically and iteratively identify and optimize the model to fit the trustworthiness series data. Experiments conducted on a large-scale real-world data set show that our method can effectively evaluate and predict the trustworthiness of Web services, which helps users to reuse Web services.

The contributions of this paper are as follows:

- We propose a novel and practical method to evaluate and predict Web services trustworthiness, which is based on classic time series analysis theories.
- The effectiveness of our approach has been validated with experiments conducted on a large-scale real-world data set. The results of our approach has been used in real systems, including CoWS[1] and TSR[2].
- The data set, including 17,832 Web services and millions of trustworthy evidences, is publicly available. This is the largest Web service trustworthiness evaluation and prediction data set to the best of our knowledge.

2   Related Work

2.1   Trustworthiness Evaluation and Prediction Methods

Many approaches have been proposed to evaluate Web services trustworthiness. E.M. Maximilien et al.[10] propose an decision theory-based approach. Z. Malik and A. Bouguettaya [11] propose a set of decentralized techniques to evaluate trustworthiness with users feedbacks. As most Web services are delivered by third parties over unreliable Internet, it is reasonable and useful to predict the trustworthiness of Web services in the future. Collaborative filtering-based prediction, e.g. [9] and [8], is a widely used prediction method. Another important category of prediction methods is based on time series analysis theories, which include [7] and [6], etc. There are several problems with previous approaches, which has been discussed in Sect. 1.

2.2   Time Series Analysis

Time series analysis have been widely applied in diverse fields including econometrics, mathematical finance, signal processing, etc. A time series can be defined

---

[1] http://www.cowebservices.com
[2] http://tsr.trustie.net

as a sequence of random variables indexed according to the order they are obtained in time [12]. Generally, the time series can be classified into two groups: stationary time series and non-stationary time series [12].

Time series prediction, also named as time series forecasting, is one of the most important parts of time series analysis. Different prediction strategies may be applied. Autoregressive moving average (ARMA) model and autoregressive integrated moving average (ARIMA) model are used to fit and forecast stationary and non-stationary time series respectively. ARIMA model can be converted to ARMA model by differencing.

3   Approach

There are three main steps in our approach: Internet-based trustworthy evidences collection, trustworthiness evaluation, and trustworthiness prediction.

3.1   Internet-Based Trustworthy Evidences Collection

We apply different strategies to collect comprehensive trustworthy evidences from the Internet. Both objective evidences (e.g. QoS attributes) and subjective (e.g. reputation) evidences are collected. We implement a third-party QoS monitor to collect objective evidences on a regular basis. To collect subjective trustworthy evidences, we apply both focused crawl and open search-based approach to collect users feedbacks including ratings, comments and relevant comment segments (RCS) [2]. These feedbacks are used to calculate a services reputation separately. For more details about trustworthiness evidences collection, we refer readers to our previous work [2, 13].

3.2   Trustworthiness Evaluation

We use a light-weight mathematical model to represent the collected evidences. All the trustworthy evidences of a service are represented as a vector. Then the trustworthy evidences of all Web services can be represented as a trustworthy evidence matrix (E):

$$E = \begin{pmatrix} e_{1,1} & e_{1,2} & \cdots & e_{1,t} \\ e_{2,1} & e_{2,2} & \cdots & e_{2,t} \\ \vdots & \vdots & \ddots & \vdots \\ e_{s,1} & e_{s,2} & \cdots & e_{s,t} \end{pmatrix} \tag{1}$$

where each row of matrix E is a services trustworthy evidences, and each column is a kind of evidence.

The preferences of trustworthy evidences are represented as a weight vector $W = \langle w_1, w_2, \ldots, w_t \rangle, \sum_1^t w_t = 1$. After normalization, the trustworthiness of each Web service can be evaluated as follows:

$$T = W^T * E^* \tag{2}$$

where E^* is the normalized trustworthy evidence matrix; W^T is the transformation of the weight vector; t_i is the i-th services trustworthiness within $[0, 1]$.

3.3   Trustworthiness Prediction

A service's cumulative history trustworthiness records are represented as a time series t_i. Then we propose an ARIMA model-based multi-step Web services trustworthiness prediction process which includes four main steps (Fig. 1).

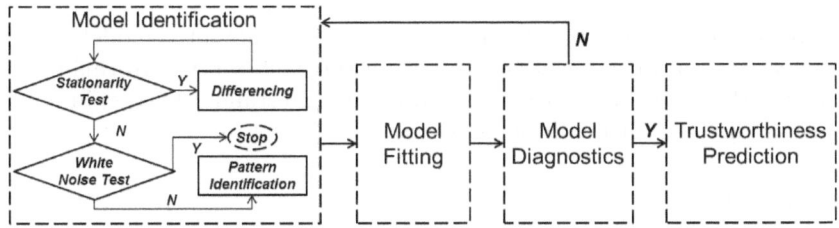

Fig. 1. Relationships of the steps of trustworthiness prediction

In **model identification**, we identify an appropriate time series model for a given trustworthiness series in the following sub steps: (1) *Stationarity Test*: Our method use sample *Autocovariance Function (ACF)* [12] to test whether a times series is a stationary series. (2) *Differencing*: If the series is identified as non-stationary in stationary test, it can be converted to a stationary series by differencing. (3) *White Noise Test*: We have to test whether the series is a white noise series, which is not worth any further analysis. The test is carried out using ACF. If the series is a white noise series, the ACF for any lag is always zero. (4) *Pattern Identification*: There are several specific patterns for ARMA model (shown in Table 1). By computing and comparing the ACF and PACF (Partial Autocorrelation Function) [12], it is possible to identify the exact pattern for the time series that passes the white noise test.

Table 1. Patterns for ARMA

	ACF	$PACF$
$AR(p)$	Tails off	Cuts off after lag p
$MA(q)$	Cuts off after lag q	Tails off
$ARMA(p,q)$	Tails off	Tails off

In **model fitting**, we try to find possible estimates of the unknown parameters within the identified model. For $ARIMA(p,d,q)$ model, there are three parameters to be determined: d is the number of differences to convert a non-stationary series into a stationary one; p and q can be determined by detecting the behaviors of ACF and PACF. For $ARMA(p,q)$ model, p and q are determined same as in $ARIMA(p,d,q)$ model.

In **model diagnostics**, we try to determine the best estimates of the parameters. First, the successive satisfying lags (10 at most) are used to construct different ARMA or ARIMA models. Second, these models are applied back to the data itself. Third, *residual test* [12] is carried out to check whether a model is significant. If the residual series is a white noise series, the model is significant; otherwise, it is not. If all the models are not significant, we return to the model identification step. Finally, we use minimized sum of squares of errors to automatically determine the best estimates of the parameters from the remaining significant models.

In **trustworthiness prediction**, we use the finally accepted model to predict the trustworthiness in the near future for a given Web service. In this research, the trustworthiness values (with plus and minus one standard error) in next five days are predicted, which will be demonstrated in Sect. 4.

4   Evaluation

By applying the Internet-based trustworthy evidences collection method, we managed to collect trustworthy evidences for 17,832 public Web services. The evidences included over 2 million objective trustworthy evidences, and over 33,000 subjective trustworthy evidences, which is the largest Web services trustworthiness data set to the best of our knowledge. We conducted several experiments on this data set to validate the effectiveness of our approach.

4.1   Case Study

First, we use a real case to demonstrate the approach proposed and its effectiveness. CDYNE IP2Geo[3] Web Service is a Web service that resolves IP address to geographic information including Network Owner Name, City, State/Province, and Country. The result of trustworthiness evaluation and prediction is shown in Fig. 2. We can see that most of the history values fall in two standard errors and are very close to the predicted values, which demonstrates that our method can effectively model the Web services trustworthiness data and predict the trustworthiness values. Due to the length limitation of the paper, more details of the case study are available at CoWS[4].

4.2   Trustworthiness Prediction Validation

In this subsection, we further studied the effectiveness of the method. We randomly selected 500 Web services from the total 17,832 collected Web services. Then we applied the prediction process on these Web services. The results showed that about 87.95% of the 500 sample Web services trustworthiness series were identified as non-stationary time series and ARIMA models were applied; the remaining 12.05% were stationary time series and ARMA models were applied. And most (about 99%) of the non-stationary trustworthiness series were converted to stationary ones by conducting differencing on the data once.

---

[3] http://ws.cdyne.com/ip2geo/ip2geo.asmx?wsdl
[4] http://www.cowebservices.com/CoWS/trust/trustIndex.jsp

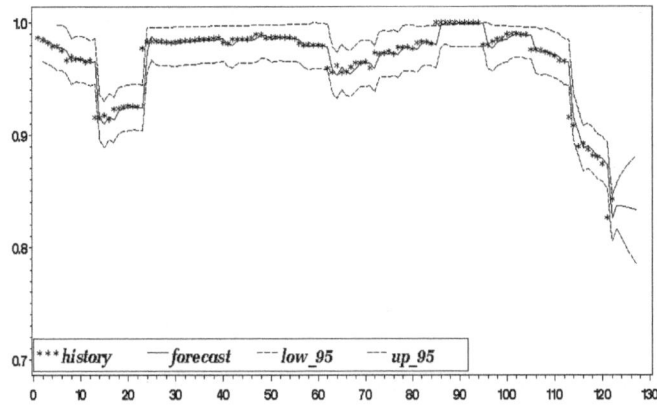

Fig. 2. Case of Web service trustworthiness evaluation and prediction: abscissa axis represents the sequence of date; vertical axis represents the trustworthiness value; * marks real values; the solid (middle) line marks the predicted vales; the dashed (up and low) lines mark two standard errors.

About 96.5% of the determined prediction models were significant, and the values predicted with these models were acceptable.

4.3   Trustworthiness Application Validation

In this subsection, we validated whether the trustworthiness evaluation and prediction results were useful to help developers to reuse Web services. The latest predicted trustworthiness values were applied in CoWS to refine and rank the service candidates as follows:

$$Score_i = \gamma * sim_i + (1 - \gamma) * t_i \tag{3}$$

where sim_i is a Web services functional similarity to the users query [2]; t_i is the predicted trustworthiness value of the service candidate; $\gamma \in [0, 1]$ is the weight and assigned to 0.5 in this experiment.

We designed a web interface as shown in Fig. 3 to compare the results returned by CoWS with and without trustworthiness, and executed ten most common queries(listed in [2]) in CoWS. Fifteen graduate students with lots of experiences of reusing Web services were invited to manually explore and grade the results returned by CoWS for each query. The services were graded one of the following values: 2 for services similar to the search query and with high trustworthiness; 1 for services similar to the search query but with low trustworthiness; 0 for other services.

We used top-k Discounted Cumulative Gain (DCG_k) to measure a search engines ability to rank the good results before bad ones.

$$DCG_k = gv_1 + \sum_{i=2}^{k} \frac{gv_i}{log_2 i} \tag{4}$$

654   M. Li et al.

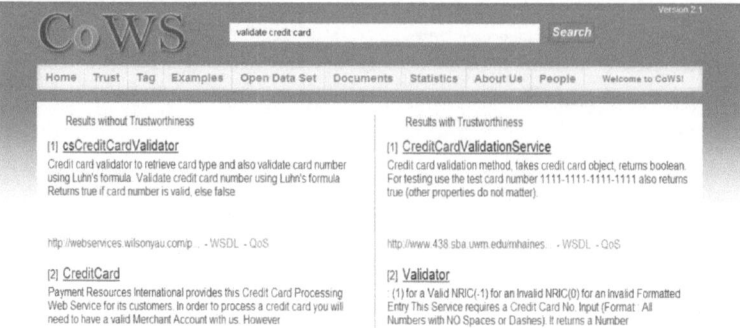

Fig. 3. Web interface to comparing the results with and without trustworthiness

where gv_i is the value of a search result graded by the graduate students. Top-5 DCG, top-10, and top-15 DCG were calculated, and the results were shown in Fig. 4. From the results we can see that Web services with higher trustworthiness were ranked toper in the result list, which would help developers to select and reuse Web services.

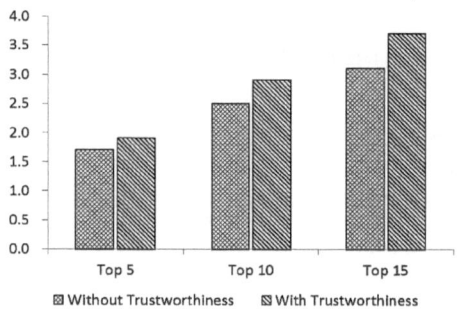

Fig. 4. DCG performance with and without trustworthiness

5 Conclusion

In this paper, we propose an ARIMA model-based approach to evaluate and predict Web services trustworthiness. Experiments conducted on a large-scale real-world data set show that our method can effectively evaluate and predict the trustworthiness of Web services, which helps users to reuse Web services.

In our future work, we will try to find and collect diverse kinds of trustworthy evidences, improve the trustworthiness evaluation and prediction method, and apply the trustworthiness in more scenarios.

Acknowledgment. This research was sponsored by the National Basic Research Program of China under Grant No. 2009CB320703; the National Natural Science Foundation of China under Grant No. 61121063, No. 60803011, No. 61103024, No. 61003072; National Department Public Benefit Research Foundation under Grant No. 2012-10256; Key National Science & Technology Specific Projects under Grant NO. 2011ZX01043-001-002; the High-Tech Research and Development Program of China, Grant No. 2012AA011202; Research & Production Combined Project of Guangdong Prov., No. 2010A090200031.

References

1. Zhang, J., Zhang, L., Chung, J.: Ws-trustworthy: a framework for web services centered trustworthy computing. In: Proceedings of the 2004 IEEE International Conference on Services Computing, SCC 2004, pp. 186–193. IEEE (2004)
2. Li, M., Zhao, J., Wang, L., Cai, S., Xie, B.: Cows: An internet-enriched and quality-aware web services search engine. In: IEEE International Conference on Web Services, ICWS 2011, pp. 419–427. IEEE (2011)
3. Al-Masri, E., Mahmoud, Q.: Understanding web service discovery goals. In: IEEE International Conference on Systems, Man and Cybernetics, SMC 2009, pp. 3714–3719. IEEE (2009)
4. Mui, L., Mohtashemi, M., Halberstadt, A.: A computational model of trust and reputation. In: Proceedings of the 35th Annual Hawaii International Conference on System Sciences, HICSS 2002, pp. 2431–2439. IEEE (2002)
5. Zhang, Y., Zheng, Z., Lyu, M.: Wsexpress: A qos-aware search engine for web services. In: IEEE International Conference on Web Services, ICWS 2010, pp. 91–98. IEEE (2010)
6. Godse, M., Bellur, U., Sonar, R.: Automating qos based service selection. In: IEEE International Conference on Web Services, ICWS 2010, pp. 534–541. IEEE (2010)
7. Solomon, A., Litoiu, M.: Business process performance prediction on a tracked simulation model. In: Proceeding of the 3rd International Workshop on Principles of Engineering Service-Oriented Systems, pp. 50–56. ACM (2011)
8. Chen, L., Feng, Y., Wu, J., Zheng, Z.: An enhanced qos prediction approach for service selection. In: IEEE International Conference on Services Computing, SCC 2011, pp. 727–728. IEEE (2011)
9. Shao, L., Zhang, J., Wei, Y., Zhao, J., Xie, B., Mei, H.: Personalized qos prediction forweb services via collaborative filtering. In: IEEE International Conference on Web Services, ICWS 2007, pp. 439–446. IEEE (2007)
10. Maximilien, E., Singh, M.: Toward autonomic web services trust and selection. In: Proceedings of the 2nd International Conference on Service Oriented Computing, pp. 212–221. ACM (2004)
11. Malik, Z., Bouguettaya, A.: Rateweb: Reputation assessment for trust establishment among web services. The VLDB Journal 18(4), 885–911 (2009)
12. Shumway, R., Stoffer, D.: Time series analysis and its applications. Springer (2000)
13. Wang, L., Liu, F., Zhang, L., Li, G., Xie, B.: Enriching descriptions for public web services using information captured from related web pages on the internet. In: Fifth IEEE International Symposium on Service Oriented System Engineering, SOSE 2010, pp. 141–150. IEEE (2010)

Analyzing Coopetition Strategies
of Services within Communities

Babak Khosravifar[1], Mahsa Alishahi[2], Ehsan Khosrowshahi Asl[2], Jamal Bentahar[2],
Rabeb Mizouni[3], and Hadi Otrok[3]

[1] McGill University, Canada
[2] Concordia University, Canada
[3] Khalifa University, UAE
babak.khosravifar@mcgill.ca,
{m_alish, e_khosr}@encs.concordia.ca, bentahar@ciise.concordia.ca,
{rabeb.mizouni, hadi.otrak}@kustar.ac.ae

Abstract. Recently, a number of frameworks have been proposed to aggregate web services within communities for the purpose of enhancing their capabilities with respect to providing the required services. Most of the proposed frameworks suggest that web services within these communities are competing but also exhibit cooperative behavior, so web services are said to be coopetitive. However, deciding which strategy to adopt, which means competing or cooperating is still an open question. The purpose of this paper is to answer this question by discussing a mechanism web services can use to effectively choose interacting strategies which bring maximum utility. In this direction, we investigate web services' characteristics and their expected utilities over different strategies. We enable web services that are hosted in communities with reasoning capabilities to enhance their quality of strategic interacting mechanisms as decision making procedures. The ultimate objective is to analyze factors that helps web services decide about different interacting strategies. Moreover, we develop a simulated environment where we analyze different scenarios and verify the obtained theoretical results using parameters from a real web services dataset.

Keywords: Web services, Reputation, Strategies.

1 Introduction

Web services are developed to continuously interact with others that could be different types of web services or service consumers. Abstracting and associating web services with knowledge-empowered agents without changing the web services implementation benefit them from interactions that those agents are able to manage [6,12]. That means web services are no more considered as simply passive components but as intelligent entities that enjoy autonomy and selfishness, two significant properties in business settings where competition is a key factor [4,7]. Those web services follow two different strategies of cooperating or competing towards serving service consumers and increasing their utilities in terms of payoffs. Analyzing web services acting strategies in such a context in terms of deciding which strategy to choose is an open and challenging

C. Liu et al. (Eds.): ICSOC 2012, LNCS 7636, pp. 656–663, 2012.

problem. Our main contribution in this paper is to address this problem and enable web services to cope with strategic decision making in a particular situation.

There are a number of related proposals that take into account the correlation between web services and the ways these services coordinate their actions to accomplish a task. In [4,5,9,10], authors propose to rank web services based on their reputation in the system and to use this ranking as a means to facilitate cooperation of services. In those models, services rely on one another using the reputation ranking system. There are other models that facilitate cooperation mechanisms using transaction-based web services [11] and communities that host and gather web services having similar or complementary functionalities but different QoS parameters [6]. However, deciding about which strategy to choose when web services are competing but still need to cooperate to accomplish complex tasks is still an open issue. We propose analyzing those different strategies to help web services in their decision making process when these web services function within communities. The objective is to enable web services to reasonably evaluate and decide over their coopetition strategies, which means when to compete and when to cooperate.

More precisely, we propose a mechanism within which web services in the community could choose either to compete for an announced task, or to cooperate with other competing web services in the same community to accomplish some subtasks of the announced task. As intelligent entities, web services require a reasoning technique that enhances their abilities over best acting strategies and the attitude they could exhibit to yield maximum outcome. In this paper, we implement a simulation environment with a number of communities hosting a number of web services having parameters extracted from a real dataset [2][1]. This dataset represents 2507 real web services that exist on the web. It includes the QoS values of 9 parameters including availability, throughput and reliability. These QoS values were determined by monitoring the web services over a 6 day period. We equip some of those web services with our proposed strategic decision making procedure and compare the performance of the equipped services against other ordinary web services. We provide detailed discussions over the implemented environment and verify the effectiveness of the proposed mechanism.

2   The Proposed Framework

In this section, we first present the architecture of the proposed model. We explore the characteristics of intelligent web services and their network. We link this architecture to the implemented system where we investigate the services' coopetitive attitudes. We compute the involved system parameters and explain the web services' interactive strategy profiles by highlighting their coopetitive choices.

2.1   The Architecture

The proposed system consists of three types of autonomous entities with different goals.

---

[1] The implemented environment includes the QWS dataset by Eyhab Al-Masri and Qusay H. Mahmoud freely available at: www.uoguelph.ca/ qmahmoud/qws.

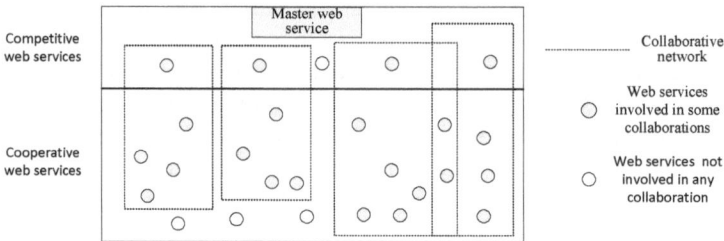

Fig. 1. Web services are partitioned into competitive and cooperative sets. Competitive web services may get tasks directly from the master web service and they can share it with other cooperative web services in their collaborative networks.

Web Services that reside inside a community which aggregates a number of functionally similar or complementary web services as a group [8]. Within the same community, each web service has a network consisting of some other web services that might get involved in a cooperative work (e.g. composition and substitution). As web services are also competing, particularly when they provide similar functionalities, each one of them aims to maximize its individual income (i.e. the payoff) by adopting a given strategy.

Master Web Service is the manager and representative of the community of web services. Among other functionalities, the master web service is responsible for allocating tasks to web services within the community. After the task being accomplished, the master rewards or penalizes the associated web service with respect to its reputation as a member of the community.

Users generate tasks with specified QoS. In our proposed system, tasks are continuously being generated and user satisfaction is abstracted since we focus on web services' interactive strategies.

Figure 1 illustrates the architecture of a typical community aggregating a number of web services with different interactive strategies. Some of them compete for the task where they directly deal with the master. Some others cooperate in the associated task where they only deal with the competed web service as the task leader and do not directly interact with the master. We highlight details of the interactive strategies in the rest of this section. In the proposed system, the master sorts the competing web services based on some parameters (such as reputation) that we explain in the rest of this section. If the web service is busy or unwilling to take a given task, the master allocates the task to the second competing web service in the list. There is a chance that some tasks being not assigned to any web service. These tasks are accumulated to the task pool to be allocated in the next task allocation round. Upon allocation of a task, the web service is responsible to offer the required QoS that is stated in the task being generated by a consumer. Afterwards, the master rewards or penalizes the competing web service by upgrading or degrading its reputation according to the offered QoS compared with the required one.

2.2   System Parameters

Task QoS (T^t_{QoS}) is the required QoS metric for a specific task at time t. Users define tasks with specific QoS requirements such as response time, availability, and accuracy [3]. We aggregate and normalize these metrics to a value between 0 and 1.

Web service QoS (QoS^t_w) is the QoS provided by the web service w after performing a task at time t. Again the metrics that contribute in computing this QoS are aggregated and normalized to a value between 0 and 1. The offered quality might or might not meet the required task quality T^t_{QoS}. In the latter case, the service user would be disappointed and a negative satisfaction feedback is expected. In our proposed system, both cases are considered when calculating the web services' reputation.

Budget (B^t_w) is the amount of money the web service w has in its disposal at time t, which helps pay for the community membership fees (ϵ) and is one of the parameters that the web service considers when deciding about getting involved in a competition or not. This parameter has been used in other service computing settings such as [3].

Reputation is a factor in any online community where trust is important. Without any trust enabling mechanism, users cannot differentiate between services, specially the ones which offer the same type of service. Reputation mechanisms usually aggregate users' experiences and in our case it strongly depends on QoS that each web service provides. Users define tasks with specific quality T^t_{QoS}; therefore, after performing a task with QoS^t_w, the reputation of w gets evaluated by the master web service. Rep^t_w refers to the reputation of w at time t. In Equation 1, we compute the reward that the master computes considering the task QoS compared with the web service offered quality QoS^t_w. In case the offered quality meets user expectations, the reward value would be positive. In this system, we consider a small value as default rewards η which the master considers together with the proportional level of satisfaction as a weighted value (by υ). In this case, the higher the offered quality is, the more weighted reward is. In case the offered quality did not meet the user expectations, the reward would be negative. In this case, we also have a default penalty value ρ (where $\rho > \eta$) together with the weighted proportional difference.

$$reward^t_w = \begin{cases} \eta + \frac{QoS^t_w}{T^t_{QoS}+QoS^t_w} * \upsilon & \text{if } T^t_{QoS} \le QoS^t_w; \\ -(\rho + \frac{T^t_{QoS}}{T^t_{QoS}+QoS^t_w} * \upsilon) & \text{otherwise.} \end{cases} \qquad (1)$$

The assigned reputation value is updated by the computed reward value. The computed reputation of web services is bounded by the minimum and maximum reputation values 0 and 1. Let $\Gamma = Rep^t_w + reward^t_w$. The updated reputation value is then computed as follows:

$$Rep^{t+1}_w = \begin{cases} \Gamma & \text{if } 0 \le \Gamma \le 1; \\ 0 & \text{if } \Gamma < 0; \\ 1 & \text{if } \Gamma > 1. \end{cases} \qquad (2)$$

Growth Factor is a parameter which declares web services' performance based on their recent strategies and activities. Growth factor is relative to web services' reputation and QoS. This parameter is the main variable a typical web service uses to decide which strategy to adopt. We use Equation 3 to compute the growth factor G^t_w of the web service w at time t. The growth factor function should be monotonically increasing in QoS_w^t, Rep_w^t and B_w^t, which is satisfied by the equation and this could be easily proven by calculating the partial derivatives of this function in 1) QoS_w^t; 2) Rep_w^t; and then 3) B_w^t and show that they are all positive. The contribution of the budget B_w^t in the calculation of the growth factor should be proportional to the ideal budget $\beta_w \times t$ where the web service receives all the offered tasks during the periods t. The parameter β_w denotes the profit obtained considering the mean received service fee μ_w and the cost of community membership ϵ. The mean service fee depends on the strategy adopted by the web service because a competitive service receives higher fees $\mu_{w,CM}$ compared to a cooperative one $\mu_{w,CO}$ ($\mu_{w,CM} > \mu_{w,CO}$).

$$G_w^t = \frac{Rep_w^t + QoS_w^t + \frac{B_w^t}{t \times \beta_w}}{3} \qquad \beta_w = \mu_w - \epsilon, \qquad \mu_w \in \{\mu_{w,CM}, \mu_{w,CO}\} \qquad (3)$$

2.3   Web Service Interactive Strategies

The main goal of each individual web service is to increase its income (payoff). This income can be earned from tasks (or requests) done by this web service. In our model, web services can decide to compete to get a task from the master web service or to cooperate with other web services in a given collaborative network (the way a collaborative network is set by a leader is based on the cooperative web services reputation and their QoS parameters that should coincide with the required QoS). Therefore, we define two types of web service strategies. On the one hand, when a web service has higher level of confidence based on its growth factor, it can compete to get a task from the master and adopts the competitive strategy. On the other hand, when it has a lower level of confidence that it does not feel able to compete to get a task, the web service waits for some other peers to cooperate with for completing the task and thus it adopts the cooperative strategy. Web services estimate the outcome of all the strategies and choose one accordingly. This decision is not static but can change over time so web services can switch from one strategy to the other and this dynamic attitude is referred to as coopetition.

3   Experimental Results

In this section, we provide an empirical analysis over the observed results regarding the characteristics of intelligent web services hosted in different communities of web services. In the implemented system, we simulate the behaviors of service consumers as request generators, web services as service providers, and master web services as community representatives. The objective is to investigate the effectiveness of the proposed strategic system on intelligent web services' overall budget. The simulation application is written in *C#* using *Visual Studio*. Developed web services are initialized with values taken from a real dataset that includes 2507 real web services functioning on the web. The dataset records the QoS values of 9 parameters including *availability*, *throughput*, and *reliability* [2].

We start our discussions with cumulative budget comparison regarding different communities within which services follow different reasoning techniques. Figure 2 part

(a) illustrates three graphs for three different communities. Each community hosts web services that follow different reasoning techniques: (1) a community that follows the interactive reasoning techniques presented in this paper (referred to as coopetive); (2) a community that follows a random reasoning technique so decisions about selecting competitive or cooperative strategies are totally random (referred to as random coopetitive); and (3) a competitive community where all services follow the competitive strategy (referred to as competitive). The proposed model's reasoning mechanism enables services to effectively select their interacting strategies and the obtained budget represents the best outcome over the strategic decision making procedure they run all the time. The procedure allows services to make decisions that maximize their utilities, so that if the web service cannot compete, the procedure would suggest to collaborate, which is better than competing and failing to obtain the task. In this case (i.e., competing and not getting the task), the service stays idle but still pays the community membership fee, which means losing utility. The developed strategic decision making mechanism leads some web services to follow cooperative strategies that overall maintain an optimal community budget. In the same figure, we observe the cumulative budget of a community where services follow random interacting strategies. The outcome is clearly lower because services at each run randomly decide over their acting strategies. This potentially influences the community budget because a low quality service if randomly selects to follow the competitive strategy, it will fail to get a task. This kind of strategy selection is totally random while the task allocation algorithm follows a logical path. The ideal system is the one that analyzes the optimal strategic path and consistently follows strategies that bring maximum outcome.

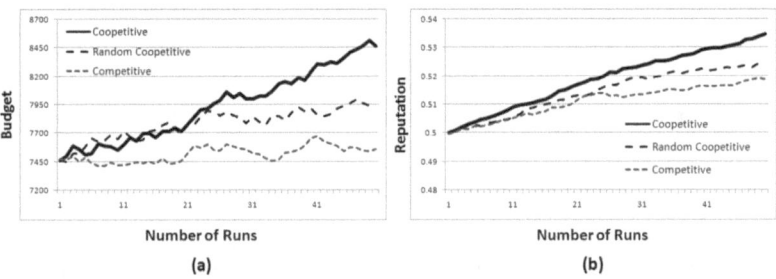

Fig. 2. Part (a): Cumulative community budget comparison. Part (b): Average community reputation comparison over different strategic decisions.

The results illustrated in Figure 2 part (a) verify the importance of the strategic decision making procedure to logically decide over the possible competitive and cooperative choices. Figure 2 part (b) illustrates communities average reputation of involved web services. The graphs represent the influence of the rewards that the master web service imposes to encourage highly capable web services to compete for a task. As for the cumulative budget, we observe that the coopetive community outperforms the random coopetitive and competitive communities in terms of average reputation. The proposed model's average reputation increases because web services follow optimal strategies where they can perform better so obtain higher rewards.

In Figure 3 parts (a) and (b), we observe the competitive and cooperative probability of four different web services where two of them (w_1 and w_3) are following optimal strategies (competitive for w_1 and cooperative for w_3) and the two others (w_2 and w_4) are following non-optimal strategies. Over elapsing runs, web services that follow optimal strategies bring best budget. In fact, the master web service rewards the high quality web service that chooses the competitive strategy, cooperates with other web services and successfully accomplishes the task. In this system, the reputation regarding such a web service is increasing over time and the possibility of allocating further tasks is increasing as well. By increasing the growth factor, such a web service (here shown as w_1) increases the probability of selecting the competitive strategy. On the other hand, the other web service (here shown as w_2) that is incapable of competing is penalized by the master web service because the offered quality might not meet the required task quality. Thus, w_2 degrades its growth factor by following the competitive strategy. As intelligent entity, this web service is encouraged to change its strategy to the cooperative one and thus, its probability of selecting the competitive strategy is decreasing over time. We have similar results in Figure 3 part (b) regarding web services w_3 and w_4 where unlike w_4, w_3 is strategically following the cooperative strategy. Therefore, w_4 is more seeking the competitive strategy where it can increase its growth factor.

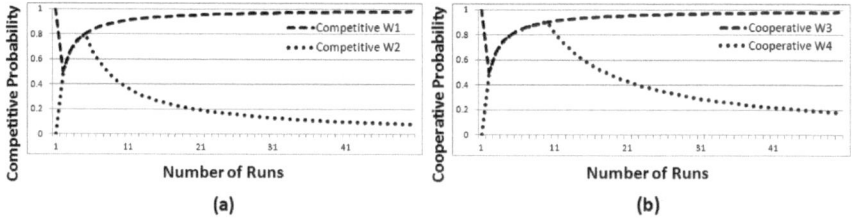

Fig. 3. Competitive and cooperative probabilities regarding four different web services

4   Related Work and Conclusion

Relevant proposals to the model presented in this paper are the ones that address service selection and task allocation mechanisms. In many frameworks proposed in the literature, service selection and task allocation are regulated based on the reputation parameter [5,11]. In [1], the authors present a dependable framework for cooperative web services that is based on the tuple space coordination model. The intrusion-tolerant perspective is emphasized in this paper where several security mechanisms are developed to enable a reliable coordination system. The proposed frameworks mostly aim to facilitate the coordination mechanism between web services. However, the opposite strategy of competing is not analyzed where web services might be more successful when competing within a same group. In fact, web services are not always willing to cooperate even if they have some common goals, particularly when they operate within groups such as communities. In such a context, web services can follow different interacting strategies and have to decide when to compete and when to cooperate so that their ultimate goal, maximizing their incomes, can be better achieved.

The contribution of this paper is the proposition of a coopetitive strategic model to analyze the interacting behavior of intelligent web services that are active within communities. We considered two acting strategies where web services expect different sort of payoffs: (1) competitive strategy where the web service claims that it can accomplish a task, and therefore can take the responsibility over the service consumer satisfaction; and (2) cooperative strategy where the web service does not take the responsibility to accomplish the task and only cooperates with other competitive web services. Our proposed model advances the state-of-the-art in cooperative systems by enabling intelligent web services to effectively choose their interacting strategies that lead to optimal outcomes. The proposed framework provides a reasoning technique that web services can use to increase their overall obtained utilities. As future work, we plan to emphasize the service consumer role in the proposed model to obtain more accurate results when consumers post their service satisfaction feedback. Moreover, we would like to enhance the reasoning technique's features to cope with different unexpected scenarios. We also need to expand the work to enable services to choose their collaboration networks.

References

1. Alchieri, E.A.P., Bessani, A.N., Fraga, J.S.: A dependable infrastructure for cooperative web services coordination. In: Proc. of the Int. Conf. on Web Services, ICWS, pp. 21–28 (2008)
2. Al-Masri, E., Mahmoud, Q.H.: Discovering the best web service. In: Proc. of the 16th Int. Conf. on World Wide Web, WWW, pp. 1257–1258 (2007)
3. Lim, E., Thiran, P., Maamar, Z., Bentahar, J.: On the analysis of satisfaction for web services selection. In: Proc. of the 9th Int. Conf. on Services Computing, SCC (2012)
4. Jurca, R., Faltings, B.: Reputation-Based Service Level Agreements for Web Services. In: Benatallah, B., Casati, F., Traverso, P. (eds.) ICSOC 2005. LNCS, vol. 3826, pp. 396–409. Springer, Heidelberg (2005)
5. Kalepu, S., Krishnaswamy, S., Loke, S.W.: A QoS metric for selecting Web services and providers. In: Proc. of the 4th Int. Conference on Web Information Systems Engineering Workshops, pp. 131–139 (2003)
6. Khosravifar, B., Bentahar, J., Moazin, A., Thiran, P.: On the reputation of agent-based web services. In: Proc. of the 24th Int. Conf. on Artificial Intelligence (AAAI), pp. 1352–1357 (2010)
7. Khosravifar, B., Bentahar, J., Clacens, K., Goffart, C., Thiran, P.: Game-Theoretic Analysis of a Web Services Collaborative Mechanism. In: Kappel, G., Maamar, Z., Motahari-Nezhad, H.R. (eds.) ICSOC 2011. LNCS, vol. 7084, pp. 549–556. Springer, Heidelberg (2011)
8. Khosravifar, B., Bentahar, J., Moazin, A., Thiran, P.: Analyzing communities of web services using incentives. Journal of Web Services Research 7(3), 30–51 (2010)
9. Malik, Z., Bouguettaya, A.: Evaluating Rater Credibility for Reputation Assessment of Web Services. In: Benatallah, B., Casati, F., Georgakopoulos, D., Bartolini, C., Sadiq, W., Godart, C. (eds.) WISE 2007. LNCS, vol. 4831, pp. 38–49. Springer, Heidelberg (2007)
10. Maximilien, E.M., Singh, M.P.: Reputation and endorsement for web services. ACM SIGEcom Exchanges 3(1), 24–31 (2002)
11. Rosario, S., Benveniste, A., Haar, S., Jard, C.: Probabilistic QoS and soft contracts for transaction based Web services. In: Proc. of the Int. Conf. on Web Services, ICWS, pp. 126–133 (2007)
12. Yassine, A., Shirehjini, A.A., Shirmohammadi, S., Tran, T.: Knowledge-empowered agent information system for privecy payoff in ecommerce. Knowledge and Information Systems (2011) doi: 10.1007/s10115-011-0415-3

Trust-Based Service Discovery
in Multi-relation Social Networks

Amine Louati, Joyce El Haddad, and Suzanne Pinson

Université Paris-Dauphine, LAMSADE CNRS UMR 7243, France
{amine.louati,elhaddad,pinson}@lamsade.dauphine.fr

Abstract. With the increasing number of services, the need to locate relevant services remains essential. To satisfy the query of a service requester, available service providers has first to be discovered. This task has been heavily investigated from both industrial and academic perspectives based essentially on registers. However, they completely ignore the contribution of the social dimension. When integrating social trust dimension to service discovery, this task will gain wider credibility and acceptance. If a service requester knows that discovered services are offered by trustworthy providers, he will be more confident. In this paper, we present a new discovery technique based on a social trust measure that ranks service providers belonging to the service requester's multi-relation social network. The proposed measure is an aggregation of three measures: the social position, the social proximity and the social similarity. To compute these measures, we take into account both semantic and structural knowledge extracted from the multi-relation social network. Semantic information includes service requestor and provider profiles and their interactions. Structural information includes among other the position of service providers in the multi-relation social network graph.

1 Introduction

Traditional *service discovery* techniques in Web services area utilize functional and non-functional properties to decide which relevant service to discover among a huge number of available services. However, with the emergence of Web 2.0 and especially *social networks*, users show the willingness to use their social networks to find services as well as to offer services. Recently, few studies tried to integrate social networking into Web service discovery [1–3]. In these works, Maamar et al. argue that using social networking at the level of Web services facilitate services discovery and composition. For authors, acquisition of interactions between services by using social networking is beneficial to organize and to extract sequences of anterior successful interactions for future needs of the user requester. Despite enhancements in the service discovery, they lack support for trust to make this task more effective. Another challenge in the service discovery task is to find providers that can be *trusted* by requesters before using their services. If a service requester knows that discovered services are offered by trustworthy providers, he will be more confident. In social networks, a particular interest have been given to trust relationship. Golbeck [4, 5] proposes a

C. Liu et al. (Eds.): ICSOC 2012, LNCS 7636, pp. 664–671, 2012.

FilmTrust site for generating predictive movie recommendations from trust in social network. The trust-based movie recommendation is founded on knowledge extracted from annotations and user ratings added in the system. The idea is to help film requesters to find the best offer from his social network. However, this approach presents some weaknesses. First, the system covers only the case of films. Second, knowledge defined in the social network can be richer than ratings and reviews and includes other kind of relevant information such as user profiles.

In this paper, our research focuses on *trustworthy service providers discovery in a Multi-Relation Social Network (MRSN) of a service requester*. We propose to compute *social trust* between the service requester and service providers by aggregating three measures: *social position, social proximity* and *social similarity*. To compute these measures, we take into account semantic and structural information extracted from the service requester MRSN. Semantic information includes service requester and provider profiles and their interactions. As stated in [6, 7], there is a strong correlation between trust and similarity of profiles: people generally prefer suggestions that come from individuals with similar profiles. Thus, the more important the similarity between two users is, the more likely a trust relationship exists between them [6]. Structural information includes among other the position of service providers in the MRSN graph. For example, a weather service provider like the national weather provider is usually more trusted than a corporate weather provider and very sought-after and subsequently is connected with a large number of requesters. In this case, such service provider occupies a central position in the social network and is considered as a trustworthy provider. The centrality measure is fundamental in a social network and participate in the computation of the social trust as proved in [8]. As far as we know, only [8, 9] combine both social dimension and trust to help users to discover appropriate services from their social network. Both of these works do not consider the multi-relation aspect of social networks.

This paper presents a new service discovery technique based on a social trust measure that takes into account both semantic and structural properties of the service requester MRSN. According to this measure, the outcome is a Trust-Relation Social Network (TRSN), that is requester centered and based on a single relation, the social trust relation that filters and ranks service providers.

The remainder of the paper is organized as follows. In the next section we describe our approach for building trust-relation social network for service providers discovery and we present our three measures as well as how to aggregate them in a single social trust measure. Experimental results are interpreted in Section 3, and Section 4 contains our concluding remarks and future work.

2 Social Trust Measure

In this section, we begin with some definitions followed by a description of our approach. We model a multi-relation social network by an undirected graph, where nodes represent users (i.e. service requesters or service providers), and an edge between two nodes indicate a symmetric social relationship between users. More formally, a multi-relation social network is defined as follows:

Definition 1 (Multi-Relation Social Network (MRSN)). *Given sets V of users and R of types of symmetric relationships with $R = \{R_1, \ldots, R_r\}$. A multi-relation social network is a connected undirected graph $G = (V, E)$, where V is the set of nodes and $E = \{E_1, \ldots, E_r\}$ is the set of edges where E_i is the set of edges with respect to the ith relationship. In other words, an edge $(u, v) \in E_i$ implies the existence of a social relationship of type R_i between nodes u and v.*

In a MRSN graph, the notion of neighborhood of a node can be expressed as follows:

Definition 2 (Neighborhood). *Given a MRSN graph $G = (V, E)$, the neighborhood of a node u regarding a type of relationship R_i, denoted $N_{R_i}(u)$, is defined as $N_{R_i}(u) = \{v \in V \mid (u, v) \in E_i\}$.*

Our approach involve two steps as outlined by Figure 1. It takes as input a MRSN, a service requester query Q, and produces a Trust-Relation Social Network (TRSN). The service requester query is defined as $Q = (G, s, U)$, where G is a MRSN graph, s is a requested service, and U is a utility function expressing the service requester preferences over types of relationships. For example, a babysitting service requester will feel most confident if a member of the family looks after his/her baby; otherwise he/she could prefer to a friend rather than a colleague. So clearly, preferences over relationship types are: $family \succeq friend \succeq colleague$. These preferences are modeled by the utility function as follow: $U(family) = a$, $U(friend) = b$, and $U(colleague) = c$, with $a \geq b \geq c$ and $a, b, c \in \mathbb{N}$. To produce the TRSN, we proceed in two steps: *social measures computing* step, and *trust computing and TRSN construction* step. Next, we describe these two steps.

2.1   Social Measures Computing

This first step consist of analyzing the MRSN to extract useful information that includes *profiles* of the service requester and service providers that contains personal data and information about their interests, and the *kind of relationships* between them. Based on the analysis of the MRSN graph and the extracted information, three measures are computed: the social position, the social proximity and the social similarity measures.

Social Position Measure. The social position of a service provider p, $SPo(p)$, represents its degree centrality which gives an indication of its social power. We do not simply compute $SPo(p)$ as the number of edges node p has, but we also consider the type of relationships connecting p with the other nodes in the MRSN graph. This measure is given by the following formula:

$$SPo(p) = \sum_{i=1, \forall p' \in V}^{|R|} w_i \cdot a^i(p, p')$$

where $a^i(p, p') = 1$ iff p and p' are directly connected according to the relationship R_i, 0 otherwise; and w_i is the weight of R_i computed as $\frac{1}{U(R_i)}$.

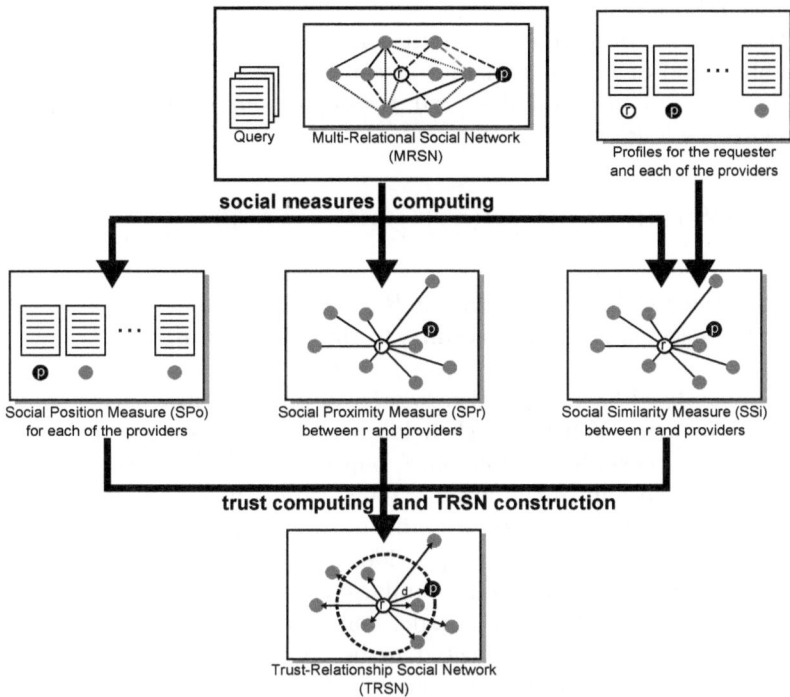

Fig. 1. Trust-Based Service Discovery Process

Social Proximity Measure. The social proximity between two nodes is computed based on the MRSN graph and service requester r preferences. $SPr(r,p)$ represents the average cost of the path, from r to service provider p, that uses the minimum number of different kind of relations regarding requester r preferences. For requester r, the cost of a path $(x_1, \ldots, x_k)$ where $x_1 = r$, $x_k = p$, and $(x_i, x_{i+1}) \in E$, to a service provider p of length $k-1$ is computed as follows:

$$SPr(r,p) = \frac{\sum_{i=1}^{k} U((x_i, x_{i+1}))}{k-1}$$

where $U((x_i, x_{i+1}))$ is the cost of the edge (x_i, x_{i+1}) given by the utility function in the requester preferences.

Social Similarity Measure. The social similarity between two nodes is computed based on their profiles and the MRSN graph. $SSi(r,p)$ is an aggregation of two measures, namely, *Degree Similarity (DS)* and *Profile Similarity (PS)*.

Degree Similarity (DS). From the MRSN graph, we propose a DS measure to find ties between requester r and provider p based on the comparison of their neighborhood. For a type of relation R_i, we count the number of nodes:

in common in both neighborhoods ($a_i = |N_{R_i}(r) \cap N_{R_i}(p)|$), in the neighborhood of r without nodes in common in both neighborhoods ($b_i = |N_{R_i}(r)| - a_i$), in the neighborhood of p without nodes in common in both neighborhoods ($c_i = |N_{R_i}(p)| - a_i$). For a pair of nodes (r, p), the degree similarity, $DS(r, p)$, can thus be calculated as follows:

$$DS(r, p) = \sum_{i=1}^{|R|} w_i \cdot \delta^i(r, p) \quad with \quad \delta^i(r, p) = \frac{1}{1 + dist^i}$$

where w_i is the weight of the relation R_i; and $dist^i = \frac{b_i + c_i}{a_i + b_i + c_i}$ is the *Jaccard distance* [10] between r and p according to the relationship R_i.

Profile Similarity (PS). In social networks, a profile consist of a set of items structured into a set of fields, each field containing one or several values (e.g. gender=[female], music-likes=[folk, jazz, pop]). In the former, the field is called a single-valued field and in the latter a multi-valued field. The aim of PS is to compare values of fields in requester profile to those in provider profile in order to determine how much requester and provider are similar. We chose the Burnaby measure [11] to evaluate the profile similarity. This choice is motivated by our interest in the neighborhood of a node, composed of nodes with which there is interactions and therefore expected to be similar. More precisely, Burnaby measure evaluates similarity between single-valued fields of two profiles as shown by the following definition.

Definition 3 (Burnaby). *Let i be a profile item consisting of a set Fd of fields. Let X_k and Y_k be the values of the kth single-valued field Fd_k respectively in profiles of service requester r and service provider p. The similarity of single-valued fields is given by:*

$$Burnaby(X_k, Y_k) = \begin{cases} 1 & if \ X_k = Y_k \\ \dfrac{\sum_{q \in A_k} 2\log(1 - \hat{p}_k(q))}{\log \frac{\hat{p}_k(X_k)\hat{p}_k(Y_k)}{(1 - \hat{p}_k(X_k))(1 - \hat{p}_k(Y_k))} + \sum_{q \in A_k} 2\log(1 - \hat{p}_k(q))} & otherwise \end{cases}$$

with

$$\hat{p}_k(x) = \frac{f_k(x)}{N}$$

where A_k denotes the set of all possible values of field Fd_k; N the total number of profiles; $f_k(x)$ the distribution of frequency of values taken by a field (i.e. the number of times a field Fd_k takes the value x), and $\hat{p}_k(x)$ the sample probability of a field Fd_k takes the value x.

Next, inspired from [12], we show how to compute the similarity between items and the similarity between profiles.

Definition 4 (Item Similarity). *Let i be an item of a profile consisting of a set Fd of fields. Let $\mathcal{V}(Fd_k^r)$ and $\mathcal{V}(Fd_k^p)$ be the set of values taken by the field Fd_k for item i in profiles of r and p respectively. Let $B_k = \{Burnaby(X_{km}, Y_{kn}), \forall X_{km} \in$*

$\mathcal{V}(Fd_k^r)$ and $\forall Y_{kn} \in \mathcal{V}(Fd_k^p)\}$ be the set of single-valued field similarity computed between all possible pairs of $\mathcal{V}(Fd_k^r)$ and $\mathcal{V}(Fd_k^v)$. Let $MaxB_k = \{bur_l \in B \mid \forall l, 1 \leq l \leq |\mathcal{V}(Fd_k^r)|, bur_l = Burnaby(X_{km}, Y_{kn})\}$ be the set of the $|\mathcal{V}(Fd_k^r)|$ biggest values in B_k. The similarity between the ith items of r and p is defined as:

$$S_i(r,p) = \frac{1}{|Fd|} \times \sum_{k=1}^{|Fd|} \frac{1}{|\mathcal{V}(Fd_k^r)|} \sum_{l=1}^{|MaxB_k|} bur_l$$

From the service requester r point of view, we define profile similarity, $PS(r,p)$, with a service provider p as follows:

$$PS(r,p) = \frac{1}{|I|} \times \sum_{i \in I} \beta_i \cdot S_i(r,p)$$

where I is the set of items in profiles; and β_i is a weight attributed to the item i reflecting its importance in the profile description.

Social Similarity (SSi). The overall measure of social similarity, $SSi(r,p)$, is the product of the two above measures defined for a service requester r and a service provider p as follows: $SSi(r,p) = DS(r,p) \times PS(r,p)$

2.2 Trust Computing and TRSN Construction

The aim of this step is to build a new social network, a TRSN that is service requester centered and based on a single relation, the *Social Trust (ST)* relation. Before building the TRSN, this step computes based on all the social measure values, generated in the first step, a single social trust value. After computing all the social measure values, a vector M_p associated to each service provider p is defined as $M_p = (SPo(p), SPr(r,p), SSi(r,p))$. By merging the vectors of all service providers, a matrix $M = (M_{pj}, p \in V \text{ and } 1 \leq j \leq 3)$ is built.To compute the value of the social trust for each service provider, we use a simple additive weighting technique that proceed in two phases. The scaling phase which aims to transform every measure value, of M_p vector, into a value M'_{pj} between 0 and 1. We obtain a matrix $M' = (M'_{pj}, p \in V \text{ and } 1 \leq j \leq 3)$.The weighting phase which aims to rank service provider according to their social trust scores. The score of social trust of a requester r in a provider p, $ST(r,p)$, is computed by using the following formula:

$$ST(r,p) = \sum_{j=1}^{3} \lambda_i \cdot M'_{pj}(r,p)$$

where λ_j is the weight of the jth social measure with $\lambda_i \in [0,1]$ and $\sum_{j=1}^{3} \lambda_i = 1$. Based on the computation of $ST(r,p)$ for every service provider p, we build a TRSN that is service requester centered and modeled by a directed weighted graph $G' = (V', E')$, where V' is the set composed by the service providers and the service requester, and E' is the set of edges. An edge $(r,p) \in E'$ implies the existence of a social trust relationship between r and p and the weight of an edge (r,p) corresponds to the degree of trust requester r has in provider p.

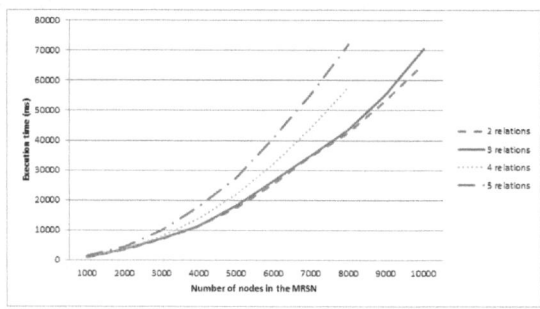

Fig. 2. Computation cost by varying the number of nodes and relations in the MRSN

3   Implementation

In this section, we present implementation and results of evaluation of our service providers discovery technique based on social trust measure on a variety of synthetic datasets. The prototype was developed in JAVA and the MRSN graph data were stored in a GML format[1]. All experiments were run on a 3.1GHz Core(TM) i5-2400 running windows 7, with 8Go of RAM.

The experiments involved a MRSN varying the number of nodes and varying the number of different kind of relations. Experimentations were done over the 10 scenarios. In the first scenario, the number of nodes in the MRSN is 1000 and the number of relation types varies from 2 to 5. In the last scenario, the number of nodes in the MRSN is 10000 and the number of relation types varies from 2 to 5. In all scenarios, the requester preferences were $U(R1) = 1$, $U(R2) = 2$, $U(R3) = 4$, $U(R4) = 8$, and $U(R5) = 16$. We randomly generate the MRSN graph. For each scenario, the experiment was executed 10 times sequentially and the average execution time was recorded. Figure 2 shows execution time (in milliseconds) of the social trust measure computing. We observe that the computation cost increases when the number of nodes in the MRSN increases. Also, the computation cost increases when the number of relations increases in the MRSN.

4   Conclusion

In this paper, we considered multi-relation social network in the service discovery task. We have proposed a new service providers discovery approach based on social trust between requester and providers computed by taking into account knowledge extracted from the requester multi-relation social network. The proposed social trust is an overall score computed from values of three measures, social position, social proximity and social similarity measures. According to the

---

[1] Graph Modelling Language, 1997, http://www.fim.uni-passau.de/en/fim/faculty/chairs/theoretische-informatik/projects.html - Extracted on Mai 2012.

social trust measure, the outcome of the proposed approach is a weighted directed graph modeling a new social network that is service requester centered and based on a single relation, the social trust relation. With this relation, we were able to rank service providers by mean of weights of an edge corresponding to the degree of trust service requester has in service provider.

As future work, we would like to investigate enhancement of service discovery by exploiting feedback of service requesters experiences. The idea is to accumulate within each service provider the history of use of its service as well as requesters past experiences with the service. We also would like to explore the extension of our trust model to find a trustworthy composition of services based on the propagation of trust among providers.

Acknowledgement. This work is supported by the Personal Information Management through Internet project (PIMI-ANR-2012-VERS-0014-03) of the French National Agency for Research.

References

1. Maamar, Z., Wives, L., Youakim, B., Said, E., Khouloud, B., Noura, F.: LinkedWS: A Novel Web Services Discovery Model Based on the Metaphor of Social Networks. Simulation Modelling Practice and Theory 19(2), 121–132 (2010)
2. Maamar, Z., Santos, P., Wives, L., Badr, Y., Faci, N., de Oliveira, J.: Using social networks for web services discovery. IEEE Internet Computing 15, 48–54 (2011)
3. Maamar, Z., Hacid, H., Huhns, M.: Why Web Services need social networks. IEEE Internet Computing 15(2), 90–94 (2011)
4. Golbeck, J.: Computing and Applying Trust in Web-Based Social Networks. PhD thesis, University of Maryland at College Park, College Park, MD, USA (2005)
5. Golbeck, J.: Generating Predictive Movie Recommendations from Trust in Social Networks. In: Stølen, K., Winsborough, W.H., Martinelli, F., Massacci, F. (eds.) iTrust 2006. LNCS, vol. 3986, pp. 93–104. Springer, Heidelberg (2006)
6. Ziegler, C., Golbeck, J.: Investigating correlations of trust and interest similarity - do birds of a feather really flock together? Decision Support Systems 43, 460–475 (2007)
7. Ziegler, C.-N., Lausen, G.: Analyzing Correlation between Trust and User Similarity in Online Communities. In: Jensen, C., Poslad, S., Dimitrakos, T. (eds.) iTrust 2004. LNCS, vol. 2995, pp. 251–265. Springer, Heidelberg (2004)
8. Bansal, S., Bansal, A., Blake, M.B.: Trust-based dynamic web service composition using social network analysis. In: 2010 IEEE International Workshop on Business Applications of Social Network Analysis, pp. 1–8 (2010)
9. Maaradji, A., Hakim, H., Daigremont, J., Crespi, N.: Towards a social network based approach for services composition. In: IEEE International Conference on Communications, ICC 2010, pp. 1–5 (2010)
10. Kaufman, L., Rousseeuw, P.: Finding Groups in Data: An Introduction to Cluster Analysis. Wiley Series in Probability and Statistics. Wiley-Interscience (2005)
11. Burnaby, T.: On a method for character weighting a similarity coefficient, employing the concept of information. Mathematical Geology 2, 25–38 (1970)
12. Akcora, C., Carminati, G., Ferrari, E.: Network and profile based measures for user similarities on social networks. In: IRI, pp. 292–298 (2011)

RETRAiN: A REcommendation Tool for Reconfiguration of RetAil BaNk Branch

Rakesh Pimplikar and Sameep Mehta

IBM Research, New Delhi, India
{rakesh.pimplikar,sameepmehta}@in.ibm.com

Abstract. Customers in many developing regions (like India) use physical bank branch as primary and preferred banking channel, resulting in high footfall in the branch. This results in high wait time of customers and high pressure on organization's resources, impacting customer satisfaction (CSAT) as well as employee satisfaction (ESAT) adversely. A naive solution to handle this is to increase the service personnel to cater to the customers. However, this is an unviable alternative because this impacts top and bottom line of the bank. Therefore, organizations are strategically looking for intelligent systems which can help in fine tuning the overall business process to maximize their business objectives while incurring zero or very less investments. Towards this end, we present a system RETRAiN to enable such calibration of various components of bank operations. Based on real time data like waiting customers, service requests, availability of service personnel and business metrics, the system provides recommendations for *reconfiguration* of the operations. The reconfiguration includes selection of *scheduling policy, number of service personnel* and *configuration of service personnel*. We present the overall system along with analysis and optimization algorithms for generating the recommendations. To showcase the efficacy and usefulness of our system, we present results based on data collected over a period of four months from multiple branches of a leading bank in India.

Keywords: Applications and Experience, Retail Banking, Services Quality.

1 Introduction

In this paper, we present a framework to optimize the business process in retail banking through use of analytic and optimization techniques. Customers in many developing countries prefer to visit bank branch for their banking needs. Even though various alternate channels like ATM, Internet banking and mobile banking have evolved significantly in the last few years, the bank branch has still retained its position as the primary service delivery channel in many emerging economies. Due to various factors like literacy rate, lack of infrastructure, legacy of public sector banks, lack of trust in e-transactions, the alternate channels have not been adopted widely. While the private banks in India have nearly 35

C. Liu et al. (Eds.): ICSOC 2012, LNCS 7636, pp. 672–687, 2012.

to 40%[1] transactions through alternate channels, this figure is in single digit for the public sector banks where the vast majority of population still bank. This results in high footfall in the bank making it difficult to maintain Customer Satisfaction (CSAT) at an acceptable level. Retail banking is one of the industries where CSAT plays a key role towards retention and growth of customer base. According to a study done by Financial Service Sector (FSS) consultants in our organization, *wait time, staff interaction, service time*, and *information availability* were discovered as important factors which influence CSAT. Of these *wait time* was found to be the most important factor. Moreover, due to huge volume of customers, the service personnel are also under constant scrutiny of customers and face tremendous pressure (often undue) to be more efficient. This affects the ESAT in an undesirable fashion. Please note that there is causal relationship between ESAT and CSAT, i.e., less pressure on employees will reflect itself in better interaction with customers, which in turn will positively impact CSAT.

A seemingly straightforward solution to the above mentioned challenges is to increase the number of service personnel. This will reduce wait time of customers (thereby increasing CSAT) as well as reduce workload for the service personnel (thereby influencing ESAT). The readers would note that every organization have multiple, sometime conflicting, business metrics. For example, even though CSAT and ESAT is important, the organizations always strive to increase gross profit. Therefore, adding personnel is an unviable solution because the bank has to incur cost for hiring, training, providing seats, procuring computers etc. Therefore, strategically, organizations are looking at intelligent integrated systems which help to meet diverse business objectives, minimize investments and increase Return on Investments (RoI).

In this paper, we provide a transformation framework **RE**commendation **T**ool for **R**econfiguration of Ret**A**il Ba**N**k Branch - **RETRAiN**, which generates various recommendations for the administrator or branch manager to reconfigure the branch operations. The framework does not change the business process associated with customer service but aims to optimize the process for various stakeholders. The system takes into account the real time information of customers, resources and service types to generate operational planning recommendations. Specifically, RETRAiN generates recommendations for the following questions: Given the real time mix of customers, service requests and resources[2]-

1. What is a *good* scheduling policy? Goodness depends on the efficacy of policy with respect to the business metrics. Our setting in non-preemptive, i.e., the customer service request is fulfilled in one go by assigned resource.
2. How many resources should be employed? The correct supply of resources helps in matching customer demand.
3. What should be the configuration of resources? Since the resources we consider are people, they display different proficiency towards different services. Therefore, given the demand, the most efficient resources should be chosen. The historical efficiency data is used for this assignment.

---

[1] This figure was quoted by bank officials during our meetings.
[2] In this article, we use resource and service personnel interchangeably.

Table 1. Comparison with BAU scenario and effect on KPM

Dimension	Current (BAU)	Proposed (RETRAIN)	Optimized KPM
Scheduling Policy	Agnostic to Demand Fixed, FIFO	Demand aware, Dynamic, non-FIFO	Profitability, Wait Time, CSAT
Number of Resources	Fixed or Ad-hoc Change	Computed	ESAT, Small Queue Customer Expectation
Resource Configuration	Universal (for all services) or Dedicated (for single service)	Any Subset of services	Reduction in Service Time

Table 1 highlights the key dimensions which are transformed by RETRAiN, comparison with Business-As-Usual (BAU) scenario and the impact on Key Performance Metrics (KPM) for a retail bank. We briefly describe the data in table.

Scheduling Policy. Currently, all banks use FIFO to schedule and serve customers. While FIFO is a fair policy but it does not lend itself to customer and service differentiation [1]. Given the number of customers coming in branch, the banks are increasingly looking at way to pay more attention to more important customers (High Networth Individuals -HNI) or high profitable services (like Demand Orders) and provide better quality service (low wait times). However, it is not always advisable to use non-FIFO policy. For example, consider the following scenarios:

Scenario 1: Only 10% of customers waiting in branch are HNI.
Scenario 2: 60% of customers waiting in branch are HNI.

It is clear that a priority based scheduling will work very well in Scenario 1 and help server HNIs in a better fashion. However, in Scenario 2, a FIFO based policy might be better because of large number of HNIs in the branch.

Number of Resources. Currently, the number of resources are fixed in the bank or resources are added after manually observing the queue in the bank. In our system, the choice of addition or removal of a resource is taken by analytically computing the impact of such action on the business metrics.

Configuration of Resources. The banks configure the service personnel in two ways either the personnel can provide all services or she provides only one service (like Account Opening or investment advice). However, our system analyzes the current demand of customers while taking into account the individual proficiencies of resources to generate a configuration which allows any subset of services to be assigned to a resource.

To re-iterate, the crux of our framework is to leverage the current customer demand, proficiencies of resources, priority of customers and profitability of services to generate recommendations by employing novel algorithms which will optimize various business metrics.

To further motivate the need and importance of such framework, we present few results derived from data which was collected from multiple branches while deploying some functionality of RETRAiN. Figure 1(a) shows the wait time of customers in each hourly slot for both FIFO as well as RETRAiN. Please note that the wait time is almost equal for both cases. Overall, the FIFO provides a slightly better performance. The wait time using FIFO is 2% less than RE-TRAiN. However, our system does provide the differentiation between customers by recommending non-FIFO based policies. Now, lets look at the number of re-sources used as shown in Figure 1(b). The number of resource hours used by our system is 29 whereas in static system the corresponding number is 40. There-fore, our system is able to reduce 25% resource hours while increasing the wait time by a mere 2%. Moreover, in few slots, our system recommended non-FIFO policy which helped in focusing on important customers and profitable services, thereby, optimizing metrics which matter the most.

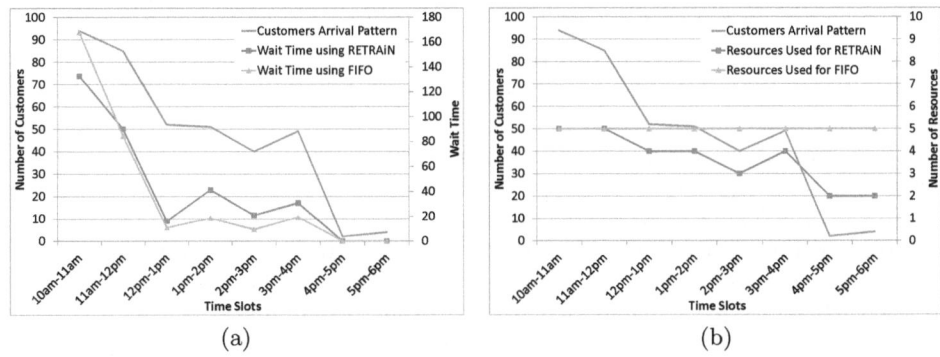

(a)   (b)

Fig. 1. Comparison of wait time and number of resources

Section 2 describes the related work in this field. Due to real time nature of the system, we chose to develop some polynomial time approximation algorithms to handle the technical challenges. We provide those details in Section 3. Finally, we present results on data in Section 4. The data was collected over a period of four months from multiple branches of a leading bank in India.

2   Related Work

In the proposed system, different (human) resources have different efficiency. The problem of scheduling in such settings is known as unrelated machine problem, which has already been proved to be NP-Hard by [2]. Since then, several approx-imation algorithms like [2–8] have been proposed for solving this problem. [9] describes scheduling on unrelated parallel machines where every job is associated with a weight. Our system also has a weight/priority assigned to every customer. But unlike the standard problem where number of machines/resources are fixed, number of resources may vary in our system. Apart from finding a *good* schedule, we also need to find *correct* number of resources to be used in the schedule. Moreover since all resources are not equally efficient, we also need to find which resources are best to be used given the real time state of the system. Our schedule depends not only on makespan but also on business metric. Therefore, solutions mentioned in above literature are not suitable for our system. We propose a polynomial time approximation algorithm for this problem. We point interested readers to some excellent surveys on scheduling [10–12].

The work most pertinent to our work is by [13]. The authors describe a hybrid scheduling policy obtained from the integration of real time scheduling algorithms. Based on the characteristics of jobs, hybrid scheduling policy gets reduced to one of the scheduling algorithms. Their choice of real time scheduling algorithms and formulation of hybrid scheduling policy are very much specific to the embedded real time monitor and control system requirements. Hence it cannot be extended for our system. Moreover, working of a scheduling policy is supposed to be unknown to our system. We need to pick the best scheduling policy based on the business metrics returned by various scheduling policies. This objective of our system overrules the idea of having a hybrid policy.

In our previous work [1], we presented a scheduling algorithm for reducing weighted average weight time of customers in a bank branch, while considering prioritization of customers based on several factors. Our system also considers a priority assigned to every customer. It additionally considers a priority assigned to every service as well requested by customers. The focus of the this paper is not on scheduling algorithm. The scheduling algorithm is one component of the our system. Currently, we use algorithm presented in [1], however, the proposed framework allows for replacing it with any other scheduling algorithm.

In commercial offerings, Adobe and IBM solutions for bank branch transformation [14] concentrates mainly on efficient processing of data and documents. It focuses on providing solutions with more secure, personalized, and compelling communications. It helps in setting up different processes in a bank branch ensuring compliance with government regulations. In the similar spirit, Oracle's Siebel Branch Teller solution [15] provides a comprehensive, customer-centric teller solution with the following features. It has 360-degree view of customer relationship which enables more relevant and targeted sales offers (up/cross sell) and improves customer experience. It streamlines transaction processing via an easy-to-use interface. It improves operational efficiencies driven by centralizing business processes and operational information that traditionally exists in each branch server. A branch transformation system by Talaris [16] focuses on maximizing revenue through increased sales of targeted financial products. It also mentions creating a branch experience to retain and develop customer relationships through exceptional service. The tool advises on strategies to position the bank branch as strategic delivery channel and their expertise assists clients to achieve specific outcomes through targeted investment. However, like our system, none of above mentioned bank branch transformation systems enhances customer experience by employing scheduling policy which is different from traditional FIFO scheduling policy.

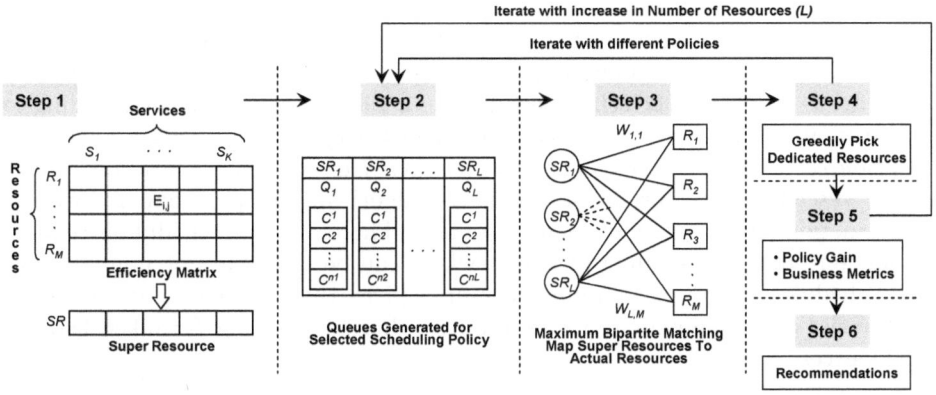

Fig. 2. Depiction of algorithm

Optimizing resource usage for better demand and supply match is not supported by the solutions. Similarly, various Queue Management Systems exist in market to enforce discipline and schedule customers in some predefined order. The solutions generally work on a static fair play principle and schedule customers in a FIFO order. However, any advanced dynamic scheduling (e.g. based on multiple service parameters) and real time decision support system is missing from these products. To best of our knowledge, the proposed framework, associated technical problems and business use cases are novel.

3   Algorithms

Notations. Let $\mathcal{C} = \{C_1, C_2, \ldots, C_N\}$ denote the customers. Assume $\mathcal{S} = \{S_1, S_2, \ldots, S_K\}$ be the list of services offered by the organization. Each customer C_i is associated with an arrival time AT_i, service request(s) $G_i \subseteq \mathcal{S}$ and a data packet D_i. The data packet can contain customer specific information like category, number of years with the bank, average quarterly balance etc. Please note that the focus of our current work is to recommend a policy and therefore, we do not delve into data requirements and the rules for individual policies. The assumption is that the abstract data packet would contain all relevant information which is needed by individual scheduling policies. For example, a policy can give more priority to customers with long running accounts. This priority can be calculated by using data packet. The list of scheduling policies is represented by $\mathcal{P} = \{P_1, P_2, \ldots, P_Q\}$. The list of M resources is denoted by $\mathcal{R} = \{R_1, R_2, \ldots, R_M\}$. E is a $M \times K$ matrix capturing the efficiency of resources. $E_{i,j}$ stores the time which R_i takes to serve a request of type S_j. Finally, $\mathcal{B} = \{B_1, B_2, \ldots, B_U\}$ represents the list of business metrics. Each policy P_i will generate a schedule for serving customers and also evaluate the generated schedule with respect to various business metrics. Some metrics which we consider are *wait time, wait time per category, wait time of important customers, wait time of customers with profitable services*, etc.

Policy Evaluation Function. This function generates a schedule Sch_{P_i} using policy P_i, subset of customers C', subset of resources R' and corresponding efficiency matrix E'. The definition is: `Sch = evalPolicy(`P_i`, C', R', E')`. If there are L resources, the schedule will have L ranked lists one corresponding to each resource. *Please note that generation of the optimal schedule, in presence of resources with different efficiencies, is a NP-Hard problem and is an area of active research.* However, in our proposed algorithm (Steps 1 and 2), we use this function with equally efficient resources. Therefore, the scheduling reduces to single resource scheduling problem (which can be solved in polynomial time) and schedule generation component simply picks the unserved customer from ranked list and assigns it to a free resource, thereby creating L ranked lists for L resources.

Schedule Evaluation Function. Given a schedule generated by P_k, this function returns values of different business metrics. The definition is `B = evalSch(`Sch_{P_k}`, R', E')`. For each resource, the corresponding ranked list is simulated by taking into account the efficiency of the resource.

Gain Evaluation Function. Given a schedule and two policies P_1 & P_2, the function computes the difference in the values of different business metrics. This difference can be construed as gain G which a candidate policy P_2 realizes over current in-use policy P_1. The function is implemented as: $\forall_{i=1}^{U} G(i) = \frac{B_i^{P_2} - B_i^{P_1}}{B_i^{P_1}}$.

3.1   Algorithms

As noted in related work, the problem of scheduling jobs on known number of unrelated machines is a NP-Hard problem. Our problem becomes much harder because the number of machines (resources) and which resources to be used are also unknown. The choice of resources depends upon the characteristics of services being requested by the customers. Moreover, due to complexity of problem arising from varying efficiency of resources, properties which could help to reduce search space do not hold. For example, P_1 can outperform P_2 on a business metric given L resources, however, with addition of one more resource, the performance may be reversed. Similarly, given customer and service data, assume we use a single resource to serve all customers. Let resource R_1 be the best performer followed by R_2 and R_3. However, the top resources together, i.e., $\{R_1, R_2\}$ can be outperformed by combination of $\{R_2, R_3\}$. This can happen if efficiency of R_2 and R_3 complement each other. We propose a solution which iterates over values of L from 1 to M, while picking best L resources and best scheduling policy every time. We recommend L along with the corresponding resources and policy, which perform the best as per the business metrics. The bottleneck here is to chose best L resources, which is a NP-Hard problem.

NP-Hardness Proof. We already know that it is a NP-Complete problem to decide if all edges of a graph can be covered by exactly $\mathcal{K}$ number of vertices.

The problem of selecting optimal set of resources in current setting can be proved to be NP-Hard by reducing Vertex Cover problem to resource selection problem in polynomial time as follows. Create a resource for every vertex in the graph. Create a customer for every edge in the graph who requires a unique service corresponding to the same edge. A resource provides a service in unit time if the vertex corresponding to the resource is one of the two vertices of the edge corresponding to the service. Otherwise resource requires infinite time to provide a service. Now we solve this resource selection problem to select exactly $\mathcal{K}$ resources so as to minimize the makespan. If the value of makespan is infinity, there is at least one customer who requires a service which is not provided by any of those $\mathcal{K}$ selected resources in unit time. It also indicates that all edges in the graph cannot be covered by exactly $\mathcal{K}$ vertices. If the value of makespan is any finite number, every customer can be served in unit time by one of the $\mathcal{K}$ selected resources. It also indicates that all edges of the graph can be covered by $\mathcal{K}$ vertices corresponding to the $\mathcal{K}$ selected resources. Thus we can use resource selection problem to solve vertex cover problem. Clearly, reduction of vertex cover to resource selection problem takes polynomial time. Hence resource selection problem is harder than vertex cover problem and can be included in NP-Hard category. Even if we are given $\mathcal{K}$ optimal resources, we cannot verify it in polynomial time. We need to enumerate all other combinations of $\mathcal{K}$ resources to verify if the given solution actually results in the smallest makespan.

Figure 2 presents the key steps of the proposed solution.

Step 1. For each service type S_j, we find the resource R_i which takes the least time to provide the service and store the service time, $E_{i,j}$, in SR. Formally, $SR_j = \min\{E_{*,j}\}$. SR can be conceived as a *Super Resource* which provides all services in minimum time possible.

Step 2. In this step, a schedule is generated given a scheduling policy $P_k \in \mathcal{P}$ and L resources where $1 \leq L \leq M$. The point to note is that all L resources are taken to be *super resources*. Moreover, with this setup we can use `evalPolicy` to generate schedule. This construction provides, hypothetically, the best performance (in terms of average wait time) which can be achieved by L resources. In next step we map the super resources to actual resources while incurring an increase in wait time. For a resource SR_i and Policy P_k, the average wait time $WT_{SR_i}^{P_k}$ of assigned customers (Q_i in Step 2 of Figure 2) as per policy P_k is computed by using `evalSch`.

Step 3. In this step we map L super resources to L actual resources while minimizing the increase in wait time. We pose this problem as a maximum bipartite matching with edge weights. Super Resources form one set of vertices while actual resources the other set. The graph is fully connected because every super resource can be replaced by any of the actual resource. The cost of replacing a super resource by actual resource is $C_{i,j} = WT_{R_j}^{P_k} - WT_{SR_i}^{P_k}$. The cost/penalty captures the increase in wait time if SR_i is replaced by R_j. Since the objective is to find maximum weight matching, the weights are computed as $W_{i,j} = max\{C_{*,*}\} - C_{i,j}+1$. We use existing algorithm proposed by [17] to find the matching. Algorithm takes $O(mn \log_{\lceil m/n+1 \rceil} n)$ where n is the number of nodes and m is the number of edges.

If all resources are equally efficient or if we can order them in decreasing order of their efficiencies such that R_i is more efficient than R_j in providing all services for $i < j$, then resources selected in step 3 are nothing but the optimal resources. Step 3 fails to get optimal resources when efficiencies of resources complement each other for different services, for example, $E_{1,1} < E_{2,1}$, but $E_{1,2} > E_{2,2}$. Step 4 provides a greedy solution to fix this problem.

Step 4. Customers are scheduled in Step 2 considering super resources. It results in service requests to be uniformly distributed among all resources. This overrules the inclusion of resources who are extremely efficient in providing one service, but equally bad in providing other services. In optimal solution, these resources might have been selected to provide that one service dedicatedly, resulting in reduction of total wait time of customers. Figure 3 represents an algorithm to greedily select such dedicated resources.

Require: $\mathcal{R}^L$, set of L resources selected in Step 3;
   $\mathcal{R}^C$, set of all available resources to be considered;
   E, efficiency matrix; RC_k, request count for service S_k;
   $RS_{i,k}$, number of requests of service S_k to be served by R_i;
   P, policy in consideration; C', waiting customers; WT_{min}, total wait time using $\mathcal{R}^L$

1: **while** $\mathcal{R}^C \neq \emptyset$ && $\max_i RC_i > 0$ **do**
2:   Find a service with maximum requests, $m \leftarrow \text{argmax}_k RC_k$
3:   Find the most efficient resource for service S_m, $d \leftarrow \text{argmin}_{i \in \mathcal{R}^C} E_{i,m}$
4:   $\mathcal{R}^C \leftarrow \mathcal{R}^C - \{R_d\}$
5:   **if** $R_d \notin \mathcal{R}^L$ **then**
6:     **for all** $R_i \in \mathcal{R}^L$ **do**
7:       Prepare a new set by replacing R_i with R_d, $\mathcal{R}^L_{new} \leftarrow (\mathcal{R}^L - \{R_i\}) \cup \{R_d\}$
8:       $Sch = \texttt{evalPolicy}(P, C', \mathcal{R}^L_{new}, E)$
9:       Compute total wait time, $WT_i = \texttt{evalSch}(Sch, \mathcal{R}^L_{new}, E)$
10:    **end for**
11:    **if** $\min_i WT_i < WT_{min}$ **then**
12:      Find a resource to be removed from $\mathcal{R}^L$, $n \leftarrow \text{argmin}_i WT_i$
13:      Update minimum total wait time, $WT_{min} \leftarrow WT_n$
14:      Replace R_n with R_d in $\mathcal{R}^L$, $\mathcal{R}^L \leftarrow (\mathcal{R}^L - \{R_n\}) \cup \{R_d\}$
15:      Decrease request count for S_m, $RC_m \leftarrow RC_m - RS_{d,m}$
16:    **end if**
17: **else**
18:    Decrease request count for S_m, $RC_m \leftarrow RC_m - RS_{d,m}$
19: **end if**
20: **end while**

Fig. 3. Algorithm to select dedicated resources

'IF' condition on line 11 ensures that whenever a resource is replaced by a new dedicate resource on line 14, our solution always results in decreased total wait time and we approach towards the optimal solution. Though we could not prove the approximation bound for our algorithm because of its complexity, it never deviated from optimal solution by a factor more than 2 during our experiments.

Steps 2-4 are repeated by keeping the resources fixed at L and changing the policy. At the end of this iteration, we would have identified L *best* resources for each P_k.

Step 5. In this step we compute the gain $\mathcal{G}$ and other business metrics for each policy and use a rule based system to generate candidate recommendations. Next, we enumerate the rules and also describe intuition behind them:

- *Rule 1.* The Gain ($\mathcal{G}$) over current configuration should be greater than θ_1 where θ_1 defines the improvement which the organization would like to witness. All policies with corresponding gain greater than θ_1 are chosen to generate candidate recommendations. In current deployment, average wait time of all customers is used to compute gain. If gain is too less, it implies that the organization is changing a business process with a new one without substantial improvements.
- *Rule 2.* RETRAiN generates configuration recommendations after every F minutes. Given policy (selected by Rule 1) and set of resources, we compute how many customers can be served in next F minutes. Subtracting this from the total waiting customers C' (used in Policy Evaluation), gives the number of unserved customers UC at the end of next F minutes. If $\frac{UC}{C'} \leq \theta_2$, then the configuration gets added to candidate recommendations.

The configurations which satisfy both rules are tagged as candidate recommendations with the following details $\{P_k, C', L, \mathcal{R}', E', \mathcal{G}, \frac{UC}{C'}\}$. If no configuration satisfies rules, then number of resources is increased by 1 and Step 2 is repeated. The process is continued till $L \leq M$.

Step 6. All the candidate recommendations are presented to the administrator to choose from. The chosen recommendation then replaces the current configuration and is used for next F minutes. At this point, we would like to share the key motivation of involving domain expert as opposed to the completely automated system. Consider an example where recommendation CR_1 results in gain of 5% whereas CR_2 shows gain of 4.9%. An automated system will choose CR_1 as new configuration. However, the domain expert can investigate respective policies and conclude that the policy used in CR_2 enforces fairness whereas CR_1 gives high preference to a set of customers. In this case, based on business logic and other real time factors, she may decide to choose CR_2. Moreover, in such scenarios, the rules itself keep changing based on state of the system including number of customers, number of available resources, time of month, special promotion season etc. Therefore, the same expert can take different decisions based on real time state of the physical system. It would be very challenging to encode and prioritize full expert knowledge base with different permutations of system state.

4   Results

The experiments are conducted on real data collected during (partial) deployment of RETRAiN at multiple branches of a leading bank in India. Over the deployment period, our system scheduled around 25000 customers. Category 2 (important customers) accounted for around 60% of customers whereas around 1500 customers were in Category 1 (most important customers). Out of 30000 service requests, around 75% were deemed to have positive value for the bank. For each branch we collected one week of data with fixed resources and FIFO policy. This data was used to learn the model and also baseline various metrics.

We demonstrate the working of our algorithm on different scenarios to showcase the efficacy of the proposed solution. We consider four different categories (priorities) of customers, denoted as $Cat_1, \ldots, Cat_4$. These categories scaled by appropriate weight vector are used in ranking customers with Weighted Shortest Job First (WSJF) policy. Different weighing vectors result in different policies. For example, weight vector (0.5, 1, 1, 1) suggests that Cat_1 customer is twice more important than any other category. Similarly, vector (0, 1, 1, 1) implies that Cat_1 customers should be served as soon as a resource is free by pushing it ahead of all other customers. Another weighing vector (1, 1 ,1, 5) captures that all customers except Cat_4 are equal and Cat_4 would have to wait much longer. Similarly we consider five different service categories as $S_1, \ldots, S_5$. For both customer and service categories, lower the category id, higher is the importance. There are five resources in our setup with different proficiencies for different services as mentioned in Table 2. Every cell represents the average time (in seconds) required by corresponding resource to provide the corresponding service. We computed the efficiency matrix from the collected data.

Table 2. Efficiency matrix

Resources\Services	S_1	S_2	S_3	S_4	S_5
R_1	258.17	275.49	250.86	180.54	236.64
R_2	199.70	201.89	185.73	145.60	191.91
R_3	312.95	548.07	309.27	189.34	317.12
R_4	453.57	300.62	123.95	240.66	253.90
R_5	308.67	312.56	220.17	168.18	135.09

Key Results. The highlights of our deployment are:

– The wait time of Cat 2 customers reduced by 30% while the most important customers (Cat 1) experienced a wait time reduction of 83%. This can be attributed to non-FIFO policies. Due to large chunk of customers (65%) in these two categories, the overall wait time over all customers went down as compared to pure FIFO policy.

- The wait time of least important customers (10% by volume) increased by 25%.
- For the above mentioned results, the number of resources were kept fixed (same as in baseline data). When the number of resources and their config-uration was optimized, we found that by using $\approx 25\%$ less resources we can maintain same wait time (within $\pm 2\%$) as in baseline data.
- We conducted an informal survey of customers to get their feedback on the system. Around 70% customers felt reduction in wait time. Around 19% cus-tomers had difficulty to understand the new system. Overall 82% customers felt system has made a positive impact and thereby increasing CSAT.
- Informally, the bank staff also acknowledged the impact of the system. The support was exemplary.

Next, we show some of the expository results. We consider FIFO as the baseline policy. Different variants of WSJF constitute the policy bank. The experiments use RETRAiN frequency F as 30 minutes. From real data we observed that during peak hours, around 60 customers come to branch in an hour. Therefore, in our experiments we use 30 customers. Please note the arrival frequency changes through the day. However, we choose the peak period because RETRAiN is motivated to help banks in peak periods. We set $\theta_1 = 0.1$, i.e., a policy with improvement of at least 10% over FIFO should be selected for the current time slot.

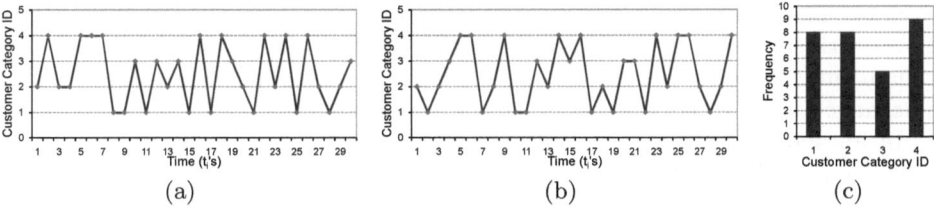

(a)   (b)   (c)

Fig. 4. Uniform ordering, (a) WSJF recommended (b) FIFO recommended (c) Cus-tomer category distribution

In our first setting we study the effect of arrival patterns of customer cate-gories on policy selection. Figure 4(a) shows a pattern where customer categories are uniformly ordered and improvement of WSJF over FIFO is computed to be 21% ($> \theta_1$). Therefore, WSJF policy is selected as a candidate recommendation. Figure 4(c) shows the histogram of different customer categories in the pattern. Figure 4(b) shows a different arrival pattern for the same frequencies of cate-gories. However, improvement of WSJF over FIFO in this case is very less, 9.3% ($< \theta_1$). Therefore, FIFO is selected. It is evident that policy selection depends on the arrival pattern of customer categories.

Consider a special case as shown in Figure 5 where there are maximum cus-tomers of the same category Cat_2 and others are distributed among other cate-gories. Table 3 shows the two different WSJF and FIFO numbers (in seconds).

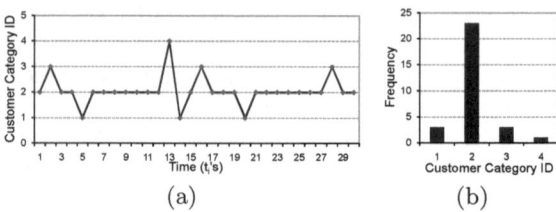

Fig. 5. Skewed distribution

Table 3. Comparison of different policies

Policy	All Customers	Cat_1	Cat_2	Cat_3	Cat_4
FIFO	309.1	309.1	309.1	309.1	309.1
WSJF$_1$	304.70	27.89	309.73	395.60	848
WSJF$_2$	309.95	235.07	304.27	384.34	511

Since FIFO does not differentiate between customers, average wait time over all customers is taken to be wait time in each category as well. WSJF$_1$ drastically improves the wait time of Cat_1 customers, however, customers in Cat_4 are penalized heavily. Moreover, the improvement in overall wait time (over FIFO) is marginal. This small improvement for Cat_1 may not justify heavy increase in the wait time for other customers. Moreover, in such scenarios, the fairness provided by FIFO also plays a role in the decision. However, WSJF$_2$ provides a viable alternative where wait time of important customers Cat_1 decreases (by 23%) with small increase for Cat_4 customers. Based on domain knowledge, the admin can choose between FIFO or WSJF$_2$. Wait time of Cat_2 remains almost unchanged in all three settings.

In an another setting, we study the effect of arrival patterns of service requests on number of resources. Figure 6(a) and Figure 6(b) show two different arrival patterns of service categories but with same frequencies as depicted in Figure 6(c). In Figure 6(a) all services are uniformly ordered over the current time slot and three best resources are suggested to be $\{R_1, R_2, R_5\}$. Proficiency matrix mentioned in Table 2 is used in selecting these resources. If we observe this matrix, services S_1 and S_2 are most time consuming. Clearly if these two services are clustered in the earlier part of the slot as shown in Figure 6(b), then overall wait time of all customers increases. To reduce this wait time, system is reconfigured and 4 resources are suggested as $\{R_1, R_2, R_4, R_5\}$ instead of just 3 in previous case. Thus order of services and time required to process them are important factors to suggest *correct* resources.

As noted in algorithm, we select minimum number of resources where $\frac{UC}{C'} \leq \theta_2$. In our setup, we have $\theta_2 = 0.1$. For a pattern shown in Figure 6(a) where three resources are suggested, unserved customers are just 3 out of 30 ($\frac{UC}{C'} = 0.1$) and average wait time is 313s. Now if we add one more resource, the average wait time decreases to 205s which is good for CSAT, but at the end of the slot all four resources remain idle for 5 to 10 minutes. To avoid this under utilization, θ_2 plays an important role.

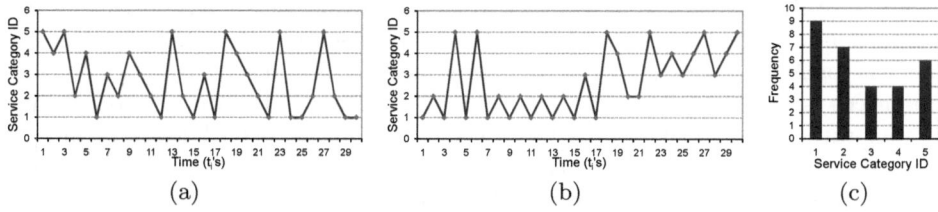

Fig. 6. (a) Uniform ordering, three resources recommended (b) Non-uniform ordering, four resources recommended (c) Service category distribution

We also present results of our system when run for an entire day over real time data. Figure 7 shows recommendations given by our system for different time slots of a day in a branch of a leading bank in India. RETRAiN frequency F is set to be 1 hour. Horizontal axis shows slot durations along with recommended policies and selected resources. Figure 7(a) shows distributions of customer categories for different time slots, while Figure 7(b) shows distributions of service categories for corresponding times slots. Initially, when customers are small in number in first slot, only two resources are selected. As we can observe services S_3 and S_4 are predominantly required by customers in first slot. So resources R_2 and R_5 are selected, because they are more efficient than others in providing S_3 and S_4, which is clear from efficiency matrix shown in Table 2. WSJF policy is recommended by our system for the first slot, as we are getting improvement greater than θ_1 over FIFO. FIFO is recommended for second and third slots, because WSJF has smaller improvement over FIFO in these slots. 4 and 5 resources are selected respectively for these slots, because our system observed increased in number of customers. When branch load decreases in later slots, resources are removed and appropriate policies are recommended. You can observe in Figure 7(b) that service S_4 is having high demand through out the day. So resource R_2 is selected for all time slots, as he is the most efficient in providing service S_4.

Thus resources are better managed by our system and now there is no need for all 5 resources to be engaged for all the slots. This directly leads to reduction of human hours from 30 to just 14 (53%).

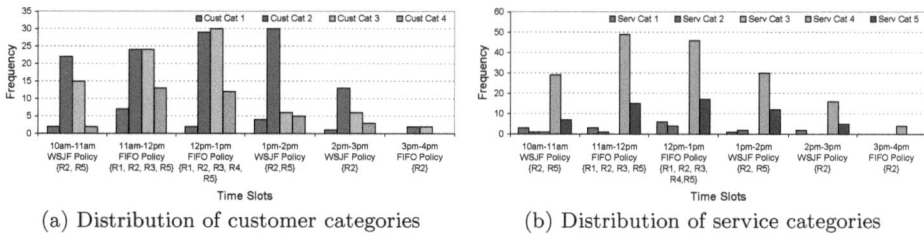

(a) Distribution of customer categories   (b) Distribution of service categories

Fig. 7. Recommendations for entire day

Algorithmic Complexity and Timing Results. Scheduling customers using a policy with a single resource is typically a sorting task. The complexity is $O(N \log N)$. Generation of actual schedule by assigning customers to super resources is $O(N \log L)$ where $1 \leq L \leq M$. Therefore, the overall complexity of generating schedule for super resources is $O(N \log N) + O(N \log M)$. Finally, we create a bipartite graph which can have maximum $M * M$ edges and $2 * M$ nodes (if $L = M$). So, complexity of finding maximum bipartite matching is $O(M^3)$ using [17]. The steps are repeated for every policy (1 to Q) and number of resources (1 to M). So overall complexity of running our algorithm is dominated by $O(Q \times M \times M^3)$. With $Q = 10$ (number of candidate policies), 90 customers and 7 resources, our system generates recommendations in approximately 2 seconds. Due to the limit on number of resources which the branch can accommodate (typically 3 to 7), M^4 is manageable. The time increases linearly with the increase in number of policies.

5 Conclusions and Future Work

In this paper, we presented an integrated system RETRAiN which analyzes the real time mix of customers, service requests and resources and recommends a good configuration for optimizing the retail bank branch operations. The system tries to use minimum resources and strives to improve business metrics. We presented an approximation algorithm which discovers how many and which resources should be used. We presented some results on real data collected from a leading bank in India. Currently, we are conducting more experiments to study the quality of our algorithm vis-a-vis optimal algorithm. The problem is modeled as math program and solved using existing solver for optimal recommendation. Solving math program for large number of instances and comparing it with our algorithm will enable us to perform a gap analysis. Finally, we are also exploring the possibility of deploying the complete RETRAiN system in live customer environment as well as other domains like call centers.

References

1. Mehta, S., Chafle, G., Parija, G.R., Kedia, V.: A system for providing differentiated qos in retail banking. In: IJCAI, pp. 2494–2499 (2011)
2. Lenstra, J.K., Shmoys, D.B., Tardos, É.: Approximation algorithms for scheduling unrelated parallel machines. Math. Program. 46, 259–271 (1990)
3. Martello, S., Soumis, F., Toth, P.: Exact and approximation algorithms for makespan minimization on unrelated parallel machines. Discrete Applied Mathematics 75(2), 169–188 (1997)
4. Jansen, K., Porkolab, L.: Improved approximation schemes for scheduling unrelated parallel machines. In: Proceedings of the Thirty-First Annual ACM Symposium on Theory of Computing, STOC 1999, pp. 408–417. ACM, New York (1999)
5. Efraimidis, Spirakis: Randomized approximation schemes for scheduling unrelated parallel machines. In: ECCCTR: Electronic Colloquium on Computational Complexity, technical reports (2000)

6. Efraimidis, Spirakis: Approximation schemes for scheduling and covering on unrelated machines. TCS: Theoretical Computer Science 359 (2006)
7. Gairing, M., Monien, B., Woclaw, A.: A faster combinatorial approximation algorithm for scheduling unrelated parallel machines. Theor. Comput. Sci. 380(1-2), 87–99 (2007)
8. Verschae, J., Wiese, A.: On the Configuration-LP for Scheduling on Unrelated Machines. In: Demetrescu, C., Halldórsson, M.M. (eds.) ESA 2011. LNCS, vol. 6942, pp. 530–542. Springer, Heidelberg (2011)
9. Chudak, F.A.: A min-sum 3/2-approximation algorithm for scheduling unrelated parallel machines. Journal of Scheduling 2, 73–77 (1999)
10. Sgall, J.: On-line Scheduling. In: Fiat, A., Woeginger, G.J. (eds.) Online Algorithms 1996. LNCS, vol. 1442, pp. 196–231. Springer, Heidelberg (1998)
11. Vazirani, V.: Approximation Algorithms. Springer (2001)
12. Karger, D., Stein, C., Wein, J.: Scheduling algorithms. In: Handbook of Algorithms and Theory of Computation. CRC Press (2010)
13. Deng, Q., Lv, M., Yu, G.: Selecting a Scheduling Policy for Embedded Real-Time Monitor and Control Systems. In: Wu, Z., Chen, C., Guo, M., Bu, J. (eds.) ICESS 2004. LNCS, vol. 3605, pp. 494–501. Springer, Heidelberg (2005)
14. Adobe, IBM: Solutions for bank branch transformation,
http://www.adobe.com/enterprise/partners/ibm/banking.html
15. Oracle: Siebel branch teller,
http://www.oracle.com/us/industries/financial-services/046715.html
16. Talaris: Branch transformation,
http://www.talaris.com/en-gb/solutions/talaris-consulting/
branch-transformation.aspx
17. Galil, Z.: Efficient algorithms for finding maximum matching in graphs. ACM Computing Surveys 18(1), 23 (1986)

Automate Back Office Activity Monitoring to Drive Operational Excellence

Miao He[1], Tao Qin[1], Sai Zeng[2], Changrui Ren[1], and Lei Yuan[3]

[1] IBM Research, China
{hmhem,qintao,rencr}@cn.ibm.com
[2] IBM T.J. Watson Research Center
saizeng@us.ibm.com
[3] IBM China Development Lab
leiycdl@cn.ibm.com

Abstract. Business process outsourcing (BPO) is growing rapidly with intensive competition. BPO providers aim to deliver high quality services with low cost. One of the key drivers is to optimize human resource utilization. It is critical to monitor and measure the activities of the practitioners in order to identify inefficient workers, unnecessary waste in operations, and non-standardized operations. Today's practices to monitor and measure the human activities are manual and error-prone. Motivated by increasing the accuracy and eliminating manual efforts for monitoring and measuring human activities, in this paper we present our research work to automatically classify and time the daily activity of a practitioner. Even though human behavior variations and noises brings substantial deviations and randomness, the developed *activity classifier and timer* handles the variations and reduces the noise to a satisfactory extent. The pilot results demonstrate 98.18% accuracy to classify transactions into the activity taxonomy, and 91.54% accuracy to find out the transaction cycle time therefore to aggregate to the time spent on each activity. The results are highly valued by our business partners, and the tool is considered as a revolutionary solution for human activity monitoring and measurement.

1 Introduction

Business process outsourcing (BPO) refers to the contracting of the operations and responsibilities of specific, mostly "non-core", business functions (or processes) to a third-party service provider. The outsourced functions can be "human resources, information technology, indirect procurement, finance, and accounting, etc" [10]. BPO is a rapidly growing offshore market with a projected annual growth rate of 60 percent according to [17], but not every provider has the chance to thrive in the undergoing industry prosperity. For instance, although Gartner forecasts a 6.3% in 2011 and 5% growth in 2012 for the worldwide market [1], it meanwhile predicts that "one-quarter of the top BPO operatives will not exist as separate entities in 2012," due to "economic risks, loss-making contracts, and inability to adapt to standardized delivery models" [5].

C. Liu et al. (Eds.): ICSOC 2012, LNCS 7636, pp. 688–702, 2012.
© Springer-Verlag Berlin Heidelberg 2012

Being aware that a wide variety of factors together drives a provider's success [3, 6, 18], this application-oriented research aims to help providers achieve *operational excellence* in their *back office* processes. More specifically, we monitor and capture the *desktop application usages* of practitioners, which account for more than 90% of their working time. Based on application usages, we further develop the *activity classifier and timer*. Let's explain two key terms, *activity* and *transaction*, which will be revisited many times in the following.

Activity	The most granular level in the process taxonomy. Each activity has a particular and unique succession of processing procedures, and different activities have different successions of processing procedures.
Transaction	A transaction is an instance of a particular activity type.

Note that "transaction" has a many-to-one relation against "activity" type. Suppose there is an activity called "hotel invoice processing," then we can have one transaction with invoice number 123, and another with invoice number 456 - same activity type, differed transaction IDs (invoice numbers).

Activity classifier and timer has dual objectives - identify the correct *activity type* for each transaction, and simultaneously find the *start* and *end time* of each transaction. In our solution, a training module first learns the sequential application usage patterns of each activity type. This module takes application events with class label (the activity type) as input and implement sequential pattern mining algorithms. Then a testing module classifies and times a practitioner's work. Handling various human behavior variations and noises in the testing phase is technically challenging, because variations and noises lead to imperfect matching between actual application usages with the patterns learnt from standard operations. Typical variations and noises include (partial) batch processing, random click on applications, incomplete processing procedures, combined or interleaved processing and so on. If not handled, these variations and noises impose significantly negative impact on accuracy of classification and timing. In our approach, we incorporate our knowledge into human behaviors to handle variations and noises, and the details can be found in Section 3.

Our approach was implemented in a tool (the activity classifier and timer) and tested in a pilot with a few rounds of result validation. Our business shareholder from a leading BPO provider, endorses four major business benefits which were never thought to be feasible in the past. The foremost important benefit is that this tool can automate today's manual activity monitoring with high accuracy. One common practice of today's activity monitoring relies on practitioners to report their time spent on daily activities, plus team leads conduct floor auditing. Our solution eliminates the manual effort of "self reporting" and "floor auditing." The second benefit is that the solution can accurately count the number of transactions processed for each activity. Thirdly, we have observed an obvious behavior change of practitioners after the tool has been deployed - they become more efficient with less waste in operations just by awareness of "being watched" by the tool. Lastly, the tool can also discover the non-standard or exceptional operations, some of which should, but not yet, be documented in the desktop procedures.

In the remaining part of this paper, we will review related work in Section 2. Section 3 describes our approach in details, especially how we handle human behavior variations and noises featured in the back office service delivery. Section 4 illustrates the results, findings and business benefits after implementing our tool to the production environment. In Section 5 we conclude our work.

2   Related Work

To the best knowledge of the authors, there are no literatures relevant to automatic timer on service cycles based on knowledge discovery or data mining. But classification, the task of assigning an input object to one of several predefined categories, has many diverse applications. To name just a few, Bozorgi et al. train linear support vector machines (SVMs) on high dimension feature vectors to classify software vulnerabilities [4]; [7] develop a two-phase classifier that caters to large-scale file categorization; and [9] train a rule-based classifier for fingerprint classification. Some of the classification works focus on service process delivery like us. For example, Tang et al. develop a classifier to label the recorded conversations into a hierarchical taxonomy of the call types for a call center [16]. [11] categorize incoming emails to the contact centers based upon their contents. The resulted classifier identifies root, inner and leaf messages to track the progress of the email interactions. Note that a root message and a leaf message is the initiation and close of an interaction respectively, while an inner message is in between.

The most common classification algorithms include, but not limited to, decision tree, rule-based classifiers, nearest neighbor classifiers, Bayesian classifiers, artificial neural network, support vector machine, etc [15]. The mentioned methods depend on features rather than *feature sequences* to construct the corresponding classifiers. However, sequential patterns in application usage does matter much in our problem. Agrawal and Srikant first introduce *sequential pattern mining* in 1995 [2], which is trying to find if there exist any specific order of the occurrence of events. Notable applications area include "customer purchase behavior, Web access patterns, scientific experiments, disease treatments, natural disasters, DNA sequences, and so on" [12]. There are two classical sets of algorithms and derivatives in this area. One thought is to base the learning process upon the "Apriori" property in association rule mining, including AprioriAll, AprioriSome, DynamicSome in [2] , GSP in [14] and SPADE in [19], etc. The other series of algorithms proposed rely on recursively projecting the data sets into mutually exclusive subsets to speed up mining by avoiding scanning the entire database, see FreeSpan [8] and PrefixSpan [12] for more details.

3   Activity Classifier and Timer

We have developed a tool called *system timer* capable of capturing the starting and ending of every *application event, machine idle* and *keyboard idle*. An event refers to a non-switching stay on one application page. For example, system timer will record the starting time as soon as one opens Facebook in IE. Upon switching to Twitter after 10 seconds stay on Facebook, the tool promptly records the ending time of the Facebook event. Obviously, the ending time of Facebook is the starting time of Twitter. Machine idle refers to a special event type when a desktop is locked and keyboard idle is also a special event type when one let the computer on with neither mouse movement nor any key striking for a while. In this way, we can capture application events at very fine granularity which serves as the basis of the activity classifier and timer.

Before delving into the approach, we would like to walk the audience through most common non-standard human behaviors as summarized in Table 1. Figure 1 provides graphical illustrations for normal processing and variations, where each distinct shape represents a distinct application page (a processing step), and shapes with the same filling forms an end-to-end transaction. Transactions are of different activity types if their shape sequences are not identical. Omitted processing steps are colored gray. We define end-to-end transaction processing that exactly follows documented desktop procedures to be normal. Patternized deviations from the normal cases are called variations, while noises are unpredictable fluctuations around the normal cases without pattern governance. Our pilot involves eight activity types, each of which has only one succession of standard processing procedures. In other words, the service delivery center defines one standard pattern for each activity type. However, it turns out to have 40 variational sequential patterns after learning.

Understanding the variations and noises we are facing, we design an effective approach as shown in Figure 2. The approach makes integrated use of knowledge

Table 1. Non-standard Human Behaviors

Human Behavior Variations

Index	Variation type	Description
Var-1	Incomplete processing	Only early or later steps of a transaction are spotted.
Var-2	Batch processing	Multiple transactions of the same activity type form a work unit, where some of the steps (featured application pages) are triggered in batch, for example, open ten invoices one after another before processing them one by one.
Var-3	Interleaved processing	Multiple transactions of different activity types form a work unit, where the required steps (featured application pages) of each transaction appear in an interleaving way.
Var-4	Combined processing	Multiple transactions of different activity types form a work unit, where not all the required steps (featured application pages) can be found for at least one of the activities.

Human Behavior Noises

Index	Noise type	Description
Noi-1	Repetitive visits	It is hard for a practitioner to complete everything on an application page without switches, and therefore non-deterministic number of visits on the same pages could occur.
Noi-2	Inadvertent clicks	It is possible to click some featured application pages of other activity types irrelevant to the transaction under processing. The inadvertent clicks put our approach in trouble to correctly label and time the actual activity being carried out.

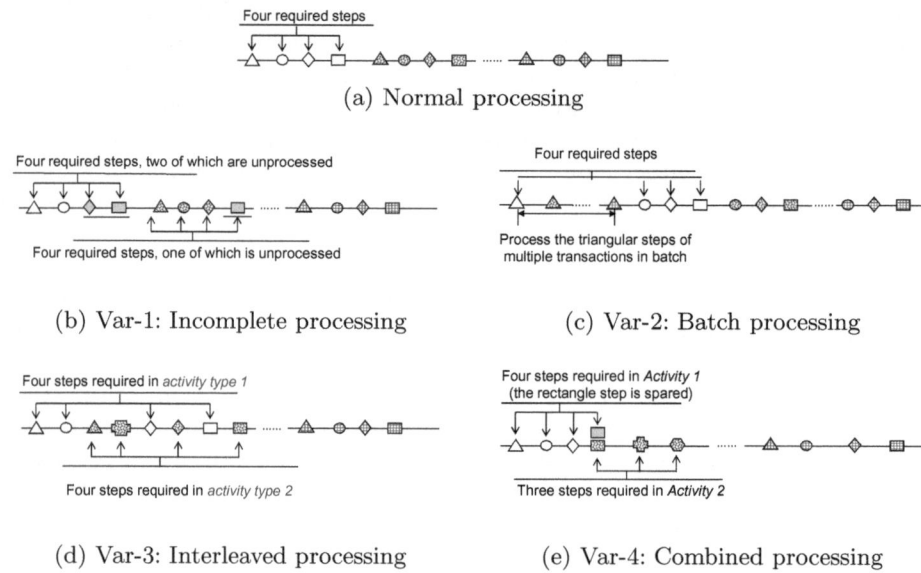

(a) Normal processing

(b) Var-1: Incomplete processing   (c) Var-2: Batch processing

(d) Var-3: Interleaved processing   (e) Var-4: Combined processing

Fig. 1. Graphical illustration of variations

discovery techniques including sequential pattern mining, scoring function, confidence interval. It follows the generic "training-testing" scheme, but attentive audience may notice that the testing phase, starting from *work unit partition*, is much more complicated than conventional approaches. The complexities result from *simultaneous classification and timing* of each transaction cycle, as well as the addressing of variations and noises as indicated in Table 1.

We also highlight that this approach embeds two sequential pattern mining modules for normal and deviated cases, respectively. Henceforth, we will use *deviated cases* to refer to *cases with human behavior variations* described in Table 1. The normal sequential pattern mining is conducted only once, with training data captured during the time veteran staffs, who strictly follow the desktop procedures, are doing their work. The training for deviated cases, on the contrary, requires iterative efforts, since it is impossible for practitioners to intentionally provide the full set of variations. We therefore incrementally expand the training data set for deviated cases with application events going through the tool but remaining unclassified. Note that practitioners usually will not diverge from the standard procedures unless shortcuts are discovered or un-documented exceptional requests enter. In the following, we are going to describe the key steps of the activity classifier and timer depicted in Figure 2.

Step 0 Initialization: The initialization includes *signature page identification* and *sequential pattern mining for normal cases*. A signature page meets two conditions. First it is a must that cannot be spared for a particular activity type, and secondly it can differentiate different transactions of the same activity type. In this work, we use the application page containing the unique transaction ID, or transaction ID page in short, as the signature page. Here we take advantage of the business process nature which is primarily transaction based. In sequential pattern mining, we always included the signature page as the first element in a pattern. We will not elaborate how we implement the "Apriopri-like" algorithm here. Interesting readers could refer to [13]. The initial sequential pattern mining extracts frequent sequential application patterns for normal transaction cycles. We initiate a toy example in the below, which will be used to demonstrate the flow of our approach, where each letter represents a different application page and letters with subscript (transaction ID) are the signature pages.

The problem setting of toy example

Normal pattern (learnt by mining)	$\{ABCD_xEFG\}$, $\{HI_xJ\}$, $\{ECD_xE\}$
Interleaved pattern (learnt by mining)	$\{ABCD_xHI_xEFGJ\}$, enclosed activities are $\{ABCD_xEFG\}$ and $\{HI_xJ\}$
Input sequence	$\{ECD_1EABCD_3HI_8EFGJ\}$

Step 1 Work unit partition: We partition the whole day application events by signature pages or signature page combinations, where the events around a signature page are considered plausible to belong to the same transaction. In our example, the three signature pages could partition the input sequence into three work units, i.e., $\{ECD_1EABC\}$, $\{EABCD_3H\}$, $\{HI_8EFGJ\}$. Alternatively, we can partition the sequence into two work units, i.e., $\{ECD_1EABC\}$ and $\{EABCD_3HI_8EFGJ\}$ since the "$D - I$" signature combination may form an interleaved work pattern learnt beforehand. Note that the applications between two signature pages (or signature page combinations) are considered possible to belong to both transactions at this phase. For instance, the $EABC$ between signature pages D_1 and D_3 are temporarily put into both work units. We point out that this step generates partitions in all the possible ways and feeds them into the following steps. In this example, we will generate partitions in two ways where one include three isolated work units, and the other include one isolated plus one interleaved work unit.

Step 2 Pattern testing and scoring: This critical step uses frequent patterns of normal and deviated cases to test if they occur around the signature pages or signature page combinations *appropriately*. The appropriateness means featured pages occur, and occur in the expected order. It is worth mentioning that we allow "partial matching," *which does not require a work unit containing 100% application pages in a pattern or arranging featured application events exactly as the pattern sequence.* We apply this principle because incomplete processing cases (Var-1) cannot have all the featured application events, while batch processing (Var-2) cannot guarantee that all the transactions contain all the featured events. In addition, this principle hedges against the risk of high generation error as a result of overfitting, which means that patterns learnt in the training phase might only work well for the training set, but are not superior for testing set.

However, "Partial matching" principle on the other hand causes the problem of having multiple candidates. It is common that activities processed by the same team (back office) are related with each other. The inherent relevance usu-

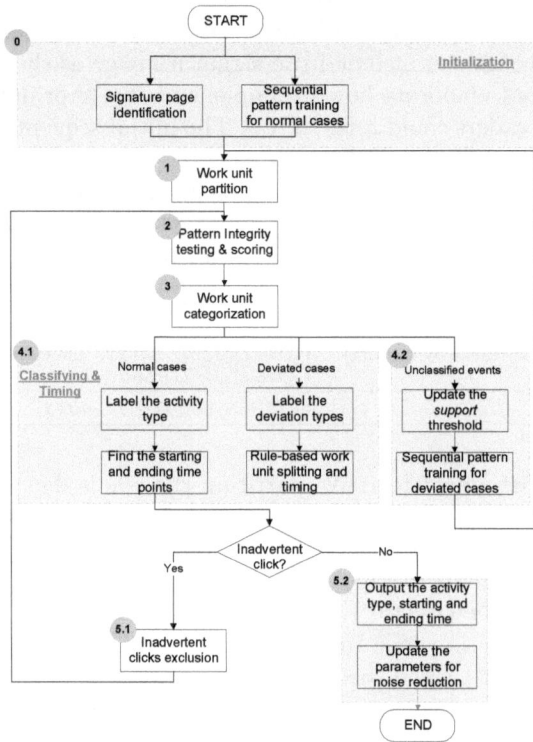

Fig. 2. The work flow

ally leads to application sharing to some extent. For example, activity "invoice auditing" is a prerequisite of activity "invoice payment," and both activities visit the same application to retrieve invoices. Therefore, Application sharing plus "partial matching" principle implies multiple candidate patterns. We design score function

$$score = \frac{\text{number of appropriately matched pages}}{\text{number of pattern pages}} \tag{1}$$

to choose the best from the candidate patterns. Returning to the toy example, we test and score each candidate pattern as shown in Table 2.

Theorem 1. *When a transaction can either be extracted from an isolated work unit or part of an interleaved (combined) work unit obtained in the partition phase, the appropriately matched application pages in the former case will always be a subset of the later.*

The way we partition work units makes the Theorem 1 self-evident. In our example, the transaction $\{HI_8J\}$ can be either extracted from the isolated work unit $\{HI_8EFGJ\}$ or the interleaved work unit $\{EABCD_3HI_8EFGJ\}$. And $\{HI_8EFGJ\}$ is a subset of $\{EABCD_3HI_8EFGJ\}$ as Theorem 1 states.

Theorem 2. *When a transaction can either be extracted from an isolated work unit or part of an interleaved (combined) work unit, it can always be split from the interleaved (combined) work unit with score not lower than score of the isolated case.*

Theorem 1 establishes that the number of appropriately matched pages split from the interleaved (combined) work unit must be equal to or more than the number of appropriately matched pages in the isolated page. Given the appropriately matched page count is the numerator in Equation (1), and the denominators are the same for both cases, we would know that Theorem 2 is valid.

Table 2. The example: pattern testing & scoring

Work unit	Pattern to test	Score
$\{ECD_1EABC\}$	$\{AB\underline{CD_x}EFG\}$	$3/7 = 42.9\%$
	$\{\underline{ECD_xE}\}$	$4/4 = 100.0\%$
$\{EABCD_3H\}$	$\{AB\underline{CD_x}EFG\}$	$4/7 = 57.1\%$
	$\{\underline{ECD_xE}\}$	$2/4 = 50.0\%$
$\{HI_8EFGJ\}$	$\{\underline{HI_xJ}\}$	$3/3 = 100.0\%$
$\{EABCD_3HI_8EFGJ\}$	$\{AB\underline{CD_xHI_xEFGJ}\}$	$10/10 = 100.0\%$

Step 3 Work unit categorization: We categorize work units by applying the below rules sequentially to compare across all the candidate patterns. Step 1 decides whether a work unit is a normal or a deviated case. Steps 2-4 defines the rules to eventually choose only one pattern which matches the work unit under concern to the best extent.

1. When a series of application events can be both a normal work unit or part of a deviated work unit, the "deviated type" will be prioritized because of Theorem 2.
2. Choose the pattern that has most number of appropriately matched application pages appear in the work unit under concern.
3. To break a tie in rule 2, select the pattern which has the highest matching score calculated via Equation (1).
4. To break a tie in rule 3, randomly select a candidate pattern.

For a normal transaction which has complete cycle, this step labels it with the activity type. For a deviated case, it points out the variation type and enclosed activities. For example, the work unit $\{EABCD_3HI_8EFGJ\}$ has variation type "interleaved work unit" and contains two interweaving activity types, $\{ABCD_xEFG\}$ and $\{HI_xJ\}$.

Let us still use the toy example for illustration. We go to rule 2 for the work unit $\{ECD_1EABC\}$ and associate pattern $\{ECD_xE\}$ with this work unit. Prioritizing $\{ABCD_xHI_xEFGJ\}$ over $\{ABCD_xEFG\}$ plus $\{HI_xJ\}$ according to rule 1, we label the work unit $\{EABCD_3HI_8EFGJ\}$ as an interleaved case.

Step 4.1 Classifying and timing for normal and deviated work units: For a normal case, we assign it with the activity type binding with the pattern selected in the step 3. To find the starting and ending time, we employ the *"farthest boundary" principle* which adopts the earliest starting page and latest ending page in the work unit to delimit the transaction cycle. This principle is designed to offset the noise brought by the fact that practitioners cannot always finish all the working on the same page without switching, or Noi-1 in Table 1. After splitting a deviated case into sub units according to signature and pattern pages, we similarly apply the "farthest boundary" principle to identify the tentative transaction starting and ending time.

Step 4.2 Label unclassified events and sequential pattern mining for deviated cases: This step invites domain experts or practitioners to look into the unclassified events to label them for training. The threshold of the support for the iterative mining is often adjusted by observing the variation frequencies. To illustrate this, let the complete cycle for activity 1 be $ABCDEFG$ and that for activity 2 be $HIJKLMN$. Assume there exist two common interleaved working styles, say, $ABCD|HIJ|EFG|KLMN$ and $ABCDE|HIJ|FG|KLMN$ which approximately make up for 75.0% and 12.3% of the interleaved cases, respectively. Then we could set the threshold of support no larger than 12.3% if the second variations deserve identification, otherwise we should raise the threshold to narrow the search space.

Table 3. Inadvertent click exclusion

For the transaction under concern, get its cycle time $cycleTime$.
If $(cycleTime > maxSpan)$
// Forward check
Set $curPage = startPage =$ the signature page.
While (A directly antecedent featured page relevant to the current activity type before $curPage$ exists)
Set it to be $startPage$.
Set $curGap$ to be time interval between $startPage$ and $curPage$
If $(curGap < maxGap)$
Set $curPage = startPage$
Else
Set $startPage = curPage$ and break **while**
End **If**
End **While**
// Backward check is similar to the forward check, except for that we are trying to find the
// $endPage$ instead of $startPage$. We omit the details for length constraint.
End **If**

Step 5.1 Inadvertent click exclusion: We introduce two adaptive parameters, $maxSpan$ and $maxGap$, to deal with the inadvertent clicking (Noi-2), given Noi-1 has been handled in Step 4.1 with the "farthest boundary" principle. Parameter $maxSpan$ restricts the cycle time of a particular activity type, while $maxGap$ confines the interval between two featured application pages under a certain threshold. A transaction cycle time exceeding $maxSpan$ calls for a double check as a result of its abnormally longer processing time, implying that

we probably incorrectly delimit or even misclassify the activity. We actuate the mechanism in Table 3 to reduce the noises. $maxSpan$ strikes a balance between solution time against accuracy. An extremely large $maxSpan$ is incapable to detect and exclude inadvertent clicks for more accurate timing, while a too small $maxSpan$ leads to case-by-case checks, which are time-demanding.

Note that excluding inadvertent clicks might change the activity type, which is rare, though. Take two activity types with sequential patterns ABC_xD and BC_xD as an example. At first we classify the working time into type 1 because of rule 2, but the noise reduction phase excludes A, for it takes 15 min to arrive at B from A while $maxGap = 3$ minutes. We thereof send the trimmed work unit to pattern testing and scoring (Step 2) for reclassification.

Step 5.2 Output and parameter update: This step outputs the class label, starting and ending time points of each transaction. Also, we update the $maxSpan$ and $maxGap$ by constructing one-sided confidence intervals and incorporating the newly identified transactions. Briefly speaking, we calculate, for each activity type i, the average cycle time $\bar{X}_i$ and the standard deviation σ_i. Let $Z = \frac{(\bar{X}_i - \mu_i)}{\sigma_i/\sqrt{n_i}}$, then $Z \sim N(0,1)$, and

$$maxSpan_i = \bar{X}_i + z_\alpha \sigma_i/\sqrt{n_i},$$

where α is the significance level, n_i is the sample size, z_α is the value that makes $P\{Z \le z_\alpha\} = 1 - \alpha$.

For $maxGap$, we need to compose it in real time in Step 5.1, since time interval between two featured pages differs among activities and applications. We calculate the upper bound for each application page similar to $maxSpan$, and sum the upper bounds of all the applications between two featured application pages to be $maxGap$ in Table 3.

4   Performance Evaluation and Business Benefits

Through a pilot deployment of the activity classifier and timer to the production environment, we evaluate the tool performance in terms of *accuracy*. Furthermore, we share multifaceted business benefits realized by the tool, some of which are pleasant surprises beyond expectation.

4.1   Pilot Introduction

The pilot took place at a service delivery center dedicating to F&A (Finance & Accounting) processes. Out of dozens of activities, we only focus test our tool with eight activity types. It last 14 working days on four desktops (four practitioners) with 768 in-scope transactions processed.

In order to monitor the working time of a practitioner, the current practice of center is to enforce the self-report by practitioners, which encompasses *volume report* and *time report*. For volume report, practitioners upload the number of processed transactions by activity type and on daily basis as shown in Table

Table 4. Sample Volume and Time Reports

Sample Volume Report

Date	Activity Type	Volume
Nov 11, 2011	Invoice processing	20
Nov 11, 2011	Invoice payment	29

Sample Time Report

Activity Type	Start Time	End Time
Invoice processing	08:12:13, Nov 11, 2011	08:49:56, Nov 11, 2011
Invoice payment	08:49:56, Nov 11, 2011	09:12:00, Nov 11, 2011
Break	09:12:00, Nov 11, 2011	09:20:04, Nov 11, 2011
Invoice processing	09:20:04, Nov 11, 2011	09:51:17, Nov 11, 2011

4 (upper part). Upon switches between activities, the practitioners will manually log the beginning of "switching-to" activity and the ending time of the "switching-from" activity. Table 4 (lower part) shows what a time report looks like. We emphasize that practitioners trigger the manual timing upon activity type changeovers rather than transaction changeovers, which means multiple "invoice payment" transactions may be processed from 08:49:56, Nov 11, 2011 to 09:12:00, Nov 11, 2011 (the second row in the Sample Time Report).

To provide the baseline for us to compare the tool performance with, our business partner offered to audit the volume and time self-reports for three working days of the four practitioners. The auditing covers 276 transactions or 518 minutes working time. 518 minutes is far less than 12 working days (three days / practitioner * four practitioners) because we only have eight activities in scope and practitioners spent time processing other out-of-scope activities, too.

4.2   Performance Evaluation

We evaluate the performance of the tool on volume count and time capture, in correspondence with the volume and time self-report. The activity classifier and timer supports automatic volume report generation by counting the distinct transaction ID of each activity type. Table 5 (left part) shows the pilot results in terms of volume count. The tool faces two sources of errors, unclassified and misclassified transactions. For transactions which were indeed processed, but no learnt pattern matches this work unit with a satisfactory degree, we will have *unclassified transactions*. When a transaction is assigned with an incorrect label, we will have *misclassified transaction*. Misclassifications further breaks into two types - *misclassification (in scope)* refers to a incorrectly labeled transaction with its true class among one of the eight activities involved in the pilot; *misclassification (beyond scope)* refers to one with its true class out of the eight activities.

We measure the performance with *accuracy*, which is defined as

$$\text{accuracy} = \frac{\text{number of objects correctly classified}}{\text{total number of objects}}.$$

Table 5. Performance of automatic volume report

Items	Volume		Time	
	Self-report	Auto-report	Self-report	Auto-report
Correctly classified	274	271	407 min	498 min
Unclassified	2	4	91 min	15 min
Misclassified (in scope)	0	1	20 min	5 min
Misclassified (beyond scope)	0	0	85 min	26 min
Accuracy	**99.28%**	**98.18%**	**67.50%**	**91.54%**
Audited volume, time	276 transactions		518 min	

Our tool achieves 98.18% accuracy, which is slightly lower than the self-report accuracy 99.27%. The automatic report accuracy drops from 100% with four unclassified and one misclassified transactions. A deep dive into the four unclassified transactions reveals that they are exceptional cases, where no signature page such as the transaction ID page will appear. The signature-page-based nature of our approach brings about the failure. This discovery uncovers the problem with the process itself. Our business partner is happy that we expose the unnoticed non-standard processing. They will follow to redesign the process and make sure each transaction to have a signature page for monitoring purpose.

Next, we share the timing performance of our tool in Table 5 (right part). The correctly classified time is 498 min while total time under concern is 544 min. We can calculate that the accuracy is 91.54%, which is a significant improvement comparing with the self-report accuracy, 67.50%. We have discussed the root causes of low accuracy of self volume reports with our business partner, who believes too frequent manual time logging distracts practitioners from their normal work flow and practitioners are reluctant to do so. We see it as an opportunity where the automatic tool helps, since the charge model of our business partner depends on working time on different activities.

The above numeric results illustrate that the activity classifier and timer performs well in terms of both automatic volume and time reports. Next, we are going to demonstrate the effectiveness of our approach design (Figure 2) with *"what-if"* scenarios.

Require complete pattern (RCP)	If a work unit do not contain all the application pages appropriately of at least one pattern, it remains unclassified.
Neglect variations (NV)	Do not handle the variations.
Neglect inadvertent clicks (NIC)	Do not address the inadvertent clicks (Nor-2).
Neglect repetitive visits (NRV)	Do not address the repetitive visits (Nor-1).

Table 6 (left part) shows the results of the above four scenarios in terms of transaction count accuracy.

We can observe that the requirement of complete pattern matching leads to more unclassified transactions, which meets our intuition. The variation neglect often results in fewer classified transactions because we fail to split the interleaved or combined work units. Very seldom misclassified cases can occur due to

Table 6. What-if analysis of automatic volume report

Items	Volume				Time			
	RCP	NV	NIC	NRV	RCP	NV	NIC	NRV
Correctly classified	215	243	271	271	422	466	503	446
Unclassified	61	32	4	4	88	40	12	68
Misclassified (in scope)	0	1	1	1	8	12	3	4
Misclassified (beyond scope)	0	0	0	0	24	28	1345	10
Accuracy	**77.9%**	**88.4%**	**98.2%**	**98.2%**	**77.9%**	**89.0%**	**27.0%**	**84.5%**
Audited volume, time	276				518 min			

unaddressed inadvertent clicks, and we do not encounter it in our pilot. Repetitive visits handling cannot improve the automatic volume report accuracy as we can expect. Hence, the performance of NIC and NRV are identical to the activity classifier and timer. With regard to timing accuracy, we also analyze the four what-if scenarios to validate our algorithm effectiveness and the indispensability of each step in Table 6 (right part).

We could observe that we have the largest amount of unclassified time due to unclassified transactions when complete pattern matching required (RCP bar). When we do not handle the variations, the unclassified time also has a slight rise which indicates the practitioners did some combined or interleaved processing during our pilot. It is interesting that if we do not exclude the advertent clicks, we end in extremely low accuracy since the tool include too many out-of-scope time because of inadvertent clicks on some featured pages. If we do not consider the possibility of visiting the same page repetitively, we will have more unclassified time because we only start from the latest starting application page and end with the earliest ending application page.

4.3 Business Benefits

Section 4.2 demonstrates the high performance of the tool in classification and timing, and how the performance will be degraded without critical steps. This section shares the business benefits we obtained. A straightforward reap by enabling the automatic tool is the time saving in manual time and volume report, which on average costs a practitioner 13.29 min per day (2.7%) assuming the total working time is 8 hours per day. We can also save the auditing time of team leads.

Next, we observe an obvious behavioral change of the practitioners who has the tool deployed. The waste (consisting of machine idle and keyboard idle) when processing the eight monitored activities is much lower than that when processing out-of-scope activities. Table 7 shows our findings. If we extrapolate the saving to an eight-hour working time, the monitored practitioners should waste about 22 minutes but unmonitored ones has about 55 minutes to squander - 30 minutes to save per person day. Additionally, the efficiency has risen for the eight in-scope activities as compared to the pre-pilot period as shown in Table

Table 7. Business Benefit: Waste and Efficiency

Waste: monitored versus unmonitored activities		
	Monitored activities	Unmonitored activities
Waste (%)	4.73%	11.48%

Efficiency: pre-pilot versus pilot period		
	Pre-pilot period	Pilot period
Efficiency (%)	90.61%	109.94%

7. The waste reduction and efficiency improvement, we believe, attributes to the practitioners' awareness of the "being watched."

Finally, the iterative training mechanism in our approach helps our business partner to unveil non-standard or exceptional processing procedures. Non-standard processing, such as processing in batch, interleaved and combined processing, tend to have strong reasons in behind. The practitioners learn to do their work faster by combining or interleaving two related activity types together to omit some steps, which we call *shortcut-driven*. It is also quite common to do batch processing, since repetition creates efficiency with familiarity to particular working contents and savings of changeover costs, which we call *familiarity-driven*. The shortcuts discovered by practitioners may motivate the business to redesign and document more efficient processing procedures. Moreover, the unclassified time implies *exceptional cases and should rouse the attention of the team leads for further investigation.*

5   Conclusions

In this paper, we present an approach and tool that automatically classifies and times the transactions processed by practitioners, based on the fine-granular application usages. This work contributes to the existing literature with a streamlined approach which comprehensively consolidates knowledge discovery & data mining techniques, and furthermore handles the typical human variations and noises in the service delivery process with domain knowledge.

A pilot with a world-class BPO provider showed a success in both technology and business. Our approach results in high accuracy in both classification and timing. The critical part is to be able to address human behavior variations and noises for service delivery. Business wise, the tool can not only eliminate the self-report efforts, it also discipline practitioners' behavior to improve efficiency and reduce waste. Lastly but not least, it can discover non-standard or exceptional operations to enforce the process standardization and business control.

References

1. Computer Business Review (2011),
   http://outsourcingbpo.cbronline.com/news/
   worldwide-bpo-market-to-grow-by-63-in-2011-gartner-230811

2. Agrawal, R., Srikant, R.: Mining sequential patterns. In: Proceedings of the 11th International Conference on Data Engineering, pp. 3–14 (1995)
3. Bharadwaj, S.S., Saxena, K.B.C., Halemane, M.D.: Building a successful relationship in business process outsourcing: An exploratory study. European Journal of Information Systems 19(2), 168–180 (2010)
4. Bozorgi, M., Saul, L.K., Savage, S., Voelker, G.M.: Beyond heuristics: Learning to classifify vulnerabilities and predict exploits. In: Proceedings of the 16th ACM SIGKDD International Conference on Knowledge Discovery and Data Mining, pp. 105–113 (2010)
5. Brown, R.H.: Business process outsourcing vendor consolidations: Is your contracts at risk? Gartner (2009)
6. Du, Z., Liao, X.: Well-defined processes and their effects on business process outsourcing vendor's success: An integrated framework. In: The 2010 International Conference on E-Business Intelligence, pp. 27–36 (2010)
7. Forman, G., Rajaram, S.: Scaling up text classification for large file systems. In: Proceedings of the 14th ACM SIGKDD International Conference on Knowledge Discovery and Data Mining, pp. 239–246 (2008)
8. Han, J., Pei, J., Mortazavi-AsI, B., Chen, Q., Dayal, U., Hsu, M.: FreeSpan: Frequent pattern-projected sequential pattern mining. In: Proceedings of the 6th ACM SIGKDD International Conference on Knowledge Discovery and Data Mining, pp. 355–359 (2000)
9. Karu, K., Jain, A.K.: Fingerprint classification. Pattern Recognition 29(3), 389–404 (1996)
10. Lacity, M.C., Willcocks, L.P., Rottman, J.W.: Global outsourcing of back office services: lessons, trends, and enduring challenges. Strategic Outsourcing 1(1), 13–34 (2008)
11. Nenkova, A., Bagga, A.: Email classification for contact centers. In: Proceedings of the 2003 ACM Symposium on Applied Computing, pp. 789–792 (2003)
12. Pei, J., Han, J., Mortazavi-AsI, B., Pinto, H., Chen, Q., Dayal, U., Hsu, M.: PrefixSpan: Mining sequential patterns efficiently by prefixed-projected pattern growth. In: Proceedings of the 17th International Conference on Data Engineering, pp. 215–224 (2001)
13. Qin, T., He, M., Zeng, S., Ren, C., Dong, J.: An effective pattern mining algorithm to support automatic process classification in contact center back office. In: Proceedings of the 2012 IEEE SOLI (2012)
14. Srikant, R., Agrawal, R.: Mining sequential patterns: Generalizations and performance improvements. In: Proceedings of the 5th International Conference on Extending Database Technology, pp. 3–17 (1996)
15. Tan, P.-N., Steinbach, M., Kumar, V.: Introduction to Data Mining. China Machine Press (2010)
16. Tang, M., Pellom, B., Hacioglu, K.: Call-type classification and unsupervised training for the call center domain. In: Proceedings of the IEEE Workshop on Automatic Speech Recognition and Understanding, pp. 204–208 (2003)
17. Tapper, D.: Worldwide and U.S. IT outsourcing services 2004-2008 forecast: A potential perfect storm. IDC # 31089 (2004)
18. Tapper, D.: U.S. customers select IBM, HP-EDS, Unisys, Accenture, Infosys, ADP, and Fedelity as top 5 ranked BPO vendors for transformation, integration, innovation and cost optimization - excerpt from IDC # 216191. IDC # 216191 (2009)
19. Zaki, M.J.: SPADE: An efficient algorithm for mining frequent sequences. Machine Learning 42(1-2), 31–60 (2001)

Collective Intelligence for Enhanced Quality Management of IT Services

Maja Vukovic and Arjun Natarajan

IBM T.J. Watson Research, 19 Skyline Drive, Hawthorne, NY 10532, USA
{maja,arjunn}@us.ibm.com

Abstract. Customer satisfaction and delivery excellence measure the overall quality of IT services. Services quality management relies on the insights obtained by extracting large volumes of tacit knowledge about processes, products and people. This knowledge is not automatically discoverable, as it is unstructured and widely distributed among the experts, making it challenging to drive quality across all these dimensions. To address these knowledge gaps needed for next level of quality management of IT services we apply collective intelligence methodology, by engaging a set of experts to discover knowledge through collaboration. We further augment enterprise data sources with uncovered human knowledge. We demonstrate the effectiveness of our approach addressing challenges in scalable knowledge discovery both as part of large-scale business transformational and on-going operational activities.

Keywords: Services Quality, IT Service Delivery, Collective Intelligence.

1   Introduction

IT outsourcing enables companies to contract out IT services, such as infrastructure management, to external providers. It attracted enterprises given a cost reduction and steep improvement in quality through aggressive service level agreements (SLAs) [1,2]. As IT outsourcing matured, quality of service became a differentiating factor for providers. To meet the quality expectations and reduce operating costs the providers need to continuously improve services quality both at front-end (e.g., client experience and satisfaction), and back-end (e.g. production and delivery).

IT outsourcing is a complex and extremely dynamic ecosystem. As shown on Fig. 1, typical IT service delivery environment consists of 1000s of products (e.g. middleware), each with 100s of instances and configurations [3]. Moreover, there are 100000s people in delivery centers globally supporting 1000s of processes, such as patch management and backup failure management. At that scale and complexity driving quality across all dimensions and in global context, becomes challenging.

Success of quality management in manufacturing relies on understanding of the back-end processes, and modularizing their operations. In contrast, IT services have experiential nature and require user practice insights. For example, while a database configuration can be automatically extracted, it is the expert who knows how it is used and its importance. Similarly, although processes document the operation flows, it is the delivery experts who understand where the bottlenecks are.

C. Liu et al. (Eds.): ICSOC 2012, LNCS 7636, pp. 703–717, 2012.

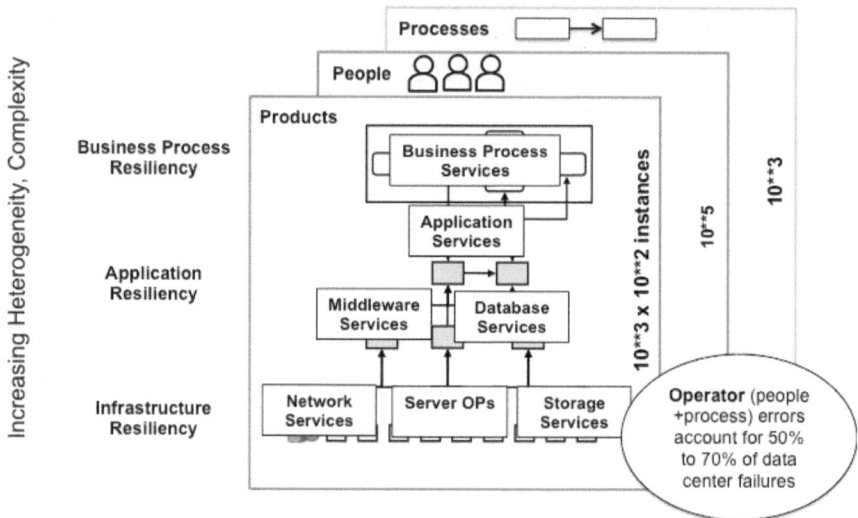

Fig. 1. IT Services Delivery - Process, Product and People [3]

Collective intelligence refers to a group of experts that through collaboration make decisions and solve problems as a (distributed) team. Xerox's Eureka system is one of the early examples of applications of collective intelligence for IT support services [4], which enabled experts to share best practices. To increase service quality in IT outsourcing, by accelerating knowledge discovery, we propose end-to-end integration of collective intelligence with existing process operations. As opposed to an "open-call" approach, we select participants based on their expertise.

In this paper we present how we integrated collective intelligence of experts using BizRay crowdsourcing service [5] with enterprise data systems, to derive quality insights about products, processes and people in IT services. Next section introduces background on IT service quality. Section 3 describes the integration of human and digital knowledge. Section 4 presents applications of our approach to harvest the knowledge about products, people and processes in IT services. Section 5 discusses results from discovering knowledge about defect prevention tools from 2300+ quality analysts, automation opportunities from 90 system administrators and compliance insights from 128 delivery staff. Section 6 puts our work in the context of state of the art in service quality and collective intelligence. Section 7 sets our future directions and concludes.

2 Complexity of IT Service and Quality Management Challenges

2.1 Background

IT outsourcing services consist of a stack of functions such as, infrastructure management and help-desk operations. An IT outsourcing provider runs operation and maintenance of client's IT environment, with the goal of improving efficiency through quality of production and delivery. In large deals the IT outsourcing provider typically takes over the entire set of client's IT functions, in contrast to smaller deals where it assumes operations of only a single function such as help-desk operations. Contract between provider and consumer outlines the outsourcing model and (quality) metrics to be continuously verified, known as Service Level Agreement (SLA).

IT services evolved from isolated environments in 1980's where there was no formal separation between the users of IT and the providers. In the 1990's services were becoming more componentized and shared, and operations formalized given the emergence of standards. In the 2000's global delivery model was widely adopted, and new challenges were introduced given the huge separation between provider and consumer, time zone differences, language barriers, etc. Complexity of service systems is evolving given the diversity of providers and consumer. This impacts how we get services to work together and how we measure them. In the 2010's we are witnessing a dramatic growth in number of service providers and granularity of services offered with inconsistent service levels, given a low barrier to entry. No single entity owns the entire service system. Lack of standard metrics and centralized ground truth source results in IT services based on inconsistent and conflicting data.

2.2   Quality of IT Services

With the increasing complexity of IT Service ecosystem and maturity of IT, quality of service became a differentiating factor for providers. Client satisfaction is an increasingly dominating choice of service provider. For example, 59% of respondents in the Accenture's study report switching from at least one provider within a year due to poor service [6].

There are two distinct aspects to measuring services quality: a service provider perspective and a service consumer perspective. Quality metrics in product industries tend to be producer centric, whereas in services the consumer perspective is as important if not dominant. Consumer perception includes the client value and SLAs. The provider quality is measured using SLA attainment, number of defects and financial aspects of operations. On the service provider side, key measure employs General Sigma approach to drive service production quality. "Defect" can be defined as an instance or event that is not a satisfactory outcome. On the consumer side, traditional Sigma approach is less understood. The consumer measure represents the difference between consumers' perception and expectation. Notion of "defect" is harder to define and carries a significant subjective component.

Consumer and provider perspective around the same service are often quite different. For example, an airline industry study revealed the despite airline baggage handling being at nearly 4 sigma[1][7], it was still the 2nd highest passenger complaint [8].

While quality engineering methodology can be adopted from established fields such as manufacturing, IT Services Quality has fundamental new dimensions related to the experiential nature and co-production of services with the client. As such it requires focus on integrated product-based process-driven, and people-centric operations.

---

[1] "Sigma" is around a specific metric. A service system has a number of metrics reflecting processes and tasks across the lifecycle. These metrics can range between 2 and 6 sigma as business criticality of individual metrics vary.

From product perspective it is important to understand how products (and tools) are used as part of IT services delivery processes. For example, in the defect prevention, addressed in Section 4.1, quality analysts rely on tools to classify and expedite the problem resolution. The quality depends on the usage and usability of available tools. Opportunities for process quality improvements are associated with automation. In Section 4.2, we investigate a set of work activities in delivery centers to identify their current levels of performance and discover further automation opportunities. Quality enhancements arising from people centric insights are two fold. First is the improved compliance posture of business described in Section 4.3. Second benefit is the ability to allocate experts more efficiently based on their expertise.

2.3   Front and Backend Elements of IT Service

Service systems can be conceptualized as a stage [9], with front-end (client-facing) and back-end (operations) functions, shown on Figure 2. A lower level, back-end stage, that focuses on consistent delivery through standardization, automaton and a learning system for continuous improvement. The middle level glues the loop between the front-stage and the back-stage. The top level, the front end, focuses on the client by developing a branded services experience and client value. Metrics at each level form a "network of metrics" determining overall quality of the service. For IT Services Delivery to take advantage of advances in manufacturing industry, a factory model has been applied to the back-end operations. This results in standardized, automated processes with adaptive dispatching (tasks sent to experts based on domain and complexity). Experts are grouped into "pools" sharing a specific competency. The delivery knowledge is captured into best practices, and real-time metrics provide sensing and response capabilities to drive continuous improvement. Finally, a learning system prevents repeat incidents leading to self-healing.

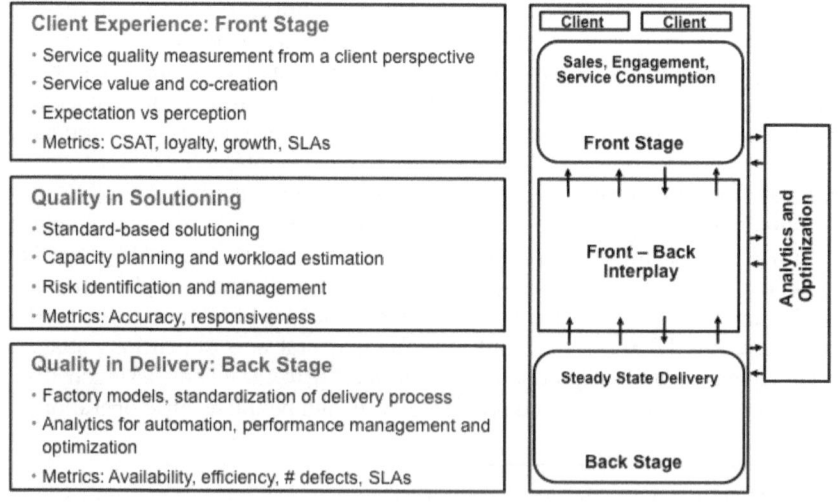

Fig. 2. Quality Characteristics of IT Services at Front and Back-end [3]

3   Approach: Integrating Digital and Collective Intelligence

Knowledge discovery is a distributed process often relying on multiple human or digital sources. Traditional techniques for knowledge discovery in enterprises such as interviews, e-mails, instant messages and Web-forms are no longer sufficient to reach out to today's globally distributed teams in large enterprises. They fall short in systematically tracing the responses, dealing with incomplete responses, and understanding the organizational relationships, with Subject Matter Experts (SMEs) moving out of organization. SMEs may forward knowledge requests to experts who took over their previous roles, yet these methods are time-consuming and intractable.

There are two critical factors that impact success of the knowledge discovery: knowing the potential source, or knowing someone who is aware of other sources. Crowdsourcing gained popularity with the emergence of Web 2.0, enabling enterprises to outsource tasks that are traditionally performed by designated human agents to an undefined large group of humans [10]. Even within the enterprise it can be applied in the form of an open call format allowing for anyone to participate. For instance, when looking for information about Apache Tomcat build procedure it may be useful to setup a forum for people interested. Yet, when seeking accurate information on a business entity, the potential contributors that may answer correctly are much smaller and may not be necessarily available for such inquiries. In this case it is easier to establish chains of inquiries.

To implement principles of collaborative knowledge discovery (Figure 3.) in Services Delivery we employ system BizRay [5]. Knowledge requests are captured in the distributed questionnaire artifact, which consists of one or more sections, each of which consists of one or more questions. BizRay manages its lifecycle, similar to a workflow system and facilitates delegation of requests and their subtasking. More than one expert (user) can complete each questionnaire instance. If the information gathered is incomplete or unidentified, the user can forward the request to another expert, asking for their help. As experts contribute their knowledge, the system keeps track of their identity resulting in the formation of micro communities around the object of that inquiry. The system also embeds capabilities to send out reminders and escalations to users who did not respond to the initial request.

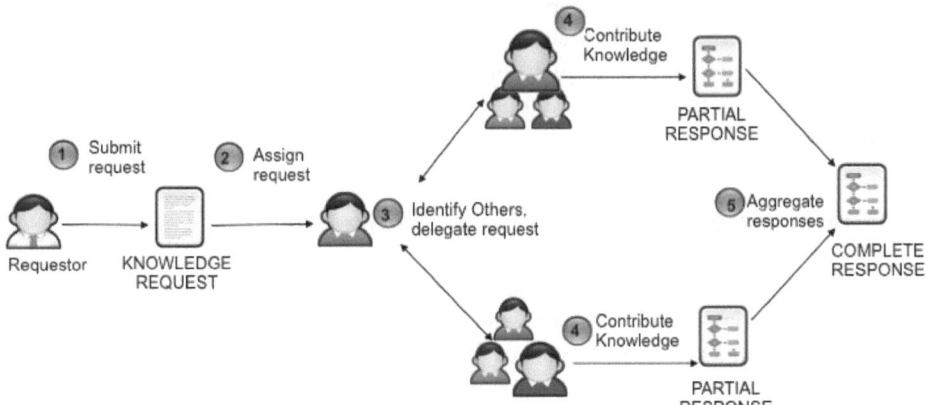

Fig. 3. Collective Intelligence Approach to Knowledge Discovery

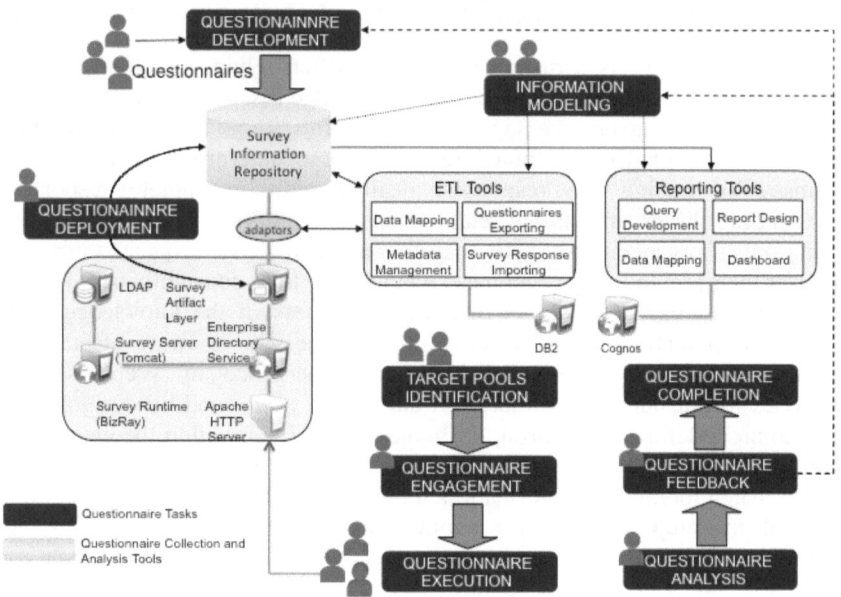

Fig. 4. Integration of Crowdsourcing Results with Enterprise Data Sources

In contrast to our prior work [5] where questionnaires were deployed as isolated instances, we integrated BizRay with existing enterprise data and reporting sources. Figure 4 shows the system architecture and lifecycle, and how we automatically processed questionnaire results, mapping them into the reports that are consumable by business analysts. The centralized information model captures the data for organization, labor, tools, automation potential, etc. Automated ETL tool maps questionnaire to this data model. Automated reporting tool, based on IBM Cognos platform, allows business users to query and view the different elements of questionnaire data. BizRay was used to manage questionnaires, tasks, delegations, status and reports. A feedback loop supports systematic refinement of questionnaires. Open source crowdsourcing solutions can be used to provide core functions, however BizRay has a unique feature that allows users to subtasks their assignments.

4   IT Service Insights for Quality Management

In this section we describe three applications of collective intelligence to IT Services Delivery operations within a global enterprise, harvesting insights and improving product, processes and people aspects of the back-end processes.

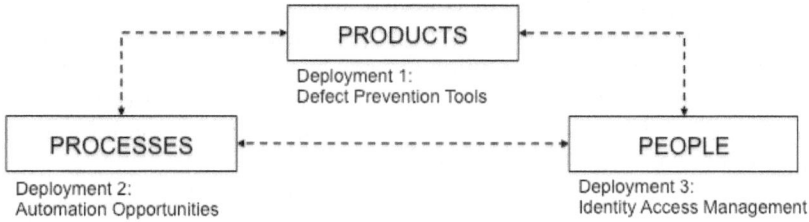

Fig. 5. Dimensions affecting IT Service Quality

4.1 Product Insights - Defect Prevention Tools

Defect prevention is the proactive and systematic methodology for improving quality and productivity by preventing the injection of defects into a service. It has three primary objectives: improving quality, improving productivity, and improving solution knowledge management. Improvements to quality in IT services are achieved by targeting defects, understanding the root cause, and eliminating defects by implementing solutions and corrective actions. Productivity improvement is achieved by removing non-value add activities that are involved in defect handling. For example, in IT Outsourcing, significant time is spent resolving recurring incidents and alert disposition. This time can be eliminated and the effort can be spent on activities that add value to the customer. Finally effective knowledge management is achieved by ensuring organizational support to effectively leverage defect knowledge across different outsourcing customers. The objective is that defect prevention leverages globally distributed teams that provide IT services to resolve problems only once and share the solutions globally, thereby improving the overall level of service quality.

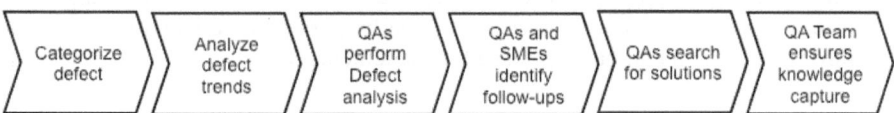

Fig. 6. Defect Prevention Process Flow: Analysis, Solution and Reuse

Figure 6. shows the main stages in defect preventions process, starting with the Quality Analysts (QAs) performing the classification and analysis of incoming issues and trends and identifying follow-up investigations. Subsequently QAs together with Subject Matter Experts (SMEs) and System Administrators (SAs), work on resolving the issues and capturing the best practices.

Defect Prevention Survey Questions		
✓		**Response**
✓	1.*	**What is the primary source of your Defect data (where you gather the data from, not what causes it)?**
		○ Account Ticketing System
		○ ISM Dispatch (Maximo)
		○ Lotus Notes Agent
		● Huddles
		○ Idea Logs
		○ Account Team or Customer
		○ Other (Please describe in Additional Detail field)

Fig. 7. Defect Prevention Collective Knowledge Request

We have applied principles of collective intelligence to 2300+ quality analysts in an effort to understand their practices, usage of available products (tools) for defect prevention and sample opportunity for novel auto-classification capabilities. The estimated time to complete the request, shown in Figure 7., was 5 minutes, and no tangible incentive was offered to participants. The campaign ran for a month, during which we obtained over 50% responses.

Within first week nearly 30% of respondents provided their responses. The rate of responses slowed down, and has resurged following a reminder that we have issued after third week. The primary value of the questionnaire is the insights obtained from respondents. It was discovered that over 60% of the QAs are still manually locating defect codes, opening up an opportunity for introducing advanced methods for auto-classification capabilities with the defect prevention process. Analysis further revealed that 25% requests were forwarded to another QA, reflecting team changed. Another 20% of respondents rejected the knowledge request altogether, claiming that they are no longer in this job function. Nevertheless, this data is enabling organization to track the size and distributions of competencies and knowledge capital (i.e. affecting people aspect of service delivery).

4.2   Process Insights – Automation Opportunities

Our objective was to discover automation opportunities for service management processes using questionnaires about accounts that are managed by pools (Figure 8) and the tools used.   From account perspective our goal was to identify variances among accounts being managed, business constraints and infrastructure prerequisites for automation. From the tool perspective, the goal was to understand the execution time for different work activities, existing automations and the estimated time reduction they introduce. Work-types performed by pool members included resolving hardware issues, patch and backup failure management, etc.

Process Maps and Account Level Assessment		
✓		Response
✓	1.	Enter the Failure Class
		(Max. 100 characters)
✓	2.	Enter the Failure Symptom
		(Max. 100 characters)
✓	3.	Enter the Failure Cause
		(Max. 100 characters)
✓	4.	Is an as-is (pre-automation) process model developed? (if yes, upload the model in the next question) ○ Yes ○ No
		Additional Detail:
		(Max. 250 characters)

Fig. 8. Account Level Questionnaire for Automation Opportunities

We were interested in performance of current processes in pools and opportunities for automation globally. As pools often develop their own productivity tools, we wanted to obtain a list of existing assets and identify their synergies. We assigned the questionnaire to SAs for 90 pools, with no explicit incentives.

Analysis of the results provided insights into variance in productivity between different pools that share business objectives, as shown in Figure 9. For work type Hardware Issues two pools report entire different duration estimates, whilst for the first three work types (backup, application and capacity system growth) they are consistent. Based on 30% of responses (other participants didn't provide this information), the mean time reduction arising from tool automation is 77.35min per SME. Section 5 discusses challenges arising from inconsistent responses, missing data, and misinterpreted requests.

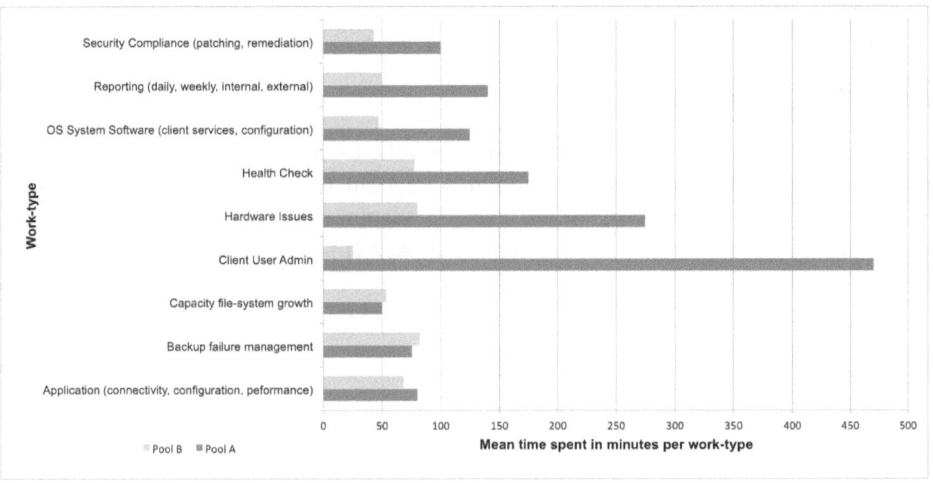

Fig. 9. Operational Insights: Variance of pool performance

4.3   People Insights – Compliance

Whilst process automation has a direct impact on the quality, regulated usage and access to customer's data and systems is of utmost concern for any enterprise, let alone IT service provider. Obtaining, managing, executing and disposing of access rights to customer's systems requires structured mechanisms that follow national and industry compliance regulations. Complexity of IT Service environment calls for new approaches to automate system access and provide fine granularity audit records [11].

To continuously improve compliance posture, adhering to a variety of regulations, enterprises require accurate and in-depth insights into employees' existing and required system access rights [12]. To generate comprehensive audit trails enterprises rely on detailed knowledge about how employees access existing systems. For that purpose we have deployed a questionnaire capturing elements of compliance in 128 pools, which were distributed to pool focals. Eighty-nine experts completed the request and twenty provided partial response. Due to the complexity questionnaire took on average 13 days to complete (measured from first time access to closure of the questionnaire in the system).

5   Discussion

5.1   Effectiveness of Collective Intelligence

Figure 10 shows the response time for three different deployments. In the simplest questionnaire (defect prevention) up to 30% responses were submitted within the first day. We observe bursts of responses as the reminders are sent. BizRay system has minimized human effort in setting up and distributing questionnaire campaigns and has enabled scaling of these activities. This has enabled us to easily reach out to 100s or 1000s of SMEs at the same cost.

5.2   Design Considerations

Scaling out campaigns impacts the accuracy levels, by introducing inconsistency and incompleteness of the gathered information (e.g. in the Automation Opportunities questionnaire we observed large variance in responses, as a result of ambiguous questions or respondents not providing the response in the correct unit of measure).

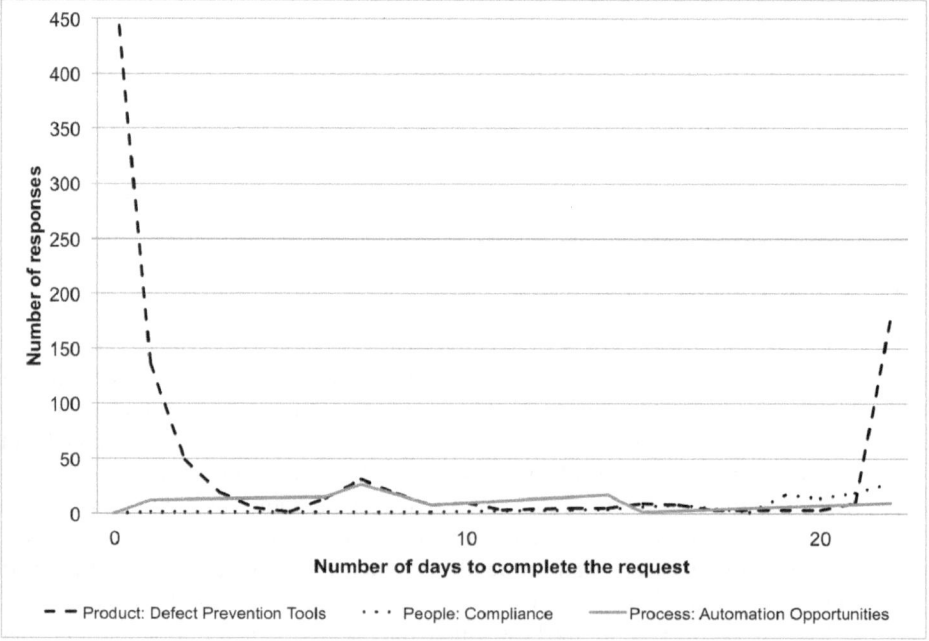

Fig. 10. Distribution of responses

For example, there was a case where a single SME reported that there is no support for "user admins", the other SME reported that "16hours were spent on supporting user admins", and yet another responded that "15mins were spent on supporting user admins". Anecdotally, the last SME did admit that they were not responsible for that issue resolution, but did spend those 15 minutes helping another colleague. Similarly, respondents may simply be in hurry and hastily respond, entering incorrect data.

However, collective intelligence approach does allow us to follow up with (selected sample) of respondents and verify their responses as part of quality assurance. The ambiguities about the questions can be overcome by facilitating communication among users and questionnaire designer, which indeed the BizRay tool supports.

We have also uncovered conflicts between responses of SMEs of the same pool, for example some were reporting that there is no for Reporting and Health Check, while another stated the names of the tools used for those activities. Normally, only one of them should be right, but here both can be right if they are SME for different accounts within the same pool. As a lesson learnt, we will capture account affiliation of the SME, and further reduce the scope of the question. In addition we discovered that respondents were collaborating on their (individual) questionnaires, and provided similar responses. This may be viewed as a notion of community driven validation.

Table 1. Use of collaborative features

Questionnaire	# Sent Requests	# of Reassignments (full and partial)	# of Full Reassignments
Product: Defect Prevention	2334	527	526
People: Compliance	128	103	98
Process: Automation Opportunities	90	6	2

5.3 Implications on Services Quality

Distributed questionnaires provided dual value: auxiliary and direct [13]. Direct output is driven by the business objectives (e.g. discover automation assets and their effectiveness). Auxiliary output is the derivative, such as discovering new Quality Analysts. Both are critical to improvement of processes (e.g. understanding current operations, and distributions of knowledge capital internally). Table 1 summarizes the usage of collaborative features In the defect prevention scenario the high number of delegations corresponds to the migration of SMEs within the enterprise departments and change in role responsibilities. The communities of experts that were uncovered can be reached out in subsequent campaigns to further expose the products used and procedures followed. This provides an enormous potential in a large global enterprise to further standardize the processes and assets used.

5.4   Effectiveness

In our initial application of BizRay for IT optimization we have demonstrated that introduces up to 30x improvement to data collection process [14]. The results were based on comparison of manually collected data using spreadsheets that were distributed and managed via e-mail. They resulted in manual follow-ups with multiple respondents. In the current work, a comparison is available for automation opportunities. Initially delivery staff was interviewed, for an hour, in person by consultants. Such sessions are often difficult to schedule, as experts need to attend to various high priority tasks. Using BizRay expert can go back multiple times to update their response. BizRay also allowed scaling of the questionnaires without increasing the cost of the effort.

6   Related Work

We position our work with respect to the state of the art in services quality. We compare our application of collective intelligence to the current state of the art in enterprise crowdsourcing and draw parallels to open source development efforts.

6.1   Services Quality

Grover et al. [1] identify high correlation between outsourcing success and system operations functions. Their results indicate that decision to outsource is driven by two types of parameters that impact the overall service quality. First is the quantifiable process improvement potential and related transaction cost. Second are the soft elements of partnership such as trust, cooperation, and communication.

Lee [15] confirms the belief that knowledge sharing is one of the major predictors for outsourcing success and impacts the soft factors of outsourcing partnership. Organizational capability to learn or acquire the needed knowledge from other organizations is a key source of successful knowledge sharing, and partnership quality, impacting the outsourcing success. Zinelid verifies that the strong competitive position is achieved through customer relationship management (CRM) and product/service quality, and proposes a new technical-functional 5 qualities model to measure the quality and loyalty [16]. This breakdown is much aligned with our approach of applying collective intelligence both in the front-end and back-end of services business. Indeed, social media techniques are becoming a prevalent method in reaching out and maintaining the relationship with the customers [17].

6.2   Collective Intelligence

Emergence of Web 2.0 and advances in social networking technologies have empowered the potential of collective intelligence to improve quality of business processes and customer relations [18,19]. Before Web 2.0 companies were engaging employees through competitions (e.g. employee of the month) to increase productivity. Similarly they employed surveys to obtain insights about the potential improvements in the workplace. Using the traditional media enterprises were reaching out to customers to sample ideas for a new product or service or quality improvements. Vukovic and Naik [20] engage enterprise online communities to capture the information required for IT optimization, such as migration to Cloud. On the customer facing side, nowadays we are witnessing a plethora of on-line communities, forums and social media applications to engage customers in product and service design decisions [21,22]. Beyond providing feedback on the service operations, end-users and customers are evolving into a virtual extension of the enterprise, by increasingly being embedded in the customer support processes [23,24].

6.3   Open Source Development

In production open source is a methodology that promotes free redistribution and access to an end product's design and implementation details. Prior work has drawn parallels between wisdom of crowd approach and open source [25], which Albers et al. [26] identify as just one of the new Internet-based learning and network collaboration paradigms. A main advantage of open-source model is the concept of concurrent yet different agendas and approaches in production, in contrast to the traditional centralized models of development and operations in enterprises. Moreover end-product, source-material, and documentation resulting from the open source method are available at no cost to the public in the open source approach. With globally distributed, virtual teams becoming the norm in the enterprises [27], the elements of open source method are being applied to internal operations.

7   Future Work and Conclusions

We have presented a collective intelligence approach to enhancing quality management processes of IT services. The main contribution of this paper is a mechanism to augment the tacit human knowledge with digital knowledge from enterprise data sources to provide enhanced enterprise insights. In contrast prior art considers collective intelligence as a stand-alone effort, disconnected from the encompassing business process.

There is very little research in the quality management of front-end processes in IT Services, opening an opportunity for unique differentiation amongst service providers. Our future work will include engaging of clients and account teams to derive insights about client processes and their quality parameters. This will enable us to close the knowledge gap arising from complexity and dynamics involved in interactions between front and back-end service elements.

Acknowledgements. We thank Jim Laredo and Sriram Rajagopal for contributions to the BizRay system, and Winnie Chang for insights from defect prevention analysis.

References

1. Grover, V., Cheon, M.J., Teng, T.C.: The Effect of Service Quality and Partnership on the Outsourcing of Information Systems Functions. Journal of Management Information Systems 12(4), 89–117 (1996)
2. Beulen, E., Van Fenema, P., Currie, W.: From Application Outsourcing to Infrastructure Management: Extending the Offshore Outsourcing Service Portfolio. European Management Journal 23(2), 133–144 (2005)
3. IBM Global Technology Outlook, Services Quality (2009)
4. Bobrow, D.G., Whalen, J.: Community Knowledge Sharing in Practice. The Eureka Story. Journal of the Society of Organizational Learning and MIT Press (2002)
5. Laredo, J., Vukovic, M., Rajagopal, S.: Scalable Knowledge Gathering for Non-Discoverable Information. In: International Conference on Service Oriented Computing (2011)
6. Accenture 2010 Global Consumer Research executive summary (2010),
   http://www.accenture.com/us-en/Pages/
   insight-accenture-customer-satisfaction-survey-2010-
   summary.aspx
7. IBM. Beyond the carousel, http://www-935.ibm.com/services/
   us/gbs/bus/pdf/g510-6592-00-baggage.pdf
8. Aviation Consumer Protection Division, http://airconsumer.ost.dot.gov
9. Teboul, J.: Service is Front Stage: Positioning Services for Value Advantage. Palgrave Macmillan (2005)
10. Howe, J.: The Rise of Crowdsourcing. Wired 14(6) (2006)
11. Bhaskaran, K., Hernandez, M., Laredo, J., Luan, L., Ruan, Y., Vukovic, M.: Privileged Identity Management in Enterprise Service-Hosting Environments. In: Proceedings of Network Operations and Management Symposium, NOMS 2012 (2012)
12. Vukovic, M., Giblin, C., Rajagopal, S.: Accelerating the Deployment of Security Service Infrastructure with Collective Intelligence and Analytics. In: IEEE Service Computing Conference, SCC 2012, Honolulu (2012)
13. Vukovic, M., Stewart, O.: Collective Intelligence Applications in IT Services Business. In: IEEE Service Computing Conference, SCC 2012, Honolulu (2012)
14. Vukovic, M., Lopez, M., Laredo, J.: PeopleCloud for the Globally Integrated Enterprise. In: Dan, A., Gittler, F., Toumani, F. (eds.) ICSOC/ServiceWave 2009. LNCS, vol. 6275, pp. 109–114. Springer, Heidelberg (2010)
15. Lee, J.-N.: The Impact of Knowledge Sharing, Organizational Capability and Partnership Quality on IS Outsourcing Success. Information Management (2001)
16. Zineldin, M.: The Royalty of Loyalty: CRM, quality and retention. Journal of Consumer Marketing 23(7), 430–437 (2006)
17. Sarner, A., Thompson, E., Dunne, M., Davies, J.: Top Use Cases and Benefits for Successful Social CRM. Gartner White Paper G00209091 (2010)
18. Surowiecki, J.: The Wisdom of Crowds. Anchor (2005)
19. Brabham, D.C.: Crowdsourced advertising: How we outperform Madison Avenue. Flow: A Critical Forum on Television and Media Culture (2009)
20. Vukovic, M., Naik, V.: Managing Enterprise IT Systems Using Online Communities. In: IEEE Services Computing Conference, SCC (2011)
21. Getsatisfacation.com Online Community Software,
    http://www.getsatisfaction.com
22. FixYa Solutions for Everything, http://www.fixya.com

23. CrowdEngineering, `http://www.crowdengineering.com`
24. giffgaff - the mobile network run by you, `http://www.giffgaff.com`
25. Brabham, D.: Crowdsourcing as a model for problem solving: An introduction and cases. Convergence: The International Journal of Research into New Media Technologies (2008)
26. Albors, J., Ramos, J.C., Hervas, J.L.: New Learning Network Paradigms: Communities of Objectives, Crowdsourcing, Wikis and Open Source. International Journal of Information Management 28(3), 194–202 (2008)
27. Malone, T.: The Future of Work. How the New Order of Business Will Shape Your Organization, Your Management Style and Your Life. Harvard Business School Press (2004)

MapReduce-Based Data Stream Processing over Large History Data

Kaiyuan Qi[1,2], Zhuofeng Zhao[1], Jun Fang[1], and Yanbo Han[1]

[1] Cloud Computing Research Center,North China University of Technology,
No.5 Jinuanzhuang Road,100144 Beijing, China
[2] Institute of Computing Technology, Chinese Academy of Sciences,
No.6 Academy South Road,100144 Beijing, China
{qikaiyuan,zhaozf}@software.ict.ac.cn, yhan@ict.ac.cn

Abstract. With the development of Internet of Things applications based on sensor data, how to process high speed data stream over large scale history data brings a new challenge. This paper proposes a new programming model RTMR, which improves the real-time capability of traditional batch processing based MapReduce by preprocessing and caching, along with pipelining and localizing. Furthermore, to adapt the topologies to application characteristics and cluster environments, a model analysis based RTMR cluster constructing method is proposed. The benchmark built on the urban vehicle monitoring system shows RTMR can provide the real-time capability and scalability for data stream processing over large scale data.

Keywords: data stream processing, large scale data processing, MapReduce.

1 Introduction

With the development of IoT (Internet of Things), real-time sensor data based data stream processing has become the key to IoT applications. When dealing with continuous data stream, processing systems must immediately react and response. Because the finite systems cannot handle the full information of infinite stream, the window mechanism is usually adopted to designate the boundary, within which the accumulated data is called history data. With the improvement of data acquisition and transmission technologies, high data stream speed makes accumulating large scale historical data in a short period possible. Meanwhile, the long-term, comprehensive and accurate requirements of current data stream processing applications also entail the enlargement of history data scale. Take the urban vehicle monitoring system as an example, which collects running vehicle information by sensor devices, and based on the data automatically identifies fake license cars and other illegal cars. These applications, in front of the data stream and historical data, should complete the computations between the both inputs in real time. And the expansion of the window, the increment of data objects (such as vehicles) and the increase of each object data (such as vehicle information), result in the large scale of historical data. With the trend, how to guarantee real-time data stream processing over large-scale historical data, i.e. to

C. Liu et al. (Eds.): ICSOC 2012, LNCS 7636, pp. 718–732, 2012.

provide scalable data stream processing for history data, became a new challenge to IoT and cloud computing.

Traditional study on scalability of data stream processing can be divided into two categories. In the centralized environments, subject to limited memory, scalability is guaranteed by sacrificing the quality of service, such as synopsis data [3] and admission control [1]. In the distributed environments, where the data stream processing network is consisting of multiple operators, scalability is supported by balancing the distribution of operators across multiple nodes [2]. However, the processing capacity is still limited by the window size a single node can handle and scalability is insufficient in the case of large scale historical data.

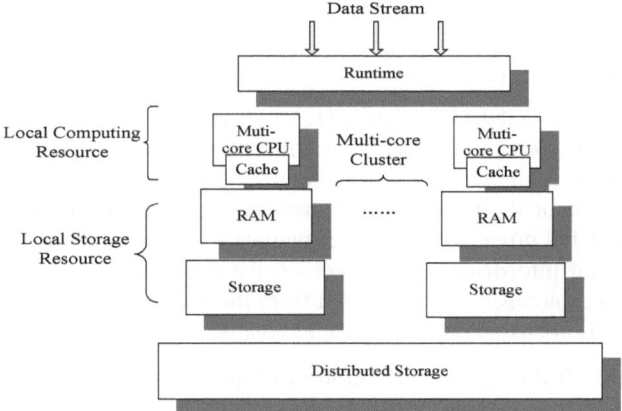

Fig. 1. Multi-core cluster architecture

Data stream processing over large scale history data needs breaking limitation of a single node. Today, in order to support large scale data processing, shared-nothing architecture is universal used, as well as 4-tier storage structure of cache, memory, storage and distributed storage. In this architecture, as shown in Fig.1, multi-core CPU forms the local computing resource, and memory and external storage forms the local storage. Under shared-nothing architecture, MapReduce [4] programming model is a core technology to solve large-scale data processing and has been widely adopted. However, the existing MapReduce methods, such as Hadoop[1] and Phoenix [5], are designed for batch processing for static persistent data. Provided continuous data is treated in this way, if the batches processed each time are small, then the system overhead is too large to fulfill real-time requirement, mainly in: 1) the runtime need to be initialized from the scratch, and history data need to be loaded and processed repeatedly, 2) there exists much synchronization and transmission overhead between Map and Reduce phases. If the batches are large, then the processing latency is added.

To support data stream processing, MapReduce should be extended by preprocessing and caching to avoid the repeated overhead on each data stream arrival, and by

---

[1] Apache Hadoop, http://hadoop.apache.org/

pipelining and localizing to reduce the synchronization overhead between stages and the data transmission cost between nodes. This paper proposes a real-time MapReduce model (RTMR) to support such kind of data processing. Furthermore, from the view of constructing RTMR cluster, there exists many possible combinations of node configurations and topologies for different applications and networks, how to build optimal architecture is a problem. This paper also proposes an adaptive RTMR cluster constructing method by establishing and analyzing the RTMR performance model.

2   Real-Time MapReduce Model

2.1   Key/value Data

In the era of big data, key/value model gradually replace the relational model to become a mainstream data processing model.

Definition 1. Key/value data is a 2-tuple $\{key,val\}$, in which key is key word and val is a set of 2-tuple $\{attr,con\}$, in which $attr$ is attribute and $cont$ is its content.

Key/value data is only related to data with the same keys, and independent of processing environment. Because of environment independence, key/value data has the nature of parallel processing and intermediate results can be saved as current state without additional information. Furthermore, the details of parallel processing, load balance and fault tolerance can be hidden from the abstract programming model, programmer can only focus on operations on key/value data.

Definition 2. Key/value algebra is a kind of abstract language used for operations on key/value data.

Similar with relational algebra, key/value data algebra also includes set operations (union, intersection and difference), special operations (Cartesian product, selection, projection, concatenation and division), comparison operation ($>$, $<$ and etc) and logic operations (not, and, or).

2.2   RTMR Theory

The definition of MapReduce model is [4]:

$$\text{Map: } k_1,v_1 \rightarrow \text{List} < k_2,v_2 >$$
$$\text{Reduce: } k_2, \text{List} < v_2 > \rightarrow list(v_2)$$

in which Map phase turns the key/value pairs $<k_1,v_1>$ into pairs $<k_2,v_2>$, and Reduce phase performs operation $list$ on the structure List$<v_2>$ of each k_2. Supposing the pending data is D, Map intermediate results for D is I, M represents the Map method, R represents the Reduce method, and $list$ represents Reduce operation, then the above process can be denoted as $MR(D)=R(M(D))=list(I)$.

MapReduce takes full advantage of key/value model: it provides sufficient semantics to parallelly process large-scale data through a simple programming interface, and shield task scheduling and data management from programmers. However, the existing batch processing based MapReduce cannot meet the real-time requirement of data stream processing. In order to extend the real-time capability of MapReduce, we prove MapReduce is no less expressive than ($\preccurlyeq$) key/value algebra at first.

Theorem 1. key/value $\preccurlyeq$ MapReduce

Proof. In MapReduce, selection and projection operators can be implemented in Map, and other key/value algebra operations can be implemented in Reduce. Therefore, MapReduce is more expressive than key/value algebra.

Definition 3. For the function $F:S\rightarrow O$, if there exists a function $P:O\times O\rightarrow O$, satisfying $F(D+\Delta)=P(F(D),F(\Delta))$, then F is mergeable.

Definition 4. For the data set D and its subsets $D_1,D_2,...,D_n$, if $D_1\cap D_2\cap...\cap D_n=\phi$ and $D_1\cup D_2\cup...\cup D_n=D$, then $D_1,D_2,...,D_n$ is called a partition on D.

Definition 5. For the key/value data set $D=\{<key,value>\}$ and the key set K, the collection $\{d\,|\,d.key\in K,d\in D\}$ is called a selection of D on K, denoted by $\sigma_K(D)$.

By the above definitions, we can see MapReduce has the following properties:

1. Map is distributive, i.e., the Map of the union of two data sets is equal to the union of the Map of the two sets, $M(D+\Delta)=M(D)+M(\Delta)$
2. Reduce is distributive, i.e., if $K_1,K_2,..,K_n$ is a partition on the key set of intermediate results I, then $list(I)=list(\sigma_{K_1}(I))+list(\sigma_{K_2}(I))+...+list(\sigma_{K_n}(I))$

In the traditional batch processing based MapReduce, overhead for repeated processing history data is the key factor to restricting real-time capability, therefore, the large-scale historical data should be preprocessed and cached.

Theorem 2. *list* is mergeable $\Leftrightarrow$ MapReduce is mergeable.

Proof. According to the properties of MapReduce, for data D and increment Δ,

$$MR(D+\Delta)$$
$$=R(M(D+\Delta))$$
$$=R(M(D)+M(\Delta))$$
$$=list(I_D+I_\Delta)$$

If *list* is mergeable, then

$$list(I_D+I_\Delta)$$
$$=list(list(I_D),list(I_\Delta))$$
$$=R(MR(D),MR(\Delta))$$

That is, if *list* is mergeable, then MapReduce is mergeable, and vice versa.

Theorem 2 shows that by caching MapReduce intermediate results of history data preprocessing, repeated processing overhead can be avoided every time data stream arrives. The above process can be denoted as $MR(D+\Delta)=$ list$(I_D+I_\Delta)=MR(\Delta|I_D)$.

In the existing MapReduce, another major factor to constraining real-time processing capability is synchronization overhead between phases, which caused by Reduce phase waiting to sort all the Map results. In fact, theorem 2 also shows that there is no data dependency between Map and Reduce phases, so synchronization can be eliminated by the asynchronous pipeline. In pipeline, Map and Reduce phases use buffers to communicate. Each Map task puts the results into buffers immediately after processing, and Reduce task obtains data asynchronously from the buffer to process. MapReduce also includes the synchronized method like Partition, Combine and Sort.

In pipeline manner, Partition and Sort can be completed respectively in Map and Reduce phase. As for Combine method, whether use it or not can be decided by the data compression effect, the algorithm will be detailed in 4.2.

In addition, the data transmission between nodes constrains the processing capability of MapReduce as well. In order to save data transmission cost, local computing resources should be fully taken advantage of to complete MapReduce.

Theorem 3. If $K_1, K_2, ..., K_n$ is a partition of key set of MapReduce intermediate results I, then the MapReduce of increment Δ over I satisfies

$$MR(\Delta|I)=MR(\Delta|\sigma_{K_1}(I))+MR(\Delta|\sigma_{K_2}(I))+...+MR(\Delta|\sigma_{K_n}(I))$$

Proof. According to the properties of MapReduce, for intermediate results I and increment Δ,

$$MR(\Delta|I)=list(I+I_\Delta)$$
$$=list(\sigma_{K_1}(I+I_\Delta))+list(\sigma_{K_2}(I+I_\Delta))+...+list(\sigma_{K_n}(I+I_\Delta))$$

For Reduce, the selection of intermediate results on K_1 is only relevant to K_1, i.e.

$$MR(\Delta|\sigma_{K_1}(I))=list(I_\Delta+\sigma_{K_1}(I))$$
$$=list(\sigma_{K_1}(I_\Delta+\sigma_{K_1}(I)))=list(\sigma_{K_1}(I_\Delta+I))$$

Similarly, $MR(\Delta|\sigma_{K_2}(I))=list(\sigma_{K_2}(I_\Delta+I))$

$$......$$
$$MR(\Delta|\sigma_{K_n}(I))=list(\sigma_{K_n}(I_\Delta+I))$$

Hence, $MR(\Delta|I)=MR(\Delta|\sigma_{K_1}(I))+MR(\Delta|\sigma_{K_2}(I))+...+MR(\Delta|\sigma_{K_n}(I))$

Theorem 3 shows that MapReduce can be localized by distributing intermediate results across the cluster. And because of avoiding data transmission, partitioning the intermediate results properly can guarantee the scalability of the cluster.

2.3   RTMR Model

Theorem 1 gives the necessary and sufficient condition that MapReduce is mergeable. However, this condition is only applies to some aggregate operations. For other operations not mergable, an intermediate results cache structure apt to randomly read and write can also be formed by grouping, sorting and indexing when preprocessing.

Definition 6. In RTMR, the [k_2,List<v_2>] and $list(v_2)$ of MapReduce model are called intermediate results.

Following the idea of Metis [6], intermediate results are stored in memory using Hash B+ tree, which is of high performance, as shown in Fig.2. In Hash B+ tree, keys k_2 with the same Hash value are grouped in the same Hash table entry as B+ tree, [k_2, $list(v_2)$] are organized as a linked list in the B+ tree leaf node, and $list(v_2)$ is stored in the B+ tree leaf node. If k_2 has a unique Hash value, Hash table can be allocated enough entries to avoid Hash conflict and tree search, then the complexity of insertion and search operation is only $O(1)$. If the Hash value of k_2 is not unique, the complexity of insertion and search is just $O(1)+O(logn)$. In order to enlarge the capacity, files

in the SSTable [7] structure are constructed at the external storage to store intermediate results. SSTable consists of an index block and several 64 KB data blocks, as
shown in Fig.3, which allocates disk space for Hash table entries in blocks. In data
stream processing, if desired intermediate result Hash entry is not in memory but in
the external storage and the memory space isn't enough, memory replacement occurs.

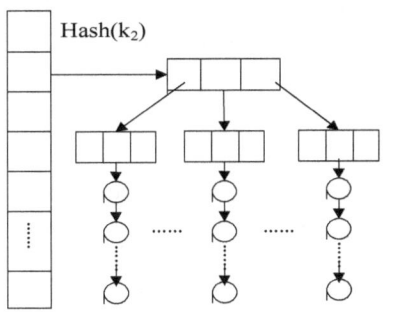

Fig. 2. Intermediate result structure   **Fig. 3.** SSTable structure

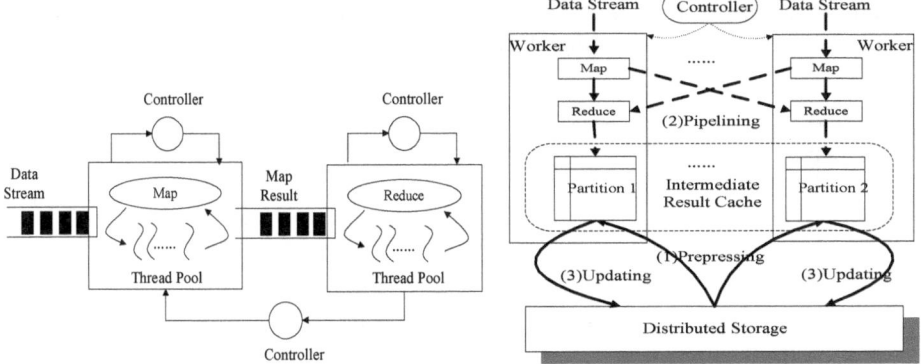

Fig. 4. RTMR architecture   **Fig. 5.** Staged pipeline

In order to support data stream processing, RTMR constructs staged pipeline between Map and Reduce phases, as shown in Fig.4. In pipeline, each stage is comprised of the thread pool, input buffer and intra-stage controller, and shared resources
such as threads are allocated by extra-stage controllers. Staged pipeline reduces the
initialization overhead on each batch processing by the thread pools, and eliminates
the synchronization between phases though event driven buffers. Furthermore, the
real-time processing capability of staged pipeline can be improved by intra-stage
batch adjustment and extra-stage thread pool control.

Based on the above designs, we propose a real-time MapReduce (RTMR) model
for data stream processing over large scale data, which works as (Fig. 5):

1. Intermediate result caching. Preprocess history data resulting in intermediate results, and partition and distribute the results across the worker nodes according to
   the Hash value on k_2.

2. Pipelining. MapReduce proceed in asynchronous way that Map phase groups the data stream by the Hash function on k_2 and transmit the data to corresponding Reduce node to compute with intermediate results according to range partitions.
3. Data updating. Update the local results to the distributed storage.

In RTMR, worker is responsible for maintaining the local cache and staged pipeline, and controller is responsible for RTMR job scheduling, fault tolerant and scalability guarantee. This paper mainly focuses on the RTMR model and architecture.

3   Adaptive RTMR Cluster

RTMR cluster architecture is decided by the Map/Reduce node configuration and topology. In RTMR, to take full advantage of local computing resource, Map nodes also act as Reduce nodes, and the architecture in the configuration of x Map nodes is called RTMR(x). For an example of 4-node cluster, the architectures RTMR(1), RTMR(2) and RTMR(4) configured 1, 2 and 4 Map node are shown in Fig.6 (a) (b) (c), respectively. Under different application characteristics, node capacities and network environments, how to construct optimal architecture is a key issue. For the data stream processing system, the goal of adaptively constructing architecture is to minimize the average data processing delay.

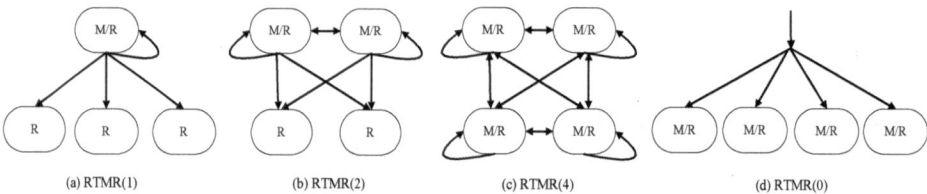

(a) RTMR(1)   (b) RTMR(2)   (c) RTMR(4)   (d) RTMR(0)

Fig. 6. RTMR architectures

3.1   RTMR Performance Model

Because the data stream arrival and processing is very similar with the queuing model, and thus queuing theory is a natural selection of the performance model of data stream system [8]. Previous work [3] and our statistics analysis on real scenarios show that data stream arrival process can be modeled as a Poisson process.

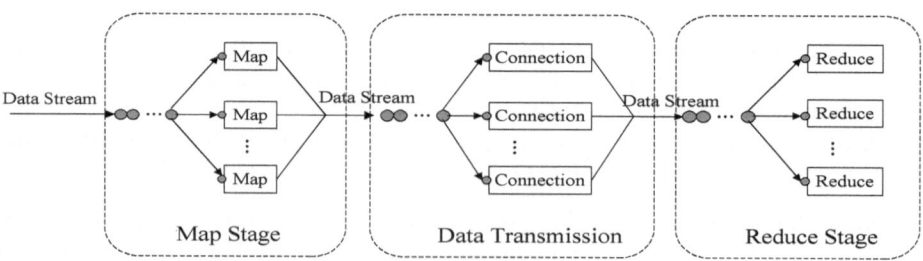

Fig. 7. RTMR performance model

Assuming that the arrival data stream is the most simple flow, the Map processing rate, network transmission speed and Reduce processing rate depends on negative exponential distribution, then RTMR cluster can be modeled as a cascade of three queuing system shown in Fig.7. Based on queuing theory [8], for the M/M/c queuing system which has c service units, when data stream speed is λ and processing rate of each unit is μ, the average processing delay is

$$L_q(c,\lambda,\mu) = \frac{(c\rho)^x \cdot \rho}{c! \cdot (1-\rho)^2} P + \frac{1}{\mu} \ , \tag{1}$$

in which

$$P = \left[\sum_{k=0}^{c-1} \frac{\rho^k}{k!} + \frac{c\rho^c}{c! \cdot (c-\rho)} \right]^{-1} .$$

$$\rho = \frac{\lambda}{\mu}$$

For a n-node RTMR cluster, supposing the number of Map nodes is x, Map processing rate of each node is μ_m, then Map stage under the data stream speed λ_m is equivalent to a M/M/x queuing system. According to equation (1), the Map stage average data processing delay is

$$L_m(x,\lambda_m,\mu_m) = L_q(x,\lambda_m,\mu_m) . \tag{2}$$

For a n-node RTMR cluster, x of n Reduce nodes shared with Map (processing rate μ_{r1}) is equivalent to a M/M/x queuing system, the other n-x exclusive Reduce node (processing rate μ_{r2}) is equivalent to an M/M/n-x queuing system. Therefore, the Reduce stage average data processing delay under data stream speed λ_r is

$$L_r(x,\lambda_r,\mu_{r1},\mu_{r2}) = \frac{x}{n} L_q(x,\frac{x}{n}\lambda_r,\mu_{r1}) + \frac{n-x}{n} L_q(n-x,\frac{n-x}{n}\lambda_r,\mu_{r2}) \ . \tag{3}$$

In RTMR(x), the output connections of each Map node are n-1, and the input connections of each Reduce node are x. If nodes is connected by the switch and the bandwidth between two nodes is μ_n, then each connection bandwidth is inversely proportional to the total number of connections, that is

$$\mu'_n = \frac{\mu_n}{x+n-1} \ .$$

On each connection, the data speed is λ_r/xn, according to the M/M/1 queuing model [10], the network delay of data stream through one Map node is

$$L_n'(x,\lambda_r,\mu_n) = \frac{1}{\dfrac{\mu_n}{x+n-1} - \dfrac{\lambda_r}{xn}} \ .$$

And the average network delay of data stream parallelly through all Map nodes is

$$L_n(x, \lambda_r, \mu_n) = \frac{L_n'(x)}{x} = \frac{1}{\dfrac{x\mu_n}{x+n-1} - \dfrac{\lambda_r}{n}} \quad . \tag{4}$$

In RTMR, too many threads will cause additional overhead such as context switching and critical resources competition. Corresponding to the connections, each pair of Map and Reduce nodes exists $n+x$-1 threads receiving and sending data. If the delay factor is ε, then the extra delay of data stream passing through 1 Map node is

$$L_e'(x) = (n+x-1) \cdot \varepsilon \quad ,$$

And the average extra delay of data stream parallelly through all Map nodes is

$$L_e(x) = \frac{L_e'(x)}{x} = \frac{(n+x-1) \cdot \varepsilon}{x} \quad . \tag{5}$$

Above all, the data stream processing delay of RTMR(x) is

$$L(x) = L_m(x, \lambda_m, \mu_m) + L_r(x, \lambda_r, \mu_{r1}, \mu_{r2}) + L_n'(x, \lambda_r, \mu_n) + L_e(x) \quad . \tag{6}$$

3.2   Model Analysis

In general, adaptive constructing RTMR is to analyze the extreme value of equation (6) to determine x. Given space limitation, instead of mentioning the solution of the extreme value of $L(x)$, two more practical architectures are discussed.

In RTMR, Combine method can be used to reduce the data transmission. If the data compression rate of Combine method is τ, then the data speed of Reduce stage is $\lambda_r' = \tau\lambda_r$, and if the Map processing rate is down to μ_m', then the data processing delay of RTMR (x) is

$$L_c(x) = L_m(x, \lambda_m, \mu_m') + L_r(x, \tau\lambda_r, \mu_{r1}, \mu_{r2}) + L_n'(x, \tau\lambda_r, \mu_n) + L_e(x) \quad .$$

Then for applications that exists Combine, whether implement Combine or not is decided by comparing $L(x)$ with $L_c(x)$.

Under the current IoT environment, the data speed is limited by acquisition terminal bandwidth, and the preliminary processing such as filtering and encoding has been completed by the communication servers, so it only occupy a small part of CPU time to accomplish the data receiving, transformation, selection and projection as well as partitioning and combining. In this case, the impact of Map Processing on Reduce performance on the shared node can be ignored, i.e. $\mu_r = \mu_{r1} \approx \mu_{r2}$. Then the Reduce stage can be considered as M/M/n system, the processing delay is

$$L_r(x, \lambda_r, \mu_{mr}) = L_q(n, \lambda_r, \mu_r) ,$$

which is independent of x. Due to equations (2) (4) (5) are monotonically decreasing functions of x. Thus, $L(x)$ is a monotone decreasing function, i.e., for a n-node cluster, RTMR(n) contributes to the minimum delay by the most highly parallel processing.

Besides, by theorem 3 we know another architecture shown in Fig.6 (d): the intermediate results are cached across distributed nodes; each node redundantly receiving the data stream, in pipeline manner, filters the data in the charge of itself at Map phase and processing the data over the local cache at Reduce phase. This architecture is defined as RTMR(0). In RTMR(0), if the existing computing and storage resources cannot satisfy the real-time requirements, the cluster can be scaled up to more nodes by repartitioning and moving the cache data. Due to avoiding data transmission and extra latency, the data stream through each node is equivalent to passing through a M/M/1 Map stage plus a M/M/1 Reduce stage, the delay of RTMR(0) is

$$L'(0) = \frac{1}{\mu_m - \lambda_m} + \frac{1}{\mu_r - \dfrac{\lambda_r}{n}} \quad .$$

And the processing delay of data stream parallelly passing through n nodes is

$$L(0) = \frac{L'(0)}{n} = \frac{1}{n\mu_m - n\lambda_m} + \frac{1}{n\mu_r - \lambda_r} \quad .$$

Apparently for these applications, adaptively constructing RTMR cluster is comparing $L(n)$ with $L(0)$.

4   Evaluation

In this section, we utilize the real-time urban traffic data processing applications as the benchmark to evaluate RTMR.

In a large city, where license plates reach 10^7, the peak will reach 10 MB/s if comprehensively capturing running vehicle data (1 KB for each item, about 10 000 items/s). Meanwhile, if the data have been stored for 1 day, history data will reach 1 TB. In the benchmark, three typical applications are adopted, which are all from real scenario of urban traffic monitoring system and can be regarded as the representative use cases out of related references[9-14].

Fake-licensed car is determined by space-time contradiction. For each item of real-time vehicle data at certain points, retrieve all the historical items at other points within the maximum time threshold, and if the time difference between the two items is less than the time threshold for the two points, the vehicle is suspected to be fake-licensed. The RTMR algorithm is implemented as: for each license plate of item, Map indexes its entry in Hash table grouped by plates; Reduce locates its list in the B+ tree, checks time difference with each historical data, and updates the list.

Traffic statistics application reports the vehicle counts of all the monitoring points, the RTMR algorithm is: for each item of real-time data occurred at certain point, Map indexes its entry in Hash table grouped by monitoring points; Reduce finds the immediate result in the B+ tree to merge and update it.

Traffic flow analysis application calculates the average travel speeds between two points to provide traffic guidance, the RTMR algorithm is: for each item of data captured at certain point, Map transforms the data into GPS coordination data and indexes its entry in Hash table grouped by monitoring points; Reduce finds the list in the

B+ tree, inserts the real-time data, eliminates the overdue data, and periodically merge immediate results within the window to compute the average travel speed.

In the above 3 RTMR algorithms, Hash function hash(k)=k mod 2^{20} can be used to group data items, and the intermediate result Hash table has 2^{20} entries, each storing data of $10^7/2^{20}\approx10$ license plates.

RTMR cluster is set up on the 2×4 cores 2.0 GHz CPU, 32 GB RAM and 250 GB disk servers, using a 4×4 cores 2.4 GHz CPU, 64 GB RAM server as control node, and the cluster is connected by 1 Gbps Ethernet and switches. Additionally, Load Runner 9.0 is deployed in a dual-core 3.0 GHz CPU and 4 GB RAM server to simulate data stream. In order to evaluate the scalability, on the basis of random and local characteristics of vehicle data stream, we evenly partition immediate result ranges across the cluster and simulate the uniform distribution stream. The method is: First, use the decimal interval $(0,10^8]$ to simulate license plates. Second, if there exists n nodes, select n subsets on immediate result ranges of n nodes $P_1',P_2',...,P_n'$, satisfying $|P_1'|+|P_2'|+...+|P_n'|=10^5$, and then generate loads for each node cyclically. Third, for node i, select a random entry t in P_i', select a random number x in the interval$(0,10)$ and regard $2^{20}x+t$ as the license plate of the data item, at last, randomly set its point and add its timestamp.

Base on the benchmark, each experiment is conducted 10 tests, and at each test we sample results for 10 minutes at steady state of the stream processing system, taking the averages as the final results.

4.1   Adaptive Architecture Analysis

First, we analyze the adaptive architecture of the 3 applications shown in Table 1.

Table 1. Benchmark applications

Application	Map	Reduce
Traffic count	The compression rate of Combine method is effective	Merging
Fake-licensed car	No combine	Comparing and updating
Traffic flow analysis	Data transform costs much overhead, and compression rate is 0	Merging and updating

For the traffic statistics application, compression ratio can be effective to reduce the cost of data transferring, so the Combine method should be adopted.

For the fake-licensed car monitoring, because of the absence of the Combine and other operations in Map phase, satisfying $\mu_r = \mu_{r1} \approx \mu_{r2}$, then the only thing for adaption is to compare $L(n)$ with $L(0)$. Experiment 1, under a 4-node cluster, compares the data processing performance of RTMR(0),RTMR(1), RTMR(2) and RTMR(4) over different history data scale. As Fig.8 shown, no matter what scale, the processing capabilities of RTMR(1), RTMR(2) and the RTMR(4) are promoting with the increase of Map nodes. In addition, when the data speed exceeds 15 MB/s, RTMR(0) is less powerful than the other 3 architectures, this is because in the broadcast mode, when it come to high speed data stream, receiving data and processing Map stage on each node occupies too much CPU time, which reduces the CPU time for the Reduce and thereby constrains the overall performance. With the history data scaling up, performances of all the architectures decrease, when the speed drops to 15 MB/s, RTMR(0) starts to be the most powerful, this is because the receiving and Map processing overhead on each node no longer affect the Reduce stage, and meanwhile avoid the data transmission cost.

For traffic flow analysis, although there exists Combine method, it cannot reduce the data transmission significantly because its Reduce need to maintain all the data within the window. Furthermore, its Map method includes expensive GPS coordinate transformation operation, dissatisfying $\mu_r = \mu_{r_1} \approx \mu_{r_2}$. The results of the extreme value analysis of $L(x)$ under the 4-node cluster are: from 0 to 200 GB data scale, $x = 2$; from 200 to 600 GB, $x = 3$; from 600 to 800 GB, $x = 1$. Experiment 2 compares the data stream processing performance of RTMR(1), RTMR(2), RTMR(3) and RTMR(4) over different historical data scale. Fig.8 shows the empirical results are consistent with the model analysis.

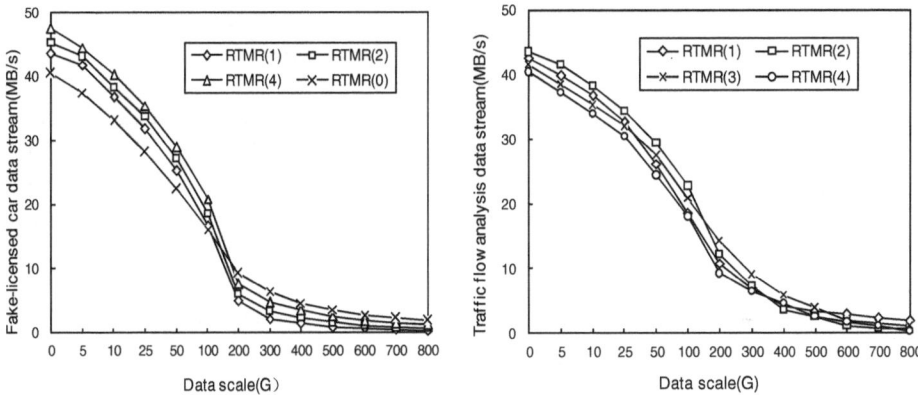

Fig. 8. Analysis of adaptive architecture

4.2 Scalability Analysis

Experiment 3 and 4 compare the scalability of RTMR(0) and RTMR(n). Experiment 3, at the fixed data stream 2 MB/s, tests historical data scale the cluster can handle when adding nodes. Fig.9 shows, the promotion trend of RTMR(0) capacity is approximately linear, which is because RTMR(0) minimize the data transmission and synchronization between nodes which affects the enhancement of parallel throughput by distributing intermediate results and localizing. And the reason why RTMR(0) doesn't achieve linear scaling is that local file read and write overhead increases when intermediate results scaling up. As for RTMT(n), as the nodes are added, data receiving and transferring cost between nodes increases significantly, thus limiting historical data scale that can be handled. Experiment 4, at the fixed intermediate results 50 GB for each node, tests the data stream the cluster can process when adding nodes.

Fig.10 shows that, as the node increases, although the data sending-receiving and transmission costs increase, but RTMR(n) is more scalable than RTMR(0) in data stream speed, this is because RTMR(n) distributes data stream to be processed parallelly across nodes, while RTMR(0) is restricted by the increasing CPU overhead of receiving data and processing Map. Specifically, when the data stream speed is less than 15 MB/s, the growth of RTMR(0) processing capability is approximately linear, and when the speed is more than 15 MB/s, the growth slows down.

From the experiences of using RTMR to solve vehicle monitoring, the data stream speed in current IoT environment, constrained by the bandwidth, is far less than 15 MB/s. In the situation of large scale history data, RTMR(0) is more adaptive.

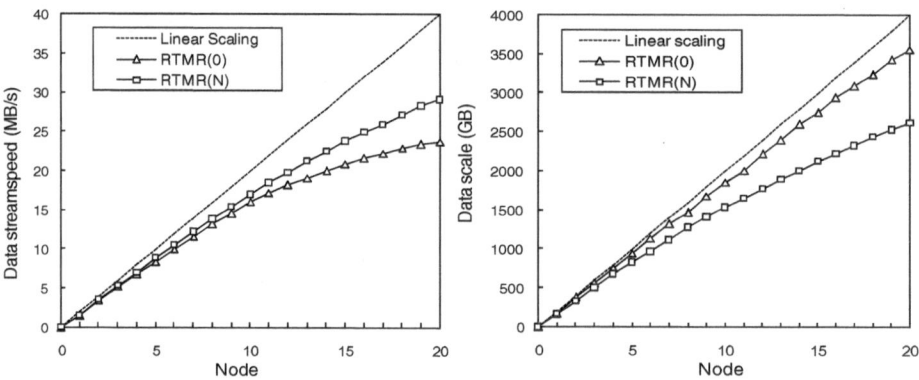

Fig. 9. Scalability analysis for data stream   **Fig. 10.** Scalability analysis for history data

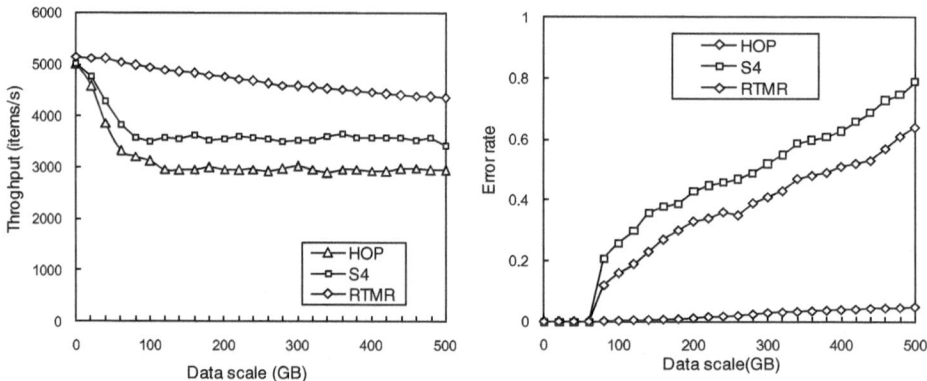

Fig. 11. Real-time capacity and Error rate

4.3   Real-Time Performance Analysis

Experiment 5 compares the real-time capacity of the architecture S4, HOP and RTMR(0). Due to the lack of preprocessing, S4 and HOP process history data repeatedly on each stream arrival. Hence, in order to compare data stream processing capacity over large-scale data, preprocessing logic is inserted into the benchmark implementation of S4 and HOP. All architectures are set up on 2 nodes, the data stream is fixed at 5 MB/s. Fig.11 show that when the scale of intermediate results is less than 32 GB, the throughputs of HOP and S4 are fairly high because a single node can accommodate all the intermediate results, while the RTMR(0) is higher due to the utilization of staged pipeline. When the intermediate results are more than 32 GB and distributed to two node memory, the throughputs of HOP and S4 decrease rapidly because of increasing data transmission and synchronization overhead between nodes, while RTMR(0) is still very high owing to localization. When the intermediate results reach 64 GB, since the scale is beyond the cache capacity, throughputs of S4 and HOP are steady and the error rates increase with the data scaling up, whereas RTMR(0) can reduce the error rate and maintain a relatively high throughput due to the expansion of local intermediate result storage.

4.4   Related Work

Real-time improvement for MapReduce has become a research hotspot. Increment processing Percolator [10] and iteration processing Twister [11] and Spark [12] promote performance of large scale data processing in the way of random storage access and intermediate result cache. However, these methods are still batch based processing for static data increment. HOP [13] and S4 [14] extends the real-time processing ability of MapReduce by pipelining and distributed processing elements respectively, but they still do not focus on large scale history data, due to the lack of the support to preprocess history data and cache immediate results, and the mechanism to adaptively configure the cluster instead of relying on experience or experiment way.

5   Conclusions

The difficult of data stream processing over large scale historical data is guaranteeing both real-time capacity and scalability. And the contributions of this paper are:

- Improving the real-time data stream processing performance of MapReduce by caching, pipelining and localizing.
- Proposing a model analysis based RTMR cluster constructing method which can configure the Map/Reduce nodes and topologies adaptively according to application characteristics and network environments.
- Showing that RTMR(0) is practically effective to support data stream processing over large scale data in current IoT environment.

Programming model and cluster architecture is the basis of RTMR, and in addition, load skew is another key factor to restrict the scalability of the RTMR cluster. So the next work is to guarantee load balance of RTMR by static history data distribution and dynamic date stream load adaption.

Acknowledgments. This research has been funded by the National Natural Science Foundation of China under Grant No. 60903137, No. 61033006.

References

1. Motwani, R., Widom, J., Arasu, A., et al.: Query processing, resource management, and approximation in a data stream management system. In: 1st Biennial Conference on Innovative Data Systems Research, pp. 176–187. ACM Press, New York (2003)
2. Abadi, D.J., Ahmad, Y., Balazinska, M., et al.: The design of the Borealis stream processing engine. In: 2nd Biennial Conference on Innovative Data Systems Research, pp. 277–289. ACM Press, New York (2005)
3. Jin, C.Q., Qian, W.N., Zhou, A.Y.: Analysis and management of streaming data: A survey. Journal of Software 15(8), 1172–1181 (2004)
4. Dean, J., Ghemawat, S.: MapReduce: Simplified data processing on large clusters. ACM Communication 51(1), 107–113 (2008)
5. Ranger, C., Raghuraman, R., Penmetsa, A., et al.: Evaluating MapReduce for multi-core and multiprocessor systems. In: 13th International Conference on High Performance Computer Architecture, pp. 13–24. IEEE Computer Society, Washington (2007)
6. Kaashoek, F., Morris, R., Mao, Y.: Optimizing MapReduce for multicore architectures. Technical Report, MIT Computer Science and Artificial Intelligence Laboratory (2010)
7. Chang, F., Dean, J., Ghemawat, S., et al.: Bigtable: A distributed storage system for structured data. In: 7th Symposium on Operating Systems Design and Implementation, pp. 205–218. USENIX Association, Berkeley (2006)
8. Diao, Z.J., Zheng, H.D., Liu, J.Z., et al.: Operational Research. Higher Education Press, Beijing (2010)
9. Shah, M.A., Hellerstein, J.M., Chandrasekaran, S., et al.: Flux: An adaptive partitioning operator for continuous query systems. In: 19th International Conference on Data Engineering, pp. 25–36. IEEE Computer Society, Washington (2003)
10. Peng, D., Dabek, F.: Large-scale incremental processing using distributed transactions and notifications. In: 9th USENIX Symposium on Operating Systems Design and Implementation, pp. 251–264. USENIX Association, Berkeley (2010)
11. Ekanayake, J., Li, H., Zhang, B., et al.: Twister: A runtime for iterative MapReduce. In: 19th ACM International Symposium on High Performance Distributed Computing, pp. 810–818. ACM Press, New York (2010)
12. Zaharia, M., Chowdhury, N.M., Franklin, M., et al.: Spark: Cluster competing with working sets. In: 2nd USENIX Conference on Hot Topics in Cloud Computing, pp. 1–10. USENIX Association, Berkeley (2010)
13. Condie, T., Conway, N., Alvaro, P., et al.: MapReduce online. In: 7th USENIX Symposium on Networked Systems Design and Implementation, pp. 313–328. USENIX Association, Berkeley (2010)
14. Neumeyer, L., Robbins, L., Nair, A., et al.: S4: Distributed stream computing platform. In: 10th IEEE International Conference on Data Mining Workshops, pp. 170–177. IEEE Computer Society, Washington (2010)

An Efficient Data Dissemination Approach
for Cloud Monitoring

Xingjian Lu, Jianwei Yin, Ying Li*,
Shuiguang Deng, and Mingfa Zhu

College of Computer Science and Technology,
Zhejiang University, 310027 Hangzhou, China
{zjulxj,zjuyjw,cnliying,dengsg}@zju.edu.cn, brucezmf@gmail.com

Abstract. Cloud computing brings dynamic resource scalability, pay-per-use billing model and simplified developing platforms, however, the monitoring of cloud today is still confronted with the flexibility, scalability, efficiency and performance problems, especially when the scale of cloud platform is being constantly expanding recent years. In this paper, we first present an efficient and intelligent monitoring architecture for cloud platform based on Data Distribution Service(DDS) and Complex Event Processing(CEP), in order to cope with these challenging issues. Then we mainly focus on the monitoring data dissemination, give more details on how DDS is used in this architecture and propose a comprehensive data delivery algorithm to achieve better accuracy and efficiency.

Keywords: Cloud Monitoring, Data Distribution Service, Complex Event Processing.

1   Introduction

As one of the hottest topics in current internet systems, cloud computing has transferred the delivery of IT services to new level that brings comfort of traditional utilities such as water, electricity to its users by dynamically scaling the service provision. Such dynamic scalability and service level agreement (SLA) negotiability of cloud computing result in a strong demand for monitoring.

Resource monitoring, which has been widely used for software optimization, profiling, performance evaluation, etc [1], is the premise of many major operations such as fault detecting, network analysis, job scheduling, and load balancing in cloud systems [2]. Organizations that are using right mix of technologies for cloud monitoring are more likely to enjoy following business benefits: prevention and resolution of performance issues in a timely manner, ability to support changes in business demand, ability to optimize spending decisions, etc [3].

However, monitoring the cloud at runtime is very challenging. Firstly, much more monitoring concerns need to be covered in clouds than in traditional software system, and individual monitoring schemas and mechanisms need to be

---

* Corresponding author.

C. Liu et al. (Eds.): ICSOC 2012, LNCS 7636, pp. 733–747, 2012.

designed and implemented respectively, due to the heterogeneity of components in the cloud. An integral cloud monitoring system should cover all the concerns, for satisfying the needs of different roles in the cloud.

Furthermore, each monitoring technique needs to consume some computing resources to take effect. Therefore, it will lead to some undesired runtime overhead to a running cloud. It is a challenging issue to keep such overhead within an acceptable range. Although the weaker the monitoring ability is, the lower the runtime overhead is, enough monitoring ability is still required to ensure the healthy operation for a running cloud. Consequently, how to balance the tradeoff between monitoring ability and runtime overhead is one of the most important issues in cloud monitoring system.

Lastly, due to the large number of services and end users in cloud, monitoring applications have to process a massive amount of runtime information for sending alerts or triggering some actions once something noteworthy happens. Usually, this information is provided in a steady stream of separate events which are detected by certain monitoring sensors. As a result, an efficient and robust communication infrastructure is required, for facilitating the dissemination of monitoring events with high throughput and low latency. Additionally, it will also need to apply real-time intelligence to the management of your cloud infrastructure through making automated decisions. For example, we can anticipate upcoming peak loads and provide the necessary capacity in advance to avoid performance slowdowns through cloud monitoring.

Therefore, in order to deal with these difficulties, an efficient and intelligent monitoring architecture for cloud platform is first proposed in this paper. In this architecture, an efficient and robust data dissemination framework is implemented to transmit the monitoring information reliably with high throughput and low latency based on Data Distribution Service (DDS)[5]. An intelligent cloud action platform is also developed to deal with infinite dynamic event stream based on Complex Event Processing (CEP) [6]. So it can filter out the meaningful information from the event flood to support decision making.

Then, in this paper, we mainly focus on monitoring data dissemination, after describing how DDS is used in this monitoring architecture, an extended comprehensive data delivery algorithm Papx is proposed to achieve better accuracy and efficiency based on the theory of temporal locality. Through this algorithm, the agent of our monitoring architecture can perform well on the balance between runtime overhead and monitoring capability with the adaptive updating frequency regulation.

The organization of this paper is as follows: section 2 gives an overview of the efficient and intelligent monitoring architecture for cloud platform. Then in section 3, details of how DDS is used in this architecture and the concrete implementation of Papx are presented. After that, section 4 shows the experimental evaluation results of the proposed algorithm. In section 5, relevant work concerning cloud monitoring is introduced. Finally, we summarize conclusions.

2   Efficient and Intelligent Monitoring Architecture for Cloud Platform

The scale of cloud computing platform has being constantly expanding recent years. According to reports, Google cloud computing platform already has more than one million servers. Amazon, IBM, Microsoft, Yahoo and other companies each also has hundreds of thousands of servers for their cloud computing. Besides the powerful computing and storage capacity, this kind of fairly large scale also brings some challenging issues for cloud monitoring.

One one hand, how to transmit the huge monitoring data to the server with high throughput and low latency is one of the most challenging issues, especially when it deals with thousands to millions physical servers. On the other hand, due to large amount of real-time data will be generated in this large scale cloud monitoring system, how to extract user required information from these confused data to provide strong support for decision making is also one of the most challenging issues in cloud monitoring.

In order to deal with these challenges, an efficient and intelligent monitoring architecture for cloud platform is proposed based on DDS and CEP in this section. As described in Fig. 1, different types of monitoring facilities are contained in a monitoring agent to collect runtime information from entities of each level of the cloud in timely manner. Then these runtime information will be encapsulated to events, so as to be delivered to the server by DDS efficiently and timely. After that, on the one hand, for facilitating manual control, analysis and display, monitoring server will save these data in database and system logs for persistency and then show to cloud operators, service developers and end users through different views. On the other hand, the cloud action platform will do a variety of complex checking and statistics to trigger related operations through CEP, in order to provide intelligent decisions for cloud management system.

Why and how we use DDS to transmit the huge monitoring information will be described more details in section 3. Due to space limitation, we just give an overview of the cloud action platform in this paper. The core component of the cloud action platform is a CEP engine, which can coordinate and refine the simple events to abstract the complex event for intelligent decision according to the monitoring rules and event schemas [8].

In addition, for reducing the coupling of event rules and decision actions and making the code reading and maintain easy, a portal that can help users configure the complex events based on customized monitoring rules is also developed in this cloud action platform. In this way, users or the third-party systems can define their own complex events conveniently, and they can also modify the rules dynamically when users' requirements or system runtime status changed.

3   Efficient Data Dissemination for Cloud Monitoring

As the number of nodes in clouds reaches a high value, vast runtime information will be send to monitoring server. It is likely to cause network congestion and

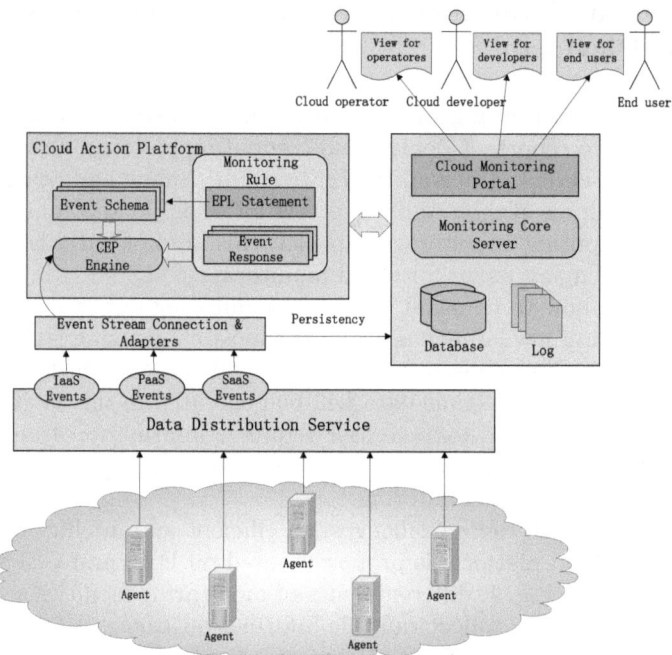

Fig. 1. Efficient and Intelligent Monitoring Architecture for Cloud Platform

make system throughput decline. For neutralizing the impact of this challenge, DDS will be used to delivery these huge monitoring data. Furthermore, an extended data delivery algorithm that can deal with the balance between runtime overhead and monitoring capability will be made to cope with this challenge too.

3.1 Data Dissemination Based on DDS

DDS is an emergent platform-independent standard that defines a data centric publish/subscribe interaction paradigm. It particularly addresses the needs of real-time applications that require deterministic information exchange, low memory footprints and high robustness requirements.

Design of the Data Model. Entities required to be monitored in cloud system can be classified into five categories: hardware, virtualization, middleware, application and interaction [4]. However, due to the tradeoff between efficient data transfer and flexible interpretation of these data, the data of each entity are not published as a whole in our cloud monitoring architecture. We divide the monitoring data of each entity into three categories: *EntityBasicInfo*, *EntityStatus* and *EntityEvent*. Note that the entities of interaction can be subsumed to a specific *EntityEvent*.

The category of *EntityBasicInfo* contains the basic information of each monitored entity. These basic information are often published to initialize the entity and rarely to be modified during the runtime. Below an example is provided for the data structure for virtual machine basic information. Each attribute is defined with a data type and a name.

```
struct   VMBasicInfo   {
    long vm_id;      long pm_id;
    int cpu_amount;    int memory_size;
    int disk_size;    string owner;
}
```

The category of *EntityStatus* defines all the runtime status information for each entity. This information come from various monitoring metrics and will be published periodically. As an example, the data structure for virtual machine status is provided below.

```
struct   VMStatus   {
    long vm_id;      string status;
    double cpu_util;    double disk_util;
    double memory_util;
}
```

The event data occurs in a running cloud will be pushed to the server immediately. Furthermore, this kind of events occurs as not frequently as the status updates, so we make it independent from the data type of entity status. There maybe serval kinds of event data types for one entity, while each entity has only one data type for the basic information and status. For example, there are *create, start, user_login, shutdown, delete* events for some specific application. Due to the different causes and participants of these events, all of them will be modeled as a data type individually in our cloud monitoring architecture.

Design of the Topic Structure. Topics, which hold one specific type of object defined by one data type, play an important part when designing a distributed publish/subscribe system [7]. In a DDS application, publishers write to topics while subscribers read from them. For our cloud monitoring architecture, a lot of topics will be defined, and each of them is bound to one data type. So we classified them into five categories which are described in Fig. 2.

In the centre of this figure, data topic categories are displayed and the corresponding data types are provided in brackets. The arrow directions indicate whether a participant is a publisher or subscriber with respect to a certain topic. When the monitoring system initializes, agents will publish data into the topic category *BasicInfoInitiation* to register the entities. If required you can publish data into the topic *BasicInfoModification* to modify these basic information. Then during runtime, all the status information are published periodically into the topic category *EntityStatusUpdate* to update the runtime information for each entity, while the event information are published into the topic category *EntityEventReport* to report these kinds of information in timely manner. In addition, server can publish the command data into the topic category *Command* to control or configure the agent dynamically.

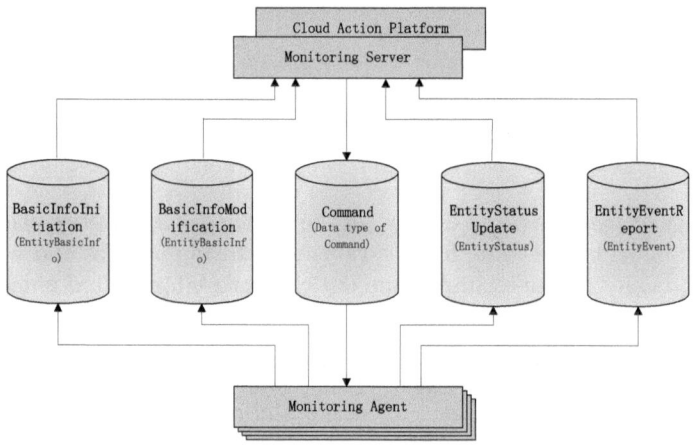

Fig. 2. Topic structure of cloud monitoring system

3.2   Comprehensive Data Delivery Algorithm

As one of the most challenging issues of cloud monitoring, the balance between runtime overhead and monitoring capability has caught the attention of researchers. In addition to dynamically adding or subtracting monitoring facilities of the agent to achieve this balance, a comprehensive data delivery model that combines the pull-based model and push-based model is proposed to deal with cloud monitoring in [2], for decreasing updating times and costs.

However, the Pap algorithm proposed in [2] is inadequate in some respects. First, User Tolerant Degree (UTD) proposed to describe how tolerant a user is to the status inaccuracy, depends on specific application environment and can not vary with the current runtime status dynamically. On the other hand, the increased or decreased pull interval in the pull algorithm is fixed and can not be adjusted according to the current change degree of pulled value.

In order to cope with these deficiencies, we extend this algorithm based on the theory of temporal locality to achieve better accuracy and efficiency in our monitoring architecture. Compared with the Pap algorithm, the extended PapX algorithm can efficiently capture the significant change of monitored values and dynamically adjust UTD and pull interval, for not losing the important updates and improving the accuracy of monitored values.

The extended PapX model consists of two mutual exclusive algorithms: Push algorithm and Pull algorithm. By comparing current change degree of monitored values with dynamic user tolerant degree, the Push and Pull models are alternated adaptively. Before introducing the details of this algorithm, let's have a look at the assumptions and definitions in the following.

Change Degree (CD), defined in Eq. (1), describes the extent of change for monitoring status value between a producer and the corresponding consumer at certain time point.

$$CD(t) = \frac{|P(t) - C(t)|}{Max - Min} \tag{1}$$

Where $P(t)$ denotes the status value of the producer at time t, while $C(t)$ represents the value maintained in the consumer at time t. Max and Min are the maximal and minimal possible value of status separately.

Additionally, in order to capture the change of monitored resource status in recent period, we maintain a sliding window of information about previous updated values for each resource status. Assume $A_0, A_1, ..., A_i, i \leq N$, represents the successive updates to the server in this window, whose size is N. Then the average amount of change (Avg_AC), which describes the average amount of change for the resource status in the sliding window, can be defined as:

$$Avg\_AC = \frac{\sum_{i=1}^{N}(|A_i - A_{i-1}| * i)}{\sum_{j=1}^{N} j} \tag{2}$$

The Dynamic User Tolerant Degree (d_UTD), defined in Eq. (3), describes how tolerant a user is to the status inaccuracy in current sliding window, when taking the average change degree of resource status in current sliding window as adjustable parameters. The value of d_UTD is initialized to user defined UTD and is dynamically calculated. If current change degree of the monitored resource status is larger than the d_UTD, the value will be updated.

$$d\_UTD = UTD \times (1 - \frac{Avg\_AC}{Max - Min}) \tag{3}$$

The core idea behind d_UTD is to decrease the value of UTD, for not losing the important updates, when status changes significantly during current sliding window. Since according to the theory of temporal locality, the larger the status change is, the more attention we should pay on these updated values.

Different from the fixed incremental of pulling interval in [2], the server periodically pull from the agents with a dynamic rate in our PapX algorithm. The pulling rate is adaptively determined based on last pull interval and current damping factor of pull interval, which depends on current average change degree in the window and the user predefined initial incremental value in our algorithm, so the dynamic pull interval (DPI) can be defined as:

$$DPI(t) = \begin{cases} \lfloor DPI(t_0) + STEP \times (1 - \frac{Avg\_AC}{Max - Min}) \rfloor, if \Delta \leq 0, \\ \lfloor DPI(t_0) - STEP \times (1 - \frac{Avg\_AC}{Max - Min}) \rfloor, if \Delta > 0. \end{cases} \tag{4}$$

$$\Delta = CD(t) - d\_UTD(t) \tag{5}$$

Where $DPI(t_0)$ is the last pull interval at time t_0, $STEP$ presents the user predefined incremental of pulling interval. Fig. 3 and Fig. 4 show details of the Push and Pull algorithm separately. In order to avoid Push and Pull operations concurrently happen in a same period, the two operation identifiers, $isPulled$ and $isPushed$ are set to be mutual exclusive to reduce updating times.

```
1   WHILE TRUE
2       set Pull operation identifier isPulled←FALSE waiting for Push_interval
3       IF isPulled equals to TRUE during Push_interval
4           update status information (s_now) that Server currently holds,
5           update the values in the sliding window(can be modeled as a Length
            Fixed Queue)
6       ELSE //check whether need to Push
7           get sensor's current value (sensor_now) at Agent,
8           calculate the value of CD(t), Avg_AC, d_UTD according to Eq. (1), (2),
9           (3) separately
10          IF CD(t)>d_UTD
11              isPushed←TRUE, s_now←sensor_now,
12              push s_now to the Server
13          ENDIF
14      ENDIF
15  ENDWHILE
```

Fig. 3. PapX-Push Algorithm

When the value of d_UTD is relatively small, the Push method dominates, because the condition at line 10 in Fig. 3 is easily to be met, and the Push operations are frequently triggered. On the other side, although the Pull algorithm is trying to minimize Pull interval's value, the PULL_INTERVAL_MIN blocks this trend when Pull interval becomes very small (line 20 to line 22 in Fig. 4).

Similarly, when the value of d_UTD is relatively large, the Pull-based method will dominates. Only when the value of d_UTD is relatively moderate, none of Push and Pull dominates and both of them act frequently. More details about the evaluation and comparison between our extend PapX algorithm and the Pap algorithm proposed in [2] will be described in Section 4.

4   Evaluation

The balance between updating times and accuracy of monitored values plays a very important role on reducing costs and improving efficiency of cloud monitoring. In this sectioon, we evaluate the key performance indexes of the proposed PapX algorithm through experimental based tests.

```
1   Initialize Pull operation's initial interval: PULL_INIT_INL,
    minimal possible interval: PULL_INL_MIN and maximal possible interval:
    PULL_INL_MAX, initial incremental interval: STEP
2   Pull_interval←PULL_INIT_INL
3   WHILE (TRUE)
4       set Push operation identifier isPushed←FLASE
5       waiting for Pull_interval
6       IF isPushed equals to TRUE
7           update status information (s_now) that Server currently holds,
8           update the values in the sliding window (can be modeled as a Length
        Fixed Queue)
9       ELSE
10          isPulled←TRUE, Pull the Agent
11          update s_now,
12          update the sliding window
13      ENDIF
14      calculate the value of CD(t) according to Eq. (1)
15      calculate the value of d_UTD according to Eq. (2) and (3)
16      calculate the value of DPI(t) according to Eq. (4)
17      IF CD(t)≤d_UTD
18          Pull_interval=min{DPI(t), PULL_INL_MAX}
19      ENDIF
20      ELSE IF CD(t)>d_UTD
21          Pull_interval =max{DPI(t), PULL_INTERVAL_MIN}
22      ENDIF
23      s_last←s_now
24  ENDWHILE
```

Fig. 4. PapX-Pull Algorithm

4.1   Experimental Environment

In this experiment, we choose two PCs as a transmission pair to evaluate the performance of our proposed PapX algorithm and the Pap algorithm proposed in [2]. One PC plays as a Producer and the other plays as a Consumer. Each PC is equipped with two Pentium(R) Dual-Core CPU E5200@2.50GHz, 2 GB memory and Ubuntu Release 10.0.4(lucid). To simplify the experiment, we use only the CPU load percentage to test performance of the two models.

This experiment aims for a high accuracy and low intrusiveness data transmission for cloud monitoring. So we analyze and evaluate the two algorithms from the two aspects. For better comparing the accuracy, we define Inaccuracy Degree (ID) to denote the degree of inaccuracy between the value holds on the server and the real value collected by the agent, the expression can be described as follows:

$$ID(t) = \frac{1}{et - st} \times \int_{st}^{et} [C(t) - P(t)]^2 dt \qquad (6)$$

where st and et represent the start and end time of monitoring separately. $C(t)$ denotes the value that the server holds at time t, while $P(t)$ denotes the value collected by agent at time t.

4.2 Experimental Analysis

For facilitating repeating the experiments to analyze the efficiency and accuracy of the two algorithms, we first collected and saved 1000 times of updating. Then in later experiments, the Push interval of the agent was set to 10s, and the server's PULL_INIT_INTERVAL, PULL_INTERVAL_MIN, and PULL_INTERVAL_MAX were set to 5s, 3s and 12s, respectively. In addition, the STEP of Pull interval increment was set to 1s.

Table 1 describes the comparative results of PapX and Pap algorithm under different window size and UTD. In this group of experiments, we set the presentative values 2, 6, 10, 20, and 50 for window size. And the value of UTD varies from 0 to 1 with an incremental interval of 0.1. For each cell of this table, the value before "/" is the result of Pap algorithm and the value after "/" is the result of PapX algorithm. Due to the limitation of space, the comparative results when UTD is 0.3 and 0.7 are ignored in this table.

Table 1. Comparative results of PapX and Pap algorithm

		0.1	**0.2**	**0.4**	**0.5**	**0.6**	**0.8**	**0.9**
2	Updates	319/310	154/152	96/99	90/93	88/88	87/88	87/88
	Inaccuracy	0.12/0.10	0.23/0.22	0.31/0.30	0.35/0.34	0.35/0.31	0.39/0.36	0.37/0.35
6	Updates	319/314	154/146	96/96	90/93	88/89	87/88	87/88
	Inaccuracy	0.12/0.12	0.23/0.24	0.31/0.29	0.35/0.32	0.35/0.32	0.39/0.36	0.37/0.34
10	Updates	319/310	154/151	96/100	90/93	88/88	87/88	87/88
	Inaccuracy	0.12/0.13	0.23/0.28	0.31/0.30	0.35/0.34	0.33/0.32	0.39/0.36	0.37/0.36
20	Updates	319/323	154/155	96/97	90/93	88/88	87/88	87/88
	Inaccuracy	0.19/0.13	0.23/0.22	0.31/0.30	0.35/0.33	0.35/0.32	0.39/0.35	0.37/0.36
50	Updates	319/326	154/158	96/97	90/94	88/88	87/88	87/88
	Inaccuracy	0.12/0.15	0.23/0.22	0.31/0.33	0.35/0.33	0.35/0.32	0.39/0.36	0.37/0.36

Now, we will analyze these data in table 1. First, we fix the window size, and vary UTD to reveal the relation between updating number and UTD. Fig. 5(a) describes the result when window size is fixed to 6 and UTD varies from 0 to 1. Overall, the total updating number decreases with UTD rising, and the Push operations' number drops dramatically, while the Pull operations' number grows slightly. The reason for this phenomenon is that the rate of Pull operations' number increasing is much less than the rate of Push operations' number decreasing. The figure also proves our analytical result described in section 3.1. That is when UTD is relatively low, most of the updating operations are push, and when UTD is relatively high, the number of Pull operations is dominant.

Also we observe the number of Push operation is not 0 but a small value when the UTD is 1 in our PapX algorithm, it is because the positive feedback effect of

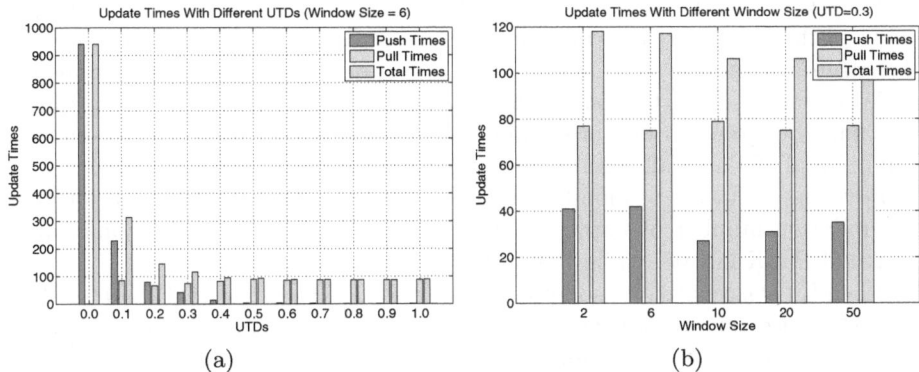

Fig. 5. Updating number of PapX at different (a)UTDs and (b)window size

dynamic UTD to the rare dramatically changes of monitoring values. In order not to lose the important updating, the PapX algorithm proposed in this paper needes to capture and transmit the significant changes even the UTD is relatively high. In addition, as UTD increases, the number of pull operation increases slowly until it to be stabilized. During this process, little fluctuations occur due to the responding result of dynamic pull interval DPI(t) to the dramatically change of monitoring information.

Fig. 5(b) shows the experimental result of PapX algorithm with different window size and a fixed UTD 0.3. From this figure, we can see that overall the differentiation of the results of different window size is small. The main reason for this phenomenon is that the average change degree of the sliding window is calculated according to the weighted moving average of the change of each two adjacent monitored values, so the influence of the window size is weakened. This is consistent with the theory of temporal locality, since the latest change of these monitored values often has the greatest impact on the eventual result.

From table 1, we also find the updating number of PapX algorithm is a little bigger than the Pap algorithm. However, the accuracy of PapX is much better than Pap. We tried to give an intuitionistic comparison of the accuracy for the two algorithms in one figure. Unluckily, the amount of the data is so large that the differences of them are not evident in one figure. So in the following experiments, we select the first 200 updates to compare the accuracy of them. Since the window size has a little influence on the eventual result, we fix it to 6.

When UTD is 0, users can not tolerant the deviation of monitored values, so the two alogorithms degenerate to the pure push algorithm, and the inaccuracy of them are both 0. When UTD is relatively low, take 0.2 (Fig. 6(a)) for example, the PapX algorithm has evident superiority than Pap algorithm on accuracy. Although the updating number of PapX and Pap algorithm are both 42, the inaccuracy degree of PapX is 0.67, while Pap is 0.74. This phenomenon is mainly caused by the dynamic UTD. When significant changes of monitored values occur, the dynamic UTD of PapX algorithm will decrease to do more push operations, so the accuracy is improved evidently in PapX.

When UTD is relatively high, take 1.0 (Fig. 6(b)) for example, the push operations of the two algorithms are not triggered in this example. However, the Pap algorithm just modifies the pull interval according to the constant incremental, while the PapX algorithm can modify the pull interval dynamically according to the change degree of monitored values. So when significant change occurs, the pull interval of PapX algorithm may decrease to a lower value immediately, and improve the accuracy of monitored values. As described in Fig. 6(b), although the updating number of PapX and Pap algorithm are both 19, the inaccuracy degree of PapX is 1.08, while Pap is 1.11.

When UTD is relatively moderate, as described in Fig. 7(a) (UTD=0.6), PapX algorithm also has evident superiority than Pap algorithm on accuracy. PapX algorithm just updates one more time and the inaccuracy degree decreases from 0.91 to 0.85. The reason for this phenomenon is mainly the combined influence by dynamic UTD and pull interval described before when significant changes occur.

Through the above logical analysis and experimental comparison, we conclude that the proposed adaptive PapX algorithm can work efficiently with the change of user requirements and monitoring status for cloud monitoring. When compared with the Pap algorithm, PapX has a higher degree of intelligence, since it can efficiently capture the mutations of monitored values to decrease the number of updating and increase the accuracy of monitored values. Fig. 7(b) shows the comparative result on updating number and accuracy for the two algorithms. From this figure, we can see that when the total updating number is low, the accuracy of PapX algorithm is much better than Pap algorithm under the same updating number. As the number of updating increases, the superiority of PapX algorithm on accuracy decreases slowly until the performance of them are analogous.

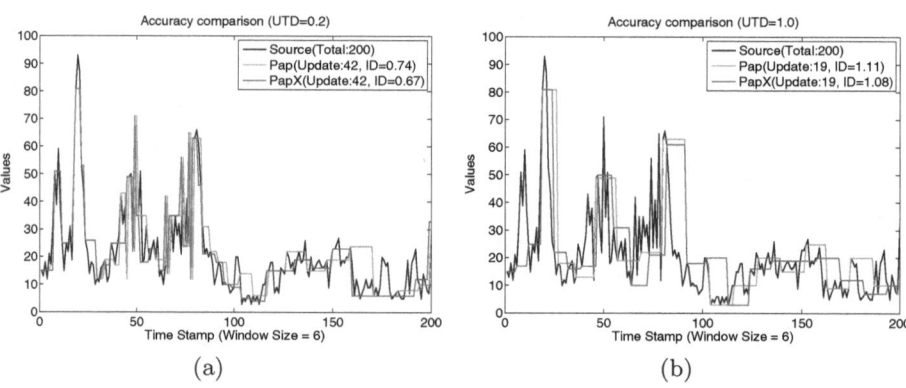

(a)   (b)

Fig. 6. Accuracy comparison between PapX and Pap when (a) UTD=0.2 and (b) UTD=1.0, window size is 6

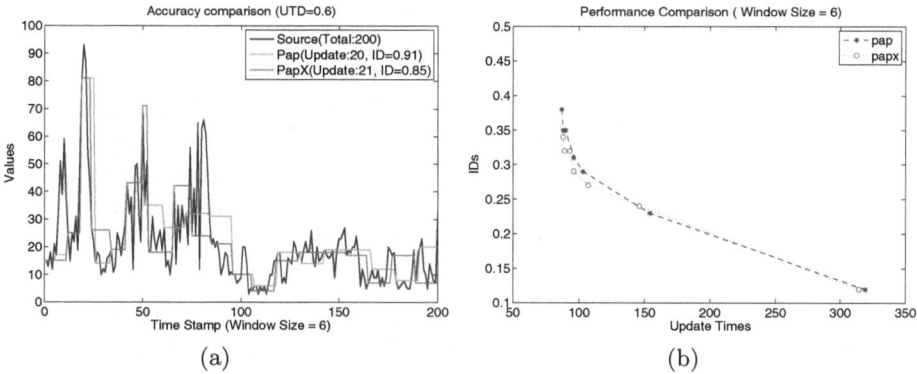

Fig. 7. (a) Accuracy comparison between PapX and Pap when UTD=0.6, window size is 6; (b) Comparison on updating number and accuracy for PapX and Pap

5   Related Work

Well-known clouds in the industry all have their own monitoring system. The representative one is App Engine System Status Dashboard, which can be used to show how the applications work in Google App Engine [11]. In addition, a third-party tool CloudStatus [12] is also developed by Hyperic Inc. to monitor Amazon service and Google App Engine.

However, research work concerned with cloud monitoring is relatively less. Due to monitoring of cloud systems typically contains three main activities: collection, dissemination and processing of monitoring information, below we will focus the discussion of related work on them respectively.

Monitoring Data Collecting: A RESTful approach is proposed in [13] to monitor and manage cloud infrastructures. Entities in the cloud are modeled with REST in a tree structure. However, such an organization of monitored information is suitable for cloud infrastructure, and other entities in the cloud can not be modeled appropriately. Therefore, in [4], the authors propose a more universal runtime model for cloud monitoring (RMCM). All the raw monitoring data gathered by multiple monitoring techniques can be organized by this model to present an intuitive representation of a cloud.

Monitoring Data Dissemination: There are two basic data delivery models for communications between consumers and producers: the pull model and the push model [14]. However, a pure push or pull model is not suited for so many different kinds of virtualized resources in cloud system. So a hybrid resource monitoring model called P&P model is proposed in [2] for cloud system. Compared with this hybrid model, our extended model PapX can achieve better suitability and efficiency for cloud monitoring, due to the dynamic UTD and pull interval based on the theory of temporal locality.

For data dissemination methods, the standards-based QoS-enabled pub/sub platforms are promising approaches to build and evolve large-scale monitoring systems. As an emergent standard for QoS-enabled pub/sub communication, DDS [5] attracts more and more attentions in mission-critical distributed real-time and embedded systems. Compared with the traditional pub/sub platforms, such as CORBA [15], SOAP [16], JMS [17], DDS perform significantly better and are well-suited for data-critical real-time systems [18]. Additionally, in [7], the authors discussed the applicability of DDS for the development of automated and modular manufacturing systems. As far as we know, we are the first to bring DDS into the data dissemination for cloud monitoring.

Monitoring Data Processing: Monitoring applications often involves processing a massive amount of data from a possibly huge number of data sources [19]. CEP [6] has evolved as the paradigm of choice to determine meaningful situations (complex events) for decision making by performing stepwise correlation over event streams in many domains, such as processing of environmental sensor data, trades in financial markets and RSS web feeds [19, 20]. In [21], a complex event language that significantly extends existing event languages to meet the needs of a range of RFID enabled monitoring applications is introduced first, then a query plan-based approach and some optimization techniques are used to efficiently implementing this language.

6   Conclusion

In this paper, an efficient and intelligent monitoring architecture for cloud platform is proposed to deal with the flexibility, scalability and efficiency challenges of cloud monitoring. In this architecture, an efficient and robust data dissemination framework is implemented to transmit the huge runtime information reliably with high throughput and low latency based on DDS. An intelligent cloud action platform is developed to provide decision making support for cloud management system based on CEP. In addition, an extended comprehensive data delivery algorithm Papx is also proposed to achieve better balance between runtime overhead and monitoring capability in this architecture.

Acknowledgment. This work was supported by National Science and Technology Supporting Program (No.2012BAH06F02, No.2011BAD21B02), Research Fund for the Doctoral Program by Ministry of Education of China (No.20110101110066), Science and Technology Program of Zhejiang Province (No.2011C14004), Zhejiang Provincial Natural Science Foundation of China under grant (No.LY12F02029), and National Technology Support Program under grant (No.2011BAH16B04).

References

1. Delgado, N., Gates, A., Roach, S.: A taxonomy and catalog of runtime software-fault monitoring tools. IEEE Transactions on Software Engineering, 859–872 (December 2004)

2. Huang, H., Wang, L.: P&P: a Combined Push-Pull Model for Resource Monitoring in Cloud Computing Environment. In: IEEE 3rd International Conference on Cloud Computing (2010)

3. White Paper from ManageEngine. Four Keys for Monitoring Cloud Services (March 2010), http://www.manageengine.com

4. Shao, J., Wei, H., Wang, Q., Mei, H.: A Runtime Model Based Monitoring Approach for Cloud. In: IEEE 3rd International Conference on Cloud Computing (2010)

5. Object Management Group. Data Distribution Service (DDS) Brief (2011)

6. Wu, E., Diao, Y., Rizvi, S.: High-Performance Complex Event Processing over Streams. In: SIGMOD 2006, Chicago, Illinois, USA, June 27-29 (2006)

7. Ryll, M., Ratchev, S.: Application of the Data Distribution Service for Flexible Manufacturing Automation. Proceedings of World Academy of Sciency, Engineering and Technology 31 (July 2008)

8. Si-Tu, F.: Event-based Monitoring and Management of the Distributed System, M.Sc. Dissertation, Shanghai Jiao Tong University, Shanghai, P.R. China (2009)

9. Baldoni, R., Bonomi, S., Lodi, G., Querzoni, L.: Data Dissemination supporting collaborative complex event processing: characteristics and open issues. In: DD4LCCI 2010, Valencia, Spain (2010)

10. Bry, F., Eckert, M., Etzion, O., Riecke, J., Paschke, A.: Event Processing Languages. Tutorial in DEBS 2009 (2009)

11. Google App Engine. Google Inc., http://code.google.com/appengine/

12. Cloudstatus. Hyperic Inc., http://www.cloudstatus.com/

13. Han, H., Kim, S., Jung, H., Yeom, H.Y., Yoon, C., Park, J., Lee, Y.: A restful approach to the management of cloud infrastructure. In: Proc. IEEE International Conference on Cloud Computing, CLOUD 2009, September 21-25 (2009)

14. Chung, W.-C., Chang, R.-S.: Chang A new mechanism for resource monitoring in Grid computing. Future Generation Computer Systems 25, 1–7 (2009)

15. Krishna, A.S., Schmidt, D.C., Klefstad, R., Corsaro, A.: Real-time CORBA Middleware. In: Mahmoud, Q. (ed.) Middleware for Communications. Wiley and Sons, New York (2003)

16. Abu-Ghazaleh, N., Lewis, M.J., Govindaraju, M.: Differential Serialization for Optimized SOAP Performance. In: Proceedings of HPDC-13: IEEE International Symposium on High Performance Distributed Computing, Honolulu, Hawaii, pp. 55–64

17. Hapner, M., Burridge, R., Sharma, R., Fialli, J., Stout, K.: Java Message Service. Sun Microsystems Inc., Santa Clara (2002)

18. Xiong, M., Parsons, J., Edmondson, J., Nguyen, H., Schmidt, D.C.: Evaluating the Performance of Publish/Subscribe Platforms for Information Management in Distributed Real-time and Embedded Systems

19. Poul, N., Migliavacca, M., Pietzuch, P.: Distributed Complex Event Processing with Query Rewriting. In: DEBS 2009, Nashville, TN, USA, July 6-9 (2009)

20. Volz, M., Koldehofe, B., Rothermel, K.: Supporting Strong Reliability for Distributed Complex Event Processing Systems. In: Proceedings of 13th IEEE International Conference on High Performance Computing and Communications (HPCC 2011), Banff, Alberta, Canada, pp. 477–486 (September 2011)

21. Wu, E., Diao, Y., Rizvi, S.: High-Performance Complex Event Processing over Streams. In: SIGMOD 2006, Chicago, Illinois, USA, June 27-29 (2006)

A Service Oriented Architecture for Exploring High Performance Distributed Power Models

Yan Liu, Jared M. Chase, and Ian Gorton

Pacific Northwest National Laboratory
Richland WA 99352
{yan.liu,jared.chase,ian.gorton}@pnnl.gov

Abstract. Power grids are increasingly incorporating high quality, high throughput sensor devices inside power distribution networks. These devices are driving an unprecedented increase in the volume and rate of available information. The real-time requirements for handling this data are beyond the capacity of conventional power models running in central utilities. Hence, we are exploring distributed power models deployed at the regional scale. The connection of these models for a larger geographic region is supported by a distributed system architecture. This architecture is built in a service oriented style, whereby distributed power models running on high performance clusters are exposed as services. Each service is semantically annotated and therefore can be discovered through a service catalog and composed into workflows. The overall architecture has been implemented as an integrated workflow environment useful for power researchers to explore newly developed distributed power models.

Keywords: Service oriented architecture, high performance computing, power grid.

1 Introduction

Electrical power grids are increasingly incorporating high quality, high throughput sensor devices in the power distribution network. These devices are driving an unprecedented increase in the volume and the rate of information available to utilities. For example, a new Phasor Measurement Unit (PMU) sensor produces up to 60 samples per second, in contrast to existing conventional Supervisory Control And Data Acquisition (SCADA) measurements generated every five seconds or longer. The dramatic growth of these high quality sensors demands new power grid models for real-time predictions, with the time to solution in the range of ten milliseconds to one second. This is a radical reduction from the current ranges of two to four minutes.

Given the sheer size of the power grid, the solution of mathematical power models requires significant time to solve. With conventional power grid operations, the core power model of state estimation can only be updated in an interval of several minutes – much slower than the measurement cycle in seconds. However, a power grid could become unstable and collapse within seconds [5]. Therefore, the current state estimation is not fast enough to predict real-time power grid behavior and respond to emergencies such as the 2003 US-Canada Blackout [6].

C. Liu et al. (Eds.): ICSOC 2012, LNCS 7636, pp. 748–762, 2012.
© Springer-Verlag Berlin Heidelberg 2012

High Performance Computing (HPC) techniques are essential to handle such a dramatic increase in data size and rate and to meet the demand of the real-time predictions. Using the Western Electricity Coordinating Council (WECC) model as an example, for state estimation, the solution time is about five seconds [7], while for contingency analysis, about a 500-times speedup was achieved with 512 processors [8][9][10]. However, HPC capabilities usually can only support the computing demand at the regional scale; while real-time predictions model for power grids requires computing resources at the continental scale. Thus, the critical issue is how to build a power model that connects HPC-enabled regional-scale distributed power grids.

Many researchers have worked on hierarchical or distributed state estimation, such as [1-4]. Their work is mainly focused on the distributed state estimation algorithms and their efficiencies. There is no such a tool that has a capability to deploy the distributed power models in a HPC-based distributed computing environment.

At Pacific Northwest National Laboratory, our research aims to design a distributed system architecture that leverages parallel computing capacities to support the demand of real-time computing for distributed power models. In our previous work, we have investigated a method to partition the overall topology of a power grid into several connected sub-areas [20]. We have also implemented a distributed state estimation algorithm that allows each sub-area to compute its local state estimation on a HPC cluster. In this algorithm, adjacent sub-areas exchange their own state estimation results so that global state beyond the local area can be computed [21].

Our previous implementation has the peer-to-peer data exchange through middleware that connects state estimators through TCP sockets [20]. Therefore the data communication logic has been hard-coded in the state estimation code, which needs to know the destination of the intermediate results. This mechanism has limitations for validating the distributed state estimation algorithm, as to study the algorithm behavior, different partitions of the same power grid network should be tested [11]. The partition may change how the sub-areas are connected and hence the peer-to-peer interactions. Hardcoding the data communication in the state estimation code is certainly not sufficiently flexible to represent the procedural steps of distributed state estimation.

In this paper, we present our solution of exposing individual state estimators as a service and connecting distributed state estimation services into a workflow. The inputs and outputs of each service are semantically defined and therefore can be registered and discovered through a service catalog. Connected services are guaranteed to match the input and output types. The overall architecture has been implemented as an integrated workflow environment, including a workbench for an engineer to compose and monitor a workflow, a service repository to register and search a matching service, and job management for launching HPC jobs in a remote cluster. This workflow environment enables power grid researchers to explore newly developed distributed power models. In this paper, we present our engineering solution to realize this service oriented design. We discuss our experience and summarize the benefit and limitation of this solution.

2   Background on HPC-Based Distributed State Estimation

We briefly introduce the distributed state estimation algorithm. A state estimator basically solves the non-linear state estimation equations as:

$$z = h(x) + e \tag{1}$$

where z is the measurement vector of dimension; x is the state vector; e corresponds to the measurement errors, and h is a vector of non-linear functions which relate states to measurements [12]. Approximately, the state estimation problem can be solved by obtaining the solution to the following equation:

$$z = Hx + e \tag{2}$$

where H is the states to measurements matrix for the entire power system. The data resources include power flow-injections and voltage magnitudes. In the distributed version, the entire power system is decomposed into m non-overlapping sub-areas and each sub-area can run its local state estimation algorithm and also exchange data with neighboring sub-areas to reevaluate its local state estimation solution. Sub-areas are connected via tie lines. Correspondingly, the matrix H and the vector z are also partitioned into m parts as follows and each part is responsible for a subsystem of the entire power system.

$$H = \begin{bmatrix} H_1 \\ H_2 \\ \vdots \\ H_m \end{bmatrix}, z = \begin{bmatrix} z_1 \\ z_2 \\ \vdots \\ z_m \end{bmatrix}, e = \begin{bmatrix} e_1 \\ e_2 \\ \vdots \\ e_m \end{bmatrix}$$

Figure 1 shows the typical tie-line of the IEEE 118-bus system [13] that is used in this paper. The specific procedural steps are as follows, assuming Area 1 as internal and Area 2 being external.

1. Perform the state estimation in individual areas not directly connected to each other (i.e., Area 1 and Area 3) to create the pseudo-measurements of the internal boundary buses connected via tie-lines to other areas (i.e., real and reactive power injection P_{inj} and Q_{inj}, and voltage V). These pseudo measurements create a network equivalent attached to the external system.
2. Run the state estimator of the external connected areas (e.g. Area 2) with measurements obtained in step 1 to calculate new tie-line data. These new data represent an equivalent network attached to external areas. They are used to resolve the influence from the external states on the internal states.
3. Run the state estimator for internal areas. Verify that the boundary buses and tie line estimates are within tolerances; otherwise re-run the external state estimator with updated tie-line information (i.e. step 2).

The data exchanges between state estimators are depicted in Fig. 2 based on the partition shown in Fig. 3. Note that the partition of a bus system affects how sub-areas are connected by tie-line buses [11] and consequently it affects the interaction between the state estimators according to the distributed state estimation algorithm above.

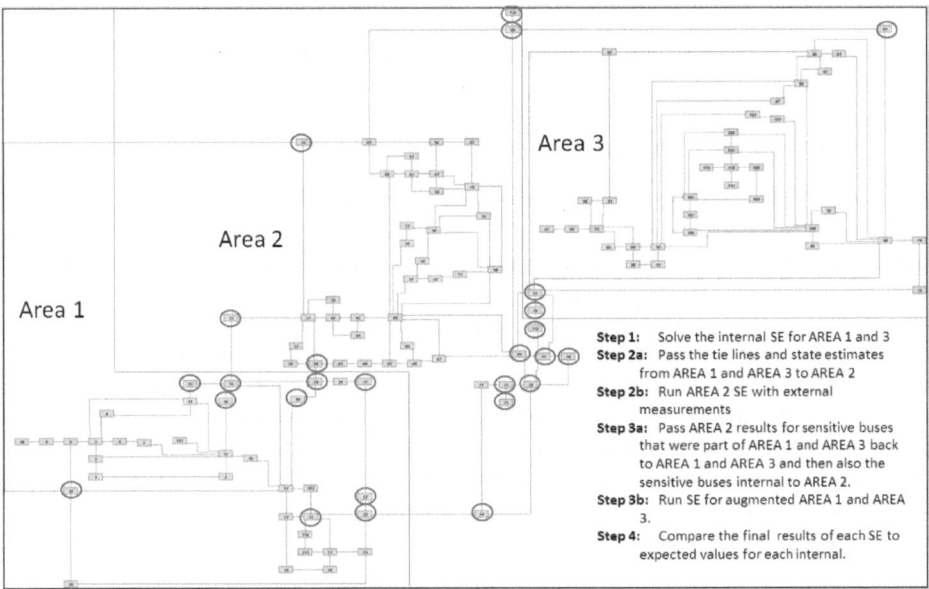

Fig. 1. Partitioning the IEEE 118-bus system into three areas

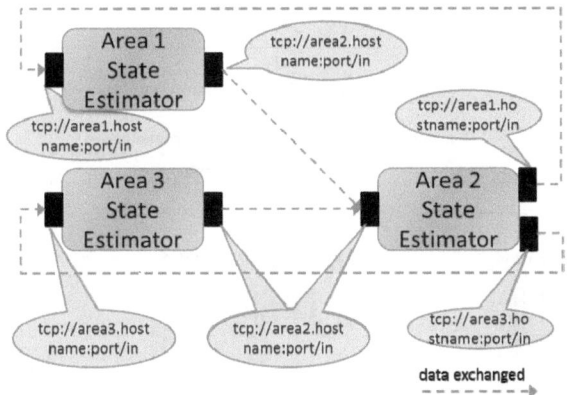

Fig. 2. Data communication between distributed state estimators

To understand the interaction, it is helpful for a power engineer to model the procedural steps of interaction as a workflow and observer the workflow execution. Thus a workflow environment allows the power engineer to examine in detail the step by step execution of the state estimation algorithm and understand not only final results but also the intermediate outputs.

For each state estimator, a Message Passing Interface (MPI)-based code is run on a computational cluster to solve the estimation metrics in (1) and (2). A master processor fetches the data from the data communication infrastructure, partitions the data, and dispatches a block of data to a number of worker processors. All the processors then run the computing tasks in parallel. The state estimation results are gathered after all the computing tasks are completed. More details can be found in our previous work [21].

3   The Service Oriented Architecture

The design of the architecture aims to make individual state estimators autonomous. This means the boundaries between state estimators are explicit, defined in terms of data inputs and outputs.   In this architecture, the state estimator does not need to deal with the data communication with its adjacent neighbors. The data communication is managed by middleware that manages individual state estimators as registered services.   Thus the state estimators can be cataloged and retrieved based on its semantic annotation (especially based on the types of inputs and outputs). The implementation of this design follows service oriented architecture principles. With this design, a power engineer who has the knowledge of the distributed state estimation algorithm can connect state estimators into a workflow aligned with the algorithm. The architecture allows the engineer to launch a state estimator on a HPC cluster and observe the data exchange between state estimators.

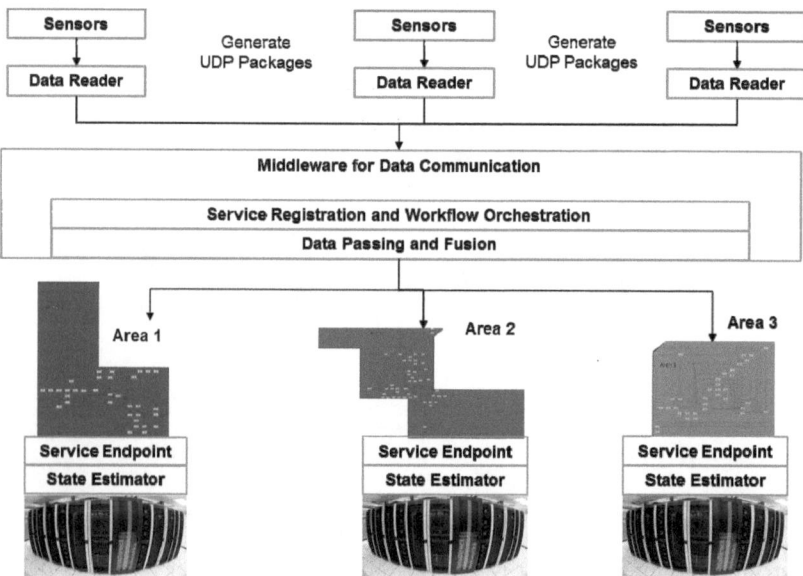

Fig. 3. Service oriented architecture of distributed state estimation

3.1   Architecture Overview

The architecture is depicted in Fig. 3. This architecture consists of three key parts: (1) reading and parsing data streams from the sensors at top of Fig. 3; (2) exposing state estimators as services and coordinating the distributed state estimation workflow in the middle of Fig. 3; (3) launching HPC jobs to run state estimation at the bottom of Fig. 3. The first part has been implemented by scripts and Java applications following the standard IEEE C37.118 protocol to extract specific measurements of bus lines for a power system. In this section, we focus on the other two parts.

3.2   Semantic Service Definition and Registration

The state estimators have been implemented as Fortran MPI programs. To expose a state estimator as a service, we need to define the input and output ports for the state estimator and provide the data type of each port. Input and output ports are defined through constructing an OWL document as follows. In the example below, the semantic type for the input port of the service at area 1 is defined in an OWL Class called Area1Input. This OWL class has one property called hasAREA1InputFilename, and it is of the type Area1InputFile.

```
<owl:Class rdf:about="#Area1Input">
  <owl:equivalentClass>
    <owl:Restriction>
      <owl:onProperty rdf:resource=" #hasAREA1InputFilename"/>
      <owl:cardinality rdf:datatype="http://www.w3.org/2001/XMLSchema#int">1</owl:cardinality>
      <owl:someValuesFrom rdf:resource="#Area1InputFile"/>
    </owl:Restriction>
  </owl:equivalentClass>
</owl:Class>
```

List 1 Semantic definition of the input port

The semantic type of resource Area1InputFile further defines that its data type is string.

```
<owl:Class rdf:about="#Area1InputFile">
  <owl:equivalentClass>
    <owl:Restriction>
      <owl:onProperty rdf:resource="#hasFilename"/>
      <owl:cardinality rdf:datatype="http://www.w3.org/2001/XMLSchema#int">1</owl:cardinality>
      <owl:someValuesFrom rdf:resource="http://www.w3.org/2001/XMLSchema#string"/>
    </owl:Restriction>
  </owl:equivalentClass>
</owl:Class>
```

List 2 Semantic definition of the data type

The purpose of defining the semantic type of a port such as Area1InputFile is to restrict the connection of two state estimator services unless they both have ports that are Area1InputFile strings. Therefore, the rules of connecting state estimators can be expressed by means of the semantic type of ports. Also, typed ports allow searching state estimator services that match the exact type of ports. For example, the resource class Area1InputFile can be used as an attribute to search with. Similarly, an output port can be defined.

After the input and output ports are defined, the next step is to define the service it-self. We use an open source system called SADI (Semantic Automated Discovery and Integration)[1] to generate the service stub code essential for wrapping a state esti-mator as a service. SADI is a framework for discovery of, and interoperability be-tween, distributed data and analytical resources. It combines simple, stateless, GET/POST-based Web Services with standards from the W3C Semantic Web initia-tive. Using SADI, a Java Servlet class is generated and annotated given the service name specified. Previously defined input and output ports are now annotated as @InputClass and @OutputClass in the service definition class.

```
@Name("Area1Part1Service")
@Description("Area 1 Part 1 Service")
@ContactEmail("jared.chase@pnnl.gov")
@InputClass("http://neptune.pnl.gov:8090/powergrid2.owl#Area1Input")
@OutputClass("http://neptune.pnl.gov:8090/powergrid2.owl#Area1Output")

public class Area1Part1Service extends SimpleSynchronousServiceServlet {
...
```

List 3 Generated service code

In this generated service definition class, the logic for launching state estimation jobs on a remote cluster is implemented in the processInput method.

```
@Override
public void processInput(final Resource input, final Resource output)
{
    final int numCores = 1;
    String filename = input.getProperty(Vocab.hasAREA1InputFilename).getString();
    final String[] inputfiles = { filename };

  try {

    JobManagerService jm = new JobManagerService();
    String[] outputfiles = jm.launchJob("node_a_part1", "local", numCores, inputfiles);

    String outputfile = outputfiles[0];
    System.out.println("Area1Part1Service " + outputfile);
    output.addLiteral(Vocab.hasAREA1OutputFilename, outputfile);

  } catch (final IOException e) {
    e.printStackTrace();
  }
}
```

List 4 Service implementation to launching state estimation job

The input and output parameters for the processInput method are passed as an RDF formatted document. To parse the RDF document and extract data of interest, we have developed a Java class Vocab using the Apache JENA[2] API. JENA is an Apache framework for building Semantic Web applications that includes a Java API for reading and writing RDF documents.

[1] http://sadiframework.org/content/
[2] http://jena.apache.org/

```
@SuppressWarnings("unused")
private static final class Vocab
{
  private static Model m_model = ModelFactory.createDefaultModel();

  public static final Property hasAREA1OutputFilename =
m_model.createProperty("http://neptune.pnl.gov:8090/powergrid2.owl#hasAREA1OutputFilename");

  public static final Property hasAREA1InputFilename =
m_model.createProperty("http://neptune.pnl.gov:8090/powergrid2.owl#hasAREA1InputFilename");

  public static final Property hasFilename =
m_model.createProperty("http://neptune.pnl.gov:8090/powergrid2.owl#hasFilename");

  public static final Resource Area1Input =
m_model.createResource("http://neptune.pnl.gov:8090/powergrid2.owl#Area1Input");

  public static final Resource Area1Output =
m_model.createResource("http://neptune.pnl.gov:8090/powergrid2.owl#Area1Output");

  public static final Resource string =
m_model.createResource("http://www.w3.org/2001/XMLSchema#string");

  public static final Resource Area1OutputFile =
m_model.createResource("http://neptune.pnl.gov:8090/powergrid2.owl#Area1OutputFile");

  public static final Resource Area1InputFile =
m_model.createResource("http://neptune.pnl.gov:8090/powergrid2.owl#Area1InputFile");
}
```

List 5 Creation of property and resource mapping

The Vocab class is developed to create property and resource instance variables to tie the input and output data according to the semantic structure of the service. As shown in List 5, the property hasAREA1InputFilename in List 1 and the resource Area1InputFile in List 2 are tied to the URLs of the OWL file. The property or resource variables of Vocab can be used to extract the input data and package the output data using a well formed RDF document representation, for example

```
String filename =
  iput.getProperty(Vocab.hasAREA1InputFilename).
  getString()
```

3.3   Job Launching

The processInput method defined in previous section invokes the job launching software we have developed. This job launcher simplifies the remote job launch, monitoring, and results handling for the state estimation scripts that are located on a remote cluster. Fig. 4 below shows a high level view of the structure and the associated steps to configure the job launcher. The first step is to configure the machine registry. The configuration files include parameters of machine name, job scheduler, installation directory of simulation code(s), number of compute nodes to use, and so on. The second step invokes the job launching function, which writes the status of the job to log files.

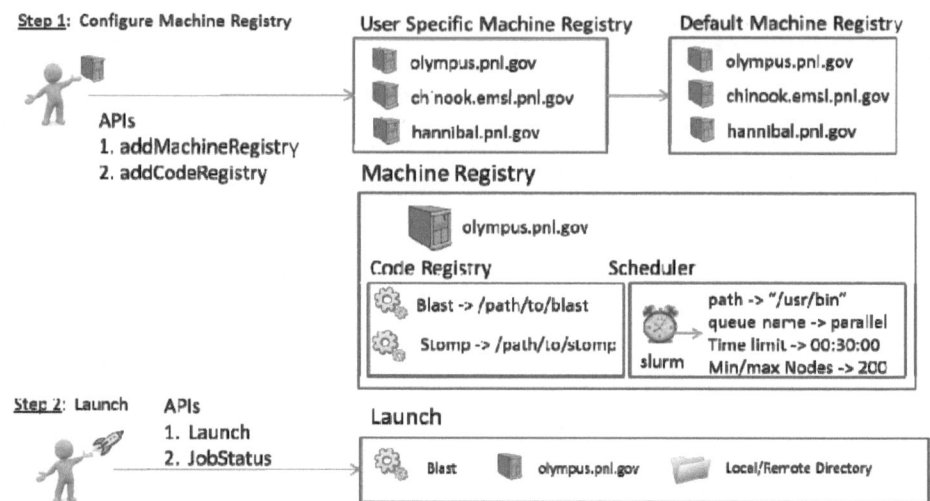

Fig. 4. Structure of job launching

The API to invoke the job launcher is the `launchJob` method in the `JobManagerService` class. The `launchJob` method takes 4 parameters.

```
JobManagerService jm = new JobManagerService();
String[] outputfiles = jm.launchJob("node_a_part1", "local", numCores, inputfiles);
```

The first parameter is Code Registry, a string that is an identifier for retrieving information from a code registry; in this case it is `node_a_part1`, a Perl script to submit an job to a cluster queue. The information that `JobManagerService` retrieves includes the submit/launch script as well as the names for the code's input and output files.

The second parameter is Machine Registry, a string that is an identifier for retrieving information from a machine registry; in this case "local". The information the `JobManagerService` retrieves includes the name of the machine, user account to launch the job with, ssh keys (if required), number of nodes, queuing system, installation location of code, time limit, and other required parameters.

The third parameter is the number of cores to use to run a simulation. This parameter is only used when launching a job through a queuing system.

The fourth parameter is an array of input files that will be used to run the job. These files are transferred from the machine that is running the SADI services to the remote cluster machine. In our example the input file is passed in this list as an argument into the state estimator.

3.4   Service Registration

Once a service is defined and implemented, it is deployed to a web application server such as Tomcat, and then registered using the SADI service registry. The SADI service registry first validates the service to make sure semantic types are correctly defined. Then the SADI service registry registers the semantic types inside the service catalog. Fig. 5 below shows the services that are registered within the SADI service registry along with the semantic types of their input and output.

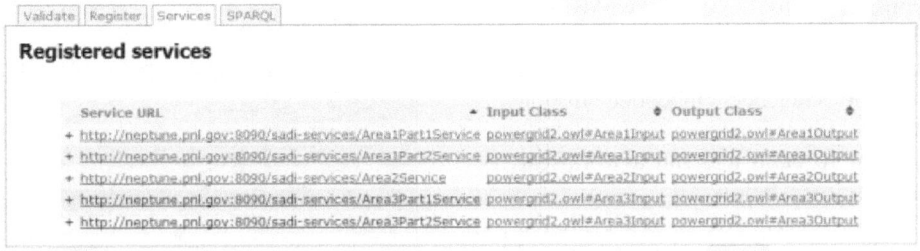

Fig. 5. Service registry

4   Composing a Workflow

Once services are created and registered for state estimators, they can be composed using workflow tools that support Web Services. In our work, we use the Taverna

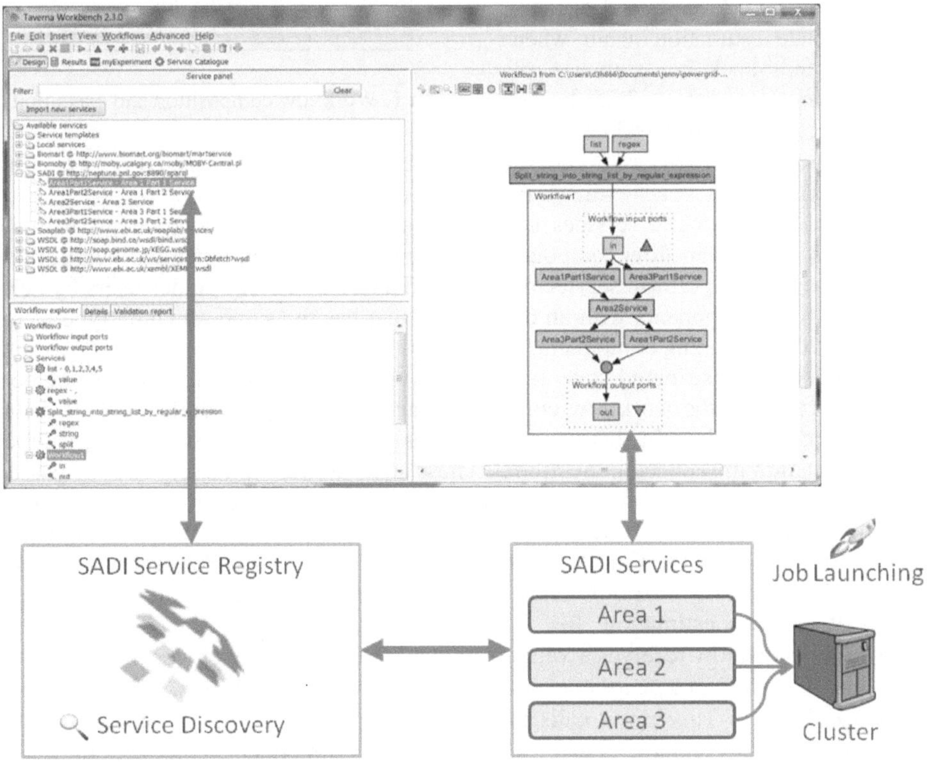

Fig. 6. Integrated Workflow Environment

Workflow Management System [3] to compose a workflow. The overall integrated workflow environment is shown in Fig. 6. This environment consists of the Taverna workbench, SADI service registry, state estimation services registered in SADI, and the job launcher embedded in the service implementation. The details of how to build and run a workflow are discussed below.

Taverna supports a SADI plugin, therefore the services that are created and registered to SADI (as described in section 3) are available in Taverna as shown in Fig. 6. Since Area 1 and Area 3 run state estimation in two separate steps: first, running its own local area state estimation, and sending its estimation of measurement on the tie-line buses to Area 2; and second, running state estimation again when Area 2 sends back its estimation of measurement on the tie-line buses. Therefore, Area 1 and Area3 have two

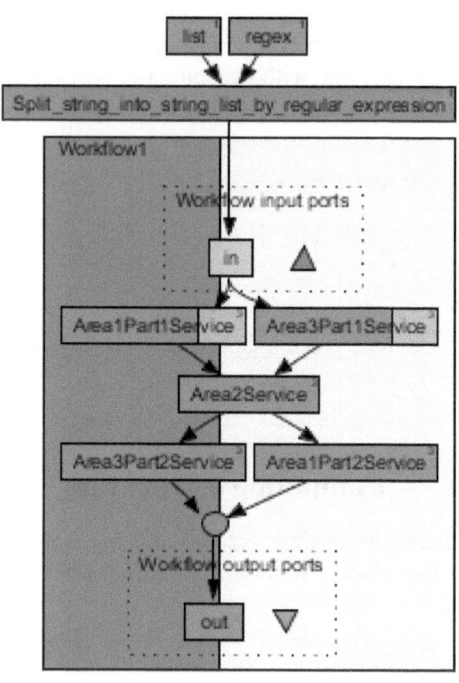

Fig. 7. Workflow composition and execution

separate services, such as `Area1Part1Service`, `Area3Part1Service` and `Area1Part2Service`,`Area3Part2Service` respectively.

Taverna allows SADI services to be used as drag-and-drop components to build workflows. Each workflow component has semantically typed input and output ports that can be used to perform service discovery. Service discovery guides users by helping them find components with an output port that has the same semantic type as the input port of an existing component.

To model the distributed state estimation workflow in Taverna, a power engineer needs to compose the workflow components according to procedural steps of distributed state estimation. In this paper, we focus on modeling the steps of distributed state estimation introduced in Section 2. These steps are run iteratively as time passes. This means for every time step of interest, these steps are invoked. Therefore, we introduce a hierarchy to the workflow. The top level of the workflow contains a list of values such as the timestamps to run the workflow steps. For each value in list is parsed, a sub-level workflow is invoked. The sub level workflow models the steps of distributed state estimation.

The sub workflow receives a value from the list in the top level workflow and triggers the `Area1Part1Service` and the `Area3Part1Service`. When a service is invoked within Taverna, it calls the `JobManagerService` to launch the state estimation jobs in a remote cluster. After both these components complete, they send

---

[3] http://www.taverna.org.uk/

their output to the `Area2Service`. After the Area2Service receives both inputs it executes and sends a separate result back to `Area1Part2Service` and `Area3Part2Service`. When both these services are finished a message is sent to the output port of the top level workflow to indicate that one iteration of the workflow is finished.

During the execution of a workflow, the result view of the Taverna workbench shows the progress of the workflow by changing colors as the workflow components execute (see Fig. 7). Once the entire workflow is finished executing, the lower result view appears populated with results data as shown in Fig. 8. Intermediate inputs and outputs for each component are available to navigate within a tree view. The separate iterations for each sub workflow execution are available.

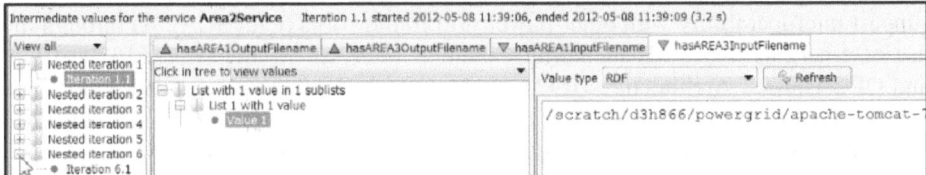

Fig. 8. Monitor workflow execution

By viewing the output file from the output port of each workflow component, a user is aware of the status of interactions between distributed state estimators. The output files in the result view allow a user to validate the distributed state estimation algorithm and identify errors of the algorithm itself.

5   Reflection and Discussions

The major benefit of using semantic services is that semantic rules for connecting services can be enforced and service discovery through the SADI service repository can be executed within an integrated workflow environment. This helps guide the user through the process of workflow composition and execution, especially when the power model evolves and consequently the data flow changes. For example, each site of the distributed state estimation involves 4 to 7 different input datasets, 2 scripts for control actions and 2 to 4 exchanges of intermediate data. For any distributed state estimation involving more than 2 sites, it is impractical to manually execute the scripts and coordinate the data flow. With this simple sematic enhancement, the workflow environment allows changing of the process through workflow composition and any violation against the composition rule is prevented.

Some of the drawbacks of using SADI services include that they use a Servlet protocol as opposed to SOAP or REST which are more common protocols used in service oriented architecture. SADI does include documentation for handling integration with SOAP services using custom code inside the SADI servlet. Another limitation is that SADI services use RDF structure data to send and receive messages. In our solution, we have developed custom code to unpackage and repackage the data specific to measurements of power grid to send to a state estimation service.

6   Related Work

The power grid is evolving to the future power grid that encompasses a business strategy within the electric utility industry for incorporating intelligence in the power distribution network. This evolution creates major challenges in the increasing complexity of the bulk power grid to respond to demand growth, support renewable energy sources and satisfy the requirements for enhanced, adaptive service quality. One of those challenges is concerned with data exchange. A service oriented architecture (SOA) has been recently adopted and reported to cope with comprehensive data exchange in layers between different stakeholders [14-16]. According to [17], SOA and Web services offer a flexible and extensible approach to integration of multiple, often autonomous, data sources and analysis procedures. Service oriented technologies support interoperability with other power grid frameworks (e.g., SCADA) through the use of emerging standards including Common Interface Model (IEC 61970/61968) and OPC Unified Architecture (IEC 62541). CIM is domain-specific data model and can be seen as a domain ontology for the utility domain. The OPC UA can be viewed as a platform for interoperability and service-based communication.

Within this background, semantic web services facilitate automation of service discovery and execution. However, the discovery could fail even if there are matching web services within the repository. For this purpose, the provision and consumption of a service should be described in a much more specific way in terms of semantics [18].

7   Conclusion

In this paper, we present a service oriented architecture for connecting distributed power models (e.g. state estimation) in a workflow environment. We define sematic services with input and output types to constrain the data exchange rules. The semantic services are mapped to state estimators running on high performance clusters. These services are registered in service repository, and discovered and composed in a workflow. Overall this integrated workflow environment separates the concerns of running individual state estimators and orchestrating their interactions in a workflow. Our future work will enhance the semantic representation of power models and support standards of CIM (IEC 61970/61968) in the service oriented architecture.

References

1. Cutsem, T.V., Howard, J.L., Ribben-Pavalla, M., El-Fattah, Y.M.: Hierachical State Estimation. International Journal of Electric Power and Energy Systems 2, 70–81 (1980)
2. Cutsem, T.V., Howard, J.L., Ribben-Pavalla, M.: A Two-level Static State Estimator for Electric Power Systems. IEEE Trans. on PAS 100, 3722–3732 (1981)

3. Cutsem, T.V., Ribbens-Pavella, M.: Critical Survey of Hierarchical Methods for State Estimation of Electrical Power Systems. IEEE Trans. on Power Apparatus and Systems 102(10), 3415–3424 (1983)
4. Habiballah, I.O., Irving, M.R.: Multipartitioning of Power System State Estimation Networks Using Simulated Annealing. Electric Power Systems Research 34, 117–120 (1995)
5. Huang, Z., Guttromson, R.T., Nieplocha, J., Pratt, R.G.: Transforming Power Grid Operations. Scientific Computing 24(5), 22–27 (2007)
6. U.S.-Canada Power System Outage Task Force, Final Report on the August 14, 2003 Blackout in the United State and Canada: Causes and Recommendations (April 2004), https://reports.energy.gov/
7. Chen, Y., Huang, Z., Liu, Y., Rice, M., Jin, S.: Computational Challenges for Power System Operation. Accepted by Hawaii International Conference on System Sciences (2012)
8. Huang, Z., Chen, Y., Nieplocha, J.: Massive Contingency Analysis with High Performance Computing. In: Proceedings of the IEEE Power Engineering Society General Meeting 2009, Calgary, Canada, July 26-30 (2009)
9. Gorton, I., Huang, Z., Chen, Y., Kalahar, B., Jin, S., Chavarría-Miranda, D., Baxter, D., Feo, J.: A High-Performance Hybrid Computing Approach to Massive Contingency Analysis in the Power Grid. In: Proceedings of the 2009 Fifth IEEE International Conference on E-Science, E-SCIENCE, December 09-11, pp. 277–283. IEEE Computer Society, Washington, DC (2009), doi: http://dx.doi.org/10.1109/e-Science.2009.46
10. Chen, Y., Huang, Z., Chavarría-Miranda, D.: Performance Evaluation of Counter-Based Dynamic Load Balancing Schemes for Massive Contingency Analysis with Different Computing Environments. IEEE PES General Meeting. PNNL-SA-69878, Pacific Northwest National Laboratory, Richland, WA (2009)
11. Bose, A., Poon, K., Emami, R.: Implementation Issues for Hierarchical State Estimators. Final Project Report (September 2010)
12. Abur, A., Expósito, A.G.: Power System State Estimation Theory and Implementation. CRC Press (2004)
13. IEEE 118-bus teset case, http://www.ee.washington.edu/research/pstca/pf118/pg_tca118bus.html (accessed November 2011)
14. Pathak, J., Li, Y., Honavar, V., McCalley, J.: A Service-Oriented Architecture for Electric Power Transmission System Asset Management. In: Georgakopoulos, D., Ritter, N., Benatallah, B., Zirpins, C., Feuerlicht, G., Schoenherr, M., Motahari-Nezhad, H.R. (eds.) ICSOC 2006. LNCS, vol. 4652, pp. 26–37. Springer, Heidelberg (2007)
15. Lalanda, P.: An E-Services Infrastructure for Power Distribution. IEEE Internet Computing 9(3), 52–59 (2005)
16. Marin, C., Lalanda, P., Donsez, D.: A MDE Approach for Power Distribution Service Development. In: Benatallah, B., Casati, F., Traverso, P. (eds.) ICSOC 2005. LNCS, vol. 3826, pp. 552–557. Springer, Heidelberg (2005)
17. Postina, M., Rohjans, S., Steffens, U., Uslar, M.: Views on Service Oriented Architectures in the Context of Smart Grids. In: First IEEE International Conference on Smart Grid Communications (SmartGridComm), pp. 25–30. IEEE Computer Society (2010)
18. Rohjans, S., Uslar, M., Juergen Appelrath, H.: OPC UA and CIM: Semantics for the smart grid. In: 2010 IEEE PES Transmission and Distribution Conference and Exposition, pp. 1–8 (2010)

19. Buyya, R., Murshed, M.: GridSim: a Toolkit for the Modeling and Simulation of Distributed Resouce Management and Scheduling for Grid Computing. Concurrency Computat. Pract. Exper. 14, 1175–1220 (2002)
20. Liu, Y., Jiang, W., Jin, S., Rice, M., Chen, Y.: Distributing Power Grid State Estimation on HPC Clusters A System Architecture Prototype. Accepted to the IEEE IPDPS Workshop on Parallel and Distributed Scientific and Engineering Computing, Shanghai, China (May 2012)
21. Jin, S., Chen, Y., Rice, M., Liu, Y., Gorton, I.: A Testbed for Deploying Distributed State Estimation in Power Grid. Accepted to IEEE Power & Energy Society General Meeting, Orlando, FL, USA (May 2012)

Business Process Extensions as First-Class Entities — A Model-Driven and Aspect-Oriented Approach

Heiko Witteborg, Anis Charfi, Mohamed Aly, and Ta'id Holmes

SAP Research Darmstadt
Bleichstr. 8, Darmstadt, Germany
`firstname.lastname@sap.com`

Abstract. To facilitate customer adaptation, extensibility constitutes an attractive design choice for providers of business software. However, most works in the context of business application extensibility are focusing on the code level. Lacking a conceptual foundation, such extensibility has shortcomings with respect to the understandability and the development of extensions. Addressing these issues, this paper presents the novel concept of business process extensions as first-class entities. We apply a model-driven approach which focuses on the business process layer and uses aspect-oriented modeling implicitly.

Keywords: process extensions, extensibility, business process modeling, model-driven.

1 Introduction

Enterprise resource planning (ERP) and customer relationship management (CRM) are examples of business applications that support a wide range of standard business processes. However, the reality shows that companies in the same activity domain (e.g., retail or service) may have their own variants of these processes. When looking at diverse domains one observes that business processes are also performed in different ways. In fact, the standard processes delivered and implemented by the business software provider mostly require to be adapted to the particular needs of a certain company running it or to those of a certain domain. The adaptation of the business applications and their underlying business processes is typically done by implementing extensions. These extensions are either built by the customer or by a third party such as an independent software vendor (ISV). In fact, there is an ecosystem of ISVs and consulting organizations around leading business software providers, which specialize in configuring base software and building extensions to it. Extensions are owned by the ISVs whereas the base software is owned by the provider of the business software.

Extending business applications is a complex task for both the application provider and the extension developer (cf. [1]). Therefore, there is a need to raise the level of abstraction in order to ease understanding, developing, and managing extensions and systems that result from base software and extensions. The lack of appropriate models for extensibility leads to further problems, which are hard to tackle on the code layer. First, it is challenging to understand a business process that results after several extensions have been applied to the base software. This is because no appropriate models of

C. Liu et al. (Eds.): ICSOC 2012, LNCS 7636, pp. 763–770, 2012.

the extensions exist in code level approaches. Second, understanding which extensions perform which activities at which points in the base business process is complicated. Therefore, it is also difficult to identify potential conflicts between extensions without looking deep into the code. The same applies to the activation and deactivation of extensions, which, in current approaches, is a topic for expert technical users through complex low-level configuration and management tools. In this paper we address some of these problems using a model-driven and aspect-oriented approach for business process extensibility.

Our contributions are three-fold: First, we present a novel approach for defining business process extensions as first-class entities. This approach focuses on the business process layer and also includes a mechanism for composing (resp. decomposing) the extension models defined by the ISVs with (resp. from) the base business processes delivered by the business software provider. Second, we present a toolset supporting the proposed approach, which includes an extension editor and model repositories. Starting from a base process, the editor supports the in-place modeling of extensions as if the end user was directly modifying the business process. Internally, the toolset extracts the deltas modeled by the extender into business process extensions. This is transparent to the modeler (implicit aspect-oriented modeling). Third, we discuss the benefits of our approach and its application areas to further address the problems mentioned above.

2   Concepts and Tools for Business Process Extensibility

We propose a model-driven and aspect-oriented approach to business process extensibility. Focusing on the process layer, it enables participants in the ecosystem of the base software provider to extend the (read-only) process models of the business application, e.g., to add new activities to the process, to match the needs of a specific domain, or to integrate with other applications. The extended process is decomposed automatically and stored in a modular way: the resulting extension encapsulates the modifications that are associated with a certain concern, ready to be reapplied, or reused in another context.

We exemplarily illustrate our approach using a common CRM process for creating and approving sales quotations, as shown in Figure 2. In our extension scenario, this process is extended to integrate customer rating data delivered through an external credit reporting agency. Based on this additional information, an online shop could lower the risk of non-payment, e.g., by appropriately setting the payment terms.

In the following, we shortly present the conceptual basis of our approach using a business process extension metamodel. After that, we describe the main steps in the extension development approach. Finally, we present the toolset supporting our approach.

2.1   Business Process Extension Metamodel

Figure 1 shows a business process extension metamodel that formalizes the concepts that enable an ISV to model process extensions as first-class entities. It consists of two packages: The package `processmodel` contains the metamodel of the process definition language used to define the base process. We present a simplistic metamodel consisting of processes, edges, and vertices to exemplarily show the generic interrelation

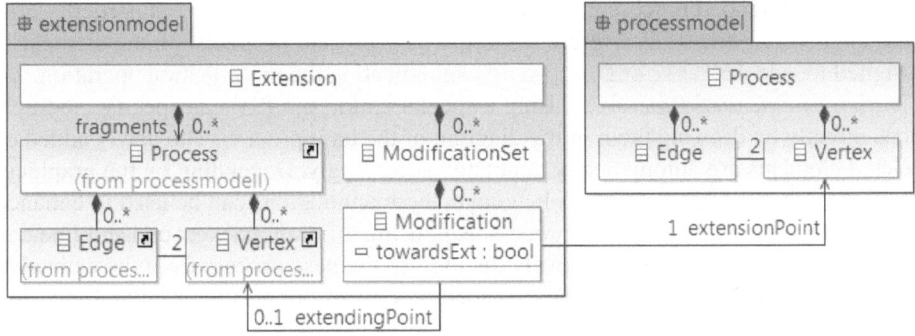

Fig. 1. Process Extension Metamodel

between our extensibility concepts and the underlying process definition language [1]. The second part of Figure 1 is the package `extensionmodel`, which defines the concepts that can be contained in an extension.

The *fragments* contain the new process elements introduced by the extension modeler. It uses the same constructs as the base process modeling language, following a symmetric approach to composition (cf. [10]), i.e., there is no conceptual distinction between base process and the extension part. This facilitates the intuitive graphical definition of extensions, and supports extension of extensions. Figure 2 shows the extended process of our motivating example, with a fragment consisting of a single task "Get external customer rating".

A *Modification* describes a single extension operation that is performed on a certain extension point. If `extendingPoint` is not specified, the modification describes a deletion. A deletion can be represented by hiding the targeted element, or by showing it grayed out. In the other case, the modification inserts and connects an extending element contained in one of the extension's fragments with the extension point contained in the base process (hereinafter called binding). Both extension point and extending point reference single identifiable nodes of the underlying process language, in our generic case, a single vertex. The binding can easily be represented as an edge in an extended process, with the `towardsExt` attribute specifying the direction of the edge.

Grouped using the *ModificationSet* concept, several bindings can be defined for the same combination of base process and fragment. In our running example, the additional task is integrated into the base process as an optional task after "Receive customer request"; thus, there is a forking edge between these two vertices and a merging edge targeting the successor vertex, as shown in Figure 2.

2.2 Extension Development Approach

The extension development is simplified by the fact that we use the same language for both the extended process and the base process. However, visualizing the extension part in the extended process, as well as extracting the extension when the process is saved

---

[1] However, our approach can be applied to any process definition language that formalizes a process as a flow of tasks, modeled as vertices interconnected via directed edges such as Business Process Modeling Notation [12] (BPMN) for example.

requires the extended process model to hold additional information [2]; in particular, for each element, `modelId` as a reference to the base process or extension the element is assigned to, and `modificationOperation` indicating the modification operation.

Creation of Extended Processes. Using a special editor, the ISV can specify modifications directly by drawing them in the diagram of the base process. The newly added or deleted elements are automatically annotated accordingly. Depending on the graphical notation of the underlying process language, these annotations can be used to enhance the visualization of the extended process, e.g., using different background and line colors. This enables the ISV to intuitively distinguish the base process from the extension parts. Figure 2 depicts the resulting extended process of our customer rating extension example.

Decomposition of Extended Processes. When an extended process is saved, the extension is extracted automatically and the base process is left unmodified. Our decomposition algorithm uses the extension annotations to retrieve the list of modified elements and derive the fragments and modification sets. Listing 1 shows the extension artifact derived by decomposing our extended example process. It consists of the extension process with a single fragment and a modification set with two modifications.

Listing 1. Customer Rating Extension

```
<?xml version="1.0" encoding="UTF-8"?>
<extensionmodel:Extension xmi:version="2.0"~xmlns:xmi="http://www.omg.org/XMI"
    xmlns:extensionmodel="http://extensionmodel/1.0"
    name="Customer Rating Extension">
  <fragments name="Customer Rating">
    <vertices name="Get external customer rating"/>
  </fragments>
  <modificationSets id="Quote2OrderModifications">
    <modifications towardsExt="true" extendingPoint="//@fragments.0/@vertices.0"
        baseProcessName="SalesQuotationCreation"
        extensionPointName="Receive customer request"/>
    <modifications extendingPoint="//@fragments.0/@vertices.0"
        baseProcessName="SalesQuotationCreation"
        extensionPointName="Check customer credit limit"/>
  </modificationSets>
</extensionmodel:Extension>
```

Composition of a Base Process and Extensions. Base processes can be (re)composed with extensions: First, the modification sets relevant for the selected base process are retrieved. The corresponding fragment is inserted and annotated as `added`, and edges are created to represent the bindings. For a deletion, the extension point is annotated accordingly. Reapplying the extracted customer rating extension (cf. Listing 1) to the "Sales Quotation Creation" process restores the extended process shown in Figure 2.

2.3 Tooling

For the accomplishment of an end-to-end solution we implemented a tool for modeling business process extensions. This tool is supported by one or more model repositories for storing the base processes and the extensions. While managing extension models

---

[2] To store this information we annotate the extended process using lightweight language-specific extension constructs. We abstract from concrete annotation implementation in the following, assuming that the additional extension information is available.

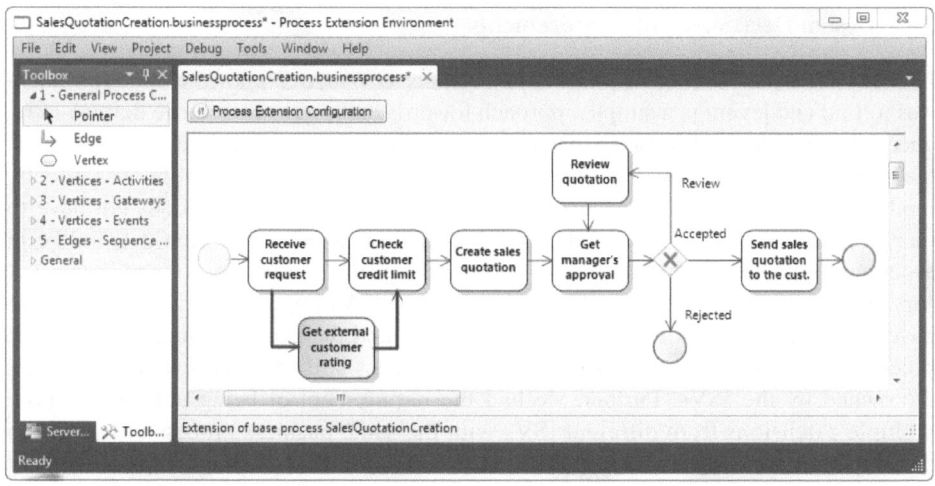

Fig. 2. Sales Quotation Creation Process with the Customer Rating Extension

as first-class artifacts in business software systems, these repositories with the tools help to bridge the gaps between various phases of the engineering lifecycle. We refer to such a setting as a Model-Aware Service Environment [11] (MORSE). Moreover, as the repositories store conceptual, platform-independent models (PIMs) they can be utilized across different products of the business software provider's portfolio. Our tooling consists of the following components:

The base business process models of one or more business applications are stored in the central *Process Model Repository*. For reference and traceability purposes each model and model element in the MORSE is identifiable by a Universally Unique Identifier. The *Extension Repository* stores business process extension models separately from the process models although it might utilize the same model repository with the access rights appropriately set. One reason for this separation is the separate ownership of the respective models: the base process models are owned by the base software vendor whereas the process extension models are owned by the ISVs.

The *Process Editor* enables the ISV to retrieve and view the base process models from the Process Model Repository, as well as extensions to be stored in the Extension Repository. Although having only read access, the editor allows to directly draw a new extension into the base process diagram or loading and editing an existing extension – in accordance with the modification restrictions defined by the base process owner. Moreover, the user can load and reuse an extension in another process context. Saving the extended process automatically triggers the extraction of the extension as a first-class entity, stored in the Extension Repository. A screenshot of the tool is shown in Figure 2.

3   Discussion

In this section, we report on relevant design decisions and give some requirements from practice. We also report on several application areas of our approach.

3.1   Design Decisions and Requirements

In-Place Extension Modeling and Implicit Aspect-Oriented Support.   One requirement was to find and leverage a simple approach towards end users. To achieve that we introduced the technique of in-place extension modeling, which means that an ISV models the extension in our editor after loading the base business process as if he was directly modifying that business process. As a result, the extension modeler does not have to know or understand the metamodel and concepts presented in Section 2.1, unlike in aspect-oriented approaches such as [8]. This reduces the complexity for end users.

Process Extensions as Modular First-Class Entities.   An important requirement was to have a strict separation of the base process model and the extension models. The base processes are owned by the provider of the business software and extension models are owned by the ISVs. Further, we had the requirement of being able to compose multiple extensions from different ISVs with the same business process model. From this requirement, which is supported through the separation of ownership, we derived the design decision to have process extensions as modular first-class entities.

3.2   Application Areas

Code and Test Generation.   The design and development process of business software extensions may start now from the process extension models. These models – possibly in conjunction with other models – can serve for generating implementation artifacts for the extension. Furthermore, the process extension models can also serve as basis for generating tests to ensure the correct interplay of the extension with the base application.

Documentation.   The process extension models also serve as a documentation of an extension. In fact, every potential customer of an extension can now understand its effects and its interplay with the base business processes (e.g., in case of an extended process containing multiple extensions).

Extension Governance and Management.   The proposed approach enables a better understanding of the business process resulting after the deployment of several extensions. For example, a customer organization may buy the basis business application and gets the respective process models. When each ISV extending that software provides a process extension model as proposed in our approach a view with the complete process including the base process and extensions can be generated for the customer organization. A sample process view created by the composition mechanism is presented in Section 2. This view not only serves the understandability but also can ease the management of extensions and their dependencies and allows the detection of potential conflicts.

4   Related Work

Reference Process Models.   Balko et al. [2,3] propose a conceptual framework using provider defined reference workflow processes with extension points. Reference processes are standard business processes that are realized by the software provider following a workflow approach. The provider defines extension points where an extender can plug in his extensions in the form of process fragments. Extensions should then be managed and called at runtime by means of an extensibility framework (similar to an extension aware BPEL engine or an aspect-aware BPEL engine as in AO4BPEL [7]). That papers remain on the conceptual level providing only a high level description of the framework without the implementation of the presented concepts.

Adaptation Techniques. Although the variety of business service types and natures is very broad (cf. [6]), a common characteristic among all services is the process of value creation between multiple parties in a flow of interaction/communication [9]. An extension of a business service therefore adds flow elements to the underlying process model, with the goal of increasing the service's business value in a specific scenario. The idea of extending, reusing, and adapting a base model to construct models for a concrete application domain is subject of the research area of reference modeling [4]. Concerning the adaptation techniques of reference models, vom Brocke [5] identifies five mechanisms such as configuration, aggregation, instantiation, specialization, and analogy. To ensure the applicability for our approach in a realistic business service network, the adaptation technique should allow (a) an automated adaptation process and (b) a maximum of flexibility for an ISV, while ensuring (c) the process owner's business need of having compliant and consistent core processes. The first requirement, an analogy-based extension is too vague to be automated. Requirement (b), both configuration and instantiation lack flexibility, because the modeler of the base process would have to foresee all potential extensions (or, at least, the extension points). For specialization, problems may arise in regard to requirement (c) as this technique empowers an ISV to fundamentally change the base process.

Aspect-Oriented Process Modeling. In a previous work [8], we defined an aspect-oriented extension to BPMN called AO4BPMN. This extension allows to model aspects in business processes. Several differences exist between that work and the work presented in this paper. In AO4BPMN aspects are modeled explicitly by an expert user whereas here process extensions are extracted automatically by the toolset behind the scenes. Moreover, AO4BPMN extends the metamodel of BPMN with aspect-oriented concepts whereas in this work the same process modeling language is used for both the base process and the extensions. AO4BPMN is a powerful language with a rich join point model and pointcut language. In the current work the extension process elements and the base process elements are related through the binding. There is no explicit pointcut and no pointcut resolution (and thus no quantification). On the other hand AO4BPMN is complex for a business user and requires an understanding of aspect-oriented concepts.

5 Conclusion

Extensibility of business applications involves several stakeholders in the ecosystem of the business software vendor such as ISVs who build extensions on top of the base software and customers who use the base software together with these extensions. All of these roles need to better understand the behavior of extensions, their effects on the base business process, and also potential conflicts between different extensions. In this paper we presented a model-driven and aspect-oriented approach and a toolset for defining business process extensions as first-class entities. Our approach addresses the limitations of state-of-the-art approaches and – through an implicit aspect-oriented modeling – makes extension development and management more accessible to business users. We also discussed several application areas that are enabled by this approach in our industrial context.

Acknowledgments. The authors would like to thank Batbold Bilegsaikhan for his implementation of the customer rating extension and Wei Wei (危巍) for his contributions to the modeling environment prototype. The work presented in this paper was performed in the context of the Software-Cluster project Emergent. It was partially funded by the German Federal Ministry of Education and Research under grant no. 01IC10S01.

References

1. Aly, M., Charfi, A., Mezini, M.: On the extensibility requirements of business applications. In: International Workshop on Next Generation Modularity Approaches for Requirements and Architecture, NEMARA. ACM, Postdam (2012)
2. Balko, S., ter Hofstede, A.H., Barros, A.P., Rosa, M.L., Adams, M.J.: Controlled flexibility and lifecycle management of business processes through extensibility. In: Proceedings of the Workshop on Enterprise Modelling and Information Systems Architectures (EMISA). GI (2009)
3. Balko, S., ter Hofstede, A.H., Barros, A.P., Rosa, M.L., Adams, M.J.: Business process extensibility. Enterprise Modelling and Information Systems Architectures Journal (July 2010)
4. Becker, J., Beverungen, D., Knackstedt, R.: The challenge of conceptual modeling for product-service systems: status-quo and perspectives for reference models and modeling languages. Inf. Syst. E-Business Management 8(1), 33–66 (2010)
5. Brocke, J.V.: Referenzmodellierung - Gestaltung und Verteilung von Konstruktionsprozessen. In: Advances in Information Systems and Management Science, vol. 4. Logos (2003)
6. Cardoso, J., Barros, A.P., May, N., Kylau, U.: Towards a unified service description language for the internet of services: Requirements and first developments. In: IEEE SCC, pp. 602–609. IEEE Computer Society (2010)
7. Charfi, A., Mezini, M.: AO4BPEL: An aspect-oriented extension to BPEL. World Wide Web Journal: Special Issue: Recent Advances in Web Services 10(3) (March 2007)
8. Charfi, A., Müller, H., Mezini, M.: Aspect-Oriented Business Process Modeling with AO4BPMN. In: Kühne, T., Selic, B., Gervais, M.-P., Terrier, F. (eds.) ECMFA 2010. LNCS, vol. 6138, pp. 48–61. Springer, Heidelberg (2010)
9. Chesbrough, H., Spohrer, J.: A research manifesto for services science. Commun. ACM 49(7), 35–40 (2006)
10. Harrison, W.H., Ossher, H.L., Tarr, P.L.: Asymmetrically vs. symmetrically organized paradigms for software composition. Tech. Rep. RC22685 (W0212-147), IBM (December 2002)
11. Holmes, T., Zdun, U., Dustdar, S.: MORSE: A model-aware service environment. In: Proceedings of the 4th IEEE Asia-Pacific Services Computing Conference (APSCC), pp. 470–477. IEEE (December 2009)
12. Object Management Group, Inc.: Business Process Model and Notation (BPMN), Version 2.0 (January 2011), http://www.omg.org/spec/BPMN/2.0 (accessed in August 2012)

Towards Dynamic Reconfiguration
for QoS Consistent Services Based Applications

Yuyu Yin[1] and Ying Li[2]

[1] College of Computer, Hangzhou Dianzi University,
Hangzhou China
Yyy718@gmail.com
[2] College of Computer Science and Technology, Zhejiang University,
Hangzhou China
cnliying@zju.edu.cn

Abstract. Original overall QoS(quality of service) constraints of services based applications may be violated due to failed services or QoS degradation of component services. Although some methods have been proposed to repair failed services and achieve original overall QoS, few works focuses on recovery of services based applications from QoS degradation of component services. In order to provide QoS consistent service based applications, the paper presents a QoS driven dynamic reconfiguration method. The key to the method lies in replacing only some component services rather than recomposing the entire service based applications. In addition, degradation factor is introduced to find the component services which are replaced to most likely achieve original overall QoS constraint. In this way, reconfiguration overheads are lowered and service disruptions may be reduced. The test shows the effectiveness of our approach.

Keywords: Services based application, Quality of service, dynamic reconfiguration.

1   Introduction

Service Computing has become one of the most promising computing paradigms in the Internet era [1]. As it is now adopted widely, great progress has been made in the research about service composition. Presently, service composition has become an increasingly important way for IT enterprises to rapidly develop their applications[3].

However, developing various service based applications is not the only critical step of service composition. To the best of our knowledge, it becomes an additionally urgent challenge how to adjust service based applications to meet highly dynamic environments (e.g. in a clouding environment) and fast changing business requirements[4,5,9,10]. Up to now, although there existed many valuable works, most of them focus on providing essential services and functions in the presence of runtime environment changes[6-9]. With the ever increasing amount of services based applications now are adopted in wide range of critical domains(such as, real time system, navigation system, and online payment system), it has become increasingly important

C. Liu et al. (Eds.): ICSOC 2012, LNCS 7636, pp. 771–778, 2012.

for enterprises to make service based applications deliver a desirable QoS. Due to many inevitable factors, such as network fault, host exception, and replacement of failed component services, delivered QoS from service based applications may not comply with their original claims at runtime. Once it happens, services based applications should be recovered immediately to continue holding original QoS. Moreover, most enterprises would like to recover their applications with lower cost and better efficiency, so that their customers may not undergo as few unexpected business shutdowns as possible. Thus, providing QoS consistent services based applications has become a huge challenge.

Although services based applications can be recovered by recomposition, service recomposition is extremely time-consuming and may lead to system shutdown, since the optimal service selection is a NP-hard problem[2]. Recently, some researchers have introduced and extended the traditional dynamic reconfiguration technology[8] to services based applications[6-8,12-14]. However, most of them still focus on the function driven dynamic reconfiguration, which is to maintain the pre-defined functions[6-8]. Few researchers[12,13] proposed dynamic reconfiguration methods to maintain the original end-to-end QoS constraints, they only limit to deal with the case of violation of some component service.

In the rest of the paper, the term component QoS and overall QoS are used to refer to QoS of a component service and QoS of an application respectively.

In this paper, to address this issue:

We propose a QoS driven dynamic reconfiguration method. When degradation of component QoS leads to violation of original overall QoS, we always try to replaced component services which have the biggest degradation factor, as long as they are reconfigured to deliver the original QoS. When some component services violate, our method replace them with new services firstly, and then repeat the above process for the rest of component services. In this way, our method can recover overall QoS with less attempts and shorter response time;

Inspired by our previous work[15], the notion of degradation factor is presented to guide us to find the component services which are replaced to most likely achieve the original overall QoS constraints;

The tests are conducted to evaluate the performance of the proposed methods.

The remainder of this paper is organizes as follows. Section 2 presents our method and gives the reconfiguration algorithms. Section 3 gives the tests to show the performance of our method. Section 4 surveys the related works. Finally, we draw a conclusion and discuss the future work in Section 5.

2   Dynamic Reconfiguration Method for Consistent QoS

We now present a QoS driven dynamic reconfiguration method. Different from previous works, our method does not limit to repair overall QoS in the case of failure of component services, it also deals with degradation of component QoS.

2.1 Dynamic Reconfiguration Algorithm

In this section, Algorithm RecQoS is to recovery the original QoS constraints. If there not exist failure component services, The algorithm first computes degradation factor of all component services in a services based application, and sorts all component services according to their degradation factor(Step 4,5). Degradation factor is introduced in Section 2.2. Then, two processes are executed as follows:

1) Single Services Replacement: we try to replace individual component service one by one in the descending order of degradation factor only if there exists some candidate service whose QoS is not worse than pre-defined QoS of the replaced service(Step 6-13). Obviously, original overall QoS constraints can also be satisfied by such replacement.

If such replacement cannot be found in the phase, then 2) Multiple Services Replacement: we begin to try to replace d component services whose degradation factor is the highest among all component services. QoS of the substitutions of the d component services is the best among their respective all candidate services. The range bound of d starts from two and increases gradually until a replacement is found to deliver original overall QoS(Step 14-24).

If there exists failure component services, Algorithm RecQoS first replace each failed service with the substitution whose QoS is the best among all candidate services of failed service(Step 27-30). If delivered overall QoS by the new services based application still do not satisfy original overall QoS, the algorithm RecDeg will be called to reconfigure the rest of component services.

Algorithm. RecQoS

Input: all replaceable component services $\{S_1,...,S_n\}$ in a services based application S.

Output: the replaced services $R_S \subseteq \{S_1,...,S_n\}$ and their substitutions $R_D \subseteq \{CS_i\}$.

Require: candidate services $CS_i = \{CS_{i1},...,CS_{im}\}$ of service S_i.

```
 1:  SET R_S = φ, R_D = φ, S_r = φ, D_g[i]=null;
 2:  IF(not existing failure service sf_i)
 3:      FOR(INT i = 0; i < n; i + +){
 4:          D_g[i]=CalDg(S_i);}/* CalDg(S_i) is to calculate degradation factor of S_i */(See Section 2.2)
 5:      S' = Sort(S); /* Sort(S) sorts S_1,..., S_n in ascending order according to D_g[]*/
 6:      SET j = n;
 7:      While(j > 0) {
 8:          S_k = Get(S'. j); /* GetS_r(j) is to get the j-th element in S'*/
 9:          IF(∃CS_kp ∈ CS_k && QoS of CS_kp  is not worse than pre-defined QoS of S_k){
10:              SET j = 0;
11:              R_S = R_S ∪ {S_k} ; R_d = R_d ∪ {CS_kp}; Goto 27;
12:              }Else{ j = j − 1;
13:          }
14:      }
15:      SET d=2;
16:      Do{
17:      FOR(INT l = 0; l < d; l ++){
18:          R_s[l] = R_s[l]  ∪ { Get(S'. j-l) };
19:          R_D[l] =R_D[l] ∪ { Select(S'.j-l) }; /*Select a service CS_kp for M[l] whose QoS is the best
         among all its candidates*/
20:          Replace M [l] with CS_kp
21:      }
```

```
22:           IF(the current QoS of S comply with the original overall QoS of S){ Goto 27;
23:               }Else{ d= d+1;
24:           }
25:       }While(d < n + 1);
26:   }ELSE{
27:       RD[l] = Select(Sfi);/*Select a service CSkp for Sfi whose QoS is the best among all its candi-
          dates*/
28:       Replace Sfi with CSkp;
29:       RD[l] = RD[l] ∪ {CSkp};
30:       Rs = Sf;
31:       IF(the current QoS of S comply with the original overall QoS of S){ Goto 35;
32:           }Else{ Goto 3;
33:       }
34:   }
35:   RETURN RS[],RD[];
```

Once it happens, no such reconfigurations can deliver original overall QoS in current given candidate services repository. A recomposition should be needed to achieve original overall QoS for services based applications. But this goes beyond our current study.

2.2   Degradation Factor

For our method, we would like to find and replace the most promising component services so that the original overall QoS can be delivered as few attempts and as soon as possible. Thus, all component services in a services based application need to be evaluated by *Degradation Factor*.

Degradation factor of a component service shows the degree of its QoS actual degradation relative to other component service. When original overall QoS constraints are violated, the bigger relative degradation value of a component service is, the bigger its contributions to the violation are.

In this paper, we calculate degradation factor of a component service by the following steps:

a)   to compute actual QoS degradation rate of a component service by Equation(1). Given a services based application Ω and its all component services $S_1,...,S_n$.

$$\overline{\Delta_K^{S_i}} = \frac{\sum_{j \le m} \Delta_{K,j}^{S_i}}{m} \times \frac{m}{n}, \tag{1}$$

Where $\overline{\Delta_K^{S_i}}$ is the actual degradation rate of QoS property $K \in \{T_{S_i}, C_{S_i}, R_{S_i}, A_{S_i}\}$ from S_i; n is the monitored time in a period of time(users defined) before violation of original overall QoS constrains; $m(m \le n)$ is the degradation time; $\Delta_{K,j}^{S_i}$ is the actual degradation value of QoS property $K \in \{T_{S_i}, C_{S_i}, R_{S_i}, A_{S_i}\}$ from S_i.

b)   to sort $S_1,...,S_n$ according to QoS actual degradation rate. Four sorts are gotten as follows: $\Delta_T[]$, $\Delta_C[]$, $\Delta_R[]$, and $\Delta_A[]$. They are the descending sorts of actual degradation value of *Response time, Cost, Reliability*, and *Availability*. And then a

$4*n$ matrix G is built by the four sorts and denoted as $[\Delta_T[], \Delta_C[], \Delta_R[], \Delta_A[]]^T$. Every column in the matrix is assigned to a weight. The weight of the j-th column is set to $(n-j+1)/n$.

c) to set effective weight of $S_1,\ldots,$ and S_n. Effective weight of S_i is a vector $WE_i=(WE_{Ti}, WE_{Ci}, WE_{Ri}, WE_{Ai})$. WE_i components are the column weights of S_i in G.

Thus, relative QoS Degradation Value DV_i of S_i equals the sum of all components of its effective weights. The formula is as follows:

$$DV_i = \frac{WE_{Ti} + WE_{Ci} + WE_{Ri} + WE_{Ai}}{4} \qquad (2)$$

3 Evaluation

In order to evaluate the efficiency and effectiveness of our proposed method, three groups of test are conducted.

We use a service test collection from JTangComponent previously built in [14] where 1056 services have been included to generate the needed application in the test. In addition, in order to support the test, QoS of candidate services is simulated and produced by the following way: *Cost* and *Response Time* are randomly generated with a uniform distribution from 1 to 100, *Availability* and *Reliability* are randomly generated with a uniform distribution from 0 to 1, are assigned to each candidate service.

In our experiment, we have generated one service based application P including sequential, parallel, choose, and loop structures in our simulation study. P includes 20 nodes and 6 structures in Fig.1. For each service node in P, we provide 10 service candidates with four randomly generated QoS values. Randomly select 1 or 2 services in P to be failure services.

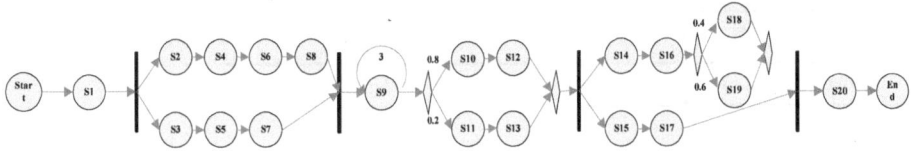

Fig. 1. Service based Application P

We compare the proposed approach with two other methods: Region-based method[12] and Random method. The idea of region-based approach is to produce reconfiguration regions that include one or more failed service. By reconfiguring only services in the selected regions, the business process will not be affected significantly. Random method is to select replaceable component services randomly and replace them. In order to study the performance of the three methods, we consider the following factors: attempt time, replaced services number, and recovery time.

Table 1 reports the performance of the three methods. In Table 1, all factors of our approach are better than other two approaches obviously in the given cases.

Table 1. Performance Comprision

Case Study	1			2		
Method	Our Method	Region based approach	Random Method	Our Method	Region based approach	Random Method
Failure services	s_1			s_{15}		
Attempt times	2	15	14	2	11	10
replaced services number	2	9	14	2	5	10
recovery time(ms)	15	105	71	11	100	57
Case Study	**3**			**4**		
Method	Our Method	Region based approach	Random Method	Our Method	Region based approach	Random Method
Failure services	s_{12}, s_{13}			s_{16}, s_{17}		
Attempt times	8	17	9	4	12	6
replaced services number	8	7	9	4	6	6
recovery time(ms)	16	88	19	22	105	9
Case Study	**5**			**6**		
Method	Our Method	Region based approach	Random Method	Our Method	Region based approach	Random Method
Failure services	s_1, s_{11}			s_9, s_{12}		
Attempt times	3	37	6	3	36	12
replaced services number	3	8	6	3	8	12
recovery time(ms)	19	349	32	10	160	22

4   Related Work

In dynamic environments, service composition needs to support to recover services based applications from unexpectable violation of not only function but also QoS. Therefore, holding the original overall QoS constraints of services based applications has proposed a big challenge that needs to be addressed.

Many works have studied QoS guarantee of service selection problem[16,17,19]. In addition, many researchers have been studied QoS optimization [18]or reoptimiaztion[11,19] of service compostion. Danilo Ardagna et al. The main difference between the above works and our work is that besides end-to-end QoS constraints, their work focuses more on service composition evolution and selection in order to optimize overall QoS, while we emphasize more on the efficiency of reconfiguration to recovery of services based applications when degradation of overall QoS.

Some researchers have studied dynamic reconfiguration of services based applications but without considering QoS[6-8,14]. Our previous work[15] also tried to dynamically reconfigure services based applications to satisfy customer's QoS constraints. But its goal is to improve overall QoS of services based applications, and it is not able to make services based applications hold their original QoS. Bo Jiang,et.al[10] proposed a statistical framework to assess component services and to identify vulnerable areas called cracks to support service adaptation. Be different than our method, their method is to find potential component services which can lead to failure of key business of services based application. But this may become one of our future research topics.

Recent works on dynamic reconfiguration for service composition has started to study in order to hold the original overall QoS constraints. T.Yu et.al.[13] presented an approach to conduct dynamic process reconfiguration under end-to-end QoS constraints. They use the replacement path idea to reconfigure a business process to avoid only one faulty service. Yanlong Zhai et al. [12] presented an approach for repairing multiple failed services by replacing them with new services and ensuring the new system satisfies the end-to-end QoS constraints. Compared to our work, their works limit to recovery when component services become faulty, while it becomes invalid when the delivered QoS of component services degrades. Furthermore, our test has shown the performance of our method is better than them.

5   Conclusion

Due to failed services or degradation of component QoS, original QoS of services based applications may be broken. Once that happens, it is undesirable to halt and recompose services based applications. Services based applications should be recovered as soon and as efficiently as possible. The paper proposes a QoS driven dynamic reconfiguration method to maintain the original QoS of services based applications. The key of our method is degradation factor of component services which can guide us to find the component services which are the most contribution to the violation of overall QoS. The results of our evaluation show that our method can recover the original overall QoS by reconfiguring only a small number of services with fewer attempts in acceptable time.

Acknoledegments. This research is partially supported by the National Technology Support Program under grant of 2012BAH16B04, Zhejiang Provincial Natural Science Foundation of China under grant of LY12F02029, and the National Natural Science Foundation of China under grant of 61100043.

References

1. Zhang, L., Zhang, J., Cai, H.: Services Computing. Springer & Tsinghua University Press (2007)
2. Zeng, L., Benatallah, B., Ngu, A.H.H., Dumas, M., Kalagnanam, J., Chang, H.: QoS-Aware Middleware for Web Services Composition. IEEE Trans. on Software Engineering 30(5), 311–327 (2004)

3. Brian Blake, M., Tan, W., Rosenberg, F.: Composition as a Service. IEEE Internet Computing (INTERNET) 14(1), 78–82 (2010)
4. Aoyama, M., Weerawarana, S., Maruyama, H., Szyperski, C., Sullivan, K., Lea, D.: Web Services Engineering: Promises and Challenges. In: Proc. ICSE 2002, Orlando, pp. 647–648 (2002)
5. Vambenepe, W., Thompson, C., Talwar, V., et al.: Dealing with Scale and Adaptation of Global Web Services Management. Int. J. Web Service Res. (3), 65–84 (2007)
6. Tsai, W.T., Song, W., Chen, Y., Paul, R.: Dynamic System Reconfiguration Via Service Composition for Dependable Computing. In: Kordon, F., Sztipanovits, J. (eds.) Monterey Workshop 2005. LNCS, vol. 4322, pp. 203–224. Springer, Heidelberg (2007)
7. Avgeriou, P.: Run-time Reconfiguration of Service-Centric Systems. In: Proceeding of the European Pattern Languages of Programming, EuroPLOP (2006)
8. Ezenwoye, O., Busi, S., Sadjadi, S.M.: Dynamically Reconfigurable Data-intensive Service Composition. In: WEBIST 2010, pp. 125–130 (2010)
9. Yan, Y., Poizat, P., Zhao, L.: Repair vs. Recomposition for Broken Service Compositions. In: Maglio, P.P., Weske, M., Yang, J., Fantinato, M. (eds.) ICSOC 2010. LNCS, vol. 6470, pp. 152–166. Springer, Heidelberg (2010)
10. Jiang, B., Chan, W.K., Zhang, Z., Tse, T.H.: Where to adapt dynamic service compositions. In: WWW 2009, pp. 1123–1124 (2009)
11. Xiong, P., Fan, Y.S., Zhou, M.C.: Web Service Configuration under Multiple Quality-of-Service Attributes. IEEE Trans. on Automation Science and Engineering, 311–321 (2008)
12. Zhai, Y.L., Zhang, J., Lin, K.-J.: SOA Middleware Support for Service Process Reconfiguration with End-to-End QoS Constraints. In: The IEEE International Conference on Web Services (ICWS), pp. 815–822 (2009)
13. Yu, T., Lin, K.J.: Adaptive algorithms for Finding Replacement Services in Autonomic Distributed Business Processes. In: Proc. of the 7th International Symposium on Autonomous Decentralized Systems (2005)
14. Yin, Y.Y., Li, Y., Yin, J.W., et al.: Ensuring Correctness of Dynamic Reconfiguration in SOA Based Software. In: 2009 Congress on SERVICES-I, pp. 599–606 (2009)
15. Li, Y., Lu, Y.L., Yin, Y.Y., et al.: Towards QoS-Based Dynamic Reconfiguration of SOA-Based Applications. In: APSCC 2010, pp. 107–114 (2010)
16. Zeng, L., Ngu, A., Benatallah, B., Podorozhny, R., Lei, H.: Dynamic composition and optimization of web services. Distrib. Parallel Databases 24(1-3), 45–72 (2008)
17. Zheng, H., Yang, J., Zhao, W.: QoS Analysis and Service Selection for Composite Services. In: IEEE SCC 2010, pp. 122–129 (2010)
18. Rosenberg, F., Müller, M.B., Leitner, P., Michlmayr, A., Bouguettaya, A., Dustdar, S.: Metaheuristic Optimization of Large-Scale QoS-aware Service Compositions. In: IEEE SCC 2010, pp. 97–104 (2010)
19. Yu, T., Zhang, Y., Lin, K.-J.: Efficient Algorithms for Web Services Selection with End-to-End QoS Constraints. ACM Transactions on the Web 1(1), 1–26 (2007)

An Ontology-Based IoT Resource Model
for Resources Evolution and Reverse Evolution[*]

Shuai Zhao, Yang Zhang, and Junliang Chen

State Key Laboratory of Networking and Switching Technology, Beijing University of Posts
and Telecommunications, Beijing 100876, China
{zhaoshuaiby,yangzhang,chjl}@bupt.edu.cn

Abstract. In view of the characteristics of Internet of Things (IoT), the current architectures could not effectively use and manage IoT resources and information.
Numerous projects in the area of IoT have proposed architectures which aim at integrating geographically dispersed and internet interconnected heterogeneous
Wireless Sensor and Actuator Networks (WSAN) systems into a homogeneous
fabric for real world information and interaction. These architectures are faced
with very similar problems in how to support the evolution of resources and maintain service continuity, how to integrate the data which comes from heterogeneous
resources. To address these issues, this paper proposes a resource model supporting dynamic evolution and reverse evolution. The resource model uses Linked
Data and extends the existing ontologies, such as W3C SSN, etc. This resource
model can express domain knowledge, event rules, and support event-based reverse evolution. Based on the resource model, our SOA-based framework can automatically access resources, generate and interpret semantic context information,
dynamically create resources, and interpret historical data and events. The validation of the resource model and framework is shown through the CCMWS (Coal
mine comprehensive monitoring and early warning system).

1 Introduction

The Internet of Things (IoT) proposed by MIT Auto-ID Center is honored as the third
IT revolution following Computer and Internet [1]. The relevant theories and technologies become the research hotspot of academia. Huge amount of resources and information are provided by the IoT, but they cannot be effectively utilized in the current
application mode. Some issues exist in the level of resource and information:

— Resource Access: Dynamic resource access, i.e. realizing the PnP (Plug-and-Play)
  of heterogeneous resources under the premise of limited resource ability and real-
  time service demands. Resource access includes three aspects: recognizing new

---

[*] This study is supported by "973" program of National Basic Research Program of China
(Grant No. 2011CB302704, 2012CB315802). National Natural Science Foundation of China
(Grant No. 61001118, 61171102, 61003067, 61132001); Program for New Century Excel-
lent Talents in University (Grant No. NECT-11-0592); Project of New Generation Broadband
Wireless Network under Grant (Grant No.2010ZX03004-001, 2011ZX03002-002-01,
2012ZX03005008-001).

resource seamlessly; interpreting and processing the information generated by the resources automatically; real-time maintaining the resource information according to the changes of resource state.

— Resource Discovery: Billions of resources provide more capabilities also bring issues in resource discovery. How to find the most appropriate resource across different platforms and networks within the acceptable time and space range?

— Resource Management: Resource management and maintenance are highly complicated due to the heterogeneity, instability and evolution of the IoT. Management framework should adapt to these characteristics to manage and track the evolution of resources; the framework should promptly perceives the changes of resource state and provides context-aware dynamic switching and scheduling mechanism of heterogeneous resource to ensure the continuity of real-time service.

— Resource Utilization: The real world can be reflected more and more realistically by the digital world with the expansion of the range and the further capability of sensing. Meanwhile, the operation and task generated in the digital world get more complicated, using a single resource is unable to be competent. How to coordinate and schedule distributed resources in a unified way according to business needs, user need context and ubiquitous resource information context?

A normative resource model and framework are the basis of addressing the issues above. Therefore, research program such as EU FP7 have been devoted to researching normative architecture of the IoT, such as PECES [2, 3], SENSEI [4], etc. This paper proposes a semantic model and resource framework which focus on the issues of resource access, resource evolution, real-world service [5] continuity, and generating context information. The model and framework have the following characteristics:

— The SOA-based framework integrates SCA (Service Component Architecture) and ESB (Enterprise Service Bus) together as the execution platform. SCA serves as the assembly standard of service components. ESB provides protocol translation, message routing, security, management functions for the interaction between components. Hot deploy and cross-platform capabilities are ensured by OSGi.

— The ontology-based semantic model can express domain knowledge and business information which are the basis of implementation the linkage (mutual influence) between model and system business logic. The model extends the current ontologies such as W3C SSN [6], OWL-S, etc. to ensure the versatility and standardization, it uses linked-data[10] to associate with functional ontologies.

— Events are generated automatically in two modes: event tree; Abductive and Deductive Reasoning (ADR). Event tree is a fast matching method and appropriate for the high real time applications. ADR is proposed by combining the improved Parsimonious Covering Theory (PCT) reasoning [7-9] with the deductive reasoning. ADR can reason out the inducement events from basic events, then forecasts what other events these inducement events can cause by deductive reasoning.

— The semantic model can be not only adapted to the evolution but also able to reverse evolution. If the model is restored to a historical state, it can restore and reproduce the real world context at that time and interpret the historical data and events. To be emphasized, the existing work only focuses on the evolution.

However, with the enhancement of real-world sensing and control ability, due to the evolution and instability of resources, tracking the evolution of the model and the capability of reverse evolution are also very important. We use graph database to store context information, use the model snapshots and archived events to track the evolution and reverse evolution.

The rest of this paper is organized as follows. Section 2 describes the semantic model and framework. Section 3 discusses the mechanism of model evolution and reverse evolution. Section 4 presents the CCMWS to validate the model and framework. Section 5 concludes the paper and discusses the further work.

2   Semantic Model and Framework

2.1   Framework

The SOA-based framework use SCA as the assembly standard and components interact with each other by service interface. The ESB provides protocol translation, message routing, security and management functions for component interaction. What's more, the underlying OSGi offers hot deploy and cross-platform capabilities.

As shown in figure 1, the framework mainly contains these components:

— Resource Adaption (RA) is used to adapt heterogeneous resources. It publishes resource description when resource accesses and wraps the Resource Interface.

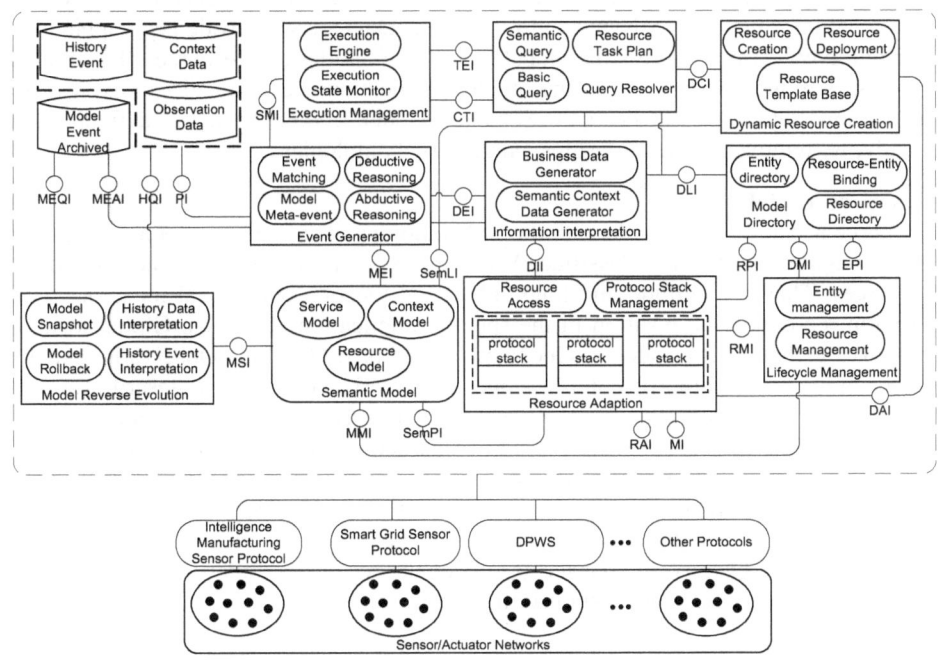

Fig. 1. Resource framework

- Model Directory, a directory of Semantic Model, is used to retrieve resources and entities efficiently.
- Lifecycle Management (LM) monitors and manages the resource lifecycle.
- Information Interpretation converts raw data to the domain data according to the definition of domain processing, promotes it to meaningful context information.
- Event Generator (EG) automatically generates events according to the event rules defined in the Context Model.
- The Persistent Component is used for persisting historical data and events.
- Execution Management (EM) executes the task plan and monitors the resource states.
- Dynamic Resource creation can create new resources based on the domain knowledge.
- Model Event Archived archives the model events using for reverse evolution.
- Reverse Evolution (RE) restores the model to a historical state based on model snapshots and events without interfering with the current model.

2.2   Semantic Model

Upper layer uses W3C SSN to describe the sensor resources and observation data, context model and domain knowledge extensions are needed. OWL-Time is used to express the time information. SemSOS O&M [11] and SENSEI O&M are extended as the observation data model. What's more, we used Linked Data to link the model to ontologies such as FOAF, GeoNames, Linked-GeoData and DBpedia[1]. OWL-S is the upper ontology for describing service. FOAF makes the Model more general and provides additional information. GeoName and Linked-GeoData are worldwide geographic location ontologies which express the global location of entities and resources. The domain ontologies in the bottom extends the ontologies mentioned above and can express domain knowledge. Figure 2 shows the Semantic Model. In order to make the figure more clearly, we removed the relationships with external ontologies.

Resource Model
Resource Model is compatible with the SSN ontology. The model is open end and can be re-classified or further classified. We use three forms to express the location of resources. They are latitude and longitude, local location and global location. Local location represents the position in the specific application scenarios. Global location links to a global position such as GeoName and Linked-GeoData. Observation Area is the resource observation or control scope. Engineering Conversion describes a conversion process which translates the raw data into available domain data. Protocol Stack describes the sensor protocol used by interacting with resources. Resource Type is a domain expert classification which is standardized and representative. It is useful in resource searching and resource-entity binding. Tag provides some information of time dimension, space dimension, capacities of the resources. Measurement Capability describes the Quality of Service (QoS) of the resources under certain conditions such as accuracy, precision, response time, delay and so on. The operation range of

---

[1] http://en.wikipedia.org/wiki/File:DBpediaLogo.svg

resources includes equipment life, battery life, transmission range and so on. Observation and Provide Service are another two attributes of the Resources. They link to the Service Model and Observation respectively. Observation mainly contains results, location, time, QoI and unit, etc.

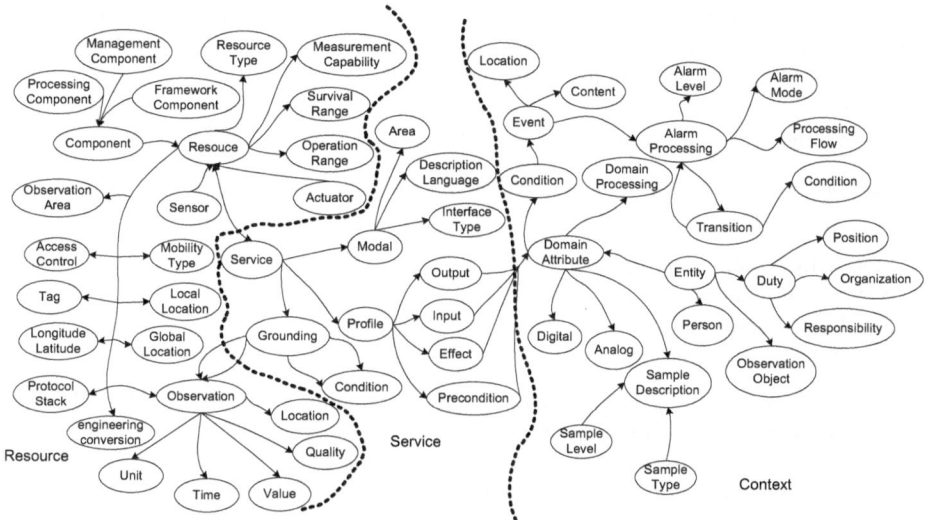

Fig. 2. Overview of the Semantic Model

Service Model

Resources are accessed by services which provide functionality to gather information about entities they are associated with or manipulate physical properties of their associated entities. Service Model describes the Real-World Service of resources which is based on the Model, Profile, Grounding concepts of the OWL-S and the service model of literature [5]. Profile has four attributes which is IOPE (input, output, precondition, effect). Input and output link to the entity attributes. Meanwhile, precondition and effect link to the entity attribute state. Model describes the service scope, service description language and service interface type. Grounding has properties such as service provider, service IOPE and so on. The input and output of the IOPE link to the Observation of Resources Model, while precondition and effect link to a SSN:Condition instance.

Context Model

Context Model includes Entity Model, Event Model and Sampling Description. Entity model consists of Person, Observation Object and Duty. Person can describe state, relations, environment information of persons. Observation Object describes the state, relationship and their relative position of the entities observed. Duty contains information such as position, responsibility and organization, etc. Event Model contains Event Tree and Alarm Disposal Process. The Event Tree makes classification on events according to location, emergency degree and theme. It also defines the relationship between events. The Alarm Disposal Process defines alarm level, alarm form, disposal process, etc. Event node associates with alarm disposal process, so the disposal process can make appropriate decisions after the event occurs. The Sampling Description includes information of sampling level, sampling type, etc. Domain attribute is linked to sample description to define the sampling rules of attributes. What's more, it is also linked to event condition to define the trigger conditions of attribute event. In our Semantic Model, the Observation of Resource Model is associated with domain attribute of Entity Model. We call this association as Resource-Entity Binding. The binding is the basis for promoting the observation data to context information. The binding can be static or dynamic and be generated automatically or manually.

2.3   Model Evolution and Reverse Evolution

In our framework, evolution has the following aspects:

— Mobility
— State(Lifecycle,   performance state,   configuration)
— New resource access
— Attributes changing
— Relationship changing

These aspects are not mutually isolated but have semantic association with each other; an evolution may lead to other evolution behaviors. For example, the mobility of resource may cause resource attribute changing, resource availability changing and the binding relationship between resource and entity changing. According to these evolution aspects, there are three main model-event types:

— Lifecycle event (resource availability changing, resource access, lifecycle state changing)
— Attribute changing event (property value, state, configuration parameter and performance parameter)
— Relationship changing event(establish, update, release)

Table 1. Example of resource evolution

| Time | Model Event | Model | | | Snapshot | Data Event |
		Entity	Resource	Relationship		
T_0		E_1, E_2	R_1, R_2	$Binding(E_1, R_1)$ $Binding(E_2, R_2)$ $Closeto(E_1, E_2)$		
T_1		E_1, E_2	R_1, R_2	$Binding(E_1, R_1)$ $Binding(E_2, R_2)$ $Closeto(E_1, E_2)$		$Event: E_1$ alarm
T_2	$Event_{l1}: R_3$ access	E_1, E_2	R_1, R_2, R_3	$Binding(E_1, R_1)$ $Binding(E_2, R_2)$ $Closeto(E_1, E_2)$		
T_3	$Event_{r1}: del\_Binding(E_1, R_1)$ $Event_{a1}: R_1\ del\_Attributes$ $Event_{l2}: R_1\ remove$	E_1, E_2	R_2, R_3	$Binding(E_2, R_2)$ $Closeto(E_1, E_2)$		
T_4	$Event_{r2}: Bind(E_1, R_3)$	E_1, E_2	R_2, R_3	$Binding(E_1, R_3)$ $Binding(E_2, R_2)$ $Closeto(E_1, E_2)$		
$\vdots$ T_{Now}	...	...	...	...	...	...

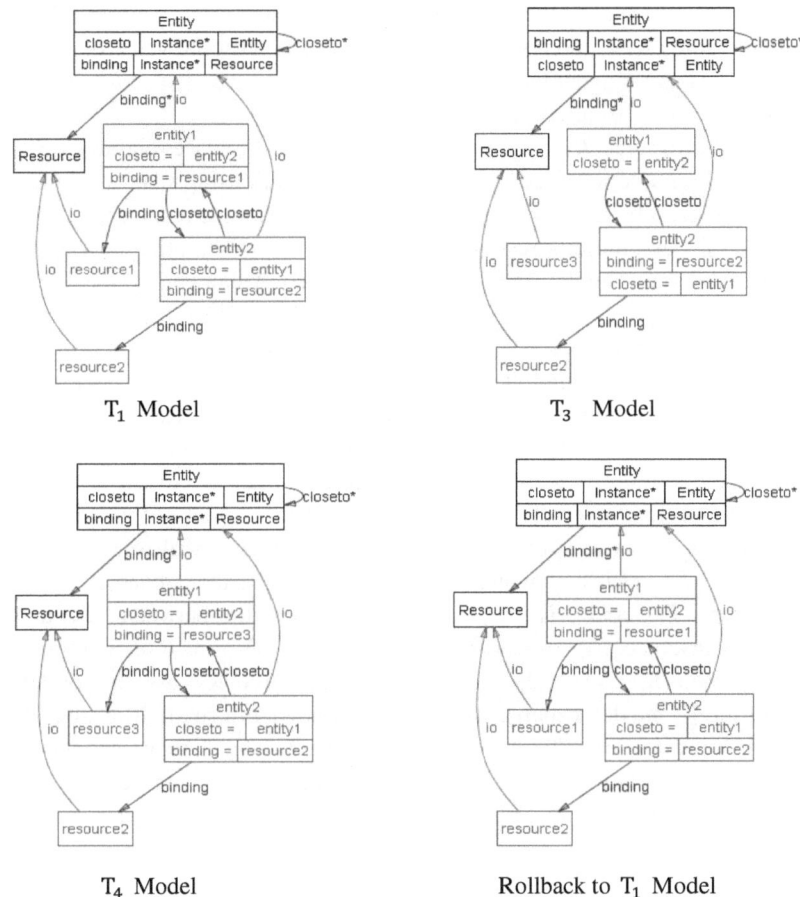

Fig. 3. Simple example of ontology evolution and reverse evolution

Model evolutions may be triggered by the underlying events from WSAN and the monitoring of resource state, or manual configurations. An evolution action often causes other evolution behaviors. For example, the sampling frequency drops lead to the performance attribute change, and the releasing of resource-entity binding if it no longer meets the requirements of entity. In order to track the evolution, EG archives the model events and Reverse Evolution (RE) snapshots the model periodically. RE rolls the model back to a historical state based on snapshots (closest to that historical moment) and events without interfering with the current model. Then, the historical model can interpret historical data and events.

Table 1 shows a simplified evolution process. Figure 3 shows the ontology which expresses the model in different time along with the evolution.

At time T_0 , there are two adjacent entities E_1 and E_2 ; resource R_1 observes the attribute value of E_1 and resource R_2 observes the attribute value of E_2 .

At time T_1 , alarm event happens on E_1 observed by R_1.

At time T_2 , new resource R_3 is accessed.

At time T_3 , resource R_1 becomes unavailable, then "release relationship", "delete attribute" and "remove resource" events occur. All relationships and attributes related to the resource must be released before removing the resource instance.

At time T_4 , assume that resource R_3 can provide observation service for entity E_1, then binding between E_1 and R_3 is established. Meanwhile, T_4 is the snapshot time.

T_{Now} is the current time.

It is unable to make a comprehensive and thorough analysis of E_1 alarm event only based on the event contents, historical model is needed. Reverse evolution mechanism can be applied to restore the model to the historical state.

For reverse evolution, system finds the snapshot which is closest to the historical time desired and then reversely does the actions in the model events which are happened in the time intervals between snapshot time and historical time. In detail, system finds the T_4 snapshot which is closest to T_1 , then reversely does the actions between T_4 and T_1 : releases the relationship between E_1 and R_3 ; adds resource instance R_1 ; restores the attributes of R_1 ; restores the binding relationship between E_1 and R_1 ; removes the resource R_3. So, the model can be restored to the T_1 model which expresses the context information at that time. The ontology restored to time T_1 is shown in figure 3. The domain knowledge along with the state and relationships of all resources and entities can be used to analyze historical data and events.

3   Implementation and Case Study

CCMWS (Coal Mine Comprehensive Monitoring and Early Warning System) is a coal mine safety application which is based on the resource model and framework. We integrated Apache Tuscany and Fuse ESB together as the service execution platform. With system implemented in Java, we store resource directory in H2 database, semantic model in AllegroGraph graph database and observation data in MySQL database. This section will show the function of system by two cases.

3.1   Dynamic Resource Creation

In the CCMWS, resource can be represented by graphic element vividly by relating resource instances to graphic element instances. Resource user can manage and use resources by dragging and dropping graphic element and these actions will be reflected in model automatically.

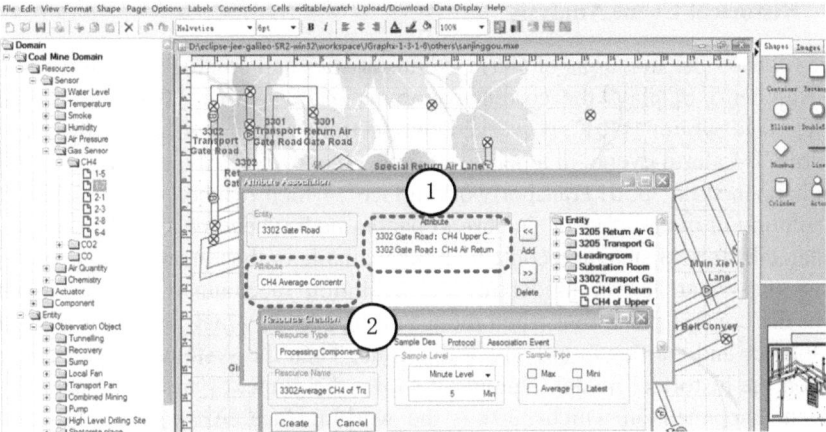

Fig. 4. Dynamic creation resource

Figure 5 shows the process of creating resource dynamically according to domain knowledge. Entity "3302TransportGateRoad" has three attributes: "CH4UpperCorner", "CH4ReturnAir" and "CH4Average". Number 1 of figure 6 shows that user defines the domain knowledge that the attribute "CH4Averagecon" can be calculated from other two attributes. Other more complicated domain processing such as "relative abundance of methane" can also be defined. "CH4UpperCorner" and "CH4ReturnAir" have been bound with resources respectively. On the basis of the conversion relationship of attributes, system can create the resource"3302TransportCH4Average" dynamically. The observation values of "CH4UpperCorner" and "CH4ReturnAir" are the inputs of the resource "3302TransportCH4Average". The resource will process the input data according to domain processing definition, the result of processing will be interpretation as the value of "CH4Average" attribute. Number 2 shows how to configure Sampling Description, Protocol Stack and Event related to the resource instance.

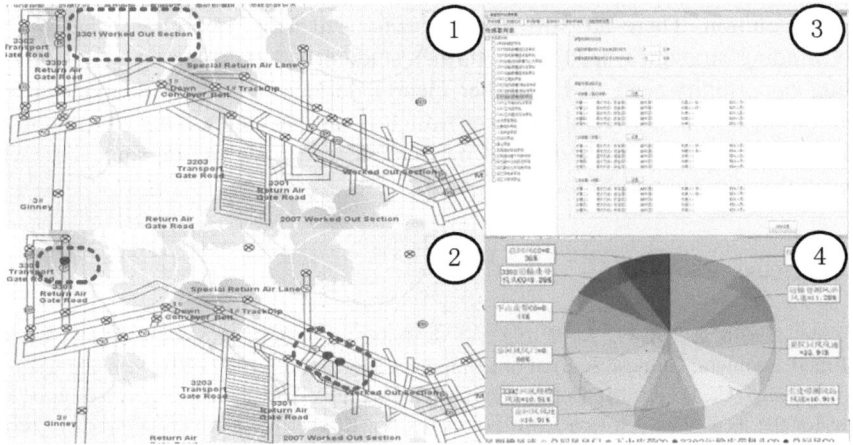

Fig. 5. Historical event analysis

3.2   Historical Event Analysis

Figure 6 shows the functions of alarm event statistics and context panorama reproduction. Number 1 displays the current panorama of coal mine, "3302" is the current working face while "3301" is worked out section. Number 4 shows the statistical result of CH4 alarm events in a period of time. According to the statistics, the highest alarm happened on "3301Transportworkingface", which reached up to 2.65%. But as the evolution of model, "3301" in current panorama has become a worked out section, the related historical state and context are unavailable in the current model. In order to analyze the event above, model reverse evolution mechanism will be applied to present the context panorama when the event happened, which can show the state of all resources and entities intuitively at that time. Then the system interprets the event based on the historical model. Number 2 shows the context panorama restored when the event happened, in which 3301 is the working face. Analysis of the historical model and panorama found that there was nothing wrong with the sensor performance and entity attribute threshold. But the "3301TransportFan" resource generated "stop working" alarm and "AirReturnLaneFeed" generated "equipment malfunction" events. So, we can determine the cause of the CH4 alarm is "power cut lead to 3301 transport fan stop working". We can also analyze the causes of "equipment malfunction" events and other hidden dangers of coal mine. Number 3 shows the analysis of the alarm disposal process executed when the alarm happened according to the historical model. The reverse evolution is very useful for failure, accident and disaster analysis.

4   Conclusion

The resource model and resource framework are the foundation of the IoT architecture, as well as the bridge between the upper layer application and the underlying WSAN. This paper proposes a SOA-based resource framework, an ontology-based resource model and proposes solutions for resource access, resource evolution and reverse evolution. There are still some aspects need to be improved. The resource-entity binding strategies need to be further studied and the binding maintainer and binding opportunity need to be further clearly defined. The current model reverse evolution method is an overall rollback which is not very effective. We plan to propose a partial rollback method based on time, space, topic and dependences, which only roll the relevant part of the model back.

References

1. Xing, L., Jin, Z., Li, G.: Modeling and verifying services of Internet of Things based on timed automata. Chinese Journal of Computers 34(8), 1365–1377 (2011) (in Chinese)
2. Villalonga, C., Bauer, M., López Aguilar, F., Huang, V., Strohbach, M.: A Resource Model for the Real World Internet. In: Lukowicz, P., Kunze, K., Kortuem, G. (eds.) EuroSSC 2010. LNCS, vol. 6446, pp. 163–176. Springer, Heidelberg (2010)

3. Haroon, M., Handte, M., Marrón, P.: Generic role assignment: a uniform middleware abstraction for configuration of pervasive systems. In: Proc. of the Pervasive Computing and Communications (PerCom's 2009), Galveston, United States, pp. 1–6 (2009)
4. Payam, B.: D3.6 Final SENSEI Architecture Framework, Public SENSEI Deliverable. CEA-LETI (2011)
5. De, S., Barnaghi, P., Bauer, M., Meissner, S.: Service modeling for the Internet of Things, pp. 949–955 (2011)
6. Semantic Sensor Network XG Final Report,
   http://www.w3.org/2005/Incubator/ssn/XGR-ssn-20110628/
7. Henson, C., Thirunarayan, K., Sheth, A., Hitzler, P.: Representation of Parsimonious Covering Theory in OWL-DL. In: Proc. of the 8th International Workshop on OWL: Experiences and Directions (OWLED 2011), San Francisco, CA, United States (2011)
8. Thirunarayan, K., Henson, C.A., Sheth, A.P.: Situation awareness via abductive reasoning from semantic sensor data: a preliminary report. In: Proc. of the International Symposium on Collaborative Technologies and Systems (CTS 2009), Balitimore, Maryland, USA, pp. 111–118 (2009)
9. Henson, C., Sheth, A., Thirunararyan, K.: Semantic Perception: A Semantic Approach to Convert Sensory Observations to Abstractions. In: Proc. of the IEEE Internet Computing (2012)
10. Bizer, C., Heath, T., Berners-Lee, T.: Linked data-the story so far. International Journal on Semantic Web and Information Systems (IJSWIS) 5(3), 1–22 (2009)
11. Henson, C.A., Pschorr, J.K., Sheth, A.P., Thirunarayan, K.: SemSOS: Semantic sensor observation service. In: Proc. of the International Symposium on Collaborative Technologies and Systems (CTS 2009), Balitimore, Maryland, USA, pp. 44–53 (2009)

Erratum: Cloud Service Selection Based on Variability Modeling

Erik Wittern[1], Jörn Kuhlenkamp[1], and Michael Menzel[2]

[1] eOrganization Research Group, Karlsruhe Institute of Technology (KIT)
Englerstr. 11, 76131 Karlsruhe, Germany
{Erik.Wittern,Joern.Kuhlenkamp}@kit.edu
http://www.eorganization.de
[2] Research Center for Information Technology
Karlsruhe Institute of Technology (KIT)
Menzel@fzi.de

C. Liu et al. (Eds.): ICSOC 2012, LNCS 7636, pp. 127–141, 2012.
© Springer-Verlag Berlin Heidelberg 2012

DOI 10.1007/978-3-642-34321-6_63

In chapter 9, Figure 1 has been given incorrectly. The correct figure should be as follows:

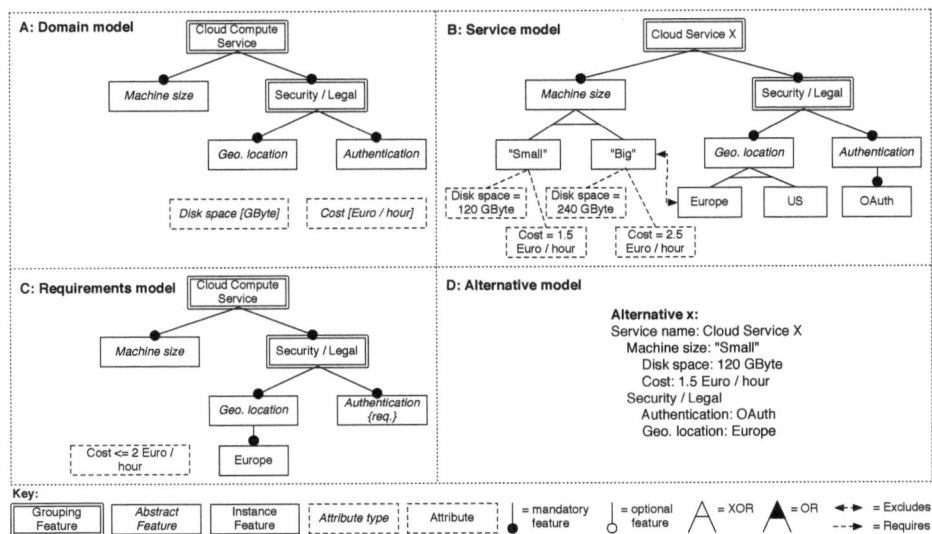

Fig. 1. Exemplary models illustrating model types and modeling elements

---

The original online version for this chapter can be found at
http://dx.doi.org/10.1007/978-3-642-34321-6_9

Author Index